Pearson New International Edition

A History of Psychology
From Antiquity to Modernity
Thomas H. Leahey
Seventh Edition

PEARSON®

Pearson Education Limited
Edinburgh Gate
Harlow
Essex CM20 2JE
England and Associated Companies throughout the world

Visit us on the World Wide Web at: www.pearsoned.co.uk

© Pearson Education Limited 2014

ISBN 10: 1-292-02797-5
ISBN 13: 978-1-292-02797-5

British Library Cataloguing-in-Publication Data
A catalogue record for this book is available from the British Library

Printed in the United States of America

Table of Contents

Introductory Essay

"Psychology is impossible."

Xam Rebew looked at his audience at Foundation Center with a mixture of anxiety and ambition. Like all Martians, Rebew had lived a long time, and wanted to do something new. He was already known as an author—a popular historian. During his compulsory military service he'd become fascinated with military history and had written a book about one of Mars's first wars, and about its greatest military hero, *Adventures with the Master Chief*. It was a big success, and after leaving the service, Rebew could afford to do just about anything.

Rebew became interested in earth when one day he looked at the royalty statement for *Adventures with the Master Chief* and saw a line he'd never noticed before, "Off-Planet Rights," which came to a huge number of marsos. He called his agent, who said, "Don't ask too many questions, but I figured out a way to wangle some lucre from our planetary neighbors. They don't read your book, but Master Chief is a big hero in their games."

As Xam learned about earthfolks, he found they had a science (or, at least they claimed to have) that compared to nothing on Mars. It was called "psychology." Translating from their languages, it meant literally "soul study," but for a Martian the phrase was meaningless. "Thing study," "life study," and "society study" made sense, but "soul study" did not—no Martian language Xam knew about had a word meaning anything like "soul." How could you study what did not exist? Perhaps he had found a subject new enough and odd enough to impress academics, even at the Foundation! He would become the anthropologist from Mars.

Marsos from his book let him study earth "psychology" at his leisure. He was even able to purchase occasional use of the time telescope (ironic that off-planet rights allowed him to spy on the past of the earthfolks).

1

Unfortunately, Xam's study was messier than he'd thought. Assuming there was no soul to study, Xam had thought he'd find a small, short-lived, esoteric group of eccentric practitioners whose group dynamics could be summarized in some impressive equations. What he found was thousands upon thousands of "psychologists" doing everything from recording the activity of a few cells in the human brain to advising elite politicians. For a while he despaired of making sense of it all, sinking into a profound depression lasting a few years. Hope returned when he noticed two things: the "science" of psychology appeared rather abruptly in human history, and the vast majority of the psychology clan worked in but one part of earth, the part earthfolks called "North America," even though that's not where it started. Perhaps some sense could be made of the mess of a science with no subject matter if one could just understand the peculiar history of earthfolks and "psychology." But the best way to make the academics at the Foundation pay attention was to start with a mystery: "Psychology is impossible."

THE SHAPE OF PSYCHOLOGY

Why did Xam say that psychology was impossible? One reason, of course, was that he wasn't sure if there was a psyche of which to have knowledge. More important, however, were his invisible anthropological trips to earth, past and present. He found "psychologists" doing so many things that he could find nothing in common between them except that they all had PhD degrees from psychology departments. Except when they didn't: Many "counseling psychologists" had EdD degrees, and among the huge clan of "clinical psychologists" were those with PsyDs. Moreover, the jobs and research of psychologists often overlapped with, and sometimes competed with, other groups of professions and sciences. The brain cell psychologists did what "biologists" did, for example, and then there were the clinical folks again, who seemed to do the same things as MD psychiatrists, licensed clinical social workers, and others. True, only MDs could write prescriptions, but the guild of the American Psychological Association (APA) was working hard to change that. Behavioral experiments were not limited to the "experimental psychologists"; there were behavioral economists and even a few experimental philosophers, too. He found it all very confusing.

Perhaps history can provide some clarification. Where had the *soi-disant* science come from? Surely psychology didn't always exist, and must have started out as a small field, more precisely defined. In addition, there was the fact that psychologists were not evenly distributed across earth, adding a sociological dimension to the problem of psychology's diversity. One might look for some features of time and place that gave rise to psychology and made it more popular in some countries than others. Whatever unity psychology now possessed might be more a function of historical and social forces external to it than its self-defined subject matter.

THE SHAPE OF HISTORY

What Is the History of Psychology About?

You might check the library and find a journal called *History of Psychology*, so there must be something for books, courses, and journals to be about. But if we look at other fields, the situation is very different. In physics, for example, there are no (that I or Xam could find) courses or textbooks on its history. There are books and resources about the history of physics, but no special texts and courses devoted to it. The history of physics is part of the larger history of natural science. The other social sciences similarly lack texts, courses, and journals. So we can add a third oddness to Xam's list: Psychologists care more about their history than other scientists or practitioners care about theirs.

In the history of science in general there have been two approaches to defining a field of study. In the natural sciences, for example, the Scientific Revolution forms an important hinge point. Older histories tended to focus on ideas about the physical world up to the Scientific Revolution, with the Revolution itself—the establishment of modern science—being the end point. Thus one learns about Aristotle's theories of motion and the earth-centered astronomy of Ptolemy, and how these were replaced by Newtonian physics and Copernican astronomy. Before the Scientific Revolution there were people who studied the topics that make up modern science, but there were no self-conscious professions or institutions of science as such until they were created in the Scientific Revolution. More recent histories tended to focus on the Scientific Revolution as the starting point when a given science became self-conscious and its formal scientific institutions were established. We might say that the older histories studied the prehistory of a field—protoscientific ideas—while the newer histories study a field after its emergence as a distinct and self-consciously scientific enterprise—a science as such.

One can apply the same scheme to psychology, defining the prehistory of psychology as concerned with ideas about mind and behavior up to the professionalization of psychology in the late nineteenth century. In fact, if one looks at the journal *History of Psychology*, the latter focus is what he or she will find. However, in the cases of the social sciences, and psychology in particular, we run into some special problems not met with in the case of the natural sciences. First, and this is unique to psychology as a science, people have their own, probably built-in, set of ideas about mind and behavior, called variously *folk psychology* (the term I'll use), *commonsense psychology*, or *theory of mind*. Thus in the prehistory phase of psychology we find not only philosophical ideas about mind and behavior developed by thinkers, such as Aristotle or John Locke, but a robust and powerful set of ideas—often only dimly articulated if at all—that ordinary people used to understand themselves and others. Moreover, unlike Ptolemaic astronomy or alchemy, which died after the Scientific Revolution, folk psychology did not go away when psychology became a science. Everybody, including psychologists, uses it every day. What will become of folk psychology is an interesting topic in cognitive science.

The other special problem for psychology is shared by the other social sciences; it goes by the relatively unhelpful word *reflexivity*. The sun has always been at the center of the solar system regardless of what people thought, and the development of scientific astronomy had no effect on the behavior of the cosmos. However, social science is about people, people can learn social science concepts—you have done so in the course of your education and also by reading books, articles, and blogs by psychologists and from TV folks like Dr. Phil—and people are influenced by them. Thus psychology can change the reality it is attempting to describe, even to the point of creating that reality.

One way to see the importance of reflexivity as a problem is to consider the work of anthropologists, Martian or human. An anthropologist studies an unfamiliar culture, and a major part of that study is talking to people about their ideas about medicine, religion, how the world works, and so on. Anthropologists listen attentively and take seriously what their people tell them, but they don't have to accept folk accounts as valid theories of disease, the gods, or nature. They respect the beliefs as sincere but not as true. But importantly for our current concern, they don't try to replace their peoples' folk beliefs. They don't say, "Your god Kador does not exist, he does not cause illness or floods." Anthropologists leave folk beliefs intact because they fear that if they challenge the beliefs they will destroy the culture they have studied because the folk web of beliefs *constitutes* the alien culture. Psychologists, however, do not act like anthropologists. They proclaim their findings and theories, shaping, if not constituting a new culture rooted in psychology's scientific theories about mind and behavior, part of a larger movement called modernity.

Modernity and Modernism

The concepts of modernity and modernism can be vexing, because the concepts are diffuse and contested, and because they can mean different things to different scholars. Even determining when "modernity" began can be difficult. On the early end, intellectual historian Michael Gillespie (2008) places the origins of modernity in fourteenth-century theology, beginning his narrative in 1326. On the other end, political historians C. A. Bayly (2004) and Paul Johnson (1992) center their narratives around 1815, Bayly ending in 1914 and Johnson in 1830. Novelist and historian A. N. Wilson (1999, p. 69) dramatically gives a univocal date, "what had been poured forth at the French Revolution [1789] was something rather more destructive than the Vials of the Apocalypse. It was the dawning of the Modern." Then, there is modern*ism*, best known as a movement in the arts, whose beginnings Joyce Medina (1995), following early critic Roger Fry (1909), locate in the inception of the late works of Paul Cézanne around 1885.

In this text I will use *modernity* and *modernism* in ways that are specific to how I see the history and prehistory of psychology. Let's begin by distinguishing a realm of ideas and a realm of everyday life. Gillespie (2008) sees the origins of modernity in an important dispute about concepts, a dispute seen even then as between the Way of Antiquity (*via antiqua*) and the Way of Modernity (*via moderna*). When I use a name such as *the White House* it's clear what I'm talking about: the individual home of the U.S. president. But when I use the generic term *house*, it's not so clear what I'm referring to. A name points to a concrete thing, but a concept does not. Puzzling about this is pretty much the origin point of cognitive psychology.

The Ancients—Greek philosophers and European theologians up to the fourteenth century—had in different ways assimilated concepts to names. They said that every particular house or cat or rock or flower or person was an instance of a fixed and unchanging ideal type of House or Cat or Flower or Person so that our words *house* or *cat* or *flower* or *person* refer to—are really the names of—those ideal types. This via antiqua was (confusingly to modern ears) called Realism, because it said that just as *the White House* refers to a *real* thing, so does *house*, even though we can't visit it. Moreover, the ability to understand these ideal types was seen as the key ability separating the human soul from animal minds.

The Moderns, for a variety of reasons, rejected Realism. They said that concepts such as house or cat were just convenient names—their view was thus called nominalism—we humans have invented to conveniently group together things that resemble each other. Ideal types are useful fictions that don't name anything outside our own thoughts. What does this have to do with modernity? It's generally agreed that a characteristic of modern life is that it's secular rather than religious: The dominant authorities today are science and government, not theology and the Church. When theology and the via antiqua reigned, to know concepts was to know God's divine Truth, for He created the ideal types of The House, The Cat, The Flower, and Everything Else. Nominalism pried apart human and divine knowledge. Concepts were human constructions, not connections to God's mind and heaven. Concepts could no longer be defined as True or False by their resemblance to divine Ideas, and philosophers searched for new bases by which to understand and justify human ideas as good or bad, eventually coming up with notions such as objectivity, peer review, and statistical significance—in short, science (Gaukroger, 2006), the authority of modernity.

The battle over nominalism began in the realm of ideas, involving only a handful of cloistered (literally) academic theologians, for whom the stakes were religious and metaphysical, such as whether there were any limits on God's power. Nevertheless, the nominalist ball that started rolling from the ivory tower of theology eventually landed on everyday life, undermining religion and creating modernity, a way of life based more on reason than revelation. The term *modernity*, then, will have two uses, an intellectual one, referring to the ideas that helped create the second use, the way of life that we live today.

There's a bottom-up influence from modernity as a way of life on intellectual thought about the human mind and man's place(s) in nature and society, bringing us to modern*ism*. The modern way of life gets noticed and intellectuals begin to think about how to respond to it. Thus Cézanne and the other modernists, including critics such as Fry, begin to reject traditional art as belonging to the premodern way of life, and rethink how art should be done in the modern world. In a sense it's the via moderna rejecting the via antiqua all over again, except that this time the moving influence is from below—life has changed and so should art (and philosophy and science) to become modern. Modernism, then, can be regarded as the ideology of modernity—a reflection by intellectuals on the modern condition, to praise it, reject it, criticize it, improve it.

And to be created by it, which brings us to psychology as a discipline. Its traditional starting date, along with Cézanne and modernism in art, is 1879. Psychology will have special and crucial roles to play in the story of the creation of modernity and the response of modernism. The Realism versus Nominalism debate was an argument in cognitive psychology about how we learn general concept terms (a debate still in progress, by the way).

There is one other aspect of modernity that I have left out and that leads to the creation of applied psychology and its importance in modern life. Figure I is possibly the most important historical graph you will ever see (from G. Clark, 2007, p. 2).

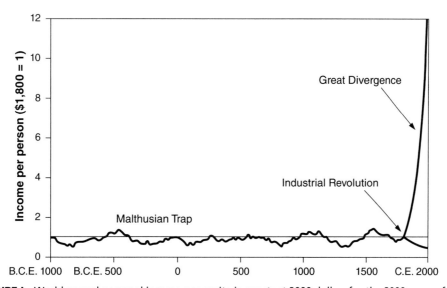

FIGURE I World annual personal income per capita in constant 2000 dollars for the 3000 years of recorded human history. *(CLARK, GREGORY; farewell to alms, © 2007 by Princeton University Press. Reprinted by permission of Princeton University Press.)*

Figure I shows that although the Vials of the Apocalypse may not have poured out in 1789, something else did: wealth. The figure shows income per person in inflation-adjusted units from 1000 B.C.E. onward. Note that there is no sustained income growth for thousands of years. Premodern people lived under what economists call Malthusian conditions, after the political economist Thomas Malthus (1768–1834), an important influence on Darwin. In the Malthusian economy, or trap, the amount of wealth was fixed and population growth was constrained only by the amount of available food. When there were occasional good times—good harvests, because the only source of wealth was agriculture—and wealth increased, so did the population, wiping out the per person increase in wealth. The other way per capita income increased was by famine, disease, or war; the same amount of wealth was distributed among fewer people. Premodern people, even relatively well off ones, lived lives of grinding poverty that ended in most cases by age 35 or so.[1]

From the standpoint of everyday life, modernity was made by the Industrial Revolution, not by nominalism or even the Scientific Revolution. What brought it about is still being investigated and debated by economic historians (G. Clark, 2007; Mokyr, 2009), but it is the biggest cause of modernity. A key development of the Industrial Revolution was the division of labor (A. Smith, 1776). People possess different skills and abilities, and if each person does what he or she does best, rather than trying to produce everything for themselves, as most farmers did, the result is increased productivity. Thus, economic output can be improved by finding the right job for the right person, the initial task of mental testing, and the foundation stone of applied, clinical, psychology. Testing is thus an example of modernism, of intellectuals reflecting on the modern way of life and seeking to improve it.

Postmodernity?

You may have heard the terms *postmodern* or *postmodernism*. Like modernism, postmodernism began as a movement in the arts, specifically architecture (Jencks, 1981). Architects became tired of the undecorated boxy structures of modern architecture that represented an austere, clean, scientifically inspired view of building as opposed to the colorful and decorated styles of premodern architecture as found in churches and ancient temples. By the way, ancient Greek and Roman art did not present the uniform pure white marble appearance as we see it today—it was vividly painted. Enabled by developments in building materials and construction techniques, postmodern architects began designing playful structures, more suited, as they saw it, to a "postmodern" way of life. Perhaps the most famous postmodern building is Frank Gehry's Guggenheim Museum in Bilbao, Spain.

What, then, was the "postmodern" life that the new architecture was supposed to express? When did it start? Not too long after postmodern architecture began, the Cold War ended with a sudden whimper in December, 1991 when the Soviet Union unexpectedly collapsed. If the French Revolution was the dawning of the modern, the collapse of the Soviet Union and communist countries of eastern Europe was perhaps the dawning of the postmodern. Whether postmodernity existed and what it was like was much debated among intellectuals (Cahoone, 1996; Fukyama, 1999; Leahey, 1997, 2001, 2008). As with modernity, we should look at changes in the nature of work to see if there's anything to the idea of the postmodern. Look at Figure I again. The growth of wealth in developed nations has been exponential, about half of it coming since about 1960. This is a quantitative change that has brought qualitative results to everyday life. When I was in college, there were no computers. I was typing, not word-processing until at least 1982. There were no iPods, iPhones

---

[1] In Clark's graph, Great Divergence refers to the fact that some nations still live under premodern, Malthusian conditions.

(or cell phones), or iPads, no Apple, no Internet, no Facebook, only chalk and blackboards in the classroom (and no Blackboard).

And the nature of work has changed, too (Drucker, 1994). The antique, premodern, and modern eras were eras of what I like to call heavy lifting. Before machines, warfare and agriculture required strong muscles, so did much factory work. In general, people worked with their bodies rather than their minds, and a premium was placed on strength. In the developed late-modern/postmodern world, however, people are information workers (Drucker, 1994), producing with their minds rather than their bodies. The productivity premium shifted to intelligence and education, and more jobs could be done equally well by both sexes. Note that the new—to me, if not to you—things I listed earlier are all information-using devices. Apple's products say they are designed in Cupertino, California, by highly educated engineers, but constructed in China, which is beginning its ascent right through modernity to postmodernity in a fraction of the time of the West.

Psychology has been changed, too (Leahey, 1997, 2001, 2008). The great explosion in the numbers of psychologists has come after World War II on an ever-upward path of growth. The APA is comprised by divisions defined by the work done and/or scholarly interest of its members. Most of the current divisions did not exist when I was an undergraduate psychology major, and, moreover, most divisions are related to applied work rather than academic work. In fact, as postmodernism was being proclaimed in architecture, the APA split in two in 1988, into the APA and the Association for Psychological Science (APS). As the name of the latter group implies, the divorce was between professional psychologists and academic scientists, which is why I called the APA a guild earlier. There was always tension between the professional and scientific branches of psychology. Fractionation of psychology is another reason why Xam said that psychology was impossible.

THE POSSIBILITY OF PSYCHOLOGY

Xam stopped talking. The holographic projector was turned off, and the Foundation auditorium brightened. After a pause, Xam concluded, "Yet as you see, seen through the lens of history, the impossible science became possible, even necessary! It may have no subject matter, but it's a vital part of contemporary human life." Xam was gratified at his standing ovation—the academics were waving all their claws and flippers! His new book, *The psychological ethic and the spirit of (post)modernism*, would be a success.

Science, History, and Psychology

From Chapter 1 of *A History of Psychology: From Antiquity to Modernity*, Seventh Edition.
Thomas Hardy Leahey. Copyright © 2013 by Pearson Education, Inc. All rights reserved.

Science, History, and Psychology

Plato observed that philosophy begins in wonder. Science also begins in wonder—wonder at the inner workings of nature—and all sciences, including psychology, were originally part of philosophy. Over the centuries, the special sciences gradually became independent of philosophy. Psychology was one of the last of the special sciences to separate from the parent, remaining part of philosophy until the nineteenth century. The founders of psychology were philosophers as well as psychologists, attempting to find scientific answers for many philosophical questions.

Psychology means *psyche–logos*, literally, the study of the soul, though the term was not coined until the seventeenth century and was not widely used until the nineteenth century. Philosophers and religious teachers around the world have wrestled with the nature of the soul: Does the soul exist? What is its nature? What are its functions? How is it related to the body? While psychologists resist the term *soul*, preferring the less religiously loaded term *mind*, they have continued to address these vexing questions. Even psychologists who define psychology not as the study of the mind but as the study of behavior have different answers to these questions.

Since the time of the ancient Greeks, philosophers have inquired into how human beings know the world. This enterprise is called **epistemology,** from the Greek words *episteme* (knowledge) and *logos* (discourse). Asking how human beings know the world involves questions about sensation, perception, memory, and thinking—the whole realm of what psychologists call *cognitive psychology.*

Ethics is another area shared by philosophers (and religious thinkers) and psychologists. Although ethics is centrally concerned with how people ought to act, practical ethics depends on a conception of human nature. Are people, by nature, good? What motives do people have? Which ones are wholesome and which should be repressed? Are people social by nature? Is there a common good life all humans ought to live? Such questions are profoundly psychological and can be informed by scientific research on human nature. Ethical concerns manifest themselves in many areas of psychology. In *scientific psychology*, we find them in the studies of motivation and emotion, social behavior, and sexual behavior. *Applied psychology*, whether in business, industry, government, or in individual clinical and counseling psychology,

Psychology in History
Was Mind Discovered, Invented, or Constructed?
Does Mind Exist?
Bibliography

is deeply involved in human ethics. People come to psychologists wanting to be happier or more productive, seeking the psychologist's scientifically informed help. The psychologist's knowledge of motivation, emotion, learning, and memory gives him or her tools to change behavior, but the psychologist must not be merely the client's servant. A business-consulting psychologist may need to tell a client that he or she is the problem in the company, and no ethical psychologist would teach a con artist how to improve his or her self-presentation skills. Science is traditionally value-neutral in pursuing the secrets of nature, but, as Francis Bacon said, "Knowledge is power," and the tools of the applied scientist must be rightly used.

Although the conceptual foundations of psychology are to be found in philosophy, the inspiration for the creation of an independent science of psychology came from biology. The idea that the functions philosophers and others ascribed to the mind depended on underlying processes of the brain had been fitfully entertained since the days of the Greeks but had attained the status of a conviction by the mid-nineteenth century. The founders of psychology hoped that, by taking a path to the mind through physiology, what had been speculative philosophy and religion might become naturalistic science. A younger branch of biology—evolution—also shaped the founding of scientific psychology. Especially in Britain and America, philosophers and psychologists began to ask what the mind was good for in the struggle for existence that was evolution by natural selection. Why should we be conscious at all? Were animals conscious? These new questions would disturb, yet animate, psychologists from the beginning. Therefore, we will be concerned not just with the abstract questions of philosophy, but with the growing understanding of the brain and nervous system from the Classical era to the present.

UNDERSTANDING SCIENCE

From the nineteenth century onward there has been general agreement that psychology is, or at least ought to be, a science. The nature of science—what psychology aspires to be—is a good starting point for understanding it.

The Image of Modern Science

People expect science to explain how and why the world, the mind, and the body work as they do. **Philosophy of science** tries to understand how science works (Rosenberg, 2005).

THE NEWTONIAN STYLE The modern style of scientific explanation began with Isaac Newton and the Scientific Revolution. Newton defined his scientific enterprise as the search for a small number of mathematical laws from which one could deduce observed regularities in nature. His domain was the physics of motion, which he proposed to explain in terms of three laws of motion and a law of gravity, and he showed how his laws could precisely account for the movement of the bodies in the solar system. As an example of the Newtonian style of explanation (Cohen, 1980), we will take the law of gravity: Between any two bodies there is a mutually attracting force whose strength is

XAM'S BLOG 1
Positivism

Hi, Xam here. I'll be popping in occasionally, blog-like (on Mars, *blog* is a type of cloud formation, not that we have many clouds) to connect things in the text to modernity/modernism.

Positivism was a self-consciously modern movement, and thus part of modern*ism* even before the term came into use. It began with a rather eccentric Frenchman named Auguste Comte (1798–1857) and his positive philosophy. It wasn't positive in the sense of your Earthfolks' "positive psychology," but positive in a philosophical way. His enemy was speculative philosophy that trucked with unseen things like gods and Forms, and he wanted to replace it with a philosophy based on directly observable—positive—facts (if there are such things). He saw human history as passing through three stages, the first two of which were based on speculative philosophy. During the *theological stage,* people thought that gods caused events and the natural rulers of society were thus priests, who supposedly understood the gods and could entreat or control them to human

advantage. The second stage was the metaphysical stage. People (or at least the elite) no longer believed that gods controlled the world, but did believe in unseen essences and forces that did. The natural rulers were thus kings and aristocrats—the elites—who understood these hidden Truths.

The last—modern—stage was the scientific stage. Gods and metaphysics were jettisoned for down-to-earth Newtonian science, which understood the genuine causes of events and which could therefore really deliver the goods for human welfare in a way that priests and aristocrats could only fake—to their own interest, rather than humanity's. The natural rulers would thus be scientists, specifically the scientists whose expertise was society itself—sociologists. Psychologists would count themselves in the number of the new elite. As founding psychologist James McKeen Cattell wrote, "Scientific men should take the place that is theirs as masters of the modern world" (quoted by Herman, 1996, p. 55).

inversely proportional to the square of the distance between them. Newton was criticized by his contemporaries for failing to provide any mechanism to explain how gravity worked; to them, action at a distance between two objects smacked of magic. Newton, however, replied, "*Hypotheses non fingo,*" "I do not feign [propose] hypotheses." Newton refused, in other words, to explain his principle of gravity; for him, it was sufficient to postulate a force from which one could predict the motions of the heavenly bodies.

POSITIVISM With Newton began a new philosophy for understanding nature that was later codified in an extreme form by Auguste Comte (1798–1857) and his followers, the *positivists,* who said science worked because of the Newtonian style of remaining as close as possible to the observable facts and as far as possible from hypothetical explanations. Thus the basic job of science is *description* rather than explanation. Scientists are supposed to closely observe nature, looking for regular occurrences and reliable correlations. On the basis of their observations, scientists would propose scientific *laws,* such as Newton's law of gravity. Extending Newton's reluctance to frame hypotheses, positivists understood scientific laws to be mathematical summaries of past observations rather than truths of nature.

From the first function of science, description, ideally summarized as laws, arises the second function, *prediction.* Using Newton's law of gravity and his three laws of motion, scientists could predict future events, such as eclipses and the return of comets. Finally, prediction from laws made *control* of nature possible. Using Newton's laws, engineers could calculate the thrust required to throw satellites into precise orbits around the earth and send probes to the distant planets. Knowledge, as Francis Bacon said, is power, and control was the ultimate rationale for science in the positivist's philosophy. Comte looked forward to the scientific rule of society, and the desire to apply scientific psychological expertise to Comte's project played an important role in shaping twentieth-century psychology.

Explanation

THE NOMOLOGICAL APPROACH Description, prediction, and control were the only three functions assigned to science by the first positivists. They regarded the human desire for explanations—answers to *why* questions—as a dangerous temptation to indulge in metaphysical and theological speculation. However, in 1948, the contemporary era of philosophical understanding of explanation began with the publication of "Studies in the Logic of Explanation" by two logical positivists, Carl Hempel and Paul Oppenheim. Their "epoch-making" (Salmon, 1989) paper showed a way of incorporating an explanatory function for science within the positivist framework, and, despite its age and defects, the Hempel–Oppenheim model of explanation remains the starting point for all subsequent studies of explanation in science.

Hempel and Oppenheim proposed that scientific explanations could be regarded as logical arguments in which the event to be explained, the *explanandum*, could be deduced from the *explanans*—relevant scientific laws and the observed initial conditions. So a physicist would explain a solar eclipse by showing that, given the relative position of sun, moon, and earth sometime before the eclipse, one could use Newton's laws of motion and gravity to deductively predict their arrival into an eclipse-producing alignment. Since Hempel and Oppenheim said that explanations are deductions from scientific laws, their scheme is called the *deductive-nomological* (from the Greek *nomos*, law) model of explanation. It is also called the **covering-law** model of explanation, since an explanation shows how an event is subsumed, or covered, under some set of scientific laws.

Certain features of the Hempel–Oppenheim model are important. First, it makes explicit a central and crucial feature of explanation that I will call the **Iron Law of Explanation:** *The explanandum may not be contained explicitly or implicitly in the explanans.* Violation of this rule renders an explanation null and void on grounds of circularity. An example borrowed from the French playwright Molière illustrates a circular explanation. Imagine asking "Why does Somitol make me sleepy?" and receiving the reply "Because it possesses the soporific power!" At first glance, this appears to be an explanation of one thing (sleepiness) in terms of another (soporific power), and indeed, stated forcefully in an advertisement, it might be able to pass itself off as one. However, when we learn that *soporific* means "sleep-inducing," we see that the proffered explanation is empty because it says, in effect, Somitol makes you sleepy because it makes you sleepy. The explanandum, causing sleep, was implicitly contained in the explanans, so the explanation was circular. The Iron Law is easy to violate because we often think when we have named something—the soporific power—that we have explained it. Because much of the mind cannot be observed, violating the Iron Law is especially easy in psychology. We may think we have explained why someone is shy and has few friends by calling him or her an "introvert," but all we have done is given a shorthand label to a person who is shy and has few friends. If introversion is to be a real explanation of being shy, it must be linked to something other than shy behavior, perhaps to a genetic predisposition.

A more controversial feature of the deductive-nomological model is that it sees prediction and explanation as the same thing. In the Hempel–Oppenheim model, explanation of an event consists of showing that it could have been predicted. Thus, an astronomer *predicts* an eclipse in the year 2010 but *explains* one in 1010. In each case, the procedure is the same—applying the laws of motion to the state of the sun, moon, and earth, and demonstrating the inevitability of the eclipse. However, the thesis that explanation and prediction are symmetrical runs into important problems. Consider a flagpole and its shadow (Rosenberg, 2000). If one knows the height of a flagpole and the position of the sun, one can deduce and so predict the length of the shadow from the laws governing light and the rules of geometry, and it seems reasonable to say that we have thereby explained the length of the shadow. By the same token, however, if we know the length of the shadow, we can deduce and so "predict" the height of the flagpole, but surely the length of the shadow does not explain the height of the flagpole.

THE CAUSAL APPROACH The covering-law model for scientific explanation deliberately avoids questions about the real causal structure of nature, preferring to focus instead on how we can predict and control nature. Usable knowledge need not pretend to be profound or true. Although how aspirin works is only now being understood, physicians have long prescribed it to relieve pain, inflammation, and fever. Following Newton, who refused to worry about why his laws of motion were true, positivists demand of scientific explanations only that they make successful predictions, not that they reveal why they do so. Discomfited by the shortcomings of the positivist approach, some philosophers want science to probe deeper, telling us not merely how nature works as it does, but why it works as it does.

The main rival to the positivist approach to explanation is the **causal approach** (e.g., Salmon, 1984). Its starting point is the difficulty of identifying explanation with prediction. Although we can deduce the height of a flagpole from the length of its shadow, shadows cannot *cause* anything, and so they should not be cited in explanations; in contrast, objects blocking rays from the sun *causally* cast shadows. The mere existence of a predictive regularity is not the same as a law of nature, no matter how reliable and useful the regularity may be. The generalization "When the reading on a barometer drops, a storm will occur" states a useful correlation, not a causal law of nature.

More importantly for the explanation of human behavior, we intuitively accept explanations that cite no laws at all. When in the last chapter of a murder mystery the detective unravels the crime, explaining who did it, how, and why, he or she will not invoke laws of nature. Instead, he or she will show how a series of particular, unique events led, one after the other, to the commission of murder. We feel satisfied to learn that Lord X was murdered by his son to pay his gambling debts, but there is no law of nature saying "All (or even most) sons with gambling debts will kill their fathers." Much explanation in everyday life and history is of this type, connecting events in a causal sequence without the mention of laws. Not all satisfying explanations fit the covering-law model.

From the causal perspective, the positivists' fear of falling into metaphysics and their consequent unwillingness ever to stray beyond the facts have led them to miss the point of science and to ignore important intuitions about the nature of explanation. Instead of shunning metaphysics, the causal approach embraces it, arguing that the goal of science is to penetrate the causal structure of reality and discover—not just invent—the laws of nature. Science is successful, they say, because it is more or less right about how nature works, and it gains predictive power and control from being true, not from being logically organized. Science protects itself from the positivists' bugaboo—superstition—by rigorously testing every hypothesis and challenging every theory.

Nevertheless, the causal view has its own weaknesses (Kitcher, 1989). For example, how can we ever be certain we have grasped the causal structure of the world when it lies, everyone concedes, beyond the reach of observation? Because we cannot directly verify our hunches about real causes, they might be a metaphysical luxury that ought not be indulged, no matter how tempting. The debate between the causal and epistemic accounts of scientific explanation is not over (Rosenberg, 2000).

REALISM: ARE GOOD EXPLANATIONS TRUE OR MERELY USEFUL? The difference between the nomological and causal approaches to explanation is a deep one, because they rest upon competing ideas about what science can achieve. Nomological theorists believe that all we can hope to do is describe the world as we find it; causal theorists believe we can go deeper, penetrating the hidden causal structure of the universe. In philosophy of science, this argument is known as the debate over *realism* in science.

The dispute may be historically illustrated by the late-nineteenth-century debate regarding the existence of atoms. Since the late eighteenth century, widespread acceptance had been gained by the theory that various observable phenomena such as the behavior of gases and the regularities governing the combination of chemical elements could best be explained by supposing that objects were composed of infinitesimally small particles called atoms. Yet, how to interpret the concept of atoms remained unclear. In one camp were the positivists, led in this battle by the distinguished physicist Ernst Mach (1838–1916), who argued that because atoms could not be seen, belief in their existence was faith, not science. He said atoms should be regarded at best as hypothetical fictions whose postulation made sense of data but whose existence could not be confirmed. The atomic camp was led by Russian chemist Dmitri Mendeleev (1834–1907), who believed atoms were real things whose properties and interactions explained the regularities of the periodic table he had invented.

Mendeleev's view is a *realist* view of inferred entities and processes: Behind observations lies a realm of unseen but real things about which science theorizes; observations are regarded as evidence for the underlying causal structure of the universe. Mach's positivist view is an *antirealist* view of science, regarding observations themselves as the only things science need explain. Antirealists come in agnostic and atheistic brands (Newton-Smith, 1981; Salmon, 1989). The most common form of antirealism is instrumentalism, which holds that scientific theories are merely tools—instruments—by which human beings come to grips with nature. If a theory predicts and explains events, we retain it as useful; if it fails to predict and explain, we discard it. We should ask no more of theories. At stake is the possibility of attaining truth in science. Realists say that science should strive to give us a true *picture* of the causal structure of the universe; antirealists say that science should strive to give us conceptual *tools* that enable us to deal with the universe. In short, the realist wants truth, the antirealist wants usefulness. Disagreement over realism lies at the heart of the nomological versus causal dispute about explanation, and the nature of scientific theories. Science explains the world with theories, whether they are regarded as true (the causal–realist view) or merely useful (the nomological–antirealist view). Savage (1990) identifies three broad approaches to theories, with many variations within: (1) the *syntactic view*, holding that theories are axiomatized collections of sentences; (2) the *semantic view*, holding that theories are counterfactual models of the world; and (3) a view we will call *naturalism*, holding that theories are amorphous collections of ideas, values, practices, and exemplars. From this mélange, I have chosen to discuss three issues of particular relevance to psychology. First, I will discuss the granddaddy of syntactic views, the Received View on Theories, which has greatly influenced psychology. Second, I will briefly consider the semantic view of theories as models, which will take us to the final topic of this section—theory testing. The naturalistic viewpoint will be taken up in the following section on rationality.

Theories about Scientific Theories

THE SYNTACTIC APPROACH: THEORIES ARE COLLECTIONS OF SENTENCES. At the end of the nineteenth century, the positivism of Comte and Mach was melded with advances in logic and mathematics to produce the movement called **logical positivism**, which dominated the philosophy of science for several decades. So great was its influence that it became known as the Received View on Theories (Suppe, 1977). The atomists had won the debate over the existence of atoms. The heirs to Comte and Mach, the logical positivists, therefore had to concede that, despite philosophical scruples, science could incorporate unseen, hypothetical concepts into its theories, and they attempted to show how it could be done without lapsing into the dangerous practices of metaphysics. Doing so, they set out a recipe for science that has had great influence.

Logical positivists divided the language of science into three sets of terms: *observation terms*, *theoretical terms*, and *mathematical terms*. Unsurprisingly, the logical positivists gave absolute priority to observation terms. The fundamental task of science remained description; observation terms referred to directly observable properties of nature and were taken to be unproblematically true. The bedrock of science was *protocol sentences*—descriptions of nature that contained only observation terms. Putative generalizations from the data—candidate laws of nature—were *axioms* that contained only theoretical terms connected by logico-mathematical terms.

The use of theoretical terms such as *atom* or *magnetic field* raised the issue of realism and, for logical positivists, the dangerous lure of metaphysical inference. They preserved the antirealism of earlier positivism by denying that theoretical terms referred to anything at all. Instead, theoretical terms were said to be given meaning and epistemological significance via *explicit*, or, more familiarly, *operational definitions*. Operational definitions were the third sort of sentences recognized by the logical positivists—mixed sentences containing a theoretical term and an observational term to which the theoretical term was linked. The resulting picture of science resembles a layer cake. On the bottom, representing the only reality for positivists, were observational terms; on top were purely hypothetical theoretical terms organized into axioms; in between were sandwiched the operational definitions connecting theory and data:

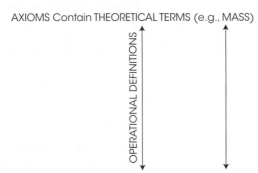

AXIOMS Contain THEORETICAL TERMS (e.g., MASS)

OPERATIONAL DEFINITIONS

PROTOCOL SENTENCES Contain OBSERVATION TERMS (e.g., WEIGHT AT SEA LEVEL)

Logical positivism's layer-cake model of scientific language.

Let us take an example from physics. An important axiom in classical physics is

$$F = M \times A$$

force equals mass times acceleration. *Force, mass*, and *acceleration* are theoretical terms. We do not observe them directly, but we must define them in terms of something we do observe—often, by some procedure—which is why operational definitions are so called. For example, mass is defined as weight of an object at sea level. Thus, in the Received View, theories are sentences (axioms) whose terms are explicitly defined by reference to observation terms. Note that, for the Received View, as for any antirealist philosophy of science, observations do not provide *evidence* for the existence and properties of inferred entities, but they *define* those entities the way a dictionary defines a word.

The Received View leads naturally to the Hempel–Oppenheim model of explanation. The laws of nature are theoretical sentences from which we logically deduce phenomena, or, more precisely, observation sentences. As we shall see, from 1930 to the 1960s psychology was greatly influenced by the ideals of logical positivism, and it remains influential through the concept of operational definition.

The Received View on Theories runs into a number of difficulties. The deepest difficulty with the Received View is its rigid separation of theory and data. Positivists always took it for granted that science was based on observation and that observation was entirely independent of theory. However, the positivist conception of perception was simplistic (Brewer & Loschky, 2005; Daston & Galison, 2007). At the very least, it's impossible to observe everything all the time; one must have some prior notion of what to observe in a given situation, some idea of which events are important and which are irrelevant, so that the significance of an event is determined by a theory. Moreover, psychologists have demonstrated how perception is influenced by people's expectations and values (Brewer & Loschky, 2005), so we know perception is never the immaculate process the positivists thought it was. Indeed, we may turn the positivist view on its head and regard the guiding of observation by theory as a virtue instead of as a sin. The point may be illustrated by a passage from the Sherlock Holmes story "Silver Blaze." We see the theoretically guided master detective triumph over the positivist policeman:

> Holmes then [descended] into the hollow, . . . [and] stretching himself upon his face and leaning his chin upon his hands he made a careful study of the trampled mud in front of him.
> "Halloa!" said he, suddenly, "what's this?" It was a wax vesta [a sort of match], half burned, which was so coated with mud that it looked at first like a little chip of wood.
> "I cannot think how I came to overlook it," said the Inspector, with an expression of annoyance.
> "It was invisible, buried in the mud. I only saw it because I was looking for it."
> "What! You expected to find it?"
> "I thought it not unlikely."

Here we see the importance of having a theory that tells investigators what to look for. Holmes found the match because he had formed a theory of the crime that led him to expect it, while the police—who had no theory—failed to find the match despite meticulous searching. To the fact-gatherer, all facts are equally meaningless and meaningful. To the theoretically guided researcher, each fact assumes its proper place in an overall framework.

THE SEMANTIC APPROACH: THEORIES ARE SIMPLIFIED MODELS OF THE WORLD The semantic approach (e.g., Suppe, 1989) builds on some highly technical developments in modern logic, but, for our purposes, the semantic approach is important for the central role it assigns to models in science, and the resulting indirect relationship between scientific theories and the world they purport to explain. The semantic approach regards theories as abstract mathematical structures that apply not to the world as it is but to an idealized world purged of irrelevant considerations.

From a theory, a scientist constructs a model of reality, a highly idealized, partial simulation of the world. It describes what the world would be like if the theory behind it were true and if the variables found in it were the only ones involved in behavior. The physical theory of particle mechanics, for example, describes a block sliding down an inclined plane as a system of three frictionless, dimensionless, point-masses—one each for the block, the plane, and the earth.

In the real world, these bodies are extended in space and there is friction between block and plane; in the model, such irrelevant or complicating factors disappear. Thus, the model is a simplified, idealized version of reality, which is all a theory can cope with. It is important to realize how limited a scientific theory is. It purports to explain only some phenomena, and only some aspects of these. A scientific theory is not about the real world as we experience it, but about abstract, idealized models.

The real world, unlike the model, is much too complex to be explained by a theory. To take a psychological example, a theory of paired associate learning describes an ideal learner as untroubled by factors such as the time of day or personal stress that surely affect the memory-performance of actual subjects. Models allow scientists to focus on and think clearly about the aspects of nature in which they are interested. To a learning theorist, while stress is a factor that surely influences learning, it is a factor to be controlled or statistically washed away. To a stress theorist, on the other hand, stress is the main concern, and he or she may use paired-associate learning as a way to study it. Each theorist will construct a model that reflects his or her theoretical concerns about the same reality—how people learn under varied conditions.

The Nature of Scientific Change

RATIONALITY: WHY AND WHEN DO SCIENTISTS CHANGE THEIR THEORIES? The ancient Greeks defined the human being as the rational animal, but this definition has become increasingly suspect (e.g., Ariely, 2008; Mele & Rawling, 2004). Science, however, is one institution that seemed to meet the Greek ideal, its success apparently proclaiming it the paragon of rationality. The issue of the rationality of science is important because rationality, like morality, is a *normative* concept. Being moral and rational is something people *ought* to be, and, over the years, philosophers have tried to establish standards of rationality to which people can be held accountable in the same way they are held accountable for moral or immoral conduct. The potential danger in abandoning standards of rationality is the same as in abandoning standards of morality: If either goes, how are we to be saved from anarchy, tyranny, and ignorance? How are we to know right from wrong and good from bad? If *science* is not rational, is anything?

Traditional philosophies of science, such as positivism and logical positivism, accepted the rationality of science and took it upon themselves to spell out the rational methodology of science in formal, logical detail. Moreover, the positivists' picture of science was *content-free*: They assumed that there is a single, logical structure to science whatever the historical period and whatever the science. Yet, the more we examine the history of science, the less it seems to be a purely rational affair following an abstract, changeless, content-free methodology. Scientists are human beings, and despite rigorous training, their perceptual and reasoning skills are subject to the same constraints and errors as other people's. Scientists are trained in and work within a community of scientists who share historically changing goals, values, and standards. In science, as in other walks of life, what seems eminently rational to one person seems like foolishness to another.

These considerations suggest that logical positivism was mistaken to look for a purely methodological account of science. Since the early 1960s, a movement in metascience (e.g., Daston & Galison, 2007) has been afoot that challenges—even denies—the assumption that science is defined by a constitutive rationality that sets it apart from other forms of human activity. Because it regards science as an institution to be examined empirically rather than dictated to philosophically, this new movement is called the *naturalistic approach* to science, and it incorporates philosophers, historians, sociologists, and psychologists of science. There are many ways of conducting a naturalistic approach to science, and in this section I will discuss two, the *Weltanschauung theorists*, led by Thomas

S. Kuhn, who have exerted direct influence on psychology in the past three decades, and theorists who regard science as a matter of intellectual *evolution* along Darwinian lines.

A NATURALISTIC APPROACH: KUHN AND PARADIGMS Thinkers who regard science as a socially constituted form of life mount the most dramatic challenge to the rational model of science. A human culture constitutes a form of life, and it shapes our perception and behavior in ways of which we are often unaware. We absorb values, practices, and ideals with little or no explicit teaching, and we take them for granted as much as we do the air we breathe. When anthropologists study a culture, they try to penetrate and describe the hidden worldview, or *Weltanschauung*, shared by its members, and to show how it works and how it changes over time. Some naturalistic students of science propose to take an anthropologist's and historian's approach to science and capture the worldviews—and revolutions in worldview—of science. Naturalistic approaches to science emerged from the field of history of science. Instead of looking at scientific theories as abstract objects, historians examine how science changes, revealing the human dimension of science.

Historian Thomas Kuhn, in his *Structure of Scientific Revolutions* (1970), gave the first and most influential expression of the Weltanschauung approach to science. Kuhn described the history of science as a repeating cycle of stages (see Figure 1) and provided an account of how scientific practice is shaped by deep assumptions of a worldview of which working scientists may be only dimly aware. One of Kuhn's innovations was to stress the social nature of science. Science is practiced by communities of scientists, not by isolated men and women. To understand working science, then, we must understand the scientific community and its shared norms, which together constitute what Kuhn called *normal science.*

For scientific research to be progressive, the scientific community in a particular research area must agree on certain basic issues. Its members must agree on the goals of their science, on the basic characteristics of the real world relevant to their subject, on what counts as a valid explanation of phenomena, and on permissible research methods and mathematical techniques. Kuhn called this agreed-on worldview a **paradigm.** Given agreement on these issues, scientists can proceed to analyze nature from a collective, unified standpoint; without such agreement, each researcher would have his or her own standpoint, and there would be much fruitless discussion at cross-purposes. Kuhn depicts a science as being like the construction of a building, requiring contributions by many hands. Cooperative effort requires that a building be constructed according to a plan and on a

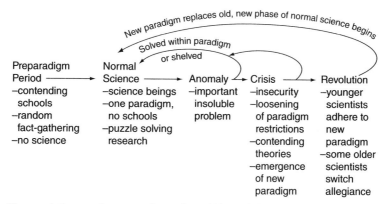

FIGURE 1 The revolutionary character of paradigm shifts and the cyclical nature of science (a schematization of Kuhn, 1970).

firm foundation. Until the blueprints and the foundation have been decided on, there can be no construction, no progress. Only when the plans are agreed on can the collective effort of construction begin. Paradigms provide the blueprints and foundations for scientific enterprises.

During periods of normal science, the blueprint is taken for granted. Experiments do not test the paradigm but are attempts to solve puzzles posed by the paradigm. If a scientist fails to solve a puzzle, the failure is the scientist's, not the paradigm's. Consider what happens in your own laboratory courses. You follow all the instructions, but the "correct" results may not occur. Nevertheless, your instructor does not conclude that existing science is wrong, but assumes that you must have erred at some point, and gives you a poor grade. This same thing occurs to scientists in normal science. The scientific community recognizes certain puzzles as ripe for solution, and—except in extraordinary circumstances—when a scientist tackles one of these problems, it is the scientist and his or her theories that are on trial, not the unstated paradigm.

Within normal science, research is progressive, as puzzle after puzzle is solved. However, Kuhn claimed that normal science is just one phase of scientific development. A paradigm is a specific historical achievement in which one or a few scientists establish a new scientific style based on an outstanding success in understanding nature. Paradigms also break down and get replaced when they cease to work well in guiding the research of a community. A science's first paradigm arises out of a prescientific phase in that science's history, and paradigms are periodically replaced during scientific revolutions.

Scientific change, according to Kuhn, is not always gradual and continuous. There are times when a science undergoes radical change in a short period of time—change so radical that those who were great individuals beforehand often become forgotten antiques, and concepts and issues that previously occupied scientists' minds simply disappear. Such change seems to constitute revolution rather than evolution and depends on principles beyond those of variation, selection, and retention. Kuhn (1959) proposed that the replacement of the ancient earth-centered cosmology of Ptolemy by the sun-centered cosmology of Copernicus constituted such a revolution, and some observers think psychology has had its own revolutions.

The picture of science drawn by Kuhn and his followers was controversial. Kuhn helped direct scholars' attention to the actual history of science, rather than to idealized versions of it. However, studies of scientific history have rendered mixed judgments on the adequacy of Kuhn's model of scientific change, especially regarding the existence of revolutions (Gutting, 1980). Some historians find little evidence that any science has ever changed in a revolutionary manner (R. Laudan, 1980), and Kuhn himself backed away from his revolutionary claims (Kuhn, 1977). On the other hand, one of the most distinguished historians of science, I. Bernard Cohen (1985), elaborated on Kuhn's theme through close case studies of successful, unsuccessful, real, and purported revolutions in science. The adequacy of Kuhn's specific historical model is unresolved, but he established without doubt that the study of science must incorporate historical, social, and personal influences lying outside scientific methodology.

A METHODOLOGICAL APPROACH: POPPER AND FALSIFICATIONISM. Philosophers who regard science as the definitively rational enterprise find naturalism distressing. The most influential critique of naturalism has come from Sir Karl Popper (1902–1994). Popper's philosophy of science is especially interesting because it tackles the question of how science changes from a normative rather than historical point of view. Popper wanted to know when scientists *ought* to change their theories (Popper, 1963).

When Popper was a young man in Vienna, he encountered many theories claiming to be scientific, including relativity theory and psychoanalysis. Popper wanted to know which theories to take seriously as science and which to dismiss as nonsense masquerading as science. He approached the problem by examining clear-cut cases of science, such as Newtonian physics, and clear-cut cases of pseudoscience, such as astrology, trying to figure out the difference between them. Positivists stressed the confirmability of theories as the test of their scientific status. That is, from a theory with properly worked-out operational definitions, we can deduce predictions whose confirmation lends credence to the theory. Pseudoscientific or metaphysical theories will not be able to operationally define their terms and so will not be able to derive predictions of events and support their claims. Good theories pile up confirmations; poor ones do not.

Popper rejected that view as naive. Pseudosciences claim many confirmations. The astrologer can point to predictions verified—raises awarded, girlfriends won—and can defend failed predictions by employing escape clauses such as neglected influences from minor planets. Nor did confirmability help with the uncertain cases, such as relativity or psychoanalysis; both could claim confirmation of their theories time after time.

In fact, by listening to psychoanalysts and comparing them to Einstein, Popper was led to formulate his **demarcation criterion,** a rule for telling real science from fake science. Popper discovered that no matter what difficulties a case seemed to raise for psychoanalysis, a good analyst, like a good astrologer, could always reinterpret it to fit analytic theory. At the same time, shortly after World War I, an expedition was mounted to test one of relativity's predictions— that light bends in the presence of a gravitational field. From photographs of stars near the edge of the sun, taken during a total eclipse, astronomers found that light rays were bent as Einstein's theory required. Although at first glance this successful test appeared consistent with the logical positivists' confirmation requirement, Popper found in it a decisive difference between relativity and psychoanalysis: Both could claim confirmation of their theory, but only relativity risked *falsification.* The important thing about Einstein's prediction was not that it might prove true, but that it might prove false. Had starlight not bent around the sun, Einstein's theory would have been in trouble. In contrast, psychoanalysis—like astrology—could readily explain everything. In other words, according to Popper, scientific rationality consists not in seeking to be proved right but in allowing for the possibility of being proved wrong—in sticking one's neck out and risking one's theory being beheaded by a fact.

Attractive as it is as a simple rule, Popper's demarcation criterion of falsifiability runs into two difficulties. First, theories are never defeated by single, decisive experiments; and second, theories compete with each other as well as with nature. Single experiments cannot decide the fate of a theory because every experiment is based on certain methodological assumptions that have nothing to do with the theory itself. Any single experiment may be flawed by choosing the wrong apparatus, sampling the wrong subjects, mishandling the statistical methods, or making some other mistake. In short, the truth of a theory may almost always be defended against falsified data by attacking the validity of those data. Additionally, Popper assumed that science was a two-sided contest between a theory and the world, but possession of a theory is so important that scientists prefer having a poor theory to having none at all. Scientific research is not a two-sided contest between a theory and the world, but a three-sided contest among two rival theories and the world.

Popper's followers have tried to refine Popper's rule (Lakatos, 1970). The criterion developed by Lakatos and, following him, by Larry Laudan (1977) is *problem-solving success.* They regard science as primarily a problem-solving—or, as Kuhn would say, puzzle- and anomaly-solving—enterprise that fails or succeeds over time rather than in a single decisive test. Theories that solve problems are scientific; those that repeatedly fail or need to protect themselves from falsification by ad-hoc fixes and evasive maneuvers are pseudoscientific. Modern falsificationism applies evolutionary logic to science. Sciences change over time as bad ideas are weeded out and more adaptive ones survive.

REDUCTION AND REPLACEMENT   When two theories clash over their ability to explain the same phenomena, there are two possible outcomes. The first is **reduction.** It may be that the two theories explain the same facts at different levels: Higher levels deal with large objects and forces, lower levels deal with more basic objects and forces. In their attempt to get a unified picture of nature, scientists try to reduce larger theories to more elementary—more basic—theories, showing that the truth of the higher theory is a consequence of the truth of the more basic theory. The reduced theory is still considered valid and useful at its level of explanation. The second possibility is **replacement** or elimination. One of the theories is right; the other is wrong, and it is discarded.

Reduction of a higher-level theory by another can be illustrated by the reduction of the classical gas laws to the kinetic theory of gases and the reduction of Mendelian genetics to molecular genetics. Physicists in the eighteenth century determined that the pressure, volume, and temperature of gases were interrelated by a mathematical equation called the *ideal gas law: $P = V \times T$.* Using this law—a paradigmatic example of a covering law—physicists could describe, predict, control, and explain the behavior of gases in precise and useful ways. The classical gas laws are an example of a high-level theory because they describe the behavior of complex objects, namely gases. One of the early triumphs of the atomic hypothesis was the kinetic theory of gases, which gave a causal explanation of the ideal gas law. The kinetic theory held that gases (like everything else) were made up of billiard-ball-like atoms, whose degree of excitation—movement—was a function of energy, particularly heat. The ideal gas law predicted, for example, that if we heat the air in a balloon it will expand, and if we cool the air it will deflate (placed in liquid nitrogen, it deflates to nothing). The kinetic theory explains why. As we heat air, the particles that compose it move around more, bouncing into the skin of the balloon, pushing it outward in expansion. As we cool air, the atoms slow down, striking the balloon's skin less vigorously, and if they slow down enough, exert no pressure at all.

Kinetic theory is a lower-level theory than the gas laws because it deals with the constituent particles of which gases are composed. It is also a more basic theory than the gas law theory because it is more general, accounting for the behavior of any object, not just gases, made up of molecules. The behavior of gases emerges as a special case of the behavior of all matter. The kinetic theory shows why the ideal gas law works by postulating an underlying causal mechanism, and so it is said that the ideal gas law is *reduced* to the kinetic theory. In principle, we could do away with the gas law, but we keep it as valid and useful in its range of application. It is still a scientific theory, but it has been unified with a broader conception of the universe.

A similar story can be told about Mendelian genetics. Mendel proposed the existence of a unit of hereditary transmission, the *gene*, which was entirely hypothetical. Mendel's concept provided the basis for population genetics, but no one ever saw a gene or knew what one might look like. However, in the early 1950s, the structure of DNA began to be unraveled, and it emerged that it was the bearer of hereditary traits. As molecular genetics has progressed, we have learned that coding sequences on the DNA model are the real "genes," and they do not always behave in the simple ways that Mendel thought. Nevertheless, Mendelian genetics remains valid for its purposes—population genetics—but, like the ideal gas law, has been reduced to and unified with molecular genetics.

In the case of reduction, the older theory is recognized as still scientific and usefully valid within its sphere of application; it simply takes a subsidiary place in the grand scheme of science. The fate of a replaced theory, on the other hand, is very different. Often, it turns out that an old theory is simply wrong and cannot be woven into the extending tapestry of scientific theory. In this case, it is abandoned and replaced by a better theory. The Ptolemaic theory of the heavens, which placed the earth at the center of the universe and described the sun, moon, and stars as revolving in complex and unlikely circles around it, was accepted by astronomers for centuries because it gave a usefully precise account of the motions of heavenly objects. Using it, they could describe, predict, and explain events such as eclipses. Despite its descriptive and predictive powers, after a long struggle the Ptolemaic view was shown to be hopelessly wrong, and it was replaced with the Copernican system, which placed the sun at the center with the rest of the solar system revolving around it. Like an old paradigm, the Ptolemaic view died off, eliminated from science.

The question of reduction or replacement is especially important in psychology (Schouten & Looren de Jong, 2007). By taking the path through physiology, psychologists tried to link psychological processes to physiological processes. But if we have a theory of some psychological process and in fact discover the underlying physiological process, will the psychological theory be reduced or replaced? Some observers believe that psychology is fated to disappear like Ptolemaic astronomy. Others hold that psychology will be reduced to physiology, becoming an outpost of biology, but some optimists among them think that at least some of human psychology can be neither reduced nor replaced by neurophysiology. We shall find that the relation of psychology to physiology has been an uneasy one.

Science as a Worldview

PARTICULAR AND UNIVERSAL KNOWLEDGE   Our everyday concerns and everyday knowledge focus on particular people, places, things, and events. In an election, for example, we gather facts about specific issues and candidates in order to decide for whom to vote. As times change, issues and candidates come and go, and we learn new facts specific to new problems and proposed solutions. In everyday life, we need to get along with particular people and we build up knowledge about them

---

XAM'S BLOG 2
What Kind of a Science Is Psychology?

One of the odd things I discovered about psychology is that people aren't sure where to put it in various classification schemes of the sciences. In most of your colleges and universities, psychology is lumped with the "social sciences," although occasionally it's called a "life science" put in with biology. In a few places it's broken up into pieces, so that, for example, there will be a department of cognitive sciences housing that part of psychology while other parts are put elsewhere. Similarly, although most graduate programs in clinical psychology are in psychology departments, sometimes they are in medical schools along with psychiatry, and counseling programs are often found in schools of education.

Libraries tell another tale. Librarians like to classify books in systematic ways, and they treat psychology differently from university department structures. Thus if a library uses the Library of Congress system, most of psychology is in the BF section, which is part of the larger B classification comprising philosophy, while a few books are in the Qs with science, the RCs with psychiatry, or the LBs in education. Psychology books are never (as far as I could tell) found in the social science, H, section. Moreover, if one picks up a book dealing with methods and theory in the social sciences, one frequently finds nothing about psychology at all! Indeed, at least one author, Peter Manicas (2006), explicitly denied that psychology is a social science, although he included it in an earlier book, Manicas (1987). This is the sort of thing that makes me wonder if there is a subject matter for all of psychology—it just doesn't fit in anywhere!

as we do about particular things and events. We seek knowledge that is useful for our immediate, practical purposes.

Science, however, seeks to answer universal questions that are true for all times and all places. Thus, physics can tell us what an electron is, and it does not matter if the electron exists in my thumb today, whether it's in the star system Tau Ceti, whether it existed in the first six minutes after the Big Bang, or exists millions of years from now. Similarly, physics seeks to characterize forces like gravity that operate all over the universe and throughout all time.

While different from practical human knowledge, science is not unique in seeking universal truths. Mathematics and geometry also seek universal truths, such as the Pythagorean Theorem, that are true regardless of time and space. Sometimes—but not always and rarely at present—philosophy has been defined as a search for universal truths. And some religions—especially the proselytizing world religions such as Christianity and Islam—claim to be true for all people.

Science differs from mathematics, philosophy, or religion by doing something that at first seems paradoxical, basing its search for universal truths on the observations of particular things and events. Mathematics' search for universal truths is based on the notion of formal proof, in which a conclusion is shown to follow ineluctably from some premises. But mathematical proofs are not proofs about the world, because one may choose different premises and create fantastic but consistent alternative mathematical systems. Religions' claims to universality rest upon revelation from God, not observation or logical proof.

Only science starts by observing particular things and events but moves to asserting general hypotheses about the nature of the world. Thus, psychologists performing an attribution experiment on attitudes about Fidel Castro did not care about Castro, or what their subjects believed about Castro, or how to change peoples' attitudes on Castro. They were trying to formulate a general theory about how people explain behavior, whatever that behavior might be: whether it's a political attitude, speculation about a friend's odd mental state, or why you think you did badly on your last math test. The goal of psychological research is to carefully study human behavior across such a wide range of circumstances that the circumstances fall away, revealing the universal mechanisms of human mind and behavior. Because science is concerned to achieve universal knowledge, apart from human thoughts and needs, the viewpoint of science is the *View from Nowhere*.

SCIENCE AS THE VIEW FROM NOWHERE   This is perhaps the oddest and most daunting part of natural science, yet it is also what has given science its purity, rigor, and power. Science searches for purely objective knowledge, for a description of the world in which people play no part at all; knowledge that has no point of view. The philosopher Thomas Nagel describes this viewpoint-that-is-not-a-viewpoint of natural science—the physical conception of objectivity—in his *The View from Nowhere* (1986):

> The development [of the view from nowhere] goes in stages, each of which gives us a more objective picture than the one before. The first step is to see that our perceptions are caused by the actions of things on us, through their effects on our bodies, which are themselves part of the physical world. The next step is to realize that since the same physical properties that cause perceptions in us through our bodies also produce different effects on other physical things and can exist without causing any perceptions at all, their true nature must be detachable from their physical appearance and need not resemble it. The third step is to try to form a conception of that true nature independent of its appearance either to us or to other types of perceivers. This means not only not thinking of the physical world from our own particular point of view, but not thinking of it from a more general human perceptual point of view

either: not thinking of how it looks, feels, smells, tastes, or sounds. These secondary qualities then drop out of our picture of the external world, and the underlying primary qualities such as size, shape, weight, and motion are thought of structurally.

This has turned out to be an extremely fruitful strategy, [making science possible]. . . . Our senses provide the evidence from which we start, but the detached character of this understanding is such that we could possess it even if we had none of our present senses, so long as we were rational and could understand the mathematical and formal properties of the objective conception of the physical world. We might even in a sense share an understanding of physics with other creatures to whom things appeared quite different, perceptually—so long as they too were rational and numerate.

The world described by this objective conception is not just centerless; it is also in a sense featureless. While the things in it have properties, none of these properties are perceptual aspects. All of those have been relegated to the mind. . . . The physical world as it is supposed to be in itself contains no points of view and nothing that can appear only to a particular point of view. (pp. 14–15)

The most important historical source of science's view from nowhere was the Cartesian conception of consciousness and its relation to the world. Descartes, in common with other early scientists, drew a radical division between consciousness (which Descartes identified with the soul) and the material world. Consciousness is subjective; it is the perspective from which each of us observes the world; it is how the world appears to me, to each of us in his or her private, subjective consciousness. Science describes the world with the soul—consciousness and subjectivity—subtracted. Science describes the natural world as it is from no perspective, as if there were no people in it at all: It is the view from nowhere.

This view from nowhere may seem strange and bizarre, but all the other special characteristics that we associate with science follow from it. Quantified measurement eliminates any one observer's or theoretician's point of view. Careful checking of papers by peers purges the originating scientist's point of view. Replicating experiments guarantees that what is true for one scientist is true for all. Proposing universal laws holding throughout the universe purges even the generic human point of view, because the same knowledge could be found by other species. The view from nowhere is critical to the success of natural science, but its applicability to the study of human beings is contentious.

UNDERSTANDING HISTORY

History of Science

The most general problem in writing history, especially scientific history, is the tension between reasons and causes in explaining human action. Imagine the investigation of a murder. The police first determine the *cause* of death; that is, they must find out what physical process (e.g., the ingestion of arsenic) caused the victim to die. Then investigators must determine the **reason** for the victim's death. They might discover that the victim's husband was having an affair with his secretary, had taken out an insurance policy on his wife, and had bought two air tickets to Rio—suggesting that the husband killed his wife in order to live in luxury with his mistress. Any given historical event may be explained in either or both of two ways, as a series of physical **causes** or of reasons. In our example, the series of physical causes is: placement of the arsenic in coffee, its ingestion by the victim, and its effect on the nervous system. The series of reasons, of rational acts carried out with intention and foresight, is: purchasing arsenic, putting it in one's intended victim's drink, setting up an alibi, and planning an escape.

Tension arises between rational and causal accounts of human action when it is unclear how much explanatory force to attribute to each. So far in our example, the causal story is relatively trivial, because we know the cause of death and fixing the guilt seems clear. However, causal considerations may enter into our evaluations of an actor's behavior. During his first term, President Ronald Reagan was shot and wounded by a young man, John Hinckley. There was no doubt that Hinckley fired the bullet and was thereby part of the cause of Reagan's wound, but there were serious doubts about whether Hinckley's act could be explained rationally. The reason given for his attack on the president was to win the love of actress Jodie Foster, but this reason seems strange, certainly stranger than murdering one's wife to run off with one's mistress. Moreover, psychiatrists offered testimony that Hinckley was psychotic: Tests showed he had abnormal brain scans. Taken together, such evidence convinced the jury that Hinckley's shooting of the president had no reasons, only causes involving Hinckley's diseased brain. Thus, he was found not guilty because where there is no reason there can be no guilt. In cases such as John Hinckley's, we feel the tension between rational and causal explanation at its highest pitch. We want to condemn a proven criminal, but we know we may only direct moral outrage at someone who chose a particular act when he or she could have done otherwise. We recognize that a person with a diseased brain cannot choose what to do and so deserves no blame.

In fact, the tension between reasons and causes arises in explaining every human action. Caesar's crossing the Rubicon (A. K. Goldsworthy, 2008) may be described either as a shrewd political move or as a result of his megalomaniacal ambitions to rule the world. One may choose to major in premed because of a desire to help people, or to make money, or because of an unconscious, neurotic need to show that one is just as good as one's older sibling.

In history of science, the tension between reasons and causes is perennial. As we have seen, science is often presented as an ideally rational enterprise. Scientific theories are supposed to be proposed, tested, accepted, or rejected on rational grounds alone. Yet, as Kuhn and others have amply shown, it is impossible to exempt scientists from the causal forces that play a part in determining human behavior. Scientists crave fame, fortune, and love as much as anyone else, and they may choose one hypothesis over another, one line of research among many, because of inner personal causes or outer sociological causes that cannot be rationally defended and may even be entirely unconscious. In every instance, the historian, including the historian of science, must consider both reasons and causes, weighing both the rational merits of a scientific idea and the causes that may have contributed to its proposal—and to its acceptance or rejection.

Traditionally, history of science has tended to overestimate reasons, producing *Whig* history and *presentism*. These failings are shared by other branches of history, too, but are most tempting to the historian of science. A Whig account of history sees history as a series of progressive steps leading up to our current state of enlightenment. A Whig history of science assumes that present-day science is essentially correct, or at least superior to that of the past, and tells the story of science in terms of how brilliant scientists discovered the truth known to us today. Error is condemned in a Whig account as an aberration of reason, and scientists whose ideas do not conform to present wisdom are either ignored or dismissed as fools.

Whig history is comforting to scientists and therefore is inevitably found in scientific textbooks. However, Whig history is fairy-tale history and is increasingly being supplanted by more adequate history of science, at least among professional historians of science. Unfortunately, because it shows scientists as human beings and science as, upon occasion, irrationally influenced by social and personal causes, good history of science is sometimes seen by practicing scientists as undermining the norms of their discipline, and therefore as dangerous. A large-scale, historical survey must be, to some degree, presentist—that is, concerned with how psychology got to be the way it is. This is not because I think psychology today is for the best, as a Whig historian would, but because I wish to use history to understand psychology's current condition.

An important dimension in history of science is *internalism–externalism.* Whig histories of science are typically internalist, seeing science as a self-contained discipline solving well-defined problems by rational use of the scientific method, unaffected by whatever social changes may be occurring at the same time. An internal history of science could be written with few references to kings and presidents, wars and revolutions, economics and social structure. Recent history of science recognizes that, although scientists might wish to be free of influence by society and social change, they cannot. Science is a social institution with particular needs and goals within the larger society, and scientists are human beings socialized within a given culture and striving for success within a certain social setting. Recent history of science therefore tends to be externalist in orientation, considering science within the larger social context of which it is a part and within which it acts.

An old historical dispute, tied up with reasons versus causes, Whig versus new history of science, and internalism versus externalism, is the dispute between those who see Great Men as the makers of history (Great Man View), and those who see history made by large, impersonal forces outside human control. In the latter *Zeitgeist* (German for "spirit of the times") view of history, people are sometimes depicted as little more than puppets.

The Great Man View was eloquently stated by the English writer Thomas Carlyle (1795–1881):

> For, as I take it, Universal History, the history of what man has accomplished in this world, is at bottom the History of the Great Men who have worked here. They were the leaders of men, these great ones; the modellers, patterns, and in a wide sense creators, of whatsoever the general mass of men contrived to do or attain; all things that we see standing accomplished in the world are properly the outer material result, the practical realization and embodiment, of Thoughts that dwelt in the Great Men sent into the world: the soul of the world's history, it may justly be considered, were the history of these. (1841/1966, p. 1)

Great Man history is stirring, for it tells of individual struggle and triumph. In science, Great Man history is the story of the research and theorizing of brilliant scientists unlocking the secrets of nature. Because Great Men are revered by later ages for their accomplishments, Great Man history is usually Whiggish and internalist, precisely because it stresses rationality and success, downplaying cultural and social causes of human thought and action.

The opposing view was first proposed by the German philosopher Georg Wilhelm Friedrich Hegel (1770–1831):

> [O]nly the study of world history itself can show that it has proceeded rationally, that it represents the rationally necessary course of the World Spirit, the Spirit whose nature is indeed always one and the same, but whose nature unfolds in the course of the world. . . . [W]orld history goes on in the realm of the Spirit. . . . Spirit, and the course of its development, is the substance of history. (1837/1953, p. 12)

Zeitgeist history tends to ignore the actions of human beings, because people are believed to be living preordained lives controlled by hidden forces working themselves out through historical process. In Hegel's original formulation, the hidden force was the Absolute Spirit (often identified with God) developing through human history. Hegel's Spirit has gone out of fashion, but Zeitgeist histories remain. Hegel's student, Karl Marx, materialized Hegel's Spirit into economics and saw human history as the development of modes of economic production. Kuhn's model of scientific history is a Zeitgeist model because it posits an entity, the paradigm that controls the research and theorizing of working scientists.

Because of its emphasis on the inevitability of progress, the Zeitgeist conception of history is Whiggish from Hegel's or Marx's perspective. Both Hegel and Marx saw human history directed toward some final end—the ultimate realization of the Spirit or God, or the ultimate achievement of socialism, the perfect economic order—and both viewed historical development as a rational process. Their history is not, however, internalist, because it places the determination of history outside the actions of men and women. The contribution of Hegel and Marx was in inventing externalism, directing historians' attention to the larger context in which people work, discovering that the context of action shapes action in ways at best dimly seen by historical actors themselves. Taking this broad perspective, externalism provides a greater understanding of history. However, contrary to Hegel or Marx, history has no discernible direction. The history of the world, or of psychology, could have been other than it has been. We humans struggle in a semidarkness of social and personal causes, not as puppets of impersonal forces.

Historiography of Psychology

The history and methodology of the field of history are called *historiography*. The historiography of science—of which history of psychology is a part—has passed through two stages (Brush, 1974). In the earlier stage, from the nineteenth century until the 1950s, history of science was mostly written by scientists themselves—typically, older scientists no longer active at the forefront of research. This is not surprising, because one of the special difficulties of writing history of science is that one must be able to understand the details of scientific theory and research in order to chronicle its story. However, beginning in the 1950s, and gaining momentum in the 1960s, a "new" history of science emerged as the field was professionalized. History of science was taken over by men and women trained as historians, although in many cases they had scientific backgrounds; Thomas S. Kuhn, for example, had been a chemist.

History of psychology underwent the same change, although a little later and still incompletely. The classic "old" history of psychology is Edwin G. Boring's magisterial *History of Experimental Psychology*, published first in 1929, with a revised edition in 1950. Boring was a psychologist, a student of introspectionist E. B. Titchener, and the psychology that Boring knew was being superseded by behaviorism and the rise of applied psychology. So, while Boring was by no means retired, he wrote his *History* as an internalist, Whiggish justification of his tradition (O'Donnel, 1979). Boring's book was the standard text for decades, but, beginning in the mid-1960s, the new, professional history of psychology began to replace the old. In 1965, a specialized journal appeared, *Journal of the History of the Behavioral Sciences*, and the American Psychological Association approved formation of a Division (26) for the history of psychology. In 1967, the first graduate program in history of psychology was begun at the University of New Hampshire, under the direction of Robert I. Watson, founder of the *Journal* (Furomoto, 1989; Watson, 1975). The development of the "new history of psychology" gathered steam in the 1970s and 1980s, until, in 1988, Laurel Furomoto could declare it fully matured and demanded its incorporation into the psychological curriculum. We should note that the change is incomplete. Although the text you are reading is one of the few to be influenced by the new history of psychology (Furomoto, 1989), I am a psychologist with no training in history. Today, an emerging niche is the psychologist-historian, who brings historical expertise to bear on psychological issues and policies (Vaughn-Blount, Rutherford, Baker, & Johnson, 2009).

Much more than who writes it is involved in the change from the old history of science (and psychology) to the new. This change coincides with a longer-term movement in historiography from "old history" to "new history" (Furomoto, 1989; Himmelfarb, 1987; Lovett, 2006). "Old history" was "history from above"; it was primarily political, diplomatic, and military, concentrating on great people and great events. Its form was the narrative, telling readable stories—frequently written for a broadly educated public, not just other historians—of nations, men, and women. **"New history"** is history from below; it attempts to describe, even re-create in words, the intimate lives of the anonymous mass of people neglected by the old history. As Peter Stearns has put it, "When the history of menarche is widely recognized as equal in importance to the history of monarchy, we [new historians] will have arrived" (quoted by Himmelfarb, 1987, p. 13). Its form is analytic rather than narrative, often incorporating statistics and analytic techniques borrowed from sociology, psychology, and other social sciences.

The new history of psychology is described by Furomoto (1989):

> The new history tends to be critical rather than ceremonial, contextual rather than simply the history of ideas, and more inclusive, going beyond the study of "great men." The new history utilizes primary sources and archival documents rather than relying on secondary sources, which can lead to the passing down of anecdotes and myths from one generation of textbook writers to the next. And finally, the new history tries to get inside the thought of a period to see issues as they appeared at the time, instead of looking for antecedents of current ideas or writing history backwards from the present context of the field. (p. 16)

Nevertheless, apart from its call for greater inclusiveness in writing history, Furomoto's description of the new history of psychology actually describes good traditional history as well.

I feel the greatest affinity for the traditional history of ideas and have not generally sought to find the causes of psychology's development in the biographies of psychologists. I believe that history is a humanity, not a science, and that when historians lean on the social sciences, they are leaning on weak reeds. I agree with Matthew Arnold that the humanities should concern themselves with the best (and most important) that has been said and done. Finally, I agree with English historian G. R. Elton that history "can instruct in the use of reason." I have tried, then, to write as narrative a history as the material allows, focusing on the leading ideas in psychological thought and aiming to instruct the young psychologist in the use of reason in psychology. A central question confronting the history of psychology—psyche-logos, the study of the soul—is the nature of the soul or mind. Does the mind exist the way atoms exist, a thing awaiting discovery, or does mind exist the way money exists, a thing constructed by humans?

Psychology in History

WAS MIND DISCOVERED, INVENTED, OR CONSTRUCTED? In 1953, the German philologist Bruno Snell published *The Discovery of the Mind: The Greek Origins of European Thought*, and his preface exemplifies the difficulties of defining the mind as an object. Despite the bold thesis proclaimed by his title, Snell was not entirely sure that the Greeks had actually discovered something that already existed. Although he asserted that "the rise of thinking among the Greeks [after Homer] was nothing less than a revolution. . . . They discovered the human mind," he hedged his claim by writing that the Greek discovery "cannot be compared with the discovery of, let us say, a new continent" (Snell, 1953, p. v). Snell wrestled with possibilities that have since loomed large in psychological metatheory. He specifically rejected the possibility (now espoused by some in cognitive science that the mind might be an artifact [see later]). The mind, Snell wrote, "was not invented, as a man would invent a tool . . . to master a certain type of problem. As a rule, inventions are arbitrarily determined; they are adapted to the purpose from which they take their cue. No objectives, no aims were involved in the discovery of the intellect" (p. viii). Snell also perceived but did not fully articulate the conception of mind favored by today's constructivists. He wrote, "[I]n spite of our statement that the Greeks discovered the intellect, we also assert that the discovery was necessary for the intellect to come into existence" (p. viii), hinting that the mind was socially constructed by Greek philosophers, poets, and dramatists during the Classical Age.

The three alternatives raised by Snell create different conceptions of the discipline of psychology and of its history. If the mind was truly discovered (or awaits discovery), then psychology, psyche-logos—the study of the soul—might be a natural science in the usual sense of the term, and its history will be similar to histories of physics and chemistry. The second possibility, that mind is a tool, an artifact, suggests that while minds exist as do hammers and modems, psychological science must be reconceived as a science of the artificial (H. Simon, 1980). Natural science concerns itself with spatiotemporal universals, objects such as electrons or quarks that are the same everywhere and everywhen. Hammers and modems are real, but as human artifacts, they do not fall under the purview of natural science. Science explains how hammers and modems work, but hammers and modems are objects of engineering, not science.

Mind as artifact shades over into the third possibility—mind as social construction. If mind is socially constructed, then it is uncertain whether there can be any science (as science is usually understood) of mind. Perhaps the study of mind is a historical, not a scientific, undertaking. As Snell (1953) remarks, "The intellect, however, comes into the world, it is 'effected,' in the process of revealing itself, i.e. in the course of history" (pp. vi–vii). Furthermore, the constructivist thesis gives rise to a darker prospect for scientific psychology. On the artifact interpretation, minds are real but lack the universality of the proper objects of science. In contrast, mind might be a social construction along the lines of the Greek gods, a profound illusion. If these social constructivist formulations of mind are correct, a history of psychology is not a history of discovery, but is a history of invention and construction, indeed a history of mind itself. If so, then the story of mind we tell in the West might be different from that told in other cultures.

Psychologists tend to take for granted the Western tradition descended from the Greeks that is traced by Snell. But other cultures have very different views of mind and self. For example, in *Selfless Selves*, Steven Collins (1982) discusses mind and personality as conceived by Theravada Buddhism. Collins, with anthropologist Clifford Geertz, agrees that the Western notion of mind, or person, is "a rather peculiar idea within the context of the world's cultures" (p. 2).

The Buddhist monk Nyanatiloka contrasts Buddhist and Western conceptions of mind (Collins, 1982):

[T]here are three teachers in the world. The first teacher teaches the existence of an eternal ego-entity outlasting death: that is the Eternalist, as for example the Christian. The second teacher teaches a temporary ego-entity which becomes annihilated at death: that is the annihilationist, or materialist. The third teacher teaches neither an eternal nor a temporary ego-entity: that is the Buddha. The Buddha teaches that what we call ego, self, soul, personality, etc., are merely conventional terms not referring to any real independent entity. And he teaches that there is only to be found this psychophysical process of existence changing from moment to moment. . . . This doctrine of egolessness of existence forms the essence of the Buddha's doctrine of emancipation. Thus with this doctrine of egolessness, or anatta, stands or falls the entire Buddhist structure. (p. 5)

Moreover, Theravada Buddhists regard the self—the mind—as a dangerous illusion from which we should free ourselves. According to the Sinhalese monk Rahula, "the idea of self is an imaginary, false belief which has no corresponding reality, and it produces harmful thoughts of 'me' and 'mine,' selfish desire, craving, attachment, hatred, ill-will, conceit, pride, egotism, and other defilements, impurities and problems. . . . In short, to this false view can be traced all the evil in the world" (Collins, 1982, p. 4). For Buddhists, it appears, psychology is the study of a no-thing, a misbegotten enterprise.

A third book title, *The Discovery of the Individual 1050–1200* (C. Morris, 1972), reminds us that more than the scientific character of psychology is at stake in the existence of mind, because possession of mind is strongly linked to personhood. In the West today, we assign supreme importance to the individual human being, bearer of inalienable rights against the state and other humans. As Morris says, "The hard core of this individualism lies in the psychological experience . . . [of] the sense of a clear distinction between my self and other people" (p. 3). Traditionally, a human being is treated as a person who transcends animal status by virtue of possessing a soul, or mind. Even in nonreligious contexts, possession of a mind is critical to one's status as a person and a citizen. A human in a persistent vegetative state may be ruled without a mind, and therefore may be deliberately allowed to die, and the death is not regarded as murder. A human being with dementia—literally, de-minded—may be stripped of civil rights and assigned a guardian or consigned to an institution. In psychology, questions of personhood manifest themselves in the study of the *self*, a less-religious term than *soul* and a more personal one than *mind*.

Western conceptions of mind began in religion before moving first to philosophy and then to science. Although there are differences in detail, religions around the world have a remarkably concordant picture of the mind, positing the existence of two immaterial souls for two distinct reasons (Onians, 1951). The first, universal, reason, is to explain the difference between living and nonliving things. Objects with souls are living; those without are nonliving. The second, less universal, reason is to explain human personality. Some religions propose that in addition to the breath of life, there is a soul that constitutes the essence of each person's personality, and sometimes this personal soul was believed to be able to survive the death of the material body, though this was not guaranteed. Christianity and Islam, for example, teach that each human being is composed of a material body and a nonmaterial soul. The soul is said to be the essence of the person, containing personal memories and personal identity. Moreover, while the body is mortal, the soul is immortal, leaving the body at death and traveling to an afterlife in Heaven or Hell.

For two reasons, psychologists have underestimated the influence of religious ideas of the soul—the *psyche* of our science—on conceptions of mind and self. First, psychology is an aggressively secular enterprise, and psychologists like to think that they put religion behind them when they assume their role as scientists. A more subtle reason concerns the dominance of historical scholarship by Christian belief. When we as psychologists read about past thinkers such as Plato and Descartes, not only do we look at them as proto-psychologists, we see them through the eyes of historians and classicists who until recently worked within a quietly but univocally held Christian framework. That framework rarely intrudes explicitly, but it filters out the rough splinters, odd conceptions, and obscure but vital disputes concerning mind and soul held from Greek times through at least Descartes. Thus, we psychologists inherit a conception of the mind subtly shaped by forces of which we know little, drain it of its specifically supernatural content (e.g., survival of bodily death), and fancy that what remains is somehow natural, and therefore a proper object of science. I will try briefly to put back some of the lost splinters, conceptions, and disputes to provide a ground against which to see the figure of mind as an object of psychological science.

DOES MIND EXIST? If "minds" are not enduring and unchanging things akin to electrons, then minds are artifacts, either naturally or socially constructed.

Mind as Natural Construction. When Snell (1953) wrote that mind "was not invented, as a man would invent a tool" he missed or passed over the possibility that mind was "invented" by nature as an adaptation to the Darwinian purpose of surviving the struggle for existence. Although psychologists since the mid-nineteenth century have asked what the mind is good for, it has only been in the last 25 years or so that genuine Darwinian analysis has been applied to the evolution and functioning of animal and human minds. In an evolutionary view, minds are spatiotemporally local adaptations to prevailing selection pressures. That is, like opposable thumbs or binocular vision, minds are solutions to problems of survival and reproduction prevailing at particular times in a particular ecosystem. Minds are therefore natural constructions, and real, but do not have fixed natures, as do electrons. The study of minds is therefore more similar to engineering—the discipline devoted to solving particular problems—than it is to science—the discipline of finding the laws that govern nature in all times and all places.

Mind as Social Construction. The idea that mind is a social construction seems at first glance to rule out the possibility that mind is a legitimate object of science. If mind is not a permanent and unchanging feature of the world, it might be a myth science should ignore, as it ignores Zeus or phlogiston, and it might be a concept just as doomed as they. However, being a social construction does not entail that something cannot be an object of science (J. R. Searle, 1995).

A good example of a social construction around which a science has been organized is money. Money is spatiotemporally local. The first coins were issued in the Near East around 700 B.C.E., and coins did not come into widespread circulation in the West until the Hellenistic period. For centuries, the value of money was tied to the medium of coinage. The value of a coin depended less on its face value than on the weight of the metal of which it was made. Inflation occurred when monarchs debased the coinage by mixing base with noble metals, or when ordinary people clipped bits of the edges off coins and passed them off as whole. Isaac Newton's first job as master of the British mint was stamping new coins with milled edges so that clipping would be immediately apparent (M. White, 1997). Paper money for a long time derived its value from governments' promise that it could be redeemed on demand for gold or silver, though this is no longer the case. More importantly, the money supply of a country is not limited to the total face value of the bills and coins in circulation at a given moment. Banks create money through lending. They take in, say, $10,000 in deposit, and then loan it out. The depositor may write checks on his or her $10,000 at the same time the borrower spends his or her $10,000. Now, there is $20,000 where there was once only $10,000, even though no coins have been minted nor bills printed. Money is an intentional object (J. R. Searle, 1995). It exists because—and as long as—people believe it exists, together with its intentional derivatives such as interest rates, bond yields, and credit-default swaps. Yet economics, however imperfect, is a science, despite the socially constructed nature of its subject matter.

Money need not be embodied in order to exist or in order to have real causal effects on human behavior. Surely, mind is the premier intentional object (J. R. Searle, 1997) and may have real causal effects on human behavior even if it cannot be reduced to or even tied to some physical reality. Mind, like money, can be a real object of a real science.

Bibliography

The literature on philosophy of science is large. Surveys include Mario Bunge, *Philosophy of science* (New Brunswick, NJ: Transaction, 1998); A. Bird, *Philosophy of science* (Montreal: McGill-Queens' University Press, 1998); and David Oldroyd, *The arch of knowledge* (New York: Methuen, 1986), S. Okasha, *Philosophy of science: A very short introduction* (Oxford University Press, 2002). A different approach to surveying the field is taken by John Losee, *A historical introduction to the philosophy of science* (Oxford: Oxford University Press, 3rd ed., 2001). An older and more technical survey, but one that is widely cited as a definitive one up to its time, is found in Frederick Suppe's long introduction to his *Structure of scientific theories* (1977). *Science and philosophy: The process of science* (Dordrecht, The Netherlands: Martinus Nijhoff, 1987), Nancy J. Nersessian, ed., contains a selection of papers by leading philosophers of science, written for nonspecialists. An important issue in today's postmodern climate is the objectivity of science. It is defended by Charles Norris, *Against relativism: Philosophy of science, deconstruction, and critical theory* (Oxford: Blackwell), and G. Couvalis, *Philosophy of science: Science and objectivity* (Thousand Oaks, CA: Sage). In *The end of science* (Reading, MA: Addison-Wesley, 1996), John Horgan argues that science is entering a postmodern period, giving up not objectivity, but the search for answers to the traditional Big Questions, which have all been answered—what remains are solving many small problems.

Many of the issues and approaches mentioned in the present text are discussed and represented in Nersessian's volume. Wesley Salmon's *Scientific explanation and the causal structure of the world* (Minneapolis: University of Minnesota Press, 1989) and *Causality and explanation* (Oxford University Press, 1998) provide outstanding, comprehensive treatments of the problem of scientific explanation by a realist. In the former volume, his friend Kitcher gives a lengthy summation of the antirealist perspective. The realism–antirealism issue is given an interesting treatment by Arthur Fine in "Unnatural attitudes: Realist and instrumentalist attachments to science,"

Mind (1986, *95:* 149–79). Fine argues that both viewpoints are flawed by mirror-image failings: "metaphysical inflationism" and "epistemological inflationism," respectively. For realism in physics, see Nick Herbert (1985), *Quantum reality* (New York: Doubleday, 1985), or John Gribben, *Schrödinger's kittens and the search for reality* (Boston: Little, Brown, 1995), wonderful introductions to modern quantum physics and its many deep puzzles. David Linley's *Where does the weirdness go?* (New York: HarperCollins, 1996) is also a good introduction to quantum physics, focusing on why the indeterminacies of quantum physics do not manifest themselves at higher levels of explanation. Moreover, the apparent solidity of physics as a science is questioned by Lee Smolin, *The trouble with physics* (Boston: Mariner Books, 2006). Peter T. Manicas defends *A realist philosophy of social science: Explanation and understanding* (Cambridge: Cambridge University Press, 2006), omitting psychology as not really a social science. However, he did briefly treat psychology as a social science in *A history and philosophy of the social sciences* (Oxford: Blackwell, 1987).

The Received View on theories is fully explicated and criticized in Suppe's introduction, already mentioned. C. W. Savage's *Scientific theories* (Minneapolis: University of Minnesota Press, 1990) contains a collection of essays (preceded by Savage's summary of all of them) on modern approaches to scientific theory, especially Bayesian considerations, and a recent paper by Kuhn that still pushes incommensurability. W. H. Newton-Smith, *The rationality of science* (London: Routledge & Kegan Paul, 1981), provides a general treatment of and argument in favor of the rationalist view of science. Ronald N. Giere, "Philosophy of science naturalized," *Philosophy of Science* (1985, *52:* 331–56), argues for the opposite point of view.

Empirical studies of science, including psychology of science, from the seventeenth century to the present are collected in R. Tweney, C. Mynatt, and D. Doherty, *On scientific thinking* (New York: Columbia University Press, 1981). A forceful set of arguments for, plus case studies of, psychology of science may be found in Gholson et al. (1989). Essays applying philosophy of science to psychology include Barry Gholson and Peter Barker, "Kuhn, Lakatos and Laudan: Applications in the history of physics and psychology," *American Psychologist* (1985, *40:* 744–69); Peter Manicas and Paul Secord, "Implications for psychology of the new philosophy of science," *American Psychologist* (1983, *38:* 399–414); and Joseph Margolis, Peter Manicas, Rom Harre, and Paul Secord, *Psychology: Designing the discipline* (Oxford, England: Basil Blackwell, 1986). J. Abrou asks, *Should psychology be a science?* (Westport, CT: Praeger, 1998), surveying the various answers and their pros and cons. An interesting study in both philosophy and history of science, Steven Shapin's *The scientific life* (Chicago: Chicago University Press, 2008) examines the public image of the scientist from the seventeenth century, when scientists were seen, like priests, to have a vocation setting them apart from ordinary people, to today's image of the scientist as entrepreneur.

Useful studies in philosophy of psychology include several surveys: Neil Bolton, ed., *Philosophical problems in psychology* (New York: Methuen, 1979); Mario Bunge and Ruben Ardila, *Philosophy of psychology* (New York: Springer, 1987); and William O'Donohue and Philip Kitchener, eds., *Philosophy of psychology* (London: Sage). For special topics, see Paul Churchland, *Matter and consciousness* (Cambridge, MA: MIT Press, 1988), which focuses on materialism and reductionism/replacement; Fred Dretske, *Explaining behavior: Reasons in a world of causes* (Cambridge, MA: MIT Press, 1988), which focuses on reasons and causes. General surveys of philosophy of mind include Peter Smith and O. R. Jones, *The philosophy of mind* (Cambridge, England: Cambridge University Press, 1986); Jenny Teichman, *Philosophy and the mind* (Oxford, England: Basil Blackwell, 1988); George Graham, *Philosophy of mind: An introduction* (Oxford: Blackwell, 1995); and Colin McGinn, *Mind and bodies: Philosophers and their ideas* (New York: Oxford University Press, 1998), and Edward Feser, *Philosophy of mind* (Oxford: Oneworld Books, 2006). The scientific status of folk psychology is considered in Garth Fletcher's *The scientific credibility of folk psychology* (Hillsdale, NJ: LEA, 1995), and rejected by Matthew Radcliffe's *Rethinking commonsense psychology: A critique of folk psychology, theory of mind, and simulation* (Houndmills, England: Palgrave/Macmillan).

The New History of psychology may be explored through Wade Pickren's and Donald Dewsbury's (Eds.) (2002) *Evolving perspective in the history of psychology* (Washington, DC: APA Books), which includes essays on historiography as well as numerous studies in the history of modern (i.e., from 1879 on) psychology.

The Legacy of Ancient Greece

INTRODUCTION

The Era of Evolutionary Adaptation

When does history begin? Traditionally, scholars distinguish between the disciplines of history, which draws on written records of human thought and behavior, and prehistory, which uses archeological finds to illuminate the past. However, this distinction is no longer viable. To begin with, the investigations of archeologists and evolutionary biologists have now invaded historians' territory, sometimes challenging traditional ideas about the past (Renfrew, 2007). For example, historians used to think that in the centuries following the fall of Rome, Europe was invaded by successive waves of peoples, each of whom displaced and replaced the previous inhabitants of different regions, eventually leading to the formation of modern European nations. Archeological discoveries have shown that most of these hypothesized mass migrations did not take place, and that cultural change, rather than ethnic cleansing, was the main driver of historical change in Late Antiquity (Heather, 2010).

More importantly—especially for the history of psychology—is the seemingly obvious point that human beings make history, and that human nature was shaped by evolution long before literacy, let alone historical writing, existed. Thus, just as psychology's founder, Wilhelm Wundt said, history is an expression of human nature and historians therefore need to attend to what evolutionary psychologists (Buss, 2011; Cosmides & Tooby, 1992) call the Era of Evolutionary Adaptation, practicing what Smail (2008) calls Deep History. Most notably, it now appears that *H. sapiens*' most important evolutionary adaptation was not bodily (upright posture and the precision grip that enable tool use), but psychological, the development of folk psychology. Humans are an intensely social species (Buss,

2011), so that individual survival depends on both cooperation—lone people are poor hunters—and competition—reproductive success depends on outwitting one's fellow humans. It became very adaptive to be able to figure out what other people were thinking and planning, and to be able to deceive others (and oneself) when useful. Folk psychology thus appears to be an innate feature of the human mind (Gangestad & Simpson, 2007). The capacity to think about other people's mental states then naturally became an object of reflective thought—of philosophy and science—giving rise to the discipline of psychology.

The Past Is Another Country

A few years ago, I visited the British Museum in London. As an undergraduate, I had narrowly chosen psychology over archeology as a career, and I was eager to visit the treasures of the past to be found in the Museum. Among the greatest are the Elgin Marbles, named after Lord Elgin, a British Hellenophile who brought them back to England for preservation. The Elgin Marbles are large, flat slabs of carved stone that were part of the decorative frieze around the top of the Parthenon on the Acropolis in Athens. In the Museum, they are rightly given a large room of their own, mounted around the walls to give the viewer some sense of the original experience of seeing them. They are marvelous works of art, but I was disappointed by how the Marbles were described by the Museum's labels. They discussed the purely formal, aesthetic properties of the Marbles, pointing out, for example, how the figures on one echoed the forms on another across the room. They did not tell what the figures and forms meant, what the people, gods, and animals were doing. At first, I thought this formal approach simply reflected the fact that archeology developed in Europe as a branch of art history and therefore stressed

The Parthenon is one of the most famous buildings in the world. Erected under the rule of Pericles in the days of Socrates and Plato, it expresses the confidence of an imperial civilization at the height of its powers. It was in Greece that the history of secular thought in Western civilization began. Psychology began there in the Greek motto "know thyself." *(Courtesy of Library of Congress)*

XAM'S BLOG 1
Forward to the Past

Looking on human life from outside as I do, it's interesting to ponder this question: Humans evolved in one environment—the grassy savannahs of east central Africa in small libertarian social bands—but have lived ever since in different environments and social structures. What kind of fit is there between evolved human nature and later human environments? Sometimes it's clear that the fit is poor. When humans evolved, food was scarce and so you evolved to eat whenever food was available. Now that food is always available, you eat all the time and there's an epidemic of obesity. In psychology, philosophers such as Colin McGinn (2000) think the human mind evolved to solve only a certain range of problems and that understanding itself isn't one of them. It will take, ahem, aliens to understand your minds.

On the other hand, the emerging way of life of late modernism or postmodernism, whatever you choose to call it, looks in many respects like the life of the Era of Evolutionary Adaptation (EEA). Of course, early *Homo sapiens* did not have iPads and BlackBerries; the similarity is in social structure. In the EEA people lived in small bands and probably mated somewhat promiscuously, mostly forming short-term mother–father bonds to care for helpless infants. People moved around to take advantage of available food and safety opportunities, traveling light with a small kit of tools and often making tools on the spot as jobs needed to be done. Agriculture changed all that. People settled down to farm and accumulated capital, especially land, that might be passed down to heirs, so that short-term mother–father bonds turned into longer-term monogamy, with

men being especially worried about adulterous wives. Women at Athens were supposed to stay home all the time, with household slaves going out to run errands. You could not move around as before but had to stay in one place to farm. You built homes and other buildings. Formal social structures arose to adjudicate disputes, and as these larger groups began to conflict with one another, states became larger and more powerful. Organized religions came into existence.

Today, only a tiny fraction of people are farmers. Increasingly, workers move from job to job, traveling light. As a character said on *CSI: New York*, "A phone isn't just a phone anymore, it's your whole life" Zuicker et al. (2010). Large libraries can be carried in a Kindle or iPad, and the World Wide Web is available from your laptop. You don't have to live in one place anymore, and like the stone tool makers of the past, can download apps as jobs need to be done. Virginity at marriage is no longer as prized as it used to be, and people expect to have had a half dozen or so sexual partners by midlife. Divorce is easier—an unhappy spouse in the age of agriculture couldn't pick up his or her part of the farm and leave; walking out with your phone and laptop is more practical. In the EEA women worked via gathering food and men hunted. In the era of agriculture women came to depend on men to do the heavy lifting of agriculture and war. Today, work rarely involves heavy lifting, even in much of the military, and women have become independent again. It may be that as evolutionary theorists would say, human nature is preadapted for the postmodern lifestyle.

aesthetic appreciation, whereas archeology developed in America as a branch of anthropology and stressed cultural interpretation. The treatment of other artifacts seemed to confirm my hypothesis.

Subsequently, however, I learned that the story was less simple: No one really knows what the Elgin Marbles mean. Traditionally, they are thought to show the Panathenaic Procession. Once a year, the leaders and citizens of Athens staged a grand parade to the Parthenon to honor their city's special god, Athena. However, detailed interpretation remains lacking (Biers, 1987), and some scholars think the marbles commemorate a legendary sacrifice by a mother of her two daughters to gain an Athenian military victory. Had she borne sons, they would have died in battle, so she gave her daughters in their stead (Adler, 1995). That the Marbles are something of a mystery is especially surprising because the Parthenon is not especially old. The Parthenon whose ruins we see today was erected in the heyday of the "glory that was Greece" era, during the leadership of Pericles (495–429 B.C.E.) and under the guidance of the great sculptor Phidias (500–432 B.C.E.), as a replacement for structures destroyed by Persian invaders. The Greeks were inventing philosophy, science, and history, yet we have no discussions of the meaning of the Parthenon frieze. People rarely write down what they take for granted.

My experience with the Elgin Marbles is an important lesson as we begin our historical journey. The job of any historian is to tell about the past, to bring alive the thoughts and actions of people who lived in earlier times, to see the world as they saw it. Yet, as the title of one book has it, *The Past Is Another Country* (Foster, 1988). Often, our grip on the past will be loose, for much quotidian detail is gone forever. We will try to think like Greeks or nineteenth-century German mandarins, and thus improve ourselves as we do by travel. The quest for historical understanding is worth the effort, but the goal of complete understanding will never be reached. No one really knows what the Elgin Marbles mean.

For the standpoint of intellectual history, another reason why the past is mysterious is that premodern writers (roughly up to the Scientific Revolution) did not always write in order to make their ideas clear, as most modern writers do. Instead, many of them wrote obscurely, masking secret (esoteric) doctrines with public (exoteric) words meant to deceive the public while leaving hints about their real beliefs for the more knowledgeable (Kennedy, 2010; Strauss, 1988). There were a number of motives for writing in the esoteric–exoteric style (Meltzer, 2007). Many ancient teachers, including Socrates, shunned writing altogether, believing that wisdom could not be plainly taught but had to emerge from personal dialogue with a challenging teacher. Later philosophers, including Plato, did write, but tried to make their readers' experience more dialogue-like by requiring them to dig for the meaning of the text.

More important for the development of social science, including psychology, was a form of elitism. Plato and many other social thinkers believed that few people are capable of handling the truth about the world, human nature, and how societies ought to be organized and run, and this belief had several consequences. First, it led to fear of persecution: Ordinary people might be outraged when their settled ideas are challenged and lash out dangerously at their critics. Plato saw his beloved Socrates tried and condemned by the Greek democracy for corrupting the youth of Athens. The charge was, in fact, arguably true, because in fact he did seek to disabuse his students of their conventional beliefs. Second, a philosopher might worry that if his ideas did become generally known, they might destabilize existing society. In the seventeenth century, when Descartes set out to doubt everything in order to find a fixed truth, he resolved to not offend conventional beliefs in public. In the eighteenth century, Kant restricted the use of reason in the private sphere, teaching that professors and prelates had a duty to teach conventional truths in public. In modern times, anthropologists don't challenge the traditional tenets of the cultures they study for fear of destroying the cultures.

A final aspect of elitism in social science came into play in the twentieth century, when social science began to become a basis for public policy. People, as objects of scientific study, are profoundly unlike physical objects. What scientists think and publish about atoms and planets has no effect on what atoms and planets do. What scientists publish about human beings can affect what people do and think they should do. Should social scientific knowledge be shared with the general public? Most social scientists think so, and write innumerable public policy and self-help books sharing their insights. But others have continued the attitude expressed in Plato's *Republic*; general knowledge of the truth of human nature might destroy society and diminish scientists' ability to control people for their own good (Thaler & Sunstein, 2008) by exposing their methods.

All this makes the history of philosophy, science, and psychology even more complex than paucity of records and the opacity of ancient presuppositions. Some of the most important premodern thinkers hid what they really thought. If we take them literally, we may misunderstand them; if we try to penetrate exoteric words to esoteric belief, we may misread them; and if we arrive at the correct interpretation, we have no sure way to confirm it. Finally, a thinker's historical influence might derive more from what he exoterically said than what he esoterically meant. Not only is the past another country—it sometimes tries to hide.

THE BRONZE (3000–1200 B.C.E.) AND DARK AGES (1200–700 B.C.E.)

The psychology of any era, scientific or folk, is inevitably affected by the society and culture that produced it. When people seek to explain human soul, mind, and behavior, their ideas rest upon unexamined assumptions about human nature and about how humans ought to live. For example, we will learn in this chapter that Classical Greeks thought the greatest goal in life was to seek eternal honor in the service of their city-state, despising anyone who pursued private self-interest. Because psychological theories reflect their time and place, I will in this text set psychological concepts in their social contexts, rather than treating them as isolated Great Ideas. Beginning this journey with the Greeks is appropriate because it was in Classical Athens that Socrates began to examine his culture's previously unexamined assumptions—and was tried and convicted for doing so.

The intellectual life of the West is deeply rooted in ancient Greece. Greek ideas were adopted by the Romans, who transmitted them around the Mediterranean and into Gaul (modern France), Germania, and Britain. The history of ancient Greece began in the Bronze Age, a royal culture that collapsed suddenly around 1200 B.C.E., leaving a Dark Age in history about which we know next to nothing. Written history appears with the Archaic Age, during which the defining Greek political and cultural order, the *polis*, was created. Then came the great cultural efflorescence of the fourth and fifth centuries B.C.E. brought to its knees by external and internal warfare and destroyed by Macedonian conquest. This Greek Classical era was followed by the Hellenistic Age, which blended into the Roman Era when, as has been said, the Romans were conquered culturally by vanquished Greece.

The Social Context: Warriors and Kings

Ancient Greek men—who totally dominated Greek society—were warriors and they ceased to be warriors only when they were conquered by Philip of Macedon and then the Romans. Their warrior ethos is the key to understanding Greek concepts of mind and behavior. Greek men prized physical strength and despised weakness and, hence, women; they prized fame and glory, not private life or the pursuit of private interest; they cultivated close, even homoerotic friendships among the members of their warrior bands. In the Bronze and Dark Ages, semi-divine kings and their supporting aristocrats ruled Greek society, and it was in this context of royal rule that the Greeks formulated their masculine warrior ethic. It was transmuted with the rise of the polis, but endured until modern times (Mansfield, 2007).

The Greek warrior ethos cast a long shadow over Greek philosophical psychology and ethics. The Bronze Age heroic conception of virtue—the good life—meant living honorably by the warriors' code and achieving immortality through prowess in battle. When a god offered young Achilles the choice between a long, quiet, private life or a short but glorious life, he chose what any Bronze Age man would—the short life of glory won in battle (which did, indeed, make his name immortal).

The Homeric concept of virtue is radically unlike ours in two important respects. First, virtue—arête—was an achievement, not a state of being; and second, as a consequence, virtue could be achieved by only a lucky few. Women, children, adolescents, slaves, the poor, and cripples (few of whom were buried) could not achieve virtue because they could not gain glory in battle. Greeks ever walked in fear of fate—*Tyche*—that might keep virtue from them. An accident of birth—being a woman, poor, or a slave—put virtue out of reach. A childhood accident or disease might cripple one, keeping one from achieving glory and, thereby, arête. Although the emphasis on glory won in battle was muted in later Classical philosophy, the idea that only those few men who attained public greatness were virtuous remained intact until the Hellenistic Age. Today, we tend to think that virtue may belong to anyone, rich or poor, man or woman, athletic or crippled, because we think of virtue as a psychological state of mind, or of the soul, not as a prize to be won by action. Our conception of virtue was developed by the philosophy of Stoicism in the last centuries B.C.E., and was incorporated into and spread by Christianity.

The pursuit of the good life is important to ancient and modern psychology. First, we want to know *what* the good life is, and answering this question requires investigating human nature. Achieving happiness depends on satisfying human motives, so we must figure out what motives humans have. Bronze Age Greeks thought that the most important motive was desire for fame and glory won on the battlefield, and they defined virtue and the good life as pursuing fulfillment of that desire. Second, we want to know *how* to achieve happiness and virtue. Bronze Age Greeks had a simple answer: Fight well. Their successors in the polis would have another, still rooted in arête: Fight well in democratic debate and lead your polis to fame and glory. Later, as conceptions of human motives changed further, various therapeutic recipes and exercises for happiness would be offered. Third, we want to know *limits* on human knowledge and happiness. Can the human mind genuinely know the world in which we act and genuinely know what the good life is? Greeks tended to be optimistic about answering both questions, but later thinkers would be less so.

The pursuit of happiness and the good life is the nexus through which society affects psychology and psychology affects society. Psychologists are born into a society that has certain conceptions about human nature, happiness, and virtue, and their research and practical projects are necessarily shaped, although not completely determined, by these conceptions. At the same time, psychologists' theories and findings are made known to their fellow citizens, whose pursuit of happiness is shaped by what experts tell them what happiness is and the most effective means to possess it.

Psychology of the Bronze Age

Our oldest window on Western psychology is opened by the Homeric poems the *Iliad* and *Odyssey*, which gave permanent voice to an oral tradition already millennia old, reaching back to the Bronze Age. Because they are tales of love and loyalty, passion and battle, they contain explanations of human behavior, indirectly revealing the oldest folk psychology of which we have record.

One object of ancient wonder was surely the difference between living and nonliving things. Only plants, animals, and humans are born, develop, reproduce, and die; only animals and humans perceive and move about. Religions all over the world mark this distinction by ascribing to living things a soul that animates their inanimate bodies, producing life. When the life-spirit is present, the body is alive, and when it departs, the body becomes a corpse. Some, but not all, religions add a second, personal soul that is the psychological essence of each person and that may survive the death of the body.

At least as recorded by Homer, Bronze Age Greek concepts of the soul are distinctive and, to a modern eye, rather odd (Bremmer, 1983; Onians, 1951; Snell, 1953). To begin with, the *Iliad* and *Odyssey* contain no word designating the mind or personality as a whole. Closest is the word *psuche* (traditionally, but misleadingly, transliterated as *psyche*, and usually translated as soul) from which the field of psychology—the study of (*logos*) the soul (psuche)—takes its name. Psuche is the breath of life, or life-spirit, because its departure from a wounded warrior means his death. However, psuche is also more than the breath of life but less than the complete individual mind or soul. During sleep or a swoon, it may leave the body and travel around, and it may survive bodily death, but it is never described as being active when a person is awake, and it is never implicated in causing behavior.

Instead, behavior is attributed to several independently operating, soul-like entities residing in different parts of the body. For example, the function of *phrenes*, located in the diaphragm, was rationally planning action. On the other hand, *thumos*, in the heart, governed action driven by emotion. *Noos* was responsible for accurate perception and clear cognition of the world, and there were other, less frequently cited mini-souls as well. None of these mini-souls survived the death of the body, giving the afterlife of the Homeric psuche a rather bizarre character. Deprived of their body-souls, psuches in the afterlife were mental cripples, deprived of feeling, thought, and speech, and incapable even of normal movement. The appearance of the psuche was exactly that of the body at death, complete with wounds. Moreover, not every psuche went to Hades, because proper burial of the body was felt necessary to effect the transition from life to afterlife. Women, children, adolescents, and the older people could not be warriors, could not, therefore, achieve arête, and so were never ritually buried. Thus, their psuches were not believed to survive death, and warriors feared death without burial—for example, by drowning at sea. On the other hand, when buried with honor, a great warrior earned arête, fame, and an exalted place in the afterlife.

THE ARCHAIC PERIOD (700–500 B.C.E.)

The end of the Dark Ages was marked by the appearance of a new form of social and political organization unique to the Greeks, the city-state, or polis. Citizens' allegiance shifted from divine kings to city-states, comprised of a small city and a few surrounding square miles of territory and governed by their citizens rather than by a king. The polis marked the beginning of rule by the people, although none of the *poleis* were democracies in our modern sense of the world. Citizenship was highly restricted: Only men born of citizens were citizens; women and slaves were excluded from citizenship. In each city-state, especially wealthy Athens, there were many noncitizens, called *metics*, who could never become citizens. Metics tended to be the economically productive backbone of the poleis, because citizens preoccupied themselves with politics and war, viewing productive work with disdain. One of Athen's most famous philosophers, Aristotle, was a metic. Moreover, the old warrior values of arête continued in the polis, though in altered form, as citizens sought glory through service to their city-state. The poleis lived by the rule of democratically enacted law but they were never liberal democracies open to participation by all (Rahe, 1994).

The Social Context: The Rise of the Polis

THE PHALANX AND THE POLIS   The Greeks were warriors, and it was a change in how Greeks fought that created the polis, maintaining while altering the warrior ethos of arête (Green, 1973; Pomeroy, Burstein, Donlan, & Roberts, 1999; Rahe, 1994). Bronze Age warriors fought as individuals. The great warrior-aristocrats were driven in chariots to the field of battle where they dismounted and engaged in single combat with their personal enemies. This form of warfare is described beautifully in the last chapters of the *Iliad*, when Achilles fights and defeats a series of

Trojan heroes, ending with Troy's battle-leader, Hector, whom Achilles denied arête by dragging his corpse around the walls of the city he died to protect. Because chariots were expensive to own and maintain, they remained aristocratic status symbols for centuries (Pomeroy et al., 1999). Bronze Age warriors also wore magnificent armor that, like the armor of the Middle Ages, signaled their aristocratic or royal status. However, during the Archaic Age, the Greeks developed a radically new form of warfare, the phalanx, composed of lightly armored soldiers called *hoplites* wielding long pikes. The phalanx democratized warfare. The hoplite did not need to afford horses and a chariot, nor expensive armor. All citizens, rich or poor, fought on foot as a closely coordinated single unit. Aristocrats lost their monopoly on military prowess, and with it their monopoly on political power. Because they fought for the polis on equal footing with aristocrats, ordinary citizens staked a claim to political power, and they became the decisive class in making political decisions.

The phalanx mentality had important effects on the values and psychology of Archaic and Classical Greece. The phalanx fought almost as a single man; the key to its success was complete coordination of the motions of the hoplites. Emphasis on unit cohesion has remained central to Western military success (Hanson, 2002, 2005). In the movie *Sands of Iwo Jima* (1949) (endorsed by the Marine Corps), the tough Sergeant John Stryker (John Wayne) tells his new recruits, "Before I'm through with you, you're going to move like one man and think like one man. If you don't, you'll be dead." This was the ethos of the phalanx.

The egalitarian ethos of the phalanx created an intense emphasis on economic equality in the poleis. Their goal was *hominoia*, a state in which every citizen had the same thoughts and served only the interests of the polis, instead of their self-interest. Accumulation of wealth was discouraged, and displays of wealth brought opprobrium. Being called a "fish-eater" was an insult because fish were rare and expensive in the eastern Mediterranean, so a person who ate fish was showing off his wealth (Davidson, 1997). There were sumptuary laws regulating what clothes one could wear, ensuring sameness of appearance. When a city-state founded a colony (the Greek world expanded from the original city-states of Greece to include Sicily, southern Italy, and the Mediterranean coast of modern Turkey), equal-sized lots of land were geometrically laid out and allotted to the colony's citizens. Laws were passed making it difficult for anyone to accumulate large landholdings. Above all, the Greeks valued the virtue they called *sophrosyne*. This word is very difficult to translate. Its simplest meaning is "self-control," but it's a self-control that springs from wisdom and honors the Greek maxims "know thyself" and "nothing in excess." It is not the self-control of a Christian or Buddhist monk who rejects the world, the flesh, and the devil, but the self-control of a person who accepts and enjoys the pleasures of the world, but is not captured by them.

Now one might think that in such an egalitarian political order, the old concept of arête would die. It did not, but was placed in service of the polis rather than individual glory. The democratic polis made it possible for any citizen, not only the wealthy aristocrats, to achieve arête; remember that metics, though residents, were not citizens. Aristotle wrote, "the city exists for the sake of noble action" (quoted by Rahe, 1994, p. 184), *action* meaning *political* action. Just as the phalanx demanded the active participation of all hoplites, the polis demanded the active participation of all citizens. Speaking of those who do not participate in politics, but preferred to live a quiet life at home—Greeks called them *idiots*—the greatest Athenian leader, Pericles, said "we judge him utterly worthless." The pursuit of fame and glory survived from the Bronze Age. Thus, Pericles also said, "The love of honor is the only thing that never grows old. . . . Turning a profit [is inferior to] . . . enjoying the respect of one's fellows" (quoted by Rahe, 1994, p. 185). The ancients never cared for the creation of wealth or economic productivity. What counted above all else was greatness of action and the fame it brought.

The Legacy of Ancient Greece

THE POLIS AT THE EXTREME: SPARTA   The ethos of the polis was carried to its extreme by the Spartans (Rahe, 1994). Each young Spartan male was allotted a farm worked by slaves called *helots*; thus Spartan males could devote themselves entirely to the service of the polis in war. They were trained to be tough, masculine, and warlike from a young age. Each warrior was annually issued a standard garment he wore at all times and in all weather, and Spartan warriors called themselves collectively *hoi hominoi*, "The Equals." When they became youths, Spartan men moved into barracks, where they lived as a band of warriors, and they perfected their warrior skills by nighttime attacks on any poor helot unfortunate enough to cross their path; indeed, one reason the Spartans had to be warlike was that the helots outnumbered the Spartans by at least 10 to 1, so that a slave revolt was a constant possibility. Even when coinage of silver and gold was introduced to the Greek world about 600 B.C.E., the Spartans forbid anyone to own coins, and used little iron bars as their only means of exchange. Greek disdain for wealth and passions for equality and service to the city-state was at the heart of the Spartan way of life, and we see that equality (the Spartan ideal) and democracy are not the same.

An important aspect of Spartan life that also illuminates Greek values more generally was the tension between the demands of the polis and the attractions of home, the *oikos*. People are naturally drawn to their spouses and children, but Spartans, like other Greeks, attempted to constrain or even eliminate the oikos. For example, every Greek infant was inspected at birth and exposed to death if physically deformed. Elsewhere, it was the male head of the family who judged the infant, but at Sparta it was a government official. Although a man might marry in his twenties, he continued to live with his messmates until age 30, mating with his wife secretly and briefly in the night. Success in warfare was the highest value for Spartans. There is a story of a soldier returning home to tell his mother that all of his fellows had been killed in battle. Rather than rejoicing that her son was alive, she threw a rock at his head and killed him for failing to die with his comrades.

Although the Spartan way of life was harsh, being designed to produce invincible soldiers, it was much admired by subsequent thinkers as an apparently successful exercise in social engineering (Pomeroy et al., 1999). Plato modeled the Guardian class of his utopian *Republic* on The Equals, and in the Enlightenment, Jean Jacques Rousseau wrote that Sparta "was a Republic of demigods rather than of men" (quoted by Pomeroy et al., 1999, p. 235.) Similarly, one of the American Revolutionaries, Samuel Adams said that the new Republic should be a "Christian Sparta" (quoted by Goetzmann, 2009, Kindle location 725). However, Sparta's exercise in social engineering was not a total success. Although Rousseau admired the Spartans, he recognized that their way of life did violence to human nature (Rahe, 1994), and they earned a reputation as hypocrites among later historians. In public they were austere, but in private they accumulated hoards of forbidden silver and gold. Self-interest and the appeal of home, spouse, and children are not easily extinguished.

Politics, Argument, Law, and Nature: Philosophy and Psychology Begin

GREEK DEMOCRACY AND THE CRITICAL TRADITION   It is difficult for people to accept criticism of their ideas or to reflect critically on them. Consequently, many systems of thought are closed. Adherents of a closed system of thought believe that they possess truths beyond criticism and improvement. If criticism is offered, the system is defended not with reason or evidence, but by attacking the character of the critic as somehow defective. Religions often become closed systems because they rest on divinely revealed dogma and persecute critics as heretics and revile outsiders as wicked infidels. Secular systems of thought may become closed, too. In psychology, psychoanalysis sometimes showed tendencies to intolerance, attacking criticisms as neuroses rather than as potentially legitimate objections.

This is the platform from which speakers addressed the Athenian assembly. Because Greek democracy rejected royal or theocratic dogma and reveled in the clash of competing ideas, it created a social space in which philosophy and science could be born and flourish. *(Michelle Grant/Dorling Kindersley)*

In Archaic Greece, however, when ordinary citizens earned a say in the conduct of their poleis, intellectual life took a different turn, unique in human history and often called the *Greek miracle*. The ancient Greek philosophers were the first thinkers to seek progress through criticism. Beginning with Thales of Miletus (flourished 585 B.C.E.), a tradition of systematic criticism arose whose aim was the improvement of ideas about the natural world. As the philosopher Karl Popper (1965, p. 151) wrote, "Thales was the first teacher who said to his pupils: 'This is how I see things—how I believe that things are. Try to improve upon my teaching.'" Thales did not teach his ideas as received Truths to be conserved, but as a set of hypotheses to be improved. Thales and his followers knew that only by making errors and then correcting them may we progress. This critical approach to philosophy is what Popper called an open system of thought. In addition, the Greek democracies achieved the fundamental basis of all free discussion, separating the character of persons from the value of their ideas. In an open system of thought, ideas are considered on their own, apart from the personality, character, ethnic background, or faith of the person who advances them. Without this separation, arguments degenerate into name-calling and heresy hunting. The critical attitude is fundamental to both philosophy and science, but it requires overcoming intellectual laziness and the natural feeling of hostility toward critics. Founding a critical tradition of thought was the major achievement of the Greek inventors of philosophy and science.

The critical tradition of philosophy and science was an outgrowth of the democratic polis (Vernant, 1982). Instead of simply obeying the orders of a king, democratic Greeks came together to argue over the best course of action, opening the debate to all citizens. Because citizens were equal, charges of bad faith or bad character became unseemly, and ideas were debated on their own merits (Clark, 1992). Law was no longer given by a king who could change it or disregard it at will, but was agreed on and written down, becoming binding on everyone equally. As Euripides wrote in *The Suppliants*, ". . . when the laws are written down, the weak/Enjoy the same protection as the rich." The idea of law governing all people eventually was mirrored in an important scientific idea: natural laws governing natural events, laws that could be discovered by human minds. This extension of law from the polis to nature first appeared in Greek myths, wherein the chief god Zeus is subjected to constraints even he cannot escape (Clark, 1992). Philosophy and science flourish only in a free society based on law.

THE FIRST NATURAL PHILOSOPHERS

Understanding the Universe: The Physicists. The earliest Greek philosophers addressed the fundamental nature of reality. Thales proposed that although the world appears to be made up of many different substances (wood, stone, air, smoke, etc.), there is in reality only one element—water—which takes on many forms. Water can be liquid, gas, or solid, and was, Thales proposed, the underlying constituent of all things. The Greek word for the single element out of which all things are made was *phusis*, and so those who followed Thales in searching for some such universal element were called *physicists*. Modern physicists continue their search, asserting that all the substances of common experience are really composed of a few elementary particles.

Besides inaugurating a critical tradition, then, Thales began a line of *physical* investigation. In doing so, he moved away from supernatural interpretations of the universe toward naturalistic explanations of how things are constituted and how they work. Thus, Thales asserted that humans could understand the world because it is made of ordinary matter and is not affected by the capricious whims of gods. Naturalism is the essential commitment of science because science seeks to explain things and events without reference to supernatural powers or entities of any kind. In psychology—the study of the soul—naturalism poses a profound challenge to dualistic conceptions of life and human personality. As scientists, psychologists seek to explain animal and human behavior without reference to soul or spirit, bringing them into conflict with an ancient and durable tradition—subscribed to by many psychologists themselves—of faith in a supernatural soul. In the rest of science, Thales's naturalism reigns; in psychology, it remains at odds with dualism. Coming to terms with this tension is a serious problem for contemporary psychology.

Thales's physicist tradition continued with Anaximander of Miletus (fl. 560 B.C.E.), who criticized Thales's hypothesis that the phusis was water, proposing instead the existence of a phusis (the *apeiron*) that was not any recognizable element but was instead something less definite that could take on many forms. Although he was a poet rather than a philosopher, Xenophanes of Colophon (fl. 530 B.C.E.) broadened the critical and naturalistic traditions by criticizing Greek religion. Xenophanes maintained that the Olympian gods were anthropomorphic constructions, behaving like human beings: lying, stealing, murdering, and philandering. Xenophanes said that if animals had gods, they would make them in their own images, inventing lion gods, cat gods, dog gods, and so on.

More directly influential on later philosophers, especially Plato, was Pythagoras of Samos (fl. 530 B.C.E.). Pythagoras was an enigmatic figure, a great mathematician, a philosopher—indeed, he coined the term, meaning "lover of wisdom," (Artz, 1980)—and, yet, the founder of a cult. He is famous for the Pythagorean Theorem, and he also formulated the first mathematical law of physics, expressing the harmonic ratios of vibrating strings of different lengths. In his geometrical reasoning, Pythagoras contributed an idea unique to Western civilization and crucial to science—the notion of *proof*. Pythagoras showed that one could argue logically step-by-step to a conclusion that must be accepted by all who followed the argument.

Mathematics, however, was more than just a tool of science for Pythagoras. He founded a cult whose devotees believed that mathematics held the keys to nature. Influenced by Eastern religions such as Hinduism, Pythagoreans introduced dualism into Western thought, drawing a sharp distinction between soul and body and believing that souls could migrate from one body to another. Not only could the soul exist without the body, but, going further, Pythagoreans considered the body a corrupting prison in which the soul was trapped. An important part of Pythagorean teaching concerned purifying the flesh—for example, by dietary restrictions—so the soul could more easily attain truth. Unlike other Greeks, for whom sex was a natural part of life, Pythagoreans viewed sexual pleasure as sin: "Pleasure is in all circumstances bad; for we come here to be punished, and we ought to be punished" (quoted by Garrison, 2000, p. 253). As we shall see, in his emphasis on the care of the soul and the purifying and transcendental character of mathematics, Plato was a follower of Pythagoras.

Being and Becoming; Appearance and Reality: Parmenides and Heraclitus. An important intellectual polarity in Western thought has been the tension between philosophies of *Being* and of *Becoming*. The first spokesman for Being was Parmenides of Elea (fl. 475 B.C.E.). Parmenides wrote his philosophy as a poem and declared it the inspiration of a goddess, suggesting, as with Pythagoras, that the line between science and religion, philosopher and shaman, was not yet clear and sharp (Clark, 1992). Parmenides's basic thesis was simply stated, "It is." Presumably influenced by the physicists, Parmenides asserted that the underlying permanent reality of the universe was an unchanging substance, a simple and immutable *It:* pure Being. Change—*Becoming*, to the Greeks—was an illusion of the human mind, because *It* simply is, beyond change or alteration. Expanded by Plato, the philosophy of Being became a moral doctrine asserting that beyond the flux of changing human opinions there are eternal Truths and Values that exist apart from humanity, truths we should seek and use to guide our lives. These Truths exist in a realm of pure Being; they exist changelessly apart from the changing physical world.

Advocates of Becoming, on the other hand, deny that any such eternal, immutable Truths, or realm of pure Being, exist. Instead, the only constant in the universe is change; things never simply *are*, but are always becoming something else. For such thinkers, moral values change as society changes. There are useful truths, but no eternal Truth. The Greek spokesman for Becoming was Heraclitus of Ephesus (fl. 500 B.C.E.). Like Parmenides, Heraclitus was as much seer as philosopher, speaking in metaphorical aphorisms that earned him the nickname "the Obscure." He asserted that the phusis was fire. This idea led to the conclusion that there is even less permanence in the world than there seems to be. What looks like a stone is really a condensed ball of everchanging fire, a reality not unlike the modern physicist's swarm of particles. Heraclitus's most famous aphorism was that no one ever steps in the same river twice. The statement aptly sums up his philosophy, in which nothing in the universe is ever the same twice. Nevertheless, Heraclitus also believed that, although change is the only constant, it is lawful rather than capricious. Thus, whatever truth philosophy and science may attain will be truth about change—Becoming—rather than about static things.

The debate between Being and Becoming was a metaphysical one, but it created an important epistemological difficulty that led to the first theory in psychology. Both Parmenides's philosophy of Being and Heraclitus's philosophy of Becoming imply a sharp difference between *Appearance* and *Reality.* For Parmenides, the Appearance was Change and the Reality was Being; for Heraclitus, it was the other way around. Parmenides made the distinction explicit, sharply distinguishing a *Way of Seeming* (Appearances) from a *Way of Truth* (Reality).

The idea that the human mind might not be able to know reality as it is jolted the Greeks into self-consciousness about how best to search for truth and promoted inquiry into the workings of the human mind, especially what today we call the cognitive functions. With regard to the first issue, how best to discover Truth, Parmenides concluded that because the senses deceive, they should not be trusted, and one should rely on logic instead. Thus was founded the approach to philosophy known as rationalism, which after being further developed and combined with Being by Plato, would emerge as a powerful general theory of the universe. Concern with the second issue, how the mind is connected to the world, resulted in the first psychological theories about sensation and perception. These psychologically minded philosophers tended to defend the accuracy of human perception against the charges of rationalism, developing the opposing viewpoint of empiricism, which maintains that the way to truth is through the senses, not logic.

The First Protopsychologists: Alcmaeon and Empedocles

When psychology was founded as a science in the nineteenth century, it took a path through physiology. The new psychology was conceived as the scientific offspring of a fruitful marriage between philosophy of mind and the science of physiology. This marriage—or alliance, as Wilhelm Wundt called it—was reflected in the careers of psychology's main founders, Wundt, William James, and Sigmund Freud, all of whom received MD degrees before becoming psychologists. However, long before psychology established itself as a science on the path through physiology, there were physician-philosophers—protopsychologists—who approached explaining mind and behavior using the methods and findings of physiology.

The first of the protopsychologists seems to have been Alcmaeon of Croton (fl. 500 b.c.e.). He was interested in philosophy and directed his attention to understanding perception. He dissected the eye and traced the optic nerves to the brain. Unlike later thinkers, such as Empedocles and Aristotle, Alcmaeon correctly believed that sensation and thought occur in the brain. Alcmaeon also proposed a view of perception that was developed into the first theory in psychology by another physician-philosopher who opposed Parmenides's rejection of the validity of experience.

The ideas of this protopsychologist, Empedocles of Acragas (fl. 450 b.c.e.), may be regarded as the forerunner of empiricism, the orientation to philosophy that finds truth in appearances and rejects reason as tending to fantasy. Following Alcmaeon, Empedocles believed that the senses are "duct[s] of understanding" through which information about the world travels to the brain (Vlastos, 1991, p. 68), and upon that basis developed a theory of perception that would justify our commonsense reliance on our senses. Empedocles proposed that objects emit "effluences," sense-modality-specific copies of themselves that enter the body through the ducts of the senses. Unlike Alcmaeon, Empedocles returned to the usual Greek location of the mind in the heart or chest, saying that the effluences get in the bloodstream where they meet and mix in the heart. The agitation of the effluences in the beating of the heart, Empedocles argued, was thinking. Although it sounds absurd, his theory was an important step for naturalism in psychology because it proposed a purely physical basis for mental activity, which was usually attributed to a soul.

A key feature of the various protopsychologists we will meet along the way to the founding of scientific psychology is that they worked in an intersection between philosophy and psychology. That is, they took up philosophical questions such as, "Do we know the world truly?" or "What is the best way for people to live?" and addressed these questions from a psychological perspective. Instead of speculating about human knowledge, they inquired into how sensation, perception, and thought actually work, using their findings to reflect back on philosophical issues about the possibilities and means of justifying knowledge. Instead of debating ethical positions, they inquired into human nature, trying to discover what motives people have and how they might be managed to attain the good life. Scientific psychologists have kept up this tradition, using scientific inquiries into human nature to address issues in epistemology, decision making, and the relations between human beings and human society (e.g., Keyes & Schwartz, 2007).

The Last Physicists: Atomism

The last Classical philosophers to be concerned primarily with the nature of physical reality were Leucippus of Miletus (fl. 430 b.c.e.) and his better-known student, Democritus of Abdera (fl. 420 b.c.e.). After them, philosophers turned to questions about human knowledge, morality, and happiness. These atomists proposed an idea that has proven immensely fruitful in physics: that all objects are composed of infinitesimally small atoms. The atomists pushed their hypothesis to its limit, supporting two ideas that have seemed dangerous to some philosophers and ordinary people: materialism and determinism. A recurring motto of Democritus was that only "atoms and [the] Void exist in reality." There is no God and no soul, only material atoms in empty space. If only atoms exist, then free will must be an illusion. Leucippus said, "Nothing happens at random; everything happens out of reason and by necessity," providing a naturalistic explanation of Tyche. Soul and free will are illusions that should be abandoned and replaced by naturalistic science. Democritus became known as the "Laughing Philosopher" for the moral conclusions he drew from his naturalism. The Hellenistic dramatist Lucian (120–200 C.E.), imagining Democritus and other philosophers put on sale by the gods, has a prospective buyer exclaim, "You're laughing at us all? You think our life's nothing?" Democritus replies, "That's right. It's just atoms moving in the infinite" (in Saunders, 1966, p. 189).

Atomism deepened the divide between Appearance and Reality. Democritus wrote, "We know nothing accurately in reality, but only as it changes according to the bodily condition and the constitution of those things that impinge upon [the body]" (Freeman, 1971, p. 93), concluding that only reason can penetrate to the reality of the atoms (Irwin, 1989). Democritus adopted a version of Empedocles's theory of cognition. Democritus said that every object gives off special kinds of atoms called *eidola*, which are copies of the object. When these reach our senses, we perceive the object indirectly through its copy. Thus, our thought processes are restricted to putting together or taking apart the *eidola*-images in our brains. Democritus also maintained an ethical doctrine that came to trouble later ethical philosophers and psychologists. A consistent materialism, denying as it does God and the soul, typically offers a sensuous guide to the conduct of life: the pursuit of pleasure and the avoidance of pain. This doctrine is called hedonism, *and will be fully developed as a psychology of motivation and political philosophy by the utilitarians of the nineteenth century.* Democritus said, "The best thing for man is to pass his life so as to have as much joy and as little trouble as may be" (Copleston, 1964, p. 93). Hedonism reduces moral values to our natural bodily experiences of pleasure and pain. To many, however, it is offensive, for if an individual's pleasure is the sole criterion of the good, what right has anyone to condemn the happy and successful criminal or tyrant? Such moral concerns were at the heart of Socrates's and Plato's thinking, and Plato once suggested burning Democritus's books.

THE CLASSICAL PERIOD (500–323 B.C.E.)

The Social Context: Empire and War

As the Greek city-states established themselves and colonized the Mediterranean, they came into conflict with the Persian Empire. In a series of campaigns, the Persians tried to capture Greece, but due to battles fought with great heroism and cleverness by the Greeks, the Persians failed. Had the Greeks lost any of the close-run battles against the Persians, the history of the world would have been changed radically. The Persian wars also revealed the great political weakness of the polis system— the Greeks never fully united against the Persians, but set up short-term alliances that encouraged jockeying for supremacy. The main rivals were Sparta, the most potent, land-based military power, and Athens, the largest and wealthiest of the poleis.

Athens's citizens numbered as many as 40,000, far more than other poleis, and its rich silver mines gave them enormous wealth. Because Athens had a port, the Piraeus, it became a great trading center, and it developed as a sea power against Sparta's formidable land power. As the Persian wars continued, Athens became the most important Greek city, developing an empire controlling most of the Greek peninsula and reaching into Persian territories as the Persians retreated. Unsurprisingly, the Athenians fell victim to the Greek sin of *hubris*—excessive pride. They styled themselves the teachers of the Greeks, and other cities came to feel threatened by Athenian hegemony. Some poleis allied with Athens's power, while others rallied around Athens's rival, Sparta, setting in motion a series of horrifically destructive civil wars known collectively as the Peloponnesian War. In the end, Sparta defeated Athens with the help of the Persians, but the devastation and loss of life and wealth were so great that no one could justly be called the victor. Greece was fatally weakened, set up for conquest by Philip of Macedon and his son, Alexander.

At its height, Athens was the cultural center of the Greek world, producing art, architecture, and philosophy whose influence lasted for millennia. It also became, for a while, a radical democracy, completely erasing status differences between the few aristocrats and the many common citizens. As the fortunes of war with Sparta ebbed and flowed, the aristocrats tried several times to seize power, only to be defeated by the partisans of democracy. The internal squabbling of Athenian citizens aided their enemies as disaffected aristocrats periodically defected to the Spartan or Persian cause. The tumults within Greece and within Athens are important to understanding the philosophy of Plato, who sought to find a world of unchanging Truth behind the appearance of chaos.

Teaching the Polis

HUMANISM: THE SOPHISTS   Because it was a democracy, the key to success in the Athenian polis was rhetoric: the art of persuasion. Gaining political power depended on effective speech in the assembly, and being a litigious people, Athenian citizens had to argue lawsuits and sit in judgment on juries. Therefore, the ability to make and critically comprehend complex arguments was a skill of great value. Naturally, then, rhetoric became an object of study, a profession, and a body of expertise to be taught. The new teachers of rhetoric were called *Sophists*, from *sophistes* (meaning expert), the source of our word *sophisticated*. The art of rhetoric arrived in Athens from Syracuse in 427 B.C.E. The sophist Gorgias came from Sicily to obtain Athenian aid for his city of Leontini against its enemy Syracuse (Davidson, 1997). Although Gorgias does not come off well in Plato's eponymous dialogue, the art of persuasion had come to stay. The Sophists were the first paid professional teachers in history, and they represent the beginnings of higher, as opposed to childhood, education (Clark, 1992). The practical concerns of the Sophists mark an important turn in philosophy from concern with physics to concern with human life and how it ought to be lived.

As hired advocates and teachers of rhetoric, the Sophists did not profess a general system of philosophy, but certain important philosophical attitudes emerged from their practice. If the Sophists had a central idea, it was stated by Protagoras (approximately 490–420 B.C.E.): "Of all things the measure is man, of things that are that they are, and of things that are not that they are not" (Sprague, 1972). Protagoras's motto suggests a range of meanings from the personal through the cultural to the metaphysical. At the center of all of them, however, is humanism, a concern with human nature and human living.

On its narrowest personal interpretation, "man is the measure of all things" endorses a *relativistic empiricism*, a humanistic preference for Appearance over Reality. Whatever may be the ultimate constituent of nature—water, fire, or atoms—the world we humans live in is the world as it appears to us in our immediate experience. Truth for us, as a practical matter, will never be the phusis, but will be the familiar world of people and things; usable truth therefore lies in Appearances, not in a speculative Reality. Yet, because truth is in Appearances, truth is relative to each perceiver: Each human being is the only qualified judge of how things appear to him or her. Two people may enter the same room, yet to one the room is warm, to the other cool, if the former has been out in a blizzard and the latter downstairs stoking the furnace. Neither perception is incorrect; each is true for its perceiver, and there is no hidden Reality of the matter.

"Man is the measure of all things" also carries a cultural, or, to use a term of today, a multicultural meaning. The Greeks were cultural chauvinists: Their word *barbarian*, with all of its negative connotations, simply meant non-Greek-speaking. For them, there is only one right way of life—the Greek way—and all others were ways of folly or wickedness. The Sophists challenged Greek thinking on this point, championing a form of cultural relativism. Just as each person knows what is true for himself or herself, so cultures may arrange their affairs in any number of equally valid and satisfying ways. Hellenes speak Greek and Romans speak Latin; neither is superior to the other. Greeks worship Zeus, the Anglo-Saxons, Wotan; each is the god of his or her people.

Finally, "man is the measure of all things" has a metaphysical meaning. If the alleged Reality of nature is unknowable, so, too, are the gods (Luce, 1992). There is no divine truth or god-given law to which human beings are subject. Right and wrong are matters for cultures, not gods, to decide. Science and philosophy ought not waste time on idle speculation about Reality or the gods, but concern itself with practical achievements conductive to human happiness and work.

The Sophists' relativism was an important innovation in the history of Western thought, but carried dangers for Greek democracy and for Western social and political thought down to the present. The Sophists sharpened the division between phusis (nature) and *nomos* (human law). By considering their way of life the best life, traditional Greeks identified phusis and nomos: The Greek way of life, their nomos, was the best,—that is, the natural (phusis) way of life, ideally suited to human nature (phusis). The Sophists denied this identification, making nomos a matter of arbitrary convention, a set of equal ways of life lived in different cultures, none superior to another. Indeed, the Sophist Antiphon elevated convention (nomos) above nature, saying that human laws bind human nature (phusis), presumably in different ways in different cultures.

Psychological inquiry is important to the dispute between traditional Athenians and the Sophists. The Sophists assumed that human nature is quite flexible, being happily adaptable to very different ways of life. Traditional Athenians saw human nature as relatively fixed, so that one culture—the free polis—was most suited to it. Submerged for a time by the dominance of Christian thought, the nature of human nature—and its implications for social policies—became a prime problem for the Enlightenment. Psychology began to be politically important in the eighteenth century, when politicians rejected traditional forms of social organization (nomos) in favor of forms rooted in a scientific understanding of human nature (*physis*). The tension between physis and nomos is as intense now as ever in the history of humankind. Is freedom the natural (physis) yearning of the human heart, justifying the overthrow of despotic regimes, or should they be left alone as nomoi different from, but no better or worse than, our own?

The immediate danger from Sophistic humanism for Athenian democracy emerged in Plato's lifetime. The aristocrat Callicles says in Plato's dialogue *Gorgias* that laws are made by the weak and inferior—but more numerous—citizens to fetter the naturally strong and superior aristocrats who ought naturally to rule over the weak masses. De Sade, Nietzsche, and, in some moods, Freud, later agreed with Callicles's position. Callicles put his claim into action, participating in an aristocratic coup against Athenian democracy. Ever since the time of the Sophists, the questions of what human nature is and what, if any, way of life is natural to it, have challenged those parts of psychology and philosophy devoted to human happiness. These challenges were first met head-on by Socrates.

ENLIGHTENMENT AND EUDAEMONIA: SOCRATES

XAM'S BLOG 2
Socrates: The First Modern

It seems silly to say that the first modern was a Greek who lived in the fourth century B.C.E., but it could be true. A big question about modernity—science, industrialization, urbanization, and spectacular economic growth—was why it occurred in Western Civilization and not in another of the world's great civilizations such as Islam or China. As one book asks, "Why does the West rule?" (Morris, 2010), one feasible answer is the Greek miracle and Socrates's place at the heart of that miracle. Socrates went around asking people why they did what they did. Most people and societies are content to just keep doing what they have been doing as long as things work out OK. But Socrates stepped back and asked people to think about and to *justify* their beliefs and actions. This can bring trouble—it brought Socrates's death—but it provokes change. Only if one thinks about why one is doing things can one then think about doing things differently, and doing things better: One can move past results that are OK to trying for better outcomes—for economic innovation and growth, not the static outcomes of the Malthusian economy. The restlessness of modernism, seeking for constant change and improvement began with the restless moral questioning of Socrates.

Much to his own liking, Socrates was a troublesome and troubling figure in his own lifetime and has remained so in the history of Western thought, esteemed the greatest of philosophers. For conventional Athenians, Socrates was a troublemaker whose deliberately provocative questions about virtue corrupted their children and undermined their morals. For Christian philosophers, and especially for people still Christian in outlook if not in faith, Socrates became an attractive figure—a poor, wandering seeker after virtue who annoyed the smug and the self-righteous—and whose reward was execution. Although a citizen of Athens and an admired soldier, Socrates, like Jesus, came from a modest background, being the son of a stonemason, and challenged the reigning values of the day, whether the aristocrat's love of power and glory or the merchant's love of money. Speaking to the jury that condemned him, Socrates said, "I go about doing nothing but persuading you, young and old, to care not for the body or money in place of it, or so much as, excellence of soul" (*Apology*, 30a, trans. R. E. Allen). For the old aristocratic class of Athens, and later for Friedrich Nietzsche and the German neo-Pagans of the turn of the century—some of whom turned to that decisive leader Hitler—Socrates and Jesus were evil teachers who clouded the minds of the naturally strong with altruistic morality and bound their hands with manacles of law passed by the weak.

Socrates, it seems, was a dangerous man, but what did he teach? In a sense, nothing. Socrates was a moral philosopher, unconcerned with physics and, though Athenians took him for one, he was not a Sophist teaching expertise for a fee. He was on a self-defined quest for the nature of true virtue and goodness, though he professed not to know what they were. In his teaching, he would closely question a young man or group of young men about some topic related to virtue. What is justice? Beauty? Courage? The Good? Socrates's interlocutors would offer conventional definitions that Socrates dismantled with clever and penetrating questions. For example, in the *Gorgias*, Callicles defines justice as "the rule of the strong," reflecting his aristocratic birth and Sophistic training. So devastating is Socrates's assault on Callicles's beliefs, however, that Callicles flees rather than give them up. Those who stayed with Socrates came to share his own mental state of *aporia*, or enlightened ignorance. With Socrates, they had to confess they were ignorant about what justice (or whatever virtue was under discussion) really was, but realized they were better off than before because they had been disabused

(Continued)

of their conventional, but wrong, beliefs. Socrates feared that in their acquisition of an empire and the hubris that it had engendered, Athenians had strayed from the path of sophrosyne, and his mission was to deflate imperial arrogance and restore traditional Greek self-control.

Although Socrates taught no positive doctrine, his philosophical approach contained several important innovations. The first was his search for the general nature of the virtues and of virtue itself. We intuitively recognize that returning a pencil and establishing a democracy are just acts, but what they have in common—what justice itself as such is—remains elusive. A spectacular sunset and a Mozart symphony are both beautiful, but what they share in common, what beauty itself is, remains likewise elusive. Moreover, Socrates took his inquiries to a higher level. Justice, beauty, honor, and so on are all good, but what they have in common, or what *good* itself is, remains elusive. In his domain of moral philosophy, Socrates began to try to understand the meaning and nature of abstract human concepts such as justice and beauty. Plato and Aristotle would broaden Socrates's quest from ethics to include the whole range of human concepts in every area, creating the field of epistemology—the search for truth itself—a central undertaking of later philosophy and cognitive psychology.

Socrates's method, a special sort of dialogue called the *elenchus*, was innovative as well. Socrates believed that everyone possesses moral truth, even if they are unaware of it. Socrates called himself a "midwife" to knowledge of virtue, bringing it out of people by questions rather than simply teaching it to them. So, for example, he would use specific cases to undermine false ideas about virtue. A young man might define courage in Bronze Age fashion, as fighting honorably and fearlessly against one's enemies, and Socrates might counter it with something like the Charge of the Light Brigade: brave but foolish, and bringing death and defeat to one's family, followers, and fellow citizens. Such questions and problems weakened and eventually—for those who stayed—dislodged false beliefs and ended in aporia. However, precisely because we can make correct intuitive judgments about right and wrong, even if we cannot say why, Socrates assumed knowledge of virtue is latently within us. We

can discover this knowledge, and become more fully virtuous, if we seek it with him, making our latent knowledge conscious and explicit. In some respects, the Socratic elenchus is the starting point of psychotherapy. With Socrates, psychotherapists maintain that we have learned false beliefs that make us ill, yet we possess hidden and liberating truths that can be found through dialogue with a personal guide.

Socrates also believed that nothing deserves the name knowledge or truth unless we are conscious of it and can explain it. A person might infallibly do the right things, but for Socrates, he or she was not truly virtuous without being able to explicitly and rationally justify his or her actions. In his quest for virtue, Socrates demanded more than good behavior or correct intuitions about right and wrong; he demanded a theory of virtue—the Greek word *theoria*, means "contemplation." In the *Symposium*, the semi-divine seeress and alleged teacher of Socrates, Diotima, says to him, "Don't you know that right opinion without ability to render an account is not knowledge—how could an unaccountable thing be knowledge?. . . Right opinion . . . is intermediate between wisdom and ignorance" (202a, trans. R. E. Allen).

Socrates's requirement that knowledge be an explicitly stated and defended theory was adopted by Plato and became a standard goal of Western philosophy, setting it off from two other forms of human thought. The first are dogmatic religions that do not allow natural reason to question divine revelation. Islam after the thirteenth century failed to develop natural philosophy and science on just this ground. In a somewhat similar way, China, too, failed to develop science because of the total control of thought by its divinely appointed emperors and their bureaucrats, the Confucian mandarins. The other traditions are those that value intuition rather than logic, such as Buddhism or western Romanticism. Within psychology today there is a movement called embodied cognition that deprecates the explicit and verbal side of knowledge and elevates the intuitive knowledge of the world we use to practically interact with it (Ratcliffe, 2007).

Finally, in his concern with virtue, Socrates raised important questions about human motivation. Central problems for any moral philosophy are providing reasons why people should do right and explaining why they so often do wrong. The first problem—why people should be virtuous—was never a difficulty for Greek and Roman philosophers because they assumed, entirely without discussion, that virtue and *eudaemonia* were deeply linked, if not identical. The usual translation of eudaemonia into English is "happiness," but eudaemonia meant more than the attainment of pleasure, though it included pleasure. It meant living well, or flourishing. Like all Greeks, Socrates assumed that the proper end of life was eudaemonia, and he believed that being virtuous would guarantee eudaemonia. Thus, he, in common with Greeks generally, assumed that because all people seek happiness, eudaemonia, they naturally seek virtue, and there was no need to provide special reasons for doing good. Plato asserts in the *Symposium* (205a, trans. R. E. Allen), ". . . the happy are happy by possession of good things, and there is no need in addition to ask further for what purpose he who wishes to be happy wishes it. On the contrary, the answer seems final." In their near-identification of happiness and virtue, the Greeks differed sharply from later ethical systems, including Christianity, which urge us to be ethical but warn that pursuing virtue often brings suffering rather than happiness. Classical Greeks also differed from Stoics (see later) and Christians in restricting moral concern to an individual's happiness and perhaps the happiness of his polis. Concern with other human beings simply because they were human beings formed no part of the Classical concept of virtue (MacIntyre, 1981).

Because Greek and Roman ethical philosophers had no problem explaining why people should behave well, they focused instead on the question of why people don't always do so. If virtue and happiness are almost the same, the existence of bad behavior—behavior that makes a person unhappy—becomes hard to explain. Because people want to be happy, they therefore ought always to act rightly. Socrates proposed a purely intellectual answer to the problem of bad behavior, maintaining that people act wrongly only when they are ignorant of the good. A thirsty person would not knowingly drink poison, but might do so on the false belief that it was pure water. Harmful acts are never chosen as such, but only when the actor is ignorant of their bad consequences.

Socrates's explanation of bad behavior was predicated on the assumption behind the elenchus that people intuitively know what virtue is, but that false beliefs acquired from their upbringing mask this knowledge and may lead them to do wrong. Once someone knows what virtue truly is, he will automatically act correctly. Thus, Callicles, having abandoned his dialogue with Socrates, participated in the aristocratic coup because he remained in the grip of the false belief that justice was the rule of the strong. In Socrates's account, Callicles was not evil, but simply misguided. Had he continued his encounter with Socrates, he would have learned that justice was not the rule of the strong, and would not have sought the overthrow of democracy. For Socrates, knowledge of the good—not a good will or virtuous character—was all that was needed to effect good behavior. Later Greek and Roman ethical philosophers, including Plato himself and the early Christians, found Socrates's intellectual solution implausible because, manifestly, some people enjoy wrongdoing, and even virtuous people sometimes knowingly do wrong because their wills are too weak to overcome temptation. Wrestling with the source of evil in human behavior became an important question for motivational psychology.

THE GREAT CLASSICAL PHILOSOPHIES

Plato: The Quest for Perfect Knowledge

Unlike his teacher, the son of a stonemason, Plato sprang from the old aristocratic class that was losing power as the Athenian polis became more democratic. When Sparta finally defeated Athens at the end of the long Peloponnesian wars, a clique of aristocrats, including two of Plato's relatives, carried out the short-lived coup against the Athenian democracy in which Callicles participated. Ironically, when the coup was defeated, Socrates was caught up in the purge of aristocrats and their supporters because so many of them, like Callicles, had been in his circle of students. Socrates was condemned to the death he chose in preference to exile from the city he loved. As a result, Plato became disenchanted with politics as he knew it. Aristocrats, even relatives, friends, and students, might selfishly sacrifice the general good to personal ambition. A democracy might fear and kill a loyal yet critical citizen because he questioned conventional ideas of virtue.

Socrates, the first moral philosopher, had tried to find an overarching idea of the Good. His student, Plato, built on and broadened Socrates's moral concerns, filling Socrates's aporia with his own philosophy. Plato dedicated his philosophy above all to the pursuit of justice both in the state and in the individual. The Greek word for justice, *dikaiosune*, had a specific, relatively narrow meaning: getting out of life what one fairly deserved, no more and no less, reflecting the Greek goal of hominoia. Fish eaters and the aristocratic junta were guilty of justice's corresponding vice, *pleonexia*, grasping for more than one is fairly due. Plato tried to lead his students from their conventional Greek understanding of justice to a new one, doing good for its own sake and not for fame and glory. Plato's new understanding of virtue would later make its way into Christianity.

COGNITION: WHAT IS KNOWLEDGE?   Socrates had tried to find a general definition of Virtue. Plato saw that Socrates's quest was part of a larger undertaking—that of finding definitions for any sort of general terms. Just as we can define *courage* apart from particular courageous actions, or *beauty* apart from particular beautiful things or people, so we can define *cat* apart from any particular cats, or *fish* apart from any particular fish.

Talk of cats and fish may seem to make Plato's quest trivial, but it is not. According to the Greeks, what sets human beings apart from animals is the capacity for abstract knowledge, while animals respond only to the concrete here-and-now. Science, including psychology, searches for general knowledge about how things are everywhere in the universe at any point in time. Psychologists run experiments on small groups of people, but build theories about human nature. In a social psychology experiment, for example, our concern is not why Bob Smith or Susan Jones failed to help a person in distress, but why people so often fail to help others in similar situations. Plato was the first thinker to inquire into how knowledge is possible and how it may be justified. In philosophy, he created the field of epistemology—the study of knowledge—that eventually gave rise to cognitive psychology.

Modern science, heir to the empiricist tradition in epistemology that Empedocles inaugurated, justifies its claims to knowledge by citing observations. However, science has learned to live with an ugly fact about generalizations based on past experience: As Plato was the first to point out, what seems true based on today's data may be overturned by tomorrow's. The truth for which Socrates died could not be so transient, so tentative, Plato thought. Truth had to be permanent and known with certainty.

Wrestling with Skepticism.   For the Platonist, then, Truth, and hence our knowledge of it, has two defining characteristics. First, a belief is True—is Knowledge—if and only if it is true in all times and all places absolutely. Socrates wanted to know what justice or beauty *is*, apart from just acts and beautiful things, and knowledge of justice or beauty itself would therefore be true of all just acts and beautiful things in the past, now, and forever. Second, for Plato, as for Socrates, knowledge had to be rationally justifiable. A judge who always judges rightly or a connoisseur of impeccable taste does not, for Plato, genuinely know the truth unless he or she can explain his or her judgments and by force of argument convince others they are correct.

Unlike the later Skeptics, who were also students of Socrates, Plato never questioned Socrates's faith that there was a Truth to replace aporia, and he accepted earlier philosophers' arguments that sense perception was not the path to knowledge. From Heraclitus, Plato took the belief that the phusis was fire, and thus the conclusion that the physical world was always in a state of becoming. Because the truth Plato sought lay in the realm of Being—eternally and unchangeably True—knowledge of it could not derive from material senses reflecting the changing material world. From the Sophists, Plato took the belief that how the world seems to each person and each culture is relative to each of them. Observation, therefore, is tainted by individual differences and the sort of cultural preconceptions that Socrates had challenged. For Plato, then, even if the copy theory of cognition was an accurate account of human perception, it was not adequate as a theory for finding eternal Truth.

Mathematics and the Theory of the Forms.   So far, Plato had not gotten past Socratic aporia; Plato was convinced that transcendental Truth exists, and that perception was not the path to knowledge. Then, in midlife, Plato studied geometry with the Pythagoreans and was transformed by it, as philosopher Thomas Hobbes and psychologist Clark Hull would be centuries later. In mathematics, Plato found not only a path to Truth but also something of the nature of Truth itself. Plato came to side with Parmenides in holding that the Way of Truth was the inward path of logic and reason rather than the outward path of Seeming, but went beyond them to indicate what Truth—Reality—was. In the *Phaedo*, Plato has Socrates conclude, "So when does the soul grasp truth? For whenever she undertakes to investigate anything with the body it is clear that she will be thoroughly deceived by the body. . . . Therefore it is in reasoning, if anywhere, that any reality becomes clearly revealed to the soul" (65b–c, trans. G. Vlastos, 1991).

Most of us have, in high school or college, done proofs in geometry, such as of the Pythagorean Theorem that the area of a square erected on the hypotenuse of a right-angled triangle is equal to the sum of the areas of squares erected on the other two sides. For Plato, the first revelation of geometry was the notion of proof. The Pythagorean Theorem was provable, and therefore True, a piece of genuine knowledge supported by logical argument rather than observation and measurement. The Socratic requirement that knowledge be justified by reason was satisfied by geometry because anyone who followed the steps of the proof is compelled to believe the theorem. Geometry supported rationalism's claim that logic was the Way of Truth.

Plato went on to assert that reason was the way to Reality and the realm of Being, too. The Pythagorean Theorem is true not merely of a triangle drawn by someone doing the proof, or of all the people who have ever done or will do the proof, but of every right-angled triangle. However, given that the Pythagorean Theorem is true, and that it is not true simply of triangles drawn by mathematicians, or a mere statistical generalization from a sample of triangles, but is a real universal proof, of what object is it true? Plato asserted that it was true of what he called the *Form* of the Right-Angled Triangle, an eternally existing, perfect right-angled triangle of no particular size.

The idea of Form helped reconcile Being and Becoming and provided a solution for Socrates's questions about Virtue that had implications beyond ethical philosophy. Forms belong to the realm of Being, subsisting eternally, while their material but ephemeral copies belong to the realm of Becoming. Similarly, in Socrates's ethical realm, every courageous act resembles the *Form of Courage*, every beautiful object resembles the *Form of Beauty*, and every just act resembles the *Form of Justice*. Courage, Beauty, and Justice—each of them being good—resemble the *Form of the Good*. Genuine knowledge then, which Socrates had sought in the moral domain, was knowledge of the Forms of things, not of physical things or events.

It is important to grasp an aspect of Plato's thinking that is alien to us. We tend to believe that thinking a sculpture or a person is beautiful is a matter of subjective, aesthetic judgment, largely shaped by what our society tells us is beautiful. Other people in other cultures might have different opinions, and like the Sophists, we accept these as mere differences rooted in culture or individual taste. From Socrates, Plato accepted that societies might instill different views of beauty and ugliness, but, unlike the Sophists, he did not conclude that judgments of beauty were therefore matters of local taste. For Plato, a person or sculpture was beautiful by resembling the Form of Beauty; a sculpture or person was ugly by departing from the Form of Beauty. Similarly, an act was good because it participated in the Form of the Good. Beauty and virtue were not subjective judgments of people and cultures, but real properties that objects actually possessed, like size or weight. If two people (or cultures) disagreed about whether a person was beautiful or an act virtuous, at least one of them was wrong because he or she was ignorant of the Form of Beauty or the Good. Socrates's goal was to find out what virtue was and teach it to people—regardless of social opinion—so they could act upon their knowledge. Plato elaborated Socrates's idea into metaphysical realism: The Forms *really* exist as *nonphysical* objects. Indeed, for Plato, the Forms were more real than their observable copies, because they were eternal, existing outside the physical realm of Becoming.

Imagining the Forms. As Plato realized, describing the Forms is difficult, if not impossible, because by their very nature they cannot be displayed. Instead, Plato offered metaphors for the Forms, descriptions of the "child of goodness" rather than Goodness itself (*Republic*, 506e, trans. R. Waterfield). Three of these similes, the Sun, the Line, and the Cave, are given in the *Republic*. A fourth, which offers a psychological path to the Forms, the Ladder of Love, occurs in the *Symposium*, probably written just before the *Republic*.

The Simile of the Sun: Illumination by the Good. In the Simile of the Sun, Plato says that the Form of the Good is to the intelligible world of the Forms what the sun is to the physical world of objects, the copies of the Forms. Plato did not think of vision as happening because light entered the eye, as we do today; that conception was developed centuries later (Lindberg, 1992). Instead, the eye was thought to have a power of seeing by sending out rays that struck physical objects. Nevertheless, because it's hard to see at night, everyone recognized that light had to be present in order for vision to occur. The light of the sun was the "other third thing" needed (in addition to the eye and an object) for vision to occur. In the intelligible realm, reason has the power to grasp the Forms as in the physical world the eye has the power to see. However, in the intelligible realm, an "other third thing" is needed to illuminate the Forms, making it possible for reason to know them. By themselves, the senses lack the power to perceive the world accurately, but need the help of divine illumination. Plato says that the "third thing—the source of divine illumination—is the Form of the Good, analogous to the light of the Sun on earth."

The Metaphor of the Line: The Hierarchy of Opinion and Knowledge. The Simile of the Sun is followed by the appropriately geometrical Metaphor of the Line. Imagine a line (Figure 1) divided into four unequal sections each of whose relative length is a measure of its degree of truth. The line is first divided into two large sections. The lower and shorter section stands for the world of Appearances and opinions—beliefs without proof—based on perception. The higher and longer section stands for the world of the Forms and provable knowledge about them. The world of Appearances line is further divided into segments for the worlds of *Imagining*, the shortest line segment of all, and of *Belief*, next shortest in length.

Apprehension of images is the most imperfect way of knowing. Imagining is the lowest level of cognition, dealing with mere images of concrete objects, such as images cast in water. Plato relegated representational art to this realm, for when we see a portrait of a man we are seeing only an image, an imperfect copy of a thing. Plato banished representational art from his utopian Republic, and his hostility to images entered some later religions. In 2002, the world looked on with horror as the Taliban of Afghanistan destroyed large statues of Buddha because they represented a

	OBJECTS	STATES OF MIND
INTELLIGIBLE WORLD	The Good	Intelligence or D Knowledge
	Forms	
	Mathematical Objects	C Thinking
WORLD OF APPEARANCES	Visible Things	B Belief
	Images	A Imagining

FIGURE 1 Plato's metaphor of the line (From Cornford, 1945).

physical human form. Better than looking at images is looking at objects themselves; Plato called this Belief. With the next, longer section of the line, *Thinking*, we move from mere opinion to real knowledge, beginning with mathematical knowledge. Proofs vouchsafe the truth of mathematical propositions, and the objects of mathematical knowledge are not observable things but Forms themselves.

Mathematics, however, while providing a model of knowledge, was recognized by Plato to be imperfect and incomplete. It is imperfect because mathematical proofs rest upon assumptions that cannot themselves be proven, falling short of the Socratic ideal of justified knowledge. For example, geometrical proofs—the form of mathematics most developed in Plato's time—depend on unproven positing of axioms that may be intuitively appealing, such as the axiom that parallel lines never meet. Plato sensed what later turned out to be correct, that if one changes the axioms, different systems of geometry emerge. To be True in Plato's sense, then, geometry needed metaphysical support, which he provided with the Forms. Mathematics is incomplete because not all knowledge concerns mathematics. Highest in importance were the moral truths sought by Socrates. The highest and longest segment of the line, then, represents the *World of the Forms*, the place of all Truth, mathematical or otherwise. Greatest among the Forms is, naturally, the Form of the Good, the ultimate object of Socrates's and Plato's quest.

The Allegory of the Cave: The Prison of Culture. The third "child of goodness" in the *Republic* is the most famous and influential, the Allegory of the Cave. Imagine people imprisoned in a deep cave, chained in such a way that they can look only at the back wall of the cave. Behind them is a fire with a short wall between it and the prisoners. Bearers walk along a path behind the wall, holding above it statues of various objects, so that the objects cast shadows on the wall for the prisoners to see. For the prisoners, "the shadows of artifacts would constitute their only reality" (515c, trans. R. Waterfield).

"Imagine that one of them has been set free and is suddenly made to stand up, to turn his head and walk, and to look toward the firelight" (515c–d). Plato (1993) goes on to tell how hard it would be for the liberated prisoner to give up his familiar reality for the greater reality of the fire and the statues. Harder still—he must be "dragged forcibly" through "pain and distress"—is the ascent past the fire out the mouth of the cave and into the world itself and the sun that illuminates it. Ultimately, he would feel joy in his new situation and look with disdain on the life he previously led, with its traditionally Greek pursuit of honor and glory. Finally, Plato asks that we imagine the prisoner returned to his old spot in the cave, not seeing well in the dark, yet knowing the Truth. "Wouldn't he make a fool of himself? Wouldn't they [the other cave dwellers] say that he'd come back from his upward journey with his eyes ruined and that it wasn't even worth trying to go up

Plato's Allegory of the Cave. *(Dorling Kindersley)*

there? And wouldn't they—if they could—grab hold of anyone who tried to set them free and take them up there and kill him?" (517a).

Plato offered the cave as an allegory of the human condition. Each soul is imprisoned in an imperfect fleshly body, forced to look through imperfect physical eyes at imperfect copies of the Forms, illuminated by the sun. Moreover, the soul is victim to the conventional beliefs of the society in which it lives. As the freed prisoner turns his head around from the shadows to reality, Plato asks us to turn our souls around from the ordinary world and our cultural presuppositions, and undertake the difficult journey to the better world of the Forms, the true Reality of which objects are but shadows. The Allegory of the Cave is at once optimistic and pessimistic (Annas, 1981). The optimism lies in the promise that, with effort, we can be liberated from ignorance and illusion. The cave is culture, the web of conventional beliefs that Socrates's elenchus brought into question. Through philosophy and right education, however, we can escape from the cave of opinion and Appearances to the realm of knowledge and Reality. We may know the truth and it shall make us free. The pessimism lies in the difficulty and dangers of the path upward. It is not, Plato says, for everyone; it is only for an elite few whose character can bear its burdens. Most people do not want to be free, he suggests, and will greet their would-be liberators with jeers and even death.

The story is also an allegory of Socrates's life. He once was a political animal and a brave soldier, but obtained a vision of Truth that he tried to share with the world to his own cost. Centuries later, when the *Republic* became known to Christians, the Allegory of the Cave and Socrates's life made powerful impressions, striking deep resonances with the story of Christ, who assumed human form, taught the truth, and was executed by disbelieving men.

The Ladder of Love: Being Drawn to the Good.   The fourth metaphor for the Forms, the Ladder of Love in the *Symposium*, describes the love of Beauty, which Plato once said was the easiest path from this world to the Forms. Through the female character Diotima, Plato describes an upward ascent from profane physical love to sacred love of the Form of Beauty itself. The introduction of Diotima into the *Symposium* is quite significant. Athenian men deprecated women. They were not citizens; they could not be warriors because they were physically weak. Athenian men looked upon women only as vehicles of procreation. They treated women much as the Wahhabi Islam does: They were to remain at home, out of sight of men; slaves went out to do shopping and other chores. The only women allowed into a symposium were the most expensive prostitutes, the *hetaera*. Yet, at the same time, if politics was the province of men, religion was the province of women. Thus, Plato suggests that Diotima's teachings on love to Socrates, and through him to his audience at the symposium, are a divine revelation rather than a philosophical argument.

The first rung of the ladder is sexual love, but it must be steered in the right direction by a philosophical guide, as Diotima was said to have led Socrates. The student "begin[s] while still young by going to beautiful bodies; and first, if his guide guides rightly, to love one single body" (201a). Understanding Plato's (1991) formulation of this first step to Truth requires understanding the conception and practice of male homoerotic love in Athens and much of the Classical world. Greek citizens—all male—spent most of their time together, shunning home life. In this atmosphere, a well-defined homoerotic culture grew up, as Greeks did not categorize people as heterosexual or homosexual (Garrison, 2000). Established citizens would take as lovers beautiful youths who had just entered puberty but whose beards were not grown and so were not yet citizens themselves. The older man became a mentor and teacher to the youth, and sometimes the relationship would last throughout life. The Greeks regarded the erotic connection between teacher and student as essential to the education of youth (Pomeroy et al., 1999) and as part of the initiation of a young man into the warrior band, especially at Sparta (Rahe, 1994). As the Greeks sequestered their women, homosexual relationships also formed among women, again especially at Sparta, whose men were rarely at home, living in their barracks or away at war. Among both men and women, homosexual relationships provided the companionship and emotional intimacy later linked to marriage in Hellenistic and Christian cultures (Pomeroy et al., 1999).

The exact nature of these relationships, especially the kind of physical intimacy that took place, remains controversial. In the highest theory of the day, the relationships were, as our saying goes, "platonic," although there is no question that sexual activity did in fact occur. Socrates, although susceptible to male beauty, condemned any sexual liaisons with his students, saying it was always bad for the young men. The *Symposium* ends with the story of Alcibiades, the most beautiful youth of his day and a student of Socrates, recounting the abject failure of his aggressive attempts to seduce Socrates. Socrates's resistance to Alcibiades's attempted seduction shows that while lust is the first step toward knowledge of the Beautiful, it must be abandoned for the love of wisdom, philosophy.

In the conception of love in the *Symposium* (1991) and most of Plato's works (his last, the *Laws*, in which Socrates is absent, condemns homosexuality outright), love of women was inferior to homosexual love. Love of women leads to procreation of children, seeking immortality through merely physical offspring doomed to die. Greek men tended to fear women as sexual temptresses who pulled their eyes from better things such as politics, war, or, for Socrates and Plato, philosophy and the pursuit of the Good. Such fear of sexuality passed over into certain strands of Christian and Islamic thought, where physical pleasure was regarded as distracting men from knowing and worshipping God. Better than physical procreation—being "pregnant with respect to the body"—Plato thought, was being "pregnant in respect to [one's] soul" (209a), seeking immortality in the soul itself and through teaching students, and having intellectual rather than physical heirs.

Having learned to love one beautiful body, the student "next, learn[s] to recognize that the beauty on any body whatever is akin to that on any other body. . . . Realizing this, he is constituted a lover of all beautiful bodies and relaxes this vehemence for one, looking down on it and believing it of small importance. After this, he must come to believe that beauty in souls is more to be valued than in the body" (201b–c). With Socrates, we move beyond the love of the body to the love of the soul, and such a man will teach ugly youths of good soul—Socrates was famously ugly—believing "bodily beauty a small thing" (201c). Now, the teacher introduces the student to other kinds of beauty in practices such as music and art, and in studies such as mathematics and philosophy.

For Plato, when properly guided, *eros* goes beyond the panting of physical love to a union with Beauty itself in the realm of the Forms where Truth is Beauty and Beauty is Truth:

> He who has been educated in the things of love up to this point, beholding beautiful things rightly and in due order, will then, suddenly, in an instant, proceeding at that point to the end of things of love, see something marvelous, beautiful in nature: it is that, Socrates, for the sake of which in fact all his previous labors existed. . . . But when someone, ascending from things here through the right love of boys, begins clearly to see that, the Beautiful, he would pretty well touch the end. For this is the right way to proceed in matters of love, or to be led by another—beginning from these beautiful things here, to ascend ever upward for the sake of that, the Beautiful, as though using the steps of a ladder; from one to two, and from two to all beautiful bodies and from beautiful bodies to beautiful practices and from practices to beautiful studies, and from studies one arrives in the end at that study which is nothing other than the study of that, the Beautiful itself, and one knows in the end, by itself, what it is to be beautiful. It is there, if anywhere, dear Socrates . . . that human life is to be lived: in contemplating the Beautiful itself. (210e–210d)

In the *Republic*, the Ladder of Love is elaborated into the lengthy and painstaking form of education laid down for the Republic's philosopher-leaders, the Guardians. As children, they receive the same moralizing form of education as all citizens. Plato proposes carefully censoring literature, including Homer, whose *Iliad* and *Odyssey* were the Greeks' Bible, replacing it with tales crafted by teachers to build proper character. Music, too, is carefully regulated so that only what is perfect and pleasant is heard. Athletics train the body as literature and music train the soul. Only the elite of the noblest souls—including women (a concept that initially shocked Plato's audience)—however, are selected for higher, academic education. Through philosophy, the Guardian elite is led out of the Cave of Opinion to knowledge of the Forms, but they are obligated to return to the best cave going, Plato's Republic, and rule disinterestedly out of their inspired wisdom. Only they know what is best for all the citizens of the Republic.

The Spartan Equals inspired Plato's Guardian class, although the Guardians were not to be warriors. The Greek tension between what is owed to the polis and what is owed to the family (oikos) was solved by Plato along Spartan lines. He extended the idea of Spartan barracks life by forbidding marriage, though not sexual union, among the Guardians. They thus had no oikos to draw their attention away from choosing what was best for their Republic. A form of testing was implicit in Plato's Republic, because offspring of the lower classes might enter the Guardian class if they were worthy, and offspring of Guardians might be demoted if found unworthy. We have seen that, at Sparta, a government official, not an infant's parents, decided if a child was to be accepted as a Spartan or exposed to death, and Plato incorporated this practice into his ideal Republic.

Learning as Remembering: Knowledge Is within Us.   In some other dialogues, a different path to the Forms is described that resembles Socrates's midwifery. From his Pythagorean education and from the Greek religion of Orphism as well as other religious influences, especially Hinduism, entering Greece from the east, Plato adopted the idea of reincarnation. For example, in the *Phaedrus*, Plato works out a detailed scheme by which souls go through a cycle of reincarnations. Souls are born in heaven, and thus see the Forms before their first incarnation in "the pollution of the walking sepulcher we call a body" (250c, trans. W. Hamilton). The future fate of a soul depends on how virtuous a life it led on earth. At death, souls are brought to judgment. The wicked "go to expiate their sins in places of judgment beneath the earth" (249a) and may come back as beasts. The virtuous, especially those who had been philosophers (who on the third straight incarnation as philosophers escape the wheel of rebirth), will ascend to the highest reaches of the heavens, and in the train of the gods see the Forms again. The less virtuous ascend less high in heaven and are more quickly reincarnated as lesser humans such as financier (third best) or farmer (seventh).

Thus, "every human soul by its very nature has beheld true being" (250a). In the sepulcher of the body, however, the "beatific vision" of the Forms is forgotten, more in bad people than in good. Knowledge of the Forms may be regained, however. As contemplation of beautiful things leads us to knowledge of Beauty itself because all beautiful things resemble Beauty, so all cats resemble the Form of the Cat, gerbils the Form of the Gerbil, just acts the Form of Justice, and so on for all universal concept terms. Because of the resemblance of things to the Forms that are within us, we can "collect out of the multiplicity of sense-impressions a unity arrived at by a process of reason. Such a process is simply the recollection of things which our soul once perceived when it took its journey with a god . . . gazing upwards toward what is truly real" (249b). Plato appealed to reincarnation to explain how Socrates could act as a moral midwife giving birth to knowledge of virtue without explicitly teaching it. Knowledge of virtue, like all knowledge, is latent in the soul, hidden by the body and conventional belief, awaiting the right stimuli to be recollected.

Perhaps the oldest enduring controversy in the history of psychology is the debate between *nativism* and *empiricism*, nature and nurture. Plato is the first great exponent of nativism, holding that our character and knowledge are innate, being carried by the soul from its vision of the Forms and its lives in previous incarnations. Learning is a process of recollecting to consciousness what we already know but of which we have become ignorant.

MOTIVATION: WHY DO WE ACT AS WE DO?   As a moral philosopher, Plato addressed questions about human motivation. Although he accepted the Greek beliefs that happiness (eudaemonia) and virtue are intimately connected and that all people naturally seek happiness, he did not accept his teacher's view that wrong deeds are the result of ignorance alone. In the *Republic* and *Phaedrus*, Plato proposed a different psychology of human motives and human action.

Plato divided the citizens of the Republic into three classes. By virtue of innate greatness of soul and the academic education it merits, the elite Guardians constitute the ruling class. Next in character are the Auxiliaries, who aid the Guardians by acting as soldiers, magistrates, and other functionaries of the Republic. The mass of the citizens makes up the least inherently virtuous Productive Class. In a way reminiscent of Homeric mini-soul psychology, Plato postulates three forms of soul present in every human being that parallel the three classes of citizens. Class membership is determined by which soul rules each citizen.

The highest form of soul, and the only immortal one, is the *rational soul*, located in the head because the soul, being perfect, must be round and thus be located in the roundest and highest part of the body. The rational soul rules in the Guardians and will be led back to the Forms from which it came by philosophical education. The second form of soul is the *spirited soul*, located in the chest and dominant in the Auxiliaries. The spirited soul represents the old Homeric virtues, being motivated by glory and fame. Because of its quest for noble things like glory and the immortality of fame, and because it can feel shame and guilt, the spirited soul is superior to the third soul, the *desiring soul*, located in the belly and genitals. The desiring soul is a disparate grab bag of irrational wants. Physical desires for food or sex, which we share with animals, are paradigm cases of the appetites of the desiring soul, but desire for money is also located there. It may be best to think of the desiring soul as the pursuit of self-interest, which the Greeks always deprecated. It dominates in the Productive Classes, who are described as unfit to rule precisely because they seek their own interests, not the general interest of the polis. The Guardians may rule because their educated reason and virtuous character places them beyond self-interest.

As in his doctrine of reincarnation, Plato's depiction of the ideal society and the mapping of its classes onto aspects of personality were probably influenced by ancient Indian theology. The Hindu Rig Veda divided society into four castes: the *Brahmans*, theologians and ultimate rulers; the *Kshatriya*, warriors and day-to-day rulers; the *Vaisa*, professionals and artisans; and the *Sudra*, laborers. In a way we've learned is characteristic of Greek thought, Plato folds the last two Hindu castes—who work rather than think or rule—into a single productive class. Like Plato, the Hindus identified each class with an aspect of the person, soul, intellect, mind, and body, and with a corresponding part of the body, head, heart, loins, and feet (Danto, 1987).

In the *Phaedrus*, the three forms of soul are described in a metaphor later alluded to by a psychologist deeply read in the classics, Sigmund Freud. Plato depicts human personality as a chariot pulled by two horses. One horse is "upright and clean limbed . . . white with black eyes" whose "thirst for honor is tempered by restraint and modesty. He is a friend to genuine renown and needs no whip, but is driven simply by the word of command. The other horse is lumbering, crooked and ill-made . . . wantonness and boastfulness are his companions and he is . . . hardly controllable even with whip and goad" (253d, trans. W. Hamilton). The first horse is the spirited soul; the second is the desiring soul. The charioteer is the rational soul, which should master the horses and drive them toward the good. Mastering the spirited soul is easy because it knows honor, and therefore, something of virtue. Mastering the desiring soul is nearly impossible; the most strenuous efforts by reason are required to break it utterly. Plato's conception of the desiring soul reflects Greek disdain for slaves. Slaves, Greeks said, are ignoble because they "observe everything from the perspective of the stomach" (quoted by Rahe, 1994, p. 19). Even when the rational soul thinks it is master, desire springs up in dreams, said Plato. In dreams, a person "doesn't stop at trying to have sex with his mother . . . he doesn't hold back from anything, however bizarre or disgusting" (*Republic*, 571d, trans. R. Waterfield). As the Spartans feared rebellion of the helots, the rational soul of the Guardians feared rebellion of the desiring soul.

According to Plato, and unlike Socrates, bad behavior may stem from more than ignorance; it may stem from insufficient mastery of the rational over the spirited and desiring souls. Foolish pursuit of honor may lead to disasters such as the Charge of the Light Brigade. Even worse are the sins committed by giving in to the demands of the body. In the *Phaedrus*, Plato vividly describes the torments of a philosophical lover for a beautiful youth. Reason knows physical consummation of love is wrong, but the desiring horse races headlong into it. Only by the strongest measures, yanking on the reins until the horse's mouth is drenched in blood and beating its haunches until they collapse to the ground, will "the wicked horse abandon its lustful ways" (254e, trans. W. Hamilton) and submit to the commands of reason.

Plato's analysis of human motivation contains, however, a profound muddle that haunted later philosophical and scientific psychology (Annas, 1981). In his explicitly psychological descriptions of human personality, reason was sharply differentiated from irrational passion. The desiring soul, and to a lesser extent the spirited soul, simply *want*, being incapable of any sort of rational calculation at all; they are all drive and no reason, providing the energy that makes the chariot go. Reason is directive, steering the motivational souls to good ends; it is all reason and no drive, providing direction but not energy.

However, when Plato described the souls operating in the citizens of his Republic, the picture becomes more complicated. Citizens of the Productive Class are supposed to be dominated by desire, but they do not dash about in a confused orgy of lust and gratification—they are productive. Merchants must be able to calculate how to buy or make goods that people want, and how to price and market them. Tailors and shoemakers must be able to design clothes and shoes and properly execute the means to make them. Plato's disdain of the Productive class reflects the disdain Athenian citizens felt for profit-seeking metics who preferred practical outcomes to the contemplation of Truth. Similarly, Auxiliaries must be able to make and carry out battle plans.

Members of the Productive and Auxiliary classes clearly can calculate means to ends, suggesting that the desiring and spirited souls themselves have some measure of reason, being not mere engines of action. Reason, for its part, does more than merely steer behavior. The souls of the Guardians seek knowledge out of a special kind of eros, drawn not to physical bodies but by love of the Good and Beautiful themselves. Reason, then, is more than a calculator; it has a motive of its own: justice.

Western thought from Plato's time to our own has wrestled with the relationship between reason on one side and emotion and motivation on the other. Most classical and Hellenistic theorists favored Plato's official theory, distrusting emotion and subordinating it to reason. The Stoics (see later) aimed to completely extirpate the emotions and live by logic alone. On the other hand, the ecstatic Greek religions distrusted reason, and found in strong emotion a pathway to the divine, as would the later Romantics such as Keats. In the Age of Reason, David Hume spoke up for emotion, saying that reason is and can only be a slave to the passions (the emotions), capable of steering them but not of initiating action on its own. Freud agreed with Hume but modified Plato's image. With the Homeric warrior virtues lost by 1900, Freud described the rational ego as a rider struggling to master the horse of the id, Plato's desiring soul. Others, however, saw more in feeling than irrational desire. Shortly before Hume, Blaise Pascal wrote that the heart has its reasons that reason does not understand; later, the Romantics revolted against cold reason, elevating feeling and intuition over scientific calculation. In our own day, we worry about the triumph of the computer—the very model of Plato's charioteer—and about computer-inspired models of the mind, for which motives to do anything are missing. Today, psychologists are discovering that Pascal was right (Damasio, 1994; Goleman, 1995).

Plato's chariot image contains another difficulty of longstanding in psychology, called the *homunculus problem* (Annas, 1981). Homunculus means "little man." Plato asks us to imagine that the driver of a person's behavior is the rational soul, a charioteer. He thus invites us to think of the rational soul as a little man inside the head, who steers the behavior of the body and manages the passions of the heart, belly, and genitals the way a charioteer steers the chariot and masters its horses. However, what accounts for the behavior of the little charioteer—reason—inside the head? Does he have inside an even smaller charioteer (an inner Mini-Me)? Who has, in turn, a still smaller charioteer? And so on, *ad infinitum?* To explain the behavior of a person by positing a small person inside is not adequate, because the actions of the inner person, the homunculus, remain unexplained, violating the Iron Law of Explanation. To what extent Plato is guilty of this mistake is unclear (Annas, 1981), but it is a mistake that will crop up in psychology from Plato's day to our own.

CONCLUSION: PLATO'S SPIRITUAL VISION Although Plato began with Socrates, he ultimately went a great deal further, constructing the first general point of view in philosophy. We must call it a point of view rather than a system, because, unlike Aristotle, Plato did not work out a set of systematically interlocking theories across the whole range of human knowledge. For example, Plato's so-called Theory of the Forms is less a theory in epistemology than a vision, tempting to some people, of a higher reality (Annas, 1981). The Forms appear in different guises in different dialogues, and appear not at all in many. In the late dialogue, the *Thaetetus,* Plato discusses knowledge without mentioning the Forms, and skeptically concludes that truth is elusive. That Platonic thought was more a point of view than a system made it easy for Christian thinkers to assimilate it during the early Middle Ages. Christians could pick and choose the most appealing parts of Plato and identify the realm of the Forms with Heaven.

Plato's ideas resonate with other religions, too. For example, the basic idea of the Ladder of Love—that one can move toward Enlightenment beginning with physical love—is found in the Hindu path of *Kama* (pleasure) and the Buddhist use of love imagery to lead the soul to the light of the *One,* although these ladders do not involve homosexuality. Many, if not most, world religions teach that, in addition to this physical world, there is an invisible world of spirits. As with love, Brahman Hindus and Buddhists teach that this world is an illusion, *Maya,* and that the soul must have as little to do with it as possible or risk more reincarnations. With Plato, they bid the charioteer of the body to discipline desire, but go beyond metaphor to prescribe practices by which the desiring soul may be broken. In the *Phaedrus,* Plato talks metaphorically about controlling lust for one's beloved. Tantric Yoga and Daoist masters provided concrete instructions on how to have sexual intercourse with perfect rational control while withholding orgasm to obtain spiritual strength (*Tantrism*) or personal health (*Daoism*).

There is often an otherworldly, religious cast to Plato's thought because his philosophy was greatly influenced by changes taking place in Greek religion (Morgan, 1992). Greek life was permeated by religion—festivals and sacrifices to the gods were an everyday affair. Greek religion was the special arena of women as politics and war were the special arenas of men. Greek beliefs and practices were pluralistic, but in the polis tradition that was on the way out, there was an emphasis on the radical separation of the human and divine worlds. The famous Greek epigram "know thyself" was not only an invitation to self-scrutiny; it was also an admonition to accept one's place in the universe. The gods are divine and immortal; we are not. The Greeks valued self-control (Davidson, 1997), making *hubris* and *pleonexia* (greed) the most important sins in Greek eyes. The tendrils of a different kind of religion first appeared in movements such as Pythagoreanism and Orphism. These religions were more mystical, teaching how to commune with the gods and teaching the existence of an immortal, reincarnating, human soul.

Following the stresses of the Peloponnesian War (431–404) and the defeat of Athens, the Greek world experienced a religious revolution (Burkert, 1985). New, mystical cults and ecstatic practices replaced the polis tradition of seeking favors from the gods by making sacrifices to them. In these new rites, worshippers used music, wine, and erotic stimulation to achieve a divine madness, *mania.* The goal was to unite with the god they worshipped (e.g., Dionysos) in a divine, transcendental moment that would purge the initiate of her or his sins. These new religions also taught that each person has a divine, immortal soul. Plato accepted the new teachings, but sought to tame their excesses (Morgan, 1992). He, too, taught that each person has an immortal soul, but that the path to salvation lay through philosophy, combining the new belief in a world beyond this one with the traditional Greek injunction to know thyself and exercise rational self-control.

Plato's otherworldliness takes us to points on which Plato changed Socrates's teachings in ways Socrates himself might have found disturbing. Once he had his own philosophy to push, Plato discarded the penetrating search of the elenchus for dialogues in which "Socrates'" students come off as toadies, saying "Oh yes, wise Socrates," and "It cannot be otherwise." Disdaining wealth and fame, Socrates was unworldly, but he was not otherworldly (Vlastos, 1991). Socrates never mentioned the Forms, and he always meant a virtuous life to be worthwhile in *this* world, not some imagined afterlife, recalling imperial Athenians to the path of sophrosyne. Socrates would converse with, and try to teach virtue to, anyone willing to undertake the elenchus. Plato was an elitist, reserving academic education for an innately wise ruling class, the Guardians, and, among them, he reserved philosophy only for the mature, over age 30, (the age at which Spartans could leave their barracks) fearing it would make the young lawless.

Plato's otherworldliness and search for eternal Being had an important effect on the history of science. Recall that theoria meant contemplation—for Plato, contemplation of the Forms—for Greeks, the highest form of knowledge. Plato, and the Greeks generally, disdained practical, useful knowledge, which they called metis (Eamon, 1994), associated with the profit-seeking tradesmen who moved to Athens because of its wealth and were *metics* rather than citizens. For many centuries to come, philosophical thought in both Europe and Islam would be identified with demonstrable, abstract knowledge rather than the active experimental inquiry into nature we associate with science today. Moreover, practical applications of science were rarely sought before the Enlightenment. As late as 1730, the British patent office rejected patents for devices that were labor-saving (Jacob, 2001). In the Greek scheme of things—which Plato polished to high perfection—Truth had little, if anything, to do with the world in which humans live. Life was something to escape, not embrace and improve.

Whatever its faults, the Platonic vision has been immensely influential. The twentieth-century philosopher and mathematician Alfred North Whitehead said, "The safest general characterization of the whole Western philosophical tradition is that it consists of a series of footnotes to Plato" (quoted by Artz, 1980, p. 15). Returning a copy of the *Republic* to Ralph Waldo Emerson, a Vermont farmer said, "That book has a great number of my ideas" (quoted by Artz, 1980, p. 16). Plato had many students, but the most important was Aristotle, who nevertheless took philosophy in a more empirical and scientific direction.

Aristotle: The Quest for Nature

Like Plato, Aristotle (384–322 B.C.E.) came from a wealthy family, but from the remote province of Macedonia. His father was a physician to a Macedonian king, and Aristotle was a biologist as well as the first truly systematic philosopher. At 17, he went to the Academy to study with Plato, and remained there for 20 years. When Plato died, Aristotle left the Academy and traveled around the Adriatic doing zoological research, until being called by King Philip II of Macedon to be tutor to his son, Alexander. Eventually, Aristotle returned to Athens and founded his own place of learning and research, the *Lyceum*. After Alexander the Great's death in 323, anti-Macedonian feeling prompted Aristotle to flee Athens, fearing that Athenians might "sin twice against philosophy." He died in the town of Chalcis soon after.

The differences between Plato and Aristotle begin with temperament. Plato never developed a systematic philosophy, but wrote dramatic and provocative dialogues laying out a stirring cosmic vision, and there was clearly about him, as about so many Greek thinkers, something of the seer and shaman. Aristotle, on the other hand, was first and foremost a scientist, an empirically inclined observer of nature as the rationalist Plato could never be. Whether writing about the soul or ethics, metaphysics or politics, dreams or art, Aristotle was always practical and down to earth. His surviving works are prose treatises, probably lecture notes. In them, we hear the voice of the first professor, reviewing the literature—fortunately for us, else we would know next to nothing about the Presocratics—before advancing his own carefully thought out and often reworked ideas. Even while philosophizing, Aristotle remained a scientist. We never find in Aristotle the otherworldly quasi-mysticism of Plato.

Instead, Aristotle was always concerned with discovering what is natural, and until the term *scientist* was coined in the nineteenth century, people who studied nature were called *natural philosophers*. Unlike Plato, for whom what is most Real exists in heavenly Being rather than on earth, Aristotle, the biologist, looked to this world to define what is. Unlike the Sophists, he drew no sharp line between phusis and nomos, believing that the human way of life should be built on what was best for human nature.

PHILOSOPHY OF SCIENCE   Aristotle worked out a comprehensive philosophical system, including the first philosophy of science. As a working scientist who was also a philosopher, Aristotle painstakingly considered the goals and methods of science, defining in large measure what science would be until the Scientific Revolution of the seventeenth century overthrew Aristotle to create the very different kind of science we know today.

The Four Fashions of Explanation.   Aristotle set out four ways by which to explain things and events. Like Plato, Aristotle tended to focus on the former more than the latter, on understanding what a thing is, rather than on the dynamics of change, the focus of modern science.

The most basic conceptual division for Aristotle was between form and matter. Aristotle's conception of matter was very different from ours. Today, we think of matter as coming in distinct types with distinct properties, as in the elements in the atomic table or the list of subatomic particles of quantum physics. However, for Aristotle, precisely because they can be distinguished and defined, such particles are already mixtures of intelligible form and raw matter. In his conception, matter was sheer, undifferentiated physical existence. The closest modern parallel to Aristotle's conception of matter is matter as it existed in the first seconds after the Big Bang, before the particles and elements had come into existence. Matter as such was unknowable, said Aristotle; for matter to be knowable—to be an object of perception and science—it has to be joined to form.

Form is a term Aristotle took from Plato, but characteristically he stripped it of its heavenly existence and demystified it; hence, in Plato it is Form; in Aristotle, form. Form is, most generally, what makes a thing that which it is, defining it and making it intelligible to us. The paradigm example of the relation of form and matter has always been a statue. Imagine a bronze statue of the type that stands on Monument Avenue in Richmond, representing a Confederate Civil War general such as Robert E. Lee or tennis champion Arthur Ashe.

The *matter* of a statue is what it is made of; in the case of a Monument Avenue statue, it is bronze. When the bronze is cast, it takes on form, becoming a likeness of Lee or Ashe. The form makes the statue what it is. The same bronze could be cast as Lee or Ashe: same matter, different form. We can also have the same form in different matter: the figure of Lee or Ashe might be rendered in plaster, clay, or plastic. What makes something a statue of Robert E. Lee or of Arthur Ashe is, then, its form, not its matter, and we know the statue through the form rather than the matter. In perception, Aristotle said, the mind receives the form of an object but not its matter.

Aristotle rejected what he called the separability of the Forms, Plato's thesis that the Forms exist in a realm of Being separate from our imperfect physical world. Aristotle's general standpoint was that the alleged eternal Forms do not explain anything. They are just glorified individuals—perfect, heavenly individuals, true—but individuals nonetheless. There is no reason to think that if an artist casts 100 identical statues there must be a separate, 101st heavenly Form of the Statue that they all resemble. Similarly, there may be thousands of cats in the world, but there is no reason to think there's an additional heavenly Form of the Cat, too. Positing one perfect Cat (or statue) does nothing to explain the nature of the physical cats (or statues) we see. We lose nothing by dropping the separate Forms.

Aristotle's concept of form, however, is more than just shape and is comprised of the other three causes. First, form defines what something is in its essence: *essential cause*. Essential cause is definition. What defines a statue as being of Lee or Ashe is form—specifically, form as essential cause. Second, form includes how things come into existence or are made: *efficient cause*. The efficient cause of a bronze statue is the process of casting the metal; of a marble statue, the processing of chipping and polishing a block of marble into the desired shape. Third, form includes the purpose for which a thing exists: *final cause*. Statues are erected to honor a great person and perpetuate his or her memory. Taking all these things together—a thing's shape and essence, its process of creation, and its purpose for being—constitutes a thing's form, why it is what it is, independent of its physical embodiment but not existing separately from it, as Plato held. Aristotle's form does not exist without being physically embodied in matter of some type.

Although as a scientist Aristotle was more concerned with the physical world than Plato had been, his philosophy of science was unlike modern science in an important methodological respect. Aristotle observed nature and offered accounts of how nature works, but he did not interrogate nature through experimentation. He continued in the Greek tradition of disdaining practical knowledge in favor of developing abstract theories that demonstrated why the world is the way it is. Finding new and useful facts and techniques was never one of his goals.

Aristotle's science is also very different from modern science with regard to his conception of causation. We think today of causation in terms of mechanisms, of how objects interact with one another by contact, by forces, or physical/chemical processes. But Aristotle thought of causes as the natural behavior of things given their essences. Thus, according to Aristotle, heavy objects fall simply because it is their inherent, essential, *nature* to fall, not because of the interaction of two masses via the force of gravity. This orientation reinforced in Aristotle the Greek tendency to contemplate nature passively. To find out what an object's nature is, one has to observe it causing as little disturbance as possible, because disturbing the object would make its behavior to some degree "unnatural," because we caused it, not its essential nature. Today we think that to understand nature we must ask it questions via experiment, but that idea came late to science, as we will see.

Finally, modern science rejects Aristotle's idea that every event has a purpose behind it. The world is seen by modern science as a machine affected by efficient causes alone. This change in the conception of the universe as being full of purpose to being a simple machine will have profound implications for psychology and modern life.

Potentiality and Actuality.   In Aristotle's philosophy, everything in the universe (with two exceptions) has both potentiality and actuality. A lump of bronze is actually a lump of bronze, but it is potentially a statue; a psychology major is actually a psychology major but potentially a cognitive psychologist. The two exceptions to the rule of potentiality and actuality are pure matter in Aristotle's sense, and his unmoved mover, whom Christians later identified with God. Sheer matter without form of any kind is pure potentiality, capable of becoming anything, as matter was at the moment of the Big Bang. If there is pure potentiality, Aristotle thought, there must logically be pure actuality, a being whose potentiality is used up, incapable of further change, perfected; this is the unmoved mover. Because it has no potentiality, the unmoved mover cannot change. Because the unmoved mover is perfect, fully actualized, other things naturally move toward it, as their potentiality becomes actuality. The unmoved mover moves by being desired, not through activity of its own, the way a beloved moves a lover by inspiring desire, as in Plato's Ladder of Love; for Aristotle, love literally made the world go round. The more fully actualized a thing is, the nearer it is to the unmoved mover. The striving for actualization creates a grand hierarchy among all things, from perfectly unformed, neutral matter in a state of pure potentiality up to the unmoved mover. Aristotle called this hierarchy the *natural scale*, but later it was called the *Great Chain of Being*.

The ideas of potentiality and actuality may be regarded as a creative solution to an important biological problem that was not fully solved until the structure of DNA was elucidated in 1953. Plant an acorn and it becomes an oak; plant a tomato seed and it becomes a tomato plant; fertilize a human ovum and it becomes a human being. Unlike the casting of a bronze statue, these changes are examples of spontaneous development. We don't sculpt the acorn and its sprout to become an oak the way we mold bronze to become a statue. Moreover, biological development is directed to a predetermined end. Acorns never become tomato plants; tomato seeds never become oaks; and human mothers never give birth to bears. Such observations led the biologist Aristotle to see purpose everywhere in nature, including nonliving things.

Something apparently guides the acorn to naturally actualize its potential oak-hood. Today we know that what guides biological development is DNA. For Aristotle, however, it was form. The purpose, or final cause, of an acorn is to become an oak, and so the striving of an acorn toward oak-hood is an aspect of its form. Plato's Forms were perfect Objects in the realm of Being. Aristotle's forms, at least in the biological world, are dynamic, directing development and constituting and controlling the life processes of living things.

PSYCHOLOGY

Soul and Body. For Aristotle, psychology was the study of the soul—that which differentiates the animate from the inanimate worlds. Aristotle defines the soul as "the form of a natural body having life potentially within it" (*On the Soul*, II, i, 412a20–1). All living things possess soul as their form, and thus it is a living thing's soul that defines its nature, what it is to be that living thing. Soul is the actuality and the actualizing, directing force of any living organism, fulfilling the body's potential *having of life*.

As the form of a living thing, soul is thus the essential, efficient, and final cause of an organism. As essential cause, the soul is what defines an animal or plant—a cat is a cat because it has a cat's soul and therefore behaves like a cat. The soul is the efficient cause of bodily growth and movement and of life processes generally. Without soul, the body is not actualized and is dead, mere matter. The soul is also the final cause of an organism, for the body serves the soul and the soul guides its purposive development and activity. To summarize, of any living organism, the material cause is the body of which the living thing is made, and the soul is the form, being the efficient cause of life processes, being the animal's essence, and being the organism's final cause, the purpose of the body.

Aristotle's view of the relation of soul to body is different from Plato's. As he rejected the separability of the forms, Aristotle rejected the separability of soul and body, the dualism of Plato, the Pythagoreans, Descartes, and of many religions. The form of a statue is not a separate thing added to bronze to make it a statue. Similarly, as the form of the body, the soul is not a separate thing added to the body. An organism is a unity. Without soul, the body is dead; without body, there is no soul, that is, no form to define the matter of the body as a particular knowable being. Aristotle put it this way in *On the Soul*, "That is why we can wholly dismiss as unnecessary the question whether the soul and the body are one: it is as meaningless to ask whether the wax and the shape given to it by the stamp are one" (II. i, 412b6–9).

Aristotle evades the ways of thinking about mind and body ushered in by Descartes. He is not a dualist with Plato, Christianity, or Descartes, because Aristotle's soul is not a separate thing made of something other than matter, a thing that may therefore exist without a body. Neither is he the dualist's modern nemesis, a materialist, denying as had the atomists the existence of soul altogether, because without a soul a body has no definition, no life, and no purpose. For Aristotle, the soul is the set of capacities of a living body. Just as seeing is the capacity of the eye, soul is the capacity of the body to act (Sorabji, 1974/1993). Without an eye, there is no seeing; without a body, there is no action, no soul.

All living things have soul, but there are different forms of living things, possessing, therefore, different forms of soul. Specifically, Aristotle distinguished three levels of soul appropriate to different levels of actualization on his natural scale. At the lowest level there is the *nutritive soul*, possessed by plants, serving three functions: (1) maintaining the individual plant through nutrition, (2) maintaining the species through reproduction, and (3) directing growth. Animals possess a more complex, *sensitive soul*, which subsumes the nutritive soul's functions while adding others, making it more fully actualized than the nutritive soul. Animals, unlike plants, are aware of their surroundings. They have sensations; hence, "sensitive soul." As a consequence of sensation, animals experience pleasure and pain and so feel desire either to seek pleasure or to avoid pain. There are two further consequences of sensation: first, imagination and memory (since experience can be imagined or recalled); and second, movement as a consequence of desire. Highest in the scale of souls comes the human or, *rational, soul*, subsuming the others and adding *mind*, the power to think and have general knowledge.

Structure and Functions of the Rational, Human Soul. According to Aristotle, gaining knowledge is a psychological process that starts with the perception of particular objects and ends with general knowledge of universals, of forms. Aristotle's analysis of the soul can be represented by a diagram showing the faculties of the soul and their interrelationships (Figure 2). In many respects, Aristotle's analysis of the sensitive and rational soul resembles that given by modern cognitive psychologists,

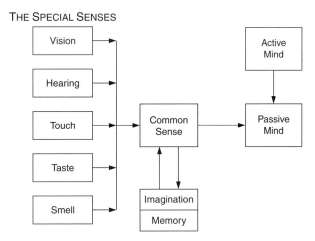

FIGURE 2 The structure of the human (sensitive and rational) soul according to Aristotle.

and I have anachronistically depicted Aristotle's theory as an information-processing flowchart of the type made familiar by cognitive psychology.

Sense Perception. Aristotle writes, "Generally, about all perception we can say that a sense is what has the power of receiving into itself the sensible forms of things without the matter, in the way in which a piece of wax takes on the impress of a signet ring without the iron or gold" (*On the Soul*, 4242a18–20). That is, if I look at a bronze statue, my eye receives the form of the statue without receiving its matter, the bronze. Perception—the starting point of knowledge—has to do with form, not matter.

The Special Senses. The first stage in perception is the reception of aspects of an object's form by the *special senses*. Each special sense is dedicated to reception of a particular kind of information about objects, which is why these senses are called "special"; a better translation might be "special-ized." Aristotle regarded the special senses as passive, simply conforming themselves to the forms of objects, and therefore reliable and unerring.

Plato, as we have seen, was a metaphysical realist. Aristotle was a perceptual realist. He rejected the Forms, but taught that in perception our minds receive the form of an object without the matter. Each of the *special sensibles*—the particular perceptual features of an object—is simply picked up in the act of perception. Thus, if we see a green sweater, we see it as green because it really is green. In the example of color, Aristotle thought that the eye-jelly takes on the color of an object, thus register-ing it in the mind. The conscious object of perception, however, was what Aristotle called a *common sensible*, and identifying it required an act of judgment. For example, you might see someone you take to be an old friend across the street, only to discover he or she is someone else. You correctly perceived the person's hair color, build, and so on, but came to an incorrect conclusion about his or her identity. Aristotle's perceptual theory allows for cognitive error, but connects the mind directly with the world.

The Interior Senses. The information provided by the special senses is passed on to faculties that deal with it in various ways. In the animal soul, these faculties are called the *interior senses* because they are not connected with the outside world, but still are dealing with experienced sensations.

The first interior sense is *common sense*. Common sense is an important faculty, being Aristotle's answer to one of the great mysteries of perception, the problem of *sensory integration*, or as it is known in cognitive neuroscience, the *binding problem*. Each special sense detects a specific kind of information about how an object looks, sounds, feels, tastes, or smells. The physical origin of each sense is quite distinct; for example, vision begins with light striking the retina; hearing with sound waves striking the eardrum. The neural path of each special sense into the brain is unique. Yet, the world as we experience it is not a jumble of disconnected sensations. We hear sounds coming from objects we see, and we expect objects to be touchable. We experience single objects—the common sensibles—with multiple facets, not a blooming, buzzing confusion of sense-impressions. Somehow, we integrate the information provided by the special senses by binding together their separate neural pathways into a single mental representation of objects.

Aristotle said the job was done by common sense (Bynum, 1987/1993). It is the place—Aristotle located it in the heart—where the inputs from the special senses are brought together and coordinated into a single, integrated picture of the world, where the sensations are held together in common. Common sense and the next faculty, *imagination*, are involved in judging what an object is. I see a red spot on a tree, but I must judge whether it is a drop of red paint or a ladybug. Thus, whereas the special sensations are infallible—there can be no doubt that I see a red spot—the judgments of common sense and imagination are fallible interpretations of special sensibles—I may wrongly think I'm seeing a ladybug.

We now know that Aristotle was right to draw a sharp distinction between sensing an object and judging what sort of object it is, because the two mental processes are performed in different parts of the brain. For example, there is the syndrome of *prosopagnosia*, in which people with certain sorts of brain damage (Aristotle was wrong about the heart) lose the ability to see faces (Gazzaniga, Ivry, & Mangun, 2002). They see the stimuli that correspond to eyes, noses, mouths, and so on, but they do not integrate the stimuli into the perception of a face, even a familiar face, as in the well-known case of the man who mistook his wife for a hat rack (Sacks, 1985).

The coherent images of objects assembled by common sense are passed on in two directions: to imagination and memory in animals and human beings and, in human beings alone, to mind. The basic function assigned to imagination by Aristotle is the ability to represent the form of an object in its absence, whether just after it has been presented to common sense, or later, after retrieval from memory. Imagination, however, is assigned other functions (Bynum, 1987/1993) that were later separated into distinct faculties by medieval physician-philosophers. As already mentioned, imagination is involved in judging what an object is—that is, in inferring from sensation what object is affecting our senses. In addition to this purely cognitive function, imagination is involved in feeling pleasure and pain and in judging whether a perceived object is good or bad for an organism, thereby causing a behavioral response. Thus, a cat sees a mouse and judges that the mouse is good for it, and so it chases the mouse. The mouse, seeing the cat, judges that it is bad for it and runs away.

The final faculty of the sensitive, or animal, soul is *memory*. Aristotle conceived of memory as a storehouse of the images created by common sense and imagination. It is thus the record of an animal's life, available to be recalled by imagination. Whereas Plato tended to treat memory as reminiscence of absolute Truth from the soul's passage through the heavens between incarnations, Aristotle treats it in a more modern way of recall of previous experiences in our earthly lives (Barash, 1997). Aristotle's memory corresponds to what modern cognitive psychologists call *episodic*, or personal, memory—the ability to recall specific events, or episodes, in one's life. The organization of memory is based on *association*, as described in many modern psychological theories. Plato hinted at the concept of the association of ideas in his proposal that, by their resemblance to the innate Forms, perceived objects lead to knowledge. Aristotle, however, discussed the processes of association more fully. Aristotle discussed three laws of association—*similarity*, *contiguity*, and *contrast*. Similar images are associatively linked, images of contiguous experiences are linked, and opposite images are linked (that is, "hot" usually elicits the association "cold"). He also hinted at the law of *causality*—causally linked experiences remind us of one another.

Cognitive scientists distinguish *episodic* memory from *semantic* memory, the ability to recall the definitions of words. Sometimes, semantic memory is called simply "knowledge" because it concerns general ideas (*universals*), not specific events or things (*particulars*). Aristotle, too, separated memory from knowledge, acquisition of the latter being the function of the uniquely human part of the soul, mind, or *nous*.

Mind.   Aristotle called the rational part of the human soul the *mind*. It is unique to human beings and is capable of acquiring knowledge of abstract universals, as opposed to the knowledge of individual things given in perception. As we experience different members of the same natural type, we note similarities and differences, forming an impression of a universal, which Aristotle believed was always an image. As one experiences a multitude of cats, one eventually forms an idea of what the essence of a cat is, an image of a cat that contains only those perceptual features shared by all cats. To borrow Platonic imagery, my memory stores the remembered forms of our cats—Silver, Theo, and Ginger—but my mind stores the universal concept of the Cat.

Within the mind there must be, as Aristotle believed there to be throughout nature, a difference between potentiality and actuality. The *passive mind* is potentiality. It has no character of its own, for it can take on the form of experienced objects. Knowledge of universals in the passive mind is actualized, or made manifest, by the operations of the active mind. The *active mind* is pure thought, acting on the contents of the passive mind to achieve rational knowledge of universals. This active mind is quite different from the other parts of the soul. As actuality, it is not acted on; rather, it acts on the contents of the passive mind. For Aristotle, this meant that the active mind was unchangeable—hence, immortal, for death is a form of change. The active mind is, therefore, separable from the body and may survive death, unlike the rest of the soul. However, the active mind is not a personal soul, for it is identical in all human beings. It is pure thought and carries nothing away from its sojourn on earth. Knowledge is realized only in the passive mind, which perishes. Active mind corresponds to the processes of abstract thought; passive mind to the contents (Wedin, 1986/1993). Later Neoplatonic, Christian, and Islamic thinkers, otherwise impressed by Aristotle's scientific treatment of the world and human life, had a very difficult time reconciling Aristotle's naturalistic treatment of the soul with their radical dualism of soul and body (Adamson, 2001).

Motivation.   Movement is characteristic of animals and thus is a function of the sensitive soul, which can experience pleasure and pain. All action is motivated by some form of desire, which Aristotle believed involved imagination. In animals, motivation is directed by an image of what is pleasurable, and the animal seeks only present pleasure or the avoidance of pain. Aristotle calls this type of motivation *appetite*. Human beings, however, are capable of reason and so can conceive of right and wrong. Therefore, we can be motivated by desire for what is good or for long-term, future benefits. This type of motivation is called *wish*. Animals experience simple motivational conflicts between opposing appetites, but humans have, in addition, the problem of moral choice.

ETHICS   Aristotle erected his ethics squarely on his psychology. Just as there is a natural goal to the growth of an acorn—it ought to become a flourishing, big oak tree—so there is a natural, proper goal to human life—namely, human flourishing. Aristotle provided a philosophical basis for the Greek idea that there is only one best way of life, only one path to eudaemonia. Just as oak trees have an inherent nature that they naturally tend to fulfill when conditions are favorable, so human beings have a nature that we tend to fulfill when conditions are favorable. Because the human soul is in its essence rational, and therefore capable of virtue, so "human good turns out to be activity of the soul in accordance with virtue" (*Nichomachean Ethics*, 1098a20).

Aristotle's Greek ethics is very different from the ethical systems of later world religions and the Enlightenment systems. Religions such as Christianity and Islam see ethics as a matter of right behavior, defined as following universal rules such as those found in the Ten Commandments. Important secular philosophers of the Enlightenment replaced Divine sanction with reason or calculations of utility, but retained the idea that morality consisted in following fixed rules binding on all rational agents. In short, they brought the epistemological search for universal knowledge to bear on morality. Aristotle did not do this. He separated epistemology from ethics, because his ethical focus was on character—virtues such as wisdom and courage—rather than on conduct. He urged people to be good and live well, not simply follow rules. Thus, for Aristotle, morality was a matter of practical reason—*phronesis*—rather than theoretical reason. The good person must balance virtues to live a life of eudaemonia: Sometimes prudence is better than courageous folly or mercy is better than righteous wrath.

Because the conditions in which a tree or human develops are so important to human flourishing, Aristotle's ethics is at the same time political science (Lear, 1988). Aristotle emphasizes that becoming virtuous requires learning and practice; one cannot flourish in a society that prevents it. So much did Aristotle emphasize a person's life circumstances in becoming virtuous, that he said that people who are wealthy and powerful are potentially more virtuous than the poor and helpless because they are better placed to cultivate virtue and do good things. In this he was very Greek, bestowing true arête only on a fortunate few. Aristotle's ethics cum political science attempted to erase the distinction between phusis and nomos that the Sophists had drawn so sharply thus returning to the standard Greek view that the two are ideally the same. Aristotle famously says that by nature (phusis) man is a social, or more precisely, political, animal. The natural life for human beings is living in society, and human flourishing, eudaemonia, depends, therefore, on living in the right kind of ordered society (nomos).

However, the ideal state described by Aristotle, like Plato's Republic, would be rejected, by and large, by modern citizens of the West. As Plato had held, only the wise and virtuous should rule because only they can set aside personal interest and govern in the interest of the state as a whole. As we might agree, a monarchy might be a good state if the king is wise and benevolent, but a better state is one ruled by law rather than the temporary virtues of a mortal king. Therefore, Aristotle's ideal state is a sort of aristocratic democracy. The citizens of the state participate in ruling it, but most members of the state are not citizens. The citizens of Aristotle's utopia are not the selected and cultivated Guardians of Plato's Republic, but men of independent means who do not work, and who therefore have no personal interests to corrupt their judgment and who have the time to devote to politics. "In the state which is best governed . . . the citizens must not lead the life of artisans or tradesmen, for such a life is ignoble and inimical to virtue. Neither must they be husbandmen [working farmers and ranchers as opposed to those who had slaves], since leisure is necessary both for the development of virtue and the performance of political duties" (*Politics*, VII.9, 1328b33–1329a2). In short, Aristotle's ideal society was an aristocratic version of the Athenian polis he knew.

CONCLUSION: THE COMMONSENSE NATURALIST Plato offered a comprehensive vision of the universe, of human nature, and of people's place in the universe. Aristotle offered a systematic natural philosophy of the universe, human nature, and people's place in the universe. It was systematic, because Aristotle used a core set of concepts to analyze everything from the fall of a rock to the proper construction of a dramatic play. More importantly for the history of science and psychology, it was naturalistic. Aristotle rejected Plato's otherworldly Forms and Plato's radical dualism of soul and body for an account of both that referred only to matter and to natural forces. Moreover, Aristotle's sciences were deeply commonsensical. In his physics, heavier objects fall faster than lighter ones, and in his psychology animals and people do things with purposes in mind. Aristotle's comprehensive yet familiar picture of our world would prove appealing to many later thinkers, but at the same time it clashed with two rival pictures.

One, Plato's spiritual picture, was already on the scene. The rise of the mystery religions of the Hellenistic period and of the world religions of Christianity and Islam reinforced Plato's vision, and naturalism withered. The Scientific Revolution's revived naturalism might have been Aristotle's friend, but its naturalism went further than Aristotle's toward a mechanistic conception of causation that had no room for purpose either in the actions of animals and people or the development of the universe. In psychology, the right understanding of purpose in explaining behavior would be bitterly contested from the Scientific Revolution through the coming of cognitive science. In neither physics nor in psychology would commonsense prevail.

Conclusion: The Greek Legacy

Ancient Greeks effected a miracle—thinking about nature and human beings through philosophy and science rather than through revelation. They began the long Western—and, perhaps, human—trek toward science, freedom, and democracy. At the same time, they glorified war and martial prowess in ways few moderns would endorse; their way of life depended upon slaves, who knew neither freedom nor dignity; and they looked upon material production with disdain.

This last point would have a lasting impact on the history of science and psychology. We are used today to thinking of science as experimental. But because the Greeks disdained interaction with the physical world, their ideal in science was *theoria*—contemplation rather than investigation of nature. It is thus no surprise that the most developed of the ancient sciences was astronomy, in which recording and contemplating the natural movements of the stars and planets is all that is empirically possible. Asking nature questions via experiment—which the early scientist Robert Bacon called "twisting the lion's tail" —did not occur to the Greeks and would take a long time to enter scientific practice. As we shall see, psychology will play an important role in making experimentation part of science and medicine.

The Greek separation of contemplation and action affects how psychologists think about the mind to the present day (Ohlsson, 2007). Plato's search for the truth ended in simply knowing what the Truth is, in contemplating the eternal Forms. He was little concerned with practical action in the world of everyday life. The Guardians contemplated Truth while the toiling masses of the Productive class actually did things. The separation of contemplation and action is found in a more technical form in Aristotle. When Aristotle initiated the field of logic in his formulation of syllogistic reasoning, he was concerned with laying down rules ensuring that we would form correct beliefs. He separated reasoning about action into his ethics, in the practical syllogism. The conclusion of a logical syllogism is a proposition, as in the famous "All men are mortal"; "Socrates is a man"; "Therefore, Socrates is mortal." The conclusion of a practical syllogism is an action and builds on desires, as in "Drinking water is essential to health"; "I want to be healthy"; "Therefore, I should drink water." A logical syllogism contemplates Truth; a practical syllogism leads to behavior.

Even today, cognitive psychology textbooks typically treat reasoning and problem solving as separate topics discussed in separate chapters. The first topic is about what to believe; the second is about how to figure out what to do (Ohlsson, 2007). Recently, a number of cognitive psychologists, philosophers, and researchers in artificial intelligence have become highly critical of the separation of thought and action, creating the embodied cognition movement, that focused on how thought is, in fact, always tightly coupled to behavior (Clark, 1998; Gibbs, 2005; Pfeiffer, Bongard, Brooks, & Iwasawa, 2006; Ratcliffe, 2007).

Nevertheless, Greek values had a long reach, appealing to people who place contemplation of the Beautiful and Good—*theoria*—above everything else. In 1891, the aesthete and author Oscar Wilde gave a talk called *The Soul of Man under Socialism*. Although Christianity had subtracted the warrior ethos of arête from European values, Wilde's socialism maintained Greek ideals:

> The chief advantage that would result from the establishment of Socialism is, undoubtedly, the fact that Socialism would relieve us from th[e] sordid necessity of living for others. . . . So while Humanity will be amusing itself, or enjoying cultivated leisure—which, and not labour, is the aim of man—or making beautiful things, or reading beautiful things, or simply contemplating the world with admiration and delight, machinery will be doing all the necessary and unpleasant work. The fact is, that civilisation requires slaves. The Greeks were quite right there. Unless there are slaves to do the ugly, horrible, uninteresting work, culture and contemplation become almost impossible. Human slavery is wrong, insecure, and demoralising. On mechanical slavery, on the slavery of the machine, the future of the world depends.

Antiquity: 323 B.C.E. to 1000 C.E.

CLASSICAL ANTIQUITY: THE HELLENISTIC (323–31 B.C.E.) AND ROMAN (31 B.C.E.–476 C.E.) WORLDS

The Social Context: Hellenism and Empire

Aristotle's pupil Alexander the Great changed the Western world. He sought to establish a universal empire that brought Greek culture to lands he conquered. He failed, but the more practical Romans, who knitted their empire together with common roads, a common language, a common culture, and a common bureaucracy (Heather, 2006), fulfilled his vision. The life of the small, democratic *polis* was destroyed, eventually replaced by the large multiethnic empire of Rome. Rootedness in small, parochial communities was replaced by the universal idea of Roman citizenship. A Roman Stoic once said that every Roman is a citizen of two cities: his place of birth and Rome—center of the known world. The idea of a universal empire of reason—of mutual trust rather than genetic altruism—that embraced yet transcended local and ethnic divisions exerted a powerful influence on the modernizers of the Enlightenment Project and the founders of the American republic (Madden, 2008).

The immediate consequence of Alexander's death, however, was a period of intense and disturbing social change known as the Hellenistic period, usually dated from his death to the final conquest of Egypt by Octavian, the future Emperor Augustus, in 31 B.C.E. Until the coming of the *pax Romana*, the eastern Mediterranean was in turmoil. Alexander's imperial center did not hold: His generals carved his hoped-for empire into personal kingdoms that they ruled like gods, and they and their heirs fought incessant wars with each other.

Having lost their beloved polis, Hellenistic men and women turned away from public life toward the pleasures of private life and home. Rejecting Homeric fame and classical

Greek politics, a Stoic said what no older Greek could ever have, that nothing in life can "compare with the companionship of a man and wife" (quoted by Barnes, 1986, p. 373). From a social perspective, the great gainers of the Hellenistic era were women, as the idea of marriage as a contract to beget heirs was replaced by ideas of love and lifelong partnership. The Cynic Crates married for love and lived in full equality with his wife, Hipparchia, in what they called their "dog marriage." Most surprising to traditionalist Greeks, they even went out to dinner together (P. Green, 1990)!

Psychologically, however, the uncertainties of the Hellenistic epoch were more disturbing. The traditional Greek fear of *Tyche* was strengthened by the travails of life under the warring kings. The leading dramatist of the era, Menander, wrote, "Stop going on about [human] intelligence. . . . It's fortune's intelligence that steers the world. . . . Human forethought is hot air, mere babble" (quoted by P. Green, 1990, p. 55). As Hellenes turned inward to their homes, they also turned inward to their souls, seeking succor from the misfortunes of the world. The more secular of them sought freedom from upset in philosophy, and the more religious, in traditional worship or in the exotic new religions that flowed from the East into the West. In between was the philosophical religion of Neoplatonism.

Therapeutic Philosophies of Happiness

In a disturbing world, people sought freedom from disturbance, a form of happiness Greeks called **ataraxia**. The Classical Greeks had sought the happiness of *eudaemonia*, human flourishing or living well. Hellenistic Greeks and the Romans who followed them lowered their sights and settled for *ataraxia*, a happiness that was within their own control. As we have learned, Greek eudaemonia depended on luck, including living in favorable circumstances. When Tyche was unfavorable, as it was during the Wars of Alexander's Successors, eudaemonia was placed out of reach. What lay within reach was the ability to quiet one's own soul, to achieve self-mastery and, thus, personal freedom from disturbance, no matter what fortune might bring.

Recipes for achieving ataraxia were offered by a new form of philosopher, the philosopher as physician. If the physician as philosopher—figures such as Alcmaeon, Empedocles, and Aristotle—begins the story of psychology as science, the philosopher as physician begins the story of psychology as psychotherapy. The Hellenistic schools of philosophy set out to create and teach a therapy of the soul (Nussbaum, 1994). Their philosophies also touched religious themes: Are there gods? Is there an afterlife? How may I be saved? By addressing these questions at a personal and philosophical level, Hellenistic philosophies downplayed the role of cult worship, helping pave the way for a religion of personal redemption, Christianity (Lane Fox, 1986).

EPICUREANISM   Epicureanism, founded by Epicurus (341–270 b.c.e.), was one of the most influential of the Hellenistic therapeutic philosophies. Epicurus spoke for all the schools when he wrote, "Empty is that philosopher's argument by which no human suffering is therapeutically treated. For just as there is no use in a medical art that does not cast out the sicknesses of bodies, so too there is no use in philosophy, unless it casts out suffering of the soul" (quoted by Nussbaum, 1994, p. 13), and when he defined pleasure, ataraxia, as "the absence of pain in the body and of trouble in the soul" (in Saunders, 1966, p. 51). Epicureanism is also known as the *philosophy of the garden* because part of Epicurus's recipe for ataraxia is literal withdrawal from the world to live a quiet life of philosophy and friendship. Epicurus taught that happiness was to be found by avoiding strong passions, including the ups and downs of erotic love, and living simply, avoiding dependence on others or the world. For Epicurus, then, "the greatest good is prudence" (in Saunders, 1966, p. 52), not *arête*, whether earned by glory in battle or serving the polis through politics.

To allay fear of death, Epicurus accepted atomism, teaching that there was no soul and thus no possibility of suffering in the afterlife. There was also a cult-like aspect of Epicureanism. Epicureans addressed Epicurus as "Leader," had to promise to accept all his teachings, and were admonished always to behave "as though Epicurus is watching" (quoted by P. Green, 1990, p. 620). The success of his Garden also depended on his wealth, the donations that supported the movement, and the slaves who tended him and his circle.

CYNICISM   The most controversial of the happiness philosophies was Cynicism. Epicureanism was part philosophy and part lifestyle; Cynicism was all lifestyle, and the Cynics were the hippies of Hellenism. Epicureans withdrew physically from the world, but Cynics remained in the world but not of it. They believed that one should live as naturally as possible, utterly rejecting worldly conventions, contemptuous of whatever opinions people might have: all *phusis* and no *nomos*. The most famous Cynic was Diogenes (400–325 b.c.e.), whose proud nickname was "The Dog," because he lived as dogs live, outside social convention. He would urinate and defecate in public, as dogs do. Found masturbating in the marketplace, his only remark was that he wished hunger could be as easily assuaged. Plato called him "Socrates gone mad." Diogenes proclaimed himself citizen of the world, and said the greatest good was free speech. To the extent that there was a therapeutic philosophy in the Cynics, it resembled Epicurus's advice to reject society, control the emotions, and avoid too much pleasure. Antisthenes said, "I would rather go mad than experience pleasure" (quoted by Vlastos, 1991, p. 208).

The Anglo-Saxon Church at Escombe, England; one of the oldest Anglo-Saxon Churches in England, still in use as an Anglican church. It is an excellent symbol of the great disruption in Western history that occurred with the fall of the Roman Empire. Many of the stones in the fabric of this church were taken from a nearby Roman fort. For the Anglo-Saxons the Romans were only a dim memory, and they literally picked up the pieces of the past to create a new way of life. *(Thomas Hardy Leahey)*

SKEPTICISM   More philosophical than either Epicureanism or Cynicism was the school of Skepticism, founded by Pyrrho of Elis (360–270 b.c.e.). Skeptics divided philosophical schools into three kinds, Dogmatists, Academics, and Skeptics, depending on the attitude each held toward the ability of humans to know the truth. Dogmatists, such as Platonists, Aristotelians, and the Skeptics chief adversaries, the Stoics ("conceited braggarts" to Skeptical eyes), claimed to know what truth was. Academics, heirs to Plato's Academy, claimed that humans could not know the truth at all, but should modestly aim at Socrates's aporia. Skeptics, said Sextus Empiricus (fl. 200 c.e.), the chief chronicler of skepticism, "keep on searching" for truth (in Saunders, 1966, p. 152).

A psychologically interesting aspect of skeptical rejection of Dogmatic assertions involved appeal to individual differences. As empiricists, skeptics rejected Plato's Forms in favor of basing knowledge in Appearances. However, they elaborated on the Sophists' observation that how things appear to another, depending on immediate circumstances of observation, the physical state and different personalities of the observers, and cultural differences between them. Moreover, Skeptics noted the different sensory abilities of animals compared to humans, such as dog's vast superiority at hearing and smelling. Thus the possibility of attaining Truth through observation of the world was daunting, although Skeptics did not conclude it was impossible, as Academics did.

Despite their development of empiricist epistemology, the goal and motivation of Skepticism was the same as the other Hellenistic happiness philosophies: "The originating cause of Skepticism is, we say, the hope of attaining quietude" (Sextus Empiricus, in Saunders, 1966, p. 154). Skeptical epistemology suggested that one should never believe one has the Truth (as Dogmatists did). Instead, Skeptics suspended judgment about "what was naturally good or bad" and did not "pursue anything eagerly." Doing so, "they [*sic*] quietude, as if by chance, followed upon their suspense, and they "were not perturbed" by what befell them (Sextus Empiricus, in Saunders, 1966, p. 158).

STOICISM   The most influential of all the therapeutic philosophies was Stoicism, founded by Zeno of Citium (333–262 b.c.e.), who taught at the painted colonnade, or *Stoa*, in Athens. Stoicism was a general and genuine philosophy that was developed for centuries by Greeks and Romans. Its appeal was considerable, cutting across social lines; it counted among its adherents—both a slave (Epictetus, 50–138 c.e.) and an Emperor (Marcus Aurelius, 121–180 c.e.), and was effectively the philosophy of the Roman ruling class. In addition to philosophy, the Stoics worked in science and made tremendous advances in logic.

Their major contribution was the development of the concepts of the proposition and of propositional logic. Earlier philosophers had thought of knowledge in terms of mental imagery. Plato's Forms and the essences stored in Aristotle's passive mind were idealized images of objects stripped of those features that did not define the Form or essence. Thus, the Form or essence of a cat was the image of a cat that did not possess a particular color, size, or even a tail (Manx cats don't have them), because these features vary from cat to cat and therefore do not define the Form or essence of a cat. Psychologically, for Plato and Aristotle, then, the contents of the mind were all images, whether particular images representing individual things we've met, or generic images representing ideal Forms and essences. Stoics moved in a dramatically different direction, defining representations linguistically, as propositions. A proposition is a statement that is either true or false. They can concern individuals, as in the proposition, "Ginger [one of our cats] is on the mat," or concern statements about universal knowledge, as in the proposition, "If a creature is a cat, then it eats meat." Logical reasoning then became a matter of properly combining sets of propositions according to logical rules, thus generating new propositions. For example, if I'm told, "If a creature is a cat, then it eats meat," and "Ginger is a cat," then I can infer that "Ginger eats meat."

The development of the concept of propositional reasoning was of tremendous long-term importance for logic, computation, and cognitive psychology. If one thinks of knowledge as imagery, it is hard to think about highly abstract concepts such as Truth or the Good. We can sort of imagine an image combining all the cats we've seen into a generic picture of a cat, but thinking of an image of Justice that includes repaying a loan, writing a constitution, and aiding the poor is difficult to the point of impossibility. Moving away from images also makes it possible to think of reasoning as a set of rules that have no concrete content at all. Thus if told "If p, then q" and "p is true," then one may infer that "q is true." It does not matter if p and q are cats, meats, dogs, planets, people, virtues, money, or just letters (the sentence before this one was an if . . . then proposition itself), if the rules are followed correctly, a valid conclusion will be reached. Thought can thus be conceived as a toolkit adaptable to any ideas whatever, not just those derived from our direct experience.

In the early twentieth century, psychologists would discover that people do not always reason with images. After World War II, the field of artificial intelligence would be created when Herbert Simon and Allen Newell (economists and psychologists) came to think of computers as propositional reasoners, not just glorified numerical calculators. They would then argue that people are propositional reasoners, too, creating the leading theory in cognitive psychology to this day, the symbol system concept of mind.

As a therapy of the soul, Stoicism taught two interconnected things: absolute determinism and the complete extirpation of the emotions. Stoics believed that whatever happens in one's life was foreordained to happen. As the Roman politician and writer Marcus Tullius Cicero (106–43 b.c.e.) put it, "The evolution of time is like the unwinding of a cable; it creates nothing new, but unfolds each event in its order" (in Saunders, 1966, p. 102). However, we are in control of our mental world, so feeling unhappy about misfortune is our fault and may be corrected with Stoic teaching. Strong positive feelings are also to be avoided because they lead to overvaluation of things and people and, thus, to potential unhappiness should they be lost. These sayings from the *Enchiridion*, or *Handbook*, of Epictetus convey the flavor of Stoicism:

V

Men are disturbed not by the things which happen, but by the opinions [Stoics regarded emotions as opinions] about the things: for example, death is nothing terrible, for if it were, it would have seemed so to Socrates; for the opinion about death, that it is terrible, is the terrible thing. When, then, we are impeded or disturbed or grieved, let us never blame others, but ourselves, that is, our opinions. It is the act of an ill-instructed man to blame others for his own bad condition; it is the act of one who has begun to be instructed, to lay the blame on himself; and of one whose instruction is completed, neither to blame another nor himself.

XLIV

These reasonings do not cohere: I am richer than you, therefore I am better than you; I am more eloquent than you, therefore I am better than you. On the contrary these rather cohere, I am richer than you, therefore my possessions are greater than yours: I am more eloquent than you, therefore my speech is superior to yours. But you are neither possession nor speech.

LII

In every thing (circumstance) we should hold these maxims ready to hand:

> *Lead me, O Zeus, and thou O Destiny,*
> *The way that I am bid by you to go:*
> *To follow I am ready.*

If I choose not, I make myself a wretch, and still must follow.
But who so nobly yields unto necessity,
We hold him wise, and skill'd in things divine.

Stoics recognized the difficulty of perfecting their path to ataraxia, recognizing that only God was perfect, and that their goal of becoming "one whose instruction is completed" can be moved toward but never quite attained, and that therefore all men are to some degree evil, no matter how far instructed. Stoics spoke of the Wise Man we should try to be: "The Wise Man never opines, never regrets, never is mistaken, never changes his mind" (Cicero, in Saunders 61).

Note in saying XLIV that Stoics rejected the old Greek concept of elite arête. Neither greatness of wealth (the virtue of the Bronze Age kings and aristocrats) nor greatness of eloquence (the virtue of the democratic polis) is really virtue at all, they are merely accidental possessions. For the Stoic, virtue was a state of mind—inner mastery of emotion. And anyone, male or female, rich or poor, slave or emperor, warrior or businessman, could achieve this inner state of mind. Stoicism thus marks a sharp break with traditional Greek ethics, anticipating and influencing Christianity.

In this connection, the Stoics created a uniquely Western idea, the idea of personal conscience, which they called *syneidesis*, translated into Latin as *conscienta* (Brett, 1963). For Stoics, right and wrong involved more than knowing and obeying the laws (nomos) of one's society, but was an inwardly felt sense of sin connected with one's inner voice of reason, or *logos*, which was in turn connected to the divine logos of the universe. In the confusing Hellenistic world, in which law and custom varied from place to place, and in the Roman world where one emperor's decrees overturned another's, the Stoic ideal of conscience held out the promise that individual people knew in their minds what was rationally right and wrong, whatever kings and emperors—and later, popes—might decree.

In many respects, Stoicism was like Christianity, and its popularity in the Roman Empire aided the reception of, and also influenced, Christian thought. Unlike earlier Greek philosophies, Stoicism was universal rather than elitist. Anyone, slave or emperor, could aspire to be a Stoic sage. Stoics thought of the universe as a living and divine being, ruled by reason, or logos, and permeated by spirit, or *pneuma*. Determinism was easier to accept if one believed that the wise universe was rationally working out an ultimately good plan, and that one's personal happiness was rationally accepting the logos of the universe. Like Christian martyrs, Stoics calmly endured pain in the service of a higher purpose. Humans had spirits, their own *pneumas*, if not souls, because Stoics held that at death one's *pneuma* simply returned to the universe's, so there was for them no personal immortality. The influence of Stoicism on Christianity is displayed in the Gospel according to John. The Stoics were masters of logic, but logos also means word, and John's Gospel begins, "In the beginning was the word . . . and the word was God."

The Religious Impulse

The therapeutic philosophies of happiness offered one way of dealing with a confusing and changing world, and we have seen that all the happiness philosophies proposed an un-polis like degree of disengagement from the world. The epicurean withdrew from the world physically; the cynic withdrew from the social world of nomos, the skeptic withdrew from strong belief of any kind; the stoic refused to let the world's troubles be disturbing. Another way of dealing with a troubling world was to turn away from it to a better, purer, transcendent one. As happiness philosophies multiplied in the Hellenistic world, so did new forms of religion.

THE GREEK MIRACLE IN REVERSE Historians speak of the "Greek miracle," investigating nature, human nature, and society through reason rather than revelation. We have studied this miracle in the history of psychology from Alcmaeon to Zeno. However, in the Hellenistic period, faith in philosophy and science faltered, and many people turned away from reason and to secret revelations as the source of truth.

Gnosticism and Hermeticism.   One sign of the search for secret revelations was a movement within Christianity (Pagels, 1979) and Judaism (Colish, 1997), called Gnosticism. In Greek, *gnosis* means knowledge, though not the philosophical knowledge of natural philosophy, but the knowledge of secret teachings or secret interpretations of sacred texts. Gnostic Christians, for example, believed in the existence of Gospels beyond the four recognized by the Catholic Church. These Gnostic Gospels, such as the Gospel of Thomas, were said to contain deeper truths than those of the synoptic Gospels. They were held in secret by Gnostic teachers and revealed to their students in a series of stages in which students were gradually initiated into what the Gnostics said were the real secrets of Christ, unknown—and dangerous—to ordinary believers. Another example of the Greek miracle in reverse was Hermeticism (Eamon, 1994). Hermeticists believed that the ancient Egyptians had unraveled all the secrets of the universe, and that they had been written down by a divine figure called Hermes Trismegitus (Hermes, a Greek god, thrice great). The Hermetic documents later turned out to have been written not in ancient Egypt but in the first centuries c.e.

Gnosticism and Hermeticism are symptoms of a profound loss of confidence in Greek culture. Hellenistic people were no longer boldly exploring nature through reason and observation, but were turning to allegedly divine revelations from gods and supposedly ancient authorities to whom powerful secrets had been revealed. Western philosophy would not regain its self-confidence until about 1000 c.e.

Neoplatonism.   As we have seen, Plato's philosophy had a strong otherworldly pull, and during the Hellenistic period, as Plato's Academy turned to Skepticism, that pull produced the philosophy of Neoplatonism, whose best-known spokesman was Plotinus (204–270 c.e.), an Egyptian Greek. Plotinus fully developed the mystical aspect of Platonism, very nearly turning that philosophy into a religion. He described the universe as a hierarchy, beginning with a supreme and unknowable God called *the One*. The One "emanates" a knowable God called *Intelligence*, which rules over Plato's realm of the Forms. From Intelligence, more divine creatures serially emanate until we reach humans, whose divine souls are imprisoned in degrading, material bodies. The physical world is an imperfect, impure copy of the divine realm.

Plotinus's concern was to turn his followers' eyes away from the corrupting temptations of the flesh and toward the spiritual world of truth, goodness, and beauty in the realm of the Forms. In his *Enneads*, Plotinus wrote: "Let us rise to [the] model . . . from which [the physical] world derives. . . . Over [it] presides pure Intelligence and incredible wisdom. . . . Everything there is eternal and immutable . . . [and] in a state of bliss." The last phrase marks the change from Platonic philosophy to the ecstatic vision of religious mystics. Like Stoicism, Neoplatonism helped pave the way for, and shaped, Christian thought. It was through Neoplatonism that Plato's philosophy came to dominate the early Middle Ages.

The tendency of Neoplatonism to become a religion is well illustrated in the remarkable life of Hypatia of Alexandria (355–415 c.e.), one of the very few women philosophers and scientists of premodern times (Dzielke, 1995). Hypatia wrote notable works on mathematics and astronomy that are now lost, but her chief claim to fame and influence lay in her teaching of Neoplatonism to numerous and eager students. In fact, she regarded her scientific works as doorways to the secrets of Neoplatonism, astronomy being "a science that opens the doors to ineffable theology" (quoted by Dzielke, p. 54), and mathematics as the fruit of the godlike Pythagoras. As was typical for teachers of Neoplatonism, Hypatia was regarded as a divine and sacred figure; as a woman, her sacred status was especially exalted by her virginity and her absolute renunciation of sexual pleasure. Also typically of

Neoplatonists—as well as Gnostics and Hermeticists—she sought to keep the divine secrets of philosophy confined to an exalted and purified elite, an aristocracy with exclusive access to "the company of the blessed lady" (quoted by Dzielke, 1995, p. 60). As a Neoplatonist, she regarded philosophy as a religious mystery, and sought to lead her students to find within themselves the "luminous child of reason," an "inner eye" that would in the end lead them to an ecstatic "merging with the One" of Plotinus (quoted by Dzielke, 1995, pp. 48–49). Links between Neoplatonism and Christianity become clear in the life and teachings of Hypatia. As a virgin, she lived the life recommended to women by St. Paul and St. Jerome, and two of her students became bishops in the Christian church. Nevertheless, the Bishop of Alexandria, Cyril, resentful of her political influence on the (Christian) governor of Alexandria, branded her a witch for teaching astrology (her astronomy), and had her murdered by his personal thugs. Her murder made her a martyr for free thought down to modern times (Dzielke, 1995).

Centuries later, Friedrich Nietzsche said that Christianity was Platonism for the people because it did for the many what elite Hellenistic philosophies had done for the elite few. It devalued the quest for office, honor, and fame, and made citizenship less important than the private purification of the soul. In his letter to the Thessalonians, Paul urges Christians to "find honor in being quiet . . . [minding] private affairs" (quoted by Rahe, 1994, p. 206). Hellenistic philosophy, religion, and Christianity overthrew ancient Greek arête.

Also overthrown were Greek ideas about sexual pleasure. Greeks reveled in sexual pleasure, provided nothing was done to excess. But, as we have seen, there was an alternative, more ascetic view of the pleasures of the flesh, begun by Pythagoras and nurtured by Plato and the Neoplatonists. They all despised the body as a tomb and sought to free the soul from the corrupting desires of the body. The classically educated Paul assimilated this attitude into Christianity. Writing to Galatians, Paul wrote, "The desires of the flesh are against the spirit and the desires of the spirit are against the flesh" (quoted by Garrison, 2000, p. 251).

Mystery Cults.   Religion, too, offered a path to ataraxia, and sometimes to something more dramatic and ecstatic. There had been a few ecstatic mystery cults in early Greece, the most famous being the mysteries of Eleusis (Burkert, 1987). Nevertheless, the influx of new mystic and ecstatic religions into the Greek world that began in Plato's time became a flood in the Hellenistic and Roman eras. The old pagan religions remained lively for centuries into the Christian era, but many people turned to one or more of the various *mystery cults* that arose in the Near East, especially Anatolia (modern Turkey), Iran, and Egypt. They were called mystery cults from the word *myster*, meaning a special rite, often held in secret and never revealed to outsiders, through which initiates had to pass in order to become full members (*mystai*) of the cult. Three popular ones were the cults of *Magna Mater* (Great Mother), Isis, and Mithras (Artz, 1980; Burkert, 1987).

The cult of Magna Mater began to enter the West from Asia Minor in the 600s B.C.E. This cult was based on the myth that, inflamed by jealousy, Magna Mater, the source of life, became infuriated at the infidelity of her lover, Attis, the god of vegetation, and slew him and emasculated him, burying him beneath a pine tree. Then she mourned him and brought him back to life. The seasons of the earth retell the story, as vegetation fades in the Fall, dies in Winter, and returns in the Spring, when the great ceremonies of Magna Mater took place. There was dancing, singing, and music. Male aspirants to the priesthood emasculated themselves with stones, repeating Attis's fate and giving their fertility to the Great Mother. Finally, a pit was dug into which initiates dressed in white robes descended. A live bull was held over them and sacrificed. Covered with blood, the initiates crawled out of the pit, being "born again" into the cult of Magna Mater.

Isis, like Magna Mater, was a female deity. An Egyptian goddess, she was sister to Osiris, the chief god of the Egyptian pantheon, who gave arts and law to human beings, and who died and was reborn with Isis' help. The cult of Isis involved a daily, weekly, and yearly cycle of rituals, including baptism in holy water, lighting of candles and incense, stately processions, and temples left open so adherents could come in and pray. That mystery cults fulfilled a therapeutic function similar to that of Hellenistic philosophies is indicated by the fact that followers of Isis were sometimes called *therapeutai*. The cults offered a "chance to break out of the enclosed and barren ways of predictable existence" [especially true for ancient women] through "doors to a secret. . . . providing the experience of a great rhythm in which the resonance of the individual psyche could be integrated through an amazing event of *sympatheia*" with the divine (Burkert, 1987, p. 114).

Isis appealed especially to women; Mithraism was reserved for men, and was a special favorite of Roman soldiers, who carried it throughout the Roman world. Mithras stemmed from Persia, and was a god of light and enemy of evil, born of a virgin. Mithras is represented as riding and slaying a bull, which represents unrestrained natural power needing to be controlled by people. His birthday was December 25, and the first day of the week was his. Devotees were baptized in water, or later in a bull-slaying ceremony borrowed from Magna Mater. They identified with him by eating a sacred meal of bread and wine, and tried to live, in imitation of Mithras, lives of morality and virtue.

By the fourth century c.e., there was a tendency for the mystery cults to converge together into a single, monotheistic religion. Ultimately, this was Christianity, based on birth and rebirth, sin and redemption, but public rather than mysterious (Artz, 1980; Lane Fox, 1986; Pagels, 1979).

Early Christian Thought

An important problem for early Christians was how to deal with classical philosophy. Some Christians wanted to suppress all pagan philosophy as dangerous to Christian faith. Quintas Septimius Florens Tertullian (160–230) wrote, "We want no curious disputation after possessing Jesus Christ, no inquisition after enjoying the Gospel! With our faith, we desire no further belief" (in Saunders, 1966, p. 344). As we have learned, a key to the open systems approach to thought characteristic of the Greek world and of modern science, politics, and philosophy is abandonment of the certitude of closed system thinking and a consequent openness to criticism, research, and belief in progress. Tertullian and like-minded Christians rejected these Greek ideals, even though they seemed consistent with Jesus' teaching, "Seek and ye shall find." Instead, Tertullian wrote, "Where shall be the end of seeking? Where the stop in believing?" (in Saunders, 1966, p. 347). The Greek answered, perhaps nowhere; Tertullian found the stopping point in religious revelation.

Other Church fathers embraced pagan philosophy, because many Greek systems espoused ideas congenial to Christianity, and so made pagans ready to receive Christ's message. For example, Clement of Alexandria (d. c. 215) wrote, "[B]efore the advent of the Lord, philosophy was necessary to the Greeks for righteousness. And now it becomes conducive to piety; being a kind of preparatory training to those who attain to faith through demonstration. . . . Philosophy, therefore, was a preparation, paving the way for him who is perfected in Christ" (in Saunders, p. 306).

Perhaps more important than Clement's willingness to entertain the ideas of Greek philosophers was the Hellenistic attitude of mind that he and others assimilated to Christian practice. Those like Tertullian basically preached the Gospel and asked pagans to take it or leave it. Clement, on the other hand, addressed pagans on their own ground of philosophical disputation, seeking to convince "those who attain to faith through demonstration" by arguing the superiority of Christian ideas, rather than simply asserting it. An excellent example of this approach to converting the pagans was a dialog addressed to pagans written by Marcus Minucius Felix (fl. c. 230) in which a Christian presents the case for Christianity without once mentioning Jesus (Saunders, 1966). Christianity thus absorbed the idea of progress through argument to be set alongside salvation by revelation.

In addition to absorbing the Classical mind-set of philosophical inquiry, by admitting the virtues of pre-Christian thought, Clement and others acknowledged that the human mind—unaided by revelation—could approach, though perhaps not quite attain, God's truth. Thus they created the possibility of preserving a sphere of secular thought in which philosophy and science could develop without Church interference. We will soon see that this was an important reason why the Scientific Revolution and the Enlightenment occurred only in Europe.

The most important and influential of the Christian thinkers who refused to totally condemn pagan philosophy was St. Augustine, bishop of Hippo in North Africa (354–430). Augustine was at once the last classic philosopher and the first Christian one, combining Stoicism, Neoplatonism, and Christian faith.

Stoicism, with its emphasis on divine wisdom and human submission, has elements that can be assimilated easily to Christian belief. Even more compatible, however, was Neoplatonism, which was a philosophy evolving into a religion. In the fourth century, Christianity was a simple faith, lacking a supporting philosophy. Augustine integrated faith and philosophy into a powerful Christian worldview that would dominate medieval theology and philosophy until the thirteenth century. The following passage illustrates Augustine's Christian Neoplatonism:

> God, of course, belongs to the realm of intelligible things, and so do these mathematical symbols, though there is a great difference. Similarly the earth and light are visible, but the earth cannot be seen unless it is illumined. Anyone who knows the mathematical symbols admits that they are true without the shadow of a doubt. But he must also believe that they cannot be known unless they are illumined by something else corresponding to the sun. About this corporeal light notice three things. It exists. It shines. It illumines. So in knowing the hidden God you must observe three things. He exists. He is known. He causes other things to be known. (St. Augustine, Soliloquies I)

Augustine assimilated a sophisticated if mystical Neoplatonic philosophy to the basic teachings of Jesus and created an overarching Christian theology of considerable appeal. While his own theology assimilated pagan philosophy, Augustine did not believe that the naturalistic inquiries of the Greeks needed to go forward, showing that the victory of those who accepted pagan thought was only partial. He wrote, "It is not necessary to probe into the nature of things, as was done by those whom the Greeks call *physici*. . . . It is enough for the Christian to believe that the only cause of all created things . . . is the One True God" (quoted by Goldstein, 1995, p. 57). Augustine also condemned curiosity as a form of lust, a "lust of the eyes." "From [this] motive men proceed to investigate the workings of nature, which is beyond our ken—things which it does no good to know and which men only want to know for the sake of knowing" (quoted by Eamon, 1994, p. 60).

While many Greek and Roman attitudes and concepts persisted in early Medieval thought, the substance of their philosophy and science was lost in Christendom, was preserved (but not developed) in Islam, and was rediscovered by Europeans only after many centuries.

Fall of the Roman Empire

The fall of the Roman Empire is, of course, the oldest and most contested question in Western history, beginning with Edward Gibbon's *Decline and Fall of the Roman Empire*, written in the eighteenth century. The leaders of the Enlightenment admired the Roman Republic and Empire for creating a rationally ordered political system that was universal in scope, transcending local ethnic and political identities. Because this was the sort of political order they themselves wanted to create, for Enlightenment thinkers the fall of the Roman Empire was a great, but perhaps instructive, tragedy. Gibbon (1737–1794) made the case that Rome's fall represented a great disruption in European history, and he gave the onset of its long decline a precise date, the accession of the Emperor Commodus (b. 161, Emperor, 180–192), as depicted in the movie *Gladiator*. Gibbon's contemporaries agreed; Johann Herder, for example, wrote that the Empire was "already dead, an exhausted body, a corpse stretched out in its own blood" (quoted by M. Grant, 1990, p. 99). Interestingly, while Gibbon and other Enlightenment authors saw the destruction of the Roman Empire as a disaster, the destruction of the first rationally governed and potentially universal government, Counter-Enlightenment Germans tended to see it as a victory for German, racially pure culture over a failed, decadent, multiethnic mishmash (Mosse, 1981).

Contemporary historians now disagree with Gibbon about the decline of the Roman Empire, but they argue among themselves about whether it fell. Some historians believe that instead of falling, the Empire went through a long and gradual transition from the Roman way of life to an equally good, but different, medieval way of life, dubbing the transition period of Late Antiquity (Brown, 1989, 2002; Wickham, 1984, 2007). On the other hand, recent scholars have challenged the notion of a peaceful Late Antiquity, arguing that while there is little evidence of economic decline or the Empire unraveling until the middle of the fifth century c.e. (the last Roman Emperor, Romulus Augustulus, died in 476 c.e.), there is evidence of a sharp break between the Roman and medieval ways of life. In particular, archeological finds suggest that the ability of people to make sophisticated pottery and houses, and to trade all over the Roman world disappeared in the late fifth century. People became poorer, impoverished, and more dependent on what they could do themselves with local means (Ward-Perkins, 2005), and literacy and culture virtually disappeared in a very short period of time (Heather, 2006). The Roman Empire, in their view, did not decline and transition into the Middle Ages; it was stressed to the breaking point by internal political conflicts and civil war (Goldsworthy, 2009) and destroyed by Germanic invaders, the Goths and the Huns. These historians also point out that the Empire as a whole did not fall in 476. Centuries earlier, the Empire was divided in two, the Western (nominally centered at Rome) and Eastern (centered at Constantinople) Empires, ruled by two emperors. The Western Empire died in 476, the Eastern endured until conquered by Islam in 1453.

From Gibbon's day to the present, historians and others have asked if Romans could have saved their empire. In a recent penetrating analysis, however, Aldo Schiavone (2000) contends that the Roman world had gone as far as it could go, locked into static modes of production and thought that could only shatter, not evolve, causing a great disruption in Western history. An important psychological aspect of great disruptions is change in prevailing mentalities, and Schiavone (2000) emphasizes them—along with related economic factors—in his analysis of the fall of the Roman Empire.

The economic key to the Greek and Roman world was slavery; the mental key was Greek and Roman attitudes to mind and work. I will begin with the second point, which turns out to be more important, as it connects the fall of Rome to attitudes Romans inherited from the Greeks, and that will play an important role in the development of Western science and technology. Schiavone's account is especially important for psychologists because he shows that ideas about soul and body can have great consequences for the nature of society. The Guardians of Plato's ideal Republic are the most familiar manifestation of the attitudes Schiavone regards as essential to the formation of the ancient economy. However, the lives of the Guardians were not an eccentric vision of Plato's, but, as we have seen, an ancient Greek ideal partially fulfilled at Sparta and commanding widespread assent among literate Greeks.

As Greek dualism radically separated soul and body, cultivation of the former became the only worthy life. We meet here an important but subtle point. We have learned that the Greeks cultivated soul and body, greatly valuing beauty and athletic and martial prowess. The important distinction for the Greeks and the Romans was not between soul and body as such (as it would be for Christians, Neoplatonists, and Cartesians) but between soul—the exercise of thought on one hand—and material production on the other. Aristotle said, "Life is action, not production." Thus, the Greeks admired the physical exploits of the athlete and soldier but denigrated the productive work of artisans and tradespeople, exploiters of *metis* rather than contemplators of philosophical *theoria*. Politics, too, was action, not production. Thus, the Guardians cultivated their noble souls through philosophy and they commanded others; economic production was relegated to the inferior souls of the lowest of Plato's three classes.

Two important consequences flowed from Greek antagonism to material production. First, for Greeks and Romans, the whole productive sphere of life—economics—was a black hole, a "dead zone," in Schiavone's phrase. They had no words that correspond with the terms of modern economics, so they did not think—could not think—about life in economic terms. Second, they neglected technology. The Roman historian Plutarch described the Hellenistic scientist Archimedes this way:

> Yet Archimedes possessed such a lofty spirit, so profound a soul . . . that although his inventions had won for him a name and fame for superhuman sagacity he would not consent to leave behind him any treatise on the subject, but regarding the work of an engineer and every art that ministers to the needs of life as ignoble and vulgar, he devoted his earnest efforts only to those studies whose subtleties and charm are unaffected by the claims of necessity.

The rise of slavery deepened Classical disdain for work, hid its resulting faults, but enabled it to last for centuries until Rome's empire shattered. Slavery had, of course, been around from the earliest times in Mediterranean civilization, but not until the Athenian empire did the number of slaves swell, making them the linchpin of Classical life. By around 400 b.c.e., slaves constituted about 30% of the Athenian population. Slaves were unfree, and their debasement further defiled economically productive work in the eyes of the Greek and Roman elite. As slaves were producers, productivity became akin to slavery. Marx did not invent the concept of the "wage slave." Writing about 100 b.c.e., Panaetius of Rhodes wrote, "the workman's wage is itself the pledge of his servitude" (quoted by Rahe, 1994, p. 25). Cicero echoed the feeling: "The work of all hired men who sell their labor and not their talents is servile and contemptible. The reason is that in their case wages actually constitute a payment for slavery. . . . No one born of free parents would have anything to do with a workshop" (quoted by Schiavone, 2000, p. 40).

Attitudes toward machines were also tainted by slavery. Aristotle regarded some men and women as slaves by nature, but he also said that slaves are "animate instruments [machines]": "The slave is an instrument endowed with a soul, and the instrument is an inanimate slave." The Roman writer Varro classified instruments into three types: the "mute" (e.g., a cart), the "semivocal" (e.g., an ox), and the "vocal," the slave (quotes from Schiavone, 2000, p. 133). Aristotle also linked slavery and machinery in an interesting anticipation of artificial intelligence: "If every tool could perform its own work when ordered, or by seeing what to do in advance . . . —if thus shuttles wove and quills played harps of themselves, master-craftsmen would have no need of assistants and masters no need of slaves" (quoted by Schiavone, 2000, p. 133). The existence of slaves made inquiry into better machinery unnecessary as well as demeaning to the elite.

War and slavery were the foundation of Rome's success, but at the same time froze the ancient world into a pattern of growth without modernization. Under the Republic—not the

Empire—a river of slaves and wealth began to flow into Rome as she conquered and taxed the peoples around her. By the end of the first century b.c.e., slaves constituted at least 35% of the population of Italy. The Roman elite could in Greek fashion devote itself to war and political rule, as Roman aristocrats managed their slave-populated estates, still fancying themselves virtuous tillers of the soil, the only labor worthy of free men. Slavery was so successful that not only did the Roman elite not labor, neither did ordinary Roman citizens. They had formerly worked on the great estates, but slaves displaced them. Hence, the famous bread (produced by slaves) and circuses (provided by slave gladiators) was what Rome needed to control the unemployed, unproductive, masses.

Schiavone concludes that Roman life was locked in a pattern of life from which there was no way out except a shattering:

> The circle between the spread of slavery, the rejection of labor, and the absence of machines, from which we began our analysis, then closed: the labor of slaves was in symmetry with and concealed behind (so to speak) the freedom of aristocratic thought, while this in turn was in symmetry with the flight from a mechanical and quantitative vision of nature. It would have been quite difficult to interrupt this kind of spiral without completely disrupting the era.

Romans did not lack technology and innovation, but they developed them in ways consistent with the mind-set described by Schiavone, taking Greek and Roman Republic technology and intensifying it (Mokyr, 1990). Their innovations were organizational and applied to the public sphere of action, both military and political. They developed clever war machines utilizing existing means, but above all, the triumph of Rome was due to its organization and order. Their army conquered not because each Roman soldier was braver or more skilled than the barbarians they defeated, but because their soldiers fought as tightly organized, highly disciplined units of professional, full-time warriors. They built roads, aqueducts, and public buildings for the ages, allowing a sophisticated, uniform culture built upon trade and shared ideas to develop and flourish. They fully developed the concept of law, and their political order was administered by intelligent, well-trained bureaucrats. But they did not seek technical inventions, and when inventions were made, they were rarely put to private, productive, use. Greek and Roman artisans, for example, developed steam engines, but they were not put to productive use, but were employed to make impressive special effects in pagan temples.

In sum, the Romans perfected a particular way of life, built upon Greek values and the labor of slaves. They often saw it themselves as a perfect way of life, and Gibbon praises it highly in the opening pages of his *Decline and Fall*. But by definition, perfection cannot change, cannot evolve; perfection must endure or die. Prior to the fifth century, the Romans had been able to absorb a steady stream of outsiders desiring the peace and wealth Rome offered. However, cracks in the Empire's perfection appeared when it was unable to assimilate huge numbers of Gothic Germans who violently pushed their way into the Western Empire in the early fifth century. The Huns, bent on conquest and pillage rather than assimilation, then delivered the hammer blow that shattered the western Roman Empire.

LATE ANTIQUITY (476–1000)

The Social Context: Picking Up the Pieces

Although tradition sets the date of the end of Classical civilization at 476 c.e., something like the medieval way of life began during the Roman Empire in the late third and fourth centuries (Wickham, 1984, 2007). Economic decline forced small farmers to become legally tied to the land, a bond that evolved into serfdom. As the control of Rome over her provinces loosened, local autonomous leadership grew, leading to feudalism. The breakdown of the Roman world was evident as a barter economy began to replace the money economy of the Empire; communication broke down; the imperial army became more and more a mercenary army of barbarians rather than a voluntary army of Roman citizens; populations declined; and the Eastern Empire with its own emperor and capital at Constantinople leached treasure and resources from the European, or Western, Empire to preserve its own cultivated and luxurious way of life. During these centuries, Europe lost access to almost all of Greek and Roman literature, which is why the Early Middle Ages are sometimes called the "Dark Ages." However, one work—Plato's *Timaeus*—remained known and exerted an important influence on medieval thinking. The *Timaeus* was Plato's one foray into natural philosophy, in which he described how the world was created by a god-like creature, the *demiurge*, following the patterns of the eternal Forms. Because the physical world was modeled after the intelligible Forms, Plato implied that the world is rationally ordered and therefore knowable by human reason without revelation from God. Medieval science would begin from this foundation (Colish, 1997; E. Grant, 1996; Huff, 1993).

An extraordinary movement of barbarians into the Empire caused the final fall of the Roman Empire. Early settlers had often come peacefully into the Empire, but later invasions were bloody and destructive. Rome itself was sacked in Augustine's time; the Emperor Romulus Augustulus, who resigned into comfortable retirement in 476, was himself only a barbarian usurper. The Empire was finally torn asunder by waves of barbarian invaders, each group fleeing the one behind it, seeking stable lives within the Empire. As each group of people settled, the Empire became less Roman and more multiethnic. Restless movements of such people did not end until the Vikings settled in Northern France as Normans around 1000 c.e. What prompted and ended the barbarian invasions remain unclear, as does the size and nature of them. The old view that there was wave upon wave of mass, violent, invasion is untenable, but neither is the more recent opposite view that peoples stayed in place and only ideas moved (Heather, 2010).

This extended period of transition from classic to medieval times, from before 475 to about 1000, is sometimes still called the Dark Ages but is now usually known to historians as the period of Late Antiquity (Heather, 2010; J. Smith, 2005; Wickham, 2007). Although recorded creative thinking declined, there were periods of intellectual development, most notably the Carolingian renaissance under Charlemagne (768–814). New political forms were developed to replace the husk of imperial government. It was even a period of technological advance. For example, the heavy plow and the modern horse-harness were invented, opening new lands for farming and improving the yield from old. Although this period brought economic, demographic, and intellectual decline, a new, creative society was arising from the imperial ashes.

An important intellectual tradition began in Europe toward the end of the Early Middle Ages—the application of philosophical reason to matters of theology. Its leading proponent was St. Anselm of Canterbury (1033–1109), who called it "faith seeking reason" (Colish, 1997). Rather than simply accepting the Bible and Church dogma as the basis of his faith, Anselm proposed purely philosophical arguments in support of Christian belief. For example, he put forward the "ontological argument" for God's existence, which (roughly) says that we can conceive of a most perfect being—God—and that this being must exist because if he did not exist he would be less than perfect. The ontological argument has always been disputed, but the important point for us is that Anselm's argument appeals to neither scripture nor authority, but to logic alone. Elsewhere, most notably in Islam, philosophically based theological thought appeared fitfully, but was marginalized in the Early Middle Ages and was finally suppressed in the fourteenth century (see the following discussion). In Europe, Anselm's free thinking became a tradition entrenched in European universities.

Psychology of Late Antiquity: Islamic Medical Psychology

He who knows his soul, knows his creator. (Proverb of the Muslim Brethren of Purity)

This proverb could stand as the motto of early and high medieval psychology. Augustine, as we have seen, wanted to know God and the soul. He believed that by turning inward and inspecting the soul, one could come to know God, who is present in every soul. In Augustine's concept of the unity of Creator and Creation, the three mental powers—memory, understanding, and will—mirror the three beings of the Holy Trinity. A philosopher looked inward to his own soul as a way to know God—not to understand himself as a unique human being, or to describe his conscious experience as the first scientific psychologists did, but to find an external order, God's order, to guide one's life. The concept of the individual did not appear until the High Middle Ages, and then it was found largely in popular culture rather than philosophy.

Nevertheless, within the Islamic world, a naturalistic, rather than religious, faculty psychology developed, based on Aristotle. This psychology was originally worked out in a Neoplatonic framework within which Aristotle was interpreted, and it combined an elaboration of Aristotle's psychology with late Roman and Islamic medicine. Over the next two centuries, as Aristotle became better known in Europe, this naturalistic faculty psychology completely replaced the older Augustinian Neoplatonic psychology.

In the Neoplatonic scheme of things, humans stand midway between God and matter. As a rational animal, a human being resembles God; as a physical being, a human resembles animals and other purely physical creatures. In this view, when allied with Aristotelian faculty psychology, the human mind itself reflects this ambiguous position: The five corporeal senses are tied to the animal body, while the active intellect—pure reason—is close to God. A person is a microcosm (a small cosmos) reflecting the universal Neoplatonic macrocosm.

Various writers developed Aristotle's psychology by elaborating on the set of faculties possessed by Aristotle's sensitive souls. Because these faculties processed sensory images passed on from the special, or exterior, senses, they were called *inward wits*, or **interior senses**. These were thought to be the exact transition point between body and soul in the chain of being. Such a scheme appears in Islamic, Judaic, and Christian thought in the Early Middle Ages. Muslims made the special contribution of placing the discussion in a physiological context. Islamic medicine carried on the Classical medical tradition, and Muslim doctors looked for brain structures that hosted the various aspects of mind discussed by philosophers. The most complete statement of the Aristotelian medical view was made by Ibn Sīnā (980–1037), known in Europe as Avicenna, who was both a doctor and a philosopher and whose works were influential in constructing high medieval philosophy and psychology.

Different lists of interior mental faculties had been drawn up by commentators on Aristotle before Ibn Sīnā. Aristotle had proposed three faculties—common sense, imagination, and memory—although the lines between them were not sharply drawn. Later writers proposed three to five faculties, but Ibn Sīnā produced a list of seven faculties that became widely influential. His list was arranged in a Neoplatonic hierarchy from the faculty closest to the senses (and the body) to the faculty closest to divine intellect. His system of description is summarized in Figure 1.

Beginning with the parts of the mind closest to the body, Ibn Sīnā's system discussed the *vegetative soul*, common to plants, humans, and animals (which he treated as did Aristotle), saying that it is responsible for the reproduction, growth, and nourishment of all living things. Next comes the *sensitive soul*, common to people and animals. At its lowest level, it comprises the five *exterior senses* or corporeal senses (again, following Aristotle). The second level of the sensitive soul comprises the *interior senses*, or mental faculties, which are at the border between our animal and angelic natures. They, too, are hierarchically arranged. First comes *common sense*, which (as in Aristotle) receives,

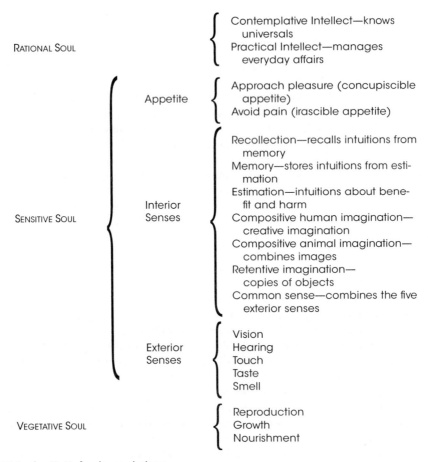

FIGURE 1 Ibn Sīnā's faculty psychology.

unites, and makes conscious the various qualities of external objects perceived by the senses. These perceived qualities are retained in the mind by the second internal sense, *retentive imagination*, for further consideration or later recall. The third and fourth internal senses are the *compositive animal imagination* and the *compositive human imagination*, which are responsible for active, creative use of mental images; they relate together (compose) the images retained by the retentive imagination into such imaginary objects as unicorns. In animals, this process is simply associative; in human beings, it may be creative—hence the distinction of two faculties. The fifth internal sense is *estimation*, a kind of natural instinct for making judgments about the "intentions" of external objects. Wolves seek sheep for they know sheep are edible; sheep avoid wolves because wolves are their predators. This power, similar to the Pavlovian conditioning of modern psychologists, "estimates" the value or harm of objects in the animal's world.

The highest internal senses are *memory* and *recollection*. Memory stores the intuitions of estimation. These intuitions are simple ideas of the object's essence, not sensible attributes of the object. Recollection is the ability to recall these intuitions at a later time. The material stored by memory and retrieved by recollection is thus not a copy of an object, for this function is performed by the retentive and compositive imaginations. Instead, the material is a set of simple but abstract ideas, or general conclusions, derived from experience. They are not, however, true universals, for only the human mind has the power to form universals.

Ibn Sīnā was a physician, and he tried to combine his explication of Aristotle's philosophical psychology with the traditional, though erroneous, Roman medical tradition stemming from Galen. By speculation, without resort to religiously forbidden dissection of the human body, Ibn Sīnā and other Muslim faculty psychologists located the internal senses in different parts—specifically, in the *ventricles* of the brain (C. D. Green, 2002). His proposals became standard medical teaching until, in the sixteenth century, Andreas Vesalius (1514–1564) dissected human bodies and proved that Classical and medieval ideas about the body were wrong, often importing animal structures into their picture of human anatomy.

The final aspect of the sensitive soul treated by Ibn Sīnā was motivation. As Aristotle had pointed out, what sets animals apart from plants is that they move. Ibn Sīnā, following Aristotle, called this motive power *appetite*, and it has two forms. Animals sense pain or danger and flee; this is called *avoidance*. On the other hand, animals sense or anticipate pleasure and move toward it; this is *approach*.

The mental powers and senses so far considered by Ibn Sīnā are tied to the body and brain and are held in common by humans and animals. With the Greeks, Ibn-Sina held that we surpass the animals because of our ability to form universal concepts. However, in Ibn-Sina's Islamic framework and in the Christian framework into which his ideas were assimilated, the ability to form universals is attributed to the human soul that transcends the material body and brain. Ibn Sīnā distinguished two faculties within the human soul: *practical intellect* and *contemplative intellect*. The lower-ranked practical intellect concerns itself with everyday affairs. It regulates the body, maintains good behavior, and protects the contemplative intellect so it may fulfill itself in knowledge of universal Truths. In this, Ibn Sīnā followed Aristotle, as he did in further distinguishing active and passive intellect. The contemplative intellect of the human soul is entirely passive (Aristotle's *passive mind*) and has the potential for knowledge, which is actualized by the active intellect, or *agent intellect*. However, Ibn Sīnā set the agent intellect outside the human soul (which Aristotle had not done). A kind of angelic intellect next up in the Neoplatonic hierarchy, it illuminates the contemplative mind and leads it to knowledge of the Forms, as in Plato and Augustine. As we shall see, the doctrine of a separate agent intellect is un-Christian as well as un-Islamic, and its entry into Europe via the Muslim philosopher Ibn Rushd precipitated the intellectual part of the crisis that ended the High Middle Ages, and would pose serious problems for Rene Descartes's struggle between his belief in a personal Christian soul and his belief that the human body is a machine.

The Individual, Mind, and Psychology

Although from a biological standpoint human nature has changed little since about 100,000 to 50,000 b.c.e., human conceptions of self, character, personality—or individuality more generally—have changed since Homeric times. Moreover, differences between cultures and philosophical traditions persist with regard to the nature and value of individual human minds (Kim & Cohen, 2010; Kim, Cohen, & Au, 2010). In political life, for example, the Anglo-American tradition places tremendous value on individual rights and responsibilities. Americans fought their Revolutionary War to defend the propositions that (Jefferson et al., 1776):

> We hold these truths to be self-evident, that all men are created equal, that they are endowed by their Creator with certain unalienable Rights, that among these are Life, Liberty, and the pursuit of Happiness. That to secure these rights, Governments are instituted among Men,

deriving their just powers from the consent of the governed. That whenever any Form of Government becomes destructive of these ends, it is the Right of the People to alter or to abolish it, and to institute new Government, having its foundation on such principles and organizing its powers in such form, as to them shall seem most likely to effect their Safety and Happiness. (p. 1)

The Declaration states that rights inhere in individuals, not in the government, and if government acts to take away human rights, it becomes illegitimate and may be justly overthrown by the people.

Other political orders, even in Europe, place less value on the free individual. In France, for example, the leaders of the French Revolution published a *Declaration of the Rights of Man and of the Citizen*, but as French law developed under Napoleon, it came to guard more closely the rights of the state and regulate the lives of French citizens. Differences between the French and American conception of the individual are also revealed in charitable giving. Americans strongly support private philanthropies, donating over 1.2% of their income per capita to charity. The French, on the other hand, see the care of the indigent as the duty of the state and give away only about 0.015% of their income per capita (Trueheart, 1998).

Psychology is the science that is concerned with the individual person. Therefore, how societies and cultures view and value individuals is important for understanding the history of psychology. On the one hand, the growth of psychology has differed from culture to culture depending on treatment of the individual. For example, although scientific psychology was first established as a recognized discipline in Germany, it grew very slowly. This was due, in part, to cultural values. German psychologists focused on a sort of Platonic Form of the Normal Mind, regarding individual differences as annoying distractions. Furthermore, Germans placed great store on being part of a larger whole, something beyond and greater than their own selves. They looked upon America with horror as a collection of atomized individuals. The German urge for wholeness would help create *Gestalt* ("whole" or "form") psychology. America's strong value of individualism created fertile soil for psychology, and it thrived here as nowhere else. On the other hand, Gestalt concepts bewildered American psychologists.

Similarly, the practice of psychology may depend upon cultural conceptions of the individual. Psychology is the study of the individual mind, but the status of mind as a natural object is unclear. The mind may have been something that existed before people thought of it and was discovered in the course of the evolution of philosophy and science. Or, the mind might be an artifact of nature, like a species, or an artifact of human invention, like a computer. Finally, mind (and individuality) might be a cultural construction that has faded into the background and is taken so for granted that we think we have discovered it in nature when, in fact, it came into existence over time and seems "natural" and "normal" to us today. Some psychologists (e.g., Spanos, 1996) argue that specific forms of abnormal mentality, such as witchcraft and demon possession, hysteria, and multiple personality disorder and repressed memory syndrome are cultural scripts—in these cases created by psychology itself—that distressed people pick up to interpret their lives.

The Yale literary critic Harold Bloom (1998) has argued that the modern conception of individual mind and character was an invention of one man, William Shakespeare. Cary (2000) argues that it should be ascribed to Augustine, while McMahon (2008) locates it in Roman literary practices. It thus is best regarded as a slow cultural construction, rather than as a solitary invention that did not come to fruition until the later Middle Ages and Renaissance. In what follows, we will sketch how people of the premodern period viewed mind and personality, as located as much outside the body as within.

CHANGING CONCEPTIONS OF THE INDIVIDUAL The growth of free cities, outside the aristocratic order, the growth of wealth, which created new kinds of jobs and ways to live, and the growth of democratic thinking led to modernity and raised the question of how to choose in a much freer world. The idea of an inner chooser—an autonomous self—became important as a new grounding for values. Observing modern earth folks I've noticed that one is supposed to be nonjudgmental: "Don't judge me" is a line I hear a lot on your TV shows. It appears that the only one capable of judging one's life is one's *self*—not the Forms, or God, or the social order. This is a quintessentially modernist notion, and if psychology is the science of the soul that becomes the secular self, then whether the self is natural or constructed becomes an issue of grave importance. For if the soul is a construction of modernity, then perhaps modernity has no foundation outside the ideas of modernism.

In the Bronze Age there was little conception of individual mind or soul. There were great and distinctive individual men and women, but little notion of the self or of mind. Changes in the direction of recognizing individuality can be traced in literature and religion. Classical Greek plays possessed strong and willful characters acting on their own rather than by the control of the gods. Religions expanded the notion of the soul and the afterlife to encompass more and more people. For example, in ancient Egypt, at first only the Pharaoh was thought to have a soul that might attain immortality, and only he was expected at death to cross over and join the divine world of the gods. Over time, however, the circle of those eligible for eternal life expanded, first embracing the Pharaoh's immediate family, and eventually including everyone who could arrange

XAM'S BLOG 1
The Self

For psychology, the existence and nature of the self is one of the two key aspects of its relation to modernity and modernism. The other is the role of psychology and the social sciences in schemes of social engineering, which we'll come to later.

In the premodern world, the self was not a big deal, at least not for philosophers, scientists, and other intellectuals who dealt with the kinds of ideas we're concerned with in your book and class. There were lots of arguments about what went on in people's heads when they perceive or think. After the coming of dualist religions like Hinduism, Christianity, and Islam (but, as your author notes, not ones such as Buddhism) there were ferocious arguments—sometimes leading to persecutions for heresy and even militant crusades—about the nature and existence of an eternal soul. But the self as a powerful, autonomous, internal being worthy of respect did not appear as an object of discourse before the eighteenth century in the West.

The reason for the change will be a shift in how people think of the ultimate grounding of values, of morality, of right and wrong, of one's place in the universe and society. In the premodern world, these things were set by an external framework. For someone like Plato, there was an external world of the Forms where dwelt the Form of the Good—the good, the true, and the beautiful were eternally defined there, not in the minds of human beings. In later, but still premodern, religious societies, God set external standards of right and wrong. Even if we put aside these metaphysical concerns, in the premodern world your place and life and as a consequence the behavior expected of you was determined by birth. A king was a king not because he chose it, but because he was born to it, and was expected to act like a king. Likewise a serf was a serf by birth and was expected to act like a serf. Choosing one's own station in life was almost—it's important to emphasize the almost (because it created modernity)—unthinkable.

a proper burial. In Egypt's Valley of the Kings, families would sometimes break in and bury one of their own in an old king's tomb, expecting him or her to thereby attain immortality. Christianity changed how Greeks and Romans treated individual misfortune. Greeks and Romans had little, if any, care for people outside their families, regarding compassion and mercy with puzzlement. Christianity, however, so deeply implanted these virtues in Europe that we take them as natural today (MacIntyre, 1981).

However, by Late Antiquity, aspects of the social understanding of individuals and of individual minds had come to resemble the old Greek Bronze Age. Again, this is not to say that there were no individuals then, for those centuries were full of strong and distinctive men and women, but there was no conception of the individual as an important object of concern or study. This lack is part of the Neoplatonic *Zeitgeist* that dictated that the human intellect knows only universals, not individuals. The rational mind of each person thus knows another person only as an essence—humanness—not as an individual defined by the characteristics that make each person unique. That was the philosophers' theory. A person's legal status as emperor, pope, king, lord, knight, or serf overwhelmingly affected his or her life. Legal status was far more important than status as an individual human being distinct from all others.

Philosophical psychology expressed this attitude. The philosopher-psychologist was interested in the sensitive soul, the will, the imagination, the intellect, and had little interest in individual differences in psychological makeup, an attitude with a long and durable history. Not until the nineteenth century do we find, among psychologists, a systematic interest in individual differences, and even then, the founder of German psychology, Wilhelm Wundt, was indifferent to them.

During Late Antiquity and the Middle Ages, the structure of everyday life was not conducive to great individuality. Serfs (peasants who were owned by the king and given to his nobles along with the castles and lands) worked the fields. Lords and ladies hunted; lords and free commoners fought in the king's wars. Nearly everyone worked the land, work that had changed little since the Neolithic. The heavy plow increased the areas of arable land; eventually the discovery of dung fertilizer and crop rotation made land stay arable longer. More productive land meant more people, but little changed. The drastic population drop caused by the plague did make life easier for many of the survivors and their descendents. To get people to work their land, lords started having to pay wages. Kings could no longer claim that they owned everything and everyone in the country, so private property rights started to develop. However, for most people life changed very little between the agricultural revolution of the late Neolithic and the Industrial Revolution, starting in the eighteenth century in Western Europe.

Medieval peoples' social roles were stereotyped, their place in the Neoplatonic order of the universe set by God, their legal rights practically nonexistent. Even the greatest lord could be summarily executed by his king upon any suspicion of treachery, just as the lord could execute or imprison anyone he did not like. The only way to change rulers was by palace coup or civil war. In England, in 1215, the barons tried to get more rights for themselves from King John by forcing him to sign the Magna Carta—setting in motion a process that eventually led to the American Declaration of Independence and Bill of Rights—but it took several more centuries before ordinary people gained political rights. Thus, for the birth of the Western conception of individualism, we must look rather to facets of popular culture and religion.

THE MIND WITHOUT This is an early example of the plays depicting saints' and martyrs' lives, or mainly deaths, that continued to be written and performed throughout Late Antiquity, the Middle Ages, and the Renaissance. This one is early enough that the accuracy of the historical setting and relatively decent treatment of the pagan torturers makes it most unusual. The characters are stereotypes, the virgins' personifications of Christian virtues, but Hrotsvitha's historical knowledge gives her six plays more that a modern reader can identify with than later plays and books of saints' and martyrs' lives are likely to do. Until the courtly romances written by clerics, these were the only literary works popular culture approved of by the Church.

By the fourteenth or fifteenth century when the Bakers' Guild of Chester, England, commissioned and performed *The Betrayal of Christ*, meant to be performed near Easter, historical context and individual characterization had been lost at the popular level, reflecting early medieval attitudes about individuality. Even as these plays were being performed, new Renaissance ideas about the individual were being written and performed by Shakespeare (see later discussion). *The Betrayal of Christ* is a passion play (about Christ's suffering, passionate death that redeemed mankind from original sin). It opens with Christ, presumably played by the Master of the Bakers' Guild, telling his disciples to go and make ready the Pascal lamb for the Easter feast, which becomes the Last Supper. There could have been no Easter feast when Jesus was alive because Easter commemorates his rising from the dead on the third day after the crucifixion. Similarly, being Himself the sacrificial, Pascal lamb of that first Easter, nobody could have known before Jesus' death that they should prepare one.

The Baker's Guild's passion play also reveals that Christian themes could be tied to pagan ones. Because Christian theology was the preserve of the literate, popular plays spoke to ordinary people in ancient language. In the Bakers' of Chester's play, Jesus describes communion wine as being "this my blood that shall be shed on a tree." The reference to a tree rather than to the Christian Cross links Jesus to the Norse god Odin. Odin hanged himself on the Worldtree and stabbed himself with his spear, making "myself a sacrifice unto myself," for nine days and nights until, screaming, he drew up the runes from chaos, bringing writing and occult knowledge, of healing and cursing, to humankind (Ellis Davidson, 1996, p. 46). Christ was thought to have been crucified on a cross made from the Tree of Knowledge, that had borne the fruit that caused mankind's fall. The convergence of Jesus and Odin, gods who had suffered on a tree to help humanity, probably helped both sides at times in the centuries over which the conversion took place.

This play has clearly lost so much touch with history that it has also lost some common sense. After this odd beginning, this play simply shows members of the Baker's Guild reenacting a simplistic version of the Last Supper, ending with Jesus instructing Judas to go and turn him in to the Romans. What little individuality the Romans, at least, were allowed by Hrotsvitha has vanished completely from high medieval passion plays. This lack of individuality in the literature remaining from this era has led some to question just how individual the people themselves could have been.

In addition to the passion plays, which were explicitly about events in the life of Jesus, there were morality plays, such as *Mankind* and *Everyman*. The morality plays are interesting in the history of psychology because they externalize what, after Descartes, would be considered personal and private operations of the mind. Morality plays are sometimes called, therefore, *psychomachia*—plays of mental machinery. Allegories, too, in which temptations are offered by Vices or Devils and argued against by Virtues and Good Angels, externalized the workings of the human mind. Courage Contagious, also called Courage Contrary, for example, is the main Vice in *Tide Tarrieth No Man* ("Time waits for no one"), written about 1576. The main character, courage, drops the unappealing second part of his name, and (en)courages a courtier to sell his estate for fine clothing to win admiration, and he (en)courages Willful Wanton to marry early and against her parents' wishes because everything about marriage is fun. In *Enough Is as Good as a Feast*, the Vice Covetous similarly encourages a formerly too-free spending man to return to his spendthrift ways because he is supposedly acquiring a reputation for being a miser. These Vices use these main characters' hopes and fears to

XAM'S BLOG 2
Penance and the Mind Without

The concept of the individual took a long time to develop in Western society, and as you've been reading, people tended in Late Antiquity to see the mind as something outside themselves. One interesting manifestation, this can be found in the concept of sin and its expiation. By the 800s, Christianity was fully entrenched in the old Roman world and was busy converting the various barbarian groups that had brought low the old empire.

An important feature of Christianity is the idea of sin as an offense against God that needs to be made right by penance. However, especially for the leaders of warring barbarian groups new to Christianity, there was a huge tension between their way of life and the pacific demands of Christianity (MacCulloch, 2009). To be successful, a barbarian leader had to be tough, ruthless, and warlike, and this meant inevitably committing many sins. The Catholic Church, primarily through the influence of Irish Christianity, had developed a system by which sins could be expiated by acts of penance. However, the sins of barbarian leaders were of such number and gravity that performing the required acts of penance was infeasible at best and impossible at worst—there was not world enough and time. But because the concept of the individual was not yet fully developed, sins were not seen as personal offences that had to be expiated by the person who had committed them. Acts of penance were required to erase the burden of sin, but the acts could be performed by anyone on behalf of the sinner, rather like a friend repaying a loan. God, like a creditor, did not care where the penance, or the money, came from, as long as it was paid. Thus aristocrats could endow monasteries and chapels to perform acts of contrition that redounded to the benefit of the sinning aristocrat.

The functioning of the whole system was aided by the concept of Purgatory, a temporary hell where sins could be worked off by a dead sinner or by penances done by his friends and family left behind on earth. That sins belonged to the person who committed them, that the sinner should feel real guilt over them, and that the sinner had to make good the offense himself required the further development of the psychological concept of the individual. The continued practice of expiating sin via good works, such as buying indulgences (roughly get-out-of-Purgatory-free tickets) was one of the Catholic practices most offensive to Martin Luther, the instigator of the Reformation.

During Late Antiquity, knowledge of Roman history and literature decreased, and the Classic and Hellenistic traditions of vividly drawn individual characters went into decline, though there was no abrupt break between ancient and medieval literature. For example, in the last quarter of the tenth century, the Saxon nun Hrotsvitha, writing apparently for an audience of not-entirely converted nobles (she was herself of noble birth) still showed clear knowledge of early Christian history—that the Emperor Diocletian had been hostile to Christianity because Christians refused to perfunctorily worship the Roman gods. Her play *Diocletian* is about the miraculously painless burning of two virgins and the shooting of another with bow and arrows. The pagan Romans are nasty, but do offer the three highborn, Christian sisters several chances to perform the sacrifice and get married. There is a comic scene based on the late Roman playwright Terrence. The virgins' Latin names translate as Holy Love, Purity, and Peace. They are repetitious stereotypes, but the pagans are quite individualistic characters.

help them make bad decisions. In many respects, plays like these recall the psychology of the *Iliad*, in which the gods manipulate human beings, and seem distant to modern people, who have internalized both temptation (Vice) and conscience (Virtue).

These plays feature realistic Hellmouths (always a crowd pleaser), white angels, and red devils, all of which are corporeal. Only one, Titivillus in *Mankind*, played as a devil carrying a net to ensnare his victims, is supposed to be invisible to the other characters, although of course the actor was clearly visible and audible to the audience. Since all temptation comes from the devil and goes into human minds, these Vices, Bad Angels, and devils are all both real and in our minds. Reality and all-in-your-mind were one and the same to the Neoplatonic, medieval mind. Such psychomachiatic theatre shows us how different medieval mentality was from ours. High-born and low all thought of people as coming in types based on social status and having minds that worked according to rules appropriate to each type.

THE END OF ANTIQUITY

We opened this chapter in the Hellenistic period, when the Western civilization was still centered on the Mediterranean Sea. Greek culture and language furnished the basis for philosophy, science, and much of everyday life. The special political institution of the polis had died, but Greek cultural hegemony continued. The Romans conquered Greece, but were themselves conquered by Greek culture, which they then spread all around the Mediterranean and into the southern parts of Europe and Great Britain. Latin replaced Greek as the universal *lingua franca* of the West. But there still was a common language, a common culture, a common stock of ideas, at least at the educated, elite levels of society. By 1000, however, the shape of the West was very different. The focus of political activity had shifted decisively to the north, to Charlemagne's France and the new Germanic peoples (Heather, 2010). Instead of a common language and culture, there were shifting movements of peoples, cultures, and languages gradually settling down into the patterns we see on maps of Europe today. The one universal institution was the Catholic (from the Greek *katholikos*, "universal") Church, which although frequently divided by arguments about what Christians should believe, provided intellectual and social structures within which thought about human nature could be proposed and debated.

The antique way of life had shattered and scattered, being slowly replaced by another premodern mode of life from which modernity finally sprang in the late eighteenth century.

Background to Psychology: Bibliography

Background to Psychology: Bibliography

A popularly written general review of what prehistory can tell us about human nature may be found in Colin Renfrew's (2007) *Prehistory: The making of the modern mind* (New York: Modern Library), Robin Dunbar's (2004) *The human story: A new history of mankind's evolution* (London: Faber & Faber), and Bernard Wood's (2005) *Human evolution: A very short introduction* (Oxford: Oxford University Press).

There are numerous works on the history of the world and of the West. Here are three: James C. Davis (2004) *The human story: From the Stone Age to today* (New York: HarperCollins) is a brief narrative covering the whole world. Barry Cunliffe (2008) *Europe between the oceans 9000 BC–AD 1000* (New Haven, CT: Yale University Press) is an unapologetic "longe duree" history of Europe. Jacques Barzun's (2000) *From dawn to decadence 1500 to the present: 500 years of Western cultural life* (New York: HarperCollins) is opinionated (as one can tell from the title) but vigorously written and the product of deep lifelong scholarship.

There are many fine books on the Classical, Hellenistic, and Roman worlds. A vigorously written history of the period to the heights of the Roman Empire is Robin Lane Fox, *The Classical world: Homer to Hadrian* (New York: Basic. 2006). On the prehistoric roots of science, Alexander Marshack's *Roots of civilization* (New York: McGraw-Hill, 1972) is fascinating. A convenient survey of ancient Greek life and history is given by Antony Andrew in *The Greeks* (New York: Norton, 1978). The outstanding historian of Greece was M. I. Finley, who published numerous works; a general one is *The ancient Greeks* (Harmondsworth, England: Penguin). See also J. V. A. Fine, *The ancient Greeks* (Cambridge, MA: Harvard University Press); and R. Sealey, *A history of the Greek city states* (Los Angeles: University of California Press). *Classical Greece: 500–323 B.C.* (R. Osborne, ed.) is a collection of up-to-date yet accessible articles by leading scholars in all areas of ancient Greek history (Oxford: Oxford University Press, 2000). In *The search for ancient Greece* (New York, Abrams, 1992), R. Etienne and F. Etienne provide a beautifully illustrated history not of ancient Greece, but of its discovery and reconstruction by scholars from the eighteenth century to the present. Pericles delivered one of the most famous political speeches in human history, and it well conveys the ethical values and psychological ideas of the Greek *polis*. It can be found at the Ancient History Sourcebook website: *www.fordham.edu/halsall/ancient/pericles-funeralspeech.html*.

On Greek philosophy, there are two excellent surveys consisting of compilations of articles by distinguished scholars: A. Kenny, ed., *The Oxford history of Western philosophy* (Oxford, England: Oxford University Press, 1994) focuses on philosophy; and J. Boardman, J. Griffin, and O. Murray, eds., *The Oxford history of the Classical world* (Oxford, England: Oxford University Press, 1986) focuses on the Classical, Hellenistic, and Roman worlds in all their aspects. Harvard University Press has issued 1,993 editions of its series on the ancient world, in five volumes: *Early Greece, Democracy and Classical Greece, The Hellenistic world, The Roman republic*, and *The later Roman Empire*. For everything there is to know about Thales, the first known scientist and philosopher see P. F. O'Grady (2002) *Thales of Miletus: The beginnings of Western science and philosophy* (Aldershot, England: Ashgate). The study of Greek homosexuality began with Kenneth Dover's, *Greek homosexuality* (Cambridge, MA: Harvard University Press, rev. ed. 1989), which is still the place to start. Dover's picture is extended by E. Cantarella, *Bisexuality in the ancient world* (New Haven, CT: Yale University Press). Greatly influential, and controversial, has been Michel Foucault's *The history of sexuality* (New York: Vintage Books, 3 vols., 1978–1986). Dover's and Foucault's books have prompted a stream of works on the "social construction of sexuality," mostly agreeing with and elaborating on their semiofficial position. However, a certain reaction has set in, suggesting that homosexual conduct was not as widely accepted as the Dover–Foucault view says. See D. Cohen, *Law, sexuality and society: The enforcement of morals in Classical Athens* (Cambridge, England: Cambridge University Press). J. Davidson (1998) is an engagingly readable survey of "the consuming passions of classical Athens." By surveying all the pleasures of the flesh, not just sexuality, Davidson offers a window onto the Greek mind and the way Greek morality worked in everyday life. Davidson has also recently published *The Greeks and Greek love: A radical reappraisal of homosexuality in ancient Greece* (London: Weidenfield & Nicholson, 2007), which lives up to its title and should be used with caution (see, for example, the review by Thomas Hubbard at *http://classicaljournal.org/reviews2009.php*). Hubbard has also collected all of the ancient writings about Greek and Roman homosexual practices, with a critical introduction, in *Homosexuality in Greece and Rome: A sourcebook of basic documents* (Berkeley: University of California Press, 2003).

On Greek psychology, see G. S. Kirk, *The nature of the Greek myths* (Harmondsworth, England: Penguin, 1974); Bruno Snell, *The discovery of the mind: The Greek origins of European thought* (New York: Harper & Row, 1960); R. B. Onians, *The origins of European thought* (Cambridge, England: Cambridge University Press, 1951); and E. R. Dodds, *The Greeks and the irrational* (Berkeley: University of California Press, 1951); which is a classic of Classical scholarship. See also Bernard Knox, *The oldest dead white European males* (New York: Norton, 1993), who rejects the idea that Bronze Age Greeks had no concept of the soul. George Sidney Brett surveys Greek and Hellenistic psychologies in *Psychology: Ancient and modern* (New York: Cooper Square, 1963). Bennett Simon examines Greek ideas about psychopathology in *Mind and madness in ancient Greece: The classical origins of modern psychiatry* (Ithaca, NY: Cornell University Press, 1978).

For the Hellenistic period, see above all Green (1992), a lively and opinionated treatment of that fascinating era in all its dimensions, with copious discussions of philosophy. Also see F. W. Walbank, *The Hellenistic world* (Sussex, England: Harvester, 1981); and Michael Grant, *From Alexander to Cleopatra: The Hellenistic world* (New York: Scribner's, 1982); the latter is especially useful on realism, art, happiness philosophies, and mystery religions. Grant has authored many other works on the ancient world, including *The rise of the Greeks* (1987); *The founders of the Western World* (1990); and *A social history of Greece and Rome* (1992), all published by Scribner's (New York). A collection of essays that survey Hellenistic philosophy and its influence on early modern philosophy is J. Miller & B. Inwood (Eds.) (2003) *Hellenistic and early modern philosophy* (New York: Cambridge University Press). D. R. Gordon and T. B. Suits (Eds.) (2003) *Epicurus: His continuing influence and contemporary relevance* (Rochester, NY: RIT Cary Arts Press) offer a similar study focusing on Epicurus. A. A. Long (2002), *Epictetus: A Stoic and Socratic guide to life* (New York: Oxford University Press) is the result of a career devoted to understanding the Stoics.

On Rome, see Donald R. Dudley, *The Romans: 850 B.C.–A.D. 337* (New York: Knopf, 1970). W. K. Klingamann's *The first century: Emperors, gods, and everyman* (New York: HarperCollins, 1990) is a broad survey

of world history of the period. Although it is unavoidably out of date, Edward Gibbon's (1776) *Decline and fall of the Roman Empire* still repays study. It is beautifully written, with some biting, ironic asides (Gibbon says history is "little more than the register of the crimes, follies and misfortunes of mankind"). Living before the age of professional history, Gibbon can get away with what every historian would like to—omitting, as he often does, everything that is neither "entertaining nor instructive." Penguin Books has published a fine, one-volume abridgment of the original (Harmondsworth, England, 1981). Gibbon and most other authors explain the fall of the Roman Empire sociologically; A. Ferrill, in *The fall of the Roman Empire* (London: Thames and Hudson, 1986), on the other hand, says military shortcomings brought about the empire's demise.

There are several valuable treatments of Classical science. An excellent, short but comprehensive work, embracing both science and philosophy, is Giorgio de Santillanas, *The origins of scientific thought* (New York: Mentor, 1961). The standard histories of science in this period are George Sarton, *A history of science*, two volumes (New York: Norton, 1952) and Marshall Clagett, *Greek science in antiquity* (New York: Collier Books, 1955). Sarton set out to write a history of all science, but he worked so thoroughly that he died before getting past the Hellenistic age. G. E. R. Lloyd's *Early Greek science: Thales to Aristotle* (New York: Norton, 1970) is a good, short introduction to the field; his *Magic, reason, and experience: Studies in the origin and development of Greek science* (Cambridge, England: Cambridge University Press, 1979) and *Science, folklore, and ideology: The life sciences in ancient Greece* (Cambridge, England: Cambridge University Press, 1983) offer more specialized and technical studies. There are more general histories of science that include the Classical period. Stephan Mason's *A history of the sciences* (New York: Collier Books, 1962) is a useful, one-volume history. The most erudite and comprehensive history is Lynn Thorndike's massive and magisterial *History of magic and experimental science*, eight volumes (New York: Columbia University Press, 1928–58). Another ambitious undertaking is Richard Olson's social history of science: *Science deified and science defied: The historical significance of science in Western culture 3500 B.C.–A.D. 1640* (Berkeley: University of California Press, 1982), with volume II (1990) taking the story to 1820. A recent award-winning book is Lindberg (1992).

Turning to philosophy, there are several comprehensive histories that include the Greek period. I have primarily consulted Frederick Copleston, *A history of philosophy*, nine volumes (Garden City, NY:

Image Books, 1962–77); Jacob Bronowski and Bruce Mazlish, *The western intellectual tradition* (New York: Harper & Row, 1960); and Bertrand Russell, *A history of western philosophy* (New York: Simon & Schuster, 1945). Copleston's history is comprehensive and detailed, though sometimes difficult. Bronowski and Mazlish's is less detailed, but more readable. Russell's history must be used with care; it is wonderfully written, but not disinterested. As a brilliant philosopher, Russell discusses his dead colleagues from his own point of view, neglecting, and sometimes distorting, various facets of the thinkers he presents.

There is a wealth of works on the Greek philosophers. Three general works are J. Burnet, *Early Greek philosophy*, 4th ed. (New York: Collins, 1957); A. H. Armstrong, *An introduction to ancient philosophy* (London: Methuen, 1980); and W. K. C. Guthrie's multivolume *History of Greek philosophy* (Cambridge, England: Cambridge University Press), summarized in *The Greek philosophers: Thales to Aristotle* (New York: Harper, 1950). In recent years, the history of philosophy has revived. Two fine works on the Greeks are Irwin (1989) and Luce (1992). The latter is shorter and informally written; the former is deeper and more reflective. More specialized works follow.

The Naturalists. Kirk and K. Raven, *The presocratic philosophers* (Cambridge, England: Cambridge University Press, 1971); Drew Hyland, *The origins of philosophy* (New York: Putnam, 1973); G. Kerferd, *The Sophistic movement* (Cambridge, England: Cambridge University Press, 1980); R. Sprague (1972).

Socrates. Vlastos (1991) is an outstanding work, the culmination of a lifetime of study of the subject. Emily Sloan Wilson (2007) uses *The death of Socrates* (Cambridge: Harvard University Press) as a dramatic vehicle for discussing Socrates's philosophy in his Greek context and for its enduring challenge to moral thought.

Plato. *The collected dialogues of Plato*, edited by Edith Hamilton and Huntington Cairns (New York: Pantheon, 1961, Bollingen Series LXXI); Georges Grube, *Plato's thought* (Boston: Beacon Press, 1958). Norman Gulley; *Plato's theory of knowledge* (London: Methuen, 1962); Erik Nis Ostenfield, *Forms, matter, and mind* (The Hague, The Netherlands: Martinus Nijhof, 1982); J. E. Raven, *Plato's thought in the making* (Cambridge, England: Cambridge University Press, 1965); T. Robinson, *Plato's psychology* (Toronto: Toronto University Press, 1970); David Ross, *Plato's theory of ideas* (Oxford, England: Oxford University Press, 1951). See Annas (1981), a fine work on the *Republic*.

Aristotle. *The basic works of Aristotle*, edited by Richard McKeon (New York: Random House, 1941); J. C. Ackrill, *Aristotle the philosopher* (Oxford, England: Oxford University Press, 1980); John Ferguson, *Aristotle* (New York: Twayne, 1972); G. E. R. Lloyd, ed., *Aristotle on mind and the senses* (Cambridge, England: Cambridge University Press, 1978); John H. Randall, *Aristotle* (New York: Columbia University Press, 1960); David Ross, *Aristotle* (London: Methuen, 1966); and Richard Sorabji, *Aristotle on memory* (Providence, RI: Brown University Press, 1972). An excellent recent work that clarified Aristotle for me is Lear (1988), M. Durrant, ed., *Aristotle's de Anima in focus* (London: Routledge & Kegan Paul, 1993); it contains most of the text of *On the soul* with accompanying reprinted articles about it. A lively controversy has arisen over Aristotle's conception of mind. Martha Nussbaum and Hilary Putnam have argued that Aristotle's idea that soul is to body as form is to matter is essentially identical to the modern thesis of functionalism that mind is to body as program is to computer. Their view was vigorously challenged by classicist Miles Burnyeat (1992), who argued that Aristotle's conception of matter was so different from ours that comparing Aristotle to artificial intelligence is comparing apples to bobsleds. Both viewpoints are represented in Nussbaum and Rorty (1992). A penetrating analysis of the dispute is offered by Christopher Green, "The thoroughly modern Aristotle: Was he really a functionalist?" *History of Psychology*, 1998, *l*, 8–20. Virtue ethics is considered in the readings in Darwall (2003), including extended extracts from Aristotle's *Nicomachean ethics*. Michael Sandel (2009) compares competing ethical systems with regard to modern social questions, generally siding with virtue ethics against its modern secular competitors, which we will meet later.

Hellenistic and Roman Philosophy. The general surveys already cited also discuss this period. A comprehensive collection of philosophical writings is J. L. Saunders (ed.), *Greek and Roman philosophy after Aristotle* (New York: The Free Press, 1966); see also A. Long, *Hellenistic philosophy: Stoics, Epicureans, Skeptics* (London: Duckworth, 1974); and Giovanni Reale, *The systems of the Hellenistic age* (Albany, NY: State University of New York Press, 1985). Epicurus gets book-length attention in David Konstanz' *A life worthy of the gods: The materialistic philosophy of Epicurus* (Las Vegas: Parmenides Publishing). R. Sorabji, in *Emotion and peace of mind: From Stoic agitation to Christian temptation* (New York: Oxford University Press) discusses Hellenistic and early Christian theories of emotion and relates them to recent psychological and neuroscientific studies of emotion.

Hellenistic and Roman Religion. There are many good works in this area. Walter Burkert is the leading authority of Greek religion; his (1985) is the standard text, and his *Ancient mystery cults* (Cambridge, MA: Harvard University Press) extends the story. See also Ramsey McMullen, *Paganism in the Roman Empire* (New Haven, CT: Yale University Press, 1981); S. Angus, *The mystery religions* (New York: Dover, 1975); and Joscelyn Godwin, *Mystery religions in the ancient world* (San Francisco: Harper & Row, 1981). Because it's a biography of a notorious emperor, *Nero*, by E. Champlin, is a readable account of some of the more outré Roman practices, such as Saturnalia, which took place near our Christmas (Cambridge, MA: Belnap Press of Harvard University Press, 2003). For Augustine, consult R. Nash, *The light of the mind: St. Augustine's theory of knowledge* (Lexington: The University of Kentucky Press, 1969). With the possible exception of the Scientific Revolution, the most important event in the history of Western civilization was the decline of paganism and the spread of Christianity. Lane Fox (1986) provides a general treatment of classical pagan religion before describing the Christian ascendancy.

R. Fletcher, *The barbarian conversion: From paganism to Christianity* (New York: Henry Holt, 1998), completes the story by describing pagan religion and conversion to Christianity in northern and western Europe. Bart Ehrman (2003) describes the bewildering multiplied and inconsistent forms taken by early Christianity in *Lost Christianities: The battles for scripture and the faiths we never knew* (New York: Oxford University Press).

The world of the scientists and philosophers was the male world of politics and war. To understand the role and importance of women in the ancient world, see S. B. Pomeroy, *Goddesses, whores, wives, and slaves: Women in classical antiquity* (New York: Schocken, 1995), a lively work and now a classic itself (it first appeared in 1975). More specialized studies are contained in E. Fantham, H. P. Foley, N. B. Kampen, S. B. Pomeroy, and H. A. Shapiro, *Women in the classical world* (New York: Oxford University Press, 1994). The life of Hypatia of Rhodes was the subject of a movie, Agora (2009), emphasizing the tension between science and religion and between the private pursuit of wisdom and the public demands of politics. Hypatia was caught in the middle.

The Premodern World 1000 C.E.–1600 C.E.

FROM ANTIQUITY TO THE SCIENTIFIC REVOLUTION

The Middle Ages 1000–1350

Following the long economic depression of Late Antiquity, the economy and population began to recover around 1000, ushering in the High Middle Ages, which lasted until about 1350. The key economic development of this period was the appearance of the first cities and the technological creativity they embraced. Cities were important for a number of reasons, each of which made European life different and more dynamic than the shattered Greco-Roman past or static societies elsewhere, such as in Islam or China. Cippola (1993, p. 120) says that the rise of European cities was "the turning point of world history." First, cities were autonomous, controlled by neither feudal lords nor the Church. Medievals said, "City air makes free": The citizen of a city owed no feudal obligations (as even great lords did to their king), and they were not serfs. The city was thus rather like the American frontier—a place people went to find liberty, and to pursue their own interests. Second, the citizens of the European cities were the first businessmen, thinking in terms of trade and profit, not *arête* as in Greece. Greeks and Romans did not think in economic terms; the burghers of the cities did, beginning to develop modern business methods such as credit and companies. Finally, in pursuit of profit and productivity, city citizens embraced technology. The ancients had despised technology—they had all the slaves they needed to do hard work. There were no slaves in the cities, and so businessmen and artisans adopted and improved machines—building mills, and looms, and clocks. The embrace of technology led to the development of great sailing ships, the growth of trade, and openness to the rest of the world as potential trading partners. It also encouraged "machine-thinking" (Cippola, 1993), helping foster

From Chapter 4 of *A History of Psychology: From Antiquity to Modernity*, Seventh Edition.
Thomas Hardy Leahey. Copyright © 2013 by Pearson Education, Inc. All rights reserved.

The well-preserved medieval city of Brugge (Bruges), Belgium. Commercial cities such as Brugge were the catalyst for economic recovery after the fall of the Roman Empire and incubator of Western science, technology, and the modern Western way of life. *(© Jim Zuckerman/Corbis)*

the idea that the world is a machine, an idea central to the Scientific Revolution. As with Anselm's "faith seeking reason," the development of cities, business, and technology was uniquely European. A small but telling example is clocks and watches. The Chinese relied on ancient water clocks until nearly modern times, and an eighteenth-century French ambassador to Islamic Turkey described the puzzled wonder with which his local guides regarded his watch (B. Lewis, 2001).

The High Middle Ages were also an enormously creative period in Western philosophy and science. Many Greek works, especially those of Aristotle, were recovered, and institutions critical to the development of modern science were created. The magnificent Romanesque and Gothic churches were constructed. Modern political forms started to develop, especially in England, with documents such as the Magna Carta (1215) limiting royal power. The recorded literary expression of individualism also increased greatly, with stereotypical dramatic and literary characters (such as Mankind) developing into very human characters, such as Chaucer's Dame Alison and the Franklin.

The Black Death—bubonic plague—dramatically marks the dividing line between the High and Late Middle Ages. The plague swept Europe, killing about a third of the population of Europe, engendering understandable fear and even panic. At the same time, conflict between secular and religious leaders intensified, and Luther's Reformation challenged the authority of the Catholic Church, which had been little questioned in earlier years. It was a turbulent period, but it did not lack creativity. Aristotle's science was developed and extended, and naturalistic investigations of nature began. The Late Middle Ages faded into the Renaissance, when the literary works of the Greeks and Romans were recovered, in addition to the philosophical and scientific works that had been translated in the High Middle Ages. It was a period of creative destruction, during which the ossified structures of feudalism and Church authority were torn down, making way for the creation of the modern way of life that began in the seventeenth century.

Medieval Psychology in the Academy

SCHOLASTIC PSYCHOLOGY IN THE HIGH MIDDLE AGES The High Middle Ages experienced an intellectual renaissance as the works of Aristotle and other Greek writers, accompanied by Muslim commentary, poured into the West through Spain, Sicily, and Constantinople, the places where Islam and Christianity intersected, sometimes peacefully, oftentimes not. Aristotle's philosophy was naturalistic and brought a fresh, unreligious approach to knowledge and human nature that was

XAM'S BLOG 1
Premodernism

I know that "premodernism" sounds like an oxymoron. I said in my speech to the Foundation that modernism was an analysis of the conditions of life in the modern world offered by thinkers who noticed and reflected on the historical changes taking place around them. They knew that they were living in modern times because in their own experience they could contrast it with premodern life. So how can there be an ideology of "premodernism"?

In one sense, of course, there can't be. No one knew in antiquity or the Middle Ages that his or her way of life wouldn't go on forever. In fact, he or she thought it would. Change was extremely rare and usually for the worse—a famine, a war, a bad king. Even good times, like bountiful harvests, sowed the seeds of their own destruction in the Malthusian economy as people responded by having more children who ate the surplus, ensuring that the poverty of subsistence living returned.

On the other hand, a sort of ideology of life emerged in the Middle Ages, based on a fusion of the ideas of Plato, the Neoplatonists, and Aristotle as filtered through Christian theology. It was an ideology based on the Great Chain of Being. It said that the universe could be described as a sort of Aristotelian hierarchy of Platonic and earthly beings, like this, in a Neoplatonic form:

THE ONE

SPIRITUAL BEINGS (called Angels by Christians)

HUMANS (a mixture of spirit, soul, and matter, body)

ANIMALS

PLANTS

INANIMATE MATTER

PRIMA MATERIA (Aristotle's pure potential matter).

The medieval ideology of life then came from extending the hierarchy to the social world, in the medieval phrase "as above, so below":

GOD

KING

ARISTOCRATS

FREEMEN

SERFS

From early on, the Catholic Church liked to see the hierarchy with POPE above KING (though below GOD), but this was a dream of theirs, never a reality, though it did stoke conflict between the Church and secular rulers.

The idea was that life on earth ought to reflect the divine order of heaven. This fit in very well with the unchanging nature of life in the Malthusian economy. Not only did things not change very much, but ideally they ought not change at all. Since most change was bad, change could be seen as departing from the ideal, static, nature of the universe and people's position in the universe. Certainly the Great Chain pleased kings, seeming to give them power to rule absolutely. Bishop J. B. Bossuet (1627–1704), King Louis IV of France's chief political spin master wrote, "Royal authority is sacred . . . God established kings as his ministers and reigns through them . . . the royal throne is not the throne of a man but the throne of God himself" (quoted by Blanning, 2007, p. 209). Efforts by parliaments and people to rule themselves were more than treason; they were offenses against God and the metaphysical order of the universe.

From our psychological perspective the thing to note is that this premodern ideology of social life differed from both the Greek way that preceded it and the modern way that followed it. The Greeks, with the partial exception of Plato, built their notions of government on their conceptions of human nature. Aristotle, recall, said that because human beings have a nature (*physis*), they should live in a society that permits and encourages human flourishing (*eudaemonia*). As you will see, while the philosophes of the Enlightenment disagreed with the Greeks, and each other, about what human nature was like, they nevertheless believed that society should be built on a right understanding—ultimately a scientific understanding—of human nature. The premodern ideology of "as above, so below" did not so much reject human nature as ignore it. It's no surprise, then, that while psychological thought continued to develop in Antiquity and the Middle Ages, it was not socially or politically important.

reconciled with Christian faith only with difficulty. St. Thomas Aquinas, who synthesized faith in God's word and reason as found in Aristotle's philosophy, only narrowly escaped a charge of heresy. This union of Christ and Aristotle, impressive though it was, was relatively sterile. The future belonged to those who, like William of Ockham, divorced faith from reason and pursued only the latter.

In the twelfth and thirteenth centuries, universities began to appear, usually linked to cathedrals, and theologian-philosophers abounded. Two of the most important were St. Bonaventure (1221–1274) and St. Thomas Aquinas (1225–1274). They stand, respectively, for the two great medieval approaches to knowledge, human nature, and God: the Platonic-Augustinian mystical way and the Aristotelian-Thomistic way of natural reason constrained by faith.

St. Bonaventure was a great voice of Christian Neoplatonic philosophy. He took a sharply dualist, Platonic view of soul and body, as had Augustine. To Bonaventure, the soul was much more than the Aristotelian form of the body. As Plato had taught, Bonaventure said the soul and body were two completely distinct substances, and the immortal soul was merely using the mortal body during its earthly existence. The essence of a person was the soul.

The soul was capable of two sorts of knowledge. First, as united with the body, it could have knowledge of the external world. Here, Bonaventure followed the empiricism of Aristotle by denying innate ideas and arguing that we build up universal concepts by abstraction from experienced individual objects. However, like Aquinas but not Aristotle, Bonaventure asserted that abstraction alone is insufficient and must be joined to divine illumination from God to achieve true knowledge.

The second source of knowledge, Bonaventure said, belonged to the soul alone: knowledge of the spiritual world, including God. The source of this knowledge was introspective meditation, which discovers the image of God illuminated in the soul, and apprehends God through interior reflection without recourse to sensation. We should emphasize again that Augustinian introspection did not have as its aim knowledge of a personal self as in psychotherapy, or of human nature as in scientific psychology. Its goal was to obtain a vision of God, not oneself.

Bonaventure distinguished four mental faculties: the vegetative faculties, the sensitive faculties, the intellect, and the will. However, Bonaventure spoke of other "aspects" of the soul, which he refused to call faculties but whose inclusion made his system resemble Ibn Sīnā's. For example, he distinguished a "higher" aspect and a "lower" aspect to the intellect, a distinction that resembles Ibn Sīnā's contemplative and practical intellects.

As Aristotle became known in the West, many thinkers struggled to reconcile his scientific naturalism with the teachings of the Catholic Church. The greatest and most influential of these thinkers was St. Thomas Aquinas. He called Aristotle "The Philosopher," the thinker who demonstrated both the power and the limits of human reason practiced without the word of God. Aquinas adopted Aristotle's system and showed that it was not incompatible with Christianity. To harmonize philosophy and theology, Aquinas distinguished sharply between them, limiting a person's reason to knowledge of the world of nature. Aquinas thus accepted Aristotle's empiricism and the consequence that reason can know only the world, not God. God can be known only by inference from His work in the world.

Aquinas set out to consider all topics, including psychology, philosophically—that is, independent of revelation, following Anslem's path of faith seeking reason. In his psychology, he closely followed Aristotle, but he also gave weight to the opinions of Islamic writers, especially Ibn Sīnā. He made few original contributions to Aristotelian psychology but refined and extended the classification of mental aspects given by the philosopher and his Islamic commentators. Figure 1 summarizes

Aquinas's picture of mind. As can be seen, most of it is similar to ideas of Aristotle and Ibn Sīnā, and most of the new points are self-explanatory.

Aquinas, more than Aristotle or his non-Christian commentators, was concerned to distinguish humans, who have souls, from animals, that do not. This concern emerges clearly in his discussions of motivation and the faculty of estimation. Unlike Ibn Sīnā, Aquinas held that there are two kinds of estimation. First, there is *estimation proper*, which is characteristic of animals and not under voluntary control: The lamb *must* flee the wolf it sees to be dangerous; the cat *must* pounce on the mouse. The second kind of estimation is under rational control. Aquinas called it *cogitava*, and it is found only in humans: We may flee the wolf if it appears dangerous or choose to approach it, perhaps to take a picture of it. One's estimative power is under the control of one's free will, for one chooses and makes judgments instead of simply responding blindly to animal instinct.

Just as there are two kinds of estimation, so there are two kinds of motivation or appetite. Sensitive, animal appetite is a compelled, natural inclination to pursue pleasurable objects and avoid harmful ones, and to overcome obstacles to that pursuit. A human being, however, has intellectual appetite, or will, which has the power to seek higher, moral goods under the guidance of reason. Animals know only pleasure or pain; humans know right and wrong.

Three other differences from Ibn Sīnā may be noted. First, Aquinas dropped compositive imagination as an unnecessary addition to retentive imagination and rational thinking. Second, by making cogitava—human estimation—a rationally guided faculty concerned with the outer world,

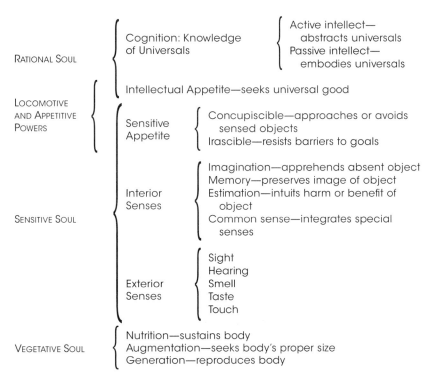

FIGURE 1 Aquinas's conception of mind.

the need for Ibn Sīnā's practical intellect vanished. Finally, Aquinas made the mind consistent with Christian theology by returning the active intellect to the human soul. Knowledge is an active product of human thinking, not a gift of divine illumination via the agent intellect.

Despite some Neoplatonic remnants, such as the hierarchic organization of faculties, Aquinas's views stand in sharp contrast to Bonaventure's. Aquinas rejected the Platonic-Augustinian tradition's radical dualism of soul and body. The body is not a tomb, a prison, or punishment; nor is it a puppet operated by the soul. A person is a whole, a mind *and* a body. Although the soul is transcendent, its natural place is in a body, which it fulfills and which fulfills it. This got Aquinas into trouble with Neoplatonized Christian orthodoxy, which looked to a disembodied life of bliss in heaven. Only by stressing the resurrection, when soul and body would be united forever, Aquinas was able to defend his Aristotelian philosophy.

Aquinas's philosophy was a heroic attempt to reconcile science—Aristotle—with revelation. However, by conceptually separating the two, he was a harbinger of the future, when reason and revelation came into open conflict. Aquinas brought a fresh naturalism to the traditional Platonic Christian framework, but he accepted that framework and worked within it, as did all medieval natural philosophers and theologians.

PSYCHOLOGY IN THE LATE MIDDLE AGES: REBIRTH OF EMPIRICISM Before the Black Death, the Late Middle Ages were remarkably creative. We will briefly examine the most influential late medieval thinker, William of Ockham, whose contribution was to revive empiricism, opening up for psychological analysis what had previously been reserved to metaphysics.

Medieval philosophers conflated psychology and ontology, the study of the nature of being or existence. Following Plato, most medieval thinkers believed that something real must correspond to each mental concept. For Plato, that something real was the Forms; for Aristotle, it was real essences; for medievals, it was the Ideas in the mind of God.

For the Greeks and medievals, the only real knowledge was knowledge of universals; indeed, it was asserted that the rational soul, or intellect, had knowledge only of universals, not of particular things. Following Aristotle, medievals held that the only certain knowledge was what could be deduced from universal propositions. This attitude persisted even in Aquinas. Although he described the process of abstraction as the way to universal knowledge, and although he held that the intellect knows only what is derived from the senses, he still maintained that the abstracted essences were metaphysically true, that they corresponded to holy Ideas.

Ockham challenged this centuries-old assumption by substituting psychology for metaphysics. He asserted that knowledge begins with acts of "intuitive cognition"—direct, infallible acquaintance with some object in the world. Intuitive cognition does not yield mere opinion, as Plato held; it yields knowledge of what is true and false about the world. From such knowledge of things, it may go on to "abstractive cognition" of universals. But universals exist only as mental concepts; they have no existence outside the mind (Kemp, 1996).

These abstract concepts may be either true or false; for example, one may form the concept of a unicorn, which does not exist. Abstractive cognition is thus wholly hypothetical. The touchstone of reality and truth is intuitive cognition. Ockham discarded the metaphysical problem that bedeviled Plato, Aristotle, and the medievals—How can each individual participate in a transcendent essence or Form? He substituted the psychological question—How do we acquire universal concepts, given that we have direct knowledge only of individuals? His answer was that the mind notes similarities among objects, and, based on the similarities, it classifies objects. Thus, universals are logical terms that apply to some objects and not others, terms that indicate relations among objects.

Unlike Aquinas and other faculty psychologists, Ockham denied the distinction of soul from its faculties. According to Ockham, the soul does not *have* the faculty of will or intellect. Rather, what we call a faculty is simply a name for a certain kind of mental act. Will describes the soul in the act of willing; intellect describes the soul in the act of thinking. Ockham always sought to simplify accounts as much as possible, ridding them of nonessentials, which is why we speak of "Ockham's razor," although the idea is Aristotle's. Ockham saw faculties as unnecessary reifications of mental acts into mental entities apart from the mind.

Habit was crucial to Ockham's view of the mind. For him, concepts were learned habits, ideas derived from experience. When he rejected the world of universals, whether Platonic Forms or divine Ideas, the status of universals was reduced to habit. These habits are what make possible the idea of a person's thinking independent of actually sensed objects. We cannot think about the Forms, for they do not exist. We think instead about derived, habitual concepts; without them, we would be animals, reduced to simple responses to external stimuli (Kemp, 1998). Ockham was the first thinker, but not the last, to put such a burden on habit; but he was not a behaviorist, for to him habits were mental concepts, not bodily responses.

Ockham drew a radical distinction, far more radical than Aquinas's, between faith and reason. Ockham pointed out that there is no ground in experience, or intuitive cognition, for believing we have an immaterial, immortal soul. As far as reason or philosophy goes, the mind may be a perishable entity dependent on the body. It is only from faith that knowledge of the immortal soul comes. This separation of faith and reason greatly weakened theology and metaphysics, but it helped bring science into being.

Most medieval philosophers believed, as did the Greeks, in the power of human reason to know eternal Truth. They went further in asserting that God's truth and philosophical truth were one and could be synthesized, as in Aquinas's *Summa theologica*. Some mystical clergymen, such as St. Bernard of Clairvaux, who denied that philosophy could say anything about God, who is known through faith alone, rejected the idea. Despite the mystics, the general trend of thought before 1300 favored the Greek view.

We saw this earlier in this chapter, when we touched on the problem of universals. Most medievals held to some form of *realism*, a belief that universal human concepts correspond to some enduring Form or essence, conceived by medievals as an Idea in the mind of God. This view was held by Plato, Aristotle, and Aquinas, despite their other differences. A few thinkers, called *nominalists*, maintained that universals were mere puffs of air emitted when we speak names (hence, nominalism). They have no transcendent reality, being nothing more than verbal behaviors.

Analysis of the problem of universal human knowledge led fourteenth-century philosophers to put severe limits on what humans may know. The first step was taken by Peter Abelard (1079–1142), the greatest medieval philosopher before the High Middle Ages (when Aristotle's works were recovered). Like Aristotle, Abelard saw the difficulty with the metaphysical-realist approach. According to realists, to say "Socrates is a man" is to relate two things: the living individual Socrates and the heavenly Form of man. Abelard saw that *man* should be considered a label—or better, a *concept* that we apply to some individual. *Man* is a mental concept applied to Socrates, not a separate thing or transcendent Form. For Abelard, concepts were purely mental images or labels, and when we discuss universals we are discussing these mental entities, not eternal Forms. Abelard's account of universals was thus logical and psychological rather than metaphysical. This position, best called conceptualism, was a forerunner of Ockham's views (discussed earlier).

In the High Middle Ages, it was thought that human knowledge and Holy Truth were coordinate, that human universals corresponded to the divine Ideas. Abelard and Ockham destroyed this self-confidence. They posed new questions about the bases of human knowledge. If universals do not reflect the divine Ideas, and if they rest on knowledge of individuals, how do we justify our knowledge and show its truth? Before Abelard and Ockham, that humans could achieve transcendental knowledge was taken for granted; after them, skepticism became an option again—perhaps all human belief was mere opinion. Philosophers had to show how knowledge and opinion could be distinguished without reference to God or Forms.

Interestingly, belief in God's omnipotence forced a skeptical attitude on fourteenth-century philosophers. Christian thinkers believed that God is omnipotent, capable of doing anything that is not self-contradictory. Therefore, if you are looking at a tree, God could destroy the tree, but maintain in you the experience of the nonexistent object. If this is so, Christian thinkers had to ask how we can be certain of any perception, or of any piece of putative knowledge.

This problem fostered a thoroughgoing critique of human knowledge by fourteenth-century philosophers. The most interesting among them was Nicholas of Autrecourt (b. 1300), a follower of Ockham. Like Ockham, he did not see psychology as metaphysics, saying that there are only acts of understanding and volition, not separate faculties of Understanding and Will. Like later empiricists, Autrecourt argued that certain knowledge lies in staying as close to appearances as possible. All we can know is what our senses tell us, so knowledge is grounded in experience, and the best knowledge is that which remains closest to experience. Making a leap from sense perception to Forms, essences, or divine Ideas he considered illegitimate.

Nicholas of Autrecourt rejected the possibility of divine intervention to maintain an illusion of perception, and he based knowledge on an assumption shared with Ockham: Whatever appears is true. This belief is necessary to any empiricist theory of knowledge, and Ockham held it implicitly. By making it explicit, Autrecourt had to ask whether it is justified. Anticipating American pragmatism, he concluded that we cannot be certain of this assumption but can only hold that it is probably true because it seems more likely than the contrary assumption that whatever appears is false. Autrecourt and others worked out the complications of Ockham's psychological account of universals by close analysis of the grounds of human knowledge. The search for a justification of human knowledge of the external world has continued ever since and is a root problem for modern cognitive science.

In addition to fostering skepticism, Ockham's thoroughgoing empiricism had another consequence. By excluding things of faith from the sphere of observation and reason, empiricism directed human eyes toward observation of the world that could be known—the physical world. Physical science experienced its birth in the fourteenth century.

Rise of the Concept of the Individual

THE INDIVIDUAL IN POPULAR PSYCHOLOGY The modern concept of the individual began to emerge in many areas during the High Middle Ages. Biographies and autobiographies were written; portraits came to reflect the individual, not merely the person's status. The development of transparent glass led to the creation of good mirrors. For the first time, people could see themselves clearly, and surely this led to self-reflection on the difference between the way they seemed to be to others and the way they felt and thought inside (Davies, 1996). Soon, Descartes would turn self-reflection into a new foundation for philosophy and, along the way, invent psychology. Most important of all was literature (Bloom, 1998).

In early Christianity, women were full participants in religion; they preached and often lived in chaste, mixed-sex monasteries. The early Middle Ages were full of strong female figures as capable and powerful as any man. However, as Christianity absorbed Classical culture, it absorbed Roman misogyny and Platonic aversion to sensual pleasure. Marriage was forbidden to priests; women were forbidden to preach or even approach holy relics. They were reduced to second-class status as helpers of men. According to St. Thomas Aquinas, "Woman was created to be man's helpmate, but her unique role is in conception . . . since for other purposes men would be better assisted by other men" (Heer, 1962, p. 322).

One especially strong source of Christian misogyny was St. Jerome (340–420), a Neoplatonist who linked womanhood to the temptation of the flesh. Medieval Christianity looked on sex as sinful, whether inside marriage or out. St. Jerome said (Pagels, 1989, p. 94), "in view of the purity of Christ's body, all sexual intercourse is unclean." Virginity was exalted; the immaculate Virgin Mary was contrasted with Eve the temptress. As the oppression of women grew, the cult of the Virgin spread throughout the Middle Ages and well into modern times, as is evident from the number of churches and schools carrying some variation of the name *Notre Dame*. This focus created an ambivalent attitude toward women. Women at their best were seen as holy vessels of God, yet men feared women as sources of temptation.

A powerful and important response to the oppression of women was the clerical and courtly invention of the literature of fin amour, an artistic and philosophical embroidering of the experience of being "madly in love" shared by many people in all societies (Jankowiak, 1995). The literature of this "courtly love" as it was renamed by a nineteenth-century librarian, focused on individual feeling, and thus helped construct the idea of people as distinct individuals to be valued in their own right. Moreover, it helped create a new conception of individuals as having within them—not in external lectures from Virtue and Vice—the causes of their own behavior.

People all over the world get struck by blind Cupid's arrows and by lust. Sex was the major topic of many folk tales, bawdy stories, and tales called *fabliaux*. It was also the main topic of the *goliards*—student poets and singers of the High Middle Ages. The most famous collection of their songs is the *Carmina Burana*, which often presents a blasphemous glorification of the pagan goddess of love, Venus, Cupid's mother. She is described in terms such as "Rose of the World," usually reserved for the Virgin Mary. (The rose, incidentally, was widely used as a symbol of both the vagina and the Virgin.)

The theme of fin amour, or courtly love, was developed by a number of medieval authors. Most were clerics from the French provinces of Aquitaine and Champagne, but some were women, most notably Marie of France, probably an Abbess in an English nunnery. In these stories, literature elaborated the idea of romantic, sexual love, and integrated it into the emerging idea of knightly honor. According to the ideals of courtly love, knights dedicated themselves to the love of one lady, for whom they promised great deeds, and from whom they hoped for great love. These songs and tales of fin amour, when not written by clerics with a moral in mind, were often written by minstrels with immoral hopes. Like many knights, the minstrels were men of too lowly origin to have any great hopes of getting their ladies into bed. In fear of these ladies' owners (husbands, fathers, or brothers), they sometimes confusingly for late readers addressed their missives to their "Lord." Such a term of address did, however, place aristocratic ladies in an uncommonly commanding position. On the other hand, aristocratic men could use it to their advantage: "Sir! I cannot have an affair with you. You are my husband's liege lord. I am but your servant!" "I'll make you my wife! Then your social rank will not count." Thus, while fin amour sometimes made men appreciate and even worship women, it did not always work to their advantage, and did nothing to change their official status as chattels of their husbands.

In the vast majority of human societies throughout history, love very rarely formed the basis of marriage. In most cultures, that relationship has been created by arrangement between the families of the husband and wife, with varying degrees of consultation with the involved parties. Unsurprisingly, adultery tends to be common (Fisher, 1992), and adulterous hopes provided the basis of fin amour literature. Still, romantic love remains an important element in popular consciousness and psychology. Theories of motivation must reckon with romantic love, or as Tennov (1979) has called it, *limerence.*

During the High Middle Ages, signs of individuality among at least the upper classes and the urban merchants became more evident. In France and Norman England, the old Celtic legends were adopted by the upper class. Adapted largely by French clerics (still trying to convert the pagans by recasting their tales), the Arthurian fin amour romances were not overloaded with plausible, individual characters. These scraps of misunderstood paganism, reworked to make Christian tales, developed such characters by copying the "how-to" dialogues known from the *Ars Amatoria* (Art of Love) by the pagan Roman author Ovid who lived in the time of Augustus. Ovid, rather tongue-in-cheek, pretended to tell aristocrats what they already knew—how to seduce and give in to seduction. This was the best, or only, model of even stereotypical love-making available to these clerics. Launcelot and Guenivere learned their cheating way from Ovid, as did Tristan and Isolde.

Ultimately, the spreading belief in romantic love (combined with the prosperity to act on it) tended to undermine the corporate nature of medieval society by making the basis of relationships personal feeling rather than appointed status. Gottfried von Strasbourg, in his *Tristan und Isolde*, one of the most enduring romantic love stories, wrote about the lovers' idyllic union in the forest this way: "Man was there with Woman, Woman there with Man. What else should they be needing?" (Heer, 1962, p. 195). Church, state, and society are dispensed within favor of the romantic, spiritual, and carnal union of two individuals.

THE INDIVIDUAL IN ACADEMIC PSYCHOLOGY In two areas, individualism did make its way into medieval academic culture—ethics and mystic religion—and even here, the movement began in popular culture. Before the twelfth century, sin was acknowledged but not felt as something personal. Penance was a mechanical procedure for expiating sin. In the twelfth century, however, people began to weigh personal intention in judging transgressions. This attitude was formalized in Peter Abelard's (1079–1142) voluntaristic ethics. Abelard held, contrary to other thinkers, that sin was entirely a matter of intention, not of action. An act is not right or wrong; what is right or wrong is the intention behind the act. Intentions are, of course, intensely personal, so Abelard's ethics were part of the growth of the individual. The medieval Catholic confessional, in which sinners recount their individual sins to a forgiving confessor, was a practical form of psychotherapy (Thomas, 1971).

Mysticism began in popular religion rather than scholastic theology. Not content with the mediation of a priest between self and God, mysticism seeks a direct connection between the two. The way to God is contemplation, not ritual. St. Francis of Assisi (1182–1226), the greatest medieval popular preacher, abandoned wealth and status in favor of communing with God through nature. St. Francis's teaching was individualistic and was perceived, correctly, as subversive by the Catholic Church. He narrowly escaped persecution as a heretic instead of canonization as a saint. Poverty was not an ideal that a rich and worldly church wished to support, and solitary contemplation threatened the complex of rituals the church claimed brought salvation. Only by absorbing St. Francis and his followers could the Church avert the threat of the rising consciousness of the individual inherent in mysticism. Thus, the idea of the individual, which would grow to great prominence in the Renaissance, was born in medieval popular culture.

This ascetic ideal is a common one in world religions. Buddha and his early followers sought release (*samsara*) from the cycle of life through meditation and asceticism. Hindu followers of Shiva have long been austere gurus—forest sages living away from society and its temptations. Early Christian hermits, living in the desert, were the first monks. Just as some Druids had been forest sages, so too Celtic Christian hermits lived in remote forest areas or on small, bleak islands.

These forest sages—Christianized by St. Francis of Assisi—were found scattered throughout the courtly romances of the High Middle Ages, too, hinting at a tie to the Albigensians of southern France. Ascetic religions focus inward for enlightenment or salvation, and psychology in the seventeenth century will be associated with English Puritanism and Counter-Reformation Catholicism. Descartes will create psychology by withdrawing from society to a lonely, stove-heated room where he will discover consciousness and prove the existence of God from the prior existence of himself as a thinking thing.

Witchcraft rooted in European paganism offered an alternative to Christianity, which had been painted over, but not vanquished, by early and medieval Christianity. Witches, female and male, were believed to be real people by the church and laity. How many such unconverted or semi-converted pagans really existed we cannot tell, though there must have been some. Eventually, the clerical conception of witches who officially sold their souls to the Devil and flew to Sabbaths seems to have caught on with the powerless. Witch-finding persecutors defined demon-possession and witchcraft in such detail that they created a social role attractive to oppressed women and servants of the wealthy (Spanos, 1996). While being a witch or the victim of a demon was socially undesirable, it nevertheless made one a center of attention and perhaps an object of fear.

The Renaissance 1350–1600

What a piece of work is man, how noble in reason,
How infinite in faculty,
In form and moving how express and admirable,
In action how like an angel,
In apprehension how like a god;
The beauty of the world, the paragon of animals.

(Shakespeare, *Hamlet*, II, ii, 300–303)

The Renaissance is rightly celebrated for its creativity in the arts. For the history of psychology, it initiated the transition from medieval to modern times. The distinctive development of the Renaissance was the reappearance of humanism: placing importance on individual human beings and their lives in this world as opposed to the medieval concern with feudal social status and the religious concern with future lives in Heaven or Hell. As psychology is the science of individual mind and behavior, it owes a debt to humanism.

THE ANCIENTS AND THE MODERNS: THE REVIVAL OF HUMANISM Although the Renaissance helped give birth to modern secular life, it began (as in the works of Francesco Petrarch [1304–1374]) by looking backward rather than forward. Renaissance writers derided the Middle Ages as dark and irrational and praised the Classical era as enlightened and full of wisdom. The "Party of the Ancients" believed that people could do no more than imitate the glories of Greece and Rome. Right through the eighteenth century—the Enlightenment and Age of Reason—the influence of the ancients lingered, as artists, architects, and political leaders looked to the Classical past for models of taste, style, and sound government. Although most Renaissance thinkers were members of the Party of the Ancients, their efforts to translate ancient works helped break Aristotle's grip on natural philosophy. Medieval thinkers knew only Aristotle's account of the universe, but Renaissance scholars recovered alternative Greek accounts, most importantly the Stoics' and the atomists' (Crombie, 1995). These rival views helped the Party of the Moderns—the makers of the Scientific Revolution—think about scientific problems in fresh ways.

Renaissance humanism turned the focus of human inquiry away from medieval preoccupations with God and heaven toward the study of nature, including human nature. Freed from medieval religious prohibitions on dissection of the human body, artists such as Leonardo da Vinci (1452–1519) and physicians such as Andreas Vesalius (1514–1564) undertook detailed anatomical studies, beginning to see the body as an intricate but understandable machine, a key to scientific psychology. Since the dawn of time, people had closely observed nature but had rarely interfered in its operations. In the Renaissance, however, a new relationship between humans and nature took shape. Led by Francis Bacon (1561–1626), scientists began to interrogate nature by means of experimentation and sought to use their knowledge to control nature. Bacon said, "Knowledge is power." Throughout the twentieth century, psychology has followed Bacon's maxim, aiming to be a means of advancing human welfare. Applied psychology began with the Italian political writer, Niccolò Machiavelli (1469–1527), who linked the study of human nature to the pursuit of political power. Though not discarding religious notions of right and wrong, Machiavelli looked unsparingly at human nature in the new naturalistic spirit, seeing humans as made more for sin than for salvation. He told princes how to exploit human nature for their own ends while avoiding tempting paths of selfishness that could harm their nations.

RENAISSANCE NATURALISM Out of Renaissance interest in understanding nature came a point of view halfway between religion and modern science—Renaissance naturalism. Magnets are mysterious: How does a special lump of metal attract and repel others? Traditional explanations cited the supernatural: The magnet is inhabited by a demon or is under the spell of a sorcerer. Renaissance naturalism, however, attributed the magnet's power to "a secret virtue, inbred by nature, and not by any conjuration." The magnet's power lay in the inherent nature of magnets, not in a demon or spell imposed on nature from without. Rejecting supernatural explanation represented a step toward science, but without an explanation of how magnetism worked, "secret virtues" remained as mysterious as demons. Renaissance naturalism was accompanied by the idea of natural magic, which meant a sort of magic that controlled or changed nature without invoking supernatural powers (Eamon, 1994). An example is discovering that food kept in a tightly sealed container would keep longer than food left lying around. It is magic only in the sense that human intervention altered the natural course of decay. Natural magic was the basis of the experimental sciences.

Greater mysteries than magnetism, however, are life and mind. Why do living things move, but not stones? How do we perceive and think? Religion said a soul dwelled in bodies, making them alive and giving them experience and the capacity for action. In Greek, *psuche* meant "breath of life." Renaissance naturalism suggested that perhaps life and mind, like magnetism, were outcomes of natural powers possessed by living bodies, not infusions into nature from the soul. With regard to the mind, Renaissance naturalism suffered from two drawbacks. As in the case of magnetism, it lacked any explanation of how the body caused mental activity. More disquieting was naturalism's implication that humans have no souls, so that our personalities will perish with our bodies. To a large degree, scientific psychology was created as scientists, beginning with Descartes, wrestled with these questions. Psychology seeks to give detailed explanations of mind and behavior without invoking a supernatural soul.

The Renaissance Party of the Ancients, which looked to the Classical past as the source of all wisdom, was challenged by the Party of the Moderns, which asserted that modern men and women were equal to the creative giants of the past. They proved they were right with the Scientific Revolution.

XAM'S BLOG 2
The First Modernist?

[Is i]t be better [for a Prince] to be loved than feared or feared than loved? It may be answered that one should wish to be both, but, because it is difficult to unite them in one person, it is much safer to be feared than loved, when, of the two, either must be dispensed with. Because this is to be asserted in general of men, that they are ungrateful, fickle, false, cowardly, covetous, and as long as you succeed they are yours entirely; they will offer you their blood, property, life and children, as is said above, when the need is far distant; but when it approaches they turn against you.

Thus wrote Machiavelli in *The Prince*. As your text notes, Machiavelli can lay claim to being the first social psychologist. He looks at human nature without moral or religious lenses, and gives practical advice, not moral lectures, to would-be rulers. This was why his contemporaries found him shocking. Traditionally, political philosophy was based on what a prince should do if he wished to be good person leading a good state. Even Bossuet, while upholding royal absolutism, said that the king was responsible to the moral judgment of God. Parliaments and people could not judge the king, but God could, and would. Machiavelli's advice, on the other hand, is meant to make a prince effective, not moral. As he also wrote, "if everything is considered carefully, it will be found that something which looks like virtue, if followed, would be his ruin; whilst something else, which looks like vice, yet followed brings him security and prosperity." Some commentators found Machiavelli's ideas so shocking that they thought he did not mean them, taking *The Prince* to be a satire, a display of what a bad ruler would look like (Berlin, 1971).

The word *Machiavellian* has entered the modern lexicon. There's even a Machiavellian personality scale (Christie & Geis, 1970; you can take it at http://www.salon.com/books/it/1999/09/13/machtest). So one might think that Machiavelli is the first modernist, proposing a proto-scientific basis for social understanding and political rule. But Machiavelli is better regarded as a reactionary. His conception of human nature, society, and politics was un-, even antireligious, but it was prereligious—pagan—rather than postreligious—modern (Berlin, 1971). His view of the state was that of the Greeks and Romans, a place wherein powerful men naturally vied for political power, and for whom the measure was success, both for themselves as politicians and for the state that they led. They were not trying to live up to a godly ideal. A good example was Julius Caesar. He was condemned by some fellow Romans as a tyrant and thus assassinated, but he worked hard for the interests of Rome as a military commander and civil leader. Even at the theater he read documents and had runners coming and going, to the consternation of the rest of the audience (Goldsworthy, 2008). Machiavelli has often been admired by moderns (including the first one), but he was not a modernist.

Popular Psychology in the Renaissance: The Mind Within

The change from an external conception of mind to a more internal and individualistic one began first in the highly individualistic Italian city-states of the High Middle Ages, which in turn gave rise to the Renaissance. The most important city-state in this connection was Florence, which produced both Machiavelli (see later discussion) and Dante.

DANTE ALIGHIERI (1265–1321)   Dante's *Divine Comedy* (1308–1320), the allegorical tale of his imaginary trip through Hell, Purgatory, and Heaven, neatly stands at the middle of the stereotype-character-divide in our psychological history of literature. (So does the imaginary nature of his trip; it may have been as mentally real to him as the Vices of the morality plays were to their audiences.) By using real, well-known people of his time as the personifications of sins in Hell (the Inferno), he achieves a uniquely realistic allegory. These people were widely known for their major vices—notorious gluttons, spendthrifts, misers, murderers, and traitors. They had in their lives been so notorious for their besetting sins that Dante uses them as personifications in his allegory.

Dante's Hell is arranged on Aristotelian lines, in strict compliance with the orthodox Catholic view of sin. Sins of the flesh are the least sinful, easily erased by penitence and penances. Those who die unrepentant, however, go to the upper levels of Hell, even though their sins are fairly minor. God created people who had to eat, after all, and ordered them to "go forth and multiply"—that is, have babies by sexual means. Having made eating and sex pleasurable, God made these sins of the flesh easy to work off. Consciously chosen sins, however, are far worse. Choosing to commit perjury (the ultimate sin "taking the Lord's name in vain"), or choosing to betray your earthly lord, or worst of all, your Heavenly Lord, are much worse sins.

Some of the sins denounced by Dante and the Middle Ages will strike modern readers as scarcely sinful. Usury, for instance, makes no sense as a sin in a country full of mortgages, car loans, and credit cards. To the medieval church, however, it was the highly unnatural act of making inert matter (gold or silver) breed. Loaning money was acceptable, unless you charged interest. Since Jews did not consider usury a sin, this provided many job openings for Jews—and much hatred and resentment.

While fin amour had its partisans, Dante provided a case study of its perils in the story of Francesca and Paulo, who because of love are eternally condemned to swirl around in the winds of Lust, in the first level of Hell.

Francesca was married off for political reasons to a deformed prince, but fell in love with his handsome younger brother, Paulo, and he with her. While reading a fin amour manuscript, Paulo and Francesca were caught kissing by the prince. He killed them then and there, which was perfectly legal. Had they lived, as a few literary fin amour couples did, and truly repented of their sin and retired to monastery and convent, they could have been saved. Instead they died in their sin still believing in fin amour, the "Love, that so soon takes hold in the gentle breast." Therefore, they wound up in the circle of lust. The prince will wind up much farther down in Hell's inverted scale of nature, in the river of boiling blood, while they, believers in genteel romantic love, are only sent to Hell's outskirts.

The aristocrat who was Dante's host and patron while he was finishing *The Divine Comedy* in his old age was a relative of Francesca and presumably not displeased with Dante's placement of her in Hell. In the story, Dante (personifying a sinful pilgrim seeking God's love) faints out of sorrow at the lovers' plight, showing that he, too, has a gentle heart. Those who say Dante populated his Hell with his enemies are only partially correct. Francesca was not the only friend he found in Hell.

Farther down, in the lowest circle of upper Hell, Dante woefully encounters his old mentor, Bruneto Latini, a neighbor who taught him much about the classics, poetry, and politics. They had both been banished when the other party came to power in Florence. Dante would have embraced his old friend, but his guide, Virgil, forbids it. Dante admits that he did not really want to share his friend's suffering. Bruneto was a sodomite, a homosexual, and he, along with others who had sex that could not possibly lead to reproduction, is running on burning sand, under a rain of fire— symbols of sterility. The usurers are seated here, too. Just as metal should not be able to breed, so too those who are equipped to breed should do so. They are two sides of the same coin—unnatural, perverse forms of breeding.

Like the sin of usury, the proper medieval placement of homosexuals in Hell will strike many modern readers as strange, even horrible. Dante, however, was certainly not homophobic. He had known what his dear friend's sexual orientation had been all along. All Florence knew, and Bruneto had been a well-respected man of learning entrusted with high political office, until his party lost. But in Dante's Hell, he illustrates the reason that he had died unrepentant of his besetting sin, and therefore represents it. He was interested during life only in his earthly reputation, not his soul, and asks Dante only to keep the memory of his poems alive. Dante writes:

> *I answered him, "Might I have had my will,*
> *Believe me, you'd not yet have been thrust apart*
> *From human life, for I keep within me still*
> *Stamped on my mind, and now stabbing my heart,*
> *The dear, benign, paternal image of you,*
> *You living, you hourly teaching me the art (poetry)*
> *By which men grow immortal; know this too:*
> *I am so grateful, that while I breathe air*
> *My tongue shall speak the thanks which are your due".*

(*Hell*, Canto XV, pp. 164, 1. 75–85)

Bruneto's request, that his fame be kept alive on earth, was a throwback to the ethics of the Greek Bronze Age, and shows why he is stuck in Hell. Having never had any regard for his immortal soul, he could not repent, and evidently did not choose monastic chastity. By choosing to live and die in his sin, he sent himself to Hell. As Francesca still cannot see that she should have pursued divine love (*agape* or *charitas*), so Bruneto still cares only about his fame on earth, and, however horribly painful his situation, does not repent his choice to abandon holy chastity. Francesca and Bruneto's inability to see their wrong choices as wrong is what has trapped them in their sins, and their being so entrapped is why Dante uses them to personify those sins in his allegory. The power of Dante's art is such that his characters transcend the stereotyping of the morality plays, but *The Divine Comedy* never quite left the world of allegory for that of real, individual characters.

GEOFFREY CHAUCER (1343–1400)   The great fourteenth-century English poet Chaucer created the first individualized, realistic characters in English. Chaucer (1343–1400) was a vintner's son, raised among the Anglo-French merchants of the wine trade in London. He had one uncle wealthy enough to buy land and live like a landed gentleman—without actually counting as a gentleman, because he had neither title nor the right to bear arms, nor to hunt. Due to young Geoffrey's proficiency in French and Italian, and his Latin education at the London Grammar School (where he would have read Dante), his father was able to get him a post as a squire to a noble of fairly high rank. Eventually he worked his way up to becoming the first poet laureate, under King Richard II. He began to write the *Canterbury Tales* around 1386, reading them out loud to entertain the royal court.

In the *Canterbury tales* (begun in 1386), Chaucer has representative, but sometimes highly realistic, members of most levels of society tell a tale to pass the time on their journey. They are on a package-tour-style pilgrimage to the new and fashionable shrine at Canterbury Cathedral, though not for overwhelmingly religious reasons. Many of the stories, and the banter in between, concern sex, love, and marriage. Probably the most memorable, and highly individual, character is Dame Alison, The Wife of Bath (a town in England).

The Wife of Bath had been very much a wife, widowed five times, and is now wealthy enough by inheritances to be on a pilgrimage. Her reason for traveling is to look for a handsome, young, sexy, and obedient sixth husband, a "boy toy" for the sexually liberated fourteenth-century woman.

She had thought she had found the perfect husband of this kind in her fifth, but he took to beating her. She is as sumptuously dressed as was allowed by the sumptuary laws—government regulations defining which people could wear particular kinds of clothing. She has been as upwardly mobile as allowed within her rank, her place in the Neoplatonic, God-given order of society. Her parents got her a start in life by marrying her off at the age of 12 (not unusual in the fourteenth century) to an old, prosperous landowner. Chaucer makes her sufficiently unattractive in both person and manner that the nobles hearing her tale could laugh at her and therefore stand to listen to her.

The story she tells was set in the times of King Arthur and his Queen Guinevere, when fairies rather than Franciscan friars roamed the land. It is a highly personalized version of the tale type known to historians as the "loathly [loathsome] damsel," a female version of the more familiar frog prince story.

The basic narrative line of this story is that Guinevere, King Arthur's Queen, sends a knightly hero on an unusual quest for unromantic reasons. He has raped a maiden who happened to catch his eye, which, as Alison informs her fellow pilgrims (and Chaucer reminds the courtiers), was punishable by death in bygone times. Upon learning of what this errant knight has done, King Arthur is about to have him beheaded. Guinevere intervenes, saying that she will grant the knight his life if he can correctly answer a question Freud would pose centuries later, "What does a woman want?"

The knight cannot answer, so the Queen grants him some time to find an answer, a quest very different from that usually undertaken by romantic knights. When his time is nearly up, the knight chances upon an ugly old hag, who asks why he looks so forlorn. She assures him that she can give him the answer—but only if he will grant her any boon she may later demand. He assents and she tells him to answer that a woman wants "the same sovereignty over her husband as over her lover; she must master him and he not be above her," a fin amour way of saying women want to be in charge. This is the correct answer to the Queen and her ladies, and the knight's life is spared.

Then the old hag demands her boon—that the knight marry her. Although he gave his word as a gentleman, and she had just saved his life, he tries in a completely ungentlemanly way to weasel out of it. Nevertheless, eventually he has to marry her. Escorted to their bedroom after the marriage service, he churlishly refuses her company and refuses to share her bed. (A churl is low class; an earl is high class.) She then makes him an offer. He can have her as an ugly, old but faithful wife, or take his chances with her as a beautiful, young wife, so beautiful that his friends will come to visit her rather than him. This last dilemma is too much for his knightly brain, and he gives up, saying that is such a hard choice he will leave it up to her. Having got him to admit that she has sovereignty over him, she becomes beautiful and is also faithful ever after.

Thus, using a covering of fin amour language and a favorite fin amour setting, Dame Alison (a Dame only by courtesy) makes her points about class and marriage. Gentilesse and courtesy—the supposedly defining traits of a fin amour gentleman—have little to do with noble blood or wealth, and much to do with good deeds (rather than rape), with respect for others, even old hags, and with keeping one's word. And Dame Alison gives a fairytale gloss to what most happily married men know—that they should love, honor, and, at times, even obey their wives.

And thus Chaucer lectured the nobility through the words of a highly individual, intelligent, strong-willed, middle-class woman, whose title "The Wife of Bath" is meant to imply a stereotype undercut by Chaucer's creativity and his none-too-high-born views on gentilesse and marriage.

WILLIAM SHAKESPEARE (1564–1616) William Shakespeare was writing and acting in his plays in the late Elizabethan and early Jacobean eras, around 1580 to 1610. He knew "little Latin and less Greek," as his friend Ben Johnson, another playwright, wrote in his eulogy of Shakespeare.

He attended only the town school in Stratford-upon-Avon, and is thus unlikely to have been much influenced by Dante, or even Chaucer, the English language having changed considerably. He would have grown up seeing passion plays and morality plays in Stratford. *Mankind* was written about 1475, around a century before Shakespeare's birth, but Courage's *The Tide Tarrieth No Man* was written when he was 11 (1576). Thus, the psychomachia of everyone's mind was still a strong element in Elizabethan folk psychology.

Shakespeare's London theatre, the Globe, was open to all who could pay. It was located in the suburbs, not then a good part of town, among the brothels, taverns, and bear-baiting rings. While patronized by the nobles and later by King James, Shakespeare wrote as much for the common people—the "groundlings" or "understanders," who bought standing-room-only tickets and stood near the stage looking up—as he did for the aristocracy. His audience, from all levels of society, was familiar with morality plays.

Othello, the Moor of Venice (performed first for King James in 1606) is one of his later tragedies, but it still shows that Shakespeare and his audience were well used to morality plays. In this play, a black general, Othello, is duped into believing that his chaste, white wife, Desdemona, is cheating on him by a very Vice-like character named *Iago*. In the first and third scenes of the first act, Iago drops many hints that he is a Devil or Vice. To Rodrigo and the audience, he says that if his speech and actions ever reflect his true intentions, " 'tis not long after/but I will wear my heart upon my sleeve/For daws to peck at; I am not what I am." (Act I, Scene 3, 1. 63–65). Some 90 lines later, Iago says that he hates Othello "as I do hell pains," which sounds like he has felt such pains. By scene 3 of Act I, he is swearing to make trouble for Othello with his wits "and all the tribe of hell," which sounds like he knows he can summon demons to his aid. Lines like these would certainly establish Iago as a Vice or Devil in the mind of Shakespeare's audience.

Iago is, however, far more individually humanlike than any previous Vice, which is what makes this play still so popular around the world when morality plays are staged only for historical reasons. Similarly, Desdemona is a believable, individual woman, and Othello a tragic hero who is easy to identify with. Their marital problems sound very modern.

Desdemona is virginal, young, urban, and white. He is a Moorish general—North African, strong but middle-aged, and used to life in rough military camps. There are certainly potential points of friction in this marriage. Desdemona has thrown away family, fortune, and hometown for Othello's sake, and might well in a few years come to regret her decision. (Divorce was practically impossible then.) He, however, has a besetting sin of jealousy, perhaps due to a sense of racial and social inferiority, but still a besetting sin. His lieutenant, Iago, (en)courages Othello's jealousy, using lying gossip to undermine Othello's faith in Desdemona. Iago, all too easily, convinces him that, right after their wedding, Desdemona is having an affair with Casio, one of Othello's officers, a Venetian gentleman whom she could have married without upsetting her family at all. This is patent nonsense, since she has just eloped with Othello. Some see Othello as very trusting and misled by lying evil. But how trusting is a man who immediately believes a lie about his bride and does not believe his bride's denial?

Othello eventually kills Desdemona and, after Iago's wife reveals his lying tricks, kills himself. Suicide and murder are both deadly sins, so Othello is bound for Hell, as surely as if Devils came and hauled him through a Hellmouth. He dies without self-understanding: "One who loved not wisely but too well," a man "not easily jealous." He sees, no more than did Francesca and Paulo, that he did not really love at all. Where they lusted in a mellow kind of way, he wanted to possess Desdemona as a prize to show off, not as an individual human being—such is the nature of jealousy. He dies unrepentant, uncomprehending (in denial, we might say), and by the violence of his own hand. Thus, the besetting sin of jealousy brings low a noble man, in an individualized psychomachia that still moves us today.

MIGUEL CERVANTES (1547–1616)   Psychologically insightful literature did not develop only in England. Cervantes's *Don Quixote* (1605–1615) is arguably the first novel, the premier literary form in which personal character, personality, and consciousness are artistically explored. Don Quixote de la Mancha is a poor Spanish knight. He has the right to bear arms, but is too poor to have good ones and is too proud of his aristocratic heritage to work. With no war in which to win glory, riches, and a wife, Don Quixote takes to reading romances, even selling off much of his land to buy more manuscripts. Finally he became so addicted to these fin amour soap operas that he read day and night that he seemed to go insane.

Having gone romantically crazy, Don Quixote proceeds to hire a flea-ridden peasant, Sancho Panza, as his squire, and goes off on errantry, seeking fame, love, and adventure. He tilts at windmills, mistaking them for giants, and takes the tavern barmaid Dulcinea as his lady. Thus, out of delusion, he takes to treating common people nicely. Eventually, word of his mad escapades spreads and a duke and duchess lay a trap for him for their aristocratic amusement. They find out where he is, bring him to their castle, and have the servants treat him as if he were indeed the star knight in an old romance. But he may not be as mad as he chooses to seem. Perhaps he is only making the best of his plight, being a knight in a time when there is no real use for knights.

After a feast, they choose to question Don Quixote rather mockingly about his quests and the adventures of which they have heard so much. He claims to have found Dulcinea transformed into an unattractive country wench by a magic spell cast by one of the evil enchanters who envy and persecute him. These enchanters want to ruin him by depriving him of his lady, whom more than anyone a true knight wanted to impress by good service. This describes the ideal of fin amour, no adultery included, the first step to *parfait* (perfect) *amour*, which leads to love of God (Mickel, 1998). This ideal is far nobler than the way the nobles are treating a poor madman.

Don Quixote's hosts go on to suggest that Dulcinea does not really exist, that he has never really seen her, that she is "a fantastic mistress, whom your worship engendered and bore in your mind." This is, of course, both true and false. There is a real Dulcinea, back at the tavern, but her ladyship is indeed a product of Don Quixote's mind. To this suggestion he gives the perfect Platonic answer, that Dulcinea is the Form of the Lady, ageless and perfect, the Lady all true knights pursue.

Such a lady would indeed be worthy of such a gentleman's loving service. But, of course, the well-bred nobles teasing him are right—and so is he. This is the ideal form of the lady, something that cannot exist on this mundane earth. Therefore, only a madman would bother to try to live up to such an exalted lady's standards. The high-born, well-bred nobles undercut his faith in good breeding, treating him so badly, but he does not notice. He is a highly eccentric individual living as much as he can in the world of his own choosing, aided by his highly realistic peasant squire.

And thus did the silly courtly romances, botched together shreds of paganism reworked by clerics and troubadours, finally achieve a truly noble form with realistic characters. The Neoplatonic ideal, in which the individual had no place, finally created the idealistic individual.

In the eighteenth century, the novel really arrived as a form of literature. Cervantes had claimed, tongue in cheek, to be telling a true tale of a real knight culled from old manuscripts. Similarly, DeFoe got in legal trouble when Robinson Crusoe turned out not to exist. The first novel openly published as a work of fiction is Richardson's *Pamela*, the tale of a serving girl whose unseducable beauty finally wins her the hand of the squire who has been trying to seduce her. The subject matter is hardly novel, but the admission that these characters are realistic individuals who did not exist was indeed novel. At this point, the concept of the individual as we conceive it had certainly arrived.

The Reformation

Although the Reformation had nothing directly to do with psychology, its general impact on European life and thought was profound, and its consequences affected psychological thinking in the seventeenth century. Christian religion in the Middle Ages was based upon performance of the Mass and upon a veritable industry of prayer (MacCulloch, 2003). Salvation was gained by regular attendance of the Mass and by prayers—not only personal prayers but prayers said for the souls of the dead. Critical to this latter practice was the medieval idea of Purgatory, a place where the souls of sinners were sent to expiate their sins rather than face eternal damnation in Hell. Thus it became possible for a dead person's relatives to do or purchase good works in aid of his or her release from Purgatory. For example, wealthy Christians endowed chantries devoted to praying for the redemption of deceased relatives, and they could sometimes buy indulgences from the Church to gain their relatives' immediate release from Purgatory. As one Dominican friar put it, "As soon as the coin in the coffer rings, the soul from Purgatory springs" (Bainton, 1995, p. 60).

The Reformation began in 1517 when Martin Luther (1483–1546) nailed his *95 Theses* to the door of Wittenberg Cathedral, challenging the Catholic hierarchy. His central claim was that salvation came from faith in redemption from sin by the death and resurrection of Jesus Christ rather than the works of prayer, or worse, the purchase of indulgences. Luther wanted a personal, intensely introspective religion, an Augustinian religion that deemphasized ritual, priesthood, and hierarchy. Catholics responded with a Counter-Reformation that fought the Protestant rebellion but that also incorporated Protestantism's new psychological inward searching for faith into its traditional emphasis on hierarchy and salvation by works. Both sides in this theological conflict also worked toward a "reformation of manners" (MacCulloch, 2003), seeking to investigate and control personal behavior—especially sexual behavior—more rigorously than before. The Reformation and Counter-Reformation divided Europe politically, as provinces and nations identified with one cause or the other and fought to create and dominate a newly unified Christendom. While the fortunes of battle swayed sometimes in favor of the Protestants and sometimes in favor of the Catholics, neither side emerged victorious. From the perspective of the history of psychology, the important outcome of the Reformation was Christianity's new emphasis on the state of the soul. Protestants and Catholics alike began to look inside themselves for signs of grace. This introspective mood would provide Rene Descartes, modern psychology's founder, with his foundational philosophical method.

SKEPTICISM AND ITS DISCONTENTS

> *Tomorrow, and tomorrow, and tomorrow*
> *Creeps in this petty pace from day to day,*
> *To the last syllable of recorded time,*
> *And all our yesterdays have lighted fools*
> *The way to dusty death. Out, out, brief candle!*
> *Life's but a walking shadow, a poor player*
> *That struts and frets his hour upon the stage*
> *And then is heard no more. It is a tale*
> *Told by an idiot, full of sound and fury,*
> *Signifying nothing.*

(Shakespeare, *Macbeth*, V, v, 17–28)

For all its creativity, the Renaissance was a time of tremendous social dislocation, misery, anxiety, and superstition. Lynn White (1974, p. 131) has written that the Renaissance was the "most psychically disturbed era in European history." The Hundred Years' War and, later, the Thirty Years' War raged, bringing destruction to much of France and Germany, as mercenary armies alternately fought each other and pillaged the countryside when they were not paid. The Black Death that began in 1348 had by 1400 reduced the population of Europe by at least one-third the population. Famines and various diseases struck year after year. The feudal order crumbled.

Everyday life reflected the anxiety engendered by stress. Europe was obsessed with death. Picnics were held under the rotting corpses of the hanged. The image of the Grim Reaper was born. Scapegoats were sought; mobs attacked Jews and "witches." At a time when humanity was being glorified by the humanists, human mortality and suffering were reaching new levels of bestiality, and the dark side of human nature was everywhere apparent. Intellectuals practiced the magical arts of occultism.

The late sixteenth century was a time of doubt and skepticism. Ambiguity about humanity is found dramatically in William Shakespeare (1564–1616). The passage from *Hamlet* quoted at the start of the Renaissance section of this chapter sums up the optimistic humanist view of humans as noble, infinite, admirable, and godlike. Yet Hamlet goes on immediately to say, "And yet to me what is this quintessence of dust? Man delights not me. . . . " The quotation from *Macbeth* at the beginning of this section is a powerful statement of disdain for humankind and life in the face of mortality, an almost existentialist expression of the seeming absurdity of life. Shakespeare's dramatic genius saw both the positive side of humans emphasized by the humanists and the negative side evident in history.

A more philosophical thinker, Michel de Montaigne (1533–1592), also felt and articulated the limits of humanity. In stark contrast to the earlier humanists, Montaigne (1580/1959, p. 194) wrote: "Of all creatures man is the most miserable and frail, and therewithal the proudest and disdainfulest." The humanists made the human the paragon of animals with a unique and godlike intellect; Montaigne denied the uniqueness of humans. People are not the lords of creation, they are part of it; they are not the highest of animals, they are on a par with them. Animals as well as humans have knowledge. Montaigne decried reason as a weak reed on which to base knowledge and argued instead for experience. But he then went on to show how deceptive and untrustworthy are the senses. In short, Montaigne toppled humans from the special place given them by medieval and Renaissance thinkers.

Montaigne pointed to the future, to a skeptical and naturalistic theory of humanity and the universe. Montaigne was, in fact, denying the worldview that held sway in Europe from Classical times. Polished and refined in the Middle Ages and Renaissance, it was ultimately to be shattered and replaced by science and an increasingly secular philosophy.

The World We Have Lost: The End of the Premodern Outlook

> *The World's a book in Folio, printed all*
> *With God's great works in letter Capital:*
> *Each creature is a Page, and each Effect*
> *A fair character, void of all defects.*
>
> (du Bartas, *Divine Weeks*)

The Renaissance perfected a worldview implicit in Classical culture and developed by the Middle Ages. Fundamental to this worldview was the idea that all things in the universe are linked in a grand order that we can decipher through resemblance. So, for example, the Renaissance physician thought skull and brain damage could be cured by the administration of walnuts, for the walnut shell resembles the skull and the nut resembles the brain.

As the poet du Bartas wrote, the world is like a book, and any being is like a page, in that it bears signs that indicate its secret meaning to others with which it shares linkage. Nature is to be understood by deciphering these signs, not through experiment but by close observation, seeking out similarities and relationships, a practice called *hermeneutics*. Hence, the medieval-Renaissance scrutiny of the classic writers: Just as the world is a book revealing nature's symbolic order, so are books collections of words, signs that should reveal universal order. This order is not the scientific order of natural law, but an order built on sympathies and analogies between things, sympathies and analogies signified by resemblance, as between walnut and brain, as in Neoplatonism.

The human being occupied the central place in this orderly web of analogies. Annibale Romei's seventeenth-century *Courtier's academy* states: "The body of man is no other than a little model of the sensible world, and his soul an image of the world intelligible [Plato's world of the Forms]." The human body is a summary analogy of the physical world, and the mind is a summary analogy of the invisible world. The human is a microcosm reflecting the natural and supernatural macrocosm. The human is at the exact midpoint of the universe. The human body is worldly flesh and the bodily passions tie humans to the animals. The human's rational soul is angelic, for angels are rational souls without bodies. In between, mediating between rational soul and worldly body are human faculties, such as imagination and common sense. These faculties in the brain are subtle animal spirits, the purest of earthly substances, which link body and soul.

This worldview was shattered in the seventeenth century and brushed away in the eighteenth. Montaigne pointed the way: The human is not the center of creation, but one animal among many. So also did Sir Francis Bacon: Nature is to be investigated by experiment and explained mechanistically. Soon, Galileo would show that the world is to be understood not by the decipherment of signs, as in language, but by the application of mathematics, which transcends particular observation.

The Scientific Revolution

From Chapter 5 of *A History of Psychology: From Antiquity to Modernity*, Seventh Edition.
Thomas Hardy Leahey. Copyright © 2013 by Pearson Education, Inc. All rights reserved.

The Scientific Revolution

Foundations of Modernity 1600–1700

The two centuries after 1600 were literally revolutionary. The period began with the Scientific Revolution of the seventeenth century and closed with political revolutions in colonial America and monarchical France. The Scientific Revolution, and the revolutions in conceptions of human nature and society that followed in its wake, laid the basis for political revolutions that implemented their ideas. In the seventeenth century, there was a general European crisis in which the old feudal order died away and began to be replaced by the modern, secular, capitalist nation-states that survive today. The transformation was completed during the eighteenth century, the Enlightenment, in which traditional ideas about human nature, society, and government were replaced by ideas that were scientific, or scientifically inspired.

To the medieval and Renaissance thinker, the cosmos was a somewhat mysterious place, organized in a grand hierarchy from God to angels to humans to the material world, where each event had a special meaning. This worldview was profoundly spiritual, as matter and soul were not sharply divided. In the seventeenth century, this view was replaced by one that was scientific, mathematical, and mechanical. Natural scientists demonstrated the mechanical nature of heavenly and earthly phenomena and then of the bodies of animals. Eventually, the mechanical approach was extended to humanity itself, and the study of humankind, from politics to psychology, was subjected to the scientific method. By 1800, both the universe and human beings were widely believed to be machines subject to natural law. In the process, the ancient view of the world as a pattern of mystically meaningful symbols disappeared.

Portrait of the English physicist and mathematician Sir Isaac Newton.
(Courtesy of Library of Congress)

THE SCIENTIFIC REVOLUTION

> The Scientific Revolution outshines everything since the rise of Christianity and reduces the Renaissance and Reformation to the rank of mere episodes, mere internal displacements, within the system of medieval Christendom. (Butterfield, 1965, p. 7)

The importance of science in the modern world cannot be doubted, and the Scientific Revolution cannot be passed over by any history of the West—especially a history of a science, even if that science (psychology, in this instance) was not part of the revolution. The outcome of the Scientific Revolution is unquestioned. It displaced the earth from the center of the universe and conceived of the universe a gigantic machine quite independent of human feelings and needs. It overthrew the Aristotelian natural philosophy of scholasticism, substituting a search for precise mathematical regularities confirmable by experiment. It substituted a new view of the universe as a machine for the older Greek and Roman views of the universe as divine being or readable book. It also proposed that people could improve their lot by the application of reason and experiment rather than by prayer and devotion (Rossi, 1975). It also created modern consciousness and its science, psychology.

Continuity or Revolution?

One of the most disputed issues in the history of science concerns the degree of continuity between ancient and medieval science on the one hand and modern science on the other. Recent scholarship is concluding that the answer to this question depends on whether we approach it from an internalist or externalist approach. Internalist history of science focuses on learning how scientists thought about the technical problems of their field, such as the dynamics of motion, and how they formulated and tested theories. The externalist history of science looks at the broader social and institutional contexts in which scientific practice is embedded. Traditional internalist histories of the Scientific Revolution have concluded that there is a sharp break between medieval and modern science; recent external histories stress continuity. As we shall learn, both views are right.[1]

---

[1]The paragraphs that follow are based on Colish, 1997; Crombie, 1995; Grant, 1996; Huff, 1993; and B. Lewis, 2001, 2002. I will give citations only for direct references.

Why did the Scientific Revolution take place in Europe? The new external histories have approached the problem by asking a civilizational question: Why did the breakthrough to modern science occur in Europe rather than one of the other great world cultures such as Islam or China? If an alien anthropologist, knowing that a Scientific Revolution had occurred, had surveyed the world around 1000 C.E., he or she would never have expected that the Revolution would have occurred in Europe. Compared to Islam, which had preserved and translated the scientific works of ancient Greece, including Aristotle, Europe would have seemed mired in ignorance. Compared to China, with its vast riches and learned culture, unified under a single emperor, Europe would have seemed impoverished, illiterate, and nearly anarchic in its feudal political structure. And these judgments would have been correct. However, in just a few hundred years European science had advanced far beyond Islamic science, and was poised to unite the world by trade and imperial conquest. The secret to European success lay not in the Scientific Revolution itself, but in larger social institutions that provided a set of social structures that made free scientific inquiry possible.[2]

We have already seen two foundations for Europe's uniqueness in the early Middle Ages, in Anselm's "faith seeking reason," and in the rise of autonomous cities. The fact that Islam failed to develop modern science, while Europe did, is due to several interrelated factors.

HOW RELIGION SPREAD Christianity spread slowly through the Roman world (Grant, 1996) as a persecuted religion that had to persuade pagans by arguments to become Christian. Islam, on the other hand, spread rapidly by military conquest across North Africa and the Middle East, holding Spain for centuries and nearly capturing Vienna. Thus, although Christians did not wholly accept pagan philosophy, and indeed lost touch with most of it, Christian philosophy and theology absorbed Hellenistic modes of thought, including respect for rational argument and the separation of speaker and idea characteristic of open systems of thought. As conquerors, Muslims could hold themselves aloof from pagans, Jews, and Christians, rejecting their ideas as contrary to the revelation of the Koran. Pagans faced the choice of conversion, death, or slavery. Jews and Christians were tolerated as fellow monotheists—Muslims consider Islam to be the perfection of the monotheism of the Torah and the Bible—but were not politically equal to Muslims. They had to pay special taxes for their toleration and lacked some of legal rights of Muslims. Nevertheless, Jews were better off in Islam than in Europe, where they faced constant persecution, occasional pogroms, and periodic expulsions from the countries in which they lived.

SEPARATION OF CHURCH AND STATE In Matthew 22.21 Jesus says, "Render therefore unto Caesar the things that are Caesar's, and unto God the things that are God's" (RSV). In this saying Jesus acknowledges that secular, nonreligious authority is valid in its own sphere, in this case, taxation. The separation of Church and state was reinforced by the European discovery and acceptance of the old Roman Corpus of Civil Law, which became the basis of secular European law. Islam recognized no separation of religious and secular authority. Muhammad was both religious prophet and conquering political ruler, as were his immediate successors, the caliphs. Later political disputes about who was the Prophet's legitimate successor divided the Islamic world into competitive sects. Today's political boundaries in the Islamic world were imposed at the end of World War I by Britain and France, breaking up the older, united, House of Islam.

CREATION OF "NEUTRAL SPACES"—THE UNIVERSITIES—FOR FREE INQUIRY Just as religious and secular authority were separate, so European law recognized the existence of autonomous,

---

[2]The paragraphs that follow are based on Colish, 1997; Crombie, 1995; Grant, 1996; Huff, 1993; and B. Lewis, 2001, 2002. I will give citations only for direct references.

self-governing corporations independent of both religious and royal or aristocratic secular power. We have met the first examples of these autonomous corporations, the free cities of Europe. More important for the history of science and philosophy were the European universities, which were also autonomous, self-governing corporations that could establish their own curricula relatively free from outside meddling. Thus, in Europe, neutral spaces (Huff, 1993) were created within which to pursue natural philosophy for its own sake with little fear of repression. The law of Islam, the *Sharia*, did not recognize corporate bodies of any sort. Islamic colleges, or *madrassas*, were oriented to the teaching of Sharia and primarily involved rote memorization of the Koran and the *hadiths*, the oral teachings of Muhammad. Thus, William of Ockham wrote, "in natural philosophy everyone should be free to say freely whatever he pleases," (quoted by Grant, 1996, p. 281), while the Islamic thinker al-Ghazali wrote, "No obligations flow from reason but from the Sharia" (quoted by Huff, 1993, p. 115).

AUTHORITY OF THE BOOK   Judaism, Christianity, and Islam are all religions of a book—the Torah, the Bible, and the Koran—and Muslims regard Islam as the final fruit of the first two. However, as the quote from al-Ghazali indicates, in Islam the Sharia—the Islamic law derived from the Koran and the hadiths—became the final and exclusive authority on every aspect of life. In Europe, on the other hand, while the Bible was revered, it was also criticized and limited in authority. William of Conches wrote, "To seek the reason of things and the laws of their origins is the great mission of the believer, which we must carry out by the fraternal association of our inquiring minds. Thus it is not the Bible's role to teach you the nature of things; that is the domain of [natural] philosophy" (quoted by Goldstein, 1995, p. 87).

RECEPTION OF ARISTOTELIAN NATURAL PHILOSOPHY   During the early Middle Ages, only the world of Islam retained and translated the works of Greek natural philosophy. In the early Middle Ages there was a movement, *Kalam*, whose aim was to reconcile natural philosophy and Islamic revelation, but creative use of Greek natural philosophy essentially ended with IbnSīnā (Avicenna). Greek sciences were called "foreign sciences," and Islamic scholars developed only those aspects of Greek mathematics and science that they found practically useful. Thus, geometry and trigonometry were studied and improved because they made it possible for believers to calculate the location of Mecca for their daily prayers, and algebra was developed because it aided in the fair apportionment of inheritances (Huff, 1993). Al-Ghazali feared that students of Greek science, mathematics, and logic would be "infected with the evil and corruption of the natural philosophers." The Islamic scholar Ibn-Khaldun wrote, "The problems of physics are of no importance for us in our religious affairs and livelihoods. Therefore, we must leave them alone" (both quoted by Grant, 1996, pp. 180–181). In contrast, European philosophers warmly embraced Greek knowledge when they learned about it from contact with Islam after 1100, and Aristotelian natural philosophy quickly became the centerpiece of the university curriculum. In contrast to al-Ghazali and Ibn-Khaldun, European philosophers and theologians regarded the ancients as moving toward God through reason, to which theologians could add Christian revelation. They strove to reconcile theology and natural philosophy into a harmonious view of the universe. Although conservative theologians made occasional attempts to ban aspects of Aristotelian science, they failed.

PUBLIC KNOWLEDGE   As we have seen, certain traditions of learning in the Hellenistic world—especially Neoplatonism—encouraged the idea of "double truth," the idea that there was one truth for the learned *cognoscenti* who gathered around teachers such as Hypatia of Alexandria, and another for the public at large. This notion prevailed in Islam, but not in Europe. For example, Islam banned printing until the nineteenth century, while books of all types, including the Bible, were in circulation in Europe from the time of Gutenberg (1400–1468) onward. In the medieval universities, disputations on philosophical and theological topics were public, whereas in Islam, teaching of philosophy was typically a secret affair carried on between a master and a student (Huff, 1993).

Making knowledge public was important in another respect, both for the Scientific Revolution and for the Industrial Revolution that followed. While secret learning died with its possessor, public recording of achieved knowledge made breakthroughs cumulative. Isaac Newton once said if he had seen farther than others it was because he stood on the shoulders of giants. Hidden learning provides no shoulders.

We can find scattered around the Islamic world little beginnings of science and technology, from the copper mines of the Near East to Islamic astronomy, but in every case these breakthroughs petered out (Gaukroger, 2006; Mokyr, 1990). A key reason these stirrings toward modernity died was institutional. They often depended on the whims and interests of powerful rulers who could support research and industry, but support typically dried up when a new, differently minded king or emperor came to power. More importantly, there were no institutions that preserved and transmitted innovative ideas and practices. Without preservation and transmission, even the greatest of ideas had little or no impact on the world. The developments of literacy and printing aided the transmission of ideas, but so did the concept that ideas ought to be shared rather than hidden as dangerous or kept as proprietary secrets. It was only in Europe in the seventeenth and eighteenth centuries that ideas were openly spread, openly debated, and openly employed, making possible the accumulation of effective knowledge and the continuous building of science and technology (Mokyr, 2002, 2009).

SECONDARY CAUSATION Aristotle ascribed all change in the universe to an unmoved mover, and naturally enough, Christian and Islamic thinkers identified the unmoved mover with their creator—God. However, a question arose that was of great importance for the development of modern scientific thinking. As the creator of the world, God was responsible for its existence, but was He responsible for every event every day? Some of Aristotle's medieval followers developed the idea of *secondary causation*. God created the world, but endowed objects with the power to affect other objects; thus, a bowling ball has the power to knock down pins. As the medieval natural philosopher Jean Buridan (c. 1300–c. 1358) wrote, "In natural philosophy we ought to accept actions and dependencies as if they always proceed in a natural way" (quoted by Grant, 1996, p. 145). Hugh of St. Victor (1096–1141) depicted the world as a self-operating machine: "The visible world is this machine, this universe, that we see with our bodily eyes" (Huff, 1993, p. 102). These sayings reflect the acceptance of Greek naturalism by European philosophers. Naturalism and secondary causation were, however, rejected in Islam in favor of a doctrine called *occasionalism* (which also made a brief appearance in seventeenth-century Europe). The theological problem with secondary causation was that it took some causal power away from God and gave it to physical objects, thus subtracting from God's omnipotence, and implying, perhaps, that God is no longer present and active in His world. Occasionalism held that in every instant of time God annihilates and re-creates the entire universe. Thus, we see the bowling ball touch the pins and then we see the pins fall down, but the ball did not cause the pins to fall down, God did. Plainly, developing a modern scientific view of the universe in which objects act upon each other in lawful, causal ways would be difficult within the worldview of occasionalism.

In summary, natural philosophy in Europe took off around 1200 C.E., at the same time scientific inquiry froze in Islam. Christian philosophers and theologians welcomed the task of reconciling faith and reason, while Muslim thinkers came to reject it. The situation in China was similar to that of Islam, although the Chinese were further hobbled in developing science by not knowing Greek natural philosophy. As in Islam, religion and state were not separated. The emperor ruled by possession of a mandate from heaven, and his rule was absolute and all-pervading. Like Islam, but unlike Europe, autonomous corporations such as cities and universities did not develop. The concept of the mandate of heaven inhibited the development of astronomy, the field whence the Scientific Revolution sprang. Emperors maintained an Imperial observatory whose job was to scan the heavens for signs of the gods' pleasure or displeasure with the emperor's actions, but this made the observatory's findings state secrets rather than public scientific data. The unique feature of Chinese intellectual life that inhibited the development of natural philosophy and science was the mandarinate. Although the emperor reigned, the reins of government lay in the hands of the elite government bureaucrats, the mandarins. Entry into and advancement within the mandarin bureaucracy depended on taking a series of civil-service examinations that assessed the candidate's mastery of classical Chinese literature. Philosophy and science formed no part of the examination system, and so there was no motive to study or develop them.

Within the medieval university, European natural philosophers and theologians began to revive the Greek miracle. They embraced Greek naturalism as embodied in Aristotle's scientific approach to the universe. Siger of Brabant (1240–1282) said, "We [natural philosophers] are not discussing God's miracles; what we have to do is to discuss what is natural in a natural way"; Nicolas Oresme (1320–1382) said, "The philosopher's work is to make marvels cease" (quoted by Eamon, 1994, p. 73). They embraced the Greek attitude of separating the character of a thinker from his ideas, making natural philosophy into an open system of thought. When theologians such as Aquinas found Aristotle in disagreement with Christian faith, they did not reject him as a heretic, but sought to reconcile his reason with Christian faith. They embraced the Greek idea of theoretical explanation, and natural philosophers such as Oresme and Jean Buridan produced innovative ideas in physics. Medieval artisans made important technical innovations such as lenses (leading to the invention of the telescope) and clocks (watches were a stunning novelty in Islam as late as 1800) (B. Lewis, 2002).

Nevertheless, the conclusion of the old internalist histories of science stands: Modern science did not grow out of medieval science. Medieval philosophers and theologians were hobbled by their reverence for authoritative texts, whether the Bible or Aristotle's. They defined their jobs as the reconciliation of conflicting authorities, and they became excellent at reading texts closely and producing subtle—sometimes over-subtle—readings of discrepant texts. Their subtlety earned the ire of the scientific revolutionaries who regarded their scholastic predecessors as worthless logic-choppers and mental gymnasts (E. Lewis, 2002). Because of their reverence for authorities, medieval natural philosophers were trapped within Aristotle's system of thought, which although admirably naturalistic, had the defect of being wrong. They tried to show how the everyday world of experience could be explained by Aristotle's science, but although they suggested many thought experiments to support their arguments, they did not actually perform any experiments. Thinking Aristotle essentially correct, they formed no notion of science as a progressive enterprise that constantly discards old, incorrect theories for newer and better ones. The upshot was that although the European universities made natural philosophy possible and taught most of the makers of the Scientific Revolution, their work took place outside the universities, where it remained until the nineteenth century.

The Mechanization of the World Picture

The Scientific Revolution took a long time and drew from many sources, but it *was* a revolution, for it profoundly and permanently altered human life and human self-understanding. The Revolution may be said to have begun in 1543 with the publication of Nicholas Copernicus's *Revolution of the Heavenly Orbs*, which proposed that the sun, not the earth, was the center of the solar system. Sigmund Freud would later call Copernicus's hypothesis the first great blow to the human ego. No longer could humans pride themselves on living at the center of the universe and being those around whom everything else revolved.

However, Copernicus's physics was Aristotelian, and his system was no better supported by the data than the old Ptolemaic one, although some found its simplicity attractive. Galileo Galilei (1564–1642) was the most effective spokesman for the new system, supporting it with his new physics, which helped make sense of the sun-centered proposal, and producing telescopic evidence that the moon and other celestial bodies were no more "heavenly" than the earth. However, Galileo, like Copernicus, could not shake the old Greek assumption that the motion of the planets had to be circular, even though his friend Johann Kepler (1571–1630) showed planetary orbits to be elliptical. The final unity of celestial and earthly physics, and the ultimate victory of the new worldview of science, came from Isaac Newton's *Principia Mathematica*, published in 1687.

Newton's laws of motion put the capstone on the idea that the universe was a machine, a celestial clockwork. The machine analogy was proposed by Kepler, Galileo, and René Descartes and quickly became a popular view of the universe. Originally, it was put forward as a support for religion against magic and alchemy: God, the master engineer, constructed a perfect machine and left it running. The only operative principles are, therefore, mechanical, not occult; magical machinations cannot affect machines. Kepler stated the new viewpoint quite forcefully. "I am much occupied with the investigation of physical causes. My aim in this is to show that the machine of the universe is not similar to a divine, animated being, but similar to a clock" (quoted by Shapin, 1996, p. 32).

The clockwork conception of the universe had important implications for psychology. In the Stoic or Aristotelian theories of the universe, every thing and every event in the universe had a purpose, a final cause. Thinking of the universe as a living thing like ourselves naturally led people to give teleological explanations of physical events the way we give teleological explanations of human and animal behavior. Just as a warrior strives for victory in battle, fire strives to join its fellow starfires in the heavens, and a rock drops from our hands, striving to return to the earth. The scientific view of the universe, however, radically separated God, a living being, from the universe, a physical machine made by Him (Shapin, 1996). A clockmaker makes a clock, and the purpose behind the clock rests in the maker; the clock itself has no purpose, moving, as Kepler, said, only by "physical causes." Nevertheless, the motions of the clockwork universe, like the motions of a clock, *appear* to have purpose behind them. As the physicist Robert Boyle (1627–1691) wrote about both clocks and the clockwork universe, "Each part performs its part in order to the various ends, for which it was contrived [by its designer], as regularly and uniformly *as if* it knew and were concerned to do its duty" (quoted by Shapin, 1996, p. 34, italics added).

Machines, scientists discovered, behaved *as if* they were moved by inner purposes, though having none. Soon, scientists, led by Descartes, proposed that animals are clockwork mechanisms—beast-machines—and that human beings are beast-machines with souls inside. Thus, just as God gives purpose to His universe, the human soul gives purpose to its body. However, animals behave in purposive ways but have no souls; like the mechanical universe, they act as if they have motives, but are, in fact, moved only by "physical causes." Such a line of thinking led inevitably to the idea that we, human beings, too, are machines that act as if we have purposes, when we are in fact simply complex machines moved only by "physical causes." As belief in a soul became less tenable, and as machines became more sophisticated—culminating in computers capable of beating the reigning human chess champion—the idea that human beings are machines possessing only "as if" teleology gained momentum. This idea is a major theme in the story of scientific psychology from the seventeenth to the twentieth century.

What Was Revolutionized? Mathematical versus Experimental Sciences

Kuhn (1976) proposed that at the time of the Scientific Revolution, two distinct scientific traditions at different states of maturity could be identified. The first, more mature tradition, consisted of what Kuhn called the mathematical or classical sciences; Kuhn called the second, less developed tradition the experimental or Baconian sciences. The classical sciences were sciences such as astronomy and optics that had been treated mathematically from the times of Greek and Roman Antiquity. The classical sciences were not experimental in the sense we understand experimentation today. As we've seen, "experiments" in ancient and medieval physics were often thought experiments not actually carried out, and in astronomy—which provided the empirical data for Newton's *Principia*— experimentation was obviously impossible. When experiments were carried out in these sciences, they were like classroom "experiments" in a modern science class: demonstrations of what is already known to be true rather than investigations meant to reveal new truths about nature. The key feature of the classical sciences, then, was that theory preceded experimentation—a mathematical theory about the movements of the planets or the behavior of light was proposed, and then a few demonstrations were offered to support the theory. Nature was not interfered with or interrogated, it was simply observed.

The experimental sciences lacked sophisticated mathematical theories, but were instead based on experimental studies of nature with little or no theoretical expectations. Kuhn called them the Baconian sciences because Sir Francis Bacon (1561–1626) developed the idea of experimentation in the modern sense as a controlled interrogation of nature. He called such inquiries "twisting the lion's tail" (quoted by Kuhn, 1976, p. 44). Classical scientists looked at nature as it was in ordinary experience. Baconian experiments created conditions that would never exist without the interference of a scientist. Bacon himself died from such an experiment. Wanting to know the effects of refrigeration on meat, he stuffed a dead chicken with snow, but caught pneumonia as a result! For Bacon, science was a hunt for new facts about nature rather than a demonstration of what was known (Eamon, 1994). Although Bacon presented his approach to science as novel, in fact it had a history as ancient as the classical sciences, except that its history was somewhat disreputable. The ancient Greeks valued *theoria*—abstract, mathematical contemplation of eternal Truth—over *metis*—the practical knowledge of artisans and merchants. The classical sciences carried all the prestige of theoria—mathematical theories about nature that could be mastered only by an elite, educated, few.

Although disdained by the elite, metis had its own ancient tradition outside elite science in books of secrets and their authors, professors of secrets (Eamon, 1994). These books of secrets contained a mishmash of recipes from two ancient, secret traditions. The first tradition was the Neoplatonic, Hermetic tradition that arose in the Hellenistic period, which gave rise to the idea of supernatural magic based on spells and the invocation of supernatural beings. The second tradition was the metis tradition of practical know-how. Guilds of artisans kept secret their practical recipes for things such as dyeing cloth in order to maintain their lucrative monopolies. Their recipes were, of course, the fruit of centuries of practical experimentation, but no theories had been developed to explain why the recipes worked. Once printing was invented, however, guild secrets soon became public knowledge in so-called books of secrets (Eamon, 1994), but these books remained outside the boundaries of reputable science because of their inclusion of the Hermetic tradition of supernatural magic.

XAM'S BLOG 1
Planning for Modernity: The First Modernist

Although born of a noble family, Francis Bacon (1561–1626) was its youngest son, inheriting nothing and so had to live by his wits, starting out as a law student but ultimately rising to become Lord Chancellor of England under King James II. He was caught in a bribery scandal typical of his age, and was banned from public life. Free to pursue his real passion—the reformation of learning, Bacon turned out a number of works foundational to the Enlightenment and modernism. In the sense I've defined modernism—reflecting on the conditions of living a modern life—Bacon cannot, of course, have been a modernist. What marks him as modernist is that unlike Machiavelli he *wanted* to live a modern life and was the first person to sketch what that life was like.

At the heart of modern life Bacon set knowledge, but he defined knowledge in a way that we take for granted but was radically innovative in his time. First, Bacon elevated scientific knowledge over other forms of knowledge. Bacon shared this ambition with early modern thinkers such as Descartes who wanted to make natural philosophy, as science was then called, first among equals (at least) in the intellectual world, more important than theology, then the Queen of the Sciences, or humanistic practices such as poetry.

More peculiar to Bacon were his emphases on practical, useful knowledge and on the pursuit of knowledge as a collective, organized, systematic, cumulative enterprise. For the Greeks, as you've learned, knowledge was contemplation, theoria. The great goal of the philosopher was Truth; for there, among the Forms, as Plato put it, was the right and best way of life. For Bacon, Truth was not enough, indeed could be beside the point. The real test of knowledge lay in control—being able to do something with one's ideas. This, for Bacon, did not mean only application to everyday life—though he did include that—it meant being able to accomplish something experimentally. Part of the idea of contemplative knowledge was its passivity—one watched nature to try figure out how it worked. Bacon insisted on interrogating nature by experiment, by proving one's ideas by active engagement with nature.

Bacon also pointed forward to the modern idea of knowledge-seeking as an organized, collective, activity. The thinkers you've met so far were mostly solitary, being in a sense more like artists than scientists. Although they sought audiences and followers, they did not think of philosophy or technology as team efforts. Philosophers tended to form schools arrayed against one another. Practical thinkers, *metics* in Greek terms, sought useful knowledge from which they could make a living, and naturally tended to keep their ideas secret.

Bacon's modernizing conception of research is seen most clearly in his short utopian work, *The New Atlantis*, which describes how shipwrecked sailors wash up on the shores of a previously unknown island, New Atlantis, and are given a rather didactic tour by its inhabitants. The most important institution of New Atlantis is Salomon's House, which is in effect a modern research university, though run on more hierarchical lines than contemporary universities. There are teams of specialized researchers, those who cull learning from books, those who try experiments on nature, and so on. The findings of these teams are then compiled and combined by other teams who seek to discover more general scientific principles, and direct the making of new experiments. All the resulting knowledge is shared and the aim is finding the small–t, usable truth, not creating schools of thought or penetrating metaphysical insights into Platonic Truth, the nature of being.

The organization of New Atlantis reflects a final aspect of Bacon's thought, the idea that knowledge is best found by working upward from facts to the forming of generalizations. From Plato onward, the ancients had stressed the certainty of deductive reasoning from axioms to the formation of proofs, as in Pythagorean geometry. You will meet this ideal of reasoning even in one of the first modern philosophers, Descartes. He searched first for a single truth, *cogito ergo sum*, from which he then proceeded to deduce the rest of his system of thought. Bacon said we should work the other way, beginning with careful observation of facts and experiments on nature, and forming general conclusions only when they were fully justified. Bacon's attitude was the foundation of positivism.

Bacon was modernist above all in his quip that *knowledge is power*, the motto of your author's junior high school. Bacon's ideas will come to fruition in the Industrial Enlightenment. Bacon died in service of his ideals, catching fatal pneumonia from stuffing a chicken with snow in order to understand the preservative power of freezing. When you thaw a pizza, think of Bacon!

The figure of the professor of secrets and the Hermetic magus was memorably captured by the German author Goethe (1749–1832) in his *Faust*. After a prologue that takes place in heaven, Faust opens the play with a summary of a medieval academic career and laments its shortcomings:

> *I have, alas, studied philosophy*
> *Jurisprudence and medicine, too*
> *And worst of all, theology*
> *With keen endeavor, through and through—*
> *And here I am, for all my lore,*
> *The wretched fool I was before.*
> *Called Master of Arts, and Doctor to boot,*
> *For ten years almost I confute*
> *And up and down wherever it goes,*
> *I drag my students by the nose—*
> *And see that for all our science and art*
> *We can know nothing. It burns my heart . . .*
> *Hence I have yielded to magic to see . . .*
> *. . . what secret force*
> *Hides in the world and rules its course.*
> *Envisage the creative blazes*
> *Instead of rummaging in phrases.*

(Goethe, 1808/1961, pp. 93–95)

Faust, master and even doctor, is at the seeming pinnacle of medieval learning. The opening lines list the available fields of study in the medieval university—all of which he has mastered—but the last line decries the useless, text-oriented basis of medieval education. Faust wants more—to know the secrets of nature and to hold power over nature. So he turns from texts to practical magic, and ultimately sells his soul to the devil to know "what secret force / Hides in the world and rules its course." Faust symbolizes the desire for practical, usable knowledge that motivated the disreputable professors of secrets. He intends to experiment on nature to learn its secrets and to "twist the lion's tail" to useful ends.

The experimental tradition in science would not come into its own until the nineteenth century. Science, as we know it today, merges Kuhn's two forms of science (Kuhn, 1976). From the classical sciences comes the idea that science must develop precise, ideally mathematical theories that explain how nature works. From the experimental sciences comes the idea that science depends on the active interrogation of nature—a hunt for its secrets (Eamon, 1994). From the experimental tradition, bolstered by Protestant Christianity, also comes the idea that science should be useful. Bacon wrote, "The rule in religion that a man should demonstrate his faith in works applies in natural philosophy as well; knowledge should be proved by its works" (quoted by Eamon,

1994, p. 324). The authority and prestige of psychology today rests largely on its claims to improve society and individual lives.

PSYCHOLOGY INVENTED: THE WAY OF IDEAS

The Transformation of Experience and the Disenchantment of the World

The makers of the Scientific Revolution created the concept of consciousness as they created a radically new theory of perception that went with their new scientific epistemology. Descartes was the most important artisan of this project, creating a definition of consciousness that ruled philosophical and scientific thought for centuries.

The Cartesian idea of consciousness as an inner mental space would have puzzled Greek or medieval philosophers (Rorty, 1979, 1991). Aristotle's realist theory of perception had been preserved and developed by the scholastic philosophers of the Middle Ages (Smith, 1990). In an act of perception, the sense organ received the form but not the matter of the object perceived. For example, if I look at the Venus de Milo, my eye receives the statue's form but does not receive the marble of which it is made. Thus, I am directly acquainted with all the features that define the Venus statue, not only its size and shape but also its color and even its beauty. According to this account, there is therefore a direct, objective connection between the formal order of the universe and my experience of it. The assertion that beauty is part of the statue's form to be simply "picked up" by the mind strongly underscores how different our post-Cartesian understanding of perception is from Aristotle's. The Venus de Milo, on his account, is objectively beautiful, while we regard beauty as a culturally informed, private judgment of the mind. Similarly, whether or not an action was moral or immoral was held to be an objective fact, not a subjective judgment.

The undoing of Aristotelian perceptual theory began with the development of rigorous logic and mathematics in the late Middle Ages and Renaissance. A conflict arose between elegant mathematical calculations applied to the universe and the messy appearances of our experience of the universe. In many respects, the essence of the Scientific Revolution was the complete subordination of the world as we experience it to the way mathematical reason conceives it. Truth came to lie in calculation rather than perception. As Galileo Galilei wrote in his *Dialogue Concerning the Two Chief World Systems*, "There is no limit to my astonishment when I reflect that Aristarchus and Copernicus were able to make reason so conquer sense that, in defiance of the latter, the former became mistress of their belief" (Smith, 1990, p. 738). The conquest of sense by reason created consciousness as an object of scientific concern, although not yet an object of scientific study.

In *The Assayer*, Galileo expresses the new scientific attitude to experience that regards the senses as deceptive and reason as the best guide to understanding the world. Here, he distinguished the *primary*, physically objective and *secondary*, subjective *sense properties*, and thus began to create the modern idea of consciousness completed by Descartes (quoted by Smith, 1990).

> Whenever I conceive any material or corporeal substance I immediately . . . think of it as bounded, and as having this or that shape; as being large or small [and] as being in motion or at rest. . . . From these conditions I cannot separate such a substance by any stretch of my imagination. But that it must be white or red, bitter or sweet, noisy or silent, and of sweet or foul odor, my mind does not feel compelled to bring in as necessary accompaniments. Without the senses as our guides, reason or imagination unaided would probably never arrive at qualities like these. Hence, I think that tastes, odors, colors, and so on . . . reside only in the consciousness [so that] if the living creature were removed all these qualities would be wiped away and annihilated. (p. 739)

The key word in this passage is *consciousness*. For ancient philosophers, there was only one world—the real physical world of which we are a part and with which we are in direct touch. But the concept of secondary sense properties created a New World, the inner world of consciousness, populated by mental objects—*ideas*—possessing sensory properties not found in objects themselves. Some of these secondary properties correspond to physical aspects of objects. For example, color corresponds to different wavelengths of light to which the cones in our retinas differentially respond. That color is not a primary property, however, is revealed by the existence of colorblind individuals, whose color perception is limited or absent. Objects are not colored, only ideas are colored. Other secondary properties, such as being beautiful or good, are more troublesome because they seem to correspond to no physical facts, but reside only in consciousness. Our modern belief that beauty and goodness are subjective judgments informed by cultural norms is one consequence of the transformation of experience wrought by the Scientific Revolution. We also find in this passage the beginning of the scientific View from Nowhere. Science aims to describe the world as it objectively is, as if no living creature dwelled upon it.

In an important sense, the distinction of primary and secondary properties created psychology, or at least the psychology of consciousness. People were now compelled to ask how and why the secondary properties originate. If experience simply reflects the world as it is, then the problem of how it does so is a legitimate but not very profound question. If, however, the world of experience is radically different from the world as it is, then the creation of that subjective world—the world we live in as human beings—becomes a more interesting and important matter. Henceforth, until the behavioral redefinition of the field around 1900, psychology was the study of the relationship between the subjective world of consciousness and the physical world of matter. Understood this way, psychology was philosophically important because its study could shed light on the scope and limits of human knowledge.

The order of human experience no longer had any reliable connection to the order of the world. Instead, experience—consciousness—needed to be corrected by mathematics, which depicts in imagination the world as it really is—a perfect machine without color, taste, aesthetic value, or moral import. The new scientific views of the mind and the world began to alienate human beings from the universe. Humans discovered that the world they experienced was not the real world after all, but something created by their minds. Bluebirds are not really blue. And beautiful things are not really beautiful and just acts are not really just. All are subjective judgments of private human minds. E. A. Burtt (1954) contrasted the old worldview, when experience and reality were harmonious, with the new scientific one:

> The scholastic scientist looked out upon the world of nature, and it appeared to him a quite sociable and human world. It was finite in extent. It was made to serve his needs. It was clearly and fully intelligible, being immediately present to the rational powers of his mind; it was composed fundamentally of, and was intelligible through, those qualities which were most vivid and intense in his own immediate experience—colour, sound, beauty, joy, heat, cold, fragrance and its plasticity to purpose and ideal. Now the world is an infinite and monotonous mathematical machine. Not only is his high place in a cosmic teleology lost, but all these things which were the very substance of the physical world to the scholastic—the thing that made it alive and lovely and spiritual—are lumped together and crowded into the small fluctuating and temporary positions of extension which we call human nervous systems. It was simply an incalculable change in the viewpoint of the world held by intelligent opinion in Europe. (pp. 123–124)

The mechanical philosophy offered a new proof of the existence of God, the Argument from Design. Just as the existence of a watch implies a watchmaker, the existence of the clockwork universe implies the existence of a Divine Watchmaker, God. However, the radical separation of God from the clockwork universe made God more distant from human life. The perfect mechanical universe having been created, it had no further need of His intervention; indeed, as Nietzsche proclaimed centuries later, He may be dead, leaving us alone in a cold, impersonal universe. Science was deadly to the old medieval conception of God as an ever-present being manifested in signs and portents, and to the lingering Stoic idea, alluded to by Kepler, that the universe is a living, rational, developing being.

Shortly after Europe was shattered by World War I, the German sociologist Max Weber[3] (1864–1920) addressed deeply dispirited German students, and linked the Scientific Revolution to their feelings of despair. He said, "The fate of our times is characterized by rationalization and intellectualization and, above all, by the 'disenchantment of the world . . .' " (Weber, 1918/1996, p. 175). Nevertheless, although Weber knew his audience yearned to reenchant the world, he said that science was the only path open to modern men and women, and he urged his listeners to stay on it with him. Because it was the science of the mind, German psychology was inevitably linked to the crisis Weber described. Gestalt psychology, as we will see, tried to reenchant the world *with* science.

Ancient science was now discredited, and so, therefore, was ancient philosophy. Sir Francis Bacon said, "There [is] but one course left—to try the whole thing anew upon a better plan, and to commence a total reconstruction of sciences, arts, and all human knowledge, raised upon the proper foundations" (quoted by Shapin, 1996, p. 66). The two most important modern foundation-layers were the Frenchman, René Descartes, and the Englishman, John Locke. Between them they created the basis for the first scientific psychology, the *Way of Ideas*. They identified a realm of consciousness detached from the realm of the physical world, thereby creating possibility that there should be a science, namely, psychology, to study the New World of the mind.

Consciousness Created: René Descartes (1596–1650)

Psychology as we know it began with Descartes. For good or ill, Descartes created a framework for thinking about mind and body within which virtually all philosophers and psychologists have worked since, even when they were busy attacking Descartes's ideas.

Descartes developed his radical new approach to psychology within a Christian worldview that had been profoundly altered by the Reformation and was being further reshaped by the Scientific Revolution. During the Middle Ages, the Catholic Church had permitted the persistence of a wide range of pagan beliefs and practices that it either tolerated or exploited (Gaukroger, 1995; Thomas, 1971). Although condemned (but meeting little practical interference) witches and cunning men, even werewolves and vampires, continued to ply their trades (Ginzburg, 1991) and people danced around maypoles. Saints were often identified with old pagan gods and churches were built on sites sacred to them. As the pagan churches had, the medieval Catholic Church stressed *orthopraxy*— correct religious practice—over *orthodoxy*—correct religious belief.

However, the new Protestant churches of the Reformation played down ritual and began to demand that their followers sincerely hold the right Christian beliefs. When the Catholic Church reformed itself during the Counter Reformation, it, too, compelled not just external behavioral submission to Christianity, but internal personal submission (Gaukroger, 1995). Magical practices such as the wearing of amulets to cure headaches were denounced; witches, Jews, and heretics were persecuted; and priests were forbidden to run taverns on the side. Despite official doctrinal differences among the sects, a single, rather austere and puritanical religious sensibility appeared in

---

[3]Asks Xam, "Hmmm. Why is this name so palindromically familiar?"

seventeenth-century Europe. The Christian God became a forbidding and remote figure whose power could not be commanded by magic. Into the vacuum stepped science, a secular, material—and effective—way of gaining power over nature. Psychologically, the situation resembled the Hellenistic period, when traditional religions that demanded only that their followers practice cult rites were challenged by philosophies and new religions that drew people into themselves introspectively, seeking inner faith, not just external conformity. Descartes's philosophy, as we shall see, was based on a radical version of such withdrawal.

Descartes was closely connected with a circle of reforming Catholics, led by the scientist and theologian Marin Mersenne (1588–1648). This group was particularly worried about the scientifically appealing but religiously dangerous ideas of Renaissance naturalism. Renaissance naturalism was scientific in that it explained the world without reference to supernatural powers, but it was suspect religiously because it seemed to grant supernatural powers to matter itself. Naturalism was especially dangerous to religious orthodoxy when applied to living things, particularly people. If a magnet had the natural power to attract metals, it seemed only a short step (taken in the eighteenth century) to saying that the brain has the power to think. Medieval and Renaissance physicians already attributed sensation, perception, common sense, imagination, memory, and other powers to the brain, so why not thought and knowledge, too? However, if all mental functions are functions of the body, as Aristotle had thought, then the existence of the Christian soul was placed in doubt.

To counter Renaissance nature philosophy, Mersenne and his followers, including Descartes, believed and taught a clockwork view of the universe. Matter was completely inert, possessing no magnetism, gravity, or any other active powers of any kind. Active power was reserved to God alone. Matter moved or changed only when physically pushed by another piece of matter. Newton's tolerance for unexplained forces—he proposed no hypothesis about how gravity worked—ultimately triumphed, but not without a struggle and with Descartes's followers on the other side.

Descartes's conception of mind and body was very carefully worked out within this religious-scientific framework, and it decisively shaped the scientific psychology that was yet to come. Descartes was committed to viewing animals as complex automata—machines whose operations could be fully explained as physical processes and without resort to vital forces of any kind. Thus, Descartes had to reject the idea that the heart was a spontaneously working pump circulating blood through the body, because its action seemed self-caused by an internal power, little different from attributing attractive power to magnets. However, the "mental" powers of the beast-machine were considerable. Everything Aristotle had attributed to the sensitive soul was included, and, to the extent people were animals, human "mental" powers had to have a purely mechanical explanation. The place of the immortal human soul in a mechanical world and a mechanical body had become a serious problem.

For our purposes, Descartes's life work can be divided into two phases. In the first phase, he focused on scientific and mathematical projects, including physics but with a growing interest in physiology. His main philosophical project during this period was working out methodological rules by which the mind ought to be governed in its search for truth. Descartes's scientific work culminated in the writing of two large books, *Le Monde* (The World), on physics, and the unfinished *L'homme* (The Human), on physiology. Then, in November 1633, on the eve of the publication of *Le Monde*, Descartes learned of the condemnation of the Copernican hypothesis by the Roman Inquisition of Galileo's advocacy. To Mersenne, Descartes wrote that he was so surprised by Galileo's fate of house arrest for life that he almost burned all his private papers because his own system of the world depended so much on Galileo's. Nevertheless, "I wouldn't want to publish a discourse which had a single word that the Church disapproved of; so I prefer to suppress it rather than publish it in mutilated form" (quoted by Gaukroger, 1995, pp. 290–291). Thus began the second, primarily philosophical, phase in Descartes's career. He decided that in order for his scientific views to win the acceptance that Galileo's had not, they needed careful and convincing philosophical justification, and he proceeded to develop the philosophy that made him famous and influential.

DESCARTES AS PHYSIOLOGICAL PSYCHOLOGIST While working on his system of physics, Descartes took up the path to psychology through physiology that had begun with Alcmaeon and Empedocles and would ultimately lead to the founding of scientific psychology. In a letter to Mersenne in December 1629, Descartes described how he studied anatomy by watching butchers slaughter cattle and taking parts back to his lodgings for his own dissections. These researches took him in a new and exciting direction. Three years later, he wrote to Mersenne that he was dissecting animal brains in order to understand the physical basis of mental functions (Gaukroger, 1995). In 1890, William James told his readers to begin their study of psychology by getting a sheep's head from the butcher shop and dissecting its brain.

It is important to understand the goal Descartes set for himself in undertaking to give physiological accounts of mental processes because it is the key to understanding the problems he later created for his own theory of human consciousness and to comprehending his complex, troubling, even contradictory, legacy to later psychology. As we have learned, from the time of Aristotle right through the religious Middle Ages, physicians, philosophers, and theologians had attributed most psychological functions to the animal soul, and therefore to the animal and human bodies. The Islamic physician-philosophers had even proposed specific locations in the brain in which imagination, memory, and so on took place. Within Descartes's renovated Christian framework, however, these older treatments of the faculties were unacceptable, precisely because they endowed matter with soul-like powers, the way Renaissance naturalism endowed matter with magical powers such as magnetic attraction. Saying that a given piece of brain tissue has "the power of memory" is not a scientific explanation at all because it does not specify any mechanism by which memories are created and retrieved. Descartes wanted to create mechanical models of mental functions that had heretofore been attributed to living organisms (Gaukroger, 1995).

In *Le Monde*, Descartes described a mechanistic universe that behaved exactly like ours, thus inviting us to believe that it *is* ours. In *L'homme*, Descartes asks us to imagine "statues or earthen machines"—indeed, a "man-machine"—whose inner operations he described in detail, thus inviting us to believe that they *are* us, except that they lack a soul (Gaukroger, 2002). His optimism that he could explain the behavior of animals (and much of that of humans) as the product of inner machinery was fed by the high artisanship of contemporary craftsmen who could build statues of animals and people that behaved in lifelike ways. Contemporary physicians were even trying to build mechanical replacement body parts. Seeing mechanical statues move and respond to stimuli helped Descartes think that animals were sophisticated machines, too.

The novelty and daring of Descartes's undertaking are perhaps hard to appreciate today. We live with machines that perceive, remember, and, perhaps, think, and because we build and program computers we can explain how they work at whatever level of mathematical or mechanical detail might be demanded. In this decade of the brain, we are learning how the brain's machinery works, down to the biophysics of single cells. Struggling to oust magical, occult powers from matter, Descartes set in motion the reduction of mental functions to physiological processes that is only now coming to fruition. Although the details of Descartes's physiological psychology are not important for our purposes here (see Gaukroger, 1995, for a full treatment), the conceptual difficulties his approach created for his treatment of the human mind are discussed in the following paragraphs.

The problems for Descartes's psychology, and therefore for all later psychologists, begin when we turn to the human soul, which Descartes as a Christian had to exempt from mechanistic explanation. Descartes's account is usually presented as clean and simple, but it is in fact slippery and elusive, a tortured attempt to preserve a Christian soul in a mechanistic universe (Gaukroger, 2002). Descartes had to avoid two heretical temptations, each of which could be traced to the difficulty of assimilating Aristotle to Christianity. One was called *Averroism*, after the Latinized name of the Islamic physician-philosopher Ibn Rushd (1126–1198) who first proposed it. Averroism resulted from splitting Aristotle's human mind off from the body and then identifying it with the Christian or Muslim soul.

The heresy of Averroism derived from the fact that the Aristotelian *mind* contained only general knowledge and was therefore not the essence of one's personality, a possibly immortal, individual soul. In a religious context, *mind* was interpreted by Averroes and others, including IbnSīnā, as a divine, inner light from God that illuminates general knowledge, but that remerges with God at death. In earlier phases of Christianity, Averroism could be resisted by emphasizing, as Aquinas did, the Resurrection, when the mind is reunited with its body, reconstituting the whole person. In Descartes's time, however, the idea of the Resurrection was fading, being replaced by the idea of immediate judgment of a soul that would live forever in Heaven or Hell. If the soul was impersonal, however, its reward or suffering became absurd. Thus, it was more important than ever that the soul be one's personal essence, not an inner light from God.

The other heretical temptation, called *Alexandrism* after Alexander of Aphrodisias (fl. 200), arose from dropping Aristotle's sharp distinction of form and matter and simply attributing to matter of the brain the power not only to perceive and remember, but to think and have knowledge. Like Averroism, Alexandrism denied the immortality of a personal soul and was becoming increasingly tempting through the influence of Renaissance naturalism.

In *L'homme*, Descartes said that the unique function of the human soul was thinking. Defining the soul by the power of thought, or reason, is, of course, entirely traditional, stretching back to the ancient Greeks. What is new is Descartes's focus on how thinking separates humans from animals in *experience*, in *behavior*, and in the *possession of language*.

First of all, thought makes human *experience* different from animal experience. Descartes never denied that animals have experience—that is, that they are aware of their surroundings. What they lack is reflective, thoughtful awareness of their own awareness. Descartes wrote (quoted by Gaukroger, 1995):

> Descartes said that animals are clearly aware of their surroundings because we can see that they respond appropriately to various stimuli, as we do when our consciousness is otherwise occupied. Our brains control our behavior, not our consciousness, and animal behavior, Descartes held, is always driven by the nervous system because animals lack reflective consciousness (Gaukroger, 1995).

Descartes *(Courtesy of Library of Congress)*

As did William James centuries later, Descartes here drew a sharp dividing line between *simple awareness* and *self-awareness*. James pointed out that much of our behavior can be carried out by simple habit and without thought. In a contemporary example, a driver can respond to a traffic light turning red, without interrupting an intense conversation with a friend. The impression of the red light on the retina causes the driver to carry out the foot movement of hitting the car's brakes. The driver experiences the light becoming red, but does not think about it because his or her mind is elsewhere, in conversation.

Secondly, thought makes human behavior more *flexible* than animal behavior. Animals, Descartes wrote, require some preset reflex or habit for every response (Gaukroger, 1995). Hitting the brakes when a traffic light turns red is a preset habit that is automatically and thoughtlessly activated by the stimulus of the red light. Descartes viewed animals as machines that always respond in such reflexive ways. Humans, on the other hand, can respond to entirely novel situations by thinking about them. Approaching an intersection where all the lights are out, a driver will drop the ongoing conversation and think carefully about what to do. An animal, lacking any stimulus to control its behavior, would be frozen into inaction or spurred by some other stimulus into inappropriate action. Behavioral flexibility became the hallmark of mind for James.

Concerning animal thought, Descartes was inconsistent. Sometimes, he denied that animals think at all. At other times, he regarded the question as empirical rather than philosophical, though he said that animal thinking, should it exist, would be quite different from human thinking (Gaukroger, 1995). After the acceptance of evolution made drawing a sharp line between human and animal more difficult, comparative psychologists tried, with controversial results, to investigate animal thought.

The third aspect of human thinking was *language*, which Descartes regarded as unique to human beings. In *L'homme*, language played a crucial role in Descartes's understanding of the human mind, being critical to human self-awareness. Although engaged in conversation, a driver reflexively applies the brakes upon seeing a red traffic light. Seeing-eye dogs are trained to stop themselves and their master when they see a red light. At this level of reflexive response, there is no difference between the driver and the dog. However, according to Descartes's analysis, only the driver, as a human being, can think about traffic lights and think the thought that the red light means stop. The trained dog stops too, but it cannot formulate the proposition "Red means stop." Being able to think about red lights in this way gives humans the ability to think about experience reflectively, rather than simply having it.

Animals do not think as we do (if they think at all) because they cannot think with linguistically stated propositions. For Descartes, the ability of the human soul to formulate propositions did not, however, depend on acquiring any particular human language. He proposed that there is an innate human language of the mind of which actual human languages are outward translations. Thus, while our driver says, "Red means stop," and a German driver says, "*Rot bedeutet halten*," at a deeper level each thinks the same thought linking the concept of "redness of traffic light" to "need to stop one's motor vehicle."

Questions concerning the role of language in thinking and its presence or absence in animals have proven enormously controversial in the centuries since Descartes. Some philosophers and psychologists have followed Descartes in closely linking language and thought, while others have strongly disagreed. In the 1960s, linguist Noam Chomsky proposed a *Cartesian linguistics* in which language was a unique, species-specific property of the human mind, and his student, Jerry Fodor, dubbed Descartes's universal inner language "mentalese." Cartesian linguistics played a large role in the downfall of behaviorism—which saw no essential dividing line between human and beast—and in the creation of the field of cognitive science, which aligns humans with language-using computers instead of nonlanguage-using animals. In 1748, a French philosopher suggested teaching language to apes as a way of defeating Descartes's belief in the soul (a project carried out with uncertain results by behaviorists defending themselves from Chomsky's belief in the mind).

Unfortunately, Descartes never completed the part of *L'homme* in which he planned to give a scientific treatment of the human soul. In 1633, as he suppressed publication of *Le Monde*, he abandoned the study of physiology and the writing of *L'homme*. Faced with the possibility that his science might be condemned like Galileo's, he turned to providing it with an unshakable, philosophical foundation (Gaukroger, 1995). For the development of psychology, Descartes's new direction was fateful. It created the concept of consciousness, the definition of psychology as the science that studies consciousness, and a set of deep, perhaps intractable, problems with which psychology has struggled to the present day (Dennett, 1991; Searle, 1994).

DESCARTES AS PHILOSOPHER   As an early scientist, Descartes was concerned with philosophical issues, most importantly a project of discovering or creating methodological rules that should guide scientific thinking. As Aristotle's physics crumbled before the research of the Scientific Revolution, it became widely believed that he had gone astray because he had relied on poor methods for theorizing about and investigating nature. Descartes wanted the new science to be guided by a better methodology, and for some years he fitfully worked on writing *Rules for the Direction of the Mind*. Eventually, he abandoned it, but it was published posthumously in 1684. In 1635, he returned to giving science its epistemological foundation in *Discourse on the Method of Rightly Conducting One's Reason and Seeking Truth in the Sciences* (1637), and the briefer but more influential *Meditations on First Philosophy* (1641/1986).

Here began a new psychological style of philosophizing that remained influential for centuries. Descartes investigated his own mind in order to develop a foundational philosophy. Plato and Platonism wanted to move through the mind and then away from it to the transcendental Forms. Aristotle, believing in a realist theory of perception, thought to find philosophical truths, including truths about morality, in nature itself. Descartes had the new realm of consciousness to explore, and he plunged into it in search of philosophical truth. From now on, psychological investigations of the human mind will be the basis for philosophical proposals about knowledge and morality.

In the *Discourse*, Descartes described how he found his philosophy. Returning home after military service at the coronation of the Holy Roman Emperor Ferdinand II, he spent one day, possibly November 10, 1619, in a stove-heated room meditating on his own thoughts and formulating the basic principles of his philosophy. Descartes wanted to find a firm, philosophical foundation for the apparently dangerous science he was developing, and to find his foundation he adopted a method of radical doubt. He resolved to systematically doubt every belief he had—even those no sane person would doubt—until he found something so self-evidently true that it could not be doubted. His aim was not to actually cast doubt on commonsense truths, but to force himself to find sound reasons for believing them. In a sense, Descartes was subjecting himself to Socrates's *elenchus*, seeking explicit reasons for holding intuitively obvious beliefs and thereby providing a foundation for his scientific investigations.

Descartes found he could doubt the existence of God, the validity of his own sensations, and the existence of his body. He continued in this way until he found one thing he could not doubt: his own existence as a self-conscious, thinking thing (*res cogitans*). One cannot doubt that one doubts, for in doing so, one makes real the very action supposedly in doubt. Doubting is an act of thinking, and Descartes expressed his first indubitable truth as the famous "*Cogito, ergo sum*" (I think, therefore I am). I am a thing that thinks, and that is all. The soul, the thinking thing, was a spiritual substance wholly without matter, not occupying space (unextended) and completely separate from the body. Descartes proposed a radical new dualism in which soul and body are completely different, sharing neither matter nor form. Nor is the soul conceived as the form of the body. Instead, the soul dwells within the mechanical body as a sort of ghost, receiving sensations from it and commanding it by acts of will.

Descartes's *dualism* of soul and body was a way of explaining the dualism of secondary and primary sense properties. According to Descartes, the material world was made of *corpuscles*, or *atoms*, which possess only the properties of extension in space and physical location. In addition to that material world, which includes the body, there is a subjective world of *consciousness* and *mind*. Perhaps this second world is spiritual as well, for God and the soul are not material. In any case, as far as human knowledge is concerned, Descartes concluded there are two worlds: an objective, scientifically knowable, mechanical-material world—the world as it really is—and a subjective world of human consciousness known through introspection—the world of a person as a thinking being.

Descartes was not the first to prove his own existence from mental activity. St. Augustine had said, "If I am deceived, I exist," and Parmenides had said, "For it is the same thing to think and to be." What was new and carried profound implications was Descartes's radical reflexivity (Taylor, 1989)—his focus on the self and his invention of consciousness as a thing that could be studied. Augustine had turned inward and found *God*. Descartes turned inward and found only *himself*. It is a momentous point in the history of psychology and philosophy, and we need to examine it and its implications carefully.

Descartes's argument of the cogito created consciousness as an object of scrutiny by radically dividing the self from conscious experience. Prior to the Scientific Revolution, people had assumed that the world was as it seemed to be, and had simply lived in and through experience. However, the division of the primary and secondary sense properties destroyed the traditional, naive belief in the validity of experience. Descartes built on this distinction by claiming that we can step back from our experience and examine it as a collection of objects—sensations—that are not part of the self.

Imagine you are looking at a green leaf. Now I ask you to look at the green more closely. In the older, naive view, you would simply take yourself to be carefully inspecting the green that the leaf really is. Descartes, however, asks you to do something different—to think about your sensation of *green* and how greenness appears in consciousness. Looked at this way, you are no longer inspecting the leaf—you are *introspecting a bit of consciousness, the sensation of green*.

A useful way to think of the model of experience Descartes is setting up has been suggested by Daniel Dennett (1991). He calls Descartes's model of mind the *Cartesian Theater*. A viewer, the inner self, the existence of which Descartes has (apparently) proved by the cogito, looks at a screen on which the visual stimuli from the retina are projected. Naively, when we see the image of a leaf, we believe we are seeing an actual leaf outside us. If, however, the Cartesian Theater is true, what the self actually sees is not a leaf but the projected *image* of a leaf. Introspection then consists of thinking of the image as an image and of then inspecting the image without reference to the object outside.

In *L'homme* Descartes provides a physiological model of the Cartesian Theater, revealing important features of the new conception of consciousness that would deeply inform psychological research and theory for centuries to come. An illustration shows the brain, the eyes, and the nerves carrying information from the eyes inward to the brain as the eye/brain looks at an archer's arrow. The image of the arrow is projected by light rays onto the retina. From the retina, nerves carry the image inward to the brain, and the image is then cast on the surface of the pineal gland, the location of interaction between soul and body according to Descartes. Descartes' model of visual perception makes two important points. First, it provides a physiological—and thus for Descartes, mechanical—explanation of the new representational theory of perception created by the Scientific

Revolution. We—our non-mechanical, non-physical souls—do not see the world directly, but only as a projection on a physical screen, specifically the pineal gland. Second, the image we see is a composite of sensations, not a whole meaningful object. The illustration tracks certain points of physical stimulation via rays of light projecting onto the corresponding sensation-points on each retina. These retinal point-stimulations are each carried by separate nerves to the pineal gland, where they create projected pixel-like points on the surface of the pineal gland. This suggests that our idea of any object is a collection of associated smaller ideas of particular stimulus properties such as color and luminance. Descartes' model will be developed by important thinkers in the 18th century, and will provide the standard view of consciousness among early psychologists until the Gestalt movement in the early 20th century.

Consider a newspaper photograph. Showing a space shuttle on the launch pad, you might say, "I see the shuttle." But, in fact, you are seeing an image of the shuttle, not the shuttle itself, and closer examination will reveal the image to be much fuzzier than you first thought. Look even more closely, and you will see the picture is made up of gray and black dots that you didn't notice when you first naively "saw" the shuttle. Descartes says conscious experience is like a theater or a photograph, an image the self naively takes to be real, but an image that can be examined as a thing—consciousness itself—through a special kind of inward observation called *introspection*.

With the Cartesian Theater, the psychology of consciousness was born, although it was not yet a science. After Descartes, it was generally taken for granted that consciousness is a collection of sensations projected to the mind; the self can then reflectively examine them. Natural science continued to examine the world naively as a collection of objects to be carefully observed and about which theories might be propounded and tested. Psychological science became defined as the reflective, introspective study of sensations qua sensations. By submitting experience to experimental control, sensations could be carefully observed, and theories about them might be propounded and tested. Thinking of experience as an object—consciousness—apart from the things causing it, gave rise in the mid-nineteenth century to both scientific psychology and modern art. Modern art began when painters rebelled against the idea of art as representation and asked viewers to look at the surface of the canvas. Traditional art, like traditional theories of perception, focused on the thing represented. The goal of a landscape, for example, was to show how a mountain or lake really was. Modern artists, however, wanted viewers to look at the canvas, seeing not what the artist saw, but the subjective impression created in the artist by the mountain or lake.

Along with consciousness, the Cartesian Theater created the modern "pointlike" self (Taylor, 1989; Taylor actually uses the word *punctual*, but I regard it as misleading). According to Descartes, the soul was like a *mathematical point* located in, but not actually occupying any, space, and doing but one thing, thinking. Thinking of the soul as a point was radically new. For the Greeks and others, including Christians such as Aquinas, a person had been taken to be the embodied soul, including the faculties of the animal soul, that was directly connected to the world outside by experience. According to the argument of the cogito, on the other hand, our essence is a small, self-aware point of pure thought, dwelling in the Cartesian Theater, detached from the body and even from experience, which it receives secondhand via projection on the screen of the Cartesian Theater.

Such a small self became easy to erase, and, paradoxically, to inflate. Augustine looked inside himself and found God. Descartes looked inside himself and seemed to find himself. However, the leading British philosopher of the eighteenth century, David Hume, looked inside himself and found sensations and images from the world and the body, but no self. Rejecting this alarming conclusion, the leading German philosopher, Kant, could not find a self either, but posited it as a logical necessity. He then imbued it with enormous powers, and his followers, the German idealists, said that the invisible self is so powerful it creates the universe.

In the psychology of consciousness, the pointlike self was called on to control, observe, and precisely report on experience. In the psychology of the unconscious, the pointlike self became the *ego*, only partly able to manage the ferocious desires of the animal *id*. In the psychology of adaptation, following in the footsteps of Hume, the soul began to disappear, merging with the screen of consciousness itself. In the twentieth century, behaviorism and cognitive science have done without consciousness and self altogether, content to study what we do rather than what we are.

By splitting off experience from the self and making it a thing—consciousness—to be studied, Descartes made psychology possible—and philosophically important. As a philosopher and scientist, Descartes wanted to know how the world really is. For traditional philosophies, this was not a problem; experience was thought to reveal the world directly to us. However, in Descartes's scheme, the thinking self is trapped in the Cartesian Theater, seeing only a projection of the world, not the world itself. Consciousness was indelibly subjective, a presentation of how the world is for us. For it to be the basis of science and of knowledge more generally, it had to be purged of its subjectivity. This made it imperative to study *us*—to practice psychology—so that the subjective contributions to experience might be subtracted, leaving only objective truth (Gaukroger, 1995). In the next century, during the Enlightenment, psychology became even more important, as philosophers moved to base ethics, politics, and the definition of a good society on the study of human nature.

DIFFICULTIES WITH CARTESIAN PHILOSOPHY AND PSYCHOLOGY   Descartes's radically new conception of soul and body was in tune with the Scientific Revolution, which had begun to question the validity of perception and to think of the world as a machine. His psychology and his followers' variants of it quickly swept over the intellectual world of Europe, becoming the starting point from which virtually every psychologist and philosopher began, even when they disagreed with the details of Descartes's theory. Nevertheless, Cartesian dualism faced a number of difficulties—some old, some new. One old problem remained from earlier dualistic conceptions of the soul such as Plato's—the *homunculus* problem. Other difficulties emerged in the later course of psychological research. Descartes himself addressed two new ones.

The first new problem was how mind (or soul) and body interact. Descartes attempted to create a physiological mechanism by which the interaction takes place. He proposed that the pineal gland was not only the site of the Cartesian Theater, but also furnished the means by which the soul controlled the body. Being at the base of the brain, the pineal gland was, Descartes thought, the place where the nerve-tubes from the body enter the brain. The soul could cause the pineal gland to tilt this way and that, directing the movements of the animal spirits in the nerves and commanding the motions of the body.

Descartes's theory of interaction was eventually rendered wildly implausible by advances in the study of the brain, but it always had a philosophical problem it never surmounted. The problem was perhaps first noticed by one of Descartes's most prolific correspondents and acute critics, Princess Elizabeth of Bohemia (1615–1680), to whom he later dedicated his *Principles of Philosophy*. She pointed out that it was difficult to conceive how a purely spiritual substance, the soul, could possibly act upon a purely material substance, the body. Descartes offered two rather vague responses, and the problem of how mind and body interact was left unresolved as a problem to bedevil psychology for centuries to come. Descartes replied with a vague argument about the "unity" of mind and body. In her next letter, Elizabeth restated her perplexity over soul-body interaction, but Descartes never replied because their letters turned to her ill health.

The first patches to Descartes's psychology were sewn in an effort to answer Elizabeth's question of how an immaterial ghost can push the material pineal gland or be affected by it. Eventually, as we will see, instead of dumping the Cartesian Theater, philosophers and psychologists kept the pointlike mind, but denied that mind and body interact, violating Elizabeth's natural intuition that "the soul moves the body."

The second new difficulty with Descartes's position is called by philosophers "the problem of other minds." If my mind is a pointlike, thinking substance locked up in the body, how do I know mine is not the only soul in the universe? I know I have a soul from the argument of the cogito, but how do I know that you or Leonardo Dicaprio has one? As he had in his scientific works, Descartes responded by pointing to language. From my own self-awareness, I know that I think and that I express my thoughts in language. Therefore, any creature that possesses language—all human beings, and only human beings, possess language—thinks, and so has a mind. As suggested earlier, the problems for Descartes's analysis were not long in coming. If soulless animals could learn language, perhaps people also lacked souls; evolution undermined Descartes's radical discontinuity between human and animals; and today, computers, mere machines, may soon speak as we do.

Along with his dualism and emphasis on reason, Descartes's nativism links him to Plato. Descartes found in himself ideas that derived from experience, such as of trees or rocks, and ideas that the mind invented, such as "sirens and hippogriffs." But he also found in himself ideas that could not be traced to any sensation, and which, being universal ideas, he did not think he could have invented. These included such ideas as those of God, the mind, and mathematical objects (Gaukroger, 1995). Descartes list of innate ideas was, in other words, Plato's innate ideas of the Forms. Descartes proposed that these ideas come not from the senses but from "certain germs of truth which exist naturally in our souls," implanted by God. Thus, the indubitable, principal truths are innate. As for Plato, they are potential ideas only; they require activation by experience.

CONCLUSION It is generally recognized today that Descartes's philosophy failed to negotiate its way between the heresies he wished to avoid. Specifically, by denying personal memory to the soul, he fell into Averroism, and his works were, in fact, placed on the Catholic Church's Index of prohibited books in 1663. At the popular level, Descartes was often identified with Faust, who sold his soul to the devil for knowledge (see earlier discussion). A story, entirely false, began to circulate in the eighteenth century that Descartes had built a mechanical girl in the image of his own illegitimate daughter Francine, and it was said to be so lifelike that the two could not be told apart. There were intimations that he had sexual relations with the doll. By then, some thinkers had taken the controversial step that Descartes never took—proclaiming that humans were mere machines like the animals—and the story no doubt arose as a response to such a shocking idea (Gaukroger, 1995). Today, Descartes's psychology is under assault (e.g., Dennett, 1991; Searle, 1994). By reducing mind to a point; by making experience a mysterious, subjective thing called *consciousness*; by assuming there is a point in the brain where experience happens; and by creating the problem of other minds and the issue of interaction, it appears that Descartes dug a hole from which psychology is only now escaping. Cartesian dualism also introduced a paranoid streak to modern thinking (Farrell, 1996). Descartes did not mean for his method of radical doubt to actually cast doubt on beliefs in the external world or God. However, by introducing the notion that the mind is only acquainted with its own ideas (as Locke put it), Descartes invited later thinkers to doubt that ideas represent the world at all. In the eighteenth century, philosophical psychologists would come to doubt the existence of the external world, the possibility of human knowledge, and the foundations of morality. In the nineteenth century, Freud led people to doubt the sincerity of their own motives, introducing paranoia to the inner world of the mind that Descartes thought was the sole reservoir of truth.

However, because the hole Descartes dug was deep, Descartes's influence cannot be denied. His framework created the idea of psychology as the study of consciousness and made the search for self-understanding an important one. Interestingly, a variation on Descartes's framework was more immediately influential. It was more commonsensical, more intuitive, less encumbered with metaphysics, and informed by Newton's *Principia*, published 37 years after Descartes's death. It was the attempt at scientific psychology made by the physician-philosopher John Locke.

Consciousness Quantified: Gottfried Wilhelm Leibniz (1646–1716)

Leibniz was a mathematician, logician, and metaphysician. He independently invented calculus and dreamed of a formal conceptual calculus that would do for verbal reasoning what mathematics had done for the sciences. His metaphysics is extremely difficult. Briefly, he conceived of the universe as composed of an infinity of geometrical-point entities called *monads*, each of which is to some extent living and possesses some degree of consciousness. Animals and people are made up of monads that subserve a most conscious and, hence, most dominant, monad. Leibniz proposed a solution to the mind–body problem that was widely adopted by early scientific psychologists and set up a framework for thinking about consciousness that suggested conscious experience could be measured, making possible the first scientific research in psychology—Fechner's psychophysics.

MIND AND BODY: PSYCHOPHYSICAL PARALLELISM Leibniz's theory of monads led to a solution to the mind–body problem that became increasingly popular over the next two centuries. Descartes had said that mind and body interact. However, because it was unclear how spirit could act on matter and vice versa, a theory of mind and body based on *occasionalism* (see earlier discussion) emerged, in which God saw to it that when a bodily event occurred, so did a mental event and vice versa. This, too, has its difficulties, with God running around keeping mind and body coordinated. Leibniz proposed an answer that has since been called mind–body (or psychophysical) *parallelism*. Leibniz argued that God had created the universe (the infinitude of monads) such that there is a preestablished harmony among the monads. Leibniz used an analogy of two identical and perfect clocks, both set to the same time and started at the same moment. From then on, the clocks would always agree with, and mirror, one another, but they would not be causally connected. Each would run in an identical but parallel—not interacting—course of development. Just so, the mind and body. Consciousness (mind) mirrors exactly what happens in the body but only because of God's preestablished harmony, not because of a causal connection. In fact, Leibniz extended this neo-occasionalist scheme to the whole universe, holding that monads never interact but stay coordinated in their pictures of the universe because of God's perfect harmony. Although the metaphysical basis of psychophysical parallelism was dropped later, the doctrine itself caught on as physiological knowledge of the body and the growth of physics rendered both interactionism and occasionalism implausible.

Leibniz also upheld innate ideas. Like Descartes, Leibniz believed that many ideas, such as God and mathematical truths, could not be derived from experience for they are too abstract. Such ideas must be innate. Leibniz expressed his conception by a statue metaphor. The mind at birth is likened to a block of marble. Marble is veined, and it may be that the veins outline the form of Hercules in the marble, for example. Certain activities are required to bring out the statue, but in a sense Hercules is "innate" in the marble. Similarly, an infant's innate dispositions to certain kinds of knowledge must be activated, either by experience or by the infant's own reflection on mental life.

SENSATION, PERCEPTION, AND ATTENTION For psychology, Leibniz's most important ideas concerned his account of perception. Leibniz laid the ground for both psychophysics and Wundt's founding psychology (McRae, 1976). First, Leibniz distinguished *petite perception* from *perception*. *Petite perception* is a stimulus event (to borrow a modern term) so weak it is not perceived. To use Leibniz's most usual metaphor, one does not hear the sound of a single drop of water hitting a beach; this is a petite perception. A wave crashing on the beach is thousands of drops hitting the beach, and this we do hear. Thus, our perception of the wave's crash is made up of many petite perceptions; each is too small to be heard, but together they make a conscious experience. This doctrine points the way to psychophysics, the systematic study of the quantitative relation between stimulus intensity and experience. Leibniz's account also implies the existence of a more complex unconscious, or, as Leibniz writes, "changes in the soul itself of which we are not conscious."

Leibniz also distinguished perception from *sensation*. A *perception* is a raw, confused idea, not really conscious, which animals, as well as humans, may possess. However, a person can refine and sharpen perceptions and become reflectively aware of them in consciousness. They then become sensations. This refining process is called *apperception*. Apperception also seems to be involved in uniting petite perceptions to become perceptions. This uniting process, stressed Leibniz, is not a process of mere aggregation. Perceptions, rather, are emergent properties coming from masses of petite perceptions. If we combine blue and yellow lights, for example, we do not experience blue and yellow separately but instead green, an emergent experience not present in the simpler, constituent lights.

Attention is the major component of apperception for Leibniz, and he distinguished two types: passive and active. If we are absorbed in some activity, we may not notice another stimulus, such as a friend speaking to us, until that stimulus grows so strong that it automatically draws our attention. Here, the shift in attention is passive, for the new stimulus captures attention. Attention may also be voluntary, as when we focus it on one person at a party to the exclusion of others. Sometimes, Leibniz tied apperception closely to voluntary attention, for he saw apperception as an act of will. Leibniz's doctrine of active mental apperception would be Wundt's central theoretical concept.

PSYCHOLOGY AND HUMAN AFFAIRS

In the wake of the Scientific Revolution, it became clear that humanity's place in nature would have to be reevaluated. As religion began to lose its authority and science began to assume its own authority, new answers to the traditional questions of philosophy, psychology, politics, and values were demanded. The task of reworking human self-understanding and human life within the framework of science is an enterprise in which psychology is intimately involved, and it is one that continues in our own day. Science raises important questions about the springs of human conduct, about the place of values in a world of facts, about moral responsibility, about the proper forms of human government, and about the place of feelings in worldviews founded on scientific reason. In the seventeenth century, philosophers began to wrestle with these problems and to offer solutions that still inspire or infuriate us today.

The Laws of Social Life: Thomas Hobbes (1588–1679)

Hobbes's importance derives from being the first to comprehend and express the new scientific view of humans and their place in the universe. Hobbes wrote: "For seeing life is but a motion of limbs . . . why may we not say, that all *automata* . . . have an artificial life? For what is the *heart*, but a spring; and the *nerves*, but so many strings; and the *joints*, but so many wheels, giving motion to the whole body" (Bronowski & Mazlish, 1960, p. 197, italics in original). Hobbes's contemporary, Descartes, believed animals, but not humans, were entirely machines. Hobbes went considerably further, claiming that spiritual substance is a meaningless idea. Only matter exists, and the actions of people, no less than those of animals, are fully determined by material, never spiritual, causes. Thinking, he said, in anticipation of later computational conceptions of mental activity, could as well be carried out by a machine as by a soul (Dascal, 2007).

On one point Hobbes and Descartes agreed: Philosophy should be constructed after the model of geometry. Indeed, Hobbes's accidental exposure, at age 40, to the elegant proofs of Euclid led him to philosophize. Hobbes believed that all knowledge is ultimately rooted in sense-perception. He upheld extreme nominalism, seeing in universals no more than convenient names grouping remembered sense-perceptions. He dismissed arguments over metaphysics as scholastic wrangling about meaningless concepts. He rigidly separated philosophy, which is rational and meaningful, from theology, which is irrational and meaningless. His most interesting psychological doctrine is that language and thinking are closely related, perhaps even identical. In his major work, *Leviathan* (Hobbes, 1651/1962), Hobbes wrote: "Understanding is nothing else but conception caused by speech." Further, he stated that "children are not endowed with reason at all, till they have attained the use of speech." Hobbes was the first in the long, and still living, line of philosophers who equate right thinking with right use of language.

Hobbes's greatest importance lies in thinking about the relation between human nature and human society. He was the first to ask the question, "What would people be like in a state of nature, without government?" This question was the beginning of the Enlightenment Project of the eighteenth century and remains with us still. Once one abandons the idea that government exists to enforce God's laws and adopts a scientific view of humankind, it seems that government and society need to be constructed around human nature. Psychology, the study of human nature, becomes important to those who desire or need to govern and manage human beings.

Hobbes thought he had learned what humans were like in the absence of government, having experienced the chaotic anarchy of the English Civil War, in which government did, in fact, break down. In *Leviathan*, Hobbes began with a commonplace of modern liberalism, that persons are created roughly equal in physical and mental powers. However, without the external control of government, each person would seek his or her own interest against fellow humans. Outside of organized society, Hobbes wrote: "*There is always war of every one against every one . . . and the life of man is solitary, nasty, brutish, and short*" (italics in original). The solution is for people to recognize that their rational self-interest lies in a regulated state that will provide security, the fruits of industry, and other benefits. This means recognizing the existence of Laws of Nature—for example, that each person should give up the total liberty and equal right to all things that breed war, and "be contented with so much liberty against other men, as he would allow other men against himself." The best state for securing such liberties, Hobbes went on to argue, is an absolute despotism, in which all members of society contract their rights and powers to a sovereign, whether king or parliament, who will then rule and protect them, uniting their many wills into one will. Hobbes was not, however, the father of modern totalitarianism. For him, the authoritarian state would establish the peaceful conditions within which people could freely do what they like as long as it did not harm others. Later totalitarians such as Hitler and Stalin wanted the state to control every aspect of citizens' lives, including their thoughts.

Hobbes's idea that Natural Law would apply to people is of considerable importance to psychology. He said that there are laws inherent in nature, existing apart from humanity's recognition of them, that govern everything from the planetary machine of the solar system to the biological machines of the animals, including humans. Hobbes's attitude, however, is not fully scientific, for he says that we rationally consent to follow Natural Laws. Only in times of security must we follow them; they may be broken should government or other persons try to compel anyone to personal ruin. The planets cannot choose to obey or not obey Newton's laws of motion, and in this respect Hobbes's Natural Laws are not like the laws of physics.

Determinism Extended: Baruch Spinoza (1632–1677)

Spinoza was a thinker out of step with his own time. Born a Jew, but excommunicated for his disbelief in Yahweh, he articulated a philosophy that identified God with nature and saw the state as merely a revocable social agreement. He was spurned by the people of his birth and denounced by Christians, and his works were suppressed even in the liberal state of Holland where he lived. In the Enlightenment, he was admired for his independence but rejected for his pantheistic philosophy. Later, the Romantics venerated his apparent mysticism, and scientists saw in him a naturalist.

Spinoza's philosophy begins with metaphysics and ends with a radical reconstruction of human nature. Spinoza argued that God is essentially nature. Without the existing natural world, nothing would exist, so that God (nature) is the supporter and creator of all things. But God is not a separate being apart from nature; all things are a part of God without exception, and God is no more than the totality of the universe. Hence, Spinoza was thought to be an atheist. Furthermore, nature (God) was held to be entirely deterministic. Spinoza argued that to understand anything means to unravel its efficient causes. Spinoza denied the existence of final causes, believing teleology to be a projection of humanity's feelings of purpose onto nature, applied only to events we cannot explain with efficient—that is, deterministic—causes.

Spinoza extended his deterministic analysis to human nature. Mind is not something separate from body but is produced by brain processes. Mind and body are one but may be viewed from two aspects: as physiological brain processes or as mental events—thoughts. Spinoza did not deny that mind exists, but he saw it as one aspect of a fundamentally material nature. Thus, for Spinoza, mental activity is as deterministic as bodily activity. Spinoza rejected Cartesian dualism, and so for him there is no problem of interaction. We feel we are free, but this is only an illusion. If we properly understood the causes of human behavior and thinking, we would see we are not free. Just as no blame can be attached to the river that floods and destroys a town, so no blame can be attached to a multiple murderer. Society can act to control the river or the killer, to prevent future devastation, but this is a pragmatic consideration rather than a moral one. Spinoza's account of responsibility thus calls for a psychological science to unravel the causes of human behavior, and it bears a striking resemblance to B. F. Skinner's.

Spinoza, however, went on to describe an ethics of self-control that transcended materialistic determinism and, to some degree, conflicted with the rest of his thought. He argued that right action and thinking depend on the control of bodily emotions by reason. The wise person is one who follows the dictates of reason rather than the dictates of the momentary and conflicting passions arising from the body. Reason will lead one to act out of enlightened self-interest—helping others as one would want to be helped. Spinoza's ethics and his views of humanity are quite Stoic. The physical universe is beyond our control, but our passions are not. Thus, wisdom is rational self-control, rather than a futile effort to control nature or God. Spinoza also argued that governments should allow freedom of thought, conscience, and speech, for each person should be free to order his or her mind as he or she sees fit.

Wagering on God: Blaise Pascal (1623–1662)

Blaise Pascal was a remarkable figure. He participated significantly in the Scientific Revolution by investigating something traditional physics said could not exist, a vacuum. As a mathematician, he was a child prodigy, constructing at age 19 an early mechanical calculator. Although its purpose was humble—to help his father, a tax official, do calculations—its implication was profound. Pascal wrote: "The arithmetical machine produces effects which approach nearer to thought than all the actions of animals" (Bronowski & Mazlish, 1960). Pascal was the first to sense that the human mind could be conceived as an information processor capable of being mimicked by a machine, a concept central to contemporary cognitive psychology.

Yet at the same time, Pascal prefigures the worried intellectuals of the nineteenth century who mourned at God's funeral (Wilson, 1999) and the anguished existentialist of the twentieth century (Sartre, 1943). For Descartes, doubt led to the triumphant certainty of reason; for Pascal, doubt led to worse doubt. Wrote Pascal: I am "engulfed in the infinite immensity of spaces whereof I know nothing and which know nothing of me, I am terrified" (Bronowski & Mazlish, 1960). Pascal detested Descartes's excessive rationalism and derived solace and truth from his faith in God. For Pascal, what is essential in humans is not natural reason, but will and the capacity for faith—that is, the heart. Pascal thus resembles earlier Christian skeptics such as Montaigne. But Pascal is Cartesian in the value he places on self-consciousness, as shown by his statement in the *Pensées*: "Man knows that he is wretched. He is wretched, then, because he is wretched; but he is great, because he knows it. . . . Man is only a reed, the frailest thing in nature; but he is a thinking reed." Pascal doubted a person's capacity to fathom nature or to understand self—humanity is wretched. Yet, a human's unique self-consciousness lifts him or her above nature and the animals, offering salvation through faith in the Christian God.

Pascal's most important contribution to the modern world was his launching a new way of thinking about belief and action. People have to make decisions based on uncertain and incomplete information. Archeology tells us that humans were gambling about as soon as symbols could be etched onto bones, making simple dice. However, the idea of calculating probabilities and relating these to proposed wagers in order to bet rationally did exist until Pascal came along. Modern economics and finance would be impossible without Pascal's remarkable work (Glimcher, 2003), as would things such as scientific agriculture industrial quality control, and statistical experimentation in psychology (Gigerenzer et al., 1989).

Interestingly, this work began for Pascal with trying to convince unbelievers to accept the existence of God. He asked atheists to consider the following bet akin to betting on the flip of a coin. Either God exists or He does not exist. Your choice is to believe in—bet on—the existence of God, or to disbelieve in—bet against—the existence of God. Now we must consider the outcomes of each choice. If you believe in God and He does not exist, you have lost nothing. If you disbelieve in God and he does not exist, you have lost nothing. If you believe in God, and he exists, you reap the infinite and eternal rewards of heaven. If you disbelieve in God and He exists, you suffer the infinite and eternal sufferings of Hell. Even if the probability of God's existence is extremely small—anything other than zero, if fact, the rational choice is to believe in God.

Pascal is creating here a general framework for making any sort of decision, or as it is technically known today, decision making or judgment under uncertainty. What one should do is list his or her options, quantify the value of each combination of choice and possible outcome, estimate the probability of each outcome, and multiply the outcome's value with its probability to get what's called the expected value of each choice. Then you should make the choice with the greatest expected value. In the case of Pascal's wager with the atheist, the expected value of betting on God's existence > the expected value of God's nonexistence unless p (God exists) = 0. Try doing this exercise with one of your state's lottery games. The card tells you the possible prizes and their probabilities, so all you have to do is the math of multiplying one by the other to get the expected values. In this case you have to also figure in the cost of buying the lottery ticket. Thus if a ticket costs $5.00, the value of losing is $-$5.00, the value of not playing is $0, whether or not the number you would have gotten wins, and the value of winning is the stated prize minus $5.00. The structure of a psychological experiment is similar. The experimental and control groups are the two bets, the measured outcomes are the values of the bet, and statistical inference tells you whether you should, before running the experiment, have "bet" on the null hypothesis or the experimental hypothesis.

Other mathematicians and scientists built on Pascal's ideas, constructing sophisticated systems for making decisions of all sorts (e.g., it's what hedge fund managers do). For us here, there are two points to note. What Pascal and his followers did was to turn risk-taking into a quantifiable affair. Fundamental to modernity is risk-taking entrepreneurship and the related field of insuring against risk. Without this work the modern world could not have come into existence. More psychologically, belief has now been connected to action—behavior—in a powerful way. Philosophers had traditionally ended their psychological inquiries with the establishment of certain belief, as for example in Aristotle's human *mind*. Pascal's work goes beyond this to link belief—even less than certain belief—to actions and consequences in the outside world. In psychology, this line of thinking would culminate in American pragmatism, an important modernist philosophy, and through the pragmatists, most importantly William James and John Dewey, in the movements of functional psychology and behaviorism, wherein belief *becomes* action.

Still, in Pascal's time, and to someone with his sensibilities, the implication that thought might be material calculation both in his computer and his brain was frightening, for it meant that reason—which Descartes exempted from his mechanical system—could not be so exempted. Perhaps animals, wholly mechanical creatures according to Descartes, *do* reason. Pascal then declared that a human's free will, not reason, is what distinguishes humans from animals. He was the first modern to assert the claim of the heart and the emotions against the claims of intellectual rationality, writing, "The heart has its reasons that reason does not understand." Note that he is setting two kinds of reason against one another. He does not say that emotions are irrational and we should follow them anyway, rather that emotion has its own sort of reason that should be heeded. In this, Pascal anticipates strands of research into decision making that conclude that feeling is often the cause of good decision making, not its opponent (Glimcher, 2003; Lehrer, 2009). It is the heart, not the brain, that makes a human being human.

CONCLUSION: THE THRESHOLD OF MODERNITY

The seventeenth century laid the foundations for the Enlightenment of the eighteenth century. The Newtonian-Cartesian mechanical universe had no room for miracles, oracles, visions, or Descartes's soul. In the eighteenth century, science and reason would further replace religion as the chief intellectual institution of modern society. Human beings would be proclaimed soulless machines, and societies would be overthrown in the name of material happiness. Moreover, science's powerful grasp of the laws of nature would make possible the technology created by the Industrial Revolution, and science's mode of investigation—the steady accumulation, transmission, an application of systematically gained knowledge—created the mind-set of modernity.

The triumph of reason in the Age of Reason was at hand. Yet, a different undercurrent lurked just below the surface. The voyages of discovery had found strange, primitive cultures. To Hobbes and Locke, these wild men represented humanity in an uncivilized and unhappy state of Nature. Locke wrote in his *Second Treatise on Government*: "In the beginning all the world was America." Yet, were the Indians unhappy? Close to nature and unfettered by artifice, they lived according to natural instinct. Perhaps happiness lies in giving up reason, with its abstract, artificial ways, and returning to the instinct of the happy savage. A reaction against reason was about to set in. The poet Chaulieu wrote in 1708 that reason is an "inexhaustible source of errors, poison that corrupts the natural feelings" (Hazard, 1963, p. 396). Jean-Jacques Rousseau wrote that reason "feeds our mad pride . . . continually masking us from ourselves." Asked Rousseau: "Which is the least barbarous . . . reason which leads you astray, or instinct which guides [the Indian] truly?" Chaulieu said he came "to destroy the altars which have been raised to thee [Reason]." Here the seed is sown for the Romantic Rebellion against reason and for the concept of the Noble Savage. The tension between the individual and society, so poignantly felt by Sigmund Freud, was increasing as reason demanded more and more of men and women.

The Enlightenment 1700–1815

THE ENLIGHTENMENT

What Was the Enlightenment?

> Enlightenment is man's release from his self-incurred
> tutelage. Tutelage is man's inability to make use
> of his understanding without direction from an-
> other. . . . Sapere aude! Have courage to use your own
> reason—that is the motto of enlightenment. . . . If
> we are asked, "Do we now live in an enlightened
> age?" the answer is, "No," but we do live in an age of
> enlightenment. (Kant, 1784/1995. pp. 1, 5)

Who were the "others"—Kant called them guardians—who
wanted to direct our thinking? They were the traditional
leaders of European society, priests (or ministers), and aristocrats. Replacing these guardians defined the mission of
the Enlightenment: applying reason and scientific knowledge to human life, and replacing the static view of society
defined by biblical truths and traditional beliefs with a dynamic, progressive vision of history (Porter, 2000). The aim
was to replace religion (the priest) and tradition (the aristocrat) with the study of nature—science—and the result of
the Enlightenment was the beginning of the secularization
of European thought (Porter, 2000; R. Smith, 1995).

The lamp of the Enlightenment was Isaac Newton.
As Alexander Pope had written in eulogy of Newton, now
carved over the fireplace in the room where Newton was
born, "Nature and nature's laws lay hid in night/God said
let NEWTON be, and there was light." Newton provided
the light of the Enlightenment, and the philosophes set out
to do for human affairs what Newton had done for the affairs of the universe. During the course of the eighteenth
century, literacy spread, and as it did so, books of popular
science and novels replaced works of theology as best sell-
ers (Outram, 2005): Ordinary people became able to heed

From Chapter 6 of *A History of Psychology: From Antiquity to Modernity*, Seventh Edition.
Thomas Hardy Leahey. Copyright © 2013 by Pearson Education, Inc. All rights reserved.

The State Capital Building in Richmond, Virginia, designed by Thomas Jefferson. The American Founders were deeply influenced by the classical world, and this is an outstanding example of Greek Revival architecture. It recalls the Parthenon as an expression of selfconfidence, in this time of a new society just making its way along a radically democratic path. It was in the eighteenth century that the idea of a science of human nature began, and it would be in America that it would flourish. The classical revival poet Alexander Pope linked the eras in his Essay on Man, "Know then thyself/Presume not God to scan/The proper study of Mankind is Man." *(ELIZABETH LEAHEY MARTINEZ/Thomas Hardy Leahey)*

Kant's admonition to *sapere aude!* In short, the Enlightenment is the hinge between the old world and the modern world (Blanning, 2000a).

Enlightenment played out differently in different countries (Jacob, 2001; Outram, 2005; Porter, 2001). Histories of the Enlightenment used to focus on France as the center of the Enlightenment, claiming that as one moved away from Paris the light got dimmer (Porter, 2001), but this picture has been rejected. The Enlightenment effectively began in Britain (Porter, 2000) with the writings of John Locke (see later). There, the reign of medieval absolutism was gradually replaced by a constitutional monarchy and a parliamentary democracy. Enlightenment intellectuals were not persecuted nor were their writings suppressed or censored. British philosophers did not denounce religion. Locke wrote a book called *The Reasonableness of Christianity*, and while David Hume (see later discussion) was an atheist and skeptical of religious miracles, he did not regard religion as sinister.

In Prussia, the leading German state, Enlightenment allied with the existing autocratic government of Frederick the Great. Frederick created a rationally ordered, bureaucratic government in which he was more chief bureaucrat than divine king. Prussians applied Newton's mechanical model of the universe to the state. Johann von Justi, a leading political theorist, wrote, "A properly constituted state must be exactly analogous to a machine in which the wheels and gears are precisely adjusted to one another" and subject to the will of one man (quoted by Outram, 2005, p. 96). The example of Prussia shows that Enlightenment thinkers were not always partisans of democratic government but of rational, scientifically based government. They cared more that governments govern well than that they govern by consent of the governed (Porter, 2001).

Among Britain's North American colonies, Enlightenment philosophes such as Thomas Jefferson and James Madison were able to create a new, rationally ordered government on what amounted to a Lockean political blank slate. Separated from kings and aristocrats by the Atlantic Ocean, and home to a congeries of Protestant denominations—none of whom could become a dominant established church—the American founders in the Constitution and Declaration of Independence wrought a secular, philosophically justified "New order of the ages" (see the back of a dollar bill under the pyramid). In doing so, they created a uniquely individualistic form of society that would be especially receptive to psychology. In Russia, Czars Peter the Great and Catherine the Great tried to impose enlightenment on the Prussian model, but it never developed deep roots in Russian culture (Pipes, 1995).

Rather than being the standard setter for Enlightenment, France was the anomaly because there, Enlightenment was alienated from political power (Porter, 2001). The Bourbon monarchy subjected all publications to strict censorship, and unlike in Britain or Germany, intellectuals were excluded from positions of political influence. There was no parliament to act as a check on royal power or to speak for ordinary people. The Catholic Church—itself a hierarchical institution—was the official Church, and French philosophes developed a strong hatred of religion as a baneful institution that tried to keep its believers in a state of ignorance—the enemy of Kant's dare to know. French thinkers similarly regarded tradition as "the stupid veneration of the peoples for ancient laws and customs," as Claude Helvetius put it (quoted by Hampson, 1982, p. 126), another means by which to keep the populace in tutelage. As a result, French philosophes tended to push Cartesian, Newtonian, and Lockean ideas to extremes not found elsewhere. French philosophes had intellectual brilliance and fame, but they had little stake in existing social institutions, and so wanted to tear them down, which happened, bloodily and temporarily, in the French Revolution. The radical utopianism of the French Enlightenment is well conveyed in this passage from the Marquis de Condorcet's (1743–1794) Sketch for a Historical Picture of the Human Mind:

> The time will come when the sun will shine only on free men who know no master but their reason. . . . How consoling for the philosopher who laments the errors, the crimes, the injustices which still pollute the earth and of which he is often the victim, is this view of the human race, emancipated from its shackles, released from the empire of fate and from that of the enemies of progress, advancing with a firm and sure step along the path of truth, virtue and happiness. (Condorcet 1793/1995, p. 30)

Condorcet was an early leader of the French Revolution, but even his radicalism was too moderate for the leaders of the later Revolution, when it sank into terror. He lost his political position and was hounded by the Revolution until he committed suicide. Nevertheless, Condorcet's Sketch was the "great essay" that guided American Progressivism according to its leading philosopher and early president of the APA, John Dewey (1917).

The key Enlightenment concept was nature (Porter, 2000), often written Nature to suggest it might replace God. Especially important was human nature. The Abbé de Mably wrote,

"Let us study man as he is in order to teach him what he should be" (quoted by Smith, 1995, p. 88), and Denis Diderot (1713–1784) wrote, "Man is the single place from which we must begin and to which we must refer everything" (quoted by Smith, 1995, p. 102). In order to reform society along scientific lines, it was necessary to inquire scientifically into human nature. Once human nature was understood, society and government could be reordered to suit human nature, and virtue and happiness would follow. In the eighteenth century, the human sciences began to become socially important because their findings would be used by reformers and revolutionaries to construct better societies. Psychology was no longer a mere philosophical inquiry into the human mind—though it remained that, too—it became the basis for social engineering.

Unfortunately, these "Newtons of the Mind" (Gay, 1966/1969), as many of them styled themselves, did not agree on what human nature was, raising troubling questions about human knowledge and human morals. Pursuing epistemology within the new framework of the Way of Ideas, philosophical psychologists came to question whether we could know the world as it is, or even if we could know with certainty that there is a reality outside the Cartesian Theater. Pursuing the study of social and moral behavior in the spirit of Newton and discarding centuries of religious and traditional teachings, philosophical psychologists disagreed about whether human beings were innately evil (as Hobbes had suggested), were innately virtuous, or whether there was any human nature at all outside what society made of it.

The epistemological and moral questions are interrelated. If we cannot know anything with certainty, then we cannot know right from wrong with certainty. By the end of the century, especially after the horrors of the French Revolution, some thinkers began to worry about the dangers of rational inquiry into human nature and society. As Plato had suggested, if skepticism is correct, then not only is nature mysterious, so is morality. Bishop Joseph Butler (1692–1752) saw the practical danger in rethinking morality: "Foundations of morality are like all other foundations; if you dig too much about them the structure will come tumbling down" (quoted by Dworkin, 1980, p. 36). The philosophes made it possible for a sophisticated young man to say to his father, "The point is, father, that in the last resort the wise man is subject to no laws. . . . the wise man must judge for himself when to submit and when to free himself from them." Stripped of the certainties of religion and tradition, the father could only reply, "I should not be too worried if there were one or two people like you in the town, but if they all thought that way I should go and live somewhere else" (quoted by Hampson, 1982, p. 190).

The Industrial Enlightenment

The modern world, and thus modernity—our modern way of life—is rooted in the Industrial Revolution that created the cornucopia of wealth and personal possibilities we enjoy today. In the developed world, few people must seriously worry about having enough to eat to survive to tomorrow; nor are our lives constrained by the static social roles of premodern times. Historians and economists have investigated the causes of the Industrial Revolution almost since it began. We have already touched on some of the alleged causes, such as the rise of free cities and Europe that stood outside the feudal system and encouraged entrepreneurship. Others include the rise of institutions such as banking and insurance, the shift from animal sources of power to coal, and even the spread of entrepreneurial genes (Clark, 2007). Recently, attention has shifted to the role ideas played in the making of the Industrial Revolution, to what Mokyr (2002, 2009) calls the Industrial Enlightenment, and to a shift in social values from noble *arête* to bourgeois self-control (McCloskey, 2010).

What changed in human life about 1780 was the tremendous growth in wealth. Sometimes the origin of this new wealth has been ascribed to trade, which certainly did increase in the eighteenth century. However, profitable trade was carried on by humans from the beginning of time (Ridley, 2010), and therefore while trade was important to the spread of wealth, it was less important to its generation. Instead, the key to wealth creation was technologically driven innovation (Mokyr, 2009).

In this respect the prior Scientific Revolution was important to the Industrial Revolution, but not in the way it is often explained. Scientific research did not lead to critical technological advances, such as the invention of the steam engine or the water pump; they were clever inventions devised by nonscientists. However, the possibility of technological breakthroughs was encouraged by modes of thought brought into being by the Scientific Revolution, especially as expounded by Francis Bacon and first brought into effect in Bacon's home country Britain, where the Industrial Revolution began. Almost alone at the beginning of the Scientific Revolution, Bacon emphasized that the point of inquiry into nature was to gain power over it. Ancient philosophers and proto-scientists had viewed natural philosophy as a rather passive affair, observing nature closely in order to contemplate nature's transcendent Truth. Experimentation was frowned upon as ignoble, associated with slaves and merchants, not academic philosopher-kings and leisured aristocrats. Bacon, on the other hand, emphasized experimentation, bending nature to human will, and application, using scientific knowledge to improve the human condition. He emphasized the accumulation and constant sifting and proofing of scientific ideas, and the dissemination of these ideas as widely as possible. In other times and places, discoveries tended to be kept secret and not made known for others to build upon. It was Bacon's new scientific attitude that created the Scientific Enlightenment and thus the Industrial Revolution, not the new theories of the early scientists such as Newton. In the nineteenth century, as the Industrial Revolution spread to the rest of Europe, scientific discovery eventually came to play the role it has in today's economy, vastly increasing the sum of human wealth in the Second Industrial Revolution of 1860 and later (Mokyr, 2009).

A key psychological and sociological change also occurred in the eighteenth century, the collapse of the aristocratic set of values built up by the ancient Greeks. As late as the American Revolution, elite values reflected ancient Greek ideals of arête. In 1776, the legislature of the state of Virginia almost adopted as the motto for its state seal the phrase, *Deus nobis haec otia fecit*, "God bestowed upon us this leisure" (Wood, 2009, Kindle location 676). Such a motto reflected the antique notion that the natural rulers of society were people who did not have to work for a living, whose duty, therefore was to tend to the nation's interest rather than their personal interest or the interest of their occupation. Politically ambitious people who had made their own fortunes rather than inheriting them in the aristocratic way typically got out of business as quickly as they could, bought land and built country houses, wore aristocratic clothes, and cultivated aristocratic tastes. They regarded themselves as "the better sort," and looked down upon "the meaner sort," "the ruder sort," and "the lower sort."

They also looked down upon "the middling sort," but the middling sorts were the rising makers of the Industrial Revolution who were beginning to achieve self-consciousness and to reject the ancient Greek value of noble arête, aiming to bring "gentlemen . . . down to our level" so that "all ranks and conditions would come in for their just share of the wealth" (Wood, 2009, Kindle location 712). This new and rising middle class adopted and above all made respectable (McCloskey, 2010) a new set of virtues quite different from ancient arête. It stressed acquisitiveness and upward social mobility, not conformity to a static, God-ordained social hierarchy; it stressed work, not leisure; it stressed thrift, not the conspicuous display of riches; it stressed education in the practical arts and sciences for all, not education in fine art and philosophy for a few. In short, the modern middle-class virtues turned arête upside down. As historian Roy Porter (2001) put it, people stopped asking how to be good (arête) and asked instead, How to be happy? As we will soon see, the utilitarian calculus of happiness is a psychological key to the modern world.

Speaking for the new American Republic, the revolutionary Thomas Paine (1737–1809) really spoke for the emerging Enlightened world when he wrote, "We see with other eyes; we hear with other ears; and think with other thoughts, then those we formerly used. . . . The mind once enlightened cannot again become dark" (quoted by Wood, 2009, Kindle location 880). As Paine implies, the great change taking place was less material than psychological, and seeing with new eyes raised new challenges for the emerging science of human nature, resulting in new conceptions of human mind and behavior.

THE SKEPTICAL QUESTION: IS KNOWLEDGE ATTAINABLE?

When the philosophers of the eighteenth century investigated human nature in the spirit of Newtonian science, they reopened the old Greek problem of the possibility of human knowledge in a new naturalistic context. Is the human mind endowed by nature with the power to know truth, or are we limited to opinion, as the skeptics said? An irony of the Scientific Revolution is that while it represented a great triumph of human reason, it nevertheless cast doubt on the very possibility of human knowledge. In Newton's wake came philosopher-psychologists such as John Locke who examined the human mind and human nature in the light of Newtonian reason and concluded that no human opinion was free from the possibility of error, and that the very existence of the physical world was open to doubt. These were the conclusions of the British philosophers George Berkeley and David Hume, and they were, unsurprisingly, stoutly resisted by philosophers loathe to give up the possibility of secure human knowledge. Against the skepticism of Hume, the Scottish followers of Thomas Reid asserted commonsense faith in human cognition and religious faith in God, who made men and women so that they might know God's world. In Germany, Immanuel Kant responded to Hume's skepticism by asserting the old claim that metaphysics was science's true foundation, but in doing so created mysteries of his own.

Human Understanding: John Locke (1632–1704)

John Locke was a friend of the scientists Isaac Newton and Robert Boyle (in whose laboratory he assisted), a member of the Royal Society, adviser and tutor to noble politicians, and, at times, a practicing physician. As we might expect, therefore, Locke brought a practical and empirical bent to his philosophy. His major work in psychology was *An Essay Concerning Human Understanding* (1690), which he started writing in 1671. Like Descartes, Locke wanted to understand how the human mind works—the sources of its ideas and the limitations of human knowledge. Locke, however, as befits a physician and practical politician, was less in the grip of a comprehensive metaphysical system than was Descartes. His picture of the mind was straightforward and, to English-speakers who follow after him, commonsensical. Nevertheless, the picture of the mind painted by Locke differs from Descartes's only in details.

Locke (1690/1975) asked what the human mind knows and then answered, "Since the Mind, in all its thoughts and Reasonings, hath no other immediate Object but its own *Ideas* . . . it is evident, that our Knowledge is only conversant about them." Like Descartes, Locke revived the copy theory of cognition, holding that ideas are mental representations of objects. The mind does not know Forms or Essences, or even objects themselves, but its own ideas only. Where do our ideas come from? "To this I answer, in one word, From Experience: In that, all our knowledge is founded and derived. Our Observation employed either about *external, sensible objects; or about the internal*

XAM'S BLOG 1
Who's Modern? Descartes and Locke

I've noticed that in your philosophy courses and text, "modern philosophy" begins with Descartes as the founder of modern rationalism and Locke as the founder of modern empiricism. But the differences between are very deep, notwithstanding the fact that their pictures of the mind are variations on the theme of ideas. I think of them as bookends on different shelves of a library. Descartes is the bookend that closes out premodern thought, and Locke is the bookend sitting at the beginning of modern thought.

Descartes participated in the early decades of the Scientific Revolution, but died well before its triumph in Newton's *Principia Mathematica*. Indeed, he probably would have disapproved of Newton's apparent backsliding into premechanistic thinking in his treatment of gravity as an unseen force acting mysteriously at a distance. This disapproval is, in fact, a facet of Descartes's living at the interface between premodern and modern. He had to fight hard for the new scientific, mechanistic worldview, and like a politician driven by an ideology he would have found it hard to tolerate any compromise with the past. Newton, living later and in a more tolerant country, simply posed a theory that met his needs without worrying about metaphysics. Descartes tried to look the future, but always remained focused on old metaphysical and religious issues such as the nature of the soul.

Locke, on the other hand, was the founding thinker of the Enlightenment (Porter, 2000). He was a friend of Newton, a physician, a tutor, and, most importantly, an adviser to the politicians who made the first modern political revolution, England's Glorious Revolution of 1688. Instead of being concerned to settle the universe's metaphysical hash (as William James once put it about himself), he set himself the more modest and practical goal of describing human nature as it was so that a government could be built around it. These days it's easy to see for yourself. Find an online text of Descartes's *Meditations* and a text of Locke's *Essay*, and see which feels more comfortable.

Operations of our Minds . . . is that which supplies our Understandings with all the materials of thinking. These two are the Fountains of Knowledge, from whence all the *Ideas* we have, or can naturally have, do spring" (pp. 104–105; italics in original). The first fountain of knowledge, or kind of experience, was *sensation*, resulting in ideas about the objects that cause sensations, including pleasures and pain. The second fountain of experience was *reflection*, observation of our own mental processes.

In positing the process of reflection, Locke tackled an important question about the mind that had been left open by Descartes. Descartes's radical reflexivity created the Cartesian Theater, which distanced the self from the experience that was projected to it on the screen of the pineal gland. According to Descartes, the self could observe and critically scrutinize the projected objects of consciousness. However, the degree to which the self could examine itself was unclear. Descartes was certain that he was a thinking thing (*res cogitans*), but he did not say that he knew *how* he thought. The two are not the same. Just as a high-wire walker knows that he or she can walk on a narrow wire without knowing how he or she does it, so it is possible that Descartes might know that he thinks without knowing how he thinks. Locke proposed that in addition to observing its own experience of the outside world—sensation—the self can observe its own mental processes—reflection.

The existence and trustworthiness of reflection have become an enduring problem for psychology. Immanuel Kant later answered Descartes's implicit question about self-knowledge in the negative, denying that reflection is possible at all. David Hume, on the other hand, failing to find a self, simply denied it existed, concluding that the mind was simply the sum total of its ideas. From psychology's founding as a science, research and theory have continued to divide on when, if ever, the mind can accurately observe its own operations. If it can, as Locke thought, then the task of psychology is simplified because hypotheses about mental processes can be directly tested by observation in the form of reflection. If it cannot, as most psychologists now believe (Kahneman, 2011), then hypotheses about mental processes can be tested only indirectly. It may be, then, that the inner workings of the human mind can never be known with certainty or that, perhaps, there are no mental processes at all, only functions of the brain.

If Descartes is usually held to be the father of modern rationalist philosophy, Locke is said to be the father of empiricism because he stated the empiricist principle that knowledge derives from experience alone. He proposed the famous simile for the mind—the *tabula rasa*, or piece of white paper, on which experience writes ideas. Locke, however, was not attacking Descartes's conception of innate ideas. Rather, he opposed a large number of English writers who believed in innate *moral principles*, seeing in them the foundations of Christian morality. Thus, these writers could say that it was God's law, implanted in the soul, that a person should believe in God; anyone who did not believe was depraved and as much a moral monster as a three-legged baby would be a physical monster. Indeed, Locke himself was widely denounced as a dangerous atheist for denying innate moral truths. Locke believed the idea of innate moral and metaphysical truths to be a pillar of dogmatism. The schools of his day used rote maxims as the basis of teaching. Students were to accept them and then prove them. Locke advocated a discovery principle. Students should keep open minds, discovering truth through experience and following their own talents, instead of being forced into the straitjacket of scholastic maxims.

The difference between Locke and Descartes on innate ideas was small. Descartes maintained that he found in himself ideas that he could not trace to experience, and so he concluded they were innate. But he did not insist that they be innate as fully formed ideas. Instead, he thought it was also possible that people share mental faculties that lead them to the same universal ideas (Gaukroger, 1995). This was certainly Locke's view. There is moreover a great deal of innate, active mental machinery in Locke's "empty" mind. For example, with Descartes, Locke said that language is a human, species-specific trait. He wrote in his *Essay*: "God having designed Man for a sociable Creature . . . furnished him also with language. . . . Parrots, and general other Birds, may be taught to make articulate sounds distinct enough, which yet, by no means, are capable of Language." Only humans can use articulate sounds to represent ideas. In his works on education, Locke held that much of a child's personality and abilities is innate. Man's basic motives, to seek happiness and avoid misery, are likewise "innate practical principles," although, of course, they have nothing to do with truth.

For Locke, the mind was not merely an empty room to be furnished by experience; rather, it was a complex, information-processing device prepared to convert the materials of experience into organized human knowledge. Direct experience provides us with simple ideas, which the mental machinery then elaborates on and combines into complex ideas. Knowledge comes about as we inspect our ideas and see how they agree or disagree. The bedrock of knowledge for Locke, as for Descartes, was intuitively self-evident propositions. For example, we know directly and intuitively, without possibility of error, that the colors black and white are not the same (they "disagree"). More complex forms of knowledge arise as we deduce consequences from self-evident propositions. Like Descartes, Locke believed that, in this way, all human knowledge, even ethics and aesthetics, could be systematized.

Locke also addressed an increasingly pressing problem as the scientific view that the world, and possibly people, are machines became more plausible. Do we have free will? As we have seen, thinkers such as Hobbes and Spinoza denied that we do, saying we are unfree. Locke first proposed an answer that has been popular ever since. Locke said that asking if the *will* is free is asking the wrong question. The proper question is whether *we* are free. Seen this way, the answer seemed to Locke straightforward. We are free when we are able to do what we want, but we do not consciously will our desires. Locke offered a parable in explanation. Imagine you have gone to a room to talk to someone fascinating. While you are in conversation, someone locks the door from the outside. In a sense, you are not free to leave, but as long as you do not want to leave, you never feel unfree. What matters, then, is freedom of action, not freedom of the will. We simply want what we want, and we all want happiness. As long as we are happy, getting what we wish, we feel free and do not worry about supposed "unfreedom of the will." The self, however, ought to control desire, for, in the long run, happiness will be determined by our lot in Heaven or Hell. The economist John Maynard Keynes repudiated Locke's long-range thinking when he said, "In the long run we are all dead."

Locke's version of the rational self radically separated from experience, which it can critically scrutinize as consciousness, proved enormously influential both in Britain, where later British philosophers built on it, and in France, where it was popularized by Voltaire as a less metaphysical, more straightforward picture of the mind than Descartes's. Nevertheless, in their psychological essentials, these two modern philosophies were strikingly alike, possessing differences of nuance, not substance.

Is There a World? Bishop George Berkeley (1685–1753)

BERKELEY'S IDEALISM　As a philosopher, Berkeley, like Descartes and Locke, wanted to place philosophy on new, secure foundations; but as a religious man, he feared that Newtonian materialism imperiled faith in God. He admired Locke and believed Locke had taken the correct road toward knowledge. However, Berkeley saw that the Cartesian-Lockean Way of Ideas opened the door to skepticism. Locke and Descartes believed in the existence of "real" objects that cause our perceptions, but Berkeley saw that their belief was really a matter of unjustifiable faith. The existence of the secondary sense properties casts doubt on the appealing assumption that ideas in consciousness simply reflect objects in the world. The skeptic might ask how we know that ideas, supposed copies of objects, resemble their originals in any respect at all. Perhaps the world is completely, not partially, different from the world of consciousness. Berkeley took the bold step of asserting that ideas were not copies of anything at all. They, not things, were the ultimate reality.

Berkeley believed that the skeptic's challenge derived from another assumption we all make—that matter, things, exist apart from our perceptions of them. For example, as I am sitting here word processing, I know my computer exists because I see and feel it. But when I leave the room, what grounds have I for asserting that the computer still exists? All I can say is that if I went back I would see it, or if someone else looks for it, he or she will see it. Ultimately, then, I know the computer exists only when I or someone else sees it. More strongly, Berkeley asserted that the computer exists only when it is perceived. Berkeley's famous motto was "*Esse est percipi*" (To exist is to be perceived). Berkeley thus refuted skepticism by an astoundingly simple assertion. Locke said that all we know are our ideas. Berkeley added that therefore ideas are all that exist. The question of how ideas correspond to "real objects" does not arise if there are no "real objects" at all. Furthermore, Berkeley's philosophy rebuts atheism, for God may now be introduced as the omniscient perceiver who sees all things and so continues their existence.

In a work on the history of psychology, we do not want to get embroiled in philosophical questions about what exists. It is best to view Berkeley as asking about the material world what Descartes asked about other minds. Descartes did not want us to give up our belief that other people have minds; Berkeley did not want us to give up our belief that the physical world exists. Thinking that only I have a mind and that everything else vanishes when I'm not around is impractical to the point of madness. Instead, as Descartes tried to figure out the psychological basis for our belief in other minds outside ours, Berkeley tried to figure out the psychological basis for our belief in a physical world outside our minds. Both engaged in radically reflexive introspection and set agendas for later psychological research.

WHY DO WE SEE THE WORLD IN THREE, NOT TWO, DIMENSIONS?   In this respect, Berkeley's analysis of depth perception is especially significant. An important ground for our belief in external objects is that we see objects in three dimensions, including a dimension of depth—a distance away from us; yet the retinal image, the immediate (or "proper") object of vision, is only two-dimensional, lacking depth. So, for example, as a friend walks away from you, you see him or her getting farther and farther away, but if we were to examine your retinal image, we would find only that the image of the friend gets smaller and smaller. You may observe that indeed your friend looks smaller, but your subjective experience is that he or she is only going farther away, not shrinking. The problem arises: How does one perceive three dimensions when one can only see (on the retina) two dimensions?

Berkeley's answer was that other sensations that do give cues about distance are available. For example, as an object approaches, we move the pupils of the eyes close together as we follow it; as it recedes, we move them apart. Thus, there is a regular association between an object's distance from us and the degree to which we cross our eyes to focus on it. (Berkeley and others found many additional distance cues.) So far, Berkeley's analysis of how we see depth is the foundation of modern analyses of depth perception. However, Berkeley went on to make the empiricist claim that the association must be learned. According to Berkeley's reasoning, infants would not know that a person was receding as the person walked away; infants would simply see the figure shrink. Berkeley's claim that depth perception must be learned was countered later by Immanuel Kant, who asserted that depth perception is innate. The controversy between the nativist and empiricist views continued for decades; not until the 1960s did experiments with infants show that Kant was reasonably correct (Bower, 1974).

The importance of Berkeley's argument becomes clearer if we generalize the problem to all visual experience. If you hold a blue book at right angles to your eyes, what do you see? The naive answer is to say "a book," yet, as Berkeley would argue, all you really see is a rectangular patch of blue, an idea, or mental object. If you rotate the book to a 45-degree angle, what do you see? Again, you want to say, "a book," and in fact you would still believe the book to be a rectangle. But Berkeley would say that what you are really seeing is a blue patch-idea that now has the shape of a truncated pyramid. Berkeley's argument is that all anyone ever sees is a collection of colored patches—ideas. One must learn to "see" them as books, people, cats, cars, and so on. One must learn to believe one is still seeing a rectangular book when, in fact, one is seeing a truncated-pyramid blue patch.

Berkeley's analysis of vision supported his idealism. One's sensory and ideational world is just a collection of sensations, and one believes in the permanence of objects only because certain collections of sensations are regularly associated. Belief in matter is therefore a learned inference only, for matter is not directly perceived.

Berkeley's philosophy of the mind became the basis for at least one important psychology of consciousness—E. B. Titchener's structuralism. Berkeley had said that we are born seeing the world as isolated sensations on a two-dimensional Cartesian screen of consciousness. Titchener's research aimed to describe the Cartesian screen as it is, without inferring the existence of objects. He taught students never to commit the "stimulus error," reporting as the object of introspection the thing that caused the stimuli they were to report. Instead, subjects were to describe pure consciousness as lines, curves, and color patches—pure sensations, the basic Berkeleyan building blocks of experience. Titchener also tried to show how we learn to associate stimuli together into complex ideas, such as a book or a person, in line with Berkeley's associative psychology.

Berkeley had established the ultimate in skepticism. He showed that belief in a physical world of permanent objects outside consciousness is not one that can be rationally justified, but is a psychological inference we learn to make. How, then, are we to get on with our lives, with philosophy, morality, and politics, if there are no certainties? An answer was found in human nature itself by the Scottish philosopher David Hume (Norton, 1982).

Living with Skepticism: David Hume (1711–1776)

> It is evident that all the sciences have a relation, greater or less, to human nature. . . . To explain the principles of human nature, we in effect propose a complete system of the sciences, built on a foundation almost entirely new, and the only one upon which they can stand with any security . . . and the only solid foundation we can give to this science itself must be laid on experience and observation. (Hume, 1817, *Treatise of Human Nature*, p. 172)

Locke began the attempt to replace metaphysics with psychology as the foundation for the other sciences, and Hume carried out the task in a rigorously Newtonian manner. Hume analyzed human nature as he found it in himself and in the behavior of others. Hume's aim was to replace metaphysics with psychology, his "science of human nature." He wound up showing that reason alone—the Cartesian essence of the human mind—was powerless to construct usable knowledge of the world. Hume has long been depicted as the great skeptic, the man who showed we can know nothing at all with certainty. It is better to regard him as the first postskeptical philosopher (Norton, 1993b). He believed that skepticism had been established by Berkeley and others, and wanted to move beyond skepticism to a practical philosophy that allowed us to live our lives without the certainties that Plato, Aristotle, and religion had pretended to give us. In essence, Hume taught that the philosophical quest for absolute certainty was a fool's errand, that human nature itself was enough on which to build fallible science and fallible morals.

CONTENTS OF THE MIND Hume began his inquiry into human nature by categorizing the contents of our minds somewhat as Locke and Descartes had. They had spoken of the contents of our minds as "ideas," for which Hume, following the Scottish moral philosopher Francis Hutcheson (1694–1746), substituted "perceptions." Perceptions are then divided into two types: impressions and ideas. Impressions are essentially what we today call sensations, and ideas were for Hume less vivid copies of impressions. Thus, you have an immediate impression of the book before you, an impression you may recall later on as an idea, a less vivid copy of the actual experience. Both impressions and ideas come either through sensation of external objects or through reflection, by which Hume meant our emotional experiences (or what Hume also called the *passions*). Passions are of two sorts: the violent passions, such as love, hate, and the other emotions we ordinarily call passions; and the calm passions, such as aesthetic and moral feelings. Figure 1 summarizes Hume's categories.

Finally, Hume distinguished *simple* and *complex* perceptions. A simple impression is a single, unanalyzable sensation, such as a blue spot of ink. Most impressions are complex because our senses are usually exposed to many simple sensations at once. Simple ideas are copies of simple impressions, and complex ideas are aggregates of simple ideas. This means that complex ideas may not exactly correspond to some complex impression; you may imagine a unicorn, which of course you have never seen. However, complex ideas may always be broken down into simple ideas, which are copies of simple impressions. Your complex idea of a unicorn combines the impression or idea of a horse

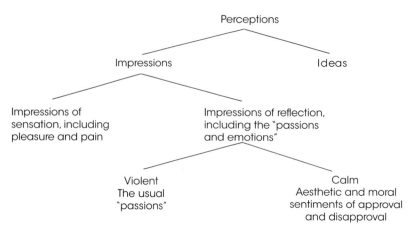

FIGURE 1 Hume's categorization of the contents of the human mind. *(Adapted from THE PHILOSOPHY OF DAVID, Smith, 1941; Macmillan, London.)*

with the impression or idea of a horn, both of which you have experienced. Before considering how complex perceptions are formed, two important conclusions can already be drawn from Hume's category of mental content. First, Hume gave priority to impressions over ideas. Impressions bring us directly in touch with reality by perception, but ideas can be false, corresponding to nothing (such as the unicorn). Truth is to be determined by tracing ideas to impressions, and whatever ideas are found to have no empirical content, such as the ideas of metaphysics and theology, are to be expunged. The second important conclusion is that Hume assigned priority to simple perceptions over complex ones. All complex perceptions are built up from our experiences of simple ones and can be completely analyzed into simple components. Hume was a psychological atomist, holding that complex ideas are built up out of simple sensations.

ASSOCIATION: THE GRAVITY OF THE MIND When we turn to how complex perceptions are built up out of elementary ones, we come to what Hume himself thought was his central contribution to the science of human nature: his doctrine of the *association* of ideas. The concept of association was not new with Hume. We have found it in Plato, Aristotle, Hobbes, and Berkeley; the phrase *association of ideas* was coined by Locke. However, they had used it in only a limited way—Locke, for example, saw in association an obstacle to clear thinking and sound education. What Hume prized was his use of association to inquire into fundamental philosophical and psychological questions. It was the chief theoretical tool of his new science.

Hume (1777/1962) wrote in his essay *An Inquiry Concerning Human Understanding*, "To me there appear to be only three principles of connection among ideas, namely, Resemblance, Contiguity in time or place, and Cause [and] Effect." In his *Abstract of a Treatise of Human Nature* (1740/1777/1962, p. 38), Hume (1740/1962, p. 302) exemplified each: "'resemblance'—a [portrait] naturally makes us think of the man it was drawn for; 'contiguity'—when St. Denis is mentioned, the idea of Paris naturally occurs; 'causation' when we think of the son we are likely to carry our attention to the father . . . [T]hese are the only links that bind the parts of the universe together or connect us with any person or object exterior to ourselves." At least, said Hume, "so far as regards the mind."

Hume's wording reveals the influence of Newton on eighteenth-century psychological thought. For Newton, gravity was the attractive force that binds the atomic parts of the universe together. For Hume, association "is a kind of attraction which in the mental world will be found to have as extraordinary effects as in the natural" (1817), and the laws of association "are really to us the cement of the universe" (1740/1777/1962, p. 302) as experienced. Thus, for Hume, complex human experience (complex ideas) is at root simple ideas (derived from impressions) united together by the principle of association. As Newton did with gravity, Hume thus made association into an ultimate principle that could not be reduced further.

Hume then proceeded to investigate human knowledge in light of these three (soon to be two) laws. Cause and effect is the most important law underlying most everyday reasoning. You will to lift your arm; it rises. You knock one billiard ball into another; the second one moves. You turn off a light switch; the light goes out. Cause and effect even lies at the root of the inference that a material world exists; for one assumes the world acts on the senses so as to cause one to perceive it. However, Hume asked, whence comes our knowledge of causation? Causes are never directly perceived. Rather, we perceive a regular conjoining of two events: the feeling of intention with the subsequent movement of the arm; the motion of one ball with the subsequent motion of the second; the flipping of the switch with the subsequent extinguishing of the light; the opening of the eyes with the appearance of things. Furthermore, no rational argument can be produced to prove causation. Hume argued that belief in causes is learned through experience. As a child experiences many regular conjunctions of events, a "propensity" of the child's mind leads to the firm conviction that the first event caused the second. This propensity also brings along a feeling of necessity. Causation is not simply correlation for Hume; it is a feeling of necessity between two events. This means, of course, that cause and effect is not a basic principle of association because it is reducible to contiguity plus the feeling of necessity.

Hume generalized his argument to all generalizations. When one claims "All swans are white," it is on the basis of experiencing a number of swans, all of which were white. One then assumes that future swans in one's experience will also be white and one therefore draws the conclusion. It is quite like assuming—based on past experiences—the light will go out when one flips the switch. In neither case, however, can the generalizations be given a rational justification, for they are based on experience, not on reason. No principle of reason underlies empirical generalizations. But we do make them, and Hume wanted to explain how we do so, in order to have a complete theory of human nature.

The principle Hume employed is the principle of custom or habit. In *Inquiry*, Hume (1740/1777/1962, p. 61) wrote: "For whenever the repetition of any particular act or operation produces a propensity to renew the same act or operation without being impelled by any reasoning or process of the understanding, we always say that this propensity is the effect of custom. . . . All inferences from experience . . . are effects of custom [habit], not of reasoning."

HUME'S ADAPTIVE SKEPTICISM   It was, and is, frequently assumed by Hume's readers that, by reducing causation and inductive generalization to habit, he is denying their validity, and that he must have been a total skeptic, surprised each morning to find that the sun had risen. This assumption is wrong (Smith, 1941). Hume wrote more as a psychologist than a philosopher, trying to find out *how* we reach causal and inductive conclusions rather than being concerned with their validity. He discovered that reason is not involved; but he did not therefore have to deny the validity of causation and induction. In fact, Hume (1740/1777/1962, p. 72) wrote, "as this operation from the mind, by which we infer effects from causes, and vice versa is so essential to the subsistence of all human creatures, it is not probable that it could be trusted to the fallacious deductions of our reason, which is slow . . . appears not, in any degree, during . . . infancy, and, at best, is . . . extremely liable to error and mistake." Further, the "wisdom of nature" has implanted in us this "instinct or mechanical tendency" that is "infallible in its operation" and appears at birth. Thus, the ability to form general conclusions, or habits, is founded on association, on our propensity to generalize from limited instances, and on our propensity to feel causes necessarily linked to effects. This ability to generalize is innate and "infallible," and of its operations we are "ignorant." Habit is a surer guide to the world than reason.

In support of this conclusion, Hume noted that the same generalizing tendency is present in animals. Their practical knowledge of the world is nearly faultless, yet they do not possess reason. Animals learn habits, and, according to Hume (1740/1777/1962, p. 111) "any theory by which we explain the operations of the understanding . . . in man will acquire additional authority if we find the same theory is requisite to explain the same phenomenon in other animals." Other philosophers had stressed humans' uniqueness, but Hume here stressed their similarity to animals, implying the value of a comparative approach to human and animal mind.

As a consequence of his views, Hume made a statement that seems startling coming from a philosopher in the Age of Reason. He writes in *A Treatise of Human Nature* (1817): "Reason is, and ought only to be the slave of the passions, and can never pretend to any other office than to serve and obey them." This is quite natural, given Hume's position. Reason is helpless to know reality; it must serve experience and the instinct for generalization, which reflect the world as it is. For Hume, morality is a matter of feeling (passion). We approve and disapprove the actions of ourselves and others according to how we feel about them, and reason must thus serve our moral sentiments.

Hume resisted skepticism by relying on human nature. As he and others pointed out, the most extreme skeptic never behaves according to his beliefs; he always assumes there will be a tomorrow. Hume (1740/1777/1962, p. 158) wrote in his *Inquiry*: "[N]o durable good can ever result from excessive skepticism," nor can it hope that "its influence will be beneficial to society." Hume preferred a moderate skepticism, one that accepts the limits of reason, properly values animal nature, and knows that general conclusions may be false (after all, there are black swans). Such a skepticism is practical (it does not doubt the accumulated wisdom of experience) and useful (it preaches toleration and provides a science of human nature for the proper founding of the other sciences).

Hume's system epitomized one of the two main ways of thinking about the mind that dominated the next century: associative empiricism. The other is Kantian idealism, which we shall meet presently. In Hume's version of the Cartesian Theater, the mind is all surface, the screen upon which sensations and images appear. Empiricists hold that one ought not believe in things that cannot be observed, and in this spirit Hume went searching for his self. However, he could find nothing in consciousness except sensations of the world and the body, and as a good empiricist, Hume concluded that like God, the self was an illusion. He was never happy with this conclusion, but could see no way around it. Thus, in Hume's view, the mind is a collection of sensations bound together by association. The job of psychology, then, was to catalog the sensory elements of the mind and describe how the laws of association bind them together as gravity binds together physical elements.

In Hume's work, we also see the first glimmerings of the psychology of adaptation. At bottom, human knowledge is habit, whether mental as with Hume, or behavioral as with the behaviorists. Hume stressed the practical knowledge of the everyday world that lets us adapt to our environment, as would post-Darwinian American and British psychologists. Hume appealed to human continuity with animals, as would psychologists after Darwin, especially the behaviorists. Hume viewed feeling—the passions—as an essential part of human nature. A person is not a pure rational soul locked in a material, passionate body, as Plato held. Finally, in preferring one theory to another because of its social and practical utility, Hume also anticipated those American psychologists for whom one defect of structuralism was its avowed practical inutility.

As had Socrates, the Sophists, and the atomists, Hume annoyed minds incapable of living without at least the possibility of knowing fixed and eternal truths. Although Hume simply taught how to live in a world without absolute certainties, his critics took him to be much more dangerous. For them, Hume was at worst an atheistical advocate of skepticism, reveling in the destruction of knowledge, or at best a dead end, demonstrating by his skepticism the necessary futility of empiricist philosophy. In reply, Hume's critics cited God-given common sense or alleged proofs of the necessary character of all experience.

Associationism

The doctrine of association of ideas as developed by Locke, Berkeley, and Hume, provided a simple, potentially scientific, yet flexible theory of the human cognitive processes. David Hartley's (1705–1757) *Observations on Man* (1749/1971) further developed associationism as a psychological doctrine and provided a speculative neurophysiological theory to explain the mental laws of association, taking a step toward the uniting of mental and medical science. Although Hartley's psychological ideas often resembled Hume's, Hartley developed them from the work of John Gay (1699–1745). In typical Enlightenment fashion, Hartley strove to see the mind through Newtonian eyes, and even adopted Newton's own proposals about the operations of the nerves.

Hartley believed in a close correspondence between mind and brain, and he proposed parallel laws of association for both. He was not a strict parallelist like Leibniz, however, for he believed that mental events causally depend on neural events. Beginning with the mental sphere, Hartley built up the mind from simple atomic units of sensation, as did Hume. Our sensory contact with a perceivable quality (what Hartley called an *impression*) causes a sensation (similar to Hume's impression) to arise in the mind. If the mind copies the sensation, this constitutes a simple idea of sensation (comparable to Hume's simple ideas), which may be compounded via association to form complex intellectual ideas (comparable to Hume's complex ideas). Turning to the physiological substrate of association formation, Hartley adopted Newton's theory of nervous vibrations, which said that the nerves contain submicroscopic particles whose vibrations pass along through the nerves and constitute neural activity. An impression started the sensory nerve-substance vibrating, and this vibration passed to the brain where it brought a sensation to the mind. Repeated occurrence created a tendency in the cortex to permanently copy this vibration as a smaller vibration, or vibratiuncle, corresponding to an idea.

Hartley's associationism was quite popular. Joseph Priestley (1733–1804), a great chemist and the co-discoverer of oxygen, propounded it to the public and defended it against critics. It was also quite influential in artistic and literary circles, because it deeply affected the critical sensibility of turn-of-the-century artists, especially the romantics. (Coleridge named his eldest son David Hartley.) In the long run, associationism eventually gave rise to analysis of behavior in terms of associated habits. Because Hartley said pleasure and pain accompanied sensations and so affected thought and action, associationism linked up with utilitarianism.

**Associationism: David Hartley's (1706–1757)
Physiological Theory**

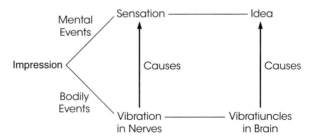

FIGURE 2 Associationism: David Hartley's (1706–1757) Physiological Theory

The Reassertion of Common Sense: The Scottish School

Some of Hume's philosophical countrymen regarded Hume as having falling victim to a sort of "metaphysical lunacy"—total skepticism. These philosophers asserted the claims of the common person against the abstruse speculations of philosophy. "I despise philosophy, and renounce its guidance—let my soul dwell with Common Sense," wrote Thomas Reid, the founder of the movement. In addition to Reid (1710–1796), other members of the Scottish School included James Beattie (1735–1803), popularizer and polemicist against Hume, and Reid's student, Dugald Stewart (1753–1828).

REVIVING REALISM Reid did not object to scientifically inquiring into the workings of the human mind, writing, "it must be by an anatomy of the mind that we can discover its powers and principles (quoted by Porter, 2000, p. 163). But Reid did believe that philosophy had begun to go astray with the creation of the Cartesian Theater (though he did not use the term) and the Way of Ideas (his phrase). According to the model of Descartes and Locke, the mind is not acquainted with objects themselves, but only with their copies—ideas—projected into consciousness. Here, Reid thought, was the first step toward skepticism, because if the mind works as Descartes and Locke say, then there is no way of ensuring that ideas are veridical copies of objects; we can never inspect objects themselves and compare them to their representations. In a contemporary parallel, imagine inserting into a copying machine an original document that we have not seen, and are then allowed to look only at the copies. We assume that the copies resemble the original, but because we cannot look at the original itself, we cannot justify our assumption. Had Berkeley seen the same problem, he would have responded by saying there was no original document. For Berkeley, the "copy machine," the mind itself, made the "copies" out of bits and pieces of sensations, but the "copies" correspond to no original. As long as the machine of the mind produced stable and coherent experience, we could study it and build science on it.

Reid founded *commonsense philosophy* by eliminating the copier; he returned to the older, intuitively appealing, Aristotelian view that perception simply records the world as it is. He maintained that there are three, not four, elements in perception: the perceiver, the act of perception, and the real object. There is no separate stage of representation as in the Cartesian Theater. Our perceptual acts make direct contact with objects, not only with their representative ideas. We know the world in a direct, unmediated way that is consistent with what each of us believes without the misleading tutoring of philosophy. This view is known to philosophers as direct *realism*, in contradistinction to Descartes's, Locke's, and Hume's representational realism and Berkeley's and Kant's *idealism*.

Reid also raised two issues that were important to later psychology. First, Reid rejected the theory found in Berkeley, Locke, Hume, and Kant that conscious experience is manufactured out of bits and pieces of sensations. Because we directly experience objects as they are, there is no need to posit a gravity of the mind or force of sensation that holds complex impressions and ideas together. Reid acknowledged that one can artificially analyze complex impressions into simple ones, but he denied that doing so returned one to the raw material of experience, pure sensations. For Reid, the raw material of experience is objects themselves. Most later psychologists would follow Hume or Kant in seeing experience as manufactured out of simpler bits. But realism was kept alive by Franz Brentano, the Gestalt psychologists, and the phenomenologists in Germany and by William James in America. They, like the Scots, refused to think of the mind as a "machine shop" manufacturing experience out of pieces of "mind stuff" (James, 1890). As modern roboticist Rodney Brooks (1991/1997) puts it, "you don't need representations in a cognitive system because the world is its own best representation."

As a realist, Reid believed that perception is always meaningful. Concepts are mental symbols that stand for something real. Perception is thus like language. Like the medievals, Reid believed we get knowledge by reading the "book of the world," which tells us the meaning of reality as surely as reading a book tells us its meaning. Complex experience cannot be reduced to atomic sensations without robbing it of something vital—its meaning.

REID'S NATIVISM   The second general point central to Reid's philosophy is his own brand of nativism. According to Reid, we are naturally endowed with certain innate faculties and principles of mind that allow us to know the world accurately and furnish us with essential truths as well. Reid (1764/1785/1975) wrote:

> Such original and natural judgments are, therefore, a part of that furniture which Nature had given to the human understanding. They are the inspiration of the Almighty . . . they serve to direct us in the common affairs of life, where our reasoning faculty would leave us in the dark . . . and all the discoveries of reason are grounded upon them. They make up what is called the common sense of mankind. . . . When a man suffers himself to be reasoned out of the principles of common sense, by metaphysical arguments, we may call this metaphysical lunacy. (pp. 118–119)

Knowledge of the world is secure because of the God-given human constitution that delivers it. We are constructed by God to know His world.

If we set aside his rejection of the Way of Ideas, we find that Reid's philosophy resembles Hume's in important respects. Both of them looked, in the characteristic Enlightenment way, to human nature in their treatment of philosophical problems. Both looked upon science and philosophy as products of the human mind, which therefore had to be studied and erected upon a prior theory of human nature. Hume's theory was rather simpler than Reid's, but their goals and methods were quite similar. The most serious difference between them as advancers of the Enlightenment Project was religious. A curious aspect of the nativism-empiricism debates of the eighteenth century often escapes the modern, secular eye. Following Darwin, we now assume that native constitution is the product of natural selection. Our ability to see depth, for example, stems from our having descended from originally arboreal apes for whom binocular vision was adaptive. However, most philosophers before Darwin believed in God and assumed that, because God made human beings, whatever ideas or principles he implanted must be true, unless God is a deceiver. Thus, Locke, staunch opponent of innate truths, never used the best counterclaim to so-called innate principles—namely, to show that they may not be true—because Locke assumed that whatever God did implant must be true. Hume was an atheist, and his moderate skepticism was an inevitable result. Our faculties, not being God-given, may err. Reid, however, avoided skepticism by asserting that the Almighty implanted in us first principles, necessarily valid because of their source. Thomas Reid was a clergyman—perhaps a clergyman first and a philosopher second. Reid's version of the Enlightenment Project stayed within the boundaries of religion; Hume's did not.

Among the Scots, an important step toward psychology was taken by Reid's student, Dugald Stewart. Stewart, who was more reconciled to Hume than was Reid, abandoned the term *common sense* and used associative concepts extensively. His basic work, *Elements of Philosophy of the Human Mind* (1792), reads like an introductory psychology text based on everyday experience instead of laboratory experiments. There are sections on attention, association (learning), memory, imagination, and dreaming. Stewart wrote charmingly about magicians, jugglers, and acrobats to illustrate his points. His discussions of attention and memory have a contemporary air about them, with Stewart making some distinctions found in modern information-processing psychology, and citing everyday experiences to support them. Stewart followed Reid in dissecting the mind into component faculties, each of which is assigned its role in mental life and knowledge. Influenced by Bacon, Stewart devoted 62 pages to showing the practical value of the study of psychology.

In all, Stewart's work is engaging and attractive. Through Stewart especially, Scottish philosophy became quite influential, especially in America. Some of America's earliest college founders were adherents of the Scottish School, as were some important college presidents in the nineteenth century. In the hands of later writers (beginning with Stewart), Scottish philosophy became a readily acceptable psychology, intuitively appealing and consistent with Christianity. Most American colleges were (and many still are) religious, and in the nineteenth-century Scottish faculty, psychology was part of the "moral sciences" taught to students. The content of their moral thought we shall come to presently.

The Transcendental Pretense: Immanuel Kant (1724–1804)

Kant wrote, "Two things awe me most, the starry sky above me and the moral law within me." As Plato had been offended by the apparent cognitive and moral relativism of the Sophists, Kant was offended by the apparent cognitive relativism of Hume and the apparent moral relativism of the French naturalists. In his new metaphysics, Kant attempted to refute Hume's skepticism and rescue the certainty of Newton's grand scheme by which gravity rules the starry sky. In his new ethics, to which we will return, Kant rebutted moral skepticism by grounding moral judgment in cognitively formed formal rules that govern a stern moral will.

KANTIAN PHILOSOPHY: REASSERTING METAPHYSICS   Kant said that Hume's skeptical arguments roused him from his "dogmatic slumbers." Before reading Hume, Kant had been a follower of Leibniz through his teacher, Christian Wolff (1679–1754). However, Hume's skepticism disturbed Kant's Leibnizian "dogmatism." Like Plato with regard to the Sophists, Kant saw Hume's conclusions as undermining the possibility of human knowledge. With Plato, Kant sought transcendent Truth, and was not content with merely useful truths. To rescue Truth, Kant deployed metaphysical arguments about the mind rather than Hume's empirical ones. He realized that the old, speculative metaphysics about God and humankind's spiritual substance was no longer viable. However, Kant could not accept Hume's merely psychological analysis of knowledge, and wanted to prove the validity of human knowledge quite apart from any empirical facts about human habit formation. He thus reasserted the claim of philosophical metaphysics, over psychology, to be the foundation of the other sciences.

Kant began, as Hume had, with the basic Cartesian framework, but developed it in a very different way. Kant called the world of experience—the world as perceived in the Cartesian Theater—*phenomena*. The world of things-in-themselves he called the *noumena*. Like almost everyone else in the eighteenth century, Kant took Newtonian physics as the paradigm of genuine human knowledge. Science rests on observations and is therefore necessarily tested against experience, that is, against phenomena. Framed this way, the question of human knowledge of Truth depends upon the nature of phenomena, not the nature of noumena. Kant then investigated how phenomena arise in the mind, asserting that the mind necessarily structures experience in universal ways that make claims to Truth potentially valid.

Kant thought that empiricist philosophy went astray because it made the natural and intuitive assumption that external, noumenal objects impose themselves on understanding, which conforms itself to them. Hume's concept of impression expresses this assumption clearly: In perception, objects impose themselves on the mind the way a signet ring imposes a pattern on wax. For Kant, Hume's philosophy demonstrated that there must be something wrong with the naive assumption that the mind conforms itself to objects, because it issues in skepticism. Kant turned Hume's hidden assumption on its head: Instead of the mind passively conforming itself to objects, Kant proposed that objects conform themselves to the mind, which actively imposes innate, *a priori*, categories on experience. For example, Hume could find no justification for the assertion that every event has a cause because causes themselves elude observation. Kant asserted that while in noumena this may be true, in phenomena—the world we know and which science deals with—every event does indeed have a cause because the mind imposes causality on experience.

The *Wizard of Oz* can be used to illustrate Kant's point. Oz is known as the Emerald City, but the movie does not reveal why. In the book, everyone who enters Oz is issued green spectacles that must be worn at all times. The spectacles make everything appear to be a shade of green, and thus Oz is the Emerald City. Now, imagine that the citizens of Oz had green lenses implanted in their eyes at birth, but that the operation was kept a secret. The Ozzites would grow up seeing everything as a shade of green, and would naturally conclude that (as empiricists say), because objects impress themselves on the mind, everything appears green because everything is, in fact, green. We know, on the other hand, that things appear green to the Ozzites because of the altered nature of their eyes. In their case, objects conform themselves to the mind because the Ozzite mind imposes itself on objects. Observe, now, that Ozzites can assert at least one Truth that cannot be falsified in the realm of phenomena, "Everything (meaning every phenomenon) is green."

Kant's idea is that the human mind, or more precisely the human Transcendental Ego, or Self, imposes certain Transcendental Categories of Understanding on experience, such as three-dimensional space, number, and causality. In Kant's usage, *transcendental* means logical and necessary. He believed he had proved that his Categories were logically necessary preconditions for any kind of experience whatsoever by any conscious being whatsoever. Thus, with regard to phenomena—the realm of what human beings can know—we can assert certain Truths, such as "Every event has a cause," or "Objects exist in three-dimensional space." Hume's skepticism about the possibility of unrefutable knowledge is thus rebutted. On the other hand, certain questions that seem at first glance to be straightforward, were, Kant held, questions that have no answers because they cannot be addressed within the realm of phenomena. The oft-contested question of the existence of God is one of these because God exists outside the realm of phenomena. Arguments for and against God's existence are of equal validity or invalidity. Kant did not assert, as Hume did, that because we cannot perceive God, God does not exist, but that God's existence or nonexistence is a question that the human mind cannot answer. Kant set limits on skepticism, but he did not entirely defeat it.

Kant thought he had proved the transcendental validity of his innate concepts, but, from a modern perspective, these concepts, if they exist, are evolutionary designs, not metaphysically necessary conditions of all consciousness. Kant's explanation is therefore just as psychological as Hume's or as physiological as Reid's. In other words, what applied to Reid as against Hume applies to Kant as well. The major difference between Hume, on the one hand, and Reid and Kant, on the other, is the amount and nature of innate equipment humans come with. The verdict of history is mixed on this score. Kant has been supported by findings that perception of three-dimensional space is innate, but he has been undermined by modern quantum physics (in which not all events have causes) and the construction of non-Euclidean geometries (which Kant implied were inconceivable). Kant's philosophy directly influenced the Swiss psychologist Jean Piaget. Kant taught a form of idealism, maintaining that the world of experience is constructed by the transcendental categories of perception. Piaget studied the process by which the categories and the construction of the world develop in growing children. Indeed, one of his works was entitled *The Construction of Reality by the Child*, and other works study each Kantian category in turn: *The Child's Conception of Space, The Child's Conception of Time,. . . of Number*, and so on.

KANT ON SCIENTIFIC PSYCHOLOGY Given his disdain for Hume's psychological account of knowledge, Kant cared little for psychology. Kant believed that psychology, defined as the introspective study of the mind, could not be a science for two reasons. First, he did not think that enough aspects of consciousness could be measured quantitatively to make possible Newtonian equations about the mind. Second, according to Kant, any science has two parts—the empirical part, involving observation and research, and the rational or metaphysical part, comprising the philosophical foundations that justify the empirical science's claim to produce knowledge. Kant believed that he had provided the metaphysical grounding of physical science in his account of human experience, the *Critique of Pure Reason*. There he showed that the basic assumptions of physics, such as universal causality, were necessarily true of human experience. Hence, physics is a complete science.

Kant argued, however, that rational psychology is an illusion. The object of rational psychology is the thinking substance, or soul—Descartes's "I think." However, we do not experience the soul—the Transcendental Ego—directly; it has no content, being pure thought, and has only noumenal, not phenomenal, existence. In Lockean terms, Kant asserted that there is no introspective power of reflection because the self cannot observe its own thought. There is an empirical ego, of course, the sum total of our sensations or mental content, and we can study it through introspection. However, this empirical psychology, unlike empirical physics, cannot be a science; because it lacked its rational counterpart, Kant thought little of it.

Nevertheless, Kant believed in a science, or at least a discipline, concerned with humanity; he called it *anthropology*, the study (*logos*) of humans (*anthropos*). Kant's anthropology was psychology, not modern anthropology, being the study of human intellectual faculties, human appetite, and human character, not the cross-cultural study of societies. Kant delivered a very popular series of lectures, published as *Anthropology from a Pragmatic Point of View* (1798/1974). If Kant's philosophy is similar to Reid's, his *Anthropology* is similar to Stewart's psychology, complete with an enumeration of faculties. Kant's lectures are accessible, full of shrewd observations of everyday behavior, charming and even funny anecdotes, and popular prejudice. In short, *Anthropology* is Kant's commonsense psychology and bears some attention.

Kant distinguished physiological anthropology, concerned with the body and its effect on mind, and pragmatic anthropology, concerned with the person as a morally free agent and citizen of the world. Wundt's later division of psychology into physiological and social branches was like Kant's division of anthropology. The goal of pragmatic anthropology was to improve human behavior and so was grounded not in the metaphysics of experience, but in the metaphysics of morals. Pragmatic anthropology's methods were many. First, we have some introspective knowledge of our own minds and, by extension, of others' minds. Kant was aware of the pitfalls of introspection, however. When we introspect, we change the state of our minds, so what we find is unnatural and of limited value; the same holds for trying to observe our own behavior. Kant even went so far as to say that excessive reflection on one's own mind may drive one insane. Similarly, when we observe others, they will act unnaturally if they know we are watching. Anthropology must be an interdisciplinary study embracing these methods—but using them with care—and also calling on history, biography, and literature for information about human nature.

Anthropology is a rich work. Kant discusses everything from insanity (which he felt was innate) to the nature of women (they are weaker but more civilized than men), and to how to give a dinner party for philosophers. Just one of Kant's many topics will be presented here, however, for it occurs in Wundt's psychology in much the same form. Kant discussed "ideas that we have without being aware of them." If we examine our awareness, we will find that some perceptions are clear—the ones we are attending to—while others are obscure. As Kant put it, "Our mind is like an immense map, with only a few places illuminated." This view of consciousness as a field with clear and obscure areas is identical to Wundt's. The obscure ideas are those we are not clearly aware of, so obviously Kant's doctrine is not Freud's view of repression into the unconscious. However, Kant does say we can be subtly affected by obscure ideas. He observes that we often unthinkingly judge persons by the clothes they wear, without being conscious of the connection between the clothes and our feelings for the wearer. Kant also offers pragmatic advice to writers: Make your ideas a little obscure so that when a reader clarifies them you will make him or her feel clever.

In addition to his conception of consciousness, many of Kant's other ideas influenced Wundt, the founder of the psychology of consciousness. By Wundt's time, ways to experiment on and quantify mind had become available, and so Wundt was able to show that a scientific empirical psychology was possible without a rational companion. Wundt thus could abandon the Transcendental Ego altogether. However, it still lived in Wundt's system in modified form. Wundt emphasized how apperception gives unity to conscious experience, a role Kant assigned to the Transcendental Ego. In addition, Wundt put thinking beyond the reach of introspection, as did Kant, holding that it could be investigated only indirectly through a study of people in society, similar to Kant's *Anthropology*. Wundt's psychology had two parts: the laboratory study of experience via introspection (Kant's empirical psychology made into a science despite him), and the study of the higher mental processes via the comparative study of culture, similar to Kant's *Anthropology* (although Wundt did not use the label). Wundt also modified Kant's view of introspection. Wundt said good scientific introspection was not the intense scrutiny of the soul, which Kant found dangerous, but only the self-observations of one's experience, which even Kant said was possible.

THE MORAL QUESTION: IS SOCIETY NATURAL?

"It has seemed to me that one must treat ethics like all the other sciences and construct experimental ethics in the same way as experimental physics," wrote the philosophe Claude Helvetius in *De L'esprit* (1758; quoted by Hampson, 1982, p. 124). Here is the heart of the Enlightenment Project: finding the ideal human way of life by scientific research and constructing it by applied scientific technology. However, constructing experimental ethics proved more daunting and more perilous than experimental physics. Hobbes had approached human nature in a scientific spirit and found that humans were vicious and dangerous creatures, apt to be at each other's throats without the stern control of an authoritarian government. Thinkers of the French Enlightenment undertook their project in an optimistic spirit of improving everyone's life through science, but ended up in their Revolution apparently confirming Hobbes's pessimism. As scientific epistemology eventually resulted in a skeptical crisis, so scientific ethics resulted in a moral crisis. In Scotland, the commonsense philosophers resisted the moral crisis in ways that were especially important to American thought. Moreover, a reaction against the Enlightenment began to set in at the very time Helvetius wrote *De L'esprit*.

Experimental Ethics: French Naturalism

In France, the Enlightenment project was pursued more radically and ruthlessly than in Britain. There were two major sources for the philosophes' naturalism (Vartanian, 1953). One was John Locke's empirical psychology. In eighteenth-century France, there was a mania for things English, especially Newton's science and Locke's psychology. The supreme philosophe, Voltaire, wrote in his philosophical letters: "So many philosophers having written the romance of the soul, a sage has arrived who has modestly written its history. Locke sets forth human reason just as an excellent anatomist explains the parts of the human body. He everywhere takes the light of Newton's physics for his guide" (Knight, 1968, p. 25). The other source of naturalism was native to France, Descartes's mechanistic physiology.

CARTESIAN MATERIALISM Immediately after Descartes proposed that animals are simply machines but humans are not machines (and so escape science, by virtue of having souls), many of his religious opponents saw the trap he had unwittingly set. For if animals, which behave in such diverse and often sophisticated ways, are but machines, is not the next logical step to say that a person, too, is but a machine? They believed that Descartes was a secret materialist who only intimated what he hoped others might later say openly. Defenders of religion said these things to ridicule Descartes's system as subversive of faith; but in the irreligious eighteenth century, there were those who said them in earnest, proclaiming materialism.

Although there were materialists since the Greek atomists, they were few and silent during the Middle Ages. However, in the Age of Reason, their numbers multiplied and they became more open and vocal. They spoke up first in anonymous pamphlets, fearing persecution, but they soon grew bolder.

The most outspoken and complete extension of Descartes's beast-machine into the human-machine was made by the physician-philosopher Julien Offray de La Mettrie (1709–1751), whose major work was *L'homme Machine (Man a Machine)* (1748/1961). Interestingly, La Mettrie, too, thought Descartes was a secret materialist, but he praised Descartes for it. La Mettrie wrote: "He was the first to prove completely animals are pure machines," a discovery of such importance that one must "pardon all his errors." La Mettrie took the step feared by religionists: "Let us boldly conclude that man is a machine," that the soul is but an empty word.

As a physician, La Mettrie held that only a physician may speak on human nature, for only a physician knows the mechanism of the body. La Mettrie went into some detail to show how the state of the body affects the mind—for example, in the effects of drugs, disease, and fatigue. Against Descartes's insistence on the uniqueness of human language, La Mettrie suggested that apes might be made into "little gentlemen" by teaching them language the way the deaf are taught. La Mettrie remained a Cartesian, however, in asserting that language is what makes a person human. He denied only that language is innate, claiming that we can make the ape human, too, via language.

In general, La Mettrie gives the impression not of lowering humans to the level of animals, but of raising animals to near-human status. This intent emerges most clearly in his discussion of natural moral law. La Mettrie argued that animals share with humans moral sentiments such as grief and regret, so that morality is inherent in the natural biological order. Having said this, however, La Mettrie left the door open to sheer hedonism by stating that the point of living is to be happy.

La Mettrie adopted an uncompromisingly scientific, anti-teleological attitude to his subject. He denied finalism or any Godly act of intentional creation. For example, the animal eye was not created by God to make seeing possible, but arose by evolution because seeing was important to creatures' biological survival. La Mettrie here stated a doctrine called *transformism*, which was increasingly popular in the later eighteenth century and which marks the beginning of evolutionary thought. According to transformism, the universe was not created by God but emerged from primordial matter as a result of the action of natural law. The development of the physical and, La Mettrie implied, biological universe is a necessary consequence of the way nature is organized. Voltaire's Creator is no more necessary than the Christian God.

When it came to discussing living creatures, La Mettrie returned to the view of the Renaissance nature philosophers Descartes had rejected and attributed special powers to living matter. He thought biological tissue to be capable, at least, of self-generation and motion. La Mettrie cited contemporary physiological research to prove his point. Polyps cut in two regenerate their missing halves; muscles of a dead animal still move when stimulated; the heart can beat after removal from the body. Matter is alive; it is vital, not dead; and it is precisely this natural vitality that made La Mettrie's human-machine plausible. In the twentieth century, vitalism became the great enemy of scientific biologists, but it was an important step in the founding of biology as a coherent field apart from physics. La Mettrie's vitalism again attests that his materialism was not meant to degrade humanity, to make of a human being a cold, metallic machine (the image we have today of the machine), but rather to make of a human a vital, living, dynamic machine, an integral part of a living nature. Descartes's human being—like Plato's and Christianity's, was torn between nature and heaven. La Mettrie's was simply part of nature.

We should conclude this summary as La Mettrie did his book. Like a good philosopher, and like B. F. Skinner much later, La Mettrie urged the progressive nature and moral goodness of accepting materialism, of giving up vain speculation and religious superstition to live pleasurable lives. Recognizing ourselves to be part of nature, we can then revere, honor, and never destroy nature. Our behavior toward others will improve. Wrote La Mettrie (1748/1961):

> Full of humanity we will love human character even in our enemies . . . in our eyes they will be but mismade men . . . we will not mistreat our kind. . . . Following the natural law given to all animals we will not wish to do to others what we would not wish them to do to us. . . . Such is my system, or rather the truth, unless I am much deceived. It is short and simple. Dispute it now who will. (pp. 148–149)

With this passage, La Mettrie closed *L'homme Machine*. Although his "truth" was not acceptable to all philosophes in its extreme form, and Christians hotly disputed it, materialism was a growing doctrine. It was reluctantly and partially accepted by Voltaire himself and by Denis Diderot, conceiver of the Encyclopedia, and espoused in extreme form by Baron Paul d'Holbach (1723–1789), who worked out its deterministic and atheistic implications. We will see its link to the moral crisis shortly.

FRENCH EMPIRICISM   The other route to naturalism was through Locke's empiricism, which inspired France's *soi-disant* "Newtons of the mind." The general tendency of their thought was toward *sensationism*, deriving the mind entirely from sensations, denying the existence of autonomous mental faculties and the power of reflection found in Locke's psychology. The French commentators thought they were purifying and improving Locke's philosophy.

The first important French Lockean was Etienne Bonnot de Condillac (1715–1780). Condillac dismissed everyone but Locke ("Immediately after Aristotle comes Locke") and to his first book, *An Essay on the Origin of Human Knowledge* (1746/1974), he gave the subtitle *Being a Supplement to Mr. Locke's Essay on Human Understanding*. Like Berkeley, Condillac believed Locke had not pursued his own empiricism far enough, but in his *Essay* he followed Locke closely. Only in a later work, *Treatise on Sensations* (1754/1982), did Condillac really fulfill his earlier promise to "reduce to a single principle whatever relates to the human understanding." That principle is sensation.

Locke had allowed the mind certain autonomous powers: the power of reflection on itself, and mental faculties or acts, such as attention and memory. Condillac strove to see the mind in a more purely empiricist way. He denied the existence of reflection and tried to derive all mental faculties from simple sensation. His motto might have been, "I sense, therefore I am." Condillac asked his readers to imagine a statue that is endowed with each sense in turn, starting with smell. Condillac then endeavored to build up complex mental activity from these senses. For example, memory arises when a sensation is experienced for a second time and recognized. We should observe that here Condillac cheated, for he assumed an inner power or faculty to store the first sensation, an innate power indistinguishable from memory. Attention is reduced to the strength of one sensation to dominate, in the mind, other weaker sensations. In his *Essay*, Condillac had followed Locke and said attention was a mental act (as will Wundt a century later); but in the *Treatise*, his sensationism is consistent and he anticipates Titchener's identical sensationist revision of Wundt's theory.

In short, Condillac attempted to work out an empiricist theory of mind. However, on one point he remained a good Cartesian. At the end of Condillac's thought experiment about the statue, although it had acquired every mental faculty and every human sense, the statue still lacked the essential Cartesian human trait: It could not speak. Condillac said, with Descartes, that it could not speak because it lacked reason. Its mind was passive, not active; it lacked the power of thought. In Condillac's scheme, as in Descartes's, the statue and animals are set off from human beings. Condillac simplified the emerging picture of the animal soul, showing how it might be built up without the innate faculties that had been attributed to it since the time of Aristotle. He left the human soul as Descartes had left it—as the power to think. Condillac, a Christian, left the stripping of human beings of their soul, the seat of reason, to more radical men who were more willing to embrace La Mettrie's materialism and to work out its consequences.

CONSEQUENCES OF FRENCH MATERIALISM AND EMPIRICISM   One of these more radical thinkers was Claude Helvetius (1715–1771), who accepted Condillac's empiricism and a mechanical version of La Mettrie's materialism. Following Locke's statement that the infant mind was "white paper or wax to be moulded and fashioned as one pleases" (quoted by Porter, 2000, p. 340), Helvetius proclaimed a complete environmentalism, in which humans have neither a divine soul nor a complex biological structure. The human possesses only senses, a passive mind able to receive sensations, and a body capable of certain actions. This mind is passively built up through watching the effects of a person's own and others' actions and observing the ways of the world. For Helvetius, then, the mind at birth is both blank and powerless; everything a person becomes is the result of the environment. Helvetius found cause for optimism in the malleability of the mind, holding out the hope that improved education would lead to improved people. In this tenet, he presaged the radical behaviorists, who believe human behavior is similarly malleable. Such beliefs, however, have a negative potential as well—an effective dictatorship can be founded on brainwashing.

We now come to the moral crisis created by the Enlightenment Project. Is it possible to have scientific ethics as Helvetius hoped? With few exceptions in the history of the West up to this time, including Descartes, Locke, and Kant, reason had been assigned the job of imposing moral behavior on humans' natural tendencies toward pleasure. Ironically, however, in the Age of Reason the scope of reason had been reduced and belief in a transcendent moral order, whether Platonic, Stoic, or Christian, had been shattered. All that remained was human nature as a guide to right and wrong.

The problem was finding good in human nature. La Mettrie said pleasure is the natural cause for our existence; nature made us to pursue pleasure. Condillac, too, reduced reason to desire, or need. If each sensation produces pleasure or pain, then our thinking, built up out of our sensations by association, is determined by their affective quality and directed by our momentary, animal needs. Hence, empiricism undercuts the autonomy of reason. For the rationalist, reason is prior to, and independent of, sensation, so hedonism is only a temptation to be overcome. The empiricist, however, constructing reason out of affectively charged sensations, makes hedonism the directing force behind all thought. Seeing happiness entirely as physical pleasure, not *eudaemonia* (living well), La Mettrie turned Socrates on his head. Socrates had always said that the moral life is the happy life. But La Mettrie wrote, in his *Anti-Seneque* (1750; quoted by Hampson, 1982):

> Since the pleasures of the mind are the real source of happiness, it is perfectly clear that, from the point of view of happiness, good and evil are things quite indifferent in themselves and he who obtains greater satisfaction from doing evil will be happier than the man who obtains

less satisfaction from doing good. This explains why so many scoundrels are happy in this life and shows that there is a kind of individual felicity which is to be found, not merely without virtue, but even in crime itself. (p. 123)

Here we see the fundamental crisis of naturalism, which was first confronted by the philosophes and which became acute after Darwin. If we are only machines, destined to pursue pleasure and avoid pain, what can be the ground of moral value and of meaning in our lives? The early philosophes assumed, as humanists, that the world was made for humans by a beneficent, if non-Christian, Creator. As the century progressed, however, it became increasingly evident that this optimism was unjustified. The great 9.0 Lisbon earthquake and tsunami of 1755, for example, blotted out over 40,000 lives and destroyed 85% of the city's buildings. Newton's universe seemed to be a machine indifferent to human life, which was a mere speck of no consequence. Moreover, the extension of materialism, determinism, and hedonism to human beings, while intellectually persuasive, was hard to accept emotionally. Diderot, for example, wrote in a letter, "I am maddened at being entangled in a devilish philosophy that my mind can't help approving and my heart refuting" (Knight, 1968, p. 115). The whole dilemma thus came down to a question of feelings—feelings of freedom and dignity versus a natural desire to seek pleasure and avoid pain.

There is a remarkably existentialist sentence in La Mettrie's *L'homme Machine*: "Who can be sure that the reason for man's existence is not simply the fact that he exists?" He continued: "Perhaps he was thrown by chance on some spot on the earth's surface, nobody knows how or why, but simply that he must live and die, like the mushrooms which appear from day to day." La Mettrie stated the possibility of a meaningless world, the abyss of moral nihilism that every philosophe saw and tried to avoid.

However, one man cheerfully jumped into that abyss, proclaiming the autonomy of pleasure, the illusion of morals, the rule of the strong, and a pleasurable life of crime. The Marquis de Sade (1740–1814) wrote, in *History of Juliette*, this description of why the strong, in the pursuit of happiness, should dominate the weak (quoted and translated by Crocker, 1959):

[T]he strong,. . . in despoiling the weak, that is to say in enjoying all the rights he has received from nature, in giving them the greatest possible extension, finds pleasure in proportion to this extension. The more atrociously he harms the weak, the more voluptuously he is thrilled; injustice is his delectation, he enjoys the tears that his oppression snatches from the unfortunate wretch; the more he grieves him, the more he oppresses him, the happier he is . . . this truly delicious gratification never establishes itself better for the fortunate man than when the misery he produces is complete. . . . Let him pillage then, let him burn, let him ravage, let him not leave the wretch more than the breath to prolong a life whose existence is necessary for the oppressor . . . whatever he does will be in nature, whatever he invents will be only the active use of the forces which he has received from her, and the more he exercises his forces, the more he will experience pleasure, the better he will use his faculties, and the better, consequently, he will have served nature. (pp. 212–213)

If pleasure is the only goal in life that naturalism can find, then we should each seek it uninhibited by morals or the opinions of society, according to Sade. In doing so, we will be fulfilling natural law. The strong not only must, but should, triumph over the weak. Sade extended comparative psychology to morals. Animals prey on one another without compunction; they have no moral law. We are animals, so we should act in the same way. Moral law is a metaphysical illusion. The philosophes first struggled with the problem of a world ruled only by efficient causes and hedonism and tried to avoid Sade's logical extrapolation of naturalism. In the twentieth century, the problem has remained unsolved, and in our own time we have seen moral nihilism proclaimed again, while modern existential humanists seek to restore humanity's dignity. The problem became acute in the nineteenth century when Darwin cut away all reason for believing that humans transcend nature. In Darwin's universe, too, the strong destroy the weak. Sade was a harbinger of the moral nihilism that stared Victorians in the face and posed for their therapist, Freud, his deepest problem.

Enlightened Ethical Philosophies

Naturalistic thinking about human nature, human society, and human ethics from Hobbes through the French naturalists starkly challenged existing ethical theories. If human nature was as depraved as Hobbes suggested or so thin as to be nearly nonexistent as the French naturalists suggested, then Aristotle's virtue ethics had no foundation at all. If there are no inherent human virtues to be allowed to flourish, then human happiness depended solely on material satisfaction and the suppression of human selfishness, though de Sade's wickedly argued things the other way round: human flourishing was exactly to be found in violence and oppression. Naturalistic theories, especially in France, did without God, so that Christian ethics based on following God's commands commanded no assent from atheists. Nietzsche would drive this point home in the nineteenth century.

As a result of these challenges and the waning of religious authority in the later eighteenth century, philosophers proposed two new forms of ethical thought and sought to revise and revive virtue ethics. What all three had in common was a psychological turn of thought. It seemed that rules for right living could no longer be derived from sources outside human nature, whether in metaphysics as Plato had argued or in God, as Christians urged, but had to be found within human beings themselves, in their happiness, their reason, or their feelings. The first new ethical system was what philosophers call consequentialism: Right action is that which has the best outcomes, that is consequences. The second was what philosophers call deontological ethics: Right action is that which stems from the rule governed (hence, deontological from the Greek word for rule, *deon*) choices of the moral will. A third group of philosophers took the most psychological course of all, proposing a form of virtue ethics (though rarely labeled as such) that saw morality as rooted in innate human feelings of moral approval and disapproval of right and wrong actions.

ETHICS OF OUTCOMES: UTILITARIANISM   There are various forms of consequentialist ethics, but the most important was, and remains, utilitarianism, which, in one form or another, has powerfully influenced all of the social sciences. It proposed a simple and potentially quantifiable theory of human motivation—*hedonism*. First advanced by Greeks such as Democritus, hedonism proposes that people are moved solely by the pursuit of pleasure and the avoidance of pain. Part of the appeal of utilitarianism is its flexibility. Although the principle of utility is simple, it respects individual differences and the quite varied kinds of pleasures and pains that people pursue or avoid. The principle of utility is fundamental to most theories in economics. In psychology, it provided the motivational doctrines of behaviorism and continues to influence theories of decision making and choice.

Turning hedonism into a practical, quantitative scientific theory was an enterprise of an English reformer and Newton of the mind, Jeremy Bentham (1748–1832). He opened his *Introduction to the Principles of Morals and Legislation* (1789/1973, p. 1) with a forceful statement of utilitarian hedonism: "Nature has placed mankind under the governance of two sovereign masters, pain and pleasure. It is for them alone to point out what we ought to do, as well as to determine what we shall do. . . . They govern us in all we do, in all we say, in all we think." Typical of an Enlightenment philosophe, Bentham's claim fused a scientific hypothesis about human nature with an ethical canon about how people ought to live. Not only do pleasure and pain "govern us in all we do" (the scientific hypothesis), they "ought" to do so as well (the moral canon). Previous thinkers had certainly recognized the temptation of hedonism, but they had hoped that it might be controlled by some other motive—for example, by the Scottish philosophers' moral sense. What made Bentham daring was his rejection of motives other than utility as superstitious nonsense, and his attempt to erect an ethics on that rejection. Bentham's definition of utility, was, however, not limited to mere sensual pleasures and pains. Bentham also recognized the pleasures of wealth, power, piety, and benevolence, to name only a few.

Bentham's Newtonian proposal that pleasure and pain might be quantified made his principle of utility scientifically important. The strength of Newtonian physics was its mathematical precision, and Bentham hoped to bring similar precision to the human sciences. His "felicific calculus" (calculus of happiness) attempted to measure units of pleasure and pain so that they might be entered into equations that would predict behavior or could be used by decision makers to make correct— that is, the most happiness-maximizing—choices. In economics, prices provide a convenient stand- in for Bentham's measures of happiness. Economists can readily determine how much people will pay for pleasures—whether cookies, concerts, cannabis, or cars—and how much they will pay to avoid pain—buying security systems, health insurance, or aspirin—and they have developed a highly mathematical science based on the principle of utility. In psychology, attempts to directly measure units of pleasure and pain have proved controversial, but nevertheless continue. For example, in the emerging field of behavioral economics, equations have been developed based on how much rats or pigeons will "pay" in terms of operant responses for various economic "goods" such as food, water, or electrical stimulation (Leahey & Harris, 2004).

As a social reformer, Bentham wanted legislators—the audience Bentham aimed at in his *Principles*—to employ the felicific calculus in making the laws. Their goal should be "the greatest happiness for the greatest number." That is, legislators should try to figure out how many happiness units and how many pleasure units would be generated in the country as a whole by any given act of government, and they should therefore always act to maximize the net amount of utility experienced by the nation as a whole. Because he believed that what is pleasurable and painful varies from person to person, Bentham generally advocated minimal government. In the utilitarian or now known view, people ought to be left alone to do what makes them happy, not dictated to by a meddling govern- ment pursuing its own utility function.

ETHICS OF DUTY: KANT Just as he could not abide the cognitive blank slate of British empiricism, Kant could not abide the moral blank slate of the French empiricists or the consequentialist ethics of the utilitarians. The problem was that traditional systems of ethics do not delve deeply enough in their inquiries about what we *ought* to do as a matter of moral duty. Instead, they tell us about how we ought to behave within an unexamined framework of assumptions about our goals. Thus, the ancient Greeks said that *if* you seek happiness—eudaemonia—*then* you ought to behave in certain ways, such as telling the truth and being brave. Thus, Greek moral reasoning was about the best means to achieving an already presupposed end, happiness. They took eudaemonia for granted. Hedonistic theories, especially in their extreme French form, were even worse, because compared to Greek eudaemonia, their notion of human happiness—the pursuit of pleasure—was cramped and thin, suggesting that playing cards was just as morally worthy as creating art if it brought the same amount of pleasure to the card player and the artist. Moreover, Kant wanted to do for morals what he had done for science. It was not enough for him that Newton's theory worked beautifully as an account of physical nature; he wanted to show that Newton's theory was necessarily, metaphysically, true. So he was unhappy with moral theories that located morality in what happened to be true about human beings. He wanted an account of morality rooted in the demands of pure reason, not the vagaries of human nature, aiming to free the study of morality from "the niggardly provision of our stepmother, nature" (quoted by Scruton, 2001, p. 88).

Moral commands are imperatives—they say what you ought to do. In Kant's terminology, previous moral philosophers had discussed only *hypothetical*, or conditional, imperatives that tell one what to do to achieve a certain goal. Kant wanted to formulate a *categorical*, or unconditional, imperative, that rationally spelled out what was right or wrong without regard to any specific goal. Psychologically, Kant wanted to honor what he found awesome: "the moral law within me." Doing what is right often seems hard and is felt as a kind of compulsion not to give into temptation. In short, doing what's right feels like a kind of duty, not simply a calculated means to a pleasurable or profitable end. One way to capture this insight is thinking of duty as obeying a law laid down by an outside authority, whether it is God—I won't cheat on my spouse because God forbids it even though I'd enjoy it—or a legislature—I as a prosecuting attorney must give exculpating evidence to the defense because the law commands it, even if I lose my case. In Kant's analysis, reason, not God or a legislature, is the ultimate lawgiver that requires moral actions.

In his metaphysics of science, Kant proposed that the universal Transcendental Ego common to all conscious beings forms experience into a knowable pattern. In his ethics, Kant proposed a law of reason that commands all rational beings, whether human or not. The categorical imperative is that I should always act "only on that maxim which I can at the same will as a universal law," always "treat[ing] humanity whether in my own self or in that of another always as an end and never as a means only" (quoted by Scruton, 2001, pp. 85–86). Here, the rational, transcendental self becomes the lawgiver for all rational beings, not just for the individual caught in a moral dilemma. Thus, if I choose to tell the truth in a difficult situation, the categorical imperative says that at the moment I choose to tell the truth, at the same time I am making telling the truth a universal law that all rational beings must follow in all circumstances necessarily, just as the law of gravity affects all physical bodies in all circumstances necessarily.

Kant is not, however, endorsing naturalistic determinism of La Mettrie's sort, the idea that choices are illusions, that everything we do is predetermined. Our moral choices are real—we can, if we choose lie, commit adultery, or conceal evidence. The categorical imperative does not make these choices impossible; it makes them morally wrong for all rational beings in all circumstances.

Kant's ethics honors one human intuition, that doing the right things can feel compelled as if by an external authority, but on the other hand Kantian ethics seems too stern, too insensitive to circumstances, and too far from human nature and real moral decision making to be plausible as an account of how people make moral decisions, or attractive as an analysis of how we ought to make moral decisions. If lying is always and everywhere and in all circumstances morally wrong, then it's wrong for me to lie to a killer about the whereabouts of his or her intended victim, or to Nazi agents seeking Anne Frank. If all humans are to be treated as equally valuable, then given the choice of saving my child or a stranger from a burning house, I should flip a coin. If I see two people donating money to charity and doing volunteer work with the poor, and find that one does so because he loves people and is moved by sympathy to help them, while the other finds the poor repulsive and repugnant and helps them out of moral duty despite the unhappiness being among the poor brings her, then I must, with Kant, conclude that only the latter person is morally worthy, because only she acts upon the demands of reason, while the former acts merely as a human animal spurred emotionally by the "provision of our stepmother, nature."

The third enlightened system of ethics rested on an understanding of human nature richer than the French and found right motives in feeling rather than reason, building morality around human nature rather than in opposition to it.

ETHICS OF SENSIBILITY: THE SCOTTISH SCHOOL OF MORAL SENSE As always, the Scotsman Hume was the anti-Kant. In his *Enquiry Concerning the Principles of Morals*, Hume wrote

> There has been a controversy started of late, much better worth examination, concerning the general foundation of MORALS; whether they be derived from REASON, or from SENTIMENT; whether we attain the knowledge of them by a chain of argument and induction, or by an immediate feeling and finer internal sense; whether, like all sound judgment of truth and falsehood, they should be the same to every rational intelligent being; or whether, like the perception of beauty and deformity, they be founded entirely on the particular fabric and constitution of the human species. (sec. 134)

Recall that in his account of the human mind, Hume included the important category of the passions, or as they were also known in the eighteenth century, the sentiments. Crucial to Hume's analysis of the concept of causality was the sentiment, or feeling, of necessity, that must hold between events if we are to call them causes. In his analysis of moral judgment, Hume again appeals to sentiment, to naturally given—arising from the "particular fabric and constitution of the human species"—moral judgments of right and wrong. Just as we immediately feel that some things are beautiful and others are ugly—Hume drew a close analogy between aesthetic and moral judgment—so we spontaneously judge some actions as right and others are wrong. Hume and his fellow Scots, in opposition to Kant, grounded human morality in human nature. For them, however, the provision of nature was anything but "niggardly."

To the horror of Kant, Hobbes and Sade seemed to set humans in a fetid swamp of violence and immorality from which there is no rescue save the arbitrary power of a police state. Kant tried to rescue morality from relativism and tyranny by arguing that within us is an imperative moral law that does not need the state to operate. However, if we move to the cooler climate of Scotland, we find its commonsense philosophers reminding us that people are not as bad as Hobbes, Sade, and their alarmed readers fear (or like) to think. Although crime and war exist, most of the time most people act decently toward one another, and when they do not, they feel guilty or ashamed. Animal mothers care for their young; animal fights rarely result in death; and many animal species live in cooperative groups, all without society or government of any kind. Surely, the Scots (including Hume [Norton, 1993a]) argue, human nature, while not always moral, tends to be moral. Scottish philosophers maintained the Enlightenment project of constructing a science of human nature, but they found in human nature a new foundation for the explanation of morality.

Thomas Reid's own teacher, George Turnbull, concisely set out the Scottish position. Turnbull aimed to do for morals what Newton did for nature, inquiring "into moral phenomena, in the same manner as we do into physical ones" (quoted by Norton, 1982, p. 156). Nature is orderly and ruled by natural laws, observed Turnbull, and the existence of Newton's physics demonstrates that God furnished human nature with mental faculties capable of knowing nature's order and discovering nature's laws. By analogy, Turnbull reasoned, human behavior is orderly and ruled by moral laws, and God has furnished us with a moral sense by which we may discover moral laws: "I am apt to think, that everyone shall immediately perceive, that he has a moral sense inherent in him, and really inseparable from him. . . . If we experience approbation and disapprobation, then we must have an approving and disapproving faculty" (p. 162). That is, we are equipped by nature so as to see that some actions are right—we approve of them—and others are wrong—we disapprove of them.

Scottish moral sense theory was important in three respects. First, it coolly rejected the extreme claims of Hobbes and the French naturalists. People are made to be sociable and to behave decently, not to be utterly vicious and selfish. People spontaneously and without coercion care for each other and try to do what is right. La Mettrie's happy criminals and Sade's sadists are exceptions, not images of what we would all be without Hobbes's authoritarian state. Second, it helps establish the science of human nature, psychology. There are principles that govern human behavior other than those imposed by governmental *nomos*, and it is possible for us to learn and use them. Finally, the Scottish School exerted great influence in psychology's modern home, the United States. Along with many Americans, Thomas Jefferson read the great Scottish philosophers. When he wrote, "We hold these truths to be self-evident, that all men are created equal . . .," he built on Reid: "Moral truths may be divided into two classes, [the first of which are] such as are self-evident to every man whose understanding and moral faculty are ripe . . ." (quoted by Wills, 1978, p. 181).

On one point the Scots were divided. They agreed that human nature was sociable and benign, and that humans possess a moral sense, but they disagreed on the source of human nature. Reid and his followers thought it came from God. Hume, the atheist, said it came from nature itself, as Kant feared. "It is needless to push our researches so far as to ask why we have humanity or fellow-feeling with others. It is sufficient, that this is experienced to be a principle in human nature" (quoted by Norton, 1993a, p. 158). Hume asked only how human nature worked and refrained from asking why it is what it is. In the next century, Darwin began to create a science that only today, as the field of evolutionary psychology, could answer Hume's unasked question (D. C. Dennett, 1995; Haidt, 2007; Pinker, 2002).

Applying Psychological Ideas: Social Engineering

From developing a science of human nature it was but a step to applying that science to the improvement of human life. One of the first and most significant attempts at social engineering was carried out by the businessman and philanthropist Robert Owen (1771–1858) at his cotton mills at New Lanark, Scotland (Porter, 2000). Owen combined the idea that humans were machines with Locke's empiricism. He said that workers were "vital machines" who needed as much care and attention as a factory's "inanimate machines," and that "Children are, without exception, passive and wonderfully contrived compounds; which, by an accurate previous and subsequent attention, *founded on a correct knowledge of the subject*, may be formed collectively to have any human character" (R. Owen, 1813). Therefore, a new, utopian society "may be arranged, on a due combination of the foregoing principles, in such a manner, as not only to withdraw vice, poverty, and, in a great degree, misery, from the world, but also to place in *every* individual under such circumstances in which he shall enjoy more permanent happiness that can be given to *any* individual under the principles which have hitherto regulated society" (R. Owen, 1813). Owen's vision was to make New Lanark into an engineered community rather than a mere factory. He provided schooling (which had not yet become a state responsibility), a museum, a music hall, and a ballroom (the premier meeting place of the turn of the century; see Jane Austen's *Pride and Prejudice*). For Owen, a benevolent employer was concerned with his workers' happiness, not only their productivity. Nevertheless, he expected that happy workers "may be easily trained and directed to procure a large increase of pecuniary gain" for their employer (R. Owen, 1813). Owen's ideas anticipate the human relations movement in business and industry of the 1930s. Owen's scheme at New Lanark was not a success, and he moved to Indiana, where he established another utopian community, New Harmony. It, too, failed, being abandoned in 1828.

Social engineering on a grander scale—a whole country—was the goal of the French Revolution. The revolutionaries put the leading ideas of the Enlightenment—and the Way of Ideas itself—into the service of building a new society and a new humanity to inhabit it. The revolutionary Fabre d'Eglantine looked to Lockean empiricism to construct the propaganda—the new "empire of images"—by which the Revolution might erase loyalty to the old regime and build affection for the new. "We conceive of nothing except by images: even the most abstract analysis or the most metaphysical formulations can only take effect through images" (quoted by Schama, 1989). Rousseau wanted to take children away from their parents, to be raised by the state. A revolutionary leader, Louis de Saint-Just (1767–1794), sought to make the scheme a reality. With Helvetius, Saint-Just looked forward to the possibility of scientific control of human behavior, which depended on denying free will, "We must form men so they can only will what we wish them to will" (quoted by Hampson, 1982, p. 281). But Saint-Just also warned that an empire of virtue was bought at a terrible price: "Those who want to do good in this world must sleep only in the tomb" (quoted by Schama, 1989, p. 767).

Saint-Just was an inadvertent prophet. The French Revolution began in an unstable stew of ancient grievances, the Enlightenment's calls for scientific reform, and the Counter-Enlightenment's reverence of emotion and action. The reforming philosophes did not realize with what social dynamite they were playing. The French people had accumulated centuries of vaguely understood but powerfully felt resentments, as the growth of the monarchical state began to weigh heavily on them. In the end, the French Revolution cast doubt on the providential hopes of the philosophes. They aimed to reform humanity, but ultimately created the violence of the Reign of Terror, which in turn invited its suppression by a military coup led by a man who would be emperor, Napoleon Bonaparte. Napoleon carried out some Prussian-style enlightened reforms, such as a complete re-writing of French law, but his egoistic drive to conquer Europe and Russia ended in disaster, and the old Bourbon kings were restored, almost as if there had been no Revolution at all.

The Enlightenment and Women

As may have become apparent, the Enlightenment was a male affair. Although the French philosophes met in *salons* hosted by aristocratic women, the philosophes themselves were men, and they addressed questions about women only occasionally. In England, Locke said that the mind had no sex (Outram, 2005; Porter, 2001) and that women might be educated as well as men. Nevertheless, most philosophes simply assumed that women were naturally inferior to men.

The one philosopher who did explicitly address women's role in society was the *Counter-Enlightenment* thinker Jean-Jacques Rousseau (see the following discussion). Rousseau believed that nature had designed men and women for separate roles in life and that their education should be constructed to accommodate, not erase, these natural differences. "A woman's education must therefore be planned in relation to man," Rousseau (1762/1995, p. 576) wrote. "To be pleasing in his sight, to win his respect and love . . . to make his life pleasant and happy, these are the duties of woman for all time, and this is what she should be taught while she is young." Rousseau admired the Spartans and echoed their attitudes to women: "Women should not be strong like men but for them, so that their sons may be strong" (Rousseau, 1762/1995, p. 577). In the end, Rousseau concluded, the natural role of women was to serve men even when they are tyrants: Women are, and should be, "formed to obey a creature so imperfect as man, a creature often vicious and always faulty, she should learn to submit to injustice and to suffer the wrongs inflicted on her by her husband without complaint. . . ." (Rousseau, 1762/1995, p. 579).

Rousseau's ideas about educating women to serve men gave rise to a bizarre experiment in behavior modification a century before the term was coined. An Englishman, Peter Day, put

Rousseau's "theory into practice by acquiring a living doll to transform, Pygmalion-fashion, into the perfect wife . . . devot[ing] herself to her husband and offspring" (Porter, 2000, p. 329). He obtained a blonde girl of 12 from an orphanage. He named her Sabrina and tried to condition her to become Rousseau's ideal Spartan wife. To teach her Spartan indifference to pain, he dropped melted wax on her arm, and to teach her Spartan indifference to fear, he fired blanks at her skirt! She flinched at the first stimulus and shrieked at the second. Day concluded that Sabrina had a weak mind, and abandoned her and his experiment (Porter, 2000).

There were opponents of Rousseau who adopted Locke's view on the educability of all minds, male or female. They argued that women's subservient place in society was not ordained by nature, but was a result of tradition and poor education. The American Judith Murray, writing under the pen name Constantia, said that the alleged superiority of men's intellect rested not in nature, but could "trace its source in the difference of education between men and women" (Constantia, 1790/1995, p. 603). Mary Wollstonecraft (1759–1797), grandmother of Mary Shelley, author of *Frankenstein*, wrote, "It is vain to expect virtue from women till they are in some degree independent of men. . . . While they are absolutely dependent on their husbands they will be cunning (Rousseau said cunning was 'a natural gift of women'), mean, and selfish" (Wollstonecraft, 1792/1995, p. 618). In France, after the early Revolutionaries proclaimed the *Rights of Man*, Olympe de Gouges (1748– 1793) demanded the adoption of a *Declaration of the Rights of Woman*. She called to her fellow women in the spirit of the French Enlightenment project: "Woman, wake up; the tocsin of reason is being heard throughout the whole universe; discover your rights. The powerful empire of nature is no longer surrounded by prejudice, fanaticism, superstition, and lies" (de Gouges, 1791/1995, p. 614).

Despite these fierce voices, the immediate future lay with Rousseau. The nineteenth century would be deeply influenced by his idea that men and women had separate spheres of influence—the male world of commerce, politics, and war versus the intimate female world of home and hearth (Porter, 2001). Freud would identify women's confinement to a separate sphere as a prime cause of their neuroses, and when Francis Galton proposed tests by which the fittest young men and women might be selected for intermarriage, beauty and skill at housewifery were among the criteria by which women were to be chosen as mates for intelligent men.

THE COUNTER-ENLIGHTENMENT: ARE THE FRUITS OF REASON POISONED?

Newton had applied human reason, logic, and mathematics to nature, and he had shown that the human mind could encompass nature's laws and bend nature to human will. The vision of the philosophes of the Enlightenment was that Newtonian reason could be applied to human affairs—to psychology, ethics, and politics. In the Newtonian scheme of the philosophes, scientific reason would banish superstition, religious revelation, and historical tradition, setting in their place laws of human conduct whose use by enlightened despots could create the perfect human society. The philosophes were intolerant of cultural diversity because cultural traditions are not products of reason, so that all existing cultures fall short of the rational ideal. The philosophes were scornful of history, regarding it as no more than gossip from the past, entirely irrelevant to understanding contemporary society and to the task of reconstructing society in the light of reason.

The philosophes' imperialism of reason and science provoked a reaction from diverse thinkers who found it horrifyingly unhuman. Against the imperialism of natural science they set the autonomy of culture, and against the excesses of reason they set the feelings of the heart.

Their horror at the mechanistic universe of the philosophes was expressed by the English poet William Blake (1757–1827; quoted by Hampson, 1982):

> I turn my eyes to the Schools and Universities of Europe
> And there behold the Loom of Locke, whose woof rages dire,
> Wash'd by the Water-wheels of Newton: black the cloth
> In heavy wreathes folds over every nation: cruel Works
> Of many Wheels I view, wheel without wheel, with cogs tyrannic
> Moving by compulsion each other. (p. 127)

The Criterion and Rule of Truth Is to Have Made It: Giambattista Vico (1668–1744)

One current of the Counter-Enlightenment began with this obscure Italian philosopher who formed his ideas even before the Enlightenment began. Neoplatonic Christian theology and Cartesian philosophy had placed the human mind in a spiritual realm beyond the reach of science. The philosophes denied that human beings stood in any respect outside Newtonian science, and looked toward a universal experimental ethics based on the idea that human nature is everywhere the same and is unchanging. If such a nature exists, it follows that science may know it and technology may construct around it a perfect society. Vico began a tradition in philosophy that respects the old Platonic and Christian intuition that human beings are radically different from the other animals, but does so without invoking an immaterial soul. Instead, followers of Vico hold that what makes humans unique is culture, and that therefore there can be no Newtonian science of human mind and behavior.

Vico began with the astonishing assertion that knowledge of nature is inferior, secondhand knowledge compared to knowledge of society and history. Vico's criterion of knowledge derived from the scholastics of the Middle Ages, who held that one cannot really know something unless one has made it. In the case of nature, only God can really know the natural world because He made it. To us humans, nature is a given, a brute fact, something we can observe only from the outside, never from the inside. People, however, make their societies in the historical process of creation. We can see our own lives from the inside and, through sympathetic understanding, we can understand the lives of men and women in other cultures and other historical times.

For Vico, then, history is the greatest science; through history, we come to know how our society, or any society we choose to study, was created. History is not gossip, said Vico, but the process of human self-creation. The Enlightenment philosophes claimed there was a universal, timeless human nature that could be known to science and on which we could build a perfect society. But, according to Vico, human beings make themselves through history, so there is no eternal human nature and each culture must be respected for the human creation it is. We understand cultures by studying what they create, especially their myths and language. Myths express the soul of a culture at a certain point of development and language shapes and expresses the thoughts of its members. To understand another time's or place's myths and language is thus to understand how men and women thought and felt then and there.

Vico anticipated a distinction that became clearer in Herder, and clearer still in nineteenth-century German historians: the distinction between *Naturwissenschaft* and *Geisteswissenschaft*. Naturwissenschaft is Newtonian natural science, built on the observation of nature from the outside, noting regularities in events and summarizing them in scientific laws. Geisteswissenschaft is much harder to translate, meaning literally "spiritual science," but more often rendered today as "human science." Human science studies the human creations of history and society. Its method is not observation from without, but sympathetic understanding from within.

XAM'S BLOG 2
Science, Modernity, and the Counter-Enlightenment

The central idea of the Enlightenment was that people should live by the light of reason alone. This meant that ultimately, cultural differences between peoples and nations were fated to melt away, and that nonrational sources of authority such as religion and tradition would be vanquished by science. The figures of the Counter-Enlightenment were skeptical that people could live by reason alone, because living by reason alone was hard—one would have to carefully think-through every decision—and because it was terrifying. Tradition and religion encoded the accumulated wisdom of millennia of human life, and created humane institutions that concealed and made bearable the necessary exercise of power. In many respects, the turning point of modernism was the French Revolution of 1789, the first political revolution carried out self-consciously in the name of reason.

The political philosopher Edmund Burke had supported the American Revolution as an assertion of traditional British rights against a tyrannical monarchy, but opposed the French Revolution for seeking to overturn tradition all together. He believed that the power of social norms, culture, derives from history, from the tradition despised by the makers of the French Revolution. Describing the execution of the Queen of France by the modernist political order arising then in France, Burke (1790) wrote:

> All the pleasing illusions which made power gentle and obedience liberal, which harmonized the different shades of life, and which, by a bland assimilation, incorporated into politics the sentiments which beautify and soften private society, are to be dissolved by this new conquering empire of light and reason. All the decent drapery of life is to be rudely torn off. All the superadded ideas, furnished from the wardrobe of a moral imagination, which the heart owns and the understanding ratifies as necessary to cover the defects of our naked, shivering nature, and to raise it to dignity in our own estimation, are to be exploded as a ridiculous, absurd, and antiquated fashion.

On this scheme of things, a king is but a man, a queen is but a woman; a woman is but an animal, and an animal not of the highest order. . . . On the scheme of this barbarous philosophy, which is the offspring of cold hearts and muddy understandings, and which is as void of solid wisdom as it is destitute of all taste and elegance, laws are to be supported only by their own terrible power.

One of the defining thinkers of modernism was Friedrich Nietzsche (1844–1900), and interestingly he agreed with Burke about the source of morality's power, but put the modernist interpretation on it. He asked a penetrating—that is, from a modernist's perspective, unmasking—question about witches, and gave it a scientific, that is, modern, answer. Most of you know about witch persecutions, and it's often said in your psychology and sociology textbooks that there were no witches, only unfortunate women and men persecuted by vicious and ignorant religious authorities. However, there were certainly people who honestly believed that they were witches, that some confessions of witchcraft were not coerced and that the witches in question felt genuine guilt for offending God's law. Should freely confessed witches feel guilt? Nietzsche asks. No, he answers, and adds, alarmingly, "Thus it is with all guilt" (Nietzsche, 1882, §250). Because there is no God, there can be no sin, and hence no guilt. The witches' feelings of guilt were coerced not by their interrogators, but by the society in which they grew up, which effectively brainwashed them into believing in God, the Devil, sorcery, and sin. From a scientific perspective, they should feel no sin. Guilt is a secondary sense property—an illusion of consciousness—conditioned into us by society. Psychologist B. F. Skinner endorsed Nietzsche's conclusion in 1971 in his *Beyond Freedom and Dignity*, in which he argued that since all behavior is strictly determined and there is no free will, that freedom, ideas of moral responsibility, and the idea of human dignity are delusions to be abandoned and replaced by scientific social management.

It is apparent that psychology straddles the divide between the two sciences. People are part of nature—things—and as such are subject in part to natural science. But people live in human cultures and as such are subject to human science. Wundt's division of psychology between experimental, "physiological" psychology of human conscious experience on the one hand, and *Völkerpsychologie*—the study, as Vico recommended, of human myth, custom, and language, on the other hand—reflected Vico as well as Kant. Within Germany, however, the distinction was challenged by Wundt's young pupils, who wanted psychology to be a science on a par with physics. Outside Germany, the division was largely unknown and psychology was assimilated, as the philosophes would have wished, to natural science and the search for universal laws of human behavior.

We Live in a World We Ourselves Create:
Johann Gottfried Herder (1744–1803)

Vico was little read outside his own circle in Italy. However, his ideas reappeared, independently asserted, in the works of Herder, who rejected the Enlightenment's worship of reason and universal truth in favor of romanticism's trust in the human heart and a historical reverence for many human truths. Herder's views are remarkably similar to Vico's, although they were formed in ignorance of Vico's works. His motto, "We live in a world we ourselves create," could have been said by Vico. Herder, too, stressed the absolute uniqueness of each living or historical culture. We should strive to fulfill ourselves and our own culture, not slavishly follow classical styles and attitudes of a bygone age. Herder is modern in his belief that each person should try to fulfill his or her potential as a total person instead of being an alienated collection of roles. Herder opposed faculty psychology for its fragmentation of the human personality. For both the individual and the individual's culture, Herder stressed organic development.

Because each culture is unique, Herder opposed any attempt to impose one culture's values on any other. He detested the tendency of the philosophes to caricature the past and hold out their own times as a universal model for humanity. Herder even went so far as to imply the degeneracy of the Age of Reason. It was artificial; it aped the Greeks and Romans; it worshipped reason and neglected spirituality.

Herder's views were highly influential, especially in Germany. Although Kant had written one of the great manifestos of the Enlightenment, *What Is Enlightenment?*, and although Prussia's Frederick the Great was the prototypical "Enlightened Despot," the ahistorical and aggressively rationalist attitudes of the philosophes did not take root in Germany, which found Herder's emphasis on historical development and profound feeling more attractive. German philosophy rejected the exaltation of individual consciousness found in the Enlightenment. Fichte wrote, "The individual life has no existence, since it has no value in itself, but must and should sink to nothing, while on the contrary the race alone exists" (quoted by Hampson, 1982, p. 278). Although Herder and Fichte defined race in terms of common language rather than the fanciful biology of the later Nazis, they helped create an environment in which Germans regarded themselves as special. As Fichte wrote, "We appear to be the elect of a universal divine plan" (p. 281). German psychology would be deeply shaped by German philosophy's alienation from the Enlightenment. German thinkers, including Wundt and even the proud Jew Freud, saw themselves as apart from and better than the supposedly shallower thinkers to their west, and in turn English-speaking psychologists would have little use for the impractical alleged profundities of German Geisteswissenschaft.

More generally, Herder helped lay the foundation for romanticism. He passionately opposed the mock-classical art of his time, calling modern critics "masters of dead learning." Instead, he advocated "Heart! Warmth! Blood! Humanity! Life!" Descartes had said, "I think, therefore I am."

Condillac implied, "I sense, therefore I am." Herder wrote "I feel! I am!" Thus ended, for many people, the rule of abstract reason, the geometric spirit, and reasonable emotion. Instead, organic development led by emphatic emotion was the base of the new romanticism.

Nature versus Civilization: Jean-Jacques Rousseau (1712–1778)

> O Almighty God, thou who holds all things in thy grasp, deliver us from the learning and destructive arts of our fathers, and give us back our ignorance, our innocence, and our poverty, the only gifts that make us happy, and are precious in thy sight. Can we forget that in the very bosom of Greece herself there arose a city which became famous through a happy ignorance, and the wisdom of her laws? A commonwealth peopled rather by demi-gods than men, so far did their virtue outshine humanity. O Sparta! thou proof of the folly of vain learning! whilst all manner of vice, led by the arts and sciences were introduced into Athens, whilst a tyrant was busy in picking up the works of the prince of poets, thou were chasing from the walls all sciences, all learning, together with their professors. (Rousseau, 1750)

In France, the Counter-Enlightenment began in 1749. In that year, the Dijon Academy of arts and sciences set an essay contest on the question "Whether the restoration of the arts and sciences has contributed to the refinement of morals." Rousseau's essay began his career as an influential writer. No clearer statement of the ideas of the Counter-Enlightenment exists than Rousseau's statements in his essay. He rejected Enlightenment, yearning to return to the days of ignorance and poverty that Enlightenment philosophes rejected because he wanted to restore the naive childhood of natural men and women. He preferred ancient Sparta, which disdained art, philosophy, and science as weak, to Athens, the home of Phidias's Parthenon, Plato's philosophy, and Aristotle's science. For Rousseau, knowledge, the light of the Enlightenment, was corrupted; it was dark, not light; bringer of evil, not happiness.

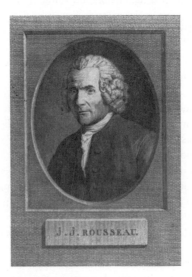

Jean-Jacques Rousseau *(Courtesy of Library of Congress)*

Rousseau argued, against the tide of Enlightened opinion, that the answer to the Academy's question was *No!* He wrote, "deliver us from the enlightenment and the fatal arts of our fathers, and give us back ignorance, innocence, and poverty, the only goods which can make our happiness." In many ways, Rousseau's complaints about the Enlightenment paralleled Herder's, although Rousseau was less conscious of history than was Herder. Rousseau said, "To exist is to feel" and "the first impulses of the heart are always right"—sentiments that recall Herder and point to romanticism. Like Herder, Rousseau rejected mechanism because it could not explain human free will.

Rousseau argued with Hobbes's conceptions of human nature and of society. Hobbes had found in the English Civil War an impression of what people without government were like: violent and warlike. In Rousseau's time, travelers from the South Pacific brought different tales of what people were like without government. They drew an idyllic picture of life unencumbered by the demands of European society. People lived without clothes, ate the food freely available on the trees, and took sexual pleasure where they found it. In the Pacific islands, it appeared, the life of humans was the opposite of being solitary, nasty, brutish, and short. These island peoples became Rousseau's famous Noble Savages. Rousseau argued that the present state of society corrupted and degraded human nature. Instead of a return to primitivism, Rousseau advocated building a new, less alienating society, and the makers of the French Revolution followed him.

Rousseau was a friend of Condillac and was similarly empiricist and interested in education. Rousseau described his ideal educational program in *Emile* (1762/1974), in which a child and his tutor retire from corrupt civilization and return to nature for education. Rousseau advocated a kind of nondirectional education, believing that a child should be allowed to express his or her native talents, and described a good education as one that cultivates the natural growth of these talents. The tutor should not impose views on the student. Nevertheless, behind the apparent freedom is firm control. At one point, Rousseau described what we would call open education: "It is rarely your business to suggest what he ought to learn; it is for him to want to learn." However, earlier, he had written: "Let him always think he is master while you are really master. There is no subjection so complete as that which preserves the forms of freedom." For Rousseau the empiricist, the corrupt state of civilization can be overcome by a proper education, which perfects the potentialities of each person. Herder believed in self-fulfillment, but he was less individualistic, seeing fulfillment in the larger context of the person's culture, which the person helped perfect while perfecting self.

Rousseau's influence has been wide. His affinities with romanticism and political revolutionaries have been alluded to. In education, he inspired those in the 1960s who supported open education of the "whole child" against those who preferred highly structured teaching of separate, basic skills. He is also behind those who want to reform society through education. In his belief in human malleability and perfectibility, he foreshadowed B. F. Skinner, who advocated a carefully controlled society whose goal is human happiness, although Skinner openly disbelieved in human freedom.

The Irrational Realm of the Unconscious: Mesmerism

The term *mesmerism* comes from the name of the movement's founder, Franz Anton Mesmer (1734–1815), a Viennese physician who attributed numerous bodily diseases to influences exerted by an impalpable fluid penetrating the entire universe. Mesmer believed that this fluid was vital to the nervous activity of the body and that physicians could cure various diseases by manipulating the fluid in a patient's body. Mesmer began by using magnets to draw the fluid away from the afflicted areas, but he soon decided that the fluid was susceptible to movements of his hands over his patients' bodies, animal magnetism, rather than to mineral magnetism. Mesmer devised a complicated and outré therapy for his patients, involving, among other things, striking the diseased parts of the body with his hands or a magic wand, tubs of water with iron rods focused on a patient's symptoms, and a "crisis room" lined with mattresses in which Mesmer's cures were effected during a kind of seizure. He specialized in what we now call "functional" illnesses—those that come from purely psychological causes. Although it was suggested at the time that at least some of the cures were a result of the patient's suggestibility, Mesmer firmly resisted any such hypothesis, insisting on his theory of animal fluids.

No single element of mesmerism was new. The curing of apparently physical diseases by inspired individuals is a staple belief of many religions. It was also practiced by such contemporaries of Mesmer as Valentine Greatraks in England and Johann Gassner in Germany. Greatraks's specialty was scrofula, or the King's Evil, so-called because the touch of the monarch was said to cure it. If Mesmer's practice was not new, neither was the hypothesis of an ineffable, universal fluid. Central to Newton's universe was the ether, a subtle fluid that carried electromagnetic waves and defined absolute space. A whole line of alchemical doctors had believed in a universal fluid essential to health, and even such a modern chemist as Robert Boyle attributed Greatraks's cures to invisible particles passing from doctor to patient. Gassner was a German priest who allegedly cast out demons. Mesmer himself investigated Gassner, concluding that Gassner's cures resulted from the natural use of animal magnetism, not religious exorcism.

Mesmer's novel approach was to try to put such cures and theorizing on a scientific basis. He attempted to convince medical establishments, first in Vienna and later in Paris, that his cures were genuine and that animal magnetism was real. Over and over again, physicians admitted that Mesmer had seemingly effected great cures, but they found his methods too bizarre, his theory unscientific. Some even intimated that he was a fraud. Mesmerism was too close to the occult—using trances, magical passes, and the trappings of the seance—to satisfy Newtonian doctors. Mesmer was eventually worn down by these repeated rebuffs and by what he felt were betrayals by some of his followers. In 1784, he left Paris to live the rest of his life detached from the movement he had started.

That movement was enormously popular. In the years before the French Revolution, it garnered far more attention from the French public than the issues of the Revolution. Mesmeric lodges sprang up all over France in the 1780s. Mesmer enlisted the Marquis de Lafayette as a patron, and corresponded briefly with George Washington. Mesmer and mesmerism seemed to fill perfectly a gap left by religion's receding influence. Science was all the rage in the late eighteenth century, and its influence grew in the nineteenth century. People were hungry for a new set of certainties to replace the old. Mesmer offered at least the trappings of science—a reasoned theory about why his cures worked, an explanation that also covered the ancient miracle workers. Yet, at the same time, Mesmer's practice, served up in mystical and magical dress, was more allowing than the austere rationalism of Newton's science. In short, Mesmer offered exactly the right pseudoscience for the times. It was scientific enough to appeal to the new rationalism, but spiritual enough to appeal to latent religious needs as well (Leahey & Leahey, 1983).

Whether Mesmer himself was a charlatan is an extremely difficult question to answer. Like Freud, he demanded absolute obedience from his followers, lest they betray his invention. His treatment sessions were lurid seances, with Mesmer attired in mystic robes and wielding an iron wand. Moreover, Mesmer drifted into genuine occultism, using animal magnetism to explain clairvoyance, telepathy, and precognition. Yet Mesmer always tried to convince the medical establishment of his validity, even when it brought him nothing but ridicule. Mesmer was at once a magician and a pioneer in abnormal psychology. Although Mesmer attributed the trance to animal magnetism, it became apparent to his critics and even to some of his followers that something simpler was involved. The trance was due to the psychological control of one person over another rather than the passing of an invisible fluid from one body to another. Once this insight was obtained, it became possible to extract the mesmeric trance from the mystical context: Mesmerism was transformed into hypnotism.

CONCLUSION: REASON AND ITS DISCONTENTS

The major theme of the period between 1600 and 1800 was the triumph of science—in particular, Newtonian science—over the old, medieval, theological worldview. In the seventeenth century, Galileo, Kepler, Descartes, and Newton demonstrated the power of a new kind of understanding of nature. The new scientific view substituted the idea of universal mathematical order for the older idea of universal meaning in nature. Humanity's view of nature changed greatly. Nature had been a book of signs revealing the invisible world beyond. Now it became an indifferent machine that could be known only in a limited way, via mathematics. Nature lost its meaningfulness, but humanity gained power over it from mathematically precise predictions.

The viewpoint of science was something fundamentally new in human history. Heretofore, thinkers had merely speculated about the nature of reality, and their speculations were comprehensive in scope but lacking in detail. Newtonian science substituted detailed analysis of concrete cases for vast speculations about cosmic order. Since Newton's time, of course, science has grown in comprehensiveness until, for many, it has entirely supplanted religion as a world picture.

No sooner had Newton propounded the new antimetaphysical science of physics, than philosophers began to see the possibility of extending it to human nature. The enterprise began with Locke and occupied almost every eighteenth-century thinker. The keynote was sounded by Hume in his call for a science of human nature to be as fundamental to science as metaphysics had been thought to be. It has emerged that natural science can get along quite well without psychology, and the average physicist would laugh at Hume's proposal. Still, the eighteenth century did move significantly toward creating a science of human nature (Fox, Porter, & Wokler, 1995). The philosophes believed in Hume's science, but they showed no more unanimity on the nature of human nature than psychologists show today.

Alexander Pope (1688–1744), the English poet, caught the spirit of the Enlightenment view of human nature before the French Revolution (Pope, *Essay on Man* [1734/1965] Epistle II, 1. 1–30):

> *Know then thyself, presume not God to scan;*
> *The proper study of Mankind is Man.*
> *Placed on this isthmus of a middle state,*
> *A being darkly wise, and rudely great:*
> *With too much knowledge for the Sceptic side,*
> *With too much weakness for the Stoic's pride,*
> *He hangs between; in doubt to act, or rest,*
> *In doubt to deem himself a God, or Beast,*
> *In doubt his Mind or Body to prefer,*
> *Born but to die, and reas'ning but to err;*
> *Alike in ignorance, his reason such,*
> *Whether he thinks too little, or too much:*
> *Chaos of Thought and Passion, all confused;*
> *Still by himself abused, or disabused;*

Created half to rise, and half to fall;
Great lord of all things, yet a prey to all;
Sole judge of Truth, in endless Error hurled:
The glory, jest, and riddle of the world!
Go, wondrous creature! mount where Science guides,
Go, measure earth, weigh air, and state the tides;
Instruct the planets in what orbs to run,
Correct old Time, and regulate the Sun;
Go, soar with Plato to th' empyreal sphere,
To the first good, first perfect, and first fair;
Or tread the maze round his follow'rs trod,
And quitting sense call imitating God;
As Eastern priests in giddy circles run,
And turn their heads to imitate the Sun.
Go, teach Eternal Wisdom how to rule—
Then drop into thyself, and be a fool!

The Ascent of Science 1815–1914

INTRODUCTION

The nineteenth century was the century in which psychology came of age as a recognized discipline. It was also a period of rapid social change. The Industrial Revolution transformed the face of Europe—working in urban factories and great department stores replaced working on farms and village stores. European GDP (gross domestic product) grew 170% in the course of the century. The population of Europe more than doubled, from 205 million people in 1800 to 414 million in 1900. Government grew even faster; in Great Britain, for example, the number of bureaucrats rose from 99,000 in 1800 to 395,000 in 1900 (Blanning, 2000). The state began to take over the roles of ancient private corporations such as guilds, religious orders, and charities in guiding peoples' lives (Tombs, 2000) as the rapid growth of cities overwhelmed the idea of the "*nightwatchman state*" of strictly limited powers, such as the power to conduct war (Burrow, 2000; Ferguson, 2000). As governments grew, they also became more democratic (Burrow, 2000) as suffrage was gradually extended from property holders to all male citizens. It would not be until well in the twentieth century that women would be able to vote in all Western countries. Because they were rapid, these changes were keenly felt (Burrow, 2000; Tombs, 2000). Nearly overwhelmed by the modern society exploding around them, social and political leaders turned to social science for the tools they needed to regain control of history. By the end of the century, psychology, the modern science for the modern age, would become a key player in shaping the modern world.

The rise of science as a new worldview that challenged religion was central to the history of the nineteenth century. The writer G. H. Lewes wrote, "Science is penetrating everywhere, and slowly changing man's conception of the world and of man's destiny" (quoted by Sheehan,

Hermann von Helmholtz *(Courtesy of Library of Congress)*

2000, p. 135). Prior to the nineteenth century, science had been respected and emulated, but it had not yet accomplished very much, nor had it become well known outside the *salons* of the philosophes. The way most people lived their lives had changed little since the invention of agriculture millennia earlier. The vast majority of people lived and worked on farms, and traveled no farther than a day or two's walk from their place of birth. Chemical dyes having not yet been invented, only aristocrats wore anything but drab clothing. People knew little of the outside world, and education past simple reading and calculating was rare; most people were completely illiterate. Social or technological change was slow, even glacial. In the nineteenth century, science increased the pace of change, deeply altering the human way of life. Industrialization revealed the power of science to dramatically control and alter the world. Electricity began to carry information on telegraph wires and to illuminate the night. Chemistry created dyes, changing profoundly how people dressed and thus how they appeared to others and in their own reflection. People began to work in factories and to move to cities. Railroads carried people great distances and brought new things to their doors. Stores opened and shopping was invented. People learned to read and they devoured books on popular science, supporting the careers of people such as T. H. Huxley and Herbert Spencer.

Unsurprisingly, as science became better known and demonstrated its world-shaking powers, it came to challenge religion. Some thinkers of the nineteenth century were so excited by science and its possibilities that it became for them a sort of religion (Burnham, 1987) with its own demands and claims of authority. The mathematician W. A. Clifford (1845–1879) wrote that people have a "universal duty of questioning all that we believe" and that "it is wrong always and everywhere, and for anyone, to believe anything upon insufficient evidence" (quoted by Burrow, 2000, p. 54); faith was no longer acceptable as a road to truth. The infallibility of the pope was challenged by the claim that "science is infallible" (H. A. Taine [see later discussion] quoted by Burrow, 2000, p. 55). At the extreme, the positivist Auguste Comte (see later discussion) wanted a scientific Religion of Humanity to replace the worship of God, but only his most devoted followers went that far. Such people, of course, did not lose their religion, they simply changed churches. Others were touched by science more deeply. They lost their old religious faith but were unsure how to replace it or if it should be replaced. For many, romanticism seemed to offer an inspiring faith based on emotion, hinting at an intuition, or at least a hope, of something beyond the material world. Other people participated in new quasi-religious movements such as spiritualism because they seemed to offer evidence that humans had souls and that there was an afterlife. And there were those who "lived on nerve" (Himmelfarb, 1995). As one Victorian agnostic put it, "I no longer believe in anything, but I mean to live and die like a gentleman." Having lost their religion, they simply chose, by sheer force of will, to act as if Christianity were true.

Psychology—*psuche-logos*—could not help but be affected by the Victorian crisis of conscience. Some people looked to psychology to continue to teach them about the soul. This tradition was especially powerful in America, where the religiously oriented Scottish psychology continued with little change until after the Civil War. On the other hand, psychology began to offer ways of thinking about the human mind and behavior that challenged religious beliefs. As science became popular, scientific and pseudoscientific psychology became popular, too. People read about phrenology, joined phrenological clubs, and sought the advice of phrenologists on whom to marry and what career to pursue. Scientific psychologists would eventually serve many of the functions served by priests and ministers, advancing the cause of applied psychology. On the other hand, some people turned to psychology, specifically psychical research, for proof that the soul existed. In sum, psychology helped deepen the Victorian crisis of conscience and began to move into areas previously dominated by religious ideas, but it was shaped by religious yearnings even as it undermined religious beliefs (Sheehan, 2000).

MOVEMENTS

The Reassertion of Emotion and Intuition: The Romantic Revolt

Although we usually think of romanticism as a movement in the arts, it was much more; it carried on the protests of the Counter-Enlightenment against the Cartesian-Newtonian worldview. As romantic poet and artist William Blake (1757–1827) prayed, "May God us keep / From Single vision and Newton's sleep." The romantics regarded Cartesian claims for the supremacy of reason as overweening, and combated them with paeans to strong feeling and nonrational intuition. Whereas some Enlightenment writers, notably Hume, had valued mild and moral "passions," the romantics were inclined to worship all strong emotions—even violent and destructive ones. Above all, the romantics fervently believed there was more in the universe than atoms and the void, and, by unleashing passion and intuition, one might reach a world beyond the material. To this end, many romantics took psychoactive drugs, hoping to escape the bonds of ordinary rational consciousness in search of higher, almost Platonic, Truth.

Unsurprisingly, the romantics' conception of the mind differed from that of the Enlightenment's "Newtons of the mind." Most Enlightenment writers concerned themselves with conscious experience; the romantics adumbrated ideas of the unconscious, the primal and chaotic home of feeling and intuition. The German philosopher Arthur Schopenhauer (1788–1860) posited Will as the noumenal reality behind appearances. Schopenhauer's Will, specifically the will to live, pushes humanity on to endless, futile striving for something better. This description of the Will foreshadows Freud's id. Schopenhauer wrote, in *Parerga*, "In the heart of every man there lives a wild beast." Intelligence tries to control the Will, but its raging inflicts pain on the self and others. Also prefiguring Freud were those writers who saw in dreams the language of the unconscious needing only to be decoded to reveal the secrets of the infinite.

In contrast to the rather bloodless and mechanical picture of the mind advanced by many philosophers, especially in Britain, the romantics depicted the mind as free and spontaneously active. The Will is a wild beast, but while that wildness implies pain, it also implies freedom of choice. Schopenhauer's philosophy thus was voluntaristic, a romantic reaction against the Enlightenment's materialistic determinism. Generally, this led the romantics to worship heroes, geniuses, and artists—those who asserted their Wills and did not bow to the way of the world. Thomas Carlyle, for instance, revered heroes who ranged from Odin to Shakespeare to Napoleon. The romantic emphasis on the mind's independent activity can be found even in the study of perception. Most philosophers followed Hume in seeing perception as a process of making "impressions" on a passive mind. Influenced by Kant, Leibniz, and the European Idealist tradition, Samuel Taylor Coleridge (1772–1834), for instance, likened the mind to a lamp. Instead of merely registering impressions, the mind casts intellectual light, actively reaching out to the world and shaping the resulting experience.

Romantics rejected the mechanical conception of society that had led to the French Enlightenment, whose beginning they applauded but whose bloody ending they lamented. If society, like physical nature, is just a machine, then, like nature, it may be rationally and scientifically controlled. Against this view, romantics such as Edmund Burke (1729–1797) held that societies were grown, not made. The customs of civil society grew slowly into a rich, interconnected set of customs, norms, and beliefs often only marginally present to consciousness. Thinking some social practice is irrational was akin to thinking the shape of a tree is irrational. Moreover, just as too much pruning and shaping can kill a tree, so scientific planning can kill a culture. As a member of Parliament, a lonely Burke applauded the American Revolution because it asserted the time-honored rights of English people against a tyrannical king. Later, however, Burke denounced the French Revolution for overturning the natural, evolved, French way of life in the name of abstract reason.

Although the romantic movement was short-lived, its legacy was a great split in psychology. Although not necessarily elevating passion and intuition, the founding psychologists all viewed the mind in the spirit of romanticism. Wundt called his psychology voluntaristic, stressing the independence of mental principles of development from physical ones. James, too, was a voluntarist, deeply committed to the reality and freedom of will. Freud, of course, picked up the notion of the unconscious, and elevated its passions over the still-small voice of reason as the causes of human thought and behavior. Nevertheless, in the English-speaking world with which we are primarily concerned, the conception of mind, and later behavior, as essentially mechanistic and driven from outside, soon replaced the romantic one, despite James's protestations. Likewise, in the twentieth century, psychologists would be deeply involved in the kinds of scientific social engineering that horrified the conservative heirs to Burke. At least in psychology, romanticism was defeated by the Continuing Enlightenment.

The Continuing Enlightenment: Developments in Utilitarianism and Associationism

Not everyone was disenchanted by the Newtonian spirit. Many important thinkers carried on the Enlightenment project, especially in England and France. Indeed, out of the Continuing Enlightenment came the central concepts of twentieth-century American psychology.

The fusing of the principle of utility with associationism began with James Mill (1773–1836), a politician turned philosopher. His associationism, a simple Tinkertoy theory of mind, was the frequent target of later, more holistic psychologists such as Wundt, James, and the Gestalt psychologists. In Mill's view, the mind is a passive, blank slate that is receptive to simple sensations (the Tinkertoy nodes) out of which complex sensations or ideas are compounded by forming associative links (the sticks linking the nodes) between atomic units.

As had Condillac, Mill (1829/1964) dispensed with the mental faculties retained by Hume, Hartley, and other previous associationists. Combined with utilitarian hedonism, the result was a completely mechanical picture of mind in which idea follows idea automatically, with no room left for voluntary control. The exercise of will is an illusion, Mill maintained. Reasoning is no more than idea following idea governed by the laws of association. Attention is simply the fact that the mind is necessarily preoccupied by current ideas that are pleasurable or painful.

Like Bentham and many others who wrote on the mind, Mill expounded his psychology for purposes of political reform. Influenced by Helvetius, as was Bentham, Mill was especially interested in education. If humans are blank slates at birth, education may be used to mold the mind. Mill put his ideas into practice by the rigorous education he gave his son, teaching him ancient Greek at age 3 and Latin at age 8. This son wrote a history of Roman law when he was 10 years old.

The son, John Stuart Mill (1806–1873), did not become the perfect utilitarian his father had expected, however. Although an early adherent of Benthamism, he experienced a nervous breakdown during which he came to find Benthamism sterile, narrow, excessively calculating and even "evil." He eventually tempered Bentham's hedonistic principles with Wordsworth's romantic vision of nature and human feeling. He endorsed the romantic preference for the grown or natural over the manufactured, and he denied that human beings are machines. He saw people as living things whose autonomous development and growth should be nurtured, a vision most fully expressed in his *On Liberty* (1859/1978), the founding document of modern political libertarian thought.

J. S. Mill was an important spokesman for the idea that the social sciences were legitimate sciences though he recognized that they might never achieve the degree of perfection attained by the natural sciences. Despite this, he believed that social sciences were not in principle different from the natural sciences, and should use the same methods. He wrote an important work on scientific method, beginning the development of the sophisticated experimental and analytic techniques psychologists use today. The influence of Mill and Comte was so great that German ideas about the methodological and theoretical differences between the natural and human sciences were rarely discussed in the English-speaking world.

In philosophical psychology, Mill modified his father's mechanical associationism by creating an analogy between chemistry and psychology. Earlier associationists, including his father, had recognized that certain associative links become so strong that the linked ideas appear inseparable. J. S. Mill went further, maintaining that elementary ideas could fuse into a whole idea with properties possessed by none of its atomic elements. In chemistry, for example, we learn that water is a wet liquid composed of two gases—hydrogen and oxygen. Similarly, complex mental ideas may be composed of sensory elements, yet have unique characteristics of their own. An example is what early psychologists called color fusion. Spin a disc divided into wedges, each colored with a primary color, and at a certain speed the experience will be of whiteness, not of spinning colors. The atomic colors on the wheel generate a new color, white, not present on the disc. Mill was influenced by the romantic' concept of coalescence, the idea that active imagination may synthesize atomic elements into a creation that is more than the sum of the atomic units themselves, as when elementary colors are mixed to make a qualitatively different one.

We must emphasize, however, that although Mill tempered his father's associationistic Benthamism with the broader conceptions of romanticism, he sought to improve utilitarianism and empiricism, not to refute them. He always detested the mystic intuitionism of Coleridge, Carlyle, and the other romantics. Nor did Mill accept romantic voluntarism. His mental chemistry, although it recognized the possible coalescence of sensations and ideas, remained an atomistic conception of mind, suggesting that scientific psychology resembled analytic chemistry, discovering the basic elements out of which mental objects are associatively compounded. Moreover, in Mill's view, it is not the mind's autonomous activity that brings about the qualitative chemical change, but the way the sensations are associated in experience. One does not choose to see the white spinning disk; the experience is forced on one's perception by the conditions of the experiment.

John Stuart Mill was the last great philosophical associationist. His associationism arose in the context of logical and metaphysical—not purely psychological—discussions. Mill believed in the possibility of Hume's science of human nature and, in fact, tried to contribute to its methodology.

A Philosophy of and for Science: Positivism

The Enlightenment philosophes venerated Newtonian science and began to apply the Newtonian spirit to the study of human nature and human affairs. These tendencies deepened in the nineteenth century, and were given clear and forceful expression in the "positive philosophy" of Auguste Comte (1798–1857). Like the philosophes, Comte was not a formal philosopher, scientist, or academician, but a public writer and lecturer who wanted to bring about political and social change rather than advance the cause of science. Unlike the philosophes, who talked among themselves in their glittering aristocratic salons and who cultivated "enlightened" despots, Comte

XAM'S BLOG 1
Modernity Described by a Frenemy

The bourgeoisie cannot exist without constantly revolutionising the instruments of production, and thereby the relations of production, and with them the whole relations of society. Conservation of the old modes of production in unaltered form was, on the contrary, the first condition of existence for all earlier industrial classes. Constant revolutionising of production, uninterrupted disturbance of all social conditions, everlasting uncertainty and agitation distinguish the bourgeois epoch from all earlier ones. All fixed, fast-frozen relations, with their train of ancient and venerable prejudices and opinions, are swept away, all new-formed ones become antiquated before they can ossify. All that is solid melts into air, all that is holy is profaned, and man is at last compelled to face with sober senses, his real conditions of life, and his relations with his kind.

—Marx and Engels, The Communist Manifesto (1848)

(1975) addressed the working classes and the women excluded from politics by the restored French aristocracy.

You all know that Marx and communists hate the bourgeoisie and capitalism and want to destroy both. But there was more to Marx than that. If you read this famous passage carefully, you will see that Marx respected and even needed the bourgeoisie and capitalism. They destroyed the static premodern past, sweeping away "ancient and venerable prejudices" replacing it with a relentless pursuit of change and improvement—"constant revolutionizing of production." They made people face the truth about themselves and society, of "the real conditions of life." They created globalization and Facebook: "The need of a constantly expanding market for its products chases the bourgeoisie over the whole surface of the globe. It must nestle everywhere, settle everywhere, establish connexions everywhere." Above all, capitalism produces wealth, "It has been the first to show what man's activity can bring about. It has accomplished wonders far surpassing Egyptian pyramids, Roman aqueducts, and Gothic cathedrals." Without the bourgeoisie and capitalism, there could be no revolution against it, and without its wealth, socialism would just be spreading poverty, not wealth, around.

Communists thought that just around the corner lay a new revolution of socialism erected on the rich rubble of capitalism. Marx did not foresee that wealth creation would continue; the *Manifesto* claims that a limit to production had been reached, just at the moment when the second Industrial Revolution of 1860 was about to take off (Clark, 2007; Mokyr, 2009). "All that is solid melts into air . . ." happened, but the socialist revolution did not. The old "fixed, fast-frozen relations" did have to be replaced, but they were replaced by social science more than social*ism*.

Positivism as Social Theory.   Comte described human history as passing through three stages, culminating, like many nineteenth-century stage theories of history, in a final, perfect stage of government. Comte's stages were defined by the characteristic way people explained events in the world around them.

The first stage was the *theological stage*. In this stage, people explained phenomena by positing unseen, supernatural entities—gods, angels, demons, souls—behind them. For example, ancient Egyptians regarded the sun, Ra, as a god, and worshipped him to ensure his arising each morning. Platonic, Cartesian, or religious dualism represents theological thinking in psychology because the soul is seen as a nonmaterial and immortal being that guides the behavior of the body.

The second stage was the *metaphysical stage*. Events were still explained by unseen entities and forces, but they were no longer anthropomorphized as divine acts or attributed to supernatural influences. In psychology, Aristotle's concept of form is at Comte's metaphysical stage. The soul of a living being is not conceived as supernatural or immortal, but as an unseen "essence" that defines and governs it. Indeed, Aristotelian thinking was a favorite target of the positivists. With its essences and entelechies, and seeing hidden purposes in all things, it committed the positivist crime of metaphysics on a grand scale.

The third stage was the *scientific stage*. In this last stage, explanations drop all references to unseen entities or forces of any type. Following Newton, positivist science feigns no hypotheses about any hidden causal structure of nature, but provides precise mathematical principles by which to gain power over nature. This stage represented the triumph of the philosophy of positivism.

According to Comte, each stage is also ruled by a characteristic form of government, depending on the reigning mode of explanation. During the theological stage, the government is run, as it was in Egypt, by priests—those who possess knowledge of the gods and so can communicate with them, propitiate them, and, to a degree, control them. The metaphysical stage is ruled by refined aristocrats such as Plato's Guardians or a philosophe elite who are in touch with the "higher" things of art and philosophy. Finally, in the scientific stage, scientists rule. In particular, a new science—sociology—would come into being. Sociologists, armed with a Newtonian science of society, would have the same precise and accurate power over society that natural scientists have over nature. With the triumph of science, superstition and religion would disappear, Comte thought, and would be replaced by a rational, naturalistic Religion of Humanity that would worship the only real creative power in the universe—*Homo sapiens*.

Positivism and Psychology.   Comte disdained psychology as it was then defined. Its very name, psuche-logos, proclaimed its dependence on an unseen construct—the soul—that was at least metaphysical and, at worst, religious. A genuine positive science of individuals—one that discarded all reference to the unseen—would have to be neurophysiological. Comte described a hierarchy of sciences, from most basic (physics) to most complex (sociology), that became the logical positivists' Unity of Science thesis. For Comte, as for J. S. Mill, all sciences used a single set of methods and aimed at a single Newtonian ideal of prediction and control. The view of Vico and Herder—that the social sciences were fundamentally different from the natural sciences—thus exerted little influence in France or the English-speaking world. In addition, Comte's insistence that science be socially useful further divided positivistic social science from the German tradition in which scientific psychology first appeared. Most German psychologists wanted psychology to be a pure science and resisted making it a practical, applied, "psychotechnics." French, English, and American psychologists, on the other hand, always wanted psychology to be socially useful.

Positivism as a Philosophy of Science.   Later, less flamboyant positivists narrowed Comte's vision to a sophisticated and influential philosophy of science. The most important of these sober positivists was Ernst Mach (1838–1916).

Mach was a German physicist who elaborated positivism as a foundational philosophy for science. He admired Berkeley and, like Berkeley, saw human consciousness as a collection of sensations, making the goal of science no more than the economical ordering of sensations. Mach stood by his austere, antirealistic philosophy during the great debate on the reality and scientific legitimacy of atoms, asking of their defenders, "Have you ever seen one?" An antirealist Mach said that human knowledge, including scientific theory, served only pragmatic functions, allowing us to adaptively predict and control nature. Theory should never commit the crime of metaphysics by aspiring to Truth. Mach also introduced a critical, historical method to the study of science. He believed that many scientific concepts had acquired metaphysical accretions in the course of their development, and that the best way to strip them off and reduce the concepts to their sensory base was to study their historical development. Echoing Comte, Mach noted that early science had grown up in the theological atmosphere of the seventeenth century, and, consequently, concepts such as force had acquired "divine" attributes as something transcending mere experience.

Though positivism was controversial, its influence on psychology was substantial. Although Wundt was very critical of positivism and postulated unperceived mental processes to explain conscious experience, many of his students, including Külpe and Titchener, were much friendlier to it. On the other hand, Freud's unconscious, with its lush but unseen mental apparatus, committed the crime of metaphysics on a large scale.

In America, however, the influence of positivism was more pervasive. William James was a great admirer of Mach, whose concept of knowledge as a practical adaptation to life is quite consistent with James's Darwinianly inspired pragmatism. Twentieth-century logical positivists wedded Comte's empiricism to modern development in logic, and they had considerable influence on behaviorism.

B. F. Skinner's radical behaviorism applied Comte's vision to psychology, culminating in grandiose schemes of scientific control of society. Skinner maintained that the single goal of science is to find lawful relations between independent and dependent variables, leading to prediction and control. Reference to unobservable "mental" processes was as much illegitimate metaphysics to Skinner as it was to Mach. Furthermore, Skinner's call for a scientifically managed, nondemocratic utopia was Comtism without Comte's implausible Religion of Humanity.

Naturalizing the Supernatural

As religious doubt deepened in the nineteenth century and the authority of science rose, many people began to turn to science to explain traditionally religious beliefs or to find support for them (Webb, 1974). Two movements resulting from these impulses bear on psychology. The first was mesmerism, which attempted to give a Newtonian scientific explanation of personal healing. The second was psychical research, which purported to give scientific evidence for the existence of a personal, immortal soul. The two are united by there being scientific versions of religious ideas. As the parapsychologist J. B. Rhine said later, they wanted to "naturalize the supernatural."

MESMERISM Whether Mesmer himself was a charlatan is an extremely difficult question to answer. Like Freud, he demanded absolute obedience from his followers, lest they betray his invention. His treatment sessions were lurid séances, with Mesmer attired in mystic robes and wielding an iron wand. Moreover, Mesmer drifted into genuine occultism, using animal magnetism to explain clairvoyance, telepathy, and precognition. Yet Mesmer always tried to convince the medical establishment of his ideas' validity, even when it brought him nothing but ridicule. Mesmer was at once a magician and a pioneer in abnormal psychology. Although Mesmer attributed the trance to animal magnetism, it became apparent to his critics and even to some of his followers that something simpler was involved. The trance was due to the psychological control of one person over another rather than the passing of an invisible fluid from one body to another. Once this insight was obtained, it became possible to extract the mesmeric trance from the mystical context: Mesmerism was transformed into hypnotism.

This transformation began in France, the locale of Mesmer's greatest successes and greatest denunciations. In 1825, the French Royal Academy of Sciences decided to look into animal magnetism again, and its report, delivered in 1831, was far more favorable than any Mesmer had received in his lifetime. Without Mesmer's secretive personality and occult theory, the magnetic trance could be viewed more objectively as an unusual mental state that was of possible use to doctors and which merited further investigation.

In the late 1830s, animal magnetism was brought to England by the Baron Dupotet de Sennevoy, who conducted a series of magnetic demonstrations. They caught the attention of a young, radical, and innovative physician named John Elliotson (1791–1868) who began to use magnetism both as a cure for various diseases and as an anesthetic drug during surgery. Like Mesmer, Elliotson was eventually drummed out of established medicine for his beliefs. He founded a journal devoted to animal magnetism and phrenology, and encouraged other physicians to use magnetism in their practices. James Esdaile (1808–1859) was another English physician who used mesmerism, especially as an anesthetic (1852). Despite his popularity with the natives of India, where he worked, the government denied support for his mesmeric hospital.

The transformation of mesmerism was completed by James Braid (1795–1860), who named it *neurohypnotism*, or more briefly hypnotism, derived from the Greek *hypnos*, meaning sleep.

Braid considered the hypnotic state to be "nervous sleep." He began as a skeptic of mesmerism, but his own investigations convinced him that the phenomena were real enough; it was the fluidic theory of animal magnetism that was incorrect. In *Neurypnology*, Braid (1843, pp. 19–20) wrote: "The phenomena of mesmerism were to be accounted for on the principle of a derangement of the state of the cerebrospinal center . . . induced by a fixed state, absolute repose of the body, [and] fixed attention. . . ." The hypnotic state, Braid wrote, depends "on the physical and psychical [mental] condition of the patient . . . not at all on the volition or passes of the operator, throwing out a magnetic fluid, or exciting into activity some mystical universal fluid or medium." Braid rescued hypnotism from the occult surroundings of mesmerism and gave it to scientific medicine. But Braid himself encountered resistance from the medical establishment. The development of chemical anesthetics rendered the use of hypnosis in surgery unnecessary.

SPIRITUALISM AND PSYCHICAL RESEARCH   The doctrine of materialism and the religion of positivism may have inspired enthusiasts of *scientism*, but many people were unsettled and even repelled by them. The crisis of naturalism got worse after Huxley proclaimed humans to be only well-developed apes. Huxley explicitly challenged not only belief in the soul but also Aristotelian final causation: The progress of science "has in all ages meant, and now than evermore means, the extension of the province of what we call matter and causation, and the concomitant gradual banishment from all regions of known thought of what we call spirit and spontaneity" (quoted by Burrow, 2000, p. 41). Traditional religion seemed to many people to be moribund; blind faith in an immortal soul had been annihilated. So, especially after 1859, many thoughtful people, including well-known scientists, turned to science itself for assurance that there was more to human life than the bodily machine. Clifford had declared that one should believe nothing without adequate evidence, so psychical researchers sought to find adequate evidence of the immortality of the soul.

"The discovery that there was a life in man independent of blood and brain would be a cardinal, a dominating fact in all science and in all philosophy." So wrote Frederic Myers (1843–1901), the leading psychical researcher of the nineteenth century. As a child he saw a dog killed by being run over by a carriage. Myers asked his mother if the dog's soul had gone to heaven. A better theologian than a mother, Myers's mother said the dog had no soul to go to heaven, and the young Myers began to fear that he, too, had no soul and so no hope of heaven. This fear was intensified when, like many Victorians, he lost his religious faith during his education. He met the philosopher Henry Sidgwick (1838–1900) who encouraged Myers to search scientifically for evidence of immortality. Sidgwick, too, had lost his faith, but he deeply believed that ethics required personal immortality for the rectification of evil on earth. Myers took up Sidgwick's challenge and gathered an enormous amount of relevant data. Sidgwick and Myers founded the Society for Psychical Research, and in 1882 their journal published Myers's findings. These were also published posthumously in two volumes in 1903.

Simply as a catalog of unusual psychological phenomena, Myers's *Human Personality and Its Survival of Bodily Death* (1903) won the respect of no less a psychologist than William James, himself once president of the Society for Psychical Research. Although from its title one might expect a collection of ghost stories, Myers in fact surveyed the realm of abnormal psychology, from sleep and hysteria to messages from departed spirits. Myers's approach to his problem was psychological. He was the first English writer to disseminate Freud's early studies of hysteria. Hysteria was an important phenomenon for Myers, for it demonstrated the power of purely mental activity over the body when physical symptoms are caused by psychological disturbances.

Indeed, Myers fixed on exactly what Freud found most instructive in his early cases, that a hysteric's symptoms express unconscious desires that the patient does not want to admit to consciousness. Like Freud, Myers formulated a theory of the unconscious, which Myers called the *subliminal self*. In Freud's hands, the unconscious was an affront to human pride, revealing the irrational, impulsive, frightening depths that underlie rational, discursive conscious thought. Myers's conception of the subliminal self, however, was romantic, Platonic, optimistic, and progressive. True, the subliminal self is irrational, said Myers, but it enables us to communicate with a spiritual world that transcends the material one. The existence of the subliminal self demonstrated for Myers the separability of soul and matter. It opened up the prospect of more than material evolution, in which the individual plays only a brief part; in spiritual, cosmic evolution, each soul perfects itself forever, actualizing mental powers hindered by our animal bodies. Although Myers scientifically investigated spiritualistic phenomena—and he was as skeptical of mediums as anyone could wish—his scientific searching was really guided by a Neoplatonic and occult view of the cosmos.

On occasion, Myers could sound like a Huxleyan naturalist, as when he wrote: "The authority of creeds and Churches will be replaced by the authority of observation and experiment," but psychical research was not well received in Huxley's circle. Huxley (1871) himself sarcastically denounced spiritualism, whose devotees believed that mediums could place them in contact with dead relatives, likening "the talk in the spiritual world" to "the chatter of old women and curates," and saying of both, "They do not interest me." Despite this hostility, the intellectuals of the Society for Psychical Research carried on, and, at the popular level, spiritualism approached a mania around the turn of the century. As quickly as debunkers (e.g., magicians Harry Houdini and John Maskelyne) exposed fake mediums, new ones sprang up. The dialectic of paranormal claim and skeptical counterclaim continues today, as illustrated by the controversy over persons such as John Edward. Psychical research, now called *parapsychology*, persists in scholarly journals and research programs, and college courses in the subject proliferate. Nevertheless, it is an even more suspect subject than hypnotism, and its very mention makes most psychologists uncomfortable (Leahey & Leahey, 1983).

TOWARD THE SCIENCE OF PSYCHOLOGY

The idea that psychology should and could be made scientific gained ground in the nineteenth century. Critical to the prospects for the creation of such a science were advances in physiology and the development of the first methods by which one might experiment on the mind. The first made it possible to seriously embark on the path through psychology through physiology that had been fitfully been taken since Greek times. The second made psychology a respectable science by bringing consciousness into the laboratory.

Understanding the Brain and Nervous System

THE BRAIN: LOCALIZATION OF FUNCTION   So far, in treating the history of psychology, we have found it to be primarily part of philosophy. Even the occasional physician-psychologists generally founded their psychologies on philosophical, not physiological, principles. Hartley is a case in point. He erected his psychology on the principles of associationist philosophy and only buttressed it with Newton's speculative account of nerve function. The separation of the physiological and philosophical portions of Hartley's psychology was so complete that his follower, Priestley, could issue an edition of Hartley's *Observations on Man, His Frame, His Duty, and His Expectations* that omitted all the physiology. Hartley wanted to create a psychology that combined philosophy and physiology, but philosophy clearly came first.

Franz Joseph Gall (1758–1828) reversed this relationship. Gall may fairly be regarded as the founder of cognitive neuroscience because he was the first to take seriously the idea that the brain is the seat of the soul. The idea was hardly new: The Hellenistic scientists of Alexandria demonstrated it; the medieval faculty psychologists located each faculty in a different portion of the brain. However, beyond encouraging materialism, the concept had little effect on psychological thought. The locations assigned to the medieval faculties were based on prior analyses of mind, not brain, and philosophical psychology had done nothing to change this. Gall, however, stated that the brain was the specific organ of mental activity, in the same way that the stomach is the organ of digestion and the lungs the organs of respiration. Therefore, the study of human nature should begin with those functions of the brain that give rise to thought and action, rather than with abstract and introspective inquiries into mind.

The philosophical background against which Gall reacted was French empiricism and associationism, especially Condillac's sensationism. Gall offered several reproaches to that philosophical approach to psychology (Young, 1970). To begin with, the empiricists claimed that experience was the proper basis of science, yet their own psychology, including Hume's science of human nature, was wholly speculative, having no reference to objective behavior or to the brain that controls it. Furthermore, the categories of analysis used by philosophers were "mere abstractions." None of the faculties proposed by philosophers—such as memory, attention, and imagination—was specific enough to explain actual human behavior and concrete individual differences. In short, the philosophers' concepts were useless for the empirical investigations that psychological science requires.

Gall's ideas brought him into conflict with empiricist philosophers in a final way. Condillac had attempted to derive every faculty of mind from sensation and association. Gall, however, believing the brain to be the organ of the mind, proposed a new version of the medical doctrine of localization of function. He said that each of his proposed faculties was innate and was located in a particular region of the brain. Gall's approach also implied comparative psychology. Given that the brains of species differ up and down the Great Chain of Being (Gall wrote before Darwin), so should the corresponding faculties differ. In fact, Gall carried out comparative anatomical studies to support this argument.

The problem for Gall, then, was to correlate specific behavioral functions with particular regions of the brain. Although he carried out detailed anatomical studies of the brain and nervous system, he found the techniques of his time too crude to answer the questions he posed, and he had moral scruples about experimenting on living but "martyrized" animals. Gall, therefore, adopted a different methodology that, unfortunately, led to the pseudoscience of phrenology. He assumed that well-developed mental faculties would correspond to well-developed parts of the brain. The "organs" corresponding to the well-developed faculties in the brain would be larger than the organs corresponding to less-developed faculties, and their relative size would be registered on the skull as bumps overlying the developed organ.

Empirically, Gall's method was to show that people possessing certain striking traits would possess skulls with bumps over the corresponding organs of the brain, and that weak traits would go with undeveloped brain organs and skull regions. Thus, Gall could observe an individual's unique behaviors and correlate them with cranial prominences. On the basis of such observations, Gall drew up a long list of faculties—destructiveness, friendship, and language, for example—and located each in a particular region of the brain. Destructiveness, for example, was located just above the ear. Later followers of Gall expanded his list to include such faculties as veneration, whose presence was believed to show that God must exist to be the object of veneration.

Certain conceptual features of Gall's approach deserve mention: It was nativistic; it compared humans with other animals; it was materialistic, although Gall himself struggled against this tendency. Gall's psychology was also behavioristic rather than introspectionistic. His system rested on the observation of behaviors and of bumps on the skull rather than on the introspection of his own mind. Gall's psychology was therefore the first objective, rather than subjective, psychology. More broadly, Gall's was a functional, almost evolutionary, psychology concerned with how the mind and its organ, the brain, actually adapt a person or animal to everyday demands. Philosophical psychology had been concerned with grand problems of epistemology rather than how the human mind copes with the world. Finally, Gall's psychology was a psychology of individual differences. He explicitly rejected the study of the generalized adult mind in favor of a study of how people differ.

Gall's conception pointed in two directions, one scientific and one pseudoscientific. Scientifically, it inspired more experimentally minded physiologists to investigate the localization of behavioral functions in particular parts of the brain. At the hands of these men, Gall's system suffered badly. His specific locations were found to be faulty. Worse, the basic assumptions that size of brain corresponds to strength of faculty and that bumps on the skull conform to the shape of the brain were found to be without foundation. The entire system was violently rejected as a sham and fraud, appealing only to credulous laypersons.

The appeal to the lay society was the other direction—the pseudoscientific direction—taken by Gall's ideas. His quondam associate, Johann Caspar Spurzheim (1776–1832) popularized Gall's ideas in the simplistic system of *phrenology*. In Spurzheim's hands, phrenology became the first popular psychology, and Spurzheim aimed to reform education, religion, and penology. His missionary activities carried him to the United States, where the ground was most fertile for phrenology. He died shortly after arriving, but his work was carried on by the English phrenologist George Combe. The features in phrenology that appealed to ordinary Americans were also those that ensured the success of evolutionary psychology in America.

Gall's major critic was a leading French physiologist, Jean-Pierre-Marie Flourens (1794–1867), a pioneer in experimental brain research. Flourens discovered the functions of the various lower parts of the brain, but, regarding the cerebral hemispheres, he parted company with Gall. Flourens ridiculed phrenology and argued on the basis of his own research—which involved lesioning or ablating parts of the brain—that the cerebral hemispheres act as a unit, containing no specialized organs for special mental faculties. In his conclusions, Flourens was more dominated by philosophical ideas than was Gall. Flourens was a Cartesian dualist who viewed the soul as residing in the cerebral hemispheres, and, said Flourens, since the soul is unitary, the action of the hemispheres must be so too. Flourens thus advocated the idea of *mass action*: The cerebrum is a single organ with a single function, thought. It acts as a mass, not a set of disparate, localized organs, as Gall held. He believed there was no organic connection between the sensory and motor functions of the lower parts of the brain and the cerebrum. Flourens's stature assured the success of his attack on Gall, and his view of the unitary action of the cerebrum remained orthodox dogma for decades.

THE NERVOUS SYSTEM: THE WAY IN AND THE WAY OUT   In 1822 François Magendie (1783–1855) announced a discovery of momentous, long-term implications for neuroscience (Cranefield, 1974). Earlier, on the basis of postmortem dissections, the English physiologist Charles Bell (1774–1842) had distinguished two sets of nerves at the base of the spinal column. Bell suggested that one set carried information to the brain (sensory, or afferent, nerves), while the other carried information from the brain to the muscles (motor, or efferent, nerves). Previously, it had been thought that nerves work in both directions. Magendie discovered the same thing independently and more conclusively because he demonstrated the different functions of the nerves in the spinal column by direct experiment on living animals. The next decade in brain physiology brought the extension of the distinction between afferent and efferent up the spinal column and into the cerebrum. Young (1970, p. 204) quotes an English physician writing in 1845, "The brain . . . is subject to the laws of reflex action, and that, in this respect it does not differ from the other ganglia of the nervous system . . . [and] must necessarily be regulated . . . by laws identical with those governing the spinal ganglia and their analogues in the lower animals."

A later breakthrough in the study of the functions of the cerebrum suggested that Gall was correct in asserting that different parts of the brain are responsible for different mental processes. This discovery was made by Pierre Paul Broca (1824–1880), who observed that a patient in his care, "Tan," with speech disorders showed, when autopsied, damage to the left frontal lobe of the brain. Broca, who rejected the study of bumps on the head, viewed his finding as limited support for Gall, although the faculty of language had not been found where Gall had predicted.

Against this view was the observation that the cerebral hemispheres seemed insensitive. They had been poked, prodded, pressed, and pricked, but no movement resulted in living animals. This supported Flourens's view that the hemispheres were not involved in action. However, in 1870, two German researchers, Gustav Fritsch and Eduard Hitzig, announced that electrical excitation of the cerebrum can elicit movement and that different parts of the brain, when stimulated, seem to regulate different movements.

The Emerging Reflex Theory of the Brain

This finding encouraged others to map out the brain, locating each sensory and motor function. Today, brain maps are remarkably precise and allow tumors to be located with great accuracy. A "new phrenology" was thus born, in which each part of the brain was assigned a discrete sensory or behavioral function. But the new localizations were different from Gall's, for they resulted from an extension of the sensorimotor nerve distinction to the cerebrum. Some parts of the brain receive sensations; others govern specific actions, and the association of sensation and action produces behavior. In this view, the brain is a complex reflex machine with the cerebral hemispheres providing associative connections between incoming stimuli and outgoing responses.

The reflex theory of the brain provided an opportunity and a serious challenge for psychology. The opportunity lay in the similarity of the new neuroscientific theory of the brain to the older Cartesian theory of consciousness, especially in its associative form. The brain connected stimuli and responses; the mind associated, or connected ideas. Thus, the reflex theory of the brain promised to fulfill the ancient ambition of the path through physiology, to connect mind with brain, and make psychology a science (see later discussion). The challenge lay in realizing how many behaviors were done by the brain alone, without consciousness. Perhaps consciousness played no role at all in causing behavior, but was simply a by-product of brain activity with no more Darwinian survival value than male nipples. This "automaton theory of the mind" was advocated by important scientists, including Huxley. Should the automaton theory of the mind be correct, a psychology of consciousness would be an exercise in futility. The nature and causal status of consciousness remain a puzzle even today (Leahey, 2005).

INVENTING METHODS FOR PSYCHOLOGY Quantitative measurement is central to the Newtonian conception of science. Without measurement, there can be no scientific laws. Of growing importance in nineteenth-century science was experimentation—manipulating nature in order to reveal its workings. Mental measurement and experimental manipulation of the mind were first achieved in the nineteenth century, laying the groundwork for the founding of psychology.

EXPERIMENTAL PSYCHOLOGY

Mental Chronometry. The first quantitative way of measuring mental processes arose in a surprising place—astronomy. An important function of astronomy is to precisely map the stars. Until the advent of modern mechanical and photographic methods in which an astronomer rarely looks through a telescope, accurately locating stars depended on the ability of him or her to note the exact moment when a star passed a point directly overhead, marked by a reticle in the telescope's field of vision. In the eye-and-ear method, the astronomer noted the exact time on a clock when a star entered the field of vision and then counted as the clock beat seconds until the star passed the reticle. Accurate notation of the exact moment of transit was critical; slight errors would be translated into immense, interstellar distances in calculating the exact positions of stars in the galaxy.

In 1795, an assistant astronomer at Greenwich Observatory lost his job when his superior discovered that his own transit times were about 0.5 second faster than his assistant's. The head astronomer naturally assumed his own times to be correct and his assistant's in error. Years later, this event came to the attention of the German astronomer F. W. Bessel (1784–1846), who began to systematically compare the transit times of different astronomers. Bessel discovered that all astronomers differed in the speed with which they reported transits. To correct this grave situation, Bessel constructed "personal equations" so that the differences among astronomers could be canceled out in astronomical calculations. For example, the "personal equation" of the two Greenwich astronomers would be Junior–Superior 0.5 sec. The observations of any pair of astronomers could be compared in these equations reflecting their personal reaction times, and calculations of star positions could be corrected accordingly. Unfortunately for astronomers, use of the personal equations assumed that individual differences were stable, which proved to be false. Indeed, experiments with artificial stars, which had known transit times, showed that sometimes observers "saw" the star intersect the cross-hair before it occurred. Only the increasing automation of observation was able to eliminate these problems.

Meanwhile, the great German physicist Hermann von Helmholtz used reaction-time measures to answer the question of the speed of nerve conduction. In 1850, Helmholtz stimulated the motor nerve of a frog's leg at points near and far from the muscle itself, measuring the time it took for the muscle to respond. Before Helmholtz's investigation, it had been widely assumed that nerve impulses traveled at infinite or at least immeasurably fast speeds. Helmholtz estimated the speed to be only 26 meters per second.

These two lines of research on reaction time came together in the work of F. C. Donders (1818–1889), a Dutch physiologist. Donders saw that the time between a stimulus and its response could be used to objectively quantify the speed of mental processes. Helmholtz had measured the simplest sort of stimulus–response (S–R) reaction, and astronomers had, for another purpose, investigated mental processes such as judgment. It was Donders's special contribution to use reaction time to infer the action of complex mental processes. So, for example, one could measure how long it takes someone to respond to a single stimulus—the turning on of a small light bulb above a response key. This is *simple reaction* time. Then, one might complicate the task by having two lights and two keys. This is *compound reaction* time. A simple reaction is still involved, but the subject must discriminate, or make a *judgment* in the philosophical parlance of the day, about which light has come on and then respond appropriately. If simple reaction takes, for example, 150 meters per second to complete, and the compound reaction takes 230 meters per second to complete, then, Donders reasoned, the mental action of judgment added to the simple reaction must take 230 meters per second, 150 meters per second, 80 meters per second. This method, which seemed to offer an objective way of measuring physiological and mental processes that could not be directly observed, was called *mental chronometry.*

The method was taken up early by Wundt and extensively used in the first psychological laboratories. Precisely because it was a quantitative method, it helped to ensure the scientific stature of experimental psychology as apart from qualitative philosophical psychology. It took the mind out of the armchair and into the laboratory. The use of reaction times has had its ups and downs in the subsequent history of psychology, but it remains an important technique today.

Psychophysics. The dean of historians of psychology, E. G. Boring, dates the founding of experimental psychology to the 1860 publication of *Elements of Psychophysics*, written by a physicist, Gustav Theodore Fechner (1801–1887). Boring's (1929/1950) claim rests on the fact that Fechner conceived and carried out the first systematic research in experimental psychology—research, moreover, that produced mathematical laws. Before Fechner, philosophers had widely assumed, following Kant, that the mind can be subjected to neither experiment nor mathematical analysis. Fechner showed these assumptions to be false. The difficulties do at first seem to be immense. In physics, we can manipulate objects and observe what they do and we can measure their position and momentum, writing mathematical laws that interrelate these variables (such as Newton's inverse-square law of gravitation). However, minds are private and no instruments can be applied to conscious experiences.

Fechner overcame these problems. He saw that the content of consciousness can be manipulated by controlling the stimuli to which a person is exposed. This control makes mental experiment possible. We can have a person lift objects of known weight, listen to tones of known pitch and volume, and so on. Even so, how do we measure the resulting conscious experiences, or sensations? The subject can assign no number to a tone or weight sensation. Fechner perceived the difficulty and got around it by quantifying sensations indirectly. We can ask a subject to say which of two weights is heavier, which of two tones is louder. By systematically varying both the absolute values of the pairs of stimuli and the differences between them, and by observing when subjects can and cannot distinguish the pairs, sensation can be indirectly quantified. Hence, we can mathematically relate stimulus magnitude (R) with the resulting strength of sensation (S). Fechner found that the strength of a sensation (S) is a logarithmic function of stimulus strength (R), that is, $S = k \log R$, where k is a constant particular to each sense modality. Stimulus differences are easier to detect when both stimuli are of moderate absolute intensity than when they are of high absolute intensity (e.g., it would be easier to distinguish a 10-ounce weight from an 11-ounce weight than a 10-pound weight from a 10-pound, 1-ounce weight).

Fechner's approach was not without antecedents. The basic method of asking subjects to distinguish stimulus differences had been pioneered by a physiologist, E. H. Weber (1795–1878). The concept of treating sensations as quantitatively varying conscious states goes back to Leibniz's monads and his doctrines of petite perception and apperception. The immediate motivation of Fechner's work was the mind–body problem. As a physicist, Fechner hoped his psychophysics would show that mind–body are related in precise and measurable ways.

Fechner was not the founder of the science of psychology because, unlike Wundt, he did not create a social institution—the university laboratory—to sustain psychology as an officially recognized field of study. Nevertheless, Fechner founded experimental psychology, for his methods, broadened to encompass more than sensations, were basic to Wundt's experimental psychology of consciousness. In Wundt's experiments, antecedent stimulus conditions were controlled, as in Fechner's, and data were provided as subjects reported the resulting conscious content. It was not Wundt's only method, but it was an important one, and it was the one most of his students carried away with them from his laboratory.

MENTAL TESTING   Another way of measuring the mind, the mental test, arose in the nineteenth century and was fundamental for the founding of applied psychology. Mental tests were not invented for scientific reasons, but in the service of public education. In the second half of the nineteenth century, governments began first to provide universal primary education and then to make it compulsory. Compulsory education was motivated by the need of the new industries and businesses for a more educated workforce and by the desire of governments to control their citizens' thoughts. A French minister of education said, "Never shall we accept that the education of the people should be a private industry" (quoted by Tombs, 2000, p. 17); education was to remain a state monopoly, resistant to privatization schemes such as vouchers. As children were inducted into the new schools, it became desirable to establish standards of achievement, to evaluate students with respect to these standards, and to measure differences in children's mental abilities. Experimental psychology studied the normal human mind, regarding individual differences as error variance to be minimized by careful experimental control. Mental testing, on the other hand, was directly concerned with carefully measuring individual differences. For mental testing, there was no normal human mind, only the average one.

Some early mental testing was based on phrenology, which had inherited from Gall the goal of determining differences in mental and personal abilities. Popular phrenology foreshadowed future developments in mental testing, ranging from personnel selection to premarital counseling, and especially in America, phrenologists tried to use their methods in the interests of educational reform. However, phrenology did not work and fell into disfavor. More scientific methods of mental testing were developed in Great Britain and in France, and the way testing developed in the two countries was influenced by the legacies of British and French philosophy.

Testing in Britain.   Sir Francis Galton (1822–1911) was a well-to-do cousin of Charles Darwin and collaborated with him on disappointing experiments on the basis of heredity. Galton became interested in the evolution of mental traits, and in his *Hereditary Genius* (1869), he "propose[d] to show that a man's natural abilities are derived by inheritance, under exactly the same limitations as are the form and physical features of the whole organic world." He traced the lineages of families in which physical abilities seemed to pass from parent to child and other families in which mental abilities did the same. Thus, for example, he would show that one family produced generations of outstanding college wrestlers while another produced outstanding lawyers and judges.

Above all, Galton wanted to measure intelligence, for him, the master mental ability. He looked at school children's examination scores to see if children who did well or badly in one subject did well or badly in all. To this end he devised the correlation coefficient, known today as the *Pearson product-moment correlation*, because Galton's student Karl Pearson (1857–1936) perfected its calculation. Galton found that there was a strong correlation among examination grades, supporting the idea that intelligence is a single mental ability. Galton's claim began the still unresolved controversy over general intelligence. Followers of Galton believe that most intelligence can be accounted for by a single psychometric factor, g. Critics believe that intelligence is composed of multiple skills: not intelligence but intelligences (Brody, 1992; Gardner, 1983).

Rather than depending on teachers' imprecise grades, Galton then tried to measure intelligence more directly and precisely. His methods were rooted in British empiricism. If the mind is a collection of ideas, as Hume taught, then a person's intelligence would depend on how precisely he or she could represent the world in consciousness. Measures of sensory acuity, then, would be measures of intelligence. The focus on consciousness was also consistent with the German introspective study of the contents of consciousness, and some of Galton's measures were adaptations of psychophysical methods. In addition, Galton also believed, as did many scientists, including Broca, that the bigger the brain the more intelligent the mind it caused. Therefore, head size would also be a measure of intelligence.

Galton established in South Kensington, a suburb of London, an anthropometric laboratory at which people could take his mental tests. A similar exhibit introduced Americans to psychology at the Columbian Exposition in 1893. Galton's anthropometric laboratory created one of three important models for the conduct of psychological work, the other two being the laboratory (see previous discussion) and the medical clinic (see later discussion) (Danziger, 1990). Galton studied ordinary people, not the highly educated, trained observers of the German introspective laboratories or the pathological subjects of the French clinics. They paid a small fee to take the tests and were called "applicants." Galton's practice probably emulated phrenology (Danziger, 1990), in which people paid fees to have their heads examined. Galton himself had at one time visited a phrenologist. Galton contributed twice to applied psychology: by inventing mental tests and by introducing the professional, rather than scientific, "fee for service," model of practice.

Although Galton was the first to try to develop tests of intelligence, as a practical matter his tests were failures (Fancher, 1985; Sokal, 1982). Sensory acuity is not the basis of intelligence, and the correlation between brain size and intelligence is extremely small (Brody, 1992). Nevertheless, Galton's approach to intelligence and his evolutionary approach to the mind proved quite influential, especially in America. Galton's methods were carried on by James McKeen Cattell (1860–1944), who coined the term *mental test*. Cattell took his degree with Wundt in Leipzig, but worked in the anthropometric laboratory under Galton, epitomizing the historian of psychology E. G. Boring's (1950) remark that although American psychologists got their brass instruments from Wundt, they got their inspiration from Galton.

Testing in France.   In Paris, Alfred Binet (1857–1911) developed a more effective and durable means of measuring intelligence. Binet was a law student turned psychologist. Typical for a French psychologist, he was introduced to the field through the medical clinic, studying with Charcot (see later discussion). His early work concerned hypnosis, he conducted studies in many areas of psychology, and he was a co-founder of the first psychological institute in France, at the Sorbonne in 1889 (Cunningham, 1996). But he is most remembered for his intelligence test.

Binet's approach to testing combined the Cartesian emphasis on the highest mental functions of the mind with the French clinical orientation (Smith, 1997). In Galton's anthropometric laboratory and in the experimental laboratories of Germany, psychologists focused on simple sensorimotor functions. Binet, in contrast, studied high-level cognitive skills such as chess. He wrote, "If one wishes to study the differences existing between two individuals it is necessary to begin with the most intellectual and complicated processes" (quoted by Smith, 1997, p. 591). Binet's roots in the clinic also shaped his psychological research. Unlike the brief and anonymous studies of the laboratory, Binet studied individuals in great depth, even publishing their photographs in his publications (Cunningham, 1996). Binet, along with coworker Victor Henri (1872–1940), defined the field of individual, as opposed to German experimental, psychology in an article, "La Psychologie Individuelle" in 1895. They announced the practical value of their form of psychology, wishing "to illuminate the practical importance . . . [the topic] has for the pedagogue, the doctor, the anthropologist, even the judge" (quoted by Smith, 1997, p. 591). Binet's article is an important early manifesto of applied psychology.

Binet's test was developed through his work on a government commission formed in 1904 to study the education of the mentally subnormal. Binet had already studied cognitive development in children and had been a founder of the Free Society for the Psychological Study of the Child in 1899 (Smith, 1997). The government's aims called for a psychological version of clinical diagnosis in medicine. Mentally subnormal children interfered with the education of normal children, and the commission was charged to come up with a way to diagnose subnormal children, especially those on the borderline of normal functioning. Binet developed a practical test based on assembling a scale of intellectual tasks that could be performed by normal children at specific ages. Then one could compare the performance of a given child to that of his or her age mates. The subnormal child was one who could not solve the problems solved by children of the same age. Subnormal children could then be detected, removed from the classroom, and given special education.

Binet's rough and ready practical test was much more useful than Galton's theoretically driven tests. American psychologist Henry Goddard (1866–1957), a teacher turned psychologist, was research psychologist at an institution that housed children with a variety of disorders such as epilepsy, autism, and mental retardation—The Vineland (New Jersey) Training School for Feebleminded Boys and Girls. An important problem for Goddard was determining which children were mentally subnormal and which were physically ill. Goddard initially tried to use Galton-like modifications of standard laboratory methods, but they proved useless. He learned about Binet's test on a visit to Europe in 1908, and introduced it to Vineland, where he found it "met our needs" (quoted by Smith, 1997, p. 595). The test was more carefully adapted into English by Lewis Terman (1877–1956), whose first encounter with psychology was when a phrenologist examined him as a child. Terman standardized his Stanford-Binet on large numbers of normal children, introducing greater scientific rigor to intelligence testing.

Educational psychology and mental testing also developed in Germany, though more slowly than elsewhere. William Stern (1871–1938) introduced the concept of the intelligence quotient, or IQ, a quantitative way of stating a child's mental standing with respect to his or her peers. Binet's test allowed one to measure the "mental age" of a child that then could be set in a ratio to his or her chronological age. Thus, if a 10-year-old child passed the items typically passed by 10-year-olds, the child's IQ was $10/10 = 1$, which Stern multiplied by 100 to eliminate decimals; hence, "normal IQ" was always 100. A subnormal child would have an IQ less than 100, and an advanced child would have an IQ above 100. Although IQ is no longer calculated this way, the term remains in use, although Stern himself came to regard its influence as "pernicious" (Schmidt, 1996).

The influence of mental testing was profound. It was the cornerstone of early applied psychology, providing a concrete method by which psychology could be applied in a variety of areas, beginning in education but soon moving to fields such as personnel placement and personality assessment. Mental testing has become an important social force—people's educational and career paths have been shaped, and sometimes even determined, by scores on mental tests. People have been ordered to be sterilized because of the results of mental tests. As a practical matter, the everyday impact of mental testing has been much greater than that of experimental psychology.

Philosophy to the Threshold of Psychology

In 1851, Alexander Bain wrote to his friend and colleague, John Stuart Mill, "There is nothing I wish more than so to unite psychology and physiology that physiologists may be made to appreciate the true ends and drift of their researches into the nervous system." Bain fulfilled his desire in two massive volumes, *The Senses and the Intellect* (1855) and *The Emotions and the Will* (1859). Bain's comprehensive survey of psychology from the standpoints of associationism and physiology embraced every psychological topic from simple sensation to aesthetics and ethics.

Bain's importance lies in his synthesis of material borrowed from others. The idea of uniting physiology and philosophical psychology was ancient. His associationism derived from Hartley and the Mills. His physiology was drawn from the sensorimotor physiology of the German physiologist, Johannes Müller (1801–1858). In his *Elements of Physiology* (1842), Müller had already proposed that the role of the brain is to associate incoming sensory information with appropriate motor responses. Bain knew the *Elements* and incorporated Müller's conception of the role of the brain into his psychology. Thus, Bain united the philosophy of associationism with sensorimotor physiology to give a unified human psychology. Even today, most general psychology texts are organized like Bain's, beginning with simple nerve function in sensation and working up to thinking and social relations. Bain's integration was quite influential. He wrote before the functions of the cerebrum were known, and his uncompromising associative view of physiology guided later English investigators to press their studies into the mysterious cerebral hemispheres.

Bain had a considerable, lasting effect on psychology. The journal *Mind*, which he founded in 1874, is still in existence as an organ of philosophical psychology. He remained, however, a philosopher. Despite his use of physiological data, he did no experiments, and although he recognized the importance of Darwin's work, his associationism remained preevolutionary. In the long run, it was his practical attitude toward psychology that mattered. Like the phrenology that had once excited him, Bain wanted to explain human action, not just consciousness. His ideas about behavior would be developed by American pragmatists.

The last notable French philosophical psychologist was Hippolyte-Adolphe Taine (1828–1893). Although most of his works were on history and literature, he was most proud of his psychological book, *On Intelligence* (1875), which William James used as his text when he first taught psychology at Harvard. In *On Intelligence*, Taine presented an associative psychology similar to Bain's, arguing that all ideas, no matter how apparently abstract, can be reduced to a collection of sensations associated with each idea's name. The business of psychology would thus be similar to chemistry's—"to decompose [compounds] into their elements to show the different groupings these elements are capable of, and to construct different compounds with them" (Taine, 1875). Following Leibniz, Taine proposed that conscious sensations are simply aggregates of weaker, more fleeting sensations that are only marginally conscious at best.

Taine also discussed the physiological substrates of sensation. He maintained a dual-aspect psychophysical parallelism, holding that every event in consciousness has a corresponding neural event. According to Taine, the reverse is not true because some neural events give rise only to unconscious sensations. Taine's neurophysiology presents the brain as an unspecialized organ associating stimulus and response: "The brain, then, is the repeater of the sensory centers." That is, the brain simply copies incoming neural information as mental images copy sensations. Mind and brain are both seen in terms similar to Hume's or Hartley's. Taine's importance lies less in the details of his psychology than in his treatment of psychology as a naturalistic discipline (Smith, 1997). He and his colleague Théodule Ribot (1839–1916) rejected the Catholic psychology that had so far dominated French psychological thinking, still seeing psychology as very much the study of the soul. They introduced British ideas as a secular counterweight to French Catholic spiritual psychology.

In Germany, philosophical psychology struggled with the mixed legacy of Kantian idealism. Certain concepts of the idealists found a place in early German psychology. Wundt studied individual consciousness; proposed a historical, genetic approach to the investigation of the higher mental processes; and stressed human will as the unifying force in mental life. All of these ideas he inherited as aspects of idealist philosophy. Freud, too, was influenced by Schopenhauer's concept of unconscious, primitive forces lurking in the personality. Nevertheless, the German idealists, following Kant, took a dim view of psychology as a would-be science. Psychology studies only a concrete individual, or a set of individuals, whereas the idealists sought transcendent Platonic knowledge of a godlike Absolute Spirit, which they took to be the noumenal reality behind physical appearances and the individual mind. Empirical research seems trivial in the idealist context, and the idealists—most forcefully, Hegel—actively opposed the development of empirical psychology (Leary, 1978, 1980).

The leading German philosophical psychologist was Hermann Lotze (1817–1881). Before he turned to philosophy, Lotze received his MD, and he was Fechner's friend and physician. In one respect, Lotze appears to be German psychology's Bain or Taine. In his *Outlines of Psychology* (1881), Lotze proposed an empiricist view of consciousness, saying, for example, with Berkeley that depth perception is learned, not innate, and experience is compounded out of simple ideas. He integrated this empiricism with the growing sensorimotor concept of brain function.

However, Lotze was not wholly dedicated to empiricism and naturalism. He insisted that, although physiology offered a valid approach to the material aspects of mind and behavior, both human beings and animals possess divinely given souls. As was typical of German philosophers, Lotze emphatically rejected materialism in favor of Cartesian dualism. By insisting on the spiritual side of humans, Lotze earned the admiration of English-speaking psychologists who were dissatisfied with the associationistic and reductive psychologies they found around them. Among them were James Ward, the English psychologist who bitterly attacked naturalism, and William James, the tender-minded psychologist who took part in psychical research.

Hermann von Helmholtz (1821–1894), probably the greatest physical scientist of the nineteenth century, was a more consistent exponent of naturalism and empiricism. For much of his career, he was occupied with physiology. We have already learned of his measurement of the speed of nerve conduction; he also conducted definitive studies of physiological optics and acoustics. But he was also a leading physicist: He formulated the law of conservation of energy when he was only 26. The law of conservation of energy struck a death-blow to interactive dualism. Because energy can neither be created nor destroyed, no spiritual "force" can affect matter.

Helmholtz's approach to the mind was essentially that of a Lockean empiricism in which ideas are interpreted as mental content. Helmholtz argued that all we know for certain are our ideas or images of the world gathered by experience. He struck a pragmatic note by acknowledging that we cannot know whether our ideas are true, but argued that this does not matter as long as they lead to effective action in the real world. Science was an example of such effective action. Although he followed Kant in holding causality to be an innate principle, Helmholtz, like the empiricists, maintained that the other Kantian categories of knowledge are acquired.

Of particular importance to psychology was Helmholtz's theory of unconscious inference. If, for example, visual perception of space is not an innate intuition as Berkeley argued, then, in the course of development we must learn to calculate the distance of objects from us. Yet, we are not aware of performing such calculations. Helmholtz theorized that these kinds of calculations, or inferences, must be unconscious and moreover must be unconsciously learned, as happens in language acquisition. Like words, ideas (including sensations) are mental contents that represent reality. Just as children learn language spontaneously and with no direct instruction, so too they spontaneously and unconsciously learn the meanings of ideas.

As we would expect of a physicist and physiologist, Helmholtz was a forceful advocate of the natural sciences. He welcomed their growth in the German universities and heaped scorn on idealist philosophers for whom natural science was the trivial study of physical reality, which was of no consequence compared to the Spirit behind physical reality. Furthermore, Helmholtz's own theory and research supported materialism. His physiological studies of sensation established the dependence of perception on fleshly matter. His theory of conservation of energy inspired some young physiologists to swear, as Helmholtz's friend Emil du Bois-Reymond put it in a letter, "a solemn oath to put in effect this truth: no other forces than the common physical-chemical ones are active within the organism" (Kahl, 1971). In his early manuscript *Psychology for neurologists*, Sigmund Freud carried this spirit of reductionism into psychology.

Helmholtz, however, was aware of the dangers of making materialism into an ideology when he wrote, in *Thought in Medicine* (1877/1971, pp. 355–356): "Our generation has had to suffer under the tyranny of spiritualistic metaphysics; the younger generation will probably have to guard against materialistic metaphysics." He continued, "Please do not forget that materialism is a metaphysical hypothesis. . . . If one forgets this, materialism becomes a dogma [compare this to the "solemn oath" discussed earlier] which hinders the progress of science and, like all dogmas, leads to violent intolerance." Helmholtz could not accept spiritualism or vitalism, but neither could he accept aggressive materialism.

Psychopathology

The final important root of organized psychology lies in medicine, in the study of disordered minds. Psychology thus impinges on psychiatry, and in France especially, psychology was linked to psychiatry and neurology, the branches of medicine that treat the "mentally" ill.

PSYCHIATRY AND NEUROLOGY   The insane have always been with us, but before the eighteenth century, they were treated very badly, even brutally. Recent historical claims, that mad people happily wandered the medieval countryside and became locked up and mistreated only in modern times, have been exposed as myths (Shorter, 1997). There were private and public asylums for the mad, but most remained with their families who, at a loss to cope, confined them and mistreated them. An Irish politician in 1817 said that when a family member goes mad, "the only way they have to manage is by making a hole in the floor of the cabin, not high enough for the person to stand up in, with a crib over it to prevent his getting up . . . and they give this wretched being his food there and there he generally dies" (quoted by Shorter, 1997, pp. 1–2).

Psychiatry was created by the Enlightenment Project, reforming asylums from places that simply warehoused the insane, treating them, if at all, with the traditional methods of premodern medicine, such as bleeding and the administration of emetics. The goal of the new field of psychiatry was to make the asylum itself a treatment for the mad. The term *psychiatry* was coined by Johann Christian Reil (1759–1813) in 1808, although just as it took the term *psychology* decades to catch on, the older term *alienist* remained widely used. Reil voiced typical Enlightenment hopes for his new field (quoted by Shorter, 1997):

> The physicians of England, France, and Germany are all stepping forward at once to improve the lot of the insane. . . . The cosmopolite sees joyously the untiring efforts of mankind to ensure the welfare of one's neighbor. The horrors of the prisons and the jails are over. . . . A bold race of men dares to take on this gigantic idea . . . of wiping from the face of the earth one of the most devastating of pestilences. (p. 8)

The transformation in the treatment of the mad that Reil greeted with such enthusiasm and hope was the introduction of "moral therapy" into a few European asylums in the late 1790s. In this context, *moral* therapy meant *mental* therapy as opposed to traditional medical therapy. Moral therapy aimed at curing rather than merely isolating the insane. Although it was not yet psychotherapy, moral therapy moved in that direction. The idea behind moral therapy was that by freeing patients from their chains, and then having them live carefully structured lives with their fellow inmates, they could regain their sanity. As one psychiatrist described it, "subject to an orderly life, to discipline, to a well-calibrated regimen, they are obliged to reflect upon the change in their life. The necessity of adjusting, of behaving well with strangers, of living together with their companions in suffering, are powerful allies in achieving restoration of their lost reason" (quoted by Shorter, 1997, p. 19). In 1801, an influential textbook by Phillipe Pinel (1745–1826) made moral therapy the gold standard for asylum psychiatry. Unfortunately, the good intentions of the first psychiatrists were overwhelmed by the rise in the number of inmates during the nineteenth century, and by the early twentieth century, asylums had again become places where the insane were warehoused—now on a huge scale—rather than treated.

Psychiatry entered the German University a little earlier than psychology, in 1865, through the efforts of Wilhelm Griesinger (1817–1868). Because of the German universities' emphasis on research, psychiatry became more scientific. The key figure in the development of modern psychiatry was Emil Kraepelin (1856–1926). A great problem facing psychiatrists was seeing through bizarre symptoms to underlying illnesses. Kraepelin was a psychiatrist who became fascinated by psychology, undertaking study in Wundt's laboratory. Thus trained as a scientist, he sifted through case histories looking for patterns of symptoms and outcomes. Out of his research came the first scientifically informed psychiatric diagnosis, *dementia praecox* (premature dementia) now known as schizophrenia. He went on to develop a nosological system that revolutionized the diagnosis and treatment of the insane. Kraepelin drew attention away from the content of psychotic symptoms—it did not matter if a paranoid's delusions concerned Satan or the state—to whether or not specific symptoms were associated with the cause and outcome of the underlying disease. American psychiatrist Adolf Meyer spoke for the psychiatric community standing in awe of Kraepelin's achievement, "The terms and traditions of over 2,000 years are overthrown" (quoted by Shorter, 1997, p. 108). Patients paid a certain price for the advancement of scientific psychology. Although Kraepelin cared deeply for his patients, many professors of psychiatry did not, seeing them only as specimens for scientific investigation.

Problems less severe than madness—the neuroses—were treated by neurologists. Neurologists supervised rest cures at spas and consulted with patients in private offices. By the end of the century, however, the two fields had become effectively merged under the rubric of psychiatry.

In both fields, there was movement toward *psychotherapy*, a term coined by two Dutch psychiatrists in 1887. In moral therapy, stress was placed on having a therapeutic, one-to-one relationship between psychiatrist and patient in addition to the structured life of the asylum. Initially, neurologists thought to cure their patients by physical means—for example, by hosing excitable patients with cold water to soothe their supposedly overexcited nerves—and by prescribing milk diets, rest, and massages. However, neurologists began to recognize with psychiatrists that talking could help patients, establishing working relationships between doctor and patient.

THEORETICAL ORIENTATIONS IN PSYCHIATRY AND NEUROLOGY Although they increasingly recognized the value of psychotherapy, most psychiatrists and neurologists believed that the causes of the disorders they treated were biological. Madness was caused by troubles in the brain; lesser syndromes such as hysteria or neurasthenia, by troubles in the nervous system. Asylum psychiatrists, in particular, recognized that the symptoms of madness were so bizarre, the suffering of their patients so great, that the cause must lie in the brain. Psychiatrists and neurologists also believed there was genetic basis to insanity, because it so often ran in families rather than breaking out at random. Some psychiatrists advanced the notion of biological "degeneration," which represented madness as sliding back down the evolutionary ladder from rational humanity to instinctive animality.

There was a rival view to the dominant neuroscientific and genetic conception of mental illness, Romantic psychiatry, so-called because it held that the causes of mental illness lay in the patient's psychological history and life circumstances, especially their emotional lives. Romantic psychiatrists were also called the "psychically oriented," distinguishing them from the biological orientation of the majority. The biological view was in part inspired by Enlightenment philosophy, seeing madness as a result of false perception and bad thinking. Romantic psychiatrists, in contrast, saw madness as stemming from passions that had slipped the bonds of rational control. In practice, romantic psychiatrists spent hours discussing their patient's emotional lives and tried to instill in them religious and moral values. Although Freud denied the connection, psychoanalytic therapy was an extension of romantic psychiatry. In psychoanalytic form, romantic psychiatry largely displaced biological psychiatry until the "biological revolution" of the 1970s, when psychiatrists again looked to the brain and the genes for the cause of psychiatric disorders (Shorter, 1997).

French Clinical Psychology

Alfred Binet (1905) sharply distinguished French psychology from the psychologies of its neighbors (quoted by Plas, 1997):

> With relatively few exceptions, the psychologists of my country have left the investigations of psychophysics to the Germans, and the study of comparative psychology to the English. They have devoted themselves almost exclusively to the study of pathological psychology, that is to say psychology affected by disease. (p. 549)

In France, psychology developed as an adjunct to medicine. German experimental psychology focused on a sort of Platonic "normal, human adult, mind." The British compared animal and human minds, and in Galton's work described the statistically average mind. French psychology concentrated on abnormal, non-Western, and developing minds. Ribot, for example, said that the ideal subjects for scientific psychology were the madman, the primitive, and the child, which he regarded as providing natural experiments of greater value than laboratory ones (Smith, 1997). Neuroscience, as we have seen, advances by both laboratory and clinical work. In clinical neuroscience, investigators use experiments of nature—damage to the brain and nervous system caused by accident and disease—to illuminate normal functioning. Ribot advocated that psychologists do the same, studying nonnormal minds as natural experiments that not only are interesting in themselves but can shed light on normal consciousness, too.

The French clinical tradition contributed to psychology the term *subject*, later ubiquitously used to describe people who participate in psychological studies (Danziger, 1990) until replaced by the contemporary term *participant*. In French medicine, the word *sujet* meant a person under treatment or observation and before that, to a corpse to be used for dissection or a candidate for a surgical procedure. Binet and other French psychologists adopted the term to describe the objects of their psychological investigations. The word *subject* was used similarly in English and was first deployed in its modern sense by Cattell in 1889. As suggested by Binet's methods, the French model of psychological investigation differed from the French and German models. French psychology was more oriented to extensive investigations of single subjects, a legacy of its medical heritage. German psychology evolved out of philosophy and addressed the idealized Mind of the philosophers. British psychology evolved out of the study of animals and mental testing, and was attuned to statistical aggregation of measurable differences between minds, whether within human minds or between various sorts of animal (and human) minds.

French psychologists devoted much of their attention to hypnotism, which they linked to and used as a treatment for hysteria. In this connection, two theories arose as to the nature of the hypnotic trance. A. A. Liebeault (1823–1904) began one school of thought in Nancy, France, which was carried on by his student Hippolyte Bernheim (1837–1919). The Nancy school held that the hypnotic state was an intensification of certain tendencies in ordinary sleep or wakefulness. Some actions, even sophisticated ones, are automatic: We all respond impulsively to some suggestions; we all hallucinate in dreams. According to the Nancy school, in hypnosis the conscious will lose its usual control over perception and action, and the orders of the hypnotist pass immediately and unconsciously into action or hallucinatory perception. The rival school of the Salpêtrière Hospital in Paris maintained that, because hypnotic suggestion could be used to remove hysteric symptoms, the hypnotic state must be an abnormal one, found in hysteric patients only. Hypnosis and hysteria were both seen as evidence of a pathological nervous system. The leading spokesman for the Salpêtrière school was Jean Martin Charcot (1825–1893), under whom Freud studied for several months. With Freud, the study of hypnotism became part of the psychology of the unconscious, for Freud used hypnosis in his early activities as a psychotherapist.

Conclusion

The nineteenth century was a century of conflicts and its conflicts are our conflicts. The Industrial Revolution brought unparalleled material progress and tremendous urban poverty. Religious revival was widespread, even as the foundations of belief were steadily eroded by science. People were inculcated with acute and ferocious sexual morality, while allowing—or causing—prostitution and crime to be endemic. The sciences and humanities flourished as never before, but the practical businessman sneered at the ivory tower intellectual. Pessimism and optimism mixed in the same mind. Wrote Carlyle: "Deep and sad as is our feeling that we stand yet in the bodeful night; equally deep, indestructible is our assurance that the morning also will not fail" (quoted in Houghton, 1957, p. 27).

Central to the nineteenth century was the conflict between the new scientific naturalism and the older beliefs in a transcendent spiritual reality. Naturalism, product of the Enlightenment, occasioned both hope and despair. It held out the hope of perpetual progress, of the perfectibility of humanity, of useful and profound knowledge of the universe. Yet it challenged the traditional religious beliefs people had accumulated and lived by for centuries. Science also threatened to dehumanize humans, reducing the individual to a collection of chemicals laboring in a vast industrial machine. It seemed to strip the world of meaning—and each person of freedom and dignity.

Proponents of naturalism did not see the conflicts. They believed that technical, scientific solutions could be found for every human problem. Their problem was to convince society of their sincerity and efficacy. Science became scientism, a new religion, most clearly seen in Comte's positivism but also present in popularizing scientists such as Huxley. The naturalists benefited from being united in a single Newtonian conception of nature, differing among themselves only in detail. Forceful, optimistic, successful, natural science came to dominate the intellectual world.

Out of the nineteenth century emerged the three founding forms of psychology. Wundt founded the *psychology of consciousness*. Freud founded the *psychology of the unconscious*. And various psychologists influenced by evolutionary thought founded the *psychology of adaptation*. All the concepts for each were in place, awaiting only the creative minds and forceful personalities needed to weld them into coherent psychological programs.

Constructing the Modern World: Bibliography

Constructing the Modern World: Bibliography

A work that is hard to place in these bibliographies is Francis Fukyama's *The origins of political order: From pre-human times to the French Revolution* (New York: Farrar, Straus, and Giroux, 2011). It traces the development of modern political orders in the great Old World civilizations, and I place it here because its end point (there's a volume to come) is in the eighteenth century.

There are several fine introductions to medieval life and history. The briefest, but still an excellent treatment, is Denys Hay, *The medieval centuries* (New York: Harper Torchbooks, 1964). Morris Bishop, *The middle ages* (New York: American Heritage Press, 1970), is an attractive, well-written book for the general reader; also for the general reader, but more detailed, is Heer (1962). Norman Cantor, one of the outstanding students of the Middle Ages, has written two good books: *The civilization of the Middle Ages*, 4th ed. (New York: HarperCollins, 1993); and *Inventing the Middle Ages* (New York: Quill, 1991); the former is a general text, the latter an entertaining work on the historians who created "the Middle Ages." The classic scholarly work on medieval social structure is Marc Bloch, *Feudal society* (Chicago: University of Chicago Press, 1961). Finally, William Brandt, *The shape of medieval history* (New York: Schocken, 1973), provides a general intellectual history of the Middle Ages. The flavor of life in one place and one time during the Middle Ages is provided in David Howarth, *1066: The year of the conquest* (Harmondsworth, England: Penguin, 1977). Three general surveys of medieval philosophy are Frederick Artz, *The mind of the Middle Ages* (Chicago: Phoenix Books, 1980); David Knowles, *The evolution of medieval thought* (New York: Vintage Books, 1962); and J. Weinberg, *A short history of medieval philosophy* (Princeton, NJ: Princeton University Press, 1964). M. Fakhry, *A history of Islamic philosophy* (New York: Columbia University Press, 1970) describes the work of medieval Islamic thinkers. This is also a good place to mention Davies's (1996), *Europe*; this is a thoroughly engrossing narrative history of Europe from ancient times to the present, but is also quite controversial—English reviewers loved it, but American critics, by and large, disliked it.

For the early Middle Ages, see W. C. Bark, *Origins of the medieval world* (Stanford: Stanford University Press, 1958); Geoffrey Barraclough, *The crucible of Europe: The ninth and tenth centuries in European history* (Berkeley: University of California Press, 1976);

Michael Grant, *Dawn of the Middle Ages* (New York: McGraw-Hill, 1981); H. St. L. B. Moss, *The birth of the Middle Ages 394–814* (New York: Oxford University Press, 1964); and R. W. Southern, *The making of the Middle Ages: Europe 972–1204* (New Haven, CT: Yale University Press, 1953). For philosophy in the period, see George Bosworth, *Early medieval philosophy* (Freeport, NY: Books for Libraries Press, 1971). For psychology, see Augustine, *Confessions* (Harmondsworth, England: Penguin, 1961); Marcia Colish, *The mirror of language* (New Haven, CT: Yale University Press, 1968), which discusses Augustine's psychology; George Mora, "Mind-body concepts in the Middle Ages: Part I. The classical background and its merging with the Judeo-Christian tradition in the early Middle Ages," *Journal of the History of the Behavioral Sciences* (1978, *14*: 344–361); and two works on medieval faculty psychology: E. Ruth Harvey, *The inward wits: Psychological theory in the Middle Ages and Renaissance* (London: The Warburg Institute, Survey VI, 1975); and Harry Austryn Wolf-son, "The internal senses in Latin, Arabic, and Hebrew philosophical texts," *Harvard Theological Review* (1935, *28*: 69–133).

Many of the general works already cited discuss popular culture in the Middle Ages; here are some other sources: C. Erickson, *The medieval vision* (New York: Oxford University Press, 1976); Georges Duby, *The knight, the lady, and the priest: The making of modern marriage in medieval France* (New York: Pantheon, 1983); Charles Homer Haskins, *The rise of the universities* (Ithaca, NY: Cornell University Press, 1923); Colin Morris, *The discovery of the individual 1050–1200* (New York: Harper & Row, 1972); Jeffrey Burton Russell, *Witchcraft in the Middle Ages* (Ithaca, NY: Cornell University Press, 1972); and Robin Briggs, *Witches and neighbors: The social and cultural context of European witchcraft* (New York: Viking, 1996). Scholarly articles on everyday life in the Middle Ages can be found in G. Duby (ed.), *A history of private life, vol. II: Revelations of the medieval world* (Cambridge, MA: Harvard University Press, 1988).

For psychology in the High Middle Ages, see the works by Harvey and Wolfson already cited; John Marenbon, *Later medieval philosophy* (New York: Routledge, 1991); and George Mora, "Mind-body concepts in the Middle Ages: Part II. The Moslem influence, the great theological systems, and cultural attitudes toward the mentally ill in the late Middle Ages,"

Journal of the History of the Behavioral Sciences (1980, *16*: 58–72). Many versions of the works of Dante, Chaucer, Shakespeare, and Cervantes are available. The passion and morality plays referred to in the text can be found in J. Gassner, ed. (1963), *Medieval and tudor drama* (New York: Bantam); for *Diocletian* and *The betrayal of Christ: The Chester Bakers' play*; and E. T. Schell and J. D. Shucter, eds. (1969), *English morality plays and moral interludes* (New York: Holt, Rhinehart, and Winston) for *Tide tarrieth no man*.

The Late Middle Ages, grim as they were, are nevertheless fascinating. The pivotal century was the fourteenth, admirably captured by Barbara W. Tuchman in *A distant mirror: The calamitous fourteenth century* (New York: Knopf, 1978). The classic work on the period is J. Huizinga, *The waning of the Middle Ages* (Garden City, NY: Doubleday, 1954). The intellectual history of the period is told by Gordon Leff in *The dissolution of the medieval outlook* (New York: Harper & Row, 1976).

The most important thinker of the Late Middle Ages was William of Ockham; a selection of his works appears in *Philosophical writings: A selection* (Indianapolis: Library of Liberal Arts, 1964); his biographer is Gordon Leff, *William of Ockham* (Manchester, England: Manchester University Press, 1975). Ockham's skeptical follower was Nicholas of Autrecourt, *The universal treatise* (Milwaukee, WI: Marquette University Press, 1971). The folk thought of the Late Middle Ages has received much attention from historians since the first edition of this book. The most important finding has been how little the Christian Neoplatonic outlook penetrated the thought of uneducated men and women. The best known of these revisionist works is Emmanuel Le Roy Ladurie, *Montaillou: The promised land of error* (New York: George Braziller, 1978), which examines the daily life of an un-Christian village in southern France. A similar book on Italy is Carlo Ginzburg's, *The cheese and the worms: The cosmos of a sixteenth century miller* (London: Routledge & Kegan Paul, 1980). A related and more general work, which tries to describe the characteristic mentality of the Late Middle Ages, is Le Roy Ladurie's *Love, death, and money in the Pays d'Oc* (New York: George Braziller, 1982). A useful commentary on the mentality works is H. C. Erik Midelfort, "Madness and the problems of psychological history in the sixteenth century," *Sixteenth Century Journal* (1981, *12*: 5–12). Peter Laslett, *The world we have lost: England before the industrial age*, 2nd ed. (New York: Scribner's, 1971) is the work that launched a new social history.

Important works on medieval science include R. Dales, *The scientific achievement of the Middle Ages* (Philadelphia: University of Pennsylvania Press, 1973); Edward Grant, "Scientific thought in fourteenth century Paris: Jean Buridan and Nicole Oresme," in M. P. Cosman and B. Chandler, eds., *Machaut's world: Science and art in the fourteenth century* (New York: New York Academy of Science, 1978); E. Moody, *Studies in medieval philosophy, science and logic* (Berkeley: University of California Press, 1975); Tina Stiefel, "The heresy of science: A twelfth century conceptual revolution," *Isis* (1977, *68*: 347–362); Nicholas H. Steneck, *Science and creation in the Middle Ages* (South Bend, IN: University of Notre Dame Press, 1975); K. Wallace, *Francis Bacon on the nature of man* (Urbana: University of Illinois Press, 1967); and Lynn White, *Medieval technology and social change* (London: Oxford University Press, 1962). Lindberg (1992) provides an excellent general history of science up to the eve of the Scientific Revolution. He carefully considers the degree to which modern science is a continuation of ancient and medieval science, concluding that although early scientists made important contributions, the Scientific Revolution was a genuine revolution, a break with the past. Continuity, however, is seen by Thomas Goldstein, *Dawn of modern science: From the ancient Greeks to the Renaissance* (New York: Da Capo Press, 1988). Colish (1992) and Edward Grant, *God and reason in the Middle Ages* (New York: Cambridge University Press, 2001), give good overviews of medieval philosophy and science, including discussion of why science developed only in Europe. Huff (1993) is a more detailed study. Bernard Lewis is a distinguished historian of Islam; although his *What went wrong?* (Lewis, 2002) was published just after the 9/11/2001 atrocities, the provocative title has nothing to do with them, but is a study of what happened in the eighteenth century when Islam discovered that it had fallen behind Europe in technical and scientific development.

On the Renaissance: The classic work is Jakob Burkhardt, *The civilization of the Renaissance in Italy* (New York: Mentor, 1862/1960); more recent works include J. R. Hale, *The civilization of Europe in the Renaissance* (New York: Athenaeum, 1994); Denys Hay, *The Italian Renaissance in its historical background* (Cambridge, England: Cambridge University Press, 1961); and Lacey Baldwin Smith, *The Elizabethan world* (Boston: Houghton Mifflin, 1972). For the Reformation, see Roland Bainton, *The Reformation of the sixteenth century* (Boston: Beacon Press, 1956). On Renaissance thought, see E. Cassirer, P. O. Kristeller, and J. H. Randall, eds., *Renaissance philosophy of man* (Chicago: University of Chicago Press, 1948); Paul Kristeller, *Renaissance thought* (New York: Harper & Row, 1961); D. Wilcox, *In search of God and self: Renaissance and Reformation thought*

(Boston: Houghton Mifflin, 1975); and, for a work emphasizing the continuity rather then the break between the Middle Ages and the Renaissance, see Walter Ullman, *Medieval foundations of Renaissance humanism* (Ithaca, NY: Cornell University Press, 1977).

For the medieval and Renaissance worldviews, see Erickson (1976), and E. M. W. Tillyard, *The Elizabethan world-picture* (New York: Vintage Books, n.d.).

The seventeenth century is recognized by historians as critical in Western history because the modern world of science and nations was created during this century. It was a period of incredible ferment in philosophy, political thought, and religion. For an overview of the century, see Christopher Hill's, who titled *The century of revolution: 1603–1714* (New York: Norton, 1966). As a Marxist, Hill has been concerned to show how deeply seventeenth-century thinkers challenged the shibboleths of their time. His main work along this line is *The world turned upside down: Radical ideas during the English revolution* (Harmondsworth, England: Pelican, 1972). Regardless of whether one agrees with Hill's politics, his works amply repay reading, for they cast new and revealing light on our attempts to understand ourselves. A general treatment of the English civil war, focussing on its cultural and social causes, is Michael Braddick, *God's fury, England's fire* (London: Penguin, 2008). Paul Hazard, *The European mind 1680–1715* (New York: New American Library, 1963), suggested that Europe experienced a "general crisis" during the seventeenth century, and his thesis has generated controversy ever since he proposed it in 1935. Theodore K. Rabb, *The struggle for stability in early modern Europe* (New York: Oxford University Press, 1975), updates Hazard's thesis; and G. Parker and L. M. Smith, eds., *The general crisis of the seventeenth century* (London: Routledge & Kegan Paul, 1978), present a symposium on the thesis. Basil Willey, *The seventeenth century background* (Garden City, NY: Doubleday, 1953), provides a general survey of society and politics in the century.

The Scientific Revolution was the most important event of the seventeenth century. Here are some general histories: Aleandre Korye, *From the close world to the infinite universe* (Baltimore: Johns Hopkins University Press, 1957; now dated but very influential on later history of science); A. Rupert Hall, *The scientific revolution 1500–1800: The formation of the modern scientific attitude*, 2nd ed. (Boston: Beacon Press, 1962); Herbert Butterfield (1965); Vern Bullough, ed., *The scientific revolution* (New York: Holt, Rinehart & Winston, 1970); Hugh Kearney, *Science and change 1500–1700* (New York: McGraw-Hill, 1971); R. S. Westfall, *The construction of modern science: Mechanisms and mechanics* (Cambridge, England: Cambridge University Press, 1977); and I. Bernard Cohen, *The Newtonian revolution* (Cambridge, England: Cambridge University Press, 1980), a book that incorporates some of the occult-versus-reason debate in the newest history of science. A popular treatment is given by Lisa Jardine in *Ingenious pursuits: Building the scientific revolution* (New York: Doubleday). Two books revise the standard picture of the Scientific Revolution found in the standard texts. Shapin (1996) deploys a largely external-ist perspective on the Revolution, to the point of deny-ing the Revolution took place (and despite his title!). John Henry, *The Scientific Revolution and the origins of modern science* (New York: St. Martin's, 1997) is a valuable treat-ment of the revolution organized around modern histori-ography of the Revolution—it thus juxtaposes the various treatments of the Revolution by most modern historians. Thomas (1971) is an invaluable source for how the puri-tanizing tendencies in Reformation religion paved the way for the Scientific Revolution. Margaret C. Jacob, *The cultural meaning of the Scientific Revolution* (New York, McGraw Hill, 1988) is another externalist perspective on the Revolution, stressing its practical impact on everyday life. In *The good life in the scientific revolution: Descartes, Pascal, Leibniz, and the cultivation of virtue* (Chicago: Chicago University Press, 2006), Matthew Jones discusses how science and mathematics were viewed as virtue-building disciplines, furnishing a sort of early modern version of the Hellenistic happiness philosophies.

Scientists have always fancied that science is a self-contained, rational enterprise, relatively free from philosophical and social influence. This assumption has come under sharp questioning and has set off historical debates on the roots of the Scientific Revolution. Burtt (1954) was the first to challenge science's philosophical purity and is, in consequence, much cited today. Richard Westfall, "Newton and the fudge factor," *Science* (1973, *179*: 751–758), showed how Newton's psychological commitment to his theory led him to bend data to suit it; see also Westfall's biography of Newton, *Never at rest* (Cambridge, England: Cambridge University Press, 1980). The most violent debates among historians of sci-ence have been over the degree to which the Scientific Revolution was influenced by the deep occultism of the Renaissance and seventeenth century. The claim that science was indebted to the occult is often known as "the Yates thesis" after historian Frances Yates—for example, her chapter on "The hermetic tradition in Renaissance science" in C. S. Singleton, ed., *Art, science, and history in the Renaissance* (Baltimore: Johns Hopkins University Press, 1968). A good collection favoring the occult connections of science is M. L. Righini Bonelli and W. R. Shea, eds., *Reason, experiment, and mysticism in the scientific revolution* (New York: Science History Publications, 1975). The sides of reason and occult influence are respectively upheld in a debate between Mary Hesse, "Reasons and evolutions in the history of science," and P. M. Rattansi, "Some evaluations of reason in sixteenth- and seventeenth-century natural philosophy," both in M. Teich and R. Young, eds., *Changing perspectives in the history of science* (London: Heinemann, 1973). The most recent symposium on the topic is B. Vickers, ed., *Occult and scientific mentalities in the Renaissance* (New York: Cambridge University Press, 1984); see also G. A. J. Rogers, "The basis of belief: Philosophy, science, and religion in seventeenth century England," *History of European Ideas* (1985, *6*: 19–39). For a case study on the influence of occult ideas on one scientist, see Betty Jo Teeter Dobbs, *The foundations of Newton's alchemy* (Cambridge, England: Cambridge University Press, 1983). William J. Bousma, *The waning of the Renaissance 1550–1640* (New Haven, CT: Yale University Press, 2000) looks at the period through a literary rather than scientific lens, telling a story of how the self was deconstructed and then reassembled in the late Renaissance and early modern period. The text is rather postmodern in orientation and has a rather porous texture, and does not connect much with the scientific treatment of the mind discussed in this chapter.

For seventeenth-century philosophy, see Bronowski and Mazlish (1960); and, with special reference to France, Edward John Kearns, *Ideas in seventeenth century France* (Manchester, England: Manchester University Press, 1983). For a comparative study of Descartes's and Locke's psychologies, see David E. Leary, "The intentions and heritage of Descartes and Locke: Toward a recognition of the moral basis of modern psychology," *Journal of General Psychology* (1980, *102*: 283–310). For the individual philosophers, see the following paragraphs. An important general source is Taylor (1989), who focuses on the development of the punctate self. I have found much insight and inspiration in this source.

Descartes. The biography by Stephen Gaukroger is first-rate; it illuminates many vexed and significant issues concerning Descartes's philosophy and psychology; my treatment of Descartes has been deeply reshaped by reading this book; Richard B. Carter, *Descartes' medical philosophy: The organic solution to the mind-body problem* (Baltimore: Johns Hopkins University Press, 1983); Desmond M. Clarke, *Descartes' philosophy of science* (University Park: Pennsylvania State University Press, 1984); and Bernard Williams, *Descartes: The project of pure inquiry* (Harmondsworth, England: Pelican, 1978). Descartes's

works have been recently retranslated. The important psychological works are contained in R. Descartes's, *The philosophical writings of Descartes* (Cambridge, England: Cambridge University Press, 1985).

Hobbes. Hobbes (1651/1962)

Pascal. Blaise Pascal, *Pensées* (New York: Washington Square Press, 1965).

Spinoza. Baruch Spinoza, *The works of Spinoza*, two volumes (New York: Dover Books, 1955); Stuart Hampshire, *Spinoza* (Harmondsworth, England: Pelican, 1962). Leibniz. G. W. Leibniz, *Leibniz: Selections* (New York: Scribner's, 1951); and Robert D. Brandom, "Leibniz and degrees of perception," *Journal of the History of Philosophy* (1981, *19*: 447–479); McRae (1976).

On the Enlightenment itself, a fine, two-volume treatment is given by Peter Gay (1966, 1969). Of special interest to the history of psychology is the second volume, subtitled *The science of freedom*, which covers the Newtons of the Mind. A selection of the philosophes' major writings has been assembled by Gay in *The Enlightenment: A comprehensive anthology* (New York: Simon & Schuster, 1973). A somewhat older book that stresses the darker side of the Enlightenment is Crocker (1959). A recent book that does for the eighteenth century what Christopher Hill did for the seventeenth in his *The world turned upside down* is Margaret C. Jacob, *The radical enlightenment: Pantheists, Freemasons and Republicans* (London: Allen & Unwin, 1981). The revolutionary consequences of the Enlightenment are discussed by Norman Hampson, *The first European revolution 1776–1815* (New York: Norton, 1969), who gives a broader picture of the Enlightenment in his 1982 work; in this connection, see also James H. Billington, *Fire in the minds of men: Origins of the revolutionary faith* (New York: Basic Books, 1980). For science in the period, see Thomas L. Hankins, *Science and the Enlightenment* (Cambridge, England: Cambridge University Press, 1985). Finally, for social histories of the period, see Richard Sennett, *The fall of public man* (New York: Vintage Books, 1978); Lawrence Stone, *The family, sex, and marriage in England 1500–1800* (New York: Harper & Row, 1982); and Neil McKendrick, John Brewer, and J. H. Plumb, *The birth of a consumer society: The commercialization of eighteenth century England* (New Haven, CT: Yale University Press, 1982), especially the last chapter, by Plumb, on how people responded to modernity.

David Fate Norton, "The myth of 'British empiricism,'" *History of European ideas* (1981, *1*: 331–344), shows that neither rationalism nor empiricism is the fixed tradition it is taken to be. Thomas Reid started the idea of empiricism versus rationalism, and his myth has been enshrined by teachers ever since. A survey of the philosophy of the period is in S. C. Brown, ed., *Philosophers of the enlightenment* (Sussex, England: Harvester Press, 1985). Two books by John Yolton discuss the central psychological ideas of the eighteenth-century philosophers: *Thinking matter*, on materialism, and *Perceptual acquaintance from Descartes to Locke*, on perception (both Minneapolis: University of Minnesota Press, 1983 and 1984, respectively).

Works on the specific philosophers follow, omitting works cited in the text.

Locke. An informally written general account of Locke's thought is given in Edward Feser (2007) Locke (Oxford: Oneworld). Feser focuses on Locke's political thought, pointing out its deep influence on Americans, but finds it wanting. Locke (1690/1975); *The Locke reader*, J. W. Yolton, compiler (Cambridge, England: Cambridge University Press, 1977); I. C. Tipton, ed., *Locke on human understanding* (Oxford, England: Oxford University Press, 1977); and J. W. Yolton, *Locke and the compass of human understanding* (Cambridge, England: Cambridge University Press, 1970). These works discuss a modern controversy on whether Locke meant ideas to be mental copies or direct acts by which the mind grasps objects in the world. As we learned, both views have their advocates in psychology, but whatever Locke meant, his successors took him to mean ideas are mental representations, not mental acts. The intimate connection between the thinking of Locke and Newton is detailed in G. A. J. Rogers, "The system of Locke and Newton," in Z. Bechler, ed., *Contemporary Newtonian research* (Dordrecht, The Netherlands: D. Reidel, 1982).

Berkeley. Berkeley's major philosophical works are *Three dialogues between Hylas and Philonus* and *A treatise concerning the principles of human knowledge* (Indianapolis: Hackett, 1979 and 1982, respectively). His analysis of perception is in *Works on vision* (Indianapolis: Bobbs-Merrill, 1963). For commentary on Berkeley, see Ian C. Tipton, *Berkeley: The philosophy of immaterialism* (London: Methuen, 1974); J. O. Urmson, *Berkeley* (Oxford, England: Oxford University Press, 1982); and G. J. Stock, *Berkeley's analysis of perception* (The Hague, The Netherlands: Mouton, 1972).

Hume. David Hume, *An inquiry concerning the principles of morals* (Indianapolis: Hackett, 1983). For commentary, David Fate Norton, *David Hume: Common sense moralist, sceptical metaphysician* (Princeton, NJ: Princeton University Press, 1982); John Passmore, *Hume's intentions* (New York: Basic Books, 1968); John P. Wright, *The skeptical realism of David Hume* (Manchester, England: Manchester University Press,

1980); and D. F. Norton, ed., *The Cambridge companion to Hume* (Cambridge, England: Cambridge University Press, 1993).

The Scots. Dugald Stewart, *Elements of the philosophy of the human mind* (London: A. Strahan & T. Caddell, 1792). For a broad view of the Scottish Enlightenment, see R. H. Campbell, ed., *The origins and nature of the Scottish Enlightenment* (Edinburgh: John Donald, 1982).

Kant. Kant's most important book is *Critique of pure reason* (New York: St. Martin's Press, 1929), but it is extraordinarily difficult to read; more accessible, and deliberately so, is *Prolegomena to any future metaphysics that will be able to come forward as science* (Indianapolis: Hackett, 1977). There is also a large amount of Kant commentary. A useful, short introduction is S. Körner, *Kant* (Harmondsworth, England: Pelican, 1955). Karl Ameriks discusses *Kant's theory of mind* (Oxford, England: Clarendon Press, 1982). Gary Hatfield, "Psychology as science and philosophy," in P. Guyer, ed., *The Cambridge companion to Kant* (Cambridge, England: Cambridge University Press, 1992, pp. 200–227), critically discusses Kant's arguments about the difficulties facing psychology's claim to be a science, arguing that his claims were limited in scope and not always persuasive. Thomas Sturm reviews arguments about Kant's views on psychological science, arguing that they are not quite as negative or unconstructive as usually made out, and resurrects some eighteenth-century attempts to measure the mind in "Is there a problem with mathematical psychology in the 18th century? A fresh look at Kant's old argument." *Journal of the History of the Behavioral Sciences* (2005, *41*: 131–49).

French Naturalism. The account of French naturalism is based largely on the cited works and on the general treatments of the period listed in the general sources, especially Gay (1966, 1969). See also Robert J. Richards, "Influence of sensationalist tradition on early theories of the evolution of behavior," *Journal of History of Ideas* (1979, *40*: 85–105). That Condillac has long been misrepresented has been demonstrated by Hans Aarslef, *From Locke to Saussure: Essays on the study of language and intellectual history* (Minneapolis: University of Minnesota Press, 1982).

Enlightenment in Germany. Again, see the general sources. Also Robert J. Richards, "Christian Wolff's prolegomena to empirical and rational psychology: Translation and commentary," *Proceedings of the American Philosophical Society* (1980, *124*: 227–1239).

The Counter-Enlightenment. Without doubt, the outstanding modern student of the Counter-Enlightenment is Isaiah Berlin. For Vico and Herder, see his *Vico and Herder: Two studies in the history of ideas* (New York: Vintage Books, 1977). Several essays in his

Against the current (Harmondsworth, England: Penguin, 1982) touch of the Counter-Enlightenment, especially "The Counter Enlightenment," which briefly but insightfully reviews the major spokesmen of the movement.

The literature on the nineteenth century is understandably vast. For social history, at least in Victorian England, see Houghton (1957); W. J. Reader, *Life in Victorian England* (New York: Capricorn, 1964); or G. M. Young, *Victorian England: Portrait of an age* (New York: Oxford University Press, 1953); and, for the late nineteenth and early twentieth centuries, Samuel Hynes, *The Edwardian turn of mind* (Princeton, NJ: Princeton University Press, 1968). For intellectual history, see Owen Chadwick, *The secularization of the European mind in the nineteenth century* (Cambridge, England: Cambridge University Press, 1975); Elie Halevy, *The growth of philosophical radicalism* (Boston: Beacon Press, 1955); Maurice Mandlebaum, *History, man, and reason: A study in nineteenth-century thought* (Baltimore: Johns Hopkins University Press, 1971); John Passmore, *A hundred years of philosophy*, rev. ed. (New York: Basic Books, 1966); W. M. Simon, *European positivism in the nineteenth century* (Ithaca, NY: Cornell University Press, 1963); and D. C. Somerville, *English thought in the nineteenth century* (New York: David McKay, 1929). Patrick L. Gardiner, ed., *Nineteenth century philosophy* (New York: Free Press, 1969) collects important writings by the major philosophers. Wilson (1999) describes the gradual erosion of religious belief among European and American intelligentsia. Wilson is a writer and critic rather than a historian, and the book is provocative rather than authoritative. Nevertheless, the chapter on James is especially interesting as a summing up of his theme. The European state of mind just before World War I, which ushered in modernism with a big bang is described in *The vertigo years: Europe 1900–1914* by Phillip Blom (New York: Basic, 2008).

The worlds of the nineteenth century are well covered in the general sources and the references. Some additional useful sources are worth noting. As a spokesman for romanticism, Edmund Burke resembles Vico and Herder; see L. Bredvold and G. Ross, eds., *The philosophy of Edmund Burke* (Ann Arbor: University of Michigan Press, 1960). Richard Holmes (2009) fuses Romanticism and science, which are usually treated as oil and water in *The age of wonder: How the Romantic generation discovered the beauty and terror of science* (New York: Pantheon). For a biography of the Mills, see Bruce Mazlish, *James and John Stuart Mill* (New York: Basic Books, 1975). Auguste Comte's own *A general view of positivism* (New York:

Robert Speller & Sons, 1975) provides a starting point for understanding the movement. Ernst Mach's most important philosophical-psychological work is *The analysis of sensations* (New York: Dover Books, 1959); a biography of him is John Blackmore's *Ernst Mach* (Berkeley: University of California Press, 1972). For the occult movements of the nineteenth century, see Thomas H. Leahey and Grace Evans Leahey, *Psychology's occult doubles: Psychology and the problem of pseudoscience* (Chicago: Nelson-Hall, 1983); the references and bibliography therein are fairly exhaustive. An important work subsequently published is Roger Cooter, *The cultural meaning of popular science: Phrenology and the organization of consent in the nineteenth century* (Cambridge, England: Cambridge University Press, 1984). Deserving special mention is Robert Darnton, *Mesmerism and the end of the Enlightenment in France* (New York: Schocken, 1968), a model of intellectual and social history. The broad cultural impact of mesmerism and hypnotism in Britain is explored in Alison Winter (1998) *Mesmerized: Powers of the mind in Victorian Britain* (Chicago: Chicago University Press).

Works by some of the important transitional figures to psychology include A. Bain, *Mental science* (New York: D. Appleton, 1868); F. C. Donders, "On the speed of mental processes: Attention and performance II," *Acta Psychologica* (1969, *30*: 412–431); G. T. Fechner, *Elements of psychophysics*, Vol. 1 (New York: Holt, Rinehart & Winston, 1966); H. Helmholtz, *A treatise on physiological optics*, partially reprinted in T. Shipley, ed., *Classics in psychology* (New York: Philosophical Library, 1961); and H. Lotze, *Outlines of psychology* (Boston: Ginn & Co., 1886). L. Hearnshaw, *A short history of British psychology 1840–1940* (New York: Barnes & Noble, 1964) covers nineteenth-century British philosophical psychology. Two papers by David Leary (1978, 1980) discuss the situation in Germany.

There are several good books on the history of neuroscience. The most easily readable is science writer Carl Zimmer's (2005) *Soul made flesh: The discovery of the brain and how it changed the world* (New York: Free Press). Also accessible are two books by Stanley Finger, *Origins of neuroscience* (Oxford, England: Oxford University Press, 1994), and *Minds behind the brain: A history of pioneers and their discoveries* (New York: Oxford University Press, 2000). More scholarly treatments include Young (1970), Gordon Shepherd (1991) *Foundations of the neuron doctrine* (New York: Oxford) and Richard Rapport (2005) *Nerve endings: The discovery of the synapse* (New York: Norton).

The Psychology of Consciousness

B y the last quarter of the nineteenth century, conditions were ripe for psychology to emerge as an autonomous science. Scientific psychology was fated to be born as the hybrid offspring of physiology and philosophy of mind, called psychology by the middle of the century. Wilhelm Wundt (1832–1920) was the physician-philosopher who established psychology as an academic discipline. He did not follow his people, the future generations of psychologists, entirely into the land of science, but he made possible psychology's recognition as an independent discipline.

SETTINGS

Psychology had diverse institutional origins. In this chapter, we are concerned primarily with the establishment of psychology as an academic discipline and as an experimental science. Although today we take the idea of experimental science for granted, it was, in fact, a novel development of the nineteenth and twentieth centuries. Newton had built physics more on observations of the heavens than on experimentation, though he was an avid experimenter in alchemy and optics. Chemistry and physiology were just emerging in the nineteenth century, and the systematic application of experimentation in medicine would not come until 1948, when the first controlled clinical trial of a drug (streptomycin) was published. It was thus a bold and daring move when Wundt proposed that psychology, traditionally the province of philosophy, become an experimental science. To understand the shape and fate of the first experimental psychology, we must examine the place of its birth, the German university, and the unique values of those educated there.

From Chapter 8 of *A History of Psychology: From Antiquity to Modernity*, Seventh Edition.
Thomas Hardy Leahey. Copyright © 2013 by Pearson Education, Inc. All rights reserved.

The German University: Wissenschaft and Bildung

Napoleon's victory over the Prussians at the Battle of Jena in 1806 changed the world, albeit not in ways that the emperor would have hoped or expected, because it led to the creation of the modern research university. Defeated on the field of battle, the Prussian Kaiser resolved to thoroughly modernize his nation, including educating its citizens. Launching his project, Frederick William III said, "The state must replace with intellectual strength what it has lost in material resources" (quoted by D. K. Robinson, 1996, p. 87). His ministry of education asked scholars to conceive and build a new model university, the University of Berlin, founded between 1807 and 1810. With the unification in 1871 of the German states in Bismarck's Second German Empire, the University of Berlin became the model for the other German universities, and eventually for the world.

Heretofore in Germany and elsewhere, higher education had mostly aimed at the training of three professionals: physicians, lawyers, and clergy. There was no recognized class of scientists and scholars, and most early scientists were supported, as artists were, by wealthy patrons or by the Royal Scientific Societies of Britain and France. Natural philosophers in European colleges and universities preferred to expand Aristotle's science rather than test it with evidence. In the United States, there were no universities before the Civil War. Instead, there were small, church-supported colleges devoted to the higher education of a few of the young men and women of a particular Christian denomination. Very few people pursued higher education anywhere, and except for those aspiring to one of the three learned professions, college was not seen as the entrance to a career pathway, but as a means of preparing for entrance into polite, educated society. The Kaiser's new university was a genuine innovation that ultimately made universities important engines of national advancement worldwide.

The plan for the new model university was drawn up by William von Humboldt (1767–1835). Humboldt proclaimed two aims for the university: *Wissenchaft* and *Bildung*. Wissenschaft is usually translated as "science," but this is misleading. Wissenschaft referred to any body of knowledge organized on definite principles, and fields such as history or philology counted as Wissenschaften along with physics or physiology. Indeed, the new university adopted its vehicle for graduate training, the seminar, from philology. In philological seminars, a few students worked closely under the direction of an established master of the field. This humanistic model became the basis for the organization of scientific research laboratories such as Wundt's.

Bildung was a uniquely German concept referring to a person's self-formation through broad, humanistic education. R. Smith (1997, p. 375) defines Bildung this way: "The word denotes the value in a person of wholeness, integration, a state in which every part of education and life contributes to the pursuit of the good, the true, and the beautiful. It is an ideal personal quality, but also the quality that makes possible the high culture of a nation." In his proposal, Humboldt referred to it as "the spiritual and moral training of the nation" (quoted by Lyotard, 1984/1996, p. 484). The products of Bildung were the Bildungsburgers—culturally educated citizens. They were perhaps the closest realization in any society of Plato's utopian vision of the Guardians, the specially educated rulers of The Republic, who defined themselves by the Forms of the Beautiful, the True, and the Good.

XAM'S BLOG 1
Modernizing the Academy

The new German university was the first institution to be fully modernized from its premodern condition, not only chronologically, but also because of how it came into being. Earlier institutions, including institutions of higher learning, had just grown haphazardly, but the new German university—the emblematic one was the University of Berlin—was self-consciously planned to be a factory of knowledge. A funny example of how knowledge just grew in medieval universities came to me in Britain, when I found that their libraries had just put books on the shelves as they came in, so that books on totally unconnected topics sat next to one another. If one wanted to search for books by topic, librarians pointed to the big Library of [the U.S.] Congress volumes that listed the titles of books according to its system. Locating a title in it, one then had to go to the shelf list of books in the British library and go hiking all over the Cambridge or Oxford campus in search of the actual books. I couldn't even use the University of Edinburgh, because it was changing from the medieval to the modern Library of Congress system and the books were in piles all over the place.

The key change associated with modernization is secularization, the decline of the authority of the Church and the rise of the authority of the state and science. In the professorial world, this change began at the University of Göttingen in the early eighteenth century, before Humboldt's massive reforms. Medieval universities were part of the Church, and theology was the queen of the sciences. But at Göttingen, theology was demoted. Academic freedom as we understand it was created there when the theology faculty lost its right to censor the work of the rest of the faculty. This moment was the "pivot for the great turn in German life, which moved its center of gravity from religion to the state" (quoted by P. Watson, 2010, Kindle location 1040). Göttingen also elevated the importance of non-theological subjects such as science and psychology was (Watson, 2010).

As in all premodern institutions, one got ahead in life through personal connections. Young faculty dined with senior professors, and one sure way to get tenure was to marry a professor's daughter. Under Prussian reforms, however, German universities became thoroughly bureaucratized. Professors' work began to be evaluated quantitatively, by counting their research publications and the number of students who took their courses (W. Clark, 2006).

Romanticism had an impact, too. Premodern professors were expected to *profess*: to lecture on the great classical texts in their field, commenting on them and on what had been said about them over the centuries. If a professor became well known, it was time to write his lifework, a textbook, that more or less summarized his lectures. A textbook of this type was seen as a contribution to the slowly accumulating body of knowledge in his field. Romanticism, however, was modernist—it sought to break with the past, to celebrate the revolutionary, the creative, the breakthrough insight. While you don't think of professors or scientists as passionate geniuses like Byron, romanticism changed the nature of university research. It became expected that scholars would do novel, revolutionary work, overturning established consensus (the opposite of the textbook model) as romantic poets had changed the concept of the poem and authors the concept of the novel (W. Clark, 2006).

There was tension between these two goals from the outset: How can the pursuit of knowledge for its own sake—scholarship and scientific research—aid the spiritual growth of the citizenry? Humboldt tried to unify the goals of research and Bildung by relating them to three coordinated aims of the new university. The first was "deriving everything from an original principle" (the goal of Wissenschaft). Second was "relating everything to an ideal" (the goal of philosophy). And the third was "unifying this ideal and this principle in a single Idea" (so that science will serve justice in the state and society, also a goal of philosophy) (quoted by Lyotard, 1984/1996, p. 485). Note the pivotal role played by philosophy in Humboldt's scheme. To the philosopher belonged the job of providing foundations for and synthesizing all knowledge, whether scientific or humanistic, into a single unified view of the world (Weltanschauung) in the service of high moral and social ideals.

Economically, the German university rested on the training of teachers for the German gymnasia—academically oriented high schools for the rising middle classes (Gundlach, 2012). To pass the difficult licensing examinations, prospective gymnasium teachers needed to be rigorously educated in all fields of study, from literature to physics, and the tuition they paid was the economic basis of the new universities. As teachers, they then contributed to the Bildung of their students. From 1866 onward, psychology was included as part of the curriculum in philosophy and pedagogy. The tension between humanistic cultivation of character and scientific and scholarly cultivation of specialized research areas became apparent in the teachers' curriculum. As the nineteenth century progressed, the curriculum shifted from emphasizing broad, humanistic education to mastery of a specific field.

The development of psychology in German universities would be strongly affected by the institutional goals of Bildung and Wissenschaft (Ash, 1980, 1981). Humboldt's stress on scientific research made the German universities uniquely open to the creation of new arenas for scientific investigation at the same time it was moving to the forefront of the second Industrial Revolution (Littman, 1979).

XAM'S BLOG 2
Psychology Takes Off in the Second Industrial Revolution

Your Google folks have just invented a new way to explore history, called Ngram Viewer. You can search for a word, a set of words, or a short phrase in thousands of books published since 1500 that Google has been digitizing from libraries around the world. Here's the Ngram Viewer for *psychology* in English:

There were two Industrial Revolutions, the first one in the late eighteenth century in Britain and a second one from about 1860, taking place in the rest of Europe and in North America. It was this second Revolution that transformed the world, creating modernity and modernism. We see that psychology as an institution or even as a concept scarcely existed prior to the middle of the nineteenth century, and that psychology was very much part of the second Industrial Revolution, its growth almost perfectly tracking the growth in wealth as found in the following figure. Psychology was a response to modernity and a shaper of modernism.

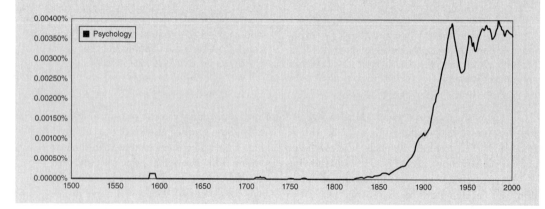

At the same time, psychology's growth in Germany would be inhibited by the tension between specialized scholarship and broad, spiritual education. Academics of Wundt's generation who built the German universities were committed to the unification of scholarship and research with humanistic Bildung. They tried to be true to Humboldt's vision, developing overarching systems of thought that coordinated philosophy, the humanities, and the sciences in the service of "a single Idea." Wundt and others saw psychology as part of philosophy, not as a natural science. However, by the turn of the century, Bildung and system building were honored more in ceremonial speeches than in actual practice. Scholars and scientists devoted themselves to specialized technical studies instead. The second generation of psychologists worked to make psychology an autonomous natural science, freeing it from being the handmaiden of philosophy. However, philosophers and humanists resented the intrusion of science into their traditional domains, and the Ministry of Education placed no great value on making psychology an autonomous science because it did not fit comfortably into the professional education of the Bildungsburger. The science of physiology belonged with medicine, whose professional aims it served. Sciences like chemistry and physics (especially chemistry) served the development of German industry. Psychology became something of an orphan, unwanted by the philosophers, but unable to find a new home anywhere else (Gundlach, 2012).

German Values: The Mandarin Bildungsburger

The historian Fritz Ringer (1969) has drawn a parallel between the cultural leaders of Germany, the Bildungsburgers, and the Mandarins who ruled Confucian China. The Mandarins were a self-defined intellectual elite based on deep education in Chinese culture, especially poetry. A young man entered the Mandarin class by passing a sort of civil service examination, but it was an examination on Chinese language and culture, not on managerial or bureaucratic skills. The Mandarins prized pure scholarship for its own sake and prided themselves on working only with their minds, not their hands, disdaining what the Bildungsburgers derided as mere "handwork." The Mandarin emphasis on scholarship inhibited in China the development of science and technology and in Germany the growth of applied psychology.

The Bildunsgburgers saw themselves as an educated elite based on deep education in German culture. Observing from England, the author Matthew Arnold (1822–1888) noted, "What I admire in Germany is, that while there, too, Industrialism . . . is making . . . most successful and rapid sort of progress, the idea of Culture, Culture of the only true sort, is in Germany a living power also" (quoted by R. Smith, 1997, p. 371). Moreover, German intellectuals saw themselves as uniquely suited to the highest forms of scholarship. Discussing the achievements of German theology in 1906, Albert Schweitzer (1875–1965) wrote, "Nowhere save in the German temperament can there be found in the same perfection the living complex of conditions and factors—of philosophic thought, critical acumen, historical insight, and religious feeling—without which no deep theology is possible" (quoted by Noll, 1994, p. 35). The values of this Mandarin elite powerfully shaped German psychology, making its ideas, though not is methods, unexportable. A revealing window on the mental world of the Bildungsburger can be found in the distinction between *Gemeinschaft*—community—and *Gesellschaft*—society—made by the German sociologist Ferdinand Tönnies (1855–1936). Gemeinschaft embraced everything the Bildungsburgers loved and valued; Gesellschaft, everything they feared and hated (Harrington, 1996).

Gemeinschaft was a genuine community of a single people sharing a common language, culture, and geographical roots, idealized by the *poleis* of ancient Greece (see Table 1). Because of these common ties, a community formed an organic whole, a single *Volk*, or race. A society was merely an agglomeration of isolated individuals lacking any common tie beyond citizenship and a superficial

TABLE 1	**The contrasting meanings of Gemeinschaft and Gesellschaft as drawn by Tonnies.**
Gemeinschaft	**Gesellschaft**
Community	Society
Culture	Civilization
Living Organism	Mechanical
Rural	Aggregate Urban
Life and Soil	Mind and Reason

veneer of merely "civilized" manners. The city, especially new cities such as Berlin, epitomized the evils of society. Cities are inhabited by strangers—immigrants who have uprooted themselves from their native places to pursue solitary, primarily commercial, ambitions.

As educated people, the Bildungsburgers did not reject mind and reason as such. Instead, they were infused with the romantic and Kantian rejection of the kind of narrow, calculating reason they saw in Newton and Hume. Indeed, for many German Mandarins, Newtonian science was the enemy of the Good, the True, and the Beautiful. It depicted the universe as a mere machine whose motions could be mathematically calculated, lacking anything spiritual or refined. Science gave rise to industrialization, and machines and factories replaced humans and organic connections to blood and soil. Moreover, composed of mere isolated parts, machines and societies can fall apart into chaos and anarchy (Burrow, 2000). The education of Bildung was meant to be an education for living in a true community. As a socialist writer put it, the purpose of Bildung was "to develop all the seeds of one's selfhood, but in the service of the whole" (quoted by Harrington, 1996, p. 24). Psychology's German founder, Wilhelm Wundt, wrote that the national state "serves ideal purposes of absolute value, purposes with respect to which the life of the individual has no value at all" (quoted by Kusch, 1999, Kindle location 3440).

As a matter of intellectual history, the values of the Bildungsburgers originated in romanticism, Kantian Idealism, and the Counter-Enlightenment of Herder. Their desire for wholeness was also rooted in the political and social experiences of nineteenth-century Germany. Before 1871, Germany was an idea, not a political state such as France or Britain. German-speaking peoples lived all over middle Europe, but lived in small, even tiny, quasi-feudal states, the largest of which was Prussia. The German people longed for unification into a greater German whole, and they placed such great value on learning German culture and cultivating the German language because these provided unification in spirit, if not in political fact. Led by Bismarck, Prussia used war to create a German empire, bringing unity to most German peoples, but not the unity the Bildungsburgers longed for. Bismarck ruled his Kaiser's new Reich by blood and iron, not by scholarship and culture (Steinberg, 2011). Ironically, the Bildungsburgers were not Mandarins in the Chinese sense because they did not rule Germany as they had hoped to do. German professors gained academic freedom by giving up their political ambitions. At the same time, urbanization and industrialization, which fueled the Prussian war machine, undermined the values of Gemeinschaft, threatening to turn the new German Reich into a Gesellschaft that might tip over into chaos. Economic development threatened to overturn traditional, rural German culture and replace it with an urban landscape of selfish, bourgeois individuals. Echoing Greek disdain for the pursuit of self-interest, German industrialist and politician Walther Rathenau (1838–1916) wrote:

Any thinking person will walk with horror through the streets and see the department stores, shops, and warehouses. . . . Most of what is stored, elegantly displayed and dearly sold is terribly ugly, serves demeaning lusts . . . and is [actually] stupid, harmful, worthless . . . meaningless and wasteful. (quoted and translated by Wiendieck, 1996, p. 516)

Part of the horror for the Bildungsburgers was precisely that such goods were popular. They were "thinking people," guided by ideals. The customers in the shops were members of the unthinking, but numerous, productive class of Plato's Republic, guided only by the utilitarian pursuit of pleasure.

World War I brought Germans hopes for unity and larger purposes to a fevered pitch of exaltation, and then, in defeat, dashed them utterly. In 1914, theologian and historian Ernst Troeltsch (1865–1923) voiced the enthusiasm he and his fellow Mandarin academics felt upon the outbreak of war, as it seemed to bring the national unity and Greek-like service of the state that the Mandarins longed for:

> The first victory we won, even before the victories on the battlefield, was the victory over ourselves. . . . A higher life seemed to reveal itself to us. Each of us . . . lived for the whole, and the whole lived in all of us. Our own ego with its personal interests was dissolved in the great historic being of the nation. The fatherland calls! The parties disappear. . . . Thus a moral elevation of the people preceded the war; the whole nation was gripped by the truth and reality of a suprapersonal, spiritual power. (quoted by Harrington, 1996, p. 30)

Wundt shared Troeltsch's enthusiasm. They and their fellow "patriots of the lectern" wrote violently anti-English and anti-American tracts, sharpening the differences between German community and the "societies" to their west. Above all, they despised America as the emblem of Gesellschaft, a nation comprising commercially minded immigrants, sharing no deep culture, no rootedness in the soil. For Wundt and other German intellectuals, Americans and their English cousins were, in the words of Werner Sombart, mere "traders" who regarded "the whole existence of man on earth as a sum of commercial transactions which everyone makes as favorably as possible for himself." Wundt excoriated them for their "egotistic utilitarianism," "materialism," "positivism," and "pragmatism" (Ringer, 1969). The German ideal, on the other hand, was "the hero," a warrior whose ideals were "sacrifice, faithfulness, openness, respect, courage, religiosity, charity and willingness to obey." The highest value of Anglo-Americans was seen as personal comfort, while that of the German was seen as sacrifice and service to a greater whole. For Wundt, the point of life was not happiness but the production of objects of intellectual value—precisely the products that he, as a German professor, churned out (Kusch, 1999).

World War I was, however, a disaster for Germany, delivering the very chaos Germans feared. As they were defeated on the battlefield, riot, revolt, and finally, revolution, broke out, replacing the Reich with a republic governed not by blood and iron but by votes. However, the Weimar Republic was forever tainted by its birth in the defeat of the Great War, and German intellectuals never fully supported it. Moreover, instead of unification, democracy brought chaos and rule by unthinking, atomized citizens divided into political factions and even private armies of disgruntled soldiers, the *Freikorps*. With such fragile foundations, the Weimar Republic failed and in 1933 was replaced by the totalitarian unity of Hitler and the Nazis: *Ein Reich, Ein Volk, Ein Führer*—One Empire, One People, One Leader.

German psychology was shaped by Bildungsburger values. Psychology is the science most directly concerned with human nature, and it was torn between its alliance with materialistic science on the one hand and, on the other, the German hope that there was more to human beings than brain, consciousness, and behavior. Wundt founded psychology as a science within philosophy, but as his career developed, he placed limits on what psychology could do as a natural science, setting uniquely human achievements such as culture and language, key aspects of Gemeinschaft, outside the purview of experimental psychology. Similarly, Wundt was torn between the atomistic view of consciousness that seemed most compatible with science, and the holistic vision of the universe he shared with his fellow Mandarins. He argued that consciousness was composed of elements, but that they were unified into larger wholes by the synthesizing power of the human will. The second and third generation of German psychologists struggled with the conflict between Mandarin values and modern life, the life of industry, and urbanization. Most psychologists wanted to move psychology completely into the realm of natural science, and some wanted psychology to become an applied field. These goals were resisted by the entrenched power of philosophy and the high value the Mandarins placed on pure scholarship. As modern life seemed to tend ever more toward the machine (industrialization) and chaos (urbanization), reconciling science and humanistic values became increasingly difficult. Nevertheless, the Gestalt psychologists attempted it, claiming to find in nature, in the brain, and in consciousness organized wholes—Gestalten—that satisfyingly transcended their atomic constituents.

WILHELM WUNDT'S PSYCHOLOGY OF CONSCIOUSNESS

Wilhelm Wundt (1832–1920)

Wilhelm Wundt was the founder of psychology as an institution. His ideas were not especially original and did not survive into the second generation of even German psychologists. He took the already-established path through physiology, accepting the Cartesian-Lockean Way of Ideas as the basis for making psychology a science, suitably linked to physiology. His enduring innovations were methodological and social rather than theoretical. He wrote a compendious text on physiological psychology that laid out in arresting detail the path through physiology for scientific psychology. He created the first academically recognized laboratory in psychology. He founded the first journal in experimental psychology. In sum, Wundt remade psychology from a fitful enterprise of solitary scholars into a genuine scientific community (Danziger, 1990).

Wilhelm Maximilian Wundt was born on August 16, 1832, in Neckarau, Baden, Germany, the fourth child of a minister, Maximilian Wundt, and his wife, Marie Frederike. He was born into the intellectual Mandarin elite. On both sides of his family were to be found intellectuals, scientists, professors, government officials, and physicians. At the age of 13, Wundt began his formal education at a Catholic gymnasium. He disliked school and failed, but he transferred to another gymnasium in Heidelberg from which he graduated in 1851. Wundt decided to go into medicine, and after an initially poor start, he applied himself and excelled in his studies. His scientific interests emerged in physiological research. He got his MD summa cum laude in 1855, and after some study with the physiologist Johannes Müller, received in 1857 the second doctorate that German universities required before one could be licensed to teach at the university level. He gave his first course in experimental physiology—to four students—in his mother's apartment in Heidelberg.

Wundt applied for and received an assistantship with Hermann von Helmholtz. Although Wundt admired Helmholtz, they were never close, and Wundt eventually rejected Helmholtz's materialism. While with Helmholtz, Wundt gave his first course in "Psychology as a Natural Science" in 1862, and his first important writings began to appear. He worked his way up the academic ladder at Heidelberg while dabbling in politics, for the first and last time, as an idealistic socialist. He got married in 1872. His publications continued, including the first edition of his fundamental work, *Grundzüge der Physiologischen Psychologie* (*Principles of Physiological Psychology*), in 1873 and 1874.

This work, in its many editions, propounded the central tenets of his experimental psychology and excited supporters of scientific psychology around the world.

After a year in a "waiting room" position in Zurich, Wundt received a chair in philosophy at Leipzig, where he taught from 1875 to 1917. At Leipzig, Wundt won a degree of independence for psychology by founding his Psychological Institute. Beginning as a purely private institute in 1879, he supported it out of his own pocket until 1881. Finally, in 1885, it was officially recognized by the university and listed in the catalogue. It began as a primitive, one-room affair and expanded over the years; in 1897, it moved to its own specially designed building, later destroyed during World War II. During the years at Leipzig, Wundt continued his extraordinary output—supervising at least 200 dissertations, teaching over 24,000 students, and writing or revising volume after volume, as well as overseeing and writing for the psychological journal he founded, *Philosophische* (later, *Psychologische*) *Studien*.

In 1900, Wundt began a massive undertaking, the publication of his *Völkerpsychologie*, which was completed only in 1920, the year of his death. In this work, Wundt developed what he believed was the other half of psychology—the study of the individual in society as opposed to the individual in the laboratory. Wundt's work continued to the last. His final undertaking was his reminiscences, *Erlebtes und Erkanntes*, which he completed only a few days before he died on August 31, 1920, at the age of 88.

Wundt's Psychology

MAKING PSYCHOLOGY A SCIENCE: THE PATH THROUGH PHYSIOLOGY   In the work that first defined scientific psychology, *Principles of Physiological Psychology* (1873), Wundt proclaimed "an alliance between two sciences." The first was physiology, which "informs us about those life phenomena that we perceive by our external senses." The second was psychology, in which "the person looks upon himself from within" (p. 157). The result of the alliance was to be a new science, physiological psychology, whose tasks were:

> first, to investigate those life processes [consciousness] that, standing midway between external and internal experience, require the simultaneous application of both methods of observation, the external and the internal; and second, to throw light upon the totality of life processes from the points of view gained by investigations of this area and in this way perhaps to mediate a total comprehension of human existence. [This new science] begins with physiological processes and seeks to demonstrate how these influence the domain of internal observation. . . . The name physiological psychology points to psychology as the real subject of our science. . . . If one wishes to place emphasis on methodological characteristics, our sciences might be called experimental psychology in distinction from the usual science of mind based purely on introspection. (1873, pp. 157–158)

Here we find Wundt transforming the Cartesian-Lockean Way of Ideas from philosophical speculation into science. Descriptively, psychology rested on introspective observation of the world of ideas, attempting to isolate and define the mental elements of which complex ideas are constituted, and the mental processes that bring the elements together into the coherent, meaningful objects of naive experience. Then, these elements and processes were to be linked to their physiological substrates.

Wundt's alliance was more than a plan for research, and a culmination of the ideas of centuries of physician-philosophers. It also provided a strategy by which his fledgling field might make its way in the academic world, serving several important functions in psychology's struggle for existence. The first functions concerned methodology, both broadly and narrowly defined. Although in Wundt's time, the word *physiology* was acquiring the biological meaning it has today, it still possessed a broader and different meaning. *Physiology* and *physics* have the same Greek root, *physis*, and in the nineteenth century, the word *physiology* was often used simply to designate taking an experimental approach to a subject. More specifically, in the case of psychology, apparatus and techniques such as reaction time measurement were taken over from physiology and put to use in psychology laboratories. Because of the important methodological aspect of the alliance, Wundt also called physiological psychology *experimental psychology*.

In the previous quoted passage, Wundt alluded to a second set of functions of the alliance between physiology and psychology. At a philosophical level, the alliance helped psychology become part of the aggressively emerging naturalistic worldview of science. Traditionally, *psychology* meant "psyche-logos," the study of the soul. But the supernatural soul had no place in naturalistic science, so continuing to pursue psychology along traditional lines would bar it from science on the grounds of unscientific dualism. However, by insisting that the nervous system is the basis of all mentality, and by defining psychology as the investigation of the physiological conditions of conscious events, the new field of physiological psychology could establish itself as a science. For example, the most important mental process in Wundt's psychology was apperception, and Wundt proposed the existence of an "apperception center" in the brain. In addition, psychologists could borrow established physiological concepts such as the threshold, and neural excitation and inhibition, and use them in psychological theories.

One theoretical possibility opened up by the creation of physiological psychology was reduction: not simply borrowing physiological concepts for psychological usage, but explaining mental and behavioral events in terms of physiological causes. To take a familiar modern example, it appears that the cause of long-term depression is disordered levels of certain neurotransmitters in the brain rather than repressed psychological conflicts. All three of the main founders of psychology—Wundt, Freud, and James—were initially attracted by the idea of jettisoning psychological theories altogether in favor of explaining consciousness as the outcome of neural causes, without positing a level of unconscious, mediating psychological processes. Ultimately, all three rejected this reductive vision because reduction might turn into replacement. Wundt moved very slowly away from reduction; Freud was briefly enchanted with the idea; and James struggled mightily with it eventually giving up psychology for philosophy. Nevertheless, the idea of reduction lived on in the succeeding generations of psychologists, sometimes hidden but never dying, and today it is reasserting itself with new vigor in the field of cognitive neuroscience.

The last function of the alliance between physiological psychology and psychology was a tactical move in the academic politics of nineteenth-century Germany. Physiology was the most recently established scientific discipline. Its practitioners, such as Hermann von Helmholtz, with whom Wundt studied, were among the world's leading scientists, and its rapid progress soon gave it enormous prestige. For an ambitious academic like Wundt, the champion of a new field seeking funds, space, and students, alliance with physiology was a way to gain respectability (Ben-David & Collins, 1966).

WUNDT'S TWO SYSTEMS OF PSYCHOLOGY: HEIDELBERG AND LEIPZIG

Conceiving Psychology. Instead of the narrow expertise expected of most modern professors, in the pursuit of Bildung the Mandarins of the nineteenth century strove to coordinate the ideas of different disciplines and to subsume them into a single, comprehensive scheme of human life. James (1875) called them "heaven-scaling Titans," and we see just a hint of Wundt as a "heaven-scaling Titan" in the opening of the 1873 edition of *Principles of Physiological Psychology*, when he offered the hope that physiological psychology might "mediate a total comprehension of human existence" (p. 158).

As a good Mandarin, Wundt was thoroughly in the grasp of the "Will to System" (Woodward, 1982) and conceived of psychology as but one component in a grand scheme of human knowledge. Although the personalities of Wundt and Freud are, in other respects, as different as night and day, they shared a trait necessary to a founder of a general system of thought: They were both ambitious hedgehogs.[1] Freud, as we shall see, called himself a conquistador; James observed that Wundt "aims at being a sort of Napoleon of the mind." For a century Freud succeeded in conquering the world in the name of a few salient ideas. Wundt, however, seemed to have no central theme; James called him "a Napoleon without genius and with no central idea which, if defeated, brings down the whole fabric in ruins. . . . Cut him up like a worm and each fragment crawls; there is no *noeud vital* [vital node] in his medulla oblongata, so you can't kill him all at once" (quoted by van Hoorn & Verhave, 1980, p. 72).

Wundt offered to the world two different systems of psychology. He formulated the first at Heidelberg but came to repudiate it later as a "sin of my youthful days" (quoted by van Hoorn & Verhave, 1980, p. 78), as Freud later repudiated and tried to suppress his early "Project for a Scientific Psychology." Wundt's second program, propounded in Leipzig, changed significantly over the years (Diamond, 1980; Graumann, 1980; van Hoorn & Verhave, 1980; Richards, 1980 but see Blumenthal, 1980a, 1980b, 1986a; Danziger, 1980a, 1980b).

What remained constant was Wundt's traditional definition of psychology as the study of the mind and the search for the laws that govern it, but his assumptions about the mind and the methods used to investigate it changed dramatically. Wundt's Heidelberg program conceived of psychology as a natural science. Echoing John Stuart Mill's sentiments, Wundt wrote that the mind could be brought within the ambit of natural science by experimental method: "It has been the experiment only that has made progress in the natural sciences possible; let us then apply the experiment to the nature of the mind" (quoted by van Hoorn & Verhave, 1980, p. 86). In his early definition of psychology, Wundt did not identify the mind with consciousness, as he did later. Rather, the goal of experimentation was to gather data permitting inferences about unconscious processes: "The experiment in psychology is the major means which guides us from the facts of consciousness to those processes which in the dark background of our mind prepare conscious life" (quoted by Graumann, 1980, p. 37).

Wundt was called to Leipzig, however, as a philosopher, to lecture in philosophy, to build a philosophical system, and to conduct psychology as part of philosophy. In the Mandarin German university system, philosophy held sway, and Wundt had to find a new place for psychology in the Mandarin scheme of knowledge. In the spirit of Herder and Vico, German intellectuals typically distinguished between *Naturwissenschaft* and *Geisteswissenschaft*. Naturwissenschaft translates straightforwardly as "natural science," the study of the physical world and the search for the laws that govern it. Geisteswissenschaft is a more difficult concept. A literal translation is "spiritual science" (*Geist* means spirit), but what was meant was a study of the human world created by human history and the search for laws governing human life, human development, and human history.

In the medieval Neoplatonic conception of the universe, human beings stood betwixt the material and the spiritual world, half bodily animal and half divine soul. In the scheme of Vico, Herder, and their followers, human beings occupied a similar position, betwixt the material world and the social world. In each case, the human body and the elementary mental functions humans

---

[1]Berlin (1957) proposes that intellectuals tend to fall into one of two types, hedgehogs and foxes. Hedgehogs are system builders like Plato or Descartes, whose thought is guided by some all-encompassing vision. Foxes think cleverly about many things, but have no single vision; Socrates was a fox.

share with animals belong to the world of matter and natural science, and the higher reaches of the human mind—the soul, for Christians; the higher mental processes, for scientific psychology—belong to the world of Geist and the Geisteswissenschaften. Thus, "psychology forms . . . the transition from the Natur- to the Geisteswissenschaften." The experimental methods of physiological psychology, which study those aspects of consciousness close to sensation and motor response, lead to an approach that "is related to the methodology of the physical sciences." On the other hand, above these elementary phenomena "rise the higher mental processes, which are the ruling forces in history as well as in society. Thus, they, on their side, require a scientific analysis, which approaches those of the special Geisteswissenschaften" (Wundt, quoted by van Hoorn & Verhave, 1980, p. 93).

Over the years, the Leipzig program changed. Solomon Diamond has translated the introductory passages of Wundt's *Principles of Physiological Psychology* from its first edition in 1873 to its last edition in 1908–1911. As edition supplanted edition, the strength of Wundt's alliance between physiology and psychology was weakened. In the early editions, psychology was linked, as we have seen, reductively as well as methodologically, to physiology. The study of the nervous system was expected to shed light on the nature of human consciousness. However, by the fourth edition, in 1893, only the methodological link remained, and physiological psychology had come to mean only experimental psychology (Wundt, 1873, 1896, 1907–1908). Like Freud and James, Wundt moved away from seeing psychology as a simple extension of physiology.

Ironically, although Wundt himself came to reject his Heidelberg system as a youthful error, his students and readers worldwide embraced its definition of psychology as an autonomous natural science. Wundt's Leipzig system, tied to the peculiar German Mandarin view of the world, the mind, and education, proved to be historical failure.

Research Methods for Psychology. Wundt carefully defined the new methods on which scientific psychology should be built. The preeminent method was introspection, but a new, experimentally controlled introspection based on the model developed by Fechner was added. Old-fashioned philosophical psychology had used armchair introspection to reveal the contents and workings of the mind, but it had fallen into bad odor among some scientists and philosophers as unreliable and subjective. Wundt agreed with these critiques of introspection, recognizing that a science of consciousness could be erected only on objective, replicable results based on standardized conditions capable of duplication and systematic variation (Wundt, 1907–1908). Precisely to achieve these aims, he introduced physiological—that is, experimental—techniques into the hitherto philosophical realm of psychology.

Wundt distinguished between two means of psychological observation whose German names were, unfortunately, both rendered into English as "introspection," giving rise to passages in which Wundt both condemns introspection and commends it as the fundamental method of psychology (Blumenthal, 1980a, 1980b, 1986a). *Innere Wahrnehmung*, or "internal perception," referred to the prescientific method of armchair subjective introspection, as practiced, for example, by Descartes and Locke. This kind of introspection is carried out in a haphazard, uncontrolled way and cannot hope to yield results useful to a scientific psychology. On the other hand, *Experimentelle Selbstbeobachtung*, "experimental self-observation," designated a scientifically valid form of introspection in which "observers" are exposed to standard, repeatable situations and are asked to describe the resulting experience. The experimenter arranges the situation and collects the observer's report of what he or she finds in consciousness, the way an astronomer's assistant might record the observations made by an astronomer peering through a telescope at Jupiter.

The rationale and limits of experimental introspection changed as Wundt's systematic definition of psychology changed. In the Heidelberg years, when Wundt believed in unconscious psychological processes, traditional introspection was rejected because it was limited to observation of consciousness and could not, by definition, reveal the workings of the unconscious. Careful experimentation, Wundt held, might reveal phenomena from which the workings of unconscious mental processes might be deduced. During this period, Wundt assigned introspective method a wider scope of application than he would later. In his Heidelberg years, Wundt stated that it is mere "prejudice" to regard it as "futile to attempt to penetrate into the realm of the higher mental processes by means of experimental methods" (quoted by van Hoorn & Verhave, 1980).

Later, when Wundt rejected the existence of the unconscious, experimentation was valued as making it possible to re-create the same experience in different observers or in the same observers at different times. This emphasis on exact duplication of experiences severely limited the realm of experimental introspection to the simplest mental processes, and Wundt duly excluded the study of the higher mental processes from physiological psychology, completely reversing his Heidelberg stance. The Leipzig restrictions on introspection were also consistent with Kantian Idealism. Kant set the Transcendental Ego outside the possibility of experience, restricting introspection, as Wundt now did, to the most superficial aspects of the mind: immediate conscious experience.

Alongside experimental introspection, Wundt recognized other methods of psychological investigation. The method of experimental introspection was, by its nature, limited to the study of normal minds of human adults—that is, the minds of experimental observers. Alongside experimental introspection, Wundt recognized *vergleichendpsychologische* (comparative-psychological) and *historisch-psychologische* (historical-psychological) methods (van Hoorn & Verhave, 1980). Both methods involved the study of mental differences. The comparative method applied to the study of consciousness in animals, children, and the "disturbed." The historical method applied to "mental differences as determined by race and nationality" (quoted by van Hoorn & Verhave, 1980, p. 92). The relations among the study of normal adult, animal, disturbed, and historically conditioned consciousness shifted over the years (van Hoorn & Verhave, 1980), but the most general change was in the importance Wundt assigned to the historical method, or Völkerpsychologie.

Wundt always believed, as did Freud, in the biogenetic law—that the development of the individual recapitulated the evolution of the species. In keeping with this notion, Wundt held that the best way to construct a theory of psychological development in individuals was to study the historical development of the human race. In his earliest program of psychology, the historical method was put forward as an adjunct to the main method of psychology—experimental introspection. However, when Wundt repositioned psychology as the crucial discipline lying between Naturwissenschaft and Geisteswissenschaft, the historical method was elevated to parity with the experimental method. The experimental method faced toward Naturwissenschaft, applying to the more strictly physiological aspects of the mind; the historical method faced toward Geisteswissenschaft, applying to the inner processes of mental creativity revealed in history, especially through language, myth, and custom. Thus, when Wundt withdrew experimental introspection from the study of the higher mental processes, consistent with the most influential German philosophy, Kantian Idealism, which denied that people have access to the Transcendental Ego, he replaced it with the historical method of Völkerpsychologie. Together, experimental method plus Völkerpsychologie would furnish a complete, albeit not completely natural-scientific, psychology.

Wundt at Work

To illustrate the nature of Wundt's psychology, we shall consider two topics taken up in the two branches of his psychology. The first applies the experimental method of physiological psychology to an old question in philosophical psychology: How many ideas can consciousness contain at a given moment? The second applies the method of the Völkerpsychologie to the question of how human beings create and understand sentences.

PHYSIOLOGICAL PSYCHOLOGY   Once one accepts the Cartesian Way of Ideas, a natural question becomes, "How many ideas can the mind hold at once?" Traditional philosophical introspection, Wundt held, can provide no reliable answers. Without experimental control, attempting to introspect the number of ideas in one's mind is futile because their content varies from time to time, and we must rely on fallible memories to give us the facts that introspection reports.

An experiment, one that would complement and perfect introspection and would yield quantitative results, was called for. The following is an updated and simplified version of Wundt's experiment. Imagine looking at a computer screen. For an instant, about 0.09 seconds, a stimulus is flashed on the screen. This stimulus is a four-column by four-row array of randomly chosen letters, and your task is to recall as many letters as possible. What you recall provides a measure of how many simple ideas you can grasp in an instant of time and so may give an answer to the original question. Wundt found that unpracticed observers could recall about four letters; experienced observers could recall up to six but no more. These figures agree with modern results on the capacity of working memory, and what Wundt discovered is now usually known as iconic memory (Leahey & Harris, 2004).

Two further important phenomena can be observed in this experiment. The first concerns whether the letters are presented as random strings, as in the previous experiment, or as words. Imagine an experiment in which each line of four letters forms a word—for example, *work*, *many*, *room*, *idea*. Under these conditions, one could probably recall all four words, or at least three, for a total of 12 to 16 letters. Similarly, one could quickly read and recall the word *miscellaneousness*, which contains 17 letters. Letters as isolated elements quickly fill up consciousness so that only four to six can be perceived in a given moment, but many more can be grasped if these elements are organized. In Wundt's terms, the letter-elements are synthesized by apperception into a greater whole, which is understood as a single complex idea and grasped as one new element. Experiments on the large differences between the numbers of letters recalled when they are presented as random strings as opposed to when they are presented as words played a revealing role in debates surrounding Gestalt psychology. Consistent with British Empiricism, American psychologists explained the superiority of word organization as the result of association. A word like *home* has been perceived so frequently that its constituent letters have become associated into a functional unit. Advocates of Gestalt psychology maintained that the word *home* was a meaningful whole in itself, perceived as such by the mind. Wundt took a middle view consistent with Kantian Idealism—that *home* was a meaningful whole, but that the whole was imposed on the elements by the organizing powers of the mind.

The second important finding revealed by Wundt's experiments concerned the perception of letters that the observers did not name. Observers reported that some letters—the ones they named—were perceived clearly and distinctly, but other letters had been presented only dimly and hazily perceived. Consciousness, it seemed, was a large field populated with ideational elements. One area of this field is in the focus of attention, and the ideas within it are clearly perceived. The elements lying outside the focal area are only faintly felt as present and cannot be identified. The focus of consciousness is where apperception works, sharpening stimuli into those seen clearly and distinctly. Items outside apperception's focus are apprehended only; they are not seen clearly.

Apperception was especially important in Wundt's system. Not only was it responsible for the active synthesis of elements into wholes, but it also accounted for the higher mental activities of analysis (revealing the parts of a whole) and of judgment. It was responsible for the activities of relating and comparing, which are simpler forms of synthesis and analysis. Apperception was the basis

A "fall" tachistiscope similar to this was used by Wundt in his letter perception experiment. The stimulus was written on a card placed in the rectangle near the bottom of the apparatus, and a system of weights and covers was used to conceal, then expose, and then conceal again the stimulus to be observed. This tachistiscope was made at Columbia University, New York City. *(Courtesy of Barnard College History of Psychology Museum)*

for all higher forms of thought, such as reasoning and use of language, and was central to Wundt's psychology in both its individual and social divisions.

Wundt's emphasis on apperception displays the voluntaristic nature of his system. When neither mind nor self referred to a special substance for Wundt, to what did he attribute our sense of self? It is the subjective feeling of the unity of experience that provides the answer. Apperception is a voluntary act of the will by which we control and give synthetic unity to our mind. The feeling of activity, control, and unity defined the self. Echoing Kant, Wundt wrote (1896, p. 234): "What we call our 'self' is simply the unity of volition plus the universal control of our mental life which it renders possible."

Wundt also studied feelings and emotions, for they are an obvious part of our conscious experience. He often used introspectively reported feelings as clues to what processes were going on in the mind at a given moment. He thought that apperception, for instance, was marked by a feeling of mental effort. Wundt proposed that feelings could be defined along three dimensions: pleasant versus unpleasant, high versus low arousal, and concentrated versus relaxed attention. He conducted a long series of studies designed to establish a physiological basis for each dimension, but the results were inconclusive, and other laboratories produced conflicting findings. Modern factor analyses of affect, however, have arrived at similar three-dimensional systems (Blumenthal, 1975). Wundt emphasized the active, synthesizing power of apperception, but he recognized the existence of passive processes as well, which he classified as various forms of association or "passive" apperception. There were, for example, assimilations, in which a current sensation is associated to an older element. When one looks at a chair, he or she knows immediately what it is by assimilation, for the current image of the perceived chair is immediately associated with the older universal element, chair. Recognition is a form of assimilation, stretched out into two steps: a vague feeling of familiarity followed by the act of recognition proper. Recollection, on the other hand, was, for Wundt, as for some contemporary psychologists, an act of reconstruction rather than reactivation of old elements. One cannot reexperience an earlier event, for ideas are not permanent. Rather, one reconstructs it from current cues and certain general rules.

Finally, Wundt considered abnormal states of consciousness. He discussed hallucinations, depression, hypnosis, and dreams. The great psychiatrist Emil Kraepelin (1856–1926) studied with Wundt and resolved to revolutionize psychiatry with scientifically based diagnoses. His first studies involved what he called *dementia praecox* (premature dementia), later called schizophrenia. In his work, Kraepelin was influenced by Wundt's theory of the disease. Wundt proposed that schizophrenia involves a breakdown in attentional processes. The schizophrenic loses the apperceptive control of thoughts characteristic of normal consciousness and surrenders instead to passive associative processes, so that thought becomes a simple train of associations rather than coordinated processes directed by volition, a theory revived in modern times.

VÖLKERPSYCHOLOGIE Especially as Wundt developed his Leipzig system, he taught that experimental individual psychology could not be a complete psychology, and he elevated the comparative-historical method to parity with the experimental method. The minds of living individuals are the products of a long course of species development of which each person is ignorant. To understand the development of the mind, then, we must have recourse to history, Wundt held. The study of animals and children is limited by their inability to introspect. History expands the range of the individual consciousness. In particular, the range of existing human cultures represents the various stages in cultural and mental evolution, from primitive tribes to civilized nation-states. Völkerpsychologie is thus the study of the products of collective life—especially of language, myth, and custom—that provides clues to the higher operations of mind. Wundt said that experimental psychology penetrates only the "outworks" of the mind; Völkerpsychologie reaches deeper, into the Transcendental Ego.

Emphasis on historical development, a legacy from Vico and Herder, was typical of German intellectuals in the nineteenth century. In the German view, every individual springs from, and has an organic relationship with, his or her natal culture. Further, cultures have complex histories that determine their forms and contents. Thus, it was generally believed that history could be used as a method for arriving at an understanding of human psychology and the different mentalities of different ethnic groups (Burrow, 2000).

Wundt's remarks on myth and custom were typical of his time. Somewhat like Comte, Wundt proposed that human civilization developed through a series of stages from primitive tribes to an age of heroes and then to the formation of states, culminating in a world state based on the concept of humanity as a whole. Many nineteenth-century scholars believed that existing societies, which varied in their degrees of economic development, revealed the historical development of humanity. To travel in geographical space from culture to culture was also to travel in time. As the English historian W. E. Lecky (1838–1903) said, "There is still so great a diversity of civilization in existing nations that traversing tracts of space is almost like traversing tracts of time, for it brings us in contact with representatives of nearly every phase of past civilization" (quoted by Burrow, 2000, p. 72). By the middle of the nineteenth century, Wundt was the most famous exponent of the idea that studying existing cultures revealed the evolution of the human mind (Burrow, 2000). It was in the study of language that he made his most substantial contribution, articulating a theory of psycholinguistics that reached conclusions similar to those of psycholinguistics in the 1960s. Language was a part of Völkerpsychologie for Wundt because, like myth and custom, it is a product of collective life. With the eighteenth-century thinker Lord Monboddo, Wundt believed that "from the study of language, if it be properly conducted, the history of the human mind is best learned" (quoted by Porter, 2000, p. 237). Wundt divided language into two aspects: outer phenomena, consisting of actually produced or perceived utterances, and inner phenomena, the cognitive processes that underlie the outer string of words. This rather Kantian division of psychological phenomena into inner and outer aspects was first adumbrated by Fechner, and was central to Wundt's psychology. The distinction between inner and outer phenomena is perhaps clearest in the case of language. It is possible to describe language as an organized, associated system of sounds that we speak or hear; this constitutes the outer form of language. However, this outer form is the surface expression of deeper cognitive processes that organize a speaker's thoughts, preparing them for utterance, and enable the listener to extract meaning from what he or she hears. These cognitive processes constitute the inner mental form of speech.

Sentence production, according to Wundt, begins with a unified idea that one wishes to express, the *Gesamtvorstellung*, or whole mental configuration. The analytic function of apperception prepares the unified idea for speech, for it must be analyzed into component elements and a given structure that retains the relationship between the parts and the whole. Consider the simple sentence: "The cat is black." The basic structural division in such a sentence is between the subject and predicate and can be represented with the tree diagram introduced by Wundt. If we let G = Gesamtvorstellung, S = subject, and P = predicate, we have the diagram:

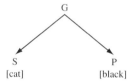

The idea of a black cat has now been divided into its two fundamental ideas and can be expressed verbally as "the cat is black" with the addition of the function words (*the*, *is*) required in our particular language. More complex ideas require more analysis and must be represented by more complex diagrams. The entire process, in all cases, can be described as the transformation of an inexpressible, organized, whole thought into an expressible, sequential structure of words organized in a sentence.

The process is reversed in comprehension of speech. Here, the synthesizing rather than the analytic function of apperception is called on. The words and grammatical structure in a heard sentence must be used by the hearer to reconstruct in his or her own mind the whole mental configuration that the speaker is attempting to communicate. Wundt supported his view of comprehension by pointing out that we remember the gist of what we hear, but only rarely the surface (outer) form, which tends to disappear in the process of constructing the Gesamtvorstellung.

We have touched on only a small portion of Wundt's discussion of language. He also wrote on gesture language; the origin of language from involuntary, expressive sounds; primitive language (based more on association than on apperception); phonology; and meaning change. Wundt has a fair claim to be the founder of psycholinguistics as well as psychology.

Nevertheless, there remains a puzzle about Wundt's Völkerpsychologie. Although he seemed in his writings to value it highly, and lectured on it, he never trained anyone in its practice (Kusch, 1995). Moreover, it was nearly unreadable and exerted little influence even in Germany (Jahoda, 1997), whose Mandarin values it reflected. Outside Germany, it was misrepresented or ignored (Jahoda, 1997).

AFTER LEIPZIG: OTHER METHODS, NEW MOVEMENTS

Although Wundt launched psychology as a recognized discipline, his Leipzig system did not represent the future of psychology. Wundt is best regarded as a transitional figure linking psychology's philosophical past to its future as a natural science and as an applied science. Educated when German universities emphasized Bildung and philosophical system building, Wundt always saw psychology as part of philosophy. His students, however, were affected by the increasing success and prestige of the natural sciences and by the tendency toward research specialization that undermined the concept of Bildung. They fought to make psychology an autonomous, natural science rather than a mere branch of philosophy. Wundt also resisted making psychology an applied science. As a good Mandarin, Wundt placed pure scholarship above practical success. On this point, too, Wundt's opinion would be overturned. Psychology's future lay with natural science and practical application.

Wundt had surprisingly little effect on the next generation of psychologists. The younger German generation established new journals and the Society for Experimental Psychology, but Wundt was conspicuous by his absence and lack of participation (Ash, 1981). At the founding of the society in 1904, Wundt was honored in a telegram, but he was called the "Nestor of experimental psychology" (Ash, 1981, p. 266). In the Iliad, Nestor, like Polonius in Hamlet, was an allegedly wise but pompous old windbag.

Wundt's successors rejected his division of psychology into a natural science, an experimental part, the physiological psychology, and the Völkerpsychologie. The generation after Wundt was much influenced by positivism (Danziger, 1979) and believed that if psychology was going to be a science erected on positive facts, the higher mental processes would have to be subjected to experimental study. As early as 1879, Hermann Ebbinghaus (1850–1909) undertook to study the higher mental process of memory. Ebbinghaus's procedure was nonintrospective, anticipating the behavioral direction of future psychology. Other psychologists, most notably Wundt's students Oswald Külpe and E. B. Titchener, attempted to observe thinking directly through "systematic introspection," a looser, more retrospective probing of consciousness that in some respects resembled psychoanalysis more than experimental psychology. The Gestalt psychologists, too, would study consciousness and behavior, perception and problem solving, endeavoring to make psychology a complete and autonomous natural science.

E. B. Titchener's Structural Psychology

Edward Bradford Titchener (1867–1927) was an Englishman who brought German psychology to America, turning British associationism into a psychological research program. He played an important role in the founding of American psychology, contrasting his extreme introspective psychology, structural psychology, with the rising tide of psychology influenced by evolution, functional psychology. To a large extent, Titchener's psychology was the system against which American psychologists defined themselves, seeing it as sterile, philosophical, and out of date. Moreover, they tended to see Titchener as Wundt's faithful apostle in the New World, missing important differences between Wundt's German psychology, influenced by Kant and Herder, and Titchener's distinctive scientific version of British psychology.

E. B. Titchener was born in 1867 in Chichester, England, and went to Oxford from 1885 to 1890. While at Oxford, his interests shifted from classics and philosophy to physiology. The conjunction of interests in philosophy and physiology naturally predisposed Titchener to psychology, and while at Oxford he translated the third edition of Wundt's massive *Principles of Physiological Psychology*. Titchener could find no one in England to train him in psychology, so in 1890 he went to Leipzig, taking his doctorate in 1892.

As an Englishman, Titchener arrived in Leipzig from the other side of the intellectual gulf separating Germany from the West. He was thoroughly versed in philosophy and was much impressed by James Mill, remarking that Mill's speculations could be empirically demonstrated. In his first systematic book, *An Outline of Psychology* (1897), he wrote: "The general standpoint of [my] book is that of the traditional English psychology." It is reasonable to expect, therefore, that Titchener may well have assimilated Wundt's German psychology into the "traditional English psychology" that Wundt rejected.

After a short stint as a biology lecturer in England, a country unreceptive to psychology, Titchener left for America to teach at Cornell, where he remained until his death in 1927. He transformed Cornell into a bastion of mentalistic psychology, even as America's focus went first functionalist and then, after 1913, behaviorist. Titchener never compromised with these movements, despite his friendships with the functionalist J. R. Angell and with John B. Watson, the founder of behaviorism. He did not participate actively in the American Psychological Association (APA), even when it met at Cornell, preferring instead his own group, the Experimental Psychologists, which he kept true to his version of psychology and which eventually became important to the movement of cognitive psychology in the 1950s and 1960s.

Titchener apparently possessed a mind in which everything had imaginal-sensational character. He even had an image for such an abstract word as meaning. Titchener (1904, p. 19) wrote: "I see meaning as the blue-grey tip of a kind of scoop, which has a bit of yellow above it . . . and which is just digging into a dank mass of . . . plastic material." Even though he recognized that not everyone had an imaginal mind, as he called it, he built his psychology on the premise that the mind was made up of sensations or images of sensation and nothing else. This led to his rejection of various Wundtian concepts such as apperception, which is inferred rather than observed directly. Titchener's psychology conformed to the Humean view of the mind as a collection of sensations rather than the Kantian view that mind was separate from its experience.

The first experimental task of Titchener's psychology was the discovery of the basic sensation elements to which all complex processes could be reduced. As early as 1897, he drew up a catalogue of elements found in the different sense departments. There were, for instance, 30,500 visual elements, 4 taste elements, and 3 sensations in the alimentary canal. Titchener defined elements as the simplest sensations to be found in experience. They were to be discovered through the systematic dissection by introspection of the contents of consciousness; when an experience could not be dissected into parts, it was declared elemental. Titchener's method of introspection was much more elaborate than Wundt's, for it was not a simple report of an experience, but a complicated retrospective analysis of that experience, not much different from the systematic introspection of the Würzburg school (see later discussion). Titchener (1901–1905) wrote: "Be as attentive as possible to the object or process which gives rise to the sensation, and, when the object is removed or the process completed, recall the sensation by an act of memory as vividly and completely as you can." Persistent application of this method would, in Titchener's view, eventually produce a complete description of the elements of human experience. The task was unfinished (and, as many thought, unfinishable) when Titchener died.

The second task of Titchener's psychology was to determine how the elementary sensations are connected to form complex perceptions, ideas, and images. These connections were not all associations, because, for Titchener, an association was a connection of elements that persisted even when the original conditions for the connection could no longer be obtained. Titchener rejected the label of associationism, not only for this reason but also because the associationists spoke of association of meaningful ideas, not of simple meaningless sensations, which was all that concerned Titchener.

The third task of Titchener's psychology was to explain the workings of mind. Introspection, according to Titchener, could yield only a description of mind. At least until about 1925, Titchener (1929/1972) believed that a scientific psychology required more than mere description. Explanation was to be sought in physiology, which would explain why the sensory elements arise and become connected. Titchener rejected Wundt's attempt to psychologically explain the operation of the mind. According to Titchener's system, all that can be found in experience are sensory elements rather than processes such as attention. Appeal to such an unobservable entity as apperception was illegitimate in Titchener's eyes—a view that betrays his positivism. He therefore sought to explain mind by reference to observable nerve physiology.

Titchener rejected as wholly unnecessary the term *apperception*, which in Wundt's psychology gave rise to attention. Attention itself Titchener reduced to sensation. One obvious attribute of any sensation is clarity, and Titchener said that "attended" sensations are simply the clearest ones. Attention was not for him a mental process, but simply an attribute of sensation—clearness—produced by certain nerve processes. What of the mental effort that Wundt says goes along with attention? This, too, Titchener reduced to sensations. Titchener (1908, p. 4) wrote: "When I am trying to attend I . . . find myself frowning, wrinkling my forehead etc. All such . . . bodily sets and movements give rise to characteristic . . . sensations. Why should not these sensations be what we call 'attention?'"

Titchener's psychology represented an attempt to turn a narrowly conceived version of British philosophical psychology into a complete science of the mind. It was never very popular or influential beyond his own circle, and is in many respects important only as a significant dead end in psychology and for misleading English-speaking psychologists about Wundt's voluntaristic ideas. Structuralism died with Titchener and has seldom been mourned since.

Phenomenological Alternatives

As the movement to make psychology into a natural science along positivist lines gained momentum, important alternative conceptions of psychology arose outside the field. Two alternatives were especially important. One came from the historian Wilhelm Dilthey. His objection to natural-science psychology grew out of the Vico-Herder distinction between the natural and human sciences that Wundt had accepted in his Leipzig system. The other came from Franz Brentano's act psychology, rooted in neo-Aristotelian perceptual realism. Both Dilthey and Brentano rejected the analytic atomism of psychologies such as Titchener's, believing that it artificially imposed pretheoretical assumptions onto to the reality of lived experience. They preferred, instead, to describe consciousness as it appears naively, without presuppositions about its nature, an undertaking called phenomenology. They also resisted the narrow specialization overtaking the natural sciences in general, including psychology, should it become one. Dilthey wrote that the rise of positivistic science was dangerous, because it would lead to "increasing skepticism, a cult of superficial, unfruitful fact-gathering, and thus the increasing separation of science from life" (quoted by Ash, 1995, p. 72).

FRANZ BRENTANO'S ACT PSYCHOLOGY Working within the Cartesian tradition, the Way of Ideas, most psychologists sought to analyze consciousness into its component pieces. Titchener's was simply the most extreme version of the practice. They took for granted the idea that just as the physical world is composed of objects that can be analyzed into atomic components, the objects of consciousness are made of mind stuff analyzable into component sensations and feelings. The analytic spirit that worked so brilliantly for physics and chemistry was simply imported into psychology with hopes for similar success. There were differences among Cartesian psychologists about the nature of psychological analysis and the forces that bound atomic units into the larger, meaningful objects of experience. Wundt, for example, regarded psychological analysis instrumentally, as a heuristic device that allowed psychology to go forward as a science. The so-called atomic sensations were imaginary, not real, he said, providing a useful framework within which to pose questions for scientific investigation by introspection (Ash, 1995). In a somewhat Kantian way, Wundt believed the mind actively synthesized the elements of experience into the objects of consciousness, assigning association a relatively minor role as the gravity of the mental universe. Associationists such as Titchener, on the other hand, believed in the reality of sensory elements and followed Hume in making association the sole source of mental organization (Külpe, 1895). Notwithstanding these differences, however, the dominant approach to consciousness was to analyze it into its component parts.

There was, however, a dissident tradition rooted in perceptual realism. If we are in more or less direct touch with the world, then there is no mind stuff to analyze into atomic constituents. Instead of analyzing experience, we should simply describe it as we find it. This approach to consciousness is called phenomenology. In America, the realist descriptive tradition was kept alive by the influence of Scottish commonsense psychology, and would be promoted in psychology by William James and in philosophy by the Neorealists.

In the German-speaking world, Franz Brentano (1838–1917) championed realism. Brentano was a Catholic theologian who broke with the Church when it proclaimed the doctrine of papal infallibility. He became a philosopher at the University of Vienna, where he supported the establishment of scientific psychology. He worked out an influential version of psychological realism that gave rise in philosophy to phenomenology and in psychology to the Gestalt movement. Unsurprisingly for a Catholic philosopher, Brentano's concept of mind was rooted in the Aristotelian realism that had been preserved and developed by medieval scholastic philosophers, but had been abandoned during the Scientific Revolution. With the Scots, Brentano regarded the Way of Ideas as an artificial imposition of a false metaphysical theory on naive experience. Inaugurating philosophical phenomenology, he tried to describe experience as it is given naively in experience. Brentano found mind consisting of mental acts directed at meaningful objects outside it. It was not a collection of complex mental objects made up of sensory atoms:

> Every mental phenomenon is characterized by what the Scholastics of the Middle Ages called the intentional (or mental) inexistence of an object, and what we might call, though not without ambiguity, reference to a content, direction toward an object. . . . Every mental phenomenon includes something as object within itself, although they do not all do so in the same way. In presentation something is presented, in judgment something is affirmed or denied, in love, loved, in hate, hated, in desire, desired, and so on. (1874/1995, p. 88)

The contrast between Brentano's description of mind and the Cartesian-Lockean analysis of mind is significant. The latter sees ideas as mental objects that represent physical objects external to us. Moreover, ideas represent objects only indirectly, because ideas are themselves composed of meaningless sensory elements such as "red sensation #113," "brown sensation #14," "brightness levels 3–26," or three "C sharps" followed by an "A flat." This is why and how Descartes introduced a degree of paranoia to philosophy, bringing on the skeptical crisis of the Enlightenment. Because the world as we experience it—consciousness—is an assemblage out of sensory bits, we have no guarantee that ideas do, in fact, correspond to objects. Hence, genuine, objective Knowledge of the world becomes doubtful—the starting point of Cartesian philosophy. Brentano, on the other hand, saw an idea as a mental act by which one grasps objects himself or herself. As acts, ideas cannot be resolved into atomic units. The mind is orderly because the world is orderly, not because of the gravity of association (Hume) or because the mind itself imposes order on the world (Kant). The mind is not, for Brentano, a mental world only incidentally connected to the physical world, but the means by which an organism actively grasps the real world outside itself.

In philosophy, Brentano's goal of describing consciousness rather than analyzing it into pieces became the phenomenological movement, beginning with his student Edmund Husserl (1859–1938). Phenomenology was further developed by Martin Heidegger (1889–1976) and Maurice Merleau-Ponty (1908–1961), and it influenced the existentialism of Jean-Paul Sartre (1905–1980). Although these thinkers' influence has been relatively slight in the English-speaking world, they are major figures in twentieth-century European philosophy. Brentano also taught psychologists, including Sigmund Freud and Christian von Ehrenfels (see the discussion later). For academic psychology, Brentano's most important student was Carl Stumpf (1848–1946), who provided the link between Brentano and Gestalt psychology. When the leading German university, the University of Berlin, established a Psychological Institute in 1894, Stumpf became its first director. There, he taught or trained the founders of Gestalt psychology, inspiring them to describe consciousness as it was, not as empiricist atomism said it must be.

WILHELM DILTHEY AND THE HUMAN SCIENCES   The historian Wilhelm Dilthey (1833–1911) linked intentionality to the distinction between the Naturwissenschaften and the Geisteswissenschaften. Explaining human actions is fundamentally different from explaining physical events. A woman shooting and killing a man is a physical event. However, understanding the event in human terms involves more than tracing the path of a bullet and showing how the bullet caused the man's death. We need to know why she shot the man, not just how she did so. Suppose the man is her husband and he was trying to quietly enter the house late at night because he has come home a day early from a trip out of town. She might have shot him because she thought he was a dangerous burglar, perhaps a rapist. Believing this, she acted, therefore, in self-defense. On the other hand, if their marriage was failing, she might have recognized him and shot him for insurance money or out of revenge for a sexual affair, or both. In either case, the physical events remain the same, but the meaning of the act—and, thus, the proper response of police and prosecutors—depends on getting inside the woman's mind. Specifically, we need to know the intentional object of her shooting. Did she aim at (the original Latin meaning of *intention* is "to aim at") a burglar or at her husband? If the former, she is at most guilty of negligence; if the latter, she is guilty of murder. Natural science cannot resolve this issue. Nor can a scientific physiological psychology, for the direction of a mental act lies not in neurons but in the subjective mind.

Dilthey said, "We explain nature; we understand psychic life" (quoted by R. Smith, 1997, p. 517). Natural scientists explain physical events to predict and control them in the future. The historian is concerned with unique human actions recorded in history and seeks to understand the reasons and motives that lie behind them. Similarly, Dilthey said, psychologists must seek to understand the motives and reasons that lie behind human actions in the here and now. The study of intentionality—of motives and reasons—means going beyond what natural science can responsibly offer. A psychology that remains limited to the study of conscious perception and physiology would truly separate itself from human life. The concept of intentionality and the status of reasons and motives remain controversial in psychology. The idea of making psychology into a purely physiological discipline is again being proposed, and its advocates want to replace intentional concepts in psychology with purely physiological ones. Cognitive science proposes that the human mind is a sort of computer program implemented in the brain and seeks to explain human thought and action as the result of computational information processing. Just as computers lack reasons and motives for what they do—although sometimes we treat them as if they didn't—perhaps human reasons and motives are convenient fictions, too.

Systematic Introspection: The Würzburg School, 1901–1909

One of Wundt's most outstanding and successful students was Oswald Külpe (1862–1915). Like most psychologists of his generation, Külpe was influenced by positivism and strove to make psychology more a complete natural science and less a branch of philosophy resting only partially in experimentation. Writing in a book aimed at philosophers, Külpe spoke for his generational colleagues: "If we define philosophy as the science of principles, we cannot call these psychological investigations philosophical. Indeed, there is general agreement on the point among experimental or physiological psychologists. . . . [Hence] it would seem well to dispense with the idea of a general philosophy of mind, or of the mental sciences, altogether" (1895, pp. 64–66).

Moreover, although he thought that historical inquiries into the mind such as Wundt's Völkerpsychologie might possibly become scientific, Külpe's definition of scientific psychology was not very different from his friend Titchener's:

> We may take it, then, that the field of psychology as a special science has now been definitely marked out. It includes: (a) the reduction of more complex facts of consciousness to more simple; (b) the determination of the relations of dependency which hold between psychical processes and the physical (neural) processes which run parallel to them; (c) the application of experiment, to obtain an objective measure of mental processes and an exact knowledge of their nature. (p. 64)

When Külpe left Leipzig for the University of Würzburg, he undertook the introspective study of thinking, championing the cause of psychology as a comprehensive natural science. In doing so, he sided with Wundt's positivistic Heidelberg system, rather than his more Kantian Leipzig system. Two important results emerged from Kulpe's research program. The first indicated that, contrary to the Way of Ideas, some contents of consciousness couldn't be traced to sensations or feelings; the second undermined associationism as an account of thinking, suggesting, with Brentano, that thoughts are acts, not passive representations.

The method Külpe developed to study thinking was called the *Ausfragen* method—the method of questions. It departed significantly from the practice of introspection at Leipzig. Wundt's experiments were quite simple, involving little more than reaction to, or a brief description of, a stimulus. Fechner's psychophysics, Donder's mental chronometry, and Wundt's apperception experiments are examples of this procedure. Under Külpe, the tasks were made more difficult and the job of introspection was more elaborate. A question of some sort was asked of the observer (hence, the name of the method). Sometimes the task was a simple one, such as giving an association to a stimulus word, and sometimes the task was quite difficult, such as agreeing or disagreeing with a lengthy passage from some philosopher. Remember that the observers in experiments in these days were not naive undergraduates, but philosophically trained professors and graduate students. The observer gave the answer in the normal way, but was supposed to attend to the mental processes that had been set in motion by the question and that solved the problem it posed. After giving the answer, the observer reported what had happened in his mind between the question and the answer—that is, he was to describe his thought processes. The method was deceptively simple, and the results were intensely controversial.

The first results were a shock to almost all psychologists: Thoughts can be imageless—that is, some of the contents of consciousness could not be traced, as the Way of Ideas said, to sensations, feelings, or images of these. This finding emerged in the first Würzburg paper by A. M. Mayer and J. Orth, published in 1901. In this experiment, the observer was instructed to respond with the first word that came to mind after hearing a stimulus word. The experimenter gave a ready signal, called out the stimulus word, and started a stopwatch; the observer gave a response and the experimenter stopped the watch. The observer then described the thinking process. Mayer and Orth reported that most thinking involved definite images or feelings associated with acts of will. However, wrote Mayer and Orth (1901), "apart from these two classes of conscious processes, we must introduce a third group. . . . The observers very frequently reported that they experienced certain conscious processes which they could describe neither as definite images nor as acts of will." For example, while serving as an observer, Mayer "made the observation that following the stimulus word 'meter' there occurred a peculiar conscious process, not further definable, which was followed by the spoken word 'trochee.'" So orthodoxy was wrong, according to Mayer and Orth; nonimaginal events in consciousness had allegedly been found.

What was to be made of imageless thought? The Würzburgers' own interpretation changed during the life of the school. Mayer and Orth did no more than discover imageless thoughts—vague, impalpable, almost indescribable "conscious states." Later on, they were identified simply as "thoughts" themselves. The final theory was that thought is actually an unconscious process, reducing the imageless thought elements to conscious indicators of thinking rather than thinking itself. However, on both sides of the Atlantic, many psychologists found the Würzburg methods, results, and interpretations to be unacceptable or at least suspect.

Writing in 1907, Wundt rebutted the Würzburgers' conclusions by rejecting their method. He argued that the Würzburg experiments were sham experiments, dangerous reversions to unreliable armchair introspection that happened to be conducted in a laboratory. According to Wundt, experimental control was entirely lacking in the thought experiments. The observer did not know exactly what task would be set. The ensuing mental process would vary from observer to observer and from trial to trial, so the results could not be replicated. Finally, said Wundt, it is difficult if not impossible for an observer to both think about the set problem and watch that process at the same time. Consequently, Wundt said, the so-called findings of imageless thought were invalid.

Sharing Külpe's expansive definition of the scope of introspection, Titchener replicated the Würzburg studies in order to refute them and defend his associationist tradition. Methodologically, Titchener echoed Wundt by claiming that observers' reports of "imageless" thought were not descriptions of consciousness at all, but fabrications based on beliefs about how one would solve the problems set in the experiments. Experimentally, Titchener's students performed thought experiments and reported that they could find no evidence of imageless thought elements; they successfully traced all conscious content to sensations or feelings (H. M. Clark, 1911). For example, according to Titchener, many superficially plausible "imageless thoughts" could be traced by Cornell observers to kinesthetic feelings of the body that had eluded the Würzburg observers. Titchener concluded that the Würzburgers had failed to accurately observe their conscious experience. They found a mental content that proved difficult to analyze further, but instead of pursuing the analysis, they gave up and called the content "imageless thought."

Other commentators offered alternative interpretations of the Würzburg results. Some suggested that certain types of minds possess imageless thought and others do not, reducing the Titchener–Külpe controversy to one of individual differences. This hypothesis was criticized as unparsimonious: Why should nature create two types of mind to attain the same end—accurate thinking? And why should one type predominate at Würzburg and the other at Cornell?

The hypothesis of unconscious thinking was rejected on the grounds that what is not conscious is not mental but physiological, and therefore not a part of psychology. As the controversy wore on, it became more and more intractable. In 1911, J. R. Angell wrote: "One feels that the differences which divide certain of the writers are largely those of mutual misunderstanding as to the precise phenomenon under discussion" (p. 306). Angell was disturbed that the combatants in the dispute had been "largely reduced to mere assertion and denial. . . . 'It is!' or 'It isn't!'" (p. 305).

In America, the most important consequence of the debate about imageless thought was the suspicion that introspection was a fragile and unreliable tool, easily prejudiced by theoretical expectations. The Würzburg observers believed in imageless thought, and they found it. Titchener's observers believed only in sensations and feelings, and they found only those. R. M. Ogden, an American supporter of imageless thought, wrote that if Wundt's and Titchener's criticisms of the Würzburg methods were valid, "may we not carry the point a step farther and deny the value of all introspection. Indeed, in a recent discussion among psychologists, this position was vigorously maintained by two among those present" (Ogden, 1911a). Ogden himself suggested that the differing results from Titchener's laboratory at Cornell and Külpe's in Würzburg betrayed "unconscious bias" based on different training (Ogden, 1911b, p. 193). The imageless thought controversy revealed difficulties with the introspective method and, by 1911, the year of Ogden's papers, we find some psychologists ready to discard it altogether. Ogden's "two among those present" were already behaviorists without the name. The imageless thought dispute tallied well with the debates over the nature of hypnosis and hysteria that were occurring in abnormal psychology at the same time. In both lines of investigation it appeared that people, whether highly motivated researchers or clinical patients, could be so influenced by suggestion as to render that reports and behavior suspect as objective scientific evidence about mind and behavior (Makris, 2008). If subjects—participants in later terminology—simply said and did what experimenters inadvertently hinted they should—it seemed that experiments were helpless to reveal human nature. Soon, in launching behaviorism as a truly objective psychology, John B. Watson would cite the imageless thought controversy as a signal failing of introspective psychology, failing to see that behavior as well subjective experienced and introspective reports could be influenced by experimenter's expectations.

The Würzburgers' second finding led them to reject associationism as an adequate account of thinking. Their key question was this: What makes one idea rather than another follow a given idea? For free association, as in Mayer and Orth's experiment, associationism has a plausible answer. If the stimulus word is *bird*, the observer may respond *canary*. The associationist can then say that the bird–canary bond is the strongest in the observer's associative network. However, this situation is complicated if we use a method of constrained association, as Henry J. Watt did in 1905. In this method, we set a specific task for the observer to carry out, such as "give a subordinate category" or "give a superordinate category." To the former task, the observer may still reply *canary*. To the second task, the correct response cannot be "canary" but instead should be "animal." However, these tasks are no longer free associations, but rather acts of directed thinking that produce propositions that may be true or false—unlike free association. So the simple associative bond bird–canary is overridden in directed thinking.

The Würzburgers argued that the force of association alone cannot explain the nature of rational thought, for something other than associative glue must direct thought along the proper lines in the associative network in order for an observer to respond correctly to such tasks as Watt's. The Würzburgers proposed that the task itself directed thinking. In their later terminology, they said that the task establishes a mental set—or a determining tendency—in the mind that properly directs the observer's use of his or her associative network. These experiments suggested unconscious thinking, for observers found that given the task "gives a superordinate category to canary," the response "bird" popped into their heads with little experienced mental activity. The Würzburgers concluded that the mental set accomplishes thinking even before the problem is given; the observer is so prepared to give a superordinate category that the actual response occurs automatically. The concept of mental set reflects the influence of Brentano's act psychology, which the Würzburgers absorbed from Husserl. Thoughts are not passive representations—mental objects—but mental acts inherently directed at other aspects of mind or at the world. As Külpe wrote, "the fundamental characteristic of thinking is referring, meaning aiming at something" (quoted by Ash, 1995, p. 79), exactly Brentano's formulation of intentionality.

As the studies of the Würzburg psychologists developed, they moved toward a psychology of function—mental acts, in Brentano's terms—from the traditional analytic psychology of content. Initially, they had been concerned to describe a new mental content, imageless thought, but in the end they found that thought as act eluded description in terms of sensory content. As Brentano held, mental activity—function—is more fundamental and psychologically real than supposed atoms of the mind. The future of psychology, especially in America, lay with the psychology of function rather than of content. The contents—the objects—of the mind proved to be ephemeral things, vastly more difficult to pin down than the substantial atoms constituting physical objects. As evolution began to affect psychology, asking how the mind acts to serve an organism's survival in the struggle for existence became a more important question than asking how many visual sensory elements there might be.

Historically, however, the systematic introspection of the Würzburg school proved a dead end (Danziger, 1990). As Wundt had intimated, the school's method was too subjective to yield replicable, scientific results. Although Würzburg-inspired work continued after 1909, the school essentially dissolved when Külpe left for the University of Bonn. No theory based on the Würzburg studies was ever published, although there is evidence that Külpe was working on such a theory when he died. It is puzzling that, from 1909 until his death, Külpe said almost nothing about the dramatic Würzburg results. No alternative psychology arose from the Würzburg school. Its methods were innovative if ultimately unfruitful, its findings stimulating if anomalous, and, in the concept of the mental set, it foreshadowed the functional psychology of the future. A more substantial offspring of Brentano's phenomenology was the Gestalt movement.

Studying Memory

The controversy ensuing from attempts to study thinking via introspection revealed the difficulties inherent in transforming introspection from a philosopher's tool into an objective scientific method, providing an argument for redefining psychology as the study of public behavior. A different higher mental process, memory, proved more amenable to scientific investigation because it could be studied quantitatively and without introspection. Unlike the study of thought, which faded from the psychological scene for decades, the study of memory—or learning—flourished during the reign of behaviorism and continued into the era of cognitive science.

The study of memory was begun by Hermann Ebbinghaus (1850–1909), a young doctor of philosophy unattached to any university when he came across a copy of Fechner's *Elements of Psychophysics* in a secondhand bookstore. He admired the scientific precision of Fechner's work on perception and resolved to tackle the "higher mental processes" that Wundt had excluded from experimental treatment. Using himself as his only subject, Ebbinghaus set out in 1879 to demonstrate that some higher useful processes could be experimentally investigated, a point Wundt (1907) later conceded. The result was his *Über das Gedächtnis* (*Memory*) of 1885, which was hailed even by

Wundt as a first-rate contribution to psychology and which helped win him a professorship at the prestigious University of Berlin.

Memory represented a necessarily small-scale but well-thought-out research program. Ebbinghaus decided to investigate the formation of associations by learning serial lists of nonsense syllables—meaningless combinations of three letters he invented for the purpose. In electing to memorize nonsense syllables, Ebbinghaus revealed the functionalist cast of his thought. He chose nonsense syllables because they are meaningless, because the sameness of their content would not differentially affect the process of learning. He wanted to isolate and study memory as the pure *function* of learning, abstracting away any effects of content.

The study of memory was further developed by Georg Elias Müller (1880–1943), the most rigorous experimentalist of the founding German psychologists (Behrens, 1997; Haupt, 1995; Kusch, 1999). Muller insisted on objectivity almost to the point of fanaticism and made a sort of factory out of his laboratory in Göttingen. Fittingly, he invented the memory drum, a machine for presenting Ebbinghaus's nonsense syllables at an objectively measurable pace. Theoretically, he insisted on association as the only mental force, rejecting the Wurzburger's notion of determining tendencies. As members of the younger generation of German academics, Ebbinghaus and Müller were less Mandarin than Wundt, never trying to develop the overarching syntheses of psychological knowledge aimed at by Wundt and other German professors. In this respect they were more like the American psychologists whose emphasis on method and minimization of theory would come to dominate twentieth-century psychology, and Americans quickly took up their methods. In 1896, Mary Calkins augmented Ebbinghaus's serial learning method with a paired-associate procedure in which the subject learns specific pairs of words or nonsense syllables.

SCIENTIFIC PHENOMENOLOGY: GESTALT PSYCHOLOGY

The leading Gestalt psychologists were Max Wertheimer (1880–1943), Wolfgang Köhler (1887–1967), and Kurt Koffka (1887–1941). Wertheimer was the founder and inspirational leader of the movement and received his PhD from Külpe at Würzburg. Köhler succeeded Stumpf as head of the prestigious Berlin Psychological Institute, and was the primary theorist and researcher of the group, having been trained in physics as well as philosophy and psychology. Koffka was the first to write up Wertheimer's ideas and spread the message of Gestalt psychology worldwide through books and articles. Of their many students and associates, the most important was Kurt Lewin (1890–1947), who devised practical applications of Gestalt theories. Inspired by Stumpf to describe rather than artificially analyze consciousness, they created a radically new approach to understanding conscious experience that rejected virtually every aspect of the Cartesian Way of Ideas.

Even before the work of the Würzburg school, it was becoming clear that the empiricist-associative theory faced formidable difficulties in explaining how meaningful, organized objects of perception are allegedly created out of meaningless sensory atoms. Christian von Ehrenfels (1859–1932), with whom Wertheimer studied, had begun to formulate a rival viewpoint, introducing the term *Gestalt* (form, or whole) to psychology. A melody, Ehrenfels said, is more than a sequence of notes. A melody can be transposed into a different key such that none of the notes—the sensory elements of which the melody is supposedly composed—remains the same, without altering our perception of it. Ehrenfels proposed that in addition to sensory elements there were form-elements—*Gestaltqualitäten*—composing the objects of consciousness. When Ehrenfels advanced this hypothesis in 1890, he left the ontological status of Gestalt qualities ambiguous. Were they imposed on sensory atoms by the mind, as Ehrenfels's own teacher, Alexius Meinong (1853–1920), proposed? Or were they something more, objective structures (not elements) that existed in the world and were picked up by consciousness, as philosophical realists and phenomenologists thought? Gestalt psychology forcefully pursued the latter possibility.

Gestalt Psychologists' Rejection of the Cartesian Framework

Gestalt psychologists were horrified by atomistic theories of consciousness and offered Gestalt psychology as a liberating revolution against psychology's ancient régime. As Köhler said in his presidential address to the APA:

> We were excited by what we found, and even more by the prospect of finding further revealing facts. Moreover, it was not only the stimulating newness of our enterprise which inspired us. There was also a great wave of relief—as though we were escaping from a prison. The prison was psychology as taught at the universities when we still were students. At the time, we had been shocked by the thesis that all psychological facts (not only those in perception) consist of unrelated inert atoms and that almost the only factors which combine these atoms and thus introduce action are associations formed under the influence of mere contiguity. What had disturbed us was the utter senselessness of this picture, and the implication that human life, apparently so colorful and so intensely dynamic, is actually a frightful bore. This was not true of our new picture, and we felt that further discoveries were bound to destroy what was left of the old picture. (1959/1978, pp. 253–254)

Gestalt theorists held that the old picture, the Way of Ideas, rested on two flawed and unexamined assumptions. The first was the bundle hypothesis (essentially associative atomism) identified by Wertheimer, which held that like chemical compounds, the objects of consciousness were made up of fixed and unchanging atomic elements. According to Wertheimer, the bundle hypothesis was a theoretical presupposition artificially imposed on experience, not a natural description of consciousness as we find it. Wertheimer wrote:

> I stand at the window and see a house, trees, sky. Theoretically I might say there were 327 brightnesses and nuances of colour. Do I have "327"? No. I have sky, house, and trees. It is impossible to achieve "327" as such. And yet even though such droll calculation were possible and implied, say, for the house 120, the trees 90, the sky 117—I should at least have this arrangement and division of the total, and not, say, 127 and 100 and 100; or 150 and 177. (1923/1938, p. 71)

The second flawed presupposition imposed on experience by the old picture was the constancy hypothesis, identified by Köhler (1947). The constancy hypothesis was the physiological side of the Way of Ideas. It held that every sensory element in consciousness corresponded to a specific physical stimulus registered by a sense organ.

In their critique of the bundle hypothesis and the constancy hypothesis, the Gestalt psychologists rejected almost the entire modern philosophy of mind. Atomism about consciousness began when Descartes severed the world of experience (ideas) from the world of physical objects. Perception became a matter of point-for-point projection of physical stimuli onto the screen of consciousness, as in a camera obscura. Only the minority tradition of philosophical realism was carried on by Gestalt psychology.

The Gestalt Research Program

As a research program, Gestalt psychology began in 1910 with investigations into apparent motion led by Wertheimer, aided by Köhler and Koffka. Apparent motion is familiar through movies, which are a series of rapidly presented still pictures that are experienced as objects in continuous, smooth motion. In Wertheimer's (1912/1961) experiments, observers viewed successive stroboscopic presentations of two vertical, black bars in two different, fixed locations on a white background. Wertheimer varied the interval between the offset of the presentation of the first stimulus and the onset of the presentation of the second stimulus. When the interval between presentations of the bars was 30 milliseconds, the observer saw two bars appearing simultaneously; when the interval was 60 milliseconds, the observer reported seeing a single bar moving from point to point.

To give this experience a name free from the sort of theoretical presuppositions he was trying to avoid, Wertheimer dubbed it the phi phenomenon. The term *apparent motion* reflected the reigning interpretation when Wertheimer did his experiments. In the grip of the bundle and constancy hypotheses, psychologists explained apparent motion as an illusion, a cognitive error, in which the observer sees two identical objects in two places and then falsely infers that a single object moved from the first to the second point. Such an explanation holds that there is no experience of motion given in consciousness; the motion is merely "apparent," and the experience is explained away. Wertheimer and his followers insisted, on the contrary, that the experience of motion was real, genuinely given in consciousness, although it did not correspond to any physical stimulus, contrary to the bundle and constancy hypotheses.

This Gestalt idea can be illustrated by the perception of illusory contours in Figure 1. One clearly perceives a triangle that is not, strictly speaking, there. Moreover, observers typically see the area enclosed by the phantom triangle as being lighter in brightness than the space outside. They thus experience a contour, a difference of light and dark, to which there is no corresponding physical stimulus.

Illusory contours also show how Gestalt study of the phi phenomenon could be brought to bear on the problem of object perception. In Figure 1, as in the perception of melodic form and in the phi phenomenon, we perceive a form—a Gestalt—to which no local physical stimulation corresponds. Objects—Wertheimer's house, trees, and sky—are immediately given in consciousness as meaningful wholes, not as collections of atomic sensations. "When we are presented with a

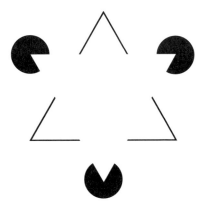

FIGURE 1   Illusory contours in the Kanizsa triangle.

FIGURE 2 The Gestalt Law of Similarity.

number of stimuli we do not as a rule experience 'a number' of individual things, this one and that," Wertheimer wrote (1923/1938, p. 78). "Instead larger wholes separated from and related to one another are given in experience. . . . Do such arrangements and divisions follow definite principles?" Wertheimer said they did, and laid down a set of "organizing principles" still cited in textbooks today. For example, following the Law of Similarity, we tend to see alternating columns of squares and circles rather than five rows of alternating squares and circles.

Later, Köhler formulated an overarching organizing law, the Law of Prägnanz—the tendency of experiences to assume the simplest shapes possible.

It is important to understand that according to Gestalt psychology, Gestalts are not imposed on experience by the mind, but are discovered in experience. Gestalts are objective, not subjective. Especially as formulated by Köhler, Gestalts were physically real, natural self-organizations in nature, in the brain, and in experience, all of them isomorphic to one another. In physics, we find that dynamic forces spontaneously organize material particles into simple elegant forms. The brain, Köhler said, is likewise a dynamic field of self-organizing force fields reflecting the physical Gestalts and giving rise to the Gestalts of experienced objects. "In a sense, Gestalt psychology has since become a kind of application of field physics to essential parts of psychology and brain physiology" (Köhler, 1967/1971, p. 115).

The conflict between atomism and Gestalt self-organization extended to the study of behavior, including animal behavior. The leading student of animal behavior at the turn of the century was Edward Lee Thorndike (1874–1949), who turned the atomistic theory of consciousness inside out into an atomistic theory of behavior. He studied cats learning to work a manipulandum in order to escape from a "puzzle box." From watching their apparently trial-and-error behavior, Thorndike concluded that animals do not form associations between ideas, but between the stimuli in the box and the response needed to escape it. A little later, Köhler studied the intelligence of apes and drew different conclusions. His apes showed insight, as problems suddenly resolved themselves into simple solutions, just as Gestalts emerge spontaneously in consciousness. According to Köhler, because the construction of the puzzle boxes hid their workings from the animal, it was reduced to trial and error by its situation, not because it was limited to forming stimulus-response associations. As the old atomistic picture of consciousness imposed its presuppositions on psychologists' understanding of perception, Thorndike's method imposed random, atomistic stimulus-response learning on his animal subjects, which would have been capable of problem-solving if given the chance. Köhler sought a phenomenology of behavior no less than a phenomenology of consciousness.

Later, Wertheimer applied the Gestalt concept of insight as self-organization of behavior to human thinking, and Kurt Lewin applied the Gestalt concept of the dynamic field to social behavior. In these studies of behavior and social psychology we see that the Gestalt psychologists shared their generation's desire that psychology be a complete natural science. However, in their emphasis on nonreducible wholes, they did not share the positivist motivation that led other German psychologists, such as Külpe and Titchener, to pursue the same goal of psychology as a natural science.

In the late nineteenth century, cultivated Germans feared atomistic conceptions of the universe. As we have seen, for them atomism was linked to the twin evils of The Machine, an object made of separable parts, and Chaos, a formless void of atoms into which machines might dissolve. Believing in real wholes—Gestalts—offered a third way in which order and meaning were inherent in nature. However, the term *Gestalt* was linked to conservative and racist strains of German thought that tended to reject modern science. For example, Houston Stewart Chamberlin said that Life is Gestalt, and that with the exception of the atomized, nationless Jews, each race was a Gestalt, the highest race-Gestalt being the Teutonic. Though not anti-Semitic, Ehrenfels voiced similar opinions, setting Gestalt (good) against Chaos (evil) and finding hope of salvation in German music. It was therefore a bold move when Wertheimer, a Jew, appropriated the term *Gestalt* for a scientific, democratic, urban movement. Rather than blaming science for the modern predicament, he hoped to use good, tough-minded science to demonstrate that the world of experience was not a lie but corresponded to a structured, organized, meaningful physical reality.

Reception and Influence of Gestalt Psychology

By the mid-1930s, Gestalt psychology was well-known around the world, a fact that briefly shielded Köhler from Nazi persecution. Nevertheless, there were significant German criticisms of Gestalt theory. The most important came from the school of Ganzheit (roughly, "holistic") psychology, led by Felix Krueger (1874–1948), Wundt's successor at Leipzig. Followers of Ganzheit found Gestalt psychology's theory that Gestalts are physically objective to be insufficiently psychological. Their motto was "No Gestalts without a Gestalter," adhering to the Kantian view that Gestalts are imposed by the mind rather than discovered.

Beginning with Koffka in 1927, the leading Gestalt psychologists left Germany for the United States. Wertheimer was one of the first Jews stripped of his professorship by the Nazis. Köhler resisted the Nazi takeover of the universities, but despite support from the Foreign Ministry (Ash, 1995)

FIGURE 3 Another ambiguous figure. Is this a young woman looking away from you or an old woman looking down to your left? This ambiguous figure was not devised by the Gestalt psychologists, but first appeared as a postcard in the early nineteenth century with the title "My wife and my mother-in-law."

also departed for America. There, the Gestalt psychologists confronted behaviorism in a society for which the concept of Gestalt had no cultural resonance. Although American psychologists respected the experimental findings of Gestalt psychology, and even elected Köhler president of the APA, they found Gestalt theory strange and bewildering. In addition, the Gestalt theorists tended not to shed their German ways and found few opportunities to train graduate students (Sokal, 1984). The exception was Kurt Lewin, who remade his personality on American lines, made sure he could train PhDs, and took up American topics such as group dynamics (Ash, 1992).

The legacy of Gestalt psychology in psychology is hard to measure. Its demonstrations and principles of organization are still found in psychology textbooks. Its greatest contribution lay in reformulating the study of perception to "carve nature at the joints." Gestalt theorists objected not to analyzing experience into parts, but to analyzing it into arbitrary parts (Henle, 1985). Perhaps because of Gestalt influence, psychologists remain wary of imposing pretheoretical assumptions on their data, and Köhler's view of the brain as a self-organizing system is returning, unacknowledged, in connectionist psychology and neuroscience. Nevertheless, Gestalt concern with wholeness and unity seems a faint voice from the now lost culture of the Bildungsburger. Perhaps the best summary of Gestalt psychology's impact is offered by one of the last surviving Gestalt psychologists, A. S. Luchins. Luchins (1975) acknowledged that Gestalt terminology is often used in contemporary, especially American, psychology but he denied that the concepts to which the terms refer have been assimilated. With its emphasis on wholes, on synthesis, and on placing psychology within a larger "total comprehension of human existence," Gestalt psychology, like Wundt's, may have been too Mandarin for export.

THE PRACTICAL TURN: APPLIED PSYCHOLOGY

By and large, academic German psychologists resisted the idea that psychology should become an applied discipline. Wundt and his generation of psychologists saw psychology as part of philosophy, but most of the next generation of psychologists wanted to make it into a pure natural science. Academic psychologists resisted making psychology a practical field for three reasons. First was the great value Mandarin Germans placed on pure scholarship undertaken for its own sake. Practical enterprises were undertaken to make money, not to cultivate the soul, and the latter was the goal of Mandarin scholarship. Stumpf, for example, feared making psychology a narrow specialization bereft of Bildung. In particular, he loathed "a certain sort of American whose whole aim is [to get a Ph.D.] in the shortest possible time with the most mechanical work possible" (quoted by Ash, 1995, p. 35). Second, German academics had achieved *Lehrfreiheit*—academic freedom to study and teach whatever one wanted—as a political bargain with Bismarck's German Reich. Academics could do whatever they wished within the confines of the academy, but they were not to interfere in social and political matters (Danziger, 1990). Third, even when German psychology turned in a functional direction—being concerned with mental processes rather than mental content, a transition we witnessed in the case of the Würzburg school—its functionalism was not tied, as American functionalism would be, to Darwinian evolution. German concerns remained philosophical, whereas Americans looked on the mind as a practical organ of adaptation to the environment. Americans thus came to focus on how the mind operates in everyday life, and hence on how to aid or improve its functioning, while German psychologists focused on the traditional epistemological question of how the mind knows the world (Ash, 1995).

Nevertheless, social forces were at work within Germany and elsewhere that promoted the growth of psychology as an applied field of study. In France, as we have noted, psychology was connected with psychiatric clinics and therefore with the practical matter of understanding and curing psychopathology, and Binet studied infants and children with a view toward improving their education.

Similarly, in Germany, William Stern (1871–1938) devised the influential concept of the intelligence quotient, or IQ. American psychology was applied almost from the outset. Even in Germany, demand for practical science, including the natural sciences, was on the rise. For example, the German chemical industry was instrumental in establishing chemistry as a science in the German universities (R. Smith, 1997). Addressing the 1912 meeting of the Society for Experimental Psychology, the mayor of Berlin virtually demanded that psychology produce practical application, implying that future government support for the new field depended on it (Ash, 1995). Commercial universities sprang up alongside state-supported universities; Wertheimer began his research on the phi phenomenon at the Frankfurt Commercial Academy (Ash, 1995). Despite the resistance of the Mandarin elite, applied psychology (or psychotechnics, as it was known in Germany; van Drunen, 1996) evolved alongside scientific psychology, including such fields as sports psychology (Bäumler, 1996), traffic psychology (Häcker & Echterhoff, 1996), and railroad psychology (Gundlach, 1996).

THE FATE OF THE PSYCHOLOGY OF CONSCIOUSNESS

What happened to the psychology of consciousness? Psychology is no longer defined as the science of consciousness, but as the science of behavior. It may, therefore, appear that the psychology of consciousness died sometime in the twentieth century. From a theoretical perspective, this is largely true. The psychological theories of Wundt, Titchener, and Külpe are no longer taught. A little bit of the Gestalt tradition lives, albeit in attenuated form. On the other hand, if we define the psychology of consciousness as a field of study within psychology—the psychology of sensation and perception—rather than as the universal definition of psychology, then the psychology of consciousness is alive and well. In the past 25 years, numerous books have been published on the nature of consciousness, and in cognitive science and cognitive neuroscience great strides have been made in explaining how humans experience the world. Our discipline today includes so much more than the study of sensation and perception that it has been lost in the plethora of subject areas that constitute contemporary psychology. The subsequent story of early psychology as an institution is a story of two nations.

Slow Growth in Germany

In Germany, the growth of psychology was greatly inhibited by the Mandarin culture of philosophical Bildung. As long as psychology remained where Wundt left it—in philosophy—psychologists had to compete with philosophers for professorships and resources. Especially as psychology became more completely experimental, it seemed to philosophers to be a rude intrusion on their traditional concerns, and they banded together to oppose its growth within psychology. Even Brentano's student Edmund Husserl, though sympathetic to Stumpf and Gestalt psychology, condemned positivistically inclined psychologists as "experimental fanatics" worshiping "the cult of the facts" (quoted by Ash, 1995, p. 44). Other philosophers agreed with younger psychologists that they should be grouped with chemists and physicists, not philosophers. However, efforts to move it elsewhere—for example, to medicine (to join physiology), as Külpe proposed—were unsuccessful.

The coming to power of the Nazis in 1933 complicated matters. They destroyed the old Mandarin system and drove from Germany its best minds. Jews and others sickened by Nazi oppression left Germany in a remarkable emigration that included outstanding intellectuals of every type, from writers such as Thomas Mann to filmmakers such as Fritz Lange to physicists such as Albert Einstein. Important psychologists were among the number, most notably the Gestalt psychologists, who moved to the United States, and Sigmund Freud, who spent his last months in England. Appallingly, many psychologists who remained in Germany turned with rapidity in the Nazi direction, in some cases providing "scientific" justification for Nazi racial policies, often invoking the concept of Gestalt. In 1935, Felix Krueger endorsed the authoritarian policies of the Nazi state: "The state's defense and jurisdiction cannot function without harshness. Imperiously it demands the sacrifice of one's own will and even one's own life, in its capacity as a Whole that must continue to exist over all else. . . . [The people] must make a sacrifice of their imperfection, by obeying their state and freely recognizing the ordered power above them" (quoted by Harrington, 1996, p. 185).

Freidrich Sander, former student of Wundt and follower of Krueger, linked psychology to the ideology of Nazism. In a 1937 public lecture, Sander said:

> He who, with believing heart and thoughtful sense, intuits the driving idea of National Socialism back to its source, will everywhere rediscover two basic motives standing behind the German movement's colossal struggles: the longing for wholeness and the will towards Gestalt. . . . Wholeness and Gestalt, the ruling ideas of the German movement, have become central concepts of German psychology. . . . Present-day German psychology and the National Socialistic world view are both oriented towards the same goal: the vanquishing of atomistic and mechanistic forms of thought. . . . In this way, though, scientific psychology is on the brink of simultaneously becoming a useful tool for actualizing the aims of National Socialism. (quoted by Harrington, 1996, p. 178)

Sander enthusiastically endorsed the extermination the Jews, to many Germans the very image of rootless, atomistic Chaos:

> Whoever would lead the German Volk . . . back to its own Gestalt, whoever wants to help the Volk soul achieve the goal it longs for: to purely express its own being—this individual must eliminate everything alienated from Gestalt; above all, he must nullify the power of all destructive foreign-racial influences. The elimination of a parasitically proliferating Jewry has its deep ethical justification in this will of the German essence to pure Gestalt, no less than does the sterilization, within their own Volk, of carriers of inferior genetic material. (pp. 184–185)

Psychology won its autonomy under the Nazi regime. The founding generation of psychologists had resisted making psychology into mere psychotechnics. Nevertheless, in 1941 German psychotechnic psychology won bureaucratic recognition as an independent field of study "because the Wehrmacht required trained psychologists to assist in the selection of officers" (Ash, 1981, p. 286; Gundlach, 2012). This proved a Faustian bargain, of course, when the Nazi regime brought upon Germany the destruction of World War II and the subsequent division of Germany into East and West. Not until the 1950s did psychology in Germany get on its feet again (Ash, 1981), and then it was in an entirely new environment, dominated by American ideas.

Transplantation to America

In one respect, German psychology flourished in America. The growth of psychology in America quickly outpaced growth in Germany or any other country. For example, the APA was founded a decade before the German Society for Experimental Psychology. In other respects, however, the psychology of consciousness in its German form could not be carried beyond the borders of Mandarin Germany. G. Stanley Hall wrote in 1912, "We need a psychology that is usable, that is dietetic, efficient for thinking, living, and working, and although

Wundtian thoughts are now so successfully cultivated in academic gardens, they can never be acclimated here, as they are antipathetic to the American spirit and temper" (quoted by Blumenthal, 1986b).

The future of psychology lay largely in America, but it would be a psychology much changed from its German roots.

Bibliography

There are several edited volumes on psychology's beginnings: Wolfgang Bringmann and Ryan D. Tweney, eds., *Wundt studies* (Toronto: Hogrefe, 1980); Josef Brozek and Ludwig Pongratz, eds., *Historiography of modern psychology* (Toronto: Hogrefe, 1980); C. Buxton, ed., *Points of view in the history of psychology* (New York: Academic Press, 1986); Eliot Hearst, ed., *The first century of experimental psychology* (Hillsdale, NJ: Erlbaum, 1979); Sigmund Koch and David Leary, eds., *A century of psychology as science* (New York: McGraw-Hill, 1985); R. W. Rieber, ed., *Wilhelm Wundt and the making of a scientific psychology* (New York: Plenum, 1980); and William W. Woodward and Mitchell G. Ash, eds., *The problematic science: Psychology in nineteenth century thought* (New York: Praeger, 1982). Many photographs of early psychologists, their laboratories, and their work may be found in Bringmann et al. (1997). Development of instruments for conducting psychological experiments was an important part of establishing the scientific credibility of early psychology. The journal *History of Psychology* devoted a special issue to the topic in 2005, *8*(1), 3–117.

An excellent introduction to the intellectual climate in nineteenth-century Germany is provided by Ringer (1969), which should be updated with Harrington (1996) and Wolf Lepenies (2006) *The seduction of culture in German history* (Princeton: Princeton University Press). A general if perhaps over-drawn account of the influence of German thought on modernity is Watson (2010).

Three papers discuss the conditions of psychology's founding: Richard Littman (1979) provides a general account of psychology's emergence as a discipline; Ash (1981) describes Germany in 1879–1941; Kurt Danziger (1990) uses sociological techniques to analyze the emergence of the human psychology experiment and contrasts the several early models of psychological research. Gundlach (2012) provides a concise discussion of the development of German psychology. Finally, an older but still useful account of psychology's beginnings, written just after it happened, is found in J. Mark Baldwin, "Sketch of the history of psychology," *Psychological Review* (1905, *12*: 144–165).

A great deal of work has been done on Wundt and his psychology. Besides Wundt (1896), the following works of his are available in English: *Outlines of psychology* (1897; reprint, St. Clair Shores: Michigan Scholarly Press, 1969); *Principles of physiological psychology*, Vol. 1, 5th ed. (New York: Macmillan, 1910); *An introduction to psychology* (1912; reprint, New York: Arno, 1973); *Elements of folk psychology* (London: Allen & Unwin, 1916); and *The language of gestures*, an excerpt from his *Völkerpsychologie* of 1900–1920 (The Hague, The Netherlands: Mouton, 1973). For Wundt's biography, see Wolfgang Bringmann, William Balance, and Rand Evans, "Wilhelm Wundt, 1832–1920: A brief biographical sketch," *Journal of the History of the Behavioral Sciences* (1975, *11*: 287–297); Wolfgang Bringmann, Norma J. Bringmann, and William Balance, "Wilhelm Maximilian Wundt 1832–74: The formative years," in Bringmann and Tweney (1980, cited earlier); and Diamond (1980). Wundt's general view of psychology and its place among the sciences, with special reference to the *Völkerpsychologie* is reviewed by Wan-chi Wong (2009) *Retracing the footsteps of Wilhelm Wundt: Explorations in the disciplinary frontiers of psychology and in Völkerpsychologie, History of Psychology, 12*, 229–65. Other sources on Wundt include Joseph Jastrow, "Experimental psychology in Leipzig," *Science* (1886, *7*: [198, Supplement]: 459–462), which describes in detail a few of Wundt's experiments, some of which are startlingly similar to current work in cognitive psychology. These parallels are discussed in my own "Something old, something new: Attention in Wundt and modern cognitive psychology," *Journal of the History of the Behavioral Sciences* 5 (1979, *15*: 242–252). Theodore Mischel discusses "Wundt and the conceptual foundations of psychology," *Philosophical and Phenomenological Research* (1970, *31*: 1–26). William R. Woodward, "Wundt's program for the new psychology: Vicissitudes of experiment, theory, and system" (in Woodward and Ash, 1982, cited earlier), presents Wundt as a typical German intellectual with a Will to System. Two papers by Kurt Danziger (1979, 1980a) correct errors in the older picture of Wundt and examine his fate in Germany. Arthur Blumenthal (1986a) provides a good general orientation to Wundt's psychology.

Titchener was a prolific writer. Important works, in addition to those cited in this chapter, include "The past decade in experimental psychology," *American Journal of Psychology* (1910, *21*: 404–421), "The scheme of introspection," *American Journal of Psychology* (1912, *23*: 485–508), "Experimental psychology: A retrospect," *American Journal of Psychology* (1925, *36*: 313–323), and *A text-book of psychology* (New York: Macmillan, 1913). In my article, "The mistaken mirror: On Wundt's and Titchener's psychologies," *Journal of the History of the Behavioral Sciences* (1981, *17*: 273–282), I show that Titchener was not, as is usually assumed, a simple follower of Wundt who faithfully reflected the master's views. Upset with the applied direction taken by the APA, Titchener formed his own scientifically focused group, as described by C. James Goodwin (2005), "Recognizing the experimentalists: The origin of the Society for Experimental Psychology," *History of Psychology*, 8, 347–361.

Some of the Würzburg school's papers are translated and excerpted in George and Jean Mandler, eds., *The psychology of thinking: From association to Gestalt* (New York: Wiley, 1964). Besides the references in the text, there were two important contemporary discussions of imageless thought: Angell (1911) and Robert S. Woodworth, "Imageless thought," *Journal of Philosophy, Psychology, and Scientific Methods* (1906, *3*: 701–708). A recent discussion is David Lindenfield, "Oswald Külpe and the Würzburg School," *Journal of the History of the Behavioral Sciences* (1978, 14: 132–141). George Humphrey, in part of his *Thinking* (New York: Science Editions, 1963), discusses the Würzburg findings, although he overestimates their damage to Wundt's psychology. The imageless thought controversy is addressed from sociology of science perspective by Kusch (1995). The development of thought-psychology and its impact on philosophy of science is discussed by Michel ter Hark, *Popper, Otto Selz, and the rise of evolutionary epistemology* (Cambridge: Cambridge University Press, 2004), and "The psychology of thinking before the cognitive revolution: Otto Selz on problems, schemas, and creativity," *History of Psychology*, 2010, *13*, 2–24. Muller's work on learning and memory is summarized in D. J. Murray, and C. A. Bandomir, (2001). G. E. Müller (1911, 1913, 1917) on memory. *Psychologie et Histoire*, *1*, 208–232.

Köhler's important works include *The mentality of apes* (New York: Liveright, 1938); *The place of value in a world of facts* (New York: Liveright, 1938); *Dynamics in psychology* (New York: Liveright, 1940); *Gestalt psychology* (New York: Mentor, 1947); and *Selected papers of Wolfgang Köhler* (New York: Liveright, 1971).

Wertheimer's *Productive thinking* (New York: Harper & Row, 1959) is recommended. Mary Henle has edited a selection of papers by the Gestaltists, *Documents of Gestalt psychology* (Berkeley: University of California Press, 1961). The most influential Gestalt psychologist in the United States was Kurt Lewin, who for some time affected social, personality, and, to a lesser extent, learning psychology; see, for example, his *Principles of topological psychology* (New York: McGraw-Hill, 1936). Julian Hochberg, "Organization and the Gestalt tradition," in E. Carterette and M. Friedman, eds., *Handbook of perception, vol. 1: Historical and philosophical roots of perception* (New York: Academic Press, 1974), discusses the Gestalt influence on perception. Mary Henle tries to explain isomorphism in "Isomorphism: Setting the record straight," *Psychological Research* (1984, *46*: 317–327). The roots of Wertheimer's ideas are discussed in Abraham S. and Edith H. Luchins, "An introduction to the origins of Wertheimer's Gestalt psychologie," *Gestalt Theory* (1982, *4*: 145–171). In a massive doctoral dissertation, Mitchell Graham Ash thoroughly documents and discusses the origin and development of Gestalt psychology in Germany in *The emergence of Gestalt theory: Experimental psychology in Germany 1890–1920*, unpublished doctoral dissertation (Cambridge, MA: Harvard University, 1982), and Ash (1995). The reception of Gestalt psychology in the United States is discussed by Michael Sokal, "The Gestalt psychologists in behaviorist America," *American Historical Review* (1984, *89*: 1240–1263). For Gestalt psychology in relation to philosophy, see T. H. Leahey, "Gestalt psychology," in T. Baldwin, ed., *The Cambridge history of philosophy, 1870–1945* (Cambridge, England: Cambridge University Press, 2003).

Brentano's basic work is *Psychology from an empirical standpoint* (New York: Humanities Press, 1973). For discussions of Brentano, see L. McAlister, ed., *The philosophy of Brentano* (Atlantic Highlands, NJ: Humanities Press, 1976). For the development of phenomenology after Brentano, see H. Philipse, "From idealism and naturalism to phenomenology and existentialism," in T. Baldwin, ed. (2003, cited earlier).

Two other books that contain good information on Gestalt psychology include W. D. Ellis, ed., *A sourcebook of Gestalt psychology* (London: Routledge & Kegan Paul, 1938); and M. Henle, ed., *Documents of Gestalt psychology* (Berkeley: University of California Press, 1961).

This text doesn't say much about social psychology, so see Gustav Jahoda (2007) *A history of social psychology from the eighteenth century Enlightenment to the Second World War* (Cambridge, England: Cambridge University Press).

The Psychology of the Unconscious

INTRODUCTION

The psychology of the unconscious was markedly different from the psychology of consciousness. Wundt and the other psychologists of consciousness focused on the normal, human, adult mind known through introspection, attempting to make an experimental science out of philosophers' traditional questions and theories. The areas of sensation/perception and cognitive psychology largely defined the field, although some attention was given to social, developmental, and animal psychology. Freud's psychology, in contrast, focused on abnormal minds and claimed to unmask consciousness—including normal consciousness—as a self-deceiving puppet of disgusting, primal impulses it dared not acknowledge. Instead of conducting experiments, Freud investigated the mind by clinically probing it, looking for the concealed springs of human conduct in unconscious, primitive residues of childhood and evolution that he claimed to find in his patients' symptoms, dreams, and therapeutic talk.

Freud's character, too, was different from that of the other German founders of psychology. Wundt, his students, and the Gestalt psychologists were, for all their differences, products of Mandarin Germany—cautious and circumspect scholars and scientists. Freud, however, rejected the Mandarin outlook, "scorn[ing] to distinguish culture and civilization" (Freud, 1930/1961). He was born a Jew—but was an atheist proud of his Jewish heritage—and lived in the shadow of oppression by the Mandarin class. Freud created psychoanalysis in part as a political challenge to the rulers of Austria-Hungary (McGrath, 1986; Schorske, 1980).

Freud wanted to be a conquering hero in the mold of Moses, bringer of disagreeable commandments to a disbelieving people. Possibly under the influence of cocaine—he

Sigmund Freud (1856–1939), the founder of psychoanalysis, in a photo taken in 1938, about the time he fled Vienna as it was being seized by the Nazis. *(Courtesy of Library of Congress)*

used it regularly in the late 1880s and 1890s (Crews, 1986)—Freud (1960) described himself to his fiancée, Martha Bernays (February 2, 1886):

> Breuer [sometime friend and collaborator] told me he had discovered that hidden under the surface of timidity there lay in me an extremely daring and fearless human being. I had always thought so, but never dared tell anyone. I have often felt as though I had inherited all the defiance and all the passions with which our ancestors defended their temple and could gladly sacrifice my life for one great moment in history. (p. 202, letter 94)

On February 1, 1899, awaiting the reception of *The Interpretation of Dreams*, Freud wrote to his intimate friend Wilhelm Fliess:

> For I am actually not at all a man of science, not an observer, not an experimenter, not a thinker. I am by temperament nothing but a conquistador—an adventurer, if you want it translated—with all the curiosity, daring, and tenacity characteristic of a man of this sort. Such people are customarily esteemed only if they have been successful, have really discovered something; otherwise they are dropped by the wayside. And that is not altogether unjust. (p. 398)

FREUD AND SCIENTIFIC PSYCHOLOGY

To the world he aimed to conquer, Freud presented psychoanalysis as a revolution. Psychoanalysis, he often said (Gay, 1989), represented the third great blow to human self-esteem. The first blow was Copernicus's demonstration that human beings did not live at the center of the universe. The second blow was Darwin's demonstration that human beings were part of nature—being animals like any other. The third blow, Freud claimed, was his own demonstration that the human ego is not master in its own house.

Freud and Academic Psychology

"Freud is inescapable": Peter Gay (1989) thus summarizes the conquistador's achievement. There can be no doubt that "we all speak Freud whether we know it or not." Freud's terminology and his essential ideas "pervade contemporary ways of thinking about human feelings and conduct" (Gay, 1989, p. xii). Nevertheless, it is both ironic and inevitable that Freud's influence should have been less in academic psychology than in any other field concerned with human affairs save economics. Psychologists of consciousness rejected the existence of the *unconscious*, Freud's indispensable hypothesis. Behaviorists rejected the existence of mind altogether. So it is unsurprising that, apart from occasional recognition of Freud's somewhat literary insights into human motives, academic psychology has largely ignored or rejected psychoanalysis. Rapprochements between academic psychology and psychoanalysis have sometimes been sought (Erdelyi, 1985; Sears, 1985) but never achieved.

Moreover, the isolation of psychoanalysis from academic psychology has been abetted by the development—over Freud's own objections—of psychoanalysis as a branch of medicine. Especially in the United States, an MD degree with specialization in psychiatry became the prerequisite for undertaking training as a psychoanalyst. Isolation became enmity with the professional rivalry that arose between psychiatry and clinical psychology. Psychiatrists have always tended to look on clinical psychologists as poorly trained interlopers in the business of medicine, and in the case of psychoanalysis, this resulted in exclusion of PhD psychologists from training in schools of psychoanalysis, a policy that remains bitterly contentious to the present day.

Freud and Experimental Method

Freud may have regarded himself as a conquistador rather than a scientist, but there is no doubt that Freud shared the goal of the other founders of psychology—to create a psychology that was a science like any other. Freud rejected the suggestion that psychoanalysis offered anything other than a scientific view of the world: "Psycho-analysis, in my opinion, is incapable of creating a *Weltanschauung* of its own. It does not need one; it is a part of science" (Freud, 1932 in Gay, 1989, p. 796). Yet, Freud did not undertake to construct an experimental psychology of the unconscious, nor did he welcome attempts to experimentally verify his ideas. In the 1930s, an American psychologist, Saul Rosenzweig, wrote to Freud about his attempts at experimental testing of psychoanalysis. Freud replied very briefly (February 28, 1934): "I have examined your experimental studies for the verification of psychoanalytic propositions with interest. I cannot put much value on such confirmation because the abundance of reliable observations on which these propositions rest makes them independent of experimental verification. Still, it can do no harm" (quoted by Rosenzweig, 1985, pp. 171–172).

The "abundance of reliable observations" on which Freud erected psychoanalysis consisted of his clinical cases. We are apt to think today of psychoanalysis as primarily a therapy, but Freud did not. Freud originally wanted to be an academic physiologist in the mold of Helmholtz, but turned to private medical practice in order to afford to marry, and he developed psychoanalysis in the context of performing psychotherapy. Nevertheless, he always meant psychoanalysis to be a science and regarded therapeutic success as his distinguishing mark of scientific truth. For Freud, a therapy would be effective if and only if the scientific theory from which it derived was true. He therefore regarded the talk of his patients as scientific data and the analytic session as a scientifically valid method of investigation. Indeed, his remarks to Rosenzweig suggest that he regarded analysis as more than the equal of experimentation as a scientific method. For Freud, successful therapy was not an end in itself, but constituted evidence that psychoanalytic theory was true.

Such dismissal of experimental methodology served to further isolate psychoanalysis from mainstream psychology. Psychoanalysts said that only someone who had been through psychoanalysis was fit to criticize it, leading academic psychologists to regard psychoanalysis more as a cult with an initiation rite than as a science open to all (Sulloway, 1991). Furthermore, reliance on clinical evidence raised more than political difficulties for psychoanalysis as a science. Fechner, Donders, Wundt, and others had introduced experiment to psychology in order to rid it of unscientific subjectivity, replacing armchair introspection with experimental rigor. Psychoanalysis sought to replace armchair introspection with couch introspection, and it could be reasonably asked whether Freud had replaced a bad method with a worse one. After all, the introspective observer in psychoanalysis is a patient: a sick individual wishing to be cured of neurosis, rather than a trained observer committed to the advancement of science. These were not and are not idle concerns, and, as we shall see, they may have played a subterranean role in Freud's greatest challenge, his *seduction error*.

THE FORMATION OF PSYCHOANALYSIS: 1884–1899

Freud and Biology

Like the other founding psychologists, Freud was initially attracted to the idea of approaching psychology through physiology. Freud's situation and ambition as a founder were in large degree the same as the other founders'. He had a medical degree and carried out important work in anatomy and physiology. Ernst Brücke, one of Helmholtz's students who had sworn themselves to reductionism, had taught Freud and influenced him considerably. Thus, Freud's psychology was likely to be physiological for the same reasons as Wundt's, but once Freud took up clinical practice and began to create psychoanalysis as both science and therapy, the path through physiology also exerted two special attractions for him.

First, one charge that could reasonably be leveled against a science built on the talk of neurotic patients was cultural parochialism. Science is supposed to discover universal truths—laws of nature that hold good across time and space. In the case of psychology, this means finding explanations of human behavior that transcend any particular culture or historical era. Living up to this standard of science was vexing enough for experimental psychologists, who could at least point to the rigor and simplicity of their experiments as warrant of their universal character, but such a claim could not plausibly be made for psychoanalytic therapy. However, if therapeutic findings were used to elaborate a neurophysiological theory of mind and behavior, then charges of cultural parochialism might be deflected (Sulloway, 1979). After all, human nervous systems exist apart from culture, so that a theory pitched at the neural level could stake a claim to universal truth.

For Freud, however, the most unique attraction of the path to science through physiology lay in his situation as a clinical neurologist. Today, the term *neurosis* is virtually synonymous with a disorder that is entirely mental ("all in your head"), but in Freud's time, neuroses were viewed as primarily neural disorders. By far the most common neurosis of the time was *hysteria*. In our post-Freudian world, hysteria is called dissociative disorder, defined as a physical symptom having a psychological cause; but in Freud's time, the physical symptoms of hysteria—such things as paralyses and failures of sense perception—were thought to stem from an unknown disorder of the nervous system (Macmillan, 1997). We will discuss the nature of hysteria more fully in the next section.

THE "PROJECT FOR A SCIENTIFIC PSYCHOLOGY" In Freud's case, the physiological path to scientific psychology found fullest expression in a manuscript he never completed, the "Project for a Scientific Psychology" (1950). It was written in a white heat of Newtonian passion (Solomon, 1974) in the fall of 1894 and the spring of 1895. On April 27, 1895, Freud wrote to Fliess, "Scientifically, I am in a bad way; namely caught up in the 'Psychology for neurologists' [Freud's working title], which regularly consumes me totally" (p. 127). On May 25: "a man like me cannot live without a hobbyhorse, without a consuming passion, without—in Schiller's words—a tyrant. I have found one. In its service I know no limits. It is psychology" (p. 129).

Freud (1985) was "tormented by two aims: to examine what shape the theory of mental functioning takes if one introduces quantitative considerations, a sort of economics of nerve forces; and second to peel off from psychopathology a gain for normal psychology" (letter to Fliess of May 25, 1895, p. 129). In the "Project" itself, Freud defined his Newtonian "intention . . . to furnish a psychology that shall be a natural science: that is, to represent psychical processes as quantitatively determinate states of specifiable material particles." He went on to develop a general theory of mind and behavior in entirely physiological and quantitative terms. For example, Freud described motivation as resulting from the buildup of tension at "barriers"—today called synapses—between neurons. This buildup is felt as unpleasure, and its eventual discharge across the barrier is felt as pleasure. Memory was explained (as it is in most neural models today) as changes to the permeability of neuronal barriers (changes in synaptic strength) resulting from repeated firing of connected neurons. In similarly quantitative-neurological ways, Freud explained the full range of "mental" functions from hallucinations to cognition.

Freud's "Project" remains one of the most fascinating but troublesome documents in the history of psychoanalysis. It is fascinating because so much of Freud's psychological theory is introduced in the "Project" in neurological guise, but it is troublesome because it is hard to evaluate Freud's final attitude toward it, or properly place it in the history of psychoanalytic thought. Because he abandoned writing it and later resisted its publication, it is fair to conclude that Freud regarded the "Project" as fatally flawed, but the question remains: Why? The standard account accepted by later Freudians is that, shortly after working on the "Project," Freud undertook a "heroic" self-analysis in which he discovered that the causes of behavior are psychological events occurring in a psychological unconscious, and he consequently abandoned the "Project" as a young man's foolishness. He remained driven by his "tyrant," psychology, but his later theories, like Wundt's, became more psychological. In his clinical work, he came to distinguish between "actual neuroses" and "psychoneuroses." The actual neuroses were true physical diseases, caused by "excess or deficiency of certain nerve-poisons," typically caused by masturbation (Freud, 1908/1953, p. 81). The psychoneuroses, including hysteria, have causes that "are psychogenic, and depend upon the operation of unconscious (repressed) ideational complexes" (p. 81).

FREUD, EVOLUTIONARY BIOLOGY, AND THE TURN TO SEXUALITY On the other hand, Sulloway (1979) has persuasively argued that regarding Freud's self-analysis as the critical event in the history of psychoanalysis is a myth. Sulloway proposes that it was put out by Freud and his followers to obscure Freud's continued reliance on biology as the secret foundation of psychoanalytic theory. Freud gave up the "Project" because he could not construct a mechanism compatible with his main guiding thesis about the origin of neurosis. Whether in the seduction theory or later, Freud always held that adult neurotic symptoms find their ultimate cause in a childhood trauma or disgusting thought. At the time, this event or thought has no pathological effect, but it lies dormant and is unconsciously reawakened, expressed as a symptom, years later.

This view of the etiology of symptoms was so dear to Freud that he gave up neurologizing, but he did not give up biology. According to Sulloway (1979, 1982), Freud turned from mechanistic physiological biology to Lamarckian evolutionary biology to explain human development. For example, most scientists of the day (including Wundt) accepted the "*biogenetic law*" of Ernst Haeckel (1834–1919), Germany's leading Darwinian. According to the biogenetic law—which we now know to be false—"ontogeny recapitulates phylogeny"; that is, the embryological development of any creature repeats its species' evolutionary path. Thus, to casual inspection, a human fetus passes through an amphibian stage, a reptile stage, a simple mammal stage, and so on, until it resembles a miniature human being. Freud simply extended the biogenetic law to include psychological development. He regarded the stages of psychosexual development as recapitulations of the sex life of our predecessor species, including latency as a recapitulation of the ice ages!

Haeckel's theory of recapitulation provided an explanation of the delay between the events that caused hysteria and its manifestation in symptoms. At this point in his career, Freud believed that hysteria was caused by sexual abuse of young children, but that the abuse caused no immediate pathology. Instead, the experience lay dormant in memory and unconsciously caused symptoms to appear in adulthood. Freud had not yet developed his theory of childhood sexuality, and he could claim that the sexual trauma had no immediate effect on the child because it was not developmentally appropriate. Because the victim was asexual, the experience meant nothing. It became meaningful when sexuality emerged in adulthood, and the repressed memory exerted a toxic effect, throwing the patient into hysteria.

Freud deployed his Haeckel-inspired theory of development as a convenient way out of many difficulties. For example, in order for a child to develop castration anxiety, he or she did not have to see that opposite-sexed people have different genitals; the knowledge was written in the genes. In Sulloway's view, then, Freud ceased to seek the cause of psychoneuroses in the physiochemical mechanics of the nervous system, but he never gave up the search for an organic basis for neurotic and normal psychological development.

Central to Freud's new biological conception of human development and behavior was the sex instinct. Sex provided a basis for constructing a truly universal and naturalistic scientific psychology because it was neither species- nor culture-specific. Following the path of the Enlightenment and going against the German Mandarins, Freud wanted a psychology shorn of scientifically irrelevant cultural factors. The ubiquity of the sex drive provided its foundation. Freud always supposed that the list of biological needs was short: hunger, thirst, self-preservation, and sex (and later, aggression). If one accepts this list as exhaustive, then one has a problem explaining much of human behavior. It is clear that animal behavior always seems to serve one of these needs, but it is equally clear that human behavior does not. Humans build cathedrals, paint pictures, write novels, think of philosophies, and conduct science, none of which immediately meets any biological need. Earlier writers on human motivation, from Plato to Franz Joseph Gall to the Scottish realists, were not faced with this problem because they supposed that human beings have special motives that lead to religion, art, philosophy, and science.

Freud, however, by taking a biologically reductive and simplifying view of motivation, accepted a short list of drives and needed to show that behavior not directly caused by them was, in reality, indirectly caused by them. It had to be the case that instincts could be redirected from their innately determined channels into other, less biological ones. Hunger, thirst, and self-preservation are poor candidates for rechanneling because satisfying them is necessary for the survival of the organism. Sexuality, on the other hand, is a powerful motive whose satisfaction can be postponed or even abandoned; the animal may be unhappy, but it lives. Sexuality, then, is the biological motive most capable of displacement from sexual satisfaction into more socially acceptable and creative activity, or into neurosis. Freud was not the first to find in sex the hidden cause of human achievement; romantic poets and philosophers such as Schopenhauer talked about the sublimation of sexuality into higher things, as did Freud's friend Fliess (Sulloway, 1979). Only Freud, however, made sublimation part of a general theory of human mind and behavior.

Moreover, the sexual drive is the one human societies take the greatest interest in regulating. Societies universally regulate the sort of person one may take as a sex partner and marry, while taking no interest in one's dining companions. It appeared to Freud, then, that society actively seeks to rechannel sex away from its native goal toward more civilized ones, but often has succeeded in making neuroses instead.

Sex played the key role in the formation of neuroses, giving Freud's science a biological foundation (Sulloway, 1979). In the case of the actual neuroses, "the sexual factor is the essential one in [their] causation" (Freud, 1908/1953), since the "nerve poisons" that cause actual neuroses are generated by wrong sexual practices such as adult masturbation or sexual abstinence (Sulloway, 1979). The situation with regard to psychoneuroses was different, with sexuality playing a more psychological role. The most purely biological factor in psychoneurosis was the prior state of the nervous system because "hereditary influence is more marked" than in the actual neuroses (Freud, 1908/1953). Sexuality came into play as the factor working on the nervous system to cause the symptoms of hysteria. In Freud's early theorizing, sexual seduction of a child provided the trauma that would later blossom into neurosis. In his later theory, childhood sexual fantasies provided the kernels of adult neuroses.

By 1905, Freud had written the founding works of psychoanalysis, *Interpretation of Dreams* and *Three Essays on the Theory of Sexuality*, and had sorted out what was biological and what was psychological in psychoanalysis:

> Some of my medical colleagues have looked upon my theory of hysteria as a purely psychological one, and have for that reason pronounced it ipso facto incapable of solving a pathological problem. . . . [But] it is the therapeutic technique alone which is purely psychological; the theory does not by any means fail to point out that neuroses have an organic basis—though it is true that it does not look for that basis in any pathological anatomical changes. . . . No one, probably, will be inclined to deny the sexual function the character of an organic factor, and it is the sexual function that I look upon as the foundation of hysteria and of the psychoneuroses in general. (1905b, in Gay, 1989, p. 372)

Freud the Sexual Reformer

Freud came to find in sex the main motive in human life. Sex furnished an organic basis for neurosis and a universal biological basis for his theoretical psychology. Another reason was his "discovery" of childhood sexuality as the root cause of neuroses (see later discussion). A third is found in social history: Men and women of Freud's day really did find sexuality hard to cope with.

Freud and other physicians found themselves presented with problems rooted in the nineteenth century's struggles with sexuality. The cause of the problem was straightforward. As societies develop economically, they experience an important demographic transition from large families to small ones. In rural and village societies, children are economic resources—hands to be put to work as soon as possible and the main support in their parents' old age. In industrially developed societies, children become economic liabilities. Costly to raise and educate before they can join the workforce, they become drains on parents' income. As standards of living rise, children become increasingly less attractive economically, and parents begin to have fewer children.

The middle classes of Victorian Europe felt most acutely the problem of controlling reproduction without modern contraceptives. To succeed economically, they had to work hard and exert enormous self-control, including control of potentially costly reproduction. They looked on the large families of rural and laboring classes, for whom children were still exploitable resources, with a mixture of horror and salacious envy. The middle class abhorred the squalor and misery of lower-class lives, but was envious of their sexual freedom. Poet George Meredith expressed both attitudes: "You burly lovers on the village green/Yours is a lower and a happier star!" (quoted by Gay, 1986). Freud, too, saw greater sexual happiness among the poor without wishing to join them. Describing for a lecture audience two imagined case histories, he said, "Sexual activity appeared to the caretaker's daughter just as natural and unproblematic in later life as it had in childhood" and is "free from neurosis," while the landlord's daughter "experienced the impact of education and acknowledged its claims," turned from sex with "distaste," and became neurotic (quoted by Gay, 1986). Yet Freud, like most educated and agnostic or atheist Victorians, continued to live on nerve, never prescribing sexual liberation. He wrote to his fiancée, Martha Bernays (August 29, 1883; Freud, 1960, letter 18, p. 50), "The rabble live without constraint while we deprive ourselves." We bourgeois do so "to maintain our integrity. . . . We keep ourselves for something, we know not what, and this habit of constantly suppressing our natural drives gives us the character of refinement" (quoted by Gay, 1986, p. 400).

There is abundant evidence that the struggle for control over sexual desires among the middle classes—from which Freud drew most of his patients—was intense:

> Where should we find that reverence for the female sex, that tenderness towards their feelings, that deep devotion of the heart to them, which is the beautiful and purifying part of love? Is it not certain that all of the delicate, the chivalric which still pervades our sentiments, may be traced to the repressed, and therefore hallowed and elevated passion?

So wrote W. R. Greg in 1850 (quoted by Houghton, 1957, p. 380). Victorians did not accept the animal part of their nature, whether sexual or simply sensual. Wrote the anonymous author of an antismoking pamphlet: "Smoking . . . is liked because it gives agreeable sensations. Now it is a positive objection to a thing that it gives agreeable sensations. An earnest man will expressly avoid what gives agreeable sensations" (p. 236). (Earnestness was a cardinal virtue to Victorians.) Victorian culture and religion thundered against pleasure, especially sexual pleasure, and Victorians were burdened by an oppressive sense of guilt. Like a medieval saint, British Liberal Prime Minister William Gladstone recorded his least sin and grieved over it. Guilt was heightened by constant temptation. Prostitution was rampant; men and women, boys and girls—all could be had for a price. The anonymous author of *My Secret Life*, a sexual autobiography, claimed to have seduced over 2,000 people of all ages and sexual orientations, and engaged in every vice. Boys at the finest private schools were sexually abused. The Victorians were caught between stern conscience and compelling temptation.

Freud (1912/1953) named as the most common cause of impotence the inability of men to love where they lusted and lust where they loved, and not only because sleeping with one's wife might beget children. Physicians often taught, and men came to believe, that women, at least middle-class women, had no sexual feelings, and men felt guilty about thrusting brutish sexuality on their wives.

The results were impotence at worst and greatly inhibited sex at best. Men could fully lust after prostitutes, but these women were degraded by their very sexuality, made unworthy of love. Middle-class women, for their part, were trapped and inhibited by being idealized and idolized. Writing to his fiancée on November 15, 1883, Freud (1960, letter 28, p. 76) wrote against feminism: "Am I to think of my delicate, sweet girl as a competitor? . . . Women's delicate natures . . . are so much in need of protection. [Emancipation would take away] the most lovely thing the world has to offer us: our ideal of womanhood." Perhaps Freud was typical of many men of his day. On October 3, 1897, at age 41, Freud wrote Fliess, "Sexual excitement, too, is no longer of use for someone like me." From about 1900, the year *Interpretation of Dreams* came out, Freud ceased having sex with his wife (Decker, 1981), but there is little evidence he took up with anyone else (Gay, 1988).

Not with standing, or perhaps because of, his own situation, Freud sided with the movement of sexual reform led by people such as Havelock Ellis. In 1905, Freud gave a deposition before a commission looking into liberalization of Austria's laws on marriage and sexuality. Freud testified in favor of "legalization of relations between the sexes outside of marriage, according a greater measure of sexual freedom and curtailing restrictions on that freedom" (Boyer, 1978, p. 100, original German; p. 92, English translation). Ten years later, Freud repeated this sentiment in a letter to one of his leading American supporters, the neurologist J. J. Putnam: "Sexual morality—as society, in its most extreme form, the American, defines it—seems to me very contemptible. I advocate an incomparably freer sexual life" (quoted by Gay, 1988, p. 143). In *"Civilized" Sexual Morality and Modern Nervousness* (1908/1953), Freud painted a devastating portrait of the effects of civilized marriage. Men become impotent, as we've seen, or "undesirably immoral" by finding sex outside marriage, but women, suffering from a double standard, are made ill:

> [Can] sexual intercourse in legitimate marriage offer full compensation for the restraint before marriage[?] The abundance of material supporting a reply in the negative is . . . overwhelming. We must above all keep in mind that our civilized sexual morality restricts sexual intercourse in marriage itself . . . and all the contraceptives available hitherto impair sexual enjoyment. . . . [The "physical tenderness" and "mental affection" between husband and wife disappear] and under the disappointments of matrimony women succumb to severe, lifelong neurosis. . . . Marital unfaithfulness would . . . be a . . . probable cure for the neurosis resulting from marriage. . . . [But] the more earnestly [a wife] has submitted to the demands of civilization, the more does she fear this way of escape, and in conflict between her desires and her sense of duty she again will seek refuge in neurosis. Nothing protects her virtue so securely as illness. (pp. 89–90)

Freud the clinician identified sex as the root of his patients' problems because, at that time and place, his patients had a hard time accommodating sex alongside their economic and moral aspirations. If Freud's emphasis on sexuality sometimes seems alien and implausible today, it may be because the sexual reforms he championed (but did not gain from) came about and because technology has improved contraception. Sex is still a problem in the era of HIV/AIDS, but not in the way it was for Freud's civilized sufferers.

Freud the Physician: Studying Hysteria

THE PUZZLE OF HYSTERIA The most common "neurotic" disorder of Freud's time was hysteria. The diagnosis was ancient, harking back to Greek times; *hyster* is the Greek word for "womb," and it was long thought that only women could be hysterical because only women have wombs. The signs and symptoms of hysteria varied greatly over the centuries, and by the nineteenth century a wide variety of them were labeled as "hysterical." Today, cases of hysteria, and its nosological descendent, conversion reaction, scarcely exist. Asking *why* is important for understanding not only Freud's thinking but also the impact of psychology on society.

In the nineteenth century, medicine, including psychiatry and neurology, was just beginning to be placed on scientific foundations, as diseases began to be linked to underlying pathologies. One of the early triumphs of scientific diagnosis, for example, was linking tuberculosis to a specific pathogenic cause, the tubercle bacillus. Many signs and symptoms of disease could not yet, however, be traced to any organic pathology. Hysteria became a sort of diagnostic dumping ground for such symptoms. For example, we will learn that in the case of Freud's patient Dora, one of her "hysterical" symptoms was a persistent cough. Some alleged cases of hysteria were almost certainly cases of diseases not yet recognized by nineteenth-century medicine. Two likely candidates are focal epilepsy (Webster, 1995) and neurosyphilis (Shorter, 1997). In focal epilepsy, only small portions of the brain are subject to seizure, resulting in transient pathologies of perception and motor control, precisely the sort of symptoms associated with "hysteria." A person infected with syphilis shows a few immediate symptoms in the genitals, but, left untreated, the spirochete lies dormant in the body, and can attack the brain and nervous system many years later causing serious psychological disorders. Because of the great time lag between infection and the appearance of psychological symptoms, connecting the two—diagnosing neurosyphilis—was difficult, and it is possible that many such patients were called "hysterical."

Whatever the underlying reality of the disease "hysteria" may have been, nineteenth-century physicians were coming to look upon hysteria as a physical disease of unknown origin. Before the advent of scientific medicine, hysteria had been viewed as a moral failing, whether a weakness of will or a possession by evil spirits. William James, who suffered from "nervous" diseases himself, spoke for enlightened medical opinion and long-suffering patients when he said, in his 1896 *Lowell Lectures* on abnormal mental states, "Poor hysterics! First treated as victims of sexual trouble . . . then of moral perversity and mendacity . . . then of imagination . . . honest disease not thought of" (quoted by Myers, 1986, ellipses in original, p. 5). Ironically, in the same year, 1896, Freud gave a paper on hysteria before the Society for Psychiatry and Neurology in which he broached for the first time his view that hysteria had a psychological—specifically sexual—etiology. Chairing the session was the greatest student of sexual psychopathology of the day, Richard von Krafft-Ebing, who pronounced it a "scientific fairytale." With James, Krafft-Ebing and the rest of the medical establishment—Freud called them "donkeys"—regarded the strictly medical view of hysteria as a great advance (Sulloway, 1979).

Unfortunately for patients, physical etiology for hysteria prescribed physical treatments, no matter how mysterious the malady. Treatments for hysteria were often "heroic" in the extreme. The leading treatment was "electrotherapy." Its milder form was "faradization," for which Freud bought the needed equipment in 1886. The patient, naked or lightly covered, was seated in water with her feet on a negative electrode, while the physician probed her body from head to foot with a positive electrode or (for "sensitive" patients) with his "electrical hand," the current passing through his own body. Treatment sessions lasted 10 to 20 minutes and were frequently repeated. Many patients had severe adverse reactions, ranging from burns to dizziness or defecation.

Other therapies included suffocation, beating with wet towels; ridicule; hard, icy showers; insertion of tubes in the rectum; application of hot irons to the spine; and, in "intractable" cases, ovariectomies and cauterization of the clitoris. Such treatments may fairly be regarded as abuse of women by powerful men, but it should also be noted that treatment for some male disorders was equally "heroic," involving, for example, cauterization of parts of the genitalia (Decker, 1991). It should also be remembered that medicine was just beginning to be based on scientific research.

Physicians had discarded ancient theories of disease, but were just beginning to develop better ones such as the germ theory. Yet, they still had to treat suffering patients, and therefore grasped any treatment that might work. A parallel may be drawn between psychiatric treatment in the nineteenth century and cancer treatment in the twenty-first century. Cancer is a horrible disease that is only now yielding up its secrets, and physicians have had to make their patients undergo painful regimes of chemotherapy, radiation therapy, and surgery, even when such treatments offer modest hopes of a cure. Some of the appeal of psychoanalysis, like some "alternative" treatments for cancer, must have resided in the alternative it offered to medical therapies. Better to lie on a couch and be shocked to discover one's sexual secrets than sit on an electrode and be shocked with electricity!

CHARCOT AND FREUD   An important change in thinking about hysteria began with Charcot, and Freud brought Charcot's new ideas back with him to Vienna after studying with him in 1885–1886. While Charcot continued to believe that there was an inherited, organic factor in hysteria, he also proposed an important psychological source for hysteria. Charcot took up the study of a class of traumatic disorders called "railway spine" (Charcot, 1873/1996). Industrial workers, mostly in the railroads—hence, the name—experienced psychological and neurological symptoms that might plausibly have been caused by on-the-job accidents such as falls. Charcot argued that many such cases were less medical in origin than they were psychological:

> [M]any of those nervous accidents designated under the name railway spine . . . whether appearing in man or in woman [are] simply hysterical manifestations. . . . It is hysteria that is at the bottom of all these nervous lesions . . . [Specifically, they are] a consequence of the psychical nervous shock resulting from the accident; frequently, moreover, they do not come on immediately after the accident but some time afterwards. (p. 98)

Charcot (1873/1996) went on to say that despite a "blow on the head, [or] a concussion" the underlying pathology in hysteria lies not in a physical lesion to the brain but a "dynamic"—that is to say, mental, lesion (p. 99). Here is the source of Freud's delayed impact theory of hysteria discussed earlier in connection with the "Project." Note that Charcot's formulation for the first time extended the diagnosis of hysteria to men.

When Charcot's work is examined more closely, we find emerging another dimension of hysteria—that it was a historically constructed disorder. Charcot believed that hysteria was a unitary disease having a single underlying pathology (traumatic shock to a hereditarily weak nervous system) and a unique set of defining systems. His model was medicine as it was then emerging, in which specific symptom clusters were being linked to specific pathogens, as in the case of tuberculosis already mentioned. Charcot thus assumed that hysteria, like tuberculosis, was a disease that existed independently of scientific medicine, awaiting precise description and effective cure.

Many historians now believe that hysteria was not a preexisting disease discovered by medicine, but a social role scripted by medicine and adopted by suggestible patients as a way of finding meaning in their lives. Hysteria is connected in the history of psychology with hypnotism. Charcot, along with French clinical psychologists, generally believed that the hypnotic trance was a genuine altered state of consciousness rooted in changes to the nervous system caused by induction of the trance. This belief would ultimately be defeated by the Nancy school of hypnosis, which regarded hypnotism as simply enhanced susceptibility to suggestion. Thus, the phenomena of hypnotism are whatever the hypnotist wants them to be and the subject expects them to be (Spanos, 1996). Similarly, the symptoms of hysteria were what doctors said they were in their diagnostic manuals and what patients expected them to be once they accepted the diagnosis of hysteria. The patient on

Charcot's arm (in the next painting) sees clearly on the wall what she is expected to do. In neither hypnotism nor hysteria was there an underlying disease entity or distinct mental, much less neurological, state.

The story of hysteria provides one of the central lessons to be learned from the history of psychology. Science is the view from nowhere that discovers and describes the world as it is apart from human wishes, hopes, or thoughts. Psychological science is the quest to discover human nature, but human nature, even human psychopathology, does not exist entirely apart from human society. In the Middle Ages, exorcists sincerely thought demons were real, and their sermons, tracts, and questions led some people to sincerely think they were demon possessed, and they acted as they thought the demon possessed should. The expectation created the reality that confirmed the expectation. In the nineteenth century, psychiatrists such as Charcot thought hysteria was a real disease, and their diagnoses and teachings led some people to believe they were hysterics, and they learned to behave as they thought hysterics should. The expectation created the reality that confirmed the expectation. We should never forget that what psychologists say is human nature may create cultural scripts that ordinary people unwittingly enact, seeming to confirm as a scientific fact what is an artifact of the theories invented by psychologists. Unlike physics or chemistry, psychology can create its own reality and mistake it for universal truth.

Portrait of Jean Martin Charcot. *(Courtesy of Library of Congress)*

Charcot's ideas about hysteria created special difficulties for Freud. We have already seen that Freud's theory of the delayed action of psychological trauma was a version of Charcot's theory of the etiology of hysteria. But Charcot's assumption that hysteria was a unitary disease entity, abetted by Freud's deep commitment to a mechanistic conception of determinism acquired from his training in the new reflex theory of the brain, caused further problems for Freud's treatment of hysteria and of the mind more generally. We may again draw a useful comparison to tuberculosis (Macmillan, 1997). Tuberculosis had recently been shown to be a unitary disease uniquely caused by a singular pathogen, the tubercle bacillus. Freud, following Charcot, assumed similarly that hysteria was a unitary disease with a single cause. We will see Freud frantically searching for a single "source of the Nile," a single cause of hysteria. He changed his mind about what that cause is, but he never doubted that there was a one-to-one match between a set of symptoms (hysteria) and a single underlying cause. Driven by scientific ambition, he did not consider that some experiences sometimes cause certain kinds of unhappiness in some people, and that alleviating such suffering is a worthy, even noble, undertaking. Instead, he forced his patients onto the Procrustean couch of his single-minded theories about the origin and cure of the neuroses, reproducing Charcot's error (Macmillan, 1997). Freud wrote to his follower Carl Jung about one long-suffering patient:

> [S]he is beyond any possibility of therapy, but it is still her duty to sacrifice herself to science. (quoted by Crews, 1990, p. 39)

STUDIES IN HYSTERIA (1895) AND ANNA O. After returning from Paris and his studies with Charcot, Freud collaborated with his Viennese mentor, Joseph Breuer (1842–1925) on investigations into hypnosis and hysteria. This work culminated in Freud's first book, *Studies in Hysteria* (1895/1966). Breuer was a distinguished general physician and physiologist who, in 1880, first treated the patient whose case starts the story of psychoanalytic therapy. Called Anna O. in *Studies*, Bertha von Pappenheim was a young, middle-class woman who, like many others, had to nurse a sick father (as Anna Freud later nursed Sigmund). She fell prey to hysteria, primarily minor paralyses and difficulties in speaking and hearing. Treating her over a period of time, Breuer found that she gained some symptomatic relief by falling into autohypnosis and talking about her symptoms, recovering, while doing so, forgotten events that had caused them. For example, her inability to drink water from a glass was traced to having seen a dog licking water from a glass, and when she recovered this memory she immediately drank from a glass again. Despite continued treatment, Anna O. showed no continued improvement and, in fact, had to be hospitalized at one point. The statement in *Studies* that she got well was false, and she did not experience a hysterical pregnancy naming Breuer as the father, as analytic legend has it.

In some respects, Anna invented psychotherapy, for she was one of a number of reported cases in the nineteenth century in which hysterical patients guided doctors to their cures (Macmillan, 1997). In Anna's case, she set her own timetable for therapy, placed herself in hypnosis, and led herself to the precipitating causes of her symptoms—a procedure she named the talking cure. She was an intelligent and forceful woman who went on to an important, influential, and successful career as the founder of social work in Germany. Despite being present at the creation, however, she never had kind words for psychoanalysis.

Freud had nothing to do with the case of Anna O., but talked Breuer into using her case as the centerpiece of a theory about the cause and cure of hysteria. The case of Anna O. was tidied up, and Freud contributed the rest of the case histories which, together with a theoretical chapter, comprise *Studies in Hysteria*. Freud and Breuer presented *Studies in Hysteria* as an extension of

"Charcot's concept of traumatic hysteria to hysteria in general. Hysterical symptoms . . . are related, sometimes clearly, sometimes in symbolic disguise, to a determined psychic trauma" (quoted by Ellenberger, 1970, p. 486). In the theoretical chapter, Breuer and Freud argued that hysterics fall ill because they "suffer mainly from reminiscences"; that is, they experience an emotional trauma that is repressed. Instead of working through the negative emotions aroused by the event, the affect is "strangulated"—repressed—along with the memory itself, but the affect survives in the unconscious and manifests itself as a symptom. Under hypnosis, the experience is relived fully: The affect is unstrangulated, or "abreacted," and the symptom connected with the event disappears. Ellenberger (1970) and Macmillan (1997) point out that, in Anna O.'s case, the abreaction described in the book never took place. Breuer's rediscovered clinical notes showed that Anna got relief from simply remembering events, not reliving them.

Freud soon found that hypnosis was not the only way to tap unconscious wishes and ideas. Patients could slowly plumb their unconscious during sessions of uninhibited talk guided by the interpretations of the therapist. In 1896, Freud first used the term *psychoanalysis* to describe his new, nonhypnotic technique (Sulloway, 1979). *Studies in Hysteria* marks the transition from Freud's strictly physiological view of the mind and of psychopathology, still on view in the "Project," to the so-called pure psychology of psychoanalysis.

In the same year, Freud's rejection of Breuer began. Breuer the scientist was too cautious for Freud the conquistador. Freud rejected Breuer because Freud was a hedgehog and Breuer a fox; he confided in a letter to Fliess on March 1, 1896 (1985):

> According to him [Breuer] I should have to ask myself every day whether I am suffering from moral insanity or *paranoia scientifica*. Yet, I regard myself as the more normal one. I believe that he will never forgive that in the *Studies* I dragged him along and involved him in something where he unfailingly knows three candidates for the position of one truth and abhors all generalizations, regarding them as presumptuous. . . . Will the two of us experience the same thing with each other? (p. 175)

For his part, Breuer agreed: "Freud is a man given to absolute and exclusive formulations; this is a psychical need which, in my opinion, leads to excessive generalization" (quoted by Crews, 1986). Breuer was the first of several friend-collaborators used and then discarded by Freud. Years later, when Breuer was an old man hobbling along the street with his daughter, they saw Freud; Breuer threw his arms out in greeting, but Freud hurried past giving no sign of recognition (Roazen, 1974). An even more bitter estrangement awaited Wilhelm Fliess.

The Seduction Error and the Creation of Psychoanalysis

It was not just sexuality but *childhood sexuality* that Freud claimed to find as the root of neuroses. If some of Freud's contemporaries found his emphasis on sex shocking, many more found shocking his postulation of childhood sexuality. Asserting the existence of sexual feelings in childhood was central to the psychoanalytic strategy for explaining human behavior. Without childhood sexual drives, there could be no *Oedipus complex*, whose happy or unhappy resolution held the key to later normality or neurosis. Childhood sexuality and the Oedipus complex are also crucial to the whole idea of depth psychology. Freud located the causes of neurosis—and, by implication, happiness—entirely in the minds of his patients. Their personal situations were not the ultimate cause of sufferers' problems, Freud said. The feelings they had had as children were. Consequently, therapy consisted of adjusting a patient's inner life, not changing the circumstances in which she or he lived. Health would come when a patient resolved the difficulties he or she had when he or she was five years old, not the difficulties he or she faced today.

The central episode in the history of psychoanalysis was Freud's abandonment of his seduction theory of hysteria—in which he had asserted that hysteria was caused by childhood sexual seductions—and its replacement by the Oedipus complex. Looking back on the history of psychoanalysis, Freud (1925) spoke of a curious, early episode in which he was told by all of his women patients that their fathers had sexually seduced them. Freud said he soon came to realize that these stories were not true. The seductions had never really happened, but reflected unconscious *phantasies*[1] of having sexual relations with the parent of the opposite sex. These phantasies were the core of the Oedipus complex, the crucible of personality in psychoanalytic theory.

In recent years, especially following the publication of the complete and unexpurgated letters of Freud to Fliess, the seduction mistake has occupied center stage in Freud scholarship, and the ensuing controversies have generated, at times, more heat than light. I will first narrate the seduction mistake episode as it unfolds in the letters Freud wrote to Fliess; Freud later tried to have these letters destroyed (Ferris, 1998). Then, I will turn to modern critics' ideas about how and why Freud committed the seduction mistake, revealing that Freud misrepresented the event in his later statements. Before starting out, it is important to observe that the very foundations of psychoanalysis are at stake. Anna Freud, daughter and loyal disciple, wrote to Jeffrey Masson, controversial critic of the seduction episode: "Keeping up the seduction theory would mean to abandon the Oedipus complex, and with it the whole importance of phantasy life, conscious or unconscious phantasy. In fact, I think there would have been no psychoanalysis afterwards" (quoted by Masson, 1984b, p. 59).

THE CURIOUS EPISODE OF THE SEDUCTION ERROR   As he was writing the "Project," Freud was equally excited by making apparent progress on the cause and cure of hysteria. Writing to Fliess on October 15, 1895, "in the throes of writing fever," he asked, "Have I revealed the great clinical secret to you . . .? Hysteria is the consequence of a presexual sexual shock. . . . The shock is . . . later transformed into [self-]reproach . . . hidden in the unconscious, . . . effective only as memories" (1985, p. 144). Five days later, Freud exclaimed, "Other confirmations concerning the neuroses are pouring in on me. The thing is really true and genuine" (p. 147). On October 31, he told Fliess that "I perpetrated three lectures on hysteria in which I was very imprudent. I am now inclined to be arrogant" (p. 148).

So, in April 1896, Freud delivered the paper that Krafft-Ebing (1840–1902) called a "scientific fairytale," containing his seduction theory of hysteria. As we have seen, in *Studies in Hysteria*, Freud and Breuer had proposed that the kernel of every hysterical symptom is a repressed traumatic event. Freud now claimed, based on the psychoanalytic recollections of his patients, that there was a single traumatic event at the heart of hysteria—seduction of sexually innocent children by their fathers. Here we see in operation Freud's commitment to finding a single cause for what he took to be the unitary disease of hysteria. Krafft-Ebing and the other "donkeys" of the medical establishment hooted at the theory for being a reversion to the prescientific conceptions of hysteria they had worked so hard to escape.

However, Freud's enthusiasm for the seduction theory turned to ashes. On September 21, 1897, Freud confessed to his friend Fliess that perhaps the seduction theory was a fairytale after all:

---

[1] When Freud wrote of a "phantasie," he meant a mental fantasy that occurred unconsciously; "fantasy" referred to the ordinary sort of conscious fantasy. Thus, when Freud said that children had "phantasies" about sex with their parents during the Oedipal period, he meant that the children never consciously experienced these desires or thoughts.

"I want to confide in you immediately the great secret that has been slowly dawning on me in the last few months. I no longer believe my neurotica [theory of the neuroses]." The stories of seduction told by his patients were untrue; they had not been seduced after all. Freud advanced four reasons for giving up the seduction theory:

1. Therapeutic failure: "disappointment in my efforts to bring a single analysis to a real conclusion; the running away [of previously successful patients]; the absence of the complete successes on which I had counted." Believing that only a true theory of the mind could cure psychopathology, Freud was prepared to abandon the seduction theory because it did not cure patients.

2. "The surprise that in all cases, the father, not excluding my own [this phrase was omitted from the 1954 edition of the Freud-Fliess letters], had to be accused of being perverse" when "surely such widespread perversions are not very probable." Hysteria was a common disorder. If child sexual abuse was the sole cause of hysteria, it must follow that sexual abuse was rampant, and Freud considered that unlikely. Moreover, Freud knew of cases in which sexually abused children had been abused but had not become hysterical, ruling out the one-to-one mapping of disease onto a singular cause.

3. "The certain insight that there are no indications of reality in the unconscious, so that one cannot distinguish between truth and [emotionally believed] fiction. . . . (Accordingly there would remain the solution that the sexual fantasy invariably seizes upon the theme of the parents)." In this sentence, Freud moves toward the concept of the Oedipus complex. The unconscious simply mistakes childhood sexual phantasies for real events, and tells them to the therapist as seductions that really took place.

4. Such stories are not found in delirium, when all mental defenses break down. In dementia, Freud believed, repressive defenses against unpleasant wishes and memories vanish. Thus, if people were regularly seduced as children, then psychotic patients, unafraid of such memories, should reveal them.

Freud was so shaken that "I was ready to give up two things: the complete resolution of neurosis and the certain knowledge of its etiology in childhood." Nevertheless, the conquistador felt no sense of "weakness" or "shame." Instead, Freud wrote, "I have more the feeling of a victory than a defeat" and he hoped that "this doubt merely represents an episode in the advance toward further insight. . . . In spite of all this I am in very good spirits" (1985, pp. 264–266).

At this point, Freud's self-analysis played its dramatic role in the tale of psychoanalysis. Freud reports the critical revelation, the discovery of his own childhood sexuality, in a letter to Fliess on October 3, 1897. Freud claimed to have remembered an event on a train trip when he was 2½ years old: "[M]y libido towards matrem was awakened . . . we must have spent the night together and there must have been an opportunity of seeing her nudam (1985, p. 268)." On October 15, Freud announced, "My self-analysis is the most essential thing I have at present and promises to become of the greatest value to me if it reaches its end" (p. 270). Further, he declared his own experience to be universal. In his "own case," Freud had learned of "being in love with my mother and jealous of my father, and I now consider it a universal event in early childhood" (p. 272). This is quite a leap of faith, from a single reconstructed memory to a claim of scientific universality!

Now, Freud concluded, we can understand the power of *Oedipus Rex* and *Hamlet*. As he suggested in his letter to Fliess, Freud now regarded the seduction stories as Oedipal fantasies from childhood, falsely recalled as memories. This resolution allowed Freud to retain his treasured view that neuroses result from the unconscious reawakening of childhood events. In the old theory, the events were childhood sexual seductions; in the new theory, the events were childhood sexual fantasies.

The psychoanalytic legend concludes by saying that Freud heroically discovered the existence of childhood sexuality and the Oedipus complex by giving up his old theory and constructing the new one out of his own, unsparingly honest, self-interrogation.

WHAT REALLY HAPPENED A consensus has begun to emerge among historians and critics of psychoanalysis about what really happened in the seduction mistake episode. It appears that Freud either bullied his patients into reporting childhood seductions or foisted such stories upon them, and he later lied about the whole seduction episode (Cioffi, 1972, 1974, 1984; Crews, 1999; Esterson, 1993; Schatzman, 1992).

A place to begin the revisionist account of the seduction episode is to examine the papers on the etiology of hysteria that Krafft-Ebing said were a scientific fairytale. The psychoanalytic legend begun by Freud says that Freud was told by his female patients of being sexually seduced by their fathers. However, in Freud's published reports, the seducers are never the parents. They are usually other children, sometimes adults such as tutors or governesses, and occasionally an unspecified adult relative, but never a parent. Either Freud misdescribed the data to his fellow psychiatrists, or there were no Oedipal-phantasy stories at all. More serious is the likelihood that Freud's patients never told him any stories of sexual abuse at all.

Freud's critics have demonstrated that, from early in his career, Freud believed in sexual causes of neurotic disorders, and we have seen that Freud believed in Charcot's traumatic theory of hysteria. The seduction mistake was the result of combining these beliefs with Freud's aggressive therapeutic techniques. Although psychoanalysis eventually became the epitome of nondirective therapy, in which the therapist says very little, offering interpretive insights only as gentle nudges to the patient, Freud's actual practice was very different. At least in his early cases, Freud was highly directive and interpretive, showering his patients with sexual interpretations of their condition, and wearing them down until they agreed with his view of their behavior (Crews, 1986; Decker, 1991; Rieff, 1979). As befits a conquistador, Freud was supremely confident of his ability to discern secrets hidden even from a patient's own consciousness: "[N]o mortal can keep a secret. If his lips are silent, he chatters with his fingertips; betrayal oozes out of him at every pore" (Freud, 1905b). Freud wrote of finding facts that "I did not hesitate to use against her [the patient Dora]" (Freud, 1905b). In the paper he gave to the Vienna Society, Freud described "boldly demand[ing] confirmation of our suspicions from the patient. We must not be led astray by initial denials" (Esterson, 1993, p. 17), and he reported having at least once "laboriously forced some piece of knowledge" on a patient (p. 18). His patients certainly resisted. "The fact is, that these patients never repeat these stories spontaneously, nor do they ever . . . present the physician with the complete recollection of a scene of this kind" (Schatzman, 1992, p. 34). Before conquering the world, Freud first conquered his patients.

Freud enjoyed forcing his patients to accept what he, Freud, regarded as the truth, and he interpreted every resistance as a sign that he was getting near a great secret. Given Freud's therapeutic technique, if he were on the path of childhood sexuality and a single traumatic cause of hysteria, as his critics show he was, surely his patients would produce stories to support it. Cioffi (1972, 1973, 1974, 1984) claims that Freud's patients invented the stories of their seductions in order to placate their conqueror, who was, no doubt, pleased to find verification of his hypotheses. Esterson (1993) and Schatzman (1992) think he "deduced" the seduction stories and forced them on his patients. In either case, it is no wonder his patients ran away.[2]

---

[2]The most widely publicized of Freud's critics is Jeffrey Masson (see bibliography and references), who says that Freud discovered childhood sexual abuse only to walk away from it, condemning abused children to psychiatrically imposed silence. Masson's theory can be easily dismissed because it rests on the premise, now discredited, that Freud was, in fact, told of parental child sexual abuse. He was not, and it is likely that he heard no stories of abuse at the hands of anyone. Moreover, Freud, like all psychiatrists of the time, was well aware that children are sexually abused. The question for Freud was not whether children are sexually abused, which he knew to be a reality, but whether such abuse causes hysteria (Cioffi, 1984).

Cioffi, Esterson, and Schatzman argue that, at some point, Freud realized that the seduction stories were false, and he was put in the position of explaining how that could be so while at the same time maintaining psychoanalytic therapy as a means for revealing scientific truth. He did so, they aver, by inventing the Oedipus complex and childhood sexuality. In the new formulation, the seduction stories about patients' outer lives as children are admitted to be false but remain wonderfully revealing about children's inner lives, displaying their Oedipal sexual fantasies about mother or father. Psychoanalysis became a doctrine concerned only with the inner life of human beings, and psychoanalytic method was said to reveal that inner life even to the earliest days of childhood. In making this move, however, Freud later had to repudiate or bury what he had believed during the original seduction episode. In his later writings, Freud depicted himself as a naive, nondirective therapist, "intentionally keeping my critical faculty in abeyance" (Esterson, 1993, p. 23), when earlier he had prided himself on discovering the seduction by "search[ing] for it single-mindedly" (p. 13). He said that he had been stunned to hear patient after patient describe being seduced by their fathers, when, in the paper of 1896, the seducers were adult strangers, older boys having sex with slightly younger sisters, or adults in whose care the child had been placed—never fathers. He even later retracted the blame he directed at his own father (Esterson, 1993; Schatzman, 1992).

Sulloway (1979) offers another motive for Freud's later distortion of the episode of the seduction mistake. Sulloway contends that the psychoanalytic legend was meant to obscure the influence of Fliess on Freud, specifically the fact that Freud got the idea of childhood sexuality from Fliess, not from his self-analysis. Sulloway calls it "the theft of the Fliessian id." Fliess is, in retrospect, a man with odd ideas from which Freud wanted to distance himself.

He believed in a theory of biorhythms, based on 23-day male and 28-day female cycles whose combination in complex permutations could explain events such as births and deaths. Freud, for a time, believed Fliess's theory wholeheartedly; his letters to Fliess, often containing calculations concerning himself and calculations concerning the birth of Anna (under a pseudonym), were used in a publication by Fliess. Fliess believed that the nose plays an important role in the regulation of human sexual life, and that surgery on the nose could cure sexual problems like masturbation. Freud himself submitted at least once to Fliess's knife.

Sulloway argues that, in the aftermath of the failure of the "Project," Freud adopted almost *in toto* Fliess's theories of sexuality and human development, while systematically concealing that he had done so. In Sulloway's account, Fliess conceived of the id and Freud took it over without acknowledgment. Fliess's influence on Freud was so thoroughgoing that it cannot be briefly summarized, but in the present context the most important borrowing is the concept of childhood sexuality. Fliess campaigned for the view that children had sexual feelings—advancing, for example, observations of his own children in support. Moreover, Fliess believed in the innate bisexuality of human beings, an important component of the biorhythm theory and, later, a central thesis in the psychoanalytic theory of psychosexual development. At what proved to be their last personal meeting, Freud boasted of his discovery of the innate, childhood bisexual nature of human beings, and Fliess tried to remind him who had the idea first. Freud persisted in claiming personal credit for the discovery, and Fliess, fearing his ideas were being stolen, withdrew from the relationship. In his last letters to Freud, Fliess has gotten wind of Freud's ideas on sexuality, and reproaches Freud for taking sole credit for them. Freud protests his innocence, and the correspondence ends.

CONSEQUENCES OF THE SEDUCTION EPISODE: PHANTASY TRUMPS REALITY In the wake of the seduction episode, Freud ceased to see the causes of neurotic suffering in his patients' lives, but located them in their mental lives. Indeed, critics of Freud, including some psychoanalysts, accuse

Freud of becoming insensitive—sometimes brutally so—to the life problems of his patients (Decker, 1981, 1991; Holt, 1982; Klein & Tribich, 1982). Two cases from Freud's practice illustrate his new attitude.

The first was a dramatic episode that was deleted from the original official publication of the Freud–Fliess letters (Masson, 1984a, 1984b). Freud had a patient named Emma Eckstein, who suffered from stomach pains and menstrual irregularities. We have already seen that Freud regarded masturbation as pathogenic, and he apparently agreed with Fliess that masturbation caused menstrual problems. Moreover, Fliess taught that nasal surgery could eliminate masturbation and hence the problems it caused. Freud brought Fliess to Vienna to perform surgery on Emma Eckstein's nose. The operation may have been Fliess's first; in any event, postoperative recovery did not go well. Eckstein suffered pain, bleeding, and discharge of pus. Freud eventually called in a Viennese doctor, who removed from Eckstein's nose a half-meter of gauze that Fleiss had incompetently left behind. At this point, Eckstein hemorrhaged, turned pale, and very nearly died. Freud was so shattered by the sight of Emma Eckstein seemingly dying that he fled, and was revived by brandy brought by the doctor's wife.

Remarkably, I think, Eckstein stayed in therapy with Freud. She continued to suffer pain and occasional, sometimes violent, bleeding from the nose. Initially, Freud recognized that her suffering was Fliess's fault. He wrote to Fliess, "So we had done her an injustice; she was not abnormal" but suffered from Fliess's mistake, and, by extension, Freud's mistake in subjecting her to Fliess's incompetent ministrations. However, eventually Freud returned to a psychological interpretation of Eckstein's bleeding. Just over a year after her brush with death, on June 4, 1896, Freud wrote that Eckstein's continued bleeding was "due to wishes." The causes of her suffering lay in her mind, not her damaged nose.

An even more revealing case is "Fragment of an Analysis of a Case of Hysteria" (1905b), describing Freud's admittedly unsuccessful treatment of an 18-year-old woman known as Dora (Ida Bauer). Shortly after the publication of *Interpretation of Dreams*, Dora's father, a successful businessman and former patient of Freud's, brought her in for therapy. Dora was suffering from symptoms Freud thought were neurotic—primarily, shortness of breath and a cough. As therapeutic sessions proceeded day by day (Freud saw his patients six days a week), Freud discovered that Dora came from a family whose tangled intrigues would do justice to a soap opera today. Dora's father's real reason for seeking Dora's treatment was to make her less unhappy about his affair with Frau K. The Ks were close friends of the Bauers, seeing each other regularly and vacationing together. On a vacation, Dora deduced the affair from her father's rearranging hotel rooms to have convenient access to Frau K. Dora's mother suffered, Freud opined, from "housewife's psychosis"—obsessive neatness— and had long since ceased having sexual relations with her husband. Dora objected most of all to the advances of Herr K.—whose wife had stopped sleeping with him—who had twice attempted to force himself on Dora, the first attempt coming when she was 13. Herr K. arranged to be alone in his place of business with Dora, ostensibly to watch a parade, but he suddenly grabbed her, pressed himself against her, and kissed her. Dora fled in disgust, tried to avoid Herr K., but nevertheless had to turn down a proposition from him two years later.

Freud's (1905b) reaction to the scene is remarkable: "This was surely just the situation to call up a distinct feeling of sexual excitement in a girl of fourteen [Freud miscalculated the age; Decker, 1991, p. 124] who had never before been approached. . . . [T]he behavior of this child of fourteen was already entirely and completely hysterical. I should without question consider a person hysterical in whom an occasion for sexual excitement elicited feelings that were preponderantly or exclusively unpleasurable." Instead of the genital sensation that would certainly have been felt by a healthy girl in such circumstances, Dora was overcome by the "unpleasurable feeling" of disgust.

Freud was especially puzzled since "I happen to know Herr K."—he came with Dora and Dora's father to Freud's office—"and he was still quite young and of prepossessing appearance" (Gay, 1989, p. 184). At this point in his career, Freud was an aggressive therapist, and he quickly used against Dora every interpretation he could. Playing with her purse during therapy represented her desire to masturbate; her cough represented hidden thoughts of Frau K. performing fellatio on her father and, therefore, Dora's secret wish to do the same. Not surprisingly, Dora was a patient who ran away. Freud ascribed his therapeutic failure to unanalyzed transference: Dora had transferred her sexual desires from Herr K., whom Freud was certain Dora secretly desired, to himself, and he had not taken due notice of it at the time. Freud said nothing about possible countertransference— from a middle-aged man no longer sleeping with his wife—to Dora, an attractive adolescent girl (Decker, 1981, 1991).

In Dora's case, we find Freud pushing all responsibility for hysteria onto his patient. Dora should have been sexually excited by Herr K.'s attentions; the disgust she felt was a symptom of her hysteria, not the cause of her distaste for the handsome Herr K. In 1895, when Freud still believed in the seduction theory, Freud had treated another young woman on whom sexual advances had been made, and he wrote of "the horror by which a virginal mind is overcome when it is faced for the first time with the world of sexuality" (quoted by Decker, 1991). In sum, the Dora case is typical of Freud's dismissal of family dynamics and other current influences on patient's troubles. Depth psychology imputed to the unconscious full sovereignty over mental health and mental illness, making patients solely responsible for their health.

PSYCHOANALYSIS GOES PUBLIC

So far, Freud had only developed his emerging psychoanalytic ideas in private, especially in his letters to Fliess. Beginning in 1900, Freud published the books and papers that quickly made psychoanalysis into an international movement far more influential than mainstream scientific psychology.

CLASSICAL PSYCHOANALYSIS (1900–1919)

The Founding Work: *The Interpretation of Dreams* (1900)

Freud regarded *The Interpretation of Dreams* as his masterpiece. In a letter to Fliess (Freud, 1985), Freud hoped that a plaque would be erected someday saying, "In this House on July 24, 1895, the Secret of Dreams was revealed to Dr. Sigmund Freud." The insight Freud valued so highly was that a dream is not a meaningless collection of experiences, but is "the royal road to the unconscious": a clue to the innermost recesses of the personality. That dreams have meaning was not a new idea, as Freud acknowledged, but it was out of step with the received academic opinion of his times. Most thinkers, including Wundt, assigned little importance to dreams, believing them to be only confused nighttime versions of waking mental processes. Freud sided instead with poets and shamans in valuing dreams as symbolic statements of a reality unavailable to waking experience.

Freud's thesis was that we all carry within ourselves repressed desires that constantly seek access to the control of behavior. As long as we are awake, our ego, or conscious self, represses these wishes; but during sleep, consciousness lapses and repression weakens. If our repressed desires ever completely eluded repression, we would awaken and reassert control. Dreaming is a compromise that protects sleep, for dreams are hallucinatory, disguised expressions of repressed ideas.

Freud said that every dream is a wish fulfillment, a disguised expression of an unconscious desire or wish. This characteristic of dreams makes them the royal road to the unconscious: If we can decipher a dream and retrieve its hidden meaning, we will have recovered a piece of the repressed material that makes us neurotic. Dreams and hysteria therefore have the same origin, because both are symbolic representations of repressed desires, and both can be understood by tracing them back to their sources. Moreover, the existence of dreams shows that no sharp line can be drawn between neurotic and normal mental lives because all human beings repress thoughts they find disgusting.

Freud's theory of dreams suggested a way to extend psychoanalysis to interpreting myths, legends, and works of art. We have already seen that in writing to Fliess about his alleged discovery of the Oedipus complex, Freud claimed to understand the enduring appeal of plays such as *Oedipus Rex* and *Hamlet*. In subsequent decades, psychoanalysis exerted great influence on literary criticism. Freud's dream theory also represented a general model of the mind as a multilayered system in which the unconscious shapes thought and behavior according to a peculiar set of rules (Sulloway, 1979) and provided the foundation for the unmasking function of psychoanalysis, so important to its hermeneutical employment by later social and literary critics. According to psychoanalysis, dreams— and, by extension, neurotic symptoms, slips of the tongue, and indeed all civilized behavior— are never what they appear to be because they are motivated by base and disgusting sexual and aggressive wishes. In the hands of literary critics, psychoanalysis could be used to argue that works of art are never what they seem, expressing yet hiding the artist's—and, if the work was popular or controversial, the audience's—deepest needs and conflicts. To social critics, psychoanalysis suggested that social practices, institutions, and values existed to enforce and, at the same time, hide rule by reprehensible value systems (usually capitalism) and reprehensible elites (usually white males). In therapy, art, and politics, the psychoanalytic line of argument placed the therapist and critic in a privileged position, beyond the subterfuges of the unconscious, uniquely capable of revealing the truth to deluded clients, audiences, and citizens.

The Classical Theory of Motivation: *Three Essays in the Theory of Sexuality* (1905)

Although Freud's ideas about childhood sexuality and the Oedipus complex were worked out in the 1890s, it was not until 1905 that Freud made them public in a set of three brief lectures, published as *Three Essays in the Theory of Sexuality*. It is in these essays that we also learn about Freud's

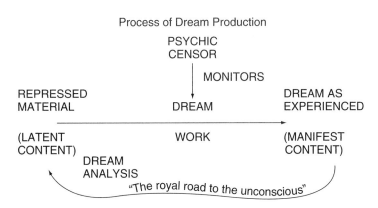

FIGURE 1 How dreams are produced according to Freud's Interpretation of Dreams.

incredibly narrow conception of human motivation. Earlier psychologists postulated a wide range of human desires, from ancient Greek desire for glory through the rich faculty psychologies of the Scots on Franz Joseph Gall. Even David Hume, a parsimonious empiricist, attributed to human beings unique motives such as moral sense, and utilitarians defined pleasure and pain very widely. Freud, however, said that human beings had no motives not shared with animals, and his list of animal motives was very short: sex, hunger, thirst, and self-defense. Later, he added aggression, but in the *Three Essays*, sex was front and center.

Freud made two points on sexual aberrations in the first essay. First: "There is indeed something innate lying behind the perversions but . . . it is something innate in everyone" (1905a/1962, p. 64). What society calls "perverse" is only a development of one component of the sexual instinct, an activity centering on an erotogenic zone other than the genitals, a zone that plays its part in "normal" sexual activity in foreplay. The second point was that "neuroses are, so to say, the negative of perversions" (p. 57). That is, all neuroses have a sexual basis and arise out of the patient's inability to deal with some aspect of his or her sexuality. Freud went so far as to say that a neurotic's symptoms are his or her sex life. The neurotic has symptoms rather than perversions or healthy sexuality.

Freud's second essay, on infantile sexuality, finally introduced the world at large to the ideas about childhood sexuality and the Oedipus concept that he had developed during the episode of the seduction mistake.

In the last essay, Freud turned to adult sexuality, which begins in puberty when maturational changes reawaken and transmute the dormant sexual instincts. At this time in the healthy person, sexual desire is directed to a person of the opposite sex, and reproductive genital intercourse becomes the goal; the instincts of childhood sexuality now serve, through the kissing and caressing of foreplay, genital drives that create the arousal necessary for actual coitus. In perverse individuals, the pleasure associated with some infantile instinct is great enough to replace genital activity altogether. The neurotic is overcome by adult sexual demands and converts his or her sexual needs into symptoms. Freud's discussion of psychosexual development suggested to his readers that raising a healthy—that is, nonneurotic and nonperverse—child was extraordinarily difficult. In this way, Freud aided the rise of applied psychology, as psychologists wrote books and dispensed advice about something that parents had been doing for millennia, but which they now feared they had been doing wrong. Parents could not, it seemed, trust their intuitions, but needed to turn to science for advice on rearing their children.

The Classical Theory of Personality

The concept of the psychological unconscious is the one truly indispensable shibboleth of psychoanalysis (Gay, 1989), the "consummation of psychoanalytic research" (Freud, 1915b). The idea did not originate with Freud, and many psychologists—including Freud in the "Project"—did not think it existed. Freud proposed two theories about the unconscious. The first has been termed the *topographical model* because it views the mind as a space in which ideas move between consciousness and unconsciousness. The topographical model was Freud's elaboration on the Way of Ideas developed by Descartes, Locke, and their philosophical successors. However, the idea of a mental unconscious was controversial in psychology. For most British philosophers, an idea was by definition conscious. Underneath consciousness lay brain processes, not unconscious thought, and Freud endorsed this position in his "Project for a Scientific Psychology." After abandoning the "Project," Freud developed a theory of mind more in keeping with the German tradition of Leibniz and Kant, for whom much of mental life lay beyond the reach of introspection. Freud was not alone; by the turn of the century, students of human affairs were increasingly regarding human behavior as being caused by processes and motives lying outside awareness (Burrow, 2000; Ellenberger, 1970; Hughes, 1958). The hypnotic trance and the power of posthypnotic suggestion, with which Freud was familiar from his studies with Charcot and his own use of hypnosis in therapy, seemed to point to a realm of mind apart from consciousness. Schopenhauer spoke of the "wild beast" within the human soul, and Nietzsche said "Consciousness is a surface" (Kaufmann, 1985). Freud acknowledged Nietzsche's grasp of unconscious dynamics in *Psychopathology of Everyday Life* (1914/1966) when he quoted Nietzsche's pithy aphorism: "'*I have done that*,' says my memory. '*I could not have done that*,' says my pride and remains inexorable. Finally, my memory yields" (Kaufmann, 1985; italics in Kaufmann).

Nevertheless, the hypothesis of unconscious mental states was not the dominant one among academic psychologists, who viewed mind as coextensive with consciousness. For them, the science of mind—psychology—was the science of consciousness. Freud's most important instructor in philosophy, Franz Brentano, rejected the unconscious (Krantz, 1990), and he was joined in his views by the preeminent American psychologist, William James (1890). Brentano and James were united in holding the doctrine called, by Brentano, the infallibility of inner perception and, by James, *esse est sentiri*. According to this view, ideas in consciousness were (*esse est*) exactly what they appeared to be (*sentiri*).

That is, ideas in consciousness were not compounded, by what James called the Kantian machine shop of the unconscious, out of simpler mental elements. The Gestalt view was similar, arguing that complex wholes were given directly in consciousness without hidden mental machinery behind the stage of experience.

It is important to realize that neither Brentano nor James denied the validity of a purely descriptive use of the term *unconscious*. They recognized that behavior or experience may be determined by factors of which humans are not aware, but they believed that the existence of unconscious causes of experience and behavior did not require the positing of unconscious mental states. They proposed a number of alternative mechanisms by which mind and behavior might be unconsciously shaped. James fully treated the problem in his *Principles of Psychology* (1890).

James pointed out that consciousness is a brain process, and we are not aware of the states of our brain. Our cerebellum keeps us balanced upright, for example, but to explain upright posture we need not suppose that the cerebellum is unconsciously computing the laws of physics. So memories not now present in consciousness exist as traces in the brain, dispositions toward consciousness awaiting activation (James, 1890). We need not posit an unconscious library of memories. Other apparently unconscious mental states may be explained as lapses in attention or memory. *Apprehended stimuli*, to use Wundt's terms, are conscious but, because they are not apperceived, they may not be remembered. If we are influenced by them, we might be disposed to think they influenced us "unconsciously," when in fact their presence in consciousness was merely no longer recollected. In 1960, George Sperling would show that, in Wundt's letter perception experiment, apprehended letters were perceived briefly but forgotten during the time it took the subjects to pronounce the letters they had seen. A dream or memory we cannot recover need not be thought to be unconscious because repressed, but "unconscious" because forgotten (James, 1890). Finally, phenomena such as hypnotism and the existence of multiple personalities may be explained by dissociation of consciousness rather than the existence of an unconscious. That is, within the brain of a single individual, two distinct consciousnesses may be present, unknown to each other, rather than a single consciousness beset by unconscious forces.

Positing an unconscious seemed to James and other psychologists to be scientifically dangerous. Because the unconscious, by definition, lies outside inspection, it can easily become a convenient vehicle by which to construct untestable theories. As James (1890, p. 163) wrote, the unconscious "is the sovereign means for believing what one likes in psychology, and of turning what might become a science into a tumbling-ground for whimsies."

Freud spelled out his conception of the unconscious mind in detail in *The Unconscious* (1915b). He offered two main arguments for postulating the existence of an unconscious mental realm. The first "incontrovertible proof" was Freud's claim for the therapeutic success of psychoanalysis. He held that a therapy will work if and only if it is based on a true theory of the mind; we have seen Freud relying on this argument as providing one reason for abandoning his seduction theory of hysteria. His second argument for belief in the existence of the unconscious was based on the philosophical issue of other minds raised by Descartes. Freud argued that just as we infer the presence of mind in other people, and perhaps animals, from "observable utterances and actions," so we should in our own individual case as well. "[A]ll the acts and manifestations which I notice in myself must be judged as if they belonged to someone else," another mind within the self. Freud acknowledged that this argument "leads logically to the assumption of another, second consciousness" within oneself, but notwithstanding James's espousal of this very hypothesis, Freud thought it unlikely to win approval from psychologists of consciousness.

Moreover, Freud asserted, this other consciousness possesses characteristics "which seem alien to us, even incredible," to the point that it is preferable to regard them as possessed not by a second consciousness but by unconscious mental processes (Gay, 1989, pp. 576–577).

Freud proceeded to distinguish several senses of the term *unconscious*. We have already recognized a descriptive usage on which Freud and psychologists of consciousness agreed—namely, that we are not always fully conscious of the causes of our behavior. Disagreement began with Freud's topographical conception of an unconscious mental space—the unconscious—where ideas and wishes live when they are not present to consciousness. Freud's scheme was like Nietzsche's: Consciousness is a surface lying over a vast and unknown realm sensed dimly, if at all. In Freud's description of the mind, all perceptions and thoughts are first registered in the unconscious, where they are tested for acceptability to consciousness. Perceptions and thoughts that pass the censorship test may become conscious; if they fail, they will not be allowed into consciousness. Applied to perception, this analysis provided the foundation for the important "New Look in Perception" movement of the 1950s. Passing the test of censorship does not directly lead to consciousness but only makes an idea "capable of becoming conscious." Ideas that are available to consciousness in this way reside in the preconscious, which Freud did not regard as importantly different from consciousness. More important and psychoanalytically interesting was the fate of ideas or wishes that did not pass muster with the mental censor. These ideas and wishes are often very powerful, constantly seeking expression. Because they are repugnant, however, they must continually be forced to remain unconscious. This dynamic unconscious is created by repression, the act of actively and forcefully opposing the entrance to consciousness of unacceptable thoughts.

REVISING AND EXTENDING PSYCHOANALYSIS: 1920–1939

Freud's ideas changed importantly from the initial formulation he gave them in the first two decades of the twentieth century. In the 1920s, he revised his theory of motivation and his theory of personality in such drastic ways that not all later analysts accepted them. In the 1930s, he wrote two very widely read books in which he applied psychoanalysis to the future of religion and the future of society.

Extensions: New Theories of Motivation and Personality

By 1905, when he wrote *Three Essays on the Theory of Sexuality*, Freud had concluded that one's becoming healthy, neurotic, or sexually "perverse" depended on childhood sexual thoughts, and, most importantly, on the resolution of the Oedipus complex. Central to his concept of the dynamic unconscious, which contained the wishes lying behind symptoms, dreams, and slips of the tongue, was repression. Yet, because repression was a continuing act of denying unacceptable sexual wishes access to consciousness, there remained a problem of explaining the source of the mental energy used to carry out repression of *libido*. Freud (1915a) proposed, as a "working hypothesis," that there exist two groups of "primal instincts": "the ego or self-preservative, instincts and the sexual instincts." The ego uses its ego-instinct energy to defend itself from—that is, repress—wishes driven by the sexual instincts. With this formulation, the mind as depicted by psychoanalysis became an arena of struggle, the compromised results of which were conscious thoughts and behavior.

In 1920, Freud revised his theory of motivation in *Beyond the Pleasure Principle*. Perhaps because of his own suffering from intractable cancer of the jaw—he endured numerous operations and his daughter Anna had to painfully replace a prosthesis in his jaw every day—and perhaps because of the carnage of World War I, Freud became increasingly pessimistic about human nature. In *Beyond the Pleasure Principle*, Freud proposed that "The aim of all life is death." Freud here gave psychoanalytic expression to an old idea—that we are born in order to die. In a sermon from 1630, John Donne had said, "Wee have a winding sheete in our Mother's wombe, which growes with us from our conception, and wee come into the world, wound up in that winding sheete, for we come to seek a grave" (quoted by Macmillan, 1997, p. 438).

Freud's argument is based on his conceptions of instincts as drives and behavior as motivated by drive reduction. Unsatisfied instincts give rise to states of arousal, which the organism seeks to reduce by engaging in behavior that satisfies the instinct. Satisfaction is only temporary, so, in time, the instinct must be gratified anew, causing a cyclical process of arousal and satisfaction that Freud called the *repetition compulsion*. It appears, then, that the optimum state sought by every living thing is complete oblivion—freedom from arousal. The wheel of the repetition compulsion is broken by death, when the aim of living—tension reduction—is permanently reached. There lies within us, Freud concluded, a drive toward death along with drives toward life. The ego instincts preserve the life of the individual, and the sexual instincts preserve the life of the species, so Freud bundled them together as the life instincts, named *Eros*, after the Greek word for "love." Opposed to the life instincts is the death instinct, or *Thanatos*, Greek for "death." Eros and Thanatos are mutually repressing. Thanatos provides the energy by which the ego, at the behest of the moralizing superego, represses sexual wishes, and Eros provides the energy to repress the death instinct from immediately fulfilling its lethal wish.

Postulation of the death wish provided a solution for the problem of aggression. In Freud's earlier theory, aggressive acts were deemed to occur out of frustrated ego or sexual needs. Thus, animals fought out of self-defense or over food, water, territory, or reproductive opportunities. In the new theory, aggression was an autonomous drive in itself. Just as sexual instincts could be rechanneled from their proper biological object, so too could the death instinct be redirected away from bringing about the death of the organism. Eros could for a time repress Thanatos' suicidal aggression, but the necessary result was aggression displaced onto others. Freud's new theory did not win universal acclaim among later analysts, many of whom preferred to accept Freud's earlier, less pessimistic, view of human nature, but both theories of aggression appear in later nonpsychoanalytic psychology. The first conception of aggression as caused by frustration surfaced in social learning theory's frustration—aggression hypothesis (Dollard, Doob, Miller, Mowrer, & Sears, 1939), and the second conception of aggression as a necessary part of nature, was reasserted by the ethologists, who stressed the adaptive value of an aggressive drive (Lorenz, 1966), if not a suicide drive.

In *The Unconscious*, Freud had worked out the descriptive, topographical, and dynamic usages of the unconscious. However, implicit in his treatment of the unconscious was an additional, structural meaning that Freud developed into a new conception of personality, not as a space but as a set of interacting structures. The unconscious was not simply a place in space (topographical use) containing readily available thoughts (the preconscious) and repressed thoughts (the dynamic unconscious). It is also a separate system of mind from consciousness, and it follows its own fantastical principles. In contrast to consciousness, it is exempt from logic, emotionally unstable, lives as much in the past as the present, and is wholly out of touch with external reality.

The systematic, or structural, conception of the unconscious became increasingly important to Freud and was central to the later restructuring of his picture of the mind (Freud, 1923/1960). The topographical model of the mind as a collection of spaces (conscious, preconscious, dynamic unconscious) was replaced by a structural model. In the new theory, personality was said to be comprised of three distinct mental systems. The first was the innate, irrational, and gratification-oriented id (the old systematic conception of the unconscious). The second was the learned, rational, reality-oriented ego (consciousness plus the preconscious). The third was the moralistically irrational superego (the censor), composed of moral imperatives inherited by Lamarckian evolution. The old dichotomy of consciousness and unconsciousness, Freud said, "begins to lose significance" with the adoption of the structural viewpoint.

Extensions: Freud's Answers to the Moral Question of the Enlightenment

In the last decade of his life, Freud began to apply psychoanalysis to large historical and cultural questions. In doing so, he took positions that one at once combined the more extreme forms of Enlightenment naturalism with currents of the Counter-Enlightenment. With Voltaire he said religion is an oppressive illusion, but with Rousseau's he said civilization is the enemy of human happiness. In the background hovers the brooding, pessimistic figure of Hobbes.

Freud echoes the French naturalists and positivists in *The Future of an Illusion* (1927). As we've seen, many philosophers from Voltaire such as Comte looked forward to religion's demise as scientific explanations of the world and human nature replaced outworn superstitious creeds. On the other hand, some sociologists and anthropologists such as Emil Durkheim (1858–1917) believed that even if religious claims about god and an afterlife were not true, religious institutions were so fundamental to human social life that religious belief would never wither away. In *Future of an Illusion*, Freud sided decisively with the first, more radical, line of thought. Freud argued that religion is an illusion, a massive attempt at wish fulfillment. Religion, he said, is based on nothing more than our infantile feelings of helplessness and the consequent desire to be protected by an all-powerful parent who becomes God. Moreover, to Freud, religion is a dangerous illusion, for its dogmatic teachings stunt the intellect, keeping humankind in a childish state. Religion is something to be outgrown as humans develop scientific resources and can stand on their own. The secret religious doubters are people who have outgrown religion but do not know it, and Freud addressed his work to them.

Hobbes and Rousseau appear in psychoanalytic form in the most widely read of all of Freud's works, *Civilization and Its Discontents* (1930). In *Future of an Illusion* Freud wrote: "Every individual is virtually an enemy of civilization . . . and people . . . feel as a heavy burden the sacrifices which civilization expects of them to make a communal life possible." Man's relation to society is the topic of *Civilization and Its Discontents*: "The sense of guilt [is] the most important problem in the development of civilization and . . . the price we pay for our advance in civilization is a loss of happiness through the heightening of a sense of guilt (p. 81)." Each person seeks happiness, and, according to Freud, the strongest feelings of happiness come from direct satisfaction of our instinctual, especially sexual, desires. Civilization, however, demands that we renounce to a large degree such direct gratification and substitute cultural activities in their stead. Such sublimated drives provide us less pleasure than direct gratification. To add to our discontents, we also internalize the demands of civilization as harsh superegos, burdening us with guilt for immoral thoughts as well as deeds. Civilized people are consequently less happy than their primitive counterparts; as civilization grows, happiness diminishes.

On the other hand, civilization has its rewards and is necessary to human social life. Along with Hobbes, Freud feared that without a means of restraining aggression, society would dissolve into a war of all against all. Civilization is therefore necessary for the survival of all but the strongest, and at least partly serves Eros. Moreover, in return for repression, civilization gives us not only security but also art, science, philosophy, and a more comfortable life through technology.

Civilization thus presents a dilemma from which Freud saw no way out. On the one hand, civilization is the protector and benefactor of humanity. On the other hand, it demands unhappiness and even neurosis as payment for its benefactions. Near the end of the book, Freud hinted that civilizations may vary in the degree of unhappiness they produce—a question he left for others to consider.

Civilization and Its Discontents has proven to be Freud's most widely read and provocative work. Some writers claimed that only Western civilization is neurotic and they anointed some utopia as savior, perhaps socialism or communism. Others taught that the only way out of Freud's dilemma was renunciation of civilization itself and a return to the simple physical pleasures of childhood. In 2012, both proposals seem from a bygone age.

THE FATE OF PSYCHOANALYSIS

Unlike the psychology of consciousness, psychoanalysis survives, though as mental disorders get traced to malfunctions of the nervous system and alternative therapies proliferate, the ranks of psychoanalysis dwindle. The young Freud alienated his friends and mentors, and the older Freud, founder and keeper of psychoanalysis, alienated independent-minded followers. Otto Rank, Alfred Adler, and Carl Jung—at one time Freud's Crown Prince—were expelled from the psychoanalytic movement for disagreeing too sharply with the founder. Schism followed schism in post-Freudian psychoanalysis, too, until the field became what it remains, a Babel of competing sects. If Freud's influence on academic psychology was limited, that of his former followers was virtually nonexistent. Peter Gay says that Freud is inescapable. Is his verb tense right? Is Freud the great hero of legend? Or is psychoanalysis "the most stupendous confidence trick of the twentieth century" as biologist Peter Medawar (quoted by Sulloway, 1979) insists? Or could Freud be a tyrant lizard—Tyrannosaurus—whose time has past?

Freudian Psychoanalysis and Science

IS PSYCHOANALYSIS A SCIENCE OR A PSEUDOSCIENCE?   The claim of psychoanalysis to be a science like any other has always been controversial. Positivists found Freudian hypotheses vague and difficult to test (Nagel, 1959). The most influential attack on the scientific status of psychoanalysis

XAM'S BLOG 1
The Party of Suspicion

As Marx noted, the modernizing revolution had two aspects. One was destructive breaking up the premodern way of life. The other was constructive, setting up new modes of production that increased wealth prodigiously. Unsurprisingly, then, modernism had a destructive aspect, too. However, the destructive forces of modernism were aimed not at the old premodern order, but at the makers of modernity, the bourgeoisie. Marx despised and fought them, and so did Freud, as one of the three leaders of what Jacques Lacan (1968), a hermeneutical psychoanalyst, called the Party of Suspicion—the others are Marx and Nietzsche—whose impact on twentieth-century thought has been immense.

The common enemy of the Party of Suspicion is the middle class. Breuer said that Freud's emphasis on sex was motivated in part by "a desire to *d'epater* [shock] le bourgeois" (quoted by Sulloway, 1979). Marx worked for the proletarian revolution that would destroy capitalism and the bourgeoisie. Nietzsche denounced middle-class morals as unfit for the *Übermensch* (literally, "Over-man," a Superman, Nietzsche's idealized man of the future). The common weapon of the Party of Suspicion was unmasking. Freud revealed depths of sexual depravity behind the seemingly innocent screen of middle-class respectability. Marx revealed self-centered greed in the aspirations of entrepreneurial capitalists. Nietzsche revealed craven cowards behind Christian martyrs.

To the Party of Suspicion, nothing is as it seems to be; in Freudian psychology, this means that no utterance, no action, is what it seems to be—everything requires interpretation. As Alasdair MacIntyre (1985) observes, the social sciences, especially psychology, are unique among the sciences because their theories might influence the subjects about which they write. As a result, psychology shapes the reality it describes, and the overinterpretative mode of life, as MacIntyre calls it, plays an important role in modern life.

"Freud made available the thought of the unacknowledged motive as an all-pervasive presence, so that each of us is encouraged to try and look behind the overt simplicities of the behavior of others to what is actually moving them and equally encouraged to respond to that hidden reality rather than to the surface appearance of the other" (MacIntyre, 1985, p. 899). Working within the overinterpretative mode of life, nothing can be believed; every statement, every action, requires an interpretative gloss. The interpretations no longer need be traditionally Freudian. To see the effects of overinterpretation, one need only consider the oddity of modern television news in which reporters, quoting experts and anonymous "insiders," tell us, the people, how a presidential speech will "play" to the people. No longer do government officials say things; they "send messages" to be decoded by pundits. Authority and sincerity have been dissolved. What Freud and the Party of Suspicion have bequeathed you is paranoia.

was mounted by Karl Popper, who regarded psychoanalysis as a pseudoscience. Popper formulated the *falsifiability* principle as the demarcation criterion separating genuine scientific viewpoints from those that merely pretended to be scientific. According to the falsifiability principle, to be worthy of science a theory must make predictions that can be proven unequivocally wrong. Popper, however, found that psychoanalysts were always able to explain any behavior, no matter how apparently inconsistent with psychoanalysis. Somewhere in the complex topography, structures, and dynamics of the mind could be found an explanation for anything at all from a woman's fiddling with her purse (symbolic masturbation) to the space race (phallic competition to build the biggest missile). In this Popperian spirit, the late philosopher Sidney Hook (1959) over a span of decades asked numerous psychoanalysts to describe what a person without an Oedipus complex would be like. He never received a satisfactory reply. Indeed, in more than one instance, he was regarded with hostility and his question met with screaming.

IS PSYCHOANALYSIS A FAILED SCIENCE? On the other hand, philosopher Adolf Grünbaum (1984, 1986) argues that Freud did after all propose tests by which psychoanalysis might be falsified, the most important of which Grünbaum calls the Tally Argument. When he offered the therapeutic success of psychoanalysis as "incontrovertible proof" of psychoanalysis, Freud said that psychoanalysis and only psychoanalysis could provide real cures for neuroses, because only psychoanalysis found the inner wishes and thoughts that "tallied" with the symptoms. Other therapies, Freud argued, could achieve only partial and temporary success because they did not go to the causes of neuroses, effecting by suggestion alone what little relief they provided.

Grünbaum believes the Talley Argument falsifiable. Therefore, psychoanalysis is a science, and the question becomes one of determining whether its claims are true or false. To be accepted as true on its own grounds, psychoanalysis must demonstrate unique therapeutic success. Unique success is vital to the Tally Argument, for if other therapeutic systems work at least as well as psychoanalysis, there is no reason to prefer the complexities of psychoanalysis to simpler theories. Behavior therapy, for example, rests on the simple principles of conditioning, and should it prove to be the equal of psychoanalysis, then, by Ockham's razor, it is scientifically preferable to psychoanalysis.

When we look into the therapeutic success of psychoanalysis, we find that although Freud boasted of success after success, he provided remarkably little data to support his claim. Freud reported only six cases in detail, one of which he did not treat and only two of which he claimed to be successes (Sulloway, 1991). The two allegedly successful cases were those of the Rat Man and the Wolf Man. The Rat Man was so-called because of his morbid fears and fantasies about rats, and the Wolf Man was named for repeatedly dreaming about seeing wolves perched in a tree. Freud's descriptions of both cases fail to stand up to scrutiny. Numerous distortions of the truth mark both reports, and neither patient seems to have been cured. After claiming success with the Rat Man in print, Freud confessed to Jung that the Rat Man was far from cured, and, like Dora, the Rat Man broke off therapy. The case of the Wolf Man is better known because he outlived Freud by many years and, near the end of life, told his story to a journalist. He stayed in analysis (for free) years after Freud's death. He told the reporter that he wrote a memoir about his case at the behest of one of his later analysts "[t]o show the world how Freud cured a seriously ill person," but "it's all false." He felt just as ill as when he went to Freud. In fact, he said, "The whole thing looks like a catastrophe" (quoted by Sulloway, 1991). Fisher and Greenberg (1977) wrote a largely sympathetic review of the status of psychoanalysis as science but concluded that Freud's own cases were "largely unsuccessful."

Later therapy outcome studies provide no evidence that psychoanalysis is a uniquely effective therapy. Gains from all forms of therapy are modest, and most forms of therapy have about equal success. Although Freud thought little of experimental attempts to verify psychoanalysis, many psychologists and analysts have carried out experiments, with highly variable results (for reviews of therapy and experimental studies, see Eysenck, 1986; Eysenck & Wilson, 1973; Farrell, 1981; Fisher & Greenberg, 1977; Grünbaum, 1984, 1986; Kline, 1981; Macmillan, 1997). Psychoanalysis seems to be caught on the horns of a dilemma. Either psychoanalysis cannot be tested, in which case it is a pseudoscience, or it can be tested, in which case it is at best a very poor science.

As a consequence, some partisans of psychoanalysis try to dissolve the dilemma by claiming that psychoanalysis is not a science at all, but a means of interpretation (Lacan, 1968; Ricoeur,

1970). This hermeneutical version of psychoanalysis maintains that the activity of psychoanalysis is more like literary criticism than science. A literary critic closely reads a text in order to discern its meaning, a meaning that may even have been hidden from the author who created it. Similarly, a psychoanalyst works with a patient to closely read the text of the patient's life, looking for or constructing the hidden meaning it holds. According to this version of psychoanalysis, the goal of therapy is to reach an interpretation with which the patient agrees and which can form the basis of a fuller life. Hermeneutics was originally the art of Bible interpretation, and hermeneutical psychoanalysis constitutes, in part, a return to the medieval conception of the world as a book containing meanings to be decoded, not causes to be discovered.

Psychoanalysis After Freud

Freud gathered disciples about him, but important ones abandoned or were expelled from psychoanalysis. Typically, dissidents rejected what they saw as Freud's excessive emphasis on sexuality. Alfred Adler (1870–1937), for example, stressed feelings of inferiority and a compensating "will to power." The most important of Freud's dissident followers was Carl Gustav Jung (1875–1961). Before studying with Freud, Jung had established himself as an internationally known psychiatrist. Freud had worried that because most of his followers were Jewish, the influence of psychoanalysis might be ghettoized, and he anointed the gentile Jung as his Crown Prince. However, Jung's thinking departed markedly from Freud's, being more sympathetic to, and influenced by, religious and moral concerns. To Jung, Freud was excessively materialistic, seeing only the darker side of human nature and oblivious to spiritual yearnings. Inevitably, Freud and Jung fell out. Jung was forced from the leadership of the psychoanalytic movement and, in their last letters, Freud and Jung traded diagnoses as insults.

Psychoanalysis as a movement, a therapy, and as a theory of mind continued to develop after the first generation of psychoanalysts died. Psychoanalysis continued to splinter into a congeries of competing sects, but two general trends can be observed. The first was the development of versions of psychoanalysis that played down the power of the instincts and came to focus more on the importance of the self, or ego (Eagle, 1984). For example, Freud had seen psychological development as driven by the inevitable unfolding of the sexual instinct through a series of genetically determined stages. In contrast, self, or object-relations, psychoanalysts propose that the key to the development of personality is differentiating the self from the not-self. Healthy people move from a state of independence from others to mature self-reliance—what Heinz Kohut calls "healthy narcissism." Pathology results when self and world are not adequately differentiated.

The other major development in psychoanalysis is the growth of systems of analysis that, in essence, accept Popper's conclusions and renounce Freud's desire that psychoanalysis must be a science. Psychoanalysis shared important tensions with experimental psychology. The most important was viewing psychoanalysis as *Naturwissenschaft* or *Geisteswissenschaft*. Freud insisted that psychoanalysis is a natural science, but his practice was more like literary interpretation than scientific investigation. For example, in what he regarded as his masterwork, *The Interpretation of Dreams* (1900/1968), Freud offered a theory of dream production rooted in the "Project." However, when interpreting dreams, Freud deployed literary methods depending on word play, allegory, and symbolism. Jung's rival "analytic psychology" openly adopted this interpretive approach to the mind, as Jung looked for universal patterns of symbolism across history and cultures. This "hermeneutic" (though not always Jungian) form of psychoanalysis is now the major force in psychoanalysis, literary criticism, and cultural studies. The same tension arose in Freud's attempt to build his science on conversations with patients. Psychotherapists know their clients as individuals—with names, life-stories, and personal problems—while scientific psychologists know their subjects as impersonal specimens of *Homo sapiens*. Freud thought he could move from particular, unique experiences to scientific generalizations about human nature everywhere and everytime. For example, having fabricated an early memory of sexually desiring his mother and fearing his father, Freud concluded it was a universal experience—the Oedipus complex. Instead of concluding that some children sometimes have these feelings, Freud's dedication to scientific universality led him to formulate a universal law from a single case. Today, many therapists reject Freud's procedure, seeing therapy as constructing a narrative of the client's life that resolves the past and enables the future.

Conclusion

Psychoanalysis powerfully shaped the twentieth century, and Freudian ideas became commonplace. The idea of psychiatry as a "talking cure" for psychiatric disorders helped lead to the creation of clinical psychology in the 1940s, although psychologists developed their own methods, such as Carl Rogers's client-centered psychotherapy and behavior therapy. To a growing number of critics, however, Freudian psychoanalysis should be regarded as a relic of nineteenth-century psychology and psychiatry.

Two fellow Viennese were never fooled by Freud. The philosopher Ludwig Wittgenstein wrote to a friend, "He is full of fishy thinking and his charm and the charm of his subject is so great that you may be easily fooled. . . . So hang on to your brains" (Schatzman, 1992, p. 34). The witty journalist Karl Kraus said, "Psychoanalysis is itself that mental illness of which it purports to be the cure" (Gay, 1988, p. 449).

Bibliography

Trying to master the scholarly literature on Freud is like trying to drink from a fire hose: One is more likely to be blasted away and drowned than to be refreshed. I have listed here only a *tiny* portion of the literature. Readers can find much more browsing in any library. Freud has become an extremely divisive figure: There are those who love him and those who hate him. These feelings, and the scholarly work attached to them, can be accessed at the Burying Freud website, www.shef.ac.uk/uni/projects/gyp/burying_freud.html. Despite its name, this website includes articles and postings that ardently defend Freud against his critics.

General Works. The standard biography of Freud is Ernest Jones's three-volume *Life and work of Sigmund Freud*, available in a one-volume abridgment (New York: Basic Books, 1961). Jones was a member of Freud's inner circle, and his biography enjoys both the benefits—privileged information—and the defects—hagiographical character—of close friendly association with its subject. More recent biographies now exist. One, Gay (1988), is by an author sympathetic to Freud. It is well written and incorporates access to some (but not all)

documents hidden from the general public (some of the Freud materials held in the Library of Congress and elsewhere cannot be published until after 2100!). Gay is a historian who underwent psychoanalysis, and he writes as something of a convert; although he criticizes Freud, Freud remains a hero for Gay. Moreover, the text hides scholarly controversies about Freud, although they are discussed in the excellent and combative bibliography. A more neutral biography, incorporating the critical literature discussed in the text and in this bibliography, is Paul Ferris (1998). Makris (2008) provides a general history of psychoanalysis from Freud through the great theoretical schisms of the 1950s. Makris's treatment of Freud himself is quite unusual compared to other recent works. While acknowledging that Freud had become a highly controversial figure (though without citations), Makris treats Freud from an entirely internalist perspective as a sober scientist seeking to solve contemporary scientific and clinical problems in a disinterested way. The background he provides on psychological research on hypnotism, suggestion, and the possibilities of scientific psychology is valuable.

My two favorite general works on Freud are Sulloway's (1979; his 1982 contribution may be regarded as a summary, and his 1991 article, a sequel) for the elegant arguments about Freud the cryptobiologist and the dissection of the myth of Freud the hero, and Rieff's (1979) for sympathetic consideration of Freud not as a doctor or a scientist or a hero, but as a moral philosopher of enormous influence. Two other biographies are philosopher Richard Wollheim's *Sigmund Freud* (New York: Viking, 1971), and professional biographer Ronald Clark's *Freud: The man and the cause* (New York: Meridian, 1980). A more critical survey, in which the cultlike nature of psychoanalysis (see also Sulloway, 1991) emerges, is Roazen (1974); one old analyst interviewed by Roazen shrieked at him, "You will never learn our secrets!" For later history of psychoanalysis, see Ellenberger (1970) and Reuben Fine, *A history of psychoanalysis* (New York: Columbia University Press, 1979). There are three collections of essays on Freud. The first two are general: S. G. M. Lee and M. Herbert, eds., *Freud and psychology* (Harmondsworth, England: Penguin, 1970), and R. Wollheim, ed., *Freud: A collection of critical essays* (Garden City, NY: Doubleday). The third, edited by Wollheim and J. Hopkins, *Philosophical essays on Freud* (Cambridge, England: Cambridge University Press, 1982), focuses on Freud as philosopher. A charmingly wicked, and even vicious, summary of recent scholarly research on Freud's character is Frederick Crews, "The unknown Freud," *New York Review of Books* (November 18, 1993, 55–66). Crews writes from the same perspective as mine, that of a deeply disenchanted former believer.

Various collections of Freud's letters have been published. However, because of the extraordinarily secretive nature of the keepers of the Freud archives, only two complete and unexpurgated sets of letters have been published: W. McGuire, ed., *The Freud–Jung letters* (Princeton, NJ: Princeton University Press, 1974), and Freud (1985), *The Freud–Fliess correspondence*. Freud began the tradition of a cultlike secrecy surrounding psychoanalysis, twice destroying collections of letters and manuscripts so his biographers could not get at them and tarnish his heroic image. The Freud–Fliess letters are extraordinarily revealing. Fliess was Freud's most intimate friend, and in the letters we find revealed the early development of Freud's thought and insights into Freud's character (the first letter was written while Freud had a woman hypnotized before him). Freud attempted to get hold of the Fliess letters when he discovered late in his life that they existed (he had destroyed Fliess's letters to him). The letters were published in a highly laundered edition together with the "Project" in 1954 (*The origins of psychoanalysis*. [New York: Basic Books]). Masson was hired to prepare Freud's complete letters for publication, but despite having been psychoanalyzed, he turned out not to be a safe choice. When he developed his version of the seduction mistake, the Freud archives fired him, and only the Freud–Fliess volume was published; I fear I shall not live to see the rest. The uproar in the analytic community was considerable: see Janet Malcolm, *In the Freud archives* (New York: Random House, 1985).

The best general work of Freud's is the pair of lectures, *A general introduction to psychoanalysis* (New York: Washington Square Press, 1924/1952), and its sequel, *New introductory lectures on psychoanalysis* (New York: Norton, 1933/1965). The bible of psychoanalysis is J. Strachey, ed., *The standard edition of the complete psychological works of Sigmund Freud*, 24 volumes (London: Hogarth Press, 1966–1974). Peter Gay (1989) has assembled a useful one-volume compilation of Freud's works based on the *Standard edition*. Complaints have often surrounded James and Alix Strachey's translations of Freud, especially by Bruno Bettleheim, *Freud and man's soul* (New York: Vintage, 1984). Light is thrown on the difficulties of translating Freud in a delightful collection of letters by the two Freudian Bloomsburians themselves, *Bloomsbury/Freud: The letters of James and Alix Strachey 1924–1925*, P. Meisel and W. Kendrick, eds. (New York: Norton, 1990).

Background. The general works listed previously provide various perspectives on the background against which to view Freud. Useful for the Viennese cultural setting are Schorske (1980), a wonderful book on the whole Viennese scene, and his student McGrath (1986), who develops Freud's situation more fully. Decker (1991) also discusses Freud in Vienna, with special attention to the history and status of the Austrian Jewish community. David Bakan, *Sigmund Freud and the Jewish mystical tradition* (Princeton, NJ: D. van Nostrand, 1958), connects Freud's thought to Jewish theology.

For the medical background, two books on the development of the concept of neurosis are available: José M. Lopez Pinero, *Historical origins of the concept of neurosis* (Cambridge, England: Cambridge University Press, 1983), and George Frederick Drinka, *The birth of neurosis: Myth, malady and the Victorians* (New York: Touchstone, 1984). For no obvious reason, the scholarly study of hysteria has proliferated in just the past few years. Mark Micale has provided guides to the literature: "Hysteria and its historiography: A review of past and present writings," *History of Science* (1989, *27*: I: 223–261, II: 319–356), and "Hysteria and its historiography: The future perspective," *History of Psychiatry* (1990, *1*: 33–124).

One of the most important of Freud's self-perpetuated myths is that his ideas met with a hostile reception; like so many other Freud stories, it isn't true (Sulloway, 1979). See the following studies of Freud's reception and influence: Hannah S. Decker, "The interpretation of dreams: Early reception by the educated German public," *Journal of the History of the Behavioral Sciences* (1975, *11*: 129–141); Hannah S. Decker, *Freud in Germany: Revolution and reaction in science, 1893–1907* (New York: International Universities Press, 1977); *Psychological Issues Monographs 11* (31), Monograph 41; Nathan Hale, *Freud and the Americans* (New York: Oxford University Press, 1971); and David Shakow, *The influence of Freud on American psychology* (New York: International Universities Press, 1964). *The path through physiology*. In addition to the cited works, especially Solomon's (1974), see Karl H. Pribram and Merton Gill, *Freud's "Project" re-assessed: Preface to contemporary cognitive theory and neuropsychology* (New York: Basic Books, 1976). Pribram was a leading neuropsychologist, and he and Gill viewed the "Project" as pioneering and prescient.

Dora and Other Cases. Decker (1991) provides a full account of what is now probably Freud's most studied case. For brief accounts and critical treatments of Freud's few published case studies, see Sulloway (1991). Mikkel Borch-Jacobsen's (1996) *Remembering Anna O: A century of mystification* (New York: Routledge) is an insightful treatment of her case history from the social constructivist perspective.

The Unconscious. The standard, massive history of the unconscious is Ellenberger (1970). Also useful are D. B. Klein, *The unconscious: Invention or discovery?* (Santa Monica, CA: Goodyear, 1977), and Lancelot Law Whyte, *The unconscious before Freud* (New York: Basic Books, 1960). Hughes (1958) shows how the concept of the unconscious came to grip social thought more generally. The view from continental hermeneutics is given in David Archard, *Consciousness and the unconscious* (La Salle, IL: Open Court, 1984). The concept of the unconscious is still controversial: see John R. Searle, "Consciousness, explanatory inversion, and cognitive science," *Behavioral and Brain Sciences* (1990, *13*: 585–642, with commentary), and Erdelyi (1985).

Victorian Sexuality. How prudish and repressed the Victorians were has become a matter of controversy between a traditional picture of uptight Victorians and Peter Gay's *The bourgeois experience: Victoria to Freud, Vol. 1: Education of the senses* (New York: Oxford University Press, 1984), picture of almost hedonistic Victorians (although in Gay, 1986, they seem more conservative). In the text, I try to steer a middle course, focusing on the

problem as Freud saw it. Herewith is a brief introduction to the enormous literature. The traditional view is that Victorians—especially women—were intensely repressed and deeply ashamed about sex. Standard sources here include Stephen Marcus, *The other Victorians* (New York: Meridian, 1964), a work I relied on; Vern and Bonnie Bullough, *Sin, sickness, and sanity: A history of sexual attitudes* (New York: Meridian, 1977), which covers periods before and after the Victorian; G. J. Barker-Benfield, *The horrors of the half-known life: Male attitudes toward women and sexuality in nineteenth-century America* (New York: Harper Colophon, 1976), which takes a feminist perspective; Ronald Pearsall, *The worm in the bud: The world of Victorian sexuality* (Harmondsworth, England: Penguin, 1983), a social history of Victorian sexuality; John S. and Robin M. Haller, *The physician and sexuality in Victorian America* (Champaign: University of Illinois Press, 1974), a fascinating study of physicians' ideas about sex and how they were translated into popular and professional "cures" for alleged sexual disorder; and Jeffrey Weeks, *Sex, politics and society: The regulation of sexuality since 1800* (New York: Longman, 1981). Victorians were especially alarmed by masturbation: see Arthur N. Gilbert, "Masturbation and insanity: Henry Maudsley and the ideology of sexual repression," *Albion* (1980, *12*: 268–282). However, revisionist historians have begun to assert that the traditional view of repressed Victorian sexuality is seriously mistaken. For example, a recently discovered unpublished sex survey—the first ever—of women who had grown up in the Victorian period suggests that they may have had orgasms with the same frequency as today's "liberated" women: Clelia Duel Mosher, *The Mosher survey: Sexual attitudes of Victorian women* (New York: Arno, 1980). Peter Gay (see *The bourgeois experience: Victoria to Freud, Vol. 1: Education of the senses.* New York: Oxford University Press, 1984) has used the Mosher survey, a diary by a sexually active young American woman, and other sources to try to debunk the "myth" of the asexual Victorian; see also Cyril Pearl, *The girl with the Swansdown seat: An informal report on some aspects of mid-Victorian morality* (London: Robin Clark, 1980), and Edmund Leites, *The Puritan conscience and human sexuality* (New Haven, CT: Yale University Press, 1986). How much of the revisionist picture is accurate, however, is still open to question. For an evaluation, see Carol Zisowitz Sterns, "Victorian sexuality: Can historians do it better?" *Journal of Social History* (1985, *18*: 625–634). Freud himself was an advocate of sexual reform. See Boyer (1978), which contains a transcript with translation of Freud's reply to a query from a commission looking into the laws regulating marriage in Austria in 1905; and Timothy McCarthy, "Freud and the problem of sexuality," *Journal of the History of the Behavioral and Social Sciences* (1981, *17*: 332–339). Other important rebels against Victorian sexual repression, assuming it existed, are described by Paul Robinson, *The modernization of sex: Havelock Ellis, Alfred Kinsey, William Masters and Virginia Johnson* (New York: Harper Colophon, 1977), and Phyllis Grosskurth, *Havelock Ellis* (New York: Knopf, 1980). For general background, see Bernard Murstein, *Love, sex, and marriage through the ages* (New York: Springer, 1974), and Lawrence Stone, *The family, sex, and marriage in England 1500–1800* (New York: Harper & Row, 1977). Although Stone's history stops before the Victorian period, he shows that a cycle of sexual repression alternating with sexual freedom was a regular feature of English history. Some of the odder byways of the understanding of female sexuality and the "disease" of hysteria are discussed by Rachel Maines (1999) *The technology of orgasm: "Hysteria, the vibrator, and women's sexual satisfaction* (Baltimore: Johns Hopkins University Press).

There are many works on the seduction error. Schatzman (1992) is a succinct but penetrating account. Crews (1998) collects several critical accounts of the event in one place, and adds other important perspective. More lengthy, and leading into the broader issue of Freud's scientific standing, is Esterson (1993). See also Crews's *The unknown Freud*, cited previously. David Livingston Smith, *Hidden conversations: An introduction to communicative psychoanalysis* (London: Tavistock/Routledge, 1991) provides a useful perspective from within modern psychoanalysis.

Other works critical of Freud appear with regularity. Here are some of them. Richard Webster, *Why Freud was wrong: Sin, science, and psychoanalysis* (New York: Basic Books, 1995). Webster's book is up-to-date and gives useful summaries of all of Freud's critics while also mentioning his defenders. More importantly, Webster carefully places Freud in the context of nineteenth-century psychiatry. Webster shows how Freud remained primarily a medical man all his life, always focusing on organic symptoms and ignoring his patients' mental distress. Webster critically describes Charcot's ideas about hysteria and demonstrates its deep influence on Freud, and argues persuasively that hysteria never existed, but was a category physicians found convenient for disposing of ill-understood disorders of the brain. That criticism of Freud still generates bitter controversy is amply demonstrated by Frederick Crews (1995). The book reprints three articles by Crews that are highly critical of Freud's character and that link him to the controversial

"repressed memory" movement, together with passionate and even vituperative defenses of Freud, the "repressed memory" movement, and Crews's response. At the very least, *Memory wars* makes lively reading. Edward Erwin (1996), *A final accounting: Philosophical and empirical issues in Freudian psychology* (Cambridge: MIT Press) sums up decades of arguments about the scientific status of Freudian psychoanalysis in a single volume. John Farrell (1996), *Freud's paranoid quest: Psychoanalysis and modern suspicion* (New York: New York University Press), uniquely connects psychoanalysis to the philosophical tradition of doubt that descends from Descartes. The best general survey of the literature on Freud is Macmillan (1997). One of the baneful effects of psychoanalysis was causing biological disorders such as schizophrenia to be treated as mental afflictions; see E. Dolnick (1998), *Madness and the couch: Blaming the victim in the heyday of psychoanalysis* (New York: Simon & Schuster). The socially constructed diagnosis of hysteria is linked to today's "epidemic" of multiple personality disorder by Spanos (1996), and J. Acocella (1998, April 6), "The politics of hysteria" (*New Yorker*, 62–79).

Webster argues that psychoanalysis became popular because it repackaged Christian religion in scientific guise while pretending to be radically new. Richard Noll, *The Jung cult: Origins of a charismatic movement* (Princeton, NJ: Princeton University Press, 1994) makes a similar argument about Freud but then concentrates on Jung. The book is excellent on the odd religious-political situation in pre-Hitler Germany and on showing how Jung thought of himself as a religious figure.

The Standing of Psychoanalysis. The text cites the most important books evaluating psychoanalysis. Freud's luster has tarnished over the years for myself and others. I came to psychology by reading Isaac Asimov's *Foundation* trilogy, and then Freud, and Freud was long one of my heroes. However, between becoming a fox and writing this revised chapter, I must confess I no longer regard Freud with much affection. For similar disenchantments, see Crews (1986) and Sulloway (1991). An interesting assessment of Freud is provided by leading literary critic Harold Bloom, "Freud, greatest modern writer," *New York Review of Books* (March 23, 1986, *1*: 26–27). Bloom makes his point by canvassing rival views of Freud, concluding that what Freud gave the world was great mythology; art, not science.

Hermeneutics. Key books are Lacan (1968) and Ricoeur (1970), works cited in the text. For a remarkably readable survey of a notoriously difficult and slippery subject, see Roy J. Howard, *Three faces of hermeneutics: An introduction to current theories of understanding* (Berkeley:

University of California Press, 1982). See also Charles D. Axelrod, *Studies in intellectual breakthrough: Freud, Simmel, Buber* (Amherst: University of Massachusetts Press, 1970); and Richard Lichtman, *The production of desire: The integration of psychoanalysis into Marxist theory* (New York: Free Press, 1982). Freud is connected to the founder of deconstructionism, Jacques Derrida, in Samuel Weber, *The legend of Freud* (Minneapolis: University of Minnesota Press, 1982). For critical views of the Party of Suspicion, I recommend R. Geuss, *The idea of a critical theory: Habermas and the Frankfurt School* (Cambridge, England: Cambridge University Press, 1971), and D. Lehman, *Signs of the times* (New York: Poseidon, 1991).

General Influence. Freud's influence has been very great in fields other than psychiatry and psychology. A collection that is especially useful for a beginner is Jonathan Miller, ed., *Freud: The man, his world, his influence* (Boston: Little, Brown, 1972); it contains essays on Freud and his time, and then a set on Freud's influence in various fields. Books on specific areas of influence follow Art: Ellen H. Spitz, *Art and psyche: A study in psychoanalysis and aesthetics* (New Haven, CT: Yale University Press, 1985). The social sciences, including anthropology, sociology, and political science: Paul Roazen, *Freud: Political and social thought* (New York: Da Capo Press, 1986); Arthur Berliner, *Psychoanalysis and society* (Washington, DC: University Press of America, 1982); Peter Bocock, *Freud and modern society: An outline of Freud's sociology* (Sunbury-on-Thames, England: Nelson, 1976); H. M. Ruitenbeek, ed., *Psychoanalysis and social science* (New York: Dutton, 1962); Melford Spiro, *Oedipus in the Trobriands* (Chicago: University of Chicago Press, 1983); and Edwin R. Wallace, *Freud and anthropology* (New York: International Universities Press, 1983). One controversial offspring of psychoanalysis is psychohistory, which is discussed and critically examined in David E. Stannard, *Shrinking history: On Freud and the failure of psychohistory* (New York: Oxford University Press, 1980).

The Psychology of Adaptation

From Chapter 10 of *A History of Psychology: From Antiquity to Modernity*, Seventh Edition.
Thomas Hardy Leahey. Copyright © 2013 by Pearson Education, Inc. All rights reserved.

The Psychology of Adaptation

The last founding psychology we will examine has proven to be the most durable and influential of them all. In the twentieth century, German psychology of consciousness quickly became an anachronistic product of nineteenth-century German thought, and it survived neither transplantation to other countries nor the destruction of its intellectual ecology by the Nazis and World War II. Psychoanalysis is an ailing and near-dead tradition. The approach that modern psychologists, first in England and later in America, have found most attractive and useful is a psychology based on evolution. With the ascendance of American psychology in the twentieth century, the psychology of adaptation in one form or another has dominated academic psychology.

THE DARWINIAN REVOLUTION

The Newtonian-Cartesian mechanical world was as changeless as the ancient one. God, or some Creator, had constructed a marvelous machine perfect in conception and endless in time. Each object, each biological species, was fixed for eternity, changelessly perfect in obedience to fixed natural laws. Such a worldview was equally consistent with Plato's Forms, Aristotle's essences, and Christian theology. In this view, change was something unusual in nature. Given the Cartesian-Newtonian concept that matter is inert, incapable of acting, and passive only, and that spontaneous change is the origin of new species, the mutation of old ones seemed impossible. Once the supreme Intelligence had acted creatively, dead matter could effect nothing new.

In the atmosphere of progress characteristic of the Enlightenment, however, this static view of nature began to change. There was an old Aristotelian-theological concept that aided acceptance of the idea of evolution, the Great Chain of Being, or Aristotle's *scala naturae*. The Chain was viewed by medievals as a measure of a creature's nearness to God and consequently its degree of spiritual perfection. To early advocates of Lamarckian evolution it became a record of the ascent of living things toward nature's crowning perfection, humankind.

The idea that living forms might change over time was also aided by the Romantic and vitalistic conception of living things that had opposed the mechanism of Mersenne and Descartes. If living things spontaneously changed in the course of their own development from life to death, and if they could give rise to new life through reproduction, then it became more plausible to think that living forms might alter themselves over great reaches of time. The vitalist, romantic concept of evolution was not mechanical, however, for it endowed matter with godlike attributes. For the Newtonian, inert matter was set in mechanical motion by an intelligent, purposeful Creator. For the vitalist, matter itself is intelligent and purposeful. Vitalism was thus a romantic view of Nature—self-perfecting and self-directing, progressively unfolding itself throughout time.

Recent discoveries in science and elsewhere also paved the way for evolutionary thought. Physicians became more knowledgeable about the development of animals, including humans, from fetus to adult form. This developmental transformation was dramatic and qualitative, a change of form, not merely of size, as ancient accounts had suggested. Thus, it became easier to think about the development of life on earth as a series of qualitative changes as one species became transformed into a new one. Voyages of exploration also helped facilitate evolutionary thinking, making it hard to fit existing species into fixed Platonic boxes. Human beings, for example, seemed different from every other living animal until visitors to Africa began to describe gorillas, orangutans, and chimpanzees. Similarity to existing creatures made it easier to accept the idea that we might have descended from them.

The idea that living things had changed during the course of life on earth—the idea of descent from modification—was becoming commonplace in scientific circles by about 1800. The remaining problem was to explain how evolution occurred. Any theory of evolution needs at least two components. The first is an *engine of change*, a mechanism that creates offspring that are in some way different from their parents. The second is a means of *preserving* the changes. If one organism's innovation cannot be passed on to its offspring, it will be lost, and evolution will not take place.

Romantic Evolution

Jean-Baptiste Lamarck (1744–1829) proposed the first important theory of evolution. Lamarck, a naturalist well known for his work in taxonomy, was the most scientific exponent of a romantic view of evolution. The engine of change proposed by Lamarck was the vitalist thesis that organic matter is fundamentally different from inorganic, linked to the romantic claim that each living species possesses an innate drive to perfect itself. Each organism strives to adapt itself to its surroundings and changes itself as it does so, developing various muscles, acquiring new physical traits or behavioral habits. Lamarck then claimed that a species preserves these acquired characteristics by somehow passing them on to its offspring. Thus, the results of each individual's striving for perfection were preserved and passed on, and, over generations, species of plants and animals would improve themselves, fulfilling their drives for perfection. Modern genetics has destroyed the romantic—*vitalist*—vision of nature. Organic matter is now known to be merely complexly arranged inorganic molecules; DNA is a collection of amino acids. The DNA chain is unchanged by modifications to an individual's body. (Certain external influences, such as drugs or radiation, can affect genetic information, but that is not what Lamarck meant.) In the absence of genetics, however, the inheritance of acquired characteristics was plausible and even Darwin from time to time accepted it, although he never accepted the vitalist view of matter.

So, by Darwin's time, evolution was a concept up for discussion, rejected only by firm religionists and a few in the biological establishment who still accepted the fixity of species. A naturalistic but romantic conception of evolution was in place. Herbert Spencer, an English Lamarckian, had already coined the phrase "survival of the fittest" in 1852. And in 1849, a decade before the publication of Darwin's *The Origin of Species* (1859/1959), Alfred, Lord Tennyson wrote in his greatest poem, *In Memoriam*, lines that foreshadowed the new view of evolution, in the struggle for survival—a view of which Tennyson disapproved (Canto 55, 1.5–8):

> Are God and Nature then at strife,
> That Nature lends such evil dreams?
> So careful of the type [species] she seems,
> So careless of the single life.

Later in the poem, in a widely quoted line, Tennyson calls nature "red in tooth and claw" (Canto 56, 1.15).

The Victorian Revolutionary: Charles Darwin (1809–1882)

Evolution did not long remain a poetic effusion, although Darwin's own grandfather, Erasmus Darwin, anticipated his grandson's theory in a scientific poem, *Zoonomia*. Nor could it remain a romantic fancy, inspiring but finally implausible. Darwin's achievement was to make evolution into a theory consistent with the rest of science by providing a nonteleological mechanism—natural selection—to replace Lamarck's romantic notion of organisms and species striving to perfect and improve themselves. Then a campaign to convince scientists and the public of the fact of evolution was needed. Darwin never campaigned himself. He was something of a hypochondriac—one biographer (Irvine, 1959) called him "the perfect patient"—and after his trip on the *H.M.S. Beagle*, he

Charles Darwin, Newton's equal as a scientific thinker. Publication of his Origin of Species in 1859 was the most important intellectual event of the nineteenth century. Darwin's theory of how and why evolution happens continues to revolutionize the life sciences, including psychology. *(Courtesy of Library of Congress)*

became a recluse, rarely leaving his country home. The struggle for the survival of natural selection was carried on by others, most spectacularly by Thomas Henry Huxley (1825–1895), "Darwin's bulldog."

SHAPING THE THEORY   Darwin was a young naturalist who had the good fortune to be included on a round-the-world scientific voyage aboard the *H.M.S. Beagle* from 1831 to 1836. Two key ideas began to emerge in Darwin's thinking during the voyage. In the South American rain forest, Darwin was deeply impressed by the sheer variety of living things—nature spontaneously throws up variations of form within and between species. For example, in each hectare of the rain forest there dwell several hundred different species of insects. On the Galapagos Island, Darwin observed the set of finch species now known in his honor as Darwin's Finches. While similar in overall shape, each species has a somewhat different beak. Moreover, each type of beak is suited to each species' means of foraging. Finches with long, thin beaks hunt for small insects in the bark of trees. Finches with shorter but sturdier beaks live off nuts or seeds that they break open. Darwin noted that it seemed likely each species had descended from a common ancestor, and each had changed over time to exploit a particular way of life. This is the central Darwinian principle of adaptation—the idea that evolution's result is to improve the fit between the species and its environment.

Then, sometime after his return to England, Darwin began to collect data on species—their variation and origin. In his *The Autobiography of Charles Darwin and Selected Letters* (1888/1958), he said that he collected facts "on a wholesale scale," on "true Baconian principles." Part of his investigation centered on artificial selection—that is, on how breeders of plants and animals improve their stocks. Darwin talked with pigeon fanciers and horticulturalists and read their pamphlets. One pamphlet he read, "The Art of Improving the Breeds of Domestic Animals," written in 1809 by John Sebright, indicated that nature, too, selected some traits and rejected others, just as breeders did: "A severe winter, or a scarcity of food, by destroying the weak and unhealthful, has all the good effects of the most skillful selection" (Ruse, 1975, p. 347). So, by the 1830s, Darwin already had a rudimentary theory of natural selection: Nature produces innumerable variations among living things, and some of these variations are selected for perpetuation. Over time, isolated populations become adapted to their surroundings. What was entirely unclear was what maintained the system of selection. Why should there be improvement in species? In the case of artificial selection, the answer is clear. Selection is made by the breeder to produce a desirable kind of plant or animal. But what force in nature parallels the breeder's ideal? Darwin could not accept Lamarck's innate drive to perfection. The cause of selection must reside outside the organism, he insisted, but where?

Darwin got his answer in 1838 while reading Thomas Malthus's (1766–1834) *Essay on the Principle of Population* (1798/1993). Malthus addressed a problem that troubled the late Enlightenment: If science and technology had progressed, why did poverty, crime, and war still exist? Malthus proposed that although human productivity had improved, population growth always outstrips growth in the supply of goods, so that life is necessarily a struggle of too many people for too few resources. In his *Autobiography*, Darwin stated he had at last "got a theory on which he could work." It was the struggle for survival that caused natural selection. Creatures struggled over scarce resources, and those who were "weak and unhealthful" could not support themselves and died without offspring. The strong and healthy survived and procreated. In this way, favorable variations were preserved and unfavorable ones were eliminated. Struggle for survival was the engine of evolution, in which only successful competitors had heirs.

Darwin need not have gone to Malthus for the concept of individual struggle for survival. As William Irvine (1959) points out, nature, in her evolutionary aspects, is almost tritely mid-Victorian. Darwin's theory "delighted mid-century optimists" who learned that "nature moved forward on the sound business principles of laissez-faire" (p. 346).

Natural selection may have offended the pious, but not the Victorian businessman of the Industrial Revolution, who knew that life was a constant struggle that rewarded failure with poverty and disgrace. The improvement of the species from the struggle of individuals was Adam Smith's "invisible hand" all over again. It was also consonant with Edmund Burke's conservative vision of societies as collections of successful practices and values.

FORMULATING THE THEORY Darwin had arrived at the essentials of his theory by 1842, at which time he first set them on paper with no thought of publication. His theory can be summarized as a logical argument (Vorzimmer, 1970). First, from Malthus, Darwin holds that there is a constant struggle for existence because of the tendency of animals to outgrow their food sources. Later, he would recognize that the key struggle is the struggle to reproduce (Darwin, 1871/1896). Not only do creatures struggle merely to exist, they must compete with others of the same sex for access to the other sex. Typically, males compete with each other for access to females, making female choice a force in evolution. Second, nature constantly produces variant forms within and between species. Some variants are better adapted to the struggle for survival than others. Consequently, organisms possessing unfavorable traits will not reproduce, causing their traits to disappear. Finally, as small adaptive change follows small adaptive change over eons, species will differentiate from a common stock as each form adapts to its peculiar environment. Furthermore, environments will change, selecting new traits for perpetuation, and as environment succeeds environment, species will diverge ever more from their parent forms. Thus, the observed diversity of nature can be explained as the result of a few mechanical principles operating over millions of years, as species evolve from species.

The theory as it stood was deficient. Without today's knowledge of genetics, the origin of variations and the nature of their transmission could not be explained. Darwin was never able to overcome these difficulties and was in fact pushed closer and closer to Lamarckism as he defended his theories against critics. It is an irony of history that while Darwin was writing and defending his *Origin of Species*, an obscure Polish monk, Gregor Mendel (1822–1884), was doing the work on heredity that eventually supplied the answer to Darwin's difficulties. Mendel's work, published and ignored in 1865, was rediscovered in 1900 and became the foundation of modern genetics. By the time Darwin died, he had earned burial in Westminster Abbey, and his thought had revolutionized the Western worldview, but not until the synthesis of genetics and natural selection into modern neo-Darwinian theory in the 1930s did evolution seriously affect biology.

Darwin set his ideas down in 1842, but it is not clear why he did not then seek to publish them. Historians have proposed a number of explanations for Darwin's delay (Richards, 1983). Some psychoanalytically influenced historians have suggested that Darwin, who had once considered becoming a minister, was made neurotic by the materialistic implications of evolution and wanted to repress his own discovery. Others have said Darwin delayed because he got involved in other, less speculative and pressing projects, such as publishing his research from the *Beagle*, and working for eight years studying barnacles. So absorbed was Darwin in his barnacle work that his young son, visiting a friend's home, asked where his father did *his* barnacles. Other theories emphasize Darwin's scientific caution. He knew the idea of evolution by natural selection was dangerous. It lacked the comforting progressive aspect of Lamarck's romantic theory, because in Darwin's formulation, evolution does not go anywhere because organisms are simply adapting to changes in their environments. If the theory was proposed prematurely, it might be rejected out of hand. He wanted to put out a complete and persuasively supported theory. Darwin also recognized that his ideas faced theoretical problems, foremost among them the existence of altruism in animals. How can altruism evolve by natural selection when altruism, by definition, involves acting to benefit another organism at some cost to itself? Altruistic genes appear, at first glance, to be suicidal. In fact, this problem was not completely solved until the formulation of the ideas of kin selection and reciprocal altruism in the 1960s and 1970s (Ridley, 1996).

PUBLISHING THE THEORY   In any event, Darwin continued to develop his theory and accumulate the empirical support it would need to gain a hearing. On June 18, 1858, Darwin's hand was forced. He was stunned to discover that someone else had discovered his theory. He received a letter from Alfred Russel Wallace (1823–1913), a fellow naturalist, but younger and bolder than Darwin. Wallace had also been to South America and had been impressed by the natural variation of life there. In southeast Asia, trapped in his tent by rain, he had read Malthus and had Darwin's insight. Writing to the foremost British biologist, Darwin (whom he did not know), Wallace attached a paper outlining his theory to Darwin to get it published.

Darwin found himself in a quandary. He wanted to be known as the discoverer of natural selection, but it would be unseemly to deny Wallace credit, too. So, Darwin and some friends arranged that Wallace's paper and one by Darwin be read on July 1, 1858, in their absence, to the Linnean Society of London, thus establishing Darwin and Wallace as codiscoverers of natural selection. Darwin rushed through a short version of his projected work on evolution, which appeared in 1859 as *The Origin of Species by Means of Natural Selection or the Preservation of Favored Races in the Struggle for Life*. It presented his theory backed by a mass of supporting detail. *The Origin* is an elegantly written book. Darwin was an acute observer of nature, and his pages are crammed with intricate descriptions of the interwoven nature of life. It was revised until its sixth edition in 1872, as Darwin tried to answer his scientific critics—unsuccessfully, as it turned out—in ignorance of genetics. Darwin wrote numerous other works, including two on the descent of humans and the expression of emotion in humans and the animals, which provided important foundations for the psychology of adaptation.

Reception and Influence of Evolution by Natural Selection

The world was well prepared for Darwin's theory. The idea of evolution was already around, and when the *Origin* was published, learned men took it seriously in all quarters. Biologists and naturalists greeted the work with varying degrees of criticism. Part of Darwin's thesis, that all living things descend from one common ancestor in the remote past, was scarcely novel and was widely accepted. Great difficulties were seen with the theory of natural selection, however, and it was still easy for scientists to hang on to some form of Lamarckism, to see the hand of God in progressive evolution, or to exempt humans from natural selection, as Darwin had, as yet, said nothing about them. Nevertheless, the implication that humans were part of nature was now hanging in the air, and Freud called Darwinism the second great blow to the human ego.

In many respects, Darwinism was not a revolution but part of the fulfillment of Enlightenment naturalism. Darwin cared only for his theory of natural selection, but others wove it into the emerging tapestry of a scientific image of humankind. Herbert Spencer, who had believed in the survival of the fittest before Darwin and applied it ruthlessly to humans and society, was one forceful proponent of metaphysical Darwinism. Another was T. H. Huxley (1825–1895), who used evolution to batter the Bible, miracles, spiritualism, and religion in general.

Huxley did much to popularize Darwinism as a naturalistic metaphysics. Darwin's theory did not begin the nineteenth-century crisis of conscience. Profound worries about the existence of God and about the meaning of life went back at least to Pascal in the seventeenth century. Darwinism was not the beginning of the scientific challenge to the old medieval–Renaissance worldview. It was the culmination of this challenge, making it most difficult to exempt human beings from immutable, determinate natural law. In *Man's Place in Nature* (1863/1954), Huxley carefully related mankind to the living apes, lower animals, and fossil ancestors, showing that we did indeed evolve from lower forms of life, that no Creation was needed. In the hands of people like Huxley, science then became not just the destroyer of illusions, but also a new metaphysics offering a new kind of salvation through science itself.

The journalist Winwood Reade wrote in *The Martyrdom of Man*: "The God of Light, the Spirit of Knowledge, the Divine Intellect is gradually spreading over the planet. . . . Hunger and starvation will then be unknown. . . . Disease will be extirpated . . . immortality will be invented. . . . Man will then be perfect . . . he will therefore be what the vulgar worship as a God" (quoted in Houghton, 1957, p. 152). This hope is similar to Comte's positivism, which Huxley called "Catholicism minus Christianity." For some, the new religion of scientific humanity was clearly at hand. Huxley (1863/1954) also boasted of science's practical fruits: "Every chemically pure substance employed in manufacture, every abnormally fertile race of plants, or rapidly growing and fattening breed of animals. . . ." Unfortunately, today Huxley's words may bring to mind today's cancerous chemicals, tasteless tomatoes, and steroid-stuffed steers.

Darwinism did not instigate Victorian doubt, but it did intensify it. Darwin effected a Newtonian revolution in biology, robbing nature of her Romantic capital N, reducing evolution to random variation and happenstance victory in the struggle for survival. The beginning of the reduction of biological nature to chemical nature that was completed with the discovery of DNA had begun. In psychology, Darwinism led to the psychology of adaptation. Assuming evolution, one may ask how mind and behavior, as distinct from bodily organs, help each creature adapt to its surroundings. Skinner carefully modeled his radical behaviorism on Darwinian variation, selection, and retention. Skinner, however, tended to underestimate the degree to which each species, including *Homo sapiens*, has a nature shaped by its evolutionary heritage. Today, evolutionary psychology (Barkow, Cosmides, & Tooby, 1994; Buss, 2011; Dunbar, Barrett, & Lycette, 2005) is developing a more complete picture of human nature.

Many, however, could not accept naturalism or were depressed by it. Huxley himself, in his last writings, said that man was unique among animals, for by his intelligence he could lift himself out of the natural Cosmic Process and transcend organic evolution. Similar sentiments, not at all uncommon among both scientists and laypeople, help account for the popularity both before and after Darwin's time of various semi- or pseudoscientific trends based on the uniqueness of humanity. Beginning with Bishop Wilberforce and continuing with William Jennings Bryan, defenders of the Bible attacked evolution, only to be crushed by such powerful personalities as T. H. Huxley and Clarence Darrow. As the authority of science increased and the authority of religion declined, many people were attracted by movements that blended science and faith.

EVOLUTION AND SCIENTIFIC PSYCHOLOGY

Any theory of evolution raises two questions that can engender psychological research programs. The first I will call the *species question*. If the body and brain are products of organic evolution, then we may ask in what ways this inheritance has shaped the thought and behavior of organisms. Hume erected his philosophical system on his science of human nature, but he did not inquire into why we have the nature we have. Darwinian evolution makes feasible asking and answering Hume's unasked question because we can ask how each aspect of human nature is adaptive in the struggle for existence. This question leads to comparative psychology, ethology, and evolutionary psychology, which study species differences in mental and behavioral capacities—differences presumably created by evolution. However, in the context of the psychology of consciousness, the first Darwinian question to be asked was: Why are we conscious at all? The second psychological question raised by evolution we may call the *individual question*. As the individual creature grows up, how can it be seen as adapting psychologically to the environment in a way analogous to organic evolution? This question leads to the study of learning, research designed to uncover how the individual adjusts to the environment.

The species question and the individual question are interrelated. If species differences are great, then different psychologies of individual adaptation will be needed for different species. If, on the other hand, species differences are small, then the same laws of individual learning will apply to all individuals, regardless of species. In this chapter, we trace the development of the psychology of adaptation and soon discover that its proponents adopt the latter line of thought. Gall's phrenology had implied a comparative psychology that looked for species differences in the possession of mental faculties. To a phrenologist, structural differences in the brain meant structural differences in the mind. However, by the middle of the nineteenth century, the sensorimotor concept of the brain had vanquished phrenology among scientists, and associationism was displacing faculty psychology among philosopher-psychologists. The view of the brain as an initially formless, associative machine and the view of the mind as a tabula rasa awaiting associations combined to cause psychologists to focus on the individual question and minimize species differences.

THE BEGINNINGS OF THE PSYCHOLOGY OF ADAPTATION IN BRITAIN

Lamarckian Psychology: Herbert Spencer (1820–1903)

In the summer of 1854, Herbert Spencer began to write a psychology whose "lines of thought had scarcely anything in common with lines of thought previously pursued" (1904). His work appeared the following year, 1855, as *Principles of Psychology*. This book gives Spencer a good claim to be the founder of the psychology of adaptation. Bain had integrated associationism and the sensorimotor conception of brain function; but, although he acknowledged the validity of Darwinian evolution, his psychology remained part of classical, preevolutionary associationism. Writing before Darwin, Spencer integrated associationism and sensorimotor physiology with Lamarckian evolution. Consequently, he anticipated the psychology of adaptation. Furthermore, not only did he raise the two evolutionary questions, but he also answered them in ways that have been basic to Anglo-American psychology until the last decade.

In 1854, Spencer wrote, "If the doctrine of Evolution is true, the inevitable implication is that Mind can be understood only by observing how Mind is evolved." Here is the starting point of the psychology of adaptation. Spencer proceeded to discuss both evolutionary psychological questions. Considering the individual, he viewed development as a process by which the connections between ideas come to mirror accurately the connections between events prevailing in the environment. The connections between ideas are built up by contiguity. Wrote Spencer (1897): "The growth of intelligence at large depends upon the law, that when any two psychical states occur in immediate succession, an effect is produced such that if the first subsequently recurs there is a certain tendency for the second to follow it." This tendency is strengthened as ideas are more frequently associated together. Like Bain, Spencer attempted to "deduce" the laws of mental association from the sensorimotor constitution of the nervous system and brain. In general, then, Spencer's analysis of the individual mind is that of atomistic associationism. He broke down the more complex phenomena of intelligence into basic elements (Spencer, 1897). What Spencer adds to Bain is the evolutionary conception, viewing the development of the mind as an adaptive adjustment to environmental conditions.

Spencer pictured the brain as a sensorimotor associative device, stating (1897) that "the human brain is an organized register of infinitely numerous experiences." His view has two important consequences. Given the Lamarckian idea of the heritability of acquired characteristics, instinct can be made acceptable to associationists and empiricists. Following the passage just quoted, Spencer described how the brain accumulates experiences "during the evolution of that series of organisms through which the human organism has been reached." Thus, innate reflexes and instincts are simply associative habits so well learned that they have become part of a species' genetic legacy. Such habits may not be acquired during an individual's life, but they are still acquired, following the laws of association, in the life of the species. Innate ideas need no longer terrify the empiricist.

The second consequence of Spencer's integration of evolution and the sensorimotor concept of nervous function is more portentous: Differences in the mental processes of different species reduce to the number of associations the brains are able to make. All brains work the same way, by association, and they differ only quantitatively in the richness of their associations. As Spencer (1897) put it, "The impressions received by inferior intelligences, even down to the very lowest, are dealt with after a like model." Thus, his answer to the species question is to deny qualitative differences among species and admit only quantitative, associational differences. This idea extends to differences within, as well as between, species; the "European inherits from twenty to thirty cubic inches more brain than the Papuan," he said. This implies that the "civilized man has also a more complex or heterogeneous nervous system than the uncivilized man," as he wrote in *First Principles* (1880/1945).

Spencer's framework shaped the psychology of adaptation for over a century. Comparative psychology would be directed toward studying associative learning in a small number of species, aimed at quantifying a single dimension of associative "intelligence" along which species could be arranged. Moreover, such studies could be performed in the laboratory, ignoring an organism's native environment. If the brain is no more than an initially empty, stimulus-response associating mechanism, then it is irrelevant whether the associations are natural or contrived; in fact, the laboratory offers greater control over the process than does naturalistic observation.

It also follows that if all organisms learn the same way, then the results of studies of simple animal learning, with their precision, replicability, and rigor, can be extended without serious modification to human learning. We will find that all of these conclusions are of fundamental importance to behaviorism, the twentieth-century psychology of adaptation. Behaviorists sought laws of learning that they thought would be valid for at least all mammals, and they extended animal findings to human psychology—often without supporting data.

Spencer applied his evolutionary ideas to contemporary social problems, producing a political theory unfortunately called Social Darwinism. He argued that natural selection should be allowed to take its course on the human species. Government should do nothing to help the poor, weak, and helpless. In nature weak animals and their maladaptive hereditary traits are weeded out by natural selection. This should be the way in human society as well, said Spencer. Government should leave the Cosmic Process alone, for it will perfect humanity by the selection of the fittest. To help human failures will only serve to degrade the species by allowing them to have children and thus pass on their hereditary tendency to fail.

When Spencer toured America in 1882, he was lionized. Social Darwinism had great appeal in a laissez-faire capitalist society where it could justify even cutthroat competition on the grounds that such competition perfected humanity. Although it promised eventual perfection of the species, Social Darwinism was profoundly conservative, for all reform was seen as tampering with nature's laws. The American Social Darwinist Edward Youmans complained bitterly about the evils of the robber barons, but when asked what he proposed to do about them, he replied, "Nothing" (quoted by Hofstadter, 1955). Only centuries of evolution could relieve human problems.

Darwinian Psychology

Spencer wrote his *Principles of Psychology* four years before Darwin published *Origin of Species*. In later editions, Spencer adjusted his text to reflect Darwin's ideas. Meanwhile, Darwin and others began to apply Darwinian thinking to animal and human psychology.

DARWIN ON HUMANS The central challenge of Darwin's *Origin of Species* concerned what Huxley called "man's place in nature." In the comprehensive, naturalistic scheme of evolution, man was made part of nature, no longer a being who transcended it. This implication was immediately seen by all, whether they agreed with it or not. Yet, *Origin* itself contains very little on human psychology. We know that in Darwin's early notebooks, dating back to the 1830s, he was concerned with these topics, but he seems to have set them aside from his initial publication as too risky. It was not until 1871 that he finally published *The Descent of Man*, which brings human nature within the scope of natural selection.

Darwin's aim in *The Descent of Man* was to show that "man is descended from some lowly organized form," a conclusion that he regretted would "be highly distasteful to many." He broadly compared human and animal behavior and concluded:

> The difference in mind between man and the higher animals, great as it is, is certainly one of degree and not of kind. We have seen that the senses and intuitions, the various emotions and faculties, such as love, memory, attention, curiosity, imitation, reason, etc., of which man boasts may be found in an incipient, or even sometimes in a well-developed condition, in lower animals. [Even the] ennobling belief in God is not universal with man. (1896)

Descent was not primarily a work of psychology; it mainly attempted to incorporate humans fully into nature. Darwin felt that Spencer had already laid the foundations for an evolutionary psychology. Yet, Darwin's work contrasts importantly with Spencer's *Principles*. Darwin followed philosophical faculty psychology, relegating association to a secondary factor in thought. Partly as a consequence, Darwin was concerned almost exclusively with the species question, for he assumed that evolution shaped the faculties. He also allowed great scope to the effects of heredity, sounding at times like an extreme nativist. For Darwin, both virtue and crime were heritable tendencies; woman is genetically inferior to man in "whatever he takes up." On the other hand, Darwin agreed with Spencer that the nature of species' differences is quantitative rather than qualitative and that well-learned habits can become innate reflexes. Lamarckian psychology and Darwinian psychology differed only in emphasis, not in content. The major difference is that Darwin's psychology is part of a materialistic, evolutionary biology. Spencer's psychology, in contrast, was part of a grand metaphysics that tended toward dualism and postulated an "Unknowable" forever beyond the reach of science. Darwin sheared off this metaphysical growth from the psychology of adaptation.

THE SPIRIT OF DARWINIAN PSYCHOLOGY: FRANCIS GALTON (1822–1911) We have already met Galton as a founder of mental testing. We now take up Galton as a psychologist of adaptation. Galton was an outstanding example of that distinct Victorian type—the gentleman dilettante. Independently wealthy, he was able to turn his inventive mind to whatever he chose. He traveled over most of Africa and wrote a manual for travelers in wild lands. He empirically investigated the efficacy of prayer. He pioneered the use of fingerprints for personal identification. He invented composite photographic portraiture. Many of his wide-ranging investigations were psychological or sociological. He once tried to understand paranoia by suspecting everyone he met of evil intentions. He canvassed the female beauties of Great Britain trying to ascertain which county had the most beautiful women. He studied twins to sort out the contributions of nature and nurture to human character, intellect, and behavior. He tried to use indirect behavioral measures (rate of fidgeting) to measure a mental state (boredom). He invented the free-association technique of interrogating memory. He used questionnaires to collect data on mental processes such as mental imagery. As we have learned, he applied anthropomorphic tests to thousands of individuals.

Galton's body of research was so eclectic that it did not add up to a research program, so he cannot be considered a psychologist in the same sense as Wundt, Titchener, or Freud. However, Galton made important contributions to the growing psychology of adaptation. He broadened psychology to encompass topics excluded by Wundt. In his *Inquiries into the Human Faculty* (1883/1907, p. 47), he wrote: "No professor of . . . psychology . . . can claim to know the elements of what he teaches, unless he is acquainted with the ordinary phenomena of idiocy, madness, and epilepsy. He must study the manifestations of disease and congenital folly, as well as those of high intellect." Wundt wanted to understand only the normal, adult mind. Galton inquired into any human mind.

Spencer began the psychology of adaptation, but Galton epitomized it. His eclectic attitude concerning both method and subject matter, and his use of statistics, would strongly characterize Darwinian psychology from this point on. Above all, his interest in individual differences points to the future: In German rationalist fashion, Wundt wanted to describe the transcendent human mind; he quite literally found the study of individual differences to be foreign and the existence of individual differences to be a nuisance. Guided by evolution, especially the concept of variation, Galton, however, was interested in all those factors that make people different. The study of individual differences is an essential part of Darwinian science, for without variation there can be no differential selection and no evolutionary improvement of the species.

Improvement of the human species was precisely Galton's aim. Underlying his various investigations was not a research program, but rather a "religious duty." He was convinced that the most important individual differences, including those of morals, character, and intellect, are not acquired. His great aim was to demonstrate that these characteristics are innate and then to measure them so that they could inform the procreative behavior of humanity. Eugenics is the selective breeding of human beings to improve the species. In his *Hereditary Genius*, Galton:

> propose[d] to show that a man's natural abilities are derived by inheritance, under exactly the same limitations as are the form and physical features of the whole organic world. Consequently, as it is easy, not withstanding these limitations, to obtain by careful selection of permanent breed of dogs or horses gifted with peculiar powers of running, or of doing anything else, so it would be quite practicable to produce a highly gifted race of men by judicious marriages during several consecutive generations. (1869/1925)

Galton's main interest was in the improvement of individuals, and he thought selective breeding would improve humanity faster than would improved education. Galton's program for selective human breeding was a form of positive *eugenics*, attempting to get especially "fit" individuals to marry one another. Galton proposed that examinations be used to discover the 10 most talented men and women in Great Britain. At a public ceremony recognizing their talent, each would be offered £5,000—a staggering sum in days when a moderately frugal person might live on a pound or so a week—as a wedding present should they choose to marry one another.

Galton's proposals gained few adherents when he first set them in 1869. Just after the turn of the century, however, Britons were more disposed to listen. In the wake of their near defeat in the Boer War in South Africa and the gradual recession of their empire, Britons began to worry that they were degenerating as a nation. In 1902, the army reported that 60% of Englishmen were unfit for military service, setting off a furious public debate on the physical deterioration (after the name of the army report) of the British people. In this atmosphere, worriers of all political stripes were excited by Galton's eugenic program for race improvement.

In 1901, Karl Pearson (1857–1936), an intimate of Galton's who had extended and perfected Galton's statistical approach to biology, pressed Galton to reenter the fray for eugenics. Pearson was a socialist who opposed conservative, laissez-faire Social Darwinism and hoped to replace it with planned, politically enforced programs of eugenics. Galton agreed, despite his advanced age, to take up the cause again, and in that year he gave a public lecture on eugenics and began to work for the establishment of eugenics policies. In 1904, he gave £1,500 to establish a research fellowship in eugenics and a eugenics record office at the University of London. In 1907, he helped found the Eugenics Education Society, which began to publish a journal, *Eugenics Review*. Eugenics appealed to people all across the political spectrum. Conservative, establishment leaders used alleged "laws of heredity and development" to support their crusade for moral, especially sexual, reform.

Social radicals could press eugenics into service as part of their programs for political and social reform. Eugenics was much talked about in the first decade of the twentieth century in Britain.

Despite the attention it received, British eugenics, in contrast to American eugenics, enjoyed only limited success in affecting public policy. Galton's program of rewards was never seriously considered. Some attention was given to laws enforcing negative eugenics—attempts to regulate the reproduction of the alleged "unfit"—but these were relatively mild measures that placed the socially incapacitated in institutions where they could receive care. British eugenicists were themselves divided on the need for government eugenics programs, the social radical eugenicists in particular urging education and voluntary control instead of legal compulsion. British eugenics was never fueled, as American eugenics was, by racism and race hysteria. British eugenicists were more concerned to encourage the reproduction of the middle and upper classes, whose birthrate had long been in decline, than to restrict spitefully the reproduction of allegedly inferior races. Although eugenics began in Britain, in the English-speaking world it was practiced mostly in America, as we shall see.

The Rise of Comparative Psychology

A psychology based on evolution should call forth research aimed at comparing the various abilities of different species of animals. Simple comparison of human and animal abilities goes back to Aristotle, and both Descartes and Hume buttressed their philosophies with such considerations. The Scottish faculty psychologists argued that humans' moral faculty distinguished them from animals. Galton studied animals and people to discover the special mental faculties of each species. The theory of evolution, however, gave comparative psychology a powerful impetus, placing it in a wider biological context and giving it a specific rationale. In the later nineteenth century, comparative psychology grew in strength until, in the twentieth century, learning theorists studied animals in preference to humans.

Modern comparative psychology may be said to have begun in 1872 with the publication of Darwin's *The Expression of the Emotions in Man and Animals*. The new approach is heralded by Darwin's statement early in the book: "No doubt as long as man and all other animals are viewed as independent creations, an effectual stop is put to our natural desire to investigate as far as possible the causes of Expression" (1872/1965, p. 12). However, he who admits "that the structure and habits of all animals have been gradually evolved" will look at the whole subject in a new and interesting light. In the rest of his book, Darwin surveyed the means of emotional expression possessed by humans and animals, noting the continuity between them and demonstrating their universality among the races of humanity. Darwin's theory of how emotional expressions evolved was Lamarckian: "Actions, which were at first voluntary, soon become habitual, and at last hereditary, and may then be performed even in opposition to the will." Darwin's theory was that our involuntary emotive expressions have gone through this development. Darwin's proposal that facial expression of emotion is universal and innate was discarded by behaviorists, but has been revived by Paul Ekman (2006).

Darwin's early work in comparative psychology was systematically carried on by his friend George John Romanes (1848–1894). In *Animal Intelligence* (1883), Romanes surveyed the mental abilities of animals from protozoa to apes. In later works, such as *Mental Evolution in Man* (1889), Romanes attempted to trace the gradual evolution of mind down the millennia. Romanes died before he could complete his comparative psychology. His literary executor was C. Lloyd Morgan (1852–1936), who, in his own *Introduction to Comparative Psychology* (1903), objected to Romanes's overestimation of animal intelligence. Romanes had quite freely attributed complex thinking to animals from analogy to his own thinking. Morgan, in formulating what has since been called *Morgan's canon*, argued that inferences of animal thinking should be no more than absolutely necessary to explain some observed behavior. The last of the early founding British comparative psychologists was the philosopher Leonard T. Hobhouse (1864–1928), who used the data of comparative psychology to construct a general evolutionary metaphysics. He also carried out some experiments on animal behavior that, in some respects, anticipated Gestalt work on animal insight and were designed to counter the artificiality of behaviorist animal experiments.

These comparative psychologists combined faculty psychology with associationism in their theories of development and collected some interesting facts. What proved important and controversial about their work, however, was their method and goal. What Romanes consciously introduced to psychology was an objective, behavioral method in contrast to the subjective method of introspection. We cannot observe the minds of animals, only their behavior; nevertheless, the theoretical goal of the British animal psychologists was never merely to describe behavior. Rather, they wanted to explain the workings of animal minds, and therefore they attempted to infer mental processes from behavior. The problems involved in this research program importantly affected the development of behavioralism, which was founded by American comparative psychologists.

Methodologically, comparative psychology began with Romanes's anecdotal method. He collected vignettes of animal behavior from many correspondents and sifted through them for plausible and reliable information from which to reconstruct the animal mind. The anecdotal method became an object of derision among the experimentally oriented Americans, especially E. L. Thorndike. The method lacked the control available in the laboratory and was felt to overestimate animal intelligence. The anecdotal method did have the virtue, largely unappreciated at the time, of observing animals in natural, uncontrived situations. We will find that animal psychology ran into real difficulties in the 1960s because of its exclusive reliance on controlled laboratory methods that overlooked the animals' ecological histories.

Theoretically, inferring mental processes from behavior presented difficulties. It is altogether too easy to attribute to animals complex mental processes they may not possess; any simple behavior can be explained (incorrectly) as the result of complex reasoning. Anyone who today reads Romanes's *Animal Intelligence* will feel that he frequently committed this error. Morgan's canon was an attempt to deal with this problem by requiring conservative inferences.

In his own treatment of animal mind, Morgan (1886) contributed a distinction that unfortunately was less known and less influential than his famous canon of simplicity. Morgan distinguished objective inferences from projective—or, as he called them in the philosophical jargon of his time, *ejective*—inferences from animal behavior to animal mind. Imagine watching a dog sitting at a street corner at 3:30 one afternoon. As a school bus approaches, the dog gets up, wags its tail, and watches the bus slow down and then stop. The dog looks at the children getting off the bus and, when one boy gets off, it jumps on him, licks his face, and together the boy and the dog walk off down the street. Objectively, Morgan would say, we can infer certain mental powers possessed by the dog. It must possess sufficient perceptual skills to pick out one child from the crowd getting off the bus, and it must possess at least recognition memory, for it responds differently to one child among all the others. Such inferences are objective because they posit certain internal, cognitive processes that we are unaware of in our own case. When you see a friend, you wave and say "Hi!" without any awareness of the face recognition process. On the other hand, we are tempted to attribute a subjective mental state—happiness—to the dog on analogy with our own consciously felt happiness when we greet a loved one who has been absent. Unlike objective inferences, projective inferences are based on analogy to our own subjective mental states because, in making them, we project our own feelings onto the animal. Objective inferences are legitimate in science, Morgan held, because they do not depend on analogy, are not emotional, and are susceptible to later verification by experiment.

Projective inferences are not scientifically legitimate because they result from attributing our own feelings to animals and cannot be more objectively assessed. Morgan did not claim that animals do not have feelings, only that their feelings, whatever they may be, fall outside the domain of scientific psychology.

Morgan's distinction is important, but it was neglected by later comparative psychologists. When Romanes's methods of anecdote and inference were challenged by American animal psychologists in the 1890s, the subjectivity of projective inference—calling rats "happy" and "carefree"—led to wholesale rejection of any discussion of animal mind. Had Morgan's distinction between objective and projective inference been heeded, however, it might have been seen that although projective inferences are scientifically worthless, objective inferences are perfectly respectable.

However, no matter how conservatively and carefully mind might be reconstructed from behavior, it remained possible for the skeptic to doubt. As Romanes put it:

> Skepticism of this kind is logically bound to deny evidence of mind, not only in the case of lower animals, but also in that of the higher, and even in that of men other than the skeptic himself. For all objections which could apply to the use of [inference] . . . would apply with equal force to the evidence of any mind other than that of the individual objector. (1883, pp. 5–6)

Such skepticism constitutes the essence of methodological behaviorism. Behaviorists admitted that he or she was conscious but refused to use mental activity to explain the behavior of animals or of human beings.

The psychology of adaptation began in England, where the modern theory of evolution was born. However, it found more fertile ground in one of Britain's former colonies: the United States. There it became the only psychology, and, as the United States came to dominate psychology, so did the psychology of adaptation.

PSYCHOLOGICAL IDEAS IN THE NEW WORLD

General Intellectual and Social Environment

America was new. Its original inhabitants were seen as savages, noble or brutish, who revealed original human nature untouched by civilization. The first settlers confidently expected to displace the Indians, replacing their primitive state with farms, villages, and churches. The wilderness found by the settlers opened up possibilities of erecting a new civilization in the New World. The Puritans came to establish a "city on a hill," a perfect Christian society, an example to be looked up to by the rest of the world. In America, there was no feudal hierarchy, no established church, no ancient universities. Instead, each person could make his or her own way in the wilderness.

This is not to say that the European settlers brought no intellectual baggage. They did (Fischer, 1989), and two traditions are particularly important: evangelical religion and Enlightenment philosophy. America was initially settled by Protestants, not Catholics. In fact, when Catholics first came to America in large numbers, they were forced to remain outside the mainstream of American life. Catholics were seen as agents of a dangerous foreign power—the pope—and anti-Catholic riots and the burning of Catholic churches were not unknown in nineteenth-century America. What emerged most strongly from the dominant American Protestantism was evangelical Christianity. This form of Christianity has little theological content, looking instead to the practical salvation of the individual soul in an emotional conversion experience when the person accepts the will of God.

An important part of the European reaction to the Newtonian spirit of the Enlightenment was romanticism. In America, however, the reaction against the Age of Reason was a religious one. America experienced revivals in the colonial period, and another took place shortly after the French Revolution. Romanticism touched America only briefly, in the Transcendental Movement. Henry David Thoreau, for example, decried industry's encroachment on romantic nature. However, more important for most people was evangelical Christianity, which rejected the antireligious skepticism of the Enlightenment.

It is no accident that many early American psychologists, including John B. Watson, the founder of behaviorism, had originally planned to become preachers. The stock-in-trade of the evangelical preacher is conversion, playing on an audience's emotions to change people from sinners to saints, modifying both soul and behavior. The goal of many American psychologists in both the functional and behavioral periods was to modify behavior—to make the person of today into the new person of tomorrow. Evangelical preachers wrote about ways to change souls through preaching; the psychologists wrote about ways to change behavior through conditioning.

Early America did possess some genuine philosophes. There was Benjamin Franklin, whose experiments on electricity were admired in Europe, who charmed France as the "natural man" of the New World, and who was enshrined as one of the leading figures of the Enlightenment, ranking even with Voltaire. Thomas Jefferson, another philosophe, is perhaps the best example of the geometric spirit in America. Jefferson attempted to apply numerical calculation to every subject, from crop rotation to human happiness. His Newtonian mechanism even blinded him to biological facts: Arguing against the possibility of Noah's flood, he "proved" from physical calculations that, in any flood, the waters cannot rise more than about 50 feet above sea level, and that consequently the fossil seashells found in America's Appalachian Mountains were just unusual rock growths (Wills, 1978).

The more radical ideas of French naturalism, however, were offensive to America's religious temperament, and only certain moderate elements of Enlightenment thought became important in America. Foremost among these acceptable ideas were those of the Scottish Enlightenment, which in fact exerted more influence on Jefferson than is commonly supposed. As we have seen, Reid's commonsense philosophy was perfectly compatible with religion. In America's religious colleges, which were the vast majority of American colleges, Scottish philosophy became the established curriculum, dominating every aspect of higher education from ethics to psychology. Scottish philosophy was American orthodoxy.

In considering the intellectual climate of the American colonies, to the influences of evangelical Christianity and a moderate Enlightenment must be added a third element, business, which interacted with the other two in important ways. America came to be a nation of business unlike any other nation on earth. There was no feudal aristocracy, no established church, and only a distant king. What remained were individual enterprise and the individual's struggle to survive in confrontation with the wilderness and in competition with other businessmen. The business of America was indeed business.

Out of this unique American mix of ideas, combined with a growing national chauvinism, several important ideas emerged. One was the supreme value placed on useful knowledge. The Enlightenment certainly held that knowledge should serve human needs and should be practical rather than metaphysical. American Protestants came to think of inventions as glorifying the ingenuity of God in creating the clever human mind. *Technology* was an American word. An unfortunate consequence of this attitude was anti-intellectualism. Abstract science was scorned as something European and degenerate. What counted was practical accomplishment that at once enriched the businessman, revealed God's principles, and advanced the American dream. The businessman valued the same hardheaded "common sense" taught in the colleges. Commonsense philosophy told the ordinary person that his or her untutored ideas were basically right, which tended to increase American anti-intellectualism.

In the use of the term *businessman*, the syllable *man* ought to be stressed. It was the men who struggled for survival in the world of business and who valued clearheaded common sense and practical achievement following Rousseau, feeling and sentiment were taken to be the special sphere of women, who in the nineteenth century were increasingly removed from the world of work, as such formerly domestic activities as baking, brewing, cheese making, spinning, and weaving became industrialized. This change stripped women of their earlier economic importance, leaving only the realm of the emotions to female rule.

Americans also tended to be radical environmentalists, greatly preferring to believe that peoples' circumstances, not their genes, were the primary cause of human characteristics and achievements. They believed that, contrary to the prejudices of Europeans, the American environment was the best in the world and would produce geniuses to surpass Newton. This belief reflected the empiricism of the Enlightenment and the flexible beliefs of the businessman. There would be no bounds on the perfectibility of humans in the New World, no bounds on the achievement of the free individual. Progress was the order of the day. A cult of self-improvement dated back to the early days of the American republic. In the 1830s, there was a monthly magazine called *The Cultivator*, "designed to improve the soil and the mind." Not only could a man improve his farm business, but he could improve his mind as well. In fact, it was expected that the good Christian would be a successful businessman or farmer.

One observer of the early American scene recognized these American trends. Alexis de Tocqueville wrote in *Democracy in America* (1850/1969), following his visit to America during 1831 and 1832: "The longer a nation is democratic, enlightened and free, the greater will be the number of these interested promoters of scientific genius, and the more will discoveries immediately applicable to productive industry confer gain, fame and even power." However, Tocqueville worried that "in a community thus organized . . . the human mind may be led insensibly to the neglect of theory." Aristocracies, on the other hand, "facilitate the natural impulse of the highest regions of thought." Tocqueville foresaw well. American psychology since its founding has neglected theory, even being openly hostile to theory at times. While Europeans such as Jean Piaget constructed grand, almost metaphysical, theories, B. F. Skinner argued that theories of learning were unnecessary.

Philosophical Psychology

THE OLD PSYCHOLOGY: PSYCHOLOGY IN RELIGION   The Puritans brought medieval faculty psychology with them to America. It perished in the early eighteenth century, however, when America's first great philosopher, Jonathan Edwards (1703–1758), read Locke. His enthusiasm for empiricism was such that his genius carried him independently in the direction of Berkeley and Hume. Like Berkeley, he denied the distinction between primary and secondary qualities and concluded that the mind knows only its perceptions, not the external world. Like Hume, he expanded the role of associations in the operation of the mind, finding, as Hume had, that contiguity, resemblance, and cause and effect are the laws of association (Jones, 1958). Finally, like Hume, he was driven toward skepticism through his recognition that generalizations about cause cannot be rationally justified, and that emotion, not reason, is the true spring of human action (Blight, 1978). Edwards, however, remained a Christian (Hume did not), and he may be regarded as more medieval than modern in this respect (Gay, 1969).

Edwards's stress on emotion as the basis of religious conversion helped pave the way for the American form of romanticism and idealism: transcendentalism. Transcendentalism was a New

England revolt against what had become a comfortable, stuffy, and dry form of Puritanism. The transcendentalists wanted to return to the lively, emotional religion of Edwards's time and to the direct, passionate encounter with God that Edwards had believed in. Such an attitude was compatible with both romanticism and post-Kantian idealism. The former prized individual feeling and communion with nature, similar to Thoreau's report of an extended, solitary sojourn in the wilderness in *Walden*. The latter believed Kant's transcendent *noumena* were knowable; similarly, George Ripley, a leading transcendentalist, wrote in *A Letter Addressed to the Congregational Church in Purchase Street* that they "believe in an order of truths which transcend the sphere of the external senses" (quoted by White, 1972). Thus, in some respects, transcendentalism was in tune with European romanticism and idealism.

In other respects, however, transcendentalism appears very American. It supported, for example, an evangelical, emotional Christianity that put the individual's feelings and conscience above hierarchical authority. Ralph Waldo Emerson (1950) preached "selfreliance," always an American ideal. He derided the radical empiricists as "negative and poisonous." Whether European or American in tone, however, transcendentalism's effect on mainstream American thought was limited. Like romanticism, its chief products were artistic rather than philosophical, and even its great art, such as Melville's *Moby-Dick*, was much less popular than other works totally forgotten today. The American intellectual establishment of the colleges viewed transcendentalism, Kant, and idealism with horror, so that budding scientists and philosophers had little contact with the movement.

A bulwark against any romantic revolt, Scottish commonsense philosophy maintained its grip on American thought. Americans, too, began to produce faculty psychology texts at an accelerating rate as the nineteenth century progressed. American texts on psychology repeated the arguments of the Scottish moral sense theorists. For example, Thomas Upham's *Elements of Mental Philosophy* (1831) taught that moral character could be built through the "thorough acquaintance with the emotions and passions" (p. 25) that psychology provided. Moral sense, which Upham called conscience, was given by God to "excite in us emotions of approval . . . [or] emotions of disapprobation" (p. 304) occasioned by seeing the actions of others. To the question, "Why should I do right?" Upham wrote that "the true source of moral obligation is in the natural impulses of the human breast" (p. 306).

PHRENOLOGY IN AMERICA   One of the most revealing episodes in the history of prescientific American psychology was the remarkable career of phrenology. Early in the nineteenth century, Gall's colleague, Johann Spurzheim, started on a triumphal tour of the United States; the rigors of the trip took his life after only a few weeks. Spurzheim was followed by the British phrenologist George Combe, who was well received by educators and college presidents. The lectures were too theoretical for American audiences, however, and phrenology fell into the hands of two industrious and businesslike brothers, Orson and Lorenzo Fowler. They minimized the scientific content of phrenology, maximized the practical applications, and set up an office in New York where clients could have their characters read for a fee. They wrote endlessly of the benefits of phrenology and published a phrenological journal that endured from the 1840s to 1911. They traveled around the country, especially the frontier areas, giving lectures and challenging skeptics. Like the great magician Houdini, they accepted any kind of test of their abilities, including blindfolded examinations of volunteers' skulls.

What made the Fowlers's phrenology so popular was its appeal to the American character. It eschewed metaphysics for practical application. It pretended to tell employers what people to hire and to advise men which wives to take. This first mental testing movement in America was Galtonian in its scrutiny of individual differences. Furthermore, it was progressive and reformist.

Gall had believed the brain's faculties to be set by heredity. The Fowlers, however, said that weak faculties could be improved by practice and overly strong ones could be controlled by efforts of will. Many people sought out the Fowlers for advice on how to lead their lives; they were the first guidance counselors. They also held out the hope that the nation and the world could be improved if only every person would be "phrenologized." Finally, the Fowlers believed they served religion and morality. They encouraged their clients to improve their moral faculties and believed that the existence of the faculty of veneration demonstrated the existence of God, because the existence of the faculty implied the existence of its object.

America's Native Philosophy: Pragmatism

THE METAPHYSICAL CLUB   In 1871 and 1872, a group of young, Harvard-educated, well-to-do Bostonians—"the very topmost cream of Boston manhood," William James called them—met as the Metaphysical Club (Menand, 2001) to discuss philosophy in the age of Darwin. Among the members of the club were Oliver Wendell Holmes (1809–1894), destined to become perhaps the United States' most distinguished jurist, and, more important for the history of psychology, Chauncey Wright (1830–1875), Charles S. Peirce, and William James. All three were important to the founding of psychology in America. Wright articulated an early stimulus-response theory of behavior, Peirce carried out the first psychological experiments in the New World, and James laid the foundations of American psychology with his book *Principles of Psychology* (1890). The immediate fruit of the Metaphysical Club was America's only homegrown philosophy, *pragmatism*, a hybrid of Bain, Darwin, and Kant. The club opposed the regnant Scottish philosophy, which was dualistic and closely connected to religion and creationism, and proposed a new naturalistic theory of mind.

From Bain they took the idea that beliefs were dispositions to behave; Bain defined belief as "that upon which a man is prepared to act." From Darwin they, like most intellectuals of the day, learned to treat mind as part of nature, not a gift from God. More important—this was Wright's contribution—they took the survival of the fittest as a model by which to understand mind. Wright combined Bain's definition with Darwin's theory of natural selection and proposed that a person's beliefs evolve just as species do. As one matures, one's beliefs compete for acceptance, so that adequate beliefs emerge "from the survival of the fittest among our original . . . beliefs." This is the essential idea of the individual approach to the psychology of adaptation—and, if we substitute "behaviors" for "beliefs," it anticipated the central ideas of B. F. Skinner's radical behaviorism. Wright also tried to show how self-consciousness, far from being a mystery to naturalism, evolved from sensorimotor habits. A habit, Wright held, was a relation between a class of stimuli and some response or responses. The cognition needed to link stimulus and response was rudimentary, involving recalled images of past experiences. Self-consciousness arose when one—or people, as compared with the animals—became aware of the connection between stimulus and response. Wright's ideas go a long way to making mind part of nature, and they point to the behavioral emphasis of American psychology, in which beliefs are important only insofar as they produce behavior.

CHARLES SAUNDERS PEIRCE (1839–1914)   Some historians and philosophers now think that Peirce was the greatest philosopher America has produced. He was trained as a physicist and worked for a time for the U.S. Coast and Geodetic Survey. As an undergraduate, he built a simple computer and may have been the first to ask if computers might be capable of emulating human thinking. A small inheritance allowed him to retire from the Survey and go to Cambridge. The inheritance was small, indeed, and the Peirces lived lives of genteel poverty. He was not an easy man to get along with, and despite the best efforts of James to find him a permanent post at Harvard, nothing but short-term appointments ensued. In contrast to James, whose writing style was fluid and forceful—it was said that his brother Henry was a novelist who wrote like a psychologist and William was a philosopher who wrote like a novelist—Peirce wrote prose that was awkward and sometimes impenetrable. Peirce's influence was also limited because he published little in his own lifetime. Nevertheless, he summarized the work of the Metaphysical Club, giving pragmatism its first formulation.

Given pragmatism's rejection of truth, it is ironic that its name derived from Kant. As a foundational philosopher, Kant had tried to lay philosophical foundations for human knowledge. Nevertheless, he recognized that men and women must act on beliefs that are not certain; a physician, for example, may not be absolutely certain of a diagnosis but must nevertheless proceed believing the diagnosis is correct. Kant called "such contingent belief which still forms the basis of the actual use of means for the attainment of certain ends, pragmatic belief." The skeptical upshot of the meditations of the Metaphysical Club was that no belief could ever be held with absolute certainty. The best that humans could hope for were beliefs that led to successful action in the world, natural selection operating to strengthen certain beliefs and weaken others as beliefs struggled for acceptance. Darwin had shown that species were not fixed, and the Metaphysical Club concluded that truth, contrary to Kant, could not be fixed either. All that remained to epistemology, then, was Kant's pragmatic belief, which Peirce refined into "the pragmatic maxim," reflecting the conclusions of the club.

In 1878, Peirce published these conclusions in a paper, "How to Make Our Ideas Clear," first read to the Metaphysical Club at the end of its life. Peirce (1878/1966) wrote that "the whole function of thought is to produce habits of action," and that what we call beliefs are "a rule of action, or, say for short, a habit." "The essence of belief," he argued, "is the establishment of a habit, and different beliefs are distinguished by the different modes of action to which they give rise." Habits must have a practical significance if they are to be meaningful, Peirce went on. "Now the identity of a habit depends on how it might lead us to act. . . . Thus we come down to what is tangible and conceivably practical as the root of every real distinction of thought . . . there is no distinction so fine as to consist in anything but a possible difference in practice." In conclusion, "the rule for attaining [clear ideas] is as follows: consider what effects, which might conceivably have practical bearings, we conceive the object of our conceptions to have. Then, our conception of these effects is the whole of our conception of the object." Or, as Peirce put it more succinctly in 1905, the truth of a belief "lies exclusively in its conceivable bearing upon the conduct of life."

Peirce's pragmatic maxim was revolutionary because it abandoned the old Platonic aim of a foundational philosophy. It admitted with Heraclitus and the post-Socratic skeptics that nothing can ever be certain and draws from Darwin the idea that the best beliefs are those that work in adapting us to our changing environment. The pragmatic maxim is also consistent with scientific practice. Peirce had been a working physicist and learned that a scientific concept was useless and therefore meaningless if it could not be translated into some observable phenomenon; thus, Peirce's pragmatic maxim anticipated the positivist concept of operational definition. Later, when James allowed emotional and ethical considerations to weigh in deciding whether a belief works, Peirce, the hardheaded physicist, refused to go along. In psychology, pragmatism represented a clear articulation of the individual-question approach to the psychology of adaptation. It took, as Skinner later would, Darwin's account of species' evolution as a model by which to understand individual learning. The pragmatic maxim also anticipated the behavioral turn in American psychology because it says that beliefs are always (if meaningful) manifested in behavior, so that reflection on consciousness for its own sake is idle.

Peirce never became a psychologist, but he did aid psychology's development in the United States. He read some of Wundt's researches in 1862 and campaigned against the continued reign of Scottish commonsense psychology and for the establishment of experimental psychology in U.S. universities. In 1877, he published a psychophysical study of color, the first experimental work to come from America. A student of his, Joseph Jastrow, became one of the leading American psychologists in the first part of the twentieth century and an early president of the American Psychological Association (APA). In 1887, Peirce asked the central question of modern cognitive science: Can a machine think like a human being? Despite these accomplishments, his influence remained remarkably limited. Pragmatism's great influence on philosophy and psychology came from his associate, William James.

AMERICA'S PSYCHOLOGIST: WILLIAM JAMES (1842–1910)

James's Principles of Psychology

James began to work out his own version of pragmatism in the 1870s and 1880s, as psychology rather than philosophy. In 1878, he contracted with the publisher Henry Holt to write a textbook on psychology, and during the 1880s, he published a series of articles that formed the core of his new psychology and were incorporated into the book, *Principles of Psychology*. Its publication in 1890 marks a watershed in the history of American psychology, for it inspired American students as neither the Scots nor Wundt could, and it set the tone for American psychology from 1890 to 1913 to the present day. James combined the usual interests of a founding psychologist: physiology and philosophy. Although as a young man James wanted to be an artist, he began his academic career with an MD and held a variety of posts at Harvard. Beginning as an instructor of physiology, he next saw to the establishment for himself of a chair in psychology; he spent his last years as a professor of philosophy. In *Principles*, James began to develop his pragmatic philosophy.

"Psychology Is the Science of Mental Life," James told his readers (1890, vol. 1, p. 1). Its primary method is ordinary introspection, accompanied by the "diabolical cunning" of German experimentalism and by comparative studies of men, animals, and savages. James rejected sensationistic atomism, the billiard ball theory also rejected by Wundt. Anticipating the Gestalt psychologists, James said, this theory takes the discernible parts of objects to be enduring objects of experience, falsely chopping up the flow of experience. Wrote James:

> Consciousness . . . does not appear to itself chopped up in bits. Such words as "chain" or "train" do not describe it fitly, as it presents itself in the first instance. It is nothing jointed; it flows. A "river" or a "stream" are the metaphors by which it is most naturally described. In talking of it hereafter let us call it the stream of thought, of consciousness, or of subjective life. (p. 239)

In Darwinian fashion, James found that what consciousness contains is less important than what it does; it is function, not content, that counts. The primary function of consciousness is to choose. He wrote: "It is always interested more in one part of its object than in another, and welcomes and rejects, or chooses, all the while it thinks" (p. 284). Consciousness creates and serves the ends of the organism, the first of which is survival through adaptation to the environment. For James, however, adaptation is never passive. Consciousness chooses, acting always toward some end. The ceaseless flow of choices affects perception as well as conduct: "The mind, in short, works on the data it receives very much as a sculptor works on his block of stone" (p. 288). James's mind is not the passive blank slate of the sensationists. It is a "fighter for ends," actively engaged with a practical world of experience.

The Challenge of Will and the Reflex Theory of the Brain

Note that there are two aspects of consciousness's adaptive nature for James. The first is that consciousness gives its bearers interests—machines do not want to survive and operate merely on preset habits. If the environment does not suit these habits, it will fail to adapt and will die because it does not care whether it lives or dies. But coping with change is the essence of evolution, and so consciousness has arisen because without it, we would not and could not adapt. The second adaptive aspect of consciousness, choice, depends on having an interest in survival. Consciousness, James taught, arises when instinct and habit cannot cope with new challenges. One can drive a familiar route without the involvement of consciousness, listening to the radio or talking to a friend. One's consciousness is "elsewhere," as Descartes said. However, should one hear on the radio that a falling tree has blocked one's usual route, one becomes immediately conscious of driving because one has to choose a new route to cope with the changed environment. For James, it was clear that without consciousness, there would be no survival, for without it we would be clockwork mechanisms, blind to the environment and uncaring about our fate.

At the same time, however, James endorsed the path to physiology, saying that psychology must be "cerebralist." It is a fundamental assumption that "the brain is the one immediate bodily condition of the mental operation," and the *Principles*, all 1,377 pages of it, is "more or less of a proof that the postulate is correct" (1890, vol. 1, p. 4). He applauded Hartley's attempt to show that the laws of association are cerebral laws, "and so far as association stands for a cause, it is between processes in the brain" (p. 554).

This seemed to involve James in a contradiction—the brain-machine must make choices. He had said that consciousness plays a positive role in human and animal life, and explicitly rejected mechanism, or what he called the "automaton theory." For James, evolutionary naturalism demanded that consciousness exist because it fulfilled a vital adaptive function. A dumb machine knows no direction, it is like "dice thrown forever on a table . . . what chance is there that the highest number will turn up oftener than the lowest?" James argued that consciousness increases the efficiency of the cerebral machine by "loading its dice." Wrote James (1890, vol. 1, p. 140): "Loading its dice would bring constant pressure to bear in favor of those of its performances" that serve the "interests of the brain's owner." Consciousness transforms survival from "mere hypothesis" into an "imperative decree. Survival shall occur and therefore organs must so work. . . . Every actually existing consciousness seems to itself at any rate to be a fighter for ends." Consciousness thus possesses survival value. Association may depend on cerebral laws, but our will can, through emphasis and reinforcement, direct chains of association to serve our interests and their direction is "all that the most eager advocate of free will need demand," for by directing association it directs thinking and, hence, action (p. 141).

The conflict between James's cerebralist view of consciousness and his belief in the behavioral efficacy of consciousness shows up clearly in his theory of emotion, the James–Lange theory of emotion, proposed independently by William James in 1884 and the Dutch physiologist Carl Lange (1834–1900) in 1885. Via its formulation in James's *Principles of Psychology*, the James–Lange theory of emotion has influenced every psychologist who has tackled the topic of emotion and is still widely discussed today.

As a psychologist of consciousness, James wanted to explain how and why emotions arise in conscious experience. He contrasted his theory of emotions with that of folk psychology, admitting that, at least at first glance, his was less plausible:

> Our natural way of thinking about . . . emotions is that the mental perception of some fact excites the mental affection called the emotion, and that this latter state of mind gives rise to the bodily expression. My theory, on the contrary, is that the bodily changes follow directly

the perception of the exciting fact, and that our feeling of the same changes as they occur is the emotion. Common-sense says, we lose our fortune, are sorry and weep; we meet a bear, are frightened and run; we are insulted by a rival, are angry and strike. The hypothesis here to be defended says that this order of sequence is incorrect, that the one mental state is not immediately induced by the other, that the bodily manifestations must first be interposed between, and that the more rational statement is that we feel sorry because we cry, angry because we strike, afraid because we tremble, and not that we cry, strike, or tremble because we are sorry, angry, or fearful, as the case may be. Without the bodily states following on the perception, the latter would be purely cognitive in form, pale, colorless, destitute of emotional warmth. We might then see the bear and judge it best to run, receive the insult and deem it right to strike, but we should not actually feel afraid or angry. Stated in this crude way, the hypothesis is pretty sure to meet with immediate disbelief. And yet neither many nor farfetched considerations are required to mitigate its paradoxical character, and possibly to produce conviction of its truth. (1892a/1992, p. 352)

In formulating his theory of emotion, James wrestled with issues that remain unresolved today. The first issue is the most basic: What *is* an emotion? Many, perhaps most, of our perceptions are "purely cognitive in form." The perceptions of my computer screen, my mouse pad, a mug of tea on my desk are "pale, colorless, destitute of emotional warmth." It is certainly true that, should I meet a bear in the woods, my perception of it will be warm (to say the least), but in what does this warmth—the *emotion* of fear—consist? What is added to consciousness in the case of the bear that is not added in the case of my mug of tea?

James's answer was virtually dictated by reflex theory of the brain. Recall that in reflex theory, the brain was seen as being rather like a telephone switchboard, providing connections between stimulus and response, but incapable of originating experience, feeling, or action on its own. James gave this rather passive view of the brain a dynamic twist, holding that any perceived stimulus acts on the nervous system to automatically bring about some adaptive bodily response, whether learned or innate. Thus, if a large animal rears up and roars at me, I possess an innate and automatic tendency to run away. When I am driving and a traffic light turns red, I have a learned and automatic tendency to step on my car's brakes.

To understand some of the later debates about consciousness, especially the motor theory of consciousness (see later), we should remember that what's evolutionarily adaptive in this sequence of events is my running away. Whatever I may subjectively feel on seeing the bear is completely irrelevant as long as I escape from its clutches. I could, as James says, see the bear and coolly reason that running away is the wise thing to do, feeling nothing at all. Robots that seek out some objects and avoid others have been built, but of course they feel neither desire nor fear.

Yet, because we humans do feel fear (and desire), it is the psychologist's job to figure out what fear (or desire)—the extra state of consciousness added to the cognitive perception of the bear—is. James proposed that the emotional something extra is the registration in consciousness of the responses of our body caused by the sight of the bear. Because he thought of the brain as a mere connecting device, James located emotions not in the brain itself but outside the brain, in the viscera (our stomach churns with fear) and the muscles that work to take us away from the bear. With regard to simple emotions like fear or lust (as opposed to subtler emotions like envy or love), James believed that the most important bodily feelings that constitute emotions arise in the viscera. In summary, according to the James–Lange theory of emotion, fear does not *cause* our intestines to churn and our legs to run, nor do churning intestines and running legs *cause* us to feel fear; instead, fear simply *is* our churning innards and running legs. Emotions are states of the body.

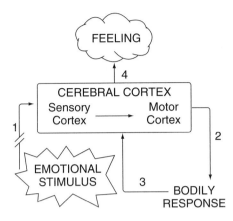

More generally, James said that mental states have two sorts of bodily effects. First, unless some inhibition is present, the thought of an act automatically leads to the execution of the act. Second, mental states cause internal bodily changes, including covert motor responses, changes in heart rate, glandular secretions, and perhaps "processes more subtle still." Therefore, James argued, "it will be safe to lay down the general law that no mental modification ever occurs which is not accompanied or followed by a bodily change" (1890, vol. 1, p. 5). The contents of consciousness are thus determined not only by sensations coming in from outside, but by kinesthetic feedback (as we call it today) from the body's motor activity. "Our psychology must therefore take account not only of the conditions antecedent to mental states, but of their resultant consequences as well. . . . The whole neural organism [is] . . . but a machine for converting stimuli into reactions; and the intellectual part of our life is knit up with but the middle or 'central' part of the machine's operations" (vol. 2, p. 372).

And here lies the rub for James. If emotions consist in our registration of the emotion-producing stimulus (e.g., the bear) and in the bodily responses automatically triggered by the stimulus (e.g., churning of the viscera and running away), then we may question if emotions actually cause behavior. If we feel afraid because we run away, then fear is not the cause of running away but a conscious state that comes along for the ride, as it were. The James–Lange theory of emotion seems to be quite consistent with the automaton theory of the brain that James rejected. Consciousness, including emotion, has no more to do with causing behavior than an automobile's color has to do with making it go. A car has to have some color, and living beings, it appears, have to have conscious experiences, but neither the car's color nor the brain's consciousness actually does anything. As a science of the causes of behavior, psychology might be able to ignore consciousness altogether.

James found himself caught in the same dilemma felt by other reluctant believers in mechanism between the heart's feeling of freedom and the intellect's scientific declaration of determinism. James was deeply committed to free will from personal experience. As a young man, he had pulled himself out of a black depression by literally willing himself to live again, and, dogged by depression his whole life, he made human will the center of his philosophy. However, in his psychology, committed to cerebralism, he found himself almost forced to accept determinism as the only scientifically acceptable view of behavior. He stoutly resisted the conclusion, denouncing mechanistic conceptions of human conduct and, as we have seen, proclaiming that consciousness decreed survival and commanded the body. After writing *Principles*, James abandoned psychology for philosophy in 1892 and developed his own brand of pragmatism. He tried to resolve the struggle between the head and the heart by setting the feelings of the heart on an equal footing with the cognitions of the head. Nevertheless, the conflict remained, and the influence of *Principles* was to lead American psychologists away from consciousness and toward behavior, and so away from James's own definition of psychology as the science of mental life.

James's Envoi to Psychology

For all its influence on psychology, James's *Principles* turned out to be for him just a diversion. In 1892, he brought out a one-volume *Briefer Course*, more suitable as a classroom text, but pronounced himself weary of psychology. In that same year, he secured a successor, Hugo Münsterberg, as Harvard's experimental psychologist and resumed his career as a philosopher, making 1892 a doubly significant year for psychology, as it also saw the founding of the APA.

James's ambiguous feeling about scientific psychology surfaced in a reply (1892b) to a negative review of his *Principles of Psychology* by George Trumbull Ladd (1842–1921). Although Ladd accepted some aspects of scientific psychology, he defended the old, religiously oriented psychology of the Scottish tradition, finding naturalistic psychology inadequate to serve human souls. James agreed that psychology was not then a science, but "a mass of phenomenal description, gossip and myth." He wrote the *Principles*, he said, wishing "by treating Psychology like a natural science to help her become one" (p. 146).

James (1890) correctly set out the new psychology's theme as a natural science. The cerebralist, reflex-action theory is invaluable because, by treating behavior as the outcome of physiologically rooted motor habits and impulses, it works toward the "practical prediction and control" that is the aim of all natural sciences. Psychology should no longer be regarded as part of philosophy but as "a branch of biology." In one important respect, James agreed with Ladd because he believed that scientific psychology could not, in fact, address many important questions concerning human life. For example, as we have seen, James believed passionately in free will. In the *Principles*, he discussed attention, an important process by which we (seem) to willfully choose to attend to one thing rather than another. He contrasted "cause" theories of attention, which say that paying attention is a willful act, with "effect" theories of attention, which say that attention is an effect produced by cognitive processes over which we have no control. James could find no way to decide between the theories on scientific grounds and concluded by endorsing cause theories on moral grounds because they accept the reality of free will and moral responsibility. However, because moral considerations lie outside science, James ended his chapter on attention without further elaboration indicating that the issue could not be decided on scientific grounds alone.

In his paper, James also touched on the future of psychology as an applied discipline. What people want, he said, is a practical psychology that tells people how to act, that makes a difference to life. "The kind of psychology which could cure a case of melancholy, or charm a chronic insane delusion away, ought certainly to be preferred to the most seraphic insight into the nature of the soul" (1892b, p. 153). Psychology should be practical, should make a difference. James not only voiced the growing practical aims of American psychologists as they organized and professionalized, but he announced his own touchstone of truth: True ideas make a difference to living. James's next task then, was the full development of the characteristically American philosophy, pragmatism.

By the mid-1890s, the outlines of a new psychology, distinctively American in character, were emerging. The interest of American psychologists was shifting away from what consciousness contains and toward what consciousness does and how it aids an organism, human or animal, in its adaptation to a changing environment. In short, mental content was becoming less important than mental function. This new functional psychology was a natural offspring of Darwinism and the new American experience. Mind, consciousness, would not exist, James had said in the *Principles*, unless it served the adaptive needs of its host; in the America of the 1890s, it was clear that consciousness's prime function was to guide adjustment to the rapid flow of change engulfing immigrant and farmer, worker and professional. In a world of constant change, ancient truths—mental content, fixed doctrines—became uncouth every day. Heraclitus's universe had at last become true, and people no longer believed in Plato's eternal Forms. In the Heraclitean flux, the only eternal constant was change, and therefore the only reality of experience—psychology's subject matter—was adjustment to change.

Jamesian Pragmatism

James went on to develop his own version of pragmatism, a more expansive and romantic pragmatism than Peirce's narrow scientific version. Pragmatism had begun with the rigorously scientific attitude of C. S. Peirce as a way of determining whether human concepts had any empirical content. But Peirce's conception was too narrowly cognitive to meet fully the everyday demands of a post-Darwinian, Heraclitean world. It had become clear that there were no Platonic permanent truths; yet people find it difficult to live without some certainty, some fixed star to steer by. James made in pragmatism a fixed star of a new sort. James offered a method for making, rather than finding, truths, and in elaborating Peirce's pragmatism he included emotional learnings that Peirce could not abide.

In a series of works beginning in 1895 and culminating in *Pragmatism* (1907/1955), James developed a comprehensive, pragmatic approach to the problems of science, philosophy, and life. He argued that ideas were worthless or, more precisely, meaningless, unless they mattered to our lives. An idea with no consequences was pointless and meaningless. As he wrote in *Pragmatism*:

> True ideas are those that we can assimilate, validate, corroborate and verify. False ideas are those that we can not. That is the practical difference it makes for us to have true ideas. . . . The truth of an idea is not a stagnant property inherent in it. Truth happens to an idea. It becomes true, is made true by events. Its verity is in fact an event, a process. (p. 133)

So far, this sounds like Peirce: a hardheaded, Darwinian approach to truth. James went beyond Peirce, however, when he said that the truth of an idea should be tested against its agreement with all of one's experience, "nothing being omitted." When Peirce had said we weigh ideas against experience, he meant experience in a narrow, cognitive sense: the scientist's apprehension of the physical world. James, however, with the romantics, saw no reason to value one kind of experience above another. Noncognitive experience—hopes, fears, loves, ambitions—were just as much part of a person's living reality as sensations of number, hardness, or mass. "Ideas," James said, "(which themselves are but parts of our experience) become true just in so far as they help us get into satisfactory relations with other parts of our experience" (p. 49, italics omitted). James's criterion of truth was thus much broader than Peirce's and could apply to any concept, no matter how seemingly fanciful or metaphysical. To the tough-minded empiricist, the ideas of God or of free will were meaningless—literally neither true nor false—because they were devoid of sensory content. To James, such ideas nevertheless could make a difference in the way we conduct our lives. If the idea of free will and its corollary, moral responsibility, lead men and women to live better, happier lives than if they believed in the automaton theory, then free will was true; or, more exactly, it was made true in the lives and experience of the people who accepted it.

James's pragmatism held no metaphysical prejudices, unlike traditional rationalism and empiricism:

> Rationalism sticks to logic and the empyrean. Empiricism sticks to the external senses. Pragmatism is willing to take anything, to follow either logic or the senses and to count the humblest and most personal experiences. She will count mystical experiences if they have practical consequences. (1907/1955, p. 61)

Against the cold, intellectual positivism of Peirce's pragmatism, James asserted the claims of the heart, so congenial to Americans since the time of Jonathan Edwards. As James recognized, his pragmatism was anti-intellectual in setting heart and head as equals in the search for truth. Compared to rationalists and searchers for perfect Truth, James wrote, "A radical pragmatist is a happy-go-lucky anarchist sort of creature" (p. 168). Functional psychologists and their heirs, the behaviorists, would likewise depreciate the intellect. Learning and problem solving, as we shall see, would soon be explained in terms of blind trial and error and resulting reward and punishment, not in terms of directed cognitive activity.

Pragmatism was a *functional* philosophy—a method, not a doctrine. It provided a way of coping with the Heraclitean flux of experience no matter what the challenge or the topic. In the fields of theology and physics, politics and ethics, philosophy and psychology, it offered a star to navigate by. Although one could not hope to find a fixed, final truth about God or matter, society or morality, metaphysics or the mind, one could at least know what questions to ask: Does this concept matter? Does it make a difference to me, to my society, to my science? Pragmatism promised that even though there were no final solutions to any problem, at least there was a method of concretely resolving problems here and now.

Heretofore, philosophers had searched for first principles, indubitable ideas on which to erect a philosophical system and a philosophy of science. James's pragmatism gave up the quest for first principles, recognizing that, after Darwin, no truth could be fixed. Instead, James offered a philosophy that worked by turning away from content (fixed truths) and toward function (what ideas do for us). As he did this, psychologists were quietly developing a psychology of function, studying not the ideas a mind contained but how the mind worked in adapting its organism to a changing environment. At the same time, they hoped that psychological science would work in the modern world, meeting the challenges of immigration and education, madness and feeblemindedness, business and politics.

FROM MENTALISM TO BEHAVIORALISM

In April 1913, the philosopher Warner Fite reviewed—anonymously, as was the custom at *The Nation*—three books on "The Science of Man." One was a text on genetics, but the other two were psychological: Hugo Münsterberg's *Psychology and Industrial Efficiency* and Maurice Parmelee's *The Science of Human Behavior*. Fite observed that psychology in 1913 seemed little concerned with consciousness; Münsterberg explicitly stated that the psychological "way of ordinary life, in which we try to understand our neighbor by entering into his mental functions . . . is not psychological analysis." Fite concluded:

> Precisely. True "psychological analysis" ignores all personal experience of mentality. The science of psychology is, then, the finished result of what we may call the conspiracy of naturalism, in which each investigator has bound himself by a strange oath to obtain all his knowledge from observation of the actions of his fellows—"as a naturalist studies the chemical

elements or the stars" [Münsterberg]—and never under any circumstances to conceive them in the light of his own experience of his living. Even the psychologist's "mental states" or "objects of consciousness" are only so many hypothetical entities read from without. . . . What is to be expected from a science of humanity which ignores all that is most distinctive of man? (1913, p. 370)

Clearly, psychology had changed since James wrote his *Principles*. James and Wundt had proclaimed a new science of mental life, the study of consciousness as such; Freud used introspection and inference to enter his patients' minds, both conscious and unconscious. But by 1913, Fite found a psychology aimed at behavior, not consciousness, based on treating people as things, not as conscious agents. The transition from mentalism, defining psychology as the scientific study of consciousness, to *behavioralism*, defining psychology as the scientific study of behavior, was the inevitable result of many historical forces.

BUILDING ON JAMES: THE MOTOR THEORY OF CONSCIOUSNESS, 1892–1896

The spirit of the new psychology in America was that of James's *Principles of Psychology*. Cattell said it "has breathed the breath of life into the dust of psychology." James himself detested the professional, even commercial, attitudes overcoming academia and harbored doubts about the validity of scientific psychology. Nevertheless, it was upon his text that American psychology was built.

Hugo Münsterberg and Action Theory

By 1892, James was weary of psychology and eager to move on to philosophy. He looked for someone to replace him as Harvard's experimental psychologist, and his attention was drawn to Hugo Münsterberg (1863–1916), who, though a student of Wundt, nevertheless disagreed with his teacher in ways James found attractive. Like James, Münsterberg addressed the problem of will in terms of feedback from automatic motor responses to stimuli. However, his "action theory" developed a more thoroughgoing *motor theory of consciousness* that did away with will altogether (a step James could never take) and reduced consciousness from an active striver for ends to a mere spectator of its bearer's actions.

In a dissertation Wundt refused to accept, Münsterberg addressed the nature of will from a psychological standpoint. In the eighteenth century, David Hume had set out to find the psychological basis of the Self, but found that it dissolved under his introspective gaze. Now Münsterberg set out to find the psychological basis of will, only to find that it, too, seemed to be more illusion than reality. will is an important concept in philosophy and folk psychology, but in what, Münsterberg asked, does it consist as a psychological experience? Moreover, Münsterberg questioned the place of any concept of free will in scientific psychology. From the time of Locke, it had been recognized that reconciling freedom of will with scientific determinism was no easy feat. James had been driven from psychology by his inability to reconcile the two. In particular, there seemed no room for will in the reflex concept of the brain then coming to full development. After the work of Fritsch and Hitzig, there seemed no place to put will: The brain produced behavior simply by associating incoming stimulus nerves with outgoing response nerves. As far as physiology went; there was no need for consciousness at all: $S \rightarrow Physiological\ Process \rightarrow R$, where S is stimulus and R is response.

Reflex theory seemed now to be a tenable conception of how behavior is produced. As Münsterberg wrote, "For the preservation of the individual, it is obviously irrelevant whether a purposeful motion is accompanied by contents of consciousness or not" (quoted by Hale, 1980, p. 41). However, there *are* conscious contents (the traditional subject matter of psychology) to explain: Why do we believe we have an effective will? Like James, Münsterberg located the source of this belief in behavior: "our ideas are the product of our readiness to act . . . our actions shape our knowledge" (quoted by Kuklick, 1977). Our feeling of will, the motor theory explains, comes about because we are aware of our behavior and our incipient tendencies to behave. Thus, I might announce that I'm going to stand up from my chair, not because I've reached a decision to stand but because the motor processes of standing have just begun and have entered consciousness. I feel my "will" to be effective because generally, the incipient tendencies to act are followed by real action, and the former triggers memories of the latter. Because the covert tendencies have usually in fact preceded overt behavior, I believe my "will" is usually carried out.

The motor theory of consciousness can be summarized as:

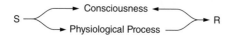

The contents of consciousness are determined by stimuli impinging upon us, by our overt behaviors, and by peripheral changes in muscles and glands produced by the physiological processes linking stimulus and response. Münsterberg, unlike James, was not afraid of the implications of the motor theory of consciousness. He concluded that consciousness is an epiphenomenon that plays no role in causing behavior. Consciousness observed the world and its body's resulting actions, falsely believing that it connected the two when in fact it was the brain that did so. In this conception, psychology must be physiological in a reductive sense, explaining consciousness in terms of underlying physiological processes, especially at the periphery. Practical, applied psychology, a field in which Münsterberg was quite active, would perforce be behavioral, explaining human action as the outcome of human circumstances.

The motor theory of consciousness was not confined to James or Münsterberg. In one form or another, it grew in influence. We have before us now the central philosophical-psychological theme of these two decades: What, if anything, does consciousness *do*? The motor theory of consciousness abetted the rise of behavioralism. If the theory is true, consciousness, in fact, does nothing. So why, except from faith in the old definition of psychology as the study of consciousness, should we study it? The study of consciousness seemed increasingly irrelevant to American psychologists building a socially and commercially useful profession.

John Dewey and the Reflex Arc

Coming under the influence of James's *Principles*, the philosopher and John Dewey (1859–1952) moved away from his youthful belief in Hegelian idealism and began to develop his own pragmatic conception of consciousness: instrumentalism. In the mid-1890s, he produced a series of important but tediously written papers that, taking the *Principles* as the footings, laid the foundations of his lifelong attempt to bring together philosophy, psychology, and ethics in a harmonious whole. These papers also furnished the central conceptions of America's native psychology: *functionalism*.

The most influential of these papers was "The Reflex Arc Concept in Psychology" (1896). Dewey criticized the traditional associationist reflex arc concept, $S \rightarrow Idea \rightarrow R$, as artificially breaking up behavior into disjointed parts. He did not deny that stimulus, sensation (idea), and response exist. He did, however, deny that they were distinct events like three beads on a string. Instead, Dewey considered stimulus, idea, and response to be divisions of labor in an overall coordination of action as the organism adjusts to its environment.

Developing his own motor theory of consciousness, Dewey regarded sensation not as passive registration of an impression but as behavior dynamically interacting with other behaviors occurring at the same time. So, to a soldier anxiously awaiting contact with the enemy, the sound of a twig snapping has one significance and fills consciousness; to a hiker in a peaceful woods, it has quite another. Indeed, the hiker may not even notice the snapping sound.

Dewey made here a decisive move whose significance, buried in his dry, abstract prose, is not immediately apparent. We might, with Wundt and James, attribute the differences in experience of the twig's snapping to willfully focused attention. The soldier is actively listening for sounds of approach; the hiker is attending to the songs of birds. But Dewey's motor theory followed Hume in dispensing with the self and followed Münsterberg in dispensing with will. It is the *current behavior*, claimed Dewey, that gives a sensation its significance, or even determines if a stimulus becomes a sensation at all. A stimulus counts as a sensation, and takes on value only if it has a relationship with our current behavior.

James had advanced a cerebralist approach to mind but had not fully drawn out the implications of this view. Dewey saw that behavior often runs off by itself, occasioning no sensations or ideas in any significant sense of the term. It is only when behavior needs to be newly coordinated to reality—that is, needs to be adjusted—that sensation and emotion arise. The hiker's behavior need not be adjusted to the snap of a twig, and his walking continues uninterrupted. The soldier urgently needs to coordinate his behavior to the snap of a twig, and its sound thus looms large in consciousness. Moreover, the soldier's emotion, fear, apprehension, and perhaps anger at the enemy are felt, Dewey argued, only because his behavior is in check; his emotions arise from feedback from his thwarted action tendencies. Emotion, said Dewey, is a sign of conflicting dispositions to act—in the soldier's case, to fight or flee. Could he do either immediately and wholeheartedly, he would feel nothing, Dewey said.

Dewey's formulation of the motor theory of consciousness was centrally important for later American psychology; in 1943, his *reflex arc* paper was chosen as one of the most important articles ever published in *Psychological Review*. Dewey showed that psychology could do away with the central willing Self of idealism, already attenuated by James. Rather than assigning the control of perception and decision to an inaccessible Transcendental Ego, it became possible to account for them in terms of coordinated, ever-changing, adaptive behaviors. So hearing was one sort of behavior, attending another, and responding a third. All were coordinated toward the end of survival in a constant, fluid stream of behavior ever in motion, not unlike the daily lives of contemporary Americans. Dewey's ideas became the commonplaces of functionalism. More broadly, Dewey began in these papers to develop the Progressive view mentioned earlier, that the self did not exist in nature but was a social construction.

FROM PHILOSOPHY TO BIOLOGY: FUNCTIONAL PSYCHOLOGY, 1896–1910

Experiments Become Functional

Traditional psychology of consciousness, while inevitably investigating mental processes such as apperception, retained an emphasis on conscious content as the subject matter of psychology; its primary novelty was subjecting consciousness to experimental control in order to capture consciousness for science. However, as we saw earlier in this chapter, William James, in his *Principles of Psychology*, shifted the interest of American psychology from content to process. As he pictured the mind, mental contents were evanescent, fleeting things—seen once and never to return; what endured were mental functions, especially the function of choosing. James's new emphasis was reinforced by the new American experience of the 1890s—old truths replaced by new ones, familiar scenes by strange ones. What remained constant was the process of adjusting to the new.

The development of the motor theory of consciousness continued the process of depreciating mental content and, by implication, the method used to access it, introspection. In the motor theory, consciousness contained sensations from the world and from motor activity but played little, if any, role in causing behavior. Although, of course, it remained possible to introspect and report conscious content—as Münsterberg continued to do in his laboratory—it could easily be seen as pointless, even irresponsible. American psychologists agreed with James: What was needed was a psychology that met the pragmatic test by being effective. Awash in change, Americans needed a psychology that did something to cope with the emerging modern world. Introspection only revealed what was; Americans needed to prepare for what *is to be*. James, Münsterberg, and Dewey were preparing for the new functional psychology by turning their attention from content to adaptive process.

At the same time, experimental psychologists shifted the focus of their research from introspective reports of conscious content to objective determinations of the correlation between stimulus and response. As developed by Wundt, the experimental method had two aspects. A standardized, controlled stimulus was presented to a subject who responded to it in some way, reporting at the same time the contents of his or her experience. Wundt, as a mentalist, was interested in the experience produced by given conditions and used objective results as clues to the processes that produced conscious content. However, in the hands of American psychologists, emphasis shifted from conscious experience to the determination of responses by stimulus conditions.

As an example, let us take an experiment on how people locate an object in space on the basis of sound (Angell, 1903a). In this experiment, a blindfolded observer—one of them, JBW, was probably John B. Watson, the founder of behaviorism—was seated in a chair at the center of apparatus that could present a sound at any point around the observer. After setting the sound generator at a given point, the experimenter made it produce a tone, and the observer pointed to where he believed the sound was coming from. Then the observer provided an introspective report of the conscious experience provoked by the sound. Watson reported seeing a mental image of the apparatus surrounding him, with the sound generator located where he pointed. Now, one could, as a mentalist would, focus on the introspective report as the data of interest, aiming to describe and explain this bit of mental content. On the other hand, one could focus on the accuracy of the pointing response, correlating the position of the sound generator with the observer's indicated position.

In the Angell experiment, although both objective data—the correlation of stimulus position with the observer's response—and introspective reports were discussed, the latter were given secondary importance. The objective findings were highlighted and extensively discussed; the introspective findings were briefly mentioned at the end of the article. Under influence of the motor theory of consciousness, introspection was becoming less important because consciousness played no causal role in determining behavior, and the same attitude affected the experiments of the time. From the inception of American psychology, introspective reports were first isolated from the objective results and then shortened or removed altogether, as "observers" became "subjects" (Danziger, 1990).

In addressing how behavior is adjusted to stimuli, American psychologists turned from the study of mental content to the study of adaptive mental functions. Another experiment, Bryan and Harter (1897), reveals a second sense in which American psychology was becoming functional— socially functional. Bryan, an experimental psychologist, and Harter, a former railroad telegrapher turned graduate student in psychology, investigated the acquisition of telegraphic skills by new railroad telegraphers. Their report contained no introspective reports at all but instead charted the students' gradual improvement over months of practice. This completely objective study was socially significant because Bryan and Harter were studying an important skill learned by people who were assuming an important role in industrialized America. As the railroads expanded and knit together the island communities of formerly rural America, railroad telegraphers were vital: They kept track of what goods were sent where, of what trains were going to what places; in short, they were the communication links that made the whole railroad system function. So important was the training of railroad telegraphers that the Union and Wabash Railroad commissioned Bryan and Harter's study. They brought psychological research to bear on a topic of real social and commercial value.

Their study is significant in another respect as well. It foreshadowed the central problem of experimental psychology 40 years later: The traditional psychology of consciousness, mentalism, had primarily investigated perception and its allied functions because it was these that produced introspectible mental contents. But in the post-Darwinian psychology of James and his followers, consciousness was important for what it does, adjusting the organism to its environment. Gradual adjustment over time is learning: finding out about the environment and then behaving in accord with it. Bryan and Harter plotted learning curves and discussed how the novice telegraphers gradually adjusted to the demands of their jobs. In its objectivism, in its concern with a socially useful problem, and in its choice of learning as subject matter, Bryan and Harter's paper was a sign of things to come. It is no wonder, therefore, that in 1943 it was voted by leading American psychologists as the most important experimental study yet published in the *Psychological Review* and one of the five most important papers of any kind.

By 1904, it was clear that the "objective" method, in which responses were correlated with stimuli, was at least as important as the introspective analysis of consciousness. Speaking before the International Congress of Arts and Science, Cattell, the American pioneer in psychology, said, "I am not convinced that psychology should be limited to the study of consciousness as such," which of course had been the definition of psychology for James and Wundt. His own work with mental tests, Cattell said, "is nearly as independent of introspection as work in physics or in zoology." Although introspection and experiment should "continually cooperate," it was obvious from "the brute argument of accomplished fact" that much of psychology now existed "apart from introspection." Although Cattell seemed to place introspection and objective measurement on an equal footing, it is clear from his tone and from his later call for applied psychology that the objective, behavioral approach to psychology was on the rise.

Functional Psychology Defined

In both theory and research, then, American psychology was moving away from the traditional psychology of conscious content and toward a psychology of mental adjustment inspired by evolutionary theory. Interestingly, it was not an American psychologist who spotted and identified this new trend but the staunchest defender of a pure psychology of content, E. B. Titchener. In his *Postulates of a Structural Psychology* (1898), Titchener cogently distinguished several kinds of psychology, and although others may have disagreed about which kind of psychology was best, his terminology endured.

Titchener drew a broad analogy among three kinds of biology and three kinds of psychology:

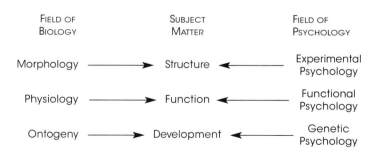

In biology, the anatomist, the student of morphology, carefully dissects the body to discover the organs that compose it, revealing the body's structure. Once an organ is isolated and described, it is the job of the physiologist to figure out its function, what it does. Finally, one might study how an organ develops in the course of embryogenesis and postnatal development and how the organ came into being in the course of evolution. Such studies constitute genetic biology.

Similarly, in psychology, the experimental psychologist—by which Titchener meant himself and his students—dissects consciousness into its component parts; this anatomy of the mind defines structural psychology. What the revealed structures do is the province of psychological physiology—functional psychology. The development of mental structures and functions is the subject matter of genetic psychology, which investigates the course of individual and phylogenetic development.

In Titchener's estimation, structural psychology logically preceded functional psychology, because only after mental structures had been isolated and described could their functions be ascertained. At the same time, Titchener noted the appeal of functional psychology. Its roots were ancient, its analysis of mind hewed close to common sense, as it employed faculty concepts such as "memory," "imagination," and "judgment," and it seemed to promise immediate practical application. Citing Dewey's reflex arc paper, Titchener also acknowledged that functional psychology was growing in influence. Nevertheless, Titchener urged psychologists to avoid the lures of functional psychology and to stick to the tough, scientific job of experimental introspective psychology. Titchener's paper marked the beginning of a struggle between *structuralism* and functionalism to control American psychology. His third kind of psychology, genetic psychology, was just underway (Baldwin, 1895; Wozniak, 1982) and offered no theoretical perspective of its own. However, because the study of development focused on mental operations rather than introspective content—and children were poor introspectors anyway—genetic psychology was a natural ally of functionalism. In the event, although Titchener set the terms of America's first war in psychological theory, his defeat was inevitable.

From Undercurrent to Main Current

In the decade following Titchener's *Postulates*, it became apparent that other psychologists found his analysis correct but reversed his priorities. In his December 1900 presidential address to the APA, Peirce's one-time collaborator, Joseph Jastrow, explored "Some Currents and Undercurrents in Psychology" (Jastrow, 1901). He declared that psychology is "the science of mental function," not content. The functional approach arose out of evolution; it "at once cast a blinding light" on dark areas of psychology long held by "dogmatism, misconception and neglect" and "breathed a new life" into "the dry bones" of psychology. Jastrow correctly observed that although concern with mental function pervaded current research, it was not the central subject of investigation but rather gave a distinctive "color tone" to American psychology. Jastrow saw functional psychology as a growing undercurrent, which he wanted to bring forward as a "main current" in the development of psychology. Functional psychology, said Jastrow, is more catholic than structural psychology. It welcomes to psychology the previously excluded topics of comparative psychology, abnormal psychology, mental testing, the study of the average person, and even psychical research, although this last topic clearly troubled him. Jastrow predicted that functional psychology would prove to have more value to practical affairs than structural psychology. Finally, he noted, as we have, that all these trends are characteristically American, and he correctly prophesied that the future would belong to functional, not structural, psychology.

Functional psychologists adopted James's conception of consciousness and moved it further toward behavioralism. Thaddeus Bolton (1902) wrote, "Mind is to be regarded as an outgrowth of conduct, a superior and more direct means of adjusting the organism to the environment," and H. Heath Bawden (1904) added, "The most fundamental statement we can make about consciousness is that it is action." Conscious content, as such, is not very important in the functionalist theory of mind, which says that mind is a set of processes whose biological value lies in its ability to be summoned forth when its organism finds itself faced with a new situation. It is not needed when instincts are adequate to the stimuli at hand or when previously learned habits are functioning smoothly.

Consciousness is a sometime thing, needed only occasionally, and it would not be long before other psychologists dispensed with mind altogether. As Frank Thilly (1905) pointed out, the functional view of consciousness retained James's fatal flaw. Along with just about everyone else, James and the functional psychologists following him held to mind-body parallelism while at the same time arguing that consciousness actively intervenes in the activities of the organism. Bolton was aware of the problem and tried to maintain that although consciousness does not affect nervous processes, it somehow plays a role in learning. This was not a happy position for functional psychologists to be in, and they would be rescued—or replaced—by the bolder behaviorists ready to chuck consciousness completely out of psychology. After all, if one can see conscious content in behavior, as Bolton maintained, why not just stick to talking about behavior?

By 1905, it was clear to contemporary psychologists that the functional tide was in. Edward Franklin Buchner, who, for some years, wrote for *Psychological Bulletin*, an annual accounting of the year's "Psychological Progress," observed "the widespread acceptance and defense of the 'functional' as over against the 'structural' view" of psychology." The replacement of the older system by a new one did have the unfortunate effect, Buchner noted, of starting the development of the field all over again, undoing cumulative progress. In the same volume, Felix Arnold raised "the great cry" of current psychologists: "WHAT IS IT [consciousness] GOOD FOR?" He praised functionalists for giving up the old view of perception Bolton had attacked and replacing it with perception conceived "as a motor process . . . determining serial reactions toward [an] object" (Arnold, 1905).

In the same year, Mary Calkins (1863–1930) took the opportunity of her APA presidential address to advance her self psychology as a way to reconcile structural and functional psychologies. If psychology is conceived as the study of a real psychological self possessing both conscious content and mental functions, each system could be viewed as contributing part of the total psychological picture. Although Calkins aggressively pushed her self psychology over the years in every forum she could find, it seems to have found few followers. The time of compromise had passed. In 1907, Buchner wrote that in 1906, "The functional point of view seem[ed] to have almost completely won out"— so much so that psychology's " 'older' (and almost consecrated) terms" were about finished. Buchner awaited the framing "of a new vocabulary of psychology for the new twentieth century."

The leading functionalist was James Rowland Angell (1869–1949), who had studied with John Dewey as an undergraduate. In 1904, Angell published an introductory textbook, *Psychology*, written from the functional standpoint. For Angell, functional psychology was more important than structural psychology. Unlike bodily organs, the structuralists' alleged mental elements were not permanent, enduring objects, but existed only at the moment of perception. That is, the functions produce the structures—the reverse of biology, in which a given organ performs a distinct function that would not exist without it. Angell also alleged that structural psychology was socially pointless and biologically irrelevant. It studied consciousness removed from "life conditions" and could therefore tell us nothing useful about how mind works in the real world. Moreover, structuralist reductionism made of consciousness an irrelevant epiphenomenon. Functional psychology, in contrast, reveals consciousness to be "an efficient agent in the furtherance of the life activities of the organism"—that is, as biologically useful and quite in accord, as Titchener himself had said, with common sense.

In his 1906 APA presidential address, "The Province of Functional Psychology," Angell (1907) directly replied to Titchener's "Postulates of a Structural Psychology." Angell's address was a milestone on the road to behavioralism. Angell conceded at the outset that functional psychology was "little more than a program" and a "protest" against the sterilities of structural psychology. But then he went on to suggest that structural psychology was a historical aberration, a brief philosophical interlude in the development of scientific, biologically oriented theories of the mind. Functional psychology only appeared new when contrasted with the introspective content psychologies of the first German laboratories. In fact, functional psychology was the true heir to psychology's past, being the fruit of an ancient line of descent running from Aristotle through Spencer, Darwin, and pragmatism.

Angell repeated the familiar distinction: Structural psychology was concerned with mental *contents*; functionalism with mental *operations*. Functionalism studies mental process as it is in the actual life of an organism; structuralism studies how mind "appears" in a "merely postmortem analysis." To this end, "modern investigations . . . dispense with the usual direct form of introspection and concern themselves . . . with a determination of what work is accomplished and what the conditions are under which it is achieved" (Angell 1907). Angell here acknowledged the trend we earlier found in his and others' research and defined the point of view of behavioralist experimentation. He justified this new research emphasis by quite correctly asserting that unlike physical organs dissected by the anatomist, "mental contents are evanescent and fleeting." What endures over time are mental functions: Contents come and go, but attention, memory, judgment—the mental faculties of the old psychology rehabilitated—"persist."

Functional psychology also brought a change in psychology's institutional relationships, Angell said. Structural psychology grew out of philosophy and remained closely allied to it. In contrast, functional psychology "brings the psychologist cheek by jowl with the general biologist," because both study the "sum total" of an organism's "organic activities"; the psychologist concentrating on the "accommodatory service" of consciousness. Angell's alliance with biology was not Wundt's. Wundt, following the ancient, pre-Darwinian *path through physiology*, linked the study of the mind to the study of the brain. Angell, more thoroughly influenced by Darwin than even James had been, linked the study of the mind to evolutionary biology, not to neurophysiology. The key idea for functionalists was viewing consciousness as an organ serving its bearer's adaptive interests. How consciousness operated at the level of brain mechanisms was less important than how it operated at the level of adaptive behavior.

This new biological orientation promised practical benefits as well, Angell averred. "Pedagogy and mental hygiene . . . await the quickening and guiding counsel" of functional psychology. Animal psychology—"the most pregnant" movement of "our generation"—finds its "rejuvenation" in the new movement because it is becoming "experimental . . . wherever possible" and "conservatively . . . non-anthropomorphic." Genetic psychology and abnormal psychology—the former barely mentioned and the latter completely ignored by Titchener—would likewise be inspired by a functional approach.

Angell endorsed the view set forth by Bawden that consciousness "supervenes on certain occasions" in the life of an organism, describing the adjustment theory as "the position now held by all psychologists of repute." But he went further than Bawden or Bolton in claiming that consciousness "is no indispensable feature of the accommodatory process." Although in a footnote Angell still held that accommodation to "the novel" is "the field of conscious activity," he has taken a further step toward behavioralism by suggesting that learning can take place without conscious intervention.

Functional psychology was "functional" in three senses. First, it considered mind to have a distinct biological function selected by Darwinian evolution: It adapts its organism to novel circumstances. Second, it described consciousness as itself a result of the physiological functioning of the organism: Mind, in this view, is itself a biological function. Third, functional psychology promised to be socially useful in improving education, mental hygiene, and abnormal states: Psychology will become functional to twentieth-century life. In 1906, Angell stood at a hinge in the development of modern psychology. His continued concern with consciousness, however interpreted, still linked functional psychology with the mentalism of the past. But at the same time, his emphasis on biology, on adaptation, and on applied psychology marks functional psychology as a "new-old movement" whose time will someday pass to "some worthier successor [to] fill its place."

By 1907, then, functional psychology had by and large replaced structural psychology as the dominant approach to the field. However, it never became more than a program and a protest. It was too inconsistent to survive, clinging to a definition of psychology as the study of consciousness, while at the same time putting forth theories of perception and learning that made consciousness less and less necessary as a concept for scientific psychology. Functional theory embodied very clearly the historical forces of the time, pushing psychology toward the study of behavior, and it helped psychologists change their fundamental conceptions of their profession without quite realizing that they were doing anything extraordinary.

Functional Psychology in Europe

Although functional psychology was strongest in America, psychologies that could be identified with functionalism also arose in Europe. Brentano's psychology, because it was labeled an "act" psychology, was often assimilated to the functional viewpoint. Similarly, the Würzburg school and the students of memory could be called "functional" because of their concern with and investigations of mental processes. In Britain, home of modern evolutionism, functional psychology found its William James in James Ward (1843–1925), sometimes called the "father of modern British psychology" (Turner, 1974). He was for a time a minister, but after a crisis of faith turned first to physiology, then psychology, and finally philosophy, exactly as James had done. His influence on British psychology came from his article on psychology in the *Encyclopedia Britannica*'s ninth edition of 1886. It was the first article by that name in the *Encyclopedia*, and Ward reworked it later into a text. Ward settled at Cambridge University, where he was active in attempts to establish a psychological laboratory.

Like James, Ward rejected atomistic analysis of the continuum of consciousness. Instead of a sensationistic atomism, Ward advocated a functional view of consciousness, the brain, and the whole organism. Ward wrote (1904, p. 615): "Functionally regarded, the organism is from first to last a continuous whole . . . the growing complexity of Psychical life is only parodied by treating it as mental chemistry." To Ward, perception was not the passive reception of sensation, but active grasping of the environment. In a Jamesian passage, Ward wrote that "not mere receptivity but creative or selective activity is the essence of subjective reality" (p. 615). He struck a Darwinian note when he said (1920, p. 607): "Psychologically regarded, then, the sole function of perception and intellection is, it is contended, to guide action and subserve volition—more generally to promote self-conservation and betterment."

Ward expounded the same kind of pragmatic, or functional, psychology that James did. For both men, consciousness is an active, choosing entity that adjusts the organism to the environment and so serves the struggle for survival. Ward resembled James in one more way: his *fin de siècle* concern with defending religion against the rising tide of Huxlean naturalism. Ward devoted his last great works to the refutation of naturalism and the support of Christianity.

Ward's influence endured for many years in English psychology. Britain retained a functionalist psychology that provided an orienting point for later cognitive psychology. Ward's antiatomism also endured, to be picked up by later antiassociationists. The Cambridge psychologist Frederick Bartlett (1887–1969), for example, explicitly rejected the attempt to study memory as the acquisition of discrete "bits" of information such as the nonsense syllables used in most memory experiments. Instead, Bartlett studied memory of everyday paragraphs. He argued that prose is not a set of atomistic ideas, but rather an embodiment of a larger meaning, which he called a *schema* (Leahey & Harris, 2004). Bartlett (1932/1967) showed, for example, that different cultures possess different schemas for organizing their experience and that, consequently, systematic distortions are introduced into one culture's member's memory of another culture's stories.

RETHINKING MIND: THE CONSCIOUSNESS DEBATE, 1904–1912

Mind's place in nature was being fundamentally revised by functional psychologists and by their colleagues in animal psychology. Mind was becoming problematic, becoming increasingly identified with adaptive behavior itself in functional psychology, and slowly disappearing altogether in animal psychology. In 1904 philosophers, too, began to reexamine consciousness.

Does Consciousness Exist? Radical Empiricism

Pragmatism was a method for finding truths to live by, not a substantive philosophical position. Having left psychology for philosophy, William James turned to the problems of metaphysics and worked out a system he called radical empiricism. He launched his enterprise in 1904 with a paper boldly titled "Does 'Consciousness' Exist?" As always; James was provocative, setting off a debate among philosophers and psychologists that reshaped their conceptions of mind. He challenged the existence of consciousness as a leftover artifact of Cartesian dualism, grown ever more attenuated by the advance of science and the compromises of philosophy:

> I believe that "consciousness," when once it has evaporated to this estate of pure diaphaneity, is on the point of disappearing altogether. It is the name of a nonentity, and has no right to a place among first principles. Those who still cling to it are clinging to a mere echo, the faint rumor left behind by the disappearing "soul" upon the air of philosophy. . . . For twenty years past I have mistrusted "consciousness" as an entity; for seven or eight years past I have suggested its non-existence to my students, and tried to give them its pragmatic equivalent in realities of experience. It seems to me that the hour is ripe for it to be openly and universally discarded.
>
> To deny plumbly that "consciousness" exists seems so absurd on the face of it—for undeniably "thoughts" do exist—that I fear some readers will follow me no farther. Let me then immediately explain that I mean only to deny that the word stands for an entity, but to insist most emphatically that it does stand for a function. . . . That function is knowing. (James, 1904, p. 477)

James argued that consciousness does not exist as a distinct, separate thing apart from experience. There simply *is* experience: hardness, redness, tones, tastes, smells. There is nothing above and beyond it called "consciousness" that possesses it and knows it. Pure experience is the stuff of which the world is made, James held. Rather than being a thing, consciousness is a function, a certain kind of relationship among portions of pure experience. James's position is complex and difficult to grasp, involving a novel form of idealism (experience is the stuff of reality) and panpsychism (everything in the world, even a desk, is conscious). For psychology, what was important was the debate James began because out of it arose two new conceptions of consciousness that supported behavioralism: the relational theory of consciousness and the functional theory of consciousness.

The Relational Theory of Consciousness: Neorealism

To some extent, the important place of consciousness in psychology and philosophy derived from the Cartesian Way of Ideas, the copy theory of knowledge. The copy theory asserts, as James put it, a "radical dualism" of object and knower. For the copy theory, consciousness contains representations of the world and knows the world only through the representations. It follows, then, that consciousness is a mental world of representations separate from the physical world of things. In this traditional definition of psychology, the science of psychology studied the world of representations with the special method of introspection, whereas natural sciences such as physics studied the world of objects constructed by observation. James's challenge to the copy theory inspired a group of young American philosophers to propose a new form of perceptual realism at about the same time the Gestalt psychologists were reviving realism in Germany.

They called themselves *neorealists*, asserting that there is a world of physical objects that we know directly, without the mediation of internal representations. Now, although this theory is epistemological in aim—asserting the knowability of a real, external, physical world—it carries interesting implications for psychology. For in this realist view, consciousness is not a special, inner world to be reported on by introspection. Rather, consciousness is a relationship between self and world—the relationship of knowing. This was the basic idea of the relational theory of consciousness, and it was developed in these years by Ralph Barton Perry (1876–1957), James's biographer and teacher of E. C. Tolman; by Edwin Bissel Holt (1873–1946), with Perry at Harvard and Münsterberg's successor as Harvard's experimental psychologist; and by Edgar Singer (1873–1954), whose papers on mind anticipated the more influential views of Gilbert Ryle.

THE MIND WITHIN AND THE MIND WITHOUT The development of the neorealist theory of mind began with Perry's (1904) analysis of the allegedly privileged nature of introspection. Since Descartes, philosophers had supposed that consciousness was a private, inward possession of representations, known only to itself; upon this idea much of Descartes's radical dualism of world and mind rested. In the traditional view, introspection was a special sort of observation of a special place, quite different from the usual sort of observation of external objects. Traditional mentalistic psychology accepted the radical dualism of mind and object and enshrined introspection as the observational technique peculiar to the study of consciousness. Perry argued that introspection was special only in trivial ways, and that the "mind within" of introspection was in no essential way different from the "mind without" exhibited in everyday behavior.

Asking me to introspect is certainly an easy way to enter my mind, Perry conceded. Only I have *my* memories, and only I know to what I am attending at any given moment. But in these instances, introspection is not specially privileged, nor is mind a private place. What I experienced in the past could, in principle, be determined by other observers present when memories were laid down. Careful observation of my current behavior will reveal to what I am paying attention. In short, contents of consciousness are not exclusively my own: Anyone can discover them. Indeed, such is the method of animal psychology, said Perry: We discover animal mind by attending to animal behavior, reading an animal's intentions and mental content by observing the way it behaves toward objects in its environment.

Another kind of knowledge that seems to make self-consciousness and introspection special sources of knowledge is knowledge of the states of one's own body. Clearly, no one else has *my* headache. Of course, in this sense, introspection is privileged. But Perry refused to see any momentous conclusion to be drawn from this circumstance. In the first place, although one does not have direct awareness of another's inner bodily states, one can easily know about them from one's own analogous states; though you do not have my headache, you do know what a headache is. Second, inner bodily processes could be better known by a properly equipped outsider. "Who is so familiar with farming as the farmer?" Perry asked. Obviously, no one; but nonetheless, a scientifically trained expert may be able to tell the farmer how to farm more efficiently. Similarly, inner bodily processes are not one's exclusive possession, being open to physiological study. Finally, to assert special introspective access to bodily states is a very trivial defense of introspective psychology, because such contents are hardly the essence of mind.

Perry implied that mentalistic psychology was misguided. Consciousness is not a private thing known only to myself and shareable only through introspection. Rather, my consciousness is a collection of sensations derived from the external world or from my own body; with James, Perry maintained that there is no entity of "consciousness" apart from experienced sensations. But because these sensations may be known by anyone else, my mind is, in fact, an open book, a public object open to scientific study. Introspection remains pragmatically useful, of course, for no one has as convenient access to my sensations, past and present, as I have; so the psychologist who wishes to open my mind should simply ask me to look within and report what I find. In Perry's view, however, introspection is not the only road to the mind because mind is always on view as behavior. In principle, then, psychology can be conducted as a purely behavioral enterprise, engaging its subjects' self-awareness when expedient, but otherwise attending only to behavior. Perry's philosophical analysis of mind coincides ultimately with the view being developed in animal psychology: Mind and behavior are, functionally, the same, and both animal and human psychology rest on the same basis—the study of behavior.

MIND AS DIRECTED BEHAVIOR   Perry claimed that anyone's consciousness could be known by a sufficiently well-informed outside observer. E. B. Holt took consciousness out of a person's head and put it in the environment with his theory of *specific response*. Holt argued that the contents of consciousness were just a cross section of the objects of the universe—past or present, distant or near—to which a person is responding. Holt offered an analogy: Consciousness is like a flashlight's beam in a darkened room, revealing the things we see while leaving others in the dark. Similarly, at any given moment, we are reacting only to some of the objects in the universe, and these are the ones of which we are conscious. So consciousness is not inside a person at all but is "out there wherever the things specifically responded to are." Even memory was treated the same way: Memory is not the recovery of some past idea stored away and recalled, but is simply the presentation before consciousness of an absent object.

Holt's view, like Perry's, rejected the alleged privacy of mind. If consciousness is no more than specific response, and its contents no more than an inventory of the objects controlling my current behavior, then anyone who turns the flashlight of consciousness on the same objects as mine will know my mind. Behavior, Holt argued, is always controlled by or directed toward some real object—that is, a goal—and behavior is to be explained by discovering the acted-toward objects. So, to do psychology, we need not ask our subjects to introspect, though of course we may. We can understand their minds by examining their behavior and the circumstances in which it occurs, abandoning mentalistic for behavioralistic psychology. Objects to which an organism reacts are those of which it is conscious, said Holt; hence, the study of consciousness and the study of behavior were essentially the same.

MIND AS REIFICATION   Although he was not formally a neorealist, E. A. Singer proposed a behavioral concept of mind consistent with Perry's and Holt's. Singer applied the pragmatic test of truth to the problem of other minds: Does it matter, or does it make a difference to our conduct whether or not other people have conscious experience or not? Singer argued that pragmatically, the "other minds" problem is meaningless because it cannot be resolved. It had been debated by philosophers and psychologists since Descartes with no sign of progress. Singer concluded that it was a pseudo-problem incapable of solution.

Singer considered a possible pragmatic objection that consciousness in others does deeply matter to our everyday behavior, being what James called a "live question." In *Pragmatism* (1907/1955), James asked us to consider an "automatic sweetheart." Suppose you are deeply in love: Every adoring glance, every gentle caress, every tender sigh you will take as signs of your sweetheart's love for you; everything she does will bespeak a love for you like yours for her. Then, one day, you discover she is only a machine, cleverly constructed to exhibit tokens of love for you; but she is not conscious being but a machine, a simulacrum of a sweetheart. Do you love her still? James thought one could not, that vital to love is not just the glances, caresses, and sighs but the conviction that behind them is a mental state called *love*, a subjective condition of fondness, affection, and commitment like one's own. In short, belief in other minds passes the pragmatic test, James concluded, for we will feel very differently about, and of course act very differently toward, a creature depending on whether or not we think it possesses a mind.

Singer tried to refute James's argument. He asked how terms such as *mind* or *soul* or *soulless* are used in practice. They are inferences from behaviors, constructions we erect out of another's conduct. Of course, these constructions may be wrong, and we discover our error when our expectations about a person's behavior are not fulfilled. In the case of the automatic sweetheart, Singer argued, discovering that she is "soulless" only means that you now fear that her behavior in the future will not be like her behavior in the past. You fall out of love with her not because she is mindless, but because you no longer can predict how she will act.

Singer argued that the concept of mind is an example of the fallacy of reification, what Ryle later called a "category mistake." We believe in an entity called consciousness only because of our tendency to think that if we can name something, it exists. Singer drew an analogy between the concept of mind and prescientific theories of heat. Before the development of the atomic theory of matter, if an object was heated by fire, it was said to absorb an invisible fluid called "caloric." Thus, a hot rock was a dualistic entity: stone plus heat. However, modern atomic physics says that heat is not a fluid but a state of molecular activity. As an object is heated, its atomic constituents move more violently, and this activity alters the object's appearance and behavior; there is no caloric fluid. Cartesian and religious dualism, said Singer, were like prescientific physics, holding that a human being is a behaving body plus an inhabiting soul. Singer concluded, "Consciousness is not something inferred from behavior, it is behavior. Or, more accurately, our belief in consciousness is an expectation of probable behavior based on observation of actual behavior, a belief to be confirmed or refuted by more observation" (1911, p. 183). In Singer's view, then, there is no mind for anyone to investigate: Mentalistic psychology was a delusion from the start. Psychology should abandon mind, then, and study what is real: behavior.

Singer's reply to James's thought experiment of the automatic sweetheart is more important now than it was then, for we can build machines that appear to think, as James's automatic sweetheart appeared to love. Do they really think? And James's own creation has been brought to life in the writings of science-fiction novelists. Can a machine, an android, love? In our age of computers and genetic engineering, these are not idle questions, and we shall meet them again in the new field of cognitive science.

Neorealism did not last long as a philosophical movement. Its primary failing was episte-mological: accounting for the problem of error. If we know objects directly and without media-tion by ideas, how is it that we have mistaken perceptions? With the copy theory, error is easy to explain by saying that copies may not be accurate. Realism finds error difficult to account for. Realism did, however, have lasting influence. The neorealists professionalized philosophy. The older generations of philosophers such as James wrote for a wide audience of interested readers, and their names were well known to educated Americans. The neorealists, however, modeled their philosophy after science, making it technical and inaccessible to nonphilosophers (Kuklick, 1977). In psychology, their relational theory of consciousness aided the development of behavioralism and behaviorism, by reworking the mentalistic concept of consciousness into something knowable from behavior, and perhaps even something identical with behavior—in which case, the concept of mind need play no role in scientific psychology, however important it might remain outside the profession.

The Functional Theory of Consciousness: Instrumentalism

The neorealists developed the relational conception of mind suggested by James (1904). Dewey and his followers developed the functional conception. Dewey's emerging philosophy was called *instru-mentalism* because of his emphasis on mind as an effective actor in the world and on knowledge as an instrument for first understanding and then changing the world. Dewey's conception of mind was thus more active than the neorealists', who still adhered to what Dewey called the "spectator theory of mind." Copy theories are spectator theories because the world impresses itself (to use Hume's term) on a passive mind, which then simply copies the impression over into an idea. Although the neorealists rejected the copy theory, they had not, in Dewey's view, gotten away from the spectator theory because in the relational theory, consciousness is still fully determined by the objects to which one is responding. So mind is still a spectator passively viewing the world, only directly rather than through the spectacles of ideas.

Dewey (1939) got rid of the spectator theory but retained a representational theory of mind. He described mind as a function of the biological organism, adapting actively to the environment, a view going back to his 1896 reflex arc paper. As he developed his instrumentalism, Dewey became more specific about what mind actually does. Mind, he proposed, is the presence and operations of meanings, ideas—or, more specifically, the ability to anticipate future consequences and to respond to them as stimuli to present behavior. So mind is a set of representations of the world that func-tion instrumentally to adaptively guide the organism in its dealings with its environment. Echoing Brentano, Dewey claimed that what makes something mental rather than physical is that it points to something else—that is, it has meaning. Postulation of meanings does not require postulation of a separate realm of mind, for ideas are to be conceived as neurophysiological functions, whose total functioning we conveniently designate "mind."

Dewey also stressed the social nature of mind, even at times coming to deny that animals had minds, a change from his 1896 paper. Dewey was impressed by Watson's claim that thinking is just speech or, more strongly, that vocalization is all thinking consists of, whether such vocalization is out loud or covert. Interestingly, this returned Dewey to Descartes's old view, seemingly rejected by functional psychologists, that animals do not think because they do not talk. Dewey reversed Descartes's priorities, though. For Descartes, thinking comes first and is only expressed in speech; for Dewey, learning to speak creates the ability to think. Descartes was an individualist, investing each human with an innately given self-consciousness endowed with thought, but forever isolated from other consciousness.

Dewey was, generally speaking, a socialist. Humans do not possess some *a priori* consciousness; because language—speech—is acquired through social interaction, it follows that thinking, perhaps all of mind, is a social construction rather than a private possession. When we think inwardly, we just talk to ourselves silently rather than out loud, using our socially given speech-reactions to adjust to changing circumstances. Dewey, the philosopher of Progressivism, always aimed at reconstructing philosophy and society on a social basis, breaking down individualism and substituting for it group consciousness and a submerging of the individual into the greater whole. By conceiving of mind as a social construction, the Cartesian privacy of the individual mind was erased. Instead, the truly mindful entity was society itself, the larger organism of which each person was a cooperative part.

ESTABLISHING AMERICAN PSYCHOLOGY

The New Psychology and the Old

In the United States, experimental psychology was called the "New Psychology," to distinguish it from the "Old Psychology" of the Scottish commonsense realists. The great majority of American colleges were controlled by Protestant denominations, and, in the 1820s, the Scottish system was installed as a safeguard against what religious leaders took to be the skeptical and atheistic tendencies of British empiricism as described by Reid. The works of Locke, Berkeley, and Hume—and, later, the German idealists—were banished from the classroom and replaced with texts by Reid, Dugald Stewart, and their American followers. Commonsense psychology was taught as a pillar of religion and Christian behavior. For the American followers of the Scots, psychology "is the science of the soul," and its method, ordinary introspection, reveals "the soul as an emanation from the Divine, and as made in the image of God" (Dunton, 1895). "Mental science, or psychology, will therefore, be [foundational] for moral science. . . . The province of psychology will . . . be to show what the faculties are; that of moral philosophy to show how they should be used for the attainment of their end" (Hopkins, 1870, quoted by Evans, 1984). Unsurprisingly, with few exceptions, adherents of the old psychology looked askance at the new psychology, which brought the mind into the laboratory and investigated the connection of mental states to nervous processes.

Nevertheless, as higher education became more secular after the Civil War, the intellectual tide turned in favor of the naturalism of the new psychology. In 1875, William James established an informal psychological laboratory at Harvard in connection with a graduate course, "The Relations between Physiology and Psychology," in the Department of Natural History. In 1887, he began to offer a course called "Psychology" in the Philosophy Department; in 1885, he had obtained recognition and funds from Harvard and had established the first official psychology laboratory in America (Cadwallader, 1980). At Yale, the old psychology of the president, Noah Porter, yielded to George Trumbull Ladd, who, though a Congregationalist minister and a psychological conservative, respected Wundt's experimental psychology and incorporated it into an influential text, *Elements of Physiological Psychology* (Ladd, 1887). At Princeton, the president, James McCosh, was a staunch Scot but recognized that "the tendency of the day is certainly towards physiology" (quoted by Evans, 1984) and taught Wundt's psychology to his students.

Harvard minted its first PhD philosopher, G. Stanley Hall (1844–1924), in 1878. A student of James, Hall was really a psychologist. He went to Johns Hopkins University, the United States' first graduate university, where he established a laboratory and a series of courses in the new psychology. Hall's psychology went well beyond Wundt, however, including, in typically American eclectic fashion, experimental studies of the higher mental processes, anthropology, and abnormal psychology, or "morbid phenomena." Hall also vigorously pursued developmental psychology, launched the child study movement, and coined the term *adolescence*. Hall led the institutionalization of American psychology; he started the *American Journal of Psychology* in 1887 and organized the founding of the APA in 1892. One of Hall's students was James McKeen Cattell (1860–1944), who later studied with Wundt and Galton and then returned to the United States to establish laboratories at the University of Pennsylvania (1887) and Columbia University (1891). When Cattell was in Leipzig, he proposed to study individual differences in reaction time, but Wundt disapprovingly called the subject *"ganz Amerikanisch"* (completely American).

It has been said that although Rome conquered Greece militarily, Rome was, in turn, captured by Greek culture. Much the same can be said about German experimental psychology in America. On the battlefields of academe, the new psychology conquered the old, turning psychology into naturalistic, objective science. However, the spirit of the old psychology profoundly transformed the new psychology away from narrow laboratory experimentation on sensation and perception to socially useful studies of the whole person (Evans, 1984). The Scots and their American followers had always emphasized mind in use—mental activity—more than mental content. Their faculty psychology was, like Aristotle's, implicitly a psychology of function. And, as Aristotle's was a biological psychology, the Scots' psychology of mental function, despite its religious connection, was ultimately compatible with modern Darwinian biology. Experiment was new in American psychology, but American psychologists have retained to the present day the Scots' concern with mental activity and with making psychology serviceable to society and the individual.

To the Future: Perception and Thinking Are Only There for Behavior's Sake

By 1892, psychology in America was well launched. In Europe, scientific psychology was making but slow headway even in Germany, the country of its birth. In the United States, by contrast, psychology expanded rapidly. In 1892, there were 14 laboratories, including one as far west as Kansas. Half of them had been founded independently of philosophy or any other discipline. Psychology would soon be what it largely remains, an American science.

But psychology in America would not be the traditional psychology of consciousness. Once psychology met evolution, the tendency to study behavior instead of consciousness became overwhelming. Traditionally, philosophers had been concerned with human knowledge, with how we form ideas and how we know they are true or false. Action resulting from ideas formed only a tiny part of their concern. However, in a biological, evolutionary context, ideas matter only if they lead to effective action. The Metaphysical Club realized this and created the pragmatic maxim. The struggle for existence is won by successful action, and any organism "sicklied o'er with the pale cast of thought," no matter how profound, is doomed to failure. The essence of the psychology of adaptation was the idea that mind matters to evolutionary success because it leads to successful action, and so is adaptive. As James said:

> If it ever should happen that [thought] led to no active measures, it would fail of its essential function, and would have to be considered either pathological or abortive. The current of life which runs in at our eyes or ears is meant to run out at our hands, feet, or lips . . . perception and thinking are only for behavior's sake. (quoted by Kuklick, 1977, p. 169)

The psychology of adaptation, from Spencer to James, remained nevertheless the science of mental life, not the science of behavior. However, much consciousness was tied up with behavior.

No matter that it was merely a way station between stimulus and response; it was real and deserved serious study because it was a vital way station. James said consciousness decreed survival; it commanded the body to behave adaptively. Underneath the main current of mentalism, however, ran an undercurrent that headed toward the study of behavior instead of the study of consciousness, and, in time, the undercurrent became the main current, and finally a flood tide, virtually erasing the Science of Mental Life.

Bibliography

As 2009 was the 150th anniversary of the publication of *Origin of species*, works on Darwin flourish. There are so many works that I refer here only to some of the older literature which might not turn up in a Google search. One invaluable resource is http://darwin-online.org.uk/, which collects not only all of his published work, but his unpublished notebooks, letters, and other documents surrounding the development and reception of his theory of natural selection. To read the first formulations of the theory by Darwin and Wallace, see their *Evolution by natural selection* (Cambridge, England: Cambridge University Press, 1958). For the background in biology, see William Coleman, *Biology in the nineteenth century: Problems of form, function, and transformation* (Cambridge, England: Cambridge University Press, 1977); or Ernst Mayr's authoritative *The growth of biological thought* (Cambridge, MA: Harvard University Press, 1984). For the specific background to Darwin's work, see Loren Eiseley, *Darwin's century* (Garden City, NY: Doubleday, 1958), a beautifully written, standard introduction to evolution. Eiseley has also drawn attention to a previously unknown forerunner and influence on Darwin in his *Darwin and the mysterious Mr. X: New light on the evolutionists* (New York: Dutton, 1979). Another very readable account of the rise of evolutionary theory is John C. Greene, *The death of Adam: Evolution and its impact on Western thought* (Ames: Iowa State University Press, 1959). Two interesting but more technical works are B. Glass, O. Temkin, and W. Straus, eds., *Forerunners of Darwin: 1745–1859* (Baltimore: Johns Hopkins University Press, 1959); and Peter J. Bowler, *Fossils and progress: Paleontology and the idea of progressive evolution in the nineteenth century* (New York: Science History Publications, 1976). Works focusing on Darwin's thinking include P. Bamler, "Malthus, Darwin, and the concept of struggle," *Journal of the History of Ideas* (1976, *37*: 631–650); Michael Ghiselin, *The triumph of the Darwinian method* (Berkeley: University of California Press, 1969); and Dov Ospovat, *The development of Darwin's theory: Natural history, natural theology, and natural selection 1838–59* (New York: Cambridge University Press, 1981). Robert J. Richards (1992) in *The meaning of evolution: The morphological construction and ideological reconstruction of Darwin's theory* (Chicago: Chicago University Press) argues that modern biologists who see Darwin as one of their own—that is, as thinking of evolution as having no direction—are mistaken. Darwin, he shows, was much influenced by the idea that embryogenesis was a recapitulation of a species' evolutionary past, and that just as embryogenesis has a direction, so does evolution, making Darwin more Lamarckian than the modern synthetic theory of evolution.

Works concentrating on the reception of evolution include Tess Cosslett, ed., *Science and religion in the nineteenth century* (Cambridge, England: Cambridge University Press, 1984), which reprints major works by nineteenth-century debaters of the subject, including Darwin himself; Gertrude Himmelfarb, *Darwin and the Darwinian revolution* (New York: Norton, 1959); D. R. Oldroyd, *Darwinian impacts: An introduction to the Darwinian revolution* (Milton Keynes, England: The Open University Press, 1980); Michael Ruse, *The Darwinian revolution: Science red in tooth and claw* (Chicago: University of Chicago Press, 1979), who, with Himmelfarb and Oldroyd, set the Darwinian revolution in broad perspective. Peter J. Bowler, *The eclipse of Darwinism* (Baltimore: Johns Hopkins University Press, 1983); David Hull, *Darwin and his critics* (Cambridge, MA: Harvard University Press, 1973); and Cynthia Eagle Russett, *Darwin in America: The intellectual response 1865–1912* (San Francisco: Freeman, 1976) focus on the more scientific aspects of Darwin's reception. J. W. Burrow, *Evolution and society: A study in Victorian social theory* (Cambridge, England: Cambridge University Press, 1966) discusses the effect of evolution on social thought and on the nascent sciences of anthropology and sociology. In a short but far-ranging paper, D. P. Crook considers "Darwinism—The political implications," *History of European Ideas* (1981, *2*: 19–34). An excellent work on Darwin and the broad implications of Darwinism is Dennett (1995), which also includes discussion of contemporary rivals to Darwin's account of adaptation by natural selection.

Samuel Hynes, *The Edwardian turn of mind* (Princeton, NJ: Princeton University Press, 1968), provides a social history of turn-of-the-century Britain; he describes the impact of the Army's *Physical deterioration report*, treating it as the dividing point between the Victorian and post-Victorian eras. The changes in psychology during these years are discussed by Reba N. Soffer, *Ethics and society in England: The revolution in the social sciences 1870–1914* (Berkeley: University of California Press, 1978). Spencer's biographer is J. Peel Herbert, *Spencer* (New York: Basic Books, 1971). Howard Gruber insightfully discusses *Darwin on man: A psychological study of scientific creativity*, 2nd ed. (Chicago: University of Chicago Press, 1981). On Galton, see F. Forest, *Francis Galton* (New York: Taplinger, 1974). For Galton and British eugenics, see Ruth Schwartz Cowan, "Nature and Nurture: The Interplay of Biology and Politics in the work of Francis Galton," in W. Coleman and C. Limoges, eds., *Studies in the history of biology*, vol. 1, 133–208 (Baltimore: Johns Hopkins University Press, 1977); Robert C. Bannister, *Social Darwinism: Science and myth in Anglo-American social thought* (Philadelphia: Temple University Press, 1979); and Daniel Kevles, *In the name of eugenics: Genetics and the uses of human heredity* (New York: Knopf, 1985). Greta Jones, *Social Darwinism in English thought: The interaction between biological and social theory* (Sussex, England: Harvester Press, 1980), discusses both Social Darwinism and eugenics during the period. In addition to the cited work, an important book by Romanes is *Mental evolution in man* (New York: D. Appleton, 1889); the only biography of Romanes is Ethel Romanes, *The life and letters of George John Romanes* (New York: Longmans, Green & Co., 1898), but Frank Miller Turner, "George John Romanes, From Faith to Faith," in F. M. Turner, *Between science and religion: The reaction to scientific naturalism in late Victorian England* (New Haven, CT: Yale University Press, 1974), provides a fine short discussion of Romanes, focusing on his part in the Victorian crisis of conscience. Morgan's major work is *An introduction to comparative psychology* (London: Walter Scott, 1894).

For a comprehensive treatment of American life in the years before 1890, see Bernard Bailyn, "Shaping the Republic to 1760," Gordon S. Wood, "Framing the Republic 1760–1820," David Brion Davis, "Expanding the Republic 1820–1860," and David Herbert Donald, "Uniting the Republic 1860–1890," in B. Bailyn, D. B. Davis, D. H. Donald, J. L. Thomas, R. H. Wiebe, and G. S. Wood, *The great republic: A history of the American people* (Boston: Little, Brown, 1977). Daniel Boorstin concentrates on intellectual and social history during the same

years in *The Americans: The colonial experience* (New York: Vintage Books, 1958) and *The Americans: The national experience* (New York: Vintage Books, 1965); both are wonderfully readable and exciting books. The best book on the American character is still Tocqueville (1850/1969); An important and fascinating survey of American colonial life is David Hackett Fischer, *Albion's seed: Four British folkways in America* (New York: Oxford University Press, 1989). *In Freedom just around the corner: A new American history 1585–1828* (2005) and *Throes of Democracy: The American Civil War era 1829–1877* (2008; both New York: Harper Collins), Walter A. McDougall tells a revisionist tale of American history viewing American citizens as first of all, hustlers. Daniel Walker Howe (2007) provides an up-to-date narrative of America in the generation after the Founders in *What hath God wrought: The transformation of America, 1815–1848* (New York: Oxford University Press). Gordon Wood (2009) emphasizes how the American Founders argued about human nature and the ideal state in *Empire of liberty: A history of the early Republic* (New York: Oxford University Press).

A valuable general intellectual history of thought in the United States is Morton White, *Science and sentiment in America: Philosophical thought from Jonathan Edwards to John Dewey* (New York: Oxford University Press, 1972). A more recent treatment is Goetzmann (2009) who gives special place to the influence of Scottish commonsense philosophy. Intellectual life in the early colonial and postrevolutionary periods is discussed by Henry Steele Commager, *The empire of reason: How Europe imagined and America realized the Enlightenment* (Garden City, NY: Doubleday, 1978); Henry May, *The Enlightenment in America* (New York: Oxford University Press, 1976); and Perry Miller, *Errand into the wilderness* (New York: Harper & Row, 1956).

For specific relevant movements of the nineteenth century, see A. Douglas, *The feminization of American culture* (New York: Knopf, 1977); Richard Hofstadter, *Anti-intellectualism in American life* (New York: Vintage Books, 1962); and R. B. Nye, *Society and culture in America 1830–1860* (New York: Harper & Row, 1974); and for American phrenology, see Thomas H. and Grace E. Leahey, *Psychology's occult doubles* (Chicago: Nelson-Hall, 1983). For American philosophy, see A. L. Jones, *Early American philosophers* (New York: Ungar, 1958); Herbert W. Schneider, *History of American philosophy* (New York: Columbia University Press, 1963); and, especially for the post–Civil War period, Kuklick (1977), from which all quotes in the Metaphysical Club section are drawn, unless otherwise indicated. The standard biography of Jonathan Edwards is Perry Miller, *Jonathan Edwards* (New York:

Meridian, 1959). On Wright, see Edward H. Madden, "Chauncy Wright's Functionalism," *Journal of the History of the Behavioral Sciences* (1974, *10*: 281–290).

For the early philosophy of pragmatism and its influences, see Philip P. Wiener, *Evolution and the founders of pragmatism* (Cambridge, MA: Harvard University Press, 1949) and Louis Menand's Pulitzer Prize winning *The Metaphysical Club: A story of ideas in America* (New York: Farrar, Straus, Giroux, 2001). Menand's unusual thesis is that the decisive influence on the pragmatists was the U.S. Civil War; for a critique of Menand's thesis and of pragmatism as a philosophy, see Paul Boghossian (Sept. 10, 2001) The gospel of relaxation, *New Republic*, *225*, 35. On Peirce, see J. K. Feibleman, *An Introduction to the philosophy of Charles S. Peirce* (Cambridge, MA: MIT Press, 1946); and Thomas S. Knight, *Charles Peirce* (New York: Twayne, 1965). For Peirce as psychologist, see Thomas Cadwallader, "Charles S. Peirce: The first American experimental psychologist," *Journal of the History of the Behavioral Sciences* (1974, *10*: 191–198). The standard biography of William James is Ralph Barton Perry, *The thought and character of William James*, two vols. (Boston: Little, Brown, 1935); Perry's biography, though still the standard, suffers somewhat from his attempt to make James into a realist like himself. A recent biography is Gay Wilson Allen, *William James* (Minneapolis: University of Minnesota Press, 1970). For James's lasting influence, see Don S. Browning, *Pluralism and personality: William James and some contemporary cultures of psychology* (Lewisburg, PA: Bucknell University Press, 1980). The most important recent biography of James is G. Myers, *William James: His life and thought* (New Haven, CT: Yale University Press, 1987). The connection between Peirce's initial proclamation of pragmatism and James's later formulation of it—mediated by G. S. Hall—is discussed in David Leary, Between Peirce (1879) and James (1898): G. Stanley Hall, the origins of pragmatism and the history of psychology, *Journal of the History of the Behavioral Sciences* (2009, *45*: 5–20).

The only comprehensive source for the establishment of American psychology is Evans (1984); related is R. Dolby, "The transmission of two new scientific disciplines from Europe to North America in the late nineteenth century," *Annals of Science* (1977, *34*: 287–310). For psychology before the new psychology, see J. W. Fay, *American psychology before William James* (New York: Octagon Books, 1966); J. R. Fulcher, "Puritans and the passions: The faculty psychology in American Puritanism," *Journal of the History of the Behavioral Sciences* (1973, *9*: 123–139); and E. Harms, "America's first major psychologist: Laurens Perseus Hickock," *Journal of the History of the Behavioral Sciences* (1972, *8*: 120–123). Two overlapping collections edited by Robert W. Rieber and Kurt Salzinger treat American psychology primarily in the old and new periods, but also after: *The roots of American psychology: Historical influences and implications for the future* (New York: New York Academy of Sciences, Annals of the New York Academy of Sciences, vol. 291, 1977), and *Psychology: Theoretical-historical perspectives* (New York: Academic Press, 1980). Josef Brozek, ed., *Explorations in the history of psychology in the United States* (Lewisburg, PA: Bucknell University Press, 1984), contains articles on both the old and the new psychologies. On the early psychologists mentioned in the text: Eugene S. Miller, *G. T. Ladd: Pioneer American psychologist* (Cleveland: Case Western Reserve University Press, 1969); Dorothy Ross, *G. Stanley Hall: Psychologist as prophet* (Chicago: University of Chicago Press, 1972). Michael Sokal has spent his career writing about James McKeen Cattell, for example: "The Unpublished Autobiography of James McKeen Cattell," *American Psychologist* (1971, *26*: 626–635), and *An education in psychology: James McKeen Cattell's journal and letters from Germany and England, 1880–1888* (Cambridge, MA: MIT Press, 1980).

One of the landmark articles in the introduction of the new psychology to the United States is John Dewey, "The new psychology," *Andover Review* (1884, *2*: 278–289); the background and influence of the piece is discussed in Morton White, *The origin of Dewey's instrumentalism* (New York: Octagon Books, 1964). Two other contemporary or near contemporary articles are useful for the history of the early laboratories in the United States: "Psychology in American universities," *American Journal of Psychology* (1892, *3*: 275–286); and Christian A. Ruckmich, "The history and status of psychology in the United States," *American Journal of Psychology* (1912, *23*: 517–531).

J. Mark Baldwin provides a more general account, with more background, in his "Sketch of the history of psychology," *Psychological Review* (1905, *12*: 144–165).

Behaviorism 1892–1956

From the time of the Greeks, psychology had been the study of the mind, *psyche-logos*. Philosophers discussed and quarreled over how mind should be defined and investigated, but they never doubted what their subject matter was. The three founding psychologies of the nineteenth century were launched as scientific versions of the ancient philosophic enterprise. However, as psychology entered the twentieth century, it began to reconceive its methods and its subject matter. Attention shifted from what mind was to what it did—cause behavior. By 1912, psychologists were well on their way to defining psychology as the science of behavior, not mind.

What brought the redefinition of psychology into sharper focus for psychologists was work in animal psychology. Because it viewed humans as having evolved from animal forms, psychologists could not exclude animals from their study, creating animal psychology as a new field of research. Explaining animal mind and behavior required psychologists to think in some detail about the definition of mind they had inherited from Descartes. Descartes had said that animals do not have minds; yet comparative psychologists were beginning to describe and explain animal minds, demonstrating that the sharp line Descartes had drawn between mechanical reflex and mindful action was no longer tenable after Darwin. Either animals had minds, in which case machines, not just souls, could think, or minds did not exist, in which case humans were soulless machines, just as La Mettrie had proposed in 1748. Behaviorism—the subject of this chapter—flirted with the second option. Cognitive science embraced the first.

From Chapter 11 of *A History of Psychology: From Antiquity to Modernity*, Seventh Edition.
Thomas Hardy Leahey. Copyright © 2013 by Pearson Education, Inc. All rights reserved.

NEW DIRECTIONS IN ANIMAL PSYCHOLOGY

Animal psychology, as Romanes had begun it, used two methods: the anecdotal method to collect data and the method of inference to interpret them. Although both methods had been challenged, discussed, and defended from their inception, they came under special scrutiny and criticism among American psychologists in the late nineteenth and early twentieth centuries. Anecdote was replaced by experiment, particularly by the techniques of E. L. Thorndike and I. P. Pavlov.

From Anecdote to Experiment

Beginning in 1898, animal psychology experienced a surge in activity and a quickening of interest. But in the new animal psychology laboratory, experiment replaced anecdotes and informal, naturalistic experiments, as psychologists investigated the behavior of species ranging from protozoa to monkeys. The aim of animal psychology, as of psychology in general, was to produce a natural science, and its practitioners felt that gentlemanly anecdote was not the path to science; as E. L. Thorndike (1898) wrote, "Salvation does not come from such a source." Although there were many psychologists experimenting on animal mind and behavior, two research programs deserve special attention because their methods became enduring ones and their theoretical conceptions embraced the whole of psychology. These programs arose at almost the same time, but in very different places and circumstances: in William James's Cambridge basement, where a young graduate student employed his mentor's children as his research assistants; and in the sophisticated laboratories of a distinguished Russian physiologist already on his way to a Nobel Prize.

THE CONNECTIONISM OF EDWARD LEE THORNDIKE (1874–1949)   Thorndike was attracted to psychology when he read James's *Principles* for a debating prize competition at his undergraduate school, Wesleyan (Connecticut). When Thorndike went to Harvard for graduate study, he eagerly took up study with James. His first research interest was children and pedagogy, but no child subjects being available, Thorndike took up the study of learning in animals. James gave him a place to work in his basement after Thorndike failed to secure official research space from Harvard. Before completing his work at Harvard, Cattell invited Thorndike to go to Columbia. At Columbia, he completed his animal research before returning to educational psychology for the remainder of his professional career. Thorndike's importance for us is his methodological and theoretical approach to animal learning and his formulation of an *S-R* psychology he called *connectionism*.

Thorndike's animal researches were summarized in *Animal Intelligence*, which appeared in 1911. It included his dissertation, "Animal Intelligence: An Experimental Study of the Associative Processes in Animals," originally published in 1898. In the introduction, Thorndike (1911/1965, p. 22) defined the usual problem of animal psychology: "to learn the development of mental life down through the phylum, to trace in particular the origin of the human faculty." However, he deprecated the value of previous animal psychology for relying on the anecdotal method. Thorndike argued that the anecdotal method overestimated animal intelligence by reporting atypical animal performances. He urged replacing anecdotes with experiments to impose order on a welter of conflicting observations of so-called animal intelligence. Thorndike's goal was by experiment to catch animals "using their minds" under controlled and repeatable conditions.

Thorndike placed a young cat in one of many "puzzle boxes," each of which could be opened by the cat in a different way, the cat being rewarded by salmon for escaping. His setup was an example of what would later be called *instrumental conditioning*: An animal makes some response, and if it is rewarded—in Thorndike's case, with escape and food—the response is learned. If the response is not rewarded, it gradually disappears.

Thorndike's results led him to renounce the older view of the anecdotal psychologists that animals reason; animals learn, he said, solely by trial and error, reward and punishment. In a passage that foreshadowed the future, Thorndike wrote that animals have no ideas to associate. There is association, but not of ideas. Wrote Thorndike (1911/1965, p. 98): "The effective part of the association [is] a direct bond between the situation and the impulse."

Thorndike's scornful remarks about traditional animal psychology were in accord with a larger campaign being conducted by American scientists against sentimental views of animals then popular in America. Magazines and books regaled readers with anecdotal accounts of animals endowed with human levels of intelligence. For example, one nature writer, William J. Long, described animals as physicians: "When a coon's foot is shattered by a bullet, he will cut it off promptly and wash the stump in running water, partly to reduce the inflammation and partly, no doubt, to make it perfectly clean" (quoted by Lutts, 1990, p. 74). Scientists such as John Burroughs regarded such stories as fantasies, crossing "the line between fact and fiction," and they worried that nature writers would "induce the reader to cross, too, and to work such a spell upon him that he shall not know he has crossed and is in the land of make-believe" (quoted by Lutts, 1990, p. 79).

Thorndike's contempt for the old animal psychology did not escape sharp replies. Wesley Mills (1847–1915), America's senior animal psychologist, attacked Thorndike for having swept away "almost the entire fabric of comparative psychology" and for regarding traditional animal psychologists as "insane." Like the nature writers assailed by Burroughs (Lutts, 1990), Mills defended anecdotal psychology by asserting that animals could be properly investigated only in their natural settings, not in the artificial confines of the laboratory. Directly addressing Thorndike's studies, Mills turned sarcastic: Thorndike "placed cats in boxes only $20 \times 15 \times 12$ inches, and then expected them to act naturally. As well enclose a living man in a coffin, lower him, against his will, into the earth, and attempt to deduce normal psychology from his behavior" (Mills, 1899, p. 266).

By 1904, however, Mills had to concede the ascendancy of "the laboratory school," led by Thorndike, "the chief agnostic of this school," who denied that animals reason or plan or imitate. But Mills, and, later, Wolfgang Köhler, maintained that animals seemed not to reason in the laboratory because their situations did not permit it, not because they were naturally incapable of thought. Köhler (1925) said that animals were forced into blind trial and error by the construction of Thorndike's puzzle boxes. Because the penned-up subject could not see how the escape mechanism worked, it simply could not reason its way out. Lacking all the pertinent information, Thorndike's poor animals were thrown back on the primitive strategy of trial and error. The method, as Flourens had said of his ablation technique, gives the results. Thorndike's method permitted only random trial and error, so that is what he found. But Thorndike's claim that all an animal is capable of is mere association was entirely unjustified, Köhler said.

Nevertheless, Thorndike developed his radically simplified theory of learning to encompass humans as well as animals. He contended that this objective method could be extended to human beings, for we can study mental states as forms of behavior. He criticized the structuralists for fabricating an artificial and imaginary picture of human consciousness. In line with Progressive calls for scientific social control, Thorndike (1911/1965, p. 15) argued that the purpose of psychology should be the control of behavior: "There can be no moral warrant for studying man's nature unless the study will enable us to control his acts." He concluded by prophesying that psychology would become the study of behavior.

Thorndike proposed two laws of human and animal behavior. The first was the law of effect (1911/1965, p. 244): "Of several responses made to the same situation, those which are accompanied or closely followed by satisfaction to the animal will, other things being equal, be more firmly connected with the situation, so that, when it recurs, they will be more likely to recur." Punishment, on the other hand, reduces the strength of the connection. Further, the greater the reward or punishment, the greater the change in the connection. Later, Thorndike abandoned the punishment part of the law of effect, retaining only reward. The law of effect became the basic law of instrumental conditioning, accepted in some form by most learning theorists. Thorndike's second law is the law of exercise (p. 244): "Any response to a situation will, all other things being equal, be more strongly connected with the situation in proportion to the number of times it has been connected with that situation, and to the average vigor and duration of the connections."

Thorndike contended that these two laws could account for all behavior, no matter how complex: It would be possible to reduce "the processes of abstraction, association by similarity and selective thinking to mere secondary consequences of the laws of exercise and effect" (1911/1965, p. 263). Like Skinner in 1957 (see later in this chapter), he analyzed language as a set of vocal responses learned because parents reward some of a child's vocalizations but not others. The rewarded ones are acquired and the nonrewarded ones are unlearned, following the law of effect.

Thorndike applied his connectionism to human behavior in *Human Learning* (1929/1968), a series of lectures delivered at Cornell in 1928 and 1929. He presented an elaborate *S–R* psychology in which many stimuli are connected to many responses in hierarchies of *S–R* associations. Thorndike asserted that each *S–R* link could be assigned a probability that *S* will elicit *R*. For example, the probability that food will elicit salivation is very near 1.00, whereas before conditioning, the probability that a tone will elicit salivation is near 0. Learning is increasing *S–R* probabilities; forgetting is lowering them. Just as animal learning is automatic, unmediated by an awareness of the contingency between response and reward, so, Thorndike argued, is human learning also unconscious. One may learn an operant response without being aware that one is doing so. As he did for animals, Thorndike reduced human reasoning to automatism and habit. He held out the promise of scientific utopia, founded on eugenics and scientifically managed education.

Notwithstanding the grand claims he made on behalf of his connectionism, Thorndike recognized a problem that haunted later behaviorism and remains troublesome for any naturalistic psychology. The problem is accounting for human behavior without referring to meaning. Animals respond to stimuli only in respect to their physical properties, such as their shape. So, we can train an animal to respond one way to the stimulus "house" and another way to "horse," but it seems implausible to suggest that an animal will ever grasp the meanings of those words. Similarly, you or I might be trained by reward to respond one way to two different Chinese ideograms without ever knowing what they mean. Meanings live in human minds and are embedded in human social lives; they have no parallel among animals, creating a serious barrier to extending to humans any theory based on animals, no matter how precise.

Glimpsing but not quite grasping the problem, Thorndike posed it as a matter of stimulus complexity more than as a problem of meaning. The objective psychologist, eschewing all reference to mind, faces difficulties defining the stimuli that control human behavior. Are all stimuli equally relevant to an act? When I am asked, for example, "What is the cube root of 64?" many other stimuli are acting on me at the same time. How can an outsider ignorant of English tell which stimulus is the relevant one? Defining the response is equally difficult. I may respond "four," but many other behaviors (such as breathing) are also occurring. How do we know which *S* is connected with which *R* without recourse to subjective, nonphysical meaning? Thorndike admitted that such questions were reasonable and that answers would have to be given eventually. About reading and listening, Thorndike (1911/1965) wrote: "In the hearing or reading of a paragraph, the connections from the words somehow cooperate to give certain total meanings." That "somehow" conceals a mystery only partially acknowledged. He realized the complexity of language when he said that the number of connections necessary to understand a simple sentence may be well over 100,000, and he conceded that organized language is "far beyond any description given by associationist psychology."

Was Thorndike a behaviorist? His biographer (Joncich, 1968) says he was, and she cited in support such statements as this: "Our reasons for believing in the existence of other people's minds are our experiences of their physical actions." He did formulate the basic law of instrumental learning, the law of effect, and the doctrine that consciousness is unnecessary for learning. Unlike Pavlov, he practiced a purely behavioral psychology without reference to physiology. On the other hand, he proposed a principle of "belongingness" that violated a basic principle of conditioning—that those elements most closely associated in space and time will be connected in learning. The sentences "John is a butcher. Harry is a carpenter. Jim is a doctor." presented in a list like this would make *butcher-Harry* a stronger bond than *butcher-John* if the associative contiguity theory were correct. However, this is clearly not the case. *John* and *butcher* "belong" together (because of the structure of the sentences) and so will be associated, and recalled, together. This principle of belongingness resembled Gestalt psychology rather than behaviorism.

Historically, Thorndike is hard to place. He did not found behaviorism, though he practiced it in his animal researches. His devotion to educational psychology quickly took him outside academic experimental psychology in which behaviorism developed. It might best be concluded that Thorndike was a practicing behaviorist but not a wholehearted one.

THE NEUROSCIENCE OF I. P. PAVLOV (1849–1936)   The other important new experimental approach to animal psychology grew from Russian objective psychology, an uncompromisingly materialistic and mechanistic conception of mind and body. The founder of modern Russian physiology was Ivan Mikhailovich Sechenov (1829–1905), who studied in some of the best physiological laboratories in Europe, including Helmholtz's. Sechenov brought Helmholtz's methods and ideas back to Russia. Sechenov believed that psychology could be scientific only if it were completely taken over by physiology and adopted physiology's objective methods. He dismissed introspective psychology as being akin to primitive superstition. Sechenov wrote:

> Physiology will begin by separating psychological reality from the mass of psychological fiction which even now fills the human mind. Strictly adhering to the principle of induction, physiology will begin with a detailed study of the more simple aspects of psychical life and will not rush at once into the sphere of the highest psychological phenomena. Its progress will therefore lose in rapidity, but it will gain in reliability. As an experimental science, physiology will not raise to the rank of incontrovertible truth anything that cannot be confirmed by exact experiments; this will draw a sharp boundary-line between hypotheses and positive knowledge. Psychology will thereby lose its brilliant universal theories; there will appear tremendous gaps in its supply of scientific data; many explanations will give place to a laconic "we do

not know"; the essence of the psychical phenomena manifested in consciousness (and, for the matter of that, the essence of all other phenomena of nature) will remain an inexplicable enigma in all cases without exception. And yet, psychology will gain enormously, for it will be based on scientifically verifiable facts instead of the deceptive suggestions of the voice of our consciousness. Its generalizations and conclusions will be limited to actually existing analogies, they will not be subject to the influence of the personal preferences of the investigator which have so often led psychology to absurd transcendentalism, and they still thereby become really objective scientific hypotheses. The subjective, the arbitrary and the fantastic will give way to a nearer or more remote approach to truth. In a word, psychology *will become a positive science. Only physiology can do all this, for only physiology holds the key to the scientific analysis of psychical phenomena.* (1973, pp. 350–351)

Sechenov's great work was *Reflexes of the Brain* (1863/1965, p. 308), in which he wrote: "All the external manifestations of brain activity can be attributed to muscular movement. . . . Billions of diverse phenomena, having seemingly no relationship to each other, can be reduced to the activity of several dozen muscles." Radical behaviorism's later dismissal of mind or brain as the cause of behavior is found in Sechenov (p. 321): "Thought is generally believed to be the cause of behavior . . . [but this is] the greatest of falsehoods: [for] the initial cause of all behavior always lies, not in thought, but in external sensory stimulation."

Sechenov's objectivism was popularized by Vladimir Michailovitch Bechterev (1867–1927), who called his system *reflexology*, a name that accurately describes its character. However, the greatest of Sechenov's followers, though not his student, was Ivan Petrovich Pavlov, a physiologist whose studies of digestion won him the Nobel Prize in 1904. In the course of this work, he discovered that stimuli other than food may produce salivation, and this led him to the study of psychology, especially to the concept of the conditioned reflex and its exhaustive investigation.

Pavlov's general attitude was uncompromisingly objective and materialistic. He had the positivist's faith in objective method as the touchstone of natural science, and consequently he rejected reference to mind. Pavlov (1957, p. 168, original paper published 1903) wrote: "For the naturalist everything lies in the method, in the chance of obtaining an unshakable, lasting truth; and solely from this point of view . . . the [concept of the] soul . . . is not only unnecessary but even harmful to his work." Pavlov rejected any appeal to an active inner agency, or mind, in favor of an analysis of the environment: It should be possible to explain behavior without reference to a "fantastic internal world," referring only to "the influence of external stimuli, their summation, etc." His analysis of thinking was atomistic and reflexive: "The entire mechanism of thinking consists in the elaboration of elementary associations and in the subsequent formation of chains of associations." His criticism of nonatomistic psychology was unremitting. He carried out replications of Köhler's ape experiments to show that "association is knowledge, . . . thinking . . . [and] insight" (p. 586, from Wednesday discussion group statements, c. 1934–1935), and he devoted many meetings of his weekly Wednesday discussion group to unfriendly analyses of Gestalt concepts. He wrongly viewed the Gestaltists as dualists who "did not understand anything" of their own experiments.

Pavlov's technical contribution to the psychology of learning was considerable. He discovered classical conditioning and inaugurated a systematic research program to discover all of its mechanisms. In the course of his Nobel Prize–winning investigation of canine salivation, Pavlov observed that salivation could later be elicited by stimuli present at the time food was presented to an animal. He originally called these learned reactions *psychical secretions*, but later he substituted the term *conditional response*.

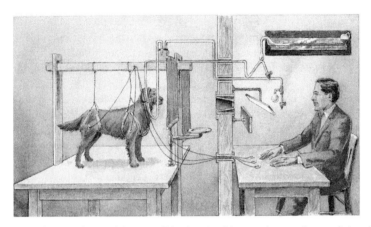

Pavlov's experimental set-up for studying conditioning. In this experiment, the conditional stimuli are tactile vibrators attached to the dog's legs. The unconditional stimuli is food placed on the rotating plate found by the dog. The response measure is amount of salivation, recorded by the device at the upper right corner. (From Pavlov, 1928, p. 271.) *(Pearson Education)*

Between them, Thorndike and Pavlov contributed important methods to psychology, methods that were to become the experimental mainstays of behaviorism. At the same time, each questioned the need for psychologists and biologists to talk about animal mind. Thorndike found only blind association forming in his animals, denying that animals reason or even imitate. Pavlov, following Sechenov, proposed to substitute physiology for psychology, eliminating talk about the mind for talk about the brain.

The Problem of Animal Mind

FINDING A CRITERION FOR CONSCIOUSNESS The trouble with animal psychology, said E. C. Sanford in his 1902 presidential address to the American Psychological Association (APA), is that it "tempts us beyond the bounds of introspection," as do the other growing elements of comparative psychology, the studies of children, the retarded, and the abnormal. But, Sanford asked, should we be "content with a purely objective science of animal or child or idiot behavior?" Sanford thought not and spelled out why, recognizing, with Romanes, the logical conclusion of an objective psychology:

> I doubt if anyone has ever seriously contemplated [a purely objective psychology] in the case of the higher animals, or could carry it to fruitful results if he should undertake it. Nor would anyone seriously propose to treat the behavior of his fellow men in the same way, i.e. to refuse to credit them with conscious experience in the main like his own, though this would seem to be required logically. (Sanford, 1903, p. 105)

However, comparative psychologists still faced Descartes's problem: If they were going to attribute mental processes to animals, they had to come up with some criterion of the mental. Just which behaviors could be explained as due to physiology alone, and which ones were caused by mental processes? Descartes had proposed a simple answer suited to Christian theology: The soul, not the body, thinks; so language, the expression of thought, is the mark of the mental. Things were not so simple for comparative psychologists, though. Having accepted phylogenetic continuity and having disposed of the soul, they found Descartes's criterion no longer plausible. It seemed clear that the higher animals possess minds and that paramecia do not (although a few animal psychologists thought they did possess very low-grade intelligence), but exactly where to draw the line was intensely problematic.

They wrestled with the problem and proposed numerous criteria, thoughtfully reviewed by Robert Yerkes (1876–1956), a leading animal psychologist, in 1905. Like Sanford, Romanes, and others, Yerkes knew the problem was important for human psychology, too, for we use inference to know other human minds just as much as to know animal minds. Indeed, "human psychology stands or falls with comparative psychology. If the study of the mental life of lower animals is not legitimate, no more is the study of human consciousness" (Yerkes, 1905).

As Yerkes saw it, "criteria of the psychic" could be divided into two broad categories. First were the structural criteria: An animal might be said to have a mind if it had a sufficiently sophisticated nervous system. More important were the functional criteria—behaviors that indicated presence of mind. Among the possible functional criteria, Yerkes found that most investigators took learning to be the mark of the mind and arranged their experiments to see if a given species could learn. Such a criterion was consistent with James's Darwinian psychology and with contemporary developments in functional psychology. As we have seen, functionalists, following James, viewed consciousness as above all an adjustive agency, so naturally, they looked for signs of adjustment in their subjects. An animal that could not learn would be regarded as a mere automaton.

Yerkes thought the search for a single criterion too simple, and he proposed three grades, or levels, of consciousness, corresponding to three classes of behavior. At the lowest level there was *discriminative* consciousness, indicated by the ability to discriminate one stimulus from another; even a sea anemone had this grade of consciousness. Next, Yerkes proposed a grade of *intelligent* consciousness, whose sign was learning. Finally, there is *rational* consciousness, which initiates behaviors rather than just responding, however flexibly, to environmental challenges.

A RADICAL SOLUTION   At least one young psychologist was coming to find the whole problem a hopeless tangle. John B. Watson (1878–1958) was a graduate student of Angell's at the University of Chicago, a stronghold of Dewey's instrumentalism and psychological functionalism. Watson disliked introspection and took up animal psychology. His dissertation, "Animal Education," which was cowritten with Angell, had very little mentalism in it and was mostly an attempt to find a physiological basis for learning. As a promising animal psychologist, Watson was one of the main reviewers of the literature in animal psychology for *Psychological Bulletin*, and there we find him becoming bored by the controversy over the criterion of the mental. In 1907, he called it "the *bête noir* of the student of behavior," and asserted, "The whole contention is tedious." However, he was still at Chicago under Angell's eye, and he defended a psychology of animal mind.

In the fall of 1908, Watson obtained a position at Johns Hopkins University; away from Angell and on his own, he became bolder. At a talk before the Scientific Association of Johns Hopkins, the newly arrived professor said that the study of animal behavior could be carried out purely objectively, producing facts on a par with the other natural sciences; no reference to animal mind was made (Swartz, 1908).

On December 31 of that same year, Watson (1909) spelled out "A Point of View in Comparative Psychology" for the Southern Society for Philosophy and Psychology, then meeting at Hopkins. He reviewed the controversy surrounding the criteria of consciousness in animals and stated (I quote E. F. Buchner, the society's secretary) "that these criteria are impossible of application and . . . have been valueless to the science" of animal behavior. Watson argued that the "facts of behavior" are valuable in themselves and do not have to be "grounded in any criteria of the psychic." Human psychology too, he said, is coming to be more objective, seeming to abandon the use of introspection and "the speech reaction." These trends away from introspection will lead psychology toward "the perfection of technique of the physical sciences." As "criteria of the psychic . . . disappear" from psychology, it will study the whole "process of adjustment" in "all of its broad biological aspects" rather than focusing narrowly on a few elements caught in a moment of introspection. Although Watson would not proclaim behaviorism as such until 1913, it is clear that the "viewpoint" he described that afternoon in McCoy Hall was behaviorism in all but name. For Watson, criteria of the mental were useless in animal psychology. Grasping the mettle of the logic of his argument, he had concluded that criteria of the mental were useless in human psychology, too.

Discarding Consciousness

By 1910, all the forces moving psychology from mentalism to behavioralism were well engaged. Philosophical idealism, which made the study of consciousness so important, had been replaced by pragmatism, realism, and instrumentalism, all of which denied consciousness a special, privileged place in the universe. The concept of consciousness had been reworked, becoming successively motor response, relation, and function, and could no longer be clearly differentiated from behavior. Animal psychologists were finding mind to be a problematic, even an unnecessary concept in their field. Psychology as a whole, especially in America, was shifting its concern from the structural study of mental content to the functional study of mental processes, at the same time shifting the focus of experimental technique from the introspective ascertaining of mental states to the objective determination of the influence of stimulus on behavior. Lurking behind all these changes was the desire of psychologists to be socially useful, implying the study of behavior—what people do in society— rather than the socially useless study of sensory contents. The shift from mentalism to behavioralism was inevitable, and it only needed to be discovered to be a *fait accompli*.

Change was in the air. Surveying the year 1910, E. R. Buchner confessed that "some of us are still struggling at initial clearness as to what psychology was about." A signal event of the year was Yerkes's discovery of the "low esteem" in which psychology was held by biologists, whom most psychologists now considered their closest disciplinary colleagues. Surveying leading biologists, Yerkes found that most of them were simply ignorant of psychology or convinced it would soon disappear into biology. Yerkes concluded that "few, if any, sciences are in worse plight than psychology," attributing its "sad plight" to a lack of self-confidence, an absence of agreed-upon principles, poor training of psychologists in physical science, and a failure to teach psychology as anything more than a set of bizarre facts or as a branch of philosophy, instead of as a natural science. Yerkes's survey was widely discussed and clearly troubled psychologists, who had labored long and hard to make of psychology a dignified scientific profession.

Psychologists were casting about for a new central concept around which to organize their science, perhaps rendering it more securely a natural science. Bawden, who was continuing to push his own program of interpreting mind "in terms of hands and feet," observed that recently, psychologists, without "being clearly conscious of what was happening," had begun to look at mind afresh, in terms of muscle movement, physiology, and "behavior." In any case, Bawden said psychology needed a general shift in methods and attitudes away from philosophical conceptions and toward biological ones.

The APA convention of 1911 was dominated by discussion of the place of consciousness in psychology, according to an observer, M. E. Haggerty (1911). He noted with some surprise that *no one* at the convention defended the traditional definition of psychology as the study of self-consciousness. Speaking at a symposium on "Philosophical and Psychological Uses of the Terms Mind, Consciousness, and Soul," Angell (1911) put his finger on the change from mentalism to behavioralism. Soul, of course, had ceased as a psychological concept when the new psychology replaced the old. But mind, too, Angell noted, was now in "a highly precarious position," and consciousness "is likewise in danger of extinction." Angell defined behavioralism as follows:

> There is unquestionably a movement on foot in which interest is centered in the *results* of conscious process, rather than in the *processes* themselves. This is peculiarly true in animal psychology; it is only less true in human psychology. In these cases interest is in what may for lack of a better term be called "behavior"; and the analysis of consciousness is primarily justified by the light it throws on behavior, rather than vice-versa. (p. 47)

If this movement should go forward, Angell concluded, psychology would become "a general science of behavior," exactly the definition of the field being offered in the latest textbooks of psychology: Parmelee's (1913), Judd's (1910), and McDougall's (1912). As early as 1908, McDougall had proposed redefining psychology as "the positive science of conduct and behavior" (p. 15).

The year 1912 proved to be pivotal. Buchner observed further confusion about the definition of mind and noted the philosophers and their psychological allies who wanted to identify mind with behavior. Knight Dunlap (1912), Watson's older colleague at Johns Hopkins, used the new relational theory of consciousness to make "the case against introspection." Introspection had value only under a copy theory of mind, Dunlap said, because introspection describes the privileged contents of consciousness. But on a relational view of mind, introspection loses its special character, becoming no more than a description of a real object under special conditions of attention. Introspection is thus not the reporting of an internal object, but merely the reporting of the stimulus currently controlling behavior. The term *introspection*, Dunlap concluded, should be restricted to the reporting of internal stimuli, which can be gotten at no other way. Introspection was not the central method of psychology.

Elliot Frost (1912) reported on European physiologists who were taking a radical new view of consciousness. These physiologists, who included Jacques Loeb, an influence on Watson at Chicago, pronounced psychological concepts "superstitions" and found no room for animal consciousness in the explanation of animal behavior. Frost tried to refute these challenges with a functional view of mind as adaptive "consciousizing" behavior.

More important for us are the reductionistic claims of these European physiologists and certain psychologists then and soon to come. Mind may be eliminated from psychology in two ways that are distinct and should be kept separate. The program of the physiologists Frost reviewed, including Pavlov, and of psychologists such as Max Meyer, another influence on Watson, called for the identification events of mental with underlying neurophysiological processes thought to cause them. Mental concepts could be eliminated from science as we learn the material causes the mentalistic terms designate, or they could be reduced to physiological processes that explain the mental ones. This reductive and perhaps eliminativist program flourishes in cognitive neuroscience.

The other program for eliminating mind was inchoate as yet, and it would be often mixed up with reductionism or physiological eliminativism for years to come. It claims that mental concepts can be replaced by behavioral ones, which themselves may not be reducible to mechanical, underlying physiological laws. We can see something of this view, perfected later by B. F. Skinner, in the relational theories of mind, especially Singer's; but it was not a distinct psychological system in 1912. The historical importance of the reductionists reviewed by Frost remains—the autonomy of consciousness and mind as central concepts in psychology was under increasing assault from every quarter.

The December 1912 meeting of the APA in Cleveland marked the final transition of psychology, with only a few holdouts, from mentalism to behavioralism. Angell (1913) identified the behavioral view in "Behavior as a Category of Psychology." Angell began by recalling his own prophecy, made at the 1910 APA meeting, that the study of behavior was overshadowing the study of consciousness. Just two years later, consciousness had become a "victim marked for slaughter" as behavior was poised to completely replace mental life as the subject matter of psychology. In philosophy, the consciousness debate questioned consciousness's very existence. In animal psychology, researchers wanted to give up reference to mind and just study behavior, matched by a "general drift" in the same direction in human psychology. This drift, Angell pointed out, is "not deliberate" and is thus likely to be "substantial and enduring."

Moreover, there were many flourishing fields concerned with human beings in which introspection offered "no adequate approach": social psychology, racial psychology, sociology, economics, development, individual differences, and others. The tendency to eliminate introspection as psychology's master method was not just a product of new topics like those mentioned, but was aided by functional psychology, which studied response more than conscious content.

Angell was not willing to completely abandon introspection. Although it could no longer be psychology's premier method, it retained an important role in providing data not otherwise obtainable. It would be a "crowning absurdity," Angell said, for the new behavioral psychology to deny any significance to the "chief distinction" of human nature: self consciousness. There was another danger in a behavioral psychology, Angell warned. By concentrating on behavior, psychologists would trespass on the territory of another science, biology; and thus there was a risk that psychology might be "swallowed up" by biology or might become a mere vassal to biology as its "overlord."

Still, there was no mistaking Angell's message. Psychology was now the study of behavior. It was a natural science closely allied to biology, forsaking its philosophical roots. Its methods were now objective, introspection serving pragmatically when needed but no longer at the center of the field. Concern with consciousness as such had been replaced by concern with the explanation, prediction, and control of behavior. The psychology viewed with such horror by Warner Fite had arrived.

THE RISE OF BEHAVIORISM

The Behaviorist Manifesto

John Broadus Watson (1878–1958) was an ambitious young animal psychologist who, as we saw earlier in this chapter, had by 1908 outlined a purely behavioral approach to animal psychology. In his autobiography, Watson says that he had broached the idea of an objective human psychology to his teachers during his days as a graduate student at Chicago, but that his proposals were greeted with such horror that he kept his own counsel. After establishing himself as a scientist, he felt emboldened to expand publicly the scope of his objective psychology. On February 13, 1913, he began a series of lectures on animal psychology at Columbia University with a lecture on "Psychology as the Behaviorist Views It." Encouraged by the editor of *Psychological Review*, Howard Warren (who for some time had been trying to get Watson to publish his new view of psychology), Watson published his lecture; in 1943, a group of eminent psychologists rated this paper as the most important one ever published in the *Review*.

XAM'S BLOG 1
J. B. Watson, Modernism in Person

The script of John Broadus Watson's life was written by modernity and modernism (Buckley, 1989), traveling in one lifetime from the rural and religious past to the urban and scientific future. He was born in the backcountry of North Carolina. His mother was a devout Baptist, and his father was a violent, ne'er-do-well Confederate veteran who was rarely home. Finally abandoned by her husband, Emma Watson left their little farm and moved to nearby Greenville, which was just becoming a factory town in the textile industry. Seeking the respectability a college education would bring, Watson attended Furman University. Although nominally a denominational Baptist college, Furman had lost its theology school, and under a modernizing president, abandoned compulsory chapel and inaugurated more scientific curricula. Young Watson encountered psychology there with teacher Gordon Moore, who had taken courses at the University of Chicago from John Dewey. Chicago and its university was the center of Progressive life and thought at the turn of the century, and after a short, unhappy stint as school principal, Watson entered the University of Chicago in 1900 undertaking graduate study under James Rowland Angell, leader of psychological functionalism, and destined to be president of Yale, where he would put social science to work solving social problems at the Institute for Human Relations during the Depression. There, in the heart of the new urbanizing America, Watson had a nervous breakdown, lost his religious faith, but acquired a driving and passionate faith in behavioristic psychology and its ability to control people.

Watson wrote innumerable popular articles and two books espousing a future ruled by behaviorists. In Watson's Utopia, behaviorists would replace government officials and the law, practicing preventive psychology to detect and treat "unstandardized sex reactions" and "unsocial ways of behaving." Indeed, in a society run by psychologists, the state itself would wither away. B. F. Skinner, just a little younger than Watson, who made a similar transition from the premodern past to scientific modernity, found inspiration in Watson's ideas, carried on Watson's faith, writing about his own state-less Utopia in Walden II, and publicizing a deterministic view of the human condition in Beyond Freedom and Dignity.

From the paper's aggressive tone, it was clear that Watson was issuing a manifesto for a new kind of psychology: behaviorism. Watson's paper may be regarded as one of many modernist manifestos issued in the first decades of the twentieth century. For example, in Watson's year of 1913, modern art came to America in the notorious Armory Show, a kind of manifesto in paint for modernism in the arts. Modern artists also issued written manifestos for various movements, such as futurism and dadaism. Watson's manifesto for behaviorism shared the goals of these modernist manifestos: to repudiate the past and set out, however incoherently, a vision of life as it might be. Watson began with a ringing definition of psychology as it might be:

> Psychology as the behaviorist views it is a purely objective branch of natural science. Its theoretical goal is the prediction and control of behavior. Introspection forms no essential part of its methods, nor is the scientific value of its data dependent on the readiness with which they lend themselves to interpretation in terms of consciousness. The behaviorist, in his efforts to get a unitary scheme of animal response, recognizes no dividing line between man and brute. The behavior of man, with all of its refinement and complexity, forms only a part of the behaviorist's total scheme of investigation. (1913a, p. 158)

CRITIQUE OF MENTALISTIC PSYCHOLOGY   In the tradition of modernist manifestos, Watson went on to repudiate psychology as it had been. He saw no difference between structuralism and functionalism. Both adopted the traditional definition of psychology as "the science of the phenomena of consciousness," and both used the traditional "esoteric" method of introspection. However, psychology so conceived had "failed to make its place in the world as an undisputed natural science." Watson felt especially constrained by traditional demands that animal psychologists discuss their subjects' minds. But animals were unable to introspect, forcing psychologists to "construct" conscious contents for them on analogy to the psychologists' own minds. Moreover, traditional psychology was anthropocentric, respecting the findings of animal psychology only insofar as they bore on questions of human psychology. Watson found this situation intolerable and aimed to reverse traditional priorities. In 1908, he had declared the autonomy of animal psychology as the study of animal behavior; now he proposed to use "human beings as subjects and to employ methods of investigation which are exactly comparable to those now employed in animal work." Earlier comparative psychologists had warned that we should not anthropomorphize animals; Watson urged psychologists not to anthropomorphize human beings.

Watson faulted introspection on empirical, philosophical, and practical grounds. *Empirically*, it failed to define questions it could convincingly answer. There was as yet no answer even to the most basic question of the psychology of consciousness: how many sensations there are and the number of their attributes. Watson saw no end to a sterile discussion (1913a, p. 164): "I firmly believe that, unless the introspective method is discarded, psychology will still be divided on the question as to whether auditory sensations have the quality of 'extension' . . . and upon many hundreds of other [questions] of like character."

Philosophically, Watson condemned mentalistic psychology for its use of the nonscientific method of introspection. In the natural sciences, good techniques provide "reproducible results," and then, when these are not forthcoming, "the attack is made upon the experimental conditions" until reliable results are obtained. In mentalistic psychology, however, we must study the private world of an observer's consciousness. This means that instead of attacking experimental conditions when results are unclear, psychologists attack the introspective observer, saying, "Your introspection is poor" or "untrained." Watson's point seemed to be that the results of introspective psychology possess a personal element not found in the natural sciences; this contention formed the basis of methodological behaviorism.

Finally, Watson condemned mentalistic psychology on practical grounds. In the laboratory, it demanded that animal psychologists find some behavioral criterion of consciousness, an issue we know involved Watson, as he reviewed it several times for the *Psychological Bulletin*. But he now argued that consciousness was irrelevant to animal work: "One can assume either the presence or absence of consciousness anywhere in the phylogenetic scale without affecting the problems of behavior one jot or one tittle." Experiments are, in fact, designed to find out what an animal will do in some novel circumstance, and its behavior is then observed; only later must the researcher attempt the "absurd," reconstructing the animal's mind as it behaved. But Watson pointed out that reconstructing the animal's consciousness added nothing at all to what had already been accomplished in the observation of behavior. With respect to applied psychology, introspective psychology was likewise irrelevant, offering no solutions to the problems facing people in modern life. Indeed, Watson reports that it was his feeling that mentalistic psychology had "no realm of application" that early on made him "dissatisfied" with it. So it is not surprising to find that the one area of existing psychology Watson praised was applied psychology: educational psychology, psychopharmacology, mental testing, psychopathology, and legal and advertising psychology. These fields were "most flourishing" because they were "less dependent on introspection." Sounding a key theme of progressivism, Watson lauded these "truly scientific" psychologies because they "are in search of broad generalizations which will lead to the control of human behavior."

On Watson's account, then, introspective psychology had nothing to recommend it and much to condemn it. "Psychology must discard all reference to consciousness." Psychology must now be defined as the science of behavior, and "never use the terms consciousness, mental states, mind, content, introspectively verifiable, imagery and the like. . . . It can be done in terms of stimulus and response, in terms of habit formation, habit integrations and the like. Furthermore, I believe that it is really worthwhile to make this attempt now" (1913a, pp. 166–167).

THE BEHAVIORIST PROGRAM The "starting point" of Watson's new psychology would be the "fact that organisms, man and animal alike, do adjust themselves to their environment"; that is, psychology would be the study of adjustive behavior, not conscious content. Description of behavior would lead to the prediction of behavior in terms of stimulus and response (1913a, p. 167): "In a system of psychology completely worked out, given the response the stimuli can be predicted; given the stimuli the response can be predicted." Ultimately, Watson aimed to "learn general and particular methods by which I may control behavior." Once control techniques become available, the leaders of society will be able to "utilize our data in a practical way." Although Watson did not cite Auguste Comte, his program for behaviorism—describe, predict, and control observable behavior—was clearly in the positivist tradition.

The methods for achieving psychology's new goals were left rather vague, as Watson (1916a) later admitted. The only thing made really clear about behavioral methodology in the manifesto is that under behaviorism, work "on the human being will be comparable directly with the work upon animals," because behaviorists "care as little about [a human subject's] 'conscious processes' during the conduct of the experiment as we care about such processes in the rat." He gave a few examples of how sensation and memory might be investigated, but they are not very convincing and would soon be replaced by Pavlov's conditioned reflex method.

Watson said some startling things about human thinking. He asserted that thinking does not involve the brain—there are no "centrally initiated processes"—but consists in "faint reinstatement of . . . muscular acts," specifically "motor habits in the larynx." "In other words, wherever there are thought processes there are faint contractions of the systems of musculature involved in the overt exercise of the customary act, and especially in the still finer systems of musculature involved in speech. . . . Imagery becomes a mental luxury (even if it really exists) without any functional significance whatever" (1913a, p. 174). Watson's claims are the logical outcome of the motor theory of consciousness (McComas, 1916). On the motor theory, consciousness merely records what we say and do without affecting either. Watson simply pointed out that because mental content has "no functional significance," there's no point in studying it save accumulated prejudice: "Our minds have been warped by fifty odd years which have been devoted to the study of states of consciousness."

In another Columbia lecture, "Image and Affection in Behavior," also published in 1913, Watson continued his assault on mental content. He considered, and rejected, the formula of methodological behaviorism, the view that "I care not what goes on in [a person's] so called mind" as long as his or her behavior is predictable. But for Watson, methodological behaviorism is a "partial defeat" he found unacceptable, preferring instead "to attack." He reiterated his view that "there are no centrally initiated processes." Instead, thinking is just "implicit behavior" that sometimes occurs between a stimulus and the resulting "explicit behavior." Most implicit behavior, he hypothesized, occurs in the larynx and is open to observation, though the technique of such observation had not been developed. The important point for Watson is that there are no functional mental processes playing causal roles in determining behavior. There are only chains of behavior, some of which are difficult to observe. Should this be true—and Watson applied his thesis to both mental images and experienced emotions, as the title states—no part of psychology could escape the behaviorist's scheme, for mind would be shown to *be* behavior; the behaviorist would concede no subject to the mentalist. Finally, Watson suggested a theme that would emerge more vividly in his later writings and shows how his behaviorism was part of a larger revolt against the cultural past, not simply a revolt against a failed introspective psychology. Watson claimed that allegiance to mentalistic psychology was at root clinging to religion in a scientific age that has made religion obsolete. Those who believe that there are centrally initiated processes—that is, behaviors begun by the brain and not by some outside stimulus—really believe in the soul. Watson said that as we know nothing about the cortex, it is easy to attribute the functions of the soul to the cortex: Both are unexplained mysteries. Watson's position was extremely radical: Not only did the soul not exist, neither did the cortex as anything other than a relay station connecting stimulus and response; soul and brain could be equally ignored in the description, prediction, and control of behavior.

The Initial Response, 1913–1918

How did psychologists receive Watson's manifesto? One might expect that behaviorism would become the rallying cry of younger psychologists and the object of denunciation by their elders, and, when Watson's manifesto later took its revered place as the starting point of behaviorism, it was thought to have been received in just such fashions. However, as Samelson (1981) has shown, published responses to "Psychology as the Behaviorist Views It" were both remarkably few and remarkably restrained.

There were a few responses in 1913. Watson's teacher, Angell, added some references to behaviorism in the published version of "Behavior as a Category of Psychology." He said he was "heartily sympathetic" to behaviorism and recognized it as a logical development of his own emphasis on behavior. Nevertheless, he did not think that introspection could ever be entirely eliminated from psychology, if only as providing useful reports on the processes connecting stimulus and response; Watson himself admitted such use of introspection, but he called it the "language method." Angell bid behaviorism "Godspeed" but counseled it to "forego the excesses of youth," which, like most counsel to youth, went unheeded. Without actually citing Watson, M. E. Haggerty agreed that the emerging laws of learning, or habit formation, reduced behavior to "physical terms," so there was no "longer any need to invoke ghosts in the form of consciousness" to explain thinking. Robert Yerkes criticized Watson for "throwing overboard" the method of self-observation that set psychology off from biology; under behaviorism, psychology would be "merely a fragment of physiology." The philosopher Henry Marshall was afraid that psychology might be "evaporating." He observed the behavioral *Zeitgeist* of which behaviorism was the latest manifestation and concluded that it contained much of value, but that to identify behavior study with psychology was an "astounding confusion of thought," for consciousness remained to be investigated whatever the achievements of behaviorism. Mary Calkins, who had earlier proposed her self-psychology as a compromise between structural and functional psychology, now proposed it as a mediator between behaviorism and mentalism. Like most of the other commentators, she agreed with much of Watson's critique of structuralism and applauded the study of behavior, but she nevertheless found introspection to be the indispensable, if sometimes troublesome, method of psychology.

The other commentaries on behaviorism in the years before World War I took much the same line as these initial responses: The deficiencies of structuralism were acknowledged, the virtues of studying behavior were conceded, but introspection was nevertheless defended as the *sine qua non* of psychology. The study of behavior was just biology; psychology, to retain its identity, had to remain introspective. A. H. Jones (1915) spoke for many when he wrote: "We may rest assured then, that whatever else psychology may be, it is at least a doctrine of awareness. To deny this . . . is to pour out the baby with the bath." Titchener (1914) also saw behavior study as biology rather than psychology. Because the facts of consciousness exist, he said, they can be studied, and such is the task of psychology. Although behaviorism might accomplish much, because it was not psychology at all, it posed no threat to introspective psychology. One of the few substantive as opposed to methodological criticisms of Watson's behaviorism was offered by H. C. McComas (1916), who correctly saw it as a natural extension of the motor theory of consciousness. McComas showed that Watson's identification of thinking with laryngeal movements stood falsified: Some people had already lost their larynxes due to disease without thereby losing the ability to think.

With the exception of McComas's paper, however, reactions to behaviorism in the prewar years tended to assert the same thing: that, although behavior study was valuable, it was really a form of biology rather than psychology because psychology was, by definition, the study of consciousness and must, perforce, use introspection as its method. Although these critics' positions were not unreasonable, they seemed not to notice that Watson might succeed in fundamentally redefining psychology altogether. As we have seen, Watson was riding the crest of behavioralism, and if enough psychologists adopted his definition of their field, it would, as a matter of historical fact, cease to be the study of the mind and would become the study of behavior.

Watson, of course, did not remain silent while his views were debated. He was chosen by a nominating committee and ratified by the members of the APA to be the president for 1916. In his presidential address (1916a), he tried to fill the most conspicuous gap in behaviorism: the method and theory by which it would study and explain behavior. Watson had tried for some years to show that thinking was just implicit speech, but he had failed. So he turned to the work of Karl Lashley, a student in Watson's laboratory, who had been replicating and extending Pavlov's conditioning techniques. Watson now presented the conditioned reflex work as the substance of behaviorism: Pavlov's method applied to humans would be behaviorism's tool of investigation, and the conditioned reflex theory would provide the basis for the prediction and control of behavior in animals and people. Watson's address set out in detail how the conditioned reflex method could be applied to both humans and animals, providing an objective substitute for introspection. Nor was Watson loath to apply the theory outside the laboratory. In another 1916 paper, he argued that neuroses were just "habit disturbances," most usually "disturbances of speech functions" (1916b). We see again that Watson's program was not merely scientific but social; even as he was first learning about and investigating conditioned reflexes, he was prepared to assert that speech and, thus, neurotic symptoms, were just conditioned reflexes—poor behavior adjustments that could be corrected by the application of behavior principles.

We have noted various reactions to Watson's manifesto. However, apart from about a dozen papers, few psychologists or philosophers wrote about it. The reason is not far to seek. A manifesto is a work of rhetoric, and when we separate Watson's rhetoric from his substantive proposals, we find that he said little that was new, but said it in especially angry tones. The behavioral approach had overcome psychology slowly and almost unnoticed in the years after 1892. What Watson did was to give behavioralism an aggressive voice, and to give it a name that stuck, *behaviorism*, however misleading that name has since become. In its time, then, his manifesto merited little attention. Older psychologists had already admitted that psychology needed to pay attention to behavior—after all, it was they who had moved the field toward behavioral-ism—but remained concerned to preserve the traditional mission of psychology, the study of consciousness. Younger psychologists of Watson's generation had already accepted behavioralism and so accepted his broad position without any sense of excitement, even if they might reject his extreme peripheralism. So no one was either outraged or inspired by Watson's manifesto of psychological modernism, for all had learned to live with modernism or were already practicing it. Watson created no revolution, but he did make clear that psychology was no longer the science of consciousness. "Psychology as the Behaviorist Views It" simply marks the moment when behavioralism became ascendant and self-conscious, creating for later behaviorists a useful "myth of origin." It provided for them a secure anchoring point in the history of psychology and a justification for the abandonment of an introspective method they found boring and sterile. But all of these things would have happened had Watson never become a psychologist.

Behaviorism Defined, 1919–1930

Along with the rest of psychology, the discussion of behaviorism was interrupted by World War I. As we shall see, psychology was much changed by its involvement with the war; when psychologists resumed their consideration of behaviorism, the grounds of the discussion were quite different from what they had been before the war. The value of objective psychology had been proved by the tests psychologists had devised to classify soldiers, and that success had brought psychology before a wider audience. After the war, the question was no longer whether behaviorism was legitimate, but what form behaviorism should take.

THE VARIETIES OF BEHAVIORISM As early as 1922, it was clear that psychologists were having trouble understanding behaviorism or formulating it in any widely agreeable way. Walter Hunter (1922), a sympathizer of Watson's, wrote "An Open Letter to the Anti-Behaviorists." He thought behaviorism was exactly what Watson preached: the definition of psychology as the study of "stimulus and response relations." He viewed the various "new formulas" for behaviorism that by then had been offered as "illegitimate offspring," making it difficult for psychologists to see what behaviorism was. Later, Hunter (1925) would try to finesse the issue by defining a new science, "anthroponomy," the science of human behavior. But Hunter's new science never caught on, leaving psychologists to redefine psychology in some new, "behavioristic" way.

Some of them, most notably Albert P. Weiss (e.g., 1924) and Zing Yang Kuo (1928), attempted to formulate behaviorism as Watson had, only more precisely. Kuo defined behaviorism as "a science of mechanics dealing with the mechanical movements of . . . organisms" and held "the duty of the behaviorist is to describe behavior in exactly the same way as the physicist describes the movements of a machine." This mechanistic, physiologically reductionist psychology, modern inheritor of La Mettrie, was most clearly and comprehensively set out by Karl Lashley (1890–1958), the student with whom Watson had studied the conditional reflex in animals and humans.

Lashley (1923) wrote that behaviorism had become "an accredited system of psychology" but, in its emphasis on "experimental method," had failed to give any satisfactory "systematic formulation" of its views. In light of behaviorism's being "so great a departure from tradition in psychology," a clearer formulation of behaviorism was needed. Heretofore, Lashley claimed, three forms of behaviorism had been advanced. The first two were scarcely distinguishable as forms of "methodological behaviorism." They allowed that "facts of conscious experience exist but are unsuited to any form of scientific treatment." It had been, according to Lashley, the beginning point of Watson's own behaviorism, but it ultimately proved unsatisfying because it conceded too much to introspective psychology. Precisely because it acknowledged the "facts of consciousness," methodological behaviorism admitted that it could never be a complete psychology and had to concede a science, or at least a study, of mind alongside the science of behavior. Opposed to methodological behaviorism was "*strict behaviorism*" (or, as Calkins [1921] and Wheeler [1923] named it, *radical behaviorism* [Schneider & Morris, 1987]), whose "extreme" view was that "the supposedly unique facts of consciousness do not exist." Such a view seems at first sight implausible, and Lashley conceded that it had not been put forward with any convincing arguments. Lashley made his own view plain:

> Let me cast off the lion's skin. My quarrel with behaviorism is not that it has gone too far, but that it has hesitated . . . that it has failed to develop its premises to their logical conclusion. To me the essence of behaviorism is the belief that the study of man will reveal nothing except

what is adequately describable in the concepts of mechanics and chemistry. . . . I believe that it is possible to construct a physiological psychology which will meet the dualist on his own ground . . . and show that [his] data can be embodied in a mechanistic system. . . . Its physiological account of behavior will also be a complete and adequate account of all the phenomena of consciousness . . . demanding that all psychological data, however obtained, shall be subjected to physical or physiological interpretation. (1923, pp. 243–244)

Ultimately, Lashley said, the choice between behaviorism and traditional psychology comes down to a choice between two "incompatible" worldviews, "scientific versus humanistic." It had been demanded of psychology heretofore that "it must leave room for human ideals and aspirations." But "other sciences have escaped this thralldom," and so must psychology escape from "metaphysics and values" and "mystical obscurantism" by turning to physiology. In physiology, it can find principles of explanation that will make of psychology a natural science, value-free, capable of addressing its "most important problems," its "most interesting and vital questions, the problems of human conduct." It would then be able to recapture the "problems of everyday life" from "sociology, education, and psychiatry," the applied fields ignored by introspective psychology. Lashley's formula for psychology was clearly La Mettrie's: the mechanistic, physiological explanation of behavior and consciousness. It was also clearly in the tradition of Comte's positivism. It preached a scientific imperialism against the humanities and questions of value, setting up instead a value-free technology claiming to solve human problems. Lashley, Weiss, Kuo, and Watson attempted to define behaviorism quite narrowly, following a behavioral version of the path through physiology, almost dismantling psychology as an independent discipline. Other psychologists and philosophical observers of psychology thought the physiologically reductive definition of behaviorism too narrow and defined a more inclusive behavioristic psychology.

The neorealist philosopher R. B. Perry (1921) saw behaviorism as nothing new, but "simply a return to the original Aristotelian view that mind and body are related as activity and organ." Adopting behaviorism did not mean denying that mind has a role in behavior. On the contrary, "If you are a behaviorist you regard the mind as something that *intervenes*" in determining behavior, and behaviorism rescues mind from the parallelistic impotence imposed on it by introspective psychology. On the other hand, the neorealist Stephen Pepper (1923), who had studied with Perry at Harvard, though similarly refusing to identify Watson's behaviorism as *the* behaviorism, nonetheless flatly contradicted Perry: For Pepper, the central contention of behaviorism was that consciousness plays no causal role in determining behavior, and that behaviorism's destiny was to bring psychology into "connection with the rest of the natural sciences." Jastrow (1927), who had been around since the beginning of psychology in America, saw nothing new in behaviorism, calling James, Peirce, and Hall "behaviorists." It was a mistake, Jastrow argued, to confuse Watson's "radical" behaviorism with the more general and moderate behaviorism held by most American psychologists.

When we set side by side the views of Lashley, Perry, Pepper, and Jastrow, it becomes clear that *behaviorism* was a term of nearly infinite elasticity. It might signify physiological reductionism, or just the study of behavior by objective means; it might mean a significant break with the past, or it might be very old; it might mean seeing mind as a causal actor in determining behavior, or it might mean the denial of mind as causal agent. Woodworth (1924) was correct when he wrote that "there is no one great inclusive enterprise" binding together the various claimants to the title "behaviorism." Woodworth saw behaviorism's "essential program" as "behavior study, behavior concepts, laws of behavior, control of behavior," not the "neuromechanistic interpretation" of psychology associated with Watson. Woodworth observed that psychology had begun as the nonintrospective study of reaction times, memory, and psychophysics, but had been sidetracked in its development as a science by Titchener, Külpe, and others around 1900. Behaviorism—or, as we have defined it here, behavioralism—was a program for psychology, not a new method. Scientific psychology was bound to become behavioralistic; Watson had wrought nothing new.

HUMAN OR ROBOT?   One point of note arose in several of the papers advocating behaviorism, connecting behavioralism with its past in functionalism and its future in cognitive science: James's "automatic sweetheart." In contrasting behaviorism with humanism, Lashley noted that "the final objection to behaviorism is that it just fails to express the vital, personal quality of experience," an objection "quite evident in James's arguments concerning the 'automatic sweetheart.'" Hunter (1923) likewise considered James's possible objection to behaviorism: It claims one's beloved is an automaton, and can one truly love a machine? With Lashley, who said descriptions of experience "belong to art, not science," Hunter dismissed worries about whether one could love, or be loved by, a machine as concerned only with the "aesthetic satisfaction" of the belief, not its scientific truth.

B. H. Bode (1918) treated the problem more fully, defending the behaviorist point of view. Bode argued that upon reflection, there is no meaningful difference between a human sweetheart and a mechanical one, because no behavioral difference between them could be discerned:

> If there is no [objectively observable] difference, then the consciousness of the spiritually animated maiden plainly makes no difference in the behavior; it is a mere concomitant or epiphenomenon . . . mechanism becomes the last word of explanation, and the mystery of the eternally feminine takes on much the same quality as the mystery of higher mathematics. (p. 451)

Finally, a critic of behaviorism, William McDougall, put the issue in the most up-to-date terms. The term *robot* had just been coined by Carel Capek in his science fiction play *R.U.R.* (Rossum's Universal Robots). MacDougall (1925) saw the critical question framed by behaviorism as "Men or robots?" Behaviorism rested on the claim that human beings are just machines—robots—but that claim was unproved. In Woodworth's opinion, it remained to be determined that robots could do anything human beings can do.

The concern over James's automatic, or robot, sweetheart raises the central problem of scientific psychology in the twentieth century: Can human beings be consistently conceived of as machines? This question transcends all the systems of psychology since James's (or even La Mettrie's) time, as it ties together functionalism, realism, behaviorism, and cognitive psychology. Following the development of computers in World War II, one of their creators would pose James's question in more intellectual terms: Can machine be said to think if you can talk to it and be fooled into believing you are talking to another person? And A. M. Turing, followed by many cognitive psychologists, would give Bode's answer: If you can't tell it's just a machine, then we're just machines, too. The prospect of the automatic sweetheart filled some psychologists with excitement, but others, such as James, with revulsion. Lashley was very likely right when he saw the battle over behaviorism not just as a battle between different ways of doing psychology, but as a much deeper battle between "mechanistic explanation and finalistic valuation": between a view of human beings as robots or as actors with purposes, values, hopes, fears, and loves.

LATER WATSONIAN BEHAVIORISM   Following World War II, in which he served unhappily in the Army working up tests for aviators, Watson moved his research and his advocacy for behaviorism in a new direction. He now intensively pursued a human psychology based on the conditioned reflex by investigating the acquisition of reflexes in infants. Watson believed that nature endowed human beings with very few unconditioned reflexes, so that the complex behavior of adults might be explained as simply the acquisition of conditioned reflexes over years of Pavlovian conditioning. Contrary to eugenicists and their followers, who believed that people inherit a great deal of their intellect, personality, and morality, Watson (1930, p. 94) asserted that "there is no such thing as inheritance of *capacity, talent, temperament, mental constitution,* and *characteristics.*" For example, Watson denied that human hand preference was innate. He could find no structural differences between babies' left and right hands and arms, nor were the different hands endowed with different strengths. So, although he remained puzzled by the fact that most people were right-handed, he put the cause of it down to social training and said there would be no harm in trying to turn apparently left-handed children into right-handers. Nothing could better demonstrate Watson's radical peripheralism: As he could find no peripheral differences between the hands' strength and structure, there could be, he concluded, no biological basis to handedness. He completely ignored the "mysterious" (Watson, 1913b) cortex of the brain, seeing it as no more than a relay station for neural impulses. We now know that the left and right hemispheres of the human brain have very different functions and that differences between right- and left-handers are determined there. To attempt to change a natural left-hander into a right-hander is to impose a very trying task, one well calculated to upset and make the left-handed child feel inferior.

In any event, to establish the truth of his equally radical environmentalism—"Give me a dozen healthy infants . . . and my own specified world to bring them up in and I'll guarantee to take any one at random and train him to become any type of specialist I might select—doctor, lawyer, artist, merchant-chief and, yes, even beggar-man and thief" (Watson, 1930, p. 104)—Watson turned to the nursery to show that humans are no more than plastic material waiting to be molded by society. The most famous of his studies with infants is "Conditioned Emotional Reactions" (Watson & Rayner, 1920). Watson carried out an experiment on an infant known as "Albert B." designed to show that people are born with only a few "instincts"—fear, rage, and sexual response—and that all other emotions are conditioned versions of these unconditioned ones. As his unconditioned stimulus (US) to produce fear (unconditioned response, UR), Watson chose a loud noise, the sound of a large metal bar being struck by a hammer; this stimulus had been determined to be one of the few that would scare little Albert. He paired the noise with a conditioned stimulus (CS), a rat whom Albert liked to pet. Now, however, when Albert touched the rat, Watson struck the bar; after seven such pairings, the child showed fear of the rat by itself. Watson claimed to have established a "conditioned emotional reaction," and he asserted that his experimental arrangement was the prototype of emotional learning by a normal human in the normal human environment. Watson believed he had demonstrated that the rich emotional life of the adult human being was, at bottom, no more than a large number of conditioned responses built up over years of human development. We should point out that Watson's claims are dubious and his ethics in this experiment questionable (E. Samelson, 1980); furthermore, the experiment is often misdescribed by secondary sources (Harris, 1979). Watson was, at least, consistent. He fell in love with graduate student collaborator Rosalie Rayner—creating a scandal that cost him his job at Johns Hopkins in 1920—and wrote to her that "every cell I have is yours singly and collectively," and that all his emotional responses "are positive and towards you . . . likewise each and every heart response" (quoted by Cohen, 1979).

Watson had always been willing to write about psychology for a popular audience. After 1920, following his expulsion from academia, he became the first modern popular psychologist (Buckley, 1984), writing, for example, a series of articles on human psychology from the behaviorist perspective in *Harper's* from 1926 to 1928. There, Watson began by laying out behaviorism as the scientific replacement for mentalistic psychology and for psychoanalysis, which had earlier captured the popular mind. According to Watson, psychoanalysis had "too little science—real science" to long command serious attention, and the traditional psychology of consciousness "never had any right to be called a science." As he often did in his popular writings, Watson connected mentalistic psychology with religion, asserting that "mind and consciousness" were but "carryovers from the church dogma of the middle ages." The mind, or soul, was, according to Watson, one of the mysteries by whose invocation "churchmen—all medicine men in fact—have kept the public under control." Psychoanalysis was just "a substitution of demonology for science," and through such "solid walls of religious protection" science was "blasting" a new path.

Watson defied the mentalist to "prove" that "there is such a thing as consciousness." To the assertion by a mentalist that he had a mental life, Watson simply replied, "I have only your unverified and unsupported word that you have" images and sensations. So the concepts of mentalism remained "mythological, the figments of the psychologist's terminology." In place of the fantastic, secretly religious, traditional mentalistic psychology, behaviorism substituted a positivistic, scientific psychology of description, prediction, and control of behavior. Watson said that behavioral psychology began with the observation of the behavior of our fellows, and issued, suitably codified by science, in "a new weapon for controlling the individual." The social use of behavioral science was made clear by Watson: "[We] can build any man, starting at birth, into any kind of social or asocial being upon order." Elsewhere, Watson (1930) said, "It is a part of the behaviorist's scientific job to be able to state what the human machine is good for and to render serviceable predictions about its future capacities whenever society needs such information." Very much in the tradition of Comte's positivism, Watson's behaviorism rejected religion and the moral control of behavior and aimed to replace these with science and the technological control of behavior through behavioral psychology. Behaviorism was well prepared to mesh with Progressivism. Because of Progressivism's interest in establishing rational control over society through scientific means, Progressive politicians and apologists found an ally in behaviorism, which seemed to promise exactly the technology Progressivism needed to replace the outworn authority of tradition.

THE GOLDEN AGE OF THEORY

By 1930, behaviorism was well established as the dominant viewpoint in experimental psychology. Watson's usage had triumphed, and psychologists called the new viewpoint "behaviorism," while recognizing that it took many forms (Williams, 1931). The stage was set for psychologists to create specific theories for predicting and explaining behavior within the new viewpoint. The central problem they would address in the coming decades would be learning (McGeoch, 1931). Functionalism had taken the ability to learn to be the criterion of animal mind, and the development of behaviorism had only magnified its importance. Learning was the process by which animals and humans adjusted to the environment, by which they were educated, and by which they might be changed in the interest of social control or therapy. So it is not surprising that what would later be regarded as the Golden Age of Theory in psychology—the years 1930 to 1950—would be golden only for theories of learning rather than perception, thinking, group dynamics, or anything else.

The other major development of these decades in experimental psychology was psychologists' increasing self-consciousness about proper scientific method. Psychologists have always felt uncertain about the scientific status of their *soidisant* "natural science" and have consequently been eager to find some methodological recipe to follow by which they could infallibly make psychology a science. In denouncing mentalism, Watson had seen its irredeemable flaw to be the "unscientific" method of introspecting, and he had proclaimed psychology's scientific salvation to be objective method, taken over from animal study. Watson's message struck home, but his own recipe was too vague and confused to provide anything more than an attitude. In the 1930s, psychologists became aware of a very specific, prestigious recipe—logical positivism—for making science. The positivist's philosophy of science codified what psychologists already wanted to do, so they accepted the recipe and determined the goals and language of psychology for decades to come. At the same time, their own original ideas were molded so subtly by logical positivism that only today can we see the molding process at work.

Psychology and the Science of Science

We have already remarked how behavioralism reflected the image of science drawn by Comtean positivism: Its goal was the description, prediction, and control of behavior, and its techniques were to be put to use as tools of social control in a rationally managed society. The early, simple positivism of Comte and physicist Ernst Mach (1838–1916) had changed, however. By the early twentieth century, it was clear that positivism's extreme emphasis on talking about only what could be directly observed, excluding from science concepts such as "atom" and "electron," could not be sustained. Physicists and chemists found that their theories could not dispense with such terms, and their research results confirmed for them, albeit indirectly, the reality of atoms and electrons (Holton, 1978). So positivism changed, and its adherents found a way to admit into science terms apparently referring to unobserved entities, without giving up the basic positivist desire to expunge metaphysics from human, or at least scientific, discourse.

This new positivism came to be called *logical positivism* because it wedded the positivist's commitment to empiricism to the logical apparatus of modern formal logic. Logical positivism was a complex and changing movement directed by many hands, but its basic idea was simple: Science had proven to be humankind's most powerful means of understanding reality, of producing knowledge, so that the task of epistemology should be to explicate and formalize the scientific method, making it available to new disciplines and improving its practice among working scientists. Thus, the logical positivists purported to provide a formal recipe for doing science, offering exactly what psychologists thought they needed. Logical positivism began with a small circle of philosophers in Vienna just after World War I, but soon became a worldwide movement aimed at the unification of science in one grand scheme of investigation orchestrated by the positivists themselves. Logical positivism had many aspects, but two have proved especially important to psychologists looking for the "scientific way," and they were adopted as talismans of scientific virtue in the 1930s: formal axiomatization of theories and the operational definition of theoretical terms.

Scientific language, the logical positivists explained, contained two kinds of terms. Most basic were *observation terms*, which referred to directly observable properties of nature: redness, length, weight, time durations, and so on. The older positivism had stressed observation and had insisted that science should contain only observation terms. Logical positivists agreed that observations provided the bedrock of science, but they recognized that theoretical terms were necessary parts of scientific vocabulary, providing explanations in addition to descriptions of natural phenomena. Science simply could not do without terms such as *force, mass, field*, and *electron*. The problem, though, was how to admit science's theoretical vocabulary as legitimate, while excluding metaphysical and religious nonsense. The solution the logical positivists arrived at was to closely tie theoretical terms to bedrock observation terms, thereby guaranteeing their meaningfulness.

The logical positivists argued that the meaning of a theoretical term should be understood to consist in procedures linking it to observation terms. So, for example, *mass* would be defined as an object's weight at sea level. A term that could not be so defined could be dismissed as metaphysical nonsense. Such definitions were called "operational definitions," following the usage of Percy Bridgman, a physicist who had independently proposed the same idea in 1927.

The logical positivists also claimed that scientific theories consisted of theoretical axioms relating theoretical terms to one another. For example, a central axiom of Newtonian physics is "force equals mass times acceleration," or $F = M \times A$. This theoretical sentence expresses a putative scientific law and can be tested by deriving predictions from it. Because each term has an operational definition, it is possible to take an operational measure of the mass of an object, accelerate it to a measurable speed, and then measure the resulting force generated by the object. Should the predicted force correspond to the measured force in the experiment, the axiom would be confirmed; should the values disagree, the axiom would be disconfirmed and would need to be revised. On the logical positivist account of theories, theories explained because they could predict. To explain an event was to show that it could have been predicted from the preceding circumstances combined with some scientific "covering law." So, to explain why a vase broke when it was dropped on the floor, one would show that given the weight of the vase (operationally defined mass) and the height it was dropped from (operationally defined acceleration in earth gravity), the resulting force would be sufficient to crack the vase's porcelain structure.

Logical positivism formalized the ideas of the earlier Comtean and Machian positivists. For both, observation yielded unquestioned truth—both forms of positivism were empiricist. The laws of science were no more than summary statements of experiences: Theoretical axioms were complex summaries of the interactions of several theoretical variables, each of which was in turn wholly defined in terms of observations. To the logical positivist it did not matter if there were atoms or forces in reality; what counted was whether or not such concepts could be systematically related to observations. Logical positivists were thus, for all their apparently tough-minded insistence on believing only what one observes, really romantic idealists (Brush, 1980), for whom ideas—sensations, observation terms—were the only ultimate reality. Nevertheless, logical positivism seemed to offer a specific recipe for doing science in any field of study: First, operationally define one's theoretical terms, be they *mass* or *hunger*; second, state one's theory as a set of theoretical axioms from which predictions can be drawn; third, carry out experiments to test the predictions, using operational definitions to link theory and observations; and finally, revise one's theory as observations warrant.

Because the logical positivists had studied science and set out their findings in explicit logical form, S. S. Stevens (1939), the psychologist who brought operational definition to psychology (Stevens, 1935a,b), called it "the Science of Science," which promised to at last make of psychology "an undisputed natural science" (as Watson had wished) and to unify it with the other sciences in the logical positivists' scheme for the "unity of science." *Operationism* was exciting to psychologists because it promised to settle once and for all fruitless disputes about psychological terminology: What does *mind* mean? "Imageless thought"? "Id"? As Stevens (1935a) put it, operationism was "the revolution that will put an end to the possibility of revolution." Operationism claimed that terms that could not be operationally defined were scientifically meaningless, and scientific terms could be given operational definitions everyone could agree on. Moreover, operationism's revolution ratified behaviorism's claim to be the only scientific psychology because only behaviorism was compatible with operationism's demand that theoretical terms be defined by linking them to observation terms (Stevens, 1939). In psychology, this meant that theoretical terms could not refer to mental entities, but only to classes of behavior. Hence, mentalistic psychology was unscientific and had to be replaced by behaviorism.

By the end of the 1930s, operationism was entrenched dogma in psychology. Sigmund Koch—by 1950, an apostate from the operationist faith—wrote in his 1939 doctoral thesis that "almost every psychology sophomore knows it is bad form if reference to 'definition' is not qualified by the adjective 'operational.' " In operationism lay psychology's scientific salvation: "Hitch the constructs appearing in your postulates to a field of scientific fact [via operational definition], and only then do you get a scientific theory" (Koch, 1941, p. 127).

At a loftier professional level, the president of the APA agreed with Koch. John F. Dashiell (1939) observed that philosophy and psychology were coming together again, not to have philosophers set psychologists' agenda—from that tyranny psychology had won "emancipation"—but to work out science's proper methods. Foremost in the "rapprochement" of philosophy and psychology were two ideas of the logical positivists. The first was operationism; the other was the demand that scientific theories be collections of mathematically stated axioms. Dashiell commended one psychologist for meeting this second requirement: In "the same positivistic vein (as operationism) Hull is urging us to look to the systematic character of our thinking" by producing a rigorous, axiomatic theory. Dashiell's admiration of Clark L. Hull as the foremost logical positivist among psychologists was, as we will see, wrong. Hull was a mechanist, believing in the physiological reality of his theoretical terms. However, Dashiell's opinion became later psychologists' myth, a comforting belief that although the specifics of their theories were mistaken, Hull and E. C. Tolman had set psychology firmly on the path toward science as the logical positivists had defined it. The true natures of their theories of learning were obscured for decades, not only from the understanding of psychologists generally, but even from the understanding of Hull and Tolman themselves. Regardless of its flaws and its distorting effect on the independent ideas of Hull and Tolman, there can be no doubt that logical positivism became psychology's official philosophy of science until at least the 1960s.

Edward Chace Tolman's Purposive Behaviorism

Although it was seldom acknowledged, behaviorism's central problem was to account for mental phenomena without invoking the mind. More liberal behavioralists might—and would eventually—leave mind in psychology as an unseen, but nevertheless causal, agent that determines behavior. But at least in its early days, and in its continuing radical strain, behaviorism has aimed to oust mind from psychology. Watson, Lashley, and the other reductive, or physiological, behaviorists tried to do so by claiming that consciousness, purpose, and cognition were myths, so that the task of psychology was to describe experience and behavior as products of the mechanistic operation of the nervous system. The motor theory of consciousness could be used to good effect in such arguments, as showing that conscious contents were just sensations of bodily movements, reporting, but not causing, behavior. E. C. Tolman and C. L. Hull took different approaches to explaining behavior without invoking the mind.

Bearing a BS in electrochemistry, E. C. Tolman (1886–1959) arrived at Harvard in 1911 to undertake graduate study in philosophy and psychology, settling on the latter as more in tune with his capacities and interests. There he studied with the leading philosophers and psychologists of the day, Perry and Holt, Münsterberg and Yerkes. For a time, reading E. B. Titchener "almost sold (him) on structuralistic introspection," but he noticed in his courses with Münsterberg that although Münsterberg "made little opening speeches to the effect that *the* method in psychology was *introspection*," the work in his laboratory was "primarily objective in nature" and that little use could be made of introspective results in writing up experimental papers. So, reading Watson's *Behavior* in Yerkes's comparative psychology course came "as a tremendous stimulus and relief" for showing that "objective measurement of behavior, not introspection, was the true method of psychology." Tolman's years at Harvard were also the great years of neorealism, just then being promulgated by Perry and Holt.

Neorealism provided the foundation for Tolman's approach to the problem of mind as he developed it after taking a position at the University of California at Berkeley in 1918. Traditionally, the evidence offered to support the existence of mind was of two sorts: introspective awareness of consciousness and the apparent intelligence and purposefulness of behavior. Following Perry, Tolman found Watson's "muscle-twitchism" (Tolman, 1959) too simple and crude to account for either kind of evidence. Neorealism implied that there was no such thing as introspection, as there were no mental objects to observe; in the neorealist view, "introspection" was only an artificially close scrutiny of an object in one's environment, in which one reported the object's attributes in great detail. Tolman allied this analysis with the motor theory of consciousness, arguing that introspection of internal states such as emotions was just the "back action" of behavior on awareness (Tolman, 1923). In either event, introspection was of no special importance to scientific psychology; in saying this, Tolman's (1922) "A New Formula for Behaviorism" was a methodological behaviorism, conceding that awareness existed, but ruling its study out of the domain of science.

Similarly, evidence of intelligent purpose in behavior could be handled from the neorealist perspective. The leading purposive psychology of the day was William McDougall's "hormic" psychology. In "Behaviorism and Purpose," Tolman (1925) criticized McDougall for handling purpose in the traditional Cartesian way: McDougall, "being a mentalist, merely *infers* purpose from (the persistence of) behavior, while we, being behaviorists, *identify* purpose with" persistence toward a goal. Following Perry and Holt, Tolman held that "purpose . . . is an objective aspect of behavior" that an observer directly perceives; it is not an inference *from* observed behavior. Tolman subjected memory to the same analysis, at once recalling the Scottish realists and anticipating B. F. Skinner: "Memory, like purpose, may be conceived . . . as a purely empirical aspect of behavior." To say that one "remembers" a nonpresent object, *X*, is just to say that one's current behavior is "causally dependent" on *X*.

In summary, then, Tolman proposed a behaviorism that excised mind and consciousness from psychology as Watson wanted to do, but retained purpose and cognition, not as powers of a mysterious "mind" inferred from behavior, but as objective, observable aspects of behavior itself. In another contrast to Watson, Tolman's behaviorism was "molar" rather than "molecular" (Tolman, 1926, 1935). In Watson's molecular view, behavior was defined as muscular responses caused by triggering stimuli, so that the appropriate strategy to adopt in predicting and controlling behavior was to analyze complex behaviors into their smallest muscular components, which in turn could be understood physiologically. Tolman, viewing behavior as ineliminably purposive, studied whole, integrated, *molar* acts.

For example, according to a molecularist, a subject who has learned to withdraw his or her finger from an electrode when a warning signal precedes shock has learned a specific conditioned muscular reflex; according to a molar behaviorist, she has learned a global avoidance response. Now turn the subject's hand over, so that the same reflex drives her finger into the electrode; the Watsonian predicts that a new molecular reflex will have to be learned, whereas Tolman predicts that the subject will immediately avoid the shock with an untrained withdrawal movement based on having learned a molar response of shock avoidance (Wickens, 1938; the results supported Tolman, unsurprisingly).

At the same time that he was treating purpose and cognition from a neorealist perspective, Tolman hinted at a different, more traditionally mentalistic approach to the problem; this approach served Tolman well following the demise of neorealism in the 1920s and is fundamental to cognitive science today. In an early paper, Tolman (1920) wrote that thoughts "can be conceived from an objective point of view as consisting in internal presentations to the organism" of stimuli not now present. Later, right alongside arguments that cognitions are "immanent" in behavior and not inferred, Tolman (1926) wrote of consciousness as providing "representations" that guide behavior. To speak of cognitions and thoughts as internal representations of the world playing a causal role in determining behavior breaks with both neorealism and behaviorism: with neorealism because representations are inferred like Lockean ideas; with behaviorism because something mental is given a place among the causes of behavior. As Tolman developed his system, he relied more and more on the concept of representation, as we shall see, becoming an inferential behavioralist committed to the real existence of mind.

In 1934, Tolman traveled to Vienna, where he came under the influence of the logical positivists, particularly Rudolph Carnap, the leader of the Vienna Circle. In Carnap's treatment of psychology, the traditional terms of mentalistic folk psychology should be understood as referring not to mental objects, but to physicochemical processes in the body. So, for example, the meaning of the statement "Fred is excited" derives from the glandular, muscular, and other bodily processes that produce excitement; Carnap's analysis is a version of the motor theory of consciousness. While awaiting the full reduction of mental terms to their true physiological referents, we must, Carnap held, compromise on a sort of behaviorism. Because we do not know the physicochemical referent of "excitement," we should understand "excitement" to refer to the behaviors that lead one to attribute excitement to someone else; this compromise is acceptable because the behaviors are "detectors" of the unknown, underlying physiology. In the long run, we should be able to eliminate behaviorism and understand mentalistic language in purely physiological terms. Carnap did recognize that in addition to its referential function, language may serve an expressive function; if I say "I feel pain," I am not just referring to some physical process within my body, I am expressing anguish. According to Carnap, the expressive function of language lies outside scientific explication and is the subject of poetry, fiction, and, more generally, art.

Carnap's psychology was not incompatible with Tolman's independently developed views, but it did give Tolman a new way to articulate his behaviorism within a philosophy of science daily growing in prestige and influence. Soon after his return to the United States, Tolman reformulated his purposive behaviorism in logical positivist language. Scientific psychology, Tolman (1935) wrote, "seeks . . . the objectively statable laws and processes governing behavior." Descriptions of "immediate experience . . . may be left to the arts and to metaphysics." Tolman was now able to be quite precise about behaviorism's research program. Behavior was to be regarded as a *dependent variable*, caused by environmental and internal (but not mental) *independent variables*. The ultimate goal of behaviorism, then, is "to write the form of the function *f* which connects the dependent variable [behavior] . . . to the independent variables—stimulus, heredity, training, and physiological" states such as hunger. Because this goal is too ambitious to be reached all at once, behaviorists introduce *intervening variables* that connect independent and dependent variables, providing equations that allow one to predict behavior given values of the independent variables. Molar behaviorism defines independent variables "macroscopically" as purposes and cognitions defined as characteristics of behavior, but eventually molecular behaviorism will be able to explain molar independent variables "in detailed neurological and glandular terms."

Tolman (1936) expanded these remarks and redefined his behaviorism as *operational behaviorism*. Operational behaviorism is cast in the mold of "the general positivistic attitude now being taken by many modern physicists and philosophers." The adjective "operational" reflects two features of his behaviorism, Tolman explained. First, it defined its intervening variables "operationally," as demanded by modern logical positivism; second, it emphasized the fact that behavior is "essentially an activity whereby the organism . . . operates on its environment." There are "two main principles" of operational behaviorism. First, "it asserts that the ultimate interest of psychology is solely the prediction and control of behavior." Second, this interest is to be achieved by a functional analysis of behavior in which "psychological concepts . . . may be conceived as objectively defined intervening variables . . . defined wholly operationally."

In these two papers, Tolman has set out clearly and forcefully the classical program of methodological behaviorism as defined under the influence of logical positivism. However, we should observe that Tolman did not get his conception of psychology from the logical positivists. Their philosophy of science meshed with what Tolman already thought and practiced, providing at most a sophisticated and prestigious justification for his own conceptions; his terms *independent, dependent,* and *intervening* variables are enduring contributions to psychological language. More important, Tolman seems quickly to have shed his operationism for psychological realism. According to operationism, theoretical terms do not refer to anything at all, but are simply convenient ways of summarizing observations. The definition of a hungry rat's intention would be its visibly persistent orientation toward the goal box in a maze. However, in his later writings (e.g., Tolman, 1948), Tolman speaks of cognitions, at least, as psychologically real entities, not just as shorthand descriptions of behavior. So "cognitive maps" were conceived as representations of the environment that a rat or person consults to guide intelligent behavior toward a goal. In the years after his return to Vienna, Tolman did not teach or even especially discuss logical positivism (Smith, 1986). It is therefore possible that his 1935 and 1936 papers, although widely read expositions of methodological behaviorism, never represented Tolman's real conception of psychology.

Finally, it is interesting to note that Tolman sometimes seemed to be fumbling for a conception of psychology that was not quite available—namely, the computational conception of cognitive science. In 1920, Tolman rejected the "slot machine" view of organisms associated with Watson. In this view, the organism was a machine in which any given stimulus elicited some reflexive response, just as putting a coin in the slot of a vending machine produces a fixed product. Rather, Tolman would prefer to think of an organism as "a complex machine capable of various adjustments such that, when one adjustment was in force," a given stimulus would produce one response, whereas under a different internal adjustment, the same stimulus would call out a different response. Internal adjustments would be caused either by external stimuli or by "automatic changes within the organism." The model Tolman wished for in 1920 was the computer, whose responses to input depend on its programming and its internal state. Similarly, Tolman anticipated the information-processing account of mind when, in 1948, he described the mind as "a central control room" in which "incoming impulses are usually worked over and elaborated . . . into a cognitivelike map of the environment."

Clark Leonard Hull's Mechanistic Behaviorism

Clark Leonard Hull (1884–1952), like so many people born in the nineteenth century, lost his religious faith as a teenager and struggled ever afterward to find a substitute faith. Hull found his in mathematics and science. Just as Thomas Hobbes had been inspired by reading the book of Euclid, so Hull could say that "the study of geometry proved to be the most important event of my intellectual life." Hull also concluded, as had Hobbes, that one should conceive of thinking, reasoning, and other cognitive powers, including learning, as quite mechanical in nature, and capable of being described and understood through the elegant precision of mathematics. His infatuation with mathematics led him first to seek a career as a mining engineer, but an attack of polio forced him to make new plans. He toyed with the idea of being a minister in the Unitarian Church—"a free, godless religion"—but "the prospect of attending an endless succession of ladies' teas" led him to abandon that calling. He sought "a field allied to philosophy in the sense of involving theory," which was so new that he might quickly "find recognition," and that would engage his penchant for machinery by allowing him "to design and work with automatic apparatus." Psychology met "this unique set of requirements," and Hull set out to "deliberately make a bid for a certain place in the history of science." He began by studying James's *Principles*, at first by having his mother read to him during his convalescence. Hull spent his undergraduate years at the University of Michigan, where for a course in logic he built a machine for displaying the logic of syllogisms. Turned down for graduate study by Yale—where he eventually spent most of his professional career—and Cornell, Hull took his PhD from the University of Wisconsin.

Hull eventually made his mark in psychology with his theory and research on learning, and his first investigations presaged the influential Hull of the 1930s. As an undergraduate, he studied learning in the insane, and he attempted to formulate mathematically precise laws to account for how they form associations (Hull, 1917). His doctoral dissertation concerned concept formation and again was very quantitative (Hull, 1920). However, circumstances led Hull to spend the next few years doing research in unrelated areas: hypnosis (an "unscientific" field, which Hull tried to improve using "quantitative methodology"); the effects of tobacco on behavior (for which Hull designed a machine through which people could smoke without inhaling tobacco's chemicals); and aptitude testing, which began to make Hull's reputation in psychology. In connection with the last, Hull designed a machine for calculating the correlations between the scores of the various tests in a test battery. Doing so confirmed for him the idea that thinking was a mechanical process that might be simulated by an actual machine; Pascal had been horrified by the same insight, but Hull found in it a hypothesis on which to work.

Like every psychologist of his era, Hull had to grapple with Watson's behaviorism. At first, although he sympathized with Watson's attacks on introspection and call for objectivity, Hull was put off by Watson's dogmatism and by "the semi-fanatical ardor with which some young people would espouse the Watsonian cause with . . . a fanaticism more characteristic of religion than of science" (1952b, pp. 153–154). Taking up an interest in Gestalt psychology, Hull as a young professor at Wisconsin managed to get Kurt Koffka to visit for a year. However, Koffka's "strikingly negative" attitude toward Watson paradoxically convinced Hull "not that the Gestalt view was sound" but that Watson's behaviorism needed improvement along the mathematical lines Hull was already inclined to follow: "Instead of converting me to *Gestalttheorie*, [I experienced] a belated conversion to a kind of neo-behaviorism—a behaviorism mainly concerned with the determination of the quantitative laws of behavior and their deductive systematization" (1952b, p. 154). In 1929, Hull moved to Yale University, where he embarked on a most influential career as the preeminent experimental psychologist of his day.

Hull's program had two components. First, as we have seen, Hull was fascinated by machinery and was convinced that machines could think, so he attempted to build machines capable of learning and thinking. The first description of such a machine came in 1929, representing, as he put it, "a direct implication of the mechanistic tendency of modern psychology. Learning and thought are here conceived as by no means necessarily a function of living protoplasm than is serial locomotion" (Hull & Baernstein, 1929). The other component of Hull's theoretical ambition represented a continuation of the geometric spirit of Hobbes and the associationism of Hume, whom Hull thought of as the first behaviorist. Around 1930, Hull says, "I came to the definite conclusion . . . that psychology is a true natural science" whose task is the discovery of "laws expressible quantitatively by means of a moderate number of ordinary equations" from which individual and group behaviors might be deduced as consequences (1952, p. 155). Given Hull's mechanistic and mathematical interests, it is unsurprising to learn that he contracted a bad case of physics envy and fancied himself the Newton of behavior. In the mid-1920s, he read Newton's *Principia*, and it became a sort of bible for him (Smith, 1986). He assigned portions of it to his seminars and placed it on his desk between himself and visitors; it represented for him the very pinnacle of scientific achievement, and he strove to emulate his hero.

The goals of building intelligent machines and of formalizing psychology according to a mathematical system were not incompatible; Newtonians had conceived of the physical universe as a machine governed by precise mathematical laws: Hull simply aimed to do the same thing for allegedly mental phenomena and behavior. During the early 1930s, Hull pursued both formal theory and learning machines in tandem, publishing increasingly mathematical treatments of complex behaviors such as the acquisition and assembling of simple S–R habits, and promising the production of "psychic machines" capable of thought and useful as industrial robots (Hull, 1930a,b, 1931, 1934, 1935). However, as the 1930s wore on, Hull's psychic machines played a less and less prominent place in his work. It appears that he feared that his preoccupation with intelligent machines would appear "grotesque" to outsiders, and that his work on them would be suppressed, as university authorities had suppressed his earlier work on hypnosis (Smith, 1986). At the same time, like Tolman and most other psychologists, Hull came under the influence of logical positivism. Its insistence on formalism and the reduction of the mental to the physical was quite consistent with Hull's own philosophy of science, so that he found increased emphasis on formal, mathematical theory to be most useful as "propaganda" by which to advance his cause (Smith, 1986).

Hull's turn from the pursuit of psychic machines and formal theories to the exclusive pursuit of the latter may be conveniently dated to 1936, the year in which he was president of the APA, and he described in his presidential address his ambitions for theoretical psychology. In his talk, Hull tackled the central problem of behaviorism: accounting for mind. He noted the same outward sign of mind as Tolman did: purposive, persistent behavior in the striving for goals. However, he proposed to account for them in a completely different way, as the outcome of mechanistic, lawful, principles of behavior: "The complex forms of purposive behavior [will] be found to derive from . . . the basic entities of theoretical physics, such as electrons and protons" (Hull, 1937). Hull recognized that traditionally such a mechanistic position had been only philosophical, and he proposed to make it scientific by applying what he took to be scientific procedure. Science, Hull stated, consisted of a set of "explicitly stated postulates" (as did Euclid's geometry) from which, "by the most rigorous logic," predictions about actual behaviors would be deduced. Just as Newton had derived the motions of the planets from a small set of physical laws, so Hull proposed to predict the motions of organisms from a (rather larger) set of behavioral laws set forth in his paper. The virtue of the scientific method, Hull claimed, was that its predictions could be precisely tested against observations, whereas the nebulous claims of philosophy, whether idealistic or materialistic, could not be.

Using his set of proposed postulates, Hull tried to show that purposive behavior could be accounted for mechanistically. Finally, he asked, "But what of consciousness?" and in answering this question articulated his own version of methodological behaviorism. Psychology could dispense with consciousness, Hull said, "for the simple reason that no theorem has been found as yet whose deduction would be facilitated in any way by including" a postulate referring to consciousness. "Moreover, we have been quite unable to find any other scientific system of behavior which . . . has found consciousness necessary" (p. 31) to deduce behavior. As did Tolman, Hull set conscious experience, the original subject matter of psychology, outside the bounds of psychology as behaviorists viewed it. Hull, like Watson, attributed continued interest in consciousness among psychologists to "the perseverative influences of medieval theology," claiming that "psychology in its basic principles is to a considerable degree in the thrall of the middle ages, and that, in particular, our prevailing systematic outlook in the matter of consciousness is largely medieval." But, concluded Hull, "fortunately the means of our salvation is clear and obvious. As ever, it ties in the application of scientific procedures. . . . For us to apply the methodology, it is necessary only to throw off the shackles of a lifeless tradition" (p. 32).

Reference to purposive robots was relegated to a footnote in which Hull mentioned "a kind of experimental shortcut to the determination of the ultimate nature of adaptive behavior." If one could build "from inorganic materials . . . a mechanism which would display" the adaptive behaviors derived from his postulates, then "it would be possible to say with assurance and a clear conscience that such adaptive behavior may be 'reached' by purely physical means" (p. 31). During his actual presentation to the APA, Hull demonstrated for the audience one of his learning machines, and some among his listeners were deeply impressed by its performance (Chapanis, 1961). Because Hull rarely mentioned his "psychic machines" again, his statement of the central thesis of cognitive science has gone unnoticed or has been dismissed as peripheral to his thinking. In fact, it is obvious that mechanical simulation of thought was central to Hull's thinking, and it gave rise to the formal theory for which he became famous and through which he became influential.

We have already seen how in the mid-1930s Tolman began to articulate his psychology with the terminology of logical positivism; the same happened to Hull. After 1937, he identified his system with "logical empiricism" and applauded the "uniting" of American behavior theory with Viennese logical positivism, which was producing "in America a behavioral discipline which will be a full-blown natural science" (Hull, 1943a). From then on, Hull bent his efforts to the creation of a formal, deductive, quantitative theory of learning and largely left his psychic machines behind, though they continued to play a heuristic, unpublished role in Hull's thinking (Smith, 1986). Adoption of positivist language obscured Hull's realism, as it did Tolman's. Hull, of course, did not believe in purposes and cognitions, as Tolman did, but he was a realist in believing that the postulates of his theories described actual neurophysiological states and processes in the nervous systems of living organisms, human or animal.

Hull set forth his postulate systems in a series of books. The first was *Mathematico-Deductive Theory of Rote Learning* (Hull et al., 1940), which offered a mathematical treatment of human verbal learning. The book was praised as "giving a foretaste of what psychology will be like when it reaches systematic, quantitative, precision" (Hilgard, 1940). The rote learning theory was a "dress rehearsal" for his major work, *Principles of Behavior* (Hull, 1943b), the expression of "the behavior system . . . which I had gradually been developing throughout my academic life," and which had formed the basis of his APA presidential address. Upon publication, the *Psychological Bulletin* accorded it a "special review" in which *Principles of Behavior* was praised as "one of the most important books published in psychology in the twentieth century" (Koch, 1944). The book promised to unify all of psychology under the *S–R* formulation, and to perform needed "radical surgery" on the "withering *corpus* of social science," saving it for real science. Hull revised his system twice more (1951, 1952a), but it was *Principles* that fulfilled his ambition of making a permanent name for himself in the history of psychology.

Tolman Versus Hull

BATTLING THEORIES   Tolman's purposive behaviorism inevitably came into conflict with Hull's mechanistic behaviorism. Tolman always believed that purpose and cognition were real, although his conception of their reality changed over time. Hull, on the other hand, sought to explain purpose and cognition as the result of mindless mechanical processes describable in logicomathematical equations. During the 1930s and 1940s, Tolman and Hull engaged in a sort of intellectual tennis match: Tolman would attempt to demonstrate that purpose and cognition were real, and Hull and his followers patched up the theory or tried to show that Tolman's demonstrations were flawed.

Let us consider an example of an experiment that contrasts the cognitive and *S–R* views. It was actually reported in 1930 (Tolman, 1932), well before the Hull–Tolman debates really got underway, but it is a simpler version of more complex experiments described in Tolman's (1948) "Cognitive Maps in Rats and Men," meant to differentially support Tolman's theory. The maze is shown in Figure 1. Rats became familiar with the entire maze because they were forced to run each

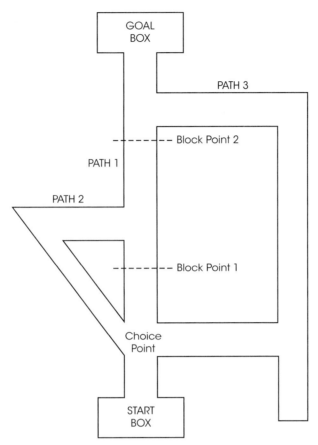

FIGURE 1 Tolman-Honzik Maze.

path in early training. Having learned the maze, a rat coming out of the start box into the choice point must pick one of the paths. How does the rat do this?

A Hullian analysis can be sketched. The choice point presents stimuli (S) to which three responses (R_s) corresponding to each path have been conditioned during initial training. For a variety of reasons, most obviously the different amounts of running that must be done in each alley, Path 1 is preferred to Path 2, which is preferred to Path 3. That is, connection S–R_1 is stronger than S–R_2, which is stronger than S–R_3. Such a state of affairs can be notated.

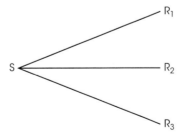

This is called a *divergent habit family hierarchy.* Now, should a block be placed at Point 1, the rat will run into it, back up, and choose Path 2. The connection S–R_1 is weakened by the block, so that S–R_2 becomes stronger and is acted on. On the other hand, if the second block is placed, the rat will retreat to the choice point and again choose Path 2 as S–R_1 is again blocked and S–R_2 becomes stronger. However, the block will be met again, S–R_2 will weaken, and finally S–R_3 will be strongest and the rat will choose Path 3. This is the Hullian prediction.

Tolman denied that what is learned is a set of responses triggered to differing degrees by the stimuli at the choice point. Instead, he held that the rat learns a mental map of the maze that guides its behavior. According to this view, the rat encountering the first block will turn around and choose Path 2, as in the S–R account, because Path 2 is shorter than Path 3. However, if it encounters Block 2, the rat will know that the same block will cut off Path 2 as well as Path 1. Therefore, the rat will show "insight": It will return and choose Path 3, ignoring Path 2 altogether. A map displays all aspects of the environment and is more informative than a set of S–R connections. The results of the experiment supported Tolman's cognitive theory of learning over Hull's S–R account.

Although Hull and Tolman differed sharply on their specific accounts of behavior, we should not forget that they shared important assumptions and goals. Both Tolman and Hull wanted to write scientific theories of learning and behavior applying to at least all mammals, including human beings. They pursued their mutual goal by experimenting on and theorizing about rats, assuming that any difference between rat and human was trivial and that results from laboratories represented naturalistic behavior as well; they followed Herbert Spencer's formula for psychology. Both Tolman and Hull rejected consciousness as the subject matter of psychology and took the description, prediction, and control of behavior as psychology's task; they were behavioralists—specifically, methodological behaviorists. Finally, both were influenced by, and seemed to endorse, logical positivism.

Psychologists have tended to assume that Tolman and Hull were slavish adherents of logical positivism and that they personally set the positivist style of modern psychology. However, such a judgment does them a disservice, obscures their independence, and depreciates their creativity. Tolman and Hull reached their conceptions of science, psychology, and behavior quite independently of logical positivism. When they encountered logical positivism in the 1930s, each found he could use this prestigious philosophy to more powerfully state his own ideas; but we must not forget that their ideas were their own. Unfortunately, because they did adopt positivist language and because positivism quickly came to be psychologists' philosophy of science, the real programs of Tolman and Hull were obscured or forgotten, resulting in some fruitless controversies in the 1950s.

RELATIVE INFLUENCE Although both Tolman and Hull were honored and influential, there is no doubt that Hull was very much more influential than Tolman. At Berkeley, Tolman filled students with enthusiasm for psychology and a healthy disrespect for scientific pomposity. He wrote lively papers and took a zestful approach to science, saying that "in the end, the only sure criterion is to have fun. And I have had fun" (Tolman, 1959). He was never a systematic theorist and had finally to confess to being a "cryptophenomenologist" who designed his experiments by imagining what he would do if he were a rat, being gratified to find that rats were as clever and commonsensical as he was. Unfortunately, this meant that although Tolman could inspire students, he could not teach them a systematic viewpoint with which to evangelize psychology. Tolman had no disciples.

Hull, however, did. Instead of valuing having fun, Hull valued the long, arduous labor of constructing postulates and deriving theorems from them. Although tedious, this gave Hull an explicit set of ideas with which to infect his students for spreading throughout the discipline. Moreover, Hull's institutional situation was ideal for building discipleship. Besides the department of psychology at

Yale, Hull was strategically placed at Yale's Institute of Human Relations (IHR), which attracted from many disciplines bright minds eager to learn the rigors of science for application to their fields and to the problems of the world (Lemov, 2005). We will later see how informal behaviorism and social learning theory emerged from Hull's seminars at the IHR. Hull found someone to continue his program in Kenneth Spence (1907–1967). Spence collaborated on Hull's books, continued his rigorous theorizing into the 1950s, created a truly positivist version of neobehaviorism and trained many leading experimental psychologists of the 1950s and 1960s: Hull's intellectual grandchildren. And, of course, Hull's rigorous theoretical system, pristinely mechanistic and eschewing any mysticism about purpose and cognition, was perfectly in tune with the naturalistic-positivistic *Zeitgeist* of American psychology after World War I.

Hull's impact on psychology was greater than Tolman's. For example, as late as the 1960s, a study of which psychologists were most often cited in the leading journals of psychology (Myers, 1970) found that the most-cited psychologist was Kenneth Spence, with Hull himself at eighth place. This is especially remarkable considering that Hull had been dead since 1952 and that his theory had been subjected to scathing criticism since the early 1950s. Despite the fact that many psychologists saw a cognitive "revolution" taking place in the 1960s, E. C. Tolman, the purposive, cognitive behaviorist, did not place in the top 60.

We're All Behaviorists Now

Hull's colleague Kenneth Spence observed in 1948 that few psychologists "ever seem to think of themselves, or explicitly refer to themselves as behaviorists," because behaviorism was "a very general point of view which has come to be accepted by almost all psychologists." Spence noted one exception to his conclusion: Tolman protested perhaps too much that he was a good behaviorist. Spence also recognized that behaviorism took many forms, so that the term *behaviorism* was rather slippery. Still, behaviorism had made progress, Spence thought, because the various neobehaviorisms had only separated themselves from Watson's early, rather crude formulation of classical behaviorism. Spence tried to tidy up the Babel of behaviorisms by formulating a behaviorist metaphysics along logical positivist lines. He hoped to create a common creed on which all behaviorists might agree. His hope was misplaced, as the Tolmanians refused to assent.

On the horizon of experimental psychology lay a newly formulated radical behaviorism that after World War II would challenge and then replace all other behaviorisms.

B. F. Skinner, a writer turned psychologist, had begun in 1931 to work out a behaviorism in the radical spirit of Watson, but with a new set of technical concepts. Skinner's influence lay in the future, when, after the war, psychologists would again lose confidence in their enterprise and begin to look for a new Newton. Before the war, however, Skinner was not taken too seriously. E. R. Hilgard (1939) wrongly prophesied that Skinner's first major theoretical statement, *Behavior of Organisms* (1938), would have little influence on psychology.

AFTER THE GOLDEN AGE

The most consciously troubled area in psychology after the war was the core of traditional scientific psychology, the study of learning. Sigmund Koch (1951a, p. 295), already becoming an effective gadfly to the pretensions of behaviorist psychology, wrote that "psychology seems now to have entered an era of total disorientation." In another (1951b) paper, Koch asserted that "since the end of World War II, psychology has been in a long and intensifying crisis . . . its core seems to be disaffection from the theory of the recent past. Never before had it seemed so evident that the development of a science is not an automatic forward movement." Koch located two causes of the "crisis" in experimental psychology, one internal and one external. Within experimental psychology, Koch saw a decade-long stagnation in the development of the prewar theoretical systems of learning theory. Outside, clinical and applied psychology were bidding for "social recognition" by abandoning theory for useful practices so they could take on "social responsibilities." In the rush toward social usefulness, theoretical psychologists had become depressed and were looking for a "new wave" to excite them again.

Koch was not a cranky prophet alone in his dissatisfaction with the state of experimental psychology, for signs of dissatisfaction abounded. In 1951, Karl Lashley, at one time Watson's student, attacked the standard *S–R* chaining theory of complex behaviors, originally proposed by Watson himself. Lashley argued on physiological grounds that chaining was impossible because of the relatively slow transmission of nervous impulses from receptor to brain and back to effector. He proposed instead that organisms possess central planning functions that coordinate sets of actions as large units, not as chains. He specifically argued that language was organized this way, raising a problem that would increasingly bedevil behaviorism. On another front in 1950, Frank Beach, a student of animal behavior, decried experimental psychologists' increasing preoccupation with rat learning. He questioned whether psychologists were interested in a general science of behavior or in only one topic—learning—in only one species, the Norway rat. Without studies of other behaviors and species, he argued, the generality of laboratory findings must remain suspect. He also pointed out the existence of species-specific behaviors such as imprinting that are not the exclusive result of either learning or instinct. Such behaviors escape all existing learning theories, which sharply divide the learned from the unlearned and then study only the latter. Problems of comparative psychology would increasingly plague the psychology of learning in the 1950s and 1960s.

Formal Behaviorism in Peril

Hull and Tolman were not professionally raised on logical positivism and operationism, but the succeeding generation of experimental psychologists coming into professional maturity after World War II was. Many of the new generation believed with Sigmund Koch that the theoretical debates of the 1930s and 1940s had led nowhere, that the problems of the psychology of learning—the heart of the adjustment process—were not being solved. So, in the later 1940s and through the early 1950s, theoretical psychologists engaged in earnest self-scrutiny, applying the tools of logical positivism and operationism to developing tactics of theory construction in psychology and applying the criteria of positivism and operationism to the theories of Hull and Tolman.

At the Dartmouth Conference on Learning Theory held in 1950, the new generation of learning theorists evaluated learning theories in light of the logical positivism they had absorbed and that they thought their teachers had followed in formulating their theories of learning. Hull's theory, as the one they believed most closely shared their positivist standards of theory construction, came in for the most devastating criticism. Sigmund Koch, the author of the report on Hull, said, "We have done what may be construed as a nasty thing. We have proceeded on a literal interpretation of some such proposition as: 'Hull has put forward a hypothetico-deductive theory of behavior.'" Proceeding on that interpretation, Koch showed that, judged by positivistic criteria, Hull's enterprise was a total failure. Koch's rhetoric was damning: Hull's theory suffered from "horrible indeterminancy" and "manifold inadequacies" in the definition of its independent variables; it was "empirically empty" and a "pseudoquantitative system"; and it failed to progress from the 1943 formulation to those of the early 1950s: "It may be said with confidence that with respect to most of the issues considered . . . there has been no evidence of constructive advance since 1943." The other theories, including those of Tolman, B. F. Skinner, Kurt Lewin, and Edwin R. Guthrie (another behaviorist), were variously criticized for failure to meet positivist criteria for good theory.

At Dartmouth it was noticed that Skinner's brand of behaviorism failed to live up to logical positivistic principles because it did not try to. Skinner had set his own standards of theoretical adequacy, and judged by them, his theory did well. Perhaps, then, change was called for in psychologists' goals, rather than in their continued pursuit of goals set by abstract philosophy. Were theories of learning needed at all?

Radical Behaviorism

By far the best known and most influential of all the major behaviorists was Burrhus Frederick Skinner (1904–1990), whose radical behaviorism, if it had been accepted, would have constituted a momentous revolution in humanity's understanding of the human self, demanding as it did no less than complete rejection of the entire intellectual psychological tradition, with the exception of the neorealists. It proposed replacing this tradition with a scientific psychology modeled on Darwinian evolutionary theory, which looked outside humans for the causes of behavior. Virtually every psychological thinker we have considered, from Wundt, James, and Freud to Hull and Tolman, intended psychology to be an explication of internal processes, however conceived—processes that produce behavior or conscious phenomena. Skinner followed Watson in placing responsibility for behavior squarely in the environment, however. For Skinner, people deserve neither praise nor blame for anything they do. The environment controls behavior so that both good and evil, if such exist, reside there, not in the person. To paraphrase Shakespeare's Julius Caesar: The fault, dear Brutus, lies in our contingencies of reinforcement, not in ourselves. Skinner defined three aspects of his work, the philosophy of radical behaviorism, the science of the experimental analysis of behavior, and the interpretation of human behavior from the perspective of radical behaviorism and the experimental analysis of behavior.

RADICAL BEHAVIORISM AS A PHILOSOPHY The heart of radical behaviorism can be approached by looking at Skinner's analysis of Freud's theory in his paper "A Critique of Psychoanalytic Concepts and Theories" (1954). For Skinner, Freud's great discovery was that much human behavior has unconscious causes. However, to Skinner, Freud's great mistake was in inventing a mental apparatus—id, ego, superego—and its attendant mental processes to explain human behavior. Skinner believed that the lesson taught by Freud's concept of the unconscious is that consciousness is irrelevant to behavior. For example, imagine a student who shows neurotic subservience to her teachers. A Freudian might explain this by asserting that the student's father was a punitive perfectionist who demanded obedience, and that his child incorporated a stern father image that now affects her behavior in the presence of authority figures. Skinner allows explaining the student's current servility by reference to punishments at the hand of a punitive father, but he would insist that the link be direct. The student cowers now because as a child she received punishment from an authority figure, but not because her superego incorporated her father's stern demands. For Skinner, the inference to an unconscious father image in the superego explains nothing that cannot be explained by simply referring current behavior to the consequences of past behavior; that is, her father's perfectionism caused her subservience to her teachers. The mental link adds nothing to an account of behavior, according to Skinner, and in fact complicates matters by requiring that the mental link itself be explained. Skinner has extended this criticism of mental entities to encompass all traditional psychologies, rejecting equally the superego, apperception, habit strength, and cognitive maps. All are unnecessary to the proper scientific explanation of behavior.

Although radical behaviorism represented a sharp break with psychology, whether scientific or common sense, its intellectual heritage can be located. It stood clearly in the empiricist camp, especially with the radical empiricism of Renaissance philosopher Francis Bacon and German physicist Ernst Mach. As a young man, Skinner read Bacon's works, and he often referred favorably to the great inductivist. Like Bacon, Skinner believed that truth is to be found in observations themselves, in "does" and "doesn't," rather than in our interpretations of our observations. Skinner's first psychological paper was an application of Mach's radical descriptive positivism to the concept of the reflex. Skinner (1931) concluded that a *reflex* is not an entity inside an animal, but merely a convenient descriptive term for a regular correlation between stimulus and response. This presaged his rejection of hypothetical entities.

Skinner's account of behavior was also heir to Darwin's analysis of evolution, as Skinner himself often suggested. Darwin argued that species constantly produce variant traits and that nature acts on these traits to select those that contribute to survival, eliminating those that do not. Similarly, for Skinner, an organism is constantly producing variant forms of behavior. Some of these acts lead to favorable consequences—are reinforced—and others do not. Those that do are strengthened, for they contribute to the organism's survival and are learned. Those that are not reinforced are not learned disappear from the organism's repertoire, just as weak species become extinct. Both Skinner's analysis of behavior and his values were Darwinian, as we shall see.

Skinner's radical behaviorism was also a straightforward extension of neorealism into psychology (Smith, 1986). By teaching that organisms perceive the physical world directly, the neorealists rejected the inner mental world posited by the Way of Ideas. Therefore, if there are no ideas, there is no such thing as private consciousness or introspection. Thus, as in Tolman's early behaviorism, an organism's behavior is a function of the environment to which the organism responds. Positing inner mental causation is unnecessary.

Like many innovative scientific thinkers, Skinner received little early training in his discipline. He took his undergraduate degree in English at Hamilton College, intending to be a writer, studying no psychology. However, a biology teacher called his attention to works by Pavlov and the mechanist physiologist Jacques Loeb. The former taught him a concern for the total behavior of an organism and the latter impressed him with the possibility of careful, rigorous, scientific research on behavior. He learned of Watson's behaviorism from some of Bertrand Russell's articles on Watson. After failing to become a writer, Skinner turned to psychology filled with the spirit of Watsonian behaviorism. He initiated a systematic research program on a new kind of behavior: the operant.

THE EXPERIMENTAL ANALYSIS OF BEHAVIOR The lodestar of Skinner's scientific work was stated in his first psychological paper and was inspired by the success of Pavlov's work with conditioned reflexes. Skinner wrote in "The Concept of Reflex in the Description of Behavior": "Given a particular part of the behavior of an organism hitherto regarded as unpredictable (and probably, as a consequence, assigned to nonphysical factors), the investigator seeks out the antecedent changes with which the activity is correlated and establishes the conditions of the correlation" (1931/1972, p. 440). The goal of psychology was thus to analyze behavior by locating the specific determinants of specific behaviors and to establish the exact nature of the relationship between antecedent influence and subsequent behavior. The best way to do this is by experiment, for only in an experiment can all the factors affecting behavior be systematically controlled. Skinner thus called his science *the experimental analysis of behavior*.

The Contingencies of Reinforcement. A behavior is explained within Skinner's framework when the investigator has identified and can control all the influences of which the behavior is a function. We refer to the antecedent influences acting on a behavior as *independent variables*, and the behavior that is a function of them, the *dependent variable*. The organism can then be thought of as a *locus* *of variables*—a place where independent variables act together to produce a behavior. There are no mental processes that intervene between independent and dependent variables, and traditional references to mental entities can be eliminated when controlling independent variables have been understood. Skinner assumed that physiology would ultimately be able to detail the physical mechanisms controlling behavior, but that analysis of behavior in terms of functional relationships among variables is completely independent of physiology. The functions will remain even when the underlying physiological mechanisms are understood.

Thus far, Skinner's account closely followed Mach. Scientific explanation is nothing more than an accurate and precise description of the relationship between observable variables; for Skinner, these are environmental variables and behavior variables. Just as Mach sought to exorcise "metaphysical" reference to unobserved causal links in physics, so Skinner sought to exorcise "metaphysical" reference to causal mental links in psychology. In his early work, Skinner emphasized the descriptive nature of his work, and it is still sometimes called *descriptive behaviorism*. We may note here the mirror-image nature of Skinnerian and Titchenerian psychology. Titchener also followed Mach by seeking only to correlate variables analyzed within an experimental framework but, of course, he wanted a description of consciousness, not behavior. Skinner sometimes conceded the possibility of such a study, but he dismissed it as irrelevant to the study of behavior, as Titchener had dismissed the study of behavior as irrelevant to the psychology of consciousness.

What separated Titchener and Skinner, besides their subject matters, was the importance of control for Skinner. Skinner was Watsonian in wanting not just to describe behavior but to control it. In fact, for Skinner, control was the ultimate test of the scientific adequacy of observationally determined functions between antecedent variables and behavior variables. Prediction alone is insufficient, for prediction may result from the correlation of two variables causally dependent on a third, but not on each other. For example, children's toe size and weight will correlate very highly: The bigger a child's toe, the heavier he or she is likely to be. However, toe size does not "cause" weight, or vice versa, for both depend on physical growth, which causes changes in both variables. According to Skinner, an investigator can be said to have explained a behavior only when, in addition to being able to predict its occurrence, he or she can *influence* its occurrence through the manipulation of independent variables. Thus, an adequate experimental analysis of behavior implies a technology of behavior, wherein behavior can be engineered for specific purposes, such as teaching. Titchener always vehemently rejected technology as a goal for psychology, but it was a concern of Skinner's that became increasingly pronounced after World War II.

In *The Behavior of Organisms*, Skinner distinguished two kinds of learned behavior, each of which had been studied before but not clearly differentiated. Skinner called the first category *respondent* behavior or learning, studied by Pavlov. This category is properly called *reflex* behavior, for a respondent is a behavior *elicited* by a definite stimulus, whether unconditioned or conditioned. It loosely corresponds to "involuntary" behavior, such as the salivary responses studied by Pavlov. Skinner called the second category *operant* behavior or learning, which corresponds loosely to "voluntary" behavior. Operant behavior cannot be elicited but is simply emitted from time to time. However, an operant's probability of occurrence may be raised if its emission is followed by an event called a *reinforcer*; after reinforcement, it will be more likely to occur again in similar circumstances. Thorndike's puzzle boxes defined an operant learning situation: The imprisoned cat emits a variety of behaviors; one of which, such as pressing a lever, leads to escape, which is *reinforcing*. With the cat placed back in the box, the probability of the correct response is now higher than before; the operant response, lever-pressing, has been strengthened. These three things—the setting in which the behavior occurs (the puzzle box), the reinforced response (lever pressing), and the reinforcer (escape)—collectively define the *contingencies of reinforcement*. The experimental analysis of behavior consists of the systematic description of contingencies of reinforcement as they occur in all forms of animal or human behavior.

These contingencies are analyzed in Darwinian fashion. Emitted behavior is parallel to random variation in species' traits. Reinforcement from the environment follows some operants and not others; the former are strengthened and the latter are extinguished. The environment's selection pressures select favorable responses through the process of operant learning, just as successful species flourish while others become extinct. Skinner considered the experimental analysis of behavior to be part of biology, concerned with explaining an individual's behavior as the product of the environment resulting from a process analogous to that which produces species. There is no room in either discipline for vitalism, mind, or *teleology*. All behavior, whether learned or unlearned, is a product of an individual's reinforcement history or his or her genetic makeup. Behavior is never a product of intention or will.

Skinner's definition of the operant and its controlling contingencies distinguished him from other behaviorists in three frequently misunderstood ways. First, operant responses are never elicited. Suppose we train a rat to press a lever in a Skinner box (or "experimental space," as Skinner called it), reinforcing the bar-press only when a certain light is on above the bar. The rat will soon come to bar-press whenever the light comes on. It may appear that the stimulus of the light elicits the response, but according to Skinner, this is not so. It merely sets the occasion for reinforcement. It enables the organism to discriminate a reinforcing situation from a nonreinforcing situation, and is thus called a *discriminative stimulus*. It does not elicit bar-pressing as an unconditioned stimulus or a conditioned stimulus elicited salivation in Pavlov's dogs. Thus, Skinner denied that he was an *S–R* psychologist, for that formula implies a reflexive link between a response and some stimulus, a link that exists only for respondents. Watson adhered to the *S–R* formula, for he applied the classical conditioning paradigm to all behavior. The spirit of radical behaviorism is so clearly Watsonian that many critics mistake Watson's analysis of behavior for Skinner's.

There is a second way in which Skinner was not an *S–R* psychologist. He said that the organism may be affected by controlling variables that need not be considered stimuli. This is clearest with respect to motivation. Motivation was seen by Hullians and Freudians as a matter of drive-stimulus reduction: Food deprivation leads to unpleasant stimuli associated with the hunger drive, and the organism acts to reduce them. Skinner sees no reason for the drive-stimuli. They are examples of mentalistic thinking that may be eliminated by directly linking food deprivation to change in behavior. Depriving an organism of food is an observable procedure that will affect an organism's behavior in lawful ways, and there is no gain in speaking of "drives" or their associated stimuli. A measurable variable, although not conceived in stimulus terms, may be causally linked to changes in observable behavior. The organism is truly a locus of variables, and whether or not the variables are stimuli of which the organism is aware is irrelevant, which renders the *S–R* formulation less applicable to Skinner.

The third important aspect of the operant concerns its definition. Behavior for Skinner was merely movement in space, but Skinner was careful not to define operants as simple movements. To begin with, an operant is not a response; it is a class of responses. The cat in the puzzle box may press the escape lever in different ways on different trials. Each is a different *response* in that its form is different at each occurrence, but all are members of the same *operant*, for each response is controlled by the same contingencies of reinforcement. Whether the cat butts the lever with its head or pushes it with its paw is unimportant—both are the same operant. Similarly, two otherwise identical movements may be instances of different operants if they are controlled by different contingencies. You may raise your hand to pledge allegiance to the flag, to swear to tell the truth in court, or to wave to a friend. The movements may be the same in each case, but each is a different operant, for the setting and reinforcement (the contingencies of reinforcement) are different in each case. This proves to be especially important in explaining verbal behavior: "Sock" is at least two operants controlled either by (1) a soft foot covering or (2) a punch in the nose. Earlier behaviorists such as Hull tried to define responses in purely physical terms as movements and were criticized for ignoring the meaning of behavior. A word, it was argued, is more than a puff of air; it has meaning. Skinner agreed, but he placed meaning in the contingencies of reinforcement, not in the speaker's mind.

These were the most important theoretical ideas that guide the experimental analysis of behavior. When Skinner asked, "Are theories of learning necessary?" and answered no, he did not intend to eschew theorizing. What he rejected was theory that refers to the unobserved hypothetical entities he considered fictions, be they ego, cognitive map, or apperception. He accepted theory in the Machian sense as being a summary of the ways in which observable variables correlate, but no more.

Operant Methodology.   Skinner also defined an innovative and radical methodology, or shared exemplar, in his *Behavior of Organisms*. First, he chose an experimental situation that preserved the fluidity of behavior, refusing to chop it up into arbitrary and artificial "trials." An organism is placed in a space and reinforced for some behavior that it may make at any time. The behavior may be closely observed as it continuously changes over time, not as it abruptly changes with each trial. Second, the experimenter seeks to exert maximal control over the organism's environment, so that the experimenter may manipulate or hold constant independent variables and thus directly observe how they change behavior. Third, a very simple, yet somewhat artificial response is chosen for study. In Skinner's own work, this was typically either a rat pressing a lever or a pigeon pecking a key to obtain food or water. Choosing such an operant makes each response unambiguous, easily observed, and easily counted by machines to produce a cumulative record of responses. Finally, Skinner defined *rate of responding* as the basic datum of analysis. It is easily quantified; it is appealing as a measure of response probability; and it has been found to vary in lawful ways with changes in independent variables. Such a simple experimental situation stands in contrast to the relative lack of control found in Thorndike's puzzle boxes or Hull's and Tolman's mazes. The situation is capable of defining precise puzzles for the investigator because it imposes so much control on the organism. The investigator need only draw on previous research to select what variables to manipulate and observe their effects on response rate. There is minimal ambiguity about what to manipulate or measure. Skinner provided a well-defined exemplar shared by all who practice the experimental analysis of behavior.

INTERPRETING HUMAN BEHAVIOR   In the 1950s, while other behaviorists were liberalizing their brands of behaviorism, Skinner began to extend his radical behaviorism to human behavior without changing any of his fundamental concepts. Skinner viewed human behavior as animal behavior not significantly different from the behavior of the rats and pigeons he had studied in the laboratory.

Skinner on Language.   Although "most of the experimental work responsible for the advance of the experimental analysis of behavior has been carried out on other species . . . the results have proved to be surprisingly free of species restrictions . . . and its methods can be extended to human behavior without serious modification." So wrote Skinner in what he considered his most important work, *Verbal Behavior* (1957, p. 3).

Verbal Behavior was a work of what he called interpretation seeking only to establish the plausibility of a radical behaviorist analysis of language, not its truth. Further, to say that he was analyzing language is misleading as conveyed by the title of his book, *Verbal Behavior*, which he defined as behavior whose reinforcement is mediated by other persons. The definition includes an animal behaving under the control of an experimenter, who together form a "genuine verbal community." The definition made no reference to the process of communication we usually assume takes place during speech. Nevertheless, *Verbal Behavior* was basically about what we ordinarily consider language, or more accurately, speech. Skinner introduced a number of technical concepts in his discussion of verbal behavior. To show the flavor of his analysis, we will briefly discuss his concept of the "tact" because it corresponds roughly to the problem of universals and because Skinner considered it the most important verbal operant.

We apply the three-term set of contingencies of reinforcement: stimulus, response, and reinforcement. A *tact* is a verbal *operant response* under the *stimulus control* of some part of the physical environment, and correct use of tacts is reinforced by the verbal community. So, a child is reinforced by parents for emitting the sound *doll* in the presence of a doll (Skinner, 1957). Such an operant "makes contact with" the physical environment and is called a *tact*. Skinner reduced the traditional notion of reference or naming to a functional relationship among a response, its discriminative stimuli, and its reinforcer. The situation is exactly analogous to the functional relation holding between a rat's bar-press in a Skinner box, the discriminative stimulus that sets the occasion for the response, and the food that reinforces it. Skinner's analysis of the tact was a straightforward extension of the experimental analysis of behavior paradigm to a novel situation.

Skinner's radical analysis of tacting raises an important general point about his treatment of human consciousness, his notion of private stimuli. Skinner believed that earlier methodological behaviorists such as Tolman and Hull were wrong to exclude private events (such as mental images or toothaches) from behaviorism simply because such events are private. Skinner held that part of each person's environment includes the world inside his or her skin, those stimuli to which the person has privileged access. Such stimuli might be unknown to an external observer, but they are experienced by the person who has them, can control behavior, and so must be included in any behaviorist analysis of human behavior. Many verbal statements, including complex tacts, are under such control. For example: "My tooth aches" is a kind of tacting response controlled by a certain kind of painful inner stimulation.

This simple analysis implied a momentous conclusion. For how do we come to be able to make such statements as the private tact? Skinner's answer was that the verbal community has trained us to observe our private stimuli by reinforcing utterances that refer to them. It is useful for parents to know what is distressing their child, so they attempt to teach a child self-reporting verbal behaviors. "My tooth aches" indicates a visit to the dentist, not the podiatrist. Such responses thus have Darwinian survival value. It is these self-observed, private stimuli that constitute consciousness. It therefore follows that human consciousness is a product of the reinforcing practices of a verbal community. A person raised by a community that did not reinforce self-description would not be conscious of anything but the sense of being awake. Descartes's and James's notion of human self-consciousness was thus for Skinner not an innate possession of humans, but a social construction of human socialization.

Self-tacting also allowed Skinner to explain apparently purposive verbal behaviors without reference to intention or purpose. For example, "I am looking for my glasses" seems to describe my intentions, but Skinner (1957, p. 145) argued: "Such behavior must be regarded as equivalent to *When I have behaved in this way in the past, I have found my glasses and have then stopped behaving in this way.*" *Intention* is a mentalistic term Skinner reduced to the physicalistic description of one's bodily state.

The last topic discussed in *Verbal Behavior* was thinking, the most apparently mental of all human activities. Skinner continued, however, to exorcise Cartesian mentalism by arguing that "thought is simply *behavior.*" Skinner rejected Watson's view that thinking is subvocal behavior, for much covert behavior is not verbal, yet can still control overt behavior in a way characteristic of "thinking": "*I think I shall be going* can be translated *I find myself going*" (1957, p. 449), a reference to self-observed, but nonverbal, stimuli.

The extreme simplicity of Skinner's argument makes it hard to grasp. Once one denies the existence of the mind, as Skinner did, all that is left is behavior, so thinking must be behavior under the control of the contingencies of reinforcement. B. F. Skinner's thought was, in his terms, simply "the sum total of his responses to the complex world in which he lived." "Thought" is simply a tact that we have learned to apply to certain forms of behavior, a tact Skinner asked people to unlearn, or at least not teach to our children. For Skinner did not merely wish to describe behavior, human or animal, he wanted to control it, control being a fundamental part of the experimental analysis of behavior. Skinner believed that current control of human behavior, based as it is on mental fictions, is ineffective at best and harmful at worst.

The Scientific Construction of Culture.   During World War II, Skinner worked on a behavioral guidance system for air-to-surface missiles called Project OrCon, for *or*ganic *con*trol. He trained pigeons to peck at a projected image of the target that the missile they were imprisoned in was to seek out. Their pecking operated controls on the missile so that it followed its target until it struck the target, destroying target and pigeons alike. Skinner achieved such complete control of the pigeons' behavior that they could carry out the most difficult tracking maneuvers during simulated attacks. The work impressed him with the possibility of a thorough control of any organism's behavior. Skinner's military funders found the project implausible, and no pigeon-guided missiles ever flew. Shortly afterward, however, Skinner wrote his most widely read book, *Walden II* (1948), a utopian novel based on the principles of the experimental analysis of behavior.

In that book, two characters represent Skinner: Frazier (an experimental psychologist and founder of Walden II, an experimental utopian community) and Burris (a skeptical visitor ultimately won over to membership in Walden II). Near the end, Frazier speaks to Burris: "I've had only one idea in my life—a true *idée fixe*. . . . The idea of having my own way. 'Control' expresses it, I think. The control of human behavior, Burris" (1948, p. 271). Frazier goes on to describe Walden II as the final laboratory and proving ground of the experimental analysis of behavior: "Nothing short of Walden II will suffice." Finally, Frazier exclaims: "Well, what do you say to the design of personalities? the control of temperament? Give me the specifications and I'll give you the man! . . . Think of the possibilities! A society in which there is no failure, no boredom, no duplication of effort. . . . Let us control the lives of our children and see what we can make of them" (p. 274). Frazier's claim to custom-make personalities recalls Watson's claim to custom-make the careers of infants. We have seen how important the desire for social control in Progressivism was to the favorable reaction to Watson's behaviorism. Skinner was heir to the Progressive desire to scientifically control human lives in the interest of society, more specifically, the survival of society, the ultimate Darwinian and Skinnerian value. He was also heir, and consciously so, to the tradition of Enlightenment optimism about human progress. Skinner asked people, in an otherwise disillusioned age, not to give up Rousseau's utopian dream, but to build a utopia on the principles of the experimental analysis of behavior. If pigeons' behavior can be controlled so that the birds guide missiles to their death, so a human being, whose behavior is likewise determined, can be controlled to be happy and productive and to feel free and dignified. *Walden II* was Skinner's first attempt to describe his vision.

Behaviorism and the Human Mind: Informal Behaviorism

While Skinner's radical behaviorism continued the Watsonian tradition of rejecting all inner causes of behavior, other behaviorists, students of Hull and Tolman, did not. After World War II, one class of inner cause, cognitive processes, received increasing attention. Psychologists treated cognition from a variety of perspectives, including neo-Hullian "liberalized" or informal behaviorism, and a variety of unrelated theories proposed by American and European psychologists. Few behaviorists were willing to agree with Skinner that organisms were "empty," that it was illegitimate to postulate, as Hull had, mechanisms taking place within the organism linking together stimulus and response. As Charles Osgood (1916–1991) put it, "Most contemporary behaviorists [can] be characterized as 'frustrated empty boxes' " (1956). They were aware of the pitfalls of "junkshop psychology," in which mental faculties or entities were multiplied as fast as the behaviors to be explained. Yet, they increasingly believed that behavior, especially "the phenomena of meaning and intention, so obviously displayed in human language behavior, entirely escape the single-stage conception" of black box S–R psychology (Osgood, 1957). It was obvious to psychologists concerned with the human higher mental processes that people possess "symbolic processes," the ability to represent the world internally, and that human responses were controlled by these symbols instead of being directly controlled by external stimulation. Their problem was avoiding "junkshop psychology": "What is the least amount of additional baggage needed to handle symbolic processes?" (Osgood, 1956).

They solved it by building on Hull's concepts of the r–g–s–g mechanism and the "pure stimulus act." The r–g–s–g mechanism, or *fractional anticipatory goal response*, was proposed to handle a special type of error made by rats that had learned a maze. Hull observed that these animals often turned into blind alleys before arriving at the last choice point before the goal. The error was always to make the correct response too soon, and with increasing likelihood as the goal was approached. So, for example, if the last correct turn was to the right, the rat's error was most likely to be a right turn one choice point before the one leading to the goal. Hull explained his findings by arguing that animals had experienced Pavlovian (classical) conditioning while eating in the goal box on earlier trials, so that the goal box stimuli produced a salivary response. By generalization, the stimuli at the last, correct choice point also elicited salivation, and by further generalization, so did other stimuli in the maze. Therefore, as a rat moved down the maze, it increasingly salivated in anticipation of the food, and the stimuli produced by salivating acted to prod the animal to turn right (in the example). Therefore, the animal would be more and more likely to turn into a blind alley before it reached the last alley to the goal box. Because the salivary response was covert (unobserved) rather than overt, Hull notated it with a small *r*, the salivary stimulus it caused by a small *s*. Because the salivary response was triggered by maze stimuli and had an effect on behavior, it could be viewed as part of an S–R behavior chain: $S \rightarrow r_{salivation} \rightarrow s_{salivary\ stimuli} \rightarrow R$.

The second of Hull's concepts leading to mediation theory was the *pure stimulus act*. Some behaviors, Hull noted, did not act on the environment, and he speculated that they occur to provide stimulus support for another behavior. For example, if you ask people to describe how they tie their shoes, they will typically go through the finger motions of shoe tying while verbally describing what they are doing. Such behavior is an example of Hull's pure stimulus act. It is not too hard to imagine these acts occurring internally, without any outward show. For example, if asked, "How many windows do you have at home?" you will likely walk through a mental house and count the windows. Such processes *mediate* between external stimuli and our responses to them. The neo-Hullian psychologists conceived of human symbolic processes as internal continuations of S–R chains: $S \rightarrow (r \rightarrow s) \rightarrow R$.

An external stimulus elicits an internal mediating response, which in turn has internal stimulus properties; it is these internal stimuli, rather than external ones, that actually elicit overt behavior. "The great advantage of this solution is that, since each stage is an S–R process, we can simply transfer all the conceptual machinery of single-stage S–R psychology into this new model without new postulation" (Osgood, 1956, p. 178). So, cognitive processes could be admitted into the body of behavior theory without giving up any of the rigor of the S–R formulation and without inventing any uniquely human mental processes. Behavior could still be explained in terms of S–R behavior chains, except that now some of the chains took place invisibly within the organism. Behavioralists now had a language with which to discuss meaning, language, memory, problem solving, and other behaviors apparently beyond the reach of radical behaviorism.

The approach described by Osgood had many practitioners. Osgood applied it to language with special reference to the problem of meaning, which he tried to measure behaviorally with his semantic differential scale. Irving Maltzman (1955) and Albert Goss (1961) applied it to problem solving and concept formation. The broadest program of human psychology in the liberalized vein was social learning theory, led by Neal Miller 1909–2002. Miller and others at Hull's Institute for Human Relations at Yale tried to construct a psychology that would do justice to Freud's insights into the human condition but remain within the objective realm of S–R psychology. They downplayed the axioms and quantification of Hull's animal work to incorporate humans within the S–R framework, and they added mediation as a way of talking about mental life in terms more precise than Freud's. Miller's (1959) description of his brand of behaviorism, including the whole neo-Hullian mediational camp, as "liberalized S–R theory" is apt. Social learning theorists did not abandon S–R theory; they only loosened its restrictions to be able to encompass human language, culture, and psychotherapy. Howard and Tracy Kendler (1962, 1975), for example, applied mediation theory to human discrimination learning, showing that differences in discrimination learning patterns among animals, children, and adult humans could be explained by claiming that animals rarely developed mediating responses and that the ability to form them developed in middle childhood.

The concept of mediation was a creative response by neo-Hullian behaviorists to the challenge of explaining human thought. However, mediationists did not leave S–R psychology intact because they had to modify Hull's strong versions of peripheralism and phylogenetic continuity to produce a theory capable of doing justice to the human higher mental processes. Hull had envisaged the fractional anticipatory goal response and the pure stimulus act as actual, if covert, motor responses that could enter into behavior chains; the mediationists, by contrast, conceived of mediation as taking place centrally, in the brain, giving up Watsonian and Hullian muscle-twitchism. Hull had wanted a single set of laws of learning to cover all forms of at least mammalian behavior; mediationists scaled back his ambition, accepting that, although in a general way, S–R theory might be universal, special allowances had to be made for species and developmental differences. Nevertheless, changes wrought by neo-Hullians were evolutionary, not revolutionary: Neal Miller was correct in asserting that they had liberalized S–R theory, not overthrown it.

Although it was a major—perhaps *the* major—theoretical position in the 1950s, mediational behaviorism ultimately proved to be no more than a bridge linking the inferential behavioralism of the 1930s and 1940s to the inferential behavioralism of the 1980s: cognitive psychology. The diagrams of mediational processes quickly became incredibly cumbersome. More important, there was no very good reason to think of processes one couldn't see as little chains of *r*s and *s*s. The mediationists' commitment to internalizing S–R language resulted primarily from their desire to preserve theoretical rigor and avoid the apparent unscientific character of "junkshop psychology." In essence, they lacked any other language with which to discuss the mental processes in a clear and disciplined fashion and took the only course they saw open to them. However, when a new language of power, rigor, and precision came along—the language of computer programming—it proved easy for mediational psychologists to abandon their *r–s* life raft for the ocean liner of information processing.

Philosophical Behaviorism

Psychological behaviorism arose out of the problems of animal psychology and in revolt against introspective mentalism. Consequently, behavioristic psychologists never addressed one of the more obvious difficulties that might be raised against their movement—namely, that ordinary people believe they possess mental processes and consciousness. There exists a folk psychology of mind that deserves attention from any psychological program departing from it. It may fairly be asked why, if there are no mental processes—as behaviorists seem to maintain—ordinary language is so rich in descriptions of mind and consciousness? Philosophical behaviorists addressed the problem of reinterpreting commonsense mentalistic psychology into acceptable "scientific" behavioristic terms as part of their more general program of linking claims about unobservables with observables.

LOGICAL BEHAVIORISM   As it is usually presented, philosophical or logical behaviorism "is a semantic theory about what mental terms mean. The basic idea is that attributing a mental state (say, thirst) to an organism is the same as saying that the organism is disposed to behave in a certain way (for example, to drink if there is water available)" (Fodor, 1981, p. 115). According to logical behaviorists, when we attribute a mental statement to a person, we're really just describing his or her actual or likely behavior in a given circumstance, not some inner mental state. In principle, then, it would be possible to eliminate mentalistic concepts from everyday psychology and replace them with concepts referring only to behavior. As stated, logical behaviorism is rather implausible. For example, according to logical behaviorism, to believe that ice on a lake is too thin for skating must mean that one is disposed not to skate on the ice and to say to others that they ought not skate on the lake. However, things are not so simple. If you see someone you thoroughly dislike about to skate out on the ice, you may say nothing, hoping that your enemy will fall through the ice and look a fool. Should you harbor real malice toward the skater—if, for example, he is blackmailing you—you may say nothing, hoping he will drown; indeed, you may direct him to the weakest ice. So the mental statement "believing the ice is thin" cannot be simply and directly translated into a behavioral disposition, because how one is disposed to behave depends on other beliefs that turn on still others—for example, that the skater *is* the blackmailer—making any direct equation of mental state and behavioral disposition impossible.

The difficulties of logical behaviorism are relevant to experimental psychology because its doctrines are the application of operationism to ordinary psychological terms. For logical behaviorism's equation of mental state and behavior or behavioral disposition provides operational definitions of "belief," "hope," fear," "being in pain," and so on. The example of the thin ice shows that one cannot give an operational definition of "believing the ice is thin," and failure to "operationalize" so simple and straightforward a concept casts doubt on the whole enterprise of operationism in psychology. The British philosopher G. E. Moore, following Ludwig Wittgenstein, refuted the logical behaviorist, operationist treatment of mental terms more bluntly: "When we pity a man for having toothache, we are not pitying him for putting his hand to his cheek" (quoted by Luckhardt, 1983).

Logical behaviorism is so obviously false that it makes an admirable straw man for philosophers of other dispositions, but it is not clear that anyone has actually held the position just sketched. It is typically attributed to Rudolph Carnap, Gilbert Ryle, and Ludwig Wittgenstein, but in fact, these philosophers held different and more interesting views on the nature of mentalistic folk psychology. We discussed Carnap's "behaviorism" earlier in this chapter in connection with E. C. Tolman, who was for a time under Carnap's influence. Carnap came closest to holding the position of logical behaviorism, but we should bear in mind that for him, it was just a temporary way station on the road to interpreting mentalistic language as talk about brain states.

THE "GHOST IN THE MACHINE"   In *The Concept of Mind* (1949), the English philosopher Gilbert Ryle (1900–1976) attacked what he called "the dogma of the Ghost in the Machine" begun by Descartes. Descartes had defined two worlds: one material and including the body; the other mental, a ghostly inner stage on which private mental events took place. Ryle accused Descartes of making a huge "category mistake," treating mind as if it were a distinct thing opposed to the body and somehow lying behind behavior. Here is Ryle's example of a category mistake: A person is taken on a tour of Oxford University and sees its college buildings, its library, its deans, its professors, and its students. At the end of the day the visitor asks, "You've showed me all these things, but where is the university?" The mistake is in supposing that because there is a name "Oxford University," it must apply to some object separate from the buildings and so on, yet be like them in being a thing. So Ryle claimed that Cartesian dualism is a category mistake. Cartesians describe behaviors with "mental" predicates such as "intelligent," "hopeful," "sincere," "disingenuous," and then assume that there must be a mental thing behind the behaviors that makes them intelligent, hopeful, sincere, or disingenuous. Here, says Ryle, lies the mistake, because the behaviors *themselves* are intelligent, hopeful, sincere, or disingenuous; no inner ghost is needed to make them so. Moreover, inventing the Ghost in the Machine accomplishes nothing because if there were an inner ghost, we would still have to explain why its operations are intelligent, hopeful, sincere, or disingenuous. Is there a Ghost in the Ghost? And a Ghost in the Ghost in the Ghost? The Ghost in the Machine, far from explaining mental life, vastly complicates our efforts to understand it.

So far, one might, as Ryle feared, put him or her down as a behaviorist claiming that mind *is* only behavior. But Ryle held that there is indeed more to mental predicates than simple descriptions of behavior. For example, when we say birds are "migrating," we see them flying south, and a behaviorist might say that "migration" is just "flying-south behavior." However, as Ryle pointed out, to say that birds are "migrating" is to say much more than that they are flying south, for the term *migration* implies a whole story about why they are flying south, how they will return later, how it happens every year, and theories about how they navigate. So to say birds are "migrating" goes *beyond* saying that they are flying south, but it does not go *behind* saying that they are flying south. Similarly, to say a behavior is "intelligent" does more than simply describe some behavior, for it brings in the various criteria we have for saying a course of action is intelligent—for example, that it is appropriate to the situation and that it is likely to be successful. But saying a person is acting intelligently does not go behind the behavior to some ghostly inner calculations that make it intelligent, however it goes much beyond a behaviorist's description of what the person is doing. Although Ryle rejected dualism, and although his analysis of mind had some similarities to behaviorism, it was rather different from either psychological behaviorism or logical, philosophical behaviorism.

MIND AS SOCIAL CONSTRUCT A difficult and subtle analysis of ordinary psychological language was made by the Viennese (later British) philosopher Ludwig Wittgenstein (1889–1951). Wittgenstein argued that Cartesian philosophers had led people to believe that there are mental objects (e.g., sensations) and mental processes (e.g., memory), whereas in fact there are neither. As an example of a mental object, consider *pain*. Quite clearly, the behaviorist is wrong in asserting that pain is behavior. The behaviorist error is in thinking that first- and third-person uses of "pain" are symmetrical. If we see someone moaning and holding his head, we say, "He is in pain"; but I do not say, "I am in pain" because I observe myself moaning and holding my head, as strict operationism requires. So the sentence "I am in pain" does not describe behavior, nor, held Wittgenstein, does it describe some inner object. An object can be known, so we can say true things about it—for example, "I know this book, *Wittgenstein*, costs $5.95." But a statement of knowledge only makes sense if we can doubt it—that is, if some other state of affairs may be true. So one can sensibly say, "I don't know if *Wittgenstein* costs $5.95." Now, "I know I'm in pain" seems to make sense and point to an inner object of description, but the statement "I don't know that I'm in pain" is simply nonsense; of course, one can have experienced bodily damage and not feel pain, but one cannot meaningfully say, "I don't know if I'm in pain." Another problem with thinking of pain as an object concerns how pains are located. Should I hold a piece of candy between my fingers and then put my fingers in my mouth, we would agree that the candy is in my mouth as well as my hand. But suppose I have a pain in my finger and put my finger in my mouth. Is the pain in my mouth? It seems odd to say so; pains are therefore not assigned location as we assign locations to ordinary objects. Wittgenstein concluded that pain is not some inner object that we know at all, and that statements about pain (or joy or ecstasy) are not descriptions of anything. Rather, they are expressions. Moaning expresses pain, it does not describe pain. Wittgenstein maintained that sentences such as "I am in pain" are learned linguistic equivalents of moaning, expressing but not describing the state of pain. Pain is perfectly real; it is not, however, a ghostly mental object.

Luckhardt (1983) introduces a useful analogy to clarify Wittgenstein's point. A painting expresses an artist's conception through the physical medium of paint on canvas. We find it beautiful (or ugly) as we interpret it. Behaviorists are like paint salespeople who point out that because the painting is made of paint, its beauty is identical with the arrangements of the paints on the canvas. However, this is obviously absurd, for a painting venerated for its beauty among academic painters and audiences in 1875 is likely to be considered tacky kitsch by modernists and their audience. Beauty depends on an interpretation of paint on canvas and is not identical with it. The painting is, again, a physical expression by an artist that is in turn interpreted by its viewers. So "I am in pain," like moans and grimaces, is a physical expression by a person that must be interpreted by those who hear it.

Likewise, mental processes do not consist in any *thing*, either, argued Wittgenstein. Consider memory. Obviously, we remember things all the time, but is there an inner mental process of remembering common to all acts of memory? Wittgenstein thought not. Malcolm (1970) gives the following example: Several hours after you put your keys in the kitchen drawer, you are asked, "Where did you put the keys?" You may remember in any of several ways:

> Nothing occurs to you, then you mentally retrace your steps earlier in the day and have an image of putting the keys in the drawer, and say, "I left them in the kitchen drawer."

> Nothing occurs to you. You have no images, but ask yourself, "Where did I put the keys?" then exclaim, "The kitchen drawer!"

> The question is asked while you are deep in conversation with another person. Without interrupting your talk, you point to the kitchen drawer.

> You are asked while writing a letter. Saying nothing, you walk over to the drawer, reach in, and hand over the keys, all the while composing the next sentence in the letter.

> Without any hesitation or doubt, you answer directly, "I put them in the kitchen drawer."

In every case, you remembered where the keys were, but each case is quite unlike the others. The behaviors are different, so there is no essential behavioral process of remembering; there is no uniform mental accompaniment to the act of remembering, so there is no essential mental process of remembering; and because there is no common behavior or conscious experience, there is no essential physiological process of remembering. In each case, there is behavior, there are mental events, and there are physiological processes, but no one of them is the same, so there is no uniform *process* of memory. We group these events together under "memory" not because of some essential defining feature of each episode, the way we define "electrons" in terms of uniform defining features, but because they share what Wittgenstein called a "family resemblance." The members of a family resemble one another, but there is no single feature all members possess. Two brothers might share similar noses, a father and son similar ears, two cousins similar hair, but there is no essential defining feature shared by all. Wittgenstein argued that terms referring to mental processes are all family-resemblance terms, having no defining essence that can be captured. "Remembering," "thinking," and "intending" are not processes, but human abilities. To the Wittgensteinian, the Würzburg psychologists' efforts to lay bare the processes of thinking had to end in failure, for there are no processes of thought to be found. Thinking, like remembering, is just something people *do* (Malcolm, 1970).

If Wittgenstein is right, the consequences for psychology would be profound. Wittgenstein (1953, II, Sec. 14) had a poor opinion of psychology: "The confusion and barrenness of psychology is not to be explained by calling it a 'young science. . . .' For in psychology there are experimental methods and *conceptual confusion.*" Psychology's conceptual confusion is to think there are mental objects and mental processes when there are not, and then to seek descriptions of the fictitious objects and processes:

> I have been trying in all this to remove the temptation to think that there "must be" a mental process of thinking, hoping, wishing, believing, etc., independent of the process of expressing a thought, a hope, a wish, etc. . . . If we scrutinize the usages which we make of "thinking," "meaning," "wishing," etc., going through this process rids us of the temptation to look for a peculiar act of thinking, independent of the act of expressing our thoughts, and stowed away in some particular medium. (Wittgenstein, 1958, pp. 41–43)

Wittgenstein's point here was related to Ryle's: There is nothing behind our acts; there is no Ghost in the Machine. There is also in Wittgenstein's analysis a broader point about science: Explanations stop somewhere (Malcolm, 1970). It is no good asking a physicist why an object once set in motion will travel in a straight line forever unless acted on by another force, because this is a basic assumption that allows physics to explain other things. No one has seen an object move that way, and the only apparently undisturbed objects we can observe moving, the planets, move (roughly) in circles; indeed, the ancients assumed that an object in space set in motion would naturally move in a circle. Similarly, a physicist cannot explain why quarks have the properties they do, only how, given those properties, their behavior can be explained. Psychologists have all along supposed that thinking, memory, wishing, and so on required explanations, but Ryle, and especially Wittgenstein, claim that they do not. They are human abilities, and thinking, remembering, and wishing are things we just *do* without there being some "inside story," mental or physiological—although they are not just behaviors, either. Psychologists went wrong when they framed their question as, "What is the process of thinking?" naturally coming up with theories about mental processes. As Wittgenstein remarks:

> We talk of processes and states and leave their nature undecided. Sometimes perhaps we shall know more about them—we think. But that is just what commits us to a particular way of looking at the matter. For we have a definite concept of what it means to learn to know a process better. The decisive movement in the conjuring trick has been made, and it was the very one that we thought quite innocent. (1953, I, paragraph 308)

To Wittgenstein, we cannot scientifically explain behavior, but we can understand it. To understand people's behavior, and the expressions of their thoughts, we must take into consideration what Wittgenstein called human "forms of life." "What has to be accepted, the given, is—so one could say—*forms of life*" (Wittgenstein, 1958). In discussing Luckhardt's painting metaphor, we pointed out that the beauty of a painting lies in its interpretation. How we interpret the painting depends on the immediate and overall context in which we meet it. The gallery-goer may have read art history and criticism, and this knowledge will shape her appreciation of the picture. She will see

Frank Stella's latest canvas against the background of Stella's previous work, the works by other artists arranged in the show, and her knowledge of the history, ambitions, and techniques of modern and postmodern painting. Simply as paint on canvas, the painting has no meaning and is neither beautiful nor ugly, meaningful or meaningless; it takes on meaning only in the eye of an interpretive viewer. All this context is a "form of life," the form of life of modernism and postmodernism in the arts. Observe that a person who knows nothing of modernism is likely to find a Stella work literally without meaning because that person does not participate in the appropriate form of life. Should he take modern art history classes, he can learn a new form of life and the painting will become meaningful.

Wittgenstein's point was that human action is meaningful only within the setting of a form of life. An untutored Westerner is likely to find practices of another culture, or another historical time, without meaning in the same way the naive gallery-goer finds the Stella painting meaningless. The reverse also is true: Some African tribesmen came to a city for the first time and were deeply shocked when, in a tall building, they saw two men go into a box and emerge a few seconds later as three women (they saw an elevator). If Wittgenstein's claim is correct, then not only can psychology not be a science because there are no mental processes and objects for it to study and explain, but psychology and the other social sciences cannot be sciences because there are no historically permanent and cross-culturally universal principles for understanding human thought and behavior. Psychology, he said, should give up the "craving for generality" and "the contemptuous attitude to the particular case" it has picked up from natural science (Wittgenstein, 1953) and accept the modest goal of explicating forms of life and explaining particular human actions within their historically given forms of life.

Cognitive Science 1956–2000

THE DECLINE OF BEHAVIORISM

Cartesian Linguistics

If anyone played Watson to the eclectic peace of the 1950s, it was the linguist Avram Noam Chomsky (1928–). Chomsky was radical in both politics and linguistics, the study of language. In politics, Chomsky was an early and outspoken critic of the war in Vietnam and of the United States' support of Israel in the Middle East. In linguistics, Chomsky revived what he took to be Descartes's rationalistic program, proposing highly formal accounts of language as the organ by which reason expresses itself and resurrecting the notion of innate ideas. Because Chomsky regarded language as a uniquely human, rational possession, he was brought into conflict with behavioral treatments of language.

THE ATTACK ON VERBAL BEHAVIOR Language was a standing challenge to behaviorism. Hull's student Spence suspected that language could not be explained by laws of learning derived from animals. In 1955, the informal behaviorist Osgood referred to the problems of meaning and perception as the "Waterloo of contemporary behaviorism" and, in response, attempted to provide a mediational theory of language, applicable only to human beings (Osgood, 1957). Behaviorist worries that Descartes may have been right about the human uniqueness of language became manifest in Chomsky's (1959) review of *Verbal Behavior*, perhaps the most influential paper in the history of psychology since Watson's manifesto for behaviorism. Chomsky attacked not only Skinner's book, but empiricist ideas in linguistics, psychology, and philosophy generally. He regarded *Verbal Behavior* as a "*reductio ad absurdum* of behaviorist assumptions" and wanted to show it up as pure "mythology" (quoted by Jakobovits & Miron, 1967).

Chomsky's basic criticism of Skinner's book was that it represented an exercise in equivocation. Skinner's

From Chapter 12 of *A History of Psychology: From Antiquity to Modernity*, Seventh Edition.
Thomas Hardy Leahey. Copyright © 2013 by Pearson Education, Inc. All rights reserved.

fundamental technical terms—*stimulus*, *response*, *reinforcement*, and so on—are well defined in animal learning experiments but cannot be extended to human behavior without serious modification, as Skinner claimed. Chomsky argued that if one attempts to use Skinner's terms in rigorous technical senses, they can be shown not to apply to language, and if the terms are metaphorically extended, they become so vague as to be no improvement on common sense. Chomsky systematically attacked all of Skinner's concepts, but we will consider only two examples: his analyses of stimulus and reinforcement.

Obviously, to any behaviorist, proper definitions of the stimuli that control behavior are important. The difficulty of defining "stimulus," however, is a notorious one for behaviorism, as Thorndike had foreseen. Are stimuli to be defined in purely physical terms, independent of behavior, or in terms of their effects on behavior? If we accept the former definition, then behavior looks unlawful, for very few stimuli in a situation ever affect behavior; if we accept the latter definition, behavior is lawful by definition, for then the behaviorist considers only those stimuli that do systematically determine behavior. Chomsky raised this problem and others specific to Skinner's *Verbal Behavior*. First, Chomsky pointed out that to say each bit of verbal behavior is under stimulus control is scientifically empty, for given any response, we can always find *some* relevant stimulus. A person looks at a painting and says, "It's by Rembrandt, isn't it?" Skinner would assert that certain subtle properties of the painting determine the response. Yet, the person could have said, "How much did it cost?" "It clashes with the wallpaper," "You've hung it too high," "It's hideous!" "I have one just like it at home," "It's forged," and so on, virtually an infinitum. No matter what is said, *some* property could be found that "controls" the behavior. Chomsky argued that there is no prediction of behavior, and certainly no serious control, in this circumstance. Skinner's system is not the scientific advance toward the prediction and control of behavior it pretends to be.

Chomsky also pointed out that Skinner's definition of stimulus becomes hopelessly vague and metaphorical at a great remove from the rigorous laboratory environment. Skinner speaks of "remote stimulus control," in which the stimulus need not impinge on the speaker at all, as when a recalled diplomat describes a foreign situation. Skinner says the suffix *-ed* is controlled by the "subtle property of stimuli we speak of as action in the past." What physical dimensions define "things in the past"? Chomsky argued that Skinner's usage here is not remotely related to his usage in his bar-pressing experiments, and that Skinner has said nothing new about the supposed "stimulus control" of verbal behavior.

Chomsky next considered *reinforcement*, another term easily defined in the usual operant learning experiment in terms of delivered food or water. Chomsky argued that Skinner's application of the term to verbal behavior was again vague and metaphorical. Consider Skinner's notion of automatic self-reinforcement. Talking to oneself is said to be automatically self-reinforcing; that is why one does it. Similarly, thinking is also said to be behavior that automatically affects the behaver and is therefore reinforcing. Also consider what we might call "remote reinforcement": A writer shunned in his own time may be reinforced by expecting fame to come much later. Chomsky (1959/1967,

p. 153) argued that "the notion of reinforcement has totally lost whatever meaning it may ever have had. . . . A person can be reinforced though he emits no response at all [thinking], and the reinforcing 'stimulus' need not impinge on the 'reinforced person' [remote reinforcement] or need not even exist [an unpopular author who remains unpopular]."

Chomsky's attitude toward Skinner was contemptuous: He was not prepared to accept Skinner's *Verbal Behavior* as a plausible scientific hypothesis and regarded the book as hopelessly muddled and fundamentally wrong. His acute and unrelenting criticism, coupled with his own positive program, was aimed at the overthrow of behaviorist psychology—not its liberalization. For Chomsky, behaviorism could not be built upon, it could only be replaced.

CHOMSKY'S INFLUENCE   Adopting a rationalist, Cartesian perspective, Chomsky (1966) claimed that no behaviorist approach to language can cope with its endless creativity and flexibility. He argued that the infinite creativity of language—excepting cliches, every sentence you hear or utter every day is new—can be understood only by recognizing that language is a rule-governed system. As part of their mental processes, persons possess a set of grammatical rules that allows them to generate new sentences by appropriately combining linguistic elements. Each person can thus generate an infinity of sentences by repeated application of the rules of grammar, just as a person can generate numbers infinitely by repeated application of the rules of arithmetic. Chomsky argued that human language will not be understood until psychology discovers the rules of grammar, the mental structures, that underlie speaking and hearing. A superficial behaviorist approach, which studies only speech and hearing but neglects the inner rules that govern speech and hearing, is necessarily inadequate.

As part of his effort to revive Cartesian rationalism in the twentieth century, Chomsky advanced a nativist theory of language acquisition to accompany his formal, rule-governed theory of adult language. Chomsky (e.g., 1959, 1966) proposed that children possess a biologically given language acquisition device that guides the acquisition of their native language between the ages of about 2 and 12 years. Thus, for Chomsky as for Descartes, language is a possession unique to the human species. In one respect, Chomsky's thesis was even more nativist than Descartes's. Descartes proposed that humans have language because they—alone among the animals—can think and express themselves in language, whereas Chomsky claims that language itself, not the more general ability to think, is a human species-specific trait. Soon after Chomsky propounded his view, behavioralist psychologists revived La Mettrie's old project of teaching language to apes via sign language, computer language, or a system of plastic tokens. The success of the projects remains a source of intense controversy (see Kenneally, 2008, for an introduction), but at present, it appears that although apes can learn crudely to communicate their desires through signs, they are unable to acquire anything remotely like human language.

Chomsky's ideas were enormously influential in psycholinguistics, rapidly and completely eclipsing behaviorist approaches, whether mediational or Skinnerian. Many psychologists became convinced that their behaviorist views were wrong and committed themselves to a renewed study of language along Chomskian lines. Chomsky's technical system, described in *Syntactic Structures* (which appeared in 1957, the year of *Verbal Behavior*), provided a new theory around which to design research. Study after study was done, so that in only a few years, Chomsky's ideas had generated much more empirical research than had Skinner's. The study of child language was similarly stimulated by Chomsky's controversial nativism. Chomsky's impact was nicely described by George Miller. In the 1950s, Miller had adhered to a behaviorist picture of language, but personal contact with Chomsky convinced him the old paradigm had to be abandoned. By 1962, he was writing: "In the course of my work I seem to have become a very old-fashioned kind of psychologist. I now believe that mind is something more than a four letter, Anglo-Saxon word—human minds exist, and it is our job as psychologists to study them" (p. 762). The mind, exorcised by Watson in 1913, had returned to psychology, brought back by an outsider, Noam Chomsky. Chomsky's emphasis on the rule-governed nature of language helped shape later information-processing theories that claim all behavior is rule-governed.

Erosion of the Spencerian Foundation: Constraints on Animal Learning

Just as Chomsky was attacking behaviorism from without, the foundations of behaviorism were crumbling from within. Watson began his career as an animal psychologist, and Tolman, Hull, and Skinner rarely studied human behavior, preferring the more controlled situations that could be imposed on animals. Animal experiments were expected to yield general behavioral laws applicable to a wide range of species, including humans, with little or no modification. Tolman spoke of cognitive maps in rats and persons, Hull of the general laws of mammalian behavior, and Skinner of the extension of animal principles to verbal behavior. It was believed that the principles that emerged from artificially controlled experiments would illuminate the ways in which all organisms learn, regardless of their evolutionary heritage. The assumption of generality was crucial to the behaviorist program, for if laws of learning are species-specific, studies of animal behavior could be pointless for understanding humanity.

Evidence accumulated in the 1960s, however, that the laws of learning uncovered with rats and pigeons were not general and that serious constraints exist on what and how an animal learns, constraints dictated by the animal's evolutionary history. This evidence came from both psychology and other disciplines. On the one hand, psychologists discovered anomalies in the application of learning laws in a variety of situations; on the other hand, ethologists demonstrated the importance of considering innate factors in explaining an animal's behavior in the natural environment its ancestors evolved in.

In developing the pigeon-guided missile, Skinner worked with a young psychologist, Keller Breland, who was so impressed by the possibilities of behavior control that he and his wife became professional animal trainers. As Skinner wrote in 1959: "Behavior could be shaped up according to specifications and maintained indefinitely almost at will . . . Keller Breland is now specializing in the production of behavior as a saleable commodity." Skinner's claim for Breland resembles Frazier's boast in *Walden II* of being able to produce human personalities to order.

However, in the course of their extensive experience in training many species to perform unusual behaviors, the Brelands found instances in which animals did not perform as they should. In 1961, they reported their difficulties in a paper whose title, "The Misbehavior of Organisms," puns on Skinner's first book, *The Behavior of Organisms*. For example, they tried to teach pigs to carry wooden coins and deposit them in a piggy bank. Although they could teach behaviors, the Brelands found that the behavior degenerated in pig after pig. The animals would eventually pick up the coin, drop it on the ground, and root it, rather than deposit it in the bank. The Brelands reported that they found many instances of animals "trapped by strong instinctive behaviors" that overwhelmed learned behaviors. Pigs naturally root for their food, and so they came to root the coins that they have been trained to collect to get food reinforcers. Breland and Breland (1961/1972) concluded that psychologists should examine "the hidden assumptions which led most disastrously to these breakdowns" in the general laws of learning proposed by behaviorism. They clearly questioned behaviorism's paradigmatic assumptions in the light of experimental anomalies.

They identified three such assumptions: "That the animal . . . [is] a virtual *tabula rasa*, that species differences are insignificant, and that all responses are about equally conditionable to all stimuli." These assumptions are fundamental to empiricism, and statements of them were made by the major behaviorists. Although limits on these assumptions had been suggested before, the Brelands's paper seemed to open the floodgates to discoveries of more anomalies under more controlled conditions.

We may mention one such line of research conducted by John Garcia (Garcia, McGowan, & Green, 1972) and his associates. Garcia was a student of I. Krechevsky, Tolman's major pupil. Garcia studied what he called "conditioned nausea," a form of classical conditioning. Standard empiricist assumptions, enunciated by Pavlov, held that any stimulus could act as a conditioned stimulus, which through conditioning could elicit any response as a conditioned response. More informally, any stimulus could be conditioned to elicit any response. Empirical studies further indicated that the conditioned stimulus and the unconditioned stimulus had to be paired within about a half-second of each other for learning to take place.

Using a variety of methods, Garcia let rats drink a novel-tasting liquid and then made the rats sick over an hour later. The question was whether rats would learn to avoid the place they were sick, the unconditioned stimulus immediately connected with their sickness, or the solution they drank, although it was remote in time from the unconditioned response. The last uniformly occurred. The usual laws of classical conditioning did not hold. Garcia argued that rats know instinctively that nausea must be due to something they ate, not stimuli present at the time of sickness. This makes good evolutionary sense, for sickness in the wild is more likely to be caused by drinking tainted water than by the bush under which a rat was sitting when it felt sick. Connecting taste with sickness is more biologically adaptive than connecting it with visual or auditory stimuli. It appears, therefore, that evolution constrains which stimuli may be associated with which responses. Garcia's research was initially greeted with extreme skepticism and was refused publication in the major journal devoted to animal behavior. However, studies by other researchers demonstrated that for many behaviors, an animal's evolutionary inheritance places distinct limits on what it can learn. Garcia's studies are now considered classics.

The findings of the Brelands, Garcia, and others demonstrated the shortcomings of the old Spencerian paradigm upon which the behaviorist research program rested. Following Spencer, behaviorists assumed that the laws of learning could be established in one or two species and then extended to others, including human beings. The new research showed that that assumption was flawed—the species question could not be ignored. Moreover, these new findings buttressed Chomsky's claim that human beings were not simply complicated rats.

EARLY THEORIES IN COGNITIVE PSYCHOLOGY

Not all psychologists interested in cognition worked within the framework of neo-Hullian mediational psychology. In Europe, a movement called *structuralism* emerged as an interdisciplinary approach to the social sciences, including psychology, and it exerted some influence on American psychology in the late 1950s and 1960s. In the United States, social psychologists had abandoned the concept of the group mind in the first decades of the twentieth century, gradually redefining it as it is today: the study of people engaged in social interaction. During the war, social psychologists had been concerned with studying attitudes, how persuasion and propaganda change attitudes, and the relation of attitudes to personality. After the war, social psychologists continued to develop theories about how people form, integrate, and act on beliefs. Finally, Jerome Bruner studied how personality dynamics shape people's perceptions of the world, and how people solve complex problems.

The New Structuralism

Structuralism in the modern sense was a movement in continental European philosophy, literary criticism, and social science. The leading exponents of structuralism, Claude Lévi-Strauss, Michel Foucault, and Jean Piaget, were French-speaking and carried on the Platonic–Cartesian rationalist attempt to describe the transcendent human mind. Structuralism was associated with the more radical cognitive psychologists, who sought a clear break with the past in American psychology; in particular, they looked to European psychology and continental European traditions in philosophy, psychology, and the other social sciences. Structuralism hoped to be a unifying paradigm for all the social sciences, and its adherents ranged from philosophers to anthropologists. Structuralists believed that human behavior patterns, whether individual or social, could be explained by reference to abstract structures of a logical or mathematical nature.

In psychology, the leading structuralist was Jean Piaget (1896–1980). Piaget was originally trained as a biologist, but his interests shifted to epistemology, which he undertook to study scientifically. He criticized philosophers for remaining content with armchair speculations about the growth of knowledge when the questions of epistemology could be empirically investigated. Genetic epistemology was his attempt to chart the development of knowledge in children. Piaget divided the growth of intellect into four stages, each of which is defined by a distinct set of logical cognitive structures. He believed intelligence does not grow quantitatively, but undergoes widespread qualitative changes as a child moves from one stage to the next. Thus, a 5-year-old not only knows less than a 12-year-old, but also thinks in a different way. Piaget traced these different kinds of intelligence, or ways of knowing the world, to changes in the logical structure of the child's mind. He attempted to describe the thinking of each stage by constructing highly abstract and formal logical models of the mental structures he believed guide intelligent behavior.

Genetic epistemology was Kantian epistemology with a developmental twist. The titles of many of Piaget's works are the names of Kant's transcendental categories: *The Child's Conception of Space*, *The Child's Conception of Number*, *The Child's Conception of Time*, and many more. Kant had asserted that the Transcendental Ego could not be fathomed, but Piaget thought that his version of it, the *epistemic subject*, revealed its nature in the course of its development and could therefore be inferred from observing children's problem-solving behavior. Piaget also shared the Mandarin tendencies of the German psychologists, aiming to formulate a broad philosophy rather than a psychological theory with practical applications. Piaget called the question of whether training can accelerate the course of cognitive growth "the American question," for it was not asked in Europe. In true pragmatic fashion, Americans wanted to make cognitive development proceed faster and more efficiently. During his long lifetime, Piaget systematically pursued his research program, paying only occasional attention to behaviorism. Thus, although he was little read before 1960, Piaget and his genetic epistemology constituted a sophisticated alternative to behaviorism ready to be picked up when behaviorism faltered.

As one might expect, given the European rationalist background of structuralism, its impact on American psychology was limited. Although American psychologists paid great attention to Piaget after 1960, few American psychologists adopted his structuralism. His logical models were viewed as too abstruse and far removed from behavior to be of any value. Moreover, subsequent research established that Piaget's stages of development were not as well defined or as rigid as he suggested, and that he tended to seriously underestimate the intelligence of young children (Leahey & Harris, 2004). Additionally, Americans are interested in individual differences and the effects of experience or training on cognitive development and did not care greatly about Piaget's idealized "epistemic subject." Today, Piaget is cited as a forerunner in the study of cognitive development, but his theory wields meager influence.

In its attempt to characterize an innate universal grammar common to all human minds, Chomsky's (1957) transformational grammar shared European structuralism's emphasis on abstract structures and indifference to individual differences, although Chomsky did not identify himself with the movement as did Piaget. Moreover, while Piaget's theory languished, Chomsky's transformational grammar remains a robust enterprise in linguistics and cognitive science. Chomsky's critique of radical behaviorism did much to create renewed interest in cognition, and his transformational grammar showed how sophisticated activities such as language could be explained as rule-governed systems. Unlike Piaget's theory, Chomsky's has remained fluid, and today's transformational grammar bears little resemblance to that of three decades ago (Pinker, 1994). Chomsky is now regarded as one of the world's foremost thinkers.

Cognition in Social Psychology

Social psychology is the study of the person as a social being, and so it has roots going back to the Greek political thinkers, Machiavelli's detached approach to practical politics, and to Hobbes's first political science. We have said little about it before because as a field, it has been exceedingly eclectic, defined by its subject matter rather than any distinctive theory about human nature. It draws our attention now because during the 1940s and 1950s it continued to employ mental concepts of a commonsense sort. We will briefly consider one theory widely influential in the 1950s and early 1960s—Leon Festinger's (1919–1989) theory of cognitive dissonance.

Festinger's theory was about a person's beliefs and their interaction. It held that beliefs may agree with one another or they may clash. When beliefs clash, they induce an unpleasant state called *cognitive dissonance*, which the person tries to reduce. For example, a nonsmoker who is persuaded that cigarettes cause lung cancer will feel no dissonance, for his or her belief that smoking causes cancer agrees with and supports his or her refusal to smoke. However, a smoker who comes to believe smoking causes cancer will feel cognitive dissonance, for the decision to smoke clashes with this new belief. The smoker will act to reduce the dissonance, perhaps by giving up smoking. However, it is quite common to manage dissonance in other ways. For example, a smoker may simply avoid anti-smoking information in order to avoid dissonance.

Festinger's theory provoked much research. One classic study appeared to challenge the law of effect. Festinger and Carlsmith (1959) devised some extremely boring tasks for subjects to perform, such as turning screws for a long time. Then the experimenter got the subject to agree to tell a waiting subject that the task was fun. Some subjects were paid $20 (about $300 today) for telling the lie; others were paid only $1. According to the theory, the $20 subjects should feel no dissonance: The large payment justified their little lie. However, the $1 subjects should feel dissonance: They were telling a lie for a paltry amount of money. One way to resolve this dissonance would be to convince oneself that the task was in fact fun, for if one believed this, telling another subject that it was fun would be no lie. After the whole experiment was over, another experimenter interviewed the subjects and discovered that the $1 subjects voted the task significantly more enjoyable than did the $20 subjects, as Festinger's theory predicted. The finding appears inconsistent with the law of effect, for we might expect that a $20 reward for saying the experiment was fun would change one's report about the enjoyability of the experiment more than a $1 reward.

What is important about the theory of cognitive dissonance for historical purposes is that it was a cognitive theory—a theory about mental entities, in this case, about a person's beliefs. It was not an informal behaviorist theory, for Festinger did not conceive of beliefs as mediating responses, but in commonsense terms, as beliefs that control behavior. In the 1950s, the theory of cognitive dissonance and other cognitive theories in social psychology constituted a vigorous cognitive psychology outside the orbit of strict behaviorism. Festinger's (1957) book, *A Theory of Cognitive Dissonance*, made no reference to behaviorist ideas. Social psychologists rarely challenged behaviorism, but their field was an alternative to it.

New Cognitive Theories of Perception and Thinking

THE "NEW LOOK" IN PERCEPTION   Shortly after the war, a "New Look" in the study of perception arose led by Jerome S. Bruner (b. 1915). The motive behind the New Look was an attempt to unify several different areas of psychology—perception, personality, and social psychology—and a desire to refute the prevalent conception, going back at least to Hume and strongly present in *S–R* behavior theory, that perception was a passive process by which a stimulus impressed (Hume's term) itself on the perceiver. Bruner and his colleagues proposed a psychoanalytic view of perception in which the perceiver takes an active role rather than being a passive register of sense data. Bruner and others did a variety of studies to support the idea that a perceiver's personality and social background play a role in affecting what the perceiver sees. The most famous and controversial of these studies concerned perceptual defense and raise the possibility of subliminal perception. Bruner and others in the New Look movement (Bruner & Postman 1947; Postman, Bruner, & McGinnies, 1948) presented words to subjects for brief intervals, as had Wundt in his studies of the span of consciousness. However, these modern researchers varied the emotional content of the words: Some were ordinary or "neutral" words, others were obscene or "taboo" words. Bruner and his associates found that longer exposures are required for a subject to recognize a taboo word than to recognize a neutral word. Their Freudian hypothesis was that the subjects unconsciously perceive the negative emotional content of a taboo word and attempt to repress its entry into awareness. Subjects therefore see the word only when the exposure is so long that they cannot help seeing it.

Research on perceptual defense was extremely controversial for many years, some psychologists arguing that subjects see taboo words as quickly as neutral words, falsely denying the experience as long as possible to avoid embarrassment. The controversy grew heated and has never been fully resolved (Leahey & Harris, 2004). What is significant for us is that the New Look in perception analyzed perception as an active mental process involving both conscious and unconscious mental activities intervening between a sensation and a person's response to it.

THE STUDY OF THINKING Concern with perception and Bruner's demonstrations that mind and personality actively shape it led him to a study of the old "higher mental processes" (Bruner, Goodnow, & Austin, 1956). Although he was not a mediational theorist and placed his own theorizing in the psychodynamic tradition, Bruner linked his own interest in cognitive processes to the new mediational S–R theories and identified a revived interest in and investigation of the cognitive processes. In the landmark book *A Study of Thinking* (1956), Bruner investigated how people form concepts and categorize new stimuli as members of different conceptual categories. Bruner and his colleagues presented subjects with arrays of geometrical figures defined along many dimensions: shape, size, color, and the like. The subject was then asked to figure out what concept the experimenter had in mind by choosing the selected examples and nonexamples. For example, the concept to be discovered might be "all red triangles," and the experimenter might begin by pointing out to the subject a large, red triangle as an example of the concept. The subject would then choose other stimuli from the array and be told whether each was or was not a member of the concept class. If the subject chose a large, red square, the subject would be told no; and if the subject chose a small, red triangle, he or she would be told yes. The subject would choose instances until he or she was prepared to guess the definition of the experimenter's concept.

Bruner, Goodnow, and Austin did not view the process of concept learning in terms of learning implicit mediational responses, although some informal behaviorists did. Rather, they looked on concept formation as an active, rather than associative, process in which the subject's choices are guided by some strategy constructed to solve the problem. Again, the details of the theory are not important for our purposes. What is important is the mentalistic nature of Bruner's theory. The subject was not seen as a passive connector between S and R or even as linking $S–r–s–R$, nor as a locus of variables. Instead, concept formation was conceived as an active intellectual process in which a subject constructs and follows certain strategies and decision procedures that guide (or fail to guide) the subject to the correct concept.

However, the most important development in reviving interest in the study of cognitive processes was the invention of machines that could, perhaps, think.

THE RISE OF COGNITIVE SCIENCE

Ever since the Scientific Revolution, philosophers and psychologists had been attracted and repelled by the similarity of human and machine. Descartes thought that all human cognitive processes save thinking were carried out by the machinery of the nervous system, and he based his sharp contrast of conscious human being versus mechanical animal on his conviction. Pascal feared that Descartes was wrong, for it seemed to him that his calculator could think, and he turned to the human heart and its faith in God to separate people from machines. Hobbes and La Mettrie embraced the idea that people are no more than animal-machines, alarming the romantics who, with Pascal, sought the secret essence of humanity in feeling rather than intellect. Leibniz dreamed of a universal thinking machine, and the English engineer Charles Babbage tried to build one (Green, 2005). William James worried about his automatic sweetheart, concluding that a machine could not feel and so could not be human. Watson, with Hobbes and La Mettrie, proclaimed that humans and animals are machines and that human salvation lay in accepting that reality and engineering a perfect future, limned by Skinner in *Walden II*. Science fiction writers and filmmakers explored the differences, if any, between human and machine in *Rossum's Universal Robots*, *Metropolis*, and *Blade-Runner*. But until World War II no one had built a machine that anyone could even hope would emulate human thinking.

The status of mind as a category of science—the *psyche* of *psyche-logos*—has always been problematic. Dualists such as Plato and Descartes, not to mention religious believers in immortal souls, seemed to set mind, and thus perhaps its study, outside science altogether. The mechanization of the world picture begun by the Scientific Revolution seemed fated to halt at the boundary between scientifically tractable machine–body on one side and ineffable soul-stuff and consciousness on the other.

The difficulties faced by the psychology of consciousness suggested as much to methodological behaviorists, who simply admitted that mind, consciousness, was not a fit topic for science, and proceeded to study behavior as if mind did not exist. Among their number Tolman thought mental processes, his cognitive maps, did exist and had to be part of psychology, but he never found a good way to ground his mentalistic hunches in scientific language. Physiological behaviorists such as Lashley sought to conquer mind by reducing it to brain processes, but at least in Lashley's time this was a program that did not have the conceptual or methodological resources to proceed. Radical behaviorists dismissed the concept of mind altogether as a bad Cartesian idea no better than the mythical fluids of phlogiston or caloric in prescientific chemistry. For them, the phenomena ordinarily regarded as mental could be more effectively treated as behavior, some of it private, but no less behavior because of that.

Nevertheless, the Way of Ideas fashioned by Descartes, Locke, and other seventeenth- and eighteenth-century philosophers offered a view of the mind that, it turned out, could be reconciled with a thoroughly mechanistic conception not only of the body but also of thought itself. Key to the Way of Ideas were two notions, rules and representations. Descartes, like Plato and the Stoics, looked at thinking as rather like doing mathematical or logical proofs, deducing new propositions from old ones by the application of rules. The concept of the idea, shared by Descartes and his empiricist rivals, and by Kant, added the notion that the rules or laws of thought applied to inner, mental representations of the world. The problem was that thought processes still seemed to be carried out in a nonphysical place, the mind, where the laws of physics did not apply.

In addition, there remained the problem of purpose that divided Tolman and Hull. Hull was fully committed to physicalism—the claim that the only forces acting in the universe were physical cause-precedes-effect ones, and thus denied that there was any such thing as purposive behavior, behavior caused by a goal not yet present to an organism. For him, all behaviors were caused by preceding stimuli. Tolman demurred, believing that at least among living things, purposes were real forces guiding behavior to wanted goals. Again, however, his hunches were hard to ground in the developing mechanistic picture of the universe.

In what follows we will learn that what psychologists and philosophers of mind needed were a few concepts developing outside their fields, in industry, mathematics, logic, and war research: feedback, information, and computation. They would revolutionize the world—the world you live in is not possible without them—and make mind again respectable in psychological science.

Purposive Machines

If the Scientific Revolution rested upon the mechanization of the world picture, the Industrial Revolution rested upon the mechanization of work, using machines in place of animals or people to do sheer physical labor. Machine work can be done more efficiently and cheaply than animal or human labor, freeing people to do less physically demanding but more productive work with their minds than their bodies. However, getting machines to produce energy poses challenges of control. A steam engine can produce enormous amounts of energy, far more than can be produced by animal bodies. Animals can't pull 100 boxcar trains or generate electricity for a city. But how to make the output of a steam engine usably regular and constant is not obvious, and in addition steam boilers can blow-up if overpressurized. In 1788 the entrepreneur and engineer James Watt (1736–1819) solved this problem, making an enormous contribution to the burgeoning Industrial Revolution. He invented the centrifugal, or Watt, governor.

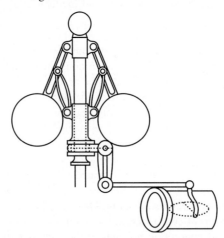

Hames Watt's centrifugal governor for controlling the output of a steam engine.

There is a shaft attached to two heavy balls. The shaft is spun by the steam in the boiler, and the higher the steam pressure, the faster the shaft rotates, and the faster the balls spin. They are mounted on a pivot, so as they spin, centrifugal force pushes them out and up away from the shaft. The position of the spinning balls controls the amount of heat allowed into the fire heating the boiler. Fast spinning balls reduce the temperature of the boiler, avoiding an explosion. As the boiler temperature goes down, the shaft rotates more slowly, the balls spin less, increasing the input of fuel into the boiler, so the temperature rises, raising the steam pressure, increasing the speed of the shaft, which lowers the temperature, in a continuous dynamic cycle that maintains the output of the boiler to a steady usable level (van Gelder, 1995).

What does this important piece of engineering have to do with psychology? Quite a lot. The issue that divided Tolman and Hull was the problem of seeing animals, including people, as machines or as pursuers of goals, as purposive organisms. But Watt's new steam engine was a purposive, goal-directed machine. The (simple) goal of the governor was to maintain safe and steady pressure in the engine's boiler, and it pursued this goal in a flexible fashion, adjusting fuel flow as the temperature in the boiler changed. Hull was right that organisms were machines, but Tolman was right that organisms are purposive. But no one knew that yet because although Watt's engine was a purposive machine, the concept he employed did not yet have a name and had not been generalized to other cases of purposive behavior. The concept was feedback, and it was not formulated until 1943.

Given the later rivalry between information-processing psychology and radical behaviorism, there is irony in the fact that the concept of feedback arose out of the same war problem that Skinner had tackled in his Pigeon project. Project OrCon had aimed at the *or*ganic *con*trol of missiles. He had solved the problem the old-fashioned way, by involving a *homunculus*, a Ghost in the Machine. He literally put a small bird, a pigeon, in the head of his missile, called the Pelican. Another team working on the same problem of guidance dissolved purpose into feedback.

In 1943, three researchers described the concept of informational feedback that lay behind their solution to guiding devices to targets, showing how purpose and mechanism could be reconciled. Rosenblueth, Wiener, and Bigelow (1943/1966) articulated feedback as a general principle applicable to all sorts of purposive systems, mechanical or alive. A good example of a system using feedback is a thermostat and a heat pump. You give the thermostat a goal when you set the temperature at which you want to keep your house. The thermostat contains a thermometer that measures the house's temperature, and when the temperature deviates from the set point, the thermostat turns on the heat pump to cool or heat the house until the set temperature is achieved. Here is a feedback loop of information: The thermostat is sensitive to the state of the room, and based on the information received by its thermometer, it takes action; the action in turn changes the state of the room, which feeds back to the thermostat, changing its behavior, which in turn influences the room temperature, and so on in an endless cycle.

In its modest way, a thermostat is a purposive device, unlike clocks, importantly changing the mechanistic view of nature (Pinker, 2002). Newtonian physics had given rise to the clockwork image of the universe, a machine blindly following the inexorable laws of physics. William James had argued that conscious, living beings could not be machines, so that consciousness had to evolve to make changeable, adaptive behavior possible. Thermostats, however, are nonconscious machines (but see Chalmers, 1996) whose behavior is adaptively responsive to their changing environment. And there is, of course, no Ghost in the Thermostat. In older times, there would have been a servant who read a thermometer and stoked the furnace when necessary, but the servant has been replaced by a mere machine, and a simple one at that. The promise of the concept of feedback was being able to treat all purposive behaviors as instances of feedback. The organism has some goal (e.g., to get food), is able to measure its distance from the goal (e.g., it's at the other end of the maze), and behaves so as to reduce and finally eliminate that distance. The Ghost in the Machine, or Tolman's cognitive map reader, could be replaced by complex feedback loops. Practically, too, machines capable of doing what before only people could do might replace servants and industrial workers.

Implicit in this concept of feedback is an even more tranformative concept, the concept of information. We are so used to the idea of information today that we take it for granted, but the notion took a long time to develop. Let's continue with the example of the thermostat. Your home thermostat probably works on the following physical principle. If you open it up, you'll see a coil of metal. It's really a thin sandwich of two metals that bend differently in response to changes in temperature. As temperature rises, the sandwich bends one way, as temperature falls, it bends the opposite way. The bending of the metal sandwich is set to turn off or on your heat pump. If the temperature goes above your target, say 75 degrees, the metal bends one way until it closes a switch that turns on the air-conditioning. As the air cools, the metal strip unbends, turning the AC off. In modern office buildings (and probably your classrooms) there are no thermostats, but sensors that relay temperature readings to a central computer that regulates airflow in each room. The important point is that the same function is being carried out by two very different physical devices. What controls both devices is information about the room, and we can explain, predict, and control the temperature of our homes and classrooms by using this information without involving ourselves with the physics a particular device instantiates to process the information.

While the devices we've looked at so far, from Watt's governor to the thermostat, show us that machines can use information to embody purpose, they are limited in that each is a single-purpose machine. People, however, are not. An individual human can do many things from playing the guitar to solving problems in calculus. The human mind is a general-purpose device. The last step toward modern cognitive science was the idea of computation, the idea that it's possible to build a machine that can do many things from guiding munitions to a target to regulating the temperature of a room to playing *Call of Duty* to simulating the world economy, and perhaps to simulate the original general-purpose device, the human mind.

REVERSE ENGINEERING THE MIND: ARTIFICIAL INTELLIGENCE So, machines could be purposive. Were they then intelligent, or at least capable of becoming intelligent? Could they emulate human intelligence? Whether computers were or could be intelligent became the central question of cognitive science, and the question was raised in its modern form by the brilliant mathematician A. M. Turing (1912–1954), who had created the concept of general-purpose computers in the 1930s and worked with them in WW II (Dyson, 2012). In 1950, Turing published a paper in *Mind*, "Computing Machinery and Intelligence," which defined the field of artificial intelligence (AI) and established the program of cognitive science. "I propose to consider the question, Can machines think?" Turing began. Because the meaning of *think* was so terribly unclear, Turing proposed to set his question more concretely "in terms of a game which we call the 'imitation game.'" Imagine an interrogator talking via computer terminal to two respondents, another human and a computer, without knowing which is which. The game consists of asking questions designed to tell which respondent is the human and which is the computer. Turing proposed that we consider a computer intelligent when it can fool the interrogator into thinking it is the human being. Turing's imitation game has since become known as the Turing Test, and it is widely (though not universally; see later discussion) taken to be the criterion of AI.

The term *artificial intelligence* was coined a few years later by the computer scientist John McCarthy, who needed a name to put on a grant proposal supporting the first interdisciplinary conference on what became cognitive science. Workers in the field of AI aim to create machines that can perform many of the same tasks previously done only by people, ranging from playing chess to assembling automobiles to exploring the surface of Mars. In "pure AI," the goal is to make computers or robots that can do what men and women do. Closer to psychology is computer simulation, which aims not simply to emulate humans but to imitate them.

A good way to understand the founding thesis of cognitive science is through the engineering concept called reverse engineering. Here's a real-life example. For many years, the Intel corporation had a monopoly on the manufacture of chips for IBM-type personal computers. Then Advanced Micro Devices decided to enter the field. But it could not simply open up and copy the existing Intel chips, because that would violate patent and copyright laws. What it could legally do, however, was to make a chip of its own that had the same input-output functions as Intel chips. So AMD could buy Intel chips, apply voltages to the chips' inputs, measure the resulting outputs, and then build chips that behaved the same way. The AI approach to intelligence is similar. Psychologists can bring people into their labs, manipulate the stimuli (inputs) to which their subjects are exposed, and measure the resulting behavior (output). Then, psychologists and AI researchers can attempt to construct computational theories about how the given stimuli bring about the resulting behavior, describing the mental processes of information processing.

This goal of reverse engineering can be pursued in two ways. In pure AI, the researcher aims to construct a system that behaves intelligently, without regard to whether or not its information processes are the same as those taking place in the human mind. Modern chess-playing programs are examples of pure AI. They play excellent chess, but the information processes they use are quite unlike those used by human grandmasters. These "brute force" programs exploit computers' ability to compute moves far faster than any humans, who have to rely on a intuitions about good and bad moves honed by playing thousands of games. It may seem that the brute force approach to intelligence has little to do with psychology, but it has been enormously useful. People think chess is hard, but we now have computers that can defeat any human. On the other hand, we think that seeing and moving around in our environment is easy—even mice can do it!—but we don't yet have robot valets. In general, AI failures to emulate human intelligence have established that what we intuitively find hard is easy to compute, but what we think is easy is hard to compute.

The other, more psychological, way to reverse engineer the mind is computer simulation. It has a much stricter requirement: Not only do we aim to build computer programs or devices that act like people (pure AI has this goal), but to carry out the same mental information processes that humans use. Pure AI aims to imitate human behavior; computer simulation aims to imitate the human mind.

The Triumph of Information Processing

DISENTANGLING MIND AND BODY, PROGRAM AND COMPUTER We have already seen that some psychologists, most notably Hull, had tried to construct learning machines, and unsurprisingly, psychologists were drawn to the computer for a model of learning and purposive behavior. In conversation with Harvard psychologist E. G. Boring, Norbert Wiener asked what the human brain could do that electronic computers could not, moving Boring (1946) to ask the same question as had Turing: What would a robot have to do to be called intelligent? After reviewing human intellectual faculties and psychologists' early attempts to mimic them with machines, Boring formulated his own version of the Turing Test: "Certainly a robot whom you could not distinguish from another student would be an extremely convincing demonstration of the mechanical nature of man and the unity of science" (p. 192). For Boring, a thinking robot could carry much metaphysical baggage because it would vindicate La Mettrie's declaration that man is a machine and promised to secure psychology a place among the natural sciences. Boring's hopes have become the expectations of contemporary cognitive scientists.

In the early 1950s, various attempts were made to create electronic or other mechanical models of learning and other cognitive processes. The English psychologist J. A. Deutsch (1953) built an "electromechanical model . . . capable of learning mazes and discrimination . . . [and insightful] reasoning." Similar models were discussed by L. Benjamin Wyckoff (1954) and James Miller (1955). Charles W. Slack (1955) used the similarities between feedback and Dewey's reflex are to attack Hullian S–R theory. Another English psychologist, Donald Broadbent (1958), proposed a mechanical model of attention and short-term memory in terms of balls being dropped into a Y-shaped tube representing various sensory "channels" of information.

In an important departure from behaviorism, Broadbent argued that psychologists should think of the input to the senses not as physical stimuli but as *information*. From the time of Descartes, the mystery of the mind lay in its nonphysical character, creating the insoluble problem of interaction: How can nonphysical mind causally interact with physical body? Psychologists such as Hull and Lashley thought that the only respectable scientific psychology was one that looked at organisms as machines in the traditional sense: as devices moved by direct physical contact between their working parts. The concept of information allowed psychologists to respect the nonphysical nature of thought without the difficulties of Cartesian dualism (Pinker, 2002). Information is real, but it is not a physical thing. What counts in reading these words is not the physical stimuli involved—black marks on white paper differentially reflecting photons to your retina—but the ideas, the nonphysical information, they convey. Similarly, the physical workings of a computer are controlled by the information contained in its running program, but the program is not a substantial soul. Thinking of the mind as information allowed psychologists to have a form of mind-body dualism that escaped the confines of physicalistic behaviorism.

Information-processing concepts were rapidly applied to human cognitive psychology. A landmark paper was George Miller's "The Magical Number Seven, Plus or Minus Two: Some Limits on Our Capacity for Processing Information" (1956). Miller was moving away from an eclectic behaviorist position on human learning and would emerge as one of the leaders of cognitive psychology in the 1960s. In the 1956 paper, he drew attention to limitations on human attention and memory and set the stage for the first massive wave of research in information-processing psychology, which concentrated on attention and short-term memory.

In all of these early papers attempting to apply computer concepts to psychology, there was some confusion about what was actually doing the thinking, because the separation of information from mechanical embodiment took some time to be worked out. Encouraged by the popular phrase for the computer, *electronic brain*, there was a strong tendency to think that it was the electronic device itself that was thinking, and that psychologists should look for parallels between the structure of the human brain and the structure of electronic computers. For example, James Miller (1955) envisioned a "comparative psychology . . . dealing not with animals but with electronic models," because the actions of computers are "in many interesting ways like living behavior." However, the identification of neural and electronic circuitry was much too simple. As Turing said in his 1950 paper, computers are general-purpose machines (the theoretically ideal general-purpose computer is called a *Turing machine*). The actual electronic architecture of a computer is unimportant because what makes a computer behave as it does is its *program*, and the same program can be run on physically different machines and different programs run on the same machine. Turing pointed out that a man in a room with an infinite supply of paper and a rulebook for transforming input symbols into output symbols could be regarded as a computer. In such circumstances, his behavior would be controlled only trivially by his neurology because the rulebook would dictate his answers to questions, and if one changed the rulebook, his behavior would change. The distinction of computer and program was crucial to cognitive psychology, for it meant that cognitive psychology was not neurology and that cognitive theories of human thinking should talk about the human mind—that is, the human program—rather than the human brain. A correct cognitive theory would be implemented by the human brain and could be run on a properly programmed computer, but the theory would be in the program, not in the brain or the computer.

What began to emerge in the 1950s was a new conception of the human being as machine and a new language in which to formulate theories about cognitive processes. People could be described, it seemed, as general-purpose computing devices, born with certain hardware and programmed by experience and socialization to behave in certain ways. The goal of psychology would be the specification of how human beings process information; the concepts of stimulus and response would be replaced by the concepts of information input and output, and theories about mediating r–s chains would be replaced by theories about internal computations and computational states. Based on the idea that the human mind was like a computer program and that the human brain was like a computer, in 1956 a conference on the new field of "artificial intelligence" was held at Dartmouth College. Its organizers proclaimed:

> Every aspect of learning or any other feature of intelligence can in principle be so precisely defined that a machine can be made to simulate it. (quoted by Crevier, 1993, p. 26)

The only attendees at the conference who had built a working AI program were Herbert Simon and Allen Newell, who were trying to theorize about human problem solving by imitating it.

SIMULATING THOUGHT　The new conception of psychology was clearly stated by Allan Newell, J. C. Shaw, and Herbert Simon in 1958 in "Elements of a Theory of Problem Solving." Since the early 1950s, they had been at work writing programs that would solve problems, beginning with a program that proved mathematical theorems, the Logic Theorist, and moving onto a more powerful program, the General Problem Solver (GPS). They had previously published their work primarily in computer engineering journals, but writing now in *Psychological Review*, they defined the new cognitive approach to psychology:

> The heart of [our] approach is describing the behavior of the system by a well-specified program, defined in terms of elementary information processes. . . . Once the program has been specified, we proceed exactly as we do with traditional mathematical systems. We attempt to deduce general properties of the system from the program (the equations); we compare the behavior predicted from the program (from the equations) with actual behavior observed . . . [and] we modify the program when modification is required to fit the facts. (pp. 165–66)

Newell, Shaw, and Simon declared special virtues for their approach to psychological theorizing. Computers are "capable of realizing programs," making possible very precise predictions about behavior. Additionally, to actually run on a computer, programs must provide "a very concrete specification of [internal] processes," ensuring that theories be precise, never vague and merely verbal. The Logic Theorist and the GPS represent, Newell, Shaw, and Simon conclude, "a thoroughly operational theory of human problem solving."

Newell, Shaw, and Simon made stronger claims for their problem-solving programs than Turing made for his hypothetical AI program. Researchers in AI wanted to write programs that would behave like people without necessarily thinking like people. So, for example, they wrote chess-playing programs that play chess but use the brute force, number-crunching ability of supercomputers to evaluate thousands of moves before choosing one, rather than trying to imitate the human chess master who evaluates many fewer alternatives, but does so more cleverly. Newell, Shaw, and Simon, however, moved from AI to *computer simulation* in claiming that not only did their programs solve problems, but they also solved problems in the same way human beings did. In a computer simulation of chess, the programmer would try to write a program whose computational steps are the same as those of a human master chess player. The distinction between AI and computer simulation is important because pure AI is not psychology. Efforts in AI may be psychologically instructive for suggesting the kinds of cognitive resources humans must possess to achieve intelligence (Leahey & Harris, 2004), but specifying how people actually behave intelligently requires actual simulation of human thought, not just behavior.

MAN THE MACHINE: IMPACT OF THE INFORMATION-PROCESSING METAPHOR   Despite the bold claims of Newell, Shaw, and Simon, GPS exerted little immediate influence on the psychology of problem solving. In 1963, Donald W. Taylor reviewed the research area of thinking and concluded that although computer simulation of thinking shows "the most promise" of any theory, "this promise, however, remains to be justified." Three years later, Davis (1966) surveyed the field of human problem solving and concluded, "There is a striking unanimity in recent theoretical orientations to human thinking and problem solving . . . that associational behavioral laws established in comparatively simple classical conditioning and instrumental conditioning situations apply to complex human learning"; Davis relegated GPS to one of three other minor theories of problem solving. Ulric Neisser, in his influential text *Cognitive Psychology* (1967), dismissed computer models of thinking as "simplistic" and not "satisfactory from the psychological point of view." On the tenth anniversary of his prediction, Simon and his colleagues quietly abandoned GPS (Dreyfus, 1972).

Yet it was acknowledged by everyone, including its opponents, that cognitive psychology was booming during the 1960s. In 1960, Donald Hebb, one of psychology's recognized leaders, called for the "Second American Revolution" (the first was behaviorism): "The serious analytical study of the thought processes cannot be postponed any longer." In 1964, Robert R. Holt said that "cognitive psychology has enjoyed a remarkable boom." The boom extended even to clinical psychology, as Louis Breger and James McGaugh (1965) argued for replacing behavioristic psychotherapy with therapy based on information-processing concepts. By 1967, Neisser could write that "a generation ago a book like this one would have needed at least a chapter of self-defense against the behaviorist position. Today, happily, the climate of opinion has changed and little or no defense is necessary," because psychologists had come to accept "the familiar parallel between man and computer." It was easy to think of people as information-processing devices that receive input from the environment (perception), process that information (thinking), and act on decisions reached (behavior). The general image of human beings as information processors was immensely exciting. So, although Simon was premature in predicting that psychological theories would be written as computer programs, the broader vision of AI and computer simulation had triumphed by 1967.

The acceptance of the information-processing perspective on cognitive psychology was aided by the existence of the large community of psychologists who fell into the mediational tradition of psychology, whether neo-Hullian or neo-Tolmanian. These psychologists already accepted the idea of processes intervening between stimulus and response, and throughout the 1950s they had "invented hypothetical mechanisms," mostly in the form of mediating r–s links holding together observable S–R connections. During the 1950s, neobehaviorist human psychology flourished (Cofer, 1978). Ebbinghaus's study of memory had been revived in the field called *verbal learning*, and, independently of computer science, verbal learning psychologists had begun by 1958 to distinguish between short-term and long-term memory. The field of psycholinguistics—an interdisciplinary combination of linguistics and psychology—had begun in the early 1950s under the auspices of the Social Science Research Council. Since the end of World War II, the Office of Naval Research had funded conferences on verbal learning, memory, and verbal behavior. A Group for the Study of Verbal Behavior was organized in 1957. It began, like Maslow's group of humanistic psychologists, as a mailing list; it became, again like the humanist group, a journal, the *Journal of Verbal Learning and Verbal Behavior*, in 1962.

These groups of early cognitive psychologists were interconnected, and they, involved with verbal behavior and thinking, took the mediational version of S–R theory for granted. For example, in psycholinguistics, the "grammars [of the pre-Chomsky linguists] and mediation theory were seen to be variations of the same line of thought" (Jenkins, 1968). While as late as 1963 Jenkins (Gough & Jenkins, 1963) could discuss "Verbal Learning and Psycholinguistics" in purely mediational terms, it was clear by 1968 that Chomsky had "dynamited the structure [of mediations psycholinguistics] at the linguistic end" (Jenkins, 1968). Chomsky convinced these psychologists that their *S–R* theories, even including mediation, were inadequate to explain human language. So they looked for a new language in which to theorize about mental processes and were naturally drawn to the language of the computer: information processing. The *S* of the *S–r–s–R* formula could become "input," the *R* could become "output," and the *r–s* could become "processing." Moreover, information-processing language could be used, even without writing computer programs, as a "global framework within which precisely stated models could be constructed for many different . . . phenomena and could be tested in quantitative fashion" (Shiffrin, 1977, p. 2). Shiffrin is describing the landmark paper of the information-processing, non-computer-programming tradition, "Human Memory: A Proposed System and Its Control Processes" (Atkinson & Shiffrin, 1968), from which virtually all later accounts of information processing descend.

Information-processing language gave mediational psychologists exactly what they needed. It was rigorous, up to date, and at least as quantitative as Hull's old theory, without having to make the implausible assumption that the processes linking stimulus and response were just the same as single-stage learning processes in animals. Psychologists could now talk about "coding," "search sets," "retrieval," "pattern recognition," and other information structures and operations with every expectation that they were constructing scientific theories. Information-processing psychology met psychologists' physics envy better than Hull's had, for information-processing psychologists could always point to computers as the working embodiment of their theories. The theories might not be computer programs, but they were *like* computer programs in regarding thinking as the formal processing of stored information. Thus, although information-processing theories were independent of computational theories in AI, they were conceptually parasitic on them, and cognitive psychologists hoped that at some future point their theories would be programs.

As Ulric Neisser (1984) said, "Models that actually run on real computers are more convincing than models that exist only as hypotheses on paper." The inspiring thing to psychologists about AI was that, as George Miller (1983) wrote, when behaviorists said that talk of mind was "moonshine," cognitive psychologists could point to AI: whose goal was building minds that actually worked. Simon's short-term prophecy failed, but his dream remained.

BEHAVIORISM DEFEATED OR MARGINALIZED During the 1960s and early 1970s, information-processing theory gradually replaced mediational theory as the language of cognitive psychology. By 1974, the venerable *Journal of Experimental Psychology* contained articles by proponents of only two theoretical orientations: information processing and radical behaviorism, the former substantially outnumbering the latter. In 1975, the journal was divided into four separate journals: two concerned with human experimental psychology, one with animal psychology, and one with long, theoretical-experimental papers; and the human journals were controlled by the information-processing point of view. During the same years, information-processing psychologists launched their own journals, including *Cognitive Psychology* (1970) and *Cognition* (1972); and the new cognitive view spread to other areas of psychology, including social psychology (Mischel & Mischel, 1976), social learning theory (Bandura, 1974), developmental psychology (Farnham-Diggory, 1972), animal psychology (Hulse, Fowler, & Honig, 1978), psychoanalysis (Wegman, 1984), and psychotherapy (Mahoney, 1977; Meichenbaum, 1977; founding of the *Journal Cognitive Therapy and Research* [1977]), and even philosophy of science (Rubinstein, 1984). Mediational behaviorism ceased to exist and the radical behaviorists were confined to a sort of "publications ghetto" comprised of three journals: *Journal of the Experimental Analysis of Behavior, Journal of Applied Behavior Analysis,* and *Behaviorism.*

In 1979, Lachman, Lachman, and Butterfield attempted in their often-cited *Cognitive Psychology and Information Processing* to describe information-processing cognitive psychology as a Kuhnian paradigm. They claimed, "Our [cognitive] revolution is now complete and the atmosphere is one of normal science" (p. 525). They defined cognitive psychology in terms of the computer metaphor: Cognitive psychology is about "how people take in information, how they recode and remember it, how they make decisions, how they transform their internal knowledge states, and how they translate these states into behavioral outputs."

Similarly, Herbert Simon (1980) declared that a revolution had occurred. Writing about the behavioral and social sciences for the centenary issue of *Science*, Simon declared, "Over the past quarter-century, no development in the social sciences has been more radical than the revolution—often referred to as the information-processing revolution—in our way of understanding the processes of human thinking." Simon dismissed behaviorism as "confining" and "preoccupied with laboratory rats" and praised information-processing theory for helping psychology achieve "a new sophistication" and for creating a "general paradigm, the information-processing paradigm," which preserved behaviorism's "operationality" while surpassing it "in precision and rigor."

The Myth of the Cognitive Revolution

The words of Lachman, Lachman, and Butterfield and of Simon suggest that, like the citizens of the United States, France, and the former Soviet Union, cognitive scientists share a myth of revolutionary origin. Proponents of information processing believe that it constitutes a Kuhnian paradigm, that behaviorism constituted another, and that in the 1960s a Kuhnian scientific revolution occurred during which information processing overthrew behaviorism. However, information-processing cognitive psychology is best viewed as the latest form of behavioralism, with strong affinities to historical forms of behaviorism. It was certainly not a return to the introspective mentalism of the founding psychology of consciousness.

Despite the fact that he wrote about "Imagery: The Return of the Ostracized," Robert R. Holt (1964) unwittingly linked the new cognitive psychology to its behavioralist forebears. He acknowledged that the concept of mediation had already brought cognitive concepts into behaviorism, and he set out the goal of cognitive psychology in terms Hull could have endorsed: constructing "a detailed working model of the behaving organism." Indeed, for Holt, an attractive feature of information-processing models was precisely that with them, one could "construct models of the psychic apparatus in which there can be processing of information without consciousness." Marvin Minsky (1968), the leader of AI at MIT, was eager to show that AI could find "mechanistic interpretations of those mentalistic notions that have real value," thereby dismissing mentalism as prescientific.

Herbert Simon, one of the founders of modern information-processing psychology, betrayed the continuity of information processing with behavioralism, and even its affinity with behaviorism, very well in his *Sciences of the Artificial* (1969, p. 25), writing: "A man, viewed as a behaving system, is quite simple. The apparent complexity of his behavior over time is largely a reflection of the complexity of the environment in which he finds himself." Simon, like Skinner, viewed human beings as largely the products of the environment that shapes them because they themselves are simple. In the same work, Simon followed Watson in dismissing the validity of mental images, reducing them to lists of facts and sensory properties associatively organized. Simon also argued that complex behaviors are assemblages of simpler behaviors.

Information-processing cognitive psychology is substantially different only from radical behaviorism because information-processing psychologists reject peripheralism. They believe complex processes intervene between stimulus (input) and response (output). Unlike Watson and Skinner, information-processing cognitive psychologists are willing to infer central mental processes from observable behavior. However, although peripheralism was part of Watson's and Skinner's behaviorisms, it was not shared by Hull, Tolman, or informal behaviorism. The information-processing adherents do not believe central processes are covert versions of S–R associations, but their theory is not far removed from Hull's or Tolman's except in complexity and sophistication.

Information-processing psychology is a form of behavioralism. It represents a continuing conceptual evolution in the psychology of adaptation, for it views cognitive processes as adaptive behavioral functions and is in a sense a reassertion of earlier American functionalism. The functionalists saw the mind as adaptive but were trapped by the limited metaphysics of the nineteenth century into espousing at the same time mind-body parallelism and the adaptive function of the mind, engendering a conflict exploited by Watson in establishing behaviorism. The cybernetic analysis of purpose, and its mechanical realization in the computer, however, vindicated the old functionalist attitude by showing that purpose and cognition were not necessarily mysterious and need not involve substantial dualism.

Watson's and Skinner's behaviorisms were extreme statements of the psychology of adaptation that attempted to circumnavigate the inaccessible—and therefore potentially mythical—reaches of the human mind. The information-processing view follows in the steps of William James, Hull, and Tolman in seeing, beneath behavior, processes to be investigated and explained. Behaviorism was one response by the psychology of adaptation to crisis; information processing was another; but in both we see a deeper continuity under the superficial changes. Perhaps to those involved, the revolt against S–R psychology was a scientific revolution, but viewed against the broader framework of history, the revolt is a period of rapid evolutionary change, not a revolutionary jump.

Cognitive scientists believe in a revolution because it provides them with an origin myth, an account of their beginnings that helps legitimize their practice of science (Brush, 1974). Kuhn provided the language of paradigm and revolution, Chomsky provided the angry voice crying for change, and the sound and fury of the alienated 1960s provided an exciting backdrop for the shift from mediational behaviorism to information processing. But there was no revolution. Behavioralism continued with a new language, a new model, and new concerns directed to its familiar end: the description, prediction, and control of behavior (Leahey, 1981, 1992).

Myths of revolution usually turn out on close examination to be misleadingly simple. The revolution of the 13 colonies against England was mainly an assertion of traditional English liberties, not a revolution at all. The French Revolution began in the name of Reason, drowned in blood, and unleashed Napoleon on Europe. The Russian Revolution traded Oriental despotism for totalitarian tyranny. The cognitive revolution was an illusion.

THE NATURE OF COGNITIVE SCIENCE

Informavores: The Subjects of Cognitive Science

The fields of AI and computer simulation psychology began to merge in the late 1970s into a new field distinct from psychology, called *cognitive science*. Cognitive scientists launched their own journal, *Cognitive Science*, in 1977 and held their first international conference a year later (Simon, 1980). Cognitive science defined itself as the science of what George Miller named *informavores* (Pylyshyn, 1984). The idea was that information-processing systems—whether made of flesh and blood, like human beings, or silicon and metal, like computers, or of whatever materials might be invented or discovered—operated according to the same principles and therefore constituted a single field of study, cognitive science, converging around the information-processing paradigm (Simon, 1980).

As defined by Simon (1980), the "long-run strategy" of human cognitive science had two goals, each of which is reductionistic in its own way. First, "human complex performance"—the old "higher mental processes"—would be connected with "the basic elementary information processes and their organization." In other words, cognitive science, like behaviorism, aimed to show that complex behavior could be reduced to assemblages of simpler behaviors. Second, "we cannot be satisfied with our explanations of human thinking until we can specify the neural substrates for the elementary information processes of the human symbol system." In other words, like the physiological behaviorism of Karl Lashley, cognitive science aimed to show that human thinking could be reduced to neurophysiology.

The convergence of AI and cognitive psychology into the field of cognitive science, and the grandiose claims of cognitive scientists, already stated by Simon, one of the first cognitive psychologists, were repeated by the Research Briefing Panel on Cognitive Science and Artificial Intelligence (Estes & Newell, 1983). According to the panel, cognitive science addresses a "great scientific mystery, on a par with understanding the evolution of the universe, the origin of life, or the nature of elementary particles" and is "advancing our understanding of the nature of mind and the nature of intelligence on a scale that is proving revolutionary."

An important part of the optimism of cognitive scientists, and the conceptual basis of the merger of cognitive psychology and AI, was the computer metaphor of mind:body:: program:computer, known as *functionalism*. For it is functionalism that allows cognitive scientists to regard people and computers as essentially similar, despite their material differences.

The Minds of Informavores: The New Functionalism

The basic thesis of functionalism derives from the activity of computer programming. Suppose I write a simple program for balancing my checkbook in a programming language such as BASIC. The program will specify a set of *computational functions*: retrieving my old balance from memory, subtracting checks written, adding deposits made, and comparing my results to the bank's. Ignoring minor formatting differences, I can enter and run this program on many different machines: an Apple, an IBM PC, a PC clone, a Sun workstation, or a mainframe computer. In each case, the same computational functions will be carried out, although the physical processes by which each computer will perform them will be different because the internal structure of each machine is different.

To be able to predict, control, and explain the behavior of a computer, it is unnecessary to know anything at all about the electronic processes involved; all one needs to understand is the higher-level computational functions in the system. I am composing these words on a program called MS Word (though I first wrote them with an old word processor called AmiPro), and because I understand the programmed functions of Word, I can use it effectively—that is, I can predict, control, and explain my computer's behavior. I know absolutely nothing about the lower-level computational functions that compose higher-level functions, such as moving paragraphs about, nor do I know much about how my PC's hardware works; but such knowledge is not necessary to use any properly programmed computer.

Functionalism simply extends the separation of program and computer to include human beings. Computers use hardware to carry out computational functions, so functionalism concludes that people use "wetware" to do the same things. When I balance my checkbook by hand, I carry out exactly the same functions as the BASIC program does. My nervous system and my PC's microchip are materially different, but both instantiate the same program in balancing my accounts. So, functionalism concludes, my mind is a set of computational functions that runs my body in exactly the same way that a computer program is a set of computational functions that controls a computer: My mind is a running program (Pinker, 2002). In this way, psychologists can hope to predict, control, and explain human behavior by understanding the human "program" and without understanding the nervous system and brain. Cognitive psychologists are thus like computer programmers asked to study an alien computer. They dare not fool with the machine's wiring, so they attempt to understand its program by experimenting with its input-output functions.

The attraction of functionalism and information processing is that they offer a solution to the behaviorist's problem: how to explain the intentionality of behavior without any residue of teleology. Within behavioralism, there were two basic approaches. Pure mechanists such as Hull tried to describe humans and animals as machines that blindly responded to whatever stimuli they happened to encounter. Tolman, after abandoning his early realism, opted for a representational strategy: Organisms build up representations of their world that they use to guide overt behavior. Each strategy was flawed and finally failed. Tolman was able to show, contrary to Hull, that animals do not simply respond to their environment; rather, they learn about it and base their behavior on more than just the currently operative stimuli, using representations stored away from earlier experience as well. Tolman's approach, however, ran into the homunculus problem: He implicitly postulated a little rat in the head of a real rat, who read the cognitive map and pulled the levers of behavior. In short, he created a Ghost in the Machine, failing to explain purpose and pushing the problem onto the mysterious Ghost. The mediational neo-Hullians tried to combine Hull's mechanistic S–R theory with Tolman's intuitively plausible representationalism by regarding mediating r–s mechanisms as representations, an interpretation countenanced by Hull's concept of the "pure stimulus act." But the mediational compromise rested on the counterintuitive notion that the brain's r–s connections follow exactly the same laws as overt S–R connections.

Functionalism preserves the virtues of Hull's and Tolman's approaches while avoiding their vices by invoking the sophisticated processes of computer programs instead of little r–s links. Computers carry out their computational functions on internal representations; in the checkbook example, the program directs the computer to manipulate representations of my previous balance, my checks, my deposits, and so on. Yet, my PC contains no little accountant bent over ledger books doing arithmetic; there is no ghostly accountant in the machine. Rather, the machine applies precisely stated formal rules to the representations, carrying out the computations in a completely mechanistic fashion. From the perspective of functionalism, both Hull and Tolman were right, but it remained for the computational approach to put their insights together. Hull was right that organisms are machines; Tolman was right that organisms build up representations from experience. According to functionalism, computer programs apply Hullian mechanistic rules to Tolmanian representations and, if functionalism is correct, so do living organisms.

COGNITIVE SCIENCE AT MATURITY: DEBATES AND DEVELOPMENTS

Uncertainties

In the 1980s, cognitive science experienced a sort of midlife crisis. Some psychologists who launched the movement became unhappy with what it had become. A few key problems resisted solution and became the subject of sometimes acrimonious debate, and a rival to the traditional system approach to cognition appeared that, for a time, threatened to slay it. These problems did not prove fatal to the enterprise of cognitive science, but they did change it.

Part of the difficulty was that the promise of AI was initially oversold. Herbert Simon was one of the chief pitchmen for the field he created. In 1956, he prophesied that by 1967, psychological theories would be written as computer programs; he also foresaw that "within ten years a digital computer will be the world's chess champion" and that "within ten years a digital computer will discover and prove an important new mathematical theorem." In 1965, he predicted that "machines will be capable, within 20 years, of doing any work that a man can do" (quoted by Dreyfus, 1972). By 2000, none of Simon's forecasts had come to pass, although the computer program Deep Blue did defeat the reigning human chess champion, Gary Kasparov, in an exhibition match in 1996. In 2003, Kasparov fought a descendant of Deep Blue, Deep Junior, to a tie.

There were signs of unhappiness within psychology. In 1981, James J. Jenkins, who had experienced the transition from mediational behaviorism to information processing, asserted that "there is a malaise in cognitive psychology, a concern with trivia, a lack of direction." He asked, and seemed to answer in the negative, "Is the field advancing as we feel sciences are supposed to advance? . . . Is the field developing and deepening our understanding of cognitive principles, processes, or facts that can contribute to the solution of real problems and generate answers to relevant questions?" Although Jenkins did not doubt that "human beings are universal machines" and was able to find "some [better] directions for cognitive psychology," he pictured a field adrift. In the same year, the editors of *Cognition*, then celebrating its tenth birthday, fretted that "in cognitive psychology, progress is [not] obvious," that since 1971 there had been in the field no "major development," that "little has really changed" (Mehler & Franck, 1981).

Even more dissatisfied with the state of cognitive psychology was Ulric Neisser, the man who had helped establish it and the information-processing approach in his *Cognitive Psychology* of 1967. In 1976, he wrote a new text, *Cognition and Reality*, which "destroyed my reputation as a mainstream cognitive psychologist" (quoted by Goleman, 1983). In the new book, Neisser said, "The actual development of cognitive psychology in the last few years has been disappointingly narrow," wondered "whether its overall direction is genuinely productive," and said he had come to "realize that the notion of *information processing* deserves a closer examination." Neisser began to argue that cognitive psychology should "take a more 'realistic' turn."

Debates

THE CHALLENGES OF INTENTIONALITY   As Lachman, Lachman, and Butterfield (1979) stated, "Information processing psychology is fundamentally committed to the concept of representation." Brentano recognized that intentionality is the criterion of mentality. Mental states such as beliefs possess "aboutness": They refer to something beyond themselves, which neurons cannot do. Tolmanian representations possess intentionality: A cognitive map is about, is a representation of, a maze.

However, although the concept of representation seems straightforward enough, it is fraught with difficulty, as Wittgenstein pointed out. Suppose I draw a stick figure:

What does it represent? At first glance, you might take it to be a man walking with a walking stick. But I might be using it to represent a fencer standing at rest, or to show how one ought to walk with a walking stick, or a man walking backward with a stick, or a woman walking with a stick, or many other things. Another example: No matter how much you might look like a portrait of Henry VIII, it remains a representation of Henry, not of you. Of course, I might use it to represent you if someone asks what you look like and you are not around. So representations don't represent by virtue of their appearance. Exactly what does make a representation a representation is a matter of debate, but functionalism has a distinctive strategy for handling the problem.

Any representation has both semantics and syntax. The semantics of a representation is its meaning; its syntax is its form. If I write the word DESK, its meaning (semantics) lies in its reference to a certain item of furniture, and its syntax is the actual structure and arrangement of the letters D, E, S, and K. From a scientific, materialistic standpoint, the mysterious thing about representations is their meaning, their intentionality; that was the original point of Brentano's concept of intentionality, showing that meaning could not be reduced to physical processes. But, as previously remarked, the goal of functionalism is to demystify intentionality, bringing behavior and mental processes within the scope of mechanistic science. It tries to do this by reducing semantics to syntax.

When I typed DESK a moment ago, did the computer understand its meaning? No; it treated those letters purely syntactically, storing them as a set of 0s and 1s in its binary machine language. However, I can ask Word to do what appear to be intelligent things, couchable in mentalistic language, with the word DESK. I can ask it to find every occurrence of DESK in a given file, and it will find both occurrences of DESK and of "desk." I can ask it to substitute CHAIR for every occurrence of DESK. Word can check the spelling of DESK and consult a thesaurus to provide words of similar meaning. Yet, although the computer can do all these things with the word DESK, it cannot be said to possess the semantic component of DESK. For in every case, the computer operates by looking for the unique machine code of 0s and 1s into which it encoded DESK and then carries out my specified operation on that register. The computer operates only on the syntax of a representation, although its behavior may be consistent with its knowing the meaning of the representation. Although from its behavior it may seem to know the semantic meaning of DESK, all it really knows is the syntax of 0s and 1s.

Another way of expressing this difficult but important point is to borrow some terminology from Daniel Dennett (1978), one of the creators of functionalism. When we play chess with a computer, we are likely to treat it as a human being, attributing to it mental dispositions: It *tries* to develop its queen early, it *wants* to capture my queen's pawn, it's *afraid* I will seize control of the center of the board. Dennett calls this adopting the *intentional stance*. We naturally adopt the intentional stance toward people, sometimes toward animals, and toward machines in certain cases. But what is going on inside the computer is not intentional at all. The layout of the pieces on the chessboard is represented internally as a complex pattern of 0s and 1s in the computer's working memory. Then the computer finds a rule that applies to the current pattern and executes the rule, changing the content of a memory register, which is displayed on a video screen as the move of a chess piece. A new input—your chess move—alters the pattern of 0s and 1s, and the computer again applies the applicable rule to the new pattern, and so on. The program does not *try*, *want*, or *fear*; it simply carries out formal computations on patterns of 0s and 1s, and you regard that as intentional behavior.

In an interview with Jonathan Miller, Dennett (1983) summarized the computational approach to intentionality this way (the dialogue is somewhat compressed):

The basic idea is that you start at the top with your whole intelligent being, with all its beliefs and desires and expectations and fears—all its information. Then you say: "How is all that going to be represented in there?" You break the whole system down into subsystems, little homunculi. Each one is a specialist, each one does a little bit of the work. Out of their cooperative endeavors emerge the whole activities of the whole system. [Miller] But isn't this another way of being unscientifically mentalistic? Yes, you do replace the little man in the brain with a committee, but the saving grace is that the members of the committee are stupider than the whole. The subsystems don't individually reproduce the talents of the whole. That would lead you to an infinite regress. Instead you have each subsystem doing a part; each is less intelligent, knows less, believes less. The representations are themselves less representational, so you don't need an inner eye to observe them; you can get away with some sort of inner process which "accesses" them in some attenuated sense (pp. 77–78).

So, although we attribute intentionality to the chess-playing computer, in fact it is only a collection of nonintentional, stupid subsystems carrying out blind computations on syntactically defined representations, following mechanistic rules.

When we take the intentional stance toward a computer, we are using an instrumental theory. We know that the game-playing computer does not really have wants and beliefs, but we treat it as if it does because doing so helps us anticipate its moves and (we hope) defeat it. Are we doing the same thing when we take the intentional stance toward people, or do people really possess wants and beliefs? If the latter is true, then intentional, folk psychology theory is a realist theory about people even if it is only instrumentally useful when applied to computers. The philosopher John Searle (1994, 1997) adopts this viewpoint and thinks that, therefore, computers will never really pass the Turing Test and that folk psychology, because it is true, will never be abandoned. Other philosophers, however, take the computational metaphor more seriously and reach a different conclusion. Stephen Stich (1983), for example, forcefully argued that the only scientifically acceptable theories in human cognitive psychology will be those that treat human information processing just like a computer's, as mechanical computation on syntactically defined representations. Therefore, folk psychology, because it is untrue, will eventually be abandoned in science and everyday life:

> The general conception of the cosmos embedded in the folk wisdom of the West was utterly and thoroughly mistaken. . . . Nor is there any reason to think that ancient camel drivers would have greater insight or better luck when the structure at hand was the structure of their own minds rather than the structure of matter or of the cosmos (pp. 229–230).

> If our science is inconsistent with the folk precepts that define who and what we are, then we are in for rough times. One or the other will have to go (p. 10). Deprived of its empirical underpinnings, our age old conception of the universe within will crumble just as certainly as the venerable conception of the external universe crumbled during the Renaissance (p. 246).

> Dennett himself (1978, 1991) tried to straddle these two views, acknowledging that in science we must ultimately treat people as machines, but that the "folk psychology" of belief and desire may be retained as an instrumental calculus for everyday use.

IS THE TURING TEST VALID?   Imagine that you are seated at a table in an empty room. On the table before you are a book and a supply of paper, and in the wall in front of the table are two slots. Out of the left-hand slot come pieces of paper on which are written Chinese characters. You know nothing about Chinese. When you receive a slip of paper, you examine the string of symbols on it and find the corresponding string in the book. The book tells you to copy out a new set of Chinese figures on one of your pieces of paper and pass them out the right-hand slot. You can do this for any string of characters that comes in the left slot. Unknown to you, Chinese psychologists on the other side of the wall are feeding into the left slot Chinese stories followed by questions about the stories, and they receive answers out of the other slot. From the psychologists' point of view, the machine beyond the wall understands Chinese because they are able to carry on a conversation with the machine, receiving plausible answers to their questions. They conclude that the machine beyond the wall understands Chinese and has passed the Turing Test.

Of course, you know that you understand nothing—you are just writing down one set of meaningless squiggles by instructed response to another set of meaningless squiggles. John Searle (1980), who proposed this thought experiment, points out that you are functioning in the "Chinese

Room" exactly as a computer functions. The computer accepts machine code input (patterns of 0s and 1s), applies syntactic rules to transform these representations into new representations (new patterns of 0s and 1s), and generates output. It is the computer user alone who calls what the computer is doing "understanding stories," "playing chess," "simulating an atomic strike," or whatever, just as it is the Chinese psychologists who say that the room "understands Chinese." Searle's argument shows that the Turing Test is not an adequate measure of intelligence because the Chinese Room passes the Turing Test without understanding anything, and its mode of operation is exactly the same as a computer's.

Searle goes on to point out an important peculiarity about cognitive simulation compared to other kinds of simulation. Meteorologists construct computer simulations of hurricanes, economists of U.S. foreign trade activity, and biologists of photosynthesis. But their computers do not develop 100-mph winds or multibillion-dollar trade deficits, or convert light into oxygen. Yet, cognitive scientists claim that when and if they simulate intelligence—that is, when a program passes the Turing Test—their machine will *really be* intelligent. In other fields, simulation and real achievement are kept separate, and Searle regards it as absurd to ignore the distinction in cognitive science.

Searle distinguishes between *weak AI* and *strong AI*. Weak AI would be maintaining the distinction between simulation and achievement and using computers as other scientists do, as wonderfully convenient calculating devices with which to use and check theories. Strong AI is the claim—refuted by the Chinese Room thought experiment—that simulation of intelligence is intelligence. Searle believes that strong AI can never succeed for the same reason that a computer cannot perform photosynthesis: It's made out of the wrong materials. In Searle's view, it is the natural biological function of certain plant structures to photosynthesize, and it is the natural biological function of brains to think and understand. Machines have no natural biological functions and so can neither photosynthesize nor understand. Computers may provide tools to help investigate photosynthesis and understanding, but they cannot, Searle concludes, ever actually do either one. Searle's argument is similar to a point made by Leibniz:

And supposing there were a machine, so constructed as to think, feel, and have perception, it might be conceived as increased in size, while keeping the same proportions, so that one might go into it as into a mill. That being so, we should, on examining its interior, find only parts which work one upon another, and never anything by which to explain a perception (quoted by Gunderson, 1984, p. 629).

Searle's Chinese Room paper has proved to be one of the most contentious in the history of AI and cognitive science, and the debate is not over. It inspires some psychologists and philosophers and absolutely infuriates others, to the point where the combatants talk past each other rather than to each other (see Searle, 1997). How any reader comes down on the issue seems to be primarily a matter of intuition and hopes and fears about our computerized future.

IS FORMALISM PLAUSIBLE? According to the Briefing Panel on Cognitive Science (Estes & Newell, 1983), because computers engage in "*symbolic* behavior" (precisely what Searle's argument denies), "we ourselves can program computers to deal with many things—anything to which we set our mind." Hidden within the panel's claim was the assumption of *formalism*. Computers can do anything that can be written as a computer program, and the panel, following Simon in claiming that computers can be programmed to do "anything a man can do," "anything to which we set our mind," implicitly asserted that anything people do is a formal procedure. Formalism in psychology represents the final development of the mechanization of the world picture. Just as physical science succeeded by analyzing nature as a machine, cognitive science hopes to succeed by analyzing human beings as machines (Dreyfus, 1972). However, Searle's Chinese Room challenged mechanistic formalism by showing that formal processing of symbols does not yield understanding of language. Another, more empirical, challenge was the *frame problem* because it questioned not only the ability of computers to imitate human intelligence, but the very possibility of achieving machine intelligence at all.

Daniel Dennett vividly presented the frame problem in this story:

> Once upon a time there was a robot, named R1 by its creators. Its only task was to fend for itself. One day its designers arranged for it to learn that its spare battery, its precious energy supply, was locked in a room with a time bomb set to go off soon. R1 located the room, and the key to the door, and formulated a plan to rescue its battery. There was a wagon in the room, and the battery was on the wagon, and R1 hypothesized that a certain action which it called PULLOUT (WAGON, ROOM) would result in the battery being removed from the room. Straightaway it acted, and did succeed in getting the battery out of the room before the bomb went off. Unfortunately, however, the bomb was also on the wagon. R1 knew that the bomb was on the wagon in the room, but didn't realize that pulling the wagon would bring the bomb out along with the battery. Poor R1 had missed that obvious implication of its planned act.
>
> Back to the drawing board. "The solution is obvious," said the designers. "Our next robot must be made to recognize not just the intended implications of its act, but also the implications about their side effects, by deducing these, implications from the descriptions it uses in formulating its plans." They called their next model the robot-deducer, R1D1. They placed R1D1 in much the same predicament that R1 had succumbed to, and as it too hit upon the idea of PULLOUT (WAGON, ROOM) it began, as designed, to consider the implications of such a course of action. It had just finished deducing that pulling the wagon out of the room would not change the color of the room's walls, and was embarking on a proof of the further implication that pulling the wagon out would cause its wheels to turn more revolutions than there were wheels on the wagon—when the bomb exploded.
>
> Back to the drawing board. "We must teach it the difference between relevant implications and irrelevant implications," said the designers, "and teach it to ignore the irrelevant ones." So they developed a method of tagging implications as either relevant or irrelevant to the project at hand, and installed the method in their next model, the robot-relevant-deducer, or R2D1 for short. When they subjected R2D1 to the test that had so unequivocally selected its ancestors for extinction, they were surprised to see it sitting, Hamlet-like, outside the room containing the ticking bomb, the native hue of its resolution sicklied o'er with the pale cast of thought, as Shakespeare (and more recently Fodor) has aptly put it. "Do something!" they yelled at it. "I am," it retorted. "I'm busily ignoring some thousands of implications I have determined to be irrelevant. Just as soon as I find an irrelevant implication, I put it on the list of those I must ignore, and . . ." the bomb went off. (1984, pp. 129–130)

R1 and his descendants are caught in the *frame problem*. How is it possible to formalize human knowledge and problem-solving skills as a set of computerized rules? It is quite obvious that people do not do what the R robots do: Somehow we just solve problems rapidly and with little conscious thought, just as the Würzburg psychologists discovered. If we did work the way the Rs did, we, like they, would have died long ago. Rather than working computationally, humans seem to work intuitionally: Solutions to problems just occur to us without thinking; adaptive behaviors happen without thought. We do not have to think to ignore all the absurdities that R2D1 had to work at ignoring because the absurd and irrelevant implications of our behavior just do not occur to us. But a computer, being a formal system, must work out all the implications of its acts and then ignore them. Escaping the frame problem now seems to involve emotion, something computers do not have (Leahey & Harris, 2004).

Developments

A NEW GAME IN TOWN: THE NEW CONNECTIONISM　　For all the doubts and difficulties of the symbol-manipulation paradigm in cognitive science, it remained for two decades "the only game in town," as philosopher Jerry Fodor liked to put it. If thinking wasn't the manipulation of formal symbols following formal rules, what else could it be? Because there was no answer to this question (except from ghettoized Skinnerians and a few other dissidents, such as Wittgensteinians), cognitive psychologists remained, perforce, in the symbol-system camp. However, in the early 1980s, a rival game set up shop under the name *connectionism*, recalling to us (but not to connectionists) the older connectionism of E. L. Thorndike.

A measure of the impact and importance of connectionism was the reception accorded the publication in 1986 of a two-volume exposition of its views and achievements, *Parallel Distributed Processing: Explorations in the Microstructure of Cognition*. The senior author and leader of the PDP (for parallel distributed processing, another name for connectionism) Research Group was David E. Rumelhart, formerly one of the leaders of symbolic paradigm AI. These volumes sold 6,000 copies the day they went on the market (Dreyfus & Dreyfus, 1988). Six thousand copies may not sound like much, but in the academic world, where 500 copies is a respectable sale for a technical book, it's enormous. Shortly afterward, Rumelhart won a MacArthur Foundation "genius grant." Soon, connectionism was being hailed as the "new wave" in cognitive psychology (Fodor & Pylyshyn, 1988).

In important respects, connectionism represented the resuscitation of traditions in both psychology and AI that seemed long dead. In psychology, there is a connectionist tradition running from Thorndike to Hull and neo-Hullian mediational theorists (Leahey, 1990). All of them banished symbols and mentalistic concepts from their theories and attempted to explain behavior in terms of the strengthening or weakening of connections between stimuli and responses: This is the central idea of Thorndike's Law of Effect and his and Hull's habit family hierarchies. Mediational psychologists introduced internal processing to Hull's connectionistic ideas by inserting covert connections—the little *r–s* connections—between external stimulus and overt response.

In AI, connectionism revived a minority tradition in computer science that competed with the symbol manipulation paradigm in the 1950s and 1960s. The symbol manipulation computer architecture is designed around a single processing unit that performs one computation at a time. Traditional computers gain their power from the ability of CPUs to perform sequential computations at enormous speeds. From the beginnings of computer science, however, there has always existed the possibility of a rival architecture built around multiple processors all hooked up together. With multiple processors working at once, sequential processing of information is replaced by *parallel processing*. Sequential architecture machines must be programmed to behave, and this is also true for many parallel-processing machines. However, some designers of parallel-processing computers hoped to build machines that could learn to act intelligently on their own by adjusting the strengths of the connections between their multiple processors according to feedback from the environment (Figure 1). The most important example of such a machine was Frank Rosenblatt's Perceptron machine of the 1960s.

Obviously, parallel-processing computers are potentially much more powerful than single CPU machines, but for a long time obstacles stood in the way of their construction. Parallel machines are more physically complex than sequential machines and they are vastly more difficult to program, as one must somehow coordinate the work of the multiple processors to avoid chaos.

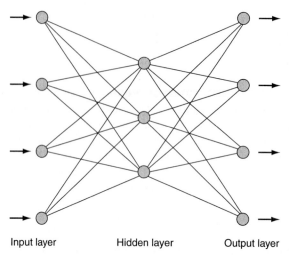

Input layer   Hidden layer   Output layer

FIGURE 1   A simple neural network composed of simple computing units connected together. This simple model has an input layer for receiving stimulation, an output layer for making responses, and a single hidden layer connecting input and output. It is a "feed forward" network because information flows only in a single direction from input to output.

With regard to self-programming machines, there is the special difficulty of figuring out how to get feedback information about the results of behavior to interior ("hidden") units lying between input and output units. Because sequential machines were great successes very early on, and the power of the parallel architecture seemed unnecessary, work on parallel-processing computers virtually ceased in the 1960s. The funeral of early connectionist AI seemed to come in 1969, when Marvin Minsky and Seymour Papert, leaders of the symbolic AI school, published *Perceptrons*, a devastating critique of Rosenblatt's work, seeming to prove mathematically that parallel machines could not learn even the simplest things.

In the 1980s, however, developments in both computer science and psychology converged to revive the fortunes of parallel-processing architectures. Although serial processors continued to gain speed, designers were pushing up against the limits of how fast electrons could move through silicon. At the same time, computer scientists were tackling jobs demanding ever greater computing speed, making a change to parallel processing desirable. For example, consider the problem of computer vision, which must be solved if robots like *Star Wars'* R2D2 are to be built. Imagine a computer graphic made up of 256×256 pixels (dots of light on a monitor). For a serial computer to recognize such an image, it would have to compute one at a time the value of $256 \times 256 = 65,536$ pixels, which might take hours. On the other hand, the Connection Machine, a parallel-processing computer containing 256×256 interconnected processors, can assign one to compute the value of a single pixel and so can process the graphic in a tiny fraction of a second (Hillis, 1987). Along with developments in hardware such as the Connection Machine came developments in programming that made it possible to coordinate the activity of independent processors, and in the case of self-modifying networks, to adjust the behavior of hidden units.

In psychology, continued failings of the symbolic paradigm made parallel, connectionist processing an attractive alternative to the old game. In addition to the difficulties with functionalism already discussed, two issues were especially important for the new connectionists. First of all, traditional AI, though it had made advances on tasks humans find intellectually taxing, such as chess playing, was persistently unable to get machines to perform the sorts of tasks that people do without the least thought, such as recognizing patterns. Perhaps most important to psychologists, the behavior that they had most intensively studied for decades—learning—remained beyond the reach of programmed computers, and the development of parallel machines that could actually learn was quite exciting.

The other shortcoming of symbolic AI that motivated the new connectionists was the plain fact that the brain is not a sequential computing device. If we regard neurons as small processors, then it becomes obvious that the brain is much more like the Connection Machine than like a PC or an Apple. The brain contains thousands of massively interconnected neurons, all of which are working at the same time. As Rumelhart and the PDP group announced in their book, they aimed to replace the computer model in psychology with the brain model. The interconnected processors of connectionist models function like neurons: Each one is activated by input and then "fires," or produces output, depending on the summed strengths of its input. Assembled properly, such a network will learn to respond in stable ways to different inputs just as organisms do: Neural nets, as such processor assemblages are often called, learn.

Connectionism suggested a new strategy for explaining intelligence. The symbol system approach depends, as we have seen, on the idea that intelligence consists in the manipulation of symbols by formal computational rules. Like the symbol system approach, connectionism is computational because connectionists try to write computer models that emulate human behavior. But connectionist systems use very different rules and representations (Dreyfus & Dreyfus, 1988; Smolensky, 1988). To understand the differences between symbol systems and connectionist systems, we need to look more closely at computational theory. Symbol system theory and connectionist theories propose different architectures of cognition, different ways of designing intelligent systems or explaining human intelligence.

Levels of Computation.   In one of the defining works in cognitive science, Marr (1982) proposed that the analysis of intelligent action must take place at three hierarchically arranged levels. In the case of AI, the levels define the job of making a mind, and in the case of psychology—which studies an already evolved intelligence—they define three levels of psychological theory. The levels are most readily described from the standpoint of AI:

- The *cognitive level* specifies the task the AI system is to perform.
- The *algorithm level* specifies the computer programming that effects the task.
- The *implementation level* specifies how the hardware device is to carry out the program instructions.

To flesh out Marr's analysis, let us consider a simple arithmetical example. At the cognitive level, the task is to add any two numbers together. At the algorithm level, we write a simple program in the BASIC language that can carry out the addition, as follows:

```
10 INPUT X
20 INPUT Y
30 LET Z = X + Y
40 PRINT Z
50 END
```

Line 10 presents a prompt on the computer screen requesting input, which it then stores as a variable called X. Line 20 repeats the process for the second number, the variable Y. Line 30 defines a variable Z, the sum of X and Y. Line 40 displays the value of Z on the screen. Line 50 says that the end of the program has been reached. If we want to repeat the process many times, we could add a new line between 40 and 50:

45 GOTO 10

This returns the program to its starting point. Loading the program into a computer and running it brings us to the implementation level. The computer takes the BASIC program and translates (the computer term is *compiles*) it into the binary language that actually controls the movement of electrons through wires and silicon chips.

Having reached the implementation level, we come to a point that is extremely important to the difference between the symbol system hypothesis and connectionism. At the cognitive level, we proceeded without considering the device that performs the addition: It could be a computer, a slide rule, a pocket calculator, or a fourth-grade child. At the algorithm level, we specified a set of rules that could also be performed by various devices, including a computer or a child, but not by a pocket calculator that cannot be programmed. Pocket calculators perform addition electronically, without being programmed with rules. However, when we reach the implementation level, the nature of the hardware (or wetware, in the case of the brain) becomes crucial because the implementation consists in actually carrying out the calculation with a real machine or real person, and different computers implement the same cognitive task in different ways.

Even the same algorithms are carried out differently by different machines. We could enter the BASIC program on any machine that understands BASIC. However, the binary machine code and the electronic processes that run the program vary from computer to computer. I could run the program on my ancient Texas Instruments TI-1000; my antique Apple IIe; my old CompuAdd 386/20, the one on which I originally wrote this sentence; CompuAdd 325TX notebook; or the one I'm now editing on, a Falcon Mach V. In every case, the electronic processes that implement the program will be different. For example, the CompuAdd 386/20 computed with an Intel 80386 microprocessor, but the 325TX used an Advanced Micro Devices AMD 386SXL chip, which emulates the Intel chip without copying its electronics—as it must in order to be legal. Thus, at the implementation level, two very similar computers run the same programs differently. One of the two main issues that separates the symbol system architecture of cognition from its connectionist rival concerns whether or not psychological theories of learning and cognition need be concerned with the implementation level. According to the symbol system view, the implementation of programs in a brain or a computer can be safely ignored at the cognitive and algorithm levels, whereas, according to the connectionist view, theorizing at higher levels must be constrained by the nature of the machine that will carry out the computations.

The second main issue concerns the algorithmic level of intelligence. William James (1890) first addressed the fundamental problem. He observed that, when we first learn a skill, we must consciously think about what to do; as we become more experienced, consciousness deserts the task and we carry it out automatically, without conscious thought. For example, consider learning to fly (Dreyfus & Dreyfus, 1990), specifically, taking off from the runway. We begin at Marr's cognitive level by describing the task to be performed as "How to take off in a small plane." Novice pilots typically talk themselves through the process of taking off by following memorized rules resembling a set of rules, which takes us to Marr's algorithm level:

1. Taxi to the flight line.
2. Set the accelerator to 100%.
3. Taxi down the runway until take-off speed is reached.
4. Pull the stick back halfway until the wheels are off the ground.
5. Retract the landing gear.

However, as the novice pilot becomes an expert, taking off becomes automatic, no longer requiring step-by-step thinking. What had formerly required conscious thought becomes intuitive, and an important question concerns what happened to the rules followed consciously by the novice pilot. What psychological change takes place when such expertise is acquired and consciousness is no longer needed for appropriate behavior to occur?

The Conscious and Intuitive Processors.   To help answer this question, Paul Smolensky (1988) analyzed the architecture of cognition from the perspective of how thoughtful processes become intuitive actions. Smolensky's framework distinguishes two levels: the conscious processor and the intuitive processor. The conscious processor is engaged when we consciously think about a task or problem, as the novice pilot does. However, as a skill becomes mastered, it moves into the intuitive processor; we just "do it" without conscious thought. Thus, experienced pilots become one with their planes and fly without conscious thought (Dreyfus & Dreyfus, 1990). Similarly, driving an automobile over a familiar route requires little if any conscious attention, which we turn over to listening to the radio, a CD, or an iPod, or having a conversation with a passenger. Moreover, not everything the intuitive processor performs was once conscious. Many of the functions of the intuitive processor are innate, such as recognizing faces or simple patterns, and some abilities can be learned without ever becoming conscious. For example, chicken sexers can identify the sex of a chick within an egg by holding it up before a light. However, they do not know how they do it, and one learns to be a chicken sexer by sitting next to a master and watching him or her work.

When it becomes automatic, a skill such as flying or driving is performed by the intuitive processor, but what happens during the transition from conscious thought to intuition is a difficult issue to resolve. To see why, we must distinguish between *rule-following* and *rule-governed* behavior.

Physical systems illustrate how rule-governed behavior need not be rule-following behavior. The earth revolves around the sun in an elliptical path governed by Newton's laws of motion and gravity. However, the earth does not follow these laws in the sense that it computes them and adjusts its course to comply with them. The computer guiding a spacecraft does follow Newton's laws, as they are written into its programs, but the motions of natural objects are governed by physical laws without following them by internal processing.

The following example suggests that the same distinction may apply to human behavior. Imagine seeing a cartoon drawing of an unfamiliar animal called a "wug." If I show you two of them, you will say, "There are two wugs." Shown two pictures of a creature called "wuk," you will say, "There are two wuks." In saying the plural, your behavior is governed by the rule of English morphology that to make a noun plural, you add an *s*. Although you probably did not apply the rule consciously, it is not implausible to believe that as a child you did. However, your behavior was also governed by a rule of English phonology that an *s* following a voiced consonant (e.g., /g/) is also voiced—wugz—and an *s* following an unvoiced consonant (such as /k/) is also unvoiced—wuks. Like the chicken sexer, it is unlikely you ever consciously knew this rule at all.

Having developed the distinction between rule-governed and rule-following behaviors, we can state the algorithm level distinction between the symbol system and the connectionist architectures of cognition. All psychologists accept the idea that human behavior is rule-governed because if it were not, there could be no science of human behavior. The issue separating the symbol system hypothesis from connectionism concerns whether and when human behavior is rule-following. According to the symbol system view, both the conscious processor and the intuitive processor are rule-following and rule-governed systems. When we think or decide consciously, we formulate rules and follow them in behaving. Intuitive thinking is likewise rule-following. In the case of behaviors that were once consciously followed, the procedures of the intuitive processor are the same as the procedures once followed in consciousness, but with awareness subtracted. In the case of behaviors such as chicken sexing, the process is truncated, with rules being formulated and followed directly by the intuitive processor. Connectionists hold that human behavior is rule-following only at the conscious level. In the intuitive processor, radically different processes are taking place (Smolensky, 1988). Advocates of the symbol system view are somewhat like Tolman, who believed that unconscious rats use cognitive maps as do conscious lost humans. Connectionists are like Hull, who believed that molar rule-governed behavior is at a lower level, the strengthening and weakening of input-output connections. After all, Thorndike called his theory "connectionism" 95 years ago.

The intuitive processor lies between the conscious mind—the conscious processor—and the brain that implements human intelligence. According to the symbol system account, the intuitive processor carries out step-by-step unconscious thinking that is essentially identical to the step-by-step conscious thinking of the conscious processor, and so Clark (1989) calls the symbol system account the *mind's-eye view* of cognition. According to connectionism, the intuitive processor carries out nonsymbolic parallel processing similar to the neural parallel processing of the brain, and Clark calls it the *brain's-eye view* of cognition.

Historically, connectionism represents more than simply a new technical approach to cognitive psychology. From the time of the ancient Greeks, Western philosophy has assumed that having knowledge is knowing rules, and that rational action consists in the following of rules. Human intuition—the key to the frame problem—has been deprecated as, at best, following rules unconsciously and, at worst, as based on irrational impulse. Consistent with this view, psychology has been the search for the rule-governed springs of human behavior, and we are advised that morally right behavior is that which follows moral rules. But connectionism could vindicate human intuition as the secret of human success and rehabilitate a dissident tradition in philosophy—represented, for example, by Friedrich Nietzsche—that scorns being bound by rules as an inferior way of life (Dreyfus & Dreyfus, 1988). In addition, psychologists and philosophers are coming to believe that emotion is wiser than pure thought (Damasio, 1994). As is so often the case in the history of psychology, what appears to be merely a technical dispute among scientists touches the deepest questions about human nature and human life.

COGNITIVE NEUROSCIENCE   In the late 1980s, connectionism and the symbol system view of learning and cognition acted as rivals, seemingly re-creating the great theoretical battles of behaviorism's Golden Age. However, around 1990, a practical *modus vivendi* reunified the field of cognitive science. The two architectures of cognition were reconciled by regarding the human mind as a hybrid of the two (Bechtel & Abrahamsen, 1991; Clark, 1989). At the neural level, learning and cognition must be carried out by connectionist-type processes because the brain is a collection of simple but massively interconnected units. Yet, as we have learned, physically different computational systems can implement the same programs. Therefore, it is possible that, although the brain is a massively parallel computer, the human mind in its rational aspects is a serial processor of representations, especially when thought is conscious. The more automatic and unconscious (intuitive) aspects of the human mind are connectionist in nature. Connectionist theories thus have a valuable role to play in being the vital interface between symbol system models of rational, rule-following thought, and intuitive, nonlinear, nonsymbolic thought.

For example, the philosopher Daniel Dennett (1991) proposed an influential Multiple Drafts Model of consciousness that relies on the idea of the mind as a hybrid of serial and parallel processing. Specifically, Dennett proposes that consciousness—Smolensky's conscious processor—is a serial virtual machine implemented in the brain's parallel architecture—Smolensky's intuitive processor. Many computer environments, such as Windows, contain virtual calculators. If you activate a calculator, an image of a real calculator appears on the computer screen. On the image, one can place the mouse's cursor on a key, click the left mouse button, and the virtual calculator will carry out the operation just like an actual calculator.

Real calculators carry out their functions by virtue of how they are wired. The calculators of Windows carry out their functions by virtue of programs written to imitate real calculators. As Turing showed, computers are general-purpose devices that can be programmed to imitate any special-purpose device. The virtual calculators seem to work just like the calculators they mimic, but the electronic work done behind the scenes is completely different. Broadly speaking, every program running on a computer implements a different *virtual machine*. The calculator programs create a virtual calculator, a flight simulator creates a virtual airplane, a chess program creates a virtual chessboard and a virtual opponent.

Dennett proposed that consciousness is a virtual machine installed by socialization on the brain's parallel processor. Most important, socialization gives us language, and in language, we think and speak one thought at a time, creating our serial-processing conscious processors. Human beings are remarkably flexible creatures, able to adapt to every environment on earth and aspiring to living in space and on distant planets. Animals are like real calculators, possessing hardwired responses that fit each one to the particular environments in which each species evolved. People are like general-purpose computers, adapting to the world not by changing their physical natures but by changing their programs. The programs are cultures that adapt to changing places and changing times. Learning a culture creates consciousness, and consciousness is adaptive because it bestows the ability to think about one's actions, to mull over alternatives, to plan ahead, to acquire general knowledge, and to be a member of one's society. It is through social interaction—not through solitary hunting, foraging, and reproduction—that individual humans and cultures survive and flourish.

The working alliance of symbol system and connectionist approaches to cognitive science was aided by the Decade of the Brain, the 1990s, when advances in techniques for studying the brain and nervous system revived the Path through Physiology that psychologists abandoned early in the twentieth century. The new Path through Physiology is called *cognitive neuroscience*. Just as the field of AI got its name out of necessity, so did cognitive neuroscience. Riding in a taxi to a meeting of scientists interested in studying "how the brain enables the mind" in the late 1970s, George Miller and Michael Gazzaniga invented the name for the fledgling enterprise (Gazzaniga, Ivry, & Mangun, 1998, p. 1). Today, connectionist models are used to bridge the gap between symbol system algorithm models of cognitive functions and studies of the brain structures that carry out cognitive processes.

REJECTING THE CARTESIAN PARADIGM: EMBODIED COGNITION There is now a movement on foot in cognitive science that rejects entirely or in part the traditional symbol-system conception of mind and mental processes, sometimes dubbed (Rowlands, 2010) Cartesian cognitive science. This new movement comprises many regiments marching under various banners, usually collected together under the umbrella term *embodied cognition*.

Proponents of these views do not always agree on which aspects of Cartesian cognitive science need to be modified or replaced, and it's not always clear if their approaches are complementary, compatible, overlapping, or redundant, but they do share deep suspicions about one or more of the four central tenets of the Cartesian paradigm:

> **Computationalism,** the claim of Simon's symbol system hypothesis that cognition consists in the digital manipulation of representations by formal logical rules.

> **Neurocentrism,** the claim that cognitive processes are located exclusively in the brain. Although connectionism challenged Simon's symbol system hypothesis, it retained the Cartesian idea that all mental processes take place in the brain.

Bodily indifference, the claim that the physical structure of a computational system has little bearing on its cognitive processes, so that cognitive processes can in principle be carried out by any appropriately programmed physical system regardless of the substance it's made of or its bodily shape. We met this idea in our discussion of feedback and Marr's levels of cognitive analysis. From which follows the **separability thesis,** the claim that mental processes are separable from the body or whatever device, such as computer, that executes them. In Descartes and religious thought the soul is regarded as an immortal substance separable from the body and capable of eternal life. The same ideas recur in materialistic Cartesian cognitive science. For example, one of the founders of computational cognitive science, Marvin Minsky (1989), regards the body as "obsolete," and looks forward to achieving immortality by having his mind transformed into a computer program and then being downloaded into a supercomputer.

It can be seen that the first assumption, computationalism, is the most basic one, as it underwrites or implies the other three. If a mind is a running computer program, it does not matter whether that program is running in a brain, a silicon chip, or whether the brain or chip is housed in a human body, an elephant's body, or a supercomputer.

We can illustrate the basic differences between Cartesian cognitive science and embodied cognitive science by returning to the Watt governor. Watt solved the problem of regulating the power output of a steam engine by designing a physical device constructed to perform that single function. However, we might attack Watt's problem from the reverse engineering point of view of AI. Let's apply Marr's levels of cognitive analysis.

- The Cognitive Level: How can we maintain steady, controlled, output from the engine?
- The Algorithm Level: What rules might be used to govern a system that maintains steady, controlled output?
- What device can we build or employ to carry out these rules?

We might then proceed as follows. Put a sensor on the boiler that samples the boiler's internal pressure every 10 seconds. This sensor then provides input to the following computational program, as in traditional symbol-system AI (each numbered line corresponds to a single computational step):

10. Input (Pressure)

20. If $P > 500$ psi then go to 40

30. If $P < 450$ psi then go to 50

40. Decrease fuel input

45. Go to 10

50. Increase fuel input

60. Go to 10.

We then enter this program into a computer—even a smartphone would do—and hook the computer to the sensor and the fuel control valve for the boiler, and the computer would do the work of the Watt governor, responding to the pressure inside the boiler by regulating the fuel input to the fire to raise or lower the temperature as needed.

In this scenario, a general-purpose information-processing device would be doing the work of Watt's noninformation-using dedicated device. The assumption of traditional AI, following the Cartesian paradigm, is that human beings are general-purpose information processors who carry out specific tasks by learning the appropriate information-processing steps. Advocates of embodied cognition believe that human beings are more like the Watt governor, being engineered by evolution to effectively engage with the world around us. Intelligence, they say, is rooted in our bodily interactions with the world. Brain processes alone—whether conceived as symbol-systems or as neural nets—do not explain animal intelligence. A body that interacts with the world is required. A Marr-type system is all thought with no relevant body except the sensor that provides input and the fuel-control valve that obeys the program's commands. Watt's governor is all body and no mind; its behavior in controlling the engine is explained by the physical laws of coupled dynamic systems (van Gelder, 1995). There are no representations, no rules, and no computations.

Advocates of embodied cognition study the role of the human body in producing intelligent behavior. Cartesian cognitive science presents a rather disembodied version of cognition, in which input is provided to the central processor where it is transformed and manipulated and where decisions are made. Experience and action are seen as merely peripheral to the intelligent decisions made in the brain. A study by Aglioti et al. (2008) casts doubt on the Cartesian view. They showed videos of elite basketball players shooting free throws, stopping the videos at various points before the ball got to the basket, asking subjects to predict whether or not the shot was good. There were three groups of subjects, skilled basketball players, basketball coaches, and sports journalists, and subjects with no special experience of basketball. If ability to compute the continued trajectory of the ball was the skill needed to succeed at this task, then experienced observers of free throws—players, coaches, and journalists alike—should all do well compared to novices, as they had seen many successful and many failed free throw attempts. However, only the skilled players were able to make accurate predictions. Most importantly, the players could predict whether a shot would be good if the video was stopped just *before* the ball left the shooter's hand, *before* there was any trajectory to compute. Skilled players essentially could feel the movement of the shooter they were watching because they had done his action many times themselves, and knew from his bodily position whether the throw would go in or not. Without the bodily experience of making and missing free throws, and without a body to mirror the movements of another player, the brain alone cannot solve this simple problem. At least in this case, the body intuitively *knows*, it does not compute.

Another flavor of embodied cognition is the thesis of the extended mind. It agrees with the symbol system hypothesis that thinking is symbol-manipulation, but it says that the human cognitive systems extend outside the brain into the larger environment (Clark, 2008). For example, the cognitive process of memory is usually located in the head, but in the modern world, much of our memory has been offloaded into smartphones and Internet services such as Google. We don't have to remember our best friend's phone number, because it's in our phones database; we don't need to know what the Magna Carta was, we can Google it. Moreover, such offloading of cognitive processes has been going on since human beings first evolved, making records on incised bones, clay tablets, notes to oneself, procedural manuals, and relying on coworkers to know critical information (Hutchins, 1995).

Embodied cognition has also developed in the field of AI, especially in robotics. The first efforts in robotics followed the symbol system approach. Robots were built that constructed internal models of their environment, and consulted them to move from one point to another, stopping periodically to update the representation to reflect new obstacles and to recompute their view of the world from their new position. However, these robots were slow and ineffective, as the cycle of consult representation → move → reconstruct representation → consult new representation → move took too long to generate effective behavior in real time. Roboticist Rodney Brooks (founder of the iRobot company, makers of Roomba and robots for the military) concluded that building representations of the world to be computed about was stupid because "*the world is its own best model*"

(Brooks, 1991, p. 417). Why go to the trouble of building a representation when you can just look at the world itself?

Brooks's statement takes us back to an old issue in philosophical and then scientific psychology, the argument between representational and realist theories of perception. The Cartesian Way of Ideas—the symbol system hypothesis—says that minds represent the world and that thinking is manipulation of those representations. Against this stood the realists from Reid onward, who said that we perceive the world directly; as Brooks remarks, we don't need representations because the world itself is available to us.

Once we ask this question, however, we return full circle to the most fundamental issue in psyche-logos, the nature of mind itself. Is mind a natural kind like the atom, awaiting discovery by science, or are they fictions like phlogiston, useful for a time in science but not real, replaceable by better concepts? Embodied cognition looks a lot like radical behaviorism. Both take a realist view of perception and both stress the importance of physical interaction between the organism and the world as the basis of adaptive behavior. The difference between them is mostly that advocates of embodied cognition assume that minds are natural kinds, really existing in nature. They say that Descartes's description of mind was wrong and needs replacing, the way that early ideas about atoms as the smallest units of matter needed to be replaced by more sophisticated theories about subatomic particles. Radical behaviorists, on the other hand, think that Descartes, aided by preexisting religious thought, invented a fictitious concept, mind, on a par with Zeus or phlogiston. The concept of "mind" should not be revised, but dropped, in their view. But embodied cognition and radical behaviorism wind up with about the same picture of psychology: the study of the organism in direct interaction with the environment, unmediated by thought. Echoing Brooks, Skinner (1977, p.6) once said, "The body responds to the world, at the point of contact; making copies would be a waste of time."

THE STUDY OF THE MIND AT THE BEGINNING OF THE NEW MILLENNIUM

The scientific study of the mind—in its new incarnation as cognitive neuroscience—flourished at the end of the second millennium and seemed poised for further success in the third. A popular treatment of cognitive neuroscience, Steven Pinker's *How the Mind Works*, and its sequel *The Blank Slate* were bestsellers, as was Nobel Prize–winning psychologist Daniel Kahneman's *Thinking, Fast and Slow* (2011), and almost every science page of the *Washington Post* (Mondays) and the *New York Times* (Wednesdays) reported some new breakthrough in the study of the brain. The founding generation's vision of a comprehensive natural science of the mind appeared to be within the grasp of psychologists armed with tools the founders only dreamed of. The only dissenter was the science writer John Horgan who argued that science in the grand mode of Newton and Einstein was coming to an end (Horgan, 1997), and suggested that cognitive science was "gee whiz" science, reporting breakthrough after breakthrough without arriving at an overarching picture of the human mind (Horgan, 2000). In this, Horgan echoed complaints about cognitive psychology discussed earlier, and sides with thinkers who believe the human brain/mind is incapable of understanding itself. He also argued at length that psychology (and psychiatry) had failed to produce any consistently effective applications of its theories. Is the glass of cognitive science half-full or half-empty?

Psychological Science in the Modern World: Bibliography

There is only one general history of behaviorism, John A. Mills's *Control: A history of behavioral psychology* (New York: NYU Press, 1998). Mills emphasizes the idea that behaviorism was a distinctly American psychology tied to American's desires for useful knowledge in general and the Progressives' desire for tools of social control in particular. Accessible discussions of logical behaviorism may be found in Fodor (1981); Arnold S. Kaufman, "Behaviorism," *Encyclopedia of the social sciences*, vol. I (New York: Macmillan, 1967, pp. 268–273); Arnold B. Levison, ed., *Knowledge and society: An introduction to the philosophy of the social sciences* (Indianapolis: Bobbs-Merrill, 1974, ch. 6); and Norman Malcolm, *Problems of mind: Descartes to Wittgenstein* (New York: Harper Torchbooks, 1971, ch. 3). Ryle's *Concept of mind* (1949), is well written, even witty, and quite readable even by someone with no previous knowledge of philosophy. Wittgenstein, on the other hand, is a notoriously difficult philosopher to understand. For our present purposes, his most important works are *The blue and brown books* (1958), a published version of Cambridge lectures delivered in 1933 and 1934, which formed the preliminary studies for the posthumously published *Philosophical investigations* (1953). Wittgenstein wrote in a sort of dialogue style, arguing with an unnamed interlocutor and, like Plato, tended to develop arguments by indirection rather than outright statement. Further difficulty understanding his philosophy arises from the fact that in an important sense, he had nothing positive to say, aiming like Socrates at clearing up misconceptions instead of offering his own conceptions. As Malcolm (1971) put it, "Philosophical work of the right sort merely unties knots in our understanding. The result is not a theory but simply—no knots!" So one should not tackle Wittgenstein without guidance. The best book-length introduction is Anthony Kenny's *Wittgenstein* (Cambridge, MA: Harvard University Press, 1973). The best treatment of Wittgenstein's philosophy of mind is Malcolm (1971). Luckhardt (1983) is also helpful and clear, especially concerning Wittgenstein's attitude to behaviorism.

Papers expounding the positivistic view of psychological theory construction nearly filled the pages of *Psychological Review* in the late 1940s and early 1950s. Some of them are collected in Melvin Marx, ed., *Theories in contemporary psychology* (New York: Macmillan, 1963). A witty reply to Kendler from the realist perspective was given by Tolman's colleague Benbow F. Ritchie, "The circumnavigation of cognition," *Psychological Review* (1953, *60*: 216–221).

Ritchie likens Kendler to an operationist geographer who defines problems of navigation purely in terms of the procedures for getting from one point to another on the earth's surface, thereby dismissing the dispute between the "flat-earth theorists" and the "ball theorists" as a pseudoissue, because both theories are operationally reducible to statements about movement on the earth's surface, rendering irrelevant any "surplus meaning" concerning the shape of the earth. The "what is learned" debate has been insightfully studied by philosopher Ron Amundson, "Psychology and epistemology: The place versus response controversy," *Cognition* (1985, *20*: 127–155). If you are interested in the many experiments done concerning "what is learned," you should consult reviews found under the heading "Learning" in the *Annual Review of Psychology*, which began publication in 1950. Also useful is Ernest R. Hilgard's (later coauthored by Gordon Bower) text, *Theories of learning*, whose first edition appeared in 1948 (New York: Appleton-Century-Crofts). For an account of the broader issues raised by operationism, see Thomas H. Leahey, "Operationism and ideology," *Journal of Mind and Behavior* (1983, *4*: 81–90), a special issue of *Theory and Psychology* (2001, *11* (1): 5–74) on operationism; Uljana Feest, "Operationism in psychology: What the debate is about, what the debate should be about," *Journal of the History of the Behavioral Sciences* (2005, *41*: 131–149). Christopher Green discusses why operationism hasn't died despite years of criticism in "Of immortal mythological beasts: Operationism in psychology," *Theory and Psychology* (1992, *2*: 291–320).

The best single book of Skinner's to read is *Science and human behavior* (New York: Macmillan, 1953), because there he discussed his philosophy of science, explained his scientific work, and went on to criticize society in light of his conclusions, offering behaviorist remedies for social ills. His autobiography, in three volumes, has been completed and published by Knopf (New York): *Particulars of my life* (1976), *The shaping of a behaviorist* (1979), and *A matter of consequences* (1983). Richard Evans has conducted two interviews with Skinner: *B. F. Skinner: The man and his ideas* (New York: Dutton, 1968) provides a good introduction to Skinner, and *A dialogue with B. F. Skinner* (New York: Praeger, 1981) provides an update. Paul Sagal discusses *Skinner's philosophy* (Washington, DC: University Press of America, 1981). Alexandra Rutherford describes the varied applications of Skinnerian behaviorism from self-help to mental health to utopia building in *Beyond the* box: *B. F. Skinner's Technology of behavior from laboratory to life, 1950s–1970s* (Toronto: University of Toronto Press, 2009). A useful defense of Skinner's treatment of language, an attack on Chomsky's treatment of it, and a brief history of the relationship between behavior analysis and cognitive psychology may be found in D. C. Palmer (2006) On Chomsky's appraisal of "Verbal Behavior: A half century of misunderstanding," *Behavior Analysis* (*29*: 253–267).

Neal Miller (1959) provides a good general introduction to informal, "liberalized" behavioralism, although he focuses on his own research and neglects the many other mediational behaviorists, such as Osgood, who were important figures in the 1950s. Miller and his associates, particularly John Dollard, developed their social learning theory over many years and in many publications, beginning with John Dollard, Leonard Doob, Neal Miller, O. Hobart Mowrer, and Robert Sears, *Frustration and aggression* (New Haven, CT: Yale University Press, 1939). Their most important books were Neal Miller and John Dollard, *Social learning and imitation* (New Haven, CT: Yale University Press, 1941), and John Dollard and Neal Miller, *Personality and psychotherapy* (New York: McGraw-Hill, 1950). As the title of the last book implies, Miller and Dollard were pioneers in behavioral psychotherapy, and an excellent summary of their therapeutic methods and comparison with other systems may be found in Donald H. Ford and Hugh B. Urban, *Systems of psychotherapy: A comparative study* (New York: McGraw-Hill, 1963). The Kendlers presented their mediational theory of reversal shift learning in many publications, but the classic paper was Howard Kendler and Tracy Kendler, "Vertical and horizontal processes in problem solving," *Psychological Review* (1962, *69*: 1–16). Their cited 1975 paper provides a retrospective on their work and shows how it turned gradually into information-processing psychology.

Jerome Bruner and George S. Klein provide an account of the beginnings and guiding concepts of the New Look in perception in "The functions of perceiving: New look retrospect," in B. Kaplan and S. Wapner, eds., *Perspectives in psychological theory: Essays in honor of Heinz Werner* (New York: International Universities Press, 1960). Jean Piaget wrote many books, most of them very difficult. A comprehensive statement of his theory for the period in question is *The psychology of intelligence* (Totowa, NJ: Rowman & Littlefield, 1948). Piaget's *Six psychological studies* (New York: Random House, 1964) collects some of his more accessible papers. Secondary sources include Alfred Baldwin, *Theories of child development*, 2nd ed. (New York: John Wiley, 1980); John Flavell, *The developmental psychology of Jean Piaget* (New York: Van Nostrand, 1963); Herbert Ginsberg and Sylvia Opper, *Piaget's theory of intellectual development* (Englewood Cliffs, NJ: Prentice-Hall, 1969); and Thomas H. Leahey and Richard J. Harris,

Human learning (Englewood Cliffs, NJ: Prentice-Hall, 1985). Finally, Howard Gruber and Jacques Voneche have compiled *The essential Piaget* (New York: Basic Books, 1977), a comprehensive anthology of extracts from all of Piaget's major works, including some rare adolescent pieces, and have added their own penetrating commentary.

Boring (1946) is the first paper I know of to address the meaning of the World War II computer revolution for psychology, and it includes a comprehensive listing of the prewar mechanical models, including Hull's. For Turing, see Alan Hodge, *Alan Turing: The enigma* (New York: Simon & Schuster, 1983). Broadbent (1958) is useful for comparing information processing and *S–R* theories. Finally, a book that doesn't fit well anywhere but that documents the revival of interest in cognition in the early 1950s is Bruner et al. (1957), a collection of papers given at the University of Colorado Symposium on Cognition in 1955. The meeting was attended by leading psychologists of cognition, including mediation theory (Charles Osgood), social psychology (Fritz Heider), psychoanalysis (David Rapaport), and Bruner himself. Only one approach was missing: artificial intelligence (AI). Its omission demonstrates that the computer revolution had not yet hit psychology, as well as how the field of AI developed entirely separately from the psychology of thinking. Crevier (1993), himself a worker in the field, provides a narrative history of AI and computer simulation research.

A history of modern computing, including AI, may be found in Dyson's (2012) *Turing's cathedral*. In *The universal computer: The road from Leibniz to Turing* (Boca Raton, FL: CRC Press, rev. ed 2011), Martin Davis provides the backstory of how thinkers gradually came to think of thinking as computing.

There are many sources to consult for embodied cognition. L. M. Osbeck (2009), "Transformations in cognitive science: Implications and issues posed," *Journal of Theoretical and Philosophical Psychology* (*29*:1, 16–33), provides a broad and brief survey. L. Shapiro (2011), *Embodied cognition* (New York: Routledge) provides a broad and critical, but evenhanded, account of the various types of embodied cognition as both philosophies and psychology. A. Chemero (2011) advocates a *Radical embodied cognitive science* (Cambridge, MA: MIT Press/Bradford) that eschews rules and representations completely.

A collection of histories of the various fields of psychology can be found in I. B. Wiener (ed.) *Handbook of psychology*, vol. 1, D. Freedheim (ed.) *History of psychology*, 2nd ed. (Hoboken, NJ: Wiley, 2012). Another approach is to tell the story of psychology organized by country, as in D. B. Baker (ed.) *The Oxford handbook of the history of psychology: Global perspectives* (Oxford: Oxford University Press, 2012).

The Rise of Applied Psychology 1892–1939

INTRODUCTION

Imagine being born in the United States in 1880. You were born in the Agricultural Age and probably would have been a farmer or a farmer's wife. Your parents probably lived their whole lives within a few miles of where they were born. However, although you were born in the Age of Agriculture, the Modern Age was beginning. When you turn just 40, in 1920, the world around you is utterly and forever changed. You probably live in a city, working in a factory or in one of the new wonders of the Modern Age, a department store. Your parents grew their own food and made their own clothes; you buy yours with money. You have a panoply of opportunities your parents never had: to work where you choose and to live where you choose, to *date* (the term was coined in 1914) and marry whom you choose. You travel farther than your parents ever could, on trains and on the newest, most revolutionary form of transportation ever invented, the automobile. The nation and the world come into your home via the radio. The United States has become a world power, helping to settle the Great War. Your grandchildren, too, are being changed by modernity. You, your parents, and your own children (now in mid- to late *adolescence*, a word coined by G. Stanley Hall) had only a few years of primary schooling and worked to support their family before forming their own. However, a new institution, the high school, is just coming into existence. Only in the 1930s will it become the central rite of passage of American teens. These opportunities and changes came with a price, creating a variety of new social stresses. Because they lived on their land making their own food and clothes, your parents had a degree of autonomy, if not freedom, which you do not. Although you can choose where to work, your livelihood now depends on people that you know dimly, if at all.

From Chapter 13 of *A History of Psychology: From Antiquity to Modernity*, Seventh Edition.
Thomas Hardy Leahey. Copyright © 2013 by Pearson Education, Inc. All rights reserved.

A busy street scene in Chicago, c. 1900. Chicago epitomized the social changes occurring in America between 1890 and 1920 would shape American psychology in a distinctive, pragmatic, and applied direction. *(Courtesy of Library of Congress)*

During this era, many people began to feel that they were losing control of their lives, and they acted in a variety of ways to assert their individual autonomy. As traditional values corroded, people looked to new forms of authority for guidance on how to live. At the same time, politicians, businessmen, and other social leaders were beginning to carry out the Enlightenment Project of a rationally managed society based on scientific rather than religious or traditional means of social control.

By 1912, Americans were truly entering a "new era of human relationships." Psychology would play a critical role in the modern world. As the study of the individual—especially in American psychology, where the study of individual differences flourished—psychology helped define personality and individuality in a new, quantitative and scientific way. Psychology would be asked to provide help in making life's new decisions: counseling psychologists to help one choose a suitable job, clinical psychologists intervening when the pursuit of happiness went awry. And psychology was looked to by America's leaders to provide scientific means of managing business and society. The future of psychology was bright, but the transformations of modernity—the creation of Wilson's "very different age"—also transformed psychology.

In this chapter, we look at psychology from a more externalist perspective. In what follows, we will see how the processes of modernization shaped psychology and how mental testing gave rise to a new, professional field of applied psychology alongside traditional academic psychology.

SCIENTIFIC, APPLIED, AND PROFESSIONAL PSYCHOLOGY

When the American Psychological Association (APA) was founded in 1892, the preamble to its bylaws declared that the association had been formed to "advance psychology as a science." When the APA was reorganized in 1945, its mission was to "advance psychology as a science, and profession, and as a means of promoting human welfare." The new phrases represented more than a desire to appeal to the American public, which valued applied over theoretical science. They represented a fundamental change in the nature of organized psychology, including the creation of a new social role, the professional psychologist, whose interests would prove to be at odds with the older academic role of psychologists.

Reflecting their Mandarin values, the founding German psychologists saw themselves as pure scientists, investigating the operations of the mind without regard for the social utility of their findings. However, as we have already seen, American psychology was destined to be more interested in useful application than in pure research. Americans wanted, as James said, a psychology that will teach them how to act. However, although the first American psychologists quickly turned to applications of their science, they remained academics and scientists. For example, when Dewey in 1899 urged psychologists to put their discipline into social practice, he did not mean that they themselves should be practitioners of a craft of applied psychology. He wanted psychologists to scientifically investigate subjects of educational importance, such as learning and reading. The results of psychologists' scientific studies would then be used by professional educators to devise teaching methods for classroom teachers. Applied psychology, in this scheme, remained scientific psychology.

However, almost from the beginning there was a tendency for psychologists themselves to deliver psychological services to institutions and individuals. Psychologists tended to move from devising intelligence and personnel tests to administering them in schools and businesses, using their results to advise parents and businesspeople on how to treat a child or potential employee. Devising tests is a scientific activity; giving and interpreting tests is a professional activity. Ultimately, professional psychologists became entrepreneurial businesspeople, providing services for a fee.

The roles of scientific/academic and professional psychologists gave rise to different social and economic interests that were not completely compatible. Scientists want to further their science through publications and conventions, and, when governments finance scientific research, through lobbying for research funds. To the extent that they depend on advances in scientific research, professionals share these interests, but add their own. Professionals want to maintain standards of training; they want to restrict the practice of their craft to those they regard as competent; thus, they seek to establish legal standards for professional licensure; they want to expand their economic horizons by creating new kinds of professional work. When medical care is paid for by insurance rather than by patients, clinical psychologists want to be included along with psychiatrists. The APA had to be reorganized in 1945 because professional psychologists had become so numerous that their demands for the APA to meet their special interests could not be ignored, and the revised preamble reflected that reality. Today, half of American psychologists are professional, primarily clinical, psychologists (Benjamin, 1996).

PSYCHOLOGY AND SOCIETY

It is appropriate to begin the history of psychology in modernity in 1892 because in that year the APA was founded. Our attention from now on will be fixed on American psychology, for although Germany granted the earliest degrees in psychology, it was in America that psychology became a profession; the German equivalent of the APA was not founded until 1904. For better or worse, modern psychology is primarily American psychology. American movements and theories have been adopted overseas—so much so that a 1980 German text in social psychology was filled with American references and made no mention of Wundt or Völkerpsychologie.

FROM ISLAND COMMUNITIES TO EVERYWHERE COMMUNITIES Society today is so professionalized—even beauticians need a license in many states— that it is easy to overlook the importance of the founding of the APA for the history of psychology. Before the formation of the APA, psychology was pursued by philosophers, physicians, and physiologists. The founders of scientific psychology necessarily began their careers in other fields, typically medicine or philosophy. But creating a recognized profession brings self-consciousness about the definition of a field and the need to decide, or even control, who may call himself or herself a member of it. To establish an organization such as the APA means to establish criteria for membership, allowing some people to call themselves "psychologists" while forbidding the name to others. If the field in question includes a profession offering services to the public, its members seek to get government to enforce the criteria, issuing licenses to properly trained professionals and attempting to stamp out those who practice the profession without a license.

The founding of the APA took place in a period of great change in American life, in which the professionalization of academic and practical disciplines played an important part. Before the Civil War, Americans were skeptical that educated expertise conferred special status or authority on anyone (Diner, 1998). During Andrew Jackson's presidency, for example, state legislatures abolished licensure requirements for physicians. During the 1890s, however, learned professions grew rapidly, and their members sought enhanced status and power by organizing professional societies that certified their members' expertise and pressured government to recognize their special authority. "Leading lawyers, engineers, teachers, social workers, and members of other professions said the same thing: expertise should confer autonomy, social status, and economic security on those who possessed it, and they alone should regulate and restrict the members of their calling" (Diner, 1998, p. 176). The new middle-class desire to advance oneself by acquiring professional expertise led to a huge increase in the number of college students, from 238,000 in 1900 to 598,000 in 1920 (p. 176).

The years between 1890 and World War I are generally recognized as critical ones in U.S. history. America in the 1880s was, in Robert Wiebe's phrase, a nation of "island communities" scattered across the immense ocean of rural America. In these small, isolated communities, people lived lives enclosed in a web of family relations and familiar neighbors; the world outside was psychologically distant and did not—indeed, could not—intrude very often on very deeply. By 1920, the United States had become a nation-state, united by the beginnings of modern media and searching for a common culture.

Part of the change was urbanization. In 1880, only 25% of the population lived in cities; by 1900, 40% did so. Cities are not island communities but collections of strangers, and this was especially true of American cities around the turn of the century. Immigration from outlying farmlands and foreign countries brought hundreds of people every day to great metropolises such as New York and Chicago. Changing from farm or village dweller to urban citizen effects psychological changes and demands new psychological skills.

Changing from island community to nation-state has, as Daniel Boorstin (1974) argues, deeply affected daily lives, widening personal horizons through education and mass media, while narrowing the range of immediate personal experience, and introducing a constant flow of change with which people must keep up. The railroad could take the rural immigrant to the big city. It could also bring to farmers and villagers the products of the city: frozen meat and vegetables, canned food, and, above all, the wonders of the Ward's and Sears-Roebuck catalogues. Previously, most men and women lived out their lives in the small radius of a few hours' walking. Now the train took them immense distances occasionally, and the trolley took them downtown every day to work and shop at the new department stores. All of this freed people from what could be the stultifying confines of small-town life. It also homogenized experience. Today we can all watch the same television programs and news, buy the same brands of foods and clothes, and travel from coast to coast, staying in the same Days Inn motel room and eating the same McDonald's hamburger.

Psychology, as the study of people, was deeply affected by this great transformation of human experience. As we move through this chapter, we see professional psychologists, no longer mere speculators about the mind, defining their job and role in society with respect to the new American scene.

The 1890s, standing as they do at the beginning of the modern era, were especially chaotic and disquieting, and Americans often felt as if they were losing control of their lives (Diner, 1998). The Panic of 1893 started a four-year depression of major proportions, bringing in its wake not only unemployment but also riots and insurrection. The "Année terrible" of 1894 to 1895 witnessed 1,394 strikes and a march on Washington by "Coxey's Army" of the unemployed, which was dispersed by troops amid rumors of revolution. The election of 1896 marked a watershed in American history, as the agrarian past gave way to the urban, industrial future. One candidate, William Jennings Bryan, was the voice of Populism; to established leaders he was also a leftist revolutionary, the leader of "hideous and repulsive vipers." His opponent was William McKinley, a dull, solid Republican. Far from being a Marxist, Bryan was really the voice of the island communities, of the farmlands and small towns, a preacher of religious morality. McKinley represented the immediate future: urban, pragmatic, the voice of big business and big labor. McKinley narrowly won and revolution was averted; reform, efficiency, and progress became the watchwords of the day. Psychology would volunteer to serve all three goals, and in doing so was transfigured from an experimental branch of philosophy to a practical, applied profession.

THE OLD PSYCHOLOGY VERSUS THE NEW PSYCHOLOGY   In psychology, too, the 1890s were a "furious decade" (Boring, 1929). To begin with, it saw the last defenses of the old religious psychology, rooted in Scottish commonsense philosophy, against the new scientific psychology, rooted in experimentation and mental measurement. The defeat of the old psychology reflected the defeat of Bryan by McKinley, the replacement of a rural, religiously inspired philosophy by a naturalistic, pragmatic science.

George Trumbull Ladd, who in his college teaching and text writing had done much to introduce the new psychology to America, loathed what psychology was becoming. He rejected the physiological, natural science conception of psychology he found in James and defended spiritualistic dualism (Ladd, 1892). In his APA presidential address, he decried the replacement of ordinary introspection by experiment and objective measurement as "absurd," finding science incompetent to treat important parts of human psychology, including, most importantly, human religious sentiments. Other adherents of the old psychology, such as Larkin Dunton (before the Massachusetts School Masters' Club in 1895), defended the old psychology as "the science of the soul," "an emanation of the Divine," furnishing the key "to moral education."

Like Bryan, Ladd, Dunton, and the old psychology represented the passing world of rural, village America, based on traditional religious truths. The Scottish commonsense psychology had been created to defend religion and would continue to do so as fundamentalists clung to it against the tide of modernism. The old psychology had a soul and taught the old moral values of an American culture being overtaken by progress.

For the decade of the 1890s was the "age of the news": the new education, the new ethics, the new woman, and the new psychology. American psychology's past had belonged to clerics; its future belonged to scientists and professionals. Chief among them was Wundt's ganz Amerikanisch student James McKeen Cattell, fourth president of the APA. Cattell (1896) described the new psychology as a rapidly advancing, quantitative science. Moreover—and this would be a key part of professional psychology in the years to come—he claimed for experimental psychology "wide reaching practical applications" in education, medicine, the fine arts, political economy, and, indeed, in the whole conduct of life. The new psychology, not the old, was in step with the times: self-confident, self-consciously new and scientific, ready to face the challenges of urbanization, industrialization, and the unceasing, ever-changing flow of American life.

PROGRESSIVISM AND PSYCHOLOGY Reform, efficiency, and progress were the actuating values of the major social and political movement following the crisis of 1896: Progressivism. During the nineteenth century, English middle-class reformers sought to tame both the decadent aristocracy and the unruly working class (as the middle class saw it) by imposing on both their own values of frugality, self-control, and hard work. Progressivism filled the same role in America, with, of course, distinctive American touches. Progressives were middle-class professionals—including the new psychologists—who aimed to reign in the rapacious American aristocracy, the Robber Barons, and the disorderly masses of urban immigrants. Not only did the Robber Barons prey on Americans through business, but also they were turning their riches to the control of politics and the living of opulent but empty lives, captured by F. Scott Fitzgerald in *The Great Gatsby*. Progressives saw the urban masses as victims exploited by corrupt political machines, which traded votes for favors and indispensable services to hopeful immigrants building new lives in a strange but opportunity-filled land.

In place of what they defined as the greedy self-interest of the moneyed class and the opportunistic self-interest of the political bosses, the Progressives sought to establish disinterested, expert, professional government—that is, government by themselves (Friedman, 2012). There can be no doubt that, especially in the cities, living conditions were often appalling as the waves of immigrants stretched American cities beyond their old bounds and beyond their ability to cope. Urban political machines were an organic, adaptive response to urban ills, providing bewildered immigrants with a helpful intermediary between them and their new society. But because the machines' help was bought with votes, middle-class Progressives, aided by academics, saw only corruption and manipulation of helpless victims by self-serving politicians. The Progressives tried to replace political corruption with the scientific management principles of the great corporations. The alleged benefactors of Progressive reform working-class people resisted it because it moved political influence from neighborhood citizen groups to distant professional, middle-class, bureaucrats (Diner, 1998).

The philosopher of Progressivism and the prophet of twentieth-century liberalism was John Dewey, elected president of the APA for the last year of the old century. Like many others, Dewey believed that the stresses of the 1890s marked the birth of a radically new, modern way of life. "One can hardly believe there has been a revolution in all history so rapid, so extensive, so complete" (quoted by Ross, 1991, p. 148). In his presidential address, "Psychology and Social Practice" (1900), Dewey connected the emerging science and profession of psychology with modernity. As we will

XAM'S BLOG 1
Psychology and Progressivism

Along with the sort of deconstruction of premodern life carried out by Freud and Watson, psychology took on the task of reconstructing society and culture along "scientific" lines. Indeed, as I suggested in my Introductory Essay, it may be argued that the modernist reconstruction of society is what created psychology as a recognized institution. As a matter of everyday life, modernity got into full swing in the late nineteenth century, as opinion leaders began to articulate the view that the past was forever lost to a new way of life. One of the leaders of the Progressive Movement—the American political movement that consciously tried to manage the transformations of modernity—was Woodrow Wilson (1856–1924; 18th president of the United States, 1913–1921), who wrote in 1912:

> We have come upon a very different age from any that preceded us. We have come upon an age when we do not do business in the way in which we used to do business,— when we do not carry on any of the operations of manufacture, sale, transportation, or communication as men used to carry them on. There is a sense in which in our day the individual has been submerged. In most parts of the country men work, not for themselves, not as partners in the old way in which they used to work, but generally as employees,—in a higher or lower grade, of great corporations. There was a time when corporations played a very minor part in our business affairs, but now they play the chief part, and most men are the servants of the corporations. . . . Yesterday, and ever since history began, men were related to one another as individuals. . . . To-day, the everyday relationships of men are largely with great impersonal concerns, with organizations, not with other individual men. Now this is nothing short of a new social age, a new era of human relationships, a new stage-setting for the drama of life. (Wilson, 2005, p. 108)

John Dewey linked psychology decisively to modernism and Progressivism in his 1899 APA

Presidential Address. With Wilson, he believed that the premodern way of life was past saving, with Burke he believed that the force of morality was tradition, with Nietzsche that tradition ought to be abolished, and with the philosophes that tradition's replacement would be science. And that is where psychology enters the picture. Dewey said

> When men derive their moral ideals and laws from custom, they also realize them through custom; but when they are in any way divorced from habit and tradition, when they are consciously proclaimed, there must be some substitute for custom as an organ of execution. We must know the method of their operation and know it in detail. . . . So long as custom reigns as tradition prevails, so long as social values are determined by instinct and habit, there is no conscious question as to the method of their achievement, and hence no need of psychology. Social institutions work of their own inertia, they take the individual up into themselves and carry him along in their own sweep. The individual is dominated by the mass life of his group. Institutions and the customs attaching to them take care of society both as to its ideals and its methods. But when once the values come to consciousness, . . . then the means, the machinery by which ethical ideals are projected and manifested, comes to consciousness also. Psychology must needs be born as soon as morality becomes reflective. . . . Moreover, psychology, as an account of the mechanism of workings of personality, is the only alternative to an arbitrary and class view of society, to an aristocratic view. . . . It is the recognition that the existing order is determined neither by fate nor by chance, but is based on law and order, on a system of existing stimuli and modes of reaction, through knowledge of which we can modify the practical outcome. (Dewey, 1900)

But Dewey did not answer the question, "What is the 'science of values' psychology should teach?" Having scraped away the life world, psychologists had to find a "natural value system," as psychologist Abraham Maslow would put it. Psychologists have tended to find it in the inner self, following the total collapse of all sources of value outside the individual. Transcendent meaning had been debunked, and society had become the enemy; truth could only be found within (Haidt, 2012). As you and I have seen, psychologists are the students of the self, and so they have (apparently) taken it upon themselves to create a new way of life based upon the self and its needs.

learn, professional, applied psychology's first market was education (Danziger, 1990), and Dewey made educational psychology the starting point of psychology's Progressive future.

Educational reform was one of the central concerns of Progressivism, and Dewey was the founder of Progressive education. According to Dewey, education as it stood was ill-suited to the needs of urban, industrial America. G. Stanley Hall had begun the reform of education with his child study movement and the idea that schools should be child-centered institutions. Nevertheless, Dewey and the Progressives urged further reform. Immigrants were perforce bringing with them alien customs and alien tongues; they, and especially their children, needed to be Americanized. Immigrants from the farm also needed to be educated in the habits appropriate to industrial work and in new skills unknown on the farm. Above all, the schools had to become the child's new community. The old values of America's island communities were disappearing and so schools had to be made into communities for children and tools for reforming American society through the adults they produced. Schooling became mandatory and school construction entered a boom time (Hine, 1999).

"The school is an especially favorable place in which to study the availability of psychology for social practice," Dewey told the assembled psychologists. Sounding the themes of the psychology of adaptation, Dewey (1900) argued that "mind [is] fundamentally an instrument of adaptation" to be improved by school experience, and that for "psychology to become a working hypothesis"—that is, to meet the pragmatic test—it would have to involve itself with the education of America's young minds. Once involved with education, Dewey continued, psychologists would inevitably be led to intervene in society at large. Above all, schools must teach values, and these values must be the values of social growth and community solidarity, the values of pragmatism and urban life. Finally, these values are not just the school's values but must become the values of every social institution; and so psychologists must naturally become engaged in the great enterprise of Progressive social reform.

Progressivism was the modern American version of the Enlightenment Project, and as such, it condemned tradition and tolerated religion, aiming to replace them with a scientific ethos under the guidance of the new educated professionals, especially social scientists. Dewey recognized that the island communities' values were maintained through custom, but that once values "are in any way divorced from habit and tradition," they must be "consciously proclaimed" and must find "some substitute for custom as an organ of their execution." Consequently, psychology, the study of mental adaptation, plays a special role in the reconstruction of society:

> The fact that conscious, as distinct from customary, morality and psychology have a historic parallel march, is just the concrete recognition of the necessary equivalence between ends consciously conceived, and interest in the means upon which the ends depend. . . . So long as custom reigns, as tradition prevails, so long as social values are determined by instinct and habit, there is no conscious question . . . and hence no need of psychology. . . . But when once the values come to consciousness . . . then the machinery by which ethical ideals are projected and manifested, comes to consciousness also. Psychology must needs be born as soon as morality becomes reflective. (Dewey, 1900/1978, pp. 77–78)

Psychology, Dewey argued, is a social analogue to consciousness. According to James, consciousness arises in an individual when adaptation to new circumstances is imperative. American society faced imperative changes, Dewey said, and psychology was rising to meet them. Only psychology offers an "alternative to an arbitrary and class view of society, to an aristocratic view" that would deny to some their full realization as human beings. Echoing the philosophes of the French Enlightenment, Dewey said, "We are ceasing to take existing social forms as final and unquestioned. The application of psychology to social institutions is . . . just the recognition of the principle of sufficient reason in the large matters of social life." The arrangements that exist among people are the results of the working of scientific laws of human behavior, and once psychologists understand these laws, they will be able to construct a more perfect society by substituting rational planning for haphazard growth. "The entire problem," Dewey concluded, "is one of the development of science, and of its applications to life." Abandoning the capricious freedom of aristocratic society, we should look forward to a scientific society, anticipating "no other outcome than increasing control in the ethical sphere." In the new society, psychology will "enable human effort to expend itself sanely, rationally, and with assurance."

In his address, Dewey touched all the themes of Progressivism, and he deepened and developed them over the course of a long career as a public philosopher. He gave Progressivism its voice; as one Progressive said, "We were all Deweyites before we read Dewey." For not only was Progressivism the politics of the moment and of the future, it reflected America's deepest traditions: distrust of aristocrats—hereditary, moneyed, or elected—and a commitment to equal treatment of all.

Where Progressivism and Dewey broke new ground was in their conceptions of the ends to be reached by society and the means to be used to reach them. As Tocqueville had observed, Americans distrusted intellect, which they associated with aristocracy, and still did nearly a century later. In 1912, the *Saturday Evening Post* attacked colleges for encouraging "that most un-American thing called class and culture. . . . There should be no such thing [in America] as a superior mind." Yet, progressivism called for government rule by a scientifically trained, managerial elite. In a progressively reformed city, the political authority of the mayor was replaced by the expertise of a university-trained city manager, whose job description was taken from big business. Progressives were obsessed by social control, the imposing of order on the disordered mass of turn-of-the-century American citizens.

Progressivism's permanent legacy is government bureaucracy. The "corrupt" politicians of the urban machine knew their constituents as individuals, to be helped or harmed insofar as they supported the machine. Bureaucracy, in contrast, is rational and impersonal: rule by the expert. Questing for fairness, it imposes anonymity; people become numbers; the poor become case files to be scientifically managed and manipulated to ensure the good of the whole. Bureaucratic social control was to rest on the findings of social scientists, including psychologists, a Comtean elite of scientist-rulers who kept their secrets to themselves, lest society dissolve. The sociologist Edward A. Ross wrote, "The secret of social order is not to be bawled from every housetop. . . . The social investigator . . . will venerate the moral system too much to uncover its nakedness. . . . He will address himself to those who administer the moral capital of society." The social scientist, Ross said, was a Nietzschean "Strong Man," guarding society (quoted by D. Ross, 1991). G. T. Ladd, for all that he disdained psychology as a natural science, agreed with Ross's goals. Ladd revived Aristotle's vision of an "aristocratic government" ruled not by the unreliable "character of the common people," but classes of "leisure, social standing, and wealth," including scientists whose rigorous training for the pursuit of truth made them disinterested "benefactors of mankind" (quoted by O'Donnell, 1985, p. 138).

The goal of society in the progressive vision was the cultivation of the individual within a supportive community that nurtures him or her. Progressives valued enduring achievements less than personal growth. As Dewey later wrote, "The process of growth, of improvement and progress, rather than . . . the result, becomes the significant thing. . . . Not perfection as a final goal, but the ever-enduring process of perfecting, maturing, refining is the aim in living. . . . Growth itself is the only moral end" (Dewey, 1920/1948/1957). Progressivism's novel goal is Lamarckian. As there is no end to progressive (i.e., Lamarckian) evolution, there should be no end to personal growth. Science had abolished God, but Dewey defined a new sin; as a Progressive enthusiast wrote: "The long disputed sin against the holy ghost has been found . . . the refusal to cooperate with the vital principle of betterment."

In Dewey's view, individuals acquire their personality and thoughts from society. There is, in reality, no individual who preexists society, nor is society a collection of separate individuals. Although the island communities were failing, Americans still craved community, and Progressives offered a new kind of rationally planned community. A leading Progressive, Randolph Bourne, argued that in the new order of things, nothing was as important as a "glowing personality"; self-cultivation "becomes almost a duty if one wants to be effective toward the great end" of reforming society. Hence, deliberate social planning would bring about individual fulfillment. As Dewey put it, the individual should be developed so "that he shall be in harmony with all others in the state, that is, that he shall possess as his own the unified will of the community. . . . The individual is not sacrificed; he is brought to reality in the state" (quoted by Ross, 1991, p. 163).

Nevertheless, despite its resonance with certain American values, Progressivism was at odds with America's individualistic, libertarian past. Following Dewey, sociologist Albion Small denounced the "preposterous [American belief in the] initial fact of the individual" (quoted by Diggins, 1994, p. 364). The scientific view of people and the scientific management of society on psychological principles had no room for individual freedom, for, of course, in naturalistic science there is no freedom. The individual should be cultivated, but in the interests of the whole state:

> Social control cannot be individually determined, but must proceed from a controlled environment which provides the individual with a uniform and constant source of stimuli. . . . The counter plea of "interference with individual liberty" should have no weight in court, for individuals have no liberties in opposition to a scientifically controlled society but find all their legitimate freedom in conformity to and furtherance of such social function. (Bernard, 1911)

The Progressive vision was not, of course, confined to psychology but was remaking all the social sciences along similar lines (Ross, 1991). The inevitable direction was behavioral because, ultimately, social control is control of behavior. And to achieve social control, psychologists would have to give up the useless and arcane practice of introspection for the practical study of behavior, aiming to discover scientific principles by which Progressives might achieve social control. As the twentieth century went on, psychologists strove to fulfill Dewey's hopes. Psychologists increasingly moved out into society, remaking its misfits, its children, its schools, its government, its businesses, and its very *psyche*. Psychology in the twentieth century would profoundly alter our conceptions of ourselves, our needs, our loved ones, and our neighbors. John Dewey, philosopher and psychologist, more than any other single person, drew the blueprint of the twentieth-century American mind.

ORIGINS OF APPLIED PSYCHOLOGY: MENTAL TESTING

We look at the origins of mental testing in more detail in this chapter. The mental test was fundamental for the founding of professional psychology and remains central to psychological practice today. Mental tests were not invented for scientific motives, but in the service of public education. In the second half of the nineteenth century, governments began first to provide universal primary education and then to make it compulsory. It became desirable to establish standards of achievement, to evaluate students with respect to the standards, and to measure differences in children's mental abilities. Experimental psychology studied the normal human mind, regarding individual differences as error variance to be minimized by careful experimental control. Mental testing, on the other hand, was directly concerned with carefully measuring individual differences. For mental testing, there was no normal human mind, only the average one.

Some early mental testing was based on phrenology, which had inherited from Gall the goal of determining differences in mental and personal abilities. Popular phrenology foreshadowed future developments in mental testing, ranging from personnel selection to premarital counseling, and especially in America, phrenologists tried to use their methods in the interests of educational reform. However, phrenology did not work and so fell into disfavor. More scientific methods of mental testing were developed in Great Britain and in France, and the way testing developed in the two countries was influenced by the legacies of British and French philosophy.

Testing in Britain: Sir Francis Galton (1822–1911)

Francis Galton was a well-to-do cousin of Charles Darwin and collaborated with him on disappointing experiments on the basis of heredity. Galton became interested in the evolution of mental traits, and in his *Hereditary Genius* (1869), he "propose[d] to show that a man's natural abilities are derived by inheritance, under exactly the same limitations as are the form and physical features of the whole organic world." He traced the lineages of families in which physical abilities seemed to pass from parent to child and in which mental abilities did, too. Thus, for example, he would show that one family produced generations of outstanding college wrestlers while another produced outstanding lawyers and judges.

Above all, Galton wanted to measure intelligence, for him the master mental ability. He looked at schoolchildren's examination scores to see if those who did well or badly in one subject did so in all. To this end, he devised the correlation coefficient, known today as the *Pearson product-moment correlation*, so named because Galton's student Karl Pearson (1857–1936) perfected its calculation. Galton found that there was a strong correlation among examination grades, supporting the idea that intelligence is a single mental ability. Galton's claim began the unresolved controversy over general intelligence. Followers of Galton believe that most intelligence can be accounted for by a single psychometric factor, *g*. Critics believe that intelligence is composed of multiple skills; not intelligence but intelligences (Gardner, 1983).

Rather than depend on teachers' imprecise grades, Galton tried to measure intelligence more precisely. His methods were rooted in British empiricism. If the mind was a collection of ideas, as Hume taught, then a person's intelligence would depend on how precisely he or she could represent the world in consciousness. Measures of sensory acuity, then, would be measures of intelligence. Focus on consciousness was also consistent with the German introspective study of the contents of consciousness, and some of Galton's measures were adaptations of psychophysical methods. In addition, Galton believed, as did many scientists, including Broca, that the bigger the brain, the more intelligent the mind it caused. Therefore, head size would also be a measure of intelligence.

Galton established in South Kensington, a suburb of London, an anthropometric laboratory at which people could take his mental tests. A similar exhibit introduced Americans to psychology at the Columbian Exposition in 1893. Galton's anthropometric laboratory created one of three important models for the conduct of psychological work, the other two being the laboratory and the medical clinic (Danziger, 1990). Galton studied ordinary people, not the highly educated, trained observers of the introspective laboratories or the pathological subjects of the clinic. They paid a small fee to take the tests, and were called "applicants." Galton's practice probably emulated phrenology (Danziger, 1990), in which people paid fees to have their heads examined. Galton himself had at one time visited a phrenologist. Galton contributed twice to applied psychology—by inventing mental tests and by introducing the professional, rather than scientific, "fee for service" model of practice.

Testing in France: Alfred Binet (1857–1911)

Although Galton was the first to try to develop tests of intelligence, as a practical matter, his tests were failures (Fancher, 1985; Sokal, 1982). Sensory acuity is not the basis of intelligence, and the correlation between brain size and intelligence is real but small (Brody, 1992; Hunt, 2011). In Paris, Alfred Binet (1905) developed a more effective and durable means of measuring intelligence. Binet was a law student turned psychologist. Typical for a French psychologist, he was introduced to the field through the medical clinic, studying with Charcot. His early work concerned hypnosis, he conducted studies in many areas of psychology, and he was a cofounder of the first psychological institute in France, at the Sorbonne in 1889 (Cunningham, 1996). But he is most remembered for his intelligence test.

Binet's approach to testing combined the Cartesian emphasis on the highest mental functions of the mind with the French clinical orientation (Smith, 1997). In Galton's anthropometric laboratory and in the experimental laboratories of Germany, psychologists focused on simple sensorimotor functions. Binet, in contrast, studied high-level cognitive skills such as chess playing. He wrote, "If one wishes to study the differences existing between two individuals it is necessary to begin with the most intellectual and complicated processes" (quoted by Smith, 1997, p. 591). Binet's roots in the clinic also shaped his psychological research. Unlike the brief and anonymous studies of the laboratory, Binet studied individuals in great depth, even publishing their photographs in his publications (Cunningham, 1996). Along with coworker Victor Henri (1872–1940), Binet defined the field of individual, as opposed to German experimental, psychology in an article, "La Psychologie Individuelle" in 1895. They announced the practical value of their form of psychology, wishing "to illuminate the practical importance . . . [the topic] has for the pedagogue, the doctor, the anthropologist, even the judge" (quoted by Smith, 1997, p. 591). Binet's article is an important early manifesto of applied psychology.

Binet's test was developed through his work on a government commission formed in 1904 to study the education of the mentally subnormal. He had already studied cognitive development in children and had been a founder of the Free Society for the Psychological Study of the Child in 1899 (Smith, 1997). The government's aims called for a psychological version of clinical diagnosis in medicine. Mentally subnormal children interfered with the education of normal children, and the commission was charged to come up with a way to diagnose subnormal children, especially those on the borderline of normal functioning.

Binet (1905) carved out a new place for psychologists in the evaluation of subnormal children. He called his method the "psychological method" to separate it from the "medical method" of physicians and the "pedagogical method" of educators, praising it as "the most direct method of all." The psychological method "aims to measure the state of intelligence as it is at the present moment" without being concerned with diagnosis, prognosis, or worries about whether the retardation is "curable or even improvable."

Binet developed a practical "measuring scale of intelligence . . . composed of a series of tests of increasing difficulty." Binet's "tests" were eclectic. Some were simple sensorimotor tasks such as grasping a seen object. Others, such as arranging weights in order, were clearly based on psychophysics. Many of the tests were verbal in nature, ranging from naming objects to filling in the missing word in a sentence such as "The crow _____ his feathers with his beak," a test suggested by Ebbinghaus. Consistent with his French emphasis on thinking as the heart of intelligence, Binet identified one test as especially important, replying to an abstract question such as "When one has need of good advice—what must one do?"

Through extensive empirical trials, Binet determined the different ages at which normal children performed each of his tests. Then one could compare the performance of a given child to those of his or her age-mates. The subnormal child was one who could not solve the problems solved by children of the same age. Subnormal children could then be detected, removed from the classroom, and given special education.

Binet's test was much more useful than Galton's. American psychologist Henry Goddard (1866–1957), a teacher turned psychologist, was research psychologist at an institution, the Vineland (New Jersey) Training School for Feeble-Minded Boys and Girls, that housed children with a variety of disorders such as epilepsy, autism, and mental retardation. An important problem was determining which children were mentally subnormal and which were physically ill. Goddard initially tried to use Galton-like modifications of standard laboratory methods, but they proved useless. He learned about Binet's test on a visit to Europe in 1908, and introduced it to Vineland, where he found it "met our needs" (quoted by Smith, 1997, p. 595).

Because his concern was practical rather than theoretical, Binet did not develop a general theory of intelligence. He did, however, touch on some perennial issues in the psychology of intelligence. First, as already noted, in contrast to the English empiricist tendency to identify intelligence with precise sensory abilities, Binet shared the French rationalist tendency to identify intelligence with the higher mental processes. He rejected the sensory approach as "wasted time," asking rhetorically, "What does it matter . . . whether the organs of sense function normally? . . . Helen Keller . . . [was] blind as well as deaf, but this did not prevent [her] from being very intelligent" (1905). On this point, Binet's approach has prevailed.

With regard to whether intelligence was a single ability, as Galton held, or a collection of abilities, Binet vacillated. He seemed to dismiss Galton's viewpoint when he wrote that intelligence "cannot be measured as linear surfaces are measured, because there are 'diverse intelligences' " (1905). On the other hand, he used the term *general intelligence* and even proposed a single ability lying behind it: "In intelligence there is fundamental faculty. . . . This faculty is judgment . . . the faculty of adapting one's self to circumstances." Indeed, the basic idea of Binet's test—to see if "one [person] rises above the other and to how many degrees"—seems to presuppose a Galtonian notion of general intelligence as an abstract ability.

Binet (1905) also shared Galton's aim to "separate natural intelligence from instruction. It is the intelligence alone that we seek to measure. . . . We believe we have succeeded in completely disregarding the acquired information of the subject. . . . It is simply the level of [the subject's] natural intelligence that is taken into account." Like the existence of general intelligence, the ability of a test to measure intelligence independent of education would prove intensely controversial within psychometric psychology, especially when doing well on standardized tests such as the SAT became crucial to educational, professional, and social advancement.

Educational psychology and mental testing also developed in Germany, though more slowly than elsewhere. Most important was the work of William Stern (1871–1938), who introduced the concept of the intelligence quotient, or IQ, a quantitative way of stating a child's mental standing with respect to his or her peers. Binet's test allowed one to measure the "mental age" of a child that then could be set in a ratio to his or her chronological age. Thus, if a 10-year-old child passed the items typically passed by 10-year-olds, the child's IQ was $10/10 = 1$, which Stern multiplied by

100 to eliminate decimals; hence, "normal" IQ was always 100. A subnormal child would have an IQ less than 100, and an advanced child would have an IQ above 100. Although IQ is no longer calculated this way, the term remains in use, though Stern himself came to regard its influence as "pernicious" (Schmidt, 1996).

The influence of mental testing was profound and continues today. It was the cornerstone of early applied psychology, providing a concrete method by which psychology could be applied in a variety of areas, beginning in education but soon moving to fields such as personnel placement and personality assessment. Mental testing has become an important social force as people's educational and career paths have been shaped, and sometimes even been determined, by scores on mental tests. People have been ordered sterilized because of the results of mental tests (see later). As a practical matter, the everyday impact of mental testing has been much greater than that of experimental psychology.

FOUNDING APPLIED PSYCHOLOGY IN THE UNITED STATES

In 1892, William James wrote: "The kind of psychology which could cure a case of melancholy, or charm a chronic insane delusion away, ought certainly to be preferred to the most seraphic insight into the nature of the soul." James identified a tension in modern psychology—especially modern American psychology—that has steadily increased throughout the twentieth century: the tension between the psychologist as scientist and the psychologist as practitioner of a craft. The tension has been most evident in the history of the APA, founded in 1892. It was founded to advance the cause of psychology as science, but very quickly its members turned to the application of their science, and the APA found itself embroiled in largely unwanted problems concerned with defining and regulating the practice of psychology as a technological profession. There was, however, especially in America, no going back on the development of professional applied psychology: Psychology's social circumstances and the ideologies of pragmatism and functionalism required it.

In nineteenth-century Germany, the academicians who controlled the gates of admission to the great universities had needed to be convinced of psychology's legitimacy as a discipline. Their leading academicians were the philosophers; in their Mandarin culture, pure knowledge was valued above technology. Naturally, Wundt and the other German psychologists founded a discipline strictly devoted to "seraphic insights into the nature of the soul." In the United States, things were very different. American universities were not institutions controlled by a few academicians working for the central state; they were a variegated collection of public and private schools subject more to local whim than central control. As Tocqueville observed, Americans valued what brought practical success and sought social and personal improvement rather than pure knowledge. So the tribunal that would pass on psychology's worthiness in America was composed of practical men of business and industry interested in techniques of social control. Naturally, then, psychologists came to stress the social and personal utility of their discipline instead of its refined scientific character.

As with phrenology, American psychology wanted to be recognized as a science, but especially as a science with practical aims. On the occasion of the 25th anniversary of the APA, John Dewey (1917) denounced the concept, characteristic of Gall or Wundt, of the mind as a creation of nature existing before society. By placing mind beyond society's control, such a view acted as a bastion of political conservatism, Dewey held. He offered his pragmatic conception of mind as a social creation as the proper foundation for experimental psychology. Because, in Dewey's view, mind was created by society, it could be deliberately molded by society, and psychology, the science of the mind, could take as its goal social control, the scientific management of society. Such a psychology would fall in with Progressivism and give American psychology the social utility Wundt's psychology lacked.

American psychologists thus offered a science with pragmatic "cash value." Pragmatism demanded that ideas become true by making a difference to human conduct; so, to be true, psychological ideas would have to show that they did matter to individuals and society. Functionalism argued that the role of mind was to adjust the behavior of the individual organism to the environment. Naturally, then, psychologists would come to be interested in how the process of adjustment played itself out in American life, and they would then move to improve the process of adjustment to make it more efficient and to repair it when it went awry. Because adjustment was the great function of mind, every sphere of human life was opened to the psychological technologist: the child's adjustment to the family, parents' adjustments to their children and to each other, the worker's adjustment to the workplace, the soldier's adjustment to the army, and so on, through every aspect of personality and behavior. No aspect of life would finally escape the clinical gaze of professional psychologists.

Testing: The Galtonian Tradition in the United States

Central to the first applications of psychology was mental testing. Galton's approach to intelligence and his evolutionary approach to the mind proved quite influential, especially in America. Galton's methods were carried to America by James McKeen Cattell (1860–1944), who coined the term *mental test* in 1890. Cattell took his degree with Wundt in Leipzig, but worked in the anthropometric laboratory under Galton, epitomizing the historian of psychology E. G. Boring's (1929/1950) remark that although American psychologists got their brass instruments from Wundt, they got their inspiration from Galton.

It was through testing that ordinary Americans first met the science of psychology when at the Columbian Exposition they entered an exhibit and took psychological tests.

When Cattell introduced the term *mental test*, he clearly saw tests as part of scientific psychology, rather than as the first step toward the development of a psychological profession. Tests were, for Cattell, a form of scientific measurement of equal value to psychological experimentation:

> Psychology cannot attain the certainty and exactness of the physical sciences, unless it rests on a foundation of experiment and measurement. A step in this direction could be made by applying a series of mental tests and measurements to a large number of individuals. The results would be of considerable scientific value in discovering the constancy of mental processes, their interdependence, and their variation under different circumstances. (1890)

As tests grew in importance to psychology, concerns arose over what kinds of tests were of greatest value. The APA appointed a committee to report on the matter (Baldwin, Cattell, & Jastrow, 1898). Modern readers, used to paper-and-pencil tests, will be surprised at early lists of psychological tests. Cattell (1890) listed ten tests he gave to "all who present themselves" to his laboratory at the University of Pennsylvania. Some of the tests were purely physical, such as "dynamometer pressure." Some were psychophysical, such as "Least noticeable difference in weight." The most "purely mental" measurement was "Number of letters remembered on once hearing," assessing what cognitive psychologists today call *short-term*, or working, memory. Similarly, the tests recommended by the APA committee included measures of "the senses," reflecting the empiricist emphasis on sensory acuity, "motor capacities," and "complex mental processes." The tests in the last category still tended to measure simple capacities, such as reaction time and association of ideas. The contrast between the Cartesian French desire to measure reasoning and the Anglo-American desire to measure sensory acuity and simple mental quickness remained.

By far the most important early American psychometrician was Lewis H. Terman (1877–1956). Binet's test of intelligence deeply impressed American psychologists such as Goddard, but only Terman was able to successfully translate and adapt Binet's test for use in American schools. The Stanford–Binet (Terman, 1916) became the gold standard in mental testing throughout the twentieth century. In introducing his test, Terman went far beyond the limited aims of Cattell and other testing pioneers, who saw testing primarily as a scientific tool. Terman linked testing to the Progressive movement, laying out grand ambitions for emerging professional psychology.

Like Dewey, Terman was interested first of all in the application of testing to education, but he expanded testing's horizons beyond the school system. Terman wrote, "The most important question of heredity is that regarding the inheritance of intelligence," and he followed Galton in believing that intelligence is determined almost completely by inheritance rather than education. Also like Galton, Terman thought that intelligence played a key role in achieving success, and that in the modern industrial world, intelligence was becoming more decisive than ever:

> With the exception of moral character, there is nothing as significant for a child's future as his grade of intelligence. Even health itself is likely to have less influence in determining success in life. Although strength and swiftness have always had great survival value among the lower animals, these characteristics have long since lost their supremacy in man's struggle for existence. For us the rule of brawn has been broken, and intelligence has become the decisive factor in success. Schools, railroads, factories, and the largest commercial concerns may be successfully managed by persons who are physically weak or even sickly. One who has intelligence constantly measures opportunities against his own strength or weakness and adjusts himself to conditions by following those leads which promise most toward the realization of his individual possibilities. (Terman, 1916)

It followed, then, that intelligence testing was important to scientific psychology—to settle the question of the heritability of intelligence—and to applied psychology to provide the means for sorting people into appropriate places in schools and work (Minton, 1997). Terman (1916) hoped that schools would make "all promotions on the basis chiefly of intellectual ability" instead of on students' mastery of the material of their current grade level. But Terman envisioned his intelligence test being used in any institution that had to manage and evaluate large numbers of people, describing the use of IQ tests in "the progressive prisons, reform schools, and juvenile courts throughout the country."

Most important to Terman was the identification and social control of people at the low and high ends of the scale of general intelligence. Genius needed to be identified and nurtured:

> The future welfare of the country hinges, in no small degree, upon the right education of these superior children. Whether civilization moves on and up depends most on the advances made by creative thinkers and leaders in science, politics, art, morality, and religion. Moderate ability can follow, or imitate, but genius must show the way. (Terman, 1916)

Later in his career, Terman launched a longitudinal study to identify the intellectually gifted and follow them throughout their lives (Cravens, 1992).

With regard to the "feeble-minded," Terman (1916) advocated the sorts of eugenics schemes that would be increasingly placed in operation after World War I. According to Terman, people with low intelligence should be feared:

> Not all criminals are feeble-minded, but all feeble-minded are at least potential criminals. That every feeble-minded woman is a potential prostitute would hardly be disputed by any one. Moral judgment, like business judgment, social judgment, or any other kind of higher thought process, is a function of intelligence. Morality cannot flower and fruit if intelligence remains infantile. (Terman, 1916)
>
> Consequently, the "feeble-minded" must be subjected to the control of the state to prevent their defective intelligence from being passed on.
>
> It is safe to predict that in the near future intelligence tests will bring tens of thousands of these high-grade defectives under the surveillance and protection of society. This will ultimately result in curtailing the reproduction of feeble-mindedness and in the elimination of an enormous amount of crime, pauperism, and industrial inefficiency.
>
> It is hardly necessary to emphasize that the high-grade cases, of the type now so frequently overlooked, are precisely the ones whose guardianship it is most important for the State to assume. (Terman, 1916)

Terman's prediction came true, as we will see later.

Articulating Applied Psychology: Hugo Münsterberg (1863–1916)

Surprisingly, the leading public advocate for the development of a distinct field of applied psychology was Hugo Münsterberg. When it came to scientific psychology, Münsterberg continued to develop the Mandarin introspective psychology he learned from Wundt. However, when he moved outside the laboratory and addressed the general public, Münsterberg put psychology to practical work.

In *On the Witness Stand: Essays on Psychology and Crime* (1908/1927), Münsterberg observed that although "there are about fifty psychological laboratories in the United States . . . the average educated man has not hitherto noticed this." Moreover, when people visited his Harvard lab, they tended to think it a place to do mental healing, demonstrate telepathy, or conduct spiritualistic seances. Münsterberg believed that it was fortunate for psychology that it should have initially developed in obscurity, because "the longer a discipline can develop itself . . . in the search for pure truth, the more solid will be its foundations." However, Münsterberg wrote, "experimental psychology has reached a stage at which it seems natural and sound to give attention to its possible service for the practical needs of life." He called for the creation of "independent experimental science which stands related to the ordinary experimental psychology as engineering to physics." Terman (1916) also suggested the creation of psychological "engineers." The first applications of applied psychology would come, Münsterberg said, in "education, medicine, art, economics, and law." The first two reflected existing realities in the application of tests in schools and in French clinical psychology, and the aim of Münsterberg's book was to apply psychology to law.

One of the books that so alarmed Warner Fite in 1918 was Münsterberg's *Psychology and Industrial Efficiency* (1913), because in it, Münsterberg retreated from defining psychology exclusively as the introspective psychology of consciousness. He also laid out a more expansive definition of applied psychology and its future role in everyday life. Münsterberg rightly identified the need of modern life for psychological services, an "increasing demand in the midst of practical life. . . . It is therefore the duty of the practical psychologist systematically to examine how far other purposes of modern society can be advanced by the new methods of experimental psychology." The goal of *Psychology and Industrial Efficiency* was to bring psychology to bear on one of these new "other purposes," aiding in the development of the new urban-industrial way of life, asking "how to find the best possible man [for a job], how to produce the best possible work, and how to secure the best possible effects."

In the book's conclusion, Münsterberg set out his vision for the future of applied psychology. Universities should create special departments of applied psychology, or independent applied laboratories should be established. "The ideal solution for the United States would be a governmental research bureau for applied psychology . . . similar to . . . the Department of Agriculture" (1913). Münsterberg worried that the ambitions of his "psychological engineers" might be caricatured, and he pooh-poohed fears that one day psychologists might demand mental testing of congressmen, or that experimental methods might be applied to "eating and drinking and love-making." Today, surrounded by psychology, it seems that Münsterberg's points of needless ridicule were really prescient predictions.

Despite fears that his proposals might seem silly, and observing that the path to it might be bumpy, Münsterberg concluded with a paean to the future psychological society:

> We must not forget that the increase of industrial efficiency by future psychological adaptation and by improvement of the psychophysical conditions is not only in the interest of the employers, but still more of the employees; their working time can be reduced, their wages increased, their level of life raised. And above all, still more important than the naked commercial profit on both sides, is the cultural gain which will come to the total economic life of the nation, as soon as every one can be brought to the place where his best energies may be unfolded and his greatest personal satisfaction secured. The economic experimental psychology offers no more inspiring idea than this adjustment of work and psyche by which mental dissatisfaction in the work, mental depression and discouragement, may be replaced in our social community by overflowing joy and perfect inner harmony. (1913)

However apt the term, professional psychologists would not be called Münsterberg's and Terman's "psychological engineers." They would be called clinical psychologists, a role quietly taking shape in Philadelphia.

PROFESSIONAL PSYCHOLOGY

CLINICAL PSYCHOLOGY As a working reality, clinical psychology—and thus professional psychology—was founded by Lightner Witmer (1867–1956) (Benjamin, 1996; Routh, 1996). After graduating from the University of Pennsylvania in 1888 and briefly teaching school, Witmer undertook graduate study. He began with Cattell, but ultimately earned his doctorate under Wundt at Leipzig. Returning to the University of Pennsylvania, Witmer's connection with education continued, as he taught child psychology courses to Philadelphia teachers; in addition to being the founder of clinical psychology, Witmer is a founder of school psychology (Fagan, 1996). In 1896, one of his students called Witmer's attention to a student of hers who, although of apparently normal intelligence, could not read. Witmer examined the boy and attempted to remedy his problem, producing the first case in the history of clinical psychology (McReynolds, 1996). Later that same year, Witmer founded his psychological clinic at the university and described it to a meeting of the APA in December (Witmer, 1897).

Witmer's clinic was not only the first formal venue for the practice of professional psychology; it provided the first graduate training program in clinical psychology. Its central function was the examination and treatment of children and adolescents from the Philadelphia school system, but soon parents, physicians, and other social service agencies took advantage of its services (McReynolds, 1996). Witmer's regimen of treatment was not yet psychotherapy as we recognize it today, but resembled the moral therapy of nineteenth-century mental hospitals. Witmer sought to restructure the child's home and school environment to change the child's behavior (McReynolds, 1996).

Witmer (1907) described his conception of clinical psychology in the first issue of the journal he founded, the *Psychological Clinic*. After recounting the founding of his pioneering clinic and training program, he observed that the term *clinical psychology* was a bit odd because the clinical psychologist did not practice the kind of one-on-one therapy people associated with physicians. "Clinical psychology" was the "best term I can find to describe the character of the method which I deem necessary for this work. . . . The term implies a method, and not a locality." For Witmer, because clinical psychology was defined by a method—mental testing—its scope of application was wide:

> I would not have it thought that the method of clinical psychology is limited necessarily to mentally and morally retarded children. These children are not, properly speaking, abnormal, nor is the condition of many of them to be designated as in any way pathological. They deviate from the average of children only in being at a lower stage of individual development.
>
> Clinical psychology, therefore, does not exclude from consideration other types of children that deviate from the average—for example, the precocious child and the genius. Indeed, the clinical method is applicable even to the so-called normal child. For the methods of clinical psychology are necessarily invoked wherever the status of an individual mind is determined by observation and experiment, and pedagogical treatment applied to effect a change, i.e., the development of such individual mind. Whether the subject be a child or an adult, the examination and treatment may be conducted and their results expressed in the terms of the clinical method. (1907)

With Terman and Münsterberg, Witmer looked forward to psychology's large-scale involvement with modern life.

Once launched, professional psychology took off. By 1914, there were 19 university-based psychological clinics like Witmer's (Benjamin, 1996). A similar institution, the child guidance clinic, was attached to the new Progressive juvenile courts. The first such clinic was attached to a juvenile court in Chicago in 1909, where psychologist Grace Fernald gave tests to children brought before the court. The first formal internship in clinical psychology was established in 1908 at the Vineland Training School for Feeble-Minded Boys and Girls, directed by Henry Goddard. As in France, clinical psychologists began to work with patients in mental asylums such as the prestigious McLean Hospital in Massachusetts. As the Progressive movement worked to keep children in school and out of the workplace, vocational bureaus were set up to issue "work certificates" to teenagers wishing to be employed rather than educated in the new high schools. Psychological testing became part of the process of issuing such certificates and placing children into suitable work (Milar, 1999).

While Hugo Münsterberg talked about psychology of business and industry, Walter Dill Scott (1869–1955) put it into action, beginning with advertising psychology in 1901 and moving into personnel selection by 1916 (Benjamin, 1997). The first tendrils of popular self-help psychology began to appear. In 1908, Clifford Beers, a former mental patient, started the mental hygiene movement with a book, *A Mind That Found Itself*, endorsed by William James himself. The movement was modeled on the great public health successes of the nineteenth century, which had eradicated ancient human scourges such as typhoid and cholera by teaching how to prevent disease by practicing good physical hygiene. The aim of the mental hygiene movement was to similarly prevent psychological disease. Psychology departments began to incorporate Mental Hygiene courses into their curricula; many are still there under titles such as Personal Adjustment or Effective Behavior. The movement also provided a further impetus to creating the child guidance clinics, which began to look for problems before they developed.

ORGANIZING PROFESSIONAL PSYCHOLOGY Professional, or clinical, psychology was a new development in psychology's short history, and its place in the world was uncertain. Existing professions disdained the mental testers even while they employed them (Routh, 1994). J. E. Wallace Wallin, for example, was employed to give Binet tests at the New Jersey Village for Epileptics (now the New Jersey Neuropsychiatric Institute) in 1910. Its superintendent was a physician who forbade Wallin to enter patients' cottages, to give a scientific paper without putting the superintendent's name on it, or even to leave the hospital's grounds without permission! At the same time, Wallin was disturbed by the fact that schoolteachers giving Binet tests were called "psychologists" (Routh, 1994).

To remedy this state of affairs, Wallin got together with other clinical and applied psychologists to organize the American Association of Clinical Psychologists (AACP) in 1917 (Resnick, 1997; Routh, 1994). Its major goal was to create a public identity for professional psychologists. The preamble of its bylaws proclaimed its goals to be improving the morale of professional psychologists, encouraging research on mental hygiene and education, providing forums for sharing ideas in applied psychology, and establishing "definite standards of professional fitness for the practice of psychology" (quoted by Routh, 1994). This last goal was the most novel because it sharply distinguished the interests of the new professional psychologists from the interests of the academic psychologists of the APA.

Although in 1915 the APA had supported clinical psychologists' desires to restrict the administration of tests to adequately trained people (Resnick, 1997; Routh, 1994), the creation of the AACP caused a stir. In 1961, Wallin recalled that news of the formation of the new group "spread rapidly and became the topic of consuming conversation" at the 1917 APA meeting. A well-attended meeting of the membership was hastily called, "characterized by a rather acrimonious debate, the majority of the speakers being bitterly opposed to the formation of another association" (quoted by Routh, 1994, p. 18).

To preserve the unity of psychology, the APA created a Clinical section to give professional psychologists a distinctive identity, and the AACP dissolved. However, the senior organization continued to resist setting standards for clinical training and practice. When the professionals of the Clinical section wrote their bylaws, the first listed goal was "to encourage and advance professional standards in the field of clinical psychology," but the APA forced its deletion (Routh, 1994). Additionally, the APA had agreed to issue certificates to the section's "consulting psychologists." Existing members of the section were to pay $35, at least $730 in 2012 dollars, and new members were supposed to undergo an examination. However, the scheme came to nothing. In 1927, F. L. Wells, who was supposed to head the certifying committee, confessed failure, observing, "One can see in this an argument for the organization of the psychological profession into a group distinct from the present one" (quoted by Routh, p. 24).

The interests of academic and professional psychologists were proving to be incompatible. The separation of the AACP from the APA was just the first divorce in the history of organized psychology.

Nevertheless, as the United States entered World War I, psychologists were actively applying their ideas and techniques—especially tests—to a wide range of social problems. Their efforts, however, were scattered and small scale. When the war came, psychologists enlisted to apply themselves to a truly massive task: the evaluation of men for fitness to serve in the U.S. Army. One year later, psychology had become a permanent part of the intellectual landscape of American life and its terminology had become part of the American vocabulary.

PSYCHOLOGISTS IN SOCIAL CONTROVERSY

The Shattering Impact of World War I

Because it has received so much less attention from Americans than World War II, the critical importance of World War I in shaping the modern world is frequently overlooked. It launched an 80-year world war that lasted from August 1914, when German troops crossed the border into Belgium, to August 1994, when the last Russian (not Soviet) troops left Germany (Fromkin, 1999). Bismarck's newly united German Empire was destroyed, replaced by an unpopular republic seized by Hitler and his Nazis, who then began World War II. The First World War created the Bolshevik Revolution in Russia, when German intelligence sent Lenin in a sealed train to Moscow, setting the stage for the cold war. To this day, the British debate whether they should have stayed out (Ferguson, 1999). World War I was incredibly bloody by any standard. One figure bespeaks the carnage: One out of every three German boys aged 19–22 at war's beginning was dead by its end (Keegan, 1999).

The Great War was an important turning point in the history of the United States. Entrance into the war marked the end of two decades of profound social change, transforming the United States from a rural country of island communities into an industrialized, urbanized nation of everywhere communities. The United States became a great power that could project military might across the Atlantic Ocean, helping to decide the outcome of a European war. Progressive politicians saw in the war a welcome chance to achieve their goals of social control, creating a unified, patriotic, efficient nation out of the mass of immigrants and scattered groups created by industrialization. Led by President Wilson, they also saw a chance to bring Progressive, rational control to the whole world. As one Progressive exclaimed, "Long live social control; social control, not only to enable us to meet the rigorous demands of the war, but also as a foundation for the peace and brotherhood that is to come" (quoted by Thomas, 1977, p. 1020).

But the Great War to End All Wars frustrated and then shattered the Progressives' dreams. The government created bureaucracies whose watchword was efficiency and whose aims were standardization and centralization, but they accomplished little. The horrors of the war, in which many European villages lost their entire male population for a few feet of foreign soil, brought Americans face to face with the irrational and left many Europeans with lifelong depression and pessimism. The victorious powers fell to dividing up the spoils of war like vultures, and Wilson became little more than a pathetic idealist ignored at Versailles and then at home, unable to bring America into his League of Nations.

The most intangible but perhaps most important legacy of the war was that it shattered beyond repair the optimism of the nineteenth century. In 1913, it was thought that war was a thing of the past. Businesspeople knew war would be bad for business; union leaders thought that the international bonds of socialist fraternity would trump petty feelings of nationalism. By 1918, such hopes were exposed as illusions. Part of the new pessimism was the death of authority. No longer would young men enthusiastically march to war, trusting their leaders not to betray them. Legislatures proved as erratic and war-prone as the kings of old. Intellectuals and social and political leaders

The Rise of Applied Psychology 1892–1939

learned the lesson that reason was not enough to achieve social control. In the aftermath of war, the lesson was underlined by the revolt of the Flaming Youth of the 1920s and the seeming breakdown of the families that had raised them. Convinced of the wisdom of science, however—for scientism still ran strong in America—American leaders turned to social science, especially psychology, to solve the problems of the postwar world, to give them the tools by which to manage the irrational masses, to reshape the family and the workplace. As Philip Rieff (1966) put it, the Middle Ages, with faith in God, ruled through the Church; the Progressive nineteenth century, with faith in reason, ruled through the legislature; the twentieth century, with faith in science tempered by recognition of the irrational, ruled through the hospital. In the twentieth century, then, psychology became one of the most important institutions in society; no wonder that psychologists' ideas became more widely applied, the latest scientific marvel read by leaders for clues to social control and by the masses for insights into the springs of their own behavior.

Psychology at War

Psychologists, like Progressives, saw the Great War as an opportunity to show that psychology had come of age as a science and could be put to service. The organizer of psychology's efforts to serve the nation at war was Robert Yerkes, the comparative psychologist. With pride he explained in his presidential address to the APA, just months after the war began:

> In this country, for the first time in the history of our science, a general organization in the interests of certain ideal and practical aims has been effected. Today, American psychology is placing a highly trained and eager personnel at the service of our military organizations. We are acting not individually but collectively on the basis of common training and common faith in the practical value of our work. (1918, p. 85)

Just as Progressives used the war to unify the country, Yerkes exhorted psychologists to "act unitedly in the interests of defense," bringing psychologists together "as a professional group in a nation-wide effort to render our professional training serviceable."

On April 6, 1917, only two days after the United States declared war, Yerkes seized the opportunity of a meeting of Titchener's "Experimentalists" to organize psychology's war efforts. Following a whirlwind of activity by Yerkes and some others—including a trip to Canada to see what Canadian psychologists were doing in their war—the APA formed 12 committees concerned with different aspects of the war, ranging from acoustic problems to recreation. Few young, male psychologists were left uninvolved; but in this war, unlike the next, only two committees really accomplished anything. One was Walter Dill Scott's APA committee on motivation, which became the Committee on Classification of Personnel of the War Department. The other was Yerkes's own committee on the psychological examination of recruits, which concentrated on the problem of eliminating the "mentally unfit" from the U.S. Army.

There was considerable tension between Yerkes and Scott from the outset. Yerkes came from experimental psychology and brought research interests to the job of testing recruits, hoping to gather data on intelligence as well as serve the needs of the military. Scott's background was industrial psychology, and he brought a practical management perspective to military testing, aiming above all at practical results, not scientific results. At the wartime organizational meeting of the APA at the Walton Hotel in Philadelphia, Scott said that he "became so enraged at [Yerkes's] points of view that I expressed myself very clearly and left the [APA] council" (quoted by von Mayrhauser, 1985). Scott believed Yerkes to be making a power play to advance his own interests in psychology, and he

458

accused Yerkes of concealing self-interest behind sham patriotism. The upshot of the quarrel was that Yerkes and Scott went their own ways in applying tests to the examination of recruits. Yerkes (who had wanted to be a physician) set up under the Surgeon General's office in the Sanitary Corps and Scott under the Adjutant General's office.

Insofar as concrete results welcomed and used by the military were concerned, Scott's committee was the more effective of the two. Drawing on his work in personnel psychology at the Carnegie Institute of Technology, Scott developed a rating scale for selecting officers. Scott convinced the army of the scale's utility, and he was allowed to form his War Department committee, which quickly became involved in the more massive undertaking of assigning the "right man to the right job" in the army. By the end of the war, Scott's committee had grown from 20 to over 175 members, had classified thousands of men, and had developed proficiency tests for 83 military jobs. Scott was awarded a Distinguished Service Medal for his work.

Yerkes's committee did little for the army—he won no medal—but it did a great deal to advance professional psychology. In this respect, its signal achievement was inventing the first group test of intelligence. Heretofore, intelligence tests had been administered to individual subjects by clinical psychologists, but, individual tests could not be administered to millions of draftees. In May 1918, Yerkes assembled leading test psychologists at the Vineland Training School to write an intelligence test that could be given to groups of men in brief periods of time. Initially, Yerkes believed that group tests of intelligence were unscientific, introducing uncontrolled factors into the test situation. He wanted to test each recruit individually, but associates of Scott's at Vineland persuaded him that individual testing was impossible under the circumstances (von Mayrhauser, 1985). Yerkes's group designed two tests, the Army Alpha test for literate recruits and the Army Beta test for presumed illiterates who did badly on the Alpha. Recruits were graded on a letter scale from A to E, just as in school; "A" men were likely officers, "D" and "E" men were considered unfit for military service.

Overcoming considerable skepticism, and following a trial period of testing at one camp, in December 1917 the army approved general testing of all recruits. Throughout the war, Yerkes's work was met with hostility and indifference by army officers, who saw Yerkes's psychologists as meddlers having no business in the army, and by army psychiatrists, who feared psychologists might assume some of their roles within the military. Nevertheless, seven hundred thousand men were tested before the program was ended in January 1919. With the invention of the group intelligence test, Yerkes and his colleagues had devised a tool that greatly expanded the potential scope of psychologists' activities and multiplied by many times the numbers of Americans who might be scrutinized by the profession.

In concluding his presidential address, Yerkes (1918), "looked ahead and attempted to prophesy future needs" for psychology. "The obvious and significant trend of our psychological military work is toward service . . . the demand for psychologists and psychological service promises, or threatens, to be overwhelmingly great." Yerkes foresaw better than he knew; although he spoke only of psychological service in the military, Yerkes's words describe the most important change in institutional psychology in the twentieth century. Before the war, applied psychologists had worked in relative obscurity in isolated settings around the country. During the war, they touched millions of lives in a self-conscious, organized, professional effort to apply psychology to a pressing social need. After the war, psychology was famous, and applied psychology grew by leaps and bounds, concerning itself with the "menace of the feebleminded," with immigrants, with troubled children, with industrial workers, with advertising, with problems of the American family. Applied psychology had arrived as an important actor on the American social scene, and its influence has never ceased to grow in the 80 years since Yerkes called psychologists to military service.

Psychology in the American Social Context

As psychologists began to concern themselves with the problems of American society, they naturally became involved in social, political, and intellectual controversies outside academia. The first important social issue to involve psychology was the so-called menace of the feebleminded, the belief held by many Americans that their collective intelligence was declining. Publication of the results of the army intelligence tests tended for a time to support this belief. Alarm over the "feebleminded" fueled public and political interest in eugenics and led to the first attempts to strictly control immigration into the United States. As professional psychology continued to grow, psychologists began to investigate and affect more and more areas of human life. Most prominent were psychologists investigating and acting in the industrial workplace and those rethinking the functions of the modern family. In the 1920s, psychology became a major American fad.

IS AMERICA SAFE FOR DEMOCRACY? THE "MENACE OF THE FEEBLEMINDED"   Progressives believed with E. L. Thorndike (1920) that "in the long run it has paid the masses to be ruled by intelligence." But the results of the Army Alpha and Beta tests suggested that there were alarmingly few intelligent Americans ("A" men) and rather too many feebleminded Americans ("D" and "E" men). Yerkes's massive report on the results of the army tests recorded a mean American mental age of 13.08. Terman's work on translating and standardizing the Binet test had set the "normal" average intelligence at a mental age of 16. Henry Goddard had coined the term *moron* to denote anyone with a mental age of less than 13, so that nearly half of the drafted white men (47.3%) would have to be considered morons. Performance by recent immigrant groups and blacks was even worse. Yerkes (1923) told readers of *Atlantic Monthly* that "racial" differences in intelligence were quite real. Children from the older immigrant stock did well on the army tests. Draftees of English descent ranked first, followed by the Dutch, Danish, Scots, and Germans. Descendants of later-arriving immigrants did badly. At the bottom of the distribution of intelligence were Turks, Greeks, Russians, Italians, and Poles. At the very bottom were African Americans, with a mental age on the army tests of just 10.41.

In retrospect, we can see that the army tests of intelligence were remarkably silly. The cartoon in Figure 1, from *The Camp Sherman News*, reprinted in *Psychological Bulletin*, 1919, expresses the ordinary soldier's experience of the tests. Groups of men were assembled in rooms and given pencils and response sheets. They had to obey shouted orders to do unfamiliar things and answer strange questions. The test items that the unfortunate recruit in the cartoon has to answer are only slight exaggerations of the real items. Stephen Jay Gould gave the Beta test to Harvard undergraduates, following the exact procedures used in the war, and found that although most students did well, a few barely made "C" level. Gould's students, of course, were greatly experienced with standardized tests, in contrast with raw draftees under great stress, many of whom had little or no education. One can only imagine how puzzled and confused the average testee was, and can sympathize with the hapless soldier at Camp Sherman.

The results appalled people who agreed with Galton that intelligence is innate. In his book's title, psychologist William McDougall (1921) asked *Is America Safe for Democracy?* and argued that unless action was taken, the answer was no: "Our civilization, by reason of its increasing complexity, is making constantly increasing demands upon the quality of its bearers; the qualities of those bearers are diminishing or deteriorating, rather than improving" (p. 168, italics deleted). Henry Goddard, who had helped construct the army tests, concluded that "the average man can manage his affairs with only a moderate degree of prudence, can earn only a very modest living, and is vastly better off when following direction than when trying to plan for himself" (quoted

From *The Camp Sherman News*

FIGURE 1 That psychological examination, 1918. In retrospect, we can see that the army tests of intelligence were remarkably silly. This cartoon, from The Camp Sherman News, reprinted in Psychological Bulletin, 1919, expresses the ordinary soldier's experience of the tests. Groups of men were assembled in rooms, given pencils and response sheets, had to obey shouted orders to do unfamiliar things, and to answer strange questions. The test items that the fortunate recruit in the cartoon has to answer are but slight exaggerations of the real items. Stephen Jay Gould gave the Beta test to Harvard undergraduates, following the exact procedures used in the war, and found that although most students did well, a few barely made "C" level. Gould's students, of course, were greatly experienced with standardized tests, in contrast with raw draftees under great stress, many of whom had little or no education. One can only imagine how puzzled and confused the average testee was, and can sympathize with the hapless soldier at Camp Sherman.

by Gould, 1981, p. 223). The Galtonian alarmists were convinced that individual and racial differences were genetic in origin and consequently incapable of being erased by education. For example, Yerkes (1923) noted that African Americans living in northern states outscored those living in the southern states by a wide margin, but he claimed that this was because smarter blacks had moved North, leaving the feebleminded behind. He could, of course, have noted that African Americans were more likely to receive an education in the North than in the South, but he did not even consider such a possibility.

There were critics of the tests and their alleged results, but for a long time, the critics were ignored. The most insightful critic was the political writer Walter Lippmann, who published a devastating critique of the alarmist interpretation of the army results in the *New Republic* in 1922 and 1923 (reprinted in Block & Dworkin, 1976). Lippmann argued that the average American cannot have a below-average intelligence. Terman's figure of a "normal" mental age of 16 was based on a reference norm of a few hundred schoolchildren in California; the army results were based on over 100,000 recruits. Therefore, it was more logical to conclude that the army results represented average American intelligence than to stick with the California sample and absurdly conclude that the American average was below average. Moreover, the classification of men into A, B, C, D, and E categories was essentially arbitrary, reflecting the needs of the army, not raw intelligence. For example, the alarmists were concerned that only 5% of the recruits were "A" men, but Lippmann pointed out that the tests were constructed so that only 5% *could* be "A" men because the army wanted to send 5% of the recruits to Officer Training School. Had the army wanted only half the number of officers, the tests would have been designed to yield 2.5% "A" men, and the alarmists would have been even more concerned. In short, Lippmann showed, there wasn't anything in the army results to get excited about. But despite his cautions, many people did get excited about the army tests. The Galtonian alarmists pressed for political action to do something about the supposed menace of the feebleminded, and as we shall shortly see, they got it.

Another, more enduring legacy of the army tests was the enhanced status given to mental tests by their application to war work. Lewis Terman, whose interest in human measurement had begun at age 10, when his "bumps" were read by an itinerant phrenologist, was elected president of the APA. In his presidential address (Terman, 1924), he argued that mental tests were equal to experiments in scientific value and that, moreover, they were capable of addressing "one of the most important [issues] humanity faces," the relative contributions of nature and nurture to intelligence. Later, Terman (1930) predicted the widespread use of tests in schools, in vocational and educational guidance, in industry, politics, and law, and even in "matrimonial clinics," where tests would be given to couples before they decided to wed. The goals of the phrenological Fowlers would be realized in Terman's world. Another leading test psychologist, Charles Spearman, grandiosely described the results from intelligence tests as having supplied the "long missing genuinely scientific foundation for psychology, . . . so that it can henceforward take its due place along with the other solidly founded sciences, even physics itself" (quoted by Gould, 1981). Test psychologists were as prone to physics envy as were experimental psychologists.

Terman's vision appeared to be well on its way to fulfillment. In his report on the army results, Yerkes spoke of "the steady stream of requests from commercial concerns, educational institutions, and individuals for the use of army methods of psychological examining or for the adaptation of such methods to special needs" (quoted in Gould, 1981). With Terman, Yerkes foresaw a bright future for applied psychology based on mental tests. He (Yerkes, 1923) called psychologists to answer the "need for knowledge of man [which] has increased markedly in our times." Because "man is just as measurable as a bar or a . . . machine," psychologists would find that "more aspects of man will become measurable . . . more social values appraisable," resulting in psychological "human engineering." In the "not remote future," applied psychology would be as precise and effective as applied physics. The goals of Progressive social control would have been reached with the tools of psychology.

MAKING AMERICA SAFE FOR DEMOCRACY: IMMIGRATION CONTROL AND EUGENICS We can have almost any kind of a race of human beings we want.

> We can have a race that is beautiful or ugly, wise or foolish, strong or weak, moral or immoral. This is not a mere fancy. It is as certain as any social fact. The whole question lies in what we can induce people to want. Greece wanted beautiful women and got them. Rome did the same thing. The Dark Ages wanted ugly men and women and got them. . . . We want ugly women in America and we are getting them in millions. For nearly a generation . . . three or four shiploads have been landing at Ellis Island every week. If they are allowed to breed the future "typical American," then the typical future American is going to be as devoid of personal beauty as this vast mass of humanity, the majority of which has never learned to love or understand woman's beauty nor man's nobility of form. And the moment we lose beauty we lose intelligence. . . . Every high period of intellectual splendor has been characterized by "fair women and brave men." The nobility of any civilization can, to a considerable extent, be measured by the beauty of its women and the physical perfection of its men. . . . No man can travel over America and not be impressed with the association between a high type of womanly beauty and a high type of art and culture. . . . As I have said, it is all a question of ideals. We can breed the race forward or backward, up or down. (Wiggam, 1924, pp. 262–263)

Galtonians regarded recent immigrants and blacks as Prospero regarded Caliban in Shakespeare's *Tempest*: as "a devil, a born devil, on whose nature, nurture can never stick." The army tests seemed to demonstrate their irredeemable stupidity, fixed in the genes, which no amount of education could improve. Because education was helpless to improve the intelligence, morality, and beauty of Americans, they concluded, something would have to be done about the stupid, the immoral, and the ugly, were America not to commit "race suicide." Specifically, according to Galtonians, inferior stock would have to be prevented from immigrating to America, and those Americans already here but cursed with stupidity or immorality would have to be prevented from breeding. Galtonians sought, therefore, to restrict immigration to what they regarded as the better sort of people and to implement negative eugenics, the prevention from reproduction of the worst sort of people. Although they were only occasionally leaders in the politics of immigration and eugenics, psychologists played an important role in support of Galtonian aims.

The worst Galtonians were outright racists. Their leader was Madison Grant, author of *The Passing of the Great Race* (1916). He divided the supposed "races" of Europe into Nordic, Alpine, and Mediterranean, the first of which, blond and Protestant, were self-reliant heroes more intelligent and resourceful than other races. The Nordics, Grant and his followers said, had founded the United States but were in danger of being swamped by the recent influx of immigrants from other racial groups. Yerkes (1923) himself endorsed Grant's fantastic racism, calling for selective immigration laws designed to keep out the non-Nordics and so fend off the "menace of race deterioration" in the United States. Yerkes wrote the foreword for psychologist Carl Brigham's *A Study of American Intelligence* (1923), which used the army results to show that due to immigration—and, worse, "the most sinister development in the history of the continent, the importation of the negro"— "the decline of American intelligence will be . . . rapid . . . [unless] public action can be aroused to prevent it. There is no reason why legal steps should not be taken which would insure a continuously progressive upward evolution. . . . Immigration should not only be restrictive but highly selective" (quoted by Gould, 1981, p. 230).

Galtonians pressed Congress for action to stanch the flow of inferior types of people in the United States. Broughton Brandenburg, president of the National Institute of Immigration, testified,

"It is not vainglory when we say that we have bred more than sixty million of the finest people the world has ever seen. Today, there is to surpass us, none. Therefore any race that we admit to our body social is certain to more or less inferior" (quoted by Haller, 1963, p. 147). The most effective propagandist for the Galtonian racist view of immigrants was A. E. Wiggam, author of *The New Decalogue of Science* and *The Fruit of the Family Tree* (1924). Following Galton, Wiggam preached race improvement as almost a religious duty, and his popular books spread his pseudoscientific gospel to thousands of readers. The passage previously quoted reveals the crass racism and intellectual snobbery pervading the whole Galtonian movement in the United States. Wiggam's cant and humbug derive not from Darwin or Mendel, but from blind prejudice. In a scientific age, bigotry adopts the language of science, for the language of heresy will no longer do.

The Galtonian arguments were fallacious, and Brigham recanted in 1930, acknowledging the worthlessness of the army data. Nevertheless, in 1924, Congress passed an immigration restriction act—altered in the 1970s and again in 1991—that limited the number of future immigrants to a formula based on the number of immigrants from each country in 1890, before the flow of non-"Nordic" immigrants increased. Racism won a great battle in a nation that 148 years before had pledged its sacred honor to the thesis that "all men are created equal." No longer would the poor, huddled masses yearning to breathe free—Polish or Italian, Mexican or Vietnamese—find free entry into the land of the free.

But what could be done about the "cacogenic" (genetically undesirable) people already in the United States? The army tests did much to further the cause of eugenics in the United States. British eugenics was concerned with class rather than race, with positive rather than negative eugenics, and had no real success in obtaining eugenics legislation. American eugenics, however, was obsessed with race, proposed aggressive programs of negative eugenics, and was remarkably successful at getting them written into law.

Eugenics in the United States began just after the Civil War. At John Humphrey Noyes's Oneida Community, one of several socialist-Utopian "heavens on earth" created in the nineteenth century, a program called "stirpiculture" was begun in 1869. Based on Noyes's interpretations of Darwin and Galton, the program involved planned matings between the most "spiritually advanced" members of the community; not surprisingly, Noyes fathered more stirpiculture babies than anyone else (Walters, 1978). In the 1890s, the sexual reformer and feminist Victoria Woodhull preached that the goal of the emancipation of women and sexual education was "the scientific propagation of the human race."

Noyes and Woodhull followed Galton in advancing voluntary positive eugenics as the best application of evolution to human betterment. The turn to negative eugenics and to compulsory control of so-called cacogenic people began with the biologist Charles Davenport. With money from the Carnegie Institution, he established a laboratory at Cold Spring Harbor, New York, in 1904, which, with the addition of his Eugenics Records Office, became the center of American eugenics. Davenport was determined to "annihilate the hideous serpent of hopelessly vicious protoplasm" (quoted in Freeman, 1983) and popularized his views with *Eugenics: The Science of Human Improvement by Better Breeding* (1910) and *Heredity in Relation to Eugenics* (1911). Davenport believed that alcoholism, feeblemindedness, and other traits were based on simple genetic mechanisms, and that they in turn caused ills such as pauperism and prostitution. Prostitutes, for example, were morons who were unable to inhibit the brain center for "innate eroticism," and so turned to a life of sex. Committed to a belief that various ethnic groups were biologically distinct races, Davenport's writings are full of derogatory ethnic stereotypes supposedly rooted in the genes: Italians were given to "crimes of personal violence"; Hebrews were given to "thieving." Davenport claimed that if immigration from southeastern Europe was not halted, future Americans would be "darker . . . smaller . . . and more given to crimes of larceny, kidnapping, assault, murder, rape, and sex-immorality." Davenport wanted to place "human matings . . . upon the same high plane as that of horse breeding."

The leading eugenicist among psychologists was Henry Goddard, superintendent of the Vineland, New Jersey, Training School for Feeble-Minded Boys and Girls. Galton had drawn up family trees of illustrious men and women; with help from Davenport's Eugenics Records Office, Goddard drew up a family tree of stupidity, vice, and crime, *The Kallikak Family: A Study in the Heredity of Feeblemindedness*. Goddard presented the Kallikaks as the "wild men of today," possessing "low intellect but strong physiques." To support his description, Goddard included photographs of Kallikaks that made them look subhuman and sinister (Gould, 1981). Like Davenport, Goddard believed that "the chief determiner of human conduct is a unitary mental process which we call intelligence . . . which is inborn . . . [and] but little affected by any later influences" (quoted by Gould, 1981). Goddard held that "the idiot is not our greatest problem. He is indeed loathsome," but he is unlikely to reproduce on his own, so "it is the moron type that makes for us our great problem." Precisely because these "high grade defectives" can pass for normal, getting married and having families, Goddard feared their influence on American intelligence. Their numbers would swamp the relatively few offspring of the well-to-do, natural American aristocracy.

Davenport, Goddard, and other Galtonian alarmists proposed various eugenics programs. One was education, aimed to promote positive eugenics. For example, in the 1920s, state fairs featured Fitter Families contests, sometimes in a "human stock" show, where eugenicists set up charts and posters showing the laws of inheritance and their application to humans. Some eugenicists favored contraception as a means of controlling cacogenics, but others feared it would promote licentiousness and be used mainly by intelligent people able to make plans—that is, the sort of people who should breed more, not less. McDougall (1921) wanted to encourage the fit to breed by giving them government subsidies to support their children. Goddard favored the segregation of morons, idiots, and imbeciles in institutions like his own, where they could live out happy lives in a setting suited to their feeblemindedness, barred only from having children.

The solution favored by Davenport and most other eugenicists was compulsory sterilization of the cacogenic. Voluntary methods were likely to fail, they feared, and permanent institutionalization was rather expensive. Sterilization was a one-time procedure that guaranteed nonreproduction of the unfit at small cost to the state. Sterilizations without legal backing had begun before the turn of the century in the Midwest; H. C. Sharp invented the vasectomy and performed hundreds on mental defectives in Indiana. Compulsory sterilization laws had also been introduced before the Great War. The first legislature to consider one was Michigan's, in 1897, but it failed to pass. In 1907, Indiana passed the first sterilization law, but it was overturned by the state supreme court in 1921 and was replaced with an acceptable law in 1923. After the war, state after state passed compulsory sterilization laws, until by 1932, over 12,000 people had been sterilized in 30 states, 7,500 of them in California. The conditions warranting sterilization ranged from feeblemindedness (the most common ground) to epilepsy, rape, "moral degeneracy," prostitution, and being a drunkard or "drug fiend."

The constitutionality of the compulsory sterilization laws was upheld with but one dissenting vote by the U.S. Supreme Court in 1927 in the case of *Buck v. Bell*, arising in the state of Virginia, second to California in the number of sterilizations performed. Carrie Buck was a 20-year-old girl living in the State Colony for Epileptics and Feebleminded in Lynchburg, Virginia, who bore an allegedly feebleminded daughter out of wedlock. An associate of Charles Davenport, Harry Laughlin, concluded, without himself examining Carrie Buck, that she was typical of "shiftless, ignorant and worthless class of anti-social whites in the South," and a typical "low-grade moron" (quoted by Quinn, 2003, p. 36). As a result of Laughlin's findings she was sterilized by court order, and she then sued the state of Virginia. Oliver Wendell Holmes, a justice noted for his sympathy with Progressivism and his willingness to listen to expert scientific opinion in deciding cases, wrote the majority opinion. He wrote: "It is better for all the world, if instead of waiting to execute degenerate offspring for crime, or to let them starve for their imbecility, society can prevent those who are manifestly unfit from continuing their kind. . . . Three generations of imbeciles are enough" (quoted by Landman, 1932).

There were critics of eugenics and especially of human sterilization. Humanists such as G. K. Chesterton denounced eugenics as a pernicious offspring of scientism, reaching toward "the secret and sacred places of personal freedom, where no sane man ever dreamed of seeing it." Catholics condemned eugenics for "a complete return to the life of the beast," seeing people as primarily animals to be improved by animal means, rather than as spiritual beings to be improved by virtue. Leading biologists, including most notably those who synthesized Darwin and Mendel, condemned eugenics as biologically stupid. For example, because 90% of all subnormally intelligent children are born to normal parents, sterilizing the subnormal would have little effect on national intelligence or the rate at which subnormal children were born. Moreover, the "feebleminded" could have normal children. Carrie Buck's child, initially called feebleminded, proved later to be normal, even bright. Civil libertarians such as Clarence Darrow denounced eugenic sterilization as a means by which "those in power would inevitably direct human breeding in their own interests." In the social sciences, the attack on eugenics was led by anthropologist Franz Boas and his followers. Boas argued that differences between human groups were not biological but cultural in origin, and he taught the "psychic unity of mankind." His teachings inspired psychologist Otto Klineberg to empirically test eugenicists' claims. He traveled to Europe and tested pure Nordics, Alpines, and Mediterraneans, finding no differences in intelligence. In the United States, he showed that northern blacks did better on intelligence tests by virtue of getting more schooling, not because they were more intelligent. In 1928, Goddard changed his mind, arguing that "feeblemindedness is *not incurable*" and that they "do not generally need to be segregated in institutions" (quoted by Gould, 1981).

By 1930, eugenics was dying. Thomas Garth (1930), reviewing "Race Psychology" for the *Psychological Bulletin*, concluded that the hypothesis that races differ on intelligence and other measures "is no nearer being established than it was five years ago. In fact, many psychologists seem practically ready for another, the hypothesis of racial equality." The leading spokesmen for eugenics among psychologists, Brigham and Goddard, had taken back their racist views. The Third International Conference of Eugenics attracted fewer than 100 people. But what finally killed eugenics was not criticism but embarrassment. Inspired by the success of eugenics laws in the United States, the Nazis began to carry out eugenic programs in deadly earnest. Beginning in 1933, Hitler instituted compulsory sterilization laws that applied to anyone, institutionalized or not, who carried some allegedly genetic defect. Doctors had to report such people to Hereditary Health Courts, which by 1936 had ordered a quarter-million sterilizations. The Nazis instituted McDougall's plan, subsidizing third and fourth children of the Aryan elite, and providing S.S. mothers, married or not, with spas at which to bear their superior children. In 1936, marriage between Aryans and Jews was forbidden. In 1939, inmates of asylums with certain diseases began to be killed by state order, including all Jews, regardless of their mental condition. At first, the Nazis' victims were shot; later, they were taken to "showers" where they were gassed. The final solution to the Nazis' eugenics desires was, of course, the Holocaust, in which 6 million Jews perished by order of the state. The Nazis enacted the final, logical conclusion of negative eugenics, and Americans, sickened by the results, simply ceased to preach and enforce negative eugenics. Many of the laws remained on the books, however. It was not until 1981 that Virginia amended its eugenics laws, following the revelation of state hospital records detailing the many instances of court-ordered sterilization. Eugenics continues as genetic counseling, in which bearers of genetically based diseases, such as sickle-cell anemia, are encouraged not to have children, or to do so under medical supervision, so that amniocentesis can be used to diagnose any undesirable condition, permitting abortion of "unfit" human beings.

Psychology and Everyday Life

PSYCHOLOGISTS AT WORK Aside from advertising psychology, which affects everyone with a radio or TV, more people have been affected by industrial psychology—the applications of psychology to business management—than by any other branch of applied psychology. As we have seen, the beginnings of industrial psychology lay before the war, but as with the rest of applied psychology, its efflorescence occurred after the war.

The goal of Progressives, in business as in government, was efficiency, and the path to efficiency in every case was thought to be through science. The first exponent of scientific management in business was Frederick Taylor (1856–1915), who developed his ideas around the turn of the century and published them in *Principles of Scientific Management* in 1911. Taylor studied industrial workers at work and analyzed their jobs into mechanical routines that could be performed efficiently by anyone, not just by the masters of a craft. In essence, Taylor turned human workers into robots, mindlessly but efficiently repeating routinized movements. Taylor was not a psychologist, and the shortcoming of his system was that it managed jobs, not people, overlooking the worker's subjective experience of work and the impact of the worker's happiness on productivity. Nevertheless, Taylor's goal was that of scientific psychology: "Under scientific management arbitrary power, arbitrary dictation ceases; and every single subject, large and small, becomes the question for scientific investigation, for reduction to law." And when these laws were understood, they could be applied in the pursuit of greater industrial efficiency.

Gradually, managers recognized that it was not enough to manage jobs; efficiency and profits could be improved only if workers were managed as people with feelings and emotional attachments to their work. After the war, in the wake of psychologists' apparent success with the large-scale personnel problems posed by the army, industrial psychology became increasingly popular in American business. Perhaps the most influential piece of research demonstrating the usefulness of applying psychology to industry—management via feelings—was carried out in the early 1920s by a group of social scientists led by psychologist Elton Mayo at the Hawthorne plant of the Western Electric Company.

The "Hawthorne Effect" is one of the best known psychological results. It seemed to demonstrate the importance of subjective factors in determining a worker's industrial efficiency. Although the experiments carried out were complex, the results from the relay assembly room are central to defining the Hawthorne Effect. A group of female workers assembling telephone relays was chosen for experimentation. The scientists manipulated nearly every aspect of the work situation, from the schedule of rest pauses to the amount of lighting. They found that virtually everything they did increased productivity, even when a manipulation meant returning to the old way of doing things. The researchers concluded that the increases in productivity were caused not by changes to the workplace, but by the activity of the researchers themselves. They felt that the workers were impressed by the fact that management cared about their welfare, and the workers' improved feelings about their jobs and about the company translated into improved output.

Following a Populist line of thought already articulated by John Dewey's prescriptions for education, Mayo (1933, 1945) thought that because of industrialization, workers had become alienated from society, having lost the intimate ties of preindustrial life that bound people together in the insular communities of the past. Unlike the nostalgic Populists, however, Mayo, like Dewey, saw that the agrarian world was irretrievably lost, and he urged business to fill the void by creating communities of workers who found meaning in their work. Various measures were instituted to meet workers' apparent emotional needs; one of the first and most obviously psychological was the creation of "personnel counseling." Workers with complaints about their jobs or about how they were being treated by their employers could go to psychologically trained peer counselors to whom they could relate their frustrations and dissatisfactions. Such programs slowly grew in numbers over the following decades.

The Hawthorne findings were reanalyzed by Bramel and Friend (1981) who concluded that the Hawthorne Effect is a myth (Bramel & Friend, 1981). There was no firm evidence that the workers in the relay room ever felt better about the company as a result of the experiments, and there was much evidence to suggest that the workers regarded the psychologists as company spies. The improved productivity of the relay assembly team was explained by Bramel and Friend (1981) as a result of the replacement in the middle of the experiment of a disgruntled, not very productive worker by an enthusiastic, productive worker. The original data from the Hawthorne studies has been reanalyzed by economists Levitt and List (2009), who also find no evidence of a "Hawthorne Effect." More broadly, radical critics of industrial psychology (Baritz, 1960; Bramel & Friend, 1981) have argued that industrial psychology produces happy robots, but robots nonetheless. Mayo's personnel counselors were to "help people think in such a way that they would be happier with their jobs"; one counselor reported being trained to "deal with attitudes toward problems, not the problems themselves" (Baritz, 1960). By using psychological manipulation, managers could deflect workers' concerns from objective working conditions, including wages, and turn them instead to preoccupations with feelings, to their adjustment to the work situation. Workers would still carry out the robotic routines laid down by Taylor, but they would do so in a happier frame of mind, prone to interpret discontent as a sign of poor psychological adjustment rather than as a sign that something was really wrong at work.

WHEN PSYCHOLOGY WAS KING The psychology of introspection did not appeal to the ordinary American. Margaret Floy Washburn (1922), a student of Titchener's, described in her APA presidential address the reaction of an intelligent janitor to her psychological laboratory: "This is queer place. It somehow gives you the impression that the thing can't be done." By the 1920s, however, psychology had gone behavioral and was proving—in industry, in schools and courts, and in war— that psychology could be done. Contemporary observers remarked on the tremendous popularity of behavioral psychology. The first historian of the 1920s, Frederick Lewis Allen (1931, p. 165), wrote: "Of all the sciences it was the youngest and least scientific which most captivated the general public and had the most disintegrating effect upon religious faith. Psychology was king. . . . One had only to read the newspapers to be told with complete assurance that psychology held the key to the problems of waywardness, divorce, and crime." Grace Adams (1934), another student of Titchener's, who had abandoned psychology for journalism and who had become quite critical of psychology, called the period from 1919 to 1929 the "Period of the Psyche." Humorist Stephan Leacock wrote in 1923 of how "a great wave of mind culture has swept over the community."

Psychology achieved its special place in public attention because of the intersection of the revolution in morals led by psychoanalytic enthusiasts (Ostrander, 1968) with the final triumph of scientism. "The word science," Allen said, "had become a shibboleth. To preface a statement with 'Science teaches us' was enough to silence argument." Religion seemed on the verge of destruction. Liberal theologian Harry Emerson Fosdick wrote: "Men of faith might claim for their positions ancient tradition, practical usefulness, and spiritual desirability, but one query could prick all such bubbles: Is it scientific?" (quoted by Allen, 1931). The faithful responded in two ways: Modernists such as Fosdick strove to reconcile science with the Bible; *fundamentalists* (the word was coined by a Baptist editor in July 1920) strove to subordinate science, especially Darwinism, to the Bible. Many other people, of course, simply lost all faith. Watson, for example, had been raised as a strict Baptist in Greenville, South Carolina, and had (like 71% of early behaviorists [Birnbaum, 1964]) chosen the ministry as his vocation, only to give it up on his mother's death. In graduate school he had a nervous breakdown and abandoned religion completely.

Science undermined religion; scientism bid to replace it. The young people of the 1920s were the first generation of Americans to be raised in the urban, industrial, everywhere communities of twentieth-century life. Cut off from the traditional religious values of the vanishing island communities, they turned to modern science for instruction in morals and rules of behavior. Postwar psychology, no longer preoccupied with socially sterile introspection, was clearly the science to consult for guidance concerning living one's life and getting ahead in business and politics.

Popular psychology simultaneously accomplished two apparently contradictory things. It provided people with a sense of liberation from the outdated religious morality of the past; this use was stressed by sexual liberationist yearning for the sexual freedom of a tropical isle. At the same time, it provided new, putatively scientific techniques for social control; this use was stressed by Progressives. As one popularizer, Abram Lipsky, wrote in *Man the Puppet: The Art of Controlling Minds*: "We are at last on the track of psychological laws for controlling the minds of our fellow men" (quoted by Burnham, 1968).

The first wave of popular psychology, and what the general public thought of as the "new psychology" (Burnham, 1968), was Freudianism which tended to dissolve Victorian religious ideals. Under the microscope of psychoanalysis, traditional morals were found to be neurosis-breeding repressions of healthy biological needs, primarily sex. Youth concluded from psychoanalytic doctrine that "the first requirement for mental health is an uninhibited sex life. As Oscar Wilde wisely counseled, 'Never resist temptation!'" (Graves & Hodge, 1940). Lady Betty Balfour, addressing the Conference of the British Educational Association in 1921, expressed the popular view of proper Freudian child rearing: She was "not sure that the moral attitude was not responsible for all the crime in the world." Children, vulgar Freudians believed, should be reared with few inhibitions, so they might grow up unrepressed, happy, and carefree, like Margaret Mead's notional Samoans (see discussion on pp. 475–476).

The second wave of popular psychology in the 1920s was behaviorism, which the general public sometimes confused with psychoanalysis. Robert Graves and Alan Hodge (1940), literate observers of the English scene, nevertheless described psychoanalysts as viewing people as "behaviouristic animals." The leading popularizer of behaviorism was Watson himself. He had turned to psychoanalysis in the wake of his nervous breakdown and, though impressed with Freud's biological emphasis, came to regard analytic psychology as "a substitution of demonology for science." The "unconscious" of psychoanalysis was a fiction, Watson held, representing no more than the fact that we do not verbalize all the influences on our behavior. If we do not talk about stimuli, we are not aware of them and so call them unconscious, according to Freudian jargon, but there is no mysterious inner realm of mind whence come hidden impulses (Watson, 1926c). According to Watson (1926a), there was "too little science—real science—in Freud's psychology" for it to be useful or enduring, and he offered behaviorism as the new claimant for popular attention.

Watson (1926a) described behaviorism as representing "a real renaissance in psychology," overthrowing introspective psychology and substituting science in its place. He consistently linked introspective psychology to religion and railed against both. Behaviorists "threw out the concepts of mind and of consciousness, calling them carryovers from the church dogma of the Middle Ages. . . . Consciousness [is] just a masquerade for the soul" (Watson, 1926a). "Churchmen—all medicine men in fact—have kept the public under control" by making the public believe in unobserved mysteries such as the soul; science, said Watson the philosopher, is "blasting" through the "solid wall of religious protection" (1926b). Having disposed of the traditional past, both social and psychological, Watson offered strong opinions and advice on the issues of the day.

Watson attacked eugenics. Belief in human instincts, he wrote, has been "strengthened in the popular view by the propaganda of the eugenists," whose programs for selective breeding are "more dangerous than Bolshevism." He maintained that there are no inferior races. Taking note of American racism, Watson said that Negroes had not been allowed to develop properly, so that even if a Negro were given $1 million a year and sent to Harvard, white society would be able to make him feel inferior anyway (1927b). A human being, Watson told readers of *Harper's*, is "a lowly piece of protoplasm, ready to be shaped . . . crying to be whipped into shape" (1927b) and promised that the behaviorist "can build any man, starting at birth, into any kind of social or asocial being upon order" (1926a).

Because there are no human instincts, and human beings could be built to order, Watson naturally had much advice to give to parents eager for scientific child-rearing techniques. Watson took a strong line, denying any influence of heredity on personality and maintaining that "the home is responsible for what the child becomes" (1926a). Homemaking, including child rearing and sexual technique, should become a profession for which girls ought to be trained. Their training would brook no nonsense about loving children, cuddling them, or putting up with their infantile demands. Watson viewed the traditional family (and the new affectionate family of other family reformers) with scorn. According to Watson, a mother lavishes affection on children out of a misplaced "sexseeking response." Her own sexuality is "starved," so she turns to cuddling and kissing her child; hence the need for training in sex.

Watson's advice on how to raise children is brutally behavioristic:

There is a sensible way of treating children. Treat them as though they were young adults. Dress them, bathe them with care and circumspection. Let your behavior always be objective and kindly firm. Never hug and kiss them, never let them sit in your lap. If you must, kiss them once on the forehead when they say good night. Shake hands with them in the

John B. Watson and Rosalie Rayner testing Little Albert for generalization of his conditioned fear of a rat.
(Professor Ben Harris, University of New Hampshire)

morning. . . . Try it out. . . . You will be utterly ashamed of the mawkish, sentimental way you have been handling it. . . .

Nest habits, which come from coddling, are really pernicious evils. The boys or girls who have nest habits deeply imbedded suffer torture when they have to leave home to go into business, to enter school, to get married. . . . Inability to break nest habits is probably our most prolific source of divorce and marital disagreements. . . .

In conclusion won't you then remember when you are tempted to pet your child that mother love is a dangerous instrument? An instrument which may inflict a never healing wound, a wound which may make infancy unhappy, adolescence a nightmare, an instrument which may wreck your adult son or daughter's vocational future and their chances for marital happiness. (1928b, pp. 81–87)

Watson's book (written with the assistance of Rosalie Rayner Watson, his second wife), *Psychological Care of Infant and Child*, from which this advice comes, sold quite well. Even Carl Rogers, founder of client-centered therapy and later a leader of humanistic psychology, tried to raise his first child "by the book of Watson." Occasionally, Watson so despaired of the ability of a mother to raise a happy child—he dedicated the child care book to the first mother to do so—that he advocated taking children away from their parents to be raised by professionals in a creche (Harris & Morawski, 1979), the solution proposed by Skinner in his utopian novel *Walden II*.

"The behaviorist, then," wrote Watson (1928a), "has given society . . . a new weapon for controlling the individual. . . . If it is demanded by society that a given line of conduct is desirable, the psychologist should be able with some certainty to arrange the situation or factors which will lead the individual most quickly and with the least expenditure of effort to perform that task." In his second career as an advertising executive, Watson had an opportunity to demonstrate the power of behavioral social control by manipulating consumers. Expelled from academia for his affair with and subsequent marriage to Rosalie Rayner, Watson was hired by the J. Walter Thompson advertising agency, which was looking for the scientific principles that would control the minds of men and women.

Central to Watson's schemes for social control was using the word as a whip to the human emotions. In evangelical preaching, words were used as whips to stir up hearers into an emotional conversion experience that would move them to Christ. To give a famous Puritan example, Jonathan Edwards's sermon, "Sinners in the Hands of an Angry God," which described people as suspended over hellfire like a spider on a single, silken thread, was constructed to appeal to his parishioners' hearts, not to their intellects. Watson was named after, and taught the views of, John Albert Broadus, a leading Baptist evangelist. Broadus taught that reason was not a secure base for morals, so that preaching had to exploit fear and anger as the emotional bases of the habits of good Christian living, and he praised Edwards's sermon. In "The Heart or the Intellect," Watson (1928a) described the need to condition the emotions in order to effect social control. The head, Watson said, cannot control the guts, making imperative the use of classical conditioning techniques to build in the habits demanded by modern society.

As evangelists had stressed fear in the training of children, so Watson's child-rearing advice always ran to the punitive. He said that people don't use their talents to the full because they have not been pushed hard enough: "The stuff [talent] is there crying out to be whipped into shape. It is a cry for getting some kind of shock or punishment . . . which will force us to develop to the limits of our capabilities" (Watson, 1927b). He repeatedly held up Little Albert B. (possibly alluding to Albert Broadus) (Creelan, 1974) as a model of proper emotional training. In adult humans, language could be used as Edwards and Broadus used it—to manipulate emotions to bring about some desired behavior. For example, in setting up an advertising campaign for baby powder, Watson used statements by medical experts to make mothers feel anxious about their infant's health and uncertain about their own competence to look after their child's hygiene. Feelings of anxiety and insecurity would then make mothers more likely to purchase a product endorsed by experts. At the same time, although Watson may not have meant to teach this message, his advertising made parents feel more dependent on experts to teach them how to raise their children. In this way, advertising helped to reinforce social scientists' message that society needed professional social scientists to solve its problems.

It is not surprising, then, that Progressives embraced Watson's behaviorism. In the New York *Herald Tribune*, Stuart Chase, who later coined the phrase *New Deal*, exclaimed that Watson's *Behaviorism* was perhaps "the most important book ever written. One stands for an instant blinded with a great hope" (quoted by Birnbaum, 1955). As Watson (1928a) had said, behaviorism gave society "a new weapon for controlling the individual," and Progressives were eager to wield it in pursuit of their dreams of social control. Watson, they thought, had correctly described the laws of conditioning governing the masses of humankind. Progressives, however, were pleased to place themselves among the "very few" individuals endowed with "creative intelligence," exempt from the laws of conditioning and able to use them as tools to escape "the voice of the herd" and to manage the herd toward Progressive ends. The "great hope" of Progressivism was always that an elite of scientific managers might be empowered to run society, and behaviorism seemed to provide exactly the techniques. Progressives needed to control the behavior, if not the minds, of men. Watson himself, it should be said, did not fall in with the Progressives' schemes. He insisted that the laws of conditioning applied to everyone, whether or not their ancestors had come over on the *Mayflower*, and that anyone could be trained to use behavioral techniques for self-control or the control of others (Birnbaum, 1964).

Watson's popularized behaviorism was welcomed by many, but others found it disturbing or shallow. Joseph Jastrow (1929) felt that psychology was degraded by Watson's popularization of himself in magazines and newspapers. What was valuable in behaviorism—the study of behavior—"will survive the 'strange interlude' of . . . behaviorism" and Watson's public antics. Grace Adams ridiculed Watson's behaviorism for sharing "most of the appealing points of psychoanalysis with few of its tedious difficulties," the resulting shallow system being "a cheering doctrine, surely—direct, objective, and completely American." Warner Fite (1918), already depressed by the experimental psychology of 1912, regarded behaviorism as the logical end product of scientism, or, as he put it, in "behavioristic psychology we behold the perfected beauty of the scientific prepossession." According to behaviorists, "Mind, in the sense of an inner, personal, spiritual experience, must be laid away, along with the immortal soul, among the discarded superstitions of an unscientific past. . . . According to them, your behavior is simply and solely what other persons are able to observe; and how you look, not to yourself, but to the world—that is all there is of you" (pp. 802–803). Lumping together the effects of psychoanalysis and behaviorism, Fite foresaw the psychological society of the later twentieth century: "Doubtless the time is coming, before we are through with the [scientific] prepossession, when all domestic and social intercourse will be made luminous and transparent by the presence of expert psychologists. In those fair days social intercourse will be untroubled by falsehood or insincerity, or even by genial exaggeration" (p. 803).

By 1930, the fad for psychology had run its course. After the crash of 1929, the popular media had more pressing economic matters to consider, and the volume of pieces written on psychology diminished noticeably. Grace Adams hoped that its influence was finished but, in fact, psychology was only in retrenchment (Sokal, 1983). Psychology continued to grow and expand its areas of application throughout the 1930s, albeit at a slower rate than in the glory years after World War I. Its reemergence on the popular stage awaited another cue of war.

FLAMING YOUTH AND THE RECONSTRUCTION OF THE FAMILY

> I learned to my astonishment that I had been involved in a momentous debauch; the campus reeked of a scandal so sulphurous it hung over our beanies for the rest of the academic year. In blazing scareheads the *Hearst Boston American* tore the veil from the excesses tolerated at Brown University dances. At these hops, it thundered, were displayed a depravity and libertinism that would have sickened Petronius, made Messalina hang her head in shame. It portrayed girls educated at the best finishing schools, crazed with alcohol and inflamed by ragtime, oscillating cheek to cheek with young ne'er-do-wells in raccoon coats and derbies. Keyed up by savage jungle rhythms, the abandonnes would then reel out to roadsters parked on Waterman Street, where frat pins were traded for kisses under cover of darkness. . . . The writer put all his metaphors into one basket and called upon outraged society to apply the brakes, hold its horses, and retrieve errant youth from under the wheels of the juggernaut. (Perelman, 1958, pp. 239–240)

Youth was in revolt during the 1920s—it was the Jazz Age and the day of the flapper—and, of course, the older generation, led by Hearst leader writers, were aghast. Youth seemed to embody the chaos of modernism described by William Butler Yeats in the poem "Second Coming." Confused and bewildered, the parents of the 1920s *Flaming Youth*—the title of a best-selling novel pandering to parents' fears, and object of Perelman's satiric pen—tried to understand what had gone wrong with their children, and, more important, they tried to learn what to do about it. The apparent crisis of the family and its youth created an opportunity for social scientists, including psychologists, to extend the realm of their concern, and of scientific social control, from the public arena of politics and business into the intimate circle of the family.

As social scientists saw it, families as traditionally conceived and organized were out-of-date in the modern world. Families had been economic units, in which father, mother, and child had distinct and productive roles to play. In the industrialized world, however, work was leaving the home, so that individuals, not families, were the economic units. Children should not be permitted to work because they needed to be in school learning the values and habits of urbanized American society. Women were "following their work out of the home" to factories and businesses. The labor of men was likewise apart from the home, being just an eight-hour job, not a way of life. The family was no longer a socially functional unit. Progressive Deweyites considered the family selfish because a parent's concern was for his or her own child, whereas in the modern, urban world it was necessary to be equally concerned for all children. The crisis of Flaming Youth was but a symptom, social scientists said, of a deeper social crisis.

The family would have to be remade, then, by professional social scientists bringing their expertise to bear on problems of family adjustment. Raising children could no longer be thought of as something anyone could do without help. The state, through professional social scientists, was to have the leading role in child rearing. As one reformer wrote: "The state is but the coordinated parentage of childhood . . . compel[ling] co-partnership, co-operation, corporate life and conscience" (quoted by Fass, 1977). In a phrase, motherhood must become "mothercraft," a profession requiring education and training. Making a profession of raising children advanced the cause of professional social science, providing an ideology that justified intervening in family life with "expert" advice not possessed by ordinary people.

Because the traditional family role as economic unit no longer existed, social scientists had to provide the new family with a new function: "The distinguishing feature of the new family will be affection. The new family will be more difficult, maintaining higher standards that test character more severely, but will offer richer fruit for the satisfying of human needs." "It does not seem probable that the family will recover the functions it has lost. But even if the family doesn't produce thread and cloth and soap and medicine and food, it can still produce happiness" (Fass, 1977). In the view of reformers, the function of the family was to produce emotional adjustment to modern life. The modern parent, then, was to become something of a psychotherapist, monitoring children's emotional states and intervening when necessary to adjust their states of mind. The ideas of the parent as professional and the family as the producer of emotional happiness were mutually reinforcing. Parents would need, at the very least, training in their new therapeutic roles, and they would probably also need a cadre of experts to call on for advice and to fall back on when acute difficulties arose. Applied psychologists would naturally find a fertile field for professional application of psychology to child rearing, child guidance, and child psychotherapy.

Meanwhile, youth were constructing a new set of values and a new social control system for themselves. As parents lost control of their children, youth found in the culture of their peers a new center for life apart from the family. They set their own values, their own style, their own goals. Central to the youth culture of the 1920s was having a "good personality," learning to be "well-rounded," and fitting in with other youth. Youth valued self-expression and sociability, attending to personal satisfaction instead of the production of objective accomplishments. Groups such as fraternities and sororities enforced conformity to the new rules of personality with therapeutic tricks of their own. Deviant youth were forced to participate in "truth sessions" in which their "objectionable traits" and weaknesses were identified and analyzed. Then the offender would make amends because "the fraternity's group consciousness is the strongest thing. One doing wrong not only disgraces oneself but his fraternity group" (Fass, 1977).

Parents and youth, then, were not so far apart, despite the ravings of Hearst's leading writers. Both were being remade by the "triumph of the therapeutic," the modern tendency to define life in psychological terms. Parents were learning that their function was therapeutic, producing emotionally well-adjusted children. The youth culture similarly valued emotional adjustment and tried to achieve it through therapeutic techniques of its own. The central values of the twentieth century were formed during the 1920s: being true to one's "real" self, expressing one's "deepest" feelings, "sharing" one's personality with a larger group.

Just as the new family and the youth culture were struggling toward a redefinition of life as centered on self-esteem, not accomplishment, an anthropologist and psychologist, Margaret Mead, came back from the South Seas bearing witness to an idyllic society in which people had little work to do and led peaceful lives of perfect adjustment, harmony, and sexual fulfillment. As in the Enlightenment, when philosophes had felt themselves emerging from centuries of religious repression, there was a longing for the free and easy life—especially the sexual life—apparently to be found in Tahiti. Committed to psychological environmentalism, the philosophers had thought that a Tahitian paradise could be constructed in Europe through social engineering. As twentieth-century intellectuals reacted against Victorian sexual morality and the excesses of eugenics, they felt themselves on the verge of a "new Enlightenment" or, as Watson put it, of a "social Renaissance, a preparation for a change in mores" (quoted by Freeman, 1983). So they were as fascinated by Mead's (1928) *Coming of Age in Samoa* as eighteenth-century readers had been by the first travelers' tales of the Pacific Islands. One reviewer of Mead's book wrote, "Somewhere in each of us, hidden among our more obscure desires and our impulses of escape, is a palm fringed South Seas island . . . a languorous atmosphere promising freedom and irresponsibility . . . Thither we run to find love which is free, easy and satisfying" (quoted by Freeman, 1983, p. 97).

Margaret Mead was a young psychologist and anthropologist who had studied under the founder of modern American anthropology, Franz Boas, whose opposition to eugenics we have already noted. Boas and his followers were convinced, with John Dewey, that human nature was, in Dewey's words, a "formless void of impulses" shaped by society into a personality. They agreed with Dewey that mind was a social construction owing nothing to nature and everything to culture. Similarly, culture was just "personality writ large," according to Ruth Benedict, another student of Boas: Personality, being entirely shaped by culture, imaged culture in the historical individual, and culture, the molder of personality, was the personality of a society. If eugenicists went to one extreme, denying nurture any influence over nature, Boasians went to the other, regarding culture as "some kind of mechanical press into which most individuals were poured to be molded." Agreeing with Watson at his most extreme, Mead wrote how the "almost unbelievably malleable" raw material of human nature was "moulded into shape by culture."

Mead traveled to American Samoa, conducted rather sloppy fieldwork, and returned with a description of a society that at once seemed to support the Deweyite and Boasian conception of an infinitely plastic human nature and to offer the ideal form of the happy society, in which people experienced "perfect adjustment" to their surroundings, their society, and each other. Mead limned a society that knew no Flaming Youth in stressful revolt against their parents; a society with no aggression, no war, no hostility; no deep attachment between parent and child, husband and wife; no competition; a society in which parents were ashamed of the outstanding child and proud of the slowest, who set the pace for the development of every other child. Most alluring was the idea that the Samoans, far from regarding sex as a sin, thought sexual relations "the pastime *par excellence*," a "fine art," making "sex [into] play, permissible in all hetero- and homosexual expression, with any sort of variation as an artistic addition." The Samoan avoidance of strong feelings and deep attachments extended to love: "Love between the sexes is a light and pleasant dance. . . . Samoans condone light love-affairs, but repudiate acts of passionate choice, and have no real place for anyone who would permanently continue . . . to prefer one woman or one man" (quoted by Freeman, 1983, p. 91). Samoans regarded jealousy as a sin and did not regard adultery as very serious, Mead reported. Before marriage, Mead wrote, adolescents experienced a free and easy promiscuity, each boy and girl engaging in many light sexual dalliances of no deep moment. There were no Flaming Youth because what Flaming Youth wanted, condemned by fuddy-duddy Hearst writers, was approved, even encouraged, by Samoan society. Samoans also lived the superficial lives of conformity to the group and average well-roundedness that Flaming Youth defined as its norm. Putting it in scientistic terms, one commentator on Mead's book remarked on "the innocent, strangely impersonal, naively mechanistic-behavioristic sexing of the lighthearted youths of far-off Samoa."

Mead's Samoans promised to resolve the nature-nurture disputes of the 1920s against the eugenicists and in favor of the Boasians. Her work also lifted up a vision of a new utopia of sexual freedom and perfect happiness, a vision that outraged Hearst's *Boston American* but became the foundation for the hedonistic philosophy of the 1960s. Finally, it gave psychologists the central role in constructing the new society. Commenting on the work of Boas and his students, Bertrand Russell, who had earlier endorsed Watson's behaviorism, asserted that "the scientific psychologist, if allowed a free run with children," could "manipulate human nature" as freely as physical scientists manipulated nature. Psychologists and other social scientists could ask, even dream, no more than this: to be the architects of a new Western civilization, well adjusted and harmonious, emotionally open and sexually liberated, warm and supporting and not in neurotic pursuit of excellence (Pinker, 2002).

Mead's Samoa, a culture entirely outside the traditions of the West, became the social scientists' Holy Grail, a blueprint for them to follow in constructing the New Man of Deweyite, Progressive idealism.

The reality behind the Flaming Youth and Samoan society was different, however, from both the Hearst writers' ravings and Mead's more prosaic depictions. Perelman's "orgy" was in fact "decorous to the point of torpor": "I spent the evening buffeting about the stag line, prayerfully beseeching the underclassmen I knew for permission to cut in on their women . . . [frequently] retiring to a cloakroom with several other blades and choking down a minute quantity of gin, warmed to body heat, from a pocket flask. Altogether, it was a strikingly commonplace experience, and I got to bed without contusions" (1958, p. 239). Derek Freeman (1983) has shown that Samoa, far from being the sexual paradise described by Mead, was obsessed with virginity and rife with rape, aggression, competition, and deep human feelings (see also Pinker, 2002).

The Psychological Society 1940–2000

PSYCHOLOGY IN WORLD WAR II

As it had just 24 years earlier, world war would profoundly affect psychology. The Great War to End All Wars had transformed a tiny, obscure academic discipline into an ambitious, visible profession. World War II provided an even greater opportunity for psychologists to act together in pursuit of social good and their own professional interests. Along the way, the war caused psychology to grow at a faster rate than ever, to reunify into a single academic-applied profession, and to invent a new professional role—the psychotherapist—which quickly became the role that defined American psychologists. After the war ended, psychology fought unsuccessfully to be included among the sciences supported by federal research money. As a profession, however, psychology was more successful. The government found itself in need of mental health professionals and embarked on a program to recruit and train a new psychological profession, requiring that psychology define itself anew and set standards for its practitioners.

Psychologists in Professional Controversy: The Clinicians Walk Out

After the Great War, the number of applied and professional psychologists increased exponentially. At the time, professional psychology was called, inappropriately, clinical psychology, because of its roots in Witmer's psychological clinic. In fact, the "clinical" psychology of these years bore little resemblance to today's clinical psychology. The term has come to mean primarily the practice of psychotherapy by psychologists, but before World War II, clinical psychology had mostly to do with giving tests to various populations: children, soldiers, workers, mental patients, and occasional individual clients.

From Chapter 14 of *A History of Psychology: From Antiquity to Modernity*, Seventh Edition.
Thomas Hardy Leahey. Copyright © 2013 by Pearson Education, Inc. All rights reserved.

The headquarters of the American Psychological Association in Washington, DC. This photograph is emblematic of the position of organized psychology today, an important institution with ready access to the corridors of political power. The three stated goals of the APA are to advance psychology "as a science, as a profession, and as a means of promoting human welfare." *(Hoachlander Davis Photography)*

In any event, clinical psychologists performed little research and were typically employed outside universities, working for companies, school systems, or as psychological consultants. The old guard of scientific psychologists who had founded the American Psychological Association (APA), for all their apparent commitment to useful psychology, was made uncomfortable by the increasing numbers of clinical psychologists. The APA, after all, had been founded to "advance psychology as a science," and it was not at all clear that clinicians were advancing scientific psychology because they did no research. Moreover, clinicians were predominantly women, and male psychologists had a hard time taking women seriously as anything more than psychological dilettantes.

During the 1920s and 1930s, the APA vacillated in its treatment of applied psychologists. Entry to the association had for some time depended on applicants having published articles in scientific journals; then a class of associate members was created for the nonscientists, who enjoyed only limited participation in the association. These clinical psychologists naturally resented their second-class status. During the same period, the APA recognized that, as the official organization of psychologists, it bore some responsibility for assuring the competence of practicing psychologists, and became concerned about charlatans and frauds passing themselves off as genuine psychologists and tarnishing the honor of the science in the eyes of the public. So for a time, the APA issued expensive certificates, badges of authenticity, to applied—or, as they were officially called, "consulting"—psychologists. The experiment was short-lived, however. Few psychologists bothered to apply for the certificates. The academicians of the APA also were unwilling to exert themselves to attain the proper ends of professionalization by enforcing standards and taking legal action against psychological frauds.

The tensions between academic and applied psychology grew to the breaking point in the late 1930s. Professional and applied psychologists realized that their interest, the creation of a socially accepted and defined practice of psychology on a par with physicians, lawyers, engineers, and other professional practitioners of a craft, could not be realized in an association devoted exclusively to psychology as an academically based science. As early as 1917, applied psychologists tried to form their own association, but the enterprise was controversial and died when the APA agreed to the creation of a clinical section within the association. In 1930, a group of applied psychologists in New York formed a national organization, the Association of Consulting Psychologists (ACP). The ACP pressed states (beginning with New York) to establish legal standards for the definition of "psychologist," wrote a set of ethical guidelines for the practice of psychology, and began its own journal, the *Journal of Consulting Psychology*, in 1937. Despite pleas by professional psychologists for the APA to get involved in defining and setting standards for practitioners of the psychological craft (e.g., Poffenberger, 1936), the association continued to fail them. So, in 1938, the unhappy psychologists of the clinical section of the APA left the parent organization and joined with the ACP to create the American Association for Applied Psychology (AAAP).

During the years between the world wars, applied psychologists groped for an identity distinct from traditional, scientific psychology. The interests of academic and professional psychologists were different and to some extent incompatible: the advancement of research versus the advancement of the legal and social status of clinicians. Academic psychologists feared the growing numbers of applied psychologists, worrying that they might lose control of the association they founded. Yet, the applied psychologists remained inextricably linked to academic psychology. They received their training in university departments of psychology and traded on the claim of psychology to be a scientific discipline. So, although applied psychologists established a professional identity by founding the AAAP, the divorce of scientific and applied psychology would, this time, be short-lived.

Reconciliation in the Crucible of War

In the 1930s, as we have seen, psychology was racked by deep divisions. Professional psychologists had formed their own organization, the AAAP, breaking with the APA in 1938. Another dissident group was the Society for the Psychological Study of Social Issues (SPSSI), formed by left-wing psychologists in 1936. Although affiliated with the APA, SPSSI psychologists, in contrast to the traditional academicians of the APA, aimed to use psychology to advance their political views. For example, SPSSI psychologists marched in New York's May Day parade carrying banners that read "Adjustment comes with jobs" (it was the depth of the Depression) and "Fascism is the world's worst behavior problem!" (Napoli, 1981). The older APA, devoted as it was to pure research and scholarly detachment, had a hard time finding a place for either the AAAP or SPSSI.

However, it seemed to many psychologists that the institutional divisions within psychology could and should be overcome. After all, the professionals of the AAAP received their educations in academic departments of psychology, and it was the scientific principles of psychology that SPSSI wished to apply to pressing social problems. So, in the years following the break between the AAAP and the APA, informal negotiations were carried on with the aim of reunifying psychologists under a single banner.

The process was greatly accelerated by the coming of World War II. In 1940, even before the United States entered the war, the APA had assembled an Emergency Committee to plan for the inevitable involvement of the United States and its psychologists in the global conflict; in 1941, several months before the Japanese attack on Pearl Harbor, the *Psychological Bulletin* devoted a whole issue to "Military Psychology." In the same year, the APA moved to remove the greatest bar to full participation by applied psychologists in the association. At the annual meeting of the APA in September, the requirement that a prospective member have published research beyond the dissertation was replaced with a requirement that to join the APA, one had to present either publications or a record of five years' "contribution" to psychology as an associate, the class of membership to which AAAP psychologists had belonged.

Once the war began, changes came at a faster pace. The annual meetings were abandoned in response to government calls to conserve vital fuels. A Committee on Psychology and War was formed, planning not only for war activities by psychologists, but for a significant postwar social role for psychology as well. The committee noted that in view of the coming world conflict, psychology should be unified, as it had been in the last war, and to this end it proposed creation of a "general headquarters" for psychology. Such headquarters came into existence as the Office of Psychological Personnel (OPP) located in Washington, DC.

Creation of the OPP as a general headquarters for psychology was a major event in the history of institutional psychology in the United States. Prior to 1941, the APA had no permanent central office; it was located in the professorial offices of whoever was its secretary in a given year. The OPP, however, became the central office of the APA, located in Washington—fount of funding and locus of lobbying—ever since. Psychologists at the OPP saw an opportunity both to reunify psychology and to advance psychology's role in American society. In 1942, Leonard Carmichael, psychology's representative on the National Research Council, reported to the APA Council that "this office [the OPP] may well mark the initiation of a central agency for psychologists which will have an important and growing effect upon the psychological profession." The head of the OPP, Stuart Henderson Britt (1943), defined the job of the OPP as more than doing useful war work, serving in addition "*the advancement of psychology as a profession*" (italics in original) and promoting "sound public relations for psychology."

There was much war work to be done. Psychologists were in great demand by the military. Uniquely among the social sciences, psychology was listed as a "critical profession" by the War Department. A survey of psychologists in December 1942, just one year after Pearl Harbor, turned up 3,918 psychologists (not all of them APA members), of whom about 25% were engaged full time in war-related activities. Many other psychologists served the war effort indirectly. E. G. Boring, for example, wrote a text on military psychology called *Psychology for the Fighting Man*, which in turn became a textbook used at West Point (Gilgen, 1982). As in World War I, psychologists served in many specialized capacities, ranging from test administration to studying the psychological demands made on human performance by new and sophisticated weapons, to the biological control of guided missiles. The war made human relations in industry more important, emphasizing the role of the psychologist in efficient industrial management. Industry faced two problems psychologists could help solve. Producing war materiel required vastly increased rates of production, while at the same time regular factory workers were drafted into the military, being replaced with new, inexperienced workers, especially women, who began for the first time to enter the workforce in large numbers. The War Production Board, alarmed by problems of low productivity, absenteeism, and high turnover, appointed an interdisciplinary team headed by Elton Mayo to apply social science techniques to retaining workers and improving their productivity. The business community came to recognize that "the era of human relations" was at hand, for "the factors that 'make a man tick' can be described and analyzed with much of the precision that would go into the dies for . . . a Sherman tank" (Baritz, 1960).

Even as the war raged, psychologists prepared for the postwar world by setting their own house in order. The Emergency Committee set up the Intersociety Constitutional Convention, a meeting of representatives of the APA, the AAAP, the SPSSI, and other psychological groups, such as the National Council of Women Psychologists. The convention created a new APA along federal lines. This new APA was to be an organization of autonomous divisions representing the various interest groups within psychology. New bylaws were written, including, in addition to the APA's traditional purpose of the advancement of psychology as a science, the advancement of psychology "as a profession, and as a means of promoting human welfare." Robert Yerkes, who did more than anyone else to create the new APA, laid out the goals of the organization to the convention: "The world crisis has created a unique opportunity for wisely planned and well directed professional activities. In the world that is to be, psychology will play a significant role, if psychologists can only unite in making their visions realities" (paraphrased by Anderson, 1943, p. 585). In the gloomiest year of the war, psychologists began to glimpse a rosy future.

In 1944, the memberships of the APA and the AAAP were polled to ratify the new bylaws. In the APA, members—the traditional academic psychologists—approved the new APA by 324 votes to 103 (out of 858 eligible voters), and among the associates (probably, members of the AAAP), the vote was 973 to 143 in favor (out of 3,806 eligible to vote). The endorsement of the new APA, especially among its traditional members, was short of ringing; nevertheless, the new bylaws were approved. The OPP became the office of the executive secretary of the APA, now permanently housed in Washington. A new journal, the *American Psychologist*, was created to serve as the voice of the new united psychology.

In this new APA there was a young and growing segment, almost entirely new: the clinical psychologist as psychotherapist.

New Prospects for Applied Psychology

"It seems as if the ivory tower had literally been blown out from under psychology" (Darley & Wolfle, 1946). Before the war, psychology had been controlled by the academicians of the APA, despite complaints from and concessions to the AAAP. The war, however, drastically altered the social role of psychologists and the balance of political power in psychology, primarily by inventing a new role for applied psychologists to fill in quickly growing numbers. During the 1930s, applied psychologists continued as they had in the 1920s, serving primarily as testers; evaluating employees, juvenile offenders, troubled children, and people seeking guidance about their intelligence or personality.

XAM'S BLOG 1
Henry Chauncey, Meritocracy, and the Big Test

Psychology, the Cinderella of the Social Sciences. The day when the prince will arrive to take her to the ball is not far off.

Unappreciated, despised

Thus wrote Henry Chauncey (1905–2002) in his diary in 1948 (Lemann, 1999, p. 68). Chauncey is not famous, but in practical terms he has probably had more influence on your life so far than any other psychologist. His patron, and perhaps psychology's prince, was Harvard President James Bryant Conant (1893–1978). Chauncey had a method, testing, and a vision, measuring human potential; Conant had a motive, destroying America's existing ruling elite. Together they created the SAT in order to replace aristocracy with meritocracy.[1]

---
[1] The Greek word *aristocracy* meant rule by the best, but had come to connote inherited rule. The British sociologist Michael Young coined the term *meritocracy* in a 1958 dystopian novel about rule by an educated elite, *The rise of the meritocracy* (Lemann, 1999). Nevertheless, the term stuck.

Colleges such as Harvard had been elite institutions since America's founding, but they were elite because of who went there, not because of the education they offered. America's leading families sent their boys to Ivy League schools for generation upon generation, polishing them for the high roles they were destined to fulfill in business and government. Academic learning was not the focus of their education; social and leadership skills were, learned through sports and extracurricular activities, not the classroom (Brooks, 2001). Conant despised them as the "Episcopacy," because so many of them were Episcopalian. Conant wanted to break their hold on power by creating a system in which talented children from high schools anywhere in the United States—not just the private northeastern schools of the Episcopacy—could have the opportunity to attend Harvard, Princeton, and Yale.

Conant turned to psychologist Henry Chauncey. Chauncey should have been a member of the Episcopacy: His family traced itself back to 1637 and the original Massachusetts Bay colony, and he was an Episcopalian. But his branch of the family had lost its wealth and he had to settle for attending Ohio State, where he became fascinated by mental testing. His thoughts mirrored Progressivism and Deweyan psychology, writing in his diary "our mores should not be derived from ethical principles which stem from religion but from a study of man in society" (quoted by Lemann, 1999, p. 68). Taking the helm of the newly created Educational Testing Service, he wrote, "What I hoped to see established is the moral equivalent of religion but based on reason and science rather than sentiment and tradition." The Progressive journalist Walter Lippman—who had sharply criticized the Army Alpha and Beta tests—nevertheless wrote in 1922 that mental testers could "occupy a position of power which no intellectual has held since the collapse of theocracy" (quoted by Lemann, 1999, p. 69).

Although today it's called the Scholastic Assessment Test, the test Chauncey created for Conant was originally called the Scholastic Aptitude Test, and was meant to be a test of general intelligence. The idea was that native talent was distributed everywhere in the United States, but could not be nurtured everywhere. The SAT was designed to find intelligent youth and bring them to the Ivy Leagues to replace the undeserving rich with the deserving talented as America's leaders. Conant aimed at a sort of American version of Plato's Republic, with high-scorers on the SAT as America's Guardian class. As college education has become increasingly important as the key to success in the modern world of knowledge workers, the impact of the SAT on American life has become greater and it has become controversial. It channels some children to elite and lucrative elite education—most Harvard students now go into Wall Street finance, a career the duty-minded Conant would abhor—while filtering other out others. If test scores are heritable, a new hereditary elite may be in the making (Murray, 2012).

REMAKING CLINICAL PSYCHOLOGY World War II created a pressing demand for a new kind of service from psychologists: psychotherapy, previously the preserve of psychiatrists. Of all the varied jobs psychologists performed in wartime, the most common, as in World War I, was testing—testing of recruits to determine for what military job they were most suited and testing soldiers returning from the front to determine if they needed psychotherapy. As late as 1944, Robert Sears could describe the role of the military psychologist in these traditional terms. However, the soldiers returning from the front needed more psychological services than anyone had anticipated or the existing psychiatric corps could provide. By the end of the war, of 74,000 hospitalized veterans, about 44,000 were hospitalized for psychiatric reasons. Psychologists had heretofore performed diagnostic duties as part of military medical teams, but faced with the overwhelming need to provide psychotherapy, psychologists—however ill-trained—began to serve as therapists, too. Even experimental psychologists were pressed into service as therapists. For example, Howard Kendler, fresh from Kenneth Spence's rigorously experimental program at the University of Iowa, wound up doing therapy at Walter Reed Army Hospital in Washington.

As the war wound down, it became clear that the desperate need for psychological services among veterans would continue. In addition to the hospitalized veterans, "normal" veterans experienced numerous adjustment difficulties. At the very least, men who had been wrenched from their prewar jobs, towns, and families desired counseling about how to make new lives in the postwar world; 65–80% of returning servicemen reported interest in such advice (Rogers, 1944). Others suffered from the World War II equivalent of posttraumatic stress syndrome. Secretary of War Stimson wrote in his diary about "a rather appalling analysis of what our infantrymen are confronting in the present war by way of psychosis. The Surgeon General tells us the spread of psychological breakdown is alarming and that it will affect every infantryman, no matter how good and strong" (quoted by Doherty, 1985, p. 30). Upon return to the United States, veterans felt a "sense of strangeness about civilian life," were often bitter about how little people at home appreciated the horrors of combat, and experienced restlessness, disturbed sleep, excessive emotionality, and marital and family disturbances. Finally, many veterans were handicapped by wounds and needed psychological as well as physical therapy (Rogers, 1944).

Spurred by the Veterans Administration (VA), the newly reunified APA, now fully emerged from the ivory tower of academe, undertook the tasks it had avoided for decades: defining the professional psychologist and setting up standards for his or her training. These tasks have not proved easy, and to this day, there is widespread disagreement among psychologists about the proper nature of training for the professional psychologist. Since World War II, the APA has established many panels and commissions to look into the matter, but no proposal has satisfied everyone, and controversy about the nature of clinical psychology has been chronic.

The most obvious model of professional training was rejected by the committees appointed after the war to set up professional training in psychology. Typically, schools that train the practitioners of a craft are separate from the scientific discipline to which they are related. Thus, physicians are trained in medical schools, not biology departments, and chemical engineers are trained in engineering schools, not chemistry departments. Of course, physicians are not ignorant of biology and chemical engineers are not ignorant of chemistry, but their schooling in basic science is considered quite distinct from their training in the crafts to which they aspire. Psychologists, however, needed to separate themselves from their very close rivals, the psychiatrists, who from the first appearance of "clinical" psychology before World War I had feared that psychologists might usurp their therapeutic duties. So, rather than define themselves as merely practitioners of a craft springing from science, as physicians had, clinical psychologists decided to define themselves as *scientist-practitioners*. That is, graduate students training to become clinical psychologists were to be taught to be scientists first— carrying out research in scientific psychology—and professionals—practitioners of a craft—second. It was as if physicians were to be trained first as biologists and only secondarily as healers. The appeal of the scheme was that it preserved for clinicians the prestige of being scientists while allowing them to fill the many jobs the VA had open for psychotherapists (Murdock & Leahey, 1986). The model of the clinical psychologist as scientist-professional was enshrined by the Boulder Conference of 1949. The Boulder model has not been without its detractors, and periodically the APA has been called on to rethink its approach to professional training. Additionally, from the very first (e.g., Peatman, 1949), academic psychologists have been afraid that their discipline would be taken over by professionals and that they would become the second-class citizens of the APA.

Whatever the trials and tribulations surrounding the redefinition of clinical psychology, it grew rapidly, becoming in the public mind the primary function of the psychologist. In 1954, during the annual meeting of the APA, Jacob Cohen and G. D. Wiebe (1955) asked the citizens of New York who "the people with the badges" were. Of the interviewees, 32% correctly identified them as psychologists, although almost as many, 25%, thought they were psychiatrists. When asked what the people with the badges did, 71% said it was psychotherapy; work scarcely done by psychologists before 1944; 24% said teachers, leaving 6% "other" (the percentages are rounded). The founders of the APA had prided themselves on being scientists and had formed their organization to advance the cause of psychology as a science. By 1954, just 62 years later, scientific psychology had largely ceased to exist in the public mind, replaced by an applied discipline with, given what even the best scientific minds in psychology—Hull, Tolman, Thorndike, Watson—had accomplished, a remarkably shallow foundation.

INVENTING COUNSELING PSYCHOLOGY The VA acted to provide the services veterans needed. To meet the need for vocational guidance, the VA established guidance centers at universities, where GIs were receiving college educations paid for by the GI bill. Psychologists working at these counseling centers continued the development of prewar applied psychology on a larger scale than before, and their activities by and large define the job of today's counseling psychologist. More disturbed veterans, especially those in VA hospitals, needed more than simple advice, and the VA set out to define a new mental health professional, the clinical psychologist, who could provide psychotherapy to the thousands of veterans who needed it. In 1946, the VA set up training programs at major universities to turn out clinical psychologists whose job would be therapy as well as diagnosis. Because it was the largest employer of clinical psychologists, the VA did much to define the job of the clinical psychologist and how he or she would be trained.

OPTIMISM IN THE AFTERMATH OF WAR

Contending for Respectability and Money at the Dawn of Big Science

Allied victory in World War II in many respects depended on the successful employment of science, primarily physics, in the pursuit of war aims. During the war, federal spending on scientific research and development went from $48 million to $500 million, from an 18% share in overall research spending to 83%. When the war ended, politicians and scientists recognized that the national interest demanded continued federal support of science and that control of research monies should not remain a monopoly of the military. Congress, of course, never allocates money without debate, and controversy over the proposed vehicles by which research dollars would be allocated centered on two problems concerning who would be eligible to apply for it.

The first problem has rarely concerned psychology but is important to understanding how research funds are doled out in the modern era of Big Science, in which huge amounts of money can be awarded to only a few of the investigators who would like to have their research supported. The problem is this: Should money be given to only the best scientists, or should it be parceled out on some other basis, perhaps allocating a certain amount of funds to each state? Progressive New Deal politicians such as Wisconsin Senator Robert La Follette pushed the latter scheme, but they were defeated by elitists in the scientific ranks and their conservative political allies who saw to it that applications for research money would be strictly competitive. As the system has evolved, most research money is "won" by a few elite institutions of higher education, while researchers at universities of lesser prestige are pressured to compete for grants they are in little position to gain. Universities value their scientists' winning grants because they get "overhead money"—money ostensibly to be spent on electricity, janitors, and other laboratory maintenance—which they in fact spend for new buildings, more staff, copiers, and many other things they would not otherwise be able to afford. In 1991, it was discovered that several universities had illegally channeled research overhead money to use for entertainment and other illegitimate purchases (Cooper, 1991). In this system of grants, scientists are not employees of their university; rather, they are its means of support. Scientists, in turn, are compelled to direct their research not to the problems they think are important, but to those the federal funding agencies think are important. Thus, scientists spend much of their time and talent trying to second-guess bureaucrats, who themselves are implementing vague congressional directives.

Of direct importance to psychology was whether or not the funding agency to be created, the National Science Foundation (NSF), should support research in the social sciences. Old Progressives and New Deal liberals included a Division of the Social Sciences in the original NSF bill, but natural scientists and conservative legislators opposed it. A leading supporter of the original bill, Senator J. William Fulbright of Arkansas, argued that the social sciences should be included because they "could lead us to an understanding of the principles of human relationships which might enable us to live together without fighting recurrent wars." Opponents argued that "there is not anything that leads more readily to isms and quackeries than so-called studies in social science unless there is eternal vigilance to protect."

In debate, even Senator Fulbright found little good to say about social science, conceding that "there are many crackpots in the field, just as there were in the field of medicine in the days of witchcraft." He was unable to give an adequate definition of social science and wound up quoting a natural scientist who said, "I would not call it a science. What is commonly called social science is one individual or group of individuals telling another group how they should live." In a letter to Congress, leading physical scientists opposed the Division of Social Science. The original bill mollified them by including special controls "to prevent the Division of Social Sciences getting out of hand," as Fulbright put it on the floor of the Senate. He also said, "It would surprise me very much if the social sciences' division got anything at all" because the NSF board would be dominated by physical scientists. The upshot of the debate was a vote of 46 to 26 senators to remove the Division of Social Sciences. As sciences, the social sciences did not command universal respect (social scientists might feel that with a friend like Fulbright, they did not need enemies), however much their concrete services, such as counseling, psychotherapy, and personnel management, might be desired.

Although the government was not yet sympathetic to supporting psychology and the other social sciences, a new foundation, the Ford Foundation, was. Prior to World War II, private research foundations, most notably the Rockefeller Foundation, had made modest grants to support social science. After the war, the Ford Foundation was established as the world's largest foundation, and it decided to fund the *behavioral sciences* (it has been said that John Dewey coined the term, but the Ford Foundation minted it) in a big way. Like Fulbright, the staff of the Ford Foundation hoped that the social sciences might be used to prevent war and ameliorate human suffering. They therefore proposed to use Ford's immense resources to give an "equal place in society" to "the study of man as to the study of the atom." At the top levels of the foundation, however, the staff's proposal met the same kind of resistance found in the Senate. Foundation president Paul Hoffman said that social science was "a good field to waste billions" in. His advisor, Robert Maynard Hutchins, president of the University of Chicago, agreed. He said that the social science research he was familiar with "scared the hell out of me." Hutchins was especially familiar with social science because the University of Chicago had established the first school devoted to it. Nevertheless, the Ford staff, led by lawyer Rowman Gaither, who had helped start the Rand Corporation, pushed ahead with their ambitious plan and got it approved. At first, the Foundation tried to give the money away as grants, but that didn't get rid of the money fast enough and took it out of Foundation control. Instead, the Foundation set up the Center for Advanced Studies in the Behavioral Sciences in California, where elite social scientists could gather to pursue theory and research in a sunny, congenial, and collegial climate free from quotidian academic chores.

Psychologists Look Ahead to the Psychological Society

By the end of the war, it was clear to psychologists that their ivory tower had indeed been destroyed. Psychology's links to its ancient roots in philosophy—to "longhaired" philosophers (Morgan, 1947)—were irrevocably severed, and for the good of psychology, according to the newest generation of American psychologists. At an APA symposium on "Psychology and Post-War Problems," H. H. Remmers (1944) observed, but did not mourn, psychology's loss of its "philosophical inheritance":

> Our philosophical inheritance has unfortunately not been an unmixed blessing. Deriving from that relatively sterile branch of philosophy known as epistemology and nurtured by a rationalistic science which tended to exalt thought at the expense of action and theory over practice, psychology has too frequently ensconced itself in the ivory tower from which pedants descended upon occasion to proffer pearls of wisdom, objectivity and logical consistency to their charges without too much concern about the nutritional adequacy of such a diet. (p. 713)

Clifford T. Morgan made the same point more bluntly at a 1947 conference on "Current Trends in Psychology" by observing that the "biggest [trend] of them all is that in the past thirty years psychology has shortened its hair, left its alleged ivory tower, and gone to work." Clearly, the world in the making demanded that psychologists be concerned less with abstruse, almost metaphysical, questions inherited from philosophy, and more with questions about how to achieve human happiness.

Psychologists entered their brave new world with anxious hope. Wayne Dennis, speaking at the Current Trends conference, proclaimed that "psychology today had unlimited potentialities [sic]." At the same time, he worried that psychology had not yet achieved the "prestige and respect" needed to earn a "successful existence as a profession. We cannot function effectively as advisers and consultants, or as researchers in human behavior, without holding the confidence and good opinion of a considerable part of the population." His worries were not misplaced, as the Senate debate on the Division of Social Sciences in the NSF demonstrated. Dennis spoke for many when he advocated further professionalization of psychology as the means of achieving public respect. Psychologists, he said, should set their own house in order, tighten requirements for training in psychology, prosecute pseudopsychologists, and establish certification and state licensing standards for professional psychologists.

Despite such worries, psychologists saw for themselves a secure and powerful place in the postwar world. Remmers (1944), reflecting the views of many psychologists, defined psychology's new, postphilosophical job: "Psychology in common with all science must have as its fundamental aim the service of society by positive contributions to the good life. . . . Knowledge for knowledge's sake is at best a by-product, an esthetic luxury." In colleges, psychology should be "placed on a par with the other sciences," and its role should be to teach the undergraduate how "to assess himself and his place in society." More broadly, psychology should help construct a "science of values" and learn to use "journalism, radio, and in the near future television" to achieve "culture control." Psychology should be more widely used in industry, education—"the most important branch of applied psychology"—gerontology, child rearing, and the solution of social problems such as racism. Remmers failed only to mention psychological psychotherapy among the potential contributions of psychology to human happiness. Psychologists were at last prepared to give people what William James had hoped for in 1892: a "psychological science that will teach them how to *act*."

Values and Adjustment

There was an unremarked irony in psychology's postwar position. The old psychology of Scottish commonsense philosophy had proudly taken as its ultimate mission the training and justification of Christian religious values. The new psychology of brass instrument experiments had, in challenging the old psychology, proudly cast off moral, especially religious, values in the name of science. With scientism becoming the new religion of the modern age, however, by 1944 Remmers could envision psychology as a "science of values." Psychology had come full circle: from serving the Christian God and teaching his values, to becoming itself, as John Burnham (1968) put it, a *deus ex clinica* representing the values of scientism.

What were psychology's new values? Sometimes psychology, in keeping with the value-free pose of science, seemed only to offer tools for social control. Watson, for example, saw conditioning as a technique by which psychology might inculcate society's values, whatever they might be, in its citizens. As Remmers put it, the "good life" to be furthered by psychology was "the homeostasis of society"; psychology would keep people from unpleasantly rocking the boat. Watson, Remmers, and other control-minded psychologists would have agreed with the motto of the 1933 World's Fair: "Science Finds, Industry Adopts, Man Conforms" (Glassberg, 1985). Emphasis on techniques of social control is symptomatic of American applied psychology's long relationship with political Progressivism, and it laid applied psychologists open to Randolph Bourne's criticism of Progressive politicians. Once a Progressive himself, Bourne came to realize that Progressives held no clear values of their own: "They have, in short, no clear philosophy of life except that of intelligent service. They are vague as to what kind of society they want, or what kind of society America needs but they are equipped with all the administrative attitudes and talents to attain it" (quoted by Abrahams, 1985, p. 7).

On the other hand, psychology sometimes held up a positive value of its own: the cult of the self. Psychology's object of study and concern is the individual human being, and its central value became encouraging the never-ending growth of individuals, furthering the tendency among Americans to set personal concerns above public ones. As Dewey had said, "Growth itself is the only moral end." American psychologists did not notice the contradiction between pretending to have no values and holding the value of individual growth because their central value was so American as to be transparent. From the time of Tocqueville, Americans had sought self-improvement more than anything else. Continuing growth and development seem as natural and necessary to Americans as God-centered stasis, the never-changing ideal divine order, had seemed to Europeans of the Middle Ages. In our world of self-made individuals, psychological techniques that fostered continual growth and change appeared value-free: What American society and psychology wanted was individualism.

However, the concept of the individual had undergone important changes since the nineteenth century. *Character* was the concept by which people had understood the individual in the nineteenth century. Emerson defined character as "moral order through the medium of individual nature," and the words used to describe character included *duty, work, golden deeds, integrity,* and *manhood*. In his or her character, then, a person had a certain relationship, good or evil, to an encompassing and transcendent moral order. Aspiring to good character demanded self-discipline and self-sacrifice. Popular psychologists of the nineteenth century such as the phrenologists offered guides to the diagnosis of one's own and others' character and gave advice on how to improve one's character. In the twentieth century, however, the moral concept of character began to be replaced by the narcissistic concept of *personality* and self-sacrifice began to be replaced by self-realization. The adjectives used to describe personality were not moral: *fascinating, stunning, magnetic, masterful, dominant, forceful*. Having a good personality demanded no conformity to moral order, but instead, fulfilled the desires of the self and achieved power over others. Character was good or bad; personality was famous or infamous. Psychologists, having shed the religious values that defined character, aided the birth of personality as a means of self-definition. Self-growth meant realizing one's potential, not living up to impersonal moral ideals. Moreover, potential—that which has not yet become actual—can be bad as well as good. Some potential is for doing bad things; developing everyone's full potential, then, can be bad for society. Thus, psychology's cultivation of individual growth was at odds with its claim to provide society with tools of social control.

Everything in twentieth-century psychology has revolved around the concept of adjustment. In experimental psychology, psychologists of learning studied how the mind and, later, behavior adjusted the individual organism to the demands of its environment. In applied psychology, psychologists developed tools to measure a person's adjustment to his or her circumstances and, should the adjustment be found wanting, tools to bring the child, worker, soldier, or neurotic back into harmony with society. In the psychological conception, sin was replaced with behavior deviation and absolute morality was replaced with statistical morality (Boorstin, 1974). In more religious times, one had a problem if one offended a moral norm standing outside oneself and society; now one had a problem if one offended society's averages as determined by statistical research. In theory, psychology placed itself on the side of individual expression, no matter how eccentric. In practice, by offering tools for social control and by stressing adjustment, it placed itself on the side of conformity.

DEVELOPING THE PSYCHOLOGICAL SOCIETY

Professional Psychology in the 1950s

American psychologists—and by the 1950s, psychology had become an American science (Reisman, 1966)—entered the 1950s with a confidence in the future shared by most other Americans. The war had ended, the Depression was only an unpleasant memory, the economy and the population were booming. To Fillmore Sanford, secretary of the APA, the future of psychology lay with professional psychology, and that future was bright indeed, because a new era had dawned, "the age of the psychological man":

> Our society appears peculiarly willing to adopt psychological ways of thinking and to accept the results of psychological research. American people seem to have a strong and conscious need for the sorts of professional services psychologists are . . . equipped to give. . . . The age of the psychological man is upon us, and . . . psychologists must accept responsibility not only for having spread the arrival of this age but for guiding its future course. Whether we like it or not, our society is tending more and more to think in terms of the concepts and methods spawned and nurtured by psychologists. And whether we like it or not, psychologists will continue to be a consequential factor in the making of social decisions and in the structuring of our culture. (1951, p. 74)

Sanford argued that psychologists had an unprecedented opportunity to "create a profession the like of which has never before been seen, either in form or content . . . the first *deliberately designed* profession in history."

By every quantitative measure, Sanford's optimism was justified. Membership in the APA grew from 7,250 in 1950 to 16,644 in 1959; the most rapid growth occurred in the applied divisions, and psychologists, by establishing various boards and committees within the APA, did deliberately design their profession, as Sanford hoped. Despite skirmishes with the other APA, the American Psychiatric Association (which was loath to give up its monopoly on mental health care and opposed the legal recognition of clinical psychology), states began to pass certification and licensing laws covering applied—primarily clinical and counseling—psychologists, defining them legally and, of course, acknowledging them as legitimate professionals (Reisman, 1966). Psychology in industry prospered as industry prospered, businesspeople recognizing that "we need not 'change human nature,' we need only to learn to control and to use it" (Baritz, 1960). Popular magazine articles on psychology began to appear regularly, often telling people how to choose genuine clinical psychologists from psychological frauds. Psychologists basked in Ernest Havemann's favorable series on psychology appearing in *Life* in 1957, and they gave him an award for his series.

HUMANISTIC PSYCHOLOGY   The broadest and most coherent theoretical movement in psychology in the 1950s was humanistic, or "Third Force" psychology. It contended against behaviorism, "First Force" psychology, but exerted little influence on experimental psychology, wherein behaviorism was being more effectively challenged by the new cognitive movements already described. Humanistic psychology was much more influential in professional, especially clinical, psychology, wherein it contended against psychoanalysis, the "Second Force."

Although humanistic psychology did not take off until the late 1950s, its immediate historical roots lay in the post–World War II period. Its most important founders were Carl Rogers (1902–1987) and Abraham Maslow (1908–1970). Although Rogers and Maslow were initially attracted to behaviorism, both became disenchanted with it and staked out similar alternative psychologies. Rogers developed his *client-centered* psychotherapy in the 1940s and used it with soldiers returning to the United States. Client-centered psychotherapy is a phenomenologically oriented technique in which the therapist tries to enter into the worldview of the client and help the client work through his or her problems so as to live the life the client most deeply desires. Rogers's client-centered therapy offered a significant alternative to the psychoanalytic methods used by psychiatrists, and thus it played an important role in the establishment of clinical and counseling psychology as independent disciplines following World War II. Because of his emphasis on empathic understanding, Rogers came into conflict with behaviorists, who, in his opinion, viewed human beings just as they viewed animals: as machines whose behavior could be predicted and controlled without reference to consciousness. In 1956, Rogers and Skinner held the first of a series of debates about the relative merits of their points of view.

Phenomenological psychology was especially appealing to the clinician, for the clinician's stock in trade is empathy, and phenomenology is the study of subjective experience. Rogers distinguished three modes of knowledge. The first is the objective mode, in which we seek to understand the world scientifically as it is. The second and third modes of knowing are subjective: The second mode is each person's personal, subjective knowledge of conscious experience, including feelings of purposiveness and freedom; the third mode is empathy, the attempt to understand another person's subjective, inner world. The clinician, of course, must master this last mode of knowing, for in Rogers's view, it is only by understanding the client's personal world and subjective self that the clinician can hope to help the client. Rogers believed that personal beliefs, values, and intentions control behavior. He hoped that psychology would find systematic ways to know the personal experience of other people, for then therapy would be greatly enhanced.

Rogers argued that behaviorism was a crippled, partial view of human nature because it limited itself to the objective mode of knowledge, seeing human beings as objects to be manipulated and controlled, not as experiencing subjects. For Rogers, behaviorism committed the Kantian sin of treating people as unfree things rather than as moral agents. In specific contradistinction to Skinner, Rogers put great emphasis on each person's experienced freedom, rejecting Skinner's purely physical conception of causality. Said Rogers (1964): "The experiencing of choice, of freedom of choice . . . is not only a profound truth, but is a very important element in therapy." As a scientist, he accepted determinism, but as a therapist, he accepted freedom: The two "exist in different dimensions" (p. 135, in discussion transcript).

Abraham Maslow was humanistic psychology's leading theorist and organizer. Beginning as an experimental animal psychologist, he turned his attention to the problem of creativity in art and science. He studied creative people and concluded that they were actuated by needs dormant and unrealized in the mass of humanity. He called these people *self-actualizers* because they made real—actualized—their human creative powers, in contrast to the great mass of people who work only to satisfy their animal needs for food, shelter, and safety. Maslow argued, however, that creative geniuses were not special human beings, but that everyone possessed latent creative talents that could be realized if it were not for socially imposed inhibitions. Maslow's and Rogers's views came together in that they both sought ways to jolt people from what they thought were comfortable but stultifying psychological ruts. A key goal of humanistic psychology was to help people realize their full potential as human beings. Thus, although humanistic psychology sometimes seemed to offer a critique of modernity, in fact it shared the tendency of modern thought to see the individual as the sole definer of values, depreciating the role of tradition and religion.

In 1954, Maslow created a mailing list for "people who are interested in the scientific study of creativity, love, higher values, autonomy, growth, self-actualization, basic need gratification, etc." (quoted by Sutich & Vich, 1969, p. 6). The number of people on Maslow's mailing list grew quickly and, by 1957, it became clear that the humanistic movement needed more formal means of communication and organization. Maslow and his followers launched the *Journal of Humanistic Psychology* in 1961 and the Association for Humanistic Psychology in 1963.

Humanistic psychologists agreed with the ancient Greek humanists, believing that "the values which are to guide human action must be found within the nature of human and natural reality itself" (Maslow, 1973, p. 4). But humanistic psychologists could not accept the naturalistic values of the behaviorists. Behaviorists treated human beings as things, failing to appreciate their subjectivity, consciousness, and free will. In the view of humanistic psychologists, behaviorists were not so much wrong as misguided. Behaviorists applied a perfectly valid mode of knowledge—Rogers's objective mode—to human beings, who could only be partially encompassed by this mode of knowing. Most especially, humanistic psychologists were distressed by behaviorists' rejection of human free will and autonomy. Where Hull, "a near saint of pre-breakthrough [i.e., prehumanistic] psychology" treated human beings as robots, humanistic psychologists proclaimed that "Man is aware . . . . Man has choice. . . . Man is intentional" (Bugental, 1964, p. 26).

Humanistic psychologists thus sought not to overthrow behaviorists and psychoanalysts, but to build on their mistakes and go beyond them. "I interpret this third psychology [humanistic psychology] to include the first and second psychologies. . . . I am Freudian and I am behavioristic and I am humanistic" (Maslow, 1973, p. 4). Humanistic psychology, then, while offering a critique of and an alternative to behaviorism, tended still to live with the eclectic spirit of the 1950s. Although it thought behaviorism was limited, it thought behaviorism nevertheless valid within its domain, and humanistic psychologists sought to add to behaviorism an appreciation of human consciousness that would round out the scientific picture of human psychology.

THE SOCIAL "REVOLUTION" OF THE 1960S Amid the prosperity and general good feelings of the 1950s there was a small but growing disturbing current, felt faintly within psychology itself and more strongly in the larger American culture: an unhappiness with the ethos and ethic of adjustment. Robert Creegan (1953) wrote in *American Psychologist* that "the job of psychology is to criticize and improve the social order . . . rather than to adjust passively . . . [and] grow fat." Sociologist C. Wright Mills deplored the application of psychology to industrial social control "in the movement from authority to manipulation, power shifts from the visible to the invisible, from the known to the anonymous. And with rising material standards exploitation becomes less material and more psychological" (Baritz, 1960). Psychoanalyst Robert Lindner (1953) attacked the ideology of adjustment as a dangerous "lie" that had reduced human beings to a "pitiful" state and threatened "to send the species into the evolutionary shadows." Lindner blamed psychiatry and clinical psychology for preserving the myth of adjustment by regarding neurotics and other unhappy humans as "sick" when in fact, according to Lindner, they were in healthy but misdirected rebellion against a stifling culture of conformity. The goal of therapy, Lindner wrote, should not be conforming the patient to a sick society but working "to transform the negative protest and rebellion of the patient into positive expression of the rebellious urge."

Outside psychology, rebellion against adjustment was more widespread and grew with the decade. In sociology, David Riesman's *The Lonely Crowd* (1950) and William H. Whyte's *The Organization Man* (1956) dissected and attacked the American culture of conformity. In politics, Peter Viereck praised *The Unadjusted Man: A New Hero for America* (1956). Novels such as J. D. Salinger's *Catcher in the Rye* (1951), Sloan Wilson's *The Man in the Grey Flannel Suit* (1955), and Jack Kerouac's *On the Road* (1957) expressed the unhappiness of people caught in a gray world of adaptation and conformity, yearning for lives less constrained and more emotional. The movie *Rebel Without a Cause* portrayed the tragic fate of one whose anxiety and unhappiness found no constructive purpose. And the fierce, restless energy of the young—whose numbers were growing rapidly—exploded in rock and roll, the only creative outlet it could find.

At the end of the decade, sociologist Daniel Bell wrote about the exhaustion of ideas during the 1950s. The beliefs of the past were no longer acceptable to young thinkers, and the middle way of adjustment was "not for [them]; it is without passion and deadening." Bell identified a "search for a cause" moved by "a deep, desperate, almost pathetic anger." The world, to many young minds, was gray and unexciting. In psychology, eclecticism could be boring, for there were no issues to fight over; no battles to be fought as before, when psychology had begun, or when functionalist had battled structuralist and behaviorist had battled introspectionist. Psychology was thriving, but to no clear end, apparently happy in its work of adjustment.

Psychologists' Critique of American Culture

Psychologists were prone to agree with and develop social science critiques of existing American society. Surveying the social attitudes of 27 leading psychologists, Keehn (1955) found that they were far more liberal than the country as a whole. Compared to most Americans, psychologists were nonreligious or even antireligious (denying that God exists, that survival of bodily death occurs, and that people need religion), were opposed to the death penalty, believed that criminals should be cured rather than punished, and supported easier divorce laws.

THE MYTH OF MENTAL ILLNESS In 1960, psychiatrist and political libertarian Thomas Szasz began an assault on the entire mental health establishment by analyzing what he called *The Myth of Mental Illness* (Szasz, 1960a,b). Szasz pointed out that the concept of mental illness was a metaphor based on the concept of physical illness, a bad metaphor with pernicious consequences. Szasz's analysis drew on Ryle's analysis of the concept of mind. Ryle had argued that the mind was a myth, the myth of the Ghost in the Machine. Szasz simply drew the conclusion that if there is no Ghost in the human machine, the Ghost—the mind—can hardly become ill. Just as, according to Ryle, we (falsely) attribute behaviors to an inner Ghost who causes them, so, Szasz said, when we find behaviors annoying, we think the Ghost must be sick and invent the (false) concept of mental illness. "Those who suffer from and complain of their own behavior are usually classified as 'neurotic'; those whose behavior makes others suffer, and about whom others complain, are usually classified as 'psychotic.' " So, according to Szasz, "Mental illness is not something a person has [there is within no sick Ghost], but is something he does or is" (1960b, p. 267).

Belief in mental illness brought evil consequences, Szasz thought. To begin with, psychiatric diagnoses are stigmatizing labels that ape the categories of physical illness, but in reality function to give political power to psychiatrists and their allies in mental health. People labeled "mentally ill" were deprived of their freedom and locked up for indeterminate periods of time, even though they may have committed no crime. While confined, they were given drugs against their will, which may not be done even to convicted felons in prison: "There is no medical, moral, or legal justification for involuntary psychiatric interventions. They are crimes against humanity" (p. 268). Making his libertarian point, Szasz argued that the concept of mental illness undermined human freedom, belief in moral responsibility, and the legal notions of guilt and innocence deriving from human freedom and moral responsibility. Instead of treating a human being who may have offended us or committed a crime as an autonomous agent, we treat him or her as a diseased thing with no will. Because the myth of mental illness is a conspiracy of kindness—we would like to excuse and help people who have done wrong—a person categorized as mentally ill, and therefore not responsible for his or her behavior, will likely come to accept his or her supposed helplessness, ceasing to view himself or herself as a morally free actor. And by contagion, as science sees all action as determined beyond self-control, everyone may cease to believe in freedom and moral responsibility. Hence, the myth of mental illness strikes at the very heart of Western civilization, committed as it is to human freedom and responsibility for one's actions.

Szasz did not say that everything called "mental illness" is a fiction, only that the concept of mental illness itself is a fiction or, more precisely, a social construction, as was hysteria in the nineteenth century. Obviously, a brain may be diseased and cause bizarre thoughts and antisocial behavior, but in such a case, there is no *mental* illness at all, but a genuine bodily disease. Szasz held that most of what are called mental illnesses are "problems of living," not true diseases. Problems of living are quite real, of course, and a person suffering from them may need professional help to solve them. Therefore, psychiatry and clinical psychology are legitimate professions: "Psychotherapy is an effective method of helping people—not to recover from an 'illness,' but rather to learn about themselves, others, and life" (Szasz, 1960a, pp. xv–xvi). Conceived medically, psychiatry is a "pseudoscience"; conceived educationally, it is a worthy vocation, concluded Szasz.

Szasz's ideas were, and remain, highly controversial. To orthodox psychiatrists and clinical psychologists he was a dangerous heretic whose "nihilistic and cruel philosophies . . . read well and offer little except justification for neglect" of the mentally ill (Penn, 1985). But to others his ideas were attractive, offering an alternative conception of human suffering that does not needlessly turn an agent into a patient. Szasz and his followers in the "antipsychiatry movement," as it was sometimes called, have had some success in changing the legal procedures by which people can be involuntarily committed to mental hospitals. In many states, such commitments are now hedged about with legal safeguards; no longer is it possible in most places to carry off someone to the local mental ward merely on the say-so of a single psychiatrist, as it was in 1960 when Szasz wrote. In addition, during the 1960s, large numbers of mental patients were released from mental hospitals because they came to be seen as prisons where people were unjustly held rather than as asylums where the mentally ill were protected and cared for.

HUMANISTIC PSYCHOLOGY AND THE CRITIQUE OF ADJUSTMENT   Part of the antipsychiatry movement was a rejection of the whole idea of adjustment. Mental patients were not sick—they refused to conform to a sick society and were locked up for their heroism. As American society became more troubled in the 1960s, by the struggle for civil rights, by riots and crime, and above all by the Vietnam War and the controversies surrounding it, the value of adaptation—conformity— was decisively rejected by increasing numbers of Americans. The roots of the discontent lay in the 1950s, as we have seen, but in the 1960s, criticism of conformity became more open and widespread.

In social science, for example, Snell and Gail J. Putney attacked conformity in *The Adjusted American: Normal Neuroses in the Individual and Society* (1964). In *Civilization and Its Discontents*, Freud had argued that civilized people are necessarily a little neurotic, the psychological price paid for civilization, so that psychoanalysis could do no more than reduce neuroses to ordinary unhappiness. According to Putney and Putney, however, "normal neuroses" are not just ordinary unhappiness but are real neuroses that can and ought to be cured. Adjusted Americans, the Putneys said, have learned to conform to a cultural pattern that deceives them about what their real needs are. Because "normalcy . . . [is] the kind of sickness or crippling or stunting that we share with everybody else and therefore don't notice" (Maslow, 1973), adjusted Americans are ignorant of their deepest yearnings and try to satisfy culturally prescribed rather than real human needs, consequently experiencing frustration and pervasive anxiety. The Putneys rejected the value of adjustment, replacing it with the value of "autonomy, [meaning] the capacity of the individual to make valid choices of his behavior in the light of his needs" (1964). Maslow (1961) thought that such views were held by most psychologists: "I would say that in the last ten years, most if not all theorists in psychology have become antiadjustment," and he endorsed the value of autonomy—self-actualization—as a replacement for adjustment.

Autonomy could be gained, humanistic psychologists said, through psychotherapy. The chief exponent of this view was Carl Rogers. His client-centered psychotherapy tried to take clients on their own terms and lead them not to adjustment to the regnant norms of society, but to insights into their real needs, and thence to an ability to meet them. A client who had been through successful psychotherapy became a Heraclitean human. By the end of successful client-centered therapy, Rogers (1958) said, "The person becomes a unity, a flow of motion . . . he has become an integrated process of changingness." Rogers's therapy centered on feelings. The person who came for help, the client (like Szasz, Rogers rejected the metaphor of mental illness and refused to call those he helped "patients"), suffered above all from inability to properly experience and fully express his or her feelings. The therapist worked with the client to open up and experience feelings fully and directly and to share these feelings with the therapist. So the "flow of motion" within the healthy human was most importantly a flow of feelings immediately and fully experienced. In the Rogerian conception, then, the unhealthy individual was one who controlled and withheld feelings; the healthy person— Maslow's self-actualizer—was one who spontaneously experienced the emotions of each moment and expressed emotions freely and directly.

Rogers, Maslow, and the other humanistic psychologists proposed new values of *growth* and *authenticity* for Western civilization. Values concern how one should live one's life and what one should treasure in life. Humanistic psychologists proposed that one should never become settled in one's ways, but instead be always in flux: the Heraclitean human. They taught that one should treasure feelings. Both values derive from psychotherapy as Rogers practiced it.

The value humanistic psychologists called "growth" was the openness to change Rogers hoped to bring about in his clients. A therapist naturally wants to change the client because, after all, the client has come seeking help to improve his or her life. Humanistic psychotherapists make change a basic human value, the goal of all living, whether within or without therapy. Humanistic psychologists agreed with Dewey that "growth itself is the only moral end."

The other new value, authenticity, concerned the open expression of feelings characteristic of the person who had been through Rogerian therapy. Maslow (1973) defined authenticity as "allowing your behavior and your speech to be the true and spontaneous expression of your inner feelings." Traditionally, people had been taught to control their feelings and to be careful in how they expressed them. Proper behavior in business and among acquaintances—manners—depended on not expressing one's immediate feelings and on telling little lies that oiled public social intercourse. Only with one's most intimate circle was free, private, emotional expression allowed, and even then, only within civilized bounds. But humanistic psychologists opposed manners with authenticity, teaching that emotional control and deceptive emotional expression—Maslow called it "phoniness"—were psychological evils, and that people should be open, frank, and honest with each other, baring their souls to any and all as they might with a psychotherapist. Hypocrisy was regarded as a sin and the ideal life was modeled on psychotherapy: The good person (Maslow, 1973) was unencumbered by hangups, experienced emotions deeply, and shared feelings freely with others.

Humanistic psychologists were clear that they were at war with traditional Western civilization and were trying to make a moral as well as a psychological revolution. Maslow (1967) denounced being polite about the drinks served at a party as "the usual kind of phoniness we all engage in" and proclaimed that, "the English language is rotten for good people." Rogers (1968) closed an article on "Interpersonal Relationships: U.S.A. 2000" by quoting "the new student morality" as propounded at Antioch College: "[We deny] that nonaffective modes of human intercourse, mediated by decency of manners, constitute an acceptable pattern of human relations."

Rogers's ideas were, of course, not new in Western civilization. Valuing emotional feeling, trusting intuition, and questioning the authority of reason can be traced back through the romantics to the Christian mystics and to the cynics and skeptics of the Hellenistic Age. Rogers, Maslow, and the others, however, gave expression to these ideas within the context of a science, psychology, speaking with the authority of science. The humanistic psychologists' prescription for *ataraxia* (feeling and sharing) began to be put into practice in the modern Hellenistic Age. As the troubles of civilization mounted, ordinary life became intolerable for many; as people had in the ancient Hellenistic world, they sought for new forms of happiness outside the accepted bounds of culture.

Humanistic psychology, a product of the modern academy, advocated a modern form of skepticism. Maslow described the "innocent cognition" of the self-actualized person this way:

> If one expects nothing, if one has no anticipations or apprehensions, if in a sense there is no future . . . there can be no surprise, no disappointment. One thing is as likely as another to happen. . . . And no prediction means no worry, no anxiety, no apprehension, no foreboding. . . . This is all related to my conception of the creative personality as one who is totally here now, one who lives without the future or the past. (1962, p. 67)

Maslow here captured the recipe for ataraxia of the Hellenistic skeptics: to form no generalizations and hence be undisturbed by what happens. The humanistic self-actualizer, like the ancient skeptic, accepts what is without disturbance, "goes with the flow," and is carried without trouble down the constantly flowing stream of change of modern American life.

The hippies were a much more visible manifestation of the new Hellenism. Like the ancient cynics, they dropped out of the conventional society they scorned and rejected. Like humanistic psychologists, they were at war with their culture, distrusted reason, and valued feeling, but they carried their anti-intellectualism and contempt for manners to greater extremes, attempting to actually live lives that were Heraclitean flows of feeling, unconstrained by intellect or manners. The hippie movement began around 1964 and quickly became a powerful cultural force, described variously as "a red warning light for the American way of life," "a quietness, an interest—something good," or "dangerously deluded" (Jones, 1967). To explore and express their feelings, hippies turned to drugs. Few had heard of Carl Rogers and Abraham Maslow, though the hippies shared their values; but they had heard of another psychologist, Timothy Leary. Leary was a young, ambitious, and successful Harvard psychologist whose personal problems drove him inward, to his feelings. He began to use drugs, at first peyote and then LSD, on himself and others to attain the Heraclitean state of being, the "integrated process of changingness" open to new experience and intensely aware of every feeling. The hippies followed Leary into the "psychedelic," mind-expanding world, using drugs (as had Coleridge and other young romantics) to erase individual, discursive consciousness (Kant's *verstand*) and replace it with rushes of emotion, strange hallucinations, and alleged cosmic, transcendental insights (*vernunft*). For the hippies, as for the post-Kantian idealists, the ultimate reality was mental, not physical, and they believed drugs would open the "doors of perception" to the greater, spiritual world of mind. Even without drugs, hippies and humanistic psychologists were not quite of this world. In a letter, Maslow wrote: "I live so much in my private world of Platonic essences . . . that I only appear to others to be living in the world" (quoted by Geiger, 1973).

By 1968, the hippie movement, and the associated movement of protest against the war in Vietnam, was at its height. The Age of Aquarius—a new Hellenistic Age—was, or seemed to be, at hand.

Giving Psychology Away

Against the background of turmoil and alienation of the late 1960s, psychology experienced an outbreak of "relevance" in 1969 (Kessel, 1980). Psychologists fretted that they were not doing enough to solve the problems of society. The most widely cited expression of psychologists' impulse to social relevance was George Miller's 1969 presidential address to the APA, in which he stated, "I can imagine nothing we could do that would be more relevant to human welfare, and nothing that could pose a greater challenge to the next generation of psychologists, than to discover how best to give psychology away."

Miller asserted that "scientific psychology is one of the most potentially revolutionary intellectual enterprises conceived by the mind of man. If we were ever to achieve substantial progress toward our stated aim—toward the understanding, prediction, and control of mental and behavioral phenomena—the implications for every aspect of society would make brave men tremble." However, Miller said, despite continuous work by applied psychologists, on the whole psychologists "have been less effective than we might have been" in providing "intellectual leadership in the search for new and better personal and social relationships." In considering how to give psychology away, Miller rejected behavioral technology for psychology's playing a part in a broad mutation of human and social values: "I believe that the real impact of psychology will be felt not through . . . technological products . . . but through its effects on the public at large, through a new and different public conception of what is humanly possible and what is humanly desirable." Miller called for "a peaceful revolution based on a new conception of human nature" based on education: "Our scientific results will have to be instilled in the public consciousness in a practical and usable form."

Miller was riding the crest of the wave of public interest in psychology. In 1967, *Psychology Today* began publication, and in 1969, *Time* inaugurated its "Behavior" department, so psychology was almost being given away in the popular media. Psychologists pushed social relevance as never before. The theme of the 1969 APA meeting was "Psychology and the Problems of Society," and the pages of *American Psychologist* began to fill with articles and notes on student activism, psychology's duty to social responsibility, and hip references to Bob Dylan, the musical poet of youth rebellion.

Not all psychologists eschewed psychological technology in solving social problems. Two years after Miller, Kenneth Clark (1971), in his APA presidential address, argued that political leaders should have "imposed" on them the "requirement" that "they accept and use the earliest perfected form of psychotechnological, biochemical intervention which would assure their positive use of power." In an article in *Psychology Today*, psychologist James McConnell (1970) proclaimed, "Somehow we've got to learn to *force* people to love one another, to *force* them to want to behave properly. I speak of psychological force." The technology was available, McConnell opined, by which society can "gain almost absolute control over an individual's behavior. . . . We should reshape our society so that we all would be trained from birth to want to do what society wants us to do." Echoing Watson's claims of the 1920s, McConnell concluded, "Today's behavioral psychologists are the architects and engineers of the Brave New World."

McConnell was not alone in his eagerness to take over and reshape traditional social functions. Harriet Rheingold (1973) urged the creation of a new psychological profession, the "Scientists of [Child] Rearing," that "must be accepted as the highest in the land." Furthermore, "parents must be taught how to rear their children," and, like clinical psychologists themselves, "parents to be must be certified." Along similar lines, Craig T. Raimey (1974) called for organized psychology to push for "the establishment of adequate services to the children of this nation." Psychological professionals would play many roles in Raimey's utopian scheme, functioning on local advisory councils, in coordinating agencies, as referral resources, and above all in schools, which would play the central role in screening, assessing, and treating unfortunate children.

Ironically, the problems that psychology sought to cure in society erupted in the APA. A ferocious debate started in the 1970s about the social value, if any, of standardized tests, especially IQ tests. It had long been known that black children did much worse than white children on IQ tests. Arthur Jensen (1969) started an uproar when, in a seeming return to old eugenic positions, he argued that the difference was genetic; blacks were inherently inferior to whites, so that the Great Society's compensatory education programs were doomed to failure. Debate among Jensen, his critics, and supporters raged for several years. At the 1968 APA convention, the Black Psychological Association presented a petition calling for a moratorium on the use of IQ tests in schools, alleging widespread abuse, specifically that tests participated in the oppression of black children by relegating them to low-achievement school tracks. The APA responded in typical academic-bureaucratic fashion: It appointed a committee. In 1975, it published its report (Cleary, Humphries, Kendrick, & Wesman, 1975), which predictably concluded, in standard academic-bureaucratic fashion, that although tests might be abused, they were basically sound.

The committee's finding was unsatisfactory to black psychologists. Speaking as chair of the Association of Black Psychologists, George D. Jackson (1975) called the report "blatantly racist" and concluded that "we need *more* than a moratorium now—we need government intervention and strict legal sanctions." The debate over testing continued and, a few school systems seriously curtailed the use of tests to track students. Nevertheless, there was an irony in organized psychology's inability to resolve problems similar to those of the society it presumed to scientifically revolutionize.

Some Americans, especially conservative ones, did not want what psychologists were giving away. In a widely quoted speech, then Vice President Spiro Agnew (1972) blasted psychologists, especially B. F. Skinner and Kenneth Clark, for proposing "radical surgery on the nation's psyche." Agnew quoted John Stuart Mill: "Whatever crushes individuality is despotism," and added, "we are contending with a new kind of despotism." Conservative columnist John Lofton (1972) contributed to a special issue of *American Psychologist* concerned with the serious overproduction and underemployment of PhD psychologists. From some informal interviews, Lofton concluded that the public believed "The tight market for Ph.D's is a good thing. There are too many people with a lot of knowledge about unimportant things" (p. 364). People were unsympathetic to psychology, Lofton said, because they were concerned about abuses of behavior modification technology and tests and felt traditional American resentment of "lordly Ph.D.'s, of whatever stripe." Academic psychology, including cognitive psychology, has been similarly castigated from outside: "The discipline continues to traffic in two kinds of propositions: those that are true but self-evident and those that are true but uninteresting. . . . [On] almost any issue that might be considered important for human existence . . . it offers pitifully little that rises above the banal" (Robinson, 1983, p. 5).

Ten years after Miller's address, a symposium was held to see what progress had been made in giving psychology away. Most of the reports were rather gloomy; even the optimists thought little had been accomplished. Two authors were especially scathing. Sigmund Koch (1980) tore Miller's speech apart, revealing its fatuities, flabby thinking, and self-contradictions. He argued that, if anything, psychology was being given away too well in pop psychotherapy and a flood of self-help books. Koch said, "In sum, I believe the most charitable thing we can do is not to give psychology away, but to take it back." Michael Scriven (1980), a philosopher-turned-program evaluator, issued psychology a failing report card. Psychology failed for being ahistorical, for not applying to itself the standards it applied to others, for fancying itself value-free, and for continuing indulgence in the Newtonian fantasy. George Miller, who was there to introduce Koch and Scriven, was depressed: "Two men who I admire enormously have just destroyed my life."

Revolt, but No Revolution

Satirist Tom Lehrer once described Gilbert and Sullivan's famous patter songs as "full of sound and fury, signifying absolutely nothing." The 1960s were full of sound and fury, and 1968 was perhaps the worst year of all: the assassinations of Martin Luther King Jr. and Robert F. Kennedy, violent eruptions from the ghettos of every major American city, the growing antiwar movement. Never did the words of Yeats's "Second Coming" seem more true: Things seemed to be falling apart, America's youth lacked all conviction—the hippies dropped out of "straight" society—or were full of passionate intensity against their parents and their nation—the Weather Underground wanted to overthrow the government with bombs and terrorism. Many citizens wondered what rough beast was slouching toward Bethlehem to be born. In its "Prairie Fire Manifesto," the Weather Underground wrongly prophesied, "We live in a whirlwind; nonetheless, time is on the side of the guerrillas." In psychology, the humanistic psychologists were at war with the culture of intellect, siding with and inspiring the hippies and their political wing, the Yippies, while cognitive psychologists cried for a Kuhnian revolution against Hull, Spence, and Skinner. But just as there was no cognitive revolution, there was no social-humanistic-hippie revolution.

Although humanistic psychology fancied that it offered a radical critique of modern American society, it was, in effect, profoundly reactionary. In his concept of self-actualization, Maslow did no more than refurbish (*tarnish* might be a better word), Aristotle's *scala naturae* with modern psychological jargon. In its cultivation of feeling and intuition, humanistic psychology harked back to the romantic rejection of the Scientific Revolution but was never honest enough to say so. Humanistic psychologists, including Maslow and Rogers, always counted themselves scientists, ignoring the deep conflict between science's commitment to natural law and determinism and their own commitment to the primacy of human purpose. Humanistic psychology traded on the good name of science to push ideas entirely at variance with modern science. In the nineteenth century, Dilthey and others of the authentic romantic tradition offered reasons for setting the human sciences, the *Geisteswissenschaften*, apart from physics, chemistry, and the other *Naturwissenschaften*, but humanistic, psychologists could only offer barely articulate protests against scientistic imperialism. If a case was to be made against the natural scientific, reductionistic image of human beings, it must come from a different, more intelligent, source.

Similarly, the hippies and their followers, far from providing a radical critique of "Amerika," as they were wont to spell it, embodied every contradiction of the American past. They worshipped simple, preurban lives, yet mostly lived in cities (which were more tolerant of deviance than were small towns) and focused their lives on drugs and electronic music, products of the industrial world they feigned to reject. With the humanistic psychologists, they valued feelings and openness to new experience, echoing the romantic poet Blake's cry, "God save us from single vision and Newton's sleep." As humanistic psychology failed to displace behavioralism, so did the hippie movement fail to overthrow straight society. In 1967, a theologian at the University of Chicago said that the hippies "reveal the exhaustion of a tradition: Western, production-oriented, problem-solving, goal-oriented and compulsive in its way of thinking" (Jones, 1967). Nor were the hippies and the humanistic psychologists the great nonconformists they made themselves out to be. The hippies lived strange lives, but they demanded conformity to their nonconformism. For them, the great sin was to be "straight," to hold to the values of one's parents and one's natal culture, to work hard, to achieve, to be emotionally "closed." A song by a pioneer rock band, Crosby, Stills, Nash, and Young, depicted a member of the counterculture resisting the temptation to cut his hair. Humanistic psychologists did not shed adaptation as a virtue. Maslow (1961) described his utopia, Eupsychia, as a place where "there would be no need to hang onto the past—people would happily adapt to changing conditions." The great therapeutic breakthrough of the humanistic psychologists was the encounter group, in which people supposedly learned to be open and authentic. As Rogers described it, members were coerced into being authentic:

> As time goes on, the group finds it unbearable that any member should live behind a mask or a front. The polite words, the intellectual understanding of each other and relationships, the smooth coin of tact and cover-up . . . are just not good enough. . . . Gently at times, almost savagely at others, the group demands that the individual be himself, that his current feelings not be hidden, that he remove the mask of ordinary social intercourse. (quoted by Zilbergeld, 1983, p. 16)

Humanistic psychologists, like the hippies, did not really question the value of adaptation and social control; they just wanted to change the standards to which people had to adapt. The legacy of the 1960s remains controversial, but as the millennium ended, hippies were quaint sights on the streets as the Dow hit 14,000, and the bursting of the dot-com bubble did not revive humanistic psychology or its quasi-romantic critique of the free worked. The atrocity of September 11, 2001, demonstrated that there were more serious things to be feared than low self-esteem.

PROFESSIONAL PSYCHOLOGY

Funding Social Science

The political relations of the social sciences, including psychology, went from disaster to apparent triumph during the 1960s. The disaster was Project Camelot, the largest social science project ever conceived. The U.S. Army, together with the CIA and other intelligence agencies, spent $6 million on social scientists at home and abroad who could pinpoint potential political trouble spots (e.g., incipient guerrilla wars) and use social scientific expertise to formulate remedies (e.g., counterinsurgency actions). However, when in 1965 Project Camelot ceased to be secret, social science was thrown under a cloud. Foreign governments viewed Project Camelot as American meddling in their internal affairs. Their complaints led to a congressional investigation and to the termination of Project Camelot in July 1965. The image of social science was tarnished because social scientists participating in Project Camelot appeared to be tools of the American government rather than disinterested investigators of social phenomena.

However, out of the Camelot debacle social science was able to finally break through to a place at the federal research grant trough. As American cities exploded with race riots and street crime in the mid-1960s, and President Lyndon Johnson launched the War on Poverty, members of Congress were moved to ask if social science could do something about race hatred, poverty, crime, and other social problems. Psychologist Dael Wolfle (1966a, p. 1177), an experienced observer of relations between science and government, wrote in *Science* that "a call for large scale support of the social sciences was a recurring theme of the 25–27 January meeting of the House of Representatives Committee on Science and Technology." Wolfle thought that the time "may be ripe for special support of the social sciences," especially in view of recent advances in "quantitative and experimental methodology," so that "within a reasonable time, these disciplines can offer substantially increased help in meeting pressing social problems." As late as 1966, out of $5.5 billion spent by the federal government on scientific research, only $221 million (less than 5%) went to social science; but by 1967, the mood in Congress "was to do something generous for the social sciences" (Greenberg, 1967).

What Congress would do, however, remained unclear (Carter, 1966; Greenberg, 1967). In the Senate, liberal Democrats were eager to give social scientists money and to make them into social planners. Fred Harris, perhaps the most liberal senator and soon to attempt a (doomed) run for the Democratic presidential nomination in 1968, introduced a bill, S.836, to the 90th Congress, authorizing the establishment of a National Social Science Foundation (NSSF) modeled on the National Science Foundation (NSF). Walter Mondale, heir to Hubert Humphrey's liberal Democratic mantle, introduced S.843, the Full Opportunity and Social Accounting Act. Its leading provision was the establishment of a Council of Social Advisers in the president's Executive Office. These advisors would carry out the "social accounting," using their presumed expertise to advise the president on the social consequences of government's action and to rationally plan America's future. In the House, Emilio Q. Daddario proposed a more conservative way to "do something generous for the social sciences" by rewriting the charter of the NSF. The NSF had been mandated to support the natural sciences, but had been permitted to support "other sciences" as well, and had in fact given small amounts to support social science ($16 million in 1966 [Carter, 1966]). Daddario's bill, H.R. 5404, charged the NSF to support social as well as natural science and to include social scientists on its governing body.

Organized psychology paid great attention to the Senate bills. *American Psychologist*, the official organ of the APA, devoted a special issue to the Harris and Mondale proposals, and Arthur Brayfield, executive secretary of the APA, submitted a long statement to Congress in support of S.836. However, individual psychologists and other social scientists had mixed reactions to the proposal to set up an NSSF. On the positive side, an NSSF would give social scientists a federal funding source under their own control and would acknowledge their importance to the country, enhancing their social prestige. On the negative side, an NSSF might create a social science ghetto, stigmatizing social science by the act of setting it off from the "real sciences" in the NSF. Moreover, it might at the same time give social science too much visibility: Project Camelot had given social scientists more publicity and controversy than they were prepared to handle. Among the psychologists who testified before Harris's committee considering the NSSF bill, two (Brayfield and Ross Stagner) were enthusiastic, two (Rensis Likert and Robert R. Sears) supported it with reservation, and one (Herbert Simon) opposed it. Wolfle, in an editorial in *Science* (1966b), supported Simon's position. There was one point of loud universal agreement among all witnesses: Social science deserved a lot more federal money than it was getting. Sears, for example, said that regardless of what agency gave it, social science funding should go up "many times" the current level.

Social scientists got their money but not the NSSF or the Council of Social Advisers. Mondale's bill, like his 1984 candidacy for president, went nowhere. Harris's bill never got out of committee. Daddario, however, got his bill to rewrite the NSF charter through the House and enlisted the support of liberal Senator Edward Kennedy, who drafted a revised version of the new NSF bill. It was passed by the Senate and signed into law by President Johnson on July 18, 1968, as Public Law 90–407. The NSF, wanting to keep its control over American science and therefore ready as always to respond to the desires of Congress (the director, Leland J. Haworth, had assured Harris that the NSF *wanted* to support social science), promised to infuse new funds into social science. Psychologists might still suffer physics envy, but the hope of federal grants took away some of the sting.

As it turned out, psychology gained nothing from the NSF's increased funding of social sciences. From 1966 to 1976, NSF spending on social sciences except psychology rose 138%, while spending on psychology *declined* 12%. Moreover, not only did the NSF continue to spend more on the natural sciences than on the social sciences, but the rate at which spending on the natural sciences increased was faster than that for the social sciences. For example, spending on physics and chemistry, the most traditional fields of natural science, rose 176% between 1966 and 1976. Why psychology fared so poorly remains unclear (Kiesler, 1977).

Clinical Psychology in the 1960s and 1970s

There was no doubt that although psychology was growing fast (Garfield, 1966), professional, especially clinical, psychology was growing faster. At the 1963 meeting of the APA, there were 670 openings in clinical psychology for only 123 applicants (Schofield, 1966). The membership in the academic divisions of the APA had grown at a 54% rate between 1948 and 1960, while the professional divisions had grown at a 149% rate and the mixed academic/professional divisions had grown 176% (Tryon, 1963). The relative success of the professional as opposed to the traditional scientific branches of psychology led to increased tension between the two classes of psychologists (Chein, 1966, who coined the labels *scientist* and *practitioner* for the two sides in what he saw as an "irrational" and "destructive" division among psychologists; Shakow, 1965). Echoing the debates of the 1930s, Leonard Small (1963) said that the greatest task facing psychology was "to obtain recognition for its competence," and he hinted that if the APA did not assist professional psychologists in achieving this, they would organize separately.

There were other disturbing developments. The first claims were made that clinical psychologists (and psychiatrists) could effectively neither diagnose (Meehl, 1954) nor treat (Eysenck, 1952) their patients. In contrast to experimental psychology, where an exciting change from behaviorism to cognitive psychology seemed to be taking place, during the decade 1958–1968, professional psychology seemed to be adrift. As Nevitt Sanford (1965) wrote: "Psychology is really in the doldrums right now. . . . The revolution in psychology that occurred during World War II . . . has been over for some time."

Professional psychologists also had reason to worry about their public image. The use of psychological tests in education, business, industry, and government had mushroomed since

World War II, including not just intelligence tests, but also instruments designed to measure personality traits and social attitudes. Many people began to feel that these tests—inquiring as they often did into sexuality, parent-child relations, and other sensitive areas—were invasions of privacy, products of the morbid curiosity of psychologists and susceptible to abuse by employers, government, or anyone looking for tools of social control. In 1963, psychologists were upset by the popularity of *The Brain Watchers*, a book by journalist Martin Gross, which assailed the use of personality and social tests by government and industry. The antitest movement culminated in 1965, when some school systems burned the results of personality tests administered to children and Congress investigated the use of personality tests by the federal government to screen possible employees, resulting in restrictions on their use. By 1967, psychologists were probably not surprised to learn that their prestige was pretty low. When parents were asked which of six professions they would most like their child to enter, they ranked them as follows, from most preferred to least: surgeon, engineer, lawyer, psychiatrist, dentist, psychologist. Most galling was the finding that parents preferred the clinical psychologist's archenemy, the psychiatrist, by 54% to 26% (Thumin & Zebelman, 1967).

CHALLENGING THE BOULDER MODEL OF CLINICAL TRAINING The Boulder Conference on clinical psychology had said that clinical psychologists were supposed to be both scientists and practitioners. However, it was becoming obvious that few clinicians were becoming scientists, opting instead for the private or institutionalized practice of psychotherapy (Blank & David, 1963; Garfield, 1966; Hoch, Ross, & Winder, 1966; Shakow, 1965). Clinical students wanted to help people and learn how to practice therapy and regarded the scientific part of their training as a boring chore. The Boulder model was increasingly challenged, and psychologists began to think about training psychologists purely as professionals, along the lines of physicians' training (Hoch, Ross, & Winder, 1966), and to reflect on their aims as both scientists and professionals (Clark, 1967). George W. Albee (1970) argued that it had been a mistake for clinical psychologists to model themselves on physicians to begin with, when in fact they should be agents of widespread social change. Other clinicians, of course, defended the Boulder model (e.g., Shakow, 1976). Faced with change that seemed to be slipping out of organized psychology's control, the APA set up another conference on clinical training.

This one met in Colorado, too, at the resort of Vail in 1973. Despite dissension, it endorsed something that Boulder and other training conferences had rejected: the recognition of a new degree in clinical psychology, the PsyD, for professionally oriented students. PsyD programs reduced the scientific demands made on students in training and openly minted practitioners rather than academicians (Strickler, 1975). Naturally, the proposals proved controversial; some clinicians welcomed the idea (Peterson, 1976), while others (Perry, 1979) denounced the PsyD and a related development, the establishment of "freestanding" professional schools, so called because they were not affiliated with a university. Despite the growth of PsyD programs and graduates in the 1980s, delegates to a national conference on clinician training in 1990 held that the scientist practitioner model was "essential" for psychology and "ideal" for practice (Belar & Perry, 1991).

COMPETITION WITH PSYCHIATRY Another problem that would not go away was clinical psychology's status anxiety. On the one hand, mainstream clinical psychologists wanted to assert their superiority over the growing horde of therapy providers who did not hold a PhD or were not trained in psychology, such as clinical social workers, marriage counselors, and psychiatric nurses. The most psychologists could do about them was to keep out of the APA anyone without a PhD. On the other hand, clinical psychologists wanted to assert their virtual equality with psychiatrists, who felt disdain for clinical psychologists. Psychiatrist Seymour Post (1985) called clinical psychologists and anyone else without an MD "barefoot doctors of mental health." "Amazingly," Post went on, "this group of laymen is now clamoring for all the privileges of being a physician, including the right to admit patients to hospitals under their direct management." Worse, he said, patients come to psychologists with symptoms as they would to a general physician or internist, but "they are not competent to play such a role. Malpractice is the rule" (p. 21). Throughout the 1980s, organized psychiatry attempted to block the full therapeutic practice of psychologists, maintaining that psychologists are not fully competent to diagnose or treat mental disorders. One psychiatrist, AMA President Paul Fink, seemingly oblivious of the fact that compared to psychiatrists, psychologists receive many more hours of therapy and diagnosis training, said that psychologists are "'not trained to understand the nuances of the mind" (anonymous, 1988, p. 4).

Naturally, psychologists resented such attitudes. Bryant Welch, head of APA's Practice Directorate, undoubtedly spoke for many clinicians in saying "organized medicine and psychiatry are a veritable menage of monopolistic personality disorders" (anonymous, 1988, p. 1). Whatever the merits of Post's arguments, however, it is certainly true that clinical psychologists were clamoring for something approaching the legal status of psychiatrists. Clinical psychologists had won the right to be licensed by the state, despite some well-placed misgivings about whether licenses really served the public interest as opposed to the private interests of psychologists (Gross, 1978). On the other hand, when a hospital accreditation committee restricted clinical psychologists to hospital practice under an MD, clinical psychologists were outraged (Dörken & Morrison, 1976). In the early 1990s, clinical psychologists fought against psychiatric resistance for the right to prescribe psychoactive medication (Squires, 1990; Wiggins, 1992). The biggest dispute between clinical psychology and psychiatry, however, naturally involved money.

Who should pay for psychotherapy? Although the obvious answer is the client or patient, in the era of managed care, most medical treatment is paid for by insurance companies or the government, and questions arise about whether or not psychotherapy should be included in third-party payment plans. A few psychiatrists and clinical psychologists (e.g., Albee, 1977b) agreed with Szasz that there is no such thing as mental illness, and logically concluded that psychotherapy is not really therapy, and so should not be covered under third-party payment schemes. Medical therapy for actual disorders of the nervous system (such as endogenous depression) would be covered. In practice, however, most therapists recognized that if psychotherapy costs had to be borne by clients, their practices would bring in a lot less income. Psychiatrists and clinical psychologists therefore agree that third parties should pay for psychotherapy, but they disagree bitterly about whom should be paid.

For many years, much to the resentment of clinical psychologists, insurance companies agreed with psychiatrists that only MDs should be paid for medical procedures, and, with certain special limitations that did not apply to organic diseases, they covered psychotherapy only if performed by a psychiatrist. Clinical psychologists rightly viewed this as a monopoly, and they pressed for "freedom of choice" legislation in the states that would force insurance companies to pay clinical psychologists, too. Of course, psychologists wanted to share the monopoly, not destroy it outright. Already faced with rising costs, insurance companies allied with psychiatry to resist the encroachments of psychology and filed suit (the test case arose in Virginia), alleging improper interference with the practice of medicine and business. Ultimately, freedom of choice laws were upheld in the courts, but the battle was long and fueled the long-standing hostility between the APA and the "other" APA, the American Psychiatric Association. The battle was refought in a new arena during the late 1970s and early 1980s, when the federal government considered passing national health insurance, then died down during the Reagan and Bush administrations, only to revive temporarily with Bill and Hillary Clinton's ambitious schemes for national health policy.

Organized psychology also had to deal with another means of controlling health care costs: managed care. The phrase *managed care* encompasses a variety of schemes by which companies and the government control patients' access to high-cost specialized care. The APA put forward its own concept of managed care for mental health, called Paradigm II (Welch, 1992). Central to Paradigm II is the direct marketing of psychological health care services to the companies who must buy health care plans for their employees to ensure that psychologists are included. Moreover, psychologists and psychiatrists also must market their skills to individuals (Gelman & Gordon, 1987).

Squabbles over insurance and managed care, and the increased marketing of health care like any other product, raised a nasty question potentially embarrassing to psychiatrist and clinical psychologist alike: Does psychotherapy *work*? Private and public health plans do not pay for quackery, so treatments must be proven safe and effective. The first person actually to investigate the outcomes of psychotherapy was the English psychologist Hans J. Eysenck in 1952. He concluded that getting therapy was no better than just *waiting* for therapy for the same period of time—the "cure" rate for spontaneous remission was as good as for therapy. This implies that psychotherapy is a fraud. Since then, psychotherapists have challenged Eysenck's conclusion and hundreds of psychotherapy outcome studies have been done. Naturally, mainstream clinical psychologists argue that psychotherapy, or at least their kind of psychotherapy, is effective, but the evidence is at best extremely mixed. A consensus emerged that psychotherapy is probably better than doing nothing for a psychological problem, although the magnitude of improvement is not very great (Landman & Dawes, 1982; Smith, Glass, & Miller, 1980). However, many studies concluded that professional psychotherapy with a trained therapist may be no more beneficial than amateur therapy or self-help (Prioleau, Murdock, & Brody, 1983; Zilbergeld, 1983).

In terms of numbers of practitioners and patients, clinical psychology was a success, but doubts about its identity, its status, and its effectiveness endure. Carl Rogers, who was the founder of modern clinical psychology, if anyone is, said, "Therapists are not in agreement as to their goals or aims. . . . They are not in agreement as to what constitutes a successful outcome of their work. They cannot agree as to what constitutes a failure. It seems as though the field is completely chaotic and divided" (quoted by Zilbergeld, 1983, p. 114).

The Turn to Service

Although Sigmund Koch and Michael Scriven had complained about the quality of the psychology that was being given away, psychologists generally seemed to be heeding George Miller's appeal to get involved with the problems of society. As the 1970s wore on, psychologists were less likely to be found in the haunts of scientific psychology's founders, the classroom and the laboratory, than in settings where they provided services. One of the major changes in the United States in the 1960s and 1970s was the change from a primarily industrial-productive economy to a service and information economy. Between 1960 and 1979, the total U.S. labor force grew by 45%, while the service sector grew by 69%. The greatest growth occurred in the social sciences, whose ranks grew by an incredible 495%; psychology grew by 435%.

Increasingly, psychologists were choosing specialties outside the old core area of experimental psychology. Between 1966 and 1980, the increase of new PhDs in experimental psychology averaged only 1.4% per year (the slowest growth of all specialty areas). Growth in applied areas was much greater. For example, clinical psychology grew about 8.1% per year, counseling 12.9%, and school psychology 17.8%. By 1980, applied psychologists made up about 61% of all doctoral psychologists and traditional experimentalists constituted only 13.5%. And new psychologists were choosing to work outside academia. In 1967, 61.9% of new doctoral psychologists took work in colleges or universities; by 1981, the figure was down to 32.6%. The most rapidly growing employment setting was self-employment as a privately practicing clinician or consultant. Self-employed psychologists were not even counted before 1970. In 1970, only 1.3% of new doctoral psychologists chose self-employment, but by 1981, 6.9% did so. Other rapidly growing employment settings were government, business, and nonprofit institutions. Even psychologists trained in research specialties were increasingly likely to be employed outside academic settings, although often nonacademic employment was forced on them by the limited number of university and college jobs. In 1975, 68.9% of new research specialty doctoral psychologists went into academic settings; in 1980, only 51.7% did so, for an average annual decline of 8%. There were offsetting increases in employment outside academia, so that there were few actually unemployed psychology PhDs.

By 1985, psychologists could be found virtually everywhere, touching millions of lives. At the Educational Testing Service (ETS), psychologists continued to refine the SAT, familiar to virtually every reader of this text, and pushed testing into new areas. You cannot become a golf pro without taking a multiple-choice ETS test (Owen, 1985). At the Stanford Research Institute, psychologists and others worked on an ambitious marketing program, the Values and Lifestyle program (VALS). VALS used a technique called "psychographics" to break American consumers into several well-defined groups, such as "I-Am-Mes," "Belongers," and "Achievers." Companies and advertising agencies paid for VALS profiles to target their products to the most receptive groups and tune their pitches to the psychological makeup of their audiences (Atlas, 1984; Novak & MacEvoy, 1990). Clinical psychologists, despite some official misgivings from the APA, were running radio call-in shows on which people could air their problems and seek advice and comfort from a psychologist (Rice, 1981). Such shows started locally, but by 1985, a nationwide radio network, Talk Radio, devoted at least six hours a day to the "psych jockeys," and in 1986, the APA created a Division of Media Psychology. People were bringing their troubles to psychologists as never before. Between 1957 and 1976, the percentage of Americans who had consulted a mental health professional rose from 4 to 14; among the college-educated, the change was from 9% to 21%. In fact, the number of people exposed to therapeutic techniques is very much greater because many self-help organizations, such as those for losing weight and stopping smoking, use such techniques (Zilbergeld, 1983). Finally, bookshops have psychology sections filled with self-help psychology books, and we can add to these most of the books in the family life sections concerning sex, intimacy, and child rearing.

Psychologists were everywhere and were taking themselves seriously as a social force. Charles Kiesler (1979), executive officer of the APA, wrote: "I see psychology, then, as a national force for the future: as a knowledgeable force on scientific issues, on the delivery of human services, and on various human concerns about which we know something."

Divorced Again: The Academics Walk Out

Within psychology, traditional experimental and theoretical psychologists were becoming unhappy with the increasing numbers and influence of applied psychologists. In 1957, a committee of the Division of Experimental Psychology polled its membership's attitudes to the APA. They found that although 55% approved of the APA, 30% were opposed to it, and they noted a growing, though still minority, desire by the experimentalists to secede from the APA (Farber, 1957).

The tensions between academic psychologists and practitioners that created the AAAP in 1938 were only papered over by the creation of the "new" APA in 1945. Indeed, tensions between the two communities got worse as the balance of practitioners to academics shifted decisively in favor of the former in the 1980s. In 1940, about 70% of APA members worked in academia; by 1985, only about 33% did. Academics viewed the APA as increasingly devoted to guild interests of practitioners, such as getting insurance payments, the ability to write prescriptions for psychoactive drugs, and hospital privileges for clinical psychologists on a par with psychiatrists. By 1965, they were pressing for a new restructuring of the APA that would increase their influence on the organization. Efforts to reorganize the APA gained momentum in the 1970s as various committees and commissions were set up to recommend changes in APA structure that would satisfy both academics and practitioners. Repeated failure of every proposal alienated academics, leading to their gradual defection from the APA and increasing the urgency felt by the reforming academics that remained.

The last attempt to reorganize came in February 1987, when an ambitious restructuring plan was rejected by the governing body of the APA, its Council. Academic reformers formed the Assembly for Scientific and Applied Psychology, whose acronym (ASAP) reflected their sense of the need for immediate change. The APA Council created another reorganizing committee, the Group on Restructuring (GOR), chaired by APA past president and ASAP member Logan Wright. For several months, GOR met in a series of meetings one member described later as the most unpleasant experience she had ever had. A clinical psychologist quit in the middle amid great acrimony and bitterness, and in December 1987, GOR approved a rather awkward restructuring scheme by a vote of 11–3.

At its winter meeting in February 1988, the APA Council debated the plan. The debate was emotional, marked by accusations of bad faith, conflict of interest, and insincerity. It was only due to backstage maneuvering that the plan was approved by Council 77–41, with a tepid recommendation to the membership to adopt it. Even the distribution of ballots to the members became a source of controversy in the campaigns to win approval or defeat. In the end, at the close of summer 1988, the GOR plan was rejected 2–1 by 26,000 of APA's 90,000 members. In the same election, Stanley Graham was elected president of APA. Graham was a private practitioner who, despite having signed the reorganization document as a member of GOR, reversed his position and campaigned against ratification. The upshot was that many academics, in the words of Logan Wright, concluded, "APA has become a guild controlled by small-business people" (quoted by Straus, 1988).

ASAP then put into action its backup plan to form a new society dedicated to academic psychologists' concerns, the American Psychological Society (APS). Starting with the initial membership of ASAP of about 500, APS had nearly 20,000 members (to the APA's 154,000) by 2000. Rancor between the organizations was strong. Attempts were made in APA Council to oust APS members from APA governance positions on grounds of conflict of interest, but after spirited and bitter debate, nothing came of them. Various APS organizers quit anyway.

As the APA celebrated its centennial in 1992, American psychology found itself divided again. The needs and desires of psychological practitioners for a professional society and of academic scientists for a learned society again proved incompatible. The first divorce of practitioners and scientists was reconciled during the heady, patriotic days of World War II. Perhaps psychology is simply too large and diverse a field to be unified.

PROFESSIONAL PSYCHOLOGY AT THE BEGINNING OF THE NEW MILLENNIUM

Professional psychology continues to struggle for equality with psychiatry and other entrenched professions, but with renewed optimism. The two main issues facing professional psychology are coping with managed care and gaining the right to prescribe drugs to treat psychological disorders (Newman, 2000). In 2002, Arizona became the first state to grant prescription-writing privileges to suitably trained clinical psychologists. Through Congress and lawsuits, psychologists were beginning to achieve recognition as psychological experts whose activities deserved third-party compensation and autonomy from micromanagement. In particular, psychologists argued that psychotherapy could be as effective as drug therapy—sometimes even more cost-effective—and that therefore psychotherapy should be a part of managed health care programs (Clay, 2000). Not hedging its bets, however, the APA continued to push state legislatures to allow appropriately trained psychologists to prescribe drugs. Of interest to students will be the required changes to clinical training programs, because in order to prescribe drugs, psychotherapists will need training similar to that of physicians in areas such as organic chemistry and psychopharmacology.

On the other hand, professional optimism needs to be tempered with concern for the state of psychotherapy outcomes and graduate training. While studies show that psychotherapy is effective, its outcomes are modest (Dawes, 1994). Moreover, almost all forms of therapy are equally effective, independent of the psychological theory on which it's based (Luborsky, Singer, & Luborsky, 1975). The key factor in psychotherapeutic success seems to be the personality of the therapist rather than her or his training. In short, therapy is an art rather than a science, and when organized psychology touts the scientific underpinnings of its practices, it is arguably guilty of misrepresenting its knowledge and practices (Dawes, 1994). Moreover, the trend in graduate training is to dilute scientific components, undermining the claim that professional psychologists are competent scientists (Maher, 1999).

Applied Psychology in the Modern World: Bibliography

For a general account of American history for the years 1912–1945, see John L. Thomas, "Nationalizing the republic" (for the period 1912–1920), and Robert H. Wiebe, "Modernizing the republic" (for the period 1920 and after), both in Bernard Bailyn et al., *The great republic* (Boston: Little, Brown, 1977). For a general account of the period with an emphasis on social history, including shrewd observations on the role of the social sciences as shapers of modern morality, see Daniel Boorstin (1973); for an emphasis on politics, see Eric F. Goldman, *Rendezvous with destiny: A history of modern American reform*, 3rd ed. (New York, Vintage, 1977).

The period between the wars has been studied a great deal, with an emphasis on the 1920s. The first book on the 1920s was Allen (1931); see also Geoffrey Perrett, *America in the twenties: A history* (New York: Touchstone, 1982). Ostrander (1968) provides a brief account of changes in morals in the 1920s. For American religion during these years, see George M. Marsden, *Fundamentalism and American culture: The shaping of twentieth-century evangelicalism 1870–1925* (Oxford: Oxford University Press, 1980). Graves and Hodge (1940) provide a wonderfully well-written account of the British scene between the wars.

On eugenics, the standard history is sure to become Daniel J. Kevles, "Annals of eugenics: a secular faith," which appeared in *The New Yorker* (October 8, 15, 22, and 29, 1984), and as a book, *In the name of eugenics: Genetics and the uses of human heredity* (New York: Knopf, 1985). Gould (1981) contains useful accounts of American hereditarian attitudes, as well as a critique of intelligence testing and an account of immigration restriction on which I relied and borrowed quotations. On the sterilization movement, the indispensable first source is Landman (1932), which contains valuable details on sterilization legislation and court decisions; Landman was sympathetic to the ideals of the negative eugenicists but quite critical of their practices. A brief popular overview of eugenics in America is Peter Quinn (2003, March). An excellent website on eugenics is run by the national laboratory Cold Spring Harbor: www.eugenicsarchive.org/eugenics. For the applications of social science to industry and other social problems, see Baritz (1960), who focuses on industrial social science, and Napoli (1981), who discusses applied psychology in all its varied roles. On Flaming Youth, see Fass (1977),

from whom the quotations in the text are drawn, who presents the problems of youth in the 1920s from the perspectives of the youth themselves, popular commentators, and social scientists. A related source is Christopher Lasch's *Haven in a heartless world: The family besieged* (New York: Basic Books, 1977), which concentrates on social scientists' views of the family. An excellent book that touches on many subjects, including American hereditarianism, the reaction against it by American social scientists, and changing conceptions of the ideal family, is Derek Freeman (1983), who dismantles Margaret Mead's romantically naive portrait of the Samoans, first by setting it in its historical context, and then by contrasting it to his own, more intimate and prolonged fieldwork. My account of the change from "character" to "personality" is based on Warren I. Susman, "'Personality' and the making of twentieth-century culture," in J. Higham and P. Conkin, eds., *New directions in American intellectual history* (Baltimore: Johns Hopkins University Press, 1979).

Moving on to works specifically on psychology, an excellent overview of applied psychology in the United States from its beginnings to the present is Ludy Benjamin and David Baker (2004) *From séance to science: A history of the profession of psychology in America* (Belmont, CA: Thomson/Wadsworth). Works on specific topics include Sokal (1983), Birnhaum (1955, 1963), and Burnham (1968) offer good broad accounts of psychology in the 1920s, focusing on psychology's social relations, especially in the case of Burnham. For the period after World War II, with some prewar background, consult Gilgen (1982). For the application of intelligence tests to World War I recruits, see Daniel J. Kevles, "Testing the army's intelligence: Psychologists and the military in World War II," *Journal of American History* (1968, *55*: 565–581); and Franz Samelson, "Putting psychology on the map: ideology and intelligence testing," in Allan R. Buss, ed., *Psychology in social context* (New York: Irvington, 1979), who draws on archival sources to demonstrate how psychologists were affected by the social and political context of the World War I and postwar years. The sources and results of the clash between Yerkes and Scott are told by von Mayrhauser (1985), part of his doctoral dissertation at the University of Chicago. There are several useful histories of clinical psychology. The broadest is John M. Reisman, *The development of clinical psychology* (New York: Appleton-Century-Crofts, 1966). More attention to professional issues is provided by Robert I. Watson, "A brief history of clinical psychology," *Psychological Bulletin* (1953, *50*: 321–346); and Virginia Staudt Sexton, "Clinical psychology: an historical survey," *Genetic Psychology Monographs* (1965, *72*: 401–434). An insider's account of the growth of clinical psychology during and immediately after World War II is given by E. Lowell Kelly, "Clinical psychology," in Dennis (1947). A brief overview of clinical psychology training issues is found in Leonard Blank, "Clinical psychology training, 1945–1962: Conferences and issues," in Leonard Blank and Henry David, eds., *Sourcebook for training in clinical psychology* (New York: Springer, 1964). On its 50th anniversary, the *American Psychologist* (2000, pp. 233–254) ran a special section on "History of psychology: The Boulder Conference," containing histories of and commentary on the scientist-practitioner model.

Now that psychotherapy is a recognized institution and social influence, its history is beginning to be written. Donald K. Freedheim, ed., *History of psychotherapy: A century of change* (Washington, DC: APA Books, 1992), is a topically organized collection of essays. More critical is Philip Cushman, *Constructing the self, constructing America: A cultural history of psychotherapy* (Reading, MA: Addison-Wesley, 1995). Cushman examines the influence of American culture on American psychotherapy and, as the title implies, the influence of psychotherapy on the American self. Bridget Murphy provides a history of "The degree that almost wasn't: The PsyD comes of age," *Monitor on Psychology* (January 2000) 52–54. A fascinating study of the impact of psychological ideas on American culture is Debbie Nathan's *Sybil exposed: The extraordinary story behind the famous multiple personality case* (New York: Free Press, 2011). Through a popular book and movie, most Americans came to believe in the existence of a dubious mental diagnosis, multiple personality disorder. Nathan shows that the case was a hoax from the beginning.

Psychologists themselves have provided periodic treatments of their immediate history. For the period in question, the broadest and most detailed treatment is given by Jerome S. Bruner and Gordon W. Allport, "Fifty years of change in American psychology," *Psychological Bulletin* (1940, *37*: 757–776), which provided the basis for Allport's APA presidential address, "The psychologist's frame of reference," *Psychological Bulletin* (1940, *37*: 1–28). Earlier relevant surveys include Robert Davis and Silas E. Gould, "Changing tendencies in general psychology," *Psychological Review* (1929, *36*: 320–331); Florence L. Goodenough, "Trends in modern psychology," *Psychological Bulletin* (1934, *31*: 81–97); and Herbert S. Langfeld, "Fifty volumes of the *Psychological Review*," *Psychological Review* (1943, *50*: 143–155). Later accounts looking back to the period in question are Kenneth E. Clark, "The APA study of psychologists," *American Psychologist* (1954, *9*: 117–120); W. A. Kaess and W. A. Bousfield, "Citation of authorities in textbooks," *American Psychologist* (1954, *9*: 144–148); Russell Becker, "Outstanding contributors to psychology," *American Psychologist* (1959, *14*: 297–298); and Kenneth Wurtz, "A survey of important psychological books," *American Psychologist* (1961, *16*: 192–194).

The narrative account of psychology's preparation for and participation in World War II, including reunification of the APA and AAAP and planning for psychology's postwar role, is based on careful reading of all the *Psychological Bulletins* for the relevant years. The reference to Carmichael (1942) is to his oral report to the meeting of the APA Council (the association did not meet because of the war) in New York on September 3, 1942, beginning in the *Bulletin* on page 713.

Two recent, complementary, works by historians concern the history of psychology in the twentieth century, with particular emphasis on World War II and after: *Psychologists on the march: Science, practice and professional identity in America, 1920–1969* (Cambridge, England: Cambridge University Press, 1999), by James Capshew, focuses on organized, institutional, psychology; Ellen Herman, *The romance of American psychology: Political culture in the age of experts* (Berkeley: University of California Press, 1995) is a broad, social history of applied psychology beginning with World War II, through the cold war, Project Camelot, and the Great Society, with some material on the 1970s and 1980s. One governmental institution that has influenced and been influenced by psychology is the NIMH. This interaction is described in a series of case studies in Wayne Pickren and Stephen Schneider (eds.), *Psychology and the National Institute of Mental Health: A historical analysis of science, practice, and policy* (Washington, DC: APA Books, 2004). A brief but broader picture of the transformation of psychology from a small science to a primarily professional field is given by Pickren (2007) "Tension and opportunity in post-World War II psychology," *History of Psychology 10*: 279–299.

A brief survey of general historical developments during the 1950s can be found in the relevant sections of Bernard Bailyn, David Davis, David Donald, John Thomas, Robert Wiebe, and Gordon Wood, *The great republic* (Boston: Little, Brown, 1977). Emphasis on the social, cultural, and intellectual history of the period is in Jeffery Hart, *When the going was good: American life in the fifties* (New York: Crown, 1982). For psychology in the 1950s, see Reisman (1966) and Albert R. Gilgen, *American psychology since World War II: A profile of the discipline* (Westport, CT: Greenwood Press, 1982). If one is interested in the conflict between the two APAs, psychological and psychiatric, one should read the professional journal of the APA, *American Psychologist*. The year of maximum conflict appears to have been 1953, when the journal was filled with articles, letters, and notes on the struggle of psychologists to win legal approval of their profession over the protests of the psychiatrists. Lindner's (1953) work should be regarded as a symptom of some psychologists' unhappiness with the ideology of adjustment rather than as offering a sound set of analyses or arguments in itself. It depends on a dubious reading of Freud and Darwin, advocates negative eugenics, and is, in general, rather hysterical in its treatment of modern life.

For histories of humanistic psychology, see Anthony J. Sutich, "Introduction," *Journal of Humanistic Psychology* (1961, *1*: vii–ix); and Sutich and Vich (1969). There are two good collections of articles from the various facets of humanistic psychology: James F. T. Bugental, *Challenges of humanistic psychology* (New York: McGraw-Hill, 1967); and Sutich and Vich, 1969). Rogers (1964) is considered by humanistic psychologists to be a representative work (Sutich & Vich, 1969); and Maslow (1973) offers a varied selection of his papers.

A critical history of humanistic psychology is provided by Joyce Milton (2002), *The road to malpsychia: Humanistic psychology and our discontents* (San Francisco: Encounter). Milton also discusses the career of Timothy Leary.

A complete "autopsy" of Project Camelot and the ensuing political fallout may be found in a special issue of *American Psychologist, 21, no. 5* (1966, May). Good accounts of the maneuvering around the founding of an NSSF as opposed to including social science in the NSF are given by Carter (1966) and Greenberg (1967). The *American Psychologist* special issue on the Harris and Mondale bills was 22, no. 11 (1967, November). It reprints both bills, articles by their sponsors (Mondale's has the earnest but mushy and soporific qualities of his presidential campaign speeches), and the testimony given before the committees considering each bill. Digests of the testimony on the NSSF bill may be found in *Transaction* (1968, 5, no. 1, Jan.–Feb., 54–76). For the legislative histories of the bill, the place to go is the *Congressional Record* for the 90th Congress, Session 2. Mondale's bill was introduced and never heard from again. Harris's bill

was discussed on the floor of the Senate, mostly by a co-sponsor, Senator Ralph Yarborough, but otherwise languished in committee.

Representative Daddario's bill to revise the NSF is fully discussed in an excellent but anonymously written report entered in the *Record* on pages 14889–14895, including complete background on the establishment of the NSF, a legislative history of Daddario's bill, and an accounting of all the changes to NSF that it made. It is interesting to observe the support of liberal Democrats for social science. Charles G. McClintock and Charles B. Spaulding, "Political affiliation of academically affiliated psychologists," *American Psychologist* (1965, *20*: 211–221), showed that until after World War II psychologists had voted with the rest of the public—Republican before FDR and Democratic afterward—but they had, unlike the rest of the voting populace, continued to become more Democratic after the war. In the 1952 and 1956 elections, American voters as a whole had supported the liberal and rather intellectual Adlai Stevenson against Eisenhower by only 44% and 42%, while psychologists had voted for Stevenson by margins of 63% and 68%. By 1960, a bare majority of voters voted for John Kennedy, yet 79% of psychologists did so. Psychologists, like their supporters in the Senate, were more liberal than the country as a whole, and social scientists benefited greatly from the rise of political liberalism from 1965 to 1980.

In 1963, *American Psychologist* (18) devoted two special issues to the problems of clinical psychology, no. 6 (June) and no. 9 (September). Alarm over Martin Gross's *The brain watchers* is found in various "Comments" in the August (no. 8) issue of the same year. Political controversies over the use and abuse of tests led to a special issue devoted to "Testing and public policy" in *20*, no. 11 (1965, November). The whole fuss was humorously captured by satirist Art Buchwald in a column published in the *Washington Post* (Sunday, June 20, 1965), in which he made up his own personality test. Since 1965, Buchwald's test has been widely circulated among psychologists, many of whom are ignorant of its origin.

Szasz's views were first presented in his book (1960a) and elaborated in many books and articles since. Although Ryle's *Concept of mind* is in Szasz's bibliography, he does not in fact derive his own argument from Ryle; nevertheless, the affinity of the two analyses is clear. For a contemporary, "straight" view of the hippie movement, see Jones (1967). However, the movement is best appreciated through its art and music, of which the most lasting has proved to be the music: the Grateful Dead and Jefferson Airplane in particular made records still likely to be accessible. Also illuminating is the

New Journalism that came out of and at first depended on the movement. My own favorites are Tom Wolfe's *The electric Kool-Aid acid test* (New York: Bantam, 1968) and anything by Hunter S. Thompson, but most relevantly *Fear and loathing in Las Vegas: A savage journey into the heart of the American dream* (New York: Popular Library, 1971). Wolfe's book is especially interesting in the present context, as it centered on the quintessential hippie group, the Merry Pranksters of Ken Kesey, author of a brilliant antipsychiatric novel, *One flew over the cuckoo's nest* (New York: New American Library, 1963). Wolfe became the outstanding observer of the new psychological Hellenistic Age.

The references provide a survey of works on the applications of psychology. On the fuss over insurance, see three special issues of *American Psychologist* devoted to the topic: September 1977 and August 1983, in the "Psychology of the public forum" section, and February 1986. The literature evaluating psychotherapy is vast, difficult, and treacherous. Probably the best place to enter the literature is Prioleau, Murdock, and Brody (1983). They do a good job of discussing the complex issues involved in evaluating therapy outcomes; the "Peer Commentary" section gives ample voice to critics who disagree with the article's contention that therapy is ineffective; and the reference section lists all the important works. Zilbergeld (1983) also discusses this literature, more readably but less precisely. See also J. Berman and N. Norton, "Does professional training make a therapist more effective?" *Psychological Bulletin* (1985, *98*: 401–407). My account of the split between the APA and the APS is based primarily on my own experience as substitute or regular representative on APA Council of Division 24 (Society for Theoretical and Philosophical Psychology) from fall 1986 to winter 1989. I have also drawn on a variety of accounts appearing in the newsletter of the APA, the *APA Monitor*, and the APS newsletter, the *APS Observer*. See also S. C. Hayes, "The gathering storm," *Behavior Analysis* (1987, *22*: 41–45); C. Holden, "Research psychologists break with APA," *Science* (1988, *241*: 1036); and C. Raymond, "18 months after its formation, psychological society proves its worth to behavioral-science researchers," *Chronicle of Higher Education* (June 27, 1990, 5: 9). I should state that I am one of the disgruntled academics of APA. Although I was not a member of ASAP, I am a charter member of APS, supporting its separation from APA. The statistics in the "Turn to Service" section are drawn from Georgine M. Pion and Mark W. Lipsey, "Psychology and Society: The Challenge of Change," *American Psychologist* (1984, *39*: 739–754). David Owen's (1985) book on the SAT should be read by everyone who has taken the SAT or is a parent of someone who will take the SAT. Owen really does "rip the lid off" an incredibly corrupt institution that serves no ends but its own and does significant social harm. Anyone who reads the book will agree with Jonathan Yardley of the *Washington Post* that the SAT "is a scam," and with Owen's conclusion that ETS should be abolished. The social consequences of the SAT are tracked by Lemann (1999).

The outstanding impressionistic portrait of the psychological society is Wolfe (1977). Another, more sardonic, tourist is Shiva Naipul, who reports in "The pursuit of wholeness," *Harper's* (April 1981): 20–27. The most scientific survey of the psychological society comes from pollster Daniel Yankelovich, "New rules in American life: Searching for self-fulfillment in a world turned upside down," *Psychology Today* (April 1981): 35–91. The term *psychological society* seems to have been coined by writer Martin L. Gross, *The psychological society: A critical analysis of psychiatry, psychotherapy, and the psychological revolution* (New York: Touchstone, 1978). Gross's book is quite good, if a little heavy-handed at times. Two related books are Peter Schrag, *Mind control* (New York: Delta, 1978), which is positively Orwellian in tone; and R. D. Rosen, *Psychobabble* (New York: Avon, 1979), which provides a witty tour of various pop psychotherapies. More scholarly is clinical psychologist Raymond Fancher's insider view in *Cultures of healing: Correcting the image of American mental health care* (New York: Freeman, 1995), and historian Jonathan Engel's broader account, including psychoanalysis, psychiatry, and social work together with psychology's own forms of therapy in *American therapy: The rise of psychotherapy in the United States* (New York: Gotham Books, 2008). Several broad critiques of the psychological society exist; I mention only those I find especially useful. First, there is an excellent but often overlooked book by Daniel Boorstin, *The image: A guide to pseudo-events in America* (New York: Harper Colophon, 1964). The first book I know of to specifically address psychology's contribution to a new moral order is Phillip Rieff, *The triumph of the therapeutic* (New York: Harper & Row, 1966). Concern with the psychological society and therapeutic sensibility grew more intense in the 1970s, producing Richard Sennett, *The fall of public man* (New York: Vintage, 1976), my own favorite of these books; and Christopher Lasch, *The culture of narcissism* (New York: W. W. Norton, 1979), which has probably had the greatest impact. An excellent book that focuses closely on the therapeutic sensibility encouraged by clinical psychology and psychiatry is Zilbergeld (1983), with the unforgettable title

The shrinking of America. Two related books bear mention. First is Alasdair MacIntyre, *After virtue: A study in moral theory* (Notre Dame, IN: University of Notre Dame Press, 1981), which takes a long view of the turn from exterior to interior standards of morality, extending back to the prephilosophic Greeks. Two recent books argue that popularized psychology has undermined traditional ideas of free will and moral responsibility: Wendy Kaminer, *I'm dysfunctional, you're dysfunctional: The recovery movement and other self-help fads* (Boston: Addison-Wesley, 1992); and Charles W. Sykes, *A nation of victims: The decay of the American character* (New York: St. Martin's Press, 1992); see also J. R. Dunlap, "Review of Sykes," *American Spectator* (December 1992, *25*: 72–73). The best actual antidote to the language of feelings is Miss Manners: Judith Martin, *Miss Manners' guide to excruciatingly correct behavior* (New York: Warner Books, 1982).

REFERENCES

Abrahams, E. (1985, May 12). Founding father of the New Republic. Review of D. W. Levy, Herbert Croly of the New Republic: The life and thought of an American Progressive. *Washington Post Book World*, 7.

Achinstein, P., & Barker, S. F. (Eds.). (1969). *The legacy of logical positivism.* Baltimore, MD: Johns Hopkins University Press.

Adams, G. (1934). The rise and fall of psychology. *Atlantic Monthly, 153,* 82–90.

Adamson, P. (2001). Aristotelianism and the soul in the Arabic Plotinus. *Journal of the History of Ideas, 62,* 211–32.

Adler, J. (1995, November 6). The gods must be hungry. *Newsweek,* p. 75.

Adler, T. (1990, April). Different sources cited in major cognitive texts. *APA Monitor,* 8.

Aglioti, S. M., Cesari, P., Romani, M., & Urgesi, C. (2008). Action anticipation and motor resonance in elite basketball players. *Nature Neuroscience, 11,* 1109–16.

Agnew, S. (1972, January). Agnew's blast at behaviorism. *Psychology Today, 5, 4,* 84, 87.

Albee, G. W. (1970). The uncertain future of clinical psychology. *American Psychologist, 25,* 1071–80.

Albee, G. W. (1977a). The protestant ethic, sex, and psychotherapy. *American Psychologist, 32,* 150–61.

Albee, G. W. (1977b). Does including psychotherapy in health insurance represent a subsidy to the rich from the poor? *American Psychologist, 32,* 719–21.

Allen, F. L. (1931). *Only yesterday: An informal history of the 1920s.* New York: Harper & Row.

Anderson, J. E. (1943). Outcomes of the intersociety constitutional convention. *Psychological Bulletin, 40,* 585–88.

Anderson, J. R. (1978). Arguments concerning representations for mental imagery. *Psychological Review, 85,* 249–77.

Anderson, J. R. (1981). Concepts, propositions, and schemata: What are the cognitive units? In J. H. Flowers (Ed.), *Nebraska symposium on motivation 1980 (vol. 28). Cognitive processes.* Lincoln, NE: University of Nebraska Press, 121–62.

Anderson, L. E. (1943). Outcomes of the intersociety constitutional convention. *Psychological Bulletin, 40,* 585–88.

Angell, J. R. (1903a). A preliminary study of the localization of sound. *Psychological Review, 10,* 1–18.

Angell, J. R. (1903b). The relation of structural and functional psychology to philosophy. *Philosophical Review, 12,* 243–71.

Angell, J. R. (1907). The province of functional psychology. *Psychological Review, 14,* 61–91.

Angell, J. R. (1908). *Psychology.* New York: Arno.

Angell, J. R. (1911a). On the imageless thought controversy. *Psychological Review, 18,* 295–323.

Angell, J. R. (1911b). Usages of the terms mind, consciousness, and soul. *Psychological Bulletin, 8,* 46–47.

Angell, J. R. (1913). Behavior as a category of psychology. *Psychological Review, 20,* 255–70.

Annas, J. (1981). *An introduction to Plato's Republic.* Oxford, England: Clarendon Press.

Anonymous. (1988, Summer). AMA and psychiatry join forces to oppose psychologists. *Practitioner Focus, 2,* 1, 4–5.

Ariely, D. (2008). *Predictably irrational: The hidden forces that shape our decisions.* New York: Harper.

Arnold, F. (1905). Psychological standpoints. *Psychological Bulletin, 2,* 369–73.

Artz, F. B. (1980). *The mind of the Middle Ages,* 3rd ed. Chicago, IL: University of Chicago Press.

Ash, M. G. (1980). Wilhelm Wundt and Oswald Külpe on the institutional status of psychology: An academic controversy in historical context. In W. Bringmann & R. D. Tweney (Eds.), *Wundt studies.* Toronto, ON: Hogrefe, 396–421.

Ash, M. G. (1981). Academic politics in the history of science: Experimental psychology in Germany, 1879–1941. *Central European History, 13,* 255–86.

Ash, M. G. (1992). Cultural contexts and scientific change in psychology: Kurt Lewin in Iowa. *American Psychologist, 47,* 198–207.

Ash, M. G. (1995). *Gestalt psychology in German culture, 1890–1967: Holism and the quest for objectivity.* Cambridge, England: Cambridge University Press.

Atkinson, R. M., & Shiffrin, R. M. (1968). Human memory: A proposed system and its control processes. *Psychology of Learning and Motivation, 2,* 89–195. Reprinted in Bower, 1977.

Atlas, J. (1984, October). Beyond demographics. *Atlantic Monthly,* 49–58.

Bainton, R. (1995). *Here I stand: A life of Martin Luther.* New York: Plume.

Baldwin, J. M. (1895). *Mental development in the child and the race.* New York: Macmillan.

Baldwin, J. M., Cattell, J. M., & Jastrow, J. (1898). Physical and mental tests. *Psychological Review, 5,* 172–79.

Bandura, A. (1974). Behavior theory and the models of man. *American Psychologist, 29,* 859–69.

Barash, J. A. (1997). The sources of memory. *Journal of the History of Ideas, 58,* 707–17.

Baritz, L. J. (1960). *The servants of power: A history of the use of social science in American industry.* Middletown, CT: Wesleyan University Press.

Barkow, J., Cosmides, L., & Tooby, J. (1994). *The adapted mind.* Oxford, England: Oxford University Press.

Barnes, J. (1986). Hellenistic philosophy and science. In J. Boardman, J. Griffin, & O. Murray *(Eds.), The Oxford history of the classical world.* Oxford, England: Oxford University Press, 385–86.

Bartlett, F. (1932/1967). *Remembering.* London: Cambridge University Press.

Baumer, F. (1977). *Modern European thought.* New York: Macmillan.

Baumgartner, E., & Baumgartner, W. (1996). Bretano: Psychology from an empirical standpoint. In W. G. Bringmann, H. E. Lück, R. Miller, & C. E. Early *(Eds.), A pictorial history of psychology.* Chicago, IL: Quintessence, 61–65.

Bäumler, G. (1996). Sports psychology. In W. G. Bringmann, H. E. Lück, R. Miller, & C. E. Early *(Eds.), A pictorial history of psychology.* Chicago, IL: Quintessence, 485–89.

Bawden, H. H. (1904). The meaning of the psychical in functional psychology. *Philosophical Review, 13,* 298–319.

Bayly, C. A. (2004). *The birth of the modern world: 1780–1914.* Malden, MA: Blackwell.

Beach, E. (1960). Experimental investigations of species-specific behavior. *American Psychologist, 15,* 1–18.

Beach, F. A. (1950). The snark was a boojum. *American Psychologist, 5,* 115–24.

Bechtel, W., & Abrahamsen, A. (1991). *Connectionism and the mind.* Cambridge, MA: Blackwell.

Beers, C. (1968/1953). *A mind that found itself.* New York: Doubleday.

Behrens, P. J. (1997). G. E. Muller: The third pillar of experimental psychology. In W. Bringmann, H. Luck, R. Miller, & C. Early *(Eds.), A pictorial history of psychology.* Chicago, IL: Quintessence, 171–81.

Belar, C. D., & Perry, N. W. (Eds.). (1991). *Proceedings: National conference on scientist-practitioner education.* Sarasota, FL: Professional Resource Exchange.

Bell, D. (1960). *The end of ideology: On the exhaustion of political ideas in the fifties.* Glencoe, IL: Free Press.

Ben-David, J., & Collins, R. (1966). Social factors in the origins of a new science: The case of psychology. *American Sociological Review, 31,* 451–65.

Benjamin, L. T. (1996). Lightner Witmer's legacy to American psychology. *American Psychologist, 51,* 235–36.

Benjamin, L. T. (1997). Wilhelm Wundt: The American connection. In W. Bringmann, H. Lück, R. Miller, & C. Early *(Eds.), A pictorial history of psychology.* Chicago, IL: Quintessence, 140–47.

Bentham, J. (1789/1973). *Introduction to the principles of morals and legislation.* Partially reprinted in *The utilitarians.* Garden City, NY: Doubleday.

Berlin, I. (1957). *The hedgehog and the fox.* New York: Mentor.

Berlin, I. (1971). A special supplement: The question of Machiavelli. *New York Review of Books.* Retrieved from http://www.nybooks.com/articles/archives/1971/nov/04/a-special-supplement-the-question-of-machiavelli/

Bernard, L. L. (1911). *The transition to an objective standard of social control.* Chicago: University of Chicago Press.

Biers, W. R. (1987). *The archaeology of Greece: An introduction,* rev. ed. Ithaca, NY: Cornell University Press.

Binet, A. (1905). New methods for the diagnosis of the intellectual level of subnormals. *L'anee Psychologique, 12,* 191–244. Translation by E. S. Kite (1916). *The development of intelligence in children.* Vineland, NJ: Publications of the Training School at Vineland. Available at Classics in Psychology Web site.

Birnbaum, L. T. (1955). Behaviorism in the 1920s. *American Quarterly, 7,* 15–30.

Birnbaum, L. T. (1964). *Behaviorism: John Broadus Watson and American social thought 1913–1933.* Unpublished doctoral dissertation, University of California, Berkeley, CA.

Blank, L., & David, H. (1963). The crisis in clinical psychology training. *American Psychologist, 18,* 216–19.

Blanning, T. (2007). *The pursuit of glory: Europe 1648–1815.* New York: Viking.

Blanning, T. C. W. (2000a). Introduction. In T. C. W. Blanning *(Ed.), The nineteenth century.* Oxford: Oxford University Press, 1–9.

Blanning, T. C. W. (2000b). Introduction. In T. C. W. Blanning *(Ed.), The eighteenth century: Europe 1688–1815.* Oxford: Oxford University Press, 1–10.

Blight, J. G. (1978, September). *The position of Jonathan Edwards in the history of psychology.* Paper presented at the annual meeting of the American Psychological Association, Toronto, ON.

Block, N. J., & Dworkin, G. (Eds.). (1976). *The I.Q. controversy: Critical readings.* New York: Pantheon.

Blom, J. J. (1978). *Descartes: His moral philosophy and psychology.* New York: New York University Press.

Bloom, H. (1998). *Shakespeare: The invention of the human.* New York: Riverhead.

Blumenthal, A. L. (1970). *Language and psychology: Historical aspects of psycholinguistics.* New York: John Wiley.

Blumenthal, A. L. (1975). A reappraisal of Wilhelm Wundt. *American Psychologist, 30,* 1081–88.

Blumenthal, A. L. (1980a). Wilhelm Wundt and early American psychology: A clash of cultures. In R. W. Rieber *(Ed.), Wilhelm Wundt and the making of a scientific psychology.* New York: Plenum.

Blumenthal, A. L. (1980b). Wilhelm Wundt: Problems of interpretation. In W. Bringmann & R. D. Tweney *(Eds.), Wundt studies.* Toronto: Hogrefe, 435–51.

Blumenthal, A. L. (1986a). Shaping a tradition: Experimentalism begins. In C. Buxton *(Ed.), Points of view in the history of psychology.* New York: Academic Press.

Blumenthal, A. L. (1986b). Wilhelm Wundt: Psychology as the propadeutic science. In C. Buxton *(Ed.), Points of view in the history of psychology.* New York: Academic Press.

Bode, B. H. (1918). Consciousness as behavior. *Journal of Philosophy, 15,* 449–53.

Boden, M. (1977). *Artificial intelligence and natural man.* New York: Basic Books.

Boden, M. (1979). The computational metaphor in psychology. In N. Bolton *(Ed.), Philosophical problems in psychology.* London: Methuen.

Bolles, R. C. (1975). Learning, motivation, and cognition. In W. K. Estes *(Ed.), Handbook of learning and the cognitive processes* (Vol. 1). Hillsdale, NJ: Erlbaum.

Bolton, T. (1902). A biological view of perception. *Psychological Review, 9,* 537–48.

Boorstin, D. J. (1974). *The Americans: The democratic experience.* New York: Vintage Books.

Boring, E. G. (1929/1950). *A history of experimental psychology,* 2nd ed. New York: Appleton-Century-Crofts.

Boring, E. G. (1946). Mind and mechanism. *American Journal of Psychology, 59,* 173–92.

Bower, T. G. R. (1974). *Development in infancy.* San Francisco: Freeman.

Bowman, J. (2007). *Honor: A history.* New York: Encounter.

Boyer, J. W. (1978). Freud, marriage, and late Viennese liberalism: A commentary from 1905. *Journal of Modern History, 50,* 72–102.

Braeman, J., Bremner, R. H., & Brody, D. (Eds.). (1968). *Change and continuity in twentieth century America:*

The 1920s. Columbus, OH: Ohio State University Press.

Braid, J. (1843). *Neurohypnology.* London: John Churchill.

Bramel, D., & Friend, R. (1981). Hawthorne, the myth of the docile worker, and class bias in American psychology. *American Psychologist, 36,* 867–78.

Breger, L. (1981). How psychoanalysis is a science—and how it is not. *Journal of the American Academy of Psychoanalysis, 9,* 261–75.

Breger, L., & McGaugh, J. L. (1965). Critique and reformulation of "learning-theory" approaches to psychotherapy and neurosis. *Psychological Bulletin, 63,* 338–58.

Breland, K., & Breland, M. (1961). The misbehavior of organisms. *American Psychologist, 16,* 681–84. Reprinted in Seligman & Hagar (1972).

Bremmer, J. N. (1983). *The early Greek concept of the soul.* Princeton, NJ: Princeton University Press.

Brentano, F. (1874/1995). *Psychology from an empirical standpoint.* London: Routledge.

Brett, G. S. (1963). *Psychology, ancient and modern.* New York: Cooper Square.

Breuer, J., & Freud, S. (1895/1966). *Studies on hysteria.* New York: Avon.

Brewer, W. F. (1974). There is no convincing evidence for operant or classical conditioning in normal, adult, human beings. In W. Weimer & D. Palermo *(Eds.), Cognition and the symbolic processes.* Hillsdale, NJ: Erlbaum, 1–42.

Brewer, W. F., & Loschky, L. (2005). Top-down and bottom-up influences on observation: Evidence from cognitive psychology and the history of science. In A. Raftopoulos *(Ed.), Cognitive penetrability of perception.* New York: Nova scientific Publications, 31–47.

Brewer, W. F., & Nakamura, G. V. (1984). The nature and functions of schemas. In R. S. Wyer & T. K. Srull *(Eds.), Handbook of social cognition.* Hillsdale, NJ: Erlbaum, 119–60.

Bridgman, P. (1927). *The logic of modern physics.* New York: Macmillan.

Brigham, C. (1923). *A study of American intelligence.* Princeton, NJ: Princeton University Press.

Bringmann, W. G., Lück, H. E., Miller, R., & Early, C. E. (1997). *A pictorial history of psychology.* Chicago, IL: Quintessence.

Britt, S. H. (1943). The office of psychological personnel: Report for the first 6 months. *Psychological Bulletin, 40,* 773–93.

Broadbent, D. E. (1957). A mechanical model for human attention and immediate memory. *Psychological Review, 64,* 205–15.

Broadbent, D. E. (1958). *Perception and communication.* Elmsford, NY: Pergamon Press.

Brody, N. (1992). *Intelligence,* 2nd ed. San Diego, CA: Academic Press.

Bronowski, J., & Mazlish, B. (1960). *The western intellectual tradition.* New York: Harper & Row.

Brook, A. (Ed.). (2007). *The prehistory of cognitive science.* Houndsmills: Palgrave/Macmillan.

Brooks, R. (1991). New approaches to robotics. *Science, 253,* 1227–32.

Brooks, D. (2001). The organization kid. *Atlantic Monthly, 287,* 40–54.

Brown, P. R. L. (1989). *The world of late antiquity: From Marcus Aurelius to Muhammad,* 2nd ed. New York: Norton.

Brown, P. R. L. (2002). *The rise of Western Christendom: Triumph and diversity, AD 200-1000,* 2nd ed. Oxford: Blackwell.

Bruner, J. S., Brunswik, E., Festinger, E., Heider, F., Muenzinger, K. E., Osgood, C. E., et al. (1957). *Contemporary approaches to cognition.* Cambridge, England: Cambridge University Press.

Bruner, J. S., Goodnow, J., & Austin, G. (1956). *A study of thinking.* New York: John Wiley.

Bruner, J. S., & Postman, L. (1947). Functional selectivity in perception and reaction. *Journal of Personality, 16,* 69–77.

Brush, S. G. (1974). Should the history of science be rated "X"? *Science, 183,* 1164–72.

Brush, S. G. (1980). The chimerical cat: Philosophy of quantum mechanics in historical perspective. *Social Studies of Science, 10,* 394–47.

Bryan, W. L. & Harter, N. (1897). Studies in the physiology and psychology of the telegraphic languages. *Psychological Review, 4,* 27–53.

Buckley, K. W. (1982). The selling of a psychologist: John Broadus Watson and the application of behavioral techniques to advertising. *Journal of the History of the Behavioral Sciences, 18,* 207–21.

Buckley, K. W. (1984). *Mechanical man: John B. Watson and the beginnings of behaviorism.* Westport, CT: Guildford Press.

Buckley, K. W. (1989). *Mechanical man: John Broadus Watson and the beginnings of behaviorism.* New York: The Guildford Press.

Bugental, J. F. T. (1964). The third force in psychology. *Journal of Humanistic Psychology, 4,* 19–26.

Burke, E. (1790). *Reflections on the revolution in France.* Retrieved from http://www.constitution.org/eb/rev_fran.htm

Burkert, W. (1985). *Greek religion* (J. Raffan, Trans.). Cambridge, MA: Harvard University Press.

Burkert, W. (1987). *Ancient mystery cults.* Cambridge, MA: Harvard University Press.

Burnham, J. C. (1968). The new psychology: From narcissism to social control. In J. Braeman, R. H. Bremner, & D. Brody *(Eds.), Change and continuity in twentieth-century America: The 1920's.* Columbus, OH: Ohio State University Press, 3451–98.

Burnham, J. C. (1987). *How superstition won and science lost: The popularization of science and health in the United States.* Bowling Green: Bowling Green University Press.

Burnyeat, M. F. (1992). Is an Aristotelian philosophy of mind still credible? In M. Nussbaum & A.-O. Rorty *(Eds.), Essays on Aristotle's de Anima.* Oxford, England: Oxford University Press, 15–26.

Burrow, J. W. (2000). *The crisis of reason: European thought, 1848–1914.* New Haven, CT: Yale University Press.

Burtt, E. A. (1954). *The metaphysical foundations of modern science.* Garden City, NY: Doubleday.

Buss, D. M. (2011). *Evolutionary psychology: The new science of the mind,* 4th ed. Boston: Allyn & Bacon.

Butterfield, H. (1965). *The origins of modern science 1300–1800.* New York: Free Press.

Bynum, T. W. (1987). A new look at Aristotle's theory of perception. *The History of Philosophy Quarterly, 4,* 163–78. Reprinted in M. Durrant *(Ed.), Aristotle's de Anima in focus,* 90–109. London: Routledge & Kegan Paul, 1993.

Cadwallader, T. C. (1980, September). *William James' Harvard psychology laboratory reconsidered.* Paper presented at the annual meeting of the American Psychological Association, Montreal.

Cahoone, L. E. (Ed.). (1996). *From modernism to postmodernism: An anthology.* Cambridge, MA: Basil Blackwell.

Calkins, M. (1896). Association: An essay analytic and experimental. *Psychological Review Monograph Supplement, 1,* 2.

Calkins, M. W. (1906). A reconciliation between structural and functional psychology. *Psychological Review, 13,* 61–81.

Calkins, M. W. (1913). Psychology and the behaviorist. *Psychological Bulletin, 10,* 288–91.

Calkins, M. W. (1921). The truly psychological behaviorism. *Psychological Bulletin, 28,* 1–18.

Campbell, D. T. (1975). On the conflicts between biological and social evolution and between psychology and moral tradition. *American Psychologist, 30,* 1103–26.

Carlyle, T. (1841/1966). *On heroes, hero-worship and the heroic in history.* Lincoln, NE: University of Nebraska Press.

Carter, L. J. (1966). Social sciences: Where do they fit in the politics of science? *Science, 154,* 488–91.

Cary, P. (2000). *Augustine's invention of the inner self.* Oxford: Oxford University Press.

Cattell, J. M. (1890). Physical and mental tests. *Mind, 15,* 373–81. Available at the Classics in Psychology Web site.

Cattell, J. M. (1896). Address of the president. *Psychological Review, 3,* 134–48.

Cattell, J. M. (1904). The conceptions and methods of psychology. *Popular Science Monthly, 66,* 176–86.

Cervantes, M. (1614/1950). *Don Quixote* (J. M. Cohen, Trans.). Harmondsworth, England: Penguin Classics.

Chalmers, D. (1996). *The conscious mind: In search of a fundamental theory.* New York: Oxford University Press.

Chapanis, A. (1961). Men, machines and models. *American Psychologist, 16,* 113–31.

Charcot, J.-M. (1873/1996). Hysteria in the male subject. Reprinted in L. Benjamin *(Ed.), A history of psychology: Main sources and contemporary research,* 2nd ed. New York: McGraw-Hill, 97–103.

Chein, I. (1966). Some sources of divisiveness among psychologists. *American Psychologist, 21,* 333–42.

Chomsky, N. (1957). *Syntactic structures.* The Hague: Mouton.

Chomsky, N. (1959). Review of B. F. Skinner's Verbal behavior. *Language, 35,* 26–58. Reprinted in Jakobovits & Miron (1967).

Chomsky, N. (1966). *Cartesian linguistics.* New York: Harper & Row.

Christie, R., & Geis, F. (1970). *Studies in Machiavellianism.* San Diego, CA: Academic Press.

Churchland, P. M. (1985). *Matter and consciousness.* Cambridge, MA: Cambridge University Press.

Churchland, P. M. (1988). The ontological status of intentional states. Nailing folk psychology to its perch. *Behavioral and Brain Sciences, 11,* 507–08.

Churchland, P. M. (1989). *A neurocomputational perspective: Toward a unified science of the mind-brain.* Cambridge, MA: MIT Press.

Churchland, P. M. (1995). *The engine of reason, the seat of the soul: A philosophical journey into the brain.* Cambridge, MA: MIT Press.

Churchland, P. M., & Churchland, P. S. (1990, January). Could a machine think? *Scientific American, 262,* 32–37.

Churchland, P. S. (1986). *Neurophilosophy.* Cambridge, MA: Cambridge University Press.

Cioffi, F. (1972). Wollheim on Freud. *Inquiry, 15,* 172–86.

Cioffi, F. (1973). Introduction. In F. Cioffi *(Ed.), Freud: Modern judgements.* London: Macmillan, 1–24.

Cioffi, F. (1974). Was Freud a liar? *The Listener, 91,* 172–74.

Cioffi, F. (1984, July 6). The cradle of neurosis. *Times Literary Supplement,* 743–44.

Cioffi, F. (Ed.). (1998). *Unauthorized Freud: Doubters confront a legend.* New York: Viking.

Cippola, M. (1993). *Before the industrial revolution: European society and economy 1000–1700,* 3rd ed. New York: Norton.

Clark, A. (1989). *Microcognition.* Cambridge, MA: MIT Press.

Clark, A. (1998). *Being there: Putting brain, body, and world together again.* Cambridge, MA: MIT Press.

Clark, A. (2008). *Supersizing the mind: Embodiment, action, and cognitive extension.* Oxford: Oxford University Press.

Clark, G. (2007). *A farewell to alms: A brief economic history of the world.* Princeton: Princeton University Press.

Clark, H. M. (1911). Conscious attitudes. *American Journal of Psychology, 22,* 214–49.

Clark, K. (1967). The scientific and professional aims of psychology. *American Psychologist, 22,* 49–76.

Clark, K. (1971). The pathos of power: A psychological perspective. *American Psychologist, 26,* 1047–57.

Clark, S. R. L. (1992). Ancient philosophy. In A. Kenny *(Ed.), The Oxford history of Western philosophy.* Oxford, England: Oxford University Press, 1–53.

Clark, W. (2006). *Academic charisma and the origin of the research university.* Chicago, IL: Chicago University Press.

Clarke, E. C., & Dewhurst, K. (1972). *An illustrated history of brain function.* Berkeley: University of California Press.

Clay, R. A. (2000, January). Psychotherapy is cost-effective. *Monitor on Psychology,* 40–41.

Cleary, T., Humphries, L., Kendrick, S., & Wesman, A. (1975). Educational uses of tests with disadvantaged students. *American Psychologist, 30,* 15–91.

Clement of Alexandria. (c. 200 CE). *The stromata.* Retrieved from http://www.newadvent.org/fathers/02101.htm

Cochran, G., & Harpending, H. (2009). *The 10,000-year explosion: How civilization accelerated human evolution.* New York: Basic Books.

Cofer, C. N. (1978). Origins of the *Journal of Verbal Learning and Verbal Behavior. Journal of Verbal Learning and Verbal Behavior, 17,* 113–326.

Cohen, D. B. (1979). *J. B. Watson: The founder of behaviorism.* London: Routledge and Kegan Paul.

Cohen, I. B. (1980). *The Newtonian revolution.* Cambridge, England: Cambridge University Press.

Cohen, I. B. (1985). *Revolution in science.* Cambridge, MA: Harvard University Press.

Cohen, J., & Wiebe, G. D. (1955). Who are these people? *American Psychologist, 10,* 84–85.

Colish, M. (1997). *Medieval foundations of the western intellectual tradition 400-1400.* New Haven: Yale University Press.

Collins, S. (1982). *Selfless persons: Imagery and thought in Theravada Buddhism.* Cambridge, England: Cambridge University Press.

Comte, A. (1975). *Comte and positivism: The essential writings.* New York: Harper & Row.

Condillac, E. B. de. (1746/1974). *An essay on the origin of human knowledge.* New York: AMS Press.

Condillac, E. B. de. (1754/1982). Treatise on sensations. *Philosophical writings.* Hillsdale, NJ: LEA.

Condorcet, M.-J.-N. de Caritat, Marquis de. (1995). The future progress of the human mind. In I. Kramnick *(Ed.), The portable enlightenment reader.* New York: Penguin, 26–38.

Constantia. (1790). On the equality of the sexes. In Kramnick *(Ed.)* (1995), 601–09.

Cooper, K. J. (1991, May 6). Universities' images stained by improper charges to government. *Washington Post,* p. A13.

Copleston, F. C. (1964). *A history philosophy* (Vol. 1). Garden City, NY: Doubleday Anchor.

Corey, L. M., & Haidt, J. (Eds.). (2003). *Flourishing: Positive psychology and the well-lived life.* Washington, DC: APA.

Cornford, F. (1945). *The Republic of Plato.* Oxford, England: Oxford University Press.

Cosmides, L., & Tooby, J. (1992). The psychological foundations of culture. In J. H. Barkow, L. Cosmides, & J. Tooby *(Eds.), The adapted mind: Evolutionary psychology and the generation of culture.* New York: Oxford University Press, 19–136.

Cranefield, P. F. (1974). *The way in and the way out: François Magendie, Charles Bell and the roots of the spinal nerve.* Mt. Kisco, NY: Futura.

Cravens, H. (1992). A scientific project lost in time: The Terman genetic studies of genius, 1920s–1950s. *American Psychologist, 47,* 183–89.

Creegan, R. (1953). Psychologist, know thyself. *American Psychologist, 8,* 52–53.

Creelan, P. G. (1974). Watsonian behaviorism and the Calvinist conscience. *Journal of the History of the Behavioral Sciences, 10,* 95–118.

Crevier, D. (1993). *AI: The tumultuous history of the search for artificial intelligence.* New York: Basic.

Crews, F. (1986). *Skeptical engagements.* New York: Oxford University Press.

Crews, F. (1990). *The memory wars.* New York: New York Review of Books.

Crews, F. (1999). *Unauthorized Freud: Doubters confront a legend.* New York: Penguin.

Crocker, L. (1959). *An age of crisis.* Baltimore: Johns Hopkins University Press.

Crombie, A. C. (1995). *The history of science from Augustine to Galileo.* New York: Dover.

Cunningham, J. L. (1996). Alfred Binet and the quest for testing higher mental functioning. In W. Bringmann, H. Lück, R. Miller, & C. Early *(Eds.), A pictorial history of psychology.* Chicago, IL: Quintessence, 309–14.

Dahlbom, B. (1993). Mind is artificial. In B. Dahlbom *(Ed.), Dennett and his critics.* Oxford: Blackwell, 161–83.

Damasio, A. (1994). *Descartes' error: Emotion, reason, and the human brain.* New York: Putnam.

Dante. (c. 1314/1950). The devine comedy (I. Hell & D. L. Sayers, Trans.). Harmondsworth, England: Penguin Classics.

Danto, R. (1987). *Mysticism and morality: Oriental thought and moral philosophy,* rev. ed. New York: Columbia University Press.

Danziger, K. (1979). The positivist repudiation of Wundt. *Journal of the History of the Behavioral Sciences, 15,* 205–30.

Danziger, K. (1980a). The history of introspection reconsidered. *Journal of the History of the Behavioral Sciences, 16,* 241–62.

Danziger, K. (1980b). Wundt and the two traditions of psychology. In R. W. Rieber *(Ed.), Wilhelm Wundt and the making of a scientific psychology.* New York: Plenum, 69–94.

Danziger, K. (1990). *Constructing the subject: Historical origins of psychological research.* Cambridge, England: Cambridge University Press.

Darley, I., & Wolfle, D. (1946). Can we meet the formidable demand for psychological services? *American Psychologist, 1,* 179–80.

Darwall, S. (Ed.). (2003). *Virtue ethics.* Oxford: Blackwell.

Darwin, C. (1859/1959). *The origin of species.* New York: Mentor.

Darwin, C. (1871/1896). *The descent of man and selection in relation to sex,* rev. ed. New York: Appleton & Co.

Darwin, C. (1872/1965). *The expression of the emotions in man and animals.* Chicago, IL: University of Chicago Press.

Darwin, C. (1888/1958). *The autobiography of Charles Darwin and selected letters* (F. Darwin, Ed.). New York: Dover Books.

Darwin, L. (1958). *Autobiography.* London: Collins.

Dascal, M. (2007). Hobbes's challenge. In A. Brook *(Ed.), The prehistory of cognitive science.* Houndsmills: Palgrave/Macmillan, 67–96.

Dashiell, J. F. (1939). Some rapprochements in contemporary psychology. *Psychological Bulletin, 36,* 1–24.

Daston, L., & Galison, P. (2007). *Objectivity.* New York: Zone Books.

Davidson, D. (1980). *Essays on actions and events.* Oxford, England: Oxford University Press at the Clarendon Press.

Davidson, J. (1997). *Courtesans and fishcakes: The consuming passions of classical Athens.* New York: St. Martin's Press, 1998.

Davies, N. (1996). *Europe: A history.* Oxford: Oxford University Press.

Davis, G. (1966). Current status of research and theory in human problem solving. *Psychological Bulletin, 66,* 36–54.

Dawes, R. (1994). *House of cards: Psychology and psychotherapy built on myth.* New York: Free Press.

Decker, H. S. (1981). Freud and Dora: Constraints on medical progress. *Journal of Social History, 14,* 445–64.

Decker, H. S. (1991). *Freud, Dora, and Vienna 1900.* New York: Free Press.

De Gouges, O. (1791). The rights of woman. In Kramnick *(Ed.)* (1995), 609–18.

Demos, J. P. (1982). *Entertaining Satan: Witchcraft and the culture of early New England.* New York: Oxford University Press.

Dennett, D. (1978). *Brainstorms.* Cambridge, MA: MIT/ Bradford.

Dennett, D. (1983). Artificial intelligence and the strategies of psychological investigation. In J. Miller *(Ed.), States of mind.* New York: Pantheon.

Dennett, D. (1984). Cognitive wheels: The frame problem of AI. In C. Hookway *(Ed.), Minds, machines, and evolution.* New York: Cambridge University Press, *129–52.*

Dennett, D. C. (1995). *Darwin's dangerous idea: Evolution and the meaning of life.* New York: Simon & Schuster.

Dennett, D. D. (1980). Where am I? In D. Dennett *(Ed.), Brainstorms.* Cambridge, MA: MIT Press, *310–23.*

Dennett, D. D. (1991). *Consciousness explained.* Boston: Little, Brown.

Dennett, D. D. (1994). Cognitive science as reverse engineering: Several meanings of "top-down" and "bottom-up." In D. Praywitz, B. Skyrms, & D. Westerstahl *(Eds.), Logic, methodology, and philosophy of science IX.* Amsterdam: Elsevier, 679–89. Reprinted in Dennett, D., *Brain children,* 249–59. Cambridge, MA: MIT Press.

Dennett, D. D. (1998). *Brain children: Essays on designing minds.* Cambridge, MA: MIT Press.

Dennis, W. (Ed.). (1947). *Current trends in psychology.* Pittsburgh: University of Pittsburgh Press.

Descartes, R. (1637). Discourse on the method. In Descartes, R. *(Ed.). The philosophical writings of Descartes* (J. Cottingham, R. Stoothoff, & D. Murdoch, Trans.). Cambridge, England: Cambridge University Press, 109–76.

Descartes, R. (1641/1986). *Meditations on first philosophy, vol. 1* (J. Cottingham, Trans.). Cambridge, England: Cambridge University Press.

Descartes, R. (1985a). *The philosophical writings of Descartes* (J. Cottingham, R. Stoothoff, & D. Murdoch, Trans.). Cambridge, England: Cambridge University Press.

Descartes, R. (1985b). Treatise on man (L'Homme). In Descartes, R. *(Ed.). The philosophical writings of Descartes* (J. Cottingham, R. Stoothoff, &

D. Murdoch, Trans.). Cambridge, England: Cambridge University Press, 99–108.

Deutsch, J. A. (1953). A new type of behavior theory. *British Journal of Psychology, 44,* 304–18.

Dewey, J. (1896). The reflex-arc concept in psychology. *Psychological Review, 3,* 357–70.

Dewey, J. (1900/1978). Psychology and social practice. *Psychological Review, 7,* 105–24. Reprinted in E. R. Hilgard *(Ed.), American psychology in historical perspective: Addresses of the Presidents of the American Psychological Association 1892–1977.* Washington, DC: APA.

Dewey, J. (1917). The need for social psychology. *Psychological Review, 24,* 266–77.

Dewey, J. (1920/1948/1957). *Reconstruction in philosophy.* Boston, MA: Beacon.

Dewey, J. (1939). In J. Ratner *(Ed.), Intelligence in the modern world: The philosophy of John Dewey.* New York: Modern Library.

Diamond, S. (1980). Wundt before Leipzig. In R. W. Rieber *(Ed.), Wilhelm Wundt and the making of a scientific psychology.* New York: Plenum, 1–68.

Diggins, J. P. (1994). *The promise of pragmatism: Modernism and the crisis of knowledge and authority.* Chicago, IL: University of Chicago Press.

Diner, S. J. (1998). *A very different age: Americans of the progressive era.* New York: Hill and Wang.

Dixon, T. R., & Horton, D. C. (Eds.). (1968). *Verbal behavior and general behavior theory.* Englewood Cliffs, NJ: Prentice Hall.

Doherty, J. C. (1985, April 30). World War II through an Indochina looking glass. *Wall Street Journal,* p. 30.

Dollard, J., Doob, L., Miller, N., Mowrer, O., & Sears, R. (1939). *Frustration and aggression.* New Haven, CT: Yale University Press.

Dorken, H., & Morrison, D. (1976). JCAH standards for accreditation of psychiatric facilities: Implications for the practice of clinical psychology. *American Psychologist, 31,* 774–84.

Dreyfus, H. (1972). *What computers can't do: A critique of artificial reason.* New York: Harper & Row.

Dreyfus, H. L., & Dreyfus, S. E. (1988). Making a mind vs. modeling the brain: Artificial intelligence back at a branchpoint. In S. R. Graubard *(Ed.), The artificial intelligence debate: False starts, real foundations.* Cambridge, MA: MIT Press.

Dreyfus, H. L., & Dreyfus, S. E. (1990). *Mind over machine: The power of human intuition and expertise in the era of the computer.* New York: Free Press.

Drucker, P. F. (1994, November). The age of social transformation. *Atlantic Monthly, 274*(5), 53–80.

Dulany, D. E. (1968). Awareness, rules, and propositional control: A confrontation with S-R behavior theory. In T. R. Dixon & D. C. Horton *(Eds.), Verbal behavior and general behavior theory.* Englewood Cliffs, NJ: Prentice-Hall.

Dunbar, R. I. M., Barett, L., & Lycette, L. (2005). *Evolutionary psychology: A beginner's guide.* London: OneWorld.

Dunlap, K. (1912). Discussion: The case against introspection. *Psychological Review, 19,* 404–12.

Dunton, L. (1895). The old psychology and the new. In L. Dunton, H. Münsterberg, W. T. Harris, & G. Stanley Hall *(Eds.), The old psychology and the new: Addresses before the Massachusetts Schoolmaster's Club, April 27, 1895.* Boston, MA: New England Publishing Co.

Durrant, M. (Ed.). (1993). *Aristotle's* de Anima *in focus.* London: Routledge.

Dworkin, G. (1980). Commentary: Ethics, foundations, and science: Response to Alaisdair MacIntyre. In H. T. Englehardt & D. Callahan *(Eds.), Knowing and valuing: The search for common roots.* Hastings-on-Hudson, NY: The Hastings Center.

Dyson, G. B. (2012). *Turing's cathedral: The origins of the digital universe.* New York: Pantheon.

Dzielke, M. (1995). *Hypatia of Alexandria.* Cambridge, MA: Harvard University Press.

Eagle, M. (1984). *Recent developments in psychoanalysis: A critical evaluation.* Cambridge, MA: Harvard University Press.

Eamon, W. (1994). *Science and the secrets of nature: Books of secrets in medieval and modern science.* Princeton, NJ: Princeton University Press.

Ebbinghaus, H. (1885/1964). *Memory.* New York: Dover.

Ekman, P. (2006). *Darwin and facial expression: A century of research in review.* New York: Malor Books.

Ellenberger, H. F. (1970). *The discovery of the unconscious.* New York: Basic Books.

Ellis Davidson, H. R. (1996). *Viking and Norse Mythology.* New York: Barnes & Noble Books.

Emerson, R. W. (1950). *Selected prose and poetry.* New York: Holt, Rinehart & Winston.

Epicurus, Letter to Menoeceus. Retrieved from http://www.epicurus.net/en/menoeceus.html

Erdelyi, M. H. (1985). *Psychoanalysis: Freud's cognitive psychology.* San Francisco: Freeman.

Ericsson, K. A., & Simon, H. (1980). Verbal reports as data. *Psychological Review, 87,* 215–51.

Esdaile, J. (1852). *Natural and mesmeric clairvoyance.* London: Hippolyte Bailliere.

Esterson, A. (1993). *Seductive mirage: An exploration of the work of Sigmund Freud.* Chicago: Open Court.

Estes, W., Koch, S., MacCorquodale, K., Meehl, K., Mueller, C., Schoenfeld, W., et al. (1954). *Modern learning theory.* New York: Appleton-Century-Crofts.

Estes, W. K., & Newell, A. (Co-chairs). (1983). Report of the research briefing panel on cognitive science and artificial intelligence. In *Research briefings 1983.* Washington, DC: National Academy Press.

Evans, R. (1984). The origins of American academic psychology. In J. Brozek *(Ed.), Explorations in the history of psychology in the United States.* Lewisburg, PA: Bucknell University Press, 17–60.

Evans, R. I. (1968). *B. F. Skinner: The man and his ideas.* New York: Dutton.

Eysenck, H. J. (1952). The effects of psychotherapy: An evaluation. *Journal of Consulting Psychology, 16,* 319–24.

Eysenck, H. J. (1986). *The decline and fall of the Freudian Empire.* Harmondsworth, England: Penguin.

Eysenck, H. J., & Wilson, G. D. (Eds.). (1973). *The experimental study of Freudian theories.* London: Methuen.

Fagan, T. K. (1996). Witmer's contribution to school psychological services. *American Psychologist, 51,* 241–43.

Fancher, R. (1985). *The intelligence men: Makers of the IQ controversy.* New York: Norton.

Farber, I. E. (1957). The division of experimental psychology and the APA. *American Psychologist, 12,* 200–202.

Farnham-Diggory, S. (Ed.). (1972). *Information processing in children.* New York: Academic Press.

Farrell, B. A. (1981). *The standing of psychoanalysis.* Oxford, England: Oxford University Press.

Farrell, J. (1996). *Freud's paranoid quest.* New York: NYU Press.

Fass, P. (1977). *The damned and the beautiful: American youth in the 1920's.* Oxford: Oxford University Press.

Ferguson, N. (1999). *The pity of war.* New York: Basic books.

Ferguson, N. (2000). The European economy, 1815–1914. In T. C. W. Blanning *(Ed.), The nineteenth century.* Oxford: Oxford University Press, 78–125.

Ferris, P. (1998). *Dr. Freud: A life.* Washington, DC: Counterpoint.

Festinger, L. (1957). *A theory of cognitive dissonance.* Stanford: Stanford University Press.

Festinger, L., & Carlsmith, J. M. (1959). Cognitive consequences of forced compliance. *Journal of Abnormal and Social Psychology, 58,* 203–10.

Fischer, D. H. (1989). *Albion's seed: Four British folkways in America.* New York: Oxford University Press.

Fisher, H. (1992). *The anatomy of love: The natural history of monogamy, adultery and divorce.* New York: Norton.

Fisher, S., & Greenberg, R. P. (1977). *The scientific credibility of Freud's theories and therapy.* New York: Basic Books.

Fite, W. (1913, April 10). The science of man. *The Nation, 96,* 368–70.

Fite, W. (1918). The human soul and the scientific prepossession. *Atlantic Monthly, 122,* 796–804.

Flowers, J. H. (Ed.). (1981). Nebraska symposium on motivation 1980. In *Cognitive processes* (Vol. 28). Lincoln, NE: University of Nebraska Press.

Fodor, J. A. (1981). The mind-body problem. *Scientific American, 294,* 114–220.

Fodor, J. A., & Pylyshyn, Z. W. (1988). Connectionism and cognitive architecture: A critical analysis. In S. Pinker & J. Mehler *(Eds.), Connections and symbols.* Cambridge, MA: Bradford Books/MIT Press, 3–72.

Foster, S. W. (1988). *The past is another country*. Berkeley: University of California Press.

Fox, C., Porter, R., & Wokler, R. (Eds.). (1995). *Inventing human science: Eighteenth century domains*. Berkeley, CA: University of California Press.

Francklin, T. (1780). *The works of Lucian, Vol. 1, The sale of philosophers*. London: T. Cadell.

Franklin, D. (1999). *The way of the world*. New York: Knopf.

Freeman, D. (1983). *Margaret Mead and Samoa: The making and unmaking of an anthropological myth*. Cambridge, MA: Harvard University Press.

Freeman, K. (1971). *Ancilla to the presocratic philosophers*. Cambridge, MA: Harvard University Press.

Freud, S. (1900/1968). *The interpretation of dreams*. New York: Avon.

Freud, S. (1905a/1962). *Three essays on the theory of sexuality*. New York: Avon.

Freud, S. (1905b). Fragment of an analysis of a case of hysteria. Partially reprinted in P. Gay (Ed.). (1989). *The Freud reader*. New York: Norton.

Freud, S. (1908/1953). "Civilized" sexual morality and modern nervousness. In *Collected papers* (Vol. 2). London: Hogarth Press.

Freud, S. (1912/1953). Contributions to the psychology of love: The most prevalent form of degradation in erotic life. In *Collected papers* (Vol. 4). London: Hogarth Press.

Freud, S. (1914/1966). *The psychopathology of everyday life*. New York: Norton.

Freud, S. (1915a). Instincts and their vicissitudes. Partially reprinted in P. Gay (Ed.), *The Freud reader*. New York: Norton, 1989.

Freud, S. (1915b). The unconscious. Partially reprinted in P. Gay (Ed.), *The Freud reader*. New York: Norton, 1989.

Freud, S. (1920/1961). *Beyond the pleasure principle*. New York: Norton.

Freud, S. (1923/1960). *The ego and the id*. New York: Norton.

Freud, S. (1925). An autobiographical study. In J. Strachey (Ed.), *The standard edition of the complete psychological works of Sigmund Freud* (Vol. 20). London: Hogarth Press, 213–22.

Freud, S. (1927/1961). *Future of an illusion*. New York: Norton.

Freud, S. (1930/1961). *Civilization and its discontents*. New York: Norton.

Freud, S. (1932). The question of a Weltanschauung. Partially reprinted in P. Gay (Ed.), *The Freud reader*. New York: Norton, 1989.

Freud, S. (1950). Project for a scientific psychology. In J. Strachey (Ed.), *The standard edition of the complete psychological works of Sigmund Freud* (Vol. 1). London: Hogarth Press, 283–346.

Freud, S. (1960). *The letters of Sigmund Freud*. New York: Basic Books.

Freud, S. (1985). *The complete letters of Sigmund Freud to Wilhelm Fliess 1887–1904* (J. M. Masson, Trans. & Ed.). Cambridge, MA: Harvard University Press.

Friedman, J. (2012). "A weapon in the hands of the people": The rhetorical Presidency in historical and conceptual context. *Critical Review, 19*, 197–240.

Fromkin, D. (1999). *The way of the world: From the dawn of civilizations to the eve of the twenty-first century*. New York: Vintage.

Frost, E. P. (1912). Can biology and physiology dispense with consciousness? *Psychological Review, 3*, 246–52.

Fry, P. (1909). Essay in aesthetics. *Art Quarterly, 2*, 171–90.

Fukyama, F. (1999). *The great disruption: Human nature and the reconstitution of social order*. New York: Free Press.

Furomoto, L. (1989). The new history of psychology. In T. S. Cohen (Ed.), *The G. Stanley hall lecture series* (Vol. 9). Washington, DC: American Psychological Association, 9–34.

Gaffan, D. (1997). Review of the mind-brain continuum. *Trends in Cognitive Sciences, 1*, 194.

Galton, F. (1869/1925). *Hereditary genius*. London: Macmillian.

Galton, F. (1883/1907). *Inquiries into the human faculty and its development*. London: J. M. Dent.

Gangestad, S. W., & Simpson, J. A. (Eds.). (2007). *The evolution of mind: Fundamental questions and controversies*. New York: Guildford Press.

Garcia, J., McGowan, B. K., & Green, K. F. (1972). Constraints on conditioning. In M. E. P. Seligman & J. L. Hager *(Eds.), Biological boundaries of learning*. New York: Appleton-Century-Crofts.

Gardner, H. (1983). *Frames of mind: The theory of multiple intelligences*. New York: Basic.

Garfield, S. L. (1966). Clinical psychology and the search for identity. *American Psychologist, 21*, 343–52.

Garrison, D. H. (2000). *Sexual culture in ancient Greece*. Norman, OK: University of Oklahoma Press.

Garth, T. R. (1930). A review of race psychology. *Psychological Bulletin, 27*, 329–56.

Gaukroger, S. (1995). *Descartes: An intellectual biography*. Oxford: Clarendon Press.

Gaukroger, S. (2002). *Descartes' system of natural philosophy*. Cambridge: Cambridge University Press.

Gaukroger, S. (2006). *The emergence of a scientific culture: Science and the shaping of modernity*. Oxford: Clarendon Press, 1210–685.

Gay, P. (1966/1969). *The enlightment: An interpretation* (2 vols.). New York: Knopf.

Gay, P. (1969). The obsolete Puritanism of Jonathan Edwards. Reprinted in J. Opie *(Ed.), Jonathan Edwards and the enlightenment*. Lexington, MA: Heath.

Gay, P. (1986). *The bourgeois experience: Victoria to Freud, Vol. 2: The tender passion*. New York: Oxford University Press.

Gay, P. (1988). *Freud: A life for our time*. New York: Norton.

Gay, P. (Ed.). (1989). *The Freud reader*. New York: Norton.

Gazzaniga, M. S., Ivry, R. B., & Mangun, G. R. (1998). *Cognitive neuroscience: The biology of the mind*. New York: Norton.

Gazzaniga, M. S., Ivry, R. B., & Mangun, G. R. (2002). *Cognitive neuroscience*, 2nd ed. New York: Norton.

Geiger, H. (1973). Introduction: A. H. Maslow. In A. Maslow *(Ed.), The farther reaches of human nature*. New York: Viking/Esalen, xv–xxxi.

Gelman, D., & Gordon, J. (1987, December 14). Growing pains for the shrinks. *Newsweek*, pp. 70–72.

Gholson, B., Shadish, W. R., Jr., Niemeyer, R., & Houts, A. (Eds.). (1989). *Psychology of science*. Cambridge, England: Cambridge University Press.

Gibbs, R. W. (2005). *Embodiment and cognitive science*. New York: Cambridge University Press.

Giere, R. N. (1988). *Exploring science: A cognitive approach*. Chicago: University of Chicago Press.

Gigerenzer, G., Swijtink, Z., Porter, T., Daston, L., Beatty, J., & Krueger, L. (1989). *The empire of chance: How probability changed science and everyday life*. Cambridge, England: Cambridge University Press.

Gilgen, A. R. (1982). *American psychology since World War II: A profile of the discipline*. Westport, CT: Greenwood Press.

Gillespie, M. A. (2008). *The theological origins of modernity*. Chicago, IL: Chicago University Press.

Ginzburg, C. (1991). *Ecstasies: Deciphering the witches' sabbath*. New York: Pantheon.

Glassberg, D. (1985, June 15). *Social science at the Chicago World's Fair of 1933–1934*. Paper presented at the annual meeting of Cheiron the Society for the History of the Behavioral Sciences, Philadelphia, PA.

Glimcher, P. W. (2003). *Decisions, uncertainty, and the brain: The science of neuroeconomics*. Cambridge, MA: MIT Press.

Goethe, J. W. (1808/1961). *Goethe's Faust* (W. Kaufmann, Trans.). New York: Anchor Books.

Goetzmann, W. H. (2009). *Beyond the revolution: A history of American thought from Paine to Pragmatism*. New York: Basic.

Goldstein, T. (1995). *Dawn of modern science: From ancient Greeks to the renaissance*. New York: Da Capo.

Goldsworthy, A. (2008). *Caesar: Life of a colossus*. New Haven, CT: Yale University Press.

Goldsworthy, A. (2009). *How Rome fell: Death of a superpower*. New Haven, CT: Yale University Press.

Goleman, D. (1983, May). A conversation with Ulric Neisser. *Psychology Today, 17*, 54–62.

Goleman, D. (1995). *Emotional intelligence*. New York: Bantam.

Goss, A. E. (1961). Verbal mediating responses and concept formation. *Psychological Review, 68,* 248–74.

Gough, P. B., & Jenkins, J. J. (1963). Verbal learning and psycholinguistics. In M. Mary *(Ed.), Theories in contemporary psychology.* New York: Macmillan.

Gould, S. J. (1981). *The mismeasure of man.* New York: W. W. Norton.

Gould, S. J., & Lewontin, R. (1979). The spandrels of San Marco and the Panglossian paradigm: A critique of the adaptationist paradigm. *Proceedings of the Royal Society, B205,* 581–98.

Grant, E. (1996). *The foundations of modern science in the Middle Ages: Their religious, institutional, and religious contexts.* Cambridge, England: Cambridge University Press.

Grant, M. (1990). *The fall of the Roman Empire.* New York: Macmillan.

Graumann, C. (1980). Experiment, statistics, history: Wundt's first program of psychology. In W. Bringmann & R. D. Tweney *(Eds.), Wundt studies.* Toronto: Hogrefe.

Graves, R., & Hodge, A. (1940). *The long week-end: A social history of Britain 1918–1939.* New York: W. W. Norton.

Green, C. D. (2002). Of immortal mythological beasts: Operationism in psychology. *Theory and Psychology, 2,* 291–320.

Green, C. D. (2005). Was Babbage's analytical engine meant to be a mechanical model of the mind? *History of Psychology, 8,* 35–45.

Green, P. (1973). *Ancient Greece: A concise history.* London: Thames and Hudson.

Green, P. (1990). *Alexander to Actium: The historical evolution of the Hellenistic Age.* Los Angeles, CA: University of California Press.

Greenberg, D. S. (1967). Social sciences: Progress slow on House and Senate bills. *Science, 157,* 660–62.

Greenspoon, J. (1955). The reinforcing effect of two spoken sounds on the frequency of two behaviors. *American Journal of Psychology, 68,* 409–16.

Gross, S. J. (1978). The myth of professional licensing. *American Psychologist, 33,* 1009–16.

Grünbaum, A. (1984). *The foundations of psychoanalysis: A philosophical critique.* Berkeley: University of California Press.

Grünbaum, A. (1986). Precis of "The foundations of psychoanalysis: A philosophical critique, with commentary." *Behavioral and Brain Sciences, 9,* 217–84.

Gunderson, K. (1984). Leibnizian privacy and Skinnerian privacy. *Behavioral and Brain Sciences, 7,* 628–29.

Gundlach, H. U. K. (1996). The mobile psychologist: Psychology in the railroads. In W. G. Bringmann, H. E. Lück, R. Miller, & C. E. Early *(Eds.), A pictorial history of psychology.* Chicago, IL: Quintessence, 506–9.

Gundlach, H. U. K. (2012). Germany. In D. B. Baker *(Ed.). The Oxford handbook of the history of psychology: Global perspectives.* Oxford: Oxford University Press, 255–88.

Gutting, G. (Ed.). (1980). *Paradigms and revolutions: Applications and appraisals of Thomas Kuhn's philosophy of science.* South Bend, IN: University of Notre Dame Press.

Häcker, H., & Echterhoff, W. (1996). Traffic psychology. In W. G. Bringmann, H. E. Lück, R. Miller, & C. E. Early *(Eds.), A pictorial history of psychology.* Chicago, IL: Quintessence, 503–5.

Haggerty, M. E. (1911). The nineteenth annual meeting of the A.P.A. *Journal of Philosophy, 8,* 204–17.

Haggerty, M. E. (1913). The laws of learning. *Psychological Review, 20,* 411–22.

Haidt, J. (2003). Elevation and the positive psychology of morality. In L. M. Corey & J. Haidt *(Eds.), Flourishing: Positive psychology and the well-lived life.* Washington, DC: APA, 275–89.

Haidt, J. (2007). The new synthesis in moral psychology. *Science, 316,* 998–1002.

Haidt, J. (2012). *The righteous mind: Why good people are divided by politics and religion.* New York: Pantheon.

Hailer, M. (1963). *Eugenics: Hereditarian attitudes in American thought.* New Brunswick, NJ: Rutgers University Press.

Hale, M. (1980). *Human science and social order.* Philadelphia, PA: Temple University Press.

Haller, M. (1963). *Eugenics: Hereditarian attitudes in American thought.* New Brunswick, NJ: Rutgers University Press.

Hampson, N. (1982). *The enlightment: An evaluation.* Harmondsworth, England: Penguin.

Hanson, V. D. (2002). *Carnage and culture: Landmark battles in the rise to Western power.* New York: Doubleday.

Hanson, V. D. (2005). *A war like no other: How the Athenians and Spartans fought the Peloponnesian war.* New York: Random House.

Harrington, A. (1996). *Reenchanted science: Holism in German culture from Wilhelm II to Hitler.* Princeton, NJ: Princeton University Press.

Harris, B. (1979). Whatever happened to Little Albert? *American Psychologist, 34,* 151–60.

Harris, B., & Morawski, I. (1979, April). *John B. Watson's predictions for 1979.* Paper presented at the 50th annual meeting of the Eastern Psychological Association, Philadelphia, PA.

Hartley, D. (1749/1971). *Observations on man, his frame, his duty, and his expectations.* Facsimile reprint. New York: Garland Press.

Haupt, E. J. (1995, August). *G. E. Müller: The shaper of experimental psychology.* Paper presented at the annual meeting of the American Psychological Association, New York.

Hayes-Roth, E. (1979). Distinguishing theories of representation. *Psychological Review, 86,* 376–82.

Hazard, P. (1963). *The European mind 1680–1715.* New York: New American Library.

Heather, P. (2006). *The fall of the Roman Empire: A new history of Rome and the barbarians.* Oxford: Oxford University Press.

Heather, P. (2010). *Empires and barbarians: The fall of Rome and the birth of Europe.* New York: Oxford University Press.

Hebb, D. O. (1960). The second American revolution. *American Psychologist, 15,* 735–45.

Heer, F. (1962). *The medieval world.* New York: Mentor.

Hegel, G. W. F. (1837/1953). *Reason in history: A general introduction to the philosophy of history* (R. Hartmann, Trans.). Indianapolis, IN: Bobbs-Merrill.

Helmholtz, H. von. (1877/1971). Thought in medicine. Reprinted in R. Kahl *(Ed.), Selected writings of Hermann von Helmholtz.* Middletown, CT: Wesleyan University Press.

Hempel, C. G., & Oppenheim, P. (1948). Studies in the logic of explanation. *Philosophy of Science, 15,* 135–75.

Reprinted in Hempel, C. (1965). *Aspects of scientific explanation.* New York: Free Press.

Henle, M. (1985). Rediscovering Gestalt psychology. In S. Koch & D. Leary *(Eds.), A century of psychology as science.* New York: McGraw-Hill.

Herbert, N. (1985). *Quantum reality: Beyond the new physics.* Garden City, NY: Doubleday.

Herman, E. (1996). *The romance of American psychology: Political culture in the age of experts.* Berkeley, CA: University of California Press.

Heyes, C. M. (1989). Uneasy chapters in the relationship between psychology and epistemology. In B. Gholson, W. R. Shadish, Jr., R. Niemeyer, & A. Houts *(Eds.), Psychology of science.* Cambridge, England: Cambridge University Press, 115–37.

Hilgard, E. R. (1939). Review of B. F. Skinner: Behavior of organisms. *Psychological Bulletin, 36,* 121–24.

Hilgard, E. R. (1940). Review of Hull, et al. *Psychological Bulletin, 37,* 808–15.

Hillis, W. D. (1987, June). The connection machine. *Scientific American, 256,* 108–15.

Himmelfarb, G. (1987). *The new history and the old.* Cambridge, MA: Harvard University Press.

Himmelfarb, G. (1995). *The de-moralization of society: From Victorian virtues to modern values.* New York: Knopf.

Hine, T. (1999). *The rise and fall of the American teenager.* New York: Avon.

Hobbes, T. (1651/1962). *Leviathan.* New York: Collier Books.

Hoch, E., Ross, A. O., & Winder, C. L. (1966). Conference on the professional preparation of clinical psychologists. *American Psychologist, 21,* 42–51.

Hofstadter, R. (1955). *Social Darwinism in American thought,* rev. ed. Boston, MA: Beacon Press.

Holding, R. (1996, June 6). Berkeley psychoanalyst loses appeal in libel suit. *San Francisco Chronicle,* p. A3.

Holt, R. R. (1964). Imagery: The return of the ostracized. *American Psychologist, 19,* 254–64.

Holt, R. R. (1982, November). Family secrets. *The Sciences, 22,* 26–28.

Holton, G. (1973). *Thematic origins of scientific thought: Kepler to Einstein.* Cambridge, MA: Harvard University Press.

Holton, G. (1978). *The scientific imagination: Case studies.* Cambridge, England: Cambridge University Press.

Holton, G. (1984, November 2). Do scientists need a philosophy? *Times Literary Supplement,* 1231–34.

Hook, S. (1959). *Psychoanalysis, scientific method, and philosophy.* New York: New York University Press.

Hookway, C. (Ed.). (1984). *Minds, machines, and programs.* New York: Cambridge University Press.

Hopkins, M. (1870). *Lectures on moral science.* Boston, MA: Gould & Lincoln.

Horgan, J. (1997). *The end of science: Facing the limits of knowledge in the twilight of the scientific age.* New York: Broadway Books.

Horgan, J. (2000). *The undiscovered mind: How the human mind defies replication, medication and explanation.* New York: Free Press.

Houghton, W. E. (1957). *The Victorian frame of mind.* New Haven, CT: Yale University Press.

Huff, T. E. (1993). *The rise of early modern science: Islam, China, and the West.* Cambridge, England: Cambridge University Press.

Hughes, H. S. (1958). *Consciousness and society: The reorientation of European social thought 1890–1930.* New York: Vintage Books.

Hull, C. (1917). The formation and retention of associations among the insane. *American Journal of Psychology, 28,* 419–35.

Hull, C. L. (1920). Quantitative aspects of the evolution of concepts. *Psychological Monographs, 28*(123).

Hull, C. L. (1930a). Simple trial and error learning: A study in psychological theory. *Psychological Review, 37,* 241–56.

Hull, C. L. (1930b). Knowledge and purpose as habit mechanisms. *Psychological Review, 37,* 511–25.

Hull, C. L. (1931). Goal attraction and directing ideas conceived as habit phenomena. *Psychological Review, 38,* 487–506.

Hull, C. L. (1934). The concept of the habit-family-hierarchy in maze learning. *Psychological Review, 41,* 33–54, 131–52.

Hull, C. L. (1935). The conflicting psychologies of learning: A way out. *Psychological Review, 42,* 491–516.

Hull, C. L. (1937). Mind, mechanism and adaptive behavior. *Psychological Review, 44,* 1–32.

Hull, C. L. (1938). The goal-gradient hypothesis applied to some "field-force" problems in the behavior of young children. *Psychological Review, 45,* 271–300.

Hull, C. L. (1943a). *Principles of behavior.* New York: Appleton-Century-Crofts.

Hull, C. L. (1943b). The problem of intervening variables in molar behavior theory. *Psychological Review, 50,* 273–88.

Hull, C. L. (1951). *Essentials of behavior.* New Haven: Yale University Press.

Hull, C. L. (1952a). *A behavior system.* New Haven: Yale University Press.

Hull, C. L. (1952b). Clark L. Hull. In E. G. Boring, H. S. Langfeld, H. Werner, & R. M. Yerkes *(Eds.), A history of psychology in autobiography* (Vol. 4). Worcester, MA: Clark University Press.

Hull, C., & Baernstein, H. (1929). A mechanical parallel to the conditioned reflex. *Science, 70,* 14–15.

Hull, C., Hovland, C., Ross, R., Hall, M., Perkins, D., & Fitch, R. (1940). *Mathematico-deductive theory of rote learning: A study in scientific methodology.* New Haven: Yale University Press.

Hulse, S., Fowler, H., & Honig, W. (Eds.). (1978). *Cognitive processes in animal behavior.* Hillsdale, NJ: Erlbaum.

Hume, D. (1740/1777/1962). Abstract of a treatise of human nature (1740), and an inquiry concerning human understanding (1777). In Anthony Flew *(Ed.), David Hume on human nature and the understanding.* New York: Collier Books.

Hume, D. (1817). *A treatise of human nature.* London: Thomas and Joseph Allman.

Hunt, E. (2011). *Human intelligence.* Cambridge: Cambridge University Press.

Hunter, W. S. (1922). An open letter to the anti-behaviorists. *Journal of Philosophy, 19,* 307–08.

Hunter, W. S. (1923). Review of A. A. Roback, "behaviorism and psychology." *American Journal of Psychology, 34,* 464–67.

Hunter, W. S. (1925). Psychology and anthroponomy. In C. Murchison *(Ed.), Psychologies of 1925.* Worcester, MA: Clark University Press.

Hutchins, E. (1995). How a cockpit remembers its speeds. *Cognitive Science, 19*, 265–88.

Huxley, T. H. (1863/1954). *Man's place in nature.* Ann Arbor, MI: University of Michigan Press.

Huxley, T. H. (1871). Letter. In London Dialectical Society *(Ed.), Report on spiritualism.* London: Longmans, Green, Reader & Dyer.

Irvine, W. (1959). *Apes, angels, and Victorians.* Cleveland, OH: Meridian Books.

Irwin, T. (1989). *Classical thought. A history of Western philosophy I.* Oxford, England: Oxford University Press.

Jackson, G. D. (1975). On the report of the ad hoc committee on educational uses of tests with disadvantaged students: Another psychological view from the Association of Black Psychologists. *American Psychologist, 30*, 88–93.

Jacob, M. C. (2001). *The enlightenment: A brief history with documents.* Boston, MA: Bedford/St. Martin's.

Jahoda, G. (1997). Wilhelm Wundt's *Völkerpsychologie.* In W. G. Bringmann, H. E. Lück, R. Miller, & C. E. Early *(Eds.), A pictorial history of psychology.* Chicago, IL: Quintessence, 148–49.

Jakobovits, L., & Miron, M. (Eds.). (1967). *Readings in the psychology of language.* Englewood Cliffs, NJ: Prentice-Hall.

James, W. (1875). Review of Grundzuge der physiologischen psychologie. *North American Review, 121*, 195–201.

James, W. (1890). *Principles of psychology* (2 vols.). New York: Holt.

James, W. (1892a/1992). *Psychology: Briefer course.* New York: Library of America.

James, W. (1892b). A plea for psychology as a natural science. *Philosophical Review, 1*, 145–53.

James, W. (1904). Does "consciousness" exist? *Journal of Philosophy, 1*, 477–91.

James, W. (1907/1955). *Pragmatism.* New York: Meridian.

Jankowiak, W. (1995). *Romantic passion: A universal experience?* New York: Columbia University Press.

Jastrow, J. (1901). Some currents and undercurrents in psychology. *Psychological Review, 8*, 1–26.

Jastrow, J. (1927). The reconstruction of psychology. *Psychological Review, 34*, 169–95.

Jastrow, J. (1929, April 26). Review of J. B. Watson: Ways of behaviorism, psychological care of infant and child, battle of behaviorism. *Science, 69*, 455–57.

Jefferson, T., et al. (1776, July 3). *Declaration of independence.* Philadelphia, PA: Continental Congress.

Jencks, C. A. (1981). *The language of postmodern architecture.* London: Academy Editions.

Jenkins, J. J. (1968). The challenge to psychological theorists. In T. R. Dixon & D. C. Horton *(Eds.), Verbal behavior and general behavior theory.* Englewood Cliffs, NJ: Prentice-Hall.

Jenkins, J. J. (1981). Can we find a fruitful cognitive psychology? In J. H. Flowers *(Ed.), Nebraska symposium on motivation 1980, Vol. 28: Cognitive processes.* Lincoln, NE: University of Nebraska Press.

Jensen, A. (1969). How much can we boost I.Q. and scholastic achievement? *Harvard Educational Review, 39*, 1–123.

Johnson, P. (1992). *The birth of the modern: World society 1815–1830.* New York: Harper Perennial.

Joncich, G. (1968). *The sane positivist: A biography of E. L. Thorndike.* Middletown, CT: Wesleyan University Press.

Jones, A. H. (1915). The method of psychology. *Journal of Philosophy, 12*, 462–71.

Jones, A. L. (1958). *Early American philosophers.* New York: Ungar.

Jones, R. (1967, July 7). Youth: The hippies. *Time*, 18–22.

Judd, C. H. (1910). *Psychology: General introduction.* New York: Scribner's.

Kahl, R. K. (Ed.). (1971). *Selected writings of Hermann von Helmholtz.* Middletown, CT: Wesleyan University Press.

Kant, I. (1784/1995). What is enlightenment? In I. Kramnick *(Ed.), The portable enlightenment reader.* New York: Penguin, 1–6.

Kant, I. (1798/1974). *Anthropology from a pragmatic point of view* (M. J. Gregor, Trans.). The Hague, The Netherlands: Martinus Nijhoff.

Kahneman, D. (2011). *Thinking, fast and slow.* New York: Farrar, Straus, and Giroux.

Kasschau, R. A., & Kessel, F. S. (Eds.). (1980). *Psychology and society: In search of symbiosis.* New York: Holt, Rinehart & Winston.

Kaufmann, W. (1985). Nietzsche as the first great (depth) psychologist. In S. Koch & D. Leary *(Eds.), A century of psychology as science.* New York: McGraw-Hill.

Keegan, J. (1999). *The First World War.* New York: Knopf.

Keehn, J. D. (1955). The expressed social attitudes of leading psychologists. *American Psychologist, 10,* 208–10.

Kemp, S. (1996). *Cognitive psychology in the middle ages.* New York: Praeger.

Kenneally, C. (2008). *The first word: The search for the origins of language.* New York: Penguin.

Kendler, H. H. (1952). "What is learned?"—A theoretical blind alley. *Psychological Review, 59,* 269–77.

Kendler, H. H., & Kendler, T. S. (1962). Vertical and horizontal processes in problem solving. *Psychological Review, 69,* 1–16. Reprinted in R. Harper *(Ed.).* (1964). *The cognitive processes: Readings.* Englewood Cliffs, NJ: Prentice-Hall.

Kendler, H. H., & Kendler, T. S. (1975). From discrimination learning to cognitive development: A neobehavioristic odyssey. In W. K. Estes *(Ed.), Handbook of learning and cognitive processes* (Vol. 1). Hillsdale, NJ: Erlbaum.

Kennedy, J. B. (2010). Plato's forms, Pythagorean mathematics, and stichometry. *Apeiron, 43,* 1–32.

Kessel, F. S. (1980). Psychology and society: In search of symbiosis. Introduction to the symposium. In R. A. Kasschau & E. S. Kessel *(Eds.), Psychology and society: In search of symbiosis.* New York: Holt, Rinehart and Winston.

Keyes, D. J., & Schwartz, B. (2007). "Leaky" rationality: How research on behavioral decision making challenges normative standards of rationality. *Perspectives on Psychological Science, 2,* 162–80.

Kiesler, C. A. (1979). Report of the executive officer 1978. *American Psychologist, 34,* 455–62.

Kiesler, S. B. (1977). Research funding for psychology. *American Psychologist, 32,* 23–32.

Kim, Y.-H., & Cohen, D. (2010). Information, perspective, and judgment about the self in face and dignity cultures. *Personality and Social Psychology Bulletin, 26,* 537–50.

Kim, Y.-H., Cohen, D., & Au, W.-T. (2010). The jury and abjury of my peers: The self in face and dignity cultures. *Journal of Personality and Social Psychology, 98,* 904–16.

Kitcher, P. (1989). Explanatory unification and the causal structure of the world. In P. Kitcher & W. S. Salmon *(Eds.), Scientific explanation. Minnesota studies in the philosophy of science* (Vol. 13). Minneapolis, MN: University of Minnesota Press, 41–506.

Kitcher, P., & Salmon, W. S. (1989). *Scientific explanation. Minnesota studies in the philosophy of science* (Vol. 13). Minneapolis, MN: University of Minnesota Press.

Klatzky, R. (1984). *Memory and awareness: An information-processing perspective.* San Francisco, CA: W H. Freeman.

Klein, M. I., & Tribich, D. (1982, November). Blame the child. *The Sciences, 22,* 14–20.

Klerman, G. L. (1979, April). The age of melancholy? *Psychology today, 12,* 36–42, 88.

Kline, P. (1981). *Fact and fantasy in Freudian theory,* 2nd ed. London: Methuen.

Knight, I. F. (1968). *The geometric spirit: The Abbé Condillac and the French enlightenment.* New Haven, CT: Yale University Press.

Koch, S. (1941). The logical character of the motivation concept. *Psychological Review, 48,* 15–38, 127–54.

Koch, S. (1944). Hull's "principles of behavior: A special review." *Psychological Bulletin, 41,* 269–86.

Koch, S. (1951a). The current status of motivational psychology. *Psychological Review, 58,* 147–54.

Koch, S. (1951b). Theoretical psychology 1950: An overview. *Psychological Review, 58,* 295–301.

Koch, S. (1980). Psychology and its human clientele: Beneficiaries or victims? In R. A. Kasschau & F. S. Kessel *(Eds.), Psychology and society: In search of symbiosis.* New York: Holt, Rinehart and Winston.

Koffka, K. (1935/1963). *Principles of Gestalt psychology.* San Diego, CA: Harcourt Brace Jovanovich.

Köhler, W. (1925). *The mentality of apes.* New York: Harcourt Brace.

Köhler, W. (1947). *Gestalt psychology: An introduction to new concepts in modern psychology.* New York: Liveright.

Köhler, W. (1959/1978). Gestalt psychology today. *American Psychologist, 14,* 727–34. Reprinted in E. R. Hilgard *(Ed.), American psychology in historical perspective: Addresses of the Presidents of the American Psychological Association.* Washington, DC: American Psychological Association, 251–63.

Köhler, W. (1967/1971). Gestalt psychology. *Psychologische Forschung, 31,* xviii–xxx. Reprinted in W. Köhler (1971). *The selected papers of Wolfgang Köhler.* New York: Liveright.

Krantz, D. L. (1973). Schools and systems: The mutual isolation of operant and non-operant psychology. In M. Henle, J. Jaynes, & J. Sullivan *(Eds.), Historical conceptions of psychology.* New York: Springer.

Krantz, S. (1990). Brentano on "unconscious consciousness." *Philosophy and Phenomenological Research, 1,* 745–53.

Krech, D. (1949). Notes toward a psychological theory. *Journal of Personality, 18,* 66–87.

Kuhn, T. S. (1959). *The Copernican revolution.* New York: Vintage Books.

Kuhn, T. S. (1970). *The structure of scientific revolutions,* rev. ed. Chicago, IL: University of Chicago Press.

Kuhn, T. S. (1976). Mathematical vs. experimental traditions in the development of physical science. *Journal of Interdisciplinary History, 7,* 1–31. Reprinted in T. S. Kuhn (1977). *The essential tension: Selected studies in scientific tradition and change.* Chicago, IL: University of Chicago Press, 31–65.

Kuhn, T. S. (1977). Second thoughts on paradigms. In F. Suppe *(Ed.), The structure of scientific theories,* 2nd ed. Urbana, IL: University of Illinois Press, 459–99.

Kuklick, B. (1977). *The rise of American philosophy: Cambridge, Massachusetts 1860–1930.* New Haven, CT: Yale University Press.

Külpe, O. (1895). *Introduction to philosophy* (W. B. Pillsbury & E. B. Titchener, Trans.). New York: Macmillan.

Kuo, Z. Y. (1928). The fundamental error of the concept of purpose and the trial and error fallacy. *Psychological Review, 35,* 414–33.

Kusch, M. (1995). Recluse, interlocutor, interrogator: Natural and social order in turn-of-the-century research schools. *Isis, 86,* 419–39.

Kusch, M. (1999). *Psychological knowledge: A social history and philosophy.* London: Routledge.

Lacan, J. (1968). *The language of the self* (A. Wilden, Trans.). Baltimore, MD: Johns Hopkins University Press.

Lachman, R., Lachman, J., & Butterfield, E. (1979). *Cognitive psychology and information processing.* Hillsdale, NJ: Erlbaum.

Ladd, G. T. (1887). *Elements of psychological psychology.* London: Longmonns Green.

Ladd, G. T. (1892). Psychology as a so-called "natural science." *Philosophical Review, 1,* 24–53.

Lakatos, I. (1970). Falsification and the methodology of scientific research programs. In I. Lakatos & A. Musgrave *(Eds.), Criticism and the growth of knowledge.* Cambridge, England: Cambridge University Press, 91–196.

Lakatos, I. (1971). History of science and its rational reconstruction. In R. Buck & R. Cohen *(Eds.), Boston studies in the philosophy of science.* Dordrecht, The Netherlands: D. Reidel.

La Mettrie, J. O. de (1748/1961). *Man a machine.* La Salle, IL: Open Court.

Landman, J. H. (1932). *Human sterilization: The history of the sexual sterilization movement.* New York: Macmillan.

Landman, J. T., & Dawes, R. (1982). Psychotherapy outcome: Smith & Glass conclusions stand up under scrutiny. *American Psychologist, 37,* 504–16.

Lane Fox, R. (1986). *Pagans and Christians.* New York: Knopf.

Langfeld, H. S. (1943). Fifty years of the psychological review. *Psychological Review, 50,* 143–55.

Lashley, K. S. (1923). The behavioristic interpretation of consciousness. *Psychological Review, 30,* Part 1: 237–72, Part 2: 329–53.

Lashley, K. S. (1951). The problem of serial order in behavior. In L. A. Jeffress *(Ed.), Cerebral mechanisms in behavior.* New York: John Wiley.

Laudan, L. (1977). *Progress and its problems.* Berkeley, CA: University of California Press.

Laudan, R. (1980). The recent revolution in geology and Kuhn's theory of scientific change. In G. Gutting *(Ed.), Paradigms and revolutions: Applications and* *appraisals of Thomas Kuhn's philosophy of science.* South Bend, IN: University of Notre Dame Press.

Leacock, S. (1923). A manual of the new mentality. *Harper's Magazine, 148,* 471–80.

Leahey, T. H. (1981, April 23). *The revolution never happened: Information processing is behaviorism.* Paper presented at the 52nd annual meeting of the Eastern Psychological Association, New York.

Leahey, T. H. (1990, August). *Three traditions in behaviorism.* Paper presented at the Annual Meeting of the American Psychological Association, Boston.

Leahey, T. H. (1992a). The mythical revolutions of American psychology. *American Psychologist, 47,* 308–18.

Leahey, T. H. (1992b). The new science of science. Review of Gholson, W. R. Shadish, Jr., Niemeyer, R. and Houts, A. (1989), *Contemporary Psychology,* in press.

Leahey, T. H. (1995). Waiting for Newton. *Journal of Mind and Behavior, 16,* 9–20.

Leahey, T. H. (1997, August). *Psychology and postmodernism.* Invited New Fellows Address, Annual meeting of the APA, Chicago, IL.

Leahey, T. H. (2001, August). *Does the past have a future? History of psychology in a postmodern age.* Division 26 Presidential Address, Annual meeting of the American Psychological Association, San Francisco, CA.

Leahey, T. H. (2005). Zombies and robots, Oh my! Twenty-two theorists in search of consciousness. *PsycCritques,* online journal.

Leahey, T. H. (2008, August 14). *Folk psychology and modernity: An exploration in deep history.* Poster presented at the 116th annual meeting of the American Psychological Association, Boston, MA.

Leahey, T. H., & Harris, R. J. (2004). *Learning and cognition,* 6th ed. Englewood Cliffs, NJ: Prentice-Hall.

Leahey, T. H., & Leahey, G. E. (1983). *Psychology's occult doubles: Psychology and the problem of pseudoscience.* Chicago, IL: Nelson-Hall.

Lear, J. (1988). *Aristotle: The desire to know.* Cambridge, England: Cambridge University Press.

Leary, D. E. (1978). The philosophical development of the conception of psychology in Germany, 1750–1850. *Journal of the History of the Behavioral Sciences, 14,* 113–21.

Leary, D. E. (1980). German idealism and the development of psychology in the nineteenth century. *Journal of the History of Philosophy, 18,* 299–317.

Lehrer, J. (2009). *How we decide.* New York: Houghton, Mifflin.

Lemann, N. (1999). *The big test: The secret history of the American meritocracy.* New York: Farrar, Straus, Giroux.

Lemov, R. (2005). *World as laboratory: Experiments with mice, mazes, and men.* New York: Hill and Wang.

Levitt, S. D., & List, J. A. (2009). *Was there really a Hawthorne effect at the Hawthorne plant? An analysis of the original illumination experiments.* National Bureau of Economic Research, Working Paper, No. 15016.

Lewis, B. (2001). *The Muslim discovery of Europe,* rev. ed. New York: Norton.

Lewis, B. (2002). *What went wrong? Western impact and the middle Eastern response.* New York: Oxford University Press.

Lewis, E. (2002). Review of E. Grant, *God and reason in the Middle Ages. Journal of the History of Ideas, 40,* 393–94.

Lindberg, D. C. (1992). *The beginnings of Western science.* Chicago, IL: University of Chicago Press.

Lindner, R. E. (1953). *Prescription for rebellion.* London: Victor Gollancz.

Littman, R. (1979). Social and intellectual origins of experimental psychology. In E. Hearst *(Ed.), The first century of experimental psychology.* Hillsdale, NJ: Erlbaum.

Llinas, R., & Churchland, P. S. (Eds.). (1996). *The mind-brain continuum.* Cambridge, MA: MIT Press.

Locke, J. (1690/1975). *An essay concerning human understanding* (Variorum ed., Peter Nidditch, Ed.). Oxford, England: Clarendon Press.

Lofton, J. (1972). Psychology's manpower: A perspective from the public at large. *American Psychologist, 27,* 364–66.

Lorenz, K. (1966). *On aggression.* San Diego, CA: Harcourt Brace Jovanovich.

Lotze, H. (1881). *Outline of psychology* (C. L. Hevrick, Ed. & Trans.). Reprint ed., 1973. New York: Arno.

Lovett, B. J. (2006). The new history of psychology: A review and critique. *History of Psychology, 9,* 17–37.

Luborsky, L., Singer, B., & Luborsky, L. (1975). Comparative studies of psychotherapy: Is it true that "everyone has won and all must have prizes"? *Archives of General Psychiatry, 32,* 995–1008.

Luce, J. V. (1992). *An introduction to Greek philosophy.* New York: Thames and Hudson.

Luchins, A. S. (1975). The place of Gestalt theory in American psychology. In S. Ertel, L. Kemmler, & M. Sadler *(Eds.), Gestalttheorie in der medernen psychologie.* Darmstadt, Germany: Dietrich Steinkopf Verlag.

Luckhardt, C. G. (1983). Wittgenstein and behaviorism. *Synthese, 56,* 319–38.

Lutts, R. H. (1990). *The nature fakers: Wildlife, science, and sentiment.* Golden, CO: Fulcrum.

Lyotard, J.-F. (1984/1996). *The postmodern condition: A report on knowledge.* (G. Bennington & B. Massumi, Trans.). Minneapolis, MN: University of Minnesota Press. Partially reprinted in L. Cahoone *(Ed.), From modernism to postmodernism: An anthology.* Cambridge, MA: Blackwell.

MacCorquodale, K., & Meehl, P. E. (1948). On a distinction between hypothetical constructs and intervening variables. *Psychological Review, 55,* 95–107.

MacCulloch, D. (2005). *The reformation.* New York: Penguin.

MacCulloch, D. (2009). *Christianity: The first three thousand years.* New York: Viking.

MacDougall, R. (1925). Men or robots? In C. Murchison *(Ed.), Psychologies of 1925.* Worcester, MA: Clark University Press.

Machiavelli, N. (1515). *The prince.* Retrieved from http://www.constitution.org/mac/prince17.htm

MacIntyre, A. (1981). *After virtue.* Notre Dame, IN: University of Notre Dame Press.

MacIntyre, A. (1985). How psychology makes itself true—or false. In S. Koch & D. Leary *(Eds.), A century of psychology as science.* New York: McGraw-Hill.

Macmillan, M. (1997). *Freud evaluated: The completed arc.* Cambridge, MA: MIT Press.

Madden, T. F. (2008). *Empires of trust: How Rome built—and America is building—a new world.* New York: Dutton.

Maher, B. T. (1999). Changing trends in doctoral training programs in psychology: A comparative analysis of research-oriented versus professional-applied programs. *Psychological Science, 10,* 475–81.

Mahoney, M. J. (1977). Reflections on the cognitive-learning trend in psychotherapy. *American Psychologist, 32,* 5–13.

Makris, G. (2008). *Revolution in mind: The creation of psychoanalysis.* New York: Harper Collins.

Malcolm, N. (1964). Behaviorism as a philosophy of psychology. In T. W. Wann *(Ed.), Behaviorism and phenomenology: Contrasting bases for modern psychology.* Chicago, IL: Chicago University Press.

Malcolm, N. (1970). Wittgenstein on the nature of mind. *American Philosophical Quarterly Monograph Series,* (4), 9–29.

Malthus, T. R. (1798/1993). *An essay on the principle of population.* Oxford, England: Oxford University Press.

Maltzman, I. (1955). Thinking: From a behavioristic point of view. *Psychological Review, 62,* 275–86.

Manicas, P. T. (1987). *A history and philosophy of the social sciences.* Oxford: Blackwell.

Manicas, P. T. (2006). *A realist philosophy of social science: Explanation and understanding.* New York: Cambridge University Press.

Mansfield, H. (2007). *Manliness.* New Haven: Yale University Press.

Marr, D. (1982). *Vision.* San Francisco, CA: Freeman.

Marshack, A. (1972). *Roots of civilization.* New York: McGraw-Hill.

Marx, K., & Engels, F. (1848). *The Communist manifesto.* Retrieved from http://www.gutenberg.org/ebooks/61

Marx, M. (1951). Intervening variable or hypothetical construct? *Psychological Review, 58,* 235–47.

Marx, M. (Ed.). (1963). *Theories in contemporary psychology.* New York: Macmillan.

Maslow, A. H. (1961). Eupsychia—The good society. *Journal of Humanistic Psychology, 1,* 1–11.

Maslow, A. H. (1962). Notes on being-psychology. *Journal of Humanistic Psychology, 2,* 47–71.

Maslow, A. H. (1967). Self-actualization and beyond. In J. R. T. Bugental *(Ed.), Challenges of humanistic psychology.* New York: McGraw-Hill.

Maslow, A. H. (1973). *The farther reaches of human nature.* New York: Viking.

Masson, J. M. (1984a, February). Freud and the seduction theory. *Atlantic Monthly,* 33–60.

Masson, J. M. (1984b). *The assault on truth: Freud's suppression of the seduction theory.* New York: Farrar, Straus & Giroux.

Mayer, A. M., & Orth, J. (1901). Experimental studies of association. Partially reprinted in G. Mandler & J. Mandler *(Eds.).* (1964). *The psychology of thinking: From associationism to Gestalt.* New York: John Wiley.

Mayo, E. (1933). *The human problems of an industrial civilization.* Cambridge, MA: Harvard University Press.

Mayo, E. (1945). *The social problems of an industrial civilization.* Cambridge, MA: Harvard Graduate School of Business Administration.

McCloskey, D. (2010). *Bourgeois dignity: Why economics can't explain the modern world.* Chicago, IL: University of Chicago Press.

McComas, H. C. (1916). Extravagances in the motor theory of consciousness. *Psychological Review, 23,* 397–406.

McConnell, J. V. (1970, April). Criminals can be brainwashed—Now. *Psychology Today, 3,* 14–18, 74.

McDougall, W. (1908). *Introduction to social psychology.* New York: Luce.

McDougall, W. (1912). *Psychology: The study of behaviour.* New York: Holt.

McDougall, W. (1921). *Is America safe for democracy?* New York: Scribner's. Reprinted. New York: Arno Press, 1977.

McDougall, W. (1977). *Is America safe for democracy?* 2nd ed. New York: Arno Press.

McGeoch, J. A. (1931). The acquisition of skill. *Psychological Bulletin, 28,* 413–66.

McGinn, C. (2000). *The mysterious flame: Conscious minds in a material world.* New York: Basic.

McGrath, W. J. (1986). *Freud's discovery of psychoanalysis: The politics of hysteria.* Ithaca, NY: Cornell University Press.

McMahon, C. (2008). Origins of the "psychological interior"—evidence from Imperial Roman literary practices and related issues. *Journal of the History of the Behavioral Sciences, 44,* 19–37.

McPherson, J. M. (1988). *The battle cry of freedom: The Civil War era.* New York: Oxford University Press.

McRae, R. (1976). *Leibniz: Perception, apperception, and thought.* Toronto, ON: University of Toronto Press.

McReynolds, P. (1996). Lightner Witmer: A centennial tribute. *American Psychologist, 51,* 237–40.

Mead, M. (1928). *Coming of age in Samoa.* New York: Morrow.

Medina, J. (1995). *Cézanne and modernism: The poetics of painting.* Albany, NY: SUNY Press.

Meehl, P. E. (1954). *Clinical vs. statistical prediction: A theoretical analysis and review of the evidence.* Minneapolis, MN: University of Minnesota Press.

Mehler, J., & Franck, S. (1981). Editorial. *Cognition, 10,* 1–5.

Meichenbaum, D. (1977). *Cognitive behavior modification: An integrative approach.* New York: Plenum.

Mele, A., & Rawling, P. (2004). *The Oxford handbook of rationality.* New York: Oxford University Press.

Meltzer, A. (2007). On the pedagogical motive for esoteric writing. *Journal of Politics, 69,* 1015–31.

Mickel, E. (1998, October 27). *Situating Marie de France: Did courtly love exist?* Paper presented at Virginia Commonwealth University, Richmond, Virginia.

Milar, K. S. (1999). "A coarse and clumsy tool": Helen Thompson Woolley and the Cincinnati Vocation Bureau. *History of Psychology, 2,* 219–35.

Mill, J. (1829/1964). Analysis of the phenomena of the human mind. Partially reprinted in J. M. Mandler & G. Mandler *(Eds.), Thinking: From association to Gestalt.* New York: John Wiley.

Mill, J. S. (1859/1978). *On liberty.* Indianapolis, IN: Hackett.

Mill, J. S. (1872/1987). *The logic of the moral sciences.* La Salle, IL: Open Court. Originally published as *Book VI. On the logic of the moral sciences,* in Mill's *A system of logic,* 8th ed. London: Longman's Green, Reader, & Dyer.

Miller, G. A. (1956). The magical number seven, plus or minus two: Some limits on our capacity for processing information. *Psychological Review, 63,* 81–97.

Miller, G. A. (1962). Some psychological studies of grammar. *American Psychologist, 17,* 748–62. Reprinted in Jakobovits and Miron (1967).

Miller, G. A. (1969). Psychology as a means of promoting human welfare. *American Psychologist, 24,* 1063–75.

Miller, G. A. (1972). *Psychology: The science of mental life.* New York: Harper & Row.

Miller, G. A. (1983). The background to modern cognitive psychology. In J. Miller *(Ed.), States of mind.* New York: Pantheon.

Miller, J. (1983). *States of mind.* New York: Pantheon.

Miller, J. G. (1955). Toward a general theory for the behavioral sciences. *American Psychologist, 10,* 513–31.

Miller, N. (1959). Liberalization of basic S-R concepts. In S. Koch *(Ed.), Psychology: Study of a science* (Vol. 2). New York: McGraw-Hill, 196–212.

Miller, N. (1962). Some psychological studies of grammar. *American Psychologist, 17,* 748–62.

Mills, W. (1899). The nature of animal intelligence. *Psychological Review, 6,* 262–74.

Minsky, M. (1968). Introduction. In M. Minsky *(Ed.), Semantic information processing.* Cambridge, MA: MIT Press.

Minsky, M. (1989, Summer). *Is the body obsolete? Whole earth review.* Retrieved April 28, 2012, from http://findarticles.com/p/articles/mi_m1510/is_n63/ai_7675133/

Minsky, M., & Papert, S. (1969). *Perceptrons: An introduction to computational geometry.* Cambridge, MA: MIT Press.

Minton, H. L. (1997). Lewis M. Terman: Architect for a psychologically stratified society. In W. Bringmann, H. Lück, R. Miller, & C. Early *(Eds.), A pictorial history of psychology.* Chicago, IL: Quintessence, 329–36.

Mischel, W., & Mischel, H. (1976). A cognitive social learning approach to morality and self-regulation. In T. Lickona *(Ed.), Moral development and behavior.* New York: Holt, Rinehart & Winston.

Mokyr, J. (1990). *The lever of riches: Technological creativity and economic progress.* New York: Oxford University Press.

Mokyr, J. (2002). *The gifts of Athena: Historical origins of the knowledge economy.* Princeton, NJ: Princeton University Press.

Mokyr, J. (2009). *The enlightened economy: An economic history of Britain 1700–1850.* New Haven, CT: Yale University Press.

Montaigne, M. de (1580/1959). *Essays.* New York: Pocket Library.

Morgan, C. L. (1886). On the study of animal intelligence. *Mind, 11,* 174–85.

Morgan, C. T. (1947). Human engineering. In W. Dennis *(Ed.), Current trends in psychology.* Pittsburgh, PA: University of Pittsburgh Press.

Morgan, M. L. (1992). Plato and Greek religion. In R. Kraut *(Ed.), The Cambridge companion to Plato.* Cambridge, England: Cambridge University Press, 227–47.

Morris, C. (1972). *The discovery of the individual 1050–1200.* New York: Harper Torchbooks.

Morris, I. (2010). *Why the West rules—For now: The patterns of history and what they reveal about the future.* New York: Farrar, Straus, and Giroux.

Mosse, G. (1981). *The crisis of German ideology: Intellectual origins of the third Reich,* rev. ed. New York: Schocken.

Münsterberg, H. (1908/1927). *On the witness stand.* Available at Classics in the History of Psychology Web site.

Münsterberg, H. (1913). *Psychology and industrial efficiency.* Available at Classics in the History of Psychology Web site.

Murdock, N., & Leahey, T. H. (1986, April). *Scientism and status: The Boulder model.* Paper presented at the annual meeting of the Eastern Psychological Association, New York.

Murray, C. (2012). *Coming apart: The state of white America 1960–2010.* New York: Random House.

Myers, C. R. (1970). Journal citations and scientific eminence in psychology. *American Psychologist, 25,* 1041–48.

Myers, F. (1903). *Human personality and its survival of bodily death,* 2 vols. London: Longmans, Green & Co.

Myers, G. E. (1986). *William James: His life and thought.* New Haven, CT: Yale University Press.

Mynatt, C. R., Doherty, M. E., & Tweney, R. D. (1978). Consequences of confirmation and disconfirmation in a simulated research environment. *Quarterly Journal of Experimental Psychology, 30*, 395–406.

Nagel, E. (1959). Methodological issues in psychoanalytic theory. In S. Hook *(Ed.)*, *Psychoanalysis, scientific method, and philosophy*. New York: New York University Press.

Nagel, T. (1986). *The view from nowhere*. New York: Oxford University Press.

Napoli, D. S. (1981). *Architects of adjustment: The history of the psychological profession in the United States*. Port Washington, NY: Kennikat Press.

Neisser, U. (1967). *Cognitive psychology*. New York: Appleton-Century-Crofts.

Neisser, U. (1976). *Cognition and reality*. San Francisco, CA: W. H. Freeman.

Neisser, U. (1982). Memory: What are the important questions? In U. Neisser *(Ed.)*, *Memory observed: Remembering in natural contexts*. San Francisco, CA: W. H. Freeman.

Neisser, U. (1984). Toward an ecologically oriented cognitive science. In T. M. Schlecter & M. P. Toglia *(Eds.)*, *New directions in cognitive science*. Norwood, NJ: Ablex.

Nersessian, N. J. (Ed.). (1987). *The process of science: Contemporary approaches to understanding scientific practice*. Dordrecht, The Netherlands: Martinus Nijhoff.

Newell, A. (1973). You can't play 20 questions with nature and win. In W. G. Chase *(Ed.)*, *Visual information processing*. New York: Academic Press, 283–308.

Newell, A., Shaw, J. C., & Simon, H. A. (1958). Elements of a theory of problem solving. *Psychological Review, 65*, 151–66.

Newman, R. (2000, January). Practice perspectives 2000. *Monitor on Psychology*, 62–65.

Newton-Smith, W. H. (1981). *The rationality of science*. London: Routledge & Kegan Paul.

Nietzsche, F. (1882). *The gay science with a prelude in rhymes and an appendix of songs* (W. Kaufmann, Trans., 1974). New York: Random House, Inc., Vintage Books.

Nisbett, R. E., & Wilson, T. D. (1977). Telling more than we can know: Verbal reports on mental processes. *Psychological Review, 84*, 231–59.

Noll, R. (1994). *The Jung cult: Origin of a charismatic movement*. Princeton, NJ: Princeton University Press.

Norton, D. F. (1982). *David Hume: Commonsense moralist, sceptic, metaphysician*. Princeton, NJ: Princeton University Press.

Norton, D. F. (1993a). Hume, human nature, and the foundations of morality. In D. F. Norton *(Ed.)*, *The Cambridge companion to Hume*. Cambridge, England: Cambridge University Press, 148–81.

Norton, D. F. (1993b). An introduction to Hume's thought. In D. F. Norton *(Ed.)*, *The Cambridge companion to Hume*. Cambridge, England: Cambridge University Press, 1–32.

Novak, T. P., & MacEvoy, B. (1990, June). On comparing alternative segmentation schemes: The list of values (LOV) and the life styles (VALS). *Journal of Consumer Research, 17*, 105–9.

Nussbaum, M. (1994). *Therapies of desire: Theory and practice in Hellenistic ethics*. Princeton, NJ: Princeton University Press.

Nussbaum, M., & Rorty, A.-O. (Eds.). (1992). *Essays on Aristotle's de anima*. Oxford: Oxford University Press.

O'Donnel, J. M. (1979). The crisis of experimentalism in the 1920's: E. G. Boring and his uses of history. *American Psychologist, 34*, 289–95.

O'Donnell, J. M. (1985). *The origins of behaviorism: American psychology, 1890-1920*. New York: New York University Press.

Ogden, R. M. (1911a). Imageless thought. *Psychological Bulletin, 8*, 183–97.

Ogden, R. M. (1911b). The unconscious bias of laboratories. *Psychological Bulletin, 8*, 330–31.

Ohlsson, S. (2007). The separation of thought and action in Western tradition. In A. Brook *(Ed.)*, *The prehistory of cognitive science*. Houndsmills: Palgrave/Macmillan, 17–37.

Onians, R. B. (1951). *The origins of European thought: About the body, the mind, the soul, the world, time, and fate*. Cambridge, England: Cambridge University Press.

Osgood, C. E. (1956). Behavior theory and the social sciences. *Behavioral Science, 1*, 167–85.

Osgood, C. E. (1957). A behaviorist analysis of perception and language as cognitive phenomena. In J. Bruner et al. *(Eds.), Contemporary approaches to cognition.* Cambridge, MA: Harvard University Press.

Ostrander, G. M. (1968). The revolution in morals. In J. Braeman, R. H. Bremner, & D. Brody *(Eds.), Change and continuity in twentieth-century America: The 1920s.* Columbus, OH: Ohio State University Press, 323–50.

Outram, D. (2005). *The enlightenment,* 2nd ed. Cambridge, England: Cambridge University Press.

Owen, D. (1985). *None of the above: Behind the myth of scholastic aptitude.* Boston, MA: Houghton Mifflin.

Owen, R. (1813). *A new view of society* (extracts). Retrieved from www.historyguide.org

Pagels, E. (1979). *The Gnostic Gospels.* New York: Random House.

Pagels, E. (1989). *Adam, Eve, and the Serpent.* New York: Vintage Books.

Palermo, D. (1971). Is a scientific revolution taking place in psychology? *Science Studies, 1,* 135–55.

Parmelee, M. (1913). *The science of human behavior.* New York: Macmillan.

Pavlov, I. P. (1957). *Experimental psychology and other essays.* New York: Philosophical Library.

Peatman, J. G. (1949). How scientific and how professional is the American Psychological Association? *American Psychologist, 4,* 486–89.

Peele, S. (1981). Reductionism in the psychology of the eighties: Can biochemistry eliminate addiction, mental illness, and pain? *American Psychologist, 36,* 807–18.

Peirce, C. S. (1878/1966). How to make our ideas clear. Partially reprinted in A. Rorty *(Ed.), Pragmatic philosophy.* Garden City, NY: Anchor Books.

Peirce, C. S. (1887). Logical machines. *American Journal of Psychology, 1,* 165–70.

Peirce, C. S. (1905/1970). What pragmatism is. In H. S. Thayer *(Ed.), Pragmatism: The classic writings.* New York: Mentor, 101–22.

Penn, I. N. (1985, June 24). The reality of mental illness [letter to the editor]. *The Wall Street Journal,* p. 33.

Pepper, S. (1923). Misconceptions regarding behaviorism. *Journal of Philosophy, 20,* 242–45.

Perelman, S. J. (1958). Sodom in the suburbs. In S. J. Perelman *(Ed.), The most of S. J. Perelman.* New York: Simon & Schuster, 211–17.

Perry, N. J. (1979). Why clinical psychology does not need alternative training models. *American Psychologist, 34,* 603–11.

Perry, R. B. (1904). Conceptions and misconceptions of consciousness. *Psychological Review, 11,* 282–96.

Perry, R. B. (1921). A behavioristic view of purpose. *Journal of Philosophy, 18,* 85–105.

Peterson, D. R. (1976). Need for the doctor of psychology degree in professional psychology. *American Psychologist, 31,* 792–98.

Pfeifer, R., Bongard, J. C., Brooks, R., & Iwasawa, S. (2006). *How the body shapes the way we think: A new view of intelligence.* Cambridge, MA: MIT Press.

Pinker, S. (1994). *The language instinct.* New York: Morrow.

Pinker, S. (1997). *How the mind works.* New York: Norton.

Pinker, S. (2002). *The blank slate: The modern denial of human nature.* New York: Norton.

Pipes, R. (1995). *Russia under the old regime,* 2nd ed. London: Penguin.

Plas, R. (1997). French psychology. In W. Bringmann, H. Lück, R. Miller, & C. Early *(Eds.), A pictorial history of psychology.* Chicago, IL: Quintessence, 548–52.

Plato. (1973). *Phaedrus and letters VII and VIII* (W. Hamilton, Trans.). London: Penguin.

Plato. (1991). *The dialogues of Plato. Volume II, the symposium* (R. E. Allen, Trans.). New Haven, CT: Yale University Press.

Plato. (1993). *Republic* (R. Waterfield, Trans.). Oxford, England: Oxford University Press.

Poffenberger, A. T. (1936). Psychology and life. *Psychological Review, 43,* 9–31.

Pomeroy, S. B., Burstein, S. M., Donlan, W., & Roberts, J. T. (1999). *Ancient Greece: A political, social and cultural history.* New York: Oxford University Press.

Pope, A. (1734/1965). *Essay on man.* Indianapolis, IN: Bobbs-Merrill.

Popper, K. (1963). *Conjectures and refutations: The growth of scientific knowledge.* London: Routledge & Kegan Paul.

Popper, K. (1965). Back to the presocratics. *In conjectures and refutations.* New York: Harper & Row.

Porter, R. (2000). *The creation of the modern world: The untold story of the British enlightenment.* New York: Norton.

Porter, R. (2001). *The enlightenment,* 2nd ed. New York: Penguin.

Post, S. C. (1985, July 25). Beware the "barefoot doctors of mental health." *The Wall Street Journal,* p. 21.

Postman, L., Bruner, S., & McGinnies, E. (1948). Personal values as selective factors in perception. *Journal of Abnormal and Social Psychology, 43,* 142–54.

Postman, L., & Sassenrath, J. (1961). The automatic action of verbal rewards and punishments. *Journal of General Psychology, 65,* 109–36.

Prioleau, L., Murdock, M., & Brody, N. (1983). An analysis of psychotherapy versus placebo studies. *Behavioral and Brain Sciences, 6,* 275–310.

Putney, S., & Putney, G. J. (1964). *The adjusted American: Normal neuroses in the individual and society.* New York: Harper Colophon.

Pylyshyn, Z. W. (1979). Validating computational models: A critique of Anderson's indeterminacy claim. *Psychological Review, 86,* 383–405.

Pylyshyn, Z. W. (1984). *Computation and cognition: Toward a foundation for cognitive science.* Cambridge, MA: MIT/Bradford.

Rahe, P. A. (1994). *Republics ancient and modern. Vol. 1, the ancién regime in classical Greece.* Chapel Hill, NC: University of North Carolina Press.

Railton, P. (1989). Explanation and metaphysical controversy. In P. Kitcher & W. S. Salmon *(Eds.), Scientific explanation. Minnesota studies in the philosophy of science* (Vol. 13). Minneapolis, MN: University of Minnesota Press, 220–52.

Raimey, C. T. (1974). Children and public policy: A role for psychologists. *American Psychologist, 29,* 14–18.

Ratcliffe, M. (2007). *Rethinking commonsense psychology: A critique of folk psychology, theory of mind, and simulation.* Basingstoke, UK: Palgrave Macmillan.

Rattansi, R. (1972). The social interpretation of science in the seventeenth century. In P. Mathias *(Ed.), Science and society 1600–1900.* Cambridge, England: Cambridge University Press.

Reid, T. (1764/1785/1975). *Thomas Reid's inquiry and essays.* In K. Lehrer & R. Beanblossom *(Eds.), Thomas Reid's inquiry and essays.* Indianapolis, IN: Bobbs-Merrill, ix–lx.

Reisman, J. M. (1966). *The development of clinical psychology.* New York: Appleton-Century-Crofts.

Remmers, H. H. (1944). Psychology—Some unfinished business. *Psychological Bulletin, 41,* 502–9.

Renfrew, C. (2007). *Prehistory: The making of the modern mind.* New York: Modern Library.

Resnick, R. J. (1997). A brief history of practice—expanded. *American Psychologist, 52,* 335–38.

Rheingold, H. (1973). To rear a child. *American Psychologist, 28,* 42–46.

Rice, B. (1981, December). Call-in therapy: Reach out and shrink someone. *Psychology Today,* 39–44, 87–91.

Richards, R. J. (1980). Wundt's early theories of unconscious inference and cognitive evolution in their relation to Darwinian biopsychology. In W. Bringmann & R. D. Tweney *(Eds.), Wundt studies.* Toronto, ON: Hogrefe, 42–70.

Richards, R. J. (1983). Why Darwin delayed, or interesting problems and models in the history of science. *Journal of the History of the Behavioral Sciences, 19,* 45–53.

Ricoeur, P. (1970). *Freud and philosophy* (B. Savage, Trans.). New Haven, CT: Yale University Press.

Ridley, M. (1996). *Evolution,* 2nd ed. Cambridge, MA: Blackwell Science.

Ridley, M. (2010). *The rational optimist: How prosperity evolves.* New York: Harper Collins.

Rieff, P. (1966). *The triumph of the therapeutic.* New York: Harper & Row.

Rieff, P. (1979). *Freud: The mind of the moralist,* 3rd ed. Chicago, IL: University of Chicago Press.

Ringer, F. K. (1969). *The decline of German Mandarins: The German academic community 1890–1933.* Cambridge, MA: Harvard University Press.

Ritchie, B. F. (1953). The circumnavigation of cognition. *Psychological Review, 60,* 216–21.

Roazen, P. (1974). *Freud and his followers.* New York: New American Library.

Robinson, D. K. (1996). Wilhelm von Humboldt and the German university. In W. G. Bringmann, H. E. Lück, R. Miller, & C. E. Early *(Eds.), A pictorial history of psychology.* Chicago, IL: Quintessence, 85–89.

Robinson, P. (1983, July 10). Psychology's scrambled egos. *Washington Post Book World, 13,* 5, 7.

Rogers, C. R. (1944). Psychological adjustments of discharged service personnel. *Psychological Bulletin, 41,* 689–96.

Rogers, C. R. (1958). A process conception of psychotherapy. *American Psychologist, 13,* 142–49.

Rogers, C. R. (1964). Toward a science of the person. In T. W. Wann *(Ed.), Behaviorism and phenomenology: Contrasting bases for modern psychology.* Chicago, IL: University of Chicago Press.

Rogers, C. R. (1968). Interpersonal relationships: U.S.A. 2000. *Journal of Applied Behavioral Science, 4,* 265–80.

Rogers, C. R., & Skinner, B. F. (1956). Some issues concerning the control of human behavior: A symposium. *Science, 124,* 1057–65.

Romanes, G. (1883). *Animal intelligence.* New York: Appleton & Co.

Romanes, G. (1889). *Mental evaluation in man.* New York: Arno.

Rorty, R. (1979). *Philosophy and the mirror of nature.* Princeton, NJ: Princeton University Press.

Rorty, R. (1991). Nonreductive physicalism. In R. Rorty *(Ed.), Objectivity, relativism, and truth. Philosophical papers.* (Vol. 1). Cambridge, England: Cambridge University Press, 113–25.

Rorty, R. (1993). Holism, intrinsicality, and the ambition of transcendence. In B. Dahlbom *(Ed.), Dennett and his critics.* Oxford: Blackwell, 184–202.

Rosch, E. (1977). Human categorization. In N. Warren *(Ed.), Studies in cross-cultural psychology.* London: Academic Press.

Rose, F. (1985). The black knight of AI. *Science, 85,* 46–51.

Rosenberg, A. (1994). *Instrumental biology: Or the disunity of science.* Chicago, IL: Chicago University Press.

Rosenberg, A. (2005). *Philosophy of science: A contemporary introduction.* New York: Routledge.

Rosenblueth, A., Wiener, N., & Bigelow, J. (1943/1966). Behavior, purpose, and teleology. Reprinted in J. V. Canfield *(Ed.),Purpose in nature.* Englewood Cliffs, NJ: Prentice-Hall.

Rosenzweig, S. (1985). Freud and experimental psychology: The emergence of idiodynamics. In S. Koch & D. Leary *(Eds.), A century of psychology as science.* New York: McGraw-Hill.

Ross, D. (1991). *The origins of American social science.* Cambridge, England: Cambridge University Press.

Rossi, P. (1975). Hermeticism, rationality, and the scientific revolution. In M. Bonelli & W. Shea *(Eds.), Reason, experiment and mysticism in the scientific revolution.* New York: Science History Publications.

Rousseau, J. J. (1750). *Discourse on the arts and sciences.* Retrieved from http://www.ucl.ac.uk/history/courses/europe1/weeks/rou1.htm

Rousseau, J. J. (1762/1974). *Emile.* New York: Dutton.

Rousseau, J. J. (1762/1995). *Emile.* Partially reprinted in I. Kramnick *(Ed.), The portable Enlightenment reader.* New York: Penguin, 568–79.

Routh, D. K. (1994). *Clinical psychology since 1917.* New York: Plenum.

Routh, D. K. (1996). Lightner Witmer and the first 100 years of clinical psychology. *American Psychologist, 51,* 244–47.

Rowlands, M. (2010). *The new science of the mind: From extended mind to embodied phenomenology.* Cambridge, MA: MIT Press.

Rubinstein, R. A. (1984). *Science as a cognitive process.* Philadelphia, PA: University of Pennsylvania Press.

Rumelhart, D. E., McClelland, J. L., & the PDP Research Group. (1986). *Parallel distributed processing: Explorations in the microstructure of cognition,* 2 vols. Cambridge, MA: Cambridge University Press.

Ruse, M. (1975). Charles Darwin and artificial selection. *Journal of the History of Ideas, 36,* 339–50.

Ryle, G. (1949). *The concept of mind.* New York: Barnes & Noble.

Sacks, O. (1985). *The man who mistook his wife for a hat.* New York: HarperCollins.

Salmon, W. S. (1984). *Scientific explanation and the causal structure of the world.* Princeton, NJ: Princeton University Press.

Salmon, W. S. (1989). Four decades of scientific explanation. In P. Kitcher & W. S. Salmon *(Eds.), Scientific explanation. Minnesota studies in the philosophy of science.* (Vol. 13). Minneapolis, MN: University of Minnesota Press, 3–219.

Samelson, F. (1980). J. B. Watson's Little Albert, Cyril Burt's twins, and the need for a critical science. *American Psychologist, 35,* 619–25.

Samelson, F. (1981). Struggle for scientific authority: The reception of Watson's behaviorism, 1913–1920. *Journal of the History of the Behavioral Sciences, 17,* 399–425.

Sanford, E. C. (1903). Psychology and physics. *Psychological Review, 10,* 105–19.

Sanford, F. H. (1951). Across the secretary's desk: Notes on the future of psychology as a profession. *American Psychologist, 6,* 74–76.

Sanford, N. (1965). Will psychologists study human problems? *American Psychologist, 20,* 192–98.

Sartre, J.-P. (1943). *Being and nothingness: An exercise in phenomenological ontology* (H. Barnes, Trans., 2001). New York: Citadel.

Saunders, J. L. (Ed.). (1966). *Greek and Roman Philosophy after Aristotle.* New York: Free Press.

Savage, W. (1990). *Scientific theories. Minnesota studies in the philosophy of science* (Vol. 14). Minneapolis, MN: University of Minnesota Press.

Schama, S. (1989). *Citizens: A chronicle of the French Revolution.* New York: Knopf.

Schatzman, M. (1992, March 21). Freud: Who seduced whom? *New Scientist,* 34–37.

Schiavone, A. (2000). *The end of the past: Ancient Rome and the modern west* (M. J. Schneider, Trans.). Cambridge, MA: Harvard University Press.

Schmidt, W. (1996). William Stern. In W. Bringmann, H. Lück, R. Miller, & C. Early *(Eds.), A pictorial history of psychology.* Chicago, IL: Quintessence, 322–25.

Schneider, S. M., & Morris, E. K. (1987). A history of the term radical behaviorism: From Watson to skinner. *The Behavior Analyst, 10,* 27–39.

Schofield, W. (1966). Clinical and counseling psychology: Some perspectives. *American Psychologist, 21,* 122–31.

Schorske, C. E. (1980). *Fin-de-siècle Vienna: Politics and culture.* New York: Knopf.

Schouton, M., & Looren de Jong, H. (Eds.). (2007). *The matter of the mind: Philosophical essays on psychology, neuroscience, and reduction.* Malden, MA: Blackwell.

Schrof, J. M., & Schultz, S. (1999, March 8). Melancholy nation. *U.S. News and World Report.* Retrieved from www.usnews.com

Scriven, M. (1980). An evaluation of psychology. In R. A. Kasschau & F. S. Kessel *(Eds.), Psychology and society: In search of symbiosis.* New York: Holt, Rinehart and Winston.

Scruton, R. (2001). *Kant: A very short introduction.* Oxford: Oxford University Press.

Searle, J. R. (1980). Minds, brains, and programs. *Behavioral and Brain Sciences, 3,* 417–24.

Searle, J. R. (1994). *The rediscovery of the mind.* Los Angeles, CA: University of California Press.

Searle, J. R. (1995). *The construction of social reality.* New York: Free Press.

Searle, J. R. (1997). *The mystery of consciousness.* New York: New York Review of Books.

Sears, R. R. (1944). Clinical psychology in the military services. *Psychological Bulletin, 41,* 502–9.

Sears, R. R. (1985). Psychoanalysis and behavior theory: 1907–1965. In S. Koch & D. Leary *(Eds.), A century of psychology as science.* New York: McGraw-Hill.

Sechenov, I. M. (1863/1965). Reflexes of the brain. Reprinted in Herrnstein & Boring (1965).

Sechenov, I. M. (1973). *Biographical sketch and essays.* New York: Arno.

Seligman, M. E. P., & Hager, J. L. (Eds.). (1972). *Biological boundaries of learning.* New York: Appleton-Century-Crofts.

Shadish, W. R., Jr. (1989). The perception and evaluation of quality in science. In B. Gholson, W. R. Shadish, Jr., R. Niemeyer, & A. Houts *(Eds.), Psychology of science.* Cambridge, England: Cambridge University Press, 383–428.

Shakow, D. (1965). Seventeen years later: Clinical psychology in the light of the 1947 committee on training in clinical psychology report. *American Psychologist, 20,* 353–67.

Shakow, D. (1976). What is clinical psychology? *American Psychologist, 31,* 553–60.

Shapin, S. (1996). *The scientific revolution.* Chicago, IL: University of Chicago Press.

Sheehan, J. J. (2000). Culture. In T. C. W. Blanning *(Ed.), The nineteenth century.* Oxford: Oxford University Press, 126–57.

Shiffrin, R. M. (1977). Commentary on "human memory: A proposed system and its control processes." In G. Bower *(Ed.), Human memory: Basic processes.* New York: Academic Press.

Shorter, E. (1997). *A history of psychiatry: From the era of the asylum to the age of Prozac.* New York: Wiley.

Shotter, J. (1981). Telling and reporting: Prospective and retrospective uses of self-ascription. In C. Antaki *(Ed.), The psychology of ordinary explanations of social behavior.* London: Academic Press, 157–81.

Simon, H. A. (1956). Rational choice and the structure of the environment. *Psychological Review, 63,* 129–38.

Simon, H. A. (1969). *The sciences of the artificial.* Cambridge, MA: MIT Press.

Simon, H. A. (1980). The social and behavioral sciences. *Science, 209,* 72–78.

Simonton, D. K. (1989). The chance-configuration theory of scientific creativity. In B. Gholson, W. R. Shadish, Jr., R. Niemeyer, & A. Houts *(Eds.), Psychology of science, 170–213.* Cambridge, England: Cambridge University Press.

Singer, E. A. (1911). Mind as observable object. *Journal of Philosophy, 8,* 180–86.

Skinner, B. F. (1931). The concept of reflex in the description of behavior. *Journal of General Psychology, 5,* 427–58. Reprinted in *Cumulative Record,* 3rd ed. Englewood Cliffs, NJ: Prentice-Hall, 1972.

Skinner, B. F. (1938). *Behavior of organisms.* New York: Appleton-Century-Crofts.

Skinner, B. F. (1948). *Walden II.* New York: Macmillan.

Skinner, B. F. (1953). *Science and human behavior.* New York: Macmillan.

Skinner, B. F. (1954). A critique of psychoanalytic concepts and theories. Reprinted in *Cumulative record,* 3rd ed. Englewood Cliffs, NJ: Prentice-Hall, 1972.

Skinner, B. F. (1957). *Verbal behavior.* New York: Appleton-Century-Crofts.

Skinner, B. F. (1959). A case history in scientific method. In S. Koch *(Ed.), Psychology: Study of a science.* New York: McGraw-Hill, 359–79.

Skinner, B. F. (1971). A lecture on "having" a poem. Reprinted in *Cumulative record,* 3rd ed. Englewood Cliffs, NJ: Prentice-Hall, 1972.

Skinner, B. F. (1977). Herrnstein and the evolution of behaviorism. *American Psychologist, 32,* 1006–12.

Slack, C. W. (1955). Feedback theory and the reflex-arc concept. *Psychological Review, 62,* 263–67.

Smail, D. L. (2008). *Deep history and the brain.* Los Angeles, CA: University of California Press.

Small, L. (1963). Toward professional clinical psychology. *American Psychologist, 18,* 558–62.

Smith, A. (1776). An inquiry into the nature and causes of the wealth of nations. Retrieved from http://econlib.org/library/Smith/smWN.html

Smith, A. M. (1990). Knowing things inside out: The scientific revolution from a medieval perspective. *American Historical Review, 95,* 726–44.

Smith, J. (2005). *Europe after Rome: A new cultural history.* Oxford: Oxford University Press.

Smith, L. J. (1986). *Behaviorism and logical positivism: A revised account of the alliance.* Stanford, CA: Stanford University Press.

Smith, M. L., Glass, G. V., & Miller, T. I. (1980). *The benefits of psychotherapy.* Baltimore, MD: Johns Hopkins University Press.

Smith, N. K. (1941). *The philosophy of David Hume.* London: Macmillan.

Smith, R. (1995). The language of human nature. In C. Fox, E. Porter, & R. Wokler *(Eds.), Inventing human science: Eighteenth century domains.* Berkeley, CA: University of California Press, 88–111.

Smith, R. (1997). *The Norton history of the human sciences.* New York: Norton.

Smith, R. (2010). Why history matters. *History and Philosophy of Psychology, 12,* 26–38.

Smolensky, P. (1988). On the proper treatment of connectionism. *Behavioral and Brain Sciences, 11,* 1–74.

Snell, B. (1953). *The discovery of the mind: The Greek origins of European thought.* Reprinted. New York: Harper & Row, 1960.

Snyder, S. H. (1980). *Biological aspects of mental disorder.* New York: Oxford University Press.

Sokal, M. M. (1982). James McKeen Cattell and the failure of anthropometric testing. In W. Woodward & M. Ash *(Eds.), The problematic science: Psychology in nineteenth-century thought.* New York: Praeger, 322–45.

Sokal, M. M. (1983). James McKeen Cattell and American psychology in the 1920s. In J. Brozek *(Ed.), Explorations in the history of psychology in the United States.* Lewisburg, PA: Bucknell University Press.

Sokal, M. M. (1984). The Gestalt psychologists in behaviorist America. *American Historical Review, 89,* 1240–63.

Solomon, R. C. (1974). Freud's neurological theory of the mind. In R. Wollheim *(Ed.), Freud: A collection of critical essays.* Garden City, NY: Doubleday.

Solomon, R. C. (1988). *Continental philosophy since 1750: The rise and fall of the self. A history of Western philosophy* (Vol. 7). Oxford: Oxford University Press.

Sorabji, R. (1974). Body and soul in Aristotle. *Philosophy: 49,* 63–89. Reprinted in M. Durrant *(Ed.), Aristotle's de Anima in focus,* 162–96. London: Routledge & Kegan Paul, 1993.

Spanos, N. (1996). *Multiple identities and false memories: A sociocognitive perspective.* Washington, DC: APA Books.

Spence, K. (1948). Postulates and methods of "behaviorism." *Psychological Review, 55,* 67–78.

Spencer, H. (1880/1945). *First principles.* London: Watts & Co.

Spencer, H. (1897). *The principles of psychology,* 3rd ed. New York: Appleton & Co.

Spencer, H. (1904). *An autobiography,* 2 vols. London: Williams & Norgate.

Spencer, T. (1966). *Shakespeare and the nature of man.* New York: Collier Books.

Sperling, G. A. (1960). The information available in brief visual presentations. *Psychological Monographs, 74,* 498.

Sprague, R. (1972). *The older Sophists.* Columbia, SC: University of South Carolina Press.

Squires, S. (1990, July 24). The quest for prescription privileges. *Washington Post, Health,* p. 7.

Steinberg, J. G. (2011). *Bismarck: A life.* Oxford: Oxford University Press.

Stevens, S. S. (1935a). The operational basis of psychology. *American Journal of Psychology, 43,* 323–30.

Stevens, S. S. (1935b). The operational definition of psychological concepts. *Psychological Review, 42,* 517–27.

Stevens, S. S. (1939). Psychology and the science of science. *Psychological Bulletin, 36,* 221–63.

Stewart, D. (1792). *Elements of the philosophy of the human mind.* Facsimile reprint, 1971. New York: Garland Press.

Stich, S. P. (1983). *From folk psychology to cognitive science: The case against belief.* Cambridge, MA: MIT/Bradford.

Stich, S. P. (1996). *The deconstruction of the mind.* Cambridge, MA: Bradford Books.

Straus, H. (1988, August 12). Psychology field finds itself of two minds: Private practice, research. *Atlanta Journal and Constitution.*

Strauss, L. (1988). *Persecution and the art of writing.* Chicago, IL: Chicago University Press.

Strickler, G. (1975). On professional schools and professional degrees. *American Psychologist, 31,* 1062–66.

Strupp, H. (1976). Clinical psychology, irrationalism, and the erosion of excellence. *American Psychologist, 31,* 561–71.

Sulloway, F. J. (1979). *Freud: Biologist of the mind.* New York: Basic Books.

Sulloway, F. J. (1982). Freud and biology: The hidden legacy. In W. R. Woodward & M. J. Ash *(Eds.), The problematic science: Psychology in nineteenth-century thought.* New York: Praeger.

Sulloway, F. J. (1991). Reassessing Freud's case histories: The social construction of psychoanalysis. *Isis, 82,* 245–75.

Suppe, F. *(Ed.).* (1977). *The structure of scientific theories,* 2nd ed. Urbana, IL: University of Illinois Press.

Suppe, F. (1989). *The semantic conception of theories and scientific realism.* Urbana, IL: University of Illinois Press.

Sutich, A. J., & Vich, M. A. (1969). Introduction. In A. J. Sutich & M. A. Vich *(Eds.), Readings in humanistic psychology.* New York: The Free Press.

Swartz, C. K. (1908). The Scientific Association of Johns Hopkins University. *Science, 28,* 814–15.

Szasz, T. S. (1960a). The myth of mental illness. *American Psychologist, 15,* 113–19.

Szasz, T. S. (1960b). *The myth of mental illness,* rev. ed.. New York: Harper Perennial Library, 974.

Taine, H. (1875). *On intelligence.* New York: Holt. (French edition 1870)

Tank, D. W., & Hopfield, J. J. (1987, December). Collective computation in neuron-like circuits. *Scientific American, 257,* 104–15.

Tart, C. (1978, August 31). *Information processing mechanisms and ESP.* Invited address presented at the annual meeting of the American Psychological Association, Toronto, Canada.

Taylor, C. (1989). *Sources of the self: The making of modern identity.* Cambridge, MA: Harvard University Press.

Taylor, D. W. (1963). Thinking. In M. Marx *(Ed.), Theories in contemporary psychology.* New York: Macmillan.

Taylor, E. (1911). *Principles of scientific management.* New York: Harper Brothers.

Tennov, D. (1979). *Love and limerence: The experience of being in love.* New York: Stein & Day.

Terman, L. M. (1916). *The measurement of intelligence.* New York: Houghton Mifflin.

Terman, L. M. (1924). The mental test as a psychological method. *Psychological Review, 31,* 93–117.

Terman, L. M. (1930). Lewis M. Terman. In C. Murchison *(Ed.), A history of psychology in autobiography* (Vol. 2). Worcester, MA: Clark University Press.

Tertullian, Q. S. F. (212 CE). *Prescription against heretics.* Retrieved from http://www.newadvent.org/fathers/0311.htm

Thagard, P. (1988). *Computational philosophy of science.* Cambridge, MA: MIT Press.

Thaler, R., & Sunstein, C. (2008). *Nudge: Improving decisions about health, wealth, and happiness.* New Haven, CT: Yale University Press.

Thilly, F. (1905). Review of Angell's psychology. *Philosophical Review, 14,* 481–87.

Thomas, K. (1971). *Religion and the decline of magic.* Harmondsworth, England: Penguin.

Thomas, L. L. (1977). Nationalizing the Republic. In B. Bailyn, D. Davis, D. Donald, L. Thomas, R. Wieber, & W. S. Wood *(Eds.), The great republic.* Boston, MA: Little, Brown, 827–1051.

Thorndike, E. L. (1898). Review of Evans' "evolution, ethics and animal psychology." *Psychological Review, 5,* 229–30.

Thorndike, E. L. (1911/1965). *Animal intelligence.* New York: Hafner.

Thorndike, E. L. (1920). Intelligence and its uses. *Harper's Magazine, 140,* 227–35.

Thorndike, E. L. (1929/1968). *Human learning.* New York: Johnson Reprint Corporation.

Thumin, F. J., & Zebelman, M. (1967). Psychology and psychiatry: A study of public image. *American Psychologist, 22,* 282–86.

Titchener, E. B. (1897). *An outline of psychology.* New York: Macmillan.

Titchener, E. B. (1898). Postulates of a structural psychology. *Philosophical Review, 7,* 449–65.

Titchener, E. B. (1901–1905). *Experimental psychology: A manual of laboratory practice,* 4 vols. New York: Macmillan.

Titchener, E. B. (1904). *Lectures on the experimental psychology of the thought processes.* New York: Macmillan.

Titchener, E. B. (1908). *Lectures on the elementary psychology of feeling and attention.* New York: Macmillan.

Titchener, E. B. (1914). On "psychology as the behaviorist views it." *Proceedings of the American Philosophical Society, 53,* 1–17.

Titchener, E. B. (1929/1972). *Systematic psychology: Prolegomena.* Ithaca, NY: Cornell University Press.

Tocqueville, A. de (1850/1969). *Democracy in America.* New York: Anchor.

Tolman, E. C. (1920). Instinct and purpose. *Psychological Review, 27,* 217–33.

Tolman, E. C. (1922). A new formula for behaviorism. *Psychological Review, 29,* 44–53.

Tolman, E. C. (1923). A behavioristic account of the emotions. *Psychological Review, 30,* 217–27.

Tolman, E. C. (1925). Behaviorism and purpose. *Journal of Philosophy, 22,* 36–41.

Tolman, E. C. (1926). A behavioristic theory of ideas. *Psychological Review, 33,* 352–69.

Tolman, E. C. (1932). *Purposive behavior in animals and men.* New York: Century.

Tolman, E. C. (1935). Psychology vs. immediate experience. *Philosophy of Science.* Reprinted in Tolman (1951/1966).

Tolman, E. C. (1936). Operational behaviorism and current trends in psychology. In E. C. Tolman *(Ed.), Behavior and psychological man.* Berkeley, CA: University of California Press.

Tolman, E. C. (1948). Cognitive maps in rats and men. *Psychological Review, 55,* 189–209.

Tolman, E. C. (1949). Discussion. *Journal of Personality, 18,* 48–50.

Tolman, E. C. (1951/1966). *Behavior and psychological man.* Berkeley, CA: University of California Press.

Tolman, E. C. (1952). Edward Chace Tolman. In E. G. Boring, H. S. Langfeld, H. Werner, & R. M. Yerkes *(Eds.), A history of psychology in autobiography* (Vol. 4). Worcester, MA: Clark University Press.

Tolman, E. C. (1959). Principles of purposive behaviorism. In S. Koche *(Ed.), Psychology: A study of a science* (Vol. 2). New York: McGraw-Hill, 92–157.

Tombs, R. (2000). Politics. In T. C. W. Blanning *(Ed.), The nineteenth century.* Oxford: Oxford University Press, 10–46.

Toulmin, S. (1961). *Foresight and understanding.* Princeton, NJ: Princeton University Press.

Toulmin, S. (1972). *Human understanding.* Princeton, NJ: Princeton University Press.

Trueheart, C. (1998, November 27). Can wintry blast melt cold Parisian hearts? Chirac appeal tests culture unused to formal charity. *The Washington Post,* p. A39.

Tryon, R. C. (1963). Psychology in flux: The academic-professional bipolarity. *American Psychologist, 18,* 134–43.

Tulving, E. (1979). Memory research: What kind of progress? In L. G. Nilsson *(Ed.), Perspectives on memory research.* Hillsdale, NJ: Erlbaum.

Turing, A. M. (1950). Computing machinery and intelligence. *Mind, 59,* 433–60.

Tweney, R. D. (1989). A framework for the cognitive psychology of science. In B. Gholson, W. R. Shadish, Jr., R. Niemeyer, & A. Houts *(Eds.), Psychology of science.* Cambridge, England: Cambridge University Press, 342–66.

Tweney, R. D., Mynatt, C. R., & Doherty, M. E. *(Eds.).* (1981). *On scientific thinking.* New York: Columbia University Press.

Upham, T. G. (1831). *Elements of mental philosophy.* Boston, MA: Hilliard, Gray & Co.

van Drunen, P. (1996). Psychotechnics. In W. G. Bringmann, H. E. Lück, R. Miller, & C. E. Early *(Eds.), A pictorial history of psychology.* Chicago, IL: Quintessence, 480–84.

van Frassen, B. C. (1980). *The scientific image.* Oxford, England: Clarendon Press.

Van Gelder, T. (1995). What might cognition be, if not computation? *Journal of Philosophy, 92,* 345–381.

van Hoorn, W., & Verhave, T. (1980). Wundt's changing conception of a general and theoretical psychology. In W. Bringmann & R. D. Tweney *(Eds.), Wundt studies.* Toronto, ON: Hogrefe.

van Strien, P. J. (1998). Early applied psychology between essentialism and pragmatism: The dynamics of theory, tools, and clients. *History of Psychology, 1,* 205–34.

Vartanian, A. (1953). *Diderot and Descartes: A study of naturalism in the enlightenment.* Princeton, NJ: Princeton University Press.

Vaughn-Blount, K., Rutherford, A., Baker, D., & Johnson, D. (2009). History's mysteries demystified: Becoming a psychologist-historian. *American Journal of Psychology, 122,* 117–29.

Vernant, J.-P. (1982). *The origins of Greek thought.* Ithaca, NY: Cornell University Press.

Viereck, P. (1956). *The unadjusted man: A new hero for modern America.* New York: Capricorn Books.

Vlastos, G. (1991). *Socrates: Ironist and moral philosopher.* Ithaca, NY: Cornell University Press.

von Mayrhauser, R. T. (1985, June 14). *Walking out at the Walton: Psychological disunity and the origins of group testing in early World War I.* Paper presented at the annual meeting of Cheiron, the Society for the History of the Behavioral Sciences, Philadelphia.

Vorzimmer, P. (1970). *Charles Darwin: The years of controversy.* Philadelphia, PA: Temple University Press.

Waldrop, M. M. (1984). The necessity of knowledge. *Science, 223,* 1279–82.

Walters, R. G. (1978). *American reformers 1815–1860.* New York: Hill and Wang.

Wann, T. W. (Ed.). (1964). *Behaviorism and phenomenology: Contrasting bases for modern psychology.* Chicago, IL: University of Chicago Press.

Ward, J. (1904). The present problems of general psychology. *Philosophical Review, 13,* 603–21.

Ward, J. (1920). *Psychological principles.* Cambridge, MA: Cambridge University Press.

Ward-Perkins, B. (2005). *The fall of Rome and the end of civilization.* Oxford: Oxford University Press.

Warren, H. (1938). Howard C. Warren. In C. Murchison *(Ed.), A history of psychology in autobiography* (Vol. 1). Worcester, MA: Clark University Press.

Washburn, M. R. (1922). Introspection as an objective method. *Psychological Review, 29,* 89–112.

Watson, J. B. (1907). Comparative psychology. *Psychological Bulletin, 4,* 288–302.

Watson, J. B. (1909). A point of view in comparative psychology. *Psychological Bulletin, 6,* 57–58.

Watson, J. B. (1913a). Image and affection in behavior. *Journal of Philosophy, 10,* 421–28.

Watson, J. B. (1913b). Psychology as the behaviorist views it. *Psychological Review, 20,* 158–77.

Watson, J. B. (1916a). Behavior and the concept of mental disease. *Journal of Philosophy, 13,* 589–97.

Watson, J. B. (1916b). The place of the conditioned reflex in psychology. *Psychological Review, 23,* 89–116.

Watson, J. B. (1926a). What is behaviorism? *Harper's Magazine, 152,* 723–29.

Watson, J. B. (1926b). How we think: A behaviorist's view. *Harper's Magazine, 153,* 40–45.

Watson, J. B. (1926c). Memory as the behaviorist sees it. *Harper's Magazine, 153,* 244–50.

Watson, J. B. (1927a). The behaviorist looks at the instincts. *Harper's Magazine, 155,* 228–35.

Watson, J. B. (1927b). The myth of the unconscious. *Harper's Magazine, 155,* 502–8.

Watson, J. B. (1928a). The heart or the intellect. *Harper's Magazine, 156,* 345–52.

Watson, J. B. (1928b). *Psychological care of infant and child.* New York: W. W. Norton.

Watson, J. B. (1930). *Behaviorism,* 2nd ed. New York: Norton (1st ed., 1925).

Watson, J. B., & Rayner, R. (1920). Conditioned emotional reactions. *Journal of Experimental Psychology, 10,* 421–28.

Watson, P. (2010). *The German genius: Europe's third Renaissance, the second scientific revolution, and the twentieth century.* New York: Harper Collins.

Watson, R. I. (1975). The history of psychology as a specialty: A personal view of its first 15 years. *Journal of the History of the Behavioral Sciences, 11,* 5–14.

Webb, J. (1974). *The occult underground.* LaSalle, IL: Open Court.

Weber, M. (1918/1996). Science as a vocation. In L. Cohoare *(Ed.), From modernism to postmodernism: An anthology.* Oxford: Blackwell, 169–76.

Webster, R. (1995). *Why Freud was wrong: Sin, science, and psychoanalysis.* New York: Basic Books.

Wedin, M. V. (1986). Tracking Aristotle's nous. In A. Donegan, A. Perovich, & M. V. Wedin *(Eds.), Human nature and natural knowledge.* Dordrecht, The Netherlands: D. Reidel, 167–97. Reprinted in M. Durrant *(Ed.). Aristotle's de Anima in focus,* 128–59. London: Routledge & Kegan Paul, 1993.

Wegman, C. (1984). *Psychoanalysis and cognitive psychology.* New York: Academic Press.

Weiss, A. P. (1924). Behaviorism and behavior. *Psychological Review, 31,* Part 1: 32–50, Part 2: 118–49.

Welch, B. L. (1992, September). Paradigm II: Providing a better model for care. *APA Monitor,* 42–43.

Wender, P. H., & Klein, D. R. (1981, February). The promise of biological psychiatry. *Psychology Today, 15,* 25–41.

Wertheimer, M. (1912/1961). Experimentelle Studien über das sehen von Bewegung. *Zeitschrift für Psychologie,* 161–265. Abbreviated translation published in T. Shipley *(Ed.), Classics in psychology.* New York: Philosophical Library, 1032–89.

Wertheimer, M. (1922/1938). The general theoretical situation. In W. D. Ellis *(Ed.), A sourcebook of Gestalt psychology.* London: Routledge & Kegan Paul.

Wertheimer, M. (1923/1938). Untersuchungen zur Lehre von der Gestalt II. *Psychologische Forschung, 4,* 301–50. In W. D. Ellis *(Ed.), A sourcebook of Gestalt psychology.* London: Routledge & Kegan Paul, 71–88. Retrieved from http://www.yorku.ca/dept/psych/classics/Wertheimer/Forms/forms.htm

Wertheimer, M. (1925/1938). Gestalt theory. In W. D. Ellis *(Ed.), A sourcebook of Gestalt psychology.* London: Routledge & Kegan Paul.

Wertheimer, M. (1978, August 31). *Max Wertheimer: Gestalt prophet.* Presidential Address to Division 26 (History), Annual meeting of the American Psychological Association, Toronto.

Westfall, R. (1975). The role of alchemy in Newton's career. In M. Bonelli & W. Shea *(Eds.), Reason, experiment and mysticism in the scientific revolution.* New York: Science History Publications.

Wheeler, R. W. (1923). Introspection and behavior. *Psychological Review, 30,* 103–15.

White, L. (1972). *Science and sentiment in America.* London: Oxford University Press.

White, L. (1974). Death and the devil. In D. S. Kinsman *(Ed.), The darker vision of the Renaissance.* Berkeley, CA: University of California Press.

White, M. (1997). *Isaac Newton: The last sorcerer.* Reading, MA: Addison-Wesley.

White, M. G. (1985). On the status of cognitive psychology. *American Psychologist, 40,* 116–19.

Wickens, D. D. (1938). The transference of conditioned extinction from one muscle group to the antagonistic muscle group. *Journal of Experimental Psychology, 22,* 101–23.

Wickham, C. (1984). The other transition: From the ancient world to feudalism. *Past and Present, 103,* 3–36.

Wickham, C. (2007). *Framing the early middle ages: Europe and the Mediterranean 400-800,* rev. ed. New York: Oxford University Press.

Wiebe, R. (1967). *The search for order 1877–1920.* New York: Hill & Wang.

Wiendieck, G. (1996). Advertising psychology. In W. G. Bringmann, H. E. Lück, R. Miller, & C. E. Early *(Eds.), A pictorial history of psychology.* Chicago, IL: Quintessence, 514–17.

Wiggam, A. E. (1924). *The fruit of the family tree.* Indianapolis, IN: Bobbs-Merrill.

Wiggins, J. G. (1992, September). Capitol comments: Time is ripe to seek prescription authority. *APA Monitor,* 3.

Wilde, O. (1891). *The soul of man under socialism.* Retrieved from http://www.classicbookshelf.com/library/oscar_wilde/the_soul_of_man/0/

Williams, K. (1931). Five behaviorisms. *American Journal of Psychology, 43,* 337–61.

Wills, G. (1978). *Inventing America: Jefferson's declaration of independence.* Garden City, NY: Doubleday.

Wilson, A. N. (1999). *God's funeral.* New York: Norton.

Wispè, L. G., & Thompson, J. N. *(Eds.).* (1976). The war between the words: Biological vs. social evolution and some related issues. *American Psychologist, 31,* 341–84.

Witmer, L. (1897). The organization of practical work in psychology. *Psychological Review, 4,* 116–17.

Witmer, L. (1907). Clinical psychology. *Psychological Clinic, 1,* 1–9. Reprinted in *American Psychologist, 51,* 248–51. Available at Classics in Psychology Web site.

Wittgenstein, L. (1953). *Philosophical investigations,* 3rd ed. New York: Macmillan.

Wittgenstein, L. (1958). *The blue and brown books.* New York: Harper Colophon.

Wolfe, T. (1977). The me decade and the third great awakening. In T. Wolfe *(Ed.), Mauve gloves and madmen, clutter and vine.* New York: Bantam Books, 111–50.

Wolfle, D. (1966a). Social problems and social science. *Science, 151,* 1177.

Wolfle, D. (1966b). Government support for social science. *Science, 153,* 485.

Wollstonecraft, M. (1792). Vindication of the rights of woman. In Kramnick, I. (1995). *The portable Enlightenment reader.* New York: Viking, 618–28.

Wolman, B. (1968). Immanuel Kant and his impact on psychology. In B. Wolman *(Ed.), Historical roots of contemporary psychology.* New York: Harper & Row.

Wood, G. (2009). *Empire of liberty: A history of the early Republic.* New York: Oxford University Press.

Woodward, W., & Ash, M. (Eds.). *The problematic science: Psychology in nineteenth-century thought.* New York: Praeger.

Woodward, W. W. (1982). Wundt's program for the new psychology: Vicissitudes of experiment, theory, and system. In W. Woodward & M. Ash *(Eds.), The problematic science: Psychology in nineteenth century thought.* New York: Praeger, 322–45.

Woodworth, R. S. (1924). Four varieties of behaviorism. *Psychological Review, 31,* 257–64.

Woodworth, R. S. (1938). *Experimental psychology.* New York: Holt, Rinehart & Winston.

Woodworth, R. S., & Schlosberg, H. (1954). *Experimental psychology,* 2nd ed. New York: Holt, Rinehart & Winston.

Wozniak, R. (1982). Metaphysics and science, reason and reality: The intellectual origins of genetic epistemology. In J. Broughton & D. Freeman Noir *(Eds.), The cognitive developmental psychology of James Mark Baldwin.* Hillsdale, NJ: Ablex.

Wright, R. (1994). *The moral animal.* New York: Pantheon.

Wundt, W. M. (1873). Principles of physiological psychology. Portions of translation by S. Diamond reprinted in R. W. Rieber *(Ed.).* (1980). Wilhelm Wundt and the making of a scientific psychology. New York: Plenum.

Wundt, W. M. (1896). *Lectures on human and animal psychology.* New York: Macmillan.

Wundt, W. M. (1907–1908). Uber Ausfrageexperimenten und über die Methoden zur Psychologie des Denkens. *Psychologischen Studien, 3,* 301–60.

Wyckoff, L. B. (1954). A mathematical model and an electronic model for learning. *Psychological Review, 61,* 89–97.

Yerkes, R. (1905). Review of Claparede, "Is comparative psychology legitimate?" *Journal of Philosophy, 2,* 527–28.

Yerkes, R. M. (1913). Comparative psychology: A question of definition. *Journal of Philosophy, 10,* 581–82.

Yerkes, R. M. (1918). Psychology in relation to the war. *Psychological Review, 25,* 85–115.

Yerkes, R. M. (1923). Testing the human mind. *Atlantic Monthly, 131,* 358–70.

Young, D. (1970). *Mind, brain, and adaptation in the nineteenth century.* Oxford, England: Clarendon Press.

Zilbergeld, B. (1983). *The shrinking of America: Myths of psychological change.* Boston, MA: Little, Brown.

Zuicker, A. E., Donohue, A., Mendelsohn, C., Silber C., & Hope, N. (Director). (May 22, 2010). Out of the sky [television series episode]. In J. Bruckheimer (Producer), CSI: New York. Los Angeles, CA: CBS Television Studios.

Index